MOLIÈRE
and the
Commonwealth
of Letters:
Patrimony and Posterity

MOLIÈRE
and the
Commonwealth
of Letters:
Patrimony and Posterity

EDITED BY

Roger Johnson, Jr.

Editha S. Neumann

and

Guy T. Trail

UNIVERSITY PRESS OF MISSISSIPPI

JACKSON

CONTENTS

PREFACE

During the course of this book's production, one of the three editors, Guy Thomas Trail, died suddenly of heart failure. He was thirty-eight years old. On his desk at the time of his death was a stack of ten essays found in this volume—half-edited, much marked, several much admired. Save for his expressed desire that this volume be dedicated specifically to Jean-Baptiste Poquelin, it would be dedicated formally to Guy Trail; but we remaining cannot in good faith contradict his energetic wishes. This book is, then, most humbly recorded in memory of perhaps the greatest comedian, whose death marked the commencement of a three-hundred-year patrimony to the commonwealth of letters. This dedication made, the remaining editors must attempt some prefatory remarks on Guy Trail and his role in the creation of this collection.

A. E. van Vogt has a character say: "In the long run, there can be no excuse for any individual's not knowing what it is possible for him to know. Why shouldn't he? Why should he stand under the sky of his planet and look up at it with stupid eyes . . . ?" The words might have been Trail's, and it is a fact that Guy Trail admired van Vogt tremendously. In a way, this book is one of the many expressions of his curiosity and will to learn. Guy Trail would and did often pose the question "Why?" in his study of world literature. Relatively certain of his own attitude toward Molière, he wished to discover in a straight-forward manner why humans loved Molière. He was too intellectually mature and too fundamentally conservative to be a Turk of literary scholarship (his foremost interest being Egyptian hieroglyphic language and literature). But he was too brilliant, skeptical, and too uninitiated to believe that Molière's appropriateness and skill could cause such sustained admiration over the years. It was Guy Trail who posed and made the rest of us pose questions of causality, and it was he who could harbor the audacity of simply asking the world why it loved Molière. A selection of answers, direct and indirect, constitutes this volume, but the book's intent and execution fall miserably short of expressing the intensity of Guy Trail's curiosity. Indeed, there is nothing known to the remaining editors that can serve as an adequate model for his curiosity; nonetheless, this is the place to attempt at least a pale abstraction of his ethic.

For him curiosity was a fortunate expression of the will to knowledge. He had what might be called a natural curiosity, but this was meager in the face of his incredible will to learn—whether tired or bored or discouraged, he pressed himself to assimilate and synthesize information. The goal was neither realization of status nor accumulation of data; it was betterment of the self and civilization. Guy Trail believed in man's future the way some small children believe in Santa Claus, not necessarily optimistically but always with the keenest anticipation. The ultimate human crime in his system of ethics was denial of the will to learn and become greater—any denial of human potential for sublimity. In its shallowest expression the crime, he said, was simply an opposition to creativity or perhaps a scorning of the noble impulse. The crime in its deepest, most treacherous and destructive form was the acceptance of death, that defacer of potentiality.

He had a gallery of heroes—Milton, Vigny, Rembrandt, Wilfred Owen, Kant, John Brown, Darwin, Hugo, Robert Lee, Shelley, Hölderlin, and Dante—and when William Faulkner died he composed a tribute to him, part of which we quote here as our best tribute to this man, Guy Thomas Trail, who came from Chicago and gave us much.

On the Death of the Poet

He came with a flourish and ruffle of spring rains,
Came drumming down his town, dreaming dawn
Into a flush and ruffle of ringing pains,
Came too late and left us thrumming alone,
Alive and pawn, isolate in our singing shown.

We remaining speak with and for him now in thanking those who offered counsel and aid to this project. We accept the shortcomings of the book as our own, for we were privy to the best of judgment: thanks to Gaston Hall and W. G. Moore for direct advice; thanks to many whose names are not to be found among the contributors but who helped to establish fruitful correspondence with interested persons; to able and dedicated assistants Rosana Cook, Rosenda del Villar, Deborah Gorney, Yutana Gulledge, Joanne Phipps, and Florence Witte. Finally, and most delightedly, the remaining editors wish to express their and Guy Trail's heartfelt gratitude to the state of Mississippi. This project was made possible through the initial efforts of R. C. Cook and William D. McCain and funded by the University of Southern Mississippi Faculty Research Council. Each year the Mississippi Legislature, through the Board of Trustees of Institutions of Higher Learning, makes money available for the Faculty Research Council to award to faculty doing research beneficial to the state of Mississippi. Work on this project was begun with such money, and it is the fervent hope of the remaining editors that this volume will prove to be of great pertinence to the people whose taxes supported its birth.

Roger Johnson, Jr.
Editha S. Neumann

Hattiesburg, Mississippi

INTRODUCTION

This volume was conceived as a tribute to Jean-Baptiste Poquelin on the tercentenary of his death. Its plan was and is not one that placed it squarely among the traditional genres of literary criticism and history. Certainly the volume comes some centuries too late to be named a *Festschrift*, which in accepted bibliographical jargon is a tomish tribute to a late or retiring colleague. Although the editors and contributors have continued to call it a *Festschrift*—partly ironically and partly because it is indeed a tribute to a man whose spiritual immortality is documented to the present—the term, if applied seriously, would only result in confusion. Nonetheless, this collection does have a peculiar correspondence to the more normal *Festschrift*; the latter often consists of a collection of essays, the authors of which have something in common—having taught with, studied under, or benefited by the person honored. The case is often that the various authors have more in common than their various articles, and this is accepted as being in the nature of *Festschriften*. This book does attempt a loose sort of relationship between individual contributions, but its editors have aspired also to uncover a hitherto unknown relationship amongst the utterly diverse contributors, namely profound interest in and knowledge of Molière as the comedian affected and added to the commonwealth of letters. Since the authors' attitudes concerning what constitutes the so-called commonwealth of letters quite naturally vary according to their backgrounds and interests, the assessment of Molière's patrimony to it must likewise vary, and in this variance there lies a beginning of the truth, a delineation of the patrimony.

It would be inappropriate, also, to call this volume a casebook, for the collection of essays in it is not pointed toward a topic specific enough in the realm of time, theme, geography, language, technique, or genre to give it the focus necessary for a casebook. Most certainly this book is not one *on* Molière. There are essays on the man, but items of a biographical nature are there to lend substance to the subsequent analyses of the man's contributions to the world of literature. Curiously, the book is also not even about the plays, although there are several readings of the plays (and a section the title of which indicates the plays as a topic). That the present collection can be none of these should be evident immediately in the stolid testimony of the book's size: had the work been intended to offer the reader a series of essays describing the man and analyzing his work, then those precious few documents incorporating original and unpublished insight would have constituted a volume of less immodest proportion. It is also not exactly a study of literary influence.

Perhaps adding confusion to scholarly disedification, the knowledge-able reader will notice that there are, among the contributors, very few *Moliéristes* and even a meager scattering of *dixseptiémistes*. While experts in Molière have participated in all phases of the production of this volume and have penned a few of the essays contained herein, the work is not theirs and can make no pretense to incorporate that which would normally be chosen by a Judd Hubert, a Will Moore, a Gaston Hall, a Marcel Gut-wirth, a Jacques Guicharnaud, or a Paul Saintogne. What, then, is this amalgamation called *Molière and the Commonwealth of Letters*?

First of all, it is a tribute to Molière, a festival of his spirit, a testimony to his participation in that mythical but well-intuited league of good fellows who left the planet a better place for their coming. Second, it is an attempt on the editors' part to apply point of view (inspired by Henry James) and spiritual geography (inspired by Dante) systematically to a problem of literary criticism and history. Here are essays and commentary by a number of persons who have come to know Molière second-hand, as it were, persons who have realized at one point or another that the French comedian had an effect within their areas of primary interest—whether these areas be the literature of Poland or their own conception of stage movement and rhythm. Here, also, are tools to assist in the exploration of novel topics relating Molière to *Weltliteratur*. The essays of this book comprise a multifaceted portrait, incorporating many points of view, of Molière's patrimony to the commonwealth of letters. It is vitally important to any historian who is not to be crippled by an ignominious provincialism that Molière has made a contribution to the literature of Hungary, the plays and thought of England, the origin of theater in Canada, and that these contributions are not the same, that all of the contributions are part of his legacy to a civilization and culture still in the forging. For those who would begin to comprehend the nature of what he gave us, it is crucial to understand in concrete terms how a play must be recreated and made to live again in the mouths and costumes of actors and in the fantastic brains of those who think of the lights and shadows exposing Don Juan to a consuming public. There is no science known to the editors to show Molière in all these facets and more; the art of compilation is not so exact and perhaps not so advanced; and here it is that the method of James produces its advantage, for James could, by showing several views of a person or event, almost magically evoke the truth of the thing. This the editors have tried to do by means of solicitation, organization, and juxtaposition.

If the object were merely to notice the skill and influence of Molière as they affected a clearly defined segment of human endeavor, then perhaps the task would be theoretically possible. But the commonwealth of letters is a nation whose borders encompass the highest and meanest of all human thought put in putatively communicable form. How odd a task to limn the world! Taking a page from Dante and his master Aristotle, the editors have begun the best way they knew to set the nature and scope of their world, the commonwealth of letters, by beginning with a breaking down of the totality into parts and then by attempting to marshall what could be gathered, piece by piece, to make clear the parts. As Dante gained finally a vision of the divine rose, its parts conjoined, so we with perhaps less to see and say gain a muted indication of the constellation of ideas which delineates the commonwealth of letters.

MOLIÈRE
and the
Commonwealth
of Letters:
Patrimony and Posterity

Molière
and his Contemporaries

Given that Molière has indeed bequeathed a patrimony to the commonwealth of letters subsequent to his own times, then it is proper to begin analysis by describing aspects of the social environment out of which the substance of the legacy originated. This first section of essays deals specifically with Jean-Baptiste Poquelin: his acquaintanceships among the court painters, especially his good friend Pierre Mignard; his fruitful and sometimes stormy collaboration with Jean-Baptiste Lully; and his encounter with the institution of marriage. While it is impossible to consider the man separate from his artistic contribution, the chief aim of these essays is to illuminate the playwright. (Other sections of this volume include discussions of particular features of the plays themselves and delineations of the literary sources Molière accepted and modified.)

MOLIÈRE AND THE COURT PAINTERS, ESPECIALLY PIERRE MIGNARD

Elizabeth Maxfield-Miller

The century of Louis XIV is rightly called *le Grand Siècle* because in the entourage of the Sun King there was a classical constellation of stars in all fields. Molière, perhaps the greatest of all, was intimately linked with leaders in the arts and sciences. He numbered among his friends[1] the musicians Lully and Charpentier, the scientist Rohault, the doctors Mauvillain and Bernier, the writers Corneille, La Fontaine, Chapelle, Boileau and Racine, and the court painters, his most intimate friend Pierre Mignard, and Nicolas Mignard, Charles Dufresnoy, Sébastien Bourdon and Charles Le Brun.

The court painters make an interesting study since their relationships with Molière shed light not only on his life, but also on the portraits they painted of him which we know from originals or from later engravings. Molière knew Bourdon and the two Mignards at the end of his years in the provinces—1656–58. He worked with the young Le Brun in 1661 in the decorations for his play *Les Fâcheux* at Fouquet's Fête de Vaux for the young king, and he was very conscious of the rivalries between Nicolas and his younger, more popular brother Pierre, as well as the life-long enmity between Le Brun and Pierre, especially in 1668–69 when Molière wrote the long poem *La Gloire du Val-de-Grâce* to defend and praise his friend's frescoes (using court painter Charles Dufresnoy's posthumous *De arte graphica* of 1668 to document his notes on the art of painting). Since Pierre Mignard (1612–95) was most intimately involved in the life of Molière and the Béjarts, he will be more fully treated here than the others.

Molière also knew two other minor court painters and members of the Académie royale, Charles-Louis Dufresne, sieur de Postel (1635–1711)

---

[1] Notes on most of these friends of Molière and their relationships with him are documented in Madeleine Jurgens and Elizabeth Maxfield-Miller: *Cent ans de recherches sur Molière, sur sa famille et sur les comédiens de sa troupe*, Archives de France, Paris, 1963. The abbreviation *Cent ans* will be used for subsequent references to it.

and Etienne Villequin (1619–88)[2] who were brothers of Molière's actors, Charles Dufresne and Edme Villequin, sieur de Brie, respectively. The actor and artist Dufresnes came from Nantes where their father, Claude Dufresne, sieur de Postel, was "peintre de son Altesse Royalle," Gaston d'Orléans, Molière's first patron 1643–45.[3] Mention should perhaps be made of three other minor painters connected with Molière. Two were apprentices of Pierre Mignard: Jean de la Borde,[4] who was in service at the time of Mignard's painting on the dome of the Val-de-Grâce and who later became a member of the Académie royale in 1683, and Zaccharie Le Masson,[5] apprenticed in 1672, about whom less is known, but whose brother Jean-Baptiste Le Masson had been baptised in 1657 in Lyon with Molière as godfather (*Cent ans*, 325–26). The third is a mysterious Jean de Courbes who appears as "peintre en l'Académie du roy" in a strange marriage contract with Geneviève Béjart (sister of Madeleine) on June 30, 1664, in which Molière is a witness. The contract was never carried out, and just five months later, Geneviève married Léonard de Loménie after a contract in which Pierre Mignard and Molière sign as witnesses.[6] There were also a number of engravers whom Molière

---

[2] The most important facts about all the painters, major and minor, treated in this article are to be found in two major art dictionaries:

   Emmanuel Bénézit: *Dictionnaire critique et documentaire des peintres, sculpteurs, dessinateurs et graveurs*, 8 vol., Paris, 1948.

   Ulrich Thieme: *Allegemeines Lexikon der bildenden Künstler von der Antike bis zum Gegenwart . . .* 37 vol. (Leipzig, 1908–1950).

The author wishes to thank Harvard University Library for the privilege of working on the given bibliographical material in Fogg Art Library, Houghton Rare Book Collection and Widener Library.

[3] Is it possible that the stops in Nantes of the Dufresne-Molière-Béjart troupe in 1646 and 1648 (*Cent ans*, 283–84, 291–92, 297–301) were encouraged by Charles Dufresne because it was his home town, even though it was a detour from Paris to their place as "comédiens du duc d'Epernon" in Guyenne?

[4] Jean de La Borde was apprenticed to Pierre Mignard, August 1, 1666 (Min. centr. XCVI, 87, discovered 1969). He has a small paragraph in the art dictionaries, although his dates of birth and death are unknown.

[5] Zaccharie (evidently named for his grandfather, the actor Montfleury—*Cent ans*, 325–6) does not appear in Bénézit or Thieme, nor in the list of members of the Académie royale. His apprenticeship to Pierre Mignard is dated April 8, 1672 (Min. centr. CXII, 141, noted in *Cent ans*, 720.)

[6] *Cent ans*, 391–93, 396–98. Did Pierre Mignard, so close to all the Béjarts, have something to do with this, denouncing "Jean de Courbes" as a pretentious impostor? The "de" was added only in this document. In others in the Minutier Central (XLII, 156 and CXVII, 70 and 71) he is just "Jean Courbes, b. de Paris" or "peintre du roi" (in an *obligation* of June 15, 1664, two contracts for several paintings to complete in two months, of August 4 and 7, 1668, and a *procuration* of Nov. 11, 1668). He does not appear on any list of members of l'Académie royale. Perhaps "peintre en l'académie du roy" is different from "peintre de l'Académie." He is too minor a painter to appear in the art dictionaries, which only list a "Jean de Courbes" engraver and "héraldiste" born in 1592 who lived mostly in England and Spain.

knew well and who engraved portraits and illustrations for the published works. Chief of these was Robert Nanteuil (1623–78), "graveur ordinaire du roi" in 1658.

This study will not treat of the minor painters and engravers but of the five court painters Molière knew best, their relations with him and their portraits of him. More space will be given to Pierre Mignard because of their many ties—personal, financial, professional—and because of the hypothesis developed briefly that Molière and some of his actors visited Rome when Pierre Mignard was there in 1651 and 1652.

In the multitude of interlocking relationships of the five court painters most involved with Molière, the following tableau presents the facts most simply:

NAMES, in chronological order with place of birth; all died in Paris.	PARIS, in the *atelier* of SIMON VOUET (1590–1649) "peintre du roy"	ROME, to work and study in *atelier* of Andrea Sacchi	MEMBERSHIP in the ACADEMIE ROYALE de PEINTURE	PARIS, years as court painters —portraits and murals
NICOLAS MIGNARD born in Troyes (1606–1668)	1627–1633	1635–1637	1663	1660–1671 after 23 years in Avignon
CHARLES-ALPHONSE DUFRESNOY born in Paris (1611–1668)	1630–1633	1633–1656	refused offer of membership	1663–1668 (asst. to Pierre Mignard)
PIERRE MIGNARD born in Troyes (1612–1695)	1633–1635	1635–1657	refused offer of membership during life of Le Brun. 1690 director	1658–1695 from 1690 to 1695 "premier peinture du roy"
SEBASTIEN BOURDON born in Montpellier (1616–1671)	1641–1642 after 3 yrs. in Rome	1638–1641	1648, one of 12 founders	1648–1652 & 1654–1671 (1652–54 court painter in Sweden)
CHARLES LE BRUN born in Paris (1619–1690)	1634–1642	1642–1646	1648, one of 12 founders; director 1662–90	1648–1690 from 1662 to 1690 "premier peinte du roy"

Jean Baptiste Poquelin Moliere

PLATE I: Portrait of Molière by Pierre Mignard, as it appears in Charles Perrault, *Hommes illustres* (Paris, 1696), between pages 89 and 90; courtesy of the Houghton Library, Harvard University.

Our tableau indicates that all these painters knew each other in Paris or in Rome, or both, as young men, and in later life in Paris and Versailles during Molière's years of triumph there (1659–73). The bitter rivalry between Charles Le Brun and Pierre Mignard dated from their student days in Vouet's *atelier*, was intensified in Rome, and lasted all their lives. Molière was directly involved in the affair with his poem on the Val-de-Grâce. In 1663 Mignard and his associate Dufresnoy refused Le Brun's invitation to become members of the Académie royale of which Le Brun had just become *directeur*. In a polite letter[7] they explained briefly they were too busy, "occupez comme nous le serons au Val-de-Grâce." Le Brun retaliated by getting a royal edict which forbade any painter not a member of the Académie royale de peinture from working for the royal family. However, because Pierre Mignard was already so immensely popular in court circles, he continued to do what he wished for his royal patrons—painting their portraits or decorating their apartments. When Louvois, who admired Mignard, took over as *surintendant* after the death of Colbert in 1683, Mignard was charged with the decoration of some of the royal apartments at Versailles, supposedly uniquely under Le Brun's control. On March 1, 1690, just two weeks after Le Brun's death on February 12, Louis XIV appointed Pierre Mignard "premier peintre du roy," and three days later the Académie royale named Pierre Mignard "agréé, membre, chancelier, recteur, et directeur de l'Académie royale de peinture et de sculpture," all in one single day! At the same time the King appointed him "directeur des manufactures des Gobelins" and director of all painting and decorating to be done in all the royal houses. How sad that Molière did not live to see the triumph he had foretold in his poem of 1668 for his friend.[8]

Molière's long poem, *La Gloire du Val-de-Grâce*[9], was written in 1668 and published in 1669 during the bitterest moments of the struggle between his independent friend Pierre Mignard and the younger, more aggressive and dictatorial Le Brun. It is not in the scope of this essay to judge the

---

[7] Letter of February 12, 1663 in ms. *Histoire de l'Académie de peinture* at the Bible. de l'Arsénal, quoted by Anatole Montauflon, *Arch. de l'art français*, I (1851), 267–8.

[8] In the long run, Mignard triumphed completely over his life-long rival. The members of the Académie were not rebellious with him as they had been with Le Brun and asked for a minature of his masterwork for the Académie. This painting is visible in the background of Mignard's self-portrait now in the Louvre.

[9] "Gloire" according to the *Dictionnaire de l'Académie*, Paris, 1694, is "en termes de peinture, la représentation du ciel ouvert avec les personnes divines, les anges et les bien-heureux." In posthumous publications, Molière's poem was entitled more correctly *La Gloire du dôme du Val-de-Grâce*, in *Oeuvres* (1674) vol. III and *Oeuvres* (1682) vol. IV.

artistic merits of these two famous painters whose work is found in most of the major art museums of Europe, but to chronicle their rivalry as background for Molière's poem. Molière had himself suffered rivalries, first with the young Racine, who robbed him of his best actress, and later with the aggressive Lully, who capitalized on their collaboration and then got a royal edict limiting use of music and musicians in Molière's plays. What emerges from all these confrontations is a character difference in men of genius. Some, like Mignard and Molière, show a warmth and humanity by which we are touched over the centuries, and others outrage us by their ruthlessness. They are no less geniuses in their fields but are less likeable as people.

The dramatic climax of the Mignard-Le Brun rivalry (which had smoldered for years) began when Charles Le Brun became "premier peintre du roy" and "directeur de l'Académie royale" in 1662. Under Le Brun, backed by Colbert, the Académie became a dictatorship regulating principles and performance of artists. In March 1663, Anne d'Autriche commissioned Pierre Mignard[10] to do the frescoes on the dome of the Val-de-Grâce.[11] In August, she approved the circular miniature, about three feet in diameter,[12] of Mignard's sketches for the dome paintings, and Loret reported it in his *Muze historique* of August 18, 1663:[13]

> De plus elle vit la peinture
> Surpassant toute mignature
> De l'excellent Monsieur Mignard
> Un des grands maîtres de son Art   Le cadet[14]
> Pour servir d'ornement au Dôme,
> Un des mieux construits du royaume.

Pierre Mignard and Charles Dufresnoy, close friends since their Roman years, completed the painting for a celebration in the church three years later,[15] as noted by the gazeteer Mayolas.

---

[10] Royal contract of March 5, 1663, mentioned in J. Guiffrey, éd.: *Comptes des bâtiments du roy*, I (1665–80), 126, when the final payment on the 33,000 livres for the dome painting was made.

[11] Church erected by Anne d'Autriche, 1645–65, in gratitude for the birth of Louis XIV after many barren years.

[12] This round painting appears in the background of Pierre Mignard's self-portrait in the Louvre.

[13] *La muze historique de Loret*, IV, 89.

[14] "Le cadet" in the margin distinguishes him from brother Nicolas, often marked "l'aîné," or "d'Avignon" in the margins of the gazette.

[15] *Lettre en vers à Son Altesse.* September 19, 1666 (*Continuateurs de Loret,* II, 301). Anne d'Autriche had died in January 1666, and Queen Marie-Thérèse had urged completion of the work.

Molière did not write anything about the project until 1668, in answer to Charles Perrault's poem *La Peintre*, which praised Le Brun extravagantly, calling him the "seul grand artiste" in France. Molière immediately composed a long poem in praise of Mignard's work on the Val-de-Grâce, comparing him to such Italian masters as Raphael and Michelangelo. He made many notes on the art of painting, especially on the difficulties of frescoes,[16] and for this he often used lines translated from Dufresnoy's *De arte graphica*, published by Pierre Mignard after Dufresnoy's death in February 1668.

On December 5, 1668, Molière got a *privilège du roi* for publication of his poem. On December 22 he read the poem aloud in the salon of his friend and able critic, Mlle Honorée de Bussy (1624–1702), niece of his old friend, the philosopher, François de la Mothe Le Vayer (1583–1672).[17] Mlle de Bussy, to insure good publicity for the coming publication of the poem, invited the gazeteer Robinet, who wrote glowingly of his hostess "une illustre de ce temps," of Mignard and his painting, as well as of Molière and his poem.

> Si noble, si brillant, si beau
> Et si digne de son cerveau,
> Sur la Gloire du Val-de-Grâce,
> Où le pinceau de Mignard trace
> Tout ce que son art de grand,
>
> . . . .
> Ce poème savant . . .
> A surpris et charmé tous ceux
> Qui l'ont ouï dans maints bons lieux,
> Où même avecque tant de grâce,
> Suivant sa mémoire à la trace,
> Son grand auteur l'a récité,
> Qu'au double on étoit enchanté.[18]

[16] Fresco painting requires more rapid execution since it is painted on wet plaster and cannot take second thoughts so readily. It is difficult because "the colors change considerably as the plaster dries out" and it requires "more advanced calculation to judge the ultimate color effect than is needed in other techniques" (Reed Kay, *The Painter's Companion*, [Cambridge, 1961], 206, with my thanks to artist Robert Harman). Boileau, who was also a close friend of Mignard's and admired the paintings, wrote: "il préférait les brusques fiertés de la fresque à la paresse de l'huile." (*Récréations littéraires*, 154–55, quoted in Molière: *Oeuvres*, éd. Grands Ecriv., IX, 53).

[17] It was said that Molière frequently read his plays to Mlle de Bussy because of her acute critical sense. He was very fond of her and her cousin, the young abbé François de La Mothe Le Vayer (1625–1664) on whose death Molière wrote a beautiful sonnet. For an interesting and well-documented biography of Honorée de Bussy, see Emile Magne: *Une amie inconnue de Molière* (Paris, 1922); pp. 72–75 treat of the poem on the Val-de-Grâce.

[18] *Lettre en vers à Madame de Robinet*, dated December 22, 1668, quoted in Molière: *Oeuvres*, éd. Grands Ecriv., IX, 522–23.

This letter of Robinet shows that the poem had already been read several times before to different groups and that it was appreciated. The poem was published early in 1669 with vignettes and *culs-de-lampe* engraved from Mignard drawings.[19] Boileau admired Molière's poem and approved his friend's versification. Even Molière's critics, objecting to the content of the poem, praised his poetry. Mlle Elisabeth Sophie Chéron, a young protégée of Colbert and pupil of Le Brun circulated in manuscript a critical poem *La Coupe du Val-de-Grâce à M. de Molière* in which the Dome speaks to Molière and chides him for exaggerated statements about Mignard and for not knowing enough about painting: "Si tu fais bien des vers, tu sçais peu la peinture." The young woman's poem was not printed for thirty years. It appeared in 1700 in *Anonimiana . . .*[20], the introduction of which gives a curious note on Molière's poem, "en faveur de M. Mignard, dont il aimait la fille." This is a very odd suggestion since Catherine Mignard was only eleven at the time of the poem.[21] There were other critical comments and occasional laudatory ones, such as a sonnet by Etienne Martin de Pichesne,[22] and the praise-filled pages of Mignard's biography by the abbé de Monville.[23] After Molière's death, friends of Le Brun sent anonymous letters to Mignard trying to hurt him, insinuating

[19] *La Gloire du Val-de-Grâce*, first edition, was published "chez Jean Ribou," Molière's regular publisher to whom he had sold the *privilège* of December 5, 1668. The second edition, also dated 1669, is published "chez Pierre le Petit" and has an added engraving on the back of the title page, taken from a Mignard drawing, showing Minerva conducting Painting to Apollo, playing his lyre and surrounded by Muses. There is a copy of this latter volume in Houghton Library at Harvard.

[20] *Anonimiana ou mélanges de poésies, d'éloquence et d'érudition* (Paris; Nicolas Pepie, 1700). 241–283.

[21] Catherine Mignard (1657–1742) was born in Rome and legitimized three years later when her parents married in Paris (St. Eustache), probably with Molière as one of the witnesses. When she was only fifteen, she was godmother to Molière's third child, Pierre Poquelin baptized October 1, 1672 (*Cent ans*, 530–31). Catherine was a very beautiful girl and modeled often for her father. A bust of her appears in the lower left hand corner of Mignard's self-portrait in the Louvre. Since Mignard often painted her as St. Catherine, it is quite possible that the "Sainte Catherine" among the paintings (all without artist's name) in Molière's *inventaire après décès* (*Cent ans*, 560) might have been a gift of his friend Mignard. She adored her father and remained single as long as he lived, but the year after his death, May 1, 1696, she married Jules Pas, comte de Feuquières. She lived a long life and gave her father's biographer most of the important information about him (some of it incorrect for obvious reasons, such as having her father marry in Rome in 1656). He published his *Vie de Mignard* (Paris, 1730), which was enlarged the following year: l'abbé Simon Philippe Mazière de Monville: *Vie de Pierre Mignard, premier peintre du roi, avec le poëme de Molière sur les peintures du Val-de-Grâce et deux dialogues de M. de Fénélon sur la peinture* (Amsterdam, 1731).

[22] *Sonnet à M. de Molière sur son poème de la Gloire du Val-de-Grâce*, published in his *Poésies héroiques ...*, Paris, 1670, and reprinted in *Le Moliériste*, V (1883), 181.

[23] See footnote 21 above.

that Molière had really been making fun of him in the poem on the Val-de-Grâce. One of these letters said:

> Vous ne trouverez plus un Molière pour prendre ce soin et pour publier que Jules Annibal, Raphael et Michel Ange ont été les Mignards de leur siècle. . . . En votre conscience, avez-vous cru ce que Molière a dit de vous et de ces grands peintres? Ne le soupçonnez-vous pas d'avoir usé en cette occasion de sa malice ordinaire, qui, par des contre-sens ingénieux et par des invectives envelopées, détruit ce qu'il voulait détruire?[24]

Mignard's son intercepted the letter and burned it, but not without having shown it to friends who might answer. One of them wrote Le Brun: "Ce qu'il [Mignard] a fait depuis la mort de Molière confirme ce que cet auteur a dit de lui. On désire partout ses ouvrages; la reine d'Espagne, le roi d'Angleterre et d'autres puissances en demandent tous les jours et ne songent pas que vous soyez au monde. Vos patrons mêmes en veulent dans leurs cabinets. Il est estimé en France aussi bien qu'ailleurs par tout ce qu'il y a de grand. Qu'a-t-il de plus à souhaiter?"[25] Nothing came of the battle of words. Pierre Mignard continued to be an independent and very successful court painter in spite of anything Le Brun could do. And when Louvois took over at Colbert's death in 1683, Le Brun's power waned until his death in 1690, when Pierre Mignard triumphantly took over all Le Brun's titles and powers.

After completing the Val-de-Grâce dome in 1666 or even before, it is possible that Mignard suggested doing a Molière portrait. Several of Mignard's portraits of Molière as a mature man seem to date from this period.[26] Shortly thereafter, Molière wrote a short comedy for the celebration at Saint-Germain-en-Laye given by Louis XIV to mark the end of a year of mourning for his mother, Anne d'Autriche. *Le Sicilien, ou l'Amour peintre* was first performed at Saint-Germain on February 14, 1667, during the festivities which lasted from December 1, 1660, to February 20, 1667, when Molière's troupe went back to Paris.[27]

Surely there is a connection between the scene of the portrait painting in *Le Sicilien* and Molière's visits to Mignard's studio, either when Mignard

---

[24] Jules Fontaine, *Académiciens d'autrefois* (Paris, 1914), 164–65.

[25] *Ibid.*, 167.

[26] See Plates I, II, and III accompanying this article and the Chantilly portrait of Molière reproduced in color on the cover of *Cent ans* in 1963.

[27] *Le Régistre de La Grange*, éd. Young, 2 vol. (Paris, 1948), I, 87–88. *Le Sicilien* was not produced in Paris until June 10, 1667, because of Molière's severe illness after Easter (with the theater closed from March 27 to May 27). Then *Le Sicilien* appeared in a double bill with Corneille's *Attila*, and later with *Rodogune* or *L'Amour médecin*. Robinet recorded in his

was painting court ladies (portraits the court called "mignardes" because of their charm) or was doing the portrait of Molière himself. In their conversations about portrait painting, Mignard must have complained about those great ladies, who did not want a true portrait but an idealization of themselves. In scene 6, Molière puts these ideas into the mouth of his charming young heroine, Isidore who speaks to her love Adraste, a French nobleman, disguised as a painter. As she sits for her portrait, she says:

> Je ne suis pas comme ces femmes qui veulent, en se faisant peindre, des portraits qui ne sont point elles, et ne sont point satisfaites du peintre s'il ne les fait toujours plus belles que le jour. Il faudroit, pour les contenter, ne faire qu'un portrait pour toutes; car toutes demandent les mêmes choses: un teint tout de lis et de roses, un nez bien fait, une petite bouche, et de grands yeux vifs, bien fendus, et surtout le visage pas plus gros que le poing, l'eussent-elles d'un pied de large. Pour moi, je vous demande un portrait qui soit moi, et qui m'oblige point à demander qui c'est.[28]

Adraste replies with graceful compliments to Isidore as he paints. Finally Dom Pèdre, Isidore's master, protests that Adraste does too much talking to his model, and Adraste answers, as Mignard himself might well have done: "J'ai toujours de coutume de parler quand je peins; et il est besoin, dans ces choses, d'un peu de conversation, pour réveiller l'esprit et tenir les visages dans la gaieté nécessaire aux personnes que l'on veut peindre." Perhaps that was the real secret of Mignard's great success as a portrait painter, for he seems to have seized not just the physical exterior of his subjects but their complete personality, which accomplishment perhaps explains why his portrait of Molière now at Chantilly is one of the most beloved of the Molière portraits.

This matter of Molière's portraits has been treated many times in the past hundred years, but there are many errors in much of the material, and it is only in the past fifteen years or so we have found, especially in

---

Lettre en vers à Madame of June 19, 1667, high praise for the play with its *jeu de mots*: "mignature," subtly noting the presence of Mignard in the background:

> Je vis à mon aise et très bien,
> Dimanche, le Sicilien.
> C'est un chef-d'œuvre, je vous jure,
> Où paroissent en mignature,
> Et comme dans leur plus beau jour,
> Et la jalousie et l'amour.

(Quoted in Molière, *Oeuvres*, éd. Grands Ecriv., VI, 211.)
[28] *Oeuvres*, éd. Grands Ecriv., VI, 263.

the articles of René-Thomas Coèle,[29] more exact material about the portraits by Sébastien Bourdon, Nicolas and Pierre Mignard. It is not in the scope of this study to give details about all of the various portraits of Molière and copies of them by engravers and sculptors then and later. However, by working over the details of the lives of the court painters Molière knew best, it is possible to make some statement about the moments in his career when such paintings might have been made.

Nineteenth-century scholars[30] recorded much incorrect data in their articles about portraits of Molière. They sometimes assigned dates to a painting when neither Molière nor the artist was in the place suggested. For instance, two of the three portraits by Bourdon, one in Montpellier and one in Montauban, are probably not of Molière at all, and the third, in the Musée Cantini in Marseille, though an authentic portrait of Molière in Roman dress, is incorrectly dated by an inscription on the back "Molière . . . en costume de théâtre à l'âge de trente ans pendant la tournée qu'il fit en Languedoc". (See Plate IV) This would mean 1652, and the date is impossible since Bourdon was in Paris (1649–52) and then court painter of Queen Christina in Sweden from October 1652 to June 1654 (when the Queen abdicated and the Bourdons returned to Paris).

Montpellier's Musée Fabre contains a Bourdon portrait of a dark young man in black. In 1882 Auguste Baluffe[31] suggested this *Portrait d'un jeune Espagnol* as it was then called, was really Molière. The great Moliériste Georges Monval[32] doubted it for many reasons even then, and today the Musée Fabre calls it simply *L'homme aux rubans noirs* and makes no mention of Molière. (See Plate V.)

Monval[33] also had doubts about the Montauban portrait attributed to Bourdon and said to be a portrait of Molière. In 1850 the painter Ingres

---

[29] Articles by René-Thomas Coèle on Molière portraits (*RHT: Revue d'histoire du théâtre*)
"Le Molière en habit de théâtre [par Bourdon] du Musée Cantini à Marseille," *RHT* (1956), 45–47;
"Madeleine Béjart et Molière, modèles des peintres Nicolas et Pierre Mignard," *RHT* (1957), 276–90;
"*La Comédie française 1680–1962* au Château de Versailles (mai-octobre 1962)," *RHT* (1962), 242–45.
[30] Paul Lacroi's *Iconographie moliéresque*, 2e éd. (Paris, 1876), is an invaluable aid in tracing material on Molière's portraits and in giving good descriptions of the paintings, even though the dates and circumstances of their origins are often incorrect.
[31] Auguste Baluffe, "Un portrait de Molière par Sébastien Bourdon," in *L'Artiste*, 52e année (1882), 267–82. Note that Baluffe is a notoriously inaccurate scholar.
[32] *Le Moliériste*, IV (1882–83), 319.
[33] *Le Moliériste*, V (1883–84), 2.

donated the painting to Montauban. An article of 1879 by Armand Cambon, director of the Musée de Montauban,[34] where the painting was hung, is full of errors about Bourdon and Molière. The engraving of the painting shows it to be very unlike other portraits of the young Molière, and Monval was quite right to question it. The putative Bourdon portrait of Molière now in the Musée Cantini in Marseille (see Plate IV) was probably painted about 1656. It shows a young Molière who resembles in face and costume the Molière of the portraits by Nicolas Mignard done in 1657: the one now owned by the Comédie-Française of Molière-Caesar in Corneille's *La Mort de Pompée*[35] (see Plate VI) and the other, now in the Musée Granet of Aix-en-Provence, (not reproduced here) where Molière-Mars is about to embrace Madeleine-Venus.

When did Molière first know Sébastien Bourdon (1616–71)? Bourdon perhaps knew Madeleine Béjart in Paris when he was a student at Simon Vouet's in 1641 and 1642, since Madeleine's aunt was related to Vouet by marriage, and since the art and theater world of the great city invariably meet. Whether or not Madeleine, and perhaps Molière, knew Bourdon earlier, it is quite possible they had contacts with him in 1649, when Bourdon was called back to Montpellier from Paris for a year on some commissions for the comte d'Aubijoux. The latter knew Molière, having seen the Molière-Dufresne troupe, "comédiens du duc d'Epernon," play in both Toulouse and Albi in July 1647 (*Cent ans*, 295–96). In 1649 Molière and the troupe played in Agen and Cadillac in residences of the duc d'Epernon, and in Toulouse for the comte du Roure, of Montpellier, Bourdon's birthplace (*Cent ans*, 302–03). However, it is more likely that Bourdon painted the Marseille portrait of Molière in 1656 or 1657. Bourdon had again left Paris for a stay in Montpellier on business from 1656 to 1658. During this time, Molière and his troupe, then called "les comédiens du prince de Conti," played for the Etats de Languedoc, presided over by the comte du Roure, in whose home Sébastien Bourdon was a frequent visitor, commissioned to make portraits for Grésinde de

---

[34] "Notice artistique sur le portrait de Molière," in Gérard de Boulan, *L'énigme d'Alceste* (Paris, 1879), i–vii.

[35] It was natural that Bourdon and Mignard should paint Molière in the Roman costume of a Corneille play, since Molière featured Corneille frequently in his programs in the Illustre Théâtre of 1643–45, in the provinces 1645–58, and in the years in Paris 1658–73. A year or so after the Mignard portraits, in May 1658, Molière and his troupe went to Rouen and visited with Pierre and Thomas Corneille, after putting on their plays in the local theater. They stayed for three months, during which time Molière went to Paris occasionally to make court contacts, perhaps through the good offices of his friend Pierre Mignard.

PLATE II: Engraving of Molière (1685) by Jean=Baptiste Nolin; based on the Mignard painting (Plate I); reproduced from *Gazette des Beaux=arts*, 3e série VIII (1892), 511.

PLATE III: Portrait of Molière by Pierre Mignard, now at the Comédie=Française, to which it was bequeathed by Samuel Scheikevitch in 1909 from his Moscow collection; from the Collection de la Comédie=Française.

PLATE IV: Molière as Caesar in Corneille's *La Mort de Pompée*, painted by Sébastien Bourdon; courtesy of the Musée Cantini, Marseille.

PLATE V: "L'Homme aux rubans noirs," portrait of an unknown young man, thought by some to be a portrait of Molière by Sébastien Bourdon, but generally accepted by experts as not being Molière; courtesy of the Musée Fabre, Monpellier.

Baudan, comtesse du Roure. "Grésinde," the unusual name of Boudon's patroness, rarely found outside of Languedoc, has led us (*Cent ans*, 131n.) to the conclusion that the comtesse du Roure, like Armand de Bourbon, prince de Conti, had some part in the christening of Armande-Grésinde-Claire-Elisabeth Béjart, Molière's future wife.[36]

Besides the one sure portrait of Molière by Sébastien Bourdon, tradition has it that Charles Le Brun also painted one. There is a profile portrait of Molière, attributed to Le Brun, in the Pushkin Museum in Moscow (see Plate VII).[37] The possibility that Molière might have sat for Le Brun, the arch enemy of Pierre Mignard, seems unlikely. And yet there was the possibility in 1661 when Molière and Le Brun worked together on the famous, ill-fated Fête de Vaux for the *surintendant* Nicolas Fouquet. Le Brun had been in charge of all the decoration for the château and was now responsible for the theatrical decorations and background for Molière's play *Les Fâcheux* and the shell which opened to let the Nymphe-

---

[36] Though somewhat outside the scope of this article, this footnote grows out of the possible connection between Molière and Bourdon, whose patroness was Grésinde de Baudan, comtesse du Roure. Whether Molière's wife, Armande-Grésinde Béjart, was the sister of Madeleine, as all legal documents say she was, or the daughter, as many persist in believing because of other evidence, is not of moment here. There is always the mystery in any case of when and where Armande was baptized. Much research in the archives of southern France in recent years has failed to unearth anything certain. However, we found frequently, especially in that region, records of a child *ondoyé*, or ritually baptized, at birth and then having a formal baptism-christening as much as ten years later. Here are three cases close to the Molière story, in Languedoc and Vaucluse:

1) The comte du Roure and his wife, Grésinde de Baudan, had several children baptized eight to ten years after birth (Arch. mun. de Montpellier).
2) A second cousin of the comte du Roure, Esprit de Rémond, comte de Mondène, who figures so prominently in the lives of Madeleine Béjart, the L'Hermite family, and even Molière, had an elaborate baptism-christening for his son Gaston-Jean-Baptiste in the Palais des Papes at Avignon, October 10, 1632, with Gaston d'Orléans as godfather, two years after the child's birth in Paris (Arch. dépt. de Vaucluse, GG Saint Genest).
3) One of Molière's actors, Pierre Réveillon de Chasteauneuf, had a son who received "l'eau de baptême" at birth in Narbonne, August 16, 1645, and who was baptised "Bernard" in Agen, March 7, 1650, with Bernard de Nogaret, duc d'Epernon (patron of Molière) as godfather (Arch. Lot et Garonne GG 1; this document speaks of the previous ceremony in 1645 in Narbonne, but I was unable to find the record in the Arch. com. de Narbonne).

Is it not logical to suppose that Armande-Grésinde Béjart, wherever she was born and no matter who her parents were, was "ondoyée" at birth, was perhaps "la petite non baptisée" of Marie Hervé's Paris document, March 10, 1643 (*Cent ans*, 643), and then given a full baptism-christening about 1653 with Armand de Bourbon, prince de Conti, as godfather and Grésinde de Baudan, comtesse du Roure, as godmother? (Suggested in our note, *Cent ans*, 131). There is still hope the document may be unearthed some day.

[37] This museum has a number of paintings by Charles Le Brun, Pierre Mignard, and Sébastien Bourdon, though none by Nicolas Mignard.

Madeleine Béjart rise and read Pellisson's prologue to the entertainment. Lacroix,[38] on the other hand, suggests it is a later portrait and might date from 1669, after Colbert intervened, prevailed on Molière not to reprint his poem *La Gloire du Val-de-Grâce*, and urged Le Brun to paint the Molière portrait to "consacrer leur repatriage."

By far the greatest number of portraits of Molière we know are engravings or other reproductions of paintings done by the two Mignard brothers, Nicolas and Pierre. The confusion concerning these portraits has been clarified in a scholarly manner by René-Thomas Coèle.[39] It is very possible that the confusion was intensified by Pierre, who outlived his brother by twenty-seven very successful years. The rivalry between the brothers in Paris court circles was very great. On May 6, 1661, Nicolas wrote a bitter letter from Paris to a friend in Avignon,[40] stating that his younger brother was taking all the best contracts for portraits of the King and Queen, was ambitiously ruthless, for instance telling the duc d'Epernon that Nicolas was not a painter, and in other ways hurting his prospects. Nicolas speaks of Pierre's ingratitude, thinking of the year in Avignon, and then writes: "Je luy pardonne comme bon chrestien et prie Dieu qu'il amande." But the hard feelings only increased when Nicolas accepted membership in the Académie royale de peinture in 1663 and became Charles Le Brun's assistant in the decoration of apartments in the Tuileries and Versailles, thereby allying himself with Pierre's bitter enemy. When Nicolas died on March 17, 1668 (probably from overwork for Le Brun), Pierre did not go to the funeral. He did, however, take into his studio Paul Mignard (1641–91), son of Nicolas, who became a painter of some note in Lyon and a member of the Académie royale in 1672.

It has been suggested that Pierre Mignard may have encouraged the confusion about their paintings, but I do not think it was done deliberately. Pierre Mignard became definitely the more famous of the two, who were equally well known in Paris and in court circles in the early 1660's. Nicolas died in 1668, and his brother continued for twenty-seven years afterward, working on Versailles and other royal palaces, as well as painting many portraits. Pierre has tended to eclipse his older brother in the minds of

---

[38] Lacroix, *Iconographie moliéresque, op. cit.*, no. 11.

[39] Article already noted (*RHT*, 1957) written with the help of Mlle Dubuisson of the Musée de Troyes, who made a catalogue of the paintings of Pierre and Nicolas Mignard for an exposition in Troyes in 1955.

[40] Bibliothèque d'Avignon, ms. 2371, fol. 77, letter to Henri de Félix, lawyer of Avignon. Adrien Marcel (in his very complete article "Mignard d'Avignon, peintre et graveur (1607–68), "*Mém. Acad. de Vaucluse*, XXXI (1931), 1–111) chronicles in detail (37–45) the rivalry between the two brothers in their professional and personal contacts.

most laymen, but even from the art critic's point of view, Nicolas is less prominent. There are no Nicolas Mignard paintings in the Louvre, or in the Pushkin Museum in Moscow, for example. The rivalry of these brothers is no longer important at this distance, so long as we can continue to enjoy their paintings of Molière which bring him to us so vividly.

The most striking of all the portraits, to my mind, is that of the young Molière and Madeleine Béjart by Nicolas Mignard now in the Musée Granet at Aix-en-Provence. Nicolas had watched Madeleine and Molière rehearsing and playing in the *jeu de paume* below his studio, and he seems to have captured the deep feeling between these two as Molière-Mars reaches out to draw into his arms the lovely Titian-blonde Madeleine-Venus. Here is the essence of that love and comradeship which endured to the very end. (On February 17, 1673, Molière could not have failed to remember that it was exactly one year to the day since Madeleine's death, and his body, worn by work, sorrow, discouragement, disillusion and dreadful illness, succombed as he mourned her.)

In this painting, Molière is wearing the same Roman costume which we see in the painting of the Molière-Caesar portrait at the Comédie-Française and in the Bourdon portrait at Marseille (Plates VI and IV). M. Coèle has noted that this same costume appears in the frontespiece[41] of Tristan L'Hermite's *La mort de Chrispé* with Madeleine-Fauste and Molière-Chrispé speaking together in the Jacques Stella engraving of 1645, when that play, premiered by the Illustre Théâtre, was first published.

A study of other portraits of Molière by the Mignard brothers shows an interesting difference, dramatically evident in the series of reproductions in the Coèle article of 1957.[42] In the Nicolas Mignard portraits the face and eyes are turned to the left side of the painting (Plate VI), and those by Pierre Mignard show the eyes front and the body somewhat turned to the right. (See Plates I, II, and III.) Until 1956, all the "Mignard" portraits at the Comédie-Française were thought to be by Pierre, but now we discover that all but one are by Nicolas. The one by Pierre Mignard was acquired in Moscow by Samuel Scheikevitch in 1891 and bequeathed to the Comédie-Française in 1909. (See Plate III.)[43] This portrait resembles somewhat the great Pierre Mignard portrait at Chantilly belonging to

---

[41] Coèle, *art. cit.*, *RHT* (1957) Plate I, between 288 and 289.

[42] *Ibid.*, a series of twelve plates, between 288 and 289.

[43] Samuel Scheikevitch, "Un portrait de Molière signé P. Mignard," in *Gazette des beaux-arts*, 3e sér. VIII (1892), 508–15 and also Coèle, *op. cit.*, *RHT* (1962).

the duc d'Aumale.[44] Not only is the facial expression the same, but even the chemise and the silk dressing gown with its soft folds of dark and light.

Besides the problem of the portraits of Molière himself, there is the matter of those paintings which were found in Molière's home at his death. In no case is the name of the artist given. We have noted above "une Saincte Catherine" (*Cent ans*, 560) as possibly a portrait of Catherine Mignard by her father, and there are two portraits among Molière's etchings: one "de la feue royne mere" and the other "du seigneur mareschal de Turenne" (*Cent ans*, 557). These are almost certainly engraved from Pierre Mignard paintings because he did several portraits of both of these people. There is a large painting "une Famille de Jésus" (*Cent ans*, 565) which might possibly be by Sébastien Bourdon since he produced a number of paintings on that subject. The fact that Molière's friend and physician, Jean-Armand de Mauvillain, had two paintings by Bourdon (a *Suzanne* and *Un Triomphe de Bacchus*)[45] in his *inventaire après décès* makes one think that perhaps one or more of the several paintings Molière owned were by Sébastien Bourdon. Could the "Famille de Jésus" of the Molière *inventaire* be the same as a *Sainte Famille* by Bourdon which turned up at a sale in Paris in 1840 with this note on the back?[46]

> Donné par mon ami Séb. Bourdon, peintre du Roy
> et Directeur de l'Académie de peinture.
> Paris ce Vingt quatriéme de Juin mil six cens septante
> J.-B.-P. Molière

It is immediately clear that this inscription is a forgery. The handwriting resembles none of Molière's signatures; Molière never used the accent on his name, never used hypthens between the initials, and his *paraphe* was never as written there.[47] Furthermore, Bourdon was never "directeur," only "recteur" of the Académie royale de peinture (very rarely called only "Académie de peinture"). The fact that the inscription on the back is a forgery[48] does not preclude the idea that this Bourdon painting itself might at one time have belonged to Molière.

---

[44] A color reproduction of this portrait was used for the cover of *Cent ans*.

[45] *Inventaire après décès* du 23 juillet 1685, Min. centr. LII, 110. Mauvillain also had a "Sainte Catherine," artist unnamed. Could it also be by Pierre Mignard?

[46] A facsimile of this is given in P. Jul. Fontaine: *Découverte d'un autographe de Molière* (Paris, 1840).

[47] See page of various signatures of Molière in *Cent ans*, 100.

[48] See also discussion of it in our article: "Etat actuel des autographes de Molière, établi par Mrs. Elizabeth Maxfield Miller . . . avec l'aide de Mme Madeleine Jurgens . . . ," in *RHT* (1955), 296–97.

PLATE VI: Molière as Caesar in Corneille's *La Mort de Pompée*, by Nicolas Mignard although long attributed to Pierre Mignard; from the Collection de la Comédie=Française.

PLATE VII: Portrait of Molière attributed to Charles Le Brun; courtesy of the Pushkin Museum of Fine Arts, Moscow.

The portraits of the mature Molière by Pierre Mignard, done in the Paris period, reveal the depth of character which he probably showed more openly to this dear friend than to any other. There were close ties here, financial, social and very personal, so that a life of either without the other, or without consideration of Madeleine Béjart, whom they both loved, is incomplete. Pierre Mignard is supposed to have met Molière for the first time in Avignon in 1657, when Molière and his troupe were playing in the *jeu de paume* belonging to Nicolas Mignard and his wife,[49] and leased to Daniel Herbouillet. Pierre Mignard had been called to Paris from Rome by the young Louis XIV because of the success of his portraits of French dignitaries passing through Rome.[50] Pierre stopped for a year in his brother's home in Avignon (where he had visited briefly in 1641, his only visit back to France in twenty-two years). Here he met Molière and went with the troupe to Lyon before going on to Paris. There Pierre was caught up in court circles, but pleasant memories of Avignon led him to ask his brother to buy for him a nearby property. Nicolas bought for him on August 9, 1658,[51] the "terre et grange de Realpanier" near Avignon from Marc-Antoine de Laurens, a cousin of Esprit de Rémond, who turns up frequently in the story of Molière and the Béjarts. In October 1658, Pierre contracted for repairs and alterations on the property. Nicolas handled Pierre's affairs in Avignon until the open break between the brothers about 1663.

Up to now, it has always been thought that Molière did not know Pierre Mignard before 1657. Catherine Mignard had mentioned the meeting then when she gave the abbé de Monville material for his biography of her father in 1730, as we have seen. But I am suggesting an interesting hypothesis—that Madeleine Béjart, whom Pierre Mignard had probably known in Paris, Molière, and two or three others of the troupe went to Rome in 1651–52 where Pierre Mignard had been living since 1635. Could Molière have gone to Rome in 1651–52 during the terrors of the Fronde and pestilence and famine which stalked the land during those two years when Molière and several of his comedians drop out of sight completely? There is nothing known about either Molière or Madeleine Béjart in the sixteen month period between April 4, 1651 (*Cent ans*, 307), when Molière signed a recept in Paris for money from his

---

[49] *Cent ans*, 116. See also Adrien Marcel, *op. cit.*

[50] When Pierre Mignard got settled in Paris, he was commissioned to paint the portrait of the young Louis XIV which was sent to Marie-Thérèse d'Autriche, his fiancée, in 1660.

[51] Arch. dépt. de Vaucluse, Fonds Vincenti 2084.

mother's estate, until August 12, 1652, in Grenoble (*Cent ans*, 307–08), when Molière was godfather and Madeleine godmother for the son of Catherine Le Clerc and her husband, Edme Villequin, sieur de Brie. These two had been separate and single actors in 1650 (she in Molière's troupe), and now they were man and wife. No document indicating time or place of their marriage has been discovered. Could they have been married in Rome?

At the end of 1650, Molière and his troupe had found themselves without a patron, for the duc d'Epernon was now to be governor of Bourgogne and had left Guyenne, where the battles of the Fronde were raging in 1651, only to find more battles in Dijon. There was unrest everywhere. There were famines and floods in Southern France. Where did Molière and his actors go? Not to Dijon to follow their patron, the duc d'Epernon, because of the Fronde which continued against him there. Not to Savoie to the court of the half-sister of their first patron, Gaston d'Orléans, since Christine de France (1606–60), duchesse de Savoie, was also having military troubles. Why not to Italy? It is an attractive possibility. Pierre Mignard, whom the Béjarts knew, had been settled in Rome since 1635, and could perhaps have helped them find a patron among the French dignitaries there.

There are many connections between Pierre and Nicolas Mignard and the entourage of Molière. The Mignard brothers were born and brought up in Troyes, about one hundred miles from Paris. It was a town where Madeleine Béjart's grandfather and Uncle François Béjart were respected *notaires*. The Béjarts and Mignards had probably known each other in Paris. The Mignard brothers studied painting with Simon Vouet, whose second wife was related by marriage to Madeleine Béjart's aunt Marguerite Béjart.[52] Pierre as a gay young art student in his twenties surely frequented the society of art and theater in Paris and probably knew the charming young red-headed actress Madeleine Béjart very well even in those days. She was six years younger than he.

Madeleine's lover in the period from 1636 until 1640 was Esprit de Rémond, seigneur and later comte de Modène, *chambellan* of Gaston d'Orléans. Their illegitimate daughter Françoise was baptised in St. Eustache, July 11, 1638 (*Cent ans*, 639). Esprit de Rémond had property near Avignon in Carpentras and the château de Modène. The reason for

---

[52] For explanation of these relationships see *Cent ans*, 73, with notes on Simon Vouet's second marriage July 1, 1640, Min. centr., VII, 29.

Nicolas Mignard's moving to Avignon in 1637 is not completely clear but may have had something to do with these Paris connections. The life of Esprit de Rémond is intricately woven with that of several people in Molière's entourage besides Madeleine Béjart. His *chambellan* was Jean-Baptiste L'Hermite (brother of Molière's playwright friend Tristan L'Hermite), whose wife Marie Courtin and daughter Madeleine L'Hermite were actresses in Molière's troupe. Marie Courtin, Madeleine Béjart's aunt, was at one point also mistress of Esprit de Rémond, and in 1666 Madeleine L'Hermite became Esprit's second wife.[53] Nicolas Mignard was involved with all these people in affairs around Avignon, and Pierre Mignard bought property nearby from a cousin of Esprit de de Rémond.[54] Madeleine Béjart handled a lot of financial matters for Esprit de Rémond and remained on good terms with him long after their liaison ended. Molière himself was directly involved with Esprit de Rémond, who was godfather (and Madeleine godmother) of Molière's daughter Esprit-Madeleine Poquelin in 1665 (*Cent ans*, 406). In 1647 Esprit de Rémond accompanied Henri, duc de Guise, to his post as governor in Naples. On the way they stopped in Rome, where Pierre Mignard painted a famous portrait of the duc de Guise.

Were there other reasons Molière might have been drawn to Rome? He admired the Eternal City, and in his poem on the Val-de-Grâce, he gave thanks to Rome for having formed his friend Mignard: "Ce grand homme, chez toi devenu tout Romain." As a devoted classicist, Molière would have wanted to see the city of Terrence and Plautus, whose comedies he admired and who profoundly influenced his own comic inventions.

Molière's plays were also greatly influenced by Italian comedies (and the *commedia dell'arte*) and by the Italian actors with whom he shared his Paris theaters from 1659 until 1673.[55] Did he perhaps know some of these Italian actors earlier in 1651–52 in Rome? Tiberio Fiorilli

---

[53] See note 36 above.

[54] Many documents in the Archives départementales de Vaucluse at Avignon.

[55] See A. Vitu: "Molière et les Italiens . . . ," in *Le Moliériste*, I (1879–80), 227–42. The two troupes shared everything: theaters, decorations, alterations, scenery, costumes, the "machiniste" Jacques Torelli (until 1661) and Torelli's servant, Marie Saint Aubin, as concierge (*Le Registre de la Grange, op. cit.* I, 6). Their friendships were close, and a contemporary, M. de Palaprat (*Oeuvres* of 1712 quoted by Vitu, *op. cit.*, 236–38) tells of regular Saturday night suppers in 1671 in Paris where Molière and Scaramouche were among the guests at the home of a Florentine painter, Antonio Verrio. The closeness of the two troupes is illustrated by a painting now owned by the Comédie-Française called "Les farceurs français et italiens depuis 60 ans, peints en 1670" (see Vitu, *op. cit.*) showing Molière (as Arnolphe) and two other French comedians with a number of the Italian actors, all on the stage of the Palais Royal.

PLATE VIII: Portrait of Molière by Pierre Mignard; courtesy of the Musée Condé, Chantilly.

(1608–94), better known as Scaramouche, greatest of them all and who was said to have been Molière's teacher of mime, was in Rome from 1649 to 1653 between two highly successful long periods of playing in Paris. In Rome at the same time was the "machiniste" Giacomo (Jacques) Torelli[56] who did not go up to Paris until 1652. Did Molière perhaps know these two in Rome in the time under question?

Many isolated facts thus juxtaposed here have led me to suggest that Molière might have gone to Rome in that mysterious undocumented period from April 1651 to August 1652, and to have known Pierre Mignard, Scaramouche and Torelli, all there at that time. It is a tempting hypothesis.[57]

Leaving our hypothesis in the realm of speculation where it belongs, let us return to the facts and the certain dates of 1657–58, when Pierre Mignard followed Molière and his troupe to Lyon as he headed for Paris. Mignard was perhaps present at the baptism of Jean-Baptiste Le Masson, December 24, 1957, in Lyon (*Cent ans* 325–26), when Molière was godfather.[58]

In 1658 Molière and the troupe came to Paris and lived not far from the residence of Pierre Mignard. It is possible that, since Pierre Mignard had been called back to Paris by Mazarin and the young King, Mignard's credit in court circles helped Molière to make connections for the patronage of the troupe and for the playing before the King. It was also helpful, of course, that Molière's previous patrons had all been members of the royal family—Gaston d'Orléans, the duc d'Epernon, and the prince de Conti,[59] as was his new patron "Monsieur," Philippe d'Anjou, brother of Louis XIV and nephew of Gaston d'Orléans, whose title he would take in 1660 when his uncle died. Monsieur remained Molière's patron until August 1665, when the company became officially "la troupe du roi" (*Cent ans*, 409).

In 1658, then, Molière and his troupe had been established in the old

---

[56] Jacques Torelli went to Paris in 1652 and was named "ingénieur du roi" in 1655. In 1661, after working on the Fête de Vaux for Fouquet, he was replaced by Charles Vigarany.

[57] Edouard Fournier makes a wonderful statement about hypotheses in a letter of October 5, 1879 to Georges Monval (in *Le Moliériste*, I (1879–80), 250): "Les hypothèses, quoiqu'on dise . . . ont du bon. Très souvent elles trouvent la piste du renseignement, et l'on n'a plus qu'à le chercher au gîte. Sans le probable, le 'prouvé' qu'il fait flairer de plus ou moins près, ne serait pas toujours déniché."

[58] As we have seen earlier in this study, the child's brother Zaccharie, born in Paris about 1660, was apprenticed to Pierre Mignard in 1672. See note 5 above.

[59] See my article: "New findings on Molière and on his first patron in Southern France: Bernard de Nogaret, duc d'Epernon," in *Romance Notes* X (1968), 94–102, especially the genealogical chart showing the relationships of the six patrons of Molière.

Théâtre du Marais, but after playing before the King on October 24, they were granted the theater of the Petit-Bourbon, in which they played alternately with the Italian troupe.

In 1659, the success of *Les Précieuses ridicules* opened doors everywhere for Molière, and with his friend Mignard he found himself in the salons of Mme de la Sablière and Ninon de Lenclos, along with Chapelle, La Fontaine, Boileau, Rohault, and his physician-friend Mauvillain. They also frequented the home of François de la Mothe Le Vayer and enjoyed the company of the latter's witty niece, Honorée de Bussy, in her salon.

When Pierre Mignard married his lovely Roman mistress Angela Avolaria, in St. Eustache, August 12, 1660 (to legitimize his two children born in Italy), Molière was probably present since his troupe was not playing that day.[60] Two years later when Molière married Armande Béjart in St. Germain l'Auxerrois, February 25, 1662, Pierre Mignard was probably one of the "autres" mentioned in the church record in addition to the immediate family who signed. It is probable that others like Chapelle, Boileau, Rohault and Mauvillain were present, as well as many of the actors of the troupe, for La Grange himself writes of it. Pierre Mignard would have gone to the wedding on account of the Béjarts as well as for Molière because he was so often intimately associated with that family. He appeared as witness in the marriage contract of Geneviève Béjart (1624–75) and Léonard de Loménie (1634–72), "bourgeois de Paris" from Limoges,[61] November 25, 1664 (*Cent ans*, 396–98). There was an earlier marriage contract for Geneviève, June 30, 1664, to a certain Jean de Courbes in which Pierre Mignard was *not* a witness. As we have seen in the study of minor painters connected with Molière, it is possible that Pierre Mignard knew some reason this painter should not marry Geneviève and the affair was dropped (*Cent ans*, 391–93).

In January 1672, Pierre Mignard was named one of the executors in Madeleine Béjart's will (*Cent ans*, 656); in March he signed the *inventaire* after her death (*Cent ans*, 505–09), and he handled many financial matters for Armande, in addition to the settlement of Madeleine's estate in which Armande was "légataire universelle."

[60] *Contrat de mariage* of August 2, 1660, found recently by Madame Jurgens in the *Archives nationales*, Min. centr. LXV, 52.

[61] Research in Limoges brought to light no documents to confirm the legend that Molière played in that town, but did uncover the birth record of Léonard de Loménie, whose parents were named in the *contrat de mariage* (*Cent ans*, 396). He was baptised in St. Maurice of Limoges, November 17, 1634 (Arch. com. de Limoges GG 7, fol. 9 r° St. Maurice) which shows he was *ten* years younger than Geneviève.

Less than five months before Molière's death, Catherine Mignard was godmother to Molière's third child, Pierre-Jean-Baptiste-Armand Poquelin, October 1, 1672 (*Cent ans*, 530–31), as we have mentioned before. Pierre Mignard was possibly present also, and it is likely he was at the funeral of the child on October 12th, trying to console his grieving friends (*Cent ans*, 532).

We shall not belabor the many connections between Molière and Mignard in Paris. They frequented the same salons and had many of the same close friends. They moved in the same court circles and were both esteemed by Louis XIV and his family. Their personal lives were very close because of their mutual involvements with the Béjart family and because of their independence of spirit in creative activity. Each gave the other moral support in difficulties. It is possible, for instance, that Pierre suggested Marc-Antoine Charpentier (1636–1704) whom he had known in Rome,[62] when Molière was looking for a musical collaborator for *Le Malade imaginaire* (1673) after Lully had abandoned him.

The last years of Molière's life were filled with the struggles of various men of genius around him against more authoritarian mentalities in the Facultés and the Académies. There were bitter rivalries in all fields, and Molière tasted the agony of it personally as he watched the growing ascendancy, to his detriment, of Jean-Baptiste Lully with Louis XIV.

Molière believed in freedom for the creative person and he backed the men around him: Boileau and La Fontaine with their hilarious *Arret burlesque* in 1671, which stopped with the arm of ridicule the Faculté's conservatives who would allow no teaching of anything not mentioned in Aristotle; Jean-Armand de Mauvillain, his dear friend and physician, who eventually triumphed against the ultraconservative *anti-circulateurs* and doctors of the Diafoirus-Purgon type, to become *doyen* of the Faculté de Médecine in 1668 and bring a more modern point of view to seventeenth-century medicine; and Pierre Mignard in his stand against Charles Le Brun and the dictatorial Académie royale de peinture, though as we have seen, Molière did not live long enough to see his friend's triumph in 1690.

---

[62] Marc-Antoine Charpentier (1636–1704) had gone to Rome to study art, had been attracted to music there and changed fields, returning to Paris to become a great composer, especially of motets, oratorios and other church music. He did all the music for *Le Malade imaginaire* (1673), including the song which Cléante sings to Angélique (Act II, sc. 5), which is the only piece of music used in most modern productions of the play, since the *ballet-intermèdes* are usually omitted and the delightful *cérémonie burlesque* at the end is spoken rather than sung.

Molière and his intimate friends reinforced and encouraged each other's creative possibilities.

Of all the five court painters with whom Molière had many contacts— Charles Dufresnoy, Sébastien Bourdon, Charles Le Brun and the Mignard brothers, Nicolas and Pierre—Pierre Mignard stands out as a case of special intimacy. Mignard and Molière were kindred spirits in the independence of their creative genius, in their appreciation of women, in their love of the social and intellectual stimulus of the salons they frequented. Their relationship was total and mutually enriching in art, in family affairs, and above all in the satisfying rewards of an abiding personal friendship.

MOLIÈRE AND LULLY
Arthur R. Harned

The most noted collaboration between playwright and musician in French history, and—if one considers the personalities involved and the scope of their influence—perhaps in all history, was that of Molière and Lully. If Molière was to become the father of French comedy, Lully was no less certain to become the father of its opera. And the collaboration advanced them both greatly in the attainment of these goals. Lasting with generally eminent success for eight years, it was responsible for just under half of all of Molière's published work, as well as profoundly influencing the rest of his contemporary and later writings.

Although most critics neglected these works as *pièces de circonstance* written for the king, unworthy, with the exception of *Le Bourgeois gentilhomme*, of serious consideration, Sainte-Beuve gave Molière credit for doing them extremely well,[1] and Pelisson, in *Les Comédies-ballets de Molière*,[2] found in them the beginnings of the social satire on doctors, lawyers, professors, and merchants which were to produce his high comedies. But the greatest influence, most seem to agree, was a new musicality in Molière's verse, furnishing him finally the suitable tool for his genial ideas.[3]

What one overlooks nowadays considering the collaboration is that during the time the most important of the collaborators was considered by far to be Lully. Already acknowledged the leading musician in France, he had been conferred French citizenship by the king with accompanying praise for his talents and genius; he had become an intimate friend of the great men of the realm, such as Colbert and *noblesse de sang*, and more important was a good friend of the king himself. Even in his most successful days, Molière was never to attain nearly this intimacy or renown. In the view of contemporaries, Molière, because of some early successes, was granted the privilege of setting words to Lully's music.

[1] Henry Prunières, "Les Comédies-ballets de Molière et de Lulli," *Revue de France*, 4 (1931), 297.
[2] Maurice Pelisson, *Les Comédies-ballets de Molière* (Paris: Hachette, 1914).
[3] Prunières, *op. cit.*, 298.

It is true that the success of the first *comédies-ballets* was greatly to increase Molière's prestige,[4] but Molière was an actor and, in the eyes of the world and of the king, on a much lower social level. Only the special intervention of the king permitted him burial in holy ground. Lully from the very beginning of his presence at court held advanced titles and was so much in favor with the king—who confided to Colbert that Lully had become indispensable to him—that whenever a controversy arose between the Italian and a Frenchman, the king invariably took Lully's part. Such controversies were frequent, and one was finally to dissolve the collaboration with Molière.

Although the king never denied the statement which Grimarest attributed to him in his biography of Molière in 1706 that the two men he could never replace were Molière and Lully, he had shown surprise that Boileau should consider Molière the leading literary light of his reign, responding to his famous "Molière, Sire" with "I should not have thought it."[5] There were never to be any such reservation about Lully. Yet Lully was the son of the Florentine miller of whom even the most recent researchers find likely the story that he was spotted in a public square in Florence in 1644 at the age of twelve, parading with a group of actors, and so intriguing his discoverer, the Chevalier de Guise (Roger de Lorraine) by his monkey-like face (which he was always to retain) and his vivacity, that the Chevalier sent him to his cousin in Paris, the Grande Mademoiselle. She, in her memoirs, explains Lully's presence in her entourage by saying she had asked her cousin for a Florentine with whom to practice her Italian.

The years at the Grande Mademoiselle were supposedly humiliating ones for Lully. His earliest biographer, Lecerf de la Viéville, writing twenty years after his death, says that he was sent directly to the kitchens and became a scullion boy, and the fictionalized accounts of Lully's life[6] explain this as the Grande Mademoiselle's disappointment in receiving such an ugly Italian. Her account of this period is lost, and when Lully is mentioned again, in 1652, he is a *garçon de la çhambre* in her household. This would have been a suitable position for him to have had, in any case, six years earlier. Nevertheless, her household did offer, with her unceasing

---

[4] Almost from the beginning they were known as "les deux grands Baptistes."

[5] Brandon Mathews, *Molière, His Life and His Works* (New York: Scribners, 1910), 149–150.

[6] Madeleine Doumerc, *Lulli, des cuisines royales à l'Opéra* (Paris: Gedalge, 1954); Théodore-Valensi, *Louis XIV et Lully* (Nice, 1951); Germaine Guillemot-Magitot, *Lully, petit violon du Roi* (Paris: G. T. Rageot, 1950).

dances, concerts, and ballets, a musical education for anyone so inclined; and Lully, evidently on his own efforts, became an accomplished violinist, as well as a composer. He said that a Franciscan monk in Florence had already taught him the rudiments of the guitar.

Then the Grande Mademoiselle joined the Frondeurs in their unsuccessful rebellion against her cousin, the king, whom she had earlier hoped to marry, and she was forced to take refuge away from Paris. According to her memoirs, Lully missed the brilliant life of the capital and asked for leave, which she granted in November 1652. Only three months later, on February 13, 1653, he is found, astonishingly enough, playing five roles in the thirteen-hour *Ballet de la nuit*, dancing alongside the king, who on March 16 made him, at twenty, *Compositeur de la musique instrumentale*. The young king of fifteen had quickly been fascinated by his humor and his talent in dancing, music and mimicry. This began his swift and never-ending rise.

Writing music for the ballet, which until then had been a joint affair of various composers, soon became his personal monopoly. And when the Venetian opera came to Paris to celebrate the marriage of Louis XIV and the Spanish princess,[7] Lully, who up until then had composed Italian-like music, made an about-face and became the defender of French music. Louis XIV in recompense made him *surintendant de la musique*.

It was at this point, when Lully stood at the height of his popularity if not yet of his power, that Molière made the claim for himself that he had invented *comédie-ballet* with *Les Fâcheux* at Vaux-le-Vicomte in 1661 and proceeded to explain the circumstances. Le Fouquet had asked Molière for a comedy and ballet for the famous *fête* with which he hoped to dazzle the king, and which was to lead to his ruin. Molière had originally intended to keep the comedy and ballet separate, but since there were not enough dancers, he dispersed the dances between the acts of the play, giving them a chance to change their costumes. Not wanting to break the thread of the comedy, he tied the ballet in with the action of the play as much as possible. He does not say who gave him the *avis* for this solution. The advisor is often thought to be Lully himself, from whom he had asked and received a *courante* for the play. (The rest of the music was by Beauchamp.)

In any case, Molière invented the term *comédie-ballet*, even if he did

---

[7] Mazarin was often criticized for his pride in Italian accomplishments and his desire to display them to the French public—particularly for the expense involved.

not realize at the time that ballet and music had already been wedded to a play on several previous occasions in Paris, particularly while he was touring the provinces and even after his return. He nevertheless sincerely felt at the time he wrote his "Avertissement" to *Les Fâcheux* that he had been the inventor of the genre and suggested that others develop it.

It turned out that he and Lully were not only to be the ones to develop it but to bring it to its greatest heights when it was suggested in 1663 that he and Lully collaborate.

In the short ensuing time, Lully, realizing that his destiny was truly French, had asked for and received naturalization papers. And with signal recognition from the king, who personally signed the marriage contract along with the queen, Colbert, and a number of important lords, Lully was married in July 1662, helping to placate the constant rumors of pederasty his enemies assailed him with. The pleased king made him, just before the marriage, *maître de la musique de la famille royale*, and at the time of the marriage made any future children inheritors of his father-in-law's position as *maître de la musique de la chambre*.[8] In the marriage contract, Lully claimed he was the son of a Florentine gentleman,[9] thus of noble birth. It was his talent and his personality that permitted him to get away with such a false claim, as well as explaining his easy friendship with so many lords. His refined Italian accent also aided in this deception. Molière too had been married shortly before the collaboration, to Armande Béjart, and although he too had a certain position at court, becoming one of the *tapissiers-valets de chambre du Roi* on the death of his father and faithfully exercising his function three months a year, his marriage received no royal recognition.

Molière had produced his first outstanding success since *Les Précieuses ridicules* with *L'Ecole des femmes*, followed by the *Critique de l'Ecole des femmes* and the *Impromptu de Versailles*. These plays increased his already growing popularity with the king and made him eligible for consideration as a co-worker of the great Lully. Their first collaboration was *Le Mariage forcé*, given at the Louvre on January 29, 1664. Both Lully and the king danced in the ballet, the king as a gypsy. Molière, following his dictum, closely connected the ballets to the comedy, and it was so successful that it was produced again at Versailles on May 13 to end the *Plaisirs de l'Ile*

---

[8] He was to lead a presumably more decorous life after his marriage, fathering annual children for six years, even if the marriage was not a particularly close one.

[9] It was only in this century that this baptismal record was found at San Giovanni in Florence, proving true the rumors during his lifetime that his father was a miller.

enchantée and was a success at Molière's own theater in the Palais Royal in the intervening months.

In fact, Molière was later to give it a number of times in 1668 as a one-act play without the ballet or music. The ease of converting it indicates that the ballet elements were not really yet essential to the structure of the play. But two important developments were already to be noted in the work. First, the almost complete disappearance of the prominent mythological elements from the ballet as it took on a more realistic turn to suit the comedy. With them went most of the popular allegorical figures as well, such as the dancing lanterns, windmills and flowerpots, and even the dancing Prétérit and Supin of the *Ballet de la grammaire*. Secondly, there was already a new lilt in Molière's prose—a new rhythm which was to become so well adapted to the musical atmosphere of these comedies and can be heard in his other work as well. The fantasy of the ballet and music had also uncovered a new comic vein and given his spirit wings. All the originality of Molière in the *comédies-ballet* is already glimpsed in this first Lully-Molière collaboration.[10]

One of the faults of several of the later works was also evident. Often the king left very little time for the production of his entertainments, and Lully was forced to keep on hand a vast quantity of composed material to suit any immediate request, fashioning them as he might to suit any particular entertainment. The Spanish *mascarade* at the end of *Le Mariage forcé* had nothing to do with the play and might have been added here to allow the Italian troupe of the Cabinet to perform in something Lully had already prepared for them.

The next collaboration was *La Princesse d'Elide*, given May 7, 1664, for the *Plaisirs de l'Ile enchantée*, certainly the most well-known and probably the most lavish of the *fêtes* which Louis XIV gave at Versailles. Although actually honoring Louise de la Vallière, who had given him his first child five months earlier and was then at the height of her popularity, it was ostensibly for his Spanish Queen and the Spanish-connected Queen Mother. Lully and Molière chose a subject from Spanish literature, Moreto's *El Desdén con el Desdén*. The transformation was, however, infelicitous. The scene being converted to ancient Greece, *précieux* sentiments and *amours galants* seemed out of place. The haste of its composition and the other changes in the play marked its inferiority to the Spanish original, and along with the uncompleted *Mélicerte* of almost three years later, it is considered the most unsuccessful play of the collaboration.

[10] See G. Michaut, *Les Luttes de Molière* (Paris: Hachette), 10.

That did not prevent its outstanding success, perhaps for its delicate *marivaudage*,[11] perhaps because Molière was particularly successful in playing the court buffoon, Moron, which role permitted him the occasion to use his rolling eyes, his grotesque grimaces, and his comic postures— always a favorite with audiences. The king sent for the troupe to play it four times in July at Fontainebleau, and the following winter it held the stage twenty-five times at the Palais Royal. Clearly anything with music and ballet was to delight the audiences, but there was yet another reason for its success. With its spectacle, it closely approached the *tragédie à machines* then very much in vogue at the Marais.

Historically, *La Princesse d'Elide* was a first, important, and perhaps inexorable step forward toward the tragedy in music—the opera—with which Lully was to end his life, a progression he continued in the collaboration later, particularly with *Les Amants magnifiques* and *Psyché*. For the first time in the collaboration, in spite of the fact that the ballets were generally restricted to the *entr'actes*, musical elements had been developed so far that the action was effaced by the spectacles, the text submerged in the music.

This was also to mark, with the satyr's song and the dialogue between Tircis and Philis, Lully's first use of the pastoral, a form which was to fascinate him and which he was to exploit further in *La Pastorale comique*, the ballets of *George Dandin*, *La Grotte de Versailles*, and *Les Amants magnifiques*. Molière could already feel himself squeezed. The ending of the play was completely Lully's, with two orchestras, and dances alternating with choruses.

How did Molière feel about this quick ascendancy of Lully? What was the actual state of the collaboration? An apparent answer is found in the preface to their next collaboration, *L'Amour médecin*. After two years of collaboration, he there speaks of "l'incomparable M. Lulli." Chiefly, Lully had a genius for understanding instantly what Molière wanted. And from his vast knowledge of the stage, he often not only elaborated Molière's ideas but brought in ideas of his own. Their minds sparked one another. In addition there were the number of Italian verses he added to the plays. Furthermore, Lully adapted his music to Molière's style. Particularly *Le Bourgeois gentilhomme* and *Monsieur de Pourceaugnac* show how thoroughly he had created a comic style suitable to the spirit of Molière's

---

[11] A number of critics have thought to find borrowings of Marivaux from this work in *Les Surprises de l'Amour*, *Les Serments indiscrets*, and *L'heureux Strategème*. See Arthur Tilley, *Molière* (Cambridge: University Press, 1921), 310.

verses. Lully never found a collaborator the equal of Molière, and it is equally true, from the musicians Molière worked with both before and after the collaboration, that no one other than Lully could have collaborated nearly so well.

But if the second effort of their collaboration was to mark the predominance of Lully, Molière made his position clear in the third, in these verses of the prologue to *L'Amour médecin*, where the comedy, the music, and and ballet dispute their priority, and where Molière gave in a certain sense the esthetics and moral of the new genre:

> Quittons, quittons notre vaine querelle,
> Ne nous disputons pas nos talents tour à tour,
> Et d'une gloire plus belle
> Piquons-nous en ce jour.
> Unissons tous trois d'une ardeur sans seconde
> Pour donner du plaisir au plus grand Roy du monde.

In fact, this *comédie-ballet*, presented at Versailles before the king on September 15, 1665, maintained a perfect balance between all three. The work was merely the familiar story of the amorous daughter, the opposing father, and the suitor who disguises himself and gets help from an accommodating *soubrette*; but the mixture was carried out with a fine delineation of character, a tender lyricism, and with a complete naturalness, as at the famous end, where the dancers in the masque prevent the father from pursuing the eloping couple.

What really was most responsible for the success of his play, however, was its satire on doctors (La Grange in his *registre* refers to the play as *Les Médecins*), including the four doctors of the king, queen, Monsieur, and Madame, all easily recognizable by the audience, either through their medical beliefs or the play on their names. It was the first time that Molière used incontestably real personalities.[12] The criticism of these doctors is without malice, although occasionally in the play Molière does criticize the whole profession on a broad scale.

Shortly before Molière wrote this play, the king had made him his actor *en titre* and had asked for this *divertissement*, which Molière, in his *avis au lecteur*, claims was "proposé, fait, appris et représenté" in five days. But this time the speed does not seem to have damaged it; and for all its broad comedy, sometimes bordering on the Rabelaisian, as well as for its delicate gallantry, the characters have been given a certain truth and complexity. The king had it played three times at Versailles, and in Paris

[12] Michaut, *op. cit.*, 197.

it was played twenty-seven times in the autumn (from September 22 to November 27). Molière quickly published the play, having the license for it by December 30.

Although he had presented it in his theater without the ballet and music, in his *avis* he conceded the value of the other arts, informing the reader that without them, "ces sortes d'ouvrages perdent des grâces dont ils ont toutes les peines du monde à se passer," and he hoped that only those would read it who could visualize "le jeu du théâtre." If it was in any way successful, he affirmed, this was due "aux airs et aux symphonies de l'incomparable M. Lulli, mêlées à la beauté des voix et à l'adresse des danseurs."

The *Ballet des Muses* was begun December 7, 1666, to be finished by carnival of the following February, as part of a gigantic fête. For it Molière began *Mélicerte*, which was never completed, and which he replaced by *La Pastorale comique*, the third ballet *entrée* in this extensive ballet. Molière's dialogue for it has been lost, but the songs have been preserved in the *livre du ballet*, the collection of verses given to the spectator. These verses, like those of the later *Amants magnifiques* (set, as was this, in the Vale of Tempe), reveal a tender, pastoral side of Molière generally little known. *La Pastorale comique* is noted principally now for a song written in the nine-syllable line, rare until Verlaine and the nineteenth century, and whose refrain Madame de Sévigné quoted in a letter to her daughter on April 20, 1690:

> Mais, hélas! quand l'âge nous glace,
> Nos beaux jours ne reviennent jamais.[13]

It was probably Lully more than Molière who was responsible for this new turn to the pastoral. Beginnings in France had already been made by others, with duets of amorous shepherds, but this was the first time that there was a complete dramatic pastoral work in France. The style of Molière is excellent, the scenes often amusing, and many of them find Lully at his best. His *entrée en scène* was as Orpheus, playing a violin concerto.

The greatest triumph of their collaboration for the *Ballet des Muses* was, however, the fourteenth and final *entrée*, *Le Sicilien*, presented on Valentine's Day, 1667. Here Molière's prose reaches a new harmony to coincide with the music of Lully, and their work together attains a delicateness and light fantasy new to the collaboration. The music forms a complete fusion with the action, and, according to Romain Rolland, "y

---

[13] Tilley, *op. cit.*, 222.

vient jeter le scintillement et la griserie d'une nuit italienne . . . d'une mascarade d'amour."[14] Almost all critics, whether viewing it from Lully's part or from Molière's, consider it the piece closest to Rossini's *Barber of Seville*, both in the skill of its execution and its plot—the old familiar one of the girl; the elder, jealous guardian; and the lover who comes in disguise to carry her off in spite of the guardian's vigilance. It even opens, as does the opera, with a serenade. The music and the verses have a delightfulness and freshness about them which make it the gem of their collaboration.

Earlier Molière had used occasional collaborators, particularly Benserade, who had written some of the earlier *ballets de cour*. In 1669 Benserade composed his last ballet, the *Ballet de Flore*, and left the scene, presumably because of Molière's success and Boileau's ridicule. It is this collaboration, as well as some of the other earlier ones, that generally serves to explain the rather un-Molière-like doggerel that one finds on occasion in the *comédies-ballets*. Afterwards Molière did most of his work alone.

Meanwhile Lully was continuing to please the king with his *musique de circonstance*, and on April 20, 1668, the king made all his titles inheritable by whichever of his sons he should designate. Molière for his part had had a success with *Amphitryon*, when he and Lully turned to collaborate again with *George Dandin*.

In spite of Molière's efforts to justify the addition of ballet to this bitter comedy—particularly difficult to do when one considers that the ballet was a series of *bergeries* forming a pastoral, as Lully continued his fascination with the genre—the ballet had absolutely nothing to do with the work and could easily have been left out. That has been its fate ever since. But the ballet did mark another advancement of Lully towards the opera. He was much praised for his contribution to the work, his ballets gradually increasing in musical and scenic effects until the grandiose finale, the ceremony of the Pythian Games, a concert for more than one hundred voices, where two choirs sang alternately to the invocation of the grand priestess. This remains one of Lully's most effective works and is already a scene from French opera. In fact, the grandiosity of the finale anticipated the religious ceremonies in his later operas. The work was given on July 18, 1668. Even this peculiar juxtaposition of the *bergeries* and the cynical farce was not enough to satisfy Lully's passion for the pastoral. He went off on his own to write other *bergeries* for *La Grotte de Versailles* at the same time.

The next collaboration found itself on solid footing. The eminently

---

[14] André Le Breton, "Les Comédies-ballets de Molière," *La Revue Bleue* (1922), p. 77.

successful *Monsieur de Pourceaugnac* was given at Chambord on October 6, 1669. Like *George Dandin*, it has been criticized for its somewhat brutal treatment of its leading character—not this time a buffoon mistreated by his wife and her family for the delight of the audience, but a provincial in Paris, equally set up for rather cruel mockery. One remembers that it is, as Voltaire said, a farce, and like *George Dandin*, must be taken in the same way. Though some of the ballets are in questionable taste, they are in themselves exceedingly clever, and were certainly found amusing by the king and court. It naturally had an equal triumph in Paris, where it opened at the Palais Royal in November. The success has been enduring, for in truth the provincial's gullibility is so extreme that it resembles M. Jourdain's credulous vanity and Argan's fear of death—reaching a sort of sublime of comic exaggeration.

As he was to do with the two characters from *Le Bourgeois gentilhomme* and *Le Malade imaginaire*, Molière had invented a new type of play in which the ridiculous side of the character assumed such fantastic proportions that it could only find its full expression in an extravaganza of song and dance—perhaps one of the unconscious effects of Lully upon Molière.

Certainly the elements in *Monsieur de Pourceaugnac* form a perfect fusion. One has only to compare the scene in which Pourceaugnac questions the lawyers who answer in music with the original comic play in *Le Mariage forcé* to see what great progress has been made in allying the music to the action. Both the music and the play are full of a prodigious joy; Lully translates the text of Molière with intelligence and with finesse. Although some of the effects may seem exaggerated in their comedy, as in the aforementioned lawyers' sung reply, "La polygamie est un cas,/Est un cas pendable," where Lully gets all the comic effect he can by holding on to the last note, the *bouffonnerie* has generally given way to fine comedy.

All reports of the time consider the work Lully's success. For the spectators, the comedy had disappeared beneath the ballet, and only Lully was spoken of. And for the first time since he had entered the king's service seventeen years earlier, although he appeared in the play as Signor Chiacchiarone (Mister Talkalot), Lully's name did not appear among the actors. This was now beneath him.

Lully also provided the Italian texts for the famous mad *sarabande* near the end of the play where the riotous band of apothecaries, brandishing their syringes like swords, chase the unfortunate M. Pourceaugnac, while the Italian singers (among them, Lully) sing:

Piglialo, sù
Signor Monsù,
Piglialo, piglialo, piglialo sù,
Che non ti farà male,
Piglialo su questo servitale.

It is Lully's verve at his very best, in the best style of *musique bouffe*.

Although Lully probably got the immediate glory for the play, its gaiety seemed to reflect the improved theatrical fortunes of Molière. The interdict had finally been removed from *Tartuffe*, and the receipts of his 1668–69 season were the greatest since that of 1663–64.

Four months after *Monsieur de Pourceaugnac*, Molière and Lully presented *Les Amants magnifiques* on February 4, 1670, in time again for carnival. Molière describes the reasons: "Sa Majesté a choisi pour sujet deux princes rivaux qui, dans le champêtre séjour de la vallée de Tempé ... régalent a l'envi une jeune princesse et sa mère de toutes les plaisanteries dont ils se peuvent aviser."

It should be stated here that Molière has often been criticized for doing work as the king's lackey, and for doing unimportant work. But the good far outweighed the ill. The king's grateful friendship and protection—already shown in the case of *Tartuffe*—stood him in good stead against the *précieuses*, the *petits marquis*, doctors, *faux dévots*, etc., and helped him produce his other work. There was likewise the new melodiousness which the musical collaboration added to Molière's voice. Nor does it really seem that Molière actually spent a great deal of time composing these works.

Except for *Les Amants magnifiques*, *Le Bourgeois gentilhomme*, and *La Comtesse d'Escarbagnas*, the king did not actually suggest any particular subject. He merely specified a certain genre, and left the rest up to Molière and Lully. The genre may not have been deep, but the stage would be much poorer without *Le Bourgeois gentilhomme* and *Le Malade imaginaire*, where the music aids in the structure of the piece and the whole spectacle together—ballet, music, and comedy—is essential to a full enjoyment of the work. Aside from this, one could take into consideration what the collaboration did for French opera. And it must be stated that *Les Amants magnifiques* clearly served Lully in this as yet uncertain goal. The play was merely a pretext for the music, almost a libretto, and, although it is essentially a comedy in five acts, there is no more material in it than would be appropriate for a one-act play. Molière was never able to revive it on his own.

It gave Lully his greatest success to date. Musically, he never surpassed himself in this genre, delighting the audiences with his varied symphonies, lavish ballets, exquisite pastoral music, and the impressive end, a chorus united with trumpets, violins, flutes, oboes, kettle drums, bells, and drums. Molière realized that they were merely flattering the taste of the king for music, dance, and machines.

Molière himself played in the work an important role, that of the court fool, Clitidon, the go-between who elicits avowals from the two young lovers. He is no longer the buffoon-like Moron of *La Princesse d'Elide*, but rather a humorous and well-bred gentleman, using the language of high comedy.

Several passages in the play seem to refer to Molière personally, as when he tells the astrologer, "Il est bien plus facile de tromper les gens que de les faire rire," afterwards adding, evidently to himself, "Vous vous émancipez trop, et vous prenez de certaines libertés qui vous joueront un mauvais tour. . . . Taisez-vous si vous etes sage." The astrologer himself was a concession to the popular interest at the court in astrology, which La Fontaine ridiculed in his fable of *L'Astrologue qui se laisse tomber dans un puits.*

Back at Chambord for the king's fall hunting, Molière and Lully presented the most triumphant of their successes on October 14, 1670, with *Le Bourgeois gentilhomme*, written to satisfy the king's request to have something with Turks in it to recall their recent visit to Paris. Molière multiplied the occasions for the music—the dance lesson, the music lesson, serenades, *air galant*, *chanson*, pastoral, drinking songs, concerts, meals with violins—not to mention the ballets with dancers, tailors, and cooks. Lully's ballet is prolonged in the dialogue to become a dream world of good spirits and humor, of bubbling fantasy and comedy brought down to earth occasionally by Molière's humanity. It is truly a "musical comedy," the first to bear the title of *comédie-ballet* in the original edition.

Lully was unfailing in his own offering. The biggest success of the evening was the scene in which M. Jourdain, played by Molière, was made a Mamamouchi, a scene Lully not only created, but in which he played the mufti with such verve that it appears to have been the part of the evening most appreciated by the king. Although the king was not particularly pleased with the entire work at its first presentation, it quickly became one of his favorites, and near the end of his life he loved to hear his musicians sing its songs.[15]

[15] Henry Prunières, *Lully* (Paris: H. Laurens, 1910), 23.

Since the ceremony seems so artificially attached to the rest of the play, even though necessary for the *dénouement*, it seems likely that it was a work which Lully held in reserve for productions on short notice and which he reworked to suit the occasion. He was equally successful with his "Ballet des Nations" which ends the play, a masterpiece in the French *bouffe* style, but there again it has nothing to do with the play, even though the play would end abruptly without it. Lully drew here, as in many of the other collaborations, on his vast knowledge of stagecraft, and if, as the mufti, he wore four or five rows of lighted candles on his turban, it was a motif found in other burlesque ballets of the time.

Molière, for his part, successfully created a character so grotesquely vain and credulous that he could be taken in by the extravagant imposture of the ceremony, or any other spectacle Lully would want to furnish. But even at its apogee the *comedie-ballet* was preparing its ruin, as it veered closer and closer to the world of spectacle, of the music and dance of opera.

Lully had now begun to solidify his wealth, speculating in property with considerable acumen, and beginning to build his impressive house, still in existence on the Rue Ste. Anne, near the Bibliothèque Nationale. For its profusion of paintings and decoration, he was forced to borrow eleven thousand *livres* from Molière—a fact which indicates that the collaboration was still on amical footing.

Their next collaboration, *Psyché*, is practically an opera. The king wished for a work to inaugurate his new theater of the Tuileries, which had been specifically designed for spectacular effects. He had in his storehouse a piece of scenery representing the underworld and asked Molière to write something in which it could be used, to be ready by Carnival of 1671. Molière chose *Psyché*, his close friend La Fontaine having made a romance of the story in 1669. Unfortunately there was not much time left to compose, and Molière was able to write only the first act and the opening scenes of the next two. Pierre Corneille finished these and the last two acts, and Quinault wrote all the verses for the ballets, except one Italian song by Lully.

The play opened the Tuileries theater with an immense success on January 17, 1671, which continued when it moved to the Palais Royal in the summer without the more spectacular mechanical effects. It played eighty times in the last two years of Molière's life, the receipts being more than double those for *Le Misanthrope*. Success was principally due to the machines, costumes, and scenery, and even more particularly to Lully's music. For a year its songs and symphonies were the rage of Paris. Louis

XIV even had them played for the inauguration of the ramparts of Dunkirk, employing seven hundred drummers, allied to the usual regimental bands and the king's chamber orchestra. Eighty cannon were fired on the last note.[16] The work lacked only the recitative to be an opera. Later on Lully converted it into an opera in only three weeks, Thomas Corneille merely putting into lyrical verses the alexandrines of Molière and of his brother Pierre. The verses of Quinault were not changed at all.[17]

Anything after this success was bound to be an anticlimax, particularly as Lully was drifting towards the opera. The last collaboration was *La Comtesse d'Escarbagnas*, given at Saint-Germain on December 2, 1671, to celebrate Monsieur's second marriage, with the Princess Palatine. It is a short play of nine scenes, only a pretext to present the *Ballet des ballets*, a selection of the best ballets of their *comédies-ballets* of the previous years.[18] The ballet is so predominant in the work that Molière made scarcely any attempt to connect them to his new comedy. The first seven scenes are given without interruption. Then follows the entertainment which the leading character, a vicomte, is giving in honor of his mistress, Julie, containing a pastoral play also written by Molière, now lost, and which was interspersed with the usual songs and dances. Next follow the last two scenes, ending with the most popular ballet from their last work, *Psyché*.[19]

Early in the following year, 1672, Lully persuaded the king to grant him the privilege of the *Académie d'opéras*, which had been granted to the Frenchman Perrin in 1669. Perrin's first opera, *Pomone*, in March, 1671, had been an enormous success. Though Cambert's music was good, Perrin's libretto was extremely poor, and Lully was astounded at the success. He nevertheless saw which way the wind was blowing and regretted he had not asked for the privilege himself. He had never genuinely believed before that opera, with no spoken dialogue at all, would really become a generally popular vogue.

In a way, the privilege fell into his hands. Perrin was a very poor businessman, and, in spite of his first success and the even better opera produced after it, also by Cambert (but with another librettist), he was

---

[16] Prunières, *Ibid.*, 24.

[17] The work, in fact, contained in its prologue the praise of the king which Lully was to place automatically in the prologue of his operas.

[18] *La Princesse d'Elide*, the *Ballet des Muses*, *George Dandin*, *Les Amants magnifiques*, *Le Bourgeois gentilhomme*.

[19] Tilley, *op. cit.*, 239–240.

imprisoned in the Conciergerie for debt. Colbert suggested to Lully that he go to the Conciergerie and ask to buy the privilege, a proposition Perrin accepted immediately and gratefully. Lully was generous in the terms, even settling Perrin with a pension. Then he approached the king for his consent. He asked for it with such determination that the king was afraid of losing him altogether, and it was then that he expressed his opinion to Colbert that he could not do without him, and, according to Charles Perrault, "qu'il fallait lui accorder tout ce qu'il demandait, ce qui fut fait dès le lendemain."[20]

That the king was reluctant to grant Lully such powers except under pressure was understandable from the already bitter disappointment of the French composers concerning Lully's monopoly of court music. There was also the fear of Lully's underlying dictatorial nature, a nature which was supposedly explained by his humiliations at the court of the Grande Mademoiselle. The fear was quickly justified. The part of the edict forbidding anyone to perform any opera without his permission was immediately enforced. Cambert left for England to direct the music at Charles II's court.

In spite of their previous collaboration, Molière was informed that his troupe—as well as that of the Hotel de Bourgogne—could not use more than six singers or twelve musicians, and none of the king's dancers were to be available for them. These were to be reserved completely for the opera. Molière, already beginning to suffer from ill health, bitterly revised his successful *Psyché* as best he could and brought out *La Comtesse d'Escarbagnas* with a completely new score by Charpentier. Lully's monopoly was actually a double blow for him. He too had observed the financial success of the opera, since even in his own theater, such a show as *Psyché* was far more financially successful than either *Le Misanthrope* or *Tartuffe*, and he was giving more and more place to the music and ballet, as his and Lully's *comédies-ballets* were rapidly approaching opera. Evidently, he did not seem ready to abandon the financial and popular success these works had brought, but rather hoped to follow Lully by producing opera himself,[21] at least to continue such a lucrative collaboration on the side. Dance and music meant a great deal to the court—the king gave as great a pension to his dance master as to Corneille—and Molière did not want to abandon that connection.

---

[20] Prunières, *Lully*, 27.
[21] This was the considered opinion of his contemporary, De Sénécé.

In fact, shortly before Lully had been granted these rights, he and Molière had agreed on a collaboration at the king's request to celebrate Louis's return in August 1672 from his first victorious campaign in Holland. But Lully soon received yet another privilege, the proprietary rights over Molière's own verses which he had set to music. This was more than Molière could stand. He turned again to Charpentier for help, and together they produced *Le Malade imaginaire* at Palais Royal on February 10, 1673, the first *comédie-ballet* that Molière presented first at his own theater instead of before the court.

Charpentier was an excellent composer, and the work was successful, even if the collaboration was not as perfect as it had often been with Lully. Molière still hoped to produce the work before the king, hoping for the same success with him that *Le Bourgeois gentilhomme* had achieved.

But at the same time Lully had received the privilege for opera, he had also received the privilege of being solely responsible for *any* work with music in it presented before the king, whether operatic (to be given in the theater), religious (to be given in the chapel), or merely to entertain at court festivities. He refused to have the work shown at court and the king acquiesced. The break between Molière and the king was complete. In his disappointment and ill health, Molière felt little spirit left for the struggle. After the third performance of *Le Malade imaginaire*, he confessed that he was ready to give up. On the fourth performance he was stricken fatally.

Shortly after his death, his troupe was forced to leave the Palais Royal, when Lully found that that theater was more suitable for his opera. But the troupe actually found nothing extraordinary in the eviction. Molière had been granted the right to play there as a personal favor, and there was no reason to expect the right to continue after his death. Nor were Lully's relations actually unfriendly with Molière's widow. Lully repaid her the debt he owed her husband, and when he was involved in the poison suit he brought against one of his enemies,[22] himself seriously believing in the truth of it, she testified in his support.

Lully went on to honor after honor, until the king promoted him to the *secrétariat*, equal to the great lords of the realm. Only to the king did Lully show any reverence. And in spite of the disapproval of the other lords of the *secrétariat*, Lully continued to play his favored comic roles in revivals,

---

[22] An actress at the opera informed Lully that her former lover and his leading rival, Guichard, had asked her to poison him. It turned out to be a case of jilted love, and Guichard was acquitted, but Lully had acted in good faith.

to please the king. But it was not alone for his entertainments that the king found Lully indispensable. Not only did Lully compose music for his rising, sleeping, eating, walking, his fanfares were the only ones to give the king a true touch of majesty. No one else could have done it with the same royal flair. His work, even the prologues of his operas, apotheosized the king. In them Louis XIV became truly Apollo, truly a king of glory and virtues, invincible and adored by his people. No one could flatter as Lully, and Lully understood this. His works are personal eulogies to the king, as were Le Brun's paintings. They glorified him and satisfied a good part of his taste for glory.

It must be said for Lully that he contributed as much to the famous collaboration as Molière had. They were both unexcelled. Lully went on to collaborate with La Fontaine, Boileau, Racine, but only with Quinault did he find it even satisfactory.[23] And although Charpentier was one of the great musicians of his epoch, there was certainly some little difficulty for Molière in working with someone for the first time; and Charpentier particularly lacked the experience of Lully.

Lully went on to establish truly French opera, with its emphasis on dramatic truth and psychologically convincing character rather than on the increasing Italian insistence on melody and musical pyrotechnics. Lully painted the delicate and moderate sentiments rather than excessive lamentation or joy. Rameau in the next century was not to stray from the lines he established, and Massenet and Debussy continued the tradition. Perhaps in the long run, Molière profited much more from the collaboration. Lully remains popularly bound in his epoch. Molière carried his new musical, flowing style, his new imagination and fantasy, into his universal triumphs.

Molière's troupe moved to the Rue Guénégaud, facing financial ruin when the *comédies-ballets*, which had been their financial stand-by, were refused to them. The actors of the Marais, equally imperilled by Lully's decrees, could not satisfactorily play their *pièces à machines*, and joined them. Together they subsisted principally on Molière's comedies.

Then in 1680 the king ordered a fusion of the Hôtel de Bourgogne and

---

[23] It was Boileau who had advised Lully to drop Quinault, but the collaboration with La Fontaine led to La Fontaine's scathing *Le Florentin* after Lully criticized his libretto, and the other collaborators fared little better, doubtless due to dogmatism on all sides. Lully had much greater success, both personally and professionally, with Quinault, to whom he later returned. But all the collaborators became his friends again after the embroilments.

the Hôtel de Guénégaud. Thus the century ended, as it had begun, with one playhouse. And the playhouse formed from these was to be La Maison de Molière. Lully's sway on Molière's apotheosis was short-lived.

MOLIÈRE: CRITIC AND VICTIM
OF THE SOCIAL INSTITUTION OF MARRIAGE
Douglas R. Hall

We know that Molière suffered from grave physical debilities during the latter part of his life. Beginning in 1666, when he was forty-four, he could drink only milk, his constitution being unable to tolerate anything stronger. His young, charming wife, Armande Béjart, known as Mademoiselle Molière, since the title "Madame" was reserved for noble ladies, unhappy in marriage to a tired, sickly, preoccupied man, only added to Molière's troubles. A genius and devoted man of the theater, but victim of a "wrong" marriage, he seems to have been destined never to taste the personal happiness which is supposed to derive from the union of two harmonious souls.

He was never good at the game of love, and yet he loved the company of women. Madeleine Béjart had been his mistress for years; and he had also been interested in other actresses, Mlle du Parc and Mlle de Brie, with whom he perhaps succeeded. Given the conditions of extreme intimacy in which actors and actresses then lived and worked, there is nothing surprising in the ease with which they passed from one lover to another. The institution of marriage was already beginning to disappear.

Mlle de Brie remained his friend even after his marriage to Armande Béjart; she probably consoled him in his marital difficulties. Molière never had what a man needs in order to be a "great lover" in the Latin tradition. He could never successfully convince the woman that he lived only for her; some part of him—his genius, certainly—always escaped her.

In the area of pure speculation simply for amusement's sake, one may chuckle with delight at the idea of Molière's briefly leaving the chamber of his beloved-of-the-moment in order to jot down ideas for a new play, while the lady languishing on the bed prepares to throw a tantrum. Indeed, he was known to treat appointments and rendezvous with considerable negligence. There can be no doubt about it, something in him made it impossible for a woman, any woman, to possess his mind and imagination entirely. The latter always lifted him from her.

Vicious tongues of the seventeenth century whispered, with typical

Gallic frankness, about Molière's personal inadequacies. Those envious of his theatrical success even had the bad taste to repeat on stage certain vulgar allusions aimed at making fun of him. After his marriage to Armande the series of now famous rumors flooded the theatrical circles of Paris: was Armande the younger sister or the daughter of Madeleine? And, especially, who was her father? Was Molière's marriage an incestuous one? In any case, it produced three children, only one of whom survived very long. But can one be sure that Molière himself was the father of them? It is a widely known fact that Armande Béjart had the power to resist the attentions of only one man—her husband. Her adultery was public.

In these trying circumstances Molière had recourse more and more to his art, in which he tended to confine himself. He allowed Armande to follow her coquettish whims, since he could not control her. With the philosophic resignation of a husband who is cuckold and knows it, he understood the young woman's needs and drives. He judged himself harshly, comparing his years with hers. His health was ruined; hers was excellent. Two years before his death, however, Armande became ill, doubtless the result of her excessive libertinage. She was away from the theater for two months but returned and was at Molière's side at the moment of his death. Her efforts at procuring hallowed ground for his body to rest in are now part of French literary history, the ever-growing Molière legend. Even the armchair in which he was placed after his attack of convulsions in *Le Malade imaginaire* can be seen today among the relics preserved by the Comédie-Française.

Molière lived to make people laugh, and he was a genius at it. For him, laughter was a serious matter. His penetrating and acute observation of human nature took expression first in simple farces, then comedies of intrigue, finally in profound studies of human types such as the sad, disillusioned Alceste of *Le Misanthrope*. Hypocrisy and affectation he surely hated, as the *Tartuffe* and *Les Précieuses ridicules* so well demonstrate.

Naturally, his considerable success attracted enemies for him. The taste and psychology of the *Ecole des femmes* were attacked in 1662. But this attack occasioned his *Critique de l'Ecole des femmes*, just as a few years later Madame de La Fayette's highly successful *Princesse de Clèves* was to elicit an attack by Valincour and then a response to the criticism by the Abbé de Charnes. And so a series of chain reactions is invoked, and no one is without his own comments on the matter. Fortunately for Molière, he had the support and admiration of Louis XIV.

But the subject at hand is Molière as a critic—and victim—of marriage, especially as he has treated this question in *L'Ecole des femmes* and *L'Ecole des maris*. This comedian-poet has been classed by Alfred Simon, in *Molière par lui-même*, as one of the world's "génies mal-aimés." Madeleine Béjart, older than he, was the object of passionate love on the part of the young Molière. And yet, strangely, he married Armande; and so his calvary began. One wonders how Madeleine reacted to the marriage. Some scholars say that she accepted and approved of it; others maintain that she watched the progress of this affair with cold fury. The question of Armande's being either her sister or her daughter will probably never be answered, but we can be certain that Madeleine Béjart's role in the unfolding of Molière's personal life was not one of pure innocence.

It is Paul Guth's *Histoire de la littérature française* which states that not only could Molière not satisfy Armande but that she also had a physical horror of his person—hence her giving herself freely to all men except her husband. The several portraits of Molière himself hardly resemble each other, as it so often happens. But Guth's description of him mentions a round-shouldered man with little or no neck, the enormous head resting almost squarely on the shoulders, a long torso supported by quite short legs, a snub nose constantly sniffing at all odors, a sensitive mouth, but especially the immense, dreamy, beautiful eyes under thick brows, eyes that do not need words in order to speak, eyes that seem to seek the revenge of a soul who knows it is not loved, eyes swimming in contemplation and regret.

How not to think of the unfortunate husband of the *Princesse de Clèves*? The same sad lucidity is present in both of them; and, in a recorded conversation between Molière and a friend, Chapelle, reported in d'Allainval's *Mémoires sur Molière*, there are amazing parallels with the text of Madame de La Fayette's famous novel:

> Marriage did not satisfy my desires, for in it I found only indifference. . . . What she felt for me was far removed from being what I would have desired in order to be happy. . . . I was determined to live with her as if she were not my wife . . . but if you knew what I suffer you would pity me. . . . My love for her is so great that I almost support her in her infidelities, if that can make her happy. . . . When I think how impossible it is for me to overcome what I feel for her, and I realize that it is just as impossible for her to overcome her flirtatious inclinations, I find myself more inclined to pity her than to blame her. . . . I have come to believe that there is only one kind of true love and that those who have not felt all the shades of it have never truly loved.

It is amorous psychology worthy of the *Princesse de Clèves's* subtle author.

L'Ecole des maris (1661) depicts a mature man, Ariste, who wishes to marry a young woman, Léonor, protected by him since childhood. Ariste's younger brother, Sganarelle, also intends to wed *his protégée*, Isabelle, Léonor's sister. Arnolphe, in *L'Ecole des femmes*, a man of about forty, has had his future wife, Agnès, raised in a convent, far from worldly temptations. Arnolphe seems pompous, lecherous and niggardly. He desires Agnès to be kept in a state of extreme ignorance and *naïveté*. Similarly, Sganarelle intends to keep Isabelle at home, busy with housework and the care of his personal effects. One wonders how men can be so unaware of, or unconcerned with, female psychology. The women, knowing nothing else, are at first content with the idea; but then they undergo the miracle of true love and, as in the case of Mme de Clèves, their eyes are at last opened to the land of the *Tendre*. Before Arnolphe's rages, Agnès, who is far from stupid, shows the strength of Joan of Arc before her judges. Isabelle demonstrates real genius in escaping from the possessive Sganarelle.

As in the case of Molière himself, the role of lover or husband becomes confused with that of father, as the difference in years predisposes Ariste and Sganarelle to act as mentor or parent to their young charges. Ariste is intelligent enough to say, "I give her free choice . . . she can marry me or choose elsewhere. And I would prefer to see her make a different marriage than to marry me against her will." And Molière himself, "father" and protector of his troup of actors, must indeed have appeared to Armande as a parent, older brother, or uncle, rather than lover. She had known him all her life. How could there be any romantic interest on her part?

Of the three fictional protagonists, Ariste alone succeeds; and what he enjoys is doubtless what Molière might have longed for in his own life: the joys of the senses mingled with the irresistible attraction of one human soul for another, but a soul clothed with a human body and possessing a sex. Unfortunately for Molière-the-man this dream could exist only in the imagination of Molière-the-playwright. His flirtatious wife had eyes that went everywhere—except to him. Victim of her coquettish ways, and of his own passion for her, victim next of his devotion to and preoccupation with his own art, Molière-the-comedian was a clown in tears. To speculate at length on what his personal life must have been is indeed tempting, but we recall that three hundred years separate us from him, and it has become difficult to discern what is fact and what is merely legend. It appears that Molière himself confessed that Armande had given him moments of true joy, mingled with the horrors of jealousy which she also created for him. Is this not often the case with passionate personal attachments?

To speak of Molière merely as a comic genius is obviously a great over-simplification. It was his trade to please and amuse. But the interior anguish of his own life is there. He was a man laughing on stage but in the wings weeping and frustrated at his own inadequacies. Where was Armande? Whom was she with? One had to dry one's eyes, touch up the dampened make-up, and get ready for the next entrance. A showman like Molière could not afford to do less than thoroughly entertain. And then there were also the enemies, those who had come not to laugh with him but at him, the mocking voices, the whispers and guffaws. Molière depicted universal man, but universal man himself fears the scorn of his peers. One can cover much with satire, but even good satire becomes cloying when overdone.

The Duke de La Rochefoucauld, in the same century, wrote, "Il y a de bons mariages; il n'y en a point de délicieux." Molière's, apparently, was neither. Marriages in the seventeenth century were contracted without love, as it was assumed that passion would grow dim and love would in-evitably pass. It appears, however, that the world has known at least a few lifelong cases of enduring passion and true love. Molière needed such a love; his sensitive nature craved it. It was not, however, meant to be. He was rather victimized by marriage. One can blame him for choosing to marry a woman young enough to be his daughter. But such mar-riages were, and still are, relatively common in France. It might be more appropriate to call Molière a failure in, rather than victim of, marriage. But he had the support of his art and went even so far as to poke fun at the pitiful Sganarelle who bitterly condemns the object of his personal failure in love. Molière doubtless knew that happiness could exist in certain mar-riages. But to him, alas! it was never given.

Molière and France

Ignoring for the moment that pronouncement concerning the fate of prophets in their own lands, one can expect that the literary patrimony of Molière would be most keenly felt and enthusiastically accepted in France. Molière's contributions to the literature of his own country are numerous: he virtually created comedy there as a serious genre by informing his plays with a profundity that never overwhelmed their potential for amusement; he may be said to have begun the literary project of cataloging his countrymen—a project that has not yet seen end but which flowered most brilliantly in the nineteenth century; he broached the topic of political and social structures and provided insights that are valid to apply to France even today; and he directed his creative talents (writing, acting, producing) against human falsity and hypocrisy under its many masks. He was, furthermore, one of the giants of that period of French literature, Classicism, which has dominated belles lettres *in France since the seventeenth century—sometimes directly by an influence dependent on literary conservatism and sometimes through the reactions of subsequent writers and thinkers to the tenets of classical drama.*

To delineate Molière's popularity, his significant admirers and detractors, and the fortunes of his various plays would be a task of considerable accomplishment and, as Professor Peyre points out, in some respects "a most uncertain undertaking." And yet the task has not been wholly ignored; this section offers the reader a sampling of essays dealing with Molière's patrimony to the French commonwealth of letters.

From the time of his death in 1673 until the French Revolution, Molière seems never to have been far offstage from the passing spectacle of French literature. The acutely drawn archetypes he left found reiteration and new nuances in the Caractères *of La Bruyère and in the plays of Marivaux. One such archetype, the* faux dévot, *is discussed in the first essay of this section, and there is further exploration of the special debt that Marivaux owes to the great comedian. Later, Voltaire, a man whose concern encompassed both Classicism and the new spirit of the eighteenth century, found much to admire in Molière, and if he chose to use the legacy of Molière as a foil against Shakespeare, then lucky for him that he had such a weapon in his native tongue. His opinions concerning Molière's plays are documented in one essay; and there is also an essayistic rationale of the somewhat less favorable, but no less energetic, reaction of Jean-Jacques Rousseau. During this general time, Molière was making his presence felt within the project of the Encyclopédie, where his comedies, theories, topics, and characters all played a role in the shaping of rationalist thought. Indeed, the very idea of an encyclopedia must have benefited from the power of analysis that Molière exemplified and passed on to posterity in his delineation of personages and social institutions. So powerful are the fictional characters of his plays that literary criticism can make good use of them in exploring the techniques of writers who do not even seem to derive specifically from Molière. Such is the case with Laclos, in whose Mme de Merteuil Baudelaire saw a "Tartuffe femelle," an observation taken up in another of the following essays. The degree of finesse evident in Molière's definition of his great comic characters is perhaps best shown by those subsequent writers who sought to recast the characters. Professor Lawrence addresses this topic specifically in an essay dealing with for versions of the* misanthrope.

THE *FAUX DÉVOT*
FROM MOLIÈRE TO MARIVAUX

Michael S. Koppisch

As the Greek root of the word indicates, a hypocrite is a stage actor, one who pretends to be something that in reality he is not. The appearance that the hypocrite presents to his public is a mask, donned in order to draw his interlocutor into a world of illusion in which the actor always has the advantage of being master of the situation. To the extent that the hypocrite succeeds in this game, the spectator becomes his dupe, existing, as it were, by the sufferance of the skillful actor. The subtle dialectic of hypocrisy, therefore, has three major components—the actor, his mask, and the other. But this other is more than a detached spectator, for he participates in the dialogue in at least two ways. If he is to be taken in by the hypocrite, the latter must choose a mask that will appeal to him. Had Tartuffe decided to pretend to be a nobleman faithful to the wishes of his king, he would probably have alienated Orgon, still anxious about his minor role in the Fronde, rather than trapped him in the act. Furthermore, the ideal spectator must eventually become an actor in the plot, granting to the hypocrite's role the status of authenticity and falling in line with its demands. In other words, the hypocrite is not a solitary figure; he is largely dependent upon his dupe. Yet, there is still another dialogue, this one between the actor and his mask, that will allow us to delineate distinctions of form and degree in the actor's hypocrisy. Just as there are different kinds of acting, there is a variety of types of hypocrisy, each with its own implications about the actor, his role, and his relationship to the others who populate his world.

In the literature of the seventeenth century, the most representative hypocrite is the *faux dévot*. Here is a character who would have others believe that he is a pious man, devoted to the precepts of religion and leading an exemplary life, when in actual fact he is neither dedicated to religious practices nor concerned with Christian ethics. His stance of piety is a mask calculated to trick others into thinking that he is what he really is not. Tartuffe is just such a character, and Molière protrays him as an impostor consciously attempting to impose his will upon Orgon

57

and his family by assuming the mask of pious behavior. If Tartuffe is a comic character, it is not just his mask, but rather the gap between the actor and his mask, that makes him laughable. An instinctively religious man might well behave in much the same way as a *faux dévot*, but what makes the hypocrite ridiculous, as the author of the *Lettre sur la comédie de l'Imposteur* demonstrates, is a "disconvenance" between what he really is and what he appears to be.[1] Whether or not it was written by Molière himself, the *Lettre*, a defense of *Panulphe* against the cabal of the *dévots* determined to have the play banned once again, elucidates one of the most crucial aspects of Molière's theater—the notion of "le ridicule."[2] "Or, si la disconvenance est l'essence du ridicule, il est aisé de voir pourquoi la galanterie de Panulphe paroît ridicule, et l'hypocrisie en général aussi; car ce n'est qu'à cause que les actions secrètes des bigots ne conviennent pas à l'idée que leur dévote grimace et l'austérité de leurs discours a fait former d'eux au public."[3] If we are to know the ridiculous, we must also know the truth from which it deviates, the source of the "actions secrètes." In the preface to *Le Tartuffe* Molière himself speaks of the hypocrites who have attacked his play in the name of religion rather than self-defense: "ils sont trop politiques pour cela et savent trop bien vivre pour découvrir le fond de leur âme . . . ils ont couvert leurs intérêts de la cause de Dieu."[4] In both the *Préface* and the *Lettre sur l'Imposteur*, then, the hypocrite is a character whose inner reality, his self—"le fond de leur âme"—is covered by a mask that is not in harmony with that self.

Although Molière has based his play precisely upon the dichotomy between the actor and his mask, precious little can be said about the actor himself. Dorine's hilarious description to Orgon of Tartuffe's behavior during Elmire's illness, the seduction scenes, and Orgon's final—if long overdue—realization of the truth prove that Tartuffe is definitively not what he appears to be. Yet, all that we know about that part of Tartuffe which lies behind the mask is that he is, as Elmire puts it, an "âme hypocrite" whose sensuality and avarice eventually lead to his undoing (IV,iv, 1374). What he is and what he wants to convince people that he is are in-

---

[1] Molière, "Lettre sur la comédie de l'Imposteur," in *Qeuvres complètes*, ed. Eugène Despois and Paul Mesnard (13 vols.; Paris: Hachette, 1873–1900), IV, 529–66.

[2] *Panulphe ou l'Imposteur* is the title of the second version (1667) of *Tartuffe*. In his *New Light on Molière* (Geneva: Droz; Paris: Minard, 1956), 2, John Cairncross has pointed out that "there is no material difference between *Panulphe* and *Tartuffe*."

[3] Molière, "Lettre sur la comédie de l'Imposteur," 560.

[4] Molière, *Le Tartuffe*, *Oeuvres complètes*, IV, 373. All in-text citations from the play refer to this edition.

dependent of each other and together make up his total character. However, Tartuffe is quite as aware of the distinction between himself as actor and himself as role as anyone in the play, or the audience. For his is a transcendent hypocrisy in the sense that it is always directed outward toward the other characters and depends to a large extent for its success on his maintaining a distance from his mask. He is always aware that he is wearing a mask and never shows any affection for his role itself. We can easily imagine him as a thoroughgoing brigand, a would-be gentleman, or a judge, were any of these roles to hold in store for him the promise of success that playing the *dévot* does. It is only important that he appear to be *dévot* so that he can accomplish other goals; the idea of piety itself holds no fascination for him. This is not true of Onuphre, La Bruyère's version of the *faux dévot*. Like many of La Bruyère's characters, Onuphre is an amateur, an amateur actor. And he is an amateur in the etymological sense of that word—he loves his role. Never taking his mask for granted, Onuphre is constantly on guard lest the public discover that his piety is just an appearance. He shares many of Tartuffe's more obvious goals, but his heightened fascination with his mask leads him to try to make his inner being correspond with it more faithfully. The gestures of devotion, which had been completely empty for Tartuffe, begin to take on more meaning for Onuphre. There is a part of him that really wants others to think that Onuphre is a *dévot*. Many of Marivaux's *faux dévots* really want nothing else. Their only goal is to convince others that they really are *dévots*. From Molière to Marivaux there is an increasing ambiguity in the situation of the *faux dévot*. Tartuffe is always aware of the reality underlying his mask of piety, but the Habert sisters in the *Paysan parvenu* seem to lose sight of it. Like Sartre's famous *garçon de café*, who carries his tray just a bit too perfectly for us to believe that the act is completely natural, they are too pious for the reader not to realize that their piety is a mask. However, they seem to have been the real dupes of the mask of devotion that, in Molière's play, was intended to trick others.

From whatever perspective we view Tartuffe, we shall witness the duality between self and mask that is at the core of his existence as a comic character. We are always aware of the breach between what he is and what he pretends to be. As Auerbach puts it, "Tartuffe is not the embodiment of an intelligent self-disciplined hypocrite, but a coarse-grained fellow with strong, crude instincts who tries to assume the attitude of a bigot because it seems to promise results and despite the fact that it is not becoming to him at all and clashes with his inner nature and outward appearance."[5] The entire first act of the play prepares the audience for the appearance of a hypocrite, and the second act reinforces this already strong impression. The audience's hostility is aroused to such a pitch that a sincere man in the shoes of Tartuffe would be unimaginable. Needless to say, we are not disappointed, for Tartuffe appears on stage speaking of his devotion in the most exaggerated terms: "Laurent, serrez ma haire avec ma discipline,/Et priez que toujours le Ciel vous illumine" (III,ii, 853–54). The rhetoric of Tartuffe's form of pious devotion is so overstated, his every attempt to appear to be a *dévot* so out of proportion with what we would expect from a truly pious man, that the audience cannot take his mask seriously. At the end of the play, we feel not the slightest sympathy for him, for we sense—and rightly so—that Tartuffe's shock at being found out has no ontological dimensions. His true identity remains intact behind the mask, so hidden that the notion of real personal suffering can never be associated with Tartuffe. The distance between self and mask is so great that we almost feel as if it were the mask that is about to be locked up.

The other characters in the play, with two notable exceptions, are equally clairvoyant in their appreciation of Tartuffe. Dorine sees the truth immediately: "Tout son fait, croyez-moi, n'est rien qu'hypocrisie" (I,i,70). Elmire and her immediate family all have first-hand proof of Tartuffe's treachery, whereas Cléante, true to his function as *raisonneur*, takes the more academic tack of reproaching his brother-in-law for not distinguishing between appearance and reality: "Hé quoi? vous ne ferez nulle distinction/Entre l'hypocrisie et la dévotion?" (I,v,331–32). Only Madame Pernelle and her son are deceived, and this does not happen by chance. Enraged at not being mistress of the household, she explains her precipitate departure in the first scene of the play: "C'est que je ne puis voir tout ce ménage-ci,/Et que de me complaire on ne prend nul souci" (I,i,7–8). Taking the side of Tartuffe becomes for Madame Pernelle the only way of experiencing power over the family, albeit a vicarious experience at best. So great are her needs to dominate that even at the end of the play, she remains unconvinced by her own son's account of Tartuffe's behavior: "Mon Dieu! le plus souvent l'apparence déçoit./Il ne faut pas toujours juger sur ce qu'on voit" (V,iii,1679–80). As for Orgon, Dorine is correct

[5] Erich Auerbach, "The 'Faux Dévot'," in *Mimesis*, trans. Willard Trask (New York: Doubleday, 1957), 317–18.

in her initial evaluation of his relationship to Tartuffe: "Enfin il en est fou; c'est son tout, son héros" (I,ii,195) and later when she describes him as "un bourru fieffé/Qui s'est de son Tartuffe entièrement coiffé" (II,iii, 627–28). What she is not cognizant of is the extent to which Orgon is in his own way using Tartuffe. He is genuinely pleased by the hypocrite's penury for the simple reason that "mon secours pourra lui donner les moyens/De sortir d'embarras et rentrer dans ses biens" (II,ii,491–92). After Damis denounces the scoundrel to his father, Orgon explicitly acknowledges the battle he is waging with his family, who would like to banish Tartuffe from the household: "Mais plus on fait effort afin de l'en bannir,/Plus j'en veux employer à l'y mieux retenir" (III,vi,1123–24). That he is using Tartuffe to assure his own supremacy is even articulated: "Ah je vous brave tous, et vous ferai connoître/Qu'il faut qu'on m'obéisse et que je suis le maître" (II, vi, 1129–30). This explains why he pleads with Tartuffe to remain with his family.[6]

What distinguishes Tartuffe from the later *faux dévots* whom we shall study is that he is himself as aware of his own lies as the other characters. He even knows that his real ends might be best served by letting his mask fall for a brief time. Professor Moore has perceptively analyzed the four points in the play when Tartuffe willingly reveals something of the reality lurking behind the mask.[7] In each of these instances, Tartuffe steps out of his role only because he deems success more likely if he puts his mask aside. His total lack of commitment to his role is revealed by his willingness to betray it at every turn. To tell Elmire that "les gens comme nous brûlent d'un feu discret" (III,iii,995) is to reveal something about the man behind the mask; but to enlarge upon the idea of this brand of discretion —"Le soin que nous prenons de notre renommée/Répond de toute chose à la personne aimée" (III,iii,997–98)—is to divulge both that he is wearing a mask and how that mask functions. The slightest desire to be what the mask represents would preclude such an admission. Perceptive though he is, Cléante seems not to have grasped the degree of Tartuffe's lack of commitment to his mask when in the fourth act he appeals to Tartuffe-*dévot*: "Sacrifiez à Dieu toute votre colère,/Et remettez le fils en grâce avec le père" (IV,i,1201–02). Having exhausted the gamut of "pious" responses to the rational arguments of his interlocutor, Tartuffe simply

---

[6] I owe much to the work of Professor Lionel Gossman—*Men and Masks* (Baltimore: The Johns Hopkins Press, 1963), 100–44—for my view of the various characters' perception of Tartuffe.

[7] W. G. Moore, *Molière: A New Criticism* (Oxford: Clarendon Press, 1949), 45–48.

withdraws: "Il est, Monsieur, trois heures et demie:/Certain devoir pieux me demande là-haut" (IV,i,1266–67). Any ploy based on Tartuffe's commitment to his role is doomed from the outset to failure.

The language of the play is calculated to emphasize the distance between Tartuffe the actor and his mask. Orgon's need for Tartuffe blinds him to the obvious fact that the *dévot* is really a hypocrite. Cléante tries to sensitize him to the difference (I,v,331–32), adding: "Vous les [hypocrisy and devotion] voulez traiter d'un semblable langage,/Et rendre même honneur au masque qu'au visage" (I,v,333–34). In his very next speech Cléante defines himself as a "raisonneur"—one who can "Du faux avec le vrai faire la différence" (I,v,354), a man who is not taken in by "le dehors plâtré d'un zèle spécieux" (I,v,360). Elmire is no less cognizant of the distance between Tartuffe the man and his mask. Her goal in the second seduction scene is to "Faire poser le masque à cette âme hypocrite" (IV,iv,1374). Of course, what none of the characters had reckoned with was Tartuffe's consciousness of the split between himself and his mask and the concomitant ability to use the mask to his own advantage. Telling Orgon the truth after he has been caught trying to seduce Elmire, Tartuffe asks: "Vous fiez-vous, mon frère, à mon extérieur?/ . . . vous vous laissez tromper à l'apparence" (III,vi,1095,1097). As the author of the *Lettre sur l'Imposteur* knew, the play is based on the unambiguous dichotomy between what Tartuffe really is and what he pretends to be. Whatever success Tartuffe has is largely due to his detachment, his ability to manipulate his mask, to be the spectator of its acts. On the other hand, it is equally true that his downfall, which is all of his own making, results from the mistakes he makes in handling his role. Nonetheless, in this form of hypocrisy, there is always a known truth, a mask devised to hide that truth, and others to be duped. Never are the three confused.

The hypocrite depicted by La Bruyère in his *Caractères* has a more complex relationship with his own role. For this very reason, some critics have seen Onuphre as little more than an exaggerated version of his illustrious predecessor. In his *Histoire de la littérature française*, Désiré Nisard condemns the portrait roundly: "Certains portraits de La Bruyère sont excessifs, moins encore par l'exagération que par le trop grand nombre de traits; chaque original en porte plus que sa charge. Ce sont les Hercules du ridicule." He goes on to attack the portrait of Onuphre as "démesurément long" and an audacious assault against Tartuffe.[8] In a

---

[8] Désiré Nisard, *Histoire de la littérature française* (4 vols.; Paris: Firmin-Didot, 1889), III, 214–15.

more recent study, Professor A. J. Krailsheimer disapproves of the excessive subtlety of the portrait, but he adds an interesting commentary: "In the event Onuphre is described in terms so indistinguishable from the true 'dévot' of La Bruyère's day that the portrait of the latter was prudently omitted from later editions."[9] Tempting though such a critical maneuver might well be, to dismiss Onuphre as an overblown copy of Tartuffe is a serious mistake. The difference between the two characters is precisely that although Tartuffe's pious behavior could only fool someone like Orgon, who needs to be convinced, Onuphre's could take us in had not La Bruyère been careful to give his reader other signs of its factitious quality. It is nonetheless true that the portrait of Onuphre is a kind of response to Tartuffe. Like Tartuffe, "S'il entre dans l'église, il observe d'abord de qui il peut être vu, et selon la découverte qu'il vient de faire il se met à genoux et prie, ou il ne songe ni à se mettre à genoux ni à prier."[10] Onuphre frequents only churches likely to be crowded because "on y est vu." Once in church, he not only prays, "mais il médite, il pousse des élans et des soupirs." Similarly, Tartuffe "faisoit des soupirs, de grands élancements,/Et baisoit humblement la terre à tous moments" (I,v,287–88). It is Orgon who has described Tartuffe's behavior in these lines, and the audience is already conditioned to assume that whatever he reports about Tartuffe pertains only to the mask of the hypocrite. Since Tartuffe has yet to appear on stage, we learn of his insincerity indirectly, from what others such as Dorine say about him and from our knowledge that whatever Orgon perceives as sincerity is really all sham. But with La Bruyère's character, the fact that "il joue son rôle" is immediately given as an integral part of the portrait.

Onuphre is also much more clever than his counterpart. "Il ne dit point: *Ma haire et ma discipline*, au contraire; il passeroit pour ce qu'il est, pour un hypocrite, et il veut passer pour ce qu'il n'est pas, pour un homme dévot." He prefers rather to convince others of his piety "sans qu'il le dise." Since it will be more difficult to make others accept him as a *dévot* without telling them verbally what it is that he wants them to perceive, Onuphre must give himself over all the more assiduously to his acting. His task is that of the mime, whose role must be more painstakingly drawn

---

[9] A. J. Krailsheimer, "La Bruyère," *Studies in Self-Interest* (Oxford: Clarendon Press, 1962), 202.

[10] Jean de La Bruyère, *Les Caractères*, in *Oeuvres complètes*, ed. Gustave Servois (4 vols.; Paris: Hachette, 1865), III, 154–59. All in-text citations from the *Caractères* refer to this edition.

because of the absence of words. Onuphre's art is a more demanding one, but the absence of language makes it less likely that he will commit the mistake of Tartuffe, who, trying to seduce Elmire, uses the language of his mask to express needs that cannot belong to the mask. Both Tartuffe and Onuphre are sensuous beings, but the latter, having insinuated himself into the household of a wealthy patron, "ne cajole point sa femme." The physical desires of the being behind the mask are never out of control, and he is above all careful never to subordinate his role to them: "Il est encore plus éloigné d'employer pour la [the wife of his patron] flatter et pour la séduire le jargon de la dévotion; ce n'est point par habitude qu'il le parle, mais avec dessein." He is preoccupied with the veracity of his mask.

However, there is more to this than virtuoso acting, for Onuphre, like many of La Bruyère's other characters, is, as we have already mentioned, an amateur. Absent is the overweening pride of Tartuffe. Whereas Onuphre "ne se persuade point que celui ou celle qui a beaucoup de bien puisse avoir tort," Tartuffe assumes that Orgon cannot possibly be right about anything. For though he is far from that true Christian humility that he affects so well, Onuphre does humble himself before his mask of piety, rather than flaunting it as Tartuffe is wont to do: "aussi ne se joue-t-il pas à la ligne directe." Onuphre's mask fascinates him: he actually wants others to think that he is a *dévot* for the sole pleasure of being thought a pious man. If he hides his evil machinations from his Prince, it is "par la crainte qu'il a d'être découvert et de paroître ce qu'il est." Tartuffe, by contrast, is never disturbed by being discovered, except insofar as this might make it impossible for him to succeed in his other goals. He is even willing on several occasions to reveal his true face. The difference between the two hypocrites is one of degree. They both have certain goals and use their mask to obtain them. But whereas Tartuffe's identity does not depend upon his mask, Onuphre actually wants to be what he is pretending to be. It is not by chance that Onuphre's taste in women goes to those who "fleurissent et qui prospèrent à l'ombre de la [fausse] dévotion." It is only natural that a hypocrite attracted by the piety that he affects would prefer women of his own type. Here we have the intimation of an accord between the desires of the man behind the mask and the mask itself, a kind of dialogue between the man and his mask in which the mask has more to offer than a success unrelated to the role in question. The distance between the mask and the man who wears it is blurred in the portrait of Onuphre:

"Onuphre n'est pas un dévot, mais *il veut être cru tel*, et par une parfaite, quoique fausse imitation de la piété, ménager sourdement ses intérêts" [emphasis added]. Tartuffe-actor's only concern is with his interests. Appearing to be a *dévot* is nothing more than a means to an end for him. But Onuphre wants to be seen as a *dévot* as well as enrich himself. His imitation must be perfect.

What is new about Onuphre is the active dialogue between what he is and what he wants other people to believe he is. His hypocrisy is of the highest order in that it has become the pivotal point not only of his behavior, but also of his thought. The dichotomy between the man and his mask now exists at the deepest level of the character's being. Onuphre's obsession with absolute perfection, that is, the resolution of the conflict between the man and his mask, can end only in the dissolution of clear distinctions between the two, if the portrait is not first brought to an arbitrary conclusion. This possibility is suggested in the seventh edition of the *Caractères* (Onuphre had appeared for the first time in the sixth edition), where La Bruyère defines a *faux dévot*: "Un dévot [*faux dévot*] est celui qui sous un roi athée, seroit athée" (*De la mode*, 21). It is not that the *faux dévot* would somehow remain true to other feelings, but rather that he would *be* an atheist. In an earlier chapter on women, La Bruyère speaks of a "fausse dévote" as "celle qui veut tromper Dieu, et qui se trompe elle-même" (*Des femmes*, 44). Now the truth has been compromised by appearances, and we are very close to the brand of hypocrisy typical of the world of Marivaux's works.

Early in Marivaux's *Paysan parvenu*, Jacob encounters his future wife, Mlle Habert. Having suffered a fainting spell on the Pont Neuf after a period of fasting, she allows Jacob to accompany her to her house, where she introduces him to her two sisters and their maid Catherine and tries to convince the former that they should hire the kindly Jacob. Catherine is charged with getting Jacob a good meal in the kitchen. Her "air d'une dévotion revêche, en colère et ardente" leads Jacob to give a description of "les dévots" and compare them unfavorably with "les gens pieux." The most striking difference between Marivaux's *dévot*s and Tartuffe or Onuphre is that the former seem to have no ends other than the appearance of piety and true devotion to God. Mlle Habert and her sisters have adopted the mode of existence that seems most congenial to them. They need the recognition of others in order to sustain the roles they are playing, but never is there a question of enriching themselves or acquiring worldly goods of any sort from their efforts as actresses. Although Marivaux makes it clear that they are playing roles—and this most brilliantly in the description of their eating habits—their identity as individuals is completely dependent upon their masks. Contradictions obvious to others reveal that these sisters are not true *dévotes*, but the sisters, unlike Tartuffe, do not seem to be aware of the contradictions. Jacob is baffled by his mistresses' self-mortifying lack of appetite and their simultaneous ability to devour an enormous meal. Finally he discovers that their apparent disgust at table, their disinterest in the food being served "m'avaient caché la sourde activité de leurs dents." However, what is most astonishing is how "elles se persuadaient être sobres en se conservant le plaisir de ne pas l'être; c'était à la faveur de cette singerie, que leur dévotion laissait innocemment le champ libre à l'intempérance."[11] They are so absorbed in their mask of piety that the reality of gluttony does not compromise their innocence. This is not the perspective of a Tartuffe carefully watching his every move.

Although such *dévots* as these "n'en [being "vrais serviteurs de Dieu"] ont que la contenance," their relationship to their mask is different from that of earlier hypocrites. They are fascinated to the point of losing themselves in the contrivances of the mask. While Tartuffe and Onuphre went to church because "on y est vu," Marivaux's hypocrites "vont à l'église simplement pour y aller, pour avoir le plaisir de s'y trouver." The very feel of devotional books in their hands is an experience full of sensuality, and, unlike their earlier counterparts, they retire into deserted corners of the church "pour y jouir superbement d'une posture de méditatifs, s'exciter à des transports pieux, *afin de croire qu'on a une âme bien distinguée*, si on en attrape" [emphasis added]. The other for whose benefit the gestures of piety had previously been intended is here made interior to such a degree that the dupe is none other than the *dévot* himself. Ultimately the mask begins to feed on itself as the character is able to experience the acutely pleasurable sensation of religious ecstasy born from his pride at having had such a feeling in the first place. So effectively does he trick himself that he returns from church "tout gonflé de respect pour soi-même."[12]

This atitude of the man tricked by the ploy he had been using to dupe others is carried over into other situations as well in Marivaux's work. When Jacob first arrives in Paris with his wagon of wine, he first stays with

---

[11] Marivaux, *Le Paysan Parvenu*, ed. Frédéric Deloffre (Paris: Garnier, 1959), 47, 53.
[12] *Ibid.*, 47, 48.

the owner of the estate worked by his family. Just as the *faux dévot* is innocent of falsehood when wearing his mask of piety, the mistress of this house is so much a coquette that she cannot really be called one: "Madame, chez elle, ne passait pas pour coquette; elle ne l'était point non plus, car elle l'était sans réflexion, sans le savoir" (p.10). She is so at home in her behavior as coquette that "elle vit dans sa coquetterie comme on vivrait dans l'état le plus décent et le plus ordinaire." Her coquettishness was "un petit libertinage de la meilleure foi du monde." Marivaux's fondness for coupling seemingly contradictory words often reflects a profound understanding of the function of his character's mask. His work is replete with characters who, like this first coquette encountered by Jacob, love virtue without hating (or avoiding) vice: "Aimant de tout son coeur la vertu, sans inimitié pour le vice" (p. 11). Jacob himself from time to time falls victim to the role he is playing. At Mme d'Alain's table Jacob is so unreservedly gay and insouciant that Mlle Habert jealously fears that he may have become interested in one of Mme d'Alain's daughters. Although he does not lie in his heated plea of his own innocence, he does try to be convincing, "avoir l'air et le ton touchant, le ton d'un homme qui pleure . . . orner un peu la vérité" (p. 92). The result is predictable: "Je fis si bien que j'en fus la dupe moi-même."

Marivaux's hypocrite differs from Onuphre in degree only. Unlike Tartuffe, these characters no longer have a well-established identity that can be relied upon to sustain itself behind a mask originally intended to deceive others. In a world of growing social and political instability, they are not possessed of a self firmly grounded in hard reality. Tartuffe was able to control his mask in a way that is not always possible in the worlds of La Bruyère and Marivaux—worlds in which appearances vie with reality rather than tacitly serve its ends. In the theater of Molière it is not possible for a bourgeois to become a "gentilhomme." However, the passage from Jacob to Monsieur de la Vallée is at times less unthinkable in Marivaux's novel. The distance between the man and his mask has been so diminished, the interaction between them so tightened, that he who would tear off the mask would risk destroying the man.

MOLIÈRE'S PRESENCE
IN SELECTED PLAYS OF MARIVAUX
Alfred Cismaru

Among the enormous scholarship available on Molière, and the more limited number of works at the disposal of Marivaux specialists, there is no book that analyzes exclusively the relationship between the two writers. In general, critics of Molière have limited themselves to parenthetical allusions to the influence the seventeenth-century writer exercised on the theater of Marivaux, while spokesmen for the eighteenth-century playwright have either minimized or denied outright any possibility of a relationship. The fact is (and a curious fact it is) that the critics for *Le Mercure de France*, when reviewing the plays of Marivaux in the 1720's and 1730's, made no mention of any possible *moliéresque* influence. Close as they were to the theater of Molière, they failed to indicate any connection between the seventeenth-century writer and Marivaux. D'Alembert himself is reported to have quoted his contemporary as follows: "J'aime mieux être humblement assis sur le dernier banc dans la petite troupe des auteurs originaux, qu'orgueilleusement placé à la première ligne dans le nombreux bétail des singes littéraires." And he commented further: "Il avait le malheur de ne pas estimer beaucoup Molière, et le malheur plus grand de ne pas s'en cacher. Il ne craignait pas même, quand on le mettait à son aise sur cet article, d'avouer naïvement qu'il ne se croyait pas inférieur à ce grand peintre de la nature."[1]

This comment proved to be quite convincing for many Anglo-Saxon critics of Marivaux, if less persuasive for French specialists. For example, the opening sentences of the most widely used popularization of Marivaux in this country, Kenneth N. McKee's book, state the following: "Marivaux was the most original French dramatist of the eighteenth century. In an age when leading dramatists . . . blindly followed the Molière tradition, Marivaux . . . dared to be different. In fact, he repudiated Molière so openly that he drew the wrath of critics and public alike."[2] E. J. H. Greene,

[1] Quoted by Marcel Arland, in *Marivaux* (Paris: Gallimard, 1950), 102–03.
[2] Kenneth N. McKee, *The Theater of Marivaux* (New York: New York University Press, 1958), 5–6.

the most recent Anglo-Saxon to have published a full length study of
Marivaux, labeled the possibility of a relationship between Molière and
the eighteenth-century playwright nothing but "a red herring."[3]

On the other hand, French scholars have been more prone to point
to similiarities, albeit unspecified, in the works of the two dramatists.
Indication of such similarities ranges all the way from minor and acceptable emulation to major and debatable accusations of plagiarism allegedly
practiced by Marivaux. While the reputable Gustave Larroumet affirms
that "Avec Marivaux, la comédie entre dans une période nouvelle. Il ne
se rattachait directement à aucun de ses devanciers. Très désireux de ne
pas les imiter, même les plus illustres . . . (but in a footnote he comments)
Telle était du moins son intention; en réalité il n'a pu se garder complètement de réminiscences de détail;"[4] and while the more recent commentator, Marcel Arland, admits

> Qu'il n'ait pas aimé Molière, c'est possible . . . . Peut-être aussi, à l'antipathie
> déclarée de Marivaux à l'égard de Molière, faut-il voir la réaction naturelle
> d'un génie qui veut se préserver d'une redoutable influence. . . . Il lui arrive
> d'ailleurs de trouver un appui chez son grand aîné, là où coïncident leurs na-
> tures, par exemple pour certaines querelles d'amoureux, certains traits de
> moeurs, de caractère, ou telle satire de l'èducation; là aussi où s'imposent,
> hors de toute nature particulière, les exigences fondamentales de la scène. Au
> demeurant, il existe entre eux un lien plus profond. . . . [5]

Molière specialists, on the contrary, have made often sweeping and even
derogatory statements concerning the influence of Molière on Marivaux.
Ferdinand Brunetière, for example, wrote: "Marivaux a voulu refaire
telles et telles pièces de Molière, et non pas *Le Sicilien* ou *Le Mariage forcé*,
mais *L'Ecole des femmes* dans son *Ecole des mères* et *Le Misanthrope* dans
Les Sincères;"[6] and Maurice Donnay asserted that "Marivaux n'a fait
que répéter, avec mille variantes, détours et subtilités, des situations senti-
mentales qui sont plus sobrement traitées et avec moins de marivaudage,
c'est certain, dans *La Princesse d'Elide*."[7]

In the face of such contradictory statements, always uncorroborated,
it is perhaps appropriate to examine closely the texts in order to determine
to what extent Molière may have influenced the work of Marivaux. The
influence of Molière on his two major novels, *La Vie de Marianne* and

---

[3] E. J. H. Greene, *Marivaux* (Toronto: University of Toronto Press, 1965), 335–36.
[4] Gustave Larroumet, *Marivaux, vie et oeuvre* (Paris: Hachette, 1881), 155–56.
[5] Arland, *Marivaux*, 103–04.
[6] Ferdinand Brunetière, *Revue des deux mondes* (April 1, 1881), 675.
[7] Maurice Donnay, *Molière* (Paris: Arthème Fayard, 1911), 309.

Le Paysan parvenu, has been already analyzed.[8] Even a superficial reading of the plays of the eighteenth-century dramatist indicates that sporadic to frequent reminiscences of Molière are present in sixteen of Marivaux's comedies. They are, in chronological order: *Le Père prudent et équitable*, *Arlequin poli par l'amour*, *La Surprise de l'amour*, *Le Dénouement imprévu*, *L'Héritier de village*, *L'Ile de la raison*, *La (Seconde) Surprise de l'amour*, *Le Triomphe de Plutus*, *Les Serments indiscrets*, *L'Ecole des mères*, *L'Heureux stratagème*, *La Mère confidente*, *Les Fausses confidences*, *Les Sincères*, *L'Epreuve* and *Félicie*. Because an examination of the relationship between Molière and Marivaux in the other plays has already been done,[9] the influence of the seventeenth-century dramatist will be discussed only in *La Surprise de l'amour*, *Le Dénouement imprévu*, *L'Héritier de village*, *L'Ile de la raison*, *Les Serments indiscrets*, *L'Heureux stratagème* and *L'Epreuve*.

It will be recalled that *La Surprise de l'amour* deals with the feigned reciprocal disdain of Lélio and the Countess who, after "much ado about nothing," confess their love for each other and marry. This play, "which established a type of comedy most closely associated with his [Marivaux's] name,"[10] contains, nevertheless, a number of *moliéresque* themes to be found in *Le Dépit amoureux*, *La Princesse d'Elide* and *Le Bourgeois gentilhomme*. The association with *Le Dépit amoureux* is not only obvious from the fact that both comedies evolve around a *dépit*, but more importantly from the fact that the latter gives rise to strikingly similar situations and dialog. For example, in both comedies master and valet discuss the proper attitude to adopt with women. To arrive at an attitude, they find it necessary in both plays to find a definition for "woman," and both settle on the word *animal*. Moreover, both valets conclude that it is best to give up on the female sex, and they express their resolution in similar phraseology; Molière has his Gros-René declare: "Et moi, je ne veux plus m'embarrasser de femme,/A toutes je renonce . . ." (IV,2), while Arlequin concludes: "Oh! voilà qui est fait! je renonce à toutes les femmes . . ." (I,2). Both valets, then, advance similar thoughts with the same words arranged differently.

---

[8] See my article, "Molière's *Le Tartuffe* in Marivaux's Work," in *Kentucky Foreign Language Quarterly*, XII, No. 3 (1965), 142–54.

[9] See my articles: "Agnès and Angélique: An Attempt To Settle the Relationship," *The French Review* (April 1962), 472–77; "The Moliéresque Origins of *Les Fausses confidences*," *Kentucky Romance Quarterly* (Spring 1968), 223–29 and "*Les Sincères* and *le Misanthrope*," *The French Review* (May 1969), 865–70.

[10] McKee, *Theater of Marivaux*, 30.

Another situation common to both plays is the quarrel and the re-conciliation of the two lovers, a theme dear to Molière and exploited by Marivaux in a number of his comedies. The similarities of tone and vocabulary could best be noted in side by side quotations, but because of space limitations, suffice it to point to the fact that in both act four, scene three of Molière's play, and act two, scene seven of Marivaux's, the lovers simulate disdain for each other and express a desire to part, followed by an inability to carry out this desire. It should also be noted that in both comedies the matter of the returning of a portrait precipitates a reconcilia-tion scene. And, seconding the principal action of the two intrigues are the quarrel and the reconciliation of the valet-soubrette couples who, under the pen of both Molière and of Marivaux, copy the moods of their respective masters.

Remarkable similarities can also be seen between *La Surprise de l'amour* and *La Princesse d'Elide*. The Princess, who despises men, expresses her scorn for love as follows: "Toutes ses larmes, tous ses soupirs, tous ces hommages, tous ces respects, sont des embûches qu'on tend à notre coeur, et qui souvent l'engagent à commettre des lâchetés . . . et je ne puis souffrir qu'une âme qui fait profession d'un peu de fierté, ne trouve pas une honte horrible à de telles faiblesses" (II, 1). Marivaux's Countess similarly re-jects love and concludes that it is not a sentiment that someone with self-respect ought to have: "Cesser d'avoir de l'amour pour un homme, c'est, à mon compte, connaître sa faute, s'en repentir, en avoir honte, sentir la misère de l'idole qu'on adorait, et rentrer dans le respect qu'une femme se doit à elle-même" (I,7). Marivaux's imitation does not stop here. The reply of a cousin of the Princess, Cynthie ("He! madame, il est de certaines faiblesses qui ne sont point honteuses, et qu'il est beau même d'avoir dans les plus hauts degrés de gloire;" [II,1]) is echoed by the Countess's servant, Colombine, in a response she addresses to her: "Soyons raisonnables; condamnez les amants déloyaux, les conteurs de sornettes, à être jetés dans la rivière une pierre au col, à merveille; enfermez les coquettes entre quatre murailles, fort bien; mais les amants fidèles, dressez-leur de belles et bonnes statues pour encourager le public" (I,7). Also, in both plays it is the man who confesses his love first, in markedly similar phraseology.

There is also an obvious resemblance between act three, scene nine of *Le Bourgeois gentilhomme* and act one, scene two of *La Surprise de l'amour*. In Molière's play, Cléonte, who has been rejected by Lucile, denounces the girl to Covielle, who, encouraged by his master, proceeds to criticize her. However, each criticism of Covielle is rejected by and answered with a praise by Cléonte. Finally, Covielle wonders how his master will be able to forget her if he still thinks she is perfect. Cléonte's reply is: "C'est en quoi ma vengeance sera plus éclatante, en quoi je veux faire mieux voir la force de mon coeur à la hair, à la quitter, toute belle, toute pleine d'attraits, toute aimable que je la trouve" (III,9). Lélio too, having been rejected, tries to persuade himself and his valet that women are harmful and should be avoided. But in so doing he only manages to show his inner dependence on the fair sex. What should have been a critical denunciation becomes a eulogy. And, like Cléonte, Lélio hopes to be able to avoid women in spite of, or perhaps because of, their infinite attractiveness. He replies to Arlequin: "Je me ressouviens qu'il y a des femmes au monde, qu'elles sont aimables, et ce ressouvenir ne va pas sans quelques émotions de coeur; mais ce sont ces émotions-là qui me rendent inébranlable dans la résolution de ne plus voir de femmes" (I,2).

While the fine gradations of love in *La Surprise de l'amour* are absent from the three plays of Molière which served Marivaux, it is nevertheless apparent from the foregoing that the eighteenth-century dramatist made use of a number of *moliéresque* devices and themes.

No critic of Marivaux has previously associated *Le Dénouement imprévu* with any of Molière's plays. This may be due to the fact that the *Dénouement imprévu* is a less known and more infrequently staged comedy. Yet, striking similarities exist between this play and scenes from *Le Tartuffe* and *Monsieur de Pourceaugnac* which point to a definite *moliéresque* influence.

When, for example, in Molière's play, Mariane is advised by her father that she is to marry Tartuffe, Dorine, the servant, is angry that her mistress does not show enough opposition:

> . . . Je vois que vous voulez
> Etre à monsieur Tartuffe; et j'aurais, quand j'y pense,
> Tort de vous détourner d'une telle alliance . . .
> Il a l'oreille rouge et le teint bien fleuri . . .
> Vous irez par la coche en sa petite ville,
> Qu'en oncles et cousins vous trouverez fertile,
> Et vous vous plairez fort à les entretenir;
> D'abord chez le beau monde on vous fera venir,
> Vour irez visiter, pour votre bienvenue,
> Madame la baillive et madame l'élue,
> Qui d'un siège pliant vous feront honorer.
> Là, dans le carnaval. . . . (II, 3)

The situation in Marivaux's comedy is similar: Mlle Argante has just been told that she is to marry Eraste instead of Dorante, whom she loves. As in *Le Tartuffe*, the servant, Lisette, tries to convince the young girl to exhibit more repugnance towards the arrangements made by her father. And Lisette's arguments are similar to those of Dorine. She proceeds to praise Eraste and the kind of life Mlle Argante will have with him, in a highly sarcastic manner, in order to convince her mistress that a less scrupulous opposition to the marriage is in order:

> Je crois qu'effectivement vous avez raison. Il vaut mieux que vous épousiez ce juene rustre que nous attendons. Que de repos vous allez avoir à sa campagne . . . il n'y a pas là que de . . . bon appétit . . . J'oubliais le meilleur. Vous aurez parfois des galants hobereaux qui viendront vous rendre hommage . . . Vous irez vous promener avec eux . . . Prenez votre parti, sinon je recommence, et je vous nomme tous les animaux de votre ferme, jusqu'à votre mari." (scene 4)

Thus the method of attack is similar: Dorine refers to the appetite of Tartuffe in "Il a l'oreille rouge et le teint bien fleuri," while Lisette says: "il n'y a pas là que de . . . bon appétit;" Dorine mentions the "petite ville" of Tartuffe, and Lisette satirizes "ce jeune rustre" and his "campagne;" Dorine anticipates with irony the entertaining Mariane will have to do in: "vous vous plairez fort à les entretenir," while Lisette forsees with sarcasm: "Vous aurez parfois des galants hobereaux qui viendront vous rendre hommage . . . Vous irez vous promener avec eux;" Dorine speaks of "le carnaval" in which Mariane will have to live, and Lisette mentions the "hobereaux"[11] and "tous les animaux de votre ferme."

There is another notable similarity between *Le Dénouement imprévu* and *Monsieur de Pourceaugnac*. In Molière's play, it will be recalled, Julie meets Monsieur de Pourceaugnac and flirts with him in a deliberate manner designed to disgust and scare away the future husband: "Qu'il est bien fait! qu'il a bon air! et que je suis contente d'avoir un tel époux! Souffrez que je l'embrasse, et que je lui témoigne . . . Que je suis aise de vous voir! et que je brûle d'impatience . . . ! [To her father] Ne voulez-vous pas que je caresse l'époux que vous m'avez choisi?" (II,6). Similarly, in Marivaux's comedy Mlle Argante meets Eraste, and with the same calculated deliberation she puts on the mask of a coquette: "Sait-il aimer? a-t-il des sentiments, de la figure? est-il grand, est-il petit? Souffrez que je l'embrasse" (scene 2).

These and other less important similarities point to Marivaux's con-

---

[11] Although the secondary meaning of this word is "gentilhommes campagnards," its primary meaning is "petits faucons, genre d'oiseaux rapaces."

tinued dependence on bits and pieces of Molière that heighten the humor of an otherwise weak and obscure comedy in the repetoire of the eighteenth-century playwright.

In the case of *L'Héritier de village*, Gustave Larroumet noted, but without textual examples: "*L'Héritier de village* rappelle à chaque instant *George Dandin* et *Le Bourgeois gentilhomme*."[12] In point of fact, *L'Héritier de village* recalls the plot of *George Dandin* more in general than in particular. While Molière's comedy deals with the consequences of one's marrying outside of one's class, Marivaux's play treats the adventures and misadventures of a peasant, Blaise, who has inherited a considerable sum of money and whose visions of grandeur and desire "de brûler l'étape," to acquire servants, and to marry his children into the nobility all collapse when he loses his fortune in the investments made for him by his *homme d'affaire*. Thus both plays share the basic situation of a social climber, with this difference: George Dandin suffers the consequences of his continued fortune, while Blaise is saved by the loss of his.

Nevertheless, there are two specific and immediately discernible similarities between Marivaux's comedy and Molière's. The first bears on an equal concern in both plays with the proper way of addressing aristocratic persons by using, not their names or such words as *belle-mère* and *beau-père*, but rather simply *Madame* and *Monsieur*. Scene four of act one in Molière's play and scenes two and three of Marivaux's bear, therefore, resemblances of tone and vocabulary which could not have occurred had Marivaux not remembered the famous *moliéresque* farce.

This is particularly plausible when one notes the resemblances between *L'Hértier de village* and *Le Bourgeois gentilhomme*, for it is possible that, while recalling in the main the latter play, Marivaux had kept in mind also certain situations in *George Dandin*. Similarities between *Le Bourgeois gentilhomme* and *L'Héritier de village* concern a number of episodes in both plays. For example, Monsieur Jourdain's preoccupation with the so-called necessity of having servants just so as to appear a *personne de qualité*:

MONSIEUR JOURDAIN: Laquais! holà, mes deux laquais!
PREMIER LAQUAIS: Que voulez-vous, monsieur?
MONSIEUR JOURDAIN: Rien. C'est pour voir si vous m'entendez bien (I, 2).

---

[12] Larroumet, *Marivaux, vie et oeuvre*, 159.

This exchange is simply reworked by Marivaux in the following dialog:

BLAISE: Eh! eh! eh! baille-moi cinq sous de monnaie, te dis-je.
CLAUDINE: Pourquoi donc?
BLAISE: Pour ce garçon qui apporte mon paquet depuis la voiture jusqu'à chez nous, pendent que je marchais tout bellement et à mon aise . . .
CLAUDINE: Et tu dépenses cinq sous en porteux de paquets?
BLAISE: Oui, par magnière de récréation. (scene 1)

Similarly, Monsieur Jourdain's obsessive concern for the clothes proper to nobility in the seventh scene of act two in Molière's play probably served to inspire scene two of Marivaux's, an episode in which Blaise exhibits a no more subtle preoccupation with the same topic. In addition, both plays deal with the mania of showing off by means of lending money to flatterers. In this connection, parts of scene seven of Marivaux's comedy are nothing but pale emulations of parts of act three, scene three of Molière's. Likewide, Monsieur Jourdain and Blaise share an equal interest in the necessity of acquiring and spending money for a mistress. Monsieur Jourdain declares: "Il n'y a point de dépense que je ne fisse, si par là je pouvais trouver le chemin de son coeur. Une femme de qualité a pour moi des charmes ravissants; et c'est un honneur que j'achèterais au prix de toutes choses" (III, 6); while Blaise reasons: "Une autre bagatelle qui est encore pour le bon air c'est que j'aurons une maîtresse qui sera queuque chiffon de femme, qui sera bian laide, et bian sotte, qui ne m'aimera point, que je n'aimerai point non pus; qui me fera des niches, maix qui me coûtera biaucoup, et qui ne vaura guère, et c'est là le pasisir" (scene 2). Thus, Blaise sees the absolute futility of having a mistress whom one does not love, although he will have one for the same reason as that of Monsieur Jourdain, namely because his new position in society requires it. Blaise, while more logical than his antecedant (he is able to anticipate what having a mistress will mean), appears more paradoxical because he will have a mistress despite his unpleasant anticipations. The clairvoyance he exhibits is not, of course, that of a peasant; rather it belongs to Marivaux, who thus bestows upon his hero a dimension not found in Molière's model. Finally, Monsieur Jourdain's affirmation, "J'ai du bien assez pour ma fille" (III, 12), pointing to his wish to buy a nobleman as a son-in-law, is repeated by Blaise who accepts the Chevalier as his daughter's husband in the conclusion: "J'achèterons de la noblesse" (scene 5).

Close examination of the texts reveals, then, that Gustave Larroumet was at least partly right in his otherwise uncorroborated suggestion that Marivaux made use of *moliéresque* themes in *L'Héritier de village*.

Like so many other of Marivaux's minor plays, *L'Ile de la raison* has received little critical attention. The dramatic situation of this comedy is somewhat original (yet not devoid of *moliéresque* influences): eight Europeans have been shipwrecked on an island where a man's size is in proportion to his reasonableness. The Europeans have been reduced to dwarf size. The natives propose to cure them, but this necessitates the abandonment of common European prejudices and customs. The members of the group are finally restored to normal height, with the exception of the Poet and the Philosopher, who are unable to become reasonable.

L'Ile de la raison can be linked to at least three of Molière's plays: *Le Bourgeois gentilhomme*, *Les Femmes savantes* and *Le Malade imaginaire*. The quarrel between the Poet and the Philosopher in Marivaux's comedy recalls, of course, the famous fourth scene of act two in Molière's *Le Bourgeois gentilhomme*. The Poet and the Philosopher poke fun at each other, try to diminish the importance of the other's discipline, and end up fighting, which is exactly what the Maître à Danser, the Maître de Musique, the Maître d'Armes and the Maître de Philosophie do in Molière's comedy. Even a superficial perusal of the texts reveals that act one, scene eight and act three, scene four of Marivaux's composition could hardly have been written (even if we grant the frequency of philosophical debates in the eighteenth century) without the famous example of Molière.

The fifth scene of act three in *Les Femmes savantes* probably contributed also to those parts of Marivaux's play which describe the argument between the Poet and the Philosopher. The quarrel between Trissotin and Vadius, relating to the former's sonnet for Uranie, contains, in germ, all the elements of the petty retorts in which Marivaux's two dwarfed personages engage. Although Molière may have drawn inspiration for similar disputes from actual living situations ("Une scène semblable à celle de Trissotin et de Vadius avait eu lieu entre Ménage et Cotin, chez Mademoiselle, fille de Gaston de France"[13]), the resemblances between the vocabulary used by Marivaux and that of Molière indicate that the eighteenth-century dramatist probably went to the printed word of his predecessor, rather than rely on indirect, hearsay information.

Fragments of *Le Malade imaginaire* may also be noted in Marivaux's comedy. It will be recalled that Molière's prolog apostrophizes doctors as follows: "Votre plus haut savoir n'est que pure chimère,/Vains et peu

---

[13] Molière, *Ouevres* (Paris: G. Charpentier, n.d.), 552.

sages médecins;/Vous ne pouvez guérir. . . . " Later in the play, Béralde attempts to demonstrate the futility of trusting doctors by saying: "C'est de la meilleure foi du monde qu'il vous expédiéra; et il ne fera, en vous tuant, que ce qu'il a fait à sa femme et à ses enfants, et ce qu'en un besoin il ferait à lui-même" (III, 3). The doctor in Marivaux's play is not only accused of, but admits the guilt imputed by Béralde in Molière's comedy:

> BLAISE: Premièrement, faut commencer par vous dire que vous êtes un sot d'être médecin.
> LE MEDECIN: Voilà un paysan bien hardi.
> BLAISE: . . . Dites-moi, sans vous fâcher, étiez-vous en ménage, aviez-vous femme?
> LE MEDECIN: Non, je suis veuf; ma femme est morte à vingt-cinq ans d'une fluxion de poitrine.
> BLAISE: Maugré la doctraine de la Faculté?
> LE MEDECIN: Il ne me fut pas possible de la réchapper.
> BLAISE: Avez-vous des enfants?
> LE MEDECIN: Non.
> BLAISE: Ni en bian ni en mal?
> LE MEDECIN: Non, vous dis-je. J'en avais trois; et ils sont morts de la petite vérole, il y a quatre ans.
> BLAISE: Peste soit du docteur! et de quoi guarissiez-vous donc le monde? (II, 2)

Thus, both Molière's and Marivaux's doctors have failed to cure their wives and children; Molière's doctors are "vains et peu sages;" Marivaux's is "sot;" finally, Molière's doctors are apostrophized with: "Vous ne pouvez guérir;" Marivaux's is asked with sarcasm: "et de quoi guarissiez-vous donc le monde?" While it is true that Molière was not the only comedy writer to satirize medicine,[14] and that irony against doctors was a commonplace at the time, Molière is most closely associated with this type of sarcasm. Moreover, there are no definite similarities between Marivaux's irony against medicine and the irony of Boursault or of Hauteroche; whereas the similarities pointed out between *Le Malade imaginaire* and *L'Ile de la raison* are quite specific.

Critics of Marivaux have not suggested any connection between *Les Sermentes indiscrets* and Molière's comedies. On the other hand, Georges Lafenestre stated clearly, but without furnishing examples, that "*La Princesse d'Elide* fournit des scènes assez nombreuses dans *Les Serments indiscrets*."[15]

The fact is that parts of Marivaux's play do indeed bear a resemblance to that of Molière. As in *La Princesse d'Elide*, *Les Serments indiscrets* deals

---

[14] Boursault wrote *Le Médecin volant* in 1664; Hauteroche wrote *Crispin médecin* in 1670, for example.
[15] Georges Lafenestre, *Molière* (Paris: Hachette, 1920), 192–93.

with the vow of two young people not to marry, although they are destined
to do so by their respective parents. The reasons advanced by Molière's
heroine: "Je ne veux point du tout me commettre à ces gens qui font les
esclaves auprès de nous pour devenir un jour nos tyrans. Toutes ces larmes,
tous ces soupirs, tous ces hommages, tous ces respects, sont des embûches"
(II, 1), are repeated by Lucille in Marivaux's comedy: "Je remarque que
les hommes ne sont bons qu'en qualité d'amants. Soumis, respectueux, et
galants . . . Mais les épousez-vous, la déesse s'humanise-t-elle, leur ido-
lâtrie finit où nos bontés commencent" (I, 2). Granted that Marivaux
might merely express here an ancient and legendary complaint of women,
it should be noted that Lucille stressed in men as *amants* the same qualities
that the Princess had noted in Molière's play, and that both realize men
become tyrants after marriage. While the Princess's and Lucille's arguments might seem similar only because they represent the standard
thinking of women on the subject, they both offer their comments as arguments against a specific marriage which they had vowed to reject.

Another instance of similarity emerges from a comparison of Molière's
and Marivaux's scenes (III, 5; IV, 9) in which both the Princess and Lucille
order their *suivant* to act on their behalf. These episodes contain resemblances of tone and of vocabulary which could hardly be coincidental.

Futhermore, act four, scene seven of Marivaux's play is a counterpart
of Molière's scene (IV, 3) in which Euryale feigns preparing to marry
Aglante in order to awaken the Princess's *dépit*. Later, in fact, the Princess
objects to the projected marriage between Euryale and Aglante by complaining to her father and by using the argument "j'ai été dédaignée" (V, 2),
and Lucille complains to her father in a comparable piece of dialog that
ends with the words: "Il m'a méprisé" (V, 2). From this point on the
endings of both plays are equally precipitous: Euryale confesses his scheme
and declares his love for the Princess, while Damis throws himself at the
feet of Lucille.

It is thus clear that certain key scenes in *La Princesse d'Elide* have their
counterpart in Marivaux's comedy. The similarities bear not only on the
general situations, but also on the tone, the temper, the vocabulary (in
several instances), and the details of the various relationships.

Le Tartuffe, too, is another comedy by Molière which has furnished at
least one of the scenes of *Les Serments indiscrets*. Gustave Larroumet in
his study of Marivaux pointed to the fact that "la scène 7, Acte III, des
Serments indiscrets, entre Damis et Lucille, est une pâle copie de la fameuse

scène du second acte de *Tartuffe* entre Marianne et Valère."[16] Molière's scene is well known: Valère and Marianne quarrel, and Dorine, the servant, attempts to effect a reconciliation of the lovers. Marivaux, in his play, follows this theme, dear to Molière, of the argument between two young persons who are brought together once more through the efforts of a servant displaying more common sense than her master. In his version, Damis's wish to leave is but an echo of Valère's movement to the same effect; Lucille's *dépit* is the reflection of Marianne's sentiments because of which she makes no effort to stop Valère; and Lisette's intervention repeats that of Dorine almost to the letter, both in gesture and in vocabulary. The only thing that is lacking is Molière's masterful development of the comic possibilities of such a scene through swift dialog, a device which escapes Marivaux's pen.

Once again, it was a Molière specialist, Georges Lafenestre, who detected the influence of *La Princesse d'Elide* on one of Marivaux's comedies: "*La Princesse d'Elide* 'lui fournit des scènes assez nombreuses dans . . . L'Heureux stratagème.'"[17] Xavier de Courville comes close to seeing this influence when he declares: "Marivaux, dans *l'Heureux stratagème*, suivra de plus près encore que dans *La Surprise* le sujet de Molière."[18] But neither of the above gives textual examples.

The basic situation in Marivaux's play is a *chassé-croisé*: Dorante, who loves the Countess and who sees the latter's attention being diverted to the Chevalier, has no recourse but to feign interest in the Marquise in order to reawaken the Countess's love for him. Although the type of *chassé-croisé* just described is a commonplace in dramatic literature, there are resemblances which are worth noting.

In Molière's play, Euryale's trouble in continuing to feign the indifference he promised to show the Princess, as well as Moron's intervention in: "Demeurez ferme, au moins, dans le chemin que vous avez pris" (III, 2) are echoed in Marivaux's comedy by Dorante's equal difficulties and by the Marquise's interference in her *tenez bon* of act two, scene two and again of act three, scene four. An additional resemblance can be pointed out between the scene in Molière's comedy in which Euryale administers the *coup de grâce* not only by announcing his marriage to Aglante but also by requesting the Princess's approval of it, and the episode in Marivaux's

[16] Larroumet, *Marivaux, vie et oeuvre*, 193.
[17] Lafenestre, *Molière*, 192.
[18] Xavier de Courville, *Le Théâtre de Marivaux* (Paris: Droz, 1945), I, 66.

play where Dorante likewise indicates his wish to marry the Marquise with the blessings of the Countess. Later in Molière's comedy Euryale confesses the pretense he had displayed and excuses it thus: "Je n'ai jamais aimé que vous . . . et tout ce que j'ai pu vous dire n'a été qu'une feinte . . . que je n'ai suivie qu'avec toutes les violences imaginables" (V, 2). The vocabulary Dorante uses to reveal the strategy employed and to apologize for it is similar: "Et n'a [he, Dorante] jamais cessé de vous aimer . . . Je ne l'ai pu [to persist in the artifice practiced] qu'à force d'amour" (III, 10).

Thus, *La Princesse d'Elide* is reorchestrated by Marivaux in still another of his plays. In justice to the eighteenth-century playwright, however, it should be pointed out that there are differences: Marivaux deals with adult, while Molière deals with young love; in Marivaux's play, the Countess is mature enough to be sorry for and confess her mistakes at the end of the play, whereas in *La Princesse d'Elide* the heroine demands time in order to decide if she will marry Euryale or not; in *L'Heureux stratagème*, at the final curtain, the Marquise and the Chevalier have not yet found happiness, whereas in Molière's comedy Aglante is promised the hand of one of the two other princes (V, 3); and although the play ends before Aglante actually marries, she is such a pale figure in the plot that the question of her happiness is not nearly so important as that of the happiness of the Marquise.

Whatever the originality of Marivaux, *La Princesse d'Elide* occupies a preponderant place in his theater. Another case in point is furnished by *L'Epreuve*. Emile Fabre noted the similarities between *L'Epreuve* and Molière's play when he declared that in this, one of the last comedies of the eighteenth-century playwright, he "mit aussi en présence des amoureux et dans chaque couple, tantôt la femme, tantôt l'homme, qui se donnent le singulier plaisir d'alarmer et de faire pleurer l'amant ou l'amante pour s'assurer de son obéissance et du don total de sa personne."[19]

As it will be recalled, *L'Epreuve* deals with the tests to which a young girl, Angélique, is submitted by her *amant*, Lucidor, who wants to make sure that he is loved for himself and not for his fortune. The tests consist in proposing to Angélique a number of prospective husbands and in contemplating the reaction of the girl each time that a *parti* is introduced. Angélique's persistent refusal to marry any of the men suggested is sufficient proof for Lucidor, who finally declares himself and provides the happy ending of the play.

---

[19] Emile Fabre, *Molière* (Paris: Gallimard, 1935), 194.

Despite the basic differences of plot, Lucidor's tests (scenes 10 and 16) can be compared to the Princess's consultation of Euryale in the matter of a pretended forthcoming marriage between herself and the Prince of Messène (IV, 1), as well as to the part in which Euryale consults the Princess on his projected marriage to Aglante (IV, 1). Another resemblance emerges from the scene in which Iphitas, the Princess's father, states that it is time she confess her love for Euryale. The spiteful Princess protests and takes the implication that she is in love as an insult (V, 2). Similarly, Angélique denies the same implication and shows her indignation when Maître Blaise, one of the men proposed and rejected by her, suggests that she is in love with Lucidor (scene 18).

It is clear that one facet or another of some Molière play is found in many of Marivaux's comedies. The influence of the seventeenth-century playwright varies, to be sure, but it is noteworthy to recall that it is present in about half of the total theatrical production of Marivaux. This should not be taken to mean that any or all of these comedies lack their own measure of originality; the fact is merely pointed out to indicate that Marivaux, despite his alleged hostile declaration concerning his predecessor, did not escape entirely from the circle of the *bétail des singes littéraires* whose stage successes depended often on the degree to which they adhered to established and proven *moliéresque* devices. While critics of the seventeenth-century dramatists have tended to depict Marivaux as a constant imitator of Molière, and critics of the former have, in general, sideswept the importance of the *moliéresque* heritage, close textual comparisons show that the instances of similarity are more than fragmentary and often concern plot, structure, and vocabulary. That Marivaux did not ignore entirely his masterful predecessor is, of course, to his credit: all French writers, as indeed all Frenchmen, *se réclament un peu de Molière*, a fact not to be overlooked on the tricentennial of his death.

LE MISANTHROPE REPRISED:
FOUR VERSIONS OF MOLIÈRE'S THEME
Francis L. Lawrence

Le Misanthrope, ensconced among Molière's masterpieces by general assent, has inspired several works, preponderantly corrective versions of Molière's play. La Bruyère inserted among his *Caractères* a misanthropic Timon, a portrait generally conceded to be a critique of Molière's Alceste.[1] La Bruyère purged his misanthrope of any comic taint by endowing him with severe politeness and complete detachment from close ties of love or friendship. The dignity of La Bruyère's misanthrope is a mild corrective in comparison to the metamorphosis which the revolutionary era required of Alceste and his friends. Fabre d'Eglantine, who was, for a time, the right hand of Danton, transformed Molière's characters into puppets for a morality play on social justice. *Le Philinte de Molière ou La Suite du Misanthrope* (1790) is a comedy only by courtesy of its author's insistence. Over a half century later, the pendulum had swung in the opposite direction. Eugène Labiche's *Le Misanthrope et l'Auvergnat* (1852) attempted to double the comic effect by making the misanthrope twice as choleric, twice as petty, and by juxtaposing him with a rustic truth-teller. Finally, Georges Courteline, in 1905, presented a short comedy that he proposed as a sixth act for Molière's play. *La Conversion d'Alceste* shows, as the title implies, a chastened Alceste ready to live at peace with the world. To draw comedy from this *tour de force*, it is necessary to turn Philinte and Célimène into conniving villains so that the trusting Alceste can be proven as ridiculous as the suspicious one. None of these versions approach the stature of Molière's play, of course, but the study of each shows how finely and with what great skill Molière treated his subject in order to avoid high melodrama, low comedy, or, simply, dullness.

The first corrective effort, La Bruyère's portrait of Timon, can conveniently be quoted in full: "Timon, ou le misanthrope, peut avoir l'âme

---

[1] La Bruyère, *Les Caractères*, "De l'homme," 155. The opinion that Timon's virtues are calculated to correct Alceste's vices is advanced by Gustave Michaut in his edition of Molière's *Oeuvres complètes*, XI (Paris, 1948), 166, and by Robert Garapon in his edition of La Bruyère's *Les Caractères* (Paris, 1962), 347.

austère et farouche; mais extérieurement il est civil et cérémonieux: il ne s'échappe pas, il ne s'apprivoise pas avec les hommes: au contraire, il les traite honnêtement et sérieusement; il emploie à leur égard tout ce qui peut éloigner leur familiarité, il ne veut pas les mieux connaître ni s'en faire des amis, semblable en ce sens à une femme qui est en visite chez une autre femme."[2] La Bruyère outlines a character impossible to portray on the stage in any conventional dramatic form. Timon is not simply an undramatic character but an antidramatic one. He deliberately refuses any but the most superficial relationships with his fellows and restricts even those relationships to empty conventional exchanges. Without love, without friendship, without conflict, Timon is La Bruyère's quintessential *honnête homme*, an impeccably gentile shell whose mask never slips. Alceste, although he rages against society, has close friends who tease him gently in the midst of his noblest transports. More drama is inherent in the misanthrope's love affair with a coquette who embodies all the social vices he professes to hate.

Fabre d'Eglantine takes some of the basic ingredients of Molière's play —a summons, a lawsuit, the friendship with Philinte, the sincerity of Eliante—to build an entirely different plot in which Alceste triumphs both in principle and in practice. The play opens on Philinte and Eliante, now married. Philinte is the Count of Valancés, owing to the influence of Eliante's uncle, newly raised to the rank of minister. He begins with two lines from Molière, avowing his tolerance, and proceeds rapidly to gainsay them, scolding Eliante in a fashion to rival Molière's Alceste at his most choleric. Alceste arrives from his country retreat pursued, as always, by the law. The affair is, again, a summons against Alceste by a nobleman he has offended but, in place of the original Alceste's trivial disagreement over the merits of a sonnet, this quarrel centers on a piece of land owned by a poor man whose cause d'Eglantine's Alceste has sustained against a rich, powerful predator.

Like the original Alceste, d'Eglantine's misanthrope rejects any proposal to aid his case. He spurns Eliante's offer to employ her uncle's influence for him and cites, as before, the justice of his cause, coupled with his determination to let innocence speak for itself. The honest lawyer whom Dubois finds to represent him is already engaged in frantic efforts to prevent a scoundrel from ruining some negligent fool who unknowingly signed a false promissory note. Alceste immediately neglects his own

[2] *Ibid.*

urgent danger to beg the assistance of Philinte for the unfortunate unknown. It is a complete reversal of Molière's situation, where Alceste was concerned only for his own wrongs. Accordingly, what was, in Molière's Philinte, generous tolerance and good-humored refusal to imitate Alceste's vocal rage over minor social vices he cannot change, becomes in Fabre d'Eglantine's Philinte a hypocritical insistence on philosophic optimism motivated by the basest self-interest. He refuses to help the honest advocate on the grounds that the fate of the foolish victim does not reduce the balance of good in the world. Actually, he refuses because he does not wish to use his credit with Eliante's uncle for any advantage but his own.

The issue is, predictably, that the intended victim is Philinte whom Alceste rescues by a series of efforts ranging from a selfless pledge of all his goods to a heroic frontal assault on the scoundrel and his lawyer. Alceste's march to the summits of virtue is matched by Philinte's descent to cowardice and dishonor. He begins with an effort to propitiate evil with an offering of part of the value of the false promissory note and ends with a wild effort to flee without the least attempt to help Alceste who was imprisoned when he identified himself to make the pledge for Philinte. The end finds Alceste at liberty, his cause having triumphed on its own merits, and finds Philinte overcome with gratitude toward his friend but spurned and confounded by the noble humanitarian. The play is a full realization of the corrective measures visualized by Jean-Jacques Rousseau, who proposed that the misanthrope ought to rage constantly against public vices while being totally unconcerned about his personal troubles. The philosopher, Philinte, should, in Rousseau's opinion, see all the disorders of society with a stoic calm while flying into a temper about the least discomfort to which he is subjected.[3] It is hardly necessary to say that the miniscule pieces of humor in this legend of the canonized Alceste have nothing to do with the main characters. Dubois, forgetful and stupid as ever, provides a grain of clumsy farce, but Alceste's anger is righteous and Philinte's humor is vicious.

While it was easy enough for Fabre d'Eglantine to destroy the comic misanthrope by stripping him of his minor vices and adding weighty reasons for his choler, Eugène Labiche set himself a much harder task: to reconstruct and intensify the comedy of misanthropy. Molière's Alceste founds his hatred of mankind on injustice in the courts, insincerity between acquaintances, libelous gossip in society, and fickleness between

---

[3] Jean-Jacques Rousseau, "Lettre à d'Alembert," *Oeuvres complètes* (Paris, 1824), II, 55.

lovers; Labiche's Chiffonet attacks the human genre on the basis of a bad shave caused by a dull razor, a store's false claims of English-speaking personnel and fixed prices, short change of a single sou, and the disappearance of one lump of sugar from his table. Alceste hedges in the practical application of his principles out of kindness. He fences with Oronte to avoid offending the amateur poet with an adverse opinion of his sonnet. Chiffonet betrays his principles for purely selfish and egoistic reasons. On his instructions, the porter lies about his residence to the national guard, and the servant Prunette lies about his whereabouts to inconvenient guests. When a friend asks for the loan of 4000 francs, Chiffonet denies that he has the money, though the exact sum is close at hand. In love, Alceste displays boorish jealousy, but he is completely honest and has every right to expect more consideration from the coquette who is fickle to him. Chiffonet in love is as great a hypocrite as he is in every other situation: he attempts to seduce his best friend's wife, and, when caught, plays out a little bedroom comedy of deceit and masquerade. Alceste's plan to expose evil and injustice in the universe is folly, but his sacrifice of a large sum of money for the sake of principle, "pour la beauté du fait avoir perdu ma cause "(I,i), has a certain mad grandeur reminiscent of the crusades of Don Quixote. As Eliante says, such behavior "a quelque chose en soi de noble et d'héroique" (IV,i). In contrast, Chiffonet's "vaste dessein" (sc.ii) is a scheme to give his friends stale, soured food and drink at his own birthday celebration. Even this petty bit of revenge on mankind fails: Chiffonet's maid, Prunette, falsifies the household accounts in order to buy decent refreshments.

There is obviously no room for a Philinte in Labiche's play; Philinte's concessions to the social amenities are minimal in comparison to Chiffonet's habitual mendacity. Labiche provides Chiffonet with his only possible foil: an honest man. L'Auvergnat, Machavoine, practices what Alceste preached, complete sincerity, the delivery of the whole truth in every situation. Chiffonet, in his second "vaste dessein" (sc.vii), hires Machavoine to discover lies in the household, a task which the employer conceives as spying on the servants and embarrassing unwary visitors. Since Chiffonet is actually the greatest liar in the house, it is his duplicity which Machavoine exposes. Chiffonet, trapped between this compulsively honest witness and a homicidally jealous husband, contrives to force Machavoine to lie for love of Prunette. The play ends with a choral tribute to the lie, led by Chiffonet and Machavoine.

The play is a passable farce, one which could, perhaps, bear comparison with one of Molière's lesser efforts on themes pertaining to obsession: for example, *Sganarelle ou le Cocu Imaginaire* or *Le Mariage Forcé*. The complete reversals of position which Labiche's characters undergo are quite common in Molière's farces, but, as several critics have pointed out, Molière's great *imaginaires,* although they may be forced to retreat on practical matters, never give up their basic illusions[4]: avarice, hypochondria, misanthropy, affectation of learning, mania for social advancement, all survive untouched. In every conceivable aspect, Labiche's comedy seems to be a systematic diminution of the comedy of misanthropy: in the triviality of the reasons adduced for hatred of mankind; in the extent to which the principle of sincerity is betrayed; in the unsuitability of the love affair; in the plan for revenge on humanity; and, finally, in the scope and tenacity of the comic illusion.

If Eugène Labiche attacked a difficult task in attempting to reassemble and transform the elements of Molière's play into a modern comedy on misanthropy, Georges Courteline set out to accomplish the impossible. In *La Conversion d'Alceste*, Courteline presents a sixth act for Molière's play, a new dénouement which supposedly takes place six months after the final events portrayed in *Le Misanthrope*. Courteline confines himself strictly to the characters of Molière with only one addition: M. Loyal from *Tartuffe* is used for a scene regarding the outcome of a new legal suit. Even the situations are, with one notable exception, simply replays of the original action developed a bit further. The verse is carefully tailored to imitate Molière's style. Courteline's intent was not parody but a serious epilogue, if we can believe the laudatory review by the author's mentor, Catulle Mendès, to whom Courteline gratefully dedicated the printed work. Mendès claims: "*La Conversion d'Alceste* n'est pas comme on pourrait le croire, un aimable pastiche du génie moliéresque: c'est le génie même de Molière évoqué. . . . Elle est comme le codicille plus féroce encore de ce testament terrible: *Le Misanthrope*."[5] This extra act for *Le Misanthrope*, written for a Molière celebration and presented at the "maison de Molière," enjoyed a great success at its first performance and was highly praised by theater critics. The accolades include: "petite pièce

---

[4] E.g., Robert J. Nelson in "The Unreconstructed Heroes of Molière," *TDR*, IV (1960), 14–37.

[5] Catulle Mendès, *Le Journal*, 16 janvier, 1905. Reprinted in Maurice Diamant-Berger, ed., *La Conversion d'Alceste. Les Oeuvres complètes de Georges Courteline* (Paris, 1925), 69–70. All citations of drama critics and of the text of the play are taken from this edition, which reproduces on pages 62–74 the reviews of the play written in January, 1905, following its first performance.

à ravir tous les lettrés"; "un morceau de choix et un régal"; "une petite comédie des plus ingénieuses"; "une manière de chef-d'oeuvre"; "un succès étourdissant"; "absolument délicieux"; "une soirée triomphale"; "une oeuvre exquise"; "suite ingénieuse et profonde."[6] The public reaction to the play was very different from that of the initial elite audience. Two days after the first performance, the play was received "dans un silence glacial,"[7] a reaction uniformly observed at every performance through the thirty-second and last. This, coupled with the fact that Flammarion was unable to sell out its fifty-copy printing in twenty years, led the editor of Courteline's complete works to observe sadly "que ce petit acte plutôt célèbre, ne fut en somme ni vu ni lu."[8] An excellent excuse for the play's poor showing was anticipated by one theater critic who feared that without an audience composed of enthusiasts who knew their Molière by heart the play might not be understood.[9] The reason is plausible, but, in actuality, the fault is not in the spectators' memories but in the play itself. Emile Faguet, while praising the play as "un ouvrage charmant," stated its overriding flaw very simply, "Tous les personnages de Molière y sont dégradés."[10]

Like *Le Misanthrope*, Courteline's play opens with a conversation between Alceste and Philinte in which a lawsuit and Célimène are discussed. Alceste has been deprived of his major grounds for misanthropy: a second lawsuit resulted in a judgment in his favor; Célimène, now married to him, has become as reasonable and even-tempered as Eliante. Alceste has repented his former excesses, "ma folie turbulence." He moralizes, "C'est le fait d'un fou que s'emporter sans cause" (sc. i). When Philinte turns out one of his nicely phrased little philosophic speeches, the former misanthrope sits enthralled, then effuses, "J'écoute./Et rends grâces au ciel qui vous mit sur ma route" (sc. i). The idea of a repentant misanthrope is comic enough and Courteline handles the actual dialog with considerable skill, giving the reformed Alceste a tone and emphasis as excessive as that of the misanthropic Alceste. The disappointing feature is that the

---

[6] The critics are, in order, Emile Faguet, *La Semaine Dramatique*, 30 janvier; Emmanuel Arène, *Le Figaro*, 16 janvier; René Doumic, *Revue des Deux Mondes*, 15 février; P. Nozière, *Gil Blas*, 16 janvier; Paul Souday, *L'Eclair*, 16 janvier; Alfred Athis, *L'Humanité*, 17 janvier; Jean Thouvenin, *Les Annales*, 22 janvier; Eugène Héros, *La Lanterne*, 18 janvier; Robert de Flers, *La Liberté*, 17 janvier.

[7] According to Maurice Diamant-Berger in his "Note sur *La Conversion d'Alceste*," p. 61 of his edition of the play.

[8] *Ibid.*

[9] Paul Souday, *L'Eclair*, 16 janvier, 1905.

[10] Emile Faguet, *La Semaine Dramatique*, 30 janvier, 1905.

motivation Courteline assigns for the conversion cheapens Alceste to the level envisaged by his severest critics. A little improvement in his personal situation has cured him: Alceste's former misanthropy is robbed of the associations of nobility and sincerity Molière gave it.

The second scene reintroduces Oronte, whose new sonnet Alceste praises so highly that Oronte demands that Alceste use his influence to have it published in the *Mercure galant*. The scene ends, as before, with a reciprocal exchange of insults. It would be a passable effort if Molière had not written it much earlier and much better. An original scene, using M. Loyal, imported from *Tartuffe*, shows Alceste that a dishonest lawyer can make him pay more for winning a suit than he formerly did for losing one. As he strays farther from Molière's text, Courteline falls into more flagrant distortions of the characters. Philinte, always concerned for Alceste's real misfortunes in Molière's play, laughs at his friend's trouble here. This little piece of callousness is an inadequate portent of the shocking transformation revealed in the scene between Philinte and Célimène.

Philinte and Célimène are lovers. It would be bad enough if it were a simple case of farcical cuckoldry. As one critic, dissenting from the general approval of the play, remarks, "Il ne nous plaît guère de voir Alceste sga-narellisé comme le simple vulgaire."[11] The case is worse than that. The wives or sweethearts of Molière's cuckolds had at least the standard justi-fication of the jealous, violent husband. Célimène and Philinte have betrayed Alceste precisely because he has become broad-minded and trusting. As a raging misanthrope, he was an exciting conquest, a demand-ing master for Célimène and an amusing companion to Philinte. They find the reformed Alceste a fool and a boor. Molière's cheating wives and lovers rationalized their actions and kept them in the comic register by playing their ingenious tricks out against a perennially suspicious domestic tyrant. The adultery of Courteline's Philinte and Célimène is a vicious affair, without reason, without ingenuity, without opposition.

Courteline carries his plot to its logical conclusion: Alceste overhears the lovers and, his former suspicions about mankind confirmed, returns to his wilderness retreat for good. Courteline's stage directions specify that Alceste weeps silently during his final speech. The hero of high comedy has become a victim of minor melodrama.

At first glance it seems curious that the most successful work of these

---

[11] F.L., *Le Rappel*, 18 janvier, 1905.

three is the one with least resemblance to Molière's play and the least successful is the one conceived as a faithful tribute, a continuation of *Le Misanthrope*. It is possible to oppose Molière rigidly and to produce, like Fabre d'Eglantine, an entirely different genre of work. It is possible to use Molière to feed one's own particular talent and to produce a lesser, still valid work, as Labiche does. It is not possible to rewrite Molière or to extend his works: Courteline's fiasco is an object lesson. In its own way, *La Conversion d'Alceste* is a successful tribute to the genius of an authentically inimitable master.

MOLIÈRE AND VOLTAIRE
Emilie P. Kostoroski-Kadish

Voltaire considered tragedy a higher form of art than comedy, and he consequently had more to say about Corneille and Racine than about Molière. But his opinions concerning the latter are nonetheless quite extensively documented, and allusions to Molière appear rather frequently in his writings. The prime source of these opinions is a *Vie de Molière* which Voltaire first published in 1739, but scattered references in his other works and in his correspondence also throw light on the subject.

We learn from these occasional remarks, for example, that all his life Voltaire professed great admiration for Molière the man and the writer. The playwright's comic universe was thoroughly familiar to him. While it is possible that a line in *Zaïre* was directly inspired by a line in *Les Fâcheux*,[1] it is indisputable that *moliéresque* phrases were often quoted or adapted to illustrate his ideas. He compared himself with La Flèche and M. de Pourceaugnac, and once he termed himself "le maître Jacques du Parnasse."[2]

Like many a contemporary, Voltaire enjoyed participating in amateur productions of plays, and Molière was part of his repertory. In 1739, during a visit with the Duc d'Arenberg at Enghien, he was Arnolphe. (Mme du Châtelet played Georgette.)[3] As late as 1763, he took the part of Trissotin in *Les Femmes savantes* (Best. 10445, 10464).

There was no doubt in Voltaire's mind that Molière far surpassed Shakespeare (Best. 14936), Plautus, and Terence (Best. 404). He was on a par only with Corneille and Racine: St. Racine, St. Corneille and St. Molière were the pride of Voltaire and the objects of his veneration (Best. 18133).

---

[1] François-Marie Arouet de Voltaire, *Oeuvres complètes*, ed. Louis Moland (Paris: Garnier frères, 1877–85), II, 566. (References are hereinafter inserted in the text.)

[2] Voltaire, *Correspondence of Voltaire*, ed. Theodore Besterman (Geneva: Institut et musée Voltaire, 1953–65), Letters 1594, 14746, 2067. (References are hereinafter inserted in the text, preceded by "Best.") For a study of Molière in the correspondence, see Arnold Ages, "The Private Voltaire: Three Studies in the Correspondence," in *Studies on Voltaire and the Eighteenth Century*, ed. Theodore Besterman (Geneva: Institut et musée Voltaire, 1971), LXXXI, 78–88.

[3] Theodore Besterman, *Voltaire* (New York: Harcourt, Brace and World, 1969), 246–47.

One suspects that, despite his priorities, Voltaire was even tempted to place Molière somewhat above the two tragedians, at least in some respects. In his "Temple du goût" (1734), his encounters with writers of the past imply an ordering in terms of excellence. Having left behind a number of plainly mediocre authors, the pilgrim Voltaire discovers within the Temple "un petit nombre de véritablement grands hommes": Fénelon, Bossuet, Corneille, Racine, La Fontaine, Boileau, Quinault, and Molière. Such an arrangement may, of course, be purely arbitrary. Yet it is curious to note in the "Défense de Louis XIV," written much later (1769), an almost identical enumeration in which a sort of climax is more clearly suggested: ". . . oui, je me regarderais comme un barbare, comme un esprit faux et bas, sans culture, sans goût, quand je pourrai [sic] oublier la force majestueuse des belles scènes de Corneille, l'inimitable Racine, les belles épîtres de Boileau, et son *Art poétique*; le nombre des fables charmantes de La Fontaine, quelques opéras de Quinault, qu'on n'a jamais pu égaler, et surtout ce génie à la fois comique et philosophique, cet homme qui en son genre est au-dessus de toute l'antiquité, ce Molière dont *le trône est vacant* (XXVIII,329)."

What are the reasons for such high praise? In the first place, Molière was the creator of French comedy, drawing it out of a state of chaos in much the same way as Corneille had created tragedy (XIV,105). Voltaire acknowledged that the analogy was not perfect; Corneille's *Menteur* had already graced the stage and Quinault's *La Mère coquette*, which Voltaire considered a model comedy of intrigue, was contemporary with Molière's first Parisian compositions (XIV,549). Still, he deserved the title of creator in that he had produced consistently a large number of fine dramatic pieces which rarely irritated Voltaire's acute literary sensitivities. Voltaire would read a book on Molière recommended by Count d'Argental (Best. 16826)[4], but he preferred Molière to reflections on Molière.

Voltaire's praise is also explained by the fact that Molière's example had been unequaled. Not only had he surpassed the ancients, he defied the moderns. Apart from Regnard, Voltaire saw no other comic writer as remotely comparable to the inimitable Molière (Best. 14524). Consequently, Molière had made a permanent and unquestionable contribution to that which was dear to Voltaire's heart, the prestige of the French nation: "le meilleur des poètes comiques de toutes les nations" (XIV, 105).[5]

---

[4] Ages states incorrectly (p. 82) that he demurred.
[5] Further attractions may have been Molière's status as a *philosophe* in both theory and

The fact that Voltaire gave to tragedy pride of place is surely the principal cause of his remarkably indulgent attitude. Corneille and even Racine, who had also greatly contributed to the prestige of French letters, did not fare so well. The question of versification is a good illustration of the difference (XVII, 418). Even in comedy, authors were expected to compose five-act plays in verse. But Voltaire had no word of reproach for *L'Avare*, written in prose. As for the other plays, he felt that certain ones—*George Dandin* and *La Comtesse d'Escarbagnac*, for example—were better in prose.[6] He was pleased that "les grandes pièces" which were "remplies de portraits, de maximes, de récits, et dont les personnages ont des caractères fortement dessinés" (*Le Misanthrope, Le Tartuffe, L'Ecole des femmes, L'Ecole des maris, Les Femmes savantes*) were rhymed, since this form made such things as the maxims all the more striking. As for the quality of Molière's verse, criticized by others, Voltaire was again rather lenient: "Il faut convenir qu'à quelques négligences près, *négligences que la comédie tolère*, Molière est plein de vers admirables, qui s'impriment facilement dans la mémoire" (XVI, 106; italics added).

In like manner, Voltaire's view on the subject of the different levels of comedy operative in Molière's theater is quite liberal. He was well aware of Boileau's famous censure of the *sac de Scapin* in his *Art poétique* (III, 393–400), but found the critic unnecessarily harsh (XVIII, 25). After all, even Raphael had deigned to paint grotesque figures at times. The author-actor had to earn a living for himself and his troupe: "il travaillait aussi pour le peuple de Paris, qui n'était pas encore décrassé; le bourgeois aimait la grosse farce, et la payait."[7] Voltaire went on to defend Molière's brand of buffoonery: "*Le Médecin malgré lui, Les Fourberies de Scapin*, ne sont pas dans le style des *Jodelets* de Scarron. Molière ne va pas rechercher des termes d'argot comme Scarron, ses personnages les plus bas n'affectent point des plaisanteries de Gilles; la bouffonnerie est dans la chose, et non dans l'expression."

---

practice (XIV, 105), a distinction not shared by Corneille, Racine, Boileau, or La Fontaine. Also, the author-actor was a prime example of France's unfair treatment of her actors (Best. 11976), especially in the circumstances of his death and burial (e.g. II, 543–44).

[6] Elsewhere (II, 314), Voltaire remarks that, due to the strength of prejudice, some of Molière's prose comedies had to be versified and that only these revised plays were now performed. But Beuchot corrects the statement in a note: of all such enterprises, only Thomas Corneille's *Le Festin de Pierre* met with success. (It remained in the repertory until 1847, during which time Molière's version was not performed.)

[7] Voltaire's compassion is laudable but his assertion is inaccurate. The contrary was often true. *Monsieur de Pourceaugnac*, for instance, was first presented as a royal diversion, and *Le Misanthrope* was first performed for audiences of the Palais-Royal.

Elsewhere, Voltaire argued that such exaggeration was necessary to comedy (Best. 2845). He even went so far as to discern in the farces passages worthy of high comedy, and to declare that Molière improved the taste of his times rather than enslaving himself to it (VII, 538). Such an affirmation does not contradict his justification of the farcical elements, as he no doubt meant that the overall effect was an improvement of public taste, in which case a few concessions might only be means to an end. For, as he said in *La Vie de Molière* when relating how *Le Médecin malgré lui* was used to retain the far less popular *Misanthrope* on the bill, "ces gentillesses frivoles servent à faire goûter des beautés sérieuses."[8]

Voltaire's defense of these occasional concessions is in sharp contrast with the diatribe of Louis-Sébastien Mercier, disciple of Diderot and advocate of *le drame*.[9] In Mercier's view, such "compromises" betrayed a lack of principle and a willingness to mock anything sacred—conjugal fidelity, paternal authority, filial respect and obedience—in order to evoke a laugh; at the same time scoundrels were made so pleasant that audiences were willing to overlook offenses for the sake of their wit. Unlike Mercier, Voltaire, for whom the question of moral instruction was also vitally important, found Molière's theater to be an eminently moral one: "Molière fut, si on ose le dire, un législateur des bienséances du monde" (XIV, 459). "Il sut nous égayer, mais en nous instruisant" (X, 158). Writing to Catherine II of Russia in 1772 (Best. 16587), he suggested that perhaps less than twenty lines of *Le Misanthrope* and less than forty of *L'Avare* would have to be altered to make them wholly acceptable for the education of the young.[10]

Not everything in Molière's theater, however, was defended by Voltaire. In "Le Temple du goût," Molière, after hearing the praise of Voltaire, expressed regret that he was sometimes obliged to exploit *le bas comique* in order to accomodate the tastes of the general public. He also considered the dénouements of his plays defective (VIII, 579). The weakness of his

---

[8] Despite his liberality, Voltaire lacked the breadth of vision of Diderot, who recognized that good farce was as difficult to achieve as any other form of comedy and that it needed no "redeeming" features: "Si l'on croit qu'il y ait beaucoup plus d'hommes capables de faire *Pourceaugnac* que *Le Misanthrope*, on se trompe." In *Oeuvres complètes*, ed. J. Assézat (Paris: Garnier, 1875–77), VII, 318.

[9] Louis-Sébastien Mercier, *Du théâtre; ou Nouvel essai sur l'art dramatique* (Amsterdam: [E. Van Harrevelt] 1773), 86–93 and *passim*.

[10] See also II, 458, XXXIII, 354. Whereas for Mercier *George Dandin* was a most dangerous play (one laughed at virtue, humiliated at the feet of insulting vice in the end), Voltaire did not see an apology for adultery. In *La Vie de Molière*, he sees Dandin as begging for trouble for having married the daughter of such a foolish nobleman.

conclusions was consistently noted by Voltaire (e.g. XXX, 354), but no examination of the issue was made beyond the simple affirmation of the fact. There were also on occasion weak plots and a certain amount of dragging (Best. 14524), and Molière was unequal in his versification (Best. 2845).

The *Vie de Molière* (XXIII, 87–126) does not contradict any of the above observations. It merely supports and expands them in concentrated fashion. It also reveals to a certain extent the attitudes of some of Voltaire's contemporaries. First of all, Voltaire's indulgent judgment of plays like *Les Fâcheux, La Princesse d'Elide*, and *Les Amants magnifiques*—the circumstances governing their composition both explain and excuse their weaknesses—is consonant with his attitude concerning the farces.[11]

With regard to the farces, Voltaire restates his position that they must be tolerated since Molière wrote them for *le peuple* out of economic necessity, and that only in these farces did he compromise his increasingly high standards.[12] Even here he makes distinctions, finding *L'Amour médecin* better than *Le Mariage forcé*; and *Le Sicilien, ou l'amour peintre* elicits considerable praise for a farce. Also, as we have already seen, certain farces—*Monsieur de Pourceaugnac, Le Malade imaginaire*—merit some esteem for the sake of a few scenes worthy of high comedy.[13] Of course the dénouements are routinely criticized (even in the concluding sentence); that of *Sganarelle, ou le cocu imaginaire* has the dubious distinction of being designated as "un des moins bien ménagés et des moins heureux." The entire fifth act of *Le Bourgeois gentilhomme* is termed a farce, "réjouissante mais trop peu vraisemblable."

The matter of choice of subject arises occasionally. That of *Dom Juan* Voltaire considers bizarre, "plus agréable au peuple qu'aux honnêtes gens." He admires the skill with which Molière handles a subject as difficult and apparently sterile as that of *Les Femmes savantes*, and in this he voices the opinion of *les connaisseurs*: "Plus on la vit (la pièce), plus on admira comment Molière avait pu jeter tant de comique sur un sujet qui paraissait fournir plus de pédanteries que d'agrément." And he enthu-

---

[11] Even here Voltaire chooses to emphasize positive thinking. See also XIV, 429: "La fête (de Vaux) fut au-dessus de celles que le cardinal Mazarin avait données, non seulement pour la magnificence, *mais pour le goût*. On y représenta pour la première fois *Les Fâcheux de Molière*" (italics added).

[12] Speaking of Boileau's attack on Scapin's *sac*, Voltaire asks: "De plus, comment Despréaux peut-il dire que 'Molière peut-être de son art eût remporté le prix'? Qui aura donc ce prix si Molière ne l'a pas?"

[13] Voltaire does not distinguish between farce and *comédie-ballet*.

siastically applauds the subjects of *Le Bourgeois gentilhomme* as one of the happiest ever conceived: whereas vanity in a person of high rank would be somewhat disguised or attenuated by his natural mannerisms and mode of expression, "ce ridicule se montre tout entier dans un bourgeois élevé grossièrement, et dont le naturel fait à tout moment un contraste avec l'art dont il veut se parer."[14]

Another point Voltaire makes is his disapproval of Molière's use of personal satire in *L'Impromptu de Versailles* (Boursault) and *Les Femmes savantes* (Ménage and Cotin). He has no pity for the victims (at least not in the second instance); if they truly deserved a fine reputation, no amount of satire would deprive them of it. But neither has he praise for the satirist: "La meilleure satire qu'on puisse faire des mauvais poètes, c'est de donner d'excellents ouvrages; Molière et Despréaux[15] n'avaient pas besoin d'y ajouter des injures." It is a curious judgment, coming from a man who excelled in satirical epigrams and whose biting tongue had no equal.

The two *Ecoles* of Molière merit special attention. Contrary to current opinion, Voltaire rated *L'Ecole des maris* much better than *L'Ecole des femmes*. He went so far as to say that if Molière had written only the former, he still would have deserved to be called an excellent comic author. Voltaire minimized Molière's indebtedness to Terence (the *Adelphi*), allowing that only the general idea represented a borrowing. He found Molière's play in every respect superior to the Latin comedy, and thought that the dénouement was Molière's best.[16]

L'Ecole des femmes, if not as good as *L'Ecole des maris*, was certainly a fine play, in Voltaire's view. He condemned, along with many others, expressions like "tarte à la crème" and "les enfants faits par l'oreille" (I,i). But he was of the opinion that such defects should not prevent one from appreciating the play's merits, in particular the handling of the plot —"toute en récits, mais ménagée avec tant d'art que tout paraît y être en action" (and, as a result, "attachante"). The principle of *la difficulté vaincue* is implied: "c'est le caractère du vrai génie de répandre sa fécondité sur un sujet stérile, et de varier ce qui semble uniforme."

Of all the comedies of Molière, two are singled out in Voltaire's esti-

---

[14] This interesting development throws light on his interpretation of *Le Misanthrope*, for he concludes thus: "C'est ce naturel grossier qui fait le plaisant de la comédie, et voilà pourquoi ce n'est jamais que dans la vie commune qu'on prend les personnages comiques."

[15] Boileau had been involved in the exchange of insults preceding the satire.

[16] Voltaire also considered *Amphitryon* and *L'Avare* superior to their Latin antecedents, the *Amphitryon* and the *Aulularia* of Plautus. Ages incorrectly attributes to him (p. 87) Frederick's opinion that Plautus's comedy was better (Best. 11074).

mation: *Le Misanthrope* and *Le Tartuffe*. The former was generally considered the masterpiece of high comedy, according to Voltaire, but he preferred the latter.[17] "Vous savez que je me fais toujours lire pendant mon dîner," he wrote to Mme du Deffand in 1769 (Best. 14891). "On m'a lu un éloge de Molière qui durera autant que la langue française: c'est *Le Tartuffe*." This favor was not belatedly bestowed, for in 1740, writing to Frederick II (Best. 2239), he had referred to *Tartuffe* as "ce chef-d'oeuvre qu'aucune nation n'a égalé."

Le Misanthrope, Voltaire commented, was more suited to an intelligent elite than to the multitude, and more fit to be read than to be staged. On the one hand, it evoked well-deserved admiration; but on the other, it did not draw large crowds when performed. Voltaire explained this admiration by the public's innate sense of justice: "Il court en foule à des comédies gaies et amusantes, mais qu'il n'estime guère; et ce qu'il admire n'est pas toujours réjouissant." The reason for this lack of response, he speculated, may well have involved the plot, ingenious and subtly developed, but also rather tenuous and not very engrossing. The conclusion likewise aroused little interest. It was predictable and acceptable but left the spectator somewhat indifferent: "En effet, le spectateur ne souhaite point beaucoup que le Misanthrope épouse la coquette Célimène, et ne s'inquiète pas beaucoup s'il se détachera d'elle."

The comedy's great asset, thought Voltaire, was its depiction of human vanity, albeit "une peinture... que les yeux vulgaires n'aperçoivent pas." Molière had not only simply appropriated the misanthrope of tradition; he had refined it in his own inimitable way: "Il s'est fait à lui-même un sujet stérile, privé d'action, dénué d'intérêt. Son Misanthrope hait les hommes encore plus par humeur que par raison."[18] In short, the comedy was a splendid accomplishment, worthy of praise in view of the *difficulté vaincue* principle. But *Tartuffe*, combining the same stylistic beauties with a far greater interest, was even more splendid.

Voltaire's predilection for *Tartuffe* was founded in large part on person-

---

[17] He also made it the favorite of his Ingénu (XXI, 279). Mercier preferred it, as well ("son chef-d'oeuvre unique" and "ouvrage étonnant, parfait et supérieur à tout"), although he objected to the interpretation given it by the actors.

[18] Mercier saw this as a decided weakness and considered the play far inferior to many others written by Molière. It is unfortunate that Voltaire did not pursue this idea further. One wonders if he would have agreed with Jules Brody's suggestion that Alceste's "rejection of the code of *politesse* has less to do with abstract moral principles than with a personal, constitutional incapacity to enact its rituals." "'Dom Juan' and 'Le Misanthrope'," *PMLA*, 84 (1969), 571–72.

al considerations. The enormous difficulties which this play had created for its author reminded him of his own skirmishes with cabals, particularly in the case of his *Mahomet* (1743), and Molière's ultimate success was an encouragement as well as a victory for the cause of truth. Voltaire refers elsewhere to his play as "l'autre Tartuffe" (Best. 2476) and "Tartuffe le grand" (Best. 2477). [19] A more profound and still personal reason was the substance of Molière's *Tartuffe*: it ridiculed fanaticism and unmasked hypocrisy, two of Voltaire's favorite foes. It was, in his own words, "l'éloge de la vertu et la satire de la seule hypocrisie."

Tartuffe had been bitterly opposed in the seventeenth century by those who were scandalized by its satire. In Voltaire's day, the play's moral lesson was calmly accepted: "On peut hardiment avancer que les discours de Cléante, dans lesquels la vertu vraie et éclairée est opposée à la dévotion imbécile d'Orgon, sont, à quelques expressions près, le plus fort et le plus élégant sermon que nous ayons en notre langue; et c'est peut-être ce qui révolta davantage ceux qui parlaient moins bien dans la chaire que Molière au théâtre." Voltaire admired all the characters of this comedy, particularly Tartuffe. He thought the plot was well developed, at least as far as the dénouement, which was, as usual, weak and artificial. But it was the play's moral content more than its technical perfection which secured his high esteem. [20]

The *Vie de Molière* concludes on a rather depressing note. Despite the merit and reputation of Molière, Voltaire notes that the theater is "deserted" when his plays are performed. Although this statement is made early in the century (1739), the description and Voltaire's explanation of the paradox continued to hold true as time went on: "la peinture de nos passions nous touche encore davantage que le portrait de nos ridicules;... l'esprit se lasse des plaisanteries, et... le coeur est inépuisable."

As early as 1716, Voltaire alludes to the diminished popularity of Molière (Best. 43). As late as 1772, he bemoans the same fact (Best. 16838, 16948). [21] In 1769, he writes to the Russian dramatist Soumarokof (Best. 14524) that he hears the plays of Molière are no longer being performed. (He supposes—perhaps ironically—this is because everyone knows them by heart and no longer needs to see them staged!) Voltaire may have been

[19] See also IV, 99; Best. 2471, 2475.
[20] In his *Lettres philosophiques* ("Sur la comédie"), Voltaire remarked that English attempts to adapt this play had failed because there were no "tartuffes" in that society, only "honnêtes hommes." See the whole of Chapter XIX (XXII, 156–62) for the English and Molière as seen by Voltaire.
[21] See also X, 128–29; Best. 2895.

exaggerating for effect, since Molière's plays were very frequently performed throughout the eighteenth century.[22] But an examination of attendance records corroborates the essence of the statement: they were often performed, but often poorly attended as well.[23]

Students of eighteenth-century French theater know that audiences were responding early to a variety of new offerings and that comedy in particular was becoming more serious, more moralizing in a heavy and obvious sense, more sentimental. Audiences wanted to become involved emotionally, and therefore the objectivity required in Molière's theater was not to their taste. *Comédies larmoyantes* and *drames* appeared to satisfy their *coeurs inépuisables* better than Molière, while providing an adequate moral experience, Jean-Jacques Rousseau's warnings to the contrary notwithstanding. Even the author of two of the century's finest comedies, Beaumarchais, expressed reservations about the relationship of comedy *à la Molière* to morality in his *Essai sur le genre dramatique sérieux.*[24]

The transformations which Maurice Descotes notes in eighteenth-century interpretations of the major characters in Molière's high comedies underscore the public's inability to appreciate or to tolerate Molière very well: "Alors que certains interprètes, fidèles selon la lettre à la tradition du franc comique, inclinent l'oeuvre vers la bouffonnerie sans mesure, la plupart des acteurs s'efforcent d'affiner le texte, de raisonner les effets comiques, de prêter aux personnages plus d'esprit et de malice que ne

[22] Figures provided in the Despois-Mesnard edition of Molière report a total of 8,331 times between 1700 and 1789. The most popular comedies, in terms of number of performances, were: *Tartuffe* (761); *Le Médecin malgré lui* (748); *L'Ecole des femmes* (593); *L'Avare* (510); *George Dandin* (497); *L'Ecole des maris* (474); *La Comtesse d'Escarbagnas* (423); *Le Misanthrope* (418); *Le Mariage forcé* (401). The statement that *Amphitryon* (354) was his most popular play (Best. 14524*n*2) is not correct, even in terms of average audience size or the first half of the century. See René Louis de Voyer de Paulmy, marquis d'Argenson, *Notices sur les oeuvres de théâtre*, ed. H. Lagrave, in *Studies on Voltaire and the Eighteenth Century*, XLII (1966), 238*n*2.

[23] The Marquis d'Argenson exaggerates somewhat when he writes that *Le Misanthrope* was splendidly performed "pour moy seul, et un seul homme aux secondes loges" (*ibid.*, 248). There were seventy-seven paying spectators at the performance (August 7, 1749). But this was indeed a small number, and such was not the fate only of *Le Misanthrope*. On December 11, 1730, only thirty paying spectators attended a performance of *L'Ecole des femmes*.

[24] Georges Lafenestra (*Molière* [Paris: Hachette, 1909], 193) explains the decline in popularity thus: "En fait, durant tout le XVIIIe siècle, jusqu'aux approches de la Révolution, avant Beaumarchais, Molière, le puissant Molière des fortes satires morales ou des bouffonneries énormes, est chez nous démodé. Il est trop franc peut-être, trop simple et naturel pour une société engouée à la fois de littérature polissonne et de déclamations sophistiques."

leur en a donnés le créateur. . . . La franchise de Molière passe volontiers pour de la crudité."[25]

Voltaire was out of place in this setting.[26] Even though he had written several sentimental comedies (*L'Enfant prodigue*, 1736; *Nanine*, 1749), he still believed that something was wrong with "le comique pleureur" (X, 158):

> Que je plains un Français quand il est sans gaîté!
> Loin de son élément le pauvre homme est jeté.
> Je n'aime point Thalie alors que sur la scène
> Elle prend gauchement l'habit de Melpomène.
> Ces deux charmantes soeurs ont bien changé de ton:
> Hors de son caractère on ne fait rien de bon.

It is still a legitimate enterprise, however, to examine Voltaire's view of Molière, if only for the sake of contrast. Yet in another sense, he *is* representative; for a distinction must be made between popularity and critical opinion. Comparisons with Mercier's thinking made here have brought out serious differences. It would be of interest to investigate the ideas of others in order to determine to what extent Voltaire does speak for the connoisseurs of his time.[27]

Voltaire's stance on Molière, it has been seen, is characterized especially by a leniency lacking in his many remarks on tragedy. But this indulgence may have been an advantage; for it permitted him to enjoy Molière as many another could not. His position can be viewed as a remnant of the past and a longing for the "good old days," as somewhat out of step with the theorizing of new generations. Yet it can also be thought of as a preview of the future, a glimpse of what Molière would again become some day in the never-ending evolution of a great writer's romance with posterity.

---

[25] Maurice Descotes, *Les grands rôles du théâtre de Molière* (Paris: Presses Universitaires de France, 1960), 255. For a brief survey of eighteenth-century opinion of Molière, seè Otis E. Fellows, *French Opinion of Molière (1800–1850)* (Providence: Brown University, 1937), 12–14.

[26] Though in one sense he was not out of place. As Virgil Topazio explains in his *Voltaire, A Critical Study of his Major Works* (New York: Random House, 1962), 87–88, his own tendency to become involved made him incapable of assuming the role of dispassionate spectator. Hence, despite his wit and sense of humor, he did not write good comedy as he would have wished.

[27] The dramatic journal of the Marquis d'Argenson provides interesting comparisons and contrasts. He agrees, for example, that Molière's *Amphitryon* is superior to that of Plautus, but finds the dénouement of *L'Ecole des maris* "bien forcé" and the play itself inferior to *L'Ecole des femmes*.

MOLIÈRE AND ROUSSEAU:
THE CONFRONTATION OF ART AND POLITICS
James F. Hamilton

The merit of Molière and the French classical theater encounters its greatest challenge in the eighteenth century with the publication of Rousseau's *Lettre à d'Alembert sur les spectacles* (1758), which disputes the establishment of the theater in his hometown, Geneva, as proposed by the encyclopedic article, "Genève." Whereas d'Alembert recommends the theater as the unique source of lessons in *goût, finesse*, and *délicatesse*—the implied cornerstones of civilization—Rousseau reacts against the priority given by French classicism to these socioaesthetic principles.[1] They are linked in his mind with inequality and injustice and reflect not absolute truths about the nature of man but the particular manners and institutions of France, once appropriate for the diversion through drama of an elite class in a monarchy.

As his prime example of the supposed incompatibility between French classical aesthetics and the ideals of a republic—*vertu, frugalité*, and *égalité*—Rousseau scrutinizes the sociopolitical implications of Molière's masterpiece, *Le Misanthrope*. The impact of his criticism in the *Lettre à d'Alembert* is confirmed by the chain of events which it unleashes—a violent debate on the value of dramatic art, the resignation of d'Alembert from the *Encyclopédie*, and its loss of printing privilege. Thereafter, Rousseau is alienated permanently from the encyclopedic party which defends Molière and the French classical theater. The question arises then as to which view of Molière (that of Rousseau or that of the encyclopedists) is more nearly correct in terms of its influence on comic theory and its consistency with the Enlightenment.

Traditionally, Rousseau's criticism of *Le Misanthrope* is rejected on aesthetic and psychological grounds. First, his moral aesthetics and political orientation to literary criticism are accused of distorting the nature of dramatic art. However, it is equally true that French classical dramatists

---

[1] See "Genève," *Encyclopédie*, ed. Diderot and d'Alembert (3rd. ed.; Genève: Pellet, 1777–79), XV, 963. All references to the *Encyclopédie* are to this edition.

justify art with moral arguments, as witnessed by the prefaces to their plays. For example, Molière characterizes *Tartuffe* as exposing "la corruption des hommes" with the intention of correcting such vices as hypocrisy, calumny, and fraud. Similarly, Racine defends *Phèdre* as dramatizing the disorder and deformity of character caused by passion, and he suggests, furthermore, that tragedy's moral instruction be accentuated in order to make it more meaningful to the religious, i.e. the Jansenists.

The commitment of French classicism to moral instruction continues into the eighteenth century, where it is politicized by the Enlightenment's most comprehensive work, the *Encyclopédie*. For instance, in the article entitled "Comédie," dramatic art is assigned the utilitarian function of enforcing correct conduct: "le théâtre est pour le vice et le ridicule ce que sont pour le crime les tribunaux où il est jugé, et les échafauds où il est puni" (VIII, 559). The dramatist as a *philosophe* is expected, as revealed in "Unité," to sacrifice "quelques beautés" for sociopolitical verities (XXXV, 691).

Because moral arguments are used traditionally to defend the French classical theater, Rousseau's moral aesthetics challenging its claims to spiritual elevation and social utility must be taken seriously. By mixing art and politics in the *Encyclopédie*, the encyclopedists (d'Alembert and Voltaire in the case of "Genève") invite Rousseau to examine the sociopolitical effects of dramatic art. So also, the second objection to his method, on psychological grounds, does not sustain scrutiny. Rousseau's criticism of *Le Misanthrope* is dismissed traditionally as exemplifying the fallacy of subjective judgment. Rousseau identifies himself too closely with the clumsy, often ridiculous conduct of Alceste in *salon* society and with his uncompromising, intolerant attitude toward the world.[2] Although there is some truth in the traditional interpretation, it fails to consider Rousseau's criticism of *Le Misanthrope* in the context of his general theory of literature.

Rousseau's literary theory, as introduced in the *Discours sur les sciences et les arts* (1750), operates in the broad perspective of art and government. These two major forces in society are meant to complement one another in rendering man a well-integrated, happy being. Their balance in power results in liberty. However, instead of offering moral examples worthy of its originally benevolent function of promoting mutual respect and under-

[2] See René Wellek, *A History of Modern Criticism* (New Haven: Yale University Press, 1955), I, 62.

standing, Rousseau feels that art has traditionally collaborated with the government in ruling the majority. Supposedly, the artist forfeits his independence for the comfort, leisure, and luxury necessary to the cult of art. In exchange for royal patronage, he not only turns his back on the general interest but blinds man as to the reality of his eroding freedom by preoccupying his mind with aesthetic illusions. The arts "étendent des guirlandes de fleurs sur les chaînes de fer."[3] Authority, both political and intellectual, is rendered absolute when art establishes its own order of aesthetically inspired values. The socioaesthetic principles of *politesse*, *bienséance*, and *goût* promote the political ambitions of government. Enforced through the king's arm in society, the *salon*, they prevent any united resistance to his will by controlling social conduct, segregating people along sociocultural lines, and by effacing the general moral system of values.[4]

If Rousseau's criticism of *Le Misanthrope* is consistent with his general theory of art, it must be explained mainly on the philosophic level of aesthetics and politics and not as a manifestation of a neurotic personality. In my opinion, his dramatic criticism evolves logically from the conspiratorial concept of literature that is evidenced by his political evaluation of comedy as "distracting the people from its miseries and making it forget its leaders in seeing comedy's clowns" (174). Similarly, Rousseau denounces tragedy on ideological grounds as being inherently antagonistic to republican truths because it teaches man that he is not free, glorifies aristocracy, and, its pity evoked through fear, proves to be a sterile aesthetic emotion which "feeds on a few tears and has never produced the slightest act of humanity" (140).

Rousseau's criticism of the French classical theater deals primarily with comedy as the more influential dramatic genre; it is a judgment shared by the encyclopedists as seen in "Comédie" (VIII, 565). In contrast to tragedy, the manners and morals portrayed by comedy enjoy a more relevant, immediate relationship with those of contemporary society; and its characters resemble men more (Rousseau, 148). Hence, it is comedy which bears the brunt of Rousseau's iconoclastic inquiry. Because comedy is defended traditionally as correcting vice through ridicule, Rousseau analyzes its means of eliciting laughter, the nature of the vices represented, the

---

[3] Rousseau, *Du Contrat social* (Paris: Garnier, 1962), 4. All references to Rousseau's works are to this edition.

[4] See my article, "A theory of Art in Rousseau's *Premier Discours*," to appear in *Studies on Voltaire and the Eighteenth Century*.

standard of conduct dramatized as desirable, and the sociomoral effects of comedy on the audience.

The definitions of vice and virtue undergo a change of value in the context of comedy according to Rousseau. Vice is reinterpreted to mean the conduct which proves unacceptable to polite society. Since the excess of virtue is considered bad taste, it becomes a social vice and fair game for the moderating forces of laughter. Consequently, Rousseau regards comedy as exposing the ridiculous rather than the vicious, for it substitutes the socioaesthetic conventions of *politesse*, *bienséance*, and *goût* for the moral criteria of *vérité* and *vertu*.

In support of his concept of comedy, Rousseau draws his examples from Molière, "le plus parfait auteur comique dont les ouvrages nous soient connus" (148). Although Rousseau professes a great admiration for Molière's talents, his method of criticism attaches primary importance to the effect of genius on society. From his sociopolitical point of view, he charges Molière with having established "une école de vices et de mauvaises mœurs" (148).

Rousseau sees Molière as the shortsighted detractor of natural authority and panderer of society's vices. Disrespect for fathers, husbands, and masters is condoned in his comedies (149). The fun which he makes of vice is not accompanied by the love of virtue (149). As an example of the prejudicial character of Molière's plays, Rousseau judges M. Jourdain as being less blameworthy than the rascally gentlemen who dupe him in *Le Bourgeois gentilhomme* (149). In the case of *L'Avare*, Rousseau maintains that the great vice of miserliness is exceeded by the son who robs and insults his father (149).

Rousseau's thesis on comedy is illustrated best by his interpretation of Molière's *Le Misanthrope*. He begins by contesting the validity of its title. The true misanthrope is a monster, in his opinion, and his portrayal would evoke horror and hatred in the spectator (150). These are not the effects which Alceste, the so-called misanthrope, excites in the audience. Rather than as the enemy of mankind, Rousseau deems Alceste to be an essentially good man who refuses to compromise with the hypocritical conventions of *salon* society. Even though Rousseau concedes the human failings and contradictions of Alceste's character, he implies that it reflects the only active moral conscience in the play. As a result, the audience retains a sympathy and certain esteem for him (152).[5]

---

[5] In d'Alembert's "Lettre à Rousseau," he approaches Rousseau's view of Alceste and

Rousseau's analysis of *Le Misanthrope* raises a valid, relative criterion of character evaluation. Rather than judging Alceste by his outbursts during moments of anger or upon an absolute correlation between his stated principles and his conduct, Rousseau compares him with the other personages of the play. In contrast with the deceit, slander, self-interest, corruption, and affectation found in Célimène's *salon*, Alceste's relative measure of virtue appears more impressive.

The level of conduct and virtue proposed by Molière's *Le Misanthrope* is represented, in Rousseau's opinion, by Alceste's friend, Philinte. Through an apparently reasonable opposition, Alceste is made to appear as the villain while Philinte embodies the desirable code of moderation (152).[6] It is based upon the socioaesthetic principles of *bienséance* rather than on moral virtue and conscience. Rousseau sees Philinte as playing the role of the amateur, *salon* philosopher who advises flattery, conformity, self-interest, and the bribery of judges. He reflects the taste of his age which lauds a false tolerance of public injustice and civil corruption.

From Rousseau's point of view, the Philintes of society aggravate social ills through their collaboration in them. Because Philinte manifests a lucid consciousness as to society's ills, his inaction makes him more guilty than the unthinking marquis. It is implied by Rousseau's reasoning that only the fanatic, such as Alceste, can shake society out of its apathy. Even if Alceste shows himself to be a fumbling, naïve social critic, his ineptitude reflects only the general mediocrity of *salon* society.

Rousseau concedes that Molière accomplishes with expertise his limited aim of entertaining the audience and perfecting the comic genre (157). The necessity of pleasing an essentially corrupt society obliges him to promote "l'homme du monde," Philinte, at the expense of ridiculing "l'honnête homme," Alceste (207). Rousseau implies that the society for which *Le Misanthrope* was created could only profit from the socioaesthetic code of Philinte, for the moral conscience of an Alceste was out of place in the *salon* and could lead only to an awkward conduct. For example, when

---

expresses dissatisfaction with Molière's portrayal of Philinte: "Il n'est personne au contraire qui ne l'estime, qui ne soit porté même à l'aimer et à la plaindre. . . . Philinte m'a paru . . . un caractère mal décidé, plein de sagesse dans ses maximes et de fausseté dans sa conduite." See *Oeuvres complètes* (Genève: Slatkine reprints, 1967), IV, 445.

[6] That the encyclopedist agrees with Rousseau is seen in "Comédie": "Molière met en opposition les mœurs corrompues de la société, et la probité farouche du Misanthrope: entre ces deux excès paroît la modération du sage, qui hait le vice & qui ne hait pas les hommes" (VIII, 557).

Alceste shows himself to be inconsistent in his hesitancy to judge Oronte's sonnet, Rousseau contends that it is out of society's disapproval of sincerity (156). Therefore, if Alceste's conduct is to be derided as inconsistent and hypocritical, it confirms merely the unnatural state of society in which honesty is impossible.

Molière's use of the love theme in *Le Misanthrope* makes the comedy, in Rousseau's opinion, both a creative work of genius and a sociopolitical failure. Alceste's love prevents him from remaining faithful to the moral dictates of his conscience. Rousseau implies that love, as portrayed in *Le Misanthrope*, conditions the spectator into accepting the defeat of his reason before passion instead of fortifying his moral resolution against an essentially destructive sentiment born of self-interest. It originates in the *salon* and necessitates intrigue and betrayal. Consequently, Rousseau judges love, as depicted in *Le Misanthrope*, to reflect alien attitudes which pose a threat to the value system and, hence, the institutions of a republic. In a society founded upon the ideal of passionate love, such as monarchist France, Rousseau contends that its true legislators become the *salon* ladies such as Célimène, who reign through taste, coquetterie, and dissimulation rather than reason and honesty in the service of the general good (161).

The significance of Rousseau's revolt against the sociopolitical implications of French classicism, as illustrated by his criticism of *Le Misanthrope*, must be evaluated first in terms of its influence on the dramatic theory and practice of comedy by succeeding generations. Although Voltaire and Diderot are rated traditionally as the foremost dramatic theorists among the major *philosophes*, the reformers of the French theater after 1760 adopt Rousseau's aesthetic relativism and sociopolitical interpretation of *Le Misanthrope*. For example, Beaumarchais includes but one direct quotation in his *Essai sur le genre dramatique sérieux* (1767); it is taken from Rousseau's attack on tragedy in the *Lettre à d'Alembert*.[7] With a similar tone of righteousness, Beaumarchais rejects the claim to moral instruction by traditional comedy, "la pièce comique," and accuses it moreover of promoting corruption in its attempt to instruct by moving the spectator to identify himself with the knave against "l'honnête homme" (*ibid.*, 11). Thus, Beaumarchais aligns himself implicitly with Rousseau's position on *Le Misanthrope*.

In the prerevolutionary generation, Rousseau's dramatic theory is con-

---

[7] Beaumarchais, *Théâtre complet*, ed. Bibliothèque de la Pléiade (Paris, 1964), 10.

tinued by Sébastien Mercier's *Du Théâtre ou Nouvel Essai sur l'art.*[8] In his criticism of Molière, Mercier refers to Rousseau's contention that "peindre les vices n'est pas les corriger" and echoes Rousseau's epigrammatic denunciation of Molière in the "Seconde Partie, Lettre XVII" of *La Nouvelle Héloïse*—"en voulant corriger la cour, il a gâté la ville" (86). In obvious reference to Alceste, Mercier reminds the reader that vice is interpreted traditionally by comedy as meaning the ridiculous rather than the vicious, which, as a cultural prejudice, is prone to blame the nonconformity of "l'homme vertueux" (55). Of foremost concern to the image of Molière in prerevolutionary France, Mercier observes that although his comedies are presented every Friday in Paris by the best actors, no one goes to see them. They no longer excite the same gaiety, he explains, for the French nation is no longer inclined to laughter (67). If Molière were writing in 1773, Mercier feels that he would have produced a more authentic *Misanthrope* (68).

Mercier's desire to see *Le Misanthrope* redone according to the demands of Rousseau's ideology is realized by Fabre d'Eglantine's comedy, five acts in verse, *Le Philinte de Molière ou la suite du Misanthrope* (1791). It attempts to portray Philinte as being incapable of friendship because of a cowardly prudence but succeeds only in animating the grotesque morality of the revolutionary in an intolerant, unphilosophic fanatic—Alceste. The literary and political careers of Fabre d'Eglantine are ended in 1794 with his execution, and the illustration of Rousseau's dramatic theory is undertaken by another disciple, Louis Picard (1769–1828), in his two comedies, *Les Amis du Collège* (1795) and *Conjectures* (1795). They fail to attain the success attributed generally to Picard's theater, the most prolific in French literature after that of Scribe.

Rousseau's influence on literary theory culminates early in the nineteenth century with the publication of Mme de Staël's *De la littérature* (1800), which systematizes Rousseau's criticism of French classicism. Although referred to often as "la fille de Rousseau," Mme de Staël's respectful attitude toward the principles of *goût, délicatesse,* and *politesse* represents an ideological retreat from Rousseau's radical repudiation of tradition. His militant rationalism is reborn with refinement in Stendhal's *Racine et Shakespeare* (1823), which in spite of its title discusses at length the comedy of Molière.

---

[8] Sébastien Mercier, *Du Théâtre ou Nouvel Essai sur l'art* (Amsterdam, 1773). All references to this work are taken from the 1967 Slatkine reprint.

Because Stendhal attributes his moral sensitivity to the reading of *La Nouvelle Héloïse*, his method of criticism with its concern for the sociopolitical effects of art is indebted no doubt to Rousseau, and it produces similar results.[9] He, also, accuses Molière of immorality which issues, in his opinion, not from *risqué* language or lessons in disrespect for parents but from his propagation of the *salon* ethic—"être comme tout le monde" and "la terreur du ridicule" (II, 198–99). These two attitudes are blamed by Stendhal for undermining the French character in its ability to act, which defect makes it vulnerable to despotism (II, 202). Stendhal's sociological approach to literary criticism, when applied to *Le Misanthrope*, sees Alceste as "un républicain" before his time whose just and severe scorn for his society almost compromises the gaiety necessary to comedy and the apolitical character of Célimène's *salon* (II, 177). Therefore, in order to retain the king's favor and to elicit laughter rather than controversy, Molière is obliged both by political and aesthetic considerations to ridicule the violent nonconformity of Alceste in favor of Philinte's circumspection (II, 177). In an evident romantic rejection of his own age, Stendhal contends that the classical ethic of conformity through fear of ridicule, as dramatized best in *Le Misanthrope* and *Les Femmes savantes*, has rendered the French incapable of understanding Alceste, the individualist, who, if sustained by a woman worthy of him, had the makings of a national hero (II, 206).

In summary, the confrontation of Molière and Rousseau concerns politics more than aesthetics, and the controversy surrounding "Genève" and the *Lettre à d'Alembert* arises from different interpretations of the Enlightenment on the part of its antagonists, the encyclopedists and Rousseau, rather than from antithetical views as to the primary function of art—the defense of progress, moral, social, and political. Their quarrel cannot be explained away as an example of the continuing contest between the forces of enlightenment and reaction. Governmental control of art for a good cause is sanctioned by the encyclopedist.[10] Consequently, both of their attitudes on comedy reflect the shortcomings of eighteenth-century philosophic literature; but the aesthetic relativism of Rousseau is trans-

---

[9] See Stendhal, *Vie de Henry Brulard* (Paris: Garnier, 1961), 178.
[10] See d'Alembert, "Réflexions sur les éloges académiques," II, 156, who invites the government to use the literary academies "à diriger les opinions vers le bien général de la nation et du souverain." Similarly, in the encyclopedic article, "Unité," Louis XII is applauded for his use of satirical dramas "contre les vices de son siècle, surtout ceux du clergé" (XXX, 124).

mitted to the nineteenth century where it is incorporated by Mme de Staël and Stendhal into the theoretical foundation of liberal romanticism.

To conclude from the broader perspective of relevancy, the eighteenth-century debate on the merit of Molière illustrates the eternal question as to the proper relationship between art and politics. Rousseau's criticism of Molière's comedies may be compared to the political demands made upon art by the modern "literature of commitment" as exemplified by the opening pages of *Situations II* where Sartre condemns the supposed "irresponsibility" of Flaubert. It is doubtful whether the ideological criterion of commitment or Rousseau's conspiratorial theory of art can adequately express the complex human condition and work of art. Furthermore, a society which is incapable of laughing at itself, as indicated by Mercier's observation on the prerevolutionary audience of Molière, would seem to be headed for disaster. Although Rousseau's negative image of Molière is adopted by nineteenth-century romanticism, his theater continues to act today as the standard for all comedy and to enjoy lively appreciation. It is a tribute to Molière and Western civilization that his comedies have survived the political demands imposed upon art by Rousseau and the eighteenth century.

PRÉSENCE DE MOLIÈRE
DANS L'*ENCYCLOPÉDIE*
Alice Rathé

En laissant une liberté entière à ses collaborateurs, l'*Encyclopédie* du 18e
siècle semblait promettre dans son "Discours préliminaire"[1] un large
évantail d'opinions sur les questions qu'elle allait traiter. Or, bien que
plusieurs gens de lettres eussent fourni des articles littéraires sur Molière,
leur optique ne variait guère. Une deuxième surprise attend celui qui examine son image dans l'*Encyclopédie*. On aurait pu s'attendre à ce que,
dépassant le cadre purement littéraire de la comédie, Molière pénétrât,
par son épicurisme, dans le domaine des idées, et, par ses luttes contre le
parti dévot, dans celui de la propagande philosophique. Il n'en est pra-
tiquement rien, et nous tenterons de déterminer les causes de cette réserve.
Molière auteur dramatique et Molière épicurien constitueront les deux
centres d'intérêt des pages qui vont suivre.

Voici, pour commencer, une liste des articles qui ont trait à Molière
dramaturge. L'abbé Edme Mallet, à qui revenait la littérature dans le
project initial, mourut après la publication du second volume, où il avait
donné l'article "Caractère dans le personnage". Prenant la relève, Jean-
François de Marmontel rédigea, pour les volumes 3 à 6, cinq articles qui in-
téressent notre propos, "Comédie", "Comique", "Critique", "Dialogue"
et "Farce". Enfin, le chevalier Louis de Jaucourt fournit deux titres,
"Comédie sainte" et "Poëte comique", et Diderot deux autres, "Gravité",
rangé parmi les articles omis du volume 17, et "Préoccupation". Mais
l'*Encyclopédie* eut un *Supplément*[2] dans lequel Molière reçut une attention
toute particulière, grâce, d'une part à Marmontel, désireux de par-
faire ce qu'il avait commencé vingt ans plus tôt, ("Acte", "Action",
"Beau", "Dénouement", "Exposition", "Intrigue", "Jargon", "Moeurs"
"Pantomime", "Poësie" et "Situation"), et d'autre part au critique d'art

---

[1] *Encyclopédie ou Dictionnaire raisonné des sciences, des arts et des métiers*, par une société
de gens de lettres (Paris: Braisson, David, Le Breton, Durand; 1751–65), I, xxxv–xxxvi.

[2] *Nouveau dictionnaire pour servir de Supplément au Dictionnaire des sciences, des arts et
des métiers*, par une société de gens de lettres (Paris: Panckoucke, Stoupe, Brunet; Amsterdam: Rey, 1776–77). Nous le désignerons désormais par le titre de *Supplément*.

allemand d'origine suisse, Johann Georg Sulzer, traduit à son insu, pour fournir la matière des articles "Comédie", "Intéressant" et "Naturel". Bien que par l'absence de Diderot ce *Supplément* se situât en dehors de l'*Encyclopédie* proprement dite, le public de l'époque eut vite fait d'associer les deux publications, et nous sommes d'autant plus autorisés à suivre son exemple que le nom de Marmontel figure dans les deux ouvrages.

L'article de l'abbé Mallet provient de son livre *Principes pour la lecture des poëtes*.[3] Ce critique d'obédience strictement classique reprend et fait siens les commentaires et les éloges de Riccoboni.[4] Il déclare préférer Molière aux Anciens, dont les caractères sont trop simples, et encore plus à ses contemporains, qui manquent, eux, de naturel. Seuls parmi ceux-ci Regnard et Destouches trouvent grâce à ses yeux pour avoir suivi les traces de Molière. Mallet n'aborde pas la question de la moralité de son théâtre, omettant ainsi la seule réserve qu'il eût formulée dans ses *Principes*.[5] Dans cette première présentation de Molière on note donc une admiration exclusive pour son oeuvre et le désir de faire oublier ses manquements à la bienséance.

Au titre "Poëte comique", Jaucourt donne une notice biographique. Ce copiste laborieux s'étant contenté de coudre ensemble des passages des *Principes de Littérature* de l'abbé Charles Batteux,[6] des vers de l' "Epître VII" de Despreaux et trois paragraphes de la *Vie de Molière* de Voltaire,[7] c'est plutôt par ce qu'il omet que son article présente un certain intérêt. Jaucourt ne tient nullement compte des scandales rapportés dans le *Dictionnaire historique et critique* de Pierre Bayle à la rubrique "Poquelin".[8] Il reproduit très rapidement un seul des commentaires subversifs de Voltaire,[9] et remplace la critique de l'abbé Batteux à l'endroit des dénouements de Molière par l'éloge suivant: "Quoi qu'il en soit, on convient généralement que Molière est le meilleur poete de toutes les nations du monde." Son intention est claire: faire de Molière à la fois un grand écrivain et un personnage irréprochable.

L'apport de ces deux écrivains étant minime, nous en avons parlé briève-

---

[3] (Paris: Durand, 1745), II, 155–88.

[4] Luigi Riccoboni, *Observations sur les comédies et le génie de Molière* (Paris: Vve Pissot, 1736).

[5] I, 231.

[6] Charles Batteux, *Principes de littérature, contenant le cours de Belles Lettres* (Gottingue et Leide, Luzac fils, 1755), I, 298–302.

[7] Voltaire, *Vie de Molière, avec des jugements sur ses ouvrages* (Paris: Prault fils, 1739).

[8] 3e édition revue par l'auteur (Rotterdam: Böhm, 1720).

[9] Voir plus bas.

ment. Avec Marmontel on rencontre enfin un critique littéraire qui a eu le loisir de présenter, dans l'*Encyclopédie* et le *Supplément*, un ensemble d'articles suffisamment cohérent pour former, plus tard, en 1787, un ouvrage indépendant, les *Eléments de littérature*, précédé d'un *Essai sur le goût*.[10] Marmontel s'est, en outre, mêlé à la querelle suscitée par la *Lettre sur les spectacles* de Rousseau, d'abord avec une *Apologie du théâtre* (1759–60),[11] puis avec un "conte moral" *Le Misanthrope corrigé* (1765).[12] L'intérêt principal de sa contribution dans l'*Encyclopédie* provient du fait qu'à travers son analyse de Molière s'exprime le point de vue du classicisme français du 18e siècle sur les questions suivantes: la légitimité morale du théâtre, la survivance de la farce, la querelle des Anciens et des Modernes et la possibilité d'un renouvellement esthétique après le grand siècle.

L'un des thèmes constants de la doctrine dramatique de Marmontel est que la comédie doit constituer une école de vertu. Précisons qu'il s'agit surtout d'une vertu mondaine permettant à l'homme de vivre en harmonie avec ses semblables. Selon Marmontel, l'oeuvre de Molière remplit parfaitement cette fonction avec ses "caractères adoucis par les égards" et ses "vices palliés par les bienséances". Elle incarne le génie d'une nation "douce et polie, où chacun se fait un devoir de conformer ses sentiments et ses idées aux moeurs de la société, où les usages sont des lois, où on est condamné à vivre seul dès qu'on veut vivre pour soi-même" ("Comédie"). Quelques vingt ans plus tard, dans le *Supplément*, on décèlera une certaine réticence. Marmontel avouera qu'à force de raffinement les Français ont perdu toute spontanéité et que Molière en est partiellement responsable: "Une éducation plus cultivée, le savoir-vivre qui est devenu notre plus sérieuse étude, l'attention si recommandée à ne blesser personne, ni l'opinion, ni les usages, la bienséance du dehors, qui du grand monde a passé au peuple, les leçons mêmes que Molière a données, soit pour saisir et relever le ridicule d'autrui, soit pour mieux déguiser les vices, ont mis la comédie en défaut" ("Poëme"). Saint Preux avait passé par là.

Dans le théâtre comique la bienséance s'est toujours heurtée à la popularité de la farce. Suivant en cela bon nombre de ses contemporains, Marmontel la qualifie d' "insipide exagération, imitation grossière d'une nature indigne d'être présentée aux yeux des honnêtes gens" ("Comique"). Il considère avec une égale horreur le théâtre italien "qu'un homme de

---

[10] Jean-François Marmontel, *Oeuvres complètes* (Paris: Verdière, 1818), XII–XV.
[11] *Ibid.*, X, 171–270.
[12] *Ibid.*, IV, 196–239.

goût ne sauroit soutenir" ("Comédie"). Mais il épargne Molière en affirmant que celui-ci n'a écrit qu'une véritable farce, *M de Pourceaugnac*. Par conséquent il n'en fait pas mention dans l'article "Farce" de l'*Encyclopédie* et, allant même plus loin, établit un contraste dans l'article du même nom du *Supplément* entre Molière et les écrivains de farce, lorsqu'il s'étonne que "la bonne comédie ayant été connue et portée au plus haut degré de perfection, les farces de Scarron aient réussi à côté des chefs-d'oeuvre de Molière."

Il est forcé toutefois d'avouer qu'il existe dans l'oeuvre de Molière des scènes et des répliques d'un goût douteux. Pour effacer l'effet de cette restriction, Marmontel s'empresse de relever les nombreux traits de bonne comédie dans des pièces contestées comme *Les Fourberies de Scapin* et, après avoir distingué le "comique bas" qui est plein de vérité et de gaîté, du "comique grossier", indigne d'un art raffiné, il s'ingénie à faire rentrer la plupart des passages réalistes de Molière dans la première catégorie ("Comédie").

De toutes ces considérations il ressort que, selon Marmontel, Molière respecte et même appuie la morale et les bienséances. Si dès le début de sa collaboration à l'*Encyclopédie* il revient là-dessus avec une telle insistance, c'est que, même avant l'intervention de Rousseau, la querelle de la moralité du théâtre persistait et qu'il importait de mettre le grand écrivain comique à l'abri de tout blâme.

Pour un classique comme Marmontel, la morale n'est pas toutefois le but de l'art mais simplement une des conditions de la doctrine du beau idéal, qui, une fois remplie, rend possible la production du chef-d'oeuvre. Il considère que le théâtre de Molière a atteint la perfection grâce à sa vérité humaine universelle et à son "coup d'oeil philosophique qui saisit non seulement les extrêmes mais le milieu des choses" ("Comédie"). Pour illustrer ses critères esthétiques, Marmontel a toujours recours à cette oeuvre, nourrie de naturel et de vraisemblance. Molière sait grouper les caractères, imiter la nature sans la forcer ("Comédie"), il offre des modèles de vérité ("Critique"), d'expositions ("Exposition" dans le *Supplément*), d'intrigues ("Acte" et, dans le *Supplément*, "Intrigue"), de situations ("Situation" dans le *Supplément*), de dialogues ("Dialogue"), de langage juste ("Jargon" dans le *Supplément*) et même de dénouements ("Dénouement" dans le *Supplément*), en dépit des avis contraires. En revanche, lorsqu'il s'agit de critiquer certaines pratiques, Marmontel choisit ses exemples chez les Anciens.

Cette admiration totale pour Molière entraîne forcément une prise de position dans la querelle des Anciens et des Modernes. Tout en blâmant l'intransigeance des Modernes du début du siècle, Marmontel leur donne raison sur le chapitre de Molière, d'abord dans son aperçu du genre ("Comédie"), et, trente ans plus tard, dans l'*Essai sur le goût*: "Aristophane et Plaute ne sont que des farceurs auprès d'un comique si vrai, si fin, si naturel. Térence est plus délicat, il est vrai, mais est-il aussi pénétrant?"[13] La réussite de Molière donne même tort aux grands théoriciens du passé, Aristote qui "n'admet les moeurs qu'à cause de l'action" alors que "la règle contraire est la nôtre" ("Pantomime" dans le *Supplément*), et Horace, qui croyait qu'une scène ne devrait comporter que trois personnages, alors que l'exposition du *Tartuffe* en compte six et reste claire ("Dialogue"). Qu'on ne s'y trompe pas, toutes minimes qu'elles semblent, ces observations marquent bien la fin du règne d'Aristote. Le classicisme français du 18ᵉ siècle a remplacé les modèles anciens par les modèles du siècle précédent.

Molière, qui incarne la réussite de l'art dramatique moderne, est pourtant solitaire dans son triomphe. Sur le théâtre étranger Marmontel se contente de lieux communs rabâchés comme "la gravité superbe des Espagnols" et l'individualisme des Anglais ("Comédie"). Même le "genre comique François" qui est "le plus parfait de tous", se résume, en fait, à l'oeuvre de Molière, si l'on excepte une brève allusion au *Menteur* de Corneille et la mention honorable accordée à Dufresny ("Comédie"). Marmontel se montre particulièrement dur envers Marivaux, dont il critique les subtilités ("Dialogue") et le langage uniforme ("Jargon" dans le *Supplément*). Assez favorable au drame bourgeois, avec son "comique attendrissant" ("Comédie"), tant qu'il collabore avec Diderot, Marmontel se raidira dans le *Supplément* ("Pantomime"), et davantage encore dans les *Eléments de littérature*, où il en minimisera la valeur, en comparant défavorablement sa portée psychologique à celle des comédies de Molière.[14] A tous ceux qui aspirent à entrer dans la carrière dramatique, il conseille d'étudier l'oeuvre de Molière et de reprendre ses méthodes, en les appliquant à d'autres types, comme l'intrigante, le bas orgueilleux, le prôneur de soi-même, etc. ("Comédie").

Toutefois le lecteur de l'*Encyclopédie* a bien l'impression qu'une telle entreprise est irréalisable. Jaucourt l'affirme en toutes lettres: "Il l'élève

---

[13] Marmontel, *Oeuvres complètes*, XX, 55.
[14] *Ibid.*, XII, 143.

[la comédie] au plus haut point de gloire et à sa mort la nature l'ensevelit avec lui" ("Comédie sainte"). Le critique plus réfléchi qu'est Marmontel, s'exprime en termes tout aussi catégoriques. Nous n'en donnerons qu'une citation : "C'est dans cet esprit et avec ce grand art que fut tissue l'intrigue de *L'Avare*, de *L'Ecole des femmes*, de *L'Ecole des maris*, du *Tartuffe*, modèles effrayants même pour le génie, et dont l'esprit et le simple talent n'approcheront jamais" ("Intrigue" dans le *Supplément*).

L'oeuvre de Molière semble, pour ces critiques, s'identifier avec le goût châtié de l'époque, qui recherche la décence, la vraisemblance et un naturel moyen et mondain dans la peinture de l'homme de société. Figés dans l'admiration du grand ecrivain, ils confondent son génie avec l'essence de la comédie qu'ils ne peuvent plus concevoir sous une autre forme.

Mais le *Supplément* offre un deuxième point de vue sur Molière, avec trois articles tirés d'une encyclopédie d'art allemande, l'*Allgemeine Theorie der schönen Künste* (1771) de Johann Georg Sulzer.[15] Bien que celui-ci connaisse les écrits de Marmontel et qu'il les cite avec considération, il ne partage pas son optique strictement classique. Muni d'un savoir cosmopolite, souvent désordonné, mais toujours curieux, il apprécie, bien mieux que le critique français à la fois la comédie antique et les innovations modernes. Il en résulte que Molière ne lui sert pas toujours de modèle dans son examen du théâtre comique, ne figurant même pas dans des articles comme "Acte" et "Poëme." Sulzer lui reconnaît, certes, la première place en France où "il mit des pièces sur la scène qui s'y soutiendront aussi longtemps que le spectacle comique subsistera" ("Comédie"). Mais sur le plan de l'art universel il ne lui accorde pas une position privilégiée : Shakespeare "peut-être le plus grand peintre des passions" ("Naturel"), Machiavel, héritier de Térence, Gray, grand peintre de moeurs dans son *Beggar's Opera*, Hegeland et d'autres Allemands excellents dans l'imitation de la nature ("Naturel"), lui font une concurrence sérieuse.

En outre, allant plus loin que les classiques français, Sulzer exige de l'art une intention morale positive : "L'artiste cependant n'accomplit de la manière la plus parfaite les devoirs de sa vocation que lorsqu'après avoir excité les forces de l'âme, il lui donne une direction advantageuse, c'est-à-dire lorsqu'il la porte constamment à la justice et à la vertu." Molière ne se mesure pas avantageusement à cet idéal, car il intéresse "trop souvent le spectateur en faveur de la fraude et du vice" ("Intéressant"). Autre critique qui concerne Molière, bien que cette fois il ne soit pas mentionné :

---

[15] Johann Georg Sulzer, *Allgemeine Theorie der schönen Künste* (Leipsic: Weidemanns, Erben und Reich, 1771–72).

"les valets bouffons et les suivantes qui agacent" répugnent à Sulzer, qui propose de les remplacer par des "personnages judicieux prêts à faire des observations sagaces" ("Comédie").

Etranger aux dogmes du classicisme français, Sulzer voit entre le tragique et le comique non pas une incompatibilité fondamentale, mais seulement une différence de degré. "La nature ne connaît point ces limites", affirme-t-il sans hésiter. Il favorise, par conséquent, la nouvelle comédie, "genre sérieux touchant, et qui donne dans le tragique", mais note, avec regret, que ce "haut comique" a de la peine à s'implanter, car "on n'est pas revenu du préjugé qui regarde la comédie comme un spectacle burlesque" ("Comédie"). Comme dans le cas des domestiques, Sulzer ne nomme pas Molière, mais il est évident que l'éclat de son oeuvre est pour beaucoup dans la résistance de la scène à tout changement radical.

Enfin, si pour l'agencement de l'intrigue et la peinture des caractères, Sulzer reste fidèle aux principes de la vraisemblance et de la mesure, il ne considère pas pour autant Molière comme un guide infaillible, et se permet, par exemple, de critiquer certaines exagérations de *L'Avare* ("Naturel" et "Comédie").

Par son silence partiel et par ses critiques incidentes, Sulzer fait bien voir que Molière n'est pas à ses yeux le maître incontesté de la comédie. Il est piquant de constater que c'est le *Supplément* et non pas l'*Encyclopédie* qui réalise la promesse du "Discours préliminaire," en présentant deux points de vue sur Molière, avec la doctrine classique de Marmontel et la doctrine du drame bourgeois de Sulzer.

Abordons, pour finir, la question suivante: pourquoi la vie et l'oeuvre de Molière sont-elles à peine exploitées par la propagande philosophique? Marmontel ne franchit jamais la frontière qui sépare la littérature de la pensée. Pourtant l'auteur du *Bélisaire* affrontait en 1767 les foudres de la censure pour s'être prononcé en faveur de la tolérance. Jaucourt effleure la question de son épicurisme: "Il apprit dans sa jeunesse la Philosophie du celèbre Gassendi, et ce fut alors qu'il commença une traduction de Lucrèce en vers français. Il n'étoit pas seulement philosophe dans la théorie, il l'étoit encore dans la pratique. C'est cependant à ce philosophe que l'archevêque de Paris, Harlay, si décrié par ses moeurs, refusa les vains honneurs de la sépulture" ("Poëte comique"). On reconnaît le style de Voltaire que Jaucourt reproduit textuellement.[16] C'est d'ailleurs la seule hardiesse qu'il se permette.

---

[16] *Siècle de Louis XIV* (Garnier-Flammarion, 1966), II, 256.

Diderot, dans l'article "Epicurisme ou épicuréisme" va beaucoup moins loin en ce qui concerne Molière. Le nom de celui-ci figure simplement dans la liste des adeptes de Gassendi et son talent littéraire ne lui vaut pas d'être distingué des "autres hommes extraordinaires qui, par un contraste de qualités agréables et sublimes, réunissent en eux l'héroisme avec la mollesse le goût de la vertu avec celui du plaisir, les qualités politiques avec les talents littéraires". Un peu plus loin, traitant de la morale épicurienne, Diderot juge qu'elle fait de la volupté le moteur naturel de toute action humaine, mais ne cite aucun exemple littéraire. Libre au lecteur de faire des rapprochements.

On trouve, d'autre part, une déclaration assez surprennate de Diderot à l'article "Gravité", publié parmi les titres omis à la fin du volume 17. Pour distinguer entre ce qui peut légitimement constituer un objet de ridicule et ce que le théâtre comique ne devrait pas toucher, Diderot propose le critère de l'utilité sociale:

> L'abus de la comédie est de jeter le ridicule sur les professions les plus sérieuses, et d'ôter à des personnages importants ce masque de *gravité* qui les défend contre l'insolence et la malignité de l'envie. Les petits-maîtres, les précieuses ridicules, et de semblables êtres inutiles et importuns à la société sont des sujets comiques. Mais les Médecins, les Avocats, et tous ceux qui exercent un ministère utile doivent être respectés. Il n'y a point d'inconvéniens à présenter *Turcaret* sur la scène, mais il y en a peut-être à jouer le *Tartuffe*. Le financier gagne à n'exciter que la risée du peuple; mais la vraie dévotion perd beaucoup au ridicule qu'on sème sur les faux dévots.

L'on est tenté d'attribuer à ces lignes une intention ambiguë, l'auteur reprenant, pour s'en moquer, les arguments de dévots du temps de Molière, d'autant plus qu'à l'article "Préoccupation" Diderot cite la réponse de Cléante pour établir une distinction entre les francs hypocrites et les vrais gens de bien. On aurait ainsi affaire, après le passage de Voltaire cité par Jaucourt, au deuxième exemple de coup fourré si typique de l'*Encyclopédie* auquel Molière fournirait des armes. C'est peu si l'on pense au potentiel de ses pièces, dont Voltaire, lui, n'avait pas hésité à se servir dans sa *Vie* du grand dramaturge.

Les motifs de cette réserve ne peuvent être estimés qu'à l'aide de conjectures. Il faut d'abord tenir compte de la personalité et des méthodes de chaque auteur. Jaucourt est conciliant, Marmontel souhaite s'établir une réputation de critique littéraire sérieux et objectif, Diderot écrit en philosophe et préfère se concentrer sur Gassendi, le vrai penseur du groupe. Deuxièmement, avant même la querelle suscitée par l'article "Genève," les encyclopédistes ont pour consigne de souligner la respectabilité du théâtre. Or présenter Molière comme agent de subversion eût été peu sage, son théâtre ayant, même à cent ans d'intervalle, de nombreux adversaires. Une troisième explication se trouve peut-être dans son oeuvre même, qui, par sa morale du juste milieu et sa répugnance à tout esprit de système, risquait de se retourner contre les philosophes remuants du 18ᵉ siècle. Mieux valait l'examiner dans la perspective de la comédie humaine éternelle.

L'esprit de réforme et de combat, auquel on pense normalement à propos de l'*Encyclopédie* ne se manifeste donc pas à tout propos et sans discernement. Sur le plan littéraire la doctrine classique domine encore, et c'est le *Supplément* qui fait preuve d'indépendance. Sur le plan de la propagande, les impératifs du moment dictent une certaine prudence et, comme dans toute guerre, la tactique joue un rôle modérateur. Il importe davantage de promouvoir le théâtre que d'exploiter l'épicurisme de Molière. Dans ce domaine, comme dans celui de la littérature, et en dépit des affirmations contraires du "Discours préliminaire," un esprit de corps anime les rédacteurs et leur impose une politique à suivre.

TARTUFFE MALE ET FEMELLE
Bernard Bray

Molière n'eut pas de successeurs, dit-on. Il est vrai que Turcaret ne saurait faire oublier Harpagon, et qu'en somme après Molière aucun poète comique n'a su créer un type littéraire qui ait la vérité et la drôlerie d'un Tartuffe, d'un Alceste, voire d'un Argan. Mais ce n'est peut-être pas au théâtre qu'il convient de rechercher les héritiers du grand comique, car la modification des conditions sociales a entraîné celle du genre lui-même : la décadence de la comédie est complète et définitive au XVIIIe siècle ; en revanche le roman se développe, son public s'étend, sa technique se perfectionne. De Gil Blas à Emma Bovary, c'est maintenant le héros de roman qui tend au lecteur ce miroir que lui offrait jadis le personnage de comédie. C'est dans les romans qu'il faut chercher, une fois ôté le masque grimaçant dont Molière les affublait, ces mêmes figures monstrueuses et fascinantes auxquelles le roman confère à son tour une illusoire réalité. Ainsi Lovelace prend la place de Don Juan. Ainsi, en Mme de Merteuil, Baudelaire voit un "Tartuffe femelle".[1] Il n'était pas le premier à proposer cette assimilation, puisqu' on la trouve sous la plume de l'auteur même des *Liaisons dangereuses*, dans les lettres qu'il échangea aussitôt après la publication de son ouvrage avec la romancière Mme Riccoboni.[2] Bien que plusieurs critiques aient tenu compte des formules que ce dialogue épistolaire a fait surgir sous la plume de Laclos à propos de son héroïne, la plupart s'y sont intéressés pour éclairer le personnage de Mme de Merteuil plutôt que celui de Tartuffe, et plus précisément encore pour étudier la validité qu'il convient d'accorder au dénouement du roman, par comparaison avec celui de la comédie ; mais aucun ne semble s'être interrogé sur la réflexion que livrent ces lignes au sujet du personnage type de l'hypocrite, identique à lui-même sous les deux avatars.[3] Il en va de même en ce qui concerne la brève note de lecture de Baudelaire : le nom de

---

[1] Laclos, *Oeuvres complètes* (Paris, Bibl. de la Pléiade, 1951), 717.
[2] *Ibid.*, 686–98.
[3] Voir surtout L. Versini, *Laclos et la tradition* (Paris, Klincksieck, 1968), 222–23 (nombreux renvois en note à la littérature critique antérieure).

Tartuffe y semble avancé comme référence à valeur implicite, et pourtant le rapprochement, comme le montrent plusieurs formules dans les pages précédentes, procède en réalité d'une vue synthétique et pessimiste de l'homme et de la société, dépassant le cadre de l'un ou de l'autre siècle. Il paraît donc opportun de revenir sur cette comparaison entre le Tartuffe mâle et le Tartuffe femelle, pour tenter d'en dégager des constantes liées à la peinture littéraire de l'hypocrite.[4]

Dans la première des lettres où Tartuffe est évoqué (lettre IV), Laclos cherche à se défendre contre l'accusation de Mme Riccoboni selon laquelle il aurait mis en scène "des caractères qui ne peuvent exister."[5] Mme de Merteuil, reconnaît-il, n'a probablement jamais vécu. Dans le cas contraire, le livre aurait été non un roman mais "un libelle," c'est-à-dire un ouvrage satirique. Mais Tartuffe lui non plus n'a jamais existé, en ce sens qu'aucun homme n'a accompli la totalité des forfaits du personnage; pourtant "cent hypocrites avaient commis séparément de semblables horreurs." En somme, l'ingénieur Laclos voit la création de Molière comme une construction géométrique, ou plutôt comme l'accumulation sur un plan théorique de traits multiples pouvant chacun résulter d'une observation vécue sur le plan pratique. Fictif dans son ensemble, Tartuffe est pourtant vrai dans le détail de ses actions, ce qui justifie son existence littéraire. Car, selon Laclos, le but ultime de Molière est moral: "livr [er le personnage] à l'indignation publique", et par là contribuer à l'épuration des moeurs, rendue possible par une meilleure connaissance de la société.[5]

Le personnage de Mme de Merteuil procède d'une technique identique. A la liste des "horreurs" accomplies par Tartuffe "sous le manteau de la religion" correspond celle des "noirceurs" que se permet Mme de Merteuil, "en couvrant [ses] vices de l'hypocrisie des moeurs". Ainsi, comme Molière, l'auteur des *Liaisons dangereuses* a pu "rassembler dans un même personnage les traits épars du même caractère".[6] Les crimes de Tartuffe et ceux de Mme de Merteuil ne sont pourtant pas exactement comparables terme à terme. Nous pourrions remarquer, il est vrai, que le "Tartuffe femelle" débauche une jeune fille (Cécile) de qui il séduit la mère (Mme de Volanges), comme l'autre compte épouser Mariane et n'en

---

[4] Nous n'oublierons pas que Baudelaire a certainement pris connaissance de la correspondance de Laclos avec Mme Riccoboni, qui fut jointe à une édition des *Liaisons dangereuses* dès 1787, car le poète, qui voulait consacrer à Laclos un travail étendu, avait procédé dans ce dessein à des lectures systématiques (voir Laclos, *Oeuvres complètes*, 903–07).

[5] Laclos, *Oeuvres complètes*, 687, 690, 691.

[6] *Ibid.*, 691.

tente pas moins la séduction d'Elmire;[7] d'autre part, que l'épisode de Prévan chassé de chez la Marquise et déshonoré[8] a des points communs avec la scène dans laquelle Orgon pour un faux motif couvre d'injures et chasse de chez lui son fils Damis;[9] puis, que la déclaration de guerre lancée par Mme de Merteuil à Valmont, à la fois son complice et sa dupe,[10] fait penser au: "C'est à vous d'en sortir, vous qui parlez en maître",[11] jeté par Tartuffe à Orgon; enfin, qu'à l'exposé de ses principes auquel se livre Tartuffe devant Elmire:

> Le scandale du monde est ce qui fait l'offense,
> Et ce n'est pas pécher que pécher en silence,[12]

semble répondre Mme de Merteuil lorsqu'elle écrit à Valmont sa fameuse lettre-programme et lui expose les règles sur lesquelles elle a fondé sa conduite hypocrite.[13] Mais ces rapprochements, bien qu'ils touchent à plusieurs personnages principaux et à la structure même des deux oeuvres, et qu'on puisse les compléter sans doute en entrant davantage dans le détail, Laclos ne semble pas avoir pris conscience de leur signification. Répondant à une lectrice, écrivain comme lui-même, qui met en doute l'existence de "pareils monstres,"[14] il s'occupe seulement de lui expliquer en quoi consiste la vérité d'un personnage littéraire, sans perdre de vue, à chaque instant de son argumentation, que l'invraisemblance qu'on lui reproche n'a pas d'autre cause que l'immoralité de la peinture, et qu'il doit donc en rejeter la responsabilité sur la société qui l'entoure s'il veut disculper sa propre personne.

Par là se trouve mise en relief la notion même d'hypocrisie. L'hypocrite, nous dit Laclos, est un type que chacun a rencontré. Or pour le reconnaître comme tel, il faut avoir percé à jour sa duplicité. Le schéma se complique si on le transpose en termes littéraires, car il faudra alors qu'un personnage-témoin supplémentaire, donné comme clairvoyant, observe l'hypocrite en

---

[7] Enumérant les actions coupables de Tartuffe, Laclos, inexactement, utilise l'expression: "Séduire la mère dont il épousait la fille." Mme Riccoboni lui fit remarquer dans sa réponse que Mariane n'est pas la fille d'Elmire. A quoi Laclos répliquera à juste titre que si le "péché" est moindre, le "procédé" est le même, ce qui entraîne une responsabilité identique de Tartuffe devant Orgon. Voir 690, 692, 696.

[8] Lettre 85.

[9] Acte III, sc. 6.

[10] Réponse à la lettre 143.

[11] Acte IV, sc. 7.

[12] Acte IV, sc. 5.

[13] Lettre 81. Voir par exemple, Laclos, 177: "dès ce moment, ma façon de penser fut pour moi seule, et je ne montrai plus que celle qu'il m'était utile de laisser voir."

[14] Laclos, 689.

train de séduire sa dupe ; ce personnage établit pour lui-même son constat ; mais la preuve de l'hypocrisie ne sera administrée qu'au dénouement, lorsque le séducteur aura levé le masque et que sa dupe, rejoignant le personnage-témoin, sera à son tour désabusée. Dans la pièce de Molière, le rôle du témoin est assumé par un groupe de personnages (Elmire, Damis, Mariane, Valère, Cléante, Dorine) : ils sont chargés de guider l'interprétation du spectateur, qui s'identifie à eux. Cette perspective triangulaire simple donne toute son efficacité à la construction de la comédie, chaque groupe étant successivement mis en opposition avec les deux autres, et le manège de l'hypocrite auprès de sa dupe étant continuellement éclairé par les jeux de scène, jeux de mots et autres effets grossissants propres au registre comique.

La structure du roman épistolaire est apparemment fort différente.[15] En particulier, le rôle du personnage-témoin est plus complexe. Théoriquement, en l'absence de toute "perspective d'auteur," le lecteur ne peut déceler l'hypocrisie de Mme de Merteuil qu'en confrontant certaines de ses lettres avec d'autres qui les contredisent expressément.[16] En fait l'héroïne ne dissimule à peu près rien de ses projets à Valmont, en sorte que les lettres qu'elle lui écrit nous révèlent déjà clairement la duplicité de sa conduite, à l'égard de Cécile ou de Prévan par exemple. Mais lorsqu'il s'agit de son rapport avec Valmont lui-même, Mme de Merteuil est moins explicite. Aussi, du drame qui se noue entre ces deux personnages, et où l'hypocrisie joue peut-être un rôle, aucun témoin ne nous aide à suivre le développement ni à dégager le sens. On peut donc considérer qu'il y a trois niveaux dans l'hypocrisie de Mme de Merteuil. Le premier niveau est éclairé par le contenu des lettres qu'elle écrit à Valmont, le second par des arrangements et juxtapositions de lettres que l'auteur a voulus clairement suggestifs, le troisième au contraire est laissé dans l'ombre. L'auteur crée ici un doute à la fois méthodologique et psychologique : l'incertitude des données épistolaires traduit l'incertitude qui s'est établie dans l'âme de Mme de Merteuil, lorsque la jalousie à l'égard de Valmont, l'orgueil, le goût de la provocation, et la passion pour Danceny, lui font oublier ses maximes de prudence[17] et la mènent à sa perte. Ainsi malgré les différences évidentes qui séparent une comédie d'un roman épistolaire, la peinture d'un caractère d'hypocrite impose ici et là des schémas de présentation comparables,

---

[15] Voir T. Todorov, *Littérature et signification* (Paris, Larousse, 1967).
[16] Voir par exemple les trois lettres écrites le 4 octobre par Mme de Merteuil à Mme de Volanges, à Cécile et à Valmont (104, 105, 106).
[17] Relatives notamment à la rédaction des lettres.

et Laclos est parfaitement en droit de rapprocher sa création du modèle
moliéresque, même si, à tort, il limite ce rapprochement au principe qui
a guidé la conception du personnage central.

　　Ce que nous venons de dire est corroboré par les hésitations et discussions qui ont marqué l'interprétation du dénouement de *Tartuffe* comme
celui des *Liaisons dangereuses*. Ces dénouements ne sont-ils que concession
à la morale publique? A Mme Riccoboni, affirmant que Tartuffe est puni
par la justice et par les lois, Laclos répond qu'au contraire le scélérat a su
se mettre à l'abri de leur action, et que seule l'arrête au dernier moment
"l'indignation du prince," c'est-à-dire une "autorité" exceptionnelle; sans
compter que "le châtiment est motivé sur d'autres actions que celles qui
se sont passées durant le cours de la pièce."[18] Ainsi le dénouement, qui
nous montre l'échec final de Tartuffe, ne saurait atténuer le caractère
inquiétant de la peinture, puisqu'en réalité cet échec n'est rien moins que
logique et inévitable. La comparaison s'impose avec la conclusion du
roman de Laclos. Et sans doute, bien qu'il n'en parle pas, l'auteur des
Liaisons dangereuses a-t-il cette conclusion à l'esprit lorsqu'il commente
à l'intention de Mme Riccoboni les dernières scènes de *Tartuffe*. Selon
l'attentive exégèse que fait M. Versini des formules du romancier, celui-ci,
en condamnant cruellement son héroïne, entend "affirmer la mission de
la littérature, mission non de police mais de dévouement à la cause de
l'honnêteté, qui met l'écrivain, chargé d'éliminer Merteuil, sur le même
plan que le prince, chargé d'éliminer Tartuffe."[19] Est-ce vraiment cela que
veut dire Laclos? C'est faire bon marché du rôle symétrique de l'écrivain
Molière. M. Versini, dans la suite de son analyse, montre le rôle de la
"facture dramatique" et celui de la "fatalité tragique" dans la conception
du dénouement, deux notions qui s'appliquent aussi bien à la comédie de
Molière qu'au roman de Laclos, surtout si l'on y joint ces "conventions
non pas seulement morales mais surtout esthétiques . . . "[20] qui régissent
dans notre littérature occidentale la présentation littéraire d'un caractère
de méchant. Nous insisterons, quant à nous, sur ces conventions esthétiques, estimant peu fondée la question de la sincérité d'un auteur de
l'époque classique quand il est amené à punir *in extremis* un hypocrite,
Don Juan ou M. de Climal (non puni mais converti: la condamnation
est la même), Tartuffe ou Mme de Merteuil. En ce qui concerne ces deux
derniers personnages, on ne peut donc s'interroger que sur le *comment*,

[18] Laclos, 692, 696, 697.
[19] Versini, 223.
[20] *Ibid.*

non sur le *pourquoi* de leur condamnation, question que ne se sont sérieusement posée ni Molière ni Laclos. Le dénouement des deux ouvrages a en réalité ici et là la même fonction dévoilante. Qu'on puisse hésiter à leur propos entre une signification de triomphe et une signification d'échec revient à s'interroger sur la nature même de l'hypocrisie, qui est une conduite double, dont le développement logique entraîne un aboutissement lui aussi double, et apparemment contradictoire.

Il nous semble que la qualification que Baudelaire applique à la Marquise de Merteuil: "Tartuffe femelle, tartuffe de moeurs, tartuffe du XVIIIe siècle", doit s'interpréter dans le même sens. Il ne peut être question d'evoquer ici en quelques lignes tout le riche contenu que Baudelaire donne au terme *femelle*. Il est pourtant évident que l'idée de perversité y est dominante. Sensuelle, la Merteuil "a d'ailleurs du bon sens et de l'esprit." Sa grandeur consiste dans l'organisation simultanée de sa double vie. Si elle se montre "toujours supérieure à Valmont," c'est qu'en elle le mensonge est plus froidement naturel que chez lui, c'est aussi qu'elle l'a pris lui-même comme objet de tromperie. Dans cette image postromantique, la Merteuil apparaît comme une nouvelle Dalila, qui épuise et trahit l'homme, sa victime. Le "Tartuffe femelle," c'est donc d'abord un être qui, comme le personnage de Molière, connaît des besoins charnels et en poursuit la satisfaction (avec, bien sûr, plus de succès que son modèle). C'est, comme le faux dévot, un imposteur. Mais, à la différence cette fois du Tartuffe mâle, c'est un être intelligent, à l'aise dans le milieu social et historique qui l'a sécrété, vainqueur de ses rivaux masculins grâce à cette prééminence de fait que les salons du XVIIIe siècle, privilégiant les techniques mondaines de la séduction amoureuse, ont dû reconnaître au sexe féminin. Tel est le sens de: "tartuffe de moeurs, tartuffe du XVIIIe siècle," deux concepts qui ne font qu'expliciter celui de "tartuffe femelle." Par là Baudelaire montre qu'à juste titre il ne saurait séparer le personnage du contexte dont l'entoure ce "livre de sociabilité" qu'est le roman de Laclos.[21]

Mme Riccoboni, "en qualité de femme [et] de Française",[22] s'indignait contre la noirceur du caractère de la Merteuil. Laclos n'eut pas de peine à réfuter cette piètre argumentation, qui tendait en réalité à refuser à l'art le privilège de peindre aucun "monstre odieux". En s'appuyant sur

---

[21] Cf. plus haut dans les *Notes* de Baudelaire: "Ici comme dans la vie, la palme de la perversité reste à [la] femme. (Saufeia.) Foemina simplex dans sa petite maison." Laclos, 715*n*, 717, 716.

[22] *Ibid.*, 689.

l'exemple de Molière, Laclos put à la fois montrer quel rapport il convient d'établir entre l'observation des moeurs contemporaines et la création d'un type littéraire, et quelle absurdité il y a, de la part des lecteurs, à refuser de croire à un personnage pour cause d'immoralité excessive. Plus profondément, on peut penser que *Tartuffe* joua pour le romancier le rôle d'un "modèle", en ce sens que Molière dans sa comédie avait déjà fixé la place de l'hypocrite entre sa dupe et les nécessaires témoins. Utilisant de façon géniale les ressources encore inexploitées de l'art du roman épistolaire, Laclos a su opérer une complète transposition du personnage, féminisé et rattaché maintenant à un monde nouveau. Mais les structures profondes des deux ouvrages se correspondent, car elles sont dictées par le sujet même, liées sous ses aspects psychologique, moral et social à l'image de l'hypocrite.

*The patrimony of Molière to the nineteenth and twentieth centuries in France is a topic of forbidding scope. The following essays certainly do not cover the subject, but they do offer a beginning, and there is further data to be gleaned in the bibliographical sources cited in notes. Constant, Hugo, Zola, Proust, Gide, and Beckett could certainly be considered in the light of Molière's legacy; but the essays available here are limited to discussions of Stendhal, Balzac, and Ionesco. The reader will find additional information concerning Molière's patrimony to the most recent times in the sections of this volume which deal with the staging of Molière's plays (*mise en scène, *French television) and with current Molière criticism.*

MOLIÈRE AND STENDHAL

Gita May

The Romantics as a whole held Molière in high esteem and were greatly preoccupied with the different aspects of his art. All were avid readers and students of Molière, and some, notably Stendhal and Balzac, even nurtured the dream of emulating the great seventeenth-century playwright.[1] Stendhal, of all the Romantics, left the most complete record of his thoughts and observations concerning Molière.

While Stendhal's lifelong interest in Molière has long been acknowledged by critics and literary historians, this has generally been done in passing or in piecemeal fashion.[2] This essay is an attempt to present a coherent synthesis of Stendhal's evolving, and at times paradoxical, atti-

---

[1] Cf. Otis Fellows, *French Opinion of Molière; 1800–1850* (Providence, Brown University, 1937).

[2] The title of Albert Thibaudet's article, "Stendhal et Molière," *La Nouvelle Revue Française* (November 1, 1924, pp. 593–606), is actually misleading, for in this essay Thibaudet begins with general considerations on the respective characteristics of the "beyliste" and the "stendhalien," and then proceeds to an analysis of Julien Sorel as a disciple of Tartuffe, only one of the many aspects of the Molière-Stendhal relationship. There are also interesting remarks concerning this relationship in V. del Litto, *La Vie intellectuelle de Stendhal* (Paris, Presses Universitaires de France, 1962).

tude toward Molière. As a resolutely subjective and highly individualistic and self-centered reader and student of literature, Stendhal consistently avoided systematizing his thoughts and reflections; hence a substantial but frequently disjointed body of references, allusions and comments which have as their unifying characteristic a pithy, lighthearted and irreverent tone—the outward sign of Henri Beyle's fierce determination not to be overwhelmed by a paralyzing admiration for one he recognized as the supreme master of the art of comedy and as a genius in penetrating and depicting the foibles of human nature.[3]

From his mother's side of the family, the Gagnons, particularly from his grandfather and his great-aunt Elisabeth, young Henri Beyle acquired a chivalrous, romantic conception of life, what he would be fond of calling his *espagnolisme*. Thus, when, as a lonely and precocious child seeking comfort and escape in books, he came upon three masters of the comic genre, Cervantes, Molière and Voltaire, his preference spontaneously went, he assures us, for the author of *Don Quixote*.[4] While Cervantes appealed to his sense of adventure and chivalry, Molière and Voltaire at first displeased him through their mercilessly satiric portrayal of human baseness and stupidity.[5]

As a rebellious youth, struggling to free himself from the constricting influence of his provincial and bourgeois surroundings, especially of his stern, conservative father, Chérubin Beyle, Henri found in Molière's plays, above all in *L'Avare* (the first work by Molière that he read), a depiction of ordinary, middle-class life that reminded him only too vividly of his own milieu, which he detested so thoroughly.

---

[3] The allusions to Molière in Stendhal's works are numerous, and not even a partial list of these would be possible within the framework of this essay. We refer the interested reader to the name index of the most complete edition of Stendhal's writings edited by Henri Martineau, in the *Oeuvres complètes* (79 vols; Paris, Le Divan, 1927–1939). Stendhal's remarks on several important Molière plays have been published by Henri Cordier in *Molière jugé par Stendhal* (Paris, Chez tous les Libraires, 1898), and, more recently, by Henri Martineau in *Molière, Shakespeare, la comédie et le rire*, in his edition of the *Oeuvres complètes*. Cf. also *Racine et Shakespeare*, ed. Pierre Martino (Paris, Champion, 1925), as well as *Oeuvres intimes*, ed. Henri Martineau (Paris, Collection de la Pléiade, 1955) and *Correspondance*, ed. Henri Martineau and V. del Litto (3 vols; Paris, Collection de la Pléiade, 1962–1968).

[4] Cf. Stendhal, *Vie de Henry Brulard*, especially in Martineau's excellent edition of the *Oeuvres intimes*. For the convenience of the English-speaking reader, however, I am using the competent translation by Jean Stewart and B. C. J. G. Knight (New York, Funk & Wagnalls, 1968), and my references will be to this edition (for a description of the effect of Cervantes, Molière and Voltaire, cf. chapter IX, 67–73).

[5] Cf. Jules C. Alciatore, "Stendhal lecteur de *La Pucelle*," *Stendhal Club* (July 15, 1960), 325–34 and, by the same author, "Stendhal et les romans de Voltaire," *Stendhal Club* (January 15, 1961), 15–23.

Stendhal is categorical when he states the age at which he discovered Molière: "From the age of seven – and this seems to be an established fact in my mind – I had resolved to write comedies like Molière." His recollection of this first encounter is vivid and detailed enough to lend credence to his retroactive dating of the event. And what reinforces Stendhal's testimony is that his initial comprehension of Molière's art was extremely rudimentary: "I found an illustrated Molière; the pictures seemed to me ridiculous and I only understood *L'Avare*." Yet Stendhal is equally insistent on the nature of his first reaction to Molière, which, he tells us, was one of shock and even revulsion: "I had a loathing for all the vulgar *bourgeois* details of which Molière made use to express his thought. These details reminded me too much of my own unhappy life."[6]

No doubt, scenes of petty dissimulation, hypocrisy, and wrangling were all too familiar to young Beyle to evoke in him wholehearted merriment. He was both far too young and too deeply involved in his own personal problems, in his own painful quest for freedom, to be objective in his appreciation of the greatest classical caricaturist of, among other things, social ambition and prejudice. As the only son of an ambitious provincial lawyer who possessed many of the unattractive traits of a M. Jourdain, a Harpagon, and a Chrysale, he was too close to the clichés, self-delusions, and blundering attempts at self-aggrandizement of such sociological types to laugh unreservedly at their obvious faux-pas.

That the middle-aged Stendhal setting down nostalgic recollections of his early years should have stressed the negative lesson derived from Molière while at the same time stating that his first ambition in life had been to become the Molière of the nineteenth century should not strike us as totally contradictory. It is important, in this connection, to remember that Stendhal never recoiled before apparent contradiction and paradox. Moreover, even when dealing with authors whom he held in greatest esteem, he rarely missed an opportunity to exercise his ironic wit and sharp critical sense at the expense of his heroes and masters. In this respect, Molière is indeed in excellent company, since Stendhal never hesitated to mistreat and castigate his most admired literary idols. The aptitude for reverence was not Stendhal's forte, and his basic antipathy for everyday ordinariness and bourgeois smugness and materialism played a major part in determining his initially negative reaction to Molière's plays.

Despite these reservations, Molière continued to occupy a very special

---

[6] Stewart and Knight, trans., *Life of Henry Brulard*, 70.

place among Stendhal's literary masters. This is made abundantly clear by numerous references and comments, spread over an entire lifetime, in the writer's diaries, notebooks, correspondence, and other works. Molière, moreover, was unfailingly included among those few select authors whose books accompanied the peripatetic Stendhal throughout his travels.[7] From the tone of his observations, it is also clear that the name of Molière remained synonymous with the kind of insight into human nature for which Stendhal had a particular appreciation.

While other youthful idols, such as Rousseau, at first far more generously praised than Molière, were eventually relegated to a less privileged position, Molière only grew in stature through the years and, as Beyle gained in intellectual and emotional maturity, was treated with ever-increasing respect. To be sure, young Beyle's *espagnolisme* caused him to equate an unadorned portrayal of the French *bourgeoisie* with a lack of true literary genius. Throughout his adult life, Stendhal evinced the same predilection for a literary view of reality that exalts our capacity for generosity, selflessness, and idealistic self-sacrifice. Yet, Stendhal remained aware that the lesson of a Molière was a salutary one, for it forced him to face contemporary society, not as he fondly like to image it, but as it was in fact.

For Stendhal Molière incarnated the painter *par excellence* of the foibles, tics and illusions of the social opportunist, a sociological type that was as prevalent in the nineteenth century, particularly under the Restoration, as it had been during the reign of Louis XIV. And when the alienated young provincial that Henri Beyle was in his native Grenoble dreamed of social and amorous conquests through literary success in Paris, he naturally looked upon Molière as a model. Through the prism of his imagination, he saw himself as the spiritual heir of Molière. Conveniently forgetting or at the time unaware of Molière's difficulties with the authorities, he viewed a career as a playwright as a passport to both personal freedom and social fame. Unbeknownst to himself, the young Stendhal was learning many lessons from Molière as he deliberately set out to vie with him as a popular and beloved playwright.

One would seek in vain for an orderly, systematic attempt on Stendhal's part to analyze the multifarious aspects of Molière's work. Characteristically, he approached Molière the way he approached all writers who eventually had a profound impact on his own aesthetics: in a resolutely, boldly subjective manner. Whenever Molière is mentioned, it is in connec-

---

[7] Cf. Ferdinand Boyer, *Les Lectures de Stendhal* (Paris, Editions du Stendhal-Club, 1925).

tion with an immediate problem that preoccupied Stendhal, never as a writer to be probed in his own right. It is symptomatic of Beyle's philosophy of enlightened egotism and relentless search for self-knowledge that Molière is envisaged as a tool, a means to gain a better understanding of human nature in general and of French social types in particular. Molière both fascinated and repelled young Beyle because his plays helped the rebellious son of a typical *bourgeois* to gain perspective in his difficult dealings with a class he held in abhorrence. For men like Chérubin Beyle, consumed with ambition and greed, the world had hardly changed since Molière had so mercilessly portrayed and caricatured their mannerisms, scheming pettiness and rigid conformism. Young Beyle wholeheartedly endorsed the high if ruthless idealism of the Jacobins and at the same time harbored admiration and sympathy for the cultured, civilized ways of a genteel and corrupt aristocracy. He felt equally at ease with men and women of the nobility and with common folk. In the *bourgeois*, however, he saw only calculating selfishness and crass materialism hiding behind a hypocritical façade of religious devotion and staunch morality. Like Molière, Stendhal would never tire of satirizing the smug and sanctimonious burghers and their stodgy ways.

Stendhal's father, with his rigidity, gaucherie, and total lack of charm, and with his single-minded devotion to social advancement and material enrichment, came to symbolize a kind of mentality which the future author of *The Red and the Black* would always hold in the profoundest contempt. Molière, therefore, who was the first to have shown young Beyle the dramatic possibilities that such seemingly unrewarding types can afford an author of real talent, was immediately equated with the adolescent's quixotic dream and ambition of embarking upon a successful career as an author of comedies that would make people laugh at the expense of the follies and stupidities of contemporary *bourgeois* types.[8] As Jean Prévost so sensitively demonstrates in his important book, Stendhal's burning desire to become the Molière of his century, although naïve and in many ways ill-conceived, contributed significantly to the writer's mastery of his craft.[9] Beyle had at first conveniently believed that, in order

[8] Cf. Jean Prévost, "Les Tentatives théâtrales en 1801" and "Le Théâtre manqué," in the excellent study *La Création chez Stendhal* (Paris, Mercure de France, 1951), 44–65. "Le seul métier possible," writes Prévost, summarizing Stendhal's youthful ambition and abortive career as a playwright, "est de faire des comédies comme Molière" (36).

[9] Cf. *supra*, note 8. Also, Paulette Trout, *La Vocation romanesque de Stendhal* (Paris, Editions universitaires, 1970), for an examination of Stendhal's unfulfilled calling as a dramatist and its positive impact on his subsequent choice of the novel as a form of literary expression.

to become a second Molière, he would merely have to unlock the basic devices and dulplicate them in a quasi-mechanical method of adaptation and transposition. Before too long, however, he became aware that this simplistic view of the problem did not take into account the complex, mysterious process by which artistic creation takes place.

Stendhal's love of the theater goes back to his Grenoble years. At the Ecole Centrale, which he attended from 1796 until 1799, he was a student of Dubois-Fontanelle, who taught French literature and the history of the literary genres, and who instilled in his pupils an appreciation not only of the Greek, Latin, and classical French authors, but also of Shakespeare and Goldoni. A native of Grenoble who had long lived in Paris and abroad, Dubois-Fontanelle had himself written plays and doubtless encouraged Henri Beyle's growing preoccupation with all aspects of dramaturgy. And it is, of course, a well-known fact that, upon his arrival in Paris late in 1799, Beyle failed to present himself for the entrance examinations at the prestigious Ecole Polytechnique, and instead aimlessly wandered through the streets, mingled with the crowds, gawked at the windows, and assiduously attended the theater, concentrating with equal intensity of interest on the play, the performance, and the reaction of the public. In order to correct his provincial Dauphinois accent, and in the hopes of meeting young actresses, he even enrolled in speech and acting classes. All this was perfectly consistent with his secret plan of achieving literary fame and worldly success by emulating Molière.

Young Stendhal paid lip service to the supreme accomplishment of French classicism, the tragedy, but was especially fascinated by comedy. Tragedy represented an esoteric distillation of human emotion, couched in noble form and in verse. The more Beyle focused on the difficult and elusive problem of laughter and comedy, the more he came to respect and admire Molière's style and technique. Through Molière young Beyle discovered the liberating role laughter and humor can play in helping the individualist and nonconformist in facing and overcoming the stupidities, prejudices, and absurdities of life. Molière differed from other authors of comedies in that he did not seek to be reassuringly cheerful or amusing. Comic genius transcends amusement.

This insight led to the next step in Stendhal's appreciation of Molière. Chamfort, French maximist and moralist of the eighteenth century, was the author, among other essays, of an *Eloge de Molière*, which Stendhal considered one of the best on comedy.[10] Through Chamfort's penetrating

---

[10] Cf. V. del Litto, *La Vie intellectuelle de Stendhal*, 449.

and corrosive comments on Molière in particular and on comedy in general, Stendhal came to the conclusion that the greatest purveyor of laughter of the French classical age died a victim of melancholy. This theory was especially attractive to one who, like young Beyle, readily admitted that melancholy was the outward manifestation of true genius and, with a touch of pride, described himself as perpetually obliged to fend off the paralyzing effects of depression and anxiety.[11]

As indicated above, Stendhal's comments on Molière are far from systematic. Yet it is worthwhile to list those plays that elicited his most detailed comments—which sometimes take the form of veritable line-by-line *explications de texte*—and to suggest what is at the heart of these *explications*.[12] The plays selected by Stendhal for special attention are *Le Misanthrope, Tartuffe, L'Avare, Les Fourberies de Scapin, George Dandin*, and *Les Femmes savantes*. Interestingly, *Dom Juan*, a play which by its combined themes of philosophical libertinism and seduction should have fascinated Stendhal, is not singled out for detailed analysis. The three plays belonging to what one might call "high comedy," *Le Misanthrope, Tartuffe* and *Les Femmes savantes*, which Beyle analyzed at some length around 1814, are especially revelatory of the future novelist's attitudes and obsessions.[13]

While recognizing that *Le Misanthrope* is overwhelmingly considered Molière's masterpiece, Beyle is curiously detached in his comments. At a performance of the play, in which Fleury and Mlle Mars were featured in the main parts, he noted that the public laughed and applauded politely, but it seemed to him that Molière had misplaced the focus of the main problem. Obviously influenced by Jean-Jacques Rousseau's famous *Lettre à d'Alembert sur les spectacles*, and its eloquent and harsh indictment of Molière as a defender of the "establishment" and of *Le Misanthrope* as a perfect example of Molière's willingness to compromise moral principles in order to please the public, Stendhal came to the conclusion that Molière had conveniently transformed Alceste's existential difficulties into the more trivial difficulties of a thwarted lover.[14]

There is no doubt that *Tartuffe* was Stendhal's favorite play. Despite

---

[11] Cf. his correspondence, and in particular his letters to his sister Pauline Beyle.

[12] Cf. Henri Cordier, *Molière jugé par Stendhal* (Paris, Chez tous les Libraires, 1898), for the complete text of these *explications*.

[13] *Ibid.*, v.

[14] For the impact of Rousseau on Stendhal, cf. Victor Brombert, "Stendhal, lecteur de Rousseau," *Revue des sciences humaines* (Oct.–Dec. 1958), 463–82. Also cf. Gita May, "Préromantisme rousseauiste et égotisme stendhalien," *L'Esprit créateur* (Summer 1966), 97–107.

minor criticisms, Stendhal was obviously immensely impressed both by the characterization and the technique, and was furthermore greatly intrigued by the main protagonist. Albert Thibaudet even went so far as to state that "la première *Défense de Tartuffe*, c'est le *Rouge et le Noir*."[15] To be sure, the theme of hypocrisy, and the way in which a superior being can exploit it to his own advantage in a society where hypocrisy is at the basis of all values, could not fail to have a powerful appeal for the son of Chérubin Beyle. There is doubtless a secret sympathy for the character of Tartuffe in young Beyle's comments on the play.

As for *Les Femmes savantes*, it permitted Beyle to take Molière to task for indulging in ridiculing serious-minded women and for treating in a flippant manner a theme worthy of more serious attention. Stendhal's sympathy for women and their difficult lot in society is clearly evidenced by his harsh remarks on Molière's play.[16]

Stendhal thoroughly enjoyed Molière's farces. Here no ideology intervened or hampered the spectator's merriment. *Les Fourberies de Scapin* and *Le Médecin malgré lui* enchanted and delighted Beyle. These plays proved to him that one could be at the same time a great comic genius, bordering on the tragic, and an author of lowly farces, a genre so thoroughly decried by Boileau.

Despite Beyle's proudly self-avowed *espagnolisme*, despite his repeated professions of admiration for the "sublime" poets and playwrights, such as Ariosto, Cervantes, Shakespeare, and Corneille, comedy continued to challenge and stimulate both his critical faculties and his creative powers. And in this connection, Molière played a key role. While he never benefited from a sense of docile reverence, he remained a steadfast guide and friend throughout Stendhal's turbulent and variegated career.

---

[15] Thibaudet, "Stendhal et Molière," 597.
[16] For a more detailed examination of this question, cf. Gita May, "Stendhal and Madame Roland," *The Romanic Review* (February 1962), 16–31.

STENDHAL AND BALZAC
AS ADMIRERS
AND FOLLOWERS OF MOLIÈRE

Henri Peyre

The posthumous fortune of the greatest of masterpieces has its ups and downs. The fame of Rembrandt, that of Dante or of Shakespeare meets with few dissenters and iconoclasts in the twentieth century. We hold libraries, museums, and other repositories of culture in too meek a reverence to even question their eminence. But historians have taught us that Rembrandt was long maligned, that Shakespeare idolatry was a relatively late occurrence in eighteenth-century Britain. In the same age, Voltaire found general assent to his famous quip about Dante who "will always be admired because no one ever reads him." Molière is no exception. Every schoolboy of the twentieth century has been told of Goethe's admiration for him, of Meredith hailing him as the embodiment of "the Comic Spirit," of Sainte-Beuve's earnest enumeration of all the benefits accruing to those who "savent aimer Molière." Nevertheless, for at least two hundred years after 1673, Molière was criticized as a poor stylist, as an unskilled bungler of plots with fake dénouements, as a vulgar bourgeois arguing for conventionality in marriage and for reasonableness in love. To him, even more fittingly than to Racine, could Boileau have addressed his epistle on the usefulness of enemies.

Strangely enough, the emergence of Molière as a universally admired figure in and outside France and the widespread conviction that audiences will always flock to performances of his plays date from the romantic era. Misled by labels and by the oversimplified formulas of textbooks, some of us used to believe that all the classical literature of France had been judged adversely by the poets, the novelists, and the bellicose critics of the Romantic era in their thundering manifestoes. In fact, only Boileau and Racine were so judged, and, in Racine's case, the hostility of Stendhal, Hugo, and Gautier was in truth directed at the would-be followers of Racinian tragedy who produced lifeless caricatures of his plays, rather than at Racine himself. But the champions of the new poetics did not attack Molière. The full history of Molière's fame has never been written, in France or in

133

other European countries. But what we know of it points to the lowest ebb
of Molière's popularity on the French stage to have occurred in the times
of Voltaire, then of the French Revolution. Marivaux in those years appeared more refined, Nivelle de la Chaussée more moving and more likely
to bring tears to the eyes of the tear-loving audiences, Beaumarchais more
relevant to a politically-minded era. The aristocrats found Molière a trifle
coarse, the middle classes thought him cool and too remote from its reforming yearnings.[1]

It is obviously a most uncertain undertaking to assess the degree of
popularity posthumously enjoyed by a playwright, and perhaps especially
by a comic author. For much is bound to depend upon the actors and
actresses who impersonate the parts of Lysistrata, Falstaff, or Célimène,
and upon a renovated "mise en scène." The number of performances
enjoyed by a certain play of Molière varies with the size of the theater, with
the actors starring in it, the publicity around it, and the public events in
the world at large. Shakespeare's *Coriolanus* unleashed a bloody riot in
Paris in February 1934; the performance of an opera by Auber, *La Muette
de Portici,* in Brussels in 1830 inspired the audience to stage a revolution
which won modern Belgium its independence. Every new wave of anti-
clericalism and of distrust of the Jesuit order has brought about a recur-
rence of popularity for *Tartuffe.* The Parisians who acclaim or those who
denigrate Molière constitute a restricted group, easily swayed by the
popularity of a theatrical star, by the reviews of a fashionable dramatic
critic who has set himself up as an arbiter of taste, or by a campaign of
moral rigorousness and of virtuous (or pharisaic) indignation engineered
by the régime then in power attempting to foster what the French politi-
cians once called "l'ordre moral." It thus appears that Napoleon the First,
having made his peace with the Church and restored much of the splendor
and not a little of the hypocrisy of the court of Louis XIV, felt markedly
cool to Molière. We know from a remark he made at St. Helena, recorded
in the *Mémorial* under the date of August 19, 1816, that, reading *Tartuffe*
over again while in exile, he was astonished by the boldness of the most
risky scene: "I do not hesitate to state that, if the play had been composed
under my reign, I would not have allowed it to be performed." Others

---

[1] Otis E. Fellows has explored part of the huge subject which the history of Molière's fame
constitutes in a thesis, *French Opinion of Molière (1800–50)* (Providence: Brown University,
1937). More recently, and for one play of Molière, Herman Prins Salomon has written a
detailed account of the play's vicissitudes over three hundred years: *Tartuffe devant l'opinion
française* (Paris: Presses Universitaires, 1962).

around him had evinced a similar dislike for the low taste and the crudeness of Molière's allusions to cuckoldry. The dramatic critic whose oracular pronouncements were all-powerful during the Empire, Julien Geoffroy, even branded Molière a bad Christian and "the outright foe of husbands, . . . the protector of lovers."

The political régime which followed Napoleon witnessed a curious change of attitude. Historical tragedy, which had enjoyed an immense vogue between 1800 and 1820, lost the favor of audiences. It was only revived when Hugo and Dumas, by freeing it from the shackles of the unities and mixing up the "genres," transformed it into romantic drama. Imitators of Racine and, to a much lesser degree, of Voltaire and of Corneille, blocked the way to a theatrical renaissance in which the new play, hailing from Shakespeare and Schiller, might be attempted. But comedy had long ago given up imitating Molière; and the author of the *Misanthrope* (a play criticized by Rousseau and redone, after a fashion, by the revolutionary poet who had rechristened the months of the new calendar, Fabre d'Eglantine) did not impede any efforts to innovate in the realm of comedy. Molière was assuming the stature of an untouchable national glory. The French sprang to his defence when August-Wilhelm Schlegel belittled him, while they proved lenient to the same critic's derogatory remarks upon Racine's *Phèdre*, judged by him far inferior to that by Euripides. One of Molière's great comedies in particular, *Tartuffe*, gained enormously in prestige when the restored French monarchy appeared to lean heavily on the clerical party and to marry the throne to the altar, denouncing Voltairianism. The reopening of the country's borders and of its educational institutions to the Jesuits in 1827 aroused the sarcastic gibes of many a writer, Stendhal, and later Michelet, among the most prominent.

The two great novelists of the first half of the nineteenth century, Stendhal and Balzac, were equally fascinated by Molière. It has oftentimes been asserted that the modern novel in France was the direct heir to the classical tragedy. That may occasionally be true for a few of the tragic novels of Balzac, and truer still for Flaubert when he stressed the value of concentrating the interest of a story, of linking the scenes and the episodes as tightly as Racine had done. But critics, always more tempted by the study of the tragic genres for which legislators of literature, from Aristotle to our contemporaries, have endeavored to formulate rules and to provide labels, have kept surprisingly shy of the more baffling comic genre. An irate and eloquent mouthpiece of Molière had already remarked upon that discrepancy in *La Critique de l'Ecole des Femmes*. Yet Stendhal and Balzac, and Flaubert himself, who proclaimed his admiration for Rabelais and Cervantes, then Proust and Sartre, have proved superb masters of comedy. But, on that essential aspect of their intentions and of their achievement relatively little has been written. The exploration of the comic element in satire, in poetry, in caricature, and in fiction appears to have daunted the audacity of most commentators. When they venture into that province of criticism, they prefer to show how tragic comedy, caricature, and laughter really are in *Le Misanthrope* (Musset's lines on the gloom behind the "mâle gaieté" of the play are fondly quoted), in Daumier, Rouault, Picasso's mournful clowns, or in the Proustian snobs whose pompous inanity is one day cruelly revealed to all onlookers.

Stendhal, born sixteen years before Balzac, also spent more years training himself for his avocation as a man of letters; Balzac realized soon enough, after his abortive attempts at a *Cromwell*, that the novel, under its multifarious avatars, was to be his empire. It took longer for Henri Beyle to reach the conclusion which he formulated thus: "Democracy having populated the theater with coarse people, incapable of understanding anything refined . . . . the novel is the comedy of the nineteenth century."[2] For several years, his reading of Molière was assiduous, critical, even severe at times, but more often inclined to admiration and envy. As early as 1809, he noted how tempting it would be to redo, in a contemporary setting, Molière's "colorful" farce on the *précieuses*. In 1813, the officer of Napoleon's Grand Army, back from the Russian retreat and expecting the invasion of the French soil, had bought a new edition of Molière on which he jotted down his comments on *Les Femmes savantes*, *Scapin*, *George Dandin*, *Tartuffe*, *Le Misanthrope*. His praise for Molière's verve, for his bold frankness in depicting Elmire's expert seduction of the sanctimonious and eloquent hypocrite, and in lending strong words to the outspoken maid Dorine is unstinted. Now and then, he blamed Molière for failing to provoke enough laughter in the audience. Puzzled by *Tartuffe*, he would, like La Bruyère once and like Balzac later, have wished to rewrite it, or to give a sequel to it. Orgon, for example, might have been presented as in love with his wife, to whom he would have confided unreservedly. But Stendhal failed to add that Orgon, in that case, would

---

[2] The sentence is a manuscript remark scribbed by Stendhal on a copy of *Le Rouge et le noir* in the Bucci library of Cività Vecchia. It was first called to the attention of the Beylists by Paul Arbelet in an article in the *Revue de Paris*, xxiv, 2 (nov. 15, 1917), 412. Henri Martineau quotes it in his introduction to Stendhal's notes on Molière and laughter: *Molière, Shakespeare, la comédie et le rire* (Paris: Le Divan, 1930), xviii.

hardly have been the stubbornly foolish man that he was, selfishly ready to sacrifice wife and daughter to the salvation of his soul. Likewise, Stendhal wished that we had witnessed Tartuffe actually plying his seducer's trade by slowly and gradually ensnaring Orgon. He did not fully realize that comedy, not altogether unlike the old farce from which much of Molière's comedy derived, had to present laughable characters full grown, ready made, and thus stiffly inflexible. If the audience were made to watch Arnolphe repeatedly jilted by women whom he would have loved, suffering from it, or Orgon trembling with fear least his soul would not be saved, or Argan gradually turning into an anxious hypochondriac and unable to face the prospect of decay and death, it could no longer laugh at them. It would be too easy for any of us to identify with those creatures and to judge them worthy of pity rather than ludicrous.

Try hard as he might, Stendhal had to concede that he lacked the sense for dramatic conflict, the clash of replicas which makes for vividness in comedy, the strong underlining of the salient features of the characters confronting each other on the stage: all necessary ingredients of a comic optics. He was too sentimental, too passionate, too much of a dreamer and of a poet to succeed in comedy. He remarked much later, in an oft-quoted sentence that, even in his fiction, he "always laid his nets much too high. Nothing low was ever caught in it." Even in his youthful notes scribbled in the margins of his copy of *L'Avare* and of *Les Femmes savantes*, he wrote that "the comic glides on Harpagon" ("le comique glisse sur lui") and, more generally, that the comic glides on, and eludes, a passionate man. "Such a man is too concerned with his quest for happiness to think of comparing himself with the ridiculous character." He dissected with great eagerness in his notes, as published by Henri Martineau, the physical, psychological, and social conditions and manifestations of laughter. But he acknowledged that he himself was closer to Alfieri and to Rousseau, who had not succeeded in producing comic effects. Perhaps he entertained too lenient an opinion of human nature. In the last but one of his fragments on laughter, he remarked: "Molière had the art of degrading ["d'avilir"] the characters at the expense of those at whom he wanted us to laugh." There may have remained throughout his life too much timid shyness in Stendhal for him to follow in the footsteps of Molière. Baudelaire, who often echoed Stendhal or happened to agree with him, submitted, in his pregnant 1855 essay on "The Essence of Laughter," that laughter often springs from the notion of one's superiority and may well have a diabolical origin. Stendhal's world, like that of Giraudoux which Sartre called "Aristotelian," is strangely free from the obsession of an indelible and original sin.[3]

Balzac had not only Dante in mind when he gave the ambitious title of "The Human Comedy" to his immense fictional enterprise. He had long envied Molière's comic genius, his comprehensive portrayal of society and his attitude as a moralist. In an early version of his novel *Les Comédiens sans le savoir* (an almost untranslatable title), which was then called "The Provincial in Paris" (1847), Balzac suggested, or dictated to a friend, Gabriel Roux, who prefaced the story with a six-page introduction, hyperbolic eulogies of his talent. That unashamed piece of self-praise ended thus:

> Among the rolls of literary talents of the different centuries who gave to the world names by which it feels most honored, we see only one name beside which we would rank M. de Balzac. And that name is that of Molière.
> Who indeed is Molière, if not the poet who depicted the eighteenth century society most truthfully? Who is M. de Balzac, if not the moralist, the philosopher who best understood and best portrayed the nineteenth century? If M. de Balzac had lived under Louis XIV, he would have composed *Les Femmes savantes*, *Tartuffe*, *Georges Dandin*, *Le Misanthrope*: If Molière were alive today, he would write *La Comédie humaine*. For which contemporary author could a similar claim be put forward? . . .[4]

Balzac's education, like that of most of his contemporaries, had stressed the Latin authors and the seventeenth century French classics. Unlike some of his age group who, fighting the battle for Romanticism, "pulled the old beards" of the masters whom their teachers had imposed upon them, Balzac never wavered in his admiration for Racine, La Fontaine, and Molière. At twenty, in 1819, he formulated his dearest wish: "To have Rousseau's Julie as a mistress, La Fontaine and Molière as friends." He railed at the Romantic poets with their inflated egos, their sonorously plaintive sighs, their pretense of scorning the body and of concentrating all their desire into their souls. He was not one to waste his pity on Chatterton's suicide, on George Sand's unsatisfied and love-hungry heroines, not even on Hugo's outlaws comparing themselves to an irresistible force rushing headlong into abysses. Both in *Les Illusions perdues* and in *Modeste Mignon* he mocked those dreamy scorners of flat reality, represented by the

---

[3] In one of the peremptory notes collected in "Mon Coeur mis à nu" under the heading Molière, Baudelaire treated the play *Tartuffe* with haughty severity as being a libelous attack rather than a comedy. Even a well-bred atheist, he asserted, would agree that "certain grave questions should not be left to the rabble."

[4] H. de Balzac, *Oeuvres* (Pléiade edition), xi, 427–28.

would-be Romantic poet Canalis, and contrasted those gloomy Romantics with the more straightforward and natural characters of Molière. In 1825, partly out of admiration for the two seventeenth-century authors to whom he felt closest, partly out of a desire to get rich quickly, Balzac undertook, with friends of his and with the publisher Urbain Canel, to launch an edition of the works of La Fontaine and of Molière. He prefaced the Molière volume with four pages of biography of the comic genius. The enterprise proved a dismal failure, as Balzac's sister had warned in a letter of April 4, 1825, reminding him of his lack of experience in business matters. The publisher became bankrupt; Balzac incurred a huge debt, turned himself into a printer to cut the expenses of bringing out his future works, lost even more money thereby. The debt incurred in that ill fated Molière venture weighed upon him for the rest of his life.

He read and reread Molière. Several hundred allusions to his life or, more often, to characters from his plays are found in his novels. Balzac's fondest dream, however, was to rival Molière as a playwright. He made several attempts, partly out of a desire to recoup his fortunes and to score a popular and a financial triumph as his friend Alexandre Dumas had repeatedly done. But he aimed higher than Dumas and, less confident in his own versatility, more anxious to impose a structure and limits to his writings, he repeatedly confided his despair to his female correspondents. To his sister, in 1834, he sadly announced that his theatrical essays were not going well. "In the realm of comedy, Molière, whom I want to follow, is a master who fills one with despair." Three years later, he told Madame Hanska how clearly he realized "what boundless judgment the comic poet needs. Each word must be a sentence rendered upon the manners of his age." The comic writer has to have a comprehensive view of society and judge men and institutions in a way which should arouse smiles or provoke laughter. Balzac failed to add that the author of a comedy cannot freely mold his form as he progresses, fly off into digressions, insert episodes from earlier works of his, multiply additions on his proofs.

Balzac composed several plays, which have been studied in at least one monograph[5] and two of which, *La Marâtre* (1848) and *Mercadet*, also entitled *Le Faiseur* (completed in 1844), have met with some success on the stage, and with a marked "succès d'estime" with a few critics. The protagonist of *Mercadet*, a play which recalls Lesage's comedy on a financier, *Turcaret*, is drawn with a power and a human depth not unworthy of

---

[5] Douchan Milatchitch, *Le Théâtre de H. de Balzac* (Paris: Hachette, 1930).

Molière. Yet Balzac's medium was not the drama, not any more than it was Flaubert's or even Zola's. The impact of Molière on his imagination proved stronger on his writing of fiction. There, less hampered by the temptation of rivalling the dialogs and the comic effects of his great predecessor, he could follow his own bent and perhaps achieve for his own age the vast portrayal of social mores which Molière had accomplished during the reign of Louis XIV.[6]

Two of Molière's characters, or types, haunted Balzac's dreams: the miser and the hypocrite. Many a schoolboy has had to exercise his wits on one of the stock parallels proposed in France by teachers: the miser in Plautus and in Molière, Ben Jonson's Volpone and Harpagon, Grandet and Harpagon. The differences between the comedy, laid in a very abstract or undefined historical and social setting, with little or no evolution in the miser's character, with scant appeal to sentiment and no agonizing threat of a fatal end, and Balzac's novel are obvious. Balzac was fond of repeating that heroes must be generalities, that is to say, types aiming at some degree of universality, and not just individuals. Molière's example incited him to endow his characters with generality. But Harpagon, through his very name suggesting in Greek the gesture of grabbing with avid hands, through the vagueness of the atmosphere conjured up around him, through the omission of all that might have enlightened the onlooker on his past, his development, the sources of his fortune, tends to be a type. At all costs, his creator had avoided stirring up sympathy for him. Miserliness is probably the most widespread of all passions, since it is but one form of our obdurate lust for possession. From early childhood on, it is the most potent means of developing our ego. Ambition, love, jealousy, the collector's greed are but some of the varied shapes which avarice may assume. Molière, through eschewing too precise a characterization of his miser in time, place, social group, prevented the many miserly, or hyperpossessive, members of his audience from feeling that they were the butt of his sarcasm.

Not so Balzac in a work of fiction which allowed of elaborate descriptions, of historical information on the revolutionary era in provincial France and on the sources of Grandet's wealth, of rich details on his wife and his daughter, his maid, his relatives, his envious friends and curious

---

[6] On Balzac's view of Molière, there are many valuable indications in a volume by P. Barrière, *Balzac et la tradition littéraire classique* (Paris: Hachette, 1928), and in a later one by Geneviève Delattre, *Les Opinions littéraires de Balzac* (Paris: Presses Universitaires, 1961).

visitors. Grandet's monomania (or that of Gobseck in one of the most arresting stories of Balzac) is truer to life, probably more human, but also more horrifying than Harpagon's. He is a more sharply delineated individual, and yet a typical representative of a certain type of nineteenth-century peasant who has accumulated the properties of a rich bourgeois, yet has remained stubbornly unwilling to shed his monomaniac's lust for gold and is incapable of any generosity and compassion. Where Molière occasionally skirted the tragic (Harpagon cursing his son) and strained every nerve to remain on the plane of the comic, Balzac, from the outset, contrived to curb laughter at the miser's tyranny over his household and to fill the reader with suspense at the inevitable impending tragedy.[7]

On January 1, 1844, in one of those boastful avowals which he occasionally made to Madame Hanska, Balzac wrote: "Molière had done avariciousness in Harpagon: I made a miser with old Grandet. Well, in *Un grand Artiste* (which was to constitute the first part of *Modeste Mignon*), I am again wrestling with him, on the theme of Tartuffe. He displayed the hypocrite in one situation only: the triumph Orgon [sic] in the bourgeoisie. But I want to portray the Tartuffe of our time, a Tartuffe who is a democrat, a philanthropist. . . . "[8]

Balzac pondered over Tartuffe long and repeatedly, and was literally obsessed by the urge to transpose the picture of hypocrisy onto a modern setting and into the framework of the novel. The limitations of the stage, the need to ward off the spectators from mistaking the hypocrite for a truly devout man and therefore to delay for two full acts his appearance on the stage, the necessity of providing a dénouement which had to be an artificial one might, in Balzac's eyes, have hampered Molière's genius. Repeatedly, the novelist who yearned to be Molière's successor and rival remarked on the advantages which the novel enjoys over a comedy. One of his mouth-pieces, in *Les Illusions perdues* (Pléiade, IV, 791), noted that "fiction has become the most immense and the most pliable of literary creations. It has set itself up as the successor to comedy which, in the modern mores, is no longer possible with its old laws." In another passage, a dedication of *Les petits Bourgeois* (Pléiade, VII, 68); he felt emboldened to hint: "A few remnants of clay, dropped by Molière at the foot of his colossal statue of

---

[7] Maurice Bardèche, in his *Balzac romancier* (Paris: Plon, 1940), Chapter x, ascribes much significance to Molière's influence on Balzac's *Eugénie Grandet* and *Père Goriot*. He writes: "Balzac's borrowing from Molière lies mostly in the broadening of the drama. . . . The memories of the classics were for Balzac a supplement, a stimulant to the inner work which was taking place inside him" (pp. 304, 306).

[8] Balzac, *Lettres à Madame Hanska* (Paris: Editions du Delta, 1968), ii, 328.

Tartuffe, have been handled here by a hand more audacious than it is skillful." In point of fact, however, Balzac never quite succeeded, or even attempted, a full delineation of a hypocrite. The hypocrite of whom he dreamt would not have been a religious one, but rather a political figure, one of the reformers (Saint-Simonian, such as he mocked in *L'Illustre Gaudissart*, or Fourierist) or one of the deputies concerned solely with their own ambitions such as the one who shamelessly utilizes Z. Marcas. Balzac somehow never drew that complete picture; *les petits Bourgeois*, where he announced his intention to compete with Tartuffe, remained unfinished. A potentially more fruitful notion that he entertained was to provide a feminine counterpart to Molière's hypocrite. In some ways, Madame Marneffe in *La Cousine Bette*, and the cousin herself, or Flore "la rabouilleuse," before she is crushed by Philippe Bridau, had some lineaments of a female Tartuffe. But the full portrayal was never achieved.

Like Stendhal, and like many a modern reader of *Tartuffe*, Balzac was puzzled by the character of Orgon. For it is too easy to dismiss Tartuffe's victim as a mere fool. It is even more facile, and altogether gratuitous, to hint that Orgon entertains for his devout guest an unavowed homosexual inclination. Credulous, gullible, unperceptive, Orgon naturally is. But he admires and loves in Tartuffe someone who fascinates him through his superior intellect, his warmth, his piety, and through the magnetism of his will power. We may surmise that his wife entertains nothing but discreet scorn for pitiful Orgon. He feels humiliated in his own home. If he is constrained to admire Elmire's cool strategy in the seduction scene, when she made him hide under a table, he cannot but have pondered, soon after, over her cool expertness. Every reader and spectator of the play wonders, once the artificial dénouement has temporarily settled some of the imbroglio, what a figure will Orgon cut in the presence of his wife and with what cool contemptuous gaze she will look upon such a mediocre husband. Balzac's dream, several times voiced in his remarks, was to compose a sequel to *Tartuffe*. He confided his vague project to Madame Hanska, and his vain hope to persuade his friends Théophile Gautier and Charles de Bernard to collaborate with him on a play in which Orgon would mourn Tartuffe's departure and would subsequently recall him and treat him as a vindicated hero. In his uncompleted novel, *Les Paysans*, near the end of his life, Balzac turned to the same theme: "Molière died too soon. He would have showed the despair of Orgon, bored by his family, harried by his children, regretting Tartuffe's flatteries and saying: 'Those were the good days' " (Pléiade, VIII, 94). The notion is indeed a tantalizing one. But would it have provided enough substance and enough dramatic possibilities for a play? For a dramatic monolog à la Browning, perhaps.

The laudatory allusions to *Le Misanthrope* are even more numerous in Balzac's novels. He praised the delineation of Alceste in *Le Père Goriot* (Pléiade, II, 914) and elsewhere, and he had evidently been moved by the pathetic betrayal of his will to be logical to which the character was led. His resigned consent to lie to himself and to believe that Célimène was true and faithful, in the face of blinding evidence to the contrary, seems to have impressed the novelist who, in depicting the slavery to his senses and the will to be duped with gross lies in Baron Hulot, developed a remotely similar character into a monomaniac in whom all sense of honor had died. Zola will travel even further along the same road in *Nana*. Balzac, however, while fully aware that novels must portray passions and that, as he wrote to a friend Hippolyte Castille, "great works survive through their passionate sides," remained a social moralist fearful of those very same passions as antisocial, as evil, because excessive. Molière's characters, Alceste like Harpagon, Orgon like Argan and M. Jourdain, are never cured of their delusions. The curtain falls and, the next day, they will relapse into their same faults of blindness and selfishness. The nineteenth-century novelist, on the other hand, appears to have entertained the notion that he could amend, and perhaps cure, people better than the seventeenth-century dramatist who paid lip service to the famous "castigat ridendo mores" had ever hoped to do.

Two other features in *Le Misanthrope* aroused his admiration: the creation of Célimène and the opposition between Philinte and Alceste. Balzac had Célimène in mind, her intelligence, her resourceful skill in keeping a number of admirers around her without becoming too attached to any, her naturalness even in her poses, when he created Diane de Maufrigneuse ("Les Secrets de la Princesse de Cadignan"). In *Le Cabinet des antiques* (Pléiade, IV, 404), he went out of his way to remark that "one of Molière's claims to glory is to have admirably depicted, from one side only, those feminine natures, in the greatest of the figures whom he carved in marble: Célimène." Philinte, used as a foil to Alceste or a spur to arouse the amorous misanthrope to the avowal of his contradictions, was hailed by Balzac as more than a dramatic device, rather as evidence of a profound philosophical mind. Several times, in particular in *Les Illusions perdues* (Pléiade, IV, 650, 652), Balzac referred to that gift for presenting the two sides: "of

envisaging everything on the right side and on the obverse, with the *pro*
and the *con*, like Rabelais, and of laughing at it all skeptically." Such an
ability to create an Alceste who says "yes" and a Philinte who says "no"
struck him as the sign of Molière's tolerant universality. True great men,
Balzac again submitted in *Modeste Mignon* (Pléiade, IV, 538), comprehend
all contradictions in themselves. They paint a Madonna and a courtesan
equally well. "Molière is right in his characters of older men and he is
equally right in those of younger ones."

Therein lay the most pregnant message which Balzac read in Molière.
From him and from Rabelais, he learned that the comic vision is not only
broader, more embracing and more compassionate than the tragic one, but
also truer to human nature and to reality. In *Les Illusions perdues*, the
long novel in which the characters most persistently debate on literary
creation, Balzac had one of them, Blondet, state the lesson which the novelist had found in Molière: "Everything is bilateral in the domain of thought.
Ideas are binary. Janus is the myth of criticism and the symbol of genius"
(Pléiade, IV, 789). Virtue itself is twofold, he remarked elsewhere. A por-
trayer of passion, of corruption, of greed, and of other soul-corroding
monomanias, a Swedenborgian mystic at times, and a believer in the
boundless power lurking in the will, Balzac could also curb his inclination
to fly away from reality or his craving for the exploration of dark and
sordid abysses. Molière reminded him of the value of simplicity in art and
of the need to strive for the universal beyond the particular.[9] Molière is
the one French author to whom he liberally granted the title of "genius."
That classical comic genius helped Balzac aim higher, encompass more
sides of human nature, and realize the full breadth of what he might
achieve in another social environment and with a different medium.

[9] In *La Maison Nucingen*, Balzac slipped another allusion to his favorite among Molière's
comedies: Bixiou is his mouthpiece. "The sublime comedy of *Le Misanthrope* proves that art
consists in erecting a palace on the point of a needle" (Pléiade, v, 625).

IONESCO AND MOLIÈRE
Sidney L. Pellissier

> J'essaie de retrouver la tradition qui n'est pas aca-
> démisme. C'est même son contraire.
> *Notes et contre-notes*

> IONESCO: J'ai aussi un peu étudié Molière.
> *L'Impromptu de l'Alma*

During the early 1950's when Eugène Ionesco was still considered to be a controversial playwright, he was perturbed by much of the criticism being written about his plays. To his consternation, he found upon reading his critics that he was being unfairly judged by men whose views he felt were either contradictory, inconsistent, or largely beside the point. Following Molière's tactics in the *guerre comique*, Ionesco mounted a counterattack on his critics in the form of a one-act comedy entitled *L'Impromptu de l'Alma*. First performed at the Studio des Champs-Elysées in 1956, the play was in part a montage of critiques of Ionesco's plays which had been published in *Le Figaro* and in journals such as *Théâtre Populaire* and *Bref*. The object was to show how ridiculous or unfounded Ionesco felt some of these opinions were. The play also presented his own views about theater and dramatic criticism, just as Molière had done in *La Critique de l'Ecole des femmes* and *L'Impromptu de Versailles*.

Although Ionesco's play is tonally quite different than either of Molière's polemical pieces, both in intent and ideology Ionesco closely parallels Molière. In an interview with Claude Bonnefoy, Ionesco explained that he had purposely set out to imitate Molière in this instance: "*L'Impromptu de l'Alma* est une pièce dans laquelle j'essaie d'imiter Molière, c'est aussi une critique de quelques critiques. Je reproche aux critiques leur dogmatisme, leur incompréhension de l'art, leur refus de comprendre le théâtre. Les critiques que je mets en scène dans cette pièce sont des critiques militants."[1] Generally Ionesco makes no attempt to imitate Molière; *L'Im-*

---

[1] Claude Bonnefoy, *Entretiens avec Eugène Ionesco* (Paris: Editions Pierre Belfond, 1966), 162.

promptu de l'Alma is clearly an exceptional case. However, Ionesco is a self-declared continuator of the classical tradition,[2] and he is a highly successful writer of comedy in the French idiom. As such, I feel that he may justifiably be compared with Molière.

My purpose here will be to elucidate some of the more salient parallels which can be established between the theater of Ionesco and of Molière, without trying to establish that Ionesco has been measurably influenced by Molière or suggesting, as did one critic, that Ionesco has a Molière complex[3]—that he wants to be the Molière of the twentieth century. Instead, I will demonstrate that Ionesco views his craft in much the same manner as did Molière and that some of his stylistic devices are *moliéresque*. Not only does Ionesco employ the same comic techniques which abound in Molière's theater, but the vision of the world which he projects onto the stage, like Molière's, is pervasively comic: virtually everything he seeks to represent in his plays, be it ludicrous, sinister, or pathetic, is cast in comic tones. Briefly then, I will demonstrate that Ionesco belongs to the great French comic tradition of which Molière is the most illustrious practitioner and an ever fertile source.

In order to create a climate favorable to the comparison of Ionesco and Molière, whose plays may appear to be more disparate than comparable, I must first examine these playwrights' concepts of dramaturgy. To do so I will have to attribute to them lines uttered by certain of their characters, remaining mindful of Henry Carrington Lancaster's admonition that "to pick out a line regardless of the context and argue from it about a dramatist's general ideas is a method worthy of the Compagnie de Saint-Sacrement."[4] Indeed, when dealing with comedy, it is exceedingly risky to try to find the author in his work. Molière has been the object of much criticism of now questionable value generated by critics who were intent upon seeing the *raisonneurs* as his *porte-parole*. Will G. Moore has demonstrated that such attribution favors the adoption of the blatantly contradictory views that Molière is both a comic genius and a mediocre man whose guiding principle is moderation in all things.[5] It is interesting to note that Ionesco, too, has had the misfortune of being mistakenly identified with

[2] See "Finalement je suis pour le classicisme," in Eugène Ionesco's *Notes et contre-notes* (Paris: Gallimard, 1962), 107–112.

[3] Philippe Bonzon, "Molière, ou Le Complexe de Ionesco," *Perspectives du Théâtre*, II (February, 1960), 7.

[4] Henry Carrington Lancaster, *A History of French Dramatic Literature in the Seventeenth Century, Part V* (Baltimore: The Johns Hopkins Press, 1942), 116.

[5] Will G. Moore, *Molière, A New Criticism* (Oxford: The Clarendon Press, 1949), 5.

some of his characters. Asked in an interview what he had meant by the remark that reality, not dreams, was capable of disintegrating into nightmares, he responded, "Je n'ai pas dit, moi, que la réalité contrairement au rêve tournait au cauchemar: c'est un de mes personnages qui a prononcé cette phrase."[6]

One must, therefore, exercise caution in interpreting the comedies of Molière and Ionesco. However, when these playwrights engage in polemics and come to the defense of their art in the face of negative criticism, when they cease to create disinterested art and use the stage primarily to debate issues rather than to entertain audiences, when they give characters their own names,[7] certainly then are we justified in attributing lines of dialog directly to the men who wrote them. Upon comparing the views expressed by the character named Ionesco in *L'Impromptu de l'Alma* with those expressed by the character named Molière in *L'Impromptu de Versailles* and by Dorante in *La Critique de l'Ecole des femmes*, of whom it is said in the play that he is Molière's loyal defender,[8] we readily see that Ionesco and Molière entertain distinctly similar notions about dramaturgy and dramatic criticism.

It may be helpful at this point to briefly describe the action of *L'Impromptu de l'Alma* since it is not as widely known as other Ionescan plays. When the curtain rises, Ionesco is discovered late at night at his work table, soon to be aroused from a deep sleep by the arrival of Bartholoméus I,[9] a learned critic who has come to inquire about our author's latest play, which is still being composed. He learns that the title of the new play is to be *Le Caméléon du berger*, that Ionesco has trouble talking about his plays, and that he considers himself to be an Aristotelian dramatist because his theater is fundamentally representational. When Bartholoméus II comes to call, the play begins again, Ionesco and he exchanging the same dialog spoken in the first scene. The play commences a third time when Bartholoméus III arrives. Finally, out of exasperation Ionesco refuses to answer

---

[6] Ionesco, *Notes et Contre-notes*, 91.

[7] Like Molière in *L'Impromptu de Versailles*, Ionesco puts himself on stage in *L'Impromptu de l'Alma*. Unlike Molière, he did not create the role in the staged version of the play.

[8] In scene 6, Lysidias says to Dorante, "Molière est bien heureux d'avoir un protecteur aussi chaud que vous."

[9] The name Bartholoméus is a thinly veiled allusion to the noted drama critic, Roland Barthes, whose theories about didactic theater and costumology seem especially simplistic to Ionesco. The other two Bartholoméuses are meant to represent the critics Dort and Jean-Jacques Gautier, whose acidic reviews have been described by Ionesco in *Notes et contre-notes* as unfounded verbal ferocity.

the door any more; then the three critics, dressed in academic robes, proceed to educate Ionesco about the theater. Gradually, their lessons disintegrate into a paroxysm of absurdity; they hang signs reading "savant" and "poète" around Ionesco's neck, don dunce caps (*bonnets d'âne*) and literally begin to bray like asses. Marie, Ionesco's maid, scolds him for listening to such nonsense and chases the three Bartholoméuses from the stage with a broom. At this point in the play, Ionesco calls the actors back on stage and begins to address them and the audience directly as did Molière at the end of *L'Impromptu de Versailles*. He explains his ideas about dramatic criticism as well as the nature of theater and the rules governing dramatic creation.

L'Impromptu de l'Alma, La Critique de l'Ecole des femmes and *L'Impromptu de Versailles,* by dint of their frankly argumentative nature, fall more within the realm of dialectic than of pure comedy. That is, in each case the playwright seems to have been less concerned with esthetics than with debate. There are hints in the plays which suggest that even their authors did not consider them wholly satisfying to create. Molière states in the fifth scene of *L'Impromptu de Versailles* that he cares to write no more plays such as this one, that he will contribute nothing more to that "sotte guerre" with his rivals. Ionesco also takes a dim view of the esthetic value of his own play, the closing lines of which clearly state that it is an exception and not the rule for him to write thus. Elsewhere he says that the piece is so pointed in its attack that he considers it merely a "mauvaise plaisanterie."[10] Even though these plays may not be as artistically pleasing as many other pieces in each author's repertory, they do afford us a wealth of insight into their creators' esthetic sense. Ionesco and Moliére do much more than counterattack their critics in these polemic plays: they also give us a lesson in the art of theater appreciation, a lesson which is at once elemental in its directness and profound in its implications.

In order to judge a play validly we are told to be receptive to the theatrical mood it evokes and to react to that mood with honesty and immediacy. Molière is explicit on this point; his Dorante says "Laissons-nous aller de bonne foi aux choses qui nous prennent par les entrailles."[11] His state-

[10] He has also written that "Quand j'écris une pièce, je n'ai aucune idée de ce qu'elle va être. J'ai des idées *après*. Au départ, il n'y a qu'un état affectif. *L'Impromptu de l'Alma* est une exception." Ionesco, *Notes et contre-notes*, 109.

[11] *La Critique de l'Ecole des femmes*, scene 6. Direct quotations of Molière's plays will be identified by scene number, or act and scene number where appropriate, and taken from the *Oeuvres complètes de Molière,* edited by Robert Jouanny (Paris: Editions Garnier Frères, 1962).

ment is not as nuanced as Ionesco's request that we strive to enter into "la propre mythologie de l'oeuvre"[12] in order to judge it well. But it implies exactly the same thing—that good theater seeks to evoke reaction and that criticism should grow out of our reaction, not precede it or preclude it.

By ridiculing the criticisms proffered by rival authors, prudes, fops, and *précieux*, Molière demonstrates that their opinions are beside the point, or misdirected, and consequently of little significance. Ionesco does likewise by mocking the academic double-talk of some of his critics. In the space of one short sequence he has the three Bartholoméuses argue: ". . . la théâtralité c'est ce qui est anti-théâtral . . ."; "Peut-être un certain théâtral est-il théâtral . . ."; "Le théâtral est dans l'antithéâtral"; "Phénoméniquement, toute théâtralité est non théâtral."[13]

It is evident that Ionesco, like Molière, is primarily concerned with the entertainment afforded by the plays he writes and is impatient with critics who bypass that factor in order to address themselves to purely theoretical considerations. He tells us in *L'Impromptu de l'Alma* that criticism should be descriptive, not normative; that the critic should not judge a play solely in the light of preconceived notions (what Molière refers to as "*prévention aveugle*" in *La Critique de l'Ecole des femmes*) but by "pénétrant dans son univers."[14] Molière with characteristic simplicity had this to say to his critics about the art of evaluating a play: " . . . la bonne façon d'en juger . . . est de se laisser prendre aux choses. . . ".[15] All other concerns of the critic are relegated to a position of negligible import and are ridiculed by both playwrights. Molière mocks Lysidias' predilection for pedantic terminology such as protasis, epitasis, and peripeteia, and Ionesco goes so far as to place dunce caps on the heads of three learned advocates of "costumologie, théâtrologie, spectato-psychologie, spectatologie."

Ionesco explains in *L'Impromptu de l'Alma* that he was inspired to write a play called *Le Caméléon du berger* because he once saw a shepherd embrace a chameleon in the street of a quiet village. This seems like pure nonsense until he elaborates that the shepherd represents a playwright (Ionesco) and the chameleon represents his career, a career which changes like the colors of a chameleon to mirror the changes in life—"car le théâtre c'est la vie. Il est changeant comme la vie. . . ."[16] Later in the play, Ionesco

---

[12] Eugène Ionesco, *Théâtre II* (Paris: Gallimard, 1958), 57.
[13] *Ibid.*, 26.
[14] *Ibid.*, 57.
[15] *La Critique de l'Ecole des femmes*, scene 5.
[16] Ionesco, *Théâtre II*, 15.

abandons figurative explanations to define a play simply as the representation of an action which takes place in a given time and place, implying
that his theater, despite appellations such as absurd, vanguard, or anti-
theatrical, is not substantially different than the theater advocated by Aristotle. Once again we see that Ionesco shares an opinion with Molière, who
feels that the playwright's task is "peindre d'après nature"[17] and that
"l'affaire de la comédie est de représenter en général tous les défauts des
hommes . . . de notre siècle."[18] For both of these playwrights, then, theater is essentially representational or mimetic art.

Ionesco and Molière express faith in the rules of dramaturgy and acknowledge their validity. However, it may be inferred from statements
made in the three polemic plays that these playwrights feel that rules must
not determine dramatic creation, but be determined by it. At the end of
his play Ionesco reproaches modern critics not for having discovered a
body of truths (rules) about the theater, but for having couched them in
pedantic verbiage. He states further that such truths become dangerous
"lorsqu'elles prennent l'allure de dogmes infaillibles et lorsque, en leur
nom, les docteurs et critiques prétendent exclure d'autres vérités et diriger,
voire tyranniser, la création artistique."[19] We are reminded of Dorante's
statement that there is nothing awesome about the rules, which are merely
"quelques observations aisées, que le bon sens a faites,"[20] and of Molière's
reservations about slavishly following the rules: "Car enfin, si les pièces qui
sont selon les règles ne plaisent pas et que celles qui plaisent ne soient selon
les règles, il faudrait de nécessité que les règles eussent été mal faites."[21]

When we proceed from the theory of theater and dramatic criticism expressed by Ionesco and Molière in their polemic plays to their actual practice of theater as a mimetic and comic art form, when we consider their
repertory as a whole, then are we immediately struck by the variety and
intensity of comic effects almost omnipresent in their work. It becomes
apparent why two dramatists concerned with representing life on stage
insist that their plays be entertaining or pleasing. This concern, of course,
is consonant with the playwrights' highly developed comic vision of the
world. Molière's often quoted opinion that "La grande règle de toutes les
règles est de plaire" takes on a wealth of new connotations if we stop to

---

[17] *La Critique de l'Ecole des femmes*, scene 6.
[18] *L'Impromptu de Versailles*, scene 4.
[19] Ionesco, *Théâtre I*, 57.
[20] *La Critique de l'Ecole des femmes*, scene 6.
[21] *Ibid.*

consider that entertainment, mimesis, and comic vision are all integral parts of his art. Ionesco has said that humor is the one effective means man has of conquering dread, the one safety valve, so to speak, which makes the human condition bearable.[22] So in his theater Ionesco, like Molière, varies the tone of his comedy from the most madcap slapstick in works such as *Scène à quatre* and *Délire à deux*, to the most subtle irony in plays like *Rhinocéros* and *Le Roi se meurt*. Whatever the tone or quality of the comedy, it is a constant in his theatrical creations.

Having established that Ionesco views his art in much the same manner as does Molière, we may now briefly consider some of the moliéresque techniques which he employs. Some striking similarities are to be noted in the manner in which Ionesco and Molière present disguised and deluded characters, characters who are involved with the essence of theatrically because they assume roles which mask their true identity. First, I must clarify my understanding of the terms delusion and disguise. Deluded characters pose no substantial threat to others because they are unaware of their delusion as such and are easily controlled by flattery. Thus, I accept the term delusion here in its broadest and most usual sense. My usage of the term disguise, however, is more specialized and restricted. Rather than treat all levels of disguise—one of which would be simple dissimulation effected by a change of voice or of costume—I shall confine discussion to the type of disguise which is willfully, consciously assumed with evil or selfish intent. Disguised characters, then, are potentially dark or sinister personages, yet both Ionesco and Molière present them as comic figures. A single example of Ionesco's treatment of a deluded character and a disguised one will be sufficient to demonstrate that he manipulates them in a moliéresque manner.

Les Chaises is a one-act comedy with a cast of three visible characters and a host of invisible ones. A very old couple living in a deserted tower-like structure, which is probably a lighthouse, receive the visit of a large number of invisible guests who have been invited there to hear an important message. Despite his self-declared potential for leadership, the old man has had a disappointing career as concierge of a deserted tower. He has been sustained, however, by a goal which has given his life meaning: he has "quelque chose dans le ventre, un message à communiquer à l'hu-

[22] Ionesco, "La Démystification par l'humour noir," *L'Avant-scène*, (February 15, 1959). See also Martin Esslin, *The Theatre of the Absurd* (New York: Anchor Books, 1961), 133 for partial translation and discussion of Ionesco's article on humour.

manité."[23] A professional orator who has been engaged to deliver the old man's message to humanity is the only other visible character, and his appearance is delayed until the final scene. As the invisible guests arrive, the old couple bring each one a chair and then engage in conversation with them. By the end of the play the stage is crowded with empty chairs; even the invisible emperor has come to the lowly old man's tower. Confident that his life will take on universal significance and that he will be immortalized, the old man declares, "Ma mission est accomplie. Je n'aurai pas vécu en vain, puisque mon message sera révélé au monde. . . ."[24] He then ends his long life by leaping into the sea, accompanied by his wife, who feels assured they will become legendary figures or at least have some street named after them. It is only after the death leap that we learn that the hired orator is a deaf mute capable only of groaning and mumbling. Thus, the old man's message, like his life, is a failure; having lived deluded, he dies deceived. A resumé makes the play seem more pathetic than comic, so it is well to point out that the stage pictures it creates are truly funny. The accumulation of empty chairs brought on stage in an ever accelerating rhythmic pattern, the reactions to and interactions of the old couple with an invisible crowd, the two elderly characters leaping out of windows, together with a comic dialog and the audience's defeated expectation at the end of the play, all stimulate laughter.

The old man in *Les Chaises* is a deluded character who may be compared on a structural level with Molière's M. Jourdain in *Le Bourgeois gentilhomme*. Such a comparison reveals that Ionesco manipulates his deluded character in much the same manner as does Molière. I hasten to add that the contention is not that Ionesco is imitating Molière in this instance, but that he uses similar techniques to render delusion comic in his play. Both the old man and M. Jourdain may be viewed as exemplifying Plato's concept of the ideal comic character, that is, one who is in some way self-ignorant and who must not be powerful enough to pose a threat to others.[25] Ionesco's character is a would-be leader of men while M. Jourdain is a would-be gentleman; both are more than simply mistaken in their evaluations of self—their self-ignorance has assumed the proportions of obssession. All their actions are governed by a fixed idea, so that their entire personality has been colored by delusion.

---

[23] Ionesco, *Théâtre I*, 132.
[24] *Ibid.*, 176.
[25] Plato, *Philebus and Epinomis*, trans. A. E. Taylor (London: Thomas Nelson and Sons, Ltd., 1956), 169.

Like a puppet on a string, M. Jourdain can be manipulated by words designed to flatter his false self image; such is also the case of the old man in *Les Chaises*. His wife can effectively bolster him simply by saying, "Tu aurais pu être Président chef, Roi chef, ou même Docteur chef, si tu avais voulu."[26] The old man has duped himself into believing that he is some sort of prophet; he has sought superiority on a spiritual plane in order to compensate for his lack of material success. Just as M. Jourdain wishes above all else to be considered a gentleman, the old man has a compulsive need to feel important. We see this need demonstrated as he gradually assumes leadership throughout the course of the play, ordering his wife to bring in chairs, telling guests where to be seated, controlling the crowd when he calls for silence or introduces new arrivals. Yet he is in control of his imagination alone, for no one is there to be led; he has imagined the whole situation.

These two characters are comic because they are unable accurately to perceive the realities of their situation. Each realizes that he is socially unsuccessful: M. Jourdain takes lessons to become gentlemanly because he feels inferior; the old man also expresses displeasure with himself, complaining, "Je suis orphelin dans la vie. . . ."[27] Being aware of their lack of social success does not render these characters comic; what they do to alleviate their dissatisfaction does. They each create a dream world in which they allow themselves to live blinded, as it were, to contingencies. M. Jourdain, for example, is delighted to learn that his father had not been a cloth merchant but a gentleman who bought cloth to be distributed among friends who reimbursed him. His acceptance of this ridiculous proposal is highly revealing, for it shows us that he is prepared to accept nonsense if it flatters his desire to become a gentleman, rather than to face up to certain aspects of reality. The old man also has a ludicrous method of coping with the world. He ignores it completely and creates his own universe peopled by an invisible crowd of admirers. We may say that these two characters are comic in the sense of Schopenhauer's appreciation of things comic, that they are not able to make accurate judgments because their mentality is out of step with reality—things are not as they perceive them.[28]

The old man and M. Jourdain are comic for yet another reason; we

---

[26] Ionesco, *Théâtre I*, 132.
[27] *Ibid.*, 136.
[28] Arthur Schopenhauer, *The World as Will and Idea*, trans. by R. B. Haldane and J. Kemp (London: Keagan Paul, Trench, Trubner and Co., Ltd., 1906), II, 272.

laugh at them because all their efforts are fruitless and result in naught. M. Jourdain falsely believes at the end of the play that he has become a Turkish nobleman, and the old man jumps to his death believing that his message is to be delivered to the world. Of course, both characters have been deceived, because nothing at all has changed for the better: M. Jourdain remains a pretentious bourgeois with an unwanted son-in-law, and the old man is only a dead concierge whose message to the world died with him. I am reminded here of Kant's contention that a strained expectation resulting in nothing is often comic.[29] Ionesco, like Molière, is careful not to allow his character to be seen as a tragically victimized or disappointed figure. Both the old man and M. Jourdain are comic in spite of their unfulfillment because they remain completely oblivious to the fact that nothing turns out well for them. In fact, one may say, only half ironically, that they even lend credence to the belief that ignorance is bliss.

To recapitulate briefly, then, I have shown grounds for thinking that Ionesco's character is comic in the same way that M. Jourdain is comic. Both characters are deluded, obsessed by the need for improvement or betterment and determined in their actions by a fixed idea. Finally, each character is unaware of his defeated expectations at the end of the play. *Les Chaises* is a comedy in which the central character is conceived and structured in much the same way as is Molière's would-be gentleman. In both plays the comedy is largely contingent upon the presentation of deluded men, or persons who play self-appointed roles.

Ionesco and Molière also use the same comic techniques in presenting a disguised villainous figure. We shall see that Ionesco employs a structural triangle of character relationships which renders his professor in *La Leçon* laughable in spite of an odious nature, and that a strikingly similar set of relationships is seen in *Le Tartuffe*.

Although the story line of *La Leçon* is rather unusual, the play is built on a conventional linear plot which incorporates an exposition (the arrival of a young girl at a professor's home to be tutored for her *doctorat total*); a development (the lesson progresses from simple mathematics to an involved investigation of comparative philology of the "Neo-Spanish" tongues); a climax (the murder of the student by her exasperated professor); and a dénouement (the maid's reprimand of the professor for having killed forty girls that day). However, Ionesco adds an additional structural

---

[29] Emmanuel Kant, *Critique of Judgement*, trans. J. H. Bernard (London: Macmillan and Co., Ltd., 1892), 223.

unit to this conventional plot sequence; another young girl knocks at the door and the play begins again. By suggesting to the audience that the action just performed is about to be repeated and that the professor is about to commit his forty-first rape and murder of the day, Ionesco underlines the comic nature of his central character without allowing us to lose sight of his monstrous nature. The professor is a power-hungry, lecherous man, yet *La Leçon* is a comedy,[30] and he is a comic figure. Why? Rape and murder are hardly the stuff of comedy if they are understood or believed literally, but such is not the case in Ionesco's play where they are intended to be performed in a highly stylized manner and meant to be seen as the figurative representation of a basic human struggle—the overpowering of a weak element by a strong one.

A major source of comedy in *La Leçon* is the professor, who is presented as a *masqué* incapable of sustaining his disguise. Ionesco's stage directions indicate that the actor playing the role of the professor must at first appear quite professorial (*très professeur*), very timid and excessively polite, but that there is to be a recurrent lubricious look in his eyes which will ultimately become too strong to be hidden by the professorial picture. Ionesco also indicates that the professor's timidity must subtly disappear as he becomes gradually more nervous, aggressive and dominating. When he finally attacks his victim, his voice is to have slowly changed from thin and flute-like to extremely loud and powerful. Once he has committed the murder, he must instantly revert to being an apparent weakling and act somewhat like a small child who is guilty of some naughty act when the maid scolds him.

A comparative structural analysis of *La Leçon* and *Le Tartuffe* may reveal that the professor and Tartuffe are similarly conceived and executed comic personages. First of all, both characters are consciously disguised with evil intent, being similar to the wolf in sheep's clothing. They try to appear something they are not, imposing a decorous façade upon a sensuous personality. Each play can be reduced structurally to a triangle of character relationships: there are (1) a disguised character with selfish motives; (2) a gullible victim; and (3) perceptive character(s) who recognize the true personality of the *masqué*. Stylistically Ionesco handles each of these three elements as did Molière in *Le Tartuffe*.

---

[30] Ionesco subtitled this play "*Farce tragique.*" When he was asked by Edith Mora if he could define his concept of comedy, he responded, "Oui...je crois que c'est une autre face du tragique" (*Notes et contre-notes*, 199).

The disguised character is forced, during the course of the play, to drop his disguise and is comic because he brings about his own downfall through an inability to control his sensuous appetites. In both plays this personage is only sketched: we know very little about him except that he has trouble keeping his mask on and that we witness his unmasking. It is interesting to note that Tartuffe and the professor have been alotted educators' roles; the former gives lessons on how to get to heaven (Orgon says of him in Act I, scene 5, "Qui suit ses leçons goûte une paix profonde. . . ."); the latter on how to distinguish the nonexistent differences between the Neo-Spanish tongues. At any rate, both are in a position of leadership as far as the gullible characters, their pupils, are concerned. Also to be observed is the fact that both of these men who assume meek attitudes are not only lusty, but have volcanic tempers: Tartuffe, in a rage because Elmire has compromised him, goes to the king to inform on Orgon, and in so doing inadvertently gives himself away; the professor warns his student, who has begun to complain of a toothache, "N'interrompez pas! Ne me mettez pas en colère! Je ne répondrai plus de moi!"[31] Indeed, both characters lose their tempers as well as their masks, and both have recourse to violence: Tartuffe would, if not foiled by a fanciful bit of *deus ex machina*, evict an entire family; the professor has raped and killed forty students. The most significant similarity in the conception and execution of these characters is that they are both potentially very dark or sinister, and yet presented in such a way as to be unfailingly comic. Fundamentally this is possible because Ionesco and Molière have allowed their audiences to penetrate the disguises assumed by the professor and Tartuffe, whose masks fall, so to speak, because of overpowering internal motivation. These characters simply cannot maintain their disguises because their sensuality prevents them from appearing consistently pious or professorial.

The victims of both plays perform a double function: they are comic in their own right because of their excessive gullibility, and they highlight the disguised characters by being willing audiences to their masquerades. In *Le Tartuffe* the victim's role is assumed by Madame Pernelle and her son, Orgon, who are gullible to a fault; they want so to believe in Tartuffe that nothing short of Elmire's near seduction will turn them from their idol. The student in *La Leçon* is also more than willing to learn from the professor; she is described in the stage directions as being "volontaire . . . jusqu'à en paraître presque agressive,"[32] and the maid's warnings to the professor

[31] Ionesco, *Théâtre I*, 83.
[32] *Ibid.*, 60.

make no apparent impression upon her. There is a charming childlike simplicity about the victims in both plays who seem to be unable to reason. Orgon cannot correlate warnings given him with evidences of Tartuffe's fraudulent behavior; the student has to memorize all the possible answers to all possible multiplication problems because she cannot understand simple mathematical principles. A significant similarity to be noted in the structuring of the victim's role in each play is the total personality transition made by the time the climax arrives: credulous Orgon becomes completely aware of Tartuffe's true nature; the avid student becomes "de plus en plus passive, jusqu'à ne plus être qu'un objet mou et inerte, semblant inanimée, entre les mains du professeur. . . ."[33] The rhythm of the personality change in Ionesco's play is quite different than in *Le Tartuffe* where Orgon's awakening is quickly effected. The student in *La Leçon* evolves very slowly from being active to becoming inert. Yet the dramatic value of both transitions is the same, for they signal perception of and reaction to the unmasking of the disguised central character of the play.

The perceptive characters, that is to say those who recognize throughout the entire play that the central character is a *masqué*, serve an important structural function. They act as a buffer zone between the audience and the disguised personage, preventing us from dreading the latter or even perhaps empathizing with him. If, for example, Molière had not carefully prepared the audience by having his perceptive characters talk about Tartuffe as a fraud, our reaction to him might be quite different. Instead of laughing at his obvious façade of excessive piety, we might fear him or pity him as a man having a deep psychological problem. Likewise, if the maid in *La Leçon* were not on hand to warn the professor that philology lessons always bring on calamity, we would be unprepared to accept the rape and murder as a comic action, which of course they are intended to be. The perceptive character is a key to the comedy, in that he prevents it from becoming melodramatic. In Molière's play, the perceptive characters, namely Elmire, Cléante, Dorine, and Damis, relate to the victim; they try to make Orgon and his mother recognize that Tartuffe is an imposter. However, in Ionesco's play the perceptive character, the maid, relates to the *masqué*, the professor, and not to his victim; she warns him against himself, for she knows what to expect after thirty-nine similar occurrences that same day. However, the dramatic function of Ionesco's perceptive character is exactly the same as that of Molière's: this personage

---

[33] *Ibid.*

is an additional indication that the central character is disguised, that his disguise is not totally effective (it has been perceived), that, in short, the *masqué* is not to be taken too seriously by the audience.

It would be unwise to conclude that Ionesco has patterned the old man in *Les Chaises* after Molière's M. Jourdain or that Tartuffe served as his model for the professor. My intention has merely been to indicate that Ionesco presents delusion and disguise in a moliéresque manner, that he uses the same structural devices to portray deluded and disguised figures. The most significant affinities of comic style to be gathered from this brief consideration of four of Molière and Ionesco's characters are implicit rather than explicit. The most obvious thing to be said about these four characters, and doubtless the most important, is that each is a dynamic example of excellent comic characterization. All four have assumed false identities, either consciously, as in the case of the disguised characters, or unconsciously, as in the case of the deluded ones. Ionesco and Molière have more than doubled the theatrical and comic impact of these characters by having them assume still other roles, for in so doing, the playwrights have drawn the audience into a creative hall of mirrors, as it were: we witness an actor playing a character who is wittingly or otherwise trying to be someone else. But more importantly, these characters cause us to sense still another affinity in the comic styles of Ionesco and of Molière, namely the vision which permits them to perceive and portray subjects which are basically pathetic, such as self-delusion, or sinister, such as willful deception, in a comic perspective. Ionesco, like Molière, has the ability to place some distance between himself and the world, to see the humor in it and to represent whatever he observes around him in comic format. Significantly, Ionesco has said, "Quand j'arrive à me détacher du monde, et à pouvoir le regarder, il me paraît comique dans son invraisemblance."[34]

In Ionesco's theater, as in Molière's, the predominant mode is comic. Density is a key factor in Ionesco's style; Richard Coe has stated that perhaps no other French writer since Molière has achieved such a consistently high degree of dramatic density in each scene.[35] That his plays are so constructed implies a high potential for the occurrence of comic effects, a potential which is fully realized by Ionesco in his plays, which afford us a wealth of comedy ranging in scope from the broadest of sight

---

[34] Ionesco, *Notes et contre-notes*, 101.
[35] Richard N. Coe, *Eugène Ionesco* (New York: Grove Press, Inc., 1961), 15.

gags to the most intricate verbal play. *La Cantatrice chauve* is one of the many excellent examples. At the present writing one production of the play is in its seventeenth consecutive season at the Théâtre de la Huchette in Paris—a strong indication that Ionesco has a solid understanding of Molière's "grande règle."

I have indicated that Ionesco and Molière entertain similar notions about stagecraft and dramatic criticism, and that they sometimes use similar structural techniques in their comedies. The two are representational artists who write primarily in a comic vein. For if Ionesco seeks to represent life as he witnesses it and Molière seeks to paint according to nature, they both are able to see the world with comic vision. It is the comic vision of these playwrights, their ability to perceive and render the ridiculous in all its multiplicity, that establishes a fundamental or internal similarity in their plays. Ionesco is, in his highly personalized manner, a continuator of the classical tradition in French comedy.

HYPNOTIC LANGUAGE AND ITS APOTHEOSES: MOLIÈRE AND IONESCO

Kenneth S. White

From the times of Molière's earliest critics to those of Ionesco's analysts in our own day, a strange reluctance has been perpetuated. Almost without exception, commentators on each playwright's artistic ingenuity have shied away from a mainspring hidden beneath the overpowering vertigo of comic *apogée*: i.e., verbal hypnotics that inspire apotheosis. Theatrical hypnosis (generated with unusual potency in Molière's *Le Bourgeois gentilhomme* and in Ionesco's *La Leçon* and *La Cantatrice chauve*) is at once less and more than literal in meaning, effect, and duration. Inventive, bedazzling language, given form by Molière and Ionesco, stuns, benumbs, immobilizes, and finally transfigures a character's anticipated reactions. Logic splinters, shatters. Unexpectedly individualized, paradoxically subtle linguistic patterning and invention disrupt the root connections of "reasonableness," the capstone of theatrical metaphor. Symptoms of total hypnotic sleep are seldom involved. Yet quite perceptible, secondary hypnotic behavior (called an "état second" by the French) emerges; it evolves into spellbinding, zany-shaped *apogées*, unforgettable whorls that realign as *dénouement*, polychromatic and partly quizzical comic resolutions.

At peaks of apotheosis (ludicrously "glorifying" Jourdain in Molière's exalting professor and pupil inhumanly in Ionesco's *La Leçon*, or idolizing King Language and his slaves, quasi-real nightmare figures that impel us with eerie sounds in *La Cantatrice chauve*) comes an ingeniously theatricalized, giddy exultation. Only a few *personae* are changed by it. A sort of mesmerism operates: more exactly, secondary hypnotic enchantments, not quite equal in species and strength to the hypnotist's bag of verbal magic. A character, caught in the eddy of such powers, may uncannily imply two divergent stances, set on planes of comic immediacy or mythic longing.

One of the most influential (and most commonly oversimplified) prototypes is Molière's buffoonish but zestful M. Jourdain, the *bourgeois gentilhomme* who prances and sings in ecstasy during the apogean Turkish ceremony. M. Jourdain progressively undergoes mesmeric (and more vitally, *kinetic*, exploratory) raptures. These endow him with a new pulse of life, acquired during memorable, though burlesque replicas of apotheosis. In double comic irony, Molière's social climber starts to tap his dormant potentialities through the fresh impetus of incipient self-discovery and self-animation. Even after Turkish bedazzlements are past, Jourdain *is* renewed. He exudes new self-awarenesses, new talent comes to the mind's surface. He *has* danced, romanced, fenced, sung, philosophized, learned "Turkish" words. The play's acute satiric edges notwithstanding, all this newness is an authentic, budding, experiential part of Jourdain.

How and why did Molière construct scenes to indicate such hypnotic forces? Few critics have attacked the problem. Robert Garapon has touched it tangentially.[1] Ionesco's extravagant sorcery with language has often been examined, his exact hypnotics rarely. Serge Doubrovsky[2] and Maurice Lecuyer[3] have delved deepest, but neither has pinpointed the mesmeric cores in Ionesco's scenes of apotheosis.

Creating laughter is by nature a strange enterprise, as Molière admitted. Three centuries later, the quizzical functioning of comic theater was rephrased in a crucial article by Ionesco, "Expérience du théâtre." Ionesco first seemed to echo Molière's concept; but he then defined a phantasmagoric power spawned, as though diabolically, in the pristine reactions provoked by theatrical mesmerism.

Incarner les fantasmes, donner la vie, c'est une aventure prodigieuse, irremplaçable, au point qu'il m'est arrivé à moi-même d'être ébloui, en voyant soudain se mouvoir sur le plateau des ages sortis de moi. J'en fus effrayé. De quel droit avais-je fait cela? Etait-ce permis?.. C'était presque diabolique... Pour s'arracher au quotidien, à l'habitude, à la paresse mentale qui nous cache l'étrangeté du réel, il faut recevoir comme un véritable coup de matraque.[4]

In figurative but crystalline terms, Ionesco discloses the sensation of a nether world's dazzling power at the instant when the playwright's ghosts

[1] Robert Garapon, *La fantasie verbale et le comique dans le théâtre français du moyen âge à fin du dix-septième siècle* (Paris: Armand Colin, 1957); and "La langue et le style des différents personnages du 'Bourgeois gentilhomme'," *Le Français moderne*, XXVI (1958), 103–12.

[2] J. S. Doubrovsky, "Ionesco and the Comedy of the Absurd," *Yale French Studies*, No. 23 (Summer 1959), 3–10. Reprinted under title "Le Rire d'Eugène Ionesco," *Nouvelle N.R.F.*, No. 86 (1 fév. 1960), 313–23.

[3] Maurice Lecuyer, "Ionesco ou la précédence du verbe," *Cahiers Renaud-Barrault*, No. 53 (fév. 1966), 3–20: and "Le Langage dans le théâtre d'Eugène Ionesco," *Rice University Studies*, Vol. 51, No. 3 (Summer 1965), 33–49.

[4] Eugène Ionesco, "Expérience du théâtre," *Nouvelle N.R.F.*, No. 62 (1958), 258–59.

take life on stage. Once they breathe as dramatic characters, speaking a strange language that deviates from the atrophied clusters of speech resounded in humdrum life, they take on fascinating, sometimes mystifying physical magnetism. Ionesco has explained his intent to strain language toward paroxysm, if not explosion. Why is this necessary? Why are language's mesmeric and explosive qualities crucial? Surfeited with jargon (bureaucratic, peer-group, mass-media) slogans, all those clinking linkages of the spurious in words used as omnipotent clubs to beat at us incessantly, Ionesco's individualists, dreamers, café-rebels, and lost souls are groping, often in frenzy, for believable ways to express their distress. In 1966, Ionesco wrote: "I have tried to show characters who would be in search of a life, in search of an essential reality."[5] In *Notes and Counternotes* he described methods he meant to use to mold "the true temper of drama" by theatricalizing the word itself to attain a level of frenzy:

> It was by plunging into banality, by draining the sense from the hollowest clichés of everyday language that I tried to render the strangeness that seems to pervade our whole existence...perhaps the unnatural can by its very violence appear natural...If one believes that "theatre" merely means the drama of the word, it is difficult to grant it can have an autonomous language of its own; it can then only be the servant of other forms of thought expressed in words, of philosophy and morals...There are means of making words more theatrical: by working them up to such a pitch that they reveal the true temper of drama, which lies in frenzy; the whole tone should be as strained as possible.[6]

A chasm separates Ionesco and Molière on the primary issue: *how* to devise power-laden theatrical language. Frenzy, claims Ionesco, embodies the true temper of drama. By straining the entire verbal ambience, the poet reaches this frantic pitch. Molière rejected any such absolutism. Even the *turquoiseries*, which inspire M. Jourdain's imaginary apotheosis, never produce complete linguistic or kinetic frenzy, as do certain unbridled scenes in Ionesco's plays, notably in *La Cantatrice chauve* and *La Leçon*.

What does Molière's invention and alliance of unexpected kinds of language (particularly Turkish and simulated Turkish) really produce in Jourdain's mind? Finally, and most essentially, is his concluding apotheosis ridiculous, or something else?

W. G. Moore proposed two challenging questions which begin to probe the unusual dynamics mobilized by the playwright's language: "How is it that speech is thus so much more meaningful in Molière than in life?...

---

[5] Ionesco, in an interview with Claude Bonnefoy, *Entretiens avec Ionesco* (Paris: Pierre Belfond, 1966), 180.

[6] Ionesco, *Notes and Counternotes* (New York: Grove, 1964), 28–29.

Do we not here approach one of the secrets of [Molière's] art, something that is not merely superficial grace but the sign of a dynamic quality?"[7] *Le Bourgeois gentilhomme* contains seeds of a solution, its unique comic sense tantalizing our wits, leading us to try untested ways of analyzing comic language. The singular forcefulness of Molière's linguistic innovations stands out, crucial in the most compelling comic effects. Yet these instances of *apogée* are comprehensible in full on one condition only; we must align our comic vision without excessively downgrading M. Jourdain's inherent potentialities. Molière's hero figuratively embodies (besides a buffoonish social-climber) a deep substratum: the mythic, overreaching dreamer-adventurer inherent in each of us. Myth, fiction and drama are replete with variants of this quitessential type, from Icarus and Ulysses to Quixote, Plume, and Walter Mitty.

Le Bourgeois gentilhomme, beaneath almost translucent comic surfaces, implies the kinetic lures and reactions entailed in sheer adventurousness, the splintering of social frameworks to participate in unlikely transfiguration. Quite early in the comedy, Jourdain is about to arrive for music and dancing lessons. His teachers precede him. They first boast how they intend to make him pay, pay, and pay. Both music and dancing master assert that their oafish pupil may still cut a good figure artistically:

> MAITRE A DANSER...je voudrois qu'avec son bien il eût encore quelque bon goût des choses.
> MAITRE DE MUSIQUE Je le voudrois aussi, et c'est à quoi nous travaillons tous deux autant que nous pouvons. . . . [8]

Comic strands are more intricate than they might seem in this caustic *répartée*. Molière's purpose is in fact split: mockery of M. Jourdain's social, worldly ambitions and his awkwardness (counterpointed by satire of predatory artistic pedagogs) but also an ambivalent guidepost; it is intimated clearly that M. Jourdain's follies *are not complete folly*. Even an oaf can learn to dance, sing, and romance.

M. Jourdain's initial apotheosis occurs early, in act two, scene four. Discovering how to emit vowels, he jubilates. This spontaneous exultation is a structural, prehypnotic presage of Jourdain's culminating linguistic ectasies during the famous ceremony with the "Turkish" potentates (acts

---

[7] W. G. Moore, "Speech" (from *Molière, a New Criticism*, Oxford: Clarendon, 1949), reprinted in part in *Molière*, ed. J. Guicharnaud (Englewood Cliffs: Prentice-Hall, 1964), 48.
[8] Molière, *Le Bourgeois gentilhomme*, in *Théâtre complet*, ed. R. Jouanny (Paris: Classiques Garnier, t. 2, I, 1), 435.

IV and V). Commencing the comedy's hypnotics, Molière slices language into babyish sounds, mesmerically simple, repetitious, irresistible to the seemingly naive mind of Jourdain. Reiterating A, E, I, O, U with shrieks of amazement, the bourgeois pupil is so entranced that he begins to change, possed by the awareness that he and contact with higher truths are One:

M. JOURDAIN

A, E, A, E. Ma foi! oui. Ah! Que cela est beau!

. . . .

A, E, I, I, I, I. Cela est vrai. Vive la science!

. . . .

O, O. Il n'y rien de plus juste. A, E, I, O, I, O. Cela est admirable! I, O, I, O.

. . . .

O, O, O. Vous avez raison. O. Ah! la belle chose, que de savoir quelque chose![9]

Renowned as one Molière's most original and most hilarious scenes, yet taken for granted because of its seeming transparence, this outburst deserves painstaking scrunity. Molière's linguistic art, disarmingly candid and direct, is also quite original. Almost infantile at first, Jourdain's awe at new sounds fuses with an adult consciousness of the impressive beauty of learning to discover *oneself* through external truths.

From ludicrous linguistic childishness has spurted knowledge of creative beauty and a possible new self, to be discovered in sound. The beauty Jourdain hears (*beau, vrai, science, juste, admirable, raison, belle*) is part of his authentic, hitherto unused exploratory being as it gushes out symbolically in elemental, sonorous shapes. The would-be gentleman, building rhythms, crude assonance and onomatopoetics with A, E, I, O, U patterns (vocalic combinations unheard in normal French prose) prefigures, in this flickering apotheosis of self-heightening, the growing consciousness of a repressed, kinetic inner being which gives mythic impact to *Le Bourgeois gentilhomme*.

In one veiled, metaphorical sense, Molière's comedy will thus celebrate, be it by indirection and laughable facsimile, exultation in social and quasi-artisitc adventure, the joyful release of yearnings at last unfettered. For Jourdain, language's charm is alluring. It promises gateways to prestige, social and personal change, pleasure. After vowels, then consonants, he joyously creates prose. An unrealistic quest (courtship of Dorimène) flounders, but not to be denied, the ever more intrepid bourgeois rebounds. Covielle tells him that the Grand Turk's son, present in Paris, wishes to marry M. Jourdain's daughter. Covielle enchants M. Jourdain with weird,

---

[9] *Ibid.*, II, 4, pp. 451–52.

melodic language, conveyed in courtship, he says, by the Grand Turk's son: "Acciam cric soler ouch alla moustaph gidelum amanahem varahini oussere carbulath."[10]

This "language" is virtually sheer Molière, invention, a comedy of sound-burdened exoticism, repetitions, and weird echoes. It contains almost nothing Turkish. The bourgeois is overjoyed, transfixed. Why? M. Jourdain's aspirations alone do not account for his rapture. Unquestionably, something in the artificial language is responsible. In part, esoteric sounds. The consonants (many strident to French ears: *cc*, the pronounced final *m*'s and *th*) and the diphthongs (*ia*, *ou*) are calculated to seem un-Gallic, weird. Even more potent mesmeric forces are the creaking alliterations and the cacaphony of the *c* sounds, which seem to call to mind foreign clamor; and the crescent echoes provoked by the *a*, with its cabalistic rhythms (*alla moustaph*, *amanahem varahini*, *carbulath*), prefiguring some exotic ceremonial chant.

M. Jourdain falls almost instantaneously under the "Turkish" spell. In a daze, he repeats Covielle's incantatory vocables: *Marababa sahem*. Outlandish alliterations, rhythms, and desires penetrate M. Jourdain's nerves like bongo drum beats. *Marababa sahem* brings to mind the insistent hypnotics and durability of an Oriental snake charmer's music. Dulcet, repeated *a*'s, liquid *r* and unexpectedly humming *m*'s combine with the insidious *s* to implant in M. Jourdain's newly activated linguistic psyche the tempos and vague dangers of an exotic East.

A blatantly incongruous invention, Covielle's word *Cacaracamouchen* is the next hypnotizing dart. It strikes Jourdain dead center. "That is really marvelous," he rejoices. Once again, Molière has devised a dazzling cascade of syllables in *ca*. A shower of scatalogical and animal allusions falls. Most importantly, the *mou* anticipates a part of the key hypnotic word, *Mamamouchi*. The richest invented term, *Cacaracamouchen*, is a primary link in Molière's thematic counterpoint, balancing burlesque illusion and the zest of artistic awakening and adventure spurred by astounding "languages."

Jourdain, enthralled, joins the "Turkish" ritual, eager to be dubbed *Mamamouchi*. The sonorous *Mamamouchi* launches the processional, amassing more and more preternatural words. These sonic creations raise M. Jourdain like a fully acquiescent human puppet toward his *apogée* in the Turkish travesty: *Ambousahim oqui boraf, Iordina, salamalequi*.

[10] *Ibid.*, IV, 4, p. 498.

Molière's favorite hypnotic vowel, *a*, insidiously repeated to strengthen its somniferous properties, occurs seven times in this brief sentence. The prominent *m* evokes mystery, mellifluousness, vibrancy. Molière, inventing the other words, transposes an Arabic greeting, "saläm alaik." Once more, he echoes the *qui* sound in his transposed term: evidence that Molière chose *qui* here, as elsewhere, to reinforce mesmerism of M. Jourdain with a sort of cutting, abrupt sonic instrument.

Turkish musicians and melodies, the Mufti, four Dervishes, dancers in native costume, all totally captivate M. Jourdain and prepare his mind for an almost Dionysiac bedazzlement. Astutely, Molière allows him to comprehend key phrases in the "Turkish" (actually an amalgam of bits of Turkish, Arabic, Sabir, Hebrew, pigeon-Turkish, French, Latin, and Molière's own admixture). The central role of "freshened" language in *Le Bourgeois gentilhomme* becomes most obvious when M. Jourdain, overwhelmed by several phrases denoting his ascendancy to *Mamamouchi*, repeats even the most difficult ones verbatim, as though hypnotized by the irresistible lures of this new idiom:

> LE MUFTI: Star bon Turca Giourdina?
> LES TURCS: Hi valla.
> LE MUFTI, *danse et chante ces mots*: Hou la ba ba la chou ba la ba ba la da.[11]

The Mufti's ultra-simple, clear syllables (spurious Turkish and inauthentic Mufti-ritual) reformulate Molière's incessant play on the sound *a* in hypnotics. Manifestly, the Mufti's childish syllables are a comic extension, in more adult form, of Jourdain's candid second-act glee at initiating the delights of vowel and consonantal sounds. Language has evolved, found fuller, more imaginative shapes; so has M. Jourdain's spirit of adventure, intellectual as well as worldly.

Mme Jourdain, arriving at ceremony's end, is incredulous. Still enraptured, her husband insists five times that she call him *Mamamouchi*. In brilliantly laughable badinage with his spouse, the bourgeois chants verbatim five crucial, psuedo-Turkish phrases. Each, we note, is dominated by the sound *a*, placed in final stressed position. Jourdain's language-induced trance is still basically unbroken. Suddenly, bursting into dance and song, he launches musically into a caricatural, Dionysiac frenzy of artistic apotheosis, of pure exultation. He now sings the apogean sense of his discovery of the noble arts, with ludicrous but genuine linguistic joy: "Hou la ba ba la chou ba la ba ba la da." (M. Jourdain *still* reproduces

---

[11] *Ibid.*, V, 1, p. 502.

the Mufti's sentence precisely.) The ecstatic bourgeois, according to the 1734 edition of the play, falls to the floor, as though exhausted by his bedazzled artistic apotheosis.

After these adventurous excesses, M. Jourdain is not belittled. On the contrary: still whirling in Turkish visions, the new *Mamamouchi* contentedly gives his daughter in marriage to her suitor, masked as a Turk. Euphoria reigns; in festive glee, the bourgeois proclaims that he will donate his wife to any man who dares take her. M. Jourdain is prepared to devise other fascinating syllables and childish escapades, foolish in degree but not in essence. Don Quixote's shadow hovers not too far.

More evident, more overtly defined than Molière's is Ionesco's hypnotism by means of rejuvenated and invented language. Simone Benmussa has declared: "Dans *La Leçon*, le langage a un but extérieur. Il doit faire basculer la témérité de l'élève en soumission et la timidité du professeur en agressivité. La parole est incisive, elle est un élément hypnotique pour réduire l'élève, elle préfigure le couteau."[12]

Only when the professor fabricates a parodied lesson in world philology does his refractory pupil start to pay attention. His wild intermingling of foreign tongues builds hypnotic lines. The girl, left alone, stares into emptiness, stupefied. Her raging toothache, in actuality, is "the final symptom," as the maid prognosticates, the indication of hypnotized stupor. Now the grisly phase occurs: violation and murder by "philological" hypnotics. The professor, claiming that he wants to regroup his Spanish, neo-Spanish, Portuguese, French, Oriental, Rumanian, Sardanapalese, and Latin knives, picks up the fatal knife, then brandishes it before his pupil. First chanting as in singsong, he forces her to imitate him, repeating *cou, teau* as she stares fixedly at the knife, inches from her face. The sounds take on terrifying hypnotic power, affecting both professor and pupil. "*Le couteau tue,*" he chants. She repeats involuntarily, as he intones his ferocious lullaby words. After the erotic assault and killing, the professor babbles incomprehensibly. He, too, has been trapped in the life-and-death theatrical spell cast by verbal incantation resembling a voodoo, deformed-academic language.

Ionesco's famed "linguistic explosion" in *The Bald Soprano* is a much more innovative and fantasmagoric technique used to create a special type of mesmerism. First, Mary's abrupt, puzzling poem, *Fire*, gives the impression of some untamed verbal rhapsody, reiterating *prit feu, prit feu*

---

[12] Simone Benmussa, *Ionesco* (Paris: Seghers, 1966), 94.

and the plural *prirent feu*. Fire is catching everywhere. In this unexpected mode, fragile, half-absurd hypnotics creep in, later to be transposed in the play's ending, when the sounds and theme of incendiary outbreak reappear as volatilized verbal fires disseminating the sparks of a new, bizarre, sound-and fury theatrical language.

In Ionesco's apotheosis of linguistic *dépassement*, an important innovation is that each character, in the final explosion, creates his own distinctive linguistic frame of invention, as it were, his own idiom. A new comic universe comes into being:

> M. Smith: Caiman!
> M. Martin: Allons gifler Ulysse.
> M. Smith: Je m'en vais habiter ma Cagna dans mes cacaoyers.
> Mme Martin: Les cacaoyers des cacaoyères donnent pas des cacahuettes, donnent du cacao! Les cacaoyers des cacaoyères donnent pas des cacahuettes, donnent du cacao. Les cacaoyers des cacaoyères donnent pas des cacahuettes, donnent du cacao.
> Mme Smith: Les souris ont des sourcils, les sourcils n'ont pas de souris.[13]

Like Molière in *Le Bourgeois gentilhomme*, Ionesco employs, for his comically hypnotic effects in *The Bald Soprano*, a dizzying repetition of the vowel *a*, esoteric diphthongs, and the hard consonantal *c*, with the mellifluous and ludicrous *ou*. The odd confluence of these almost obsessive sounds, combined by Molière and by Ionesco to accentuate the powers of mesmeric self-transformation in instances of language-induced apotheosis, functions as a significant new key to the secrets of their comic geniuses, in many other respects dissimilar.

---

[13] Ionesco, *La Cantatrice chauve* (Paris: Gallimard, éd. spéciale, 1962), 42.

Molière, Italy,
and Spain

That Italy and Spain provided much of the stuff from which Molière forged the foundation of great French comedy is not to be disputed as a generality. The Gelosi, an Italian company, played in France through most of the seventeenth century, and the commedia dell'arte *exerted its influence on the French playwright. Marinism (but apparently not Gongorism) supplied ample hyperboles for the* salons, *thus providing the verbal institution against which Molière could so effectively rail in* Les Précieuses ridicules *and other comedies. This section yields information on the fate of Molière's plays back in the countries whence came a portion of their original inspiration. (Another section of this volume deals with Molière's own reception of literary traditions and institutions.)*

The first essay gives an overview of performances, translations, adaptations, and critical receptions in Italy, from the time of the Italians' first importation of Molière until the present. A second article discusses parallels between Molière and Pirandello. For Spain, there is only one essay, a description of the current status of Molière comedies in that country.

MOLIÈRE EN ITALIE

Fiorenza Di Franco

Les liens entre Molière et l'Italie remontent à la vie de l'auteur-acteur, à son amitié avec les troupes italiennes, à son oeuvre, et à l'influence sur elle de la Commedia dell'Arte, mais cette étude va se limiter à montrer comment l'Italie a accueilli et a réagi au théâtre de Molière dès son introduction dans ce pays jusqu'à nos jours. Les faits significatifs qui seront examinés pour mettre en évidence ce rapport entre Molière et l'Italie vont être les représentations, les traductions, les imitations et les critiques de ses pièces dès le XVIIe siècle jusqu'à la période contemporaine.

Pour citer les premières représentations de Molière en Italie, je vais me servir des soigneuses recherches de Pietro Toldo dans *L'Oeuvre de Molière et sa fortune en Italie* (Torino: Loescher, 1910). Dans ce livre, Toldo étudie Molière en Italie jusqu'au commencement du XIXe siècle. Toldo a trouvé traces des représentations de pièces de Molière par des troupes françaises dès la fin du XVIIe siècle en Piémont. A cette époque pour des raisons de voisinage et parce que leur langue y était bien comprise, les comédiens français jouaient avec grand succès devant la cour et le public de Turin. Toldo cite comme la première représentation en langue française *Les Femmes savantes* en 1673. Ensuite, et toujours par des troupes françaises, les représentations suivantes:

L'hiver 1755–56, au théâtre Carignano de Turin la troupe de Delille joue: *L'Avare, Le Malade imaginaire, Tartuffe, L'Ecole des femmes, Amphitrion* (sic), *M. Poursagnac* (sic), *Le Misanthrope, L'Ecole des maris, Le Médecin malgré lui, Les Fourberies de Scapin, George Dandin, La Précieuse ridicule* (?).

L'hiver 1758–59, la troupe de Salneuve toujours au Carignano joue: *L'Ecole des femmes, Le Tartuffe, Le Misanthrope, Les Précieuses ridicules, L'Ecole des maris, Le Médecin malgré lui, L'Avare, Le Mariage forcé, Le Cocu imaginaire.*

L'hiver 1761–62, une autre troupe francaise joue *L'Ecole des femmes, L'Ecole des maris, Le Misanthrope, L'Avare, Georges D'Andin* (sic), *Le Malade imaginaire, Les Femmes savantes*, et *Le Comte des Scarbagnasse* (sic).

171

L'hiver 1774–75, les acteurs dirigés par Seviépart et Desmarés jouent au Carignano: *L'Avare, Le Dépit amoureux, Le Médecin malgré lui, Les Précieuses ridicules, Le Festin de pierre* (*sic*), *Le Misanthrope, Pourceaugnac, Les Fourberies de Scapin, Amphitryon*.

L'hiver 1776–77, les mêmes pièces sont jouées au même théâtre.

L'hiver 1778–79, la troupe avec Mme Destouches cadette joue *L'Avare, L'Ecole des maris, Le Misanthrope, Le Dépit*.

Les troupes françaises poussent jusqu'à Gênes où un scandale éclate le 15 juillet 1774 pour la représentation du *Tartuffe* que l'on bannit mais pas pour longtemps. Le magistrat auquel le sénat avait déféré l'affaire permet de nouveau la représentation.

Les troupes italiennes jouent aussi Molière; dès le commencement du XVIIIe, Toldo en a trouvé des traces dans les villes suivantes:

Sienne:

1708—A l'Institut Tolomei, un collège des Jésuites, on joue *L'ammalato immaginario ove figura la serva Tognetta* et *Mercante cavaliere ovvero Monsieur Giordano*, imitations ou traductions de Molière.

1719—*Mercante cavaliere*.

1725—*Mercante cavaliere* est joué par les Sanfirenzini.

Naples:

1708—*Medico a forza* chez le général Elbeuf.

1773—*Misantropo*.

1777—*Tartufo* (défendu).

1789—*Tartufo*.

1797—*Tartufo*.

Modène:

1727—*L'infermo immaginario, Gli infortuni, La scuola de gelosi, Le furberie di Scappino, Signor di Purcignacco, Il medico volante, Il finto medico, Il medico a suo dispetto, Il medico per forza*, etc.

Bologne:

1731—Les Accademici candidi uniti jouent avec succès *Il matrimonio per forza*.

Milan:

1735—*Porsignacco*

1739—*Arnolfo* (*L'Ecole des femmes?*).

1791—*Il medico per forza*.

Turin:

1768—La Compagnia de San Luca, detta Magliano joue au Carignano *La scuola dei maritati*.

1769–70—*Le furberie di Arlecchino* (Scapin).

1770–71—*La Scuola dei mariti.*

1772–73—*L'impostore* (*Tartuffe?*).

Pour le XIXe siècle je me suis servi, outre de Toldo, de *Enciclopedia dello Spettacolo*, Vol. VII (Firenze: Sansoni, 1960).

Turin:

1821—*Il Tartufo.*

1823–24—La Compagnia Reale Sarda joue *Il Tartufo dei Costumi, L'avaro di Molière, Il misantropo* et *Molière maritato*, pièce de Pietro Chiari.

1898—*Scuola delle mogli, Stordito, Medico per forza.*

Milan:

1800—*L'ipocondriaco.*

1844—*Tartufo.*

Parme:

1819—*Il medico per forza.*

En **1860**, une compagnie théâtrale donne dans plusieurs villes *Il Tartufo* et *L'avaro.* En **1870**, une autre compagnie donne *Il misantropo, La Scuola delle mogli, La Scuola dei mariti, Sgannarello.* En **1881**, on joue *Dispetti amorosi, Sgannarello* et en **1882**, *Giorgio Dandin.*

Pour le XXe siècle, j'ai consulté l'*Enciclopedia dello Spettacolo*, déjà cité, et un recueil de journaux de 1948 à 1969 sur les représentations de Molière en Italie.

1907—*George Dandin* est joué à *Rome.*

1923—Année exceptionnelle pour Molière. La célébration du tricentenaire en 1922 a éveillé l'attention des compagnies théâtrales italiennes. On joue dans plusieurs villes d'Italie *L'avaro, L'ammalato immaginario, Tartufo, Il medico per forza, Sgannarello, Il becco immaginario.*

1927—*Le trappolerie di Scapino* est joué à **Rome**.

Ensuite l'*Enciclopedia dello Spettacolo* dit qu'il y a eu une éclipse jusqu'à 1948, mais j'ai trouvé des pièces jouées en 1946.

1946—A **Rome** on joue *Il borghese gentiluomo* e *Il matrimonio per forza*; à **Milan** *Tartufo.*

1948—A **Milan** *Giorgio Dandini* et *Don Giovanni* à **Rome** et à **Milan**.

1950—A **Rome**, à **Milan**, à **Bologne** et à **Florence** *Il misantropo.* A **Rome** *Il Tartufo*, à **Asolo** *Amfitrione* et à **Capri** *La scuola delle mogli.*

1951—A **Milan** *Furberie di Scapino* et *Il medico volante*, à **Rome** *Le donne saccenti.*

1952—A **Rome** *Le furberie di Scapino*, à **Venise** *L'avaro*, à **Naples** *Le donne saccenti.*

1953—A **Rome** *Il borghese gentiluomo*; *Il malato immaginario*, à **Gênes**, à **Turin** et à **Rome**. A **Syracuse** *Don Giovanni*.

1954—A **Rome** *L'avaro*; à **Turin** et à **Rome** *Il Tartufo*.

1955—A **Rome** *Tartufo* (traduction de Quasimodo); à **Vicenza** et à **Rome** *L'avaro*; à **Gênes** et à **Turin** *Le donne sapienti*.

1956—A **Vicenza** *Il misantropo*.

1959—A **Rome** *Sgannarello e la figlia del re*, libre adaptation du *Médecin malgré lui* par A. Fersen.

1960—A **Rome** *Giorgio Dandin*.

1962—A **Milan** *Le donne sapienti*.

1963—A **Milan** *L'avaro*.

1964—A **Naples** *Il misantropo*.

1966—A **Rome** et à **Milan** *Don Giovanni*.

1967—A **Catane** en sicilien *Il malato immaginario*.

1968—A **Rome** *La scuola delle mogli*; à **L'Aquila** et à **Rome** *Tartufo*; à **Turin** et à **Asti** *Il misantropo*.

1969—A **Rome** *Le furberie di Scapino* et à **Vicenza** *Giorgio Dandin*.

A cette liste il faut ajouter *Il malato immaginario* jouée à la télévision italienne au mois d'août **1972**.

De même qu'au début, les troupes françaises de nos jours viennent en Italie pour jouer Molière. Jouvet en **1948**, la Comédie-Française en **1949, 1951**, et **1965**, Vilar en **1959**, la Comédie de St. Etienne en **1964**, Planchon en **1966** et **1967**, représentent des pièces de Molière en français avec grand succès.

Cette liste des représentations de Molière en Italie, malgré efforts, n'est vraisemblablement pas complète, mais elle est indicative de la présence continue de l'auteur français sur les scènes italiennes.

Molière non seulement a été joué très tôt en Italie, mais les traductions de ses pièces remontent déjà au XVIIe siècle. A l'Université de Bologne se trouve un manuscrit sûrement du XVIIe siècle qui a pour titre "Commedie del Signor de Molière tradotte da Ottaviano Annibale Giugni Stampa Fiorentino". Il contient la traduction de 31 comédies en prose. La première traduction imprimée d'une comédie est celle N. della Luna, *La Scuola delle mogli* (Bologna, 1680).

A cause du manque d'espace je vais me limiter à citer les traductions du théâtre complet ou choisi de Molière et je renvoie à Molière, *Teatro*, 2 volumes (Firenze: Sansoni, 1961) où se trouve une chronologie complète des traductions de chaque pièce.

La première traduction imprimée de toutes les pièces de Molière est celle de Nic. di Castelli (sous ce nom se cache le père Biagio Augustelli) en 4 volumes, *Le opere di G.B.P. di Molière* (Lipsia: Gledisch, 1696–98). La deuxième édition est de 1739–40. Gaspare Gozzi a signé une traduction anonyme de 24 comédies en 4 volumes, *Opere del Molière ora nuovamente tradotte nell'italiana favella* (Venezia: G. Novelli, 1756–57). Dans le recueil *Biblioteca teatrale della nazione* (Venezia, 1793–94) on trouve plusieurs comédies de Molière de même que dans *Repertorio scelto ad uso dei teatri italiani* (Milano, 1823). Pour ce dernier la traduction est de Soncini. On trouve aussi:

Molière, traduction en vers de R. Castelvecchio (R. Pullé), (Milano: Li. Ed. 1877).

Commedie scelte di Molière, traduction de A. Moretti, (Milano: Treves, 1880), 2 volumes.

Molière, *Il misantropo, Tartufo, L'avaro*, traduction de G. Brera (Milano: Il Poligono, 1947).

Molière, J. B. Poquelin, *I Capolavori del grande attore scrittore* (Torino: S.E.T., 1949).

Molière, *Commedie scelte*, traduction de S. Pons (Roma: Cremonese, 1956).

Molière, *Il teatro*, traduction par A. Moretti et F. Rigano (Editr. italiana di cultura, 1958).

La dernière traduction est celle de l'édition Sansoni que j'ai déjà citée, par C. Tumiati et A. Bartoli en 1961.

Il faut noter que les espaces d'une publication à l'autre, soit au XIXe siècle, soit au XXe sont comblés par la publication de pièces individuelles, qui sont bien nombreuses.

On ne s'est pas limité à traduire Molière dès la fin du XVIIe siècle mais aussi bien des auteurs ont essayé de l'imiter dès cette époque. Les imitateurs italiens croyaient qu'il suffisait de s'inspirer des pièces de l'auteur français, de copier les intrigues et les personnages, pour faire des oeuvres d'art, mais ils ne s'apercevaient pas que dans leurs comédies l'étude des moeurs et la satire des travers et des vices de la société restaient seulement à la surface et n'égalaient en aucune manière le génie de Molière.

Toldo trouve au XVIIe: *Il conte d'Altamura* (Firenze, 1695, Siena, 1702) d'un auteur inconnu qui ne cache pas dans la préface sont emprunt à Molière. C'est une imitation de *L'Ecole des maris*. Puis Cosimo Villifranchi qui cite comme ses sources Terrence et Ménandre pour *Hypocondriaco* (Firenze, 1695), mais dans la pièce on trouve plusieurs scènes du *Malade imaginaire*. Finalement Tommaso Stanzani qui, dans *Zelida ovvero la Scuola delle mogli* (Bologna, 1696), fait presque une copie de la pièce de Molière.

Au XVIIIe, le titre de la pièce de Cristofor Boncio parle de lui-même : *L'ammalato immaginario sotto la cura del dottor Purgon*, commedia tratta da quella di Monsu Molière et accomodata ad uso de comici italiani (Verona, 1700). Bonvincin Gioanelli traduit en venitien cette comédie en faisant quelques changements et la fait imprimer à Venise en 1701 sous son nom. Fabritio Manni écrit *La finta verità nel medico per amore* qui se trouve dans *Comedia* (Bologna, 1703), pièce très semblable au *Mariage forcé* mais avec un dénouement différent.

Trois auteurs toscans considérés comme les précurseurs de Carlo Goldoni ont aussi imité Molière. Ce sont Giovan Battista Fagiuoli (1660–1742), Girolamo Gigli (1660–1722), Iacopo Angelo Nelli (1673–1767). Fagiuoli dans ses comédies fait une analyse de caractères, mais très superficielle, ses pièces sont sans aucune philosophie. Il imite le pédant et l'avare de Molière et pour sa pièce *Inganni lodevoli* il emprunte des scènes entières de *L'Amour médecin* et du *Médecin malgré lui*. Pour *Il cicisbeo sconsolato*, il s'est inspiré de *L'Avare* et des *Fourberies de Scapin*.

Gigli emprunte à Molière la satire : il se moque de la fausse piété dans *Don Pilone ovvero il bacchettone falso* (1707) en admettant s'être inspiré du *Tartuffe*. Cette pièce est vraiment une paraphrase en prose de la comédie de Molière. Même les noms des personnages ne sont pas changés, excepté pour Orgon qui devient Monsu Buonafede et Tartuffe Don Pilone. De *L'Avare* il tire des scènes pour *La sorellina di don Pilone, ossia l'avarizia più onorata nella serva che nella padrona* (1712); pour *Il Gorgoleo*, il s'inspire de *Monsieur de Pourceaugnac*. Il écrit *Le furberie di Scapino* en admettant Molière sa source, mais il dit qu'il a ajouté du "nouveau sel" pour rendre la pièce "toute nouvelle".

Dans plusieurs pièces de Nelli on trouve des souvenirs de Molière. Il admet imiter *Les Précieuses ridicules* et *Les femmes savantes* pour *La dottoressa preziosa* mais ajoute avoir connu une femme semblable. *Le Malade imaginaire* est la source de son *Il tormentatore di se stesso*.

On arrive ainsi à Carlo Goldoni (1701–1793) que certains contemporains ont appelé "le Molière italien". De ceux qui n'étaient pas de cette opinion, Goldoni écrit dans ses *Mémoires* qu'ils étaient :

des êtres singuliers qui disoient à chacune de mes nouveautés, c'est bon, mais ce n'est pas du Molière . . . me faisaient plus d'honneur que je ne méritois; je n'avais jamais eu la prétention d'être mis en comparaison avec l'auteur François; et je savais que ceux qui prononçaient un jugement si vague et si peu motivé n'alloient au Spectacle que pour courir les loges et y faire la conversation . . . Je connoissais Molière et je savois respecter ce Maître de l'Art aussi bien que les Piémontais . . .[1]

Ailleurs Goldoni dit qu'il est "écolier de Molière", mais n'aime pas être appelé son imitateur.[2] Aujourd'hui avec plus d'objectivité on pourrait appeler Goldoni "le Molière italien"—même si la plus grande partie des critiques italiens, peut-être pour des raisons nationalistes, objecteraient cette appellation. Des rapports existent vraiment entre Molière et Goldoni. Tous deux ont été des rénovateurs, sinon des créateurs, du théâtre comique, l'un de la France et l'autre de l'Italie. Tant Molière que Goldoni ont peint la vie de la bourgeoisie et des nobles de leur temps, mais l'italien ayant un caractère optimiste, bien différent de celui de Molière, a traité avec plus d'indulgence les moeurs de son temps et les vices des hommes. Finalement on ne peut nier que dans beaucoup de pièces de Goldoni on trouve des souvenirs de Molière.

En effet plusieurs personnages du théâtre de Molière apparaissent dans les comédies de Goldoni. Harpagon est dans *La donna di maneggio*, *Il geloso avaro*, *Il vero amico*, *L'avaro fastoso*; Bélise des *Femmes savantes* est dans *Le donne di buon umore*, *Le avventure della villeggiatura*, *La sposa persiana*, *L'adulatore*, *Il vero amico*, *Il giocatore*; Tartuffe est dans *Il padre di famiglia*, *La vedova spiritosa*; Don Juan est dans *Ritorno dalla villeggiatura*, *Il vecchio bizzarro e la donna volubile*. Mais tous ces personnages deviennent plus maniérés chez Goldoni.

On trouve aussi des ressemblances entre les pièces des deux auteurs. *L'ipocondriaco* et *La serva amorosa* sont très près du *Malade imaginaire*; *Le virtuose ridicole* des *Femmes savantes*; *La finta malata* de *L'Amour mèdecin*; *Il servitor di due padroni*, *Gl'innamorati* et *Le smanie per la villeggiatura* du *Dépit*; *La conversazione* du *Misanthrope*; *Il barone Polacco interrotto nei suoi amori* du *Fâcheux* et de *Monsieur de Pourceaugnac*; *Il geloso vinto dall'avarizia* de *L'Ecole des femmes* et du *Sicilien*. Dans *Il ventaglio* on trouve des traces de *Dom Juan*, du *Malade imaginaire* et du *Dépit amoureux*.

[1] Carlo Goldoni, *Tutte le opere*, a cura di Ortolani, Vol. I (Milano: Mondadori, 1935) p. 295.
[2] *Ibid.*, p. 390.

Un contemporain de Goldoni et son rival, l'abbé Pietro Chiari a aussi puisé dans les comédies de Molière en écrivant en alexandrins. Chiari admet quelquefois ses emprunts, mais juge ses pièces meilleurs que celles qu'il a imitées. Dans *I fanatici* (1754) il copie ou traduit mot à mot des scènes entières du *Bourgeois gentilhomme*. Du *Malade imaginaire*, il fait dériver *Le sorelle rivali*. Dans plusieurs autres pièces il imite Molière, mais ses personnages sont tous des raisonneurs qui ternissent le comique de l'action.

Carlo Gozzi (1720–1806) qui s'est moqué de Chiari et de Goldoni dans le libelle *La Tartana degli influssi per l'anno bisestile 1756* en les appelant avec ironie "les nouveaux Molière", a lui-même imité *La Princesse d'Elide* avec *La principessa filosofa*.

En 1748 à Bologne un auteur anonyme publie *Il misantropo a caso maritato o sia l'orgoglio punito* en admettant dans le prologue la descendance de Molière et plus tard Giovanni De Gomerra fait de même dans la préface de *Il nuovo Tartufo* (Pisa, 1790).

On arrive ainsi au XIXe siècle et à Alberto Nota (1775–1847) qui en unissant en lui les souvenirs de Molière et de Goldoni transforme les pièces comiques en comédies larmoyantes. Les titres de certaines de ses oeuvres indiquent clairement leur source: *L'ammalato per immaginazione* et *Il nuovo ricco*. Il s'est inspiré du *Misanthrope* pour *Atrabiliare*.

Luigi Pellico, frère du fameux Silvio, imite aussi Molière avec *L'arricchito ambizioso* (*Biblioteca teatrale economica*, Vol. V, 1829) et avec *L'ipocondriaco, o sia il purgativo le Roy* (Bologna, 1825).

L'auteur romantique Vincenzo Martini (1803–62) écrit en 1853 *Il misantropo in società* (*Commedie edite e inedite*, Firenze, 1876) imitant toujours Molière, comme l'a fait aussi Angelo Brofferio (1806–66) avec *Il Tartufo* (*I miei tempi*, Vol. 8, Torino, 1904).

Au XXe siècle il est difficile de trouver des imitations de Molière, mais de nos jours on a tendance à appeler l'auteur-acteur, chef de troupe napolitain Eduardo de Filippo, le nouveau Molière. Cette appellation provient d'autres analogies entre les deux, et non pas de l'imitation.

On n'imitait pas seulement les comédies de Molière mais on les adaptait aussi à des mélodrames et à des libretti de l'Opera Buffa. Toldo a trouvé plusieurs adaptations, j'en cite quelques unes à titre d'information:

Anfitrione, tragicomedia per musica (Venezia, 1707) d'auteur anonyme (probablement Pietro Pariati) qui, cependant, dans "l'argomento" avoue les inspirations de Molière.
La confusione ne sponsali opera scenica di Monsieur Molière tradotta in

italiano (Roma, 1710). Ce n'est pas une traduction mais une imitation de *George Dandin*.

La preziosa ridicola, intermezzo musicale (Reggio Emilia 1715, Venezia 1719), avec la musique de Giuseppe Maria Orlandini.

Il matrimonio per forza, intermezzi musicali représenté à Venise en 1729 et imprimé à Naples sous le titre *Lo sposo per forza*—testo di Giuseppe Palomba, musica di Gaetano Marinelli (1792).

La maschera levata al vizio—*divertimento comico per musica* (Bologna, 1735). C'est un mélodrame inspiré du *Tartuffe* avec quelques petits changements.

L'amor pittore (1740) mis en musique par Davide Perez.

Plusieurs *librettisti* ont aussi aimé faire de la "contaminatio" en puisant dans différentes comédies. Ils croyaient ainsi de faire des pièces originales. Giovanni Bertati est l'un d'entre eux. Il unit *Le Cocu imaginaire* au *Bourgeois gentilhomme* pour écrire *Re de' Mamalucchi, dramma giocoso in musica* (Varese, 1788). Il écrit aussi *L'avaro, dramma giocoso per musica* (Firenze, 1777) où Harpagon devient Orgasmo, mais beaucoup de scènes sont reprises de Molière.

Il medico a suo dispetto avec la musique de Giuseppe Foppa (Roma, 1805) est un exemple du XIXe siècle des nombreux libretti avec le même titre. *Tartuffe* aussi a été adapté à plusieurs libretti de ce siècle.

Molière n'a pas seulement inspiré des dramaturges et des *librettisti* avec ses pièces mais, lui-même, sa vie, ont été et sont encore aujourd'hui sujet de comédies ou de drames. La première pièce sur lui en italien est une traduction: *Ombra di Molière* de Brécourt qui est incluse dans la première traduction des oeuvres complète de Molière en 1698. En 1756–57 la troupe italienne, Madebachi, joue à Turin *Moglier* (*sic*) et *Moglier geloso* (*sic*) qui étaient probablement des pièces sur Molière. Carlo Goldoni lui-même écrit *Molière* en cinq actes et en vers représentée à Turin en 1751. Goldoni dans ses *Mémoires* déclare écrire cette pièce pour montrer son grand respect pour Molière.[3] Il s'inspire de deux anecdotes de la vie de l'auteur français, l'une est son mariage avec la présumée fille de la Béjart et l'autre la défense de *Tartuffe*. Des critiques voient dans cette pièce Goldoni se cachant derrière Molière pour défendre son théâtre qui avait été ataqué par ses contemporains.

L'abbé Pietro Chiari écrit aussi une comédie en cinq actes et en vers, *Molière marito geloso* (Bologna 1759). Gaetano Barbieri traduit la pièce de Gesnoul et Naudet *Molière in famiglia* (Milano 1823). Antonio Belotti écrit un drame en quatre actes en prose *Molière* qui est dans *Poesie e Prose*

---

[3] *Ibid.*, p. 296.

(Bergamo, 1879), et Lodovico Muratori écrit *Il precettore di Molière* en un acte qui se trouve dans *Commedie* (Bari, 1902). Une pièce inédite représentée à Turin en 1902, *La fine di Molière* est de G. Ianelli. *Molière e sua moglie*, comédie en trois actes de Gerolamo Rovetta est représentée à Rome en 1909 et imprimée à Milan en 1911, et *Molière*, comédie en quatre actes de Giuseppe Calvino, se trouve dans *Commedie* (Bitonto, 1915).

La dernière pièce sur Molière que j'ai trouvée a été jouée avec grand succès à Gênes en 1971: "Il tartufo ovvero vita, amori, autocensura e morte in scena del Signor Molière nostro contemporaneo" libre adaptation de Luigi Squarzina—lui-même dramaturge—de *Tartuffe* et de *Cabala dei Bigotti, ovvero vita del Signor Molière* de Michail Bulgakov, auteur russe censuré et persécuté par Staline. Squarzina dans cette pièce analyse le rapport entre le pouvoir de l'Etat et le droit à l'existence de l'intellectuel. C'est une satire très féroce contre le moralisme de l'Etat qui décide ce qui est bien et ce qui est mal sans aucun point de référence au bien ou au mal, mais c'est aussi une triste constatation de la soumission de l'écrivain au pouvoir constitué pour continuer à vivre. C'est l'histoire des difficultés de Molière avec la censure pour représenter *Tartuffe* mais la pièce elle-même est jouée puisque tout se passe pendant les répétitions. Molière dans la pièce, malgré les concessions qu'il est obligé de faire, reste l'intellectuel, héroïque et pur.

Après les représentations, les traductions, les imitations et les pièces qui ont comme protagoniste Molière, il ne reste qu'à examiner la critique que l'auteur français a reçue en Italie, critique qui n'a pas toujours coincidé avec l'accueil enthousiaste du grand public.

Les premières rèactions des critiques, dit érudits, furent plutôt négatives. Les savants italiens, imbus des préjugés classiques, ne pouvaient pas admirer des pièces comme *Le Cocu imaginaire*, *Le Médecin malgré lui*, qui rappelaient trop *la commedia dell'arte* qu'il voulaient chasser des scènes. Les gens d'Eglise, les érudits de l'époque ne pouvaient voir d'un oeil trop favorable *Tartuffe*, ou *Dom Juan*. Ainsi Gio. Maria Crescimbene (1663–1728) dans *Istoria della Volgar Poesia* se montre nettement contraire à Molière en reprenant les jugements de Boileau et de Baillet; Lodovico Antonio Muratori fait de même dans *Della perfetta poesia italiana* (Modena, 1706).

Scipione Maffei dans *De teatri antichi e moderni* (Verona, 1753) dit que dans le théâtre de Molière le vice l'emporte et on y tourne en ridicule l'honnêteté. Giulio Cesare Becelli dans la préface de *Teatro di Scipione*

Maffei (Verona, 1730) donne aussi raison à Baillet et définit le théâtre de Molière comme un spectacle des vices heureux et triomphants. Francesco Saverio Quadrio (1695–1756) dans *Della storia della ragione di ogni poesia* accuse Molière de plagiat et d'immoralité.

La première critique favorable à l'auteur français est celle de Francesco Algarotti (1712–64). Il parle de l'oeuvre immortelle de Molière dans "Saggio sopra la lingua francese" du 10 mars 1750. Le père Giovan Battista Roberti (1719–56) embrasse dans la louange Molière et Goldoni.

On fait un retour à la critique négative avec Carlo Gozzi dans *Opere* (Venezia, 1772), mais, dix ans plus tard, l'abbé Saverio Bettinelli place le nom de Molière à coté de ceux d'Aristophane, de Plaute et de Terrence dans *Opere* (Venezia, 1782). A Naples, Signorelli, studieux du théâtre, dans *Storia critica dei teatri antichi e moderni* (Napoli, 1774), dit que Molière analyse l'homme d'aprés nature et d'aprés son temps. A propos des emprunts de l'auteur français, il ajoute qu'il a su embellir les inventions des autres, les animant d'un souffle qui fait disparaître les originaux devant ses copies.

Le Jésuite espagnol Giovanni Andrés, établi en Italie, écrit dans *Delorigine, progresso e stato attuale d'ogni letteratura* (Parma, 1795) que Molière est le vrai père du théâtre comique français. Selon Andrés, l'auteur français a remplacé la vulgarité par des situations vraisemblables et naturelles, par des dialogues spirituels, par des caractères bien formés en donnant d'agréables leçons de morale, de bon sens, et une philosophie aussi utile que douce. Pour ce Jésuite espagnol *Tartuffe* et *Les Femmes savantes* sont les chefs-d'oeuvre de Molière.

En 1780, on a de nouveau un jugement négatif sur Molière, celui de Girolamo Tiraboschi qui dans *Storia della letteratura italiana* (Modena, 1780) dit que Molière a seulement imité, mais c'est un jugement isolé. Désormais la critique officielle aussi a accepté l'auteur français et reconnu son génie.

A partir du XIXe siècle jusqu'à 1920, la liste des livres et des articles sur Molière est de dix pages dans Cesare Levi, *Studi Molierani* (Palermo: Sandron, 1922) et il est impossible de la reproduire ici. Après cette date, les livres suivants sont dédiés à Molière:

F. Picco, *Molière* (Firenze: Le Monnier, 1930).
M. Apollonio, *Molière* (Brescia: Morcelliana, 1942).
L. Sciliano, *Molière* (Milano-Venezia: Montuoro, 1947).
Molière, dans la série *I Giganti* avec la collaboration de plusieurs spécialistes (Milano: Mondadori, 1969).

Pour des études dans des oeuvres de caractères général, je cite entre autres:

Giacomo Prampolini, *Storia Universale della letteratura*, Vol. 4 (Torino: Utet, 1950).
Silvio D'Amico, *Storia del teatro drammatico* Vol. 2 (Milano: Garzanti, 1950).
Vito Pandolfi, *Storia Universale del teatro drammatico*, Vol. I. (Torino: Utet, 1964).
G. Macchia, *La letteratura francese*, tone 2 (Firenze: Sansoni, Accademia, 1970).

Finalement, pour conclure je vais citer quelques jugements de nos contemporains sur Molière. Giovanni Brera dans l'introduction à *Il misantropo, Tartufo, l'Avaro* (Milano: Poligono, 1947) dit que Molière est le "peuple" et il représente l'instinct pûr, l'instinct du peuple. Selon Brera, à Clermont, Molière se sera trouvé comme le prolétaire d'aujourd'hui, envoyé au lycée de "gras bourgeois", et plus tard dans son théâtre il ne s'est pas arrêté à la satire du personnage, mais il a visé une classe sociale; il a mis à nu l'aristocratie pour éclairer le peuple.

Pour Silvio d'Amico dans *Storia del teatro drammatico* déjà cité, Molière est le représentant de l'esprit laïque, donc bourgeois, le défenseur, l'avocat de la morale naturelle en opposition à la morale chrétienne. Pandolfi dans *Storia Universale del teatro drammatico*, aussi cité, dit que Molière est le fils typique de la bourgeoisie qui a exalté la force du bon sens et qui a donné à la bourgeoisie la conscience de sa propre dignité. Dans *I Giganti* de Mondadori dédié à Molière et déjà cité on dit que l'antirhétorique, la foi dans la "raison", l'exaltation de la jeunesse "contestatrice" donnent à Molière une place parmi les avant-gardes de notre temps.

La divergence de ces jugements a peu d'importance, l'essentiel est que Molière reste jusqu'à nos jours vivant en Italie.

THEATER OF THE THEATER:
MOLIÈRE AND PIRANDELLO

A. Richard Sogliuzzo

Over two centuries separate the careers of Molière (1622–73) and Luigi Pirandello (1867–1936), yet they shared comparable ideas regarding the art of theater, and both were influenced by the *Commedia dell 'arte*, as is evidenced in two of their plays: *L'Impromptu de Versailles*,[1] and *Questa sera si recita a soggetto*. The technique of improvised theater, characteristic of the *Commedia*, is inherent in both works. They are structured like improvisations: the action consists of the actors attempting to create their own play in the absence of a formal script. A number of the characters of the inner plays in both these works are stock types, originating in the cuckolded husbands, jealous lovers, foolish noblemen, virtuous and licentious ladies of the *Commedia*. Pirandello maintained that the *Commedia* was one of the most pervasive influences on the European theater (including his own), but stated that "Molière alone was frank enough to admit: *'je prends mon bien où je le trouve'* in answer to those who remarked that he perhaps had gone too far in appropriating not only situations and characters but entire scenes from our *Commedia dell 'arte*."[2]

Both *L'Impromptu* and *Questa sera* employ the convention of "theater of the theater," whereby the audience observes not so much the performance of an inner play, but the actual process of realizing that play on the stage. "Theater of the theater" has varied in its use throughout the history of the theater, from a simple farcical situation of putting on a play as in *A Midsummer's Night's Dream* to its complex metaphorical function in Genet's *The Blacks*, a cryptic fusion of reality and illusion.

L'Impromptu represents a simpler use of the convention: a farce based on a rehearsal in which Molière burlesques the acting styles of his rivals. *Questa sera* is another of Pirandello's dialectical explorations of the nature

---

[1] *L'Impromptu* and *La Critique de l'Ecole des femmes* were written during the Comic War (1663–65), and represent Molière's defense against the attacks of his enemies regarding his art and his morality.

[2] "Introduction to The Italian Theater," Anne Paolucci, trans., *The Genius of the Italian Theater*, ed. Eric Bentley (New York: Mentor, 1964), p. 21.

of reality and illusion, but also representing his quintessential attempt at analytically dissecting the art of the theater, providing a basis of comparison to *L'Impromptu*.[3] Plays employing the convention of "theater of the theater" are particularly valuable to historians, for they provide insights, however fragmentary, into the theatrical practices of their ages. Despite obvious differences in form and content, reflecting two centuries of dramatic evolution, *L'Impromptu* and *Questa sera* reveal surprising similarities in the playwrights' theatrical theories and practices, as well as common problems experienced in producing a play.

L'Impromptu occurs during a rehearsal; *Questa sera* begins as an evening of improvised theater but degenerates into a disordered rehearsal before a confused audience. As the plays begin, both directors are in a state of agitation. Hinkfuss, the director of *Questa sera*, rushes down the center aisle to correct the sound and light cues that have gone awry and perplexed the audience: "Ma che gong! Ma che gong! Chi ha ordinato di sonare il gong? Lo commandero io, il gong guando sarà tempo." Anxious to get his rehearsal started, Molière orders his actors on stage: "Allons donc, Messiers et Mesdames, vous moquez-vous avec votre longeur, et ne voulez-vous pas tous venir ici? La peste soit des gens. Holà ho!"

After his opening remarks to the audience, Hinkfuss is challenged by his leading actor, who refuses to be summoned by the director: "Ma no signore! Lei non presenterà me al pubblico che mi conosce. Non son mica un burattino, io, nelle sue mani." These early strident moments quickly prepare us for a major conflict in both plays—actors versus directors; they also provide Molière and Pirandello the opportunity of revealing difficulties sometimes encountered in working with actors. Molière's "Ah! les étranges animaux à conduire que des comédiens," resembles Pirandello's description of the rehearsals for the world premiere of *Questa sera* at Koenigsberg, Germany: "They are fine actors, of course, but it takes all my energy to make them understand and do the correct thing. And then there is the question of temperament. Here, they scream at the top of their lungs where we would hardly whisper, and they whisper where we would scream."[4]

---

[3] *Questa sera* is the last work of Pirandello's theatrical trilogy which he defined as "una trilogia del teatro nel treatro." "Premessa dell'autore ai tre lavori raccolti nel 1° volume dell' edizione definitiva del suo teatro," *Maschere nude*, ed., Manlio Lo Vecchio-Musti (Milano: Mondadori, 1958).

[4] Letter, April 6, 1930, *The Mountain Giant and Other Plays*, trans., Marta Abba (New York, Crown, 1958), p. 22.

Molière's *L'Impromptu* dramatizes an age old theatrical dilemma: the inability of actors to perceive the director's responsibility to an entire production because of their intense concentration on their own roles. Anxious because his company is to perform before the King in two hours, Molière orders his actors to begin the rehearsal. Since they are still memorizing their lines, they refuse, accusing him of being selfish and insensitive: "Vous n'êtes pas à plaindre: car, ayant fait la pièce, vous n'avez pas peur d'y manquer." Molière replies: "Ne comptez-vous pour rien l'inquiétude d'un succès qui ne regarde que moi seul?" Indifferent to Hinkfuss's desire to unite the production according to his personal vision, his actors demand to live their roles free of his direction. Admittedly, the problem in *Questa sera* is more complex than in *L'Impromptu*: an artistic anarchy in which each actor seeks fulfillment at the expense of the other. Molière's troupe wishes to comply, but on its own terms.

In both works, Molière and Pirandello poke fun at themselves. Molière's depiction of himself as the anxious playwright was perhaps an attempt to counter the criticism of his enemies that he was arrogant and egocentric. Instead, he characterizes himself as a simple, practical, hardworking man of the theater, naturally anxious about having to perform, on short notice, before as demanding a king as Louis XIV. Hinkfuss is partly Pirandello's self-parody. His lengthy lecture contains Pirandello's own theatrical philosophy, confirming the criticism of his detractors that he was excessively cerebral and verbose. Pirandello depicts himself as being desperately in love with the sound of his own language, and slyly gives his critics an overdose of the medicine they deplore.

Hinkfuss is also a caricature of super-directors such as Max Reinhardt[5] (1873–1943) who tended to use the playwright's script as a springboard for their own imaginative fancies. Convinced that directors are superior to dramatists, Hinkfuss merely utilizes one of Pirandello's short stories rather than a play: "Ho in questo rotoletto di poche pagine tutto quello che mi serve. Quasi niente. Una novelletta, o poco più, appena qua e là dialogata da uno scrittore a voi non ignoto." Although Pirandello demanded strict fidelity to the text, he acknowledged that in performance a play took on a unique identity: "no longer the work of the writer [which, after all, can always be preserved in some other way,] but an act of life,

---

[5] Pirandello, however, maintained the greatest respect for Reinhardt: Hinkfuss is merely an exaggerated example of what can happen when a director with a rich imagination loses sight of the author's work.

realized on the stage from one moment to the next, with the cooperation of an audience that must find satisfaction in it."[6]

In contrast to Pirandello's rigid adherence to the text, Molière is quite liberal, advising his actors to ad lib, since the play is written in prose, and they are familiar with its plot: which advice only intensifies their insecurity. Molière seems to be implying that he would welcome a Commedia-like performance from his actors: the characters are all types they have previously performed; the plot is established; all that is required is the actors' wits to create the dialogue. Pirandello's stage directions at the beginning of *Questa sera* ironically apply to Molière's problem in *L'Impromptu*: "Di mio . . . ma dove son oggi gli attori capaci di recitare a soggetto, come al loro tempo quei comici indiavolati della commedia dell'arte."[7]

The reluctance of Molière's troupe to improvise is not in the least evidenced by the actors in *Questa sera*, who are eager to have on their lips those lines that must rise from the depths of their characters, with action and gestures that are completely "natural"—echoing the beliefs of the naturalistic school of acting, particularly the school of Constantin Stanislavsky, with its reliance on improvisation as a means of training actors. However, Pirandello never believed in the possible success of a completely improvised theater (he held that there was premeditation in in the *Commedia*), and this is confirmed in *Questa sera*. The actors are thwarted in their attempts to live their roles by Hinkfuss's continual interruptions, demanding that they keep to the plot, or wait for some special scenic effect. Chasing him from the stage, the actors begin to improvise, but genuine emotion soon imbues art with life's chaos: they begin fighting amongst themselves. Ultimately, like Moliere's actors, they too demand a formal script: "Ma noi non siamo qui per questa, sa! Noi siamo qui per-recitare, imparate a memoria . . . ci vuole l'autore." Thus *Questa sera* is a formally written drama affirming Pirandello's conviction of the futility of improvised theater. Molière's actors are saved from having to improvise by the arrival of the King's messenger, informing them that Louis would be satisfied with one of their works already in repertory. Whether Molière would actually have permitted an improvised performance as suggested

---

[6] Bentley, p. 28.

[7] Pirandello's statement is even more relevant when we consider that Molière shared the Salle du Petit Bourbon with Scaramouche and his company of Italian actors. Molière admired and was influenced by Scaramouche. See John Palmer, *Molière* (New York, Benjamin Blom, 1970), pp. 130–133.

in *L'Impromptu* is uncertain, for there is no historical evidence to support such an idea. However, it would seem that under the exigencies of the moment dramatized in *L'Impromptu*, Molière might very possibly have expected his actors to rise to the occasion.

Although Pirandello was scrupulous in matters regarding the text, he respected an actor's artistic integrity, allowing him considerable freedom to experiment, willingly accepting his innovations if they enriched his characterizations. Apparently, Molière also respected his actors. In *L'Impromptu* Molière is demanding but never tyrannical, knowing precisely what he wants, but flexible and diplomatic in achieving results: flattering Mlle Du Parc to convince her to play "an affected, simpering lady," while politely but firmly correcting Brécourt's line reading. Molière reads the passage for Brécourt, but the actor interrupts him, stating "c'est assez," which can be interpreted merely as a statement of fact, or that he resents having an entire passage read for him; either is possible in the arduous process of preparing a show. Sensitive, temperamental, at times childish are the characteristics of the actors in *L'Impromptu* and *Questa sera*.

Despite the temperamental difficulties encountered with the actors, Molière is more successful than Hinkfuss, actually Pirandello's example of a bad director, one who minimizes the playwright and actors, while over-emphasizing scenic effects. Comparable to Molière's company, Pirandello's *Teatro d'arte* was a theater dedicated to playwrights and actors, not directors. Pirandello, like Molière in *L'Impromptu*, provided his actors with very provocative analyses of their roles, and his readings of the script were illuminating. However, unlike Molière, he was not an accomplished actor, and was incapable of demonstrating stage business and movement: this was usually done by one of his assistants.[8] If *L'Impromptu* is an accurate example of a Molière rehearsal, his productions must have had a consistency of style in both movement and manner that reflected his own; there is a touch of choreography in his direction.

Both Molière and Pirandello esteemed "natural" acting. In his mockery of the florid or bombastic styles of Montfleury, Mlle Beauchâteau, Hauteroche, and DeVilliers, Molière echoes Hamlet's advice to the Players: "O, it offends me to the soul to hear a robustious periwig pated fellow tear a passion to tatters, to very rags." In his discussion of the plot for a

[8] Descriptions of Pirandello's practices as a director were obtained from personal interviews with actors who worked with him in the 1920's and 1930's: Marta Abba, Eduardo de Filippo, Rina Franchetti, Carlo Tamberlani, June–July, 1971.

"Comedy of Players," Molière describes the Young Actor reading the King's part from *Nicomède* in a manner "le plus naturellment qu'il aurait été possible," displeasing the playwright, who then demonstrates his preference for Montfleury's style because he knew how to "attire l'approbation, et fait faire le brouhaha." When performing tragedy, Molière like Pirandello, sought a quiet dignity and controlled passion rather than any display of overt histrionics.[9] Pirandello's veneration of Eleonora Duse indicated his preference for actors capable of expressing powerful emotions with simplicity and conviction. However, since styles change over the centuries, it is impossible to equate Molière's and Pirandello's concepts of "natural" acting.

Consistent with their preference for "natural" acting, both Molière and Pirandello eschewed actors who relied on stock mannerisms or conventions, demanding that an actor internalize a role to make it more convincing. Molière's advice to Mlle De Briet, "entrez bien dans ce caracters," parallels Pirandello's belief that an actor "deve immedesimarsi con la sua creatura, fino a sentirle com'essa sente se stessa."[10] Both playwrights, however, maintained a distinction between art and life: actors were to get inside their roles, not themselves. When Mlle Du Parc refuses to play the role of an affected lady because she herself is so unaffected, Moliere tells her: "Cela est vrai; et c'est en quoi vous faites mieux voir que vous êtes excellente comédienne, de bien représenter un personnage qui est si contraire à votre humeur." This could have been mere flattery, but her personal qualities were unimportant. Molière expected her to have the objectivity and technical wherewithal to create a convincing characterization: "cela vous contraindra un peu, mais qu'y faire? Il faut parfois se faire violence."

Pirandello makes the same point by example in *Questa sera*: immersed in their roles, the actors lose their objectivity; reality and illusion are confused. Real emotion prevails; technique is abandoned; art suffers. In his essay on acting Pirandello stated: "devono essere intesi nell'arte l'attività pratica, la tecnica, i mezzi comunicativi della rappresentazione, il fatto fisico in rapport al fatto estetico."[11] Molière continually empha-

---

[9] However, Molière's detractors found considerable artificiality in his acting. See René Bray, *Molière: Homme de Théâtre* (Paris, Mercure, 1954), p. 184. Moreover, Molière's acting, particularly when performing farce, must have entailed comic exaggeration that could not be classified as "natural."

[10] "Illustratori, attori, e traduttori," *Saggi, poesi, scritti varii*, ed., Manlio Lo Vecchio-Musti (Milano, Mondadori, 1965), p. 215.

[11] *Saggi*, p. 211.

sizes technique in *L'Impromptu*: his actors are to observe life carefully, and then transfer it to the stage in theatrical terms. He advises Mlle Du Parc to wiggle her hips a little when playing an affected lady, and De Brécourt to play the comic marquis with the air of a stylish dandy, combing his wigs and humming a little tune. His actors obviously possessed the necessary technique to execute such physical mannerisms successfully.

Pirandello was avowedly a more philosophical playwright than Molière, a fact which he admitted was as much a fault as a virtue—a fault humorously depicted in the character of Hinkfuss, who proclaimed much of Pirandello's own theatrical philosophy. And it is Hinkfuss's philosophizing rather than directing that proves his inferiority to Molière, the theatrical practioner concentrating on the play and the actors. In *L'Impromptu*, Molière provides a sound lesson in directing comedy: laughter results from a convincing interaction of ridiculous characters, utterly serious in their absurdity.

Analogously, Pirandello realized that an audience was intellectually aroused through a truthful performance, a convincing interaction of characters in conflict. His characters were human beings, not philosophical abstractions, and he rarely discussed the philosophical meaning of a play with his actors, concentrating instead on explaining character motivation. Questions of philosophical interpretation arose whenever an actor misinterpreted a line, and Pirandello then stopped the actors and stated: "No, that idea is not clear! This is the meaning I intend." Molière was also a poet-philosopher, but even when using the stage as a platform, he knew that an audience had to be entertained, as clearly stated by Dorante in *La Critique de L'Ecole des femmes*; "Je voudrais bien savior si la grande règle de toutes les règles n'est pas de plaire, et si une pièce de théâtre qui a attrapé son but n'as pas suivi un bon chemin." Pirandello initially resented actors and directors for debasing the playwright's text, but then realized what Molière knew instinctively, stating: "The original text remains intact for anyone who may want to reread it at home, for his own edification; those who want to be entertained by it will go to the theater."[12]

In *L'Impromptu* and *Questa sera* Molière and Pirandello celebrate the essence of theater: to entertain and enlighten by combining the spontaneous and accidental art of the live performer with the ordered and predetermined art of the playwright.

[12] Bentley, p. 28.

CONTEMPORARY TRANSLATIONS AND STAGINGS OF MOLIÈRE'S PLAYS IN SPAIN

Marion P. Holt

The works of Molière have been performed with some frequency on the contemporary Spanish stage by both professional and experimental groups, and important new translations have been made of several of his plays. Of the non-Spanish dramatists of the past, only Shakespeare has commanded a comparable interest among creators of theater and translators in Spain. The productions of *El avaro* (*L'Avare*) in 1960 and in 1971, utilizing the acclaimed version by the playwright José López Rubio, and of *El Tartufo* (*Le Tartuffe*) in 1969, in a much discussed and controversial adaptation by the drama critic and translator Enrique Llovet, rank high on the list of dramatic offerings seen in Madrid in recent years. The Llovet adaptation of *Las mujeres sabias* (*Les Femmes Savantes*) was also favorably received by critics and audiences in 1967, and a revival was presented in 1972.[1]

Both the 1960 and 1971 stagings of *El avaro* were under the supervision of José Tamayo, the director of the national Teatro Español; and the noted classical actor Carlos Lemos performed the role of Harpagon in both years. The translator, López Rubio, has been a prominent figure in the post-war theatrical life of Spain as the author of some eighteen original plays and as the adaptor of numerous foreign works, ranging from the dramas of Arthur Miller to the comedies of Molière and Oscar Wilde. One of his earliest adaptations was a version of *El burgués gentilhombre* (*Le Bourgeois Gentilhomme*) which was performed in Madrid in 1948. At that time Spanish theater had shown few signs of the revitalization to which López Rubio himself was to make a personal contribution in the next decade.[2]

---

[1] The productions cited are the major ones, based on important new translations, and do not represent the totality of contemporary performances of Molière's plays in Spain. Other works performed include *Le Médecin malgré lui*, *Le Malade imaginaire*, and *Sganarelle*.

[2] Since 1950 there has been a gradual but notable improvement in all aspects of theatrical production in Spain. Although pre-censorship still prevails, the possibilities for a significant dramatic statement are far better than in the early post-civil war years.

The more recent version of *L'Avare* may be considered a model of how a translator with a fine sensitivity to nuances of speech can re-create a classic work from another language with consistency of style, intelligibility, and respect for the original. In an *antecrítica* which appeared in the Madrid daily, *ABC*, on the occasion of the première of the revival of *El avaro*, López Rubio wrote: "A while back, a provincial newspaper reproached me for fidelity in another translation of Molière. If fidelity is one of the most complete and difficult proofs of love, I'll say that I've put love for this legitimate ancestor of all the comic authors of the world into each passage from the original and I've sought with utmost care the equivalent expressions . . . to give an honest copy of *L'Avare*. Whether or not I've succeeded is another matter."[3] During rehearsals of the production, the Spanish playwright had said more concerning his fidelity to Molière. "I believe that if one translates Molière, one has to end up with Molière . . . . The opposite would be a betrayal that I have not wanted to risk. There is a retouching here and there, and I have even added a few lines to satisfy the demands of the action or because they came to my pen and I couldn't resist the temptation to include them."[4]

A close comparison of the published text of *El avaro*[5] and the original French of Molière reveals that López Rubio has indeed made a faithful version without producing a slavish duplicate in Spanish. His treatment might appropriately be called "traditional," in that his re-creation does not attempt to remove the play from the period of its composition by using anachronisms or intentional allusions to contemporary situations as Llovet has done in his *El Tartufo*. But the playwright-translator has not hesitated to expand or contract speeches discreetly when such modification does not alter the spirit of the original, and he has supplied some appropriate stage directions of his own. López Rubio's touch is most apparent in the title role of the play, where Harpagon's obsession is underscored with a line or an action added by the translator. For example, in Act IV, Scene ii, of the Spanish version, Harpagon attempts to take back the ring that he has presented to Marianne—a touch that is in keeping with the miser's nature. At the end of the play (Act V, Scene vi), López Rubio has indicated actions for Harpagon that lend a telling visual effect.

---

[3] José López Rubio, "Antecrítica," *ABC*, 2 April 1971, p. 69. For the benefit of the general reader I have translated all statements taken from Spanish publications.

[4] Angel Laborda, "*El avaro* de Molière, en versión de López Rubio," *ABC*, 2 April 1971, p. 71.

[5] *El avaro*, Colección Teatro No. 263 (Madrid: Escelicer, 1960).

In the original, Harpagon simply states that he is leaving to examine the *cassette* which contains his wealth. In the Spanish translation, Flèche comes onstage with the box, which he places on the floor; he then exits, and Harpagon kneels down before the box, opens it, and murmurs some unintelligible words. As the plays ends, the audience observes him running his fingers through the coins, caressing and kissing them, and letting them fall over his head as if he wanted to cover himself with money.

In the dialogue of *El avaro*, López Rubio maintains a sense of period without producing stilted speech. In fact, the lines are remarkably fluid and speakable—qualities characteristic of his own works for the stage. The third person singular *usted* (you) of modern Spanish is eschewed for the second person formal *vos* of classical Spanish, and the familiar *tu* is used on other occasions (where Molière has used *vous*) in order to conform to Spanish usage. However, this does not result in any verb forms that are unfamiliar in everyday speech (although the second person plural is never used singularly in modern Spanish).

After the première of *El avaro* in March 1960, the outspoken critic José Monleón wrote in *Primer Acto*: "Here is an example of 'comic theater' that is worth the bother. The presence of *El avaro* lends dignity to the theatrical fare of Madrid . . ."[6] And a few months later, when the production reopened in the fall, he added: "The version of López Rubio is good; the settings by Richart respectable, in the tradition of the Comédie-Française, and the work of Carlos Lemos has splendid moments . . . . What great theater Molière is!"[7]

Whereas the plays adapted by López Rubio are from the prose works of Molière, Llovet's two translations are based on verse plays which pose additional problems of fidelity. Several contemporary English versions of Molière works have demonstrated that successful renderings in verse can be achieved, but Llovet has elected to use prose in both of his efforts. His translation of *Les Femmes savantes* is more conservative than his later, controversial *El Tartufo*. Like López Rubio he uses the archaic *vos* in *Las mujeres sabias*, and a feeling of period is generally retained even when the dialogue itself has a modern flavor. In an introduction which accompanies the published text of the play, Llovet has noted that his translation is "respectful with the plot, the intrigue, the structure of the situations and the characters, and disrespectful with the language, which is

---

[6] "Dos meses de teatro en Madrid," *Primer Acto*, No. 13 (March-April 1960), p. 53.
[7] "El teatro en el mes de octubre," *Primer Acto*, No. 17 (Nov. 1960), p. 48.

rather contemporary."[8] However, the translator's statement should not be read too literally, for the dialogue of *Las mujeres sabias* is a reasonably faithful prose rendering of Molière's verse.

The Llovet *El Tartufo* opened at the Teatro de la Comedia on October 3, 1969, and played to capacity audiences for eight months. Federico Sainz de Robles, in his annual survey of Spanish theater, observed that the première was quite possibly the theatrical event of the year in Madrid.[9] The production was directed by Adolfo Marsillach, a relatively young actor-director who began his career as a juvenile performer some two decades ago and who is now considered one of Spain's finest talents. Marsillach also essayed the title role of the play. The quality of the production was such that it attracted considerable interest beyond the environs of the Spanish capital. The French motion picture director François Truffaut attended a performance with a copy of the original Molière in hand. Afterwards he declared himself in agreement with the staging—although at the beginning he had been surprised by the unusually brisk pace and animated movements which were quite different from the style of the Comédie-Française. Truffaut also predicted success for the production if it reached Paris.[10]

The première of *El Tartufo* triggered an immediate debate over the implications of certain allusions and *claves* in the dialogue as well as elements of the staging. Marsillach had attempted to destroy the conventional relationship of audience and actors in several ways. Before each performance the actors moved through the aisles as they put on the costumes for their roles and sang a satirical song, "*La canción de los ejecutivos*" ("The Song of the Executives"), which had originated a few years earlier in Argentina and which sharply criticised the contemporary breed of organization men.[11] The same song recurred between certain scenes of the play and at the end of the performance when the actors removed their costumes in the presence of the audience. Another innovation of the director was to give to Dorine the function of stage director within the play, to indicate light cues and movements—a further attempt to alter the

---

[8] *Las mujeres sabias*, Colección Teatro No. 571 (Madrid: Escelicer, 1968), Introducción, p. 6.

[9] *Teatro español 1969–70* (Madrid: Aguilar 1971), p. xxiv.

[10] Enrique Llovet, A. Marsillach, M. Diez Crespo, L. Nuñez Ladeveze, "Debate en torno a los valores teatrales y las significaciones del último *Tartufo*," *Primer Acto*, No. 118 (Mar. 1970), pp. 11–12.

[11] The complete text of "La canción de los ejecutivos" is included in *El Tartufo*, Colección Teatro, No. 641 (Madrid: Escelicer, 1970), pp. 9–10.

relationship of viewer and performer. (At other times the lights changed by themselves, as if a kind of invisible destiny was aiding the evil plans of Tartuffe.)[12]

Although the actual setting of the play remains in seventeenth-century France, the language of this Spanish version is essentially contemporary, and Llovet has abandoned the *vos* form of address he had employed in *Las mujeres sabias* in favor of the more modern *usted*. In the dialogue there are allusions to which audiences were quick to give political interpretations. For example, Llovet uses the word *ejecutivo* (executive) early in the play (Act I, Scene i) to describe Tartuffe, linking him with the satirical song which serves as a kind of prologue. Later, where Molière has Dorine remark on Orgon's courage while "serving his prince" (Act I, Scene ii), Llovet's Dorina tells us that Orgon has demonstrated bravery during the *guerra civil* (civil war)—a reference certain to strike a responsive note in the minds of a Spanish audience. In the same scene, Tartuffe is referred to as *nuestro espiritual ejecutivo* (our spiritual executive). Yet in Act I, Scene iv, we are reminded that we are in the seventeenth century by the retention of the reference to bleeding as a remedy for Elmire's headache.

In Act II, Scene iii, Marianne's line, *"Contre un père absolu que veux-tu que je fasse?"* ("What do you expect me to do against an unbending father?"), becomes in the Llovet version, *"¿Y qué se puede hacer frente a un padre que ha nacido para dictador?"* ("And how can one oppose a father born to be a dictator?"). Even if the line is not intended to link Orgon with any particular individual in contemporary history, the final word *dictador* does carry unavoidable associations. The lines of *El Tartufo* contain numerous other calculated phrasings of this type, especially in reference to, or in the speeches of, Tartuffe himself. Since Marsillach had instructed the actors to emphasize certain words in performance, it is hardly surprising that the public saw in the production a conscious attempt to satirize or criticize Generalisimo Franco, the technocrats of the Opus Dei, the peculiar church-state relationship in Spain, or the political uncertainties of the Spaniards in general. But Llovet has suggested—perhaps defensively—that his *Tartufo* might well be interpreted as being anti-Pompidou in France, or anti-Perón in Argentina;[13] and Marsillach maintains that there was no intention to associate the character of Tartuffe himself with any actual person. "Señor Tartuffe is not the head of

---

[12] Described by Marsillach in "Debate . . . del último *Tartufo*," p. 13.
[13] "Debate . . . del último *Tartufo*," p. 27.

anything, he is an individual who acts in his way. And wherever he turns up, we should oppose him."[14]

The polemic which accompanied the presentation of *El Tartufo* in Madrid undoubtedly helped to fill the theater for months; however, this unusual public response to Molière in modern speech does not obscure the virtues of the excellent but more traditional re-creations of other plays of Molière by both Llovet and López Rubio. What has been demonstrated in Spain in recent years by López Rubio, Tamayo, Llovet, Marsillach, and other talented professionals of the theater is that Molière's works retain their vitality and meaning for a twentieth-century audience and that they may even serve to focus attention on political, religious, or social conditions peculiar to our own time.

[14] "Debate . . . ," p. 24.

Molière, England
and Scandinavia

The topic of this section brings immediately to mind two vast problems in the establishment of Molière's patrimony: his relationship to the comedy of the Restoration period and his putative influence on Holberg. To attack these problems, in the face of a large and sometimes strict body of scholarly pronouncements, is a task of reduction and synthesis.

John Wilcox's The Relationship of Molière to Restoration Comedy *(1938) remains the study that must be taken as a point of departure for scholars looking into the effect of Molière on Dryden, Etherege, Congreve, Wycherley, Farquhar, and others of the period. Frank J. Kearful's essay, the first of this section, includes, in addition to an assessment of Molière among the English from 1660 until 1737, a sensible evaluation of the whole question of influence. His remarks, while proceeding from Wilcox, are appropriate in general for most of the essays included in this volume. H. M. Klein brings the delineation of Molière and England up through the eighteenth century, and the essay by Abraham Avni includes an analysis of Molière's legacy to the English Romantics—excluding Hazlitt, who deserves separate treatment but who constitutes one of the unfortunate lacunae in this section.*

MOLIÈRE AMONG THE ENGLISH
1660–1737

Frank J. Kearful

Among the many blessings Englishmen enjoyed as a result of the restoration of Charles II to the English throne in 1660 was the re-opening of the theaters, which had been officially closed since 1642. While *sub rosa* theatrical activity persisted throughout the Interregnum, chiefly in the form of drolls and, in the late 1650's, private operatic "entertainments," the direct links with the generations of Marlowe, Shakespeare, Jonson, Beaumont, and Fletcher had been broken. Except for Charles D'Avenant, the playwrights of the 1660's were all young men, some of whom like Wycherley had spent their formative years in France, while others, like Etherege, continued to feel as much at ease on the Continent as at home. None of the brilliant young men who were to create some of the most audacious comedies in English theatrical history had any direct knowledge of the theater, except what they may have gained in France.

For those who had not been to France, there was always, after 1660, the opportunity of seeing French troupes perform in London. During the years following Charles's return from the Continent, French companies visited London frequently, acting both at Court and in the public theaters and often remaining several months. The inveterate theatergoer Samuel Pepys, after an apparently lackluster performance by one such troupe, complained in his diary of August 30, 1661: "Then my wife and I to Drury lane to the French Comedy, which was so ill done and the Scenes and company and everything else so nasty and out of order and poor, that I was sick all the while in my mind to be there."[1] During December of the same year, a French company was performing at Court, for whose services Jean Channouveau received £300.[2] While titles of the plays they performed are lacking, it is known that one French company remained in England from December, 1672, until May, 1673, and that another came over from

---

[1] *The Diary of Samuel Pepys*, II, ed. Robert Latham and William Matthews (London: G. Bell and Sons, 1970), 164.
[2] *Cal. State Papers, Treasury Books, 1660–67*, 311, as cited in Allardyce Nicoll, *A History of Restoration Drama, 1660–1700*, 4th ed. (Cambridge: Cambridge Univ. Press, 1952), 252.

France in April or May, 1673, to perform at Court and remained until September.[3] Less is known of a French company that visited during the spring of 1677, for which the theater at Whitehall was to be specifically prepared. More casual visits also occurred, such as the one recorded in Henry Savile's letter to the Earl of Rochester on December 17, 1677: "I had allmost forgott for another argument to bring you to towne that a French troop of comaedians bound for Nimeguen were by adverse winds cast into this hospitable port and doe act at Whitehall so well that it is a thousand pittyes they should not stay, especially a young wench of fifteen, who has more beauty and sweetnesse than ever was seen upon the stage since a friend of ours left it."[4] The evidence, although scattered and frustratingly silent as regards the repertory, clearly shows that London theatergoers during the quarter-century of Charles II's reign were accustomed regularly to seeing French plays performed by French companies.

To meet such competition, English dramatists frequently adapted or imitated contemporary French plays, especially the tragedies of Corneille and Racine and the comedies of Molière. Furthermore, writing tragedies, comedies, and farces after the French manner was a way in which the young English dramatist could display his modernity and assert his independence from the Elizabethan tradition at which he might scoff but which he also found rather intimidating. His sometimes supercilious pronouncements on the "old-fashioned" drama of "the former age" may be understood as the defensive pride of a self-consciously new generation of writers seeking to find its own voice, and not at all certain how to do it. In an effort to stake out new ground, he called attention in preface, prologue, and epilogue to the novelty of his plays, and set about creating new dramatic modes. Imitation or adaptation of contemporary Continental drama was one of the obvious and more accessible ways the young English playwright could be self-consciously different from his ancestors.

Continental influence is also pervasive in the "original" dramatic modes of the period. The English rhymed heroic play, whatever it drew from native origins, could not have been written without Corneille; nor could English neoclassical tragedy have developed in the period as it did without the precedent of Racine, whose tragedies were imitated, adapted, and borrowed from well into the eighteenth century. While there has been considerable disagreement as to the extent of Molière's influence on the

[3] *The London Stage 1660–1800, Part I: 1660–1700*, ed. William Van Lennep (Carbondale: Southern Illinois Univ. Press, 1963), 197–98.
[4] *Ibid.*, 266.

development of Restoration comedy, his plays were widely known and admired, and were plundered again and again by English playwrights. If the larger question of the extent of his influence on the techniques, form, and spirit of Restoration comedy is legitimately debatable, it is safe to say that every notable English comic dramatist between 1660 and 1700 was familiar with Molière and did not hesitate to draw upon his plays whenever it suited him, sometimes by direct adaptation or imitation, more often by incorporation of characters, scenes, or plot. As Voltaire later observed, "Les Anglais ont pris, ont déguisé, ont gâté, la plupart des pièces de Molière."[5]

That the question of "influence," even more than "borrowing," is notoriously difficult to determine in literary study is nowhere better illustrated than in the attempts over the years to determine Molière's influence on Restoration comedy.[6] The first critic to draw attention to the extent of English borrowings from Molière was Gerard Langbaine, whose *Account of the English Dramatick Poets* (1691) cites twenty-five plays for plagiarism from Molière. Admittedly, not all the indicted authors had sought to hide their indebtedness. John Caryl, for example, testified in his epilogue to *Sir Salomon, or the Cautious Coxcomb* (1669):

> . . . we with Modesty our Theft avow,
> (There is some Conscience shewn in stealing too)
> And openly declare, that if our Cheer
> Does hit your Pallats, you must thank *Molliere*:
> *Molliere*, the famous Shakespear of this Age,
> Both when he Writes, and when he treads the Stage.

Succeeding histories of English drama after Langbaine's, including Charles Gildon's *Lives and Characters of the English Dramatick Poets* (1699), Giles Jacob's *Poetical Register* (1723), Theophilus Cibber's and other hands' *Lives of the Poets* (1753), David Erskine Baker's *Companion to the Playhouse* (1764), Charles Dibdin's *Complete History of the English Stage* (1800), and John Genest's *Some Account of the English Stage* (1832), generally adopted Langbaine's findings and added to them discoveries of their own.

The nineteenth century, however, saw the rise of would-be systematic

---

[5] "Sur la comédie," *Lettres sur les Anglais* (1734), *Oeuvres complètes de Voltaire*, V. (Paris: Chez Firmin Didot Frères, 1869), 34.

[6] My two-paragraph summary of the controversy from 1697 to 1938 is based largely on materials in John Wilcox, *The Relation of Molière to Restoration Comedy* (New York: Columbia Univ. Press, 1938), 1–17.

literary history, and with it an attempt not merely to cite borrowings and plagiarisms but also to assess the causal significance and "influence" of literary borrowings. Two general tendencies emerged with respect to the French influence on Restoration comedy. Some commentators, such as Scott, Hazlitt, Hallam, Hunt, and Macauley, acknowledged the general influence of French literature and culture on the Restoration, including the drama, but discounted essential influence on the form and spirit of Restoration comedy. As Macauley put it: "whatever our dramatists touched they tainted."[7] Others, wishing to ascribe the lewdness and libertinism they found in Restoration comedy to the French, like Thackeray attributed the nastiness of the times and especially the theater to the French.[8] It was the more systematic literary histories, such as Thomas Arnold's *Manual of English Literature* (rev. ed., 1876) and Henry Morley's *Manual of English Literature* (rev. ed., 1879), which enshrined the view that during the Restoration "a new school" of comedy "arose, of which the tone and form may certainly be traced to the unrivalled genius of Molière."[9] Although dissenters like Beljame, Ward, Charlanne, and Taine sought to minimize the influence of Molière on Restoration comedy, the increasingly dominant trend in the late nineteenth and early twentieth centuries was to find in French comedy, especially that of Molière, the chief source of and influence on Restoration comedy. This school of criticism, fed by several turn-of-the-century German Ph. D. dissertations, culminates in Dudley H. Miles's *The Influence of Molière on Restoration Comedy* (1910).

More recent scholarship has sought to impose more rigorous criteria for "influence," and has been more concerned to point out dissimilarities than affinities between Molière and his English contemporaries. The most notable revisionist along these lines is John Wilcox, whose study of *The Relationship of Molière to Restoration Comedy* (1938; reissued 1964) remains the standard work on the subject. In understandable reaction to the uncritical sources-and-analogues influence-studies of the late nineteenth and early twentieth centuries, Wilcox is perhaps too unwilling to grant *any* essential influence of Molière. For example, he refuses to admit "influence" except in cases wherein borrowed material has not been trans-

---

[7] *The History of England from the Accession of James the Second*, I (London, 1849), 374.
[8] See Thackeray's essay on "Congreve and Addison" in *The English Humourists of the Eighteenth Century*. The book as a whole is worth reading as an example of how most Victorians were repelled by Restoration and Augustan satirists, especially by Pope and Swift. Pope and Swift could not be blamed on the French.
[9] Arnold, 199, as cited in Wilcox, 7.

formed and has not been combined with native "influences." Wilcox's salutary reaction to his predecessors in its own way turns out to be as mechanical as their uncritical approach. Not surprisingly, it leads to the conclusion that although Molière's plays "were often used, he made no significant contribution to the type of comedy we associate with the Restoration."[10]

The reasonable conclusion to be drawn from the irreconcilable findings of scholars who have engaged, and undoubtedly will continue to engage, in the debate over Molière's influence on Restoration comedy is that their findings are predetermined not only by their methods but their conceptions of what is "essentially" the form, tone, and spirit of Molière's comedy, as well as the form, tone, and spirit of Restoration comedy. As there is even less agreement on this question concerning his English contemporaries than there is concerning Molière, a definitive study of Molière's influence on Restoration comedy is hardly to be expected. And influence will always remain hardest to describe where it is most creative. The best that can be hoped is that by continuing to raise the question, and especially by raising it in new ways, we might come to a somewhat better understanding both of Molière and his English contemporaries.

The direct aims of the present essay are modest: to put in some perspective previous analyses of the subject; to examine Dryden's *Sir Martin Mar-All* in the context of the early attempts to imitate and adapt Molière; to suggest something of Molière's most important creative influence, which was on William Wycherley; and to trace the after-life of Molière's comedies in English farce from Ravenscroft to Fielding and the re-imposition of political controls on the theaters in 1737.

Although not the first play to borrow from Molière, John Dryden's *Sir Martin Mar-All, or the Feigned Innocence* (1667) started the vogue of wholesale borrowing and direct adaptation. It was, and remained, Dryden's most popular comedy, and led to such other direct adaptations as Richard Flecknoe's *The Damoiselles à la Mode* (1668), based on *L'Ecole des maris* and *Les Précieuses ridicules*; John Lacy's *The Dumb Lady, or the Farrier Made Physician* (1669), adapted from *Le Médecin malgré lui*; John Caryll's *Sir Salomon, or the Cautious Coxcomb* (1669), adapted from *L'Ecole des femmes*; Thomas Betterton's *The Amorous Widow, or the Wanton Wife* (1670), one of whose plots derives from *George Dandin*;

---

[10] Wilcox, 200. On the question of "borrowing," as opposed to "influence," Wilcox's deliberately conservative estimate is that "altogether thirty-eight Restoration plays, nearly one in five, have some connection with Molière", 179.

Matthew Medbourne's *Tartuffe, or the French Puritan* (1670); and Shadwell's *The Miser* (1672).[11] All these appeared during Molière's lifetime, and indicate how closely English playwrights were in touch with the Paris stage. *Sir Martin Mar-All* is of particular interest not only as the first, and most popular, of the early adaptations, but also as its author was the most self-consciously European writer of his generation.

Dryden's play is typical of many Molière adaptations in its very English refusal to stick to one play as its model. To be precise, Dryden follows Quinault's *L'Amant indiscret* through the first two and one-half acts, and Molière's *L'Etourdi* in the last two and one-half. Furthermore, there is a subplot added with no previous basis in either Quinault or Molière, or their own Italian source, Barbieri's *L'Inavvertito*. And there is a comic episode added to the main plot based on a similar episode in Sorel's *Histoire comique de Francion*. The time scheme of the subplot, a suggestive seduction intrigue from which the play's subtitle *The Feigned Innocence* derives, requires (for gynecological reasons) the passage of several weeks, whereas the main plot seems to occur within something like the neo-classical twenty-four hours. Such blithe disregard of the unities, not only combining two plots of different tones but of irreconcilable time schemes, is only a slightly extreme example of how freely the English went about adapting Molière, while at the same time Englishing speech by speech entire scenes and episodes.

In the process of translating Molière's dialogue, Dryden is extraordinarily successful in turning it into idiomatic English speech, spoken by indubitably English characters. The setting, too, is thoroughly English, and localized unmistakably in Restoration London. Here again Dryden is representative of most of his fellow adapters in so entirely transforming Molière's setting, characters, and dialogue into a play as apparently English as if it had no foreign source.

There are also a number of changes in the main plot which give the play a more English flavor. The most important of these is that the feckless protagonist, Sir Martin, does not, as both Quinault's Cleandre and Molière's Lélie do, get the girl he is after. Sir Martin is an incorrigible ninny, one of those foolish asses who always end up being hoisted by their own petard in Jonsonian comedy. Although less than a tower of genius,

---

[11] Each of these is analyzed in Wilcox, 25–69. On *Sir Martin Mar-All*, including the question of the extent to which Dryden may have used materials provided him by the Duke of Newcastle, see the commentary on the play in *The works of John Dryden*, IX, ed. John Loftis and Vinton A. Dearing (Berkeley and Los Angeles: Univ. of California Press, 1966), 352–69.

Lélie is, for most of Molière's play, preposterously and thereby comically unlucky; the audience wants him to succeed and he finally does. In Dryden's play, the audience can only wonder why a bright, charming young woman like Millisent could be attracted to such a stupid nincompoop. In the end, she exhibits the independent resourcefulness characteristic of English comic heroines from Shakespeare to Shaw: she outwits both Sir Martin and his clever servant, Warner, who has been inventing a series of ever more ingenious strategems on his bungling behalf, tricking her wooer into marrying her servant and Warner into marrying herself. Just as Dryden turns Sir Martin into a Jonsonian ass who deserves gulling, with some traces of a Restoration Witwoud who deserves to lose the object of his vapid affections, so Warner acquires an essentially innocent, high-spirited charm which, modifying the calculating wit of his prototype, makes him after the English fashion worthy of a lady apparently above his station. The *dénouement*, in which it is discovered that Warner is in fact of gentle birth but has been forced because of a mortgaged estate to live in reduced circumstances, allows the frog to be ransomed by Millisent's dowry into a prince. This kind of success-story formula, of the deserving social inferior "magically" raised to wealth and status through the love of a beautiful lady, who rejects a socially acceptable but undeserving alternative suitor, is a favorite topos of English comic dramatists and novelists from Dryden to Fielding.

Sir Martin Mar-All, which Pepys thought "the most entire piece of mirth . . . that certainly was ever writ," appeared in the same year as Dryden's major critical work, *An Essay of Dramatick Poesie*. Read in conjunction with *Sir Martin Mar-All*, it casts additional light on the way English writers read, judged, and used Molière.

The essay, which is a key document in the history of comparative literary criticism, deals with the relative merits of modern and classical drama, of English and French drama, and the comparative advantages of rhymed dramatic verse and dramatic blank verse. Dryden's most important contribution in the *Essay* is a demonstrated awareness of the historical and cultural relativity of literary taste and critical judgments. Nevertheless, the *Essay* reflects a typically English critical prejudice in favor of variety, "naturalness," and "liveliness" as opposed to French regularity, artificiality, and rigidity. In view of Dryden's having written *Sir Martin Mar-All* probably not long after, one paragraph is of particular interest:

But of late years *Moliere*, the younger *Corneille*, *Quinault*, and some others, have been imitating afar off the quick turns and graces of the *English* Stage. They have mix'd their serious Plays with mirth, like our Tragicomedies, since the death of Cardinal *Richelieu*, which *Lisideius* [the spokesman for French superiority in the *Essay*] and many others not observing, have commended that in them for a virtue which they themselves no longer practice. Most of their new Plays are like some of ours, deriv'd from the *Spanish* Novells. There is scarce one of them without a vail, and a trusty *Diego*, who drolls much after the rate of the *Adventures*. But their humours, if I may grace them with that name, are so thin sown that never above one of them comes up in any Play: I dare take upon me to find more variety of them in some one Play of *Ben. Johnsons* than in all theirs together: as he who has seen the *Alchymist*, the *Silent Woman*, or *Bartholomew-Fair*, cannot but acknowledge with me.[12]

It seems a little ungracious to reverse the facts of the matter about which direction "influence" was flowing across the Channel, but the criticism of poets is not infrequently self-serving. The larger importance of the passage, borne out in the *Essay* as a whole, is that, in adapting Molière, Dryden was not rejecting as inferior his own native tradition. The *Essay*'s setting of French drama over against pre-Restoration drama in fact enabled Dryden to accord the "former age" that praise he was less comfortable in granting it, at the expense of his own, when comparing it with the new generation of English writers, of which he himself was already becoming a leading figure.

Similarly, "adaptation" of Molière for the playwrights of the 1660's and early 1670's was really a way in which they could recreate much of the older English comedy's form, spirit, and tone. Molière provided them with a way of using their own native tradition without the necessity of turning directly to the "old-fashioned" plays of Jonson and his contemporaries. When they did attempt a direct adaptation of a Shakespeare or a Jonson, their own comparative poverty of imagination was altogether too evident.[13] But under the guise of adapting a contemporary Frenchman, they were able more freely to use the older native tradition while finding their contemporary voice. Thus while none of the Molière adaptations of the early Restoration equals the achievements of the mid-1670's, they helped the playwrights to come to terms with their own tradition while creating their own "modern" drama. We need not deplore, with Wilcox,

---

[12] "An Essay of Dramatick Poesie," *The Works of John Dryden*, XVII, ed. Samuel Holt Monk and A. E. Wallace Maurer (Berkeley and Los Angeles: Univ. of California Press, 1971), 45.

[13] The grand exception which proves the rule is Dryden's *All for Love* (1678), an "Imitation" (in the special Augustan generic sense) of Shakespeare's *Antony and Cleopatra*. See Frank J. Kearful, "'Tis Past Recovery': Tragic Consciousness in Dryden's *All for Love*," *Modern Language Quarterly*, 34, (1973), 227–46.

the fact that in adapting Molière they wrote plays whose end, form, spirit, and matter "are essentially British."[14]

During the mid-1670's, especially in the major comedies of George Etherege and William Wycherley, Restoration comedy reaches its maturity. Whereas the first decade and a half was marked by uncertainty and an effort to come to terms with native and foreign traditions, the better plays of the mid-1670's display the assurance and bravura of a literary generation sure of itself, of its audience, and of its individualized stance in relation to earlier English and contemporary European drama. It is no longer so much a case of using Molière haphazardly by way of learning how to write one's own plays, as selective transformation of those elements in Molière which the English dramatist found useful in his own art. Molière's larger influence on the conception and technique of "high" Restoration comedy admits of no mechanical demonstration. Whether or not, for example, Wycherley in *The Country-Wife* "learned from Molière how to focus his implications" for maximum satiric effect remains a speculative inference.[15]

Tentative as our accounts of it must be, the most creative influence Molière exerted on Restoration comedy was unquestionably in the plays of William Wycherley. It has been frequently observed that his comedies—*Love in a Wood* (1671), *The Gentleman Dancing-Master* (1672), *The Country-Wife* (1675), and *The Plain-Dealer* (1676)—contain numerous borrowings from Molière, and critics generally emphasize Molière's influence on him as a dramatist. Attention, however, has been placed mainly on "crude" Wycherley's acquisition of more sophisticated dramaturgic techniques. What has not been appreciated is how the creative influence of Molière enabled Wycherley, in his two last plays, to engage his imagination fully in the central problem of his own dramatic vision, a conflict between the desire to vilify satirically irremediable human vice and an impulse to affirm comically the ability of human nature to recognize and to transcend its own follies.

In *The Country-Wife*, which makes important use of *L'Ecole des femmes* and *L'Ecole des maris*, the allusions to Molière throw into relief the unresolved tension between the play's satiric and comic actions. The parallel-

---

[14] Wilcox, 56. On the Englishness of English adaptation of and borrowing from Molière, see also Norman Suckling, "Molière and English Restoration Comedy," *Restoration Theatre*, ed. John Russell Brown and Bernard Harris (London: Edward Arnold, 1965), 93–107. Suckling is particularly interested in world-view differences between Molière and the English.
[15] Wilcox, 94.

ism of Arnolphe and Pinchwife, first clearly indicated in Pinchwife's Act
I paraphrases of Arnolphe's speeches on the wisdom of marrying a
complete innocent whom one may subject to one's absolute control,
underscores Pinchwife's sadistic compulsions.[16] Any complicating minor
note of sympathy or pathos is removed, while Arnolphe's essentially comic
"humor" is transformed into a repellent lustful perversion. Margery at
the outset seems as innocent as Agnès, but her unsuccessful attempt to
run away from Pinchwife (she is already married to him when the play
begins) is attempted adultery with Horner, a libertine scoundrel who is a
grotesque parallel to Horace. *The Country-Wife*'s allusions through
action, character, dialogue, and plot mechanisms to *L'Ecole des Femmes*
consistently exacerbate the savagery of Wycherley's satiric vision.

The Country-Wife also makes allusive reference, however, in its comic
subplot, the successful wooing of Alithea by Harcourt, to *L'Ecole des
maris*. Whereas in the main plot the allusions function "negatively" to
intensify satiric scorn, in the subplot they function "positively" to reinforce the joyful comic action. Wycherley takes two Molière plays essentially similar in comic action, theme, and viewpoint. One he satirically
coarsens, the other he comically deepens. Harcourt and Alithea are far
more psychologically individuated than Isabelle and Valère, as Wycherley
downplays comedy of situation and farce-contrivance in order to develop
comedy of character and theme. At the end of the play the lovers pledge
their faith to each other, in opposition to the world of the main plot. They
have also been made subject to follies and to comic exposure of their false
masks, but unlike Pinchwife, Margery, and Horner they are capable of
genuine self-knowledge, which they validate through their commitment
to each other.

The play, to the end, maintains an unresolved tension between un-
relieved satiric castigation of the Horner world and a romantic celebration
of the Alithea-Harcourt love plot. Unlike a Shakespearean romantic
comedy, even so "serious" a one as *As You Like It*, there is no comic regen-
eration of society. The comic renewal is an entirely individual one, and its
two participants never become the play's central dramatic interest. The
satiric and comic perspectives, both of which involve displacement of
tone and emphasis in Molière's parallel comedies, helped Wycherley
to define but not to resolve his own conflicting dramatic vision.

[16] On Pinchwife's sexual psychology, see David M. Vieth, "Wycherley's *The Country Wife*:
An Anatomy of Masculinity," *Papers on Language and Literature*, II (1966), 335–50.

The Plain-Dealer sharpens the conflict of perspectives to such an extent that critics of the play have never been able to convince each other as to its theme or Wycherley's viewpoint toward his protagonist, Manly. Yet virtually all have recognized its difficulty, its peculiar power, and its uniqueness among Restoration comedies. It offers both the bitterest satiric attack on human nature in Restoration drama, and the most romantically redemptive comic resolution. Both perspectives are intensified, and may be partially understood, by the way Wycherley's play counterpoints itself to Molière's *Le Misanthrope*.

Wycherley's deliberate transformations of characters, dialogue, episodes, and plot materials from *Le Misanthrope* serve to indicate the play's general satiric norms, and, more specifically, the satiric function of the protagonist.[17] As we shall see, they generally magnify the evil of the world which Manly, Alceste's counterpart, pits himself against and strengthen the integrity of his outrage. In one sense, they clarify and reinforce the play's satiric lines of attack. On the other hand, the play's comic resolution, in which satiric outrage is sublimated in comic liberation, works a *double* reversal of the parallels to *Le Misanthrope* which had seemingly locked the play into a rigidly satiric stance. Wycherley uses *Le Misanthrope*, then, both to sharpen the conflict between the satiric and comic views of human nature and to resolve them in an ironic *tertium quid* beyond the reach of his earlier comedies, or those of any of his contemporaries. That the resolution is forced, as all critics agree, is not, I suggest, a failure of the play but part of its expressive power. The uneasy balance of forces is summed up, in the final words of the play, in what Manly "will" believe:

> *I will believe, there are now in the World*
> *Good-natur'd Friends, who are not Prostitutes,*
> *And handsom Women worthy to be Friends:*
> *Yet, for my sake, let no one e're confide*
> *In Tears, or Oaths, in Love, or Friend untry'd.*[18]

Manly begins, like Alceste, as an outspoken, "plain-dealing" opponent of the duplicities of "civilized" behavior. He refuses to accept merely polite compliments; he won't flatter talentless writers; he condemns the

---

[17] See A. M. Friedson, "Wycherley and Molière: Satirical point of View in *The Plain Dealer*," *Modern Philology*, 64 (1967), 189–97. A portion of my argument parallels Friedson's.

[18] Quotations from and references to the play in my text are all based on *The Complete Plays of William Wycherley*, ed. Gerald Weales (Garden City, N.Y.: Doubleday), 1966.

hypocrisy and disguised vanity he sees everywhere; and he relishes the extent to which he is able to uncover the wickedness of his fellow human beings. In his general sentiments, outlook, and character type he closely resembles Alceste. However, the parallels which Wycherley draws to Alceste become considerably qualified in their respective contexts.

This may be seen immediately in the first scene of *The Plain-Dealer*, which draws heavily on the corresponding scene in *Le Misanthrope*. In *Le Misanthrope*, Alceste and Philinte engage in a discussion of the necessity of adapting to society's polite forms of social discourse. The discussion, initiated by Alceste's refusal to accept the "false" professions of his "seeming" friend, presents Alceste to the audience as a misanthropic, headstrong, irascible person whose mania prevents him from accepting the genuine friendship and wise counsel of Philinte. Philinte's social discretion is *not* hypocritical, but the philosophic acceptance of human nature for what it is, seen with some comic detachment.

The discussion between Alceste and Philinte is reenacted in that between Manly and Freeman, but it is preceded by a brief encounter between Manly and Lord Plausible, an egregious coxcomb who speaks "well of all Mankind" because "I hate to do a rude thing." With good reason, Manly thrusts out the fatuous Plausible, but only after the audience has been given sufficient reason to sympathize heartily with Manly's condemnation of his "*Decorums*, supercilious Forms, and slavish Ceremonies; your little Tricks, which you Spaniels of the World, do daily over and over, for, and to one another; not out of love or duty, but your servile fear" (I.i.p. 319). When Freeman enters, the audience has already been swayed to Manly's side. Furthermore, while Freeman and Manly repeat some of the argument between Philinte and Alceste, Freeman's own character is made unpleasantly suspect by his pleasure in self-serving hypocrisy, as in the following exchange:

> MANLY. I must confess, I am so much your Friend, I wou'd not deceive you, therefore must tell you (not only because my heart is taken up) but according to your rules of Friendship, I cannot be your Friend.
> FREEMAN. Why pray?
> MANLY. Because he that is (you'll say) a true Friend to a man is a Friend to all his Friends; but you must pardon me, I cannot wish well to Pimps, Flatterers, Detractors, and Cowards, stiff nodding Knaves, and supple pliant kissing Fools: now, all these I have seen you use, like the dearest Friends in the World.
> FREEMAN. Hah, hah, hah— What, you observ'd me, I warrant, in the Galleries at *Whitehall*, doing the business of the place! Pshaw, Court Professions,

like Court Promises, go for nothing, man. But, faith, cou'd you think I was a
friend to all those I hugg'd, kiss'd, flatter'd, bow'd too? Hah, ha— (I.i.p. 396.)

Philinte is essential to the design of *Le Misanthrope*, both as *raisonneur* and as a living example of disinterested friendship. In *The Plain-
Dealer* Freeman recreates Philinte's role, but he is a moral cynic whose
chief aim in the play is to trick the rich Widow Blackacre into marrying
him. He has none of Philinte's ethical credibility, and insofar as he is meant
to recall Philinte and his norms, he debases both. This parallelism with-a-
difference to *Le Misanthrope* engages increased sympathy for the one
whose "heart is taken up," makes the disillusioned satiric attack on man
as a social animal considerably stronger, and seems to deny in *this* play
the possibility of a genuine offsetting comic perspective.

The same technique of drawing parallels in order to emphasize differences in the weighting and direction of satiric attack can be seen in the
relationship of Olivia to Célimène. Célimène is disingenuous, perhaps
uncertain of her own self, and certainly inconsiderate. Her enjoyment of
the role of *coquette* is very different, however, from the behavior of Olivia,
the object of Manly's "irrational" pursuit.

The parallel with-a-difference is suggested in Olivia's first scene, with
Novel and Plausible (II.i.), which is closely modelled on that of Célimène
with Acaste and Clitandre (II.ii). Célimène's acceptance of Acaste's and
Clitandre's presence has the partial excuse that she is trying to be civil; but
Olivia has deliberately invited and encouraged Novel and Plausible, and
she is wilfully hypocritical throughout the scene. When the company turns
to raillery on absent friends and acquaintances, there are several echoes
of the corresponding raillery scene in *Le Misanthrope*. Wycherley makes
us sympathize with Manly, however, to a degree we do not with Alceste by
having him enter unnoticed during Olivia's grossly vicious caricaturing of
his honesty, courage, and candor. Manly, unlike Alceste, had never suspected his "love's" fault of gossiping; moreover, she had never given him
evidence of anything but her devotion to him. As the deluded Manly remarks in Act I: "Her tongue as well as face, ne'r knew artifice; nor ever
did her words or looks contradict her heart: She is all truth, and hates the
lying, masking, daubing World, as I do" (406–07).

The effect of such alterations is to make Olivia less charming and more
dislikable than Célimène; nor are we nearly so shocked, later, as Manly is
to discover her a scheming, promiscuous gold digger. We may not feel that
Alceste deserves Célimène any more than Célimène deserves Alceste, but
in *The Plain-Dealer* our sympathies and moral judgment are totally on the

side of Manly. Wycherley even transfers Arsinoé's hypocritical prudishness (III. iv) to Olivia (II. i. p. 419–21), to further distinguish her from her putative counterpart, Célimène.

One satellite character whose viciousness is not pointed up by comparison to his counterpart in *Le Misanthrope* is Eliza, cousin to Olivia as is Eliante to Célimène. Like Eliante she is critical of her cousin's behavior and is a spokesman for good sense. She fulfills much better the role of her prototype than Philinte does his, but she is a much more passive participant in the action than is Eliante. She is in love neither with Manly nor with Philinte, nor does she have any effect on the plot. In the world of *The Plain-Dealer* her virtues are sufficiently engaged in holding on to her own composure and decency. Insofar as she elicits the audience's sympathy, it is for one who seems to have sacrificed personal feeling in order to protect herself from the kind of disillusioned bitterness which afflicts Manly.

Wycherley, however, creates a second ectype of Eliante, who is vested with all and more of the love, faithfulness, and devotion of her Molière counterpart. Fidelia, like Eliante, is forced to see a man she loves and admires humiliated through his obsessive attachment to another woman, whom she recognizes as false and wilfully destructive. She also hopes he will free himself of his misplaced passion, and turn in genuine and reciprocal love to herself. But whereas Molière has Eliante realize the fruitlessness of her desires, and provides her an appropriate alternate suitor in Philinte, Fidelia is developed (including her disguise as a boy in Manly's service) after the fashion of Shakespeare's Viola or Beaumont and Fletcher's Bellario. That she is required by the unsuspecting Manly to woo for him an "Olivia" suggests that Wycherley meant the comic romance parallel to *Twelfth Night* to be as obtrusive as possible. Her lyrical blank verse monologues underscore further the separate perspective she introduces into the play.

Wycherley in effect divides Eliante's functions, as exemplar of practical virtue and as lover of Alceste, between two characters, Eliza and Fidelia. This specialization of functions, and the absence of Philinte, who is otherwise occupied as suitor, allows him to develop Fidelia as a romance heroine whose supra-rational love and supra-natural faithfulness are quite beyond, and are not subjected to, Eliante's realistic knowledge of herself and Alceste. Wycherley's dissociation of Eliza's self-sufficient practicality and Fidelia's transcendent fidelity suggests that the comic and ethical norms of moderation and detachment are insufficient instruments to confront the villainous world of *The Plain-Dealer*. In Wycherley's play, through Fidelia "excess" does win out, does achieve its "irrational" desire. Just as Wycherley's parallels with-a-difference exacerbated the satiric attack on the irredeemability of secular human nature, so in the comic resolution they expand the range of secular wisdom to include the super- natural. Thus Manly, who had been deceived by one who *seemed* "all truth," is redeemed from disillusionment by one whose virtue is *revealed* as "greater than I thought was in the World" (V. iii. pp. 514–15).

Wycherley, from his first play to his last, was an extremist. Molière's kind of delicately poised unity of conception and skillfully modulated manner of execution was thoroughly foreign to him. *The Plain-Dealer* is not a unified play. It offers, however, a kind of mannerist distortion of perspective in order to achieve an "unnatural," highly wrought, unsettling expression of the dissociation of the moral and comic sensibilities in a morally grotesque world.

Through an imaginative confrontation with the French playwright whose art and mind were so fundamentally different from his own, Wych- erley created two of the masterpieces of Restoration comedy. That they would never be taken for plays of Molière is an indication of the genius of both dramatists.

During the late 1670's and the 1680's two new forms of comedy arose to replace the comedy of manners, which had reached a maturity and passed beyond itself in *The Plain-Dealer*. In both the new sentimental comedy and the new vogue for farce, especially in the latter, Molière once again helped English dramatists find their own voice and manner. The key figure in the early development of Restoration sentimental drama is Thomas Shadwell. Shadwell's first use of Molière was in *The Sullen Lovers, or the Impertinents* (1668), based to some extent, as its preface indicates, on *Les Fâcheux*. It illustrates, again, how completely early Restoration plays transubstantiate Molière characters into traditional English "humor" characters populating a thoroughly English environment. *The Miser* (1672), an adaptation of *L'Avare*, is similarly skillful. Molière's *Psyché* probably had some influence on Shadwell's *Psyche* (1675), as did his *Dom Juan* upon Shadwell's *The Libertine* (1675).

With respect to the development of sentimental comedy, Molière's oblique influence was transmitted through Shadwell's *Bury Fair* (1689), based extensively on *Les Précieuses ridicules* and *Les Femmes savantes*. *Bury Fair* and Shadwell's *The Squire of Alsatia* (1688) mark a turning away from the comedy of manners emphasis on wit, libertinism, skepticism, and hard-edged satire toward a more "decent," civilized, good-natured, didactic, humane comedy. Although by no means a dominant influence at work in the new comedy, Molière did provide a precedent of and a model for genuine comedy which did not resort to the immorality and flippancy of the comedy of manners. *Bury Fair* in particular attempts to show that the English dramatist might, if he tried, write with as little scurrility and as delightful good sense as Molière. The result, according even to Wilcox, was "a play with an attitude toward life much nearer the great Frenchman's social attitude than a Restoration playwright had hitherto produced."[19]

During the 1690's Congreve successfully blended the new sentimental strain of comedy with a revived substratum of the old comedy of manners. While plot borrowings from Molière can be found in Congreve, his individual manner, conception, and style are probably less indebted to Molière than either Etherege's or Wycherley's. Perhaps Molière's more general influence on Congreve, after the commercially saccharine turn sentimental comedy had taken, was to remind him that good sense need not preclude good laughs. But where Molière's influence *is* overwhemingly apparent in the late Restoration is in quite another sort of drama from either sentimental comedy or Congreve's comedy.

From Edward Ravenscroft's *Mamamouchi, or the Citizen Turned Gentleman* (1672) to Henry Fielding's adaptations of Molière farces in the 1730's, Molière is a continuous and dominant influence on the growth and development of English farce. For some critics, it is precisely the English writers' attraction to the farcical in Molière which most indicates their blindness to and unconcern for his higher virtues and more refined techniques. Wilcox, for example, argues that "the material borrowed is so disproportionately farcical, in comparison with Molière's total production, that we may be sure it was this unimportant expression of his genius that the Restoration envied."[20] The English dramatist who must perforce bear the brunt of this critical aggravation is Edward Ravenscroft.

Mamamouchi, or the Citizen Turned Gentleman is a very funny play, so funny it makes use of farcical incidents and situations from *Monsieur de Pourceaugnac* to supplement its main source, *Le Bourgeois gentilhomme*. There are even a few bits from *L'Avare* thrown in for good measure. Critics from Langbaine to the present have resented how Ravenscroft could so adroitly and insouciantly plunder the plays of his betters, even

---

[19] Wilcox, 124.
[20] Wilcox, 198.

the great Molière's. More than anyone else, he encouraged his own and future generations of playwrights to exploit Molière as a treasury of farce materials. His most influential contribution, based mainly on *Les Four-beries de Scapin* and *Le Mariage forcé*, but with added bits from *Le Bourgeois gentilhomme* he had not found room for in *Mamamouchi*, was *Scaramouch a Philosopher, Harlequin, a Schoolboy, Bravo, Merchant, and Magician. A Comedy after the Italian Manner* (1677). For better or for worse, it inaugurated a decade of borrowing, adaptation, and plagiarism during which "the stage was flooded with farces drawn from Molière."[21]

A second flood occurred in the late 1690's and early 1700's, when the farce afterpiece became a standard feature of the theatrical program. Among the more piquant transformations of Molière's titles are Susanna Centlivre's adaptation of *Le Médecin malgré lui* as *Love's Contrivances* (1703), the adaptation of *Monsieur Pourceaugnac* by Congreve, Vanbrugh, and Walsh as *Squire Treloby* (1704), and *L'Amour médecin* turned into Swiney's *Quacks* (1705). Such Molière-based farces might follow a serious tragedy, to add variety to the theatrical program, but they were also served up in variety show productions such as the one advertised in the following bill of April 30, 1703:

> *The Cheats of Scapin. The Comical Rivals, or The School-Boy.* "Being the last time of Acting till after *May-Fair.* . . . With several Italian Sonatas by Signior *Gasperini* and others. And the *Devonshire Girl*, being now upon her Return to the City of Exeter, will perform three several Dances, particularly her last New Entry in Imitation of *Madamoiselle Subligni*, and the *Whip of* Dunboyn *by* Mr. Claxton *her Master*, being the last time of their Performance till Winter. And at the desire of several Persons of Quality (hearing that Mr. *Pinkethman* hath hired the two famous French Girls lately arriv'd from the Emperor's Court, They will peform several Dances on the Rope upon the Stage, being improv'd to that Degree, far exceeding all others in that Art. And their *Father* presents you with the *Newest Humours of Harlequin*, as perform'd by him before the Grand Signior at *Constantinople*. Also the Famous Mr. *Evans* lately arriv'd from *Vienna*, will shew you Wonders of another kind, Vaulting on the Manag'd Horse, being the greatest Master of that kind in the World. To begin at Five so that all may be done by Nine a Clock."[22]

While such an evening sounds more entertaining than the Ed Sullivan shows of early American television, it does rather illustrate how less re-verently and (*pace* Lionel Gossman) how less psycho-analytically the

---

[21] Arthur H. Scouten, "Notes toward a History of Restoration Comedy," *Philological Quarterly*, 45 (1966), 62–70.

[22] As reprinted in Emmett L. Avery and A. H. Scouten, "A Tentative Calendar of Daily Theatrical Performances in London, 1700–1701 to 1704–05," *PMLA*, 62 (1948), 127.

early eighteenth-century dramatists and producers regarded Molière than
do the generality of modern critics.

However we may choose to deplore the literary consequences, the
importance of the farce in the expansion and diversification of the theatrical program during the decade 1695–1705 has been properly emphasized
by Leo Hughes: "During this time the bill had been expanded, first to
include any catch-penny, crowd-pulling device from song and pantomime
to juggling and rope-dancing. Eventually, however, there seems to have
been every indication that the solution to the 'entertainment' problem
would be to settle upon a more consistently dramatic form, the farce."[23]
Ravenscroft had already shown how well such a product could be pack-
aged by plundering Molière, and that is precisely what the farce writers
continued to do in answer to popular demand and commercial opportunity.

To cite Molière as the source of one's farce was apparently such a drawing card that even when he was *not* a model he might be advertised as one.
Thus John Corey lyingly describes his *Metamorphosis* (1704) as "written
originally by the famous Moliere." To announce truculently that one's
play in no way derived from Molière was an alternative gambit. The same
Mrs. Centlivre mentioned for her earlier adaptation, *Love's Contrivances*
(1703), asserted in the prologue to *A Bold Stroke for a Wife* (1718):

> To-Night we come upon a bold Design,
> To try to please without one borrow'd Line:
> Our plot is new, and regularly clear,
> And not a single Tittle from *Moliere*.

Theatergoers continued, however, to hear many a "borrow'd line"
from Molière, chiefly in farces, during the following decade. But during
the 1730's farce lost ground to other "irregular" dramatic modes, notably
the ballad opera, a vogue for which had been stimulated by the success of
Gay's *Beggar's Opera* (1728). At the same time, the ballad opera often
incorporated much of the farce tradition that preceded it, as may best be
seen in the plays of Henry Fielding. In *The Mock Doctor* (1732), for example, Fielding introduces songs in ballad opera style into his otherwise
close adaptation of *Le Médecin malgré lui*. He also kept the Molière tradition alive in *The Miser* (1733), a freely adapted five-act comedy based on
L'Avare. The play had a first run of twenty-six nights—extraordinary in
the English eighteenth-century repertory system—and it was revived

---

[23] Leo Hughes, *A Century of English Farce* (Princeton: Princeton Univ. Press, 1956), 82.

frequently throughout the rest of the century. It was Fielding's most successful play (he wrote nearly thirty), and it is pleasant to record that the Molière adaptation which lasted longest in the eighteenth century was one of the best. And there is no harm in speculating how much the future novelist learned of dialogue and scene writing through his early admiration for Molière.

In 1737 political controls were re-imposed on the theaters, chiefly as a result of Fielding's satiric attacks against Walpole's administration.[24] One of the liveliest, most varied and experimental periods in English dramatic history had come to an end. Molière's influence over those nearly eighty years never produced an English Molière. For the writers of that time, he was, however, a continual inspiration. Molière was a man who knew how to write plays, and there was always something to be learned from him. In a way, he was more accessible than either Shakespeare or Jonson, by the fact that he *was* foreign. Through Molière, several generations of English playwrights learned how to write English comedy. And at least one, William Wycherley, found the way to express dramatically his own genius.

---

[24] Sheridan Baker suggests that even *The Mock Doctor* may contain covert anti-Walpole satire. See his article, "Political Allusion in Fielding's *Author's Farce, Mock Doctor,* and *Tumble-Down Dick,*" *PMLA,* 77 (1962), 221–31.

MOLIÈRE IN ENGLISH CRITICAL THOUGHT ON COMEDY TO 1800

H. M. Klein

There are numerous studies of Molière's relation to Restoration Comedy.[1] Surprisingly few studies have been made about his relation to eighteenth century Comedy.[2] And on the English opinions of Molière during the whole period to 1800 there seems to exist—apart from a chapter in Miles,[3] a few scattered remarks in other works, and a footnote by Hooker[4]—only one serious contribution[5]: K. Schmidt, *Molière in der angelsächsischen Kritik*.[6] And Schmidt manages, after the initial dictum, "Von einer englischen M-Kritik des 17. und 18. Jhdts. kann nicht die Rede sein" (15), to race through our period in under three pages before discussing the "real" Molière criticism from Scott and Prescott to his own day.

Based on letters and diaries, theatrical companions and dictionaries, prefatory matter to plays (especially translations), histories of the stage and writings on comedy, the present brief sketch aims at a revision of this impression. The relevant material is inexhaustible. However, the range of texts consulted seems broad enough for attempting such a preliminary

---

[1] References have been cut down to essentials. Unless otherwise stated, I have used the original texts (L, and some O copies). The place of publication is, if not specified, always London. For the texts of individual plays I have used the Readex Microprint series, *Three Centuries of English and American Plays*. Short titles are used and italics for all kinds of typographical emphasis.

[2] Space forbids listing the studies on Restoration comedy. For the eighteenth century I was unable to obtain J. E. Tucker, *Molière in England, 1700–1750* (Thesis, Madison, 1937). Apart from this and Tucker's article "The Eighteenth-Century Translations of Molière," *MLQ*, 3 (1942), 83–103, there seem to be mainly checklists: C. E. Jones, "Molière in England to 1775," *N&Q*, 202 (1957), 383–89; C. J[ones]., "Molière Illustrators 1666–1739: A Checklist," *N&Q*, 203 (1958), 117–18; in parts W. A. Kinne, *Revivals and Importations of French Comedies in England, 1749–1800* (New York, 1939); and E. Wray, "English Adaptations of French Drama between 1780 and 1815," *MLN*, 43 (1928), 87–90. (There are of course studies of individual authors).

[3] D. H. Miles, *The Influence of Molière on Restoration Comedy* (New York, 1910), 79–99.

[4] *The Critical Works of John Dennis*, ed. E. N. Hooker, 2 vols. (Baltimore, 1939–43), I, 444–45.

[5] Disregarding the antics of C. H. Humbert, *Molière, Shakespeare und die deutsche Kritik* (Leipzig, 1869), 63–69, and *Englands Urtheil über Molière . . .* (Bielefeld and Leipzig, 1878), *passim*.

[6] Phil. Diss. (Hamburg, 1940).

218

survey, which will try to arouse interest in the subject, to trace the fluctuations of the esteem in which Molière was held, to organise some of the main lines in the complex tangle of preoccupations and arguments in which he was discussed, and to provide a starting point for an examination of his role in critical thought on comedy in Britain from the late seventeenth to the early nineteenth centuries.

Looking at the first group of documents, one comes to the conclusion that Molière does not seem to have occupied any large space in the communications of many people of theatrical and social eminence—which is amazing perhaps, given the fact that he was highly important to English comedy at the time and that the stage played such an important part in everyday life. Instead of naming great numbers of texts that were scanned in vain,[7] it would appear to be more sensible to present one interesting document which was in fact found, a short essay by Joseph Spence on *Le Malade imaginaire*, written and amusingly corrected as a French exercise at Dijon (1731) and now in the Osborn Collection at Yale.[8]

Spence begins: "Le Malade Imaginaire . . . a des beautés très-considerables, & des fautes non médiocres," the former being due to Molière's *naturel*—perhaps the best-attuned to comedy the world has seen—the latter arising out of the necessity to please the pit. The main objection[9] is that one sees next to nothing of the "grande intrigue," the love affair and marriage of Angélique, which Spence sees as "le principal but de l'action," and that instead the imagination is constantly caught by the character of *Le Malade*. Thus, Spence argues, Molière has exactly inverted the rules of the Ancients and fashioned the entire action to serve the presentation of one character instead of making the characters subservient to the action. However, Spence is so carried away by Argan's portrait that he is prepared to cast the rules (be they Aristotle's or those of Ramus) to the winds. The essay, for all its brevity and its limitations, is a very early, perhaps the ear-

---

[7] In passing one may note the unusual if still moderate frequency of references to Molière in the letters between Horace Walpole and the Countess of Upper Ossory; cf. *The Yale Edition of Horace Walpole's Correspondence*, ed. W. S. Lewis, Vols. 32–34 (London *et al.*, 1965) and recall Dr. Johnson's remark naming Molière with Corneille and Racine as the three French poets who "go round the world"; cf. *Boswell's Life of Johnson*, ed. G. B. Hill; rev., enl. edn. by L. F. Powell (Oxford, 1934–50), V, 311.

[8] I should like to express my gratitude to James M. Osborn himself and the James Marshall and Marie-Louise Osborn Collection, Yale University Library, New Haven, Connecticut, for generously supplying a copy of, and giving me permission to use, this text to which my attention was first drawn by Osborn's note to No. 717 of the *Observations, Anecdotes and Characters* (Oxford, 1966), I, 292–93.

[9] Another objection by Spence is that Toinette occupies too much space in the play.

liest, single analysis of a Molière play written independently of French texts. Being noted down at about the same time as the most enthusiastic encomium of Molière before Scott, it serves, with its reservations and only half-hearted application of Dorante's and Uranie's theses, to illustrate the diversity of critical opinion regarding Molière which persisted throughout the century and even beyond.

Edward Phillips (1675) enters Molière only in his "Supplement." His brief description fairly illustrates the way Molière was naturally thought of, when viewed in a detached fashion, at the peak of his pre-1700 influence: "*Monsieur Moliere*, the pleasantest of French Comedians, for smart Comic wit and Mirth; and to whom our English Stage hath within a few years been not a little beholding."[10] Companions and dictionaries rarely give a place to foreign authors. Some of them, e.g. *The British Theatre* (1750, pp. 162–163) and *The Companion to the Play-house* (1764, Vol. II) include John Ozell as a translator, listing his complete translations of the plays. The real exception however, is Giles Jacob, who in his *Poetical Register* (1719) includes Molière himself under "Modern Dramatick Poets" and gives a long list of translations and adaptations of his plays (292–95).[11]

For the examination of Molière's place in dedications, prefaces, prologues and epilogues[12] Miles (81, 85, 96–98) has already presented some material, from which the following line by D'Urfey (1681) is perhaps the most interesting: "Molière is quite rifled, then how shall I write?"[13] It is common knowledge that Restoration dramatists did not often bother to indicate their sources. Thus, limiting ourselves to places where a reference to Molière could be expected, of the thirty-eight plays between 1660 and 1700 which Wilcox lists as dependent in various degrees on Molière,[14] only nine mention him at all. In the eighteenth century the practice of silent lifting and adapting does by no means cease—Cibber is a case in point—but it certainly becomes much rarer.[15]

---

[10] *Theatrum Poetarum*, facs. repr. (Hildesheim, 1970), 230.

[11] Jacob's short introductory sentence clearly shows the impact of John Ozell's translations of 1714; *vide infra*. The more usual method of simply referring to Molière as inspiration to certain plays can be observed, e.g., in Gerard Langbaine's *Momus Triumphans* (1688), intr. D. S. Rhodes, ARS, Publ. No. 150 (UCLA: W. A. Clark Mem. Lib., 1971).

[12] The scattered "famous" and "celebrated" of the theatrical advertisements now conveniently available in the volumes of *The London Stage 1600–1800* have too little substance to be seriously included here.

[13] Miles, *op. cit.*, 81.

[14] J. Wilcox, *The Relation of Molière to Restoration Comedy* (New York, 1938), 180–81.

[15] Possibly among other reasons because Molière became even more widely known and

The nine references to Molière are very mixed. Aphra Behn (1678) belittles the influence of *Le Malade imaginaire*,[16] Shadwell (1668) that of *Les Fâcheux*;[17] and in his *Miser* (1672) he tops this with the famous, uncompromising assertion of the superiority of the English playwrights, which assertion still in 1739 incensed Voltaire.[18] Whereas Shadwell obviously thought that Molière could only be improved, Richard Flecknoe (1667) already fears the original might suffer in the English rendering.[19] This attitude is much later taken up by John Ozell, the translator (1704),[20] but also by Fielding in his *Miser*:

> Happy our *English* Bard, if your Applause
> Grant h'as not injur'd the French Author's Cause,
> From that alone arises all his Fear;
> He must be safe, if he has sav'd Moliere. ("Prologue," lines 24–27)

Although it is debatable whether Shadwell or Fielding departs further from Molière in their reworking of the play, this change of attitude seems highly instructive.

Matthew Medbourne does indeed present Molière's play as "the Master-piece of Molière's Productions, or rather of all French Comedy"; but he also proudly points to the "considerable Additions" he has made to *Tartuffe* (1670).[21] Thomas Wright gives Molière his due (1693),[22] as does, significantly, Dryden in *Amphitryon*.[23] The most emphatic praise comes from John Caryll in the "Epilogue" to *Sir Salomon* (1671), where he coins the well-known phrase, "Molliere, the famous *Shakespear* of this

---

recognizable to an English audience. The remark on Cibber refers to his *Non-Juror* (1717, cf. *Tartuffe*) and *The Refusal* (1721, cf. *Les Femmes savantes*). Just as Shadwell was attacked in the preface to Settle's *Ibrahim* for his "thefts" in *The Hypocrite*, Cibber is charged with plagiarism by Collier; cf. Sr. Rose Anthony, S.C., *The Jeremy Collier Stage Controversy* (1937, repr. New York, 1966), 254, and by Dennis in *The Causes of the Decay* (1725?), ed. Hooker, II, 281.

[16] "To the Reader," *Sir Patient Fancy*.

[17] Preface, *Sullen Lovers*.

[18] "Reader," *The Miser*. Voltaire, "Vie de Molière . . .," Summary of *L'Avare*; cf. *Oeuvres complètes* (Paris, 1879), XXIII, 115. Already Voltaire suggests a comparison with Fielding's attitude.

[19] Preface, *The Damoiselles a la Mode*, acted 1666, pr. 1667.

[20] Preface, *Monsieur de Pourceaugnac, or, Squire Trelooby*.

[21] Dedication to Henry, Lord Howard of Norfolk; see also full title of the play.

[22] Dedication to Charles, Earl of Winchelsea, *The Female Vertuosos*.

[23] Dedication to Sir William Levison Gower, Bar. The *Companion to the Theatre* (2nd. edn., 1740, p. 20), incidentally, holds with the "additions" attitude so frequently met with earlier on. Langbaine's scathing and exaggerated criticism of Dryden rests on his demaskation of Dryden's "thefts" in the other plays (cf. *An Account of the English Dramatick Poets*, 1691, especially 130–77).

Age" (line 25).[24] The less often quoted continuation adds another explanation for the attitude towards Molière which manifests itself so often in this type of document: to the variously imputed guilty conscience of the plagiary which drives him either to silence or defiance, and to the genuine belief in English dramatic superiority, it adds patriotism:

> I hope this Stranger's Praise gives no pretence
> To charge us with a National Offence. (lines 27–28)[25]

This aspect is introduced, with different emphases, e.g. by Gay, Pope and Arbuthnot (1717)[26] and Mrs. Centlivre (1718) in the "Prologue" to *A Bold Stroke for a Wife*.[27] At the same time both passages are evidence supporting the statement that "if anything, translation and adaptation reached a higher level in this time than in the preceding periods."[28]

Not quite unexpectedly it seems to be in the collected translations that a general appraisal coupled with some detailed remarks first emerges in print. The series of selected or complete translations, the interrelations of which Tucker has demonstrated, begins with Ozell's (and others) *Works of Monsieur de Moliere* (1714).[29] The prefatory matter shows controlled admiration, but not yet exorbitant enthusiasm. The "Dedication" states that England and Italy can boast of several excellent comic writers, France only of Molière. The "Preface" opens with a passage of praise (which is literally translated from Grimarest):[30] "It may justly be said that *Moliere* was a happy and inimitable Genius, and that never any Man better follow'd the Precept which requires that Comedy shou'd instruct at the same Time that it diverts." He painted "after Nature"; no one has imitated Terence better; indeed, "He's call'd the *Terence* of his

---

[24] The ninth reference to Molière among this group occurs in Thomas Betterton's *The Amorous Widow*, Prologue, lines 17–18. It praises him. I have only seen the 1737 edition and could not check whether this prefatory piece by Charles Wilson actually was in the original (1670?, 1677).

[25] The importance of this Epilogue by Caryll has been vastly overestimated and this single instance generalised by A. de Mandach in his *Molière et la comédie de moeurs en Angleterre (1600–1668)* . . . (Neuchâtel, 1946), 7, 88, 90. Miles, *op. cit.*, 80–81, judges it more soberly.

[26] Prologue, *Three Hours After Marriage*.

[27] This is the famous "not one single tittle from Moliere" passage. For the whole question of patriotic feeling in prefatory matter to plays, see M. E. Knapp, *Prologues and Epilogues of the Eighteenth Century* (New Haven, 1961), "The Patriotic Prologue," 205–32.

[28] A. Nicoll, *Early Eighteenth Century Drama* (Cambridge, 1965), 143.

[29] As Tucker in his article explains, no further trace has been found of the edition entered into the *Stationers' Register* for 1693 (*op. cit.*, 83–84).

[30] I have not seen the original *Vie de Molière* but only the 2nd edn. (Amsterdam, 1705) and the *Oeuvres* (Paris, 1710). The French text in the latter corresponds word for word to Ozell's sentence quoted above.

Age: that Word includes all the Praises that can be given him." He has out-done Plautus in his *Miser* and *Amphitryon*. Even his worst plays have masterly strokes in them, and "those which are look'd upon to be the best, as the *Misantrope*, the *Tartuffe*, the *Learned Ladies*, etc., are Master-pieces that cannot be sufficiently admired." To this are added remarks on the weakness of Molière's unravellings (following Rapin);[31] other weaknesses are explained by pointing out his dependence on the king's commands and the haste in which he had to write.

If Ozell already set a high pitch for his praise, the authors of the *Select Comedies of Mr. de Moliere* (1732)[32] go much further. In the "Dedication to the Queen" (Vol. I), Molière is introduced as a model upon which both the audience's dramatic taste and the dramatists' art could be refined and improved.[33] The "Preface" to *The Miser* (probably written by James Miller)[34] opens, after a short introductory paragraph, on a new, resound-ing note which is worth comparing to the Grimarest/Ozell passage:

> It must be allowed by all who have any *Taste* for the *Drama*, or any Judgment in *Poetry*, that Moliere is the best Comic Author who ever wrote for the Stage; and this without any ways derogating from his two great *Ancestors* and *Masters* in the *Sock*, Plautus and Terence. 'Tis with their well-spun *Woof* that his beauteous *Texture* is wove, and 'twas by copying and blending *both* their Excel-lencies, that he became able to excel them *each*. He has all the *Spirit* and *Pleasantry* of *Plautus*, temper'd with the *Simplicity* and *Politeness* of *Terence*, so that he never *laughs* with the *one*, but he *thinks* with the *other*.

After more general points—Molière's knowledge of the Ancients and their rules, of philosophy and poetry, as well as his experience in life and powers of observation which enable him to draw "Men truly and fully" in the only way possible, "to copy from the Life" and to "paint" the manners "after Nature," finally his insight "into the Heart of Man"—there follows what I believe may be the first systematic and fairly detailed analysis of Molière's art, in several sections. "Characters" (strong, lively, consistent, manners adapted to character, speech, especially wit, arising naturally from the action, decent, polite—primary example, *The Miser*); "Conduct of his Fable" (probable and diverting, well managed, regular in the unities, dis-

---

[31] René Rapin, *Réflexions . . .* (1674), No. 25. Cf. also Voltaire, *op. cit.*, 98.

[32] This is the edition on which Prévost's enthusiastic impression of the "Estime des Anglois pour Molière" is based (*Le Pour et Contre . . .*, I [Paris, 1733], No. iv, 78–85).

[33] An interesting parallel to this, applied to the Italian theater, is Louis Riccoboni, *Observations sur la comédie, et sur le génie de Molière* (Paris, 1736); cf. especially iv, ix and xviii of the dedication to the Prince of Modena.

[34] According to Tucker, *op. cit.*, 88. I have unfortunately not been able to see L. P. Goggin, "Fielding and the *Select Comedies of Mr. de Moliere*," *PQ*, 21 (1952).

coveries and unravellings easy and familiar; Rapin rebutted); "*Moral*"
(most praiseworthy, noble, useful, instructive, courageous, decent); and
"*Stile*" (delicate and nervous; unfortunately he had to comply with the
customs and write in verse, against his better knowledge [sic.]). A few stoop-
ings to the vulgar are mentioned (Cf. Boileau, *L'Art poétique*, III) and
more or less condoned before the author winds up in an expansion of the
idea of Molière as a model for the improvement and re-orientation of
English comedy which at present is unnatural, diffuse and pernicious (Addison's *Drummer* and Vanbrugh's *Confederacy* excepted, which were
both, typically, demolished by the audience). To this incisive, largely neo-
classical credo, the dedications to the individual plays have little to add.
What they do add, however, are various memorable phrases; Molière
"has justly grown to the Authority of a Classic";[35] later dramatists who
have excelled "have copied *Moliere*, and therein were sure of copying
Nature";[36] in one prologue, finally, he is called "immortal *Moliere*."[37]

The enlarged, complete edition of this collection, the *Works* of 1739,
cuts down on this long preface, but retains the main opening paragraph
and some of the salient points, omitting however the entire attack on
English comedy; similar things happen to the "Preface" of the *Works* of
1748.[38] The Glasgow *Works* of 1751 do away altogether with a preface
and immediately start with the "Life," as does the Berwick edition of the
Works, 1771. It seems fairly clear that the *Select Comedies* of 1732 represents the effort of a band of devoted Molière enthusiasts (presumably with
Miller as guiding spirit), whose ideals and impulses were later watered
down by others, perhaps because they were less dedicated, or because
they felt the dramatic situation in England had changed.

The only other major collected translation is Samuel Foote's *Comic
Theatre* (1762), the fourth and fifth volumes of which are given to Molière,
who also takes up about half the "Preface." Foote, after emphasising the
didactic aspect of comedy and establishing character, or rather "that specific difference in the mind of one man, which renders him ridiculous to the
rest of his contemporaries" as the "great comic object," turns to Molière,
calling him "unquestionably the first comic poet the French have produced." But he immediately launches into a depreciation of Roman co-

---

[35] Vol. II, *The Cit turn'd Gentleman.*
[36] Vol. III, *The Blunderer.*
[37] Vol. V. (*Tartuffe*), "*Prologue*. By a *Young Gentleman* of the Academy in *Soho Square*.
Spoken by him when Acted there in the Year 1726."
[38] I have not seen the *Works* of 1755. (Tucker, *op. cit*: reprint in 1739, 1748 series).

medy and an attack on Molière for trying to imitate it in *Amphitryon* (which is improper and improbable in Foote's eyes). He also charges him, like Spence,[39] with giving too much space to the servants (except in *Le Misanthrope* and *Le Tartuffe*) and admitting them to an unrealistic familiarity with their masters. Still, he allows him "plenary possession of that first great comic requisite, character." He repeats the old charges of inadequate dénouement and popular vulgarity, but exonerates him from the charge of plagiarism by pointing out that he bettered what he borrowed.[40] In sum, this is much more limited applause compared with the *Select Comedies*.

I have up to this point concentrated on material where Molière was bound to be discussed and where a certain admiration might naturally be expected; it is essential to add a wider perspective. In the dramatic histories and in writings on comedy one meets the occasional objection to Molière on moral grounds. Examples, besides Bourdaloue and Bossuet, come from interesting quarters. There is the curious work *Maxims and Reflections upon Plays* (1699) which Sr. Rose Anthony suspects to be Collier's.[41] Here, the "Compositions of *Moliere*" are said to "abound" in "impious and scandalous Passages," and Molière is guilty of "the grossest and most nausious *Double-entendres* that ever . . . poysoned the Ears of Christians" (4-5). Surprisingly enough, although more mildly worded, moral objections are also raised by Riccoboni (1741).[42] *The Lounger*, No. L (1786) extends Bourdaloue's protest against the setting of false and misleading examples of behaviour in *Tartuffe*, and beyond that play to the *Ecole des femmes*, *George Dandin*, *Le Cocu imaginaire*, *L'Avare*, and the *Cheats of Scapin*[43] (whereas there seems to have been little echoing of Rousseau's attack on *Le Misanthrope*).

[39] Spence on Toinette; cf. note 9.
[40] This is a significant and amusing inversion of Shadwell's attitude in the *Miser* (1672).
[41] I have seen neither text in the original. Dibdin (*A Complete History of the English Stage*, ca. 1797–1800, II, 364–65) quotes at length from Father Bourdaloue's sermon. Scott in his famous review of Auger's edition, *Oeuvres* of Molière (Paris, 1819–27) and of Taschereau's monograph (Paris, 1825) originally published in *The Foreign Quarterly* for 1828 and repr. in *The Miscellaneous Prose Works*, 22 vols. (Edinburgh, 1851), XVIII, 137–215, mentions Bossuet and Bourdaloue together (171) and then, like Dibdin, quotes from the latter. The way in which the *Maxims and Reflections* argue, at least in the context of the passage on Molière, makes it clear that the English pen involved cannot have been just translating, so that Sr. Rose Anthony's surmise (*The Jeremy Collier Stage Controversy*, 157 ff) seems quite plausible.
[42] *An Historical and Critical Account of the Theatres in Europe* (1741), 157. Interestingly enough, the translator makes a footnote protesting Molière's decency.
[43] *The Lounger*, No. L (Edinburgh, Saturday Jan. 14, 1786), 197–98. *Vide infra* for Charles Dibdin's similar remarks.

However, what appears as even more important is that there are a considerable number of writers who completely pass by Molière.[44] While it is difficult to understand this lack of commentary in such cases and the slightness of references in others,[45] patriotic feelings may again explain the attitude of several authors. This applies to Dryden (1667),[46] Sir William Temple (1690),[47] and John Oldmixon,[48] to name just a few. In Temple and Oldmixon nationalistic bias is accompanied by the objection that Molière's plays are too farcical—an argument which reappears in Richard Hurd[49] and, much later, in Hazlitt,[50] to be brilliantly inverted and overcome by Scott.[51]

An equally important obstacle to the appreciation of Molière is the theory that humor is based mainly on language and nation and is therefore of necessity confined to each nation separately. Farquhar's *Discourse* (1702) is based on such thoughts,[52] although they alone are hardly responsible for his silence on Molière. James Beattie in the "Essay on Laughter and Ludicrous Composition" (1764) formulates the consequences of this approach very succinctly: "Shakespeare's humor will never be adequately relished in France, nor that of Moliere in England . . . ."[53] Hugh Blair is another representative of this opinion, although it does not

---

[44] Richard Flecknoe, "A Short Discourse of the English Stage" appended to *Love's Kingdom* (1664); James Wright, *Historia Histrionica* (1699); Charles Gildon. "An Essay on the Art, Rise and Progress of the English Stage," in Rowe's *Works* on Shakespeare (1714), IX, xlvi—lii (on Comedy); id. *The Complete Art of Poetry* (1718), I, 261–66 (on Comedy); William Whitehead, *An Essay on Ridicule* (1743); Corbyn Morris, *An Essay Toward Fixing the True Standards of Wit* . . . (1744); [John Hippisley] *A Dissertation on Comedy* (1750); anon. *An Essay on Satirical Entertainments* (1772) and others. B. Walwyn, *An Essay on Comedy* (1782), was unobtainable at the time of writing.

[45] Striking examples are Steele and Addison in the *Spectator* and Henry Home, Lord Kames, in his *Elements of Criticism* (Edinburgh, 1762).

[46] Cf. Watson's note to Neander's absurd claim that Molière and other French writers copied traits from the English dramatists: *Of Dramatic Poesy and other Critical Essays*, ed. G. Watson (London and New York, 1962), I, 57.

[47] "Of Poetry," in *The Works* (1798), edn. 1814, III, 437.

[48] *An Essay on Criticism* (1728), 54.

[49] "A Dissertation Concerning the Provinces of the Several Species of Drama" in *Q. Horatii Flacci Epistolae* . . . (1753), I, 277. He excepts, however, *Le Misanthrope* and *Le Tartuffe*. Another instance is Isaac Bickerstaffe's preface to *Doctor Last in his Chariot* (1769).

[50] *Lectures on the English Comic Writers*, Lecture I, "Introductory—On Wit and Humour" (3rd edn., 1841), 50–54.

[51] Scott, *op. cit.*, 207, (The Midas-Image).

[52] "A Discourse upon Comedy . . ." (1702), conveniently available in Scott Elledge, *Eighteenth Century Critical Essays* (Ithaca, N.Y., 1961), I, 92–93. One might also note here in passing the silence of Congreve on Molière in his various writings, including the letter to Dennis on Comedy, which was variously reprinted.

[53] *Essays* (Edinburgh, 1776), 684.

prevent him from concurring with Voltaire's assertion that "Moliere is the most eminent Comic Poet, of any age or country." He knows of "none who deserves to be preferred to him" (but nevertheless accepts the traditional strictures of the unravellings and the farcical elements).[54]

Praise of a general nature apparently becomes more frequent from the beginning of the eighteenth century onwards. In the "Original Letters of Love and Friendship" added to *Letters of Wit, Politicks and Morality* . . . (1701), there is a passage joining Jonson and Molière: "Our famous *Ben. Johnson's Silent Woman; The Fox*, and *The Alchymist*, and most of *Moliere's* Plays are the surest Standards to judge of Comedy . . ."[55] In the *Comparison Between the Two Stages* (1702) Molière and Plautus are endowed with authority.[56] Close in time to Beattie, William Cooke in his argumentation against sentimental comedy connects Shakespeare and Molière, rebutting the thesis that those two should have exhausted all viable comic characters.[57] Goldsmith links Plautus and Molière (1757).[58] In another place (1759) he varies the national and linguistic argument rather in the same way as Foote[59] in saying that the French, as opposed to the English, are fortunate in their "universal sameness of character" and draws the conclusion: "The French pictures therefore of life and manners are immediately allowed to be just, because foreigners are acquainted with the models from which they are copied. The Marquis of Moliere strikes all Europe. Sir John Falstaff, with all the merry men of Eastcheap, are entirely of England, and please the English alone."[60] A similar idea, but explaining the phenomenon of universality rather with Molière's superb powers of observing human nature, is heightened by Thomas Wilkes ("Samuel Derrick") to the statement: "His humorous

[54] *Lectures on Rhetoric and Belles Lettres* (1783), 540–41. But cf. his praise of Terence, 538. Voltaire also thought comedy to be mainly tied to nation and language; cf. *Lettres philosophiques ou Lettres anglaises*, ed. R. Naves (Paris, 1964), 115. A voice different from this fairly common conviction is Hurd, who expressly opposes Molière's Avare, as a picture of covetousness, to Racine's Nero, as a picture of a cruel man (*op. cit.*, 235 ff).

[55] Letter V, 235.

[56] Ed. by S. B. Wells as *A Late Restoration Book of the Theatre* (Princeton and London, 1942), 79.

[57] *The Elements of Dramatic Criticism* (1775), 151. Scott later placed Molière above Shakespeare in comedy (*op. cit.*, 204–05). As Shakespeare was not usually thought of as the master of comedy earlier on (that, for a long time, was Jonson), this does not strike as quite so revolutionary an innovation as it might seem at first sight.

[58] *The Monthly Review*, No. XVII (1757); in A. Friedman, ed., *Collected Works*, 5 vols. (Oxford, 1966), I, 85. Cf. also *An Enquiry into the Present State of Polite Learning in Europe* (1759), Ch. IV, ed. Friedman, I, 273.

[59] *The Roman and English Comedy Consider'd and Compar'd* (1747), 22.

[60] *An Enquiry* . . . Ch. VII, ed. Friedman, I, 293–4.

characters are neither French, Spanish, nor English: they are Citizens of
the World, and their exactness must be acknowledged by all nations."[61]
With this remark we have reached a connection to the attitude most clearly
manifested in the 1732 *Select Comedies* "Preface."

Three authors remain to be discussed, in whose thought on comedy
Molière plays a role unusual for their respective times. The first is John
Dennis, whom Garnett and Gosse called "the first English critic to do full
justice to Milton and Molière."[62] At any rate, for Dennis, Molière is an
authority of the first order, whom he uses on the most diverse occasions
and in most varied contexts.[63] Thus, when defending his *Comical Gallant*
(an adaptation of *The Merry Wives*), he states the principle that comedy
can very well prosper without a considerable love interest and adduces
Molière as an example.[64] In another place he compares Molière and
Menander; both suffered the fate of being translated by people who in
the process lost the *naïveté*, "which is a charming simplicity, dictated by
pure Nature."[65] It is well known that Dennis sided with the Moderns.
And although he expressly shares the belief that English comedy excels all
other[66] (while realizing that this fact is not known outside Britain)[67] and
puts Jonson first,[68] he gives Molière a place close to him and in fact voices
his preference for modern comedy in the phrase "Moliere and Two or
Three of our own Comic Poets."[69] The longest passage on Molière, however, occurs in the *Defence of Sir Fopling Flutter* (1722). Here he states his
principle that the subject of comedy must be ridiculous throughout, as
must the incidents and characters, at any rate the principal ones. Having
mentioned the usual Jonsonian triad (*The Silent Woman*, *The Alchymist*,
and *The Fox*), he continues: " 'Tis the very same Thing in the Masterpieces of *Moliere*; The *Misanthrope*, the *Imposter*, the *Avare*, and the
Femmes Savantes . . . ," a list of which the first two at least remained con-

[61] *A General View of the Stage* (1759), 55. Cf. a similar passage in Scott, *op. cit.*, 141, in conjunction with 206. Humbert (*Molière, Shakespeare und die deutsche Kritik*, 64) reports an
anecdote of Charles Kemble, who is said to have uttered the same sentiments in Paris, 1800.
Also, later writers refer to this story. (Cf. Schmidt, 157–58).

[62] *English Literature: An Illustrated Record* (New York, 1935), III, 178; cf. 181–82. Quoted
from Hooker's edition of Dennis (see note 4), II, lxxiv.

[63] E.g. against Cibber (ed. Hooker, II, 262) in 1723, and against Steele's Biddy Tipkin (ed.
Hooker, II, 187) in 1720.

[64] *A Large Account of the Taste in Poetry* . . . (1702), ed. Hooker, I, 284–85.

[65] *To Henry Cromwell Esq.* . . . (1717, publ. 1721), ed. Hooker, II, 161.

[66] *Remarks on a Play, Call'd, The Conscious Lovers* (1723), ed. Hooker, II, 252.

[67] *The Advancement and Reformation of Modern Poetry* (1701), ed. Hooker, I, 205.

[68] *Remarks on a Play* . . . ed. Hooker, II, 259.

[69] *The Advancement and Reformation* . . ., ed. Hooker, I, 211, 224.

stant favorites throughout the century. And he mentions fourteen other comedies of Molière in which the principal character and even the very title show "the Ridicule of Comedy."[70]

Whereas Dennis in no one place develops a coherent theory of comedy (and consequently scatters his remarks on Molière), John Aikin is one of those who do, after a fashion.[71] The interesting aspect of his "On the Province of Comedy" (pr. 1773) in the present context is that for all the loose categories of comic objects for the stage which he establishes (9-16)—improprieties of fashion, silly affectations and pedantry, superstition and priestcraft, the abuses of the professions and the singularities of character —Molière invariably furnishes him with examples, sometimes in conjunction with others.[72] He ends with preferring Molière's and Congreve's genius for comedy to that of Terence (24).

It was not unusual for dramatic histories to lead up to English drama with a purview of the ancient theater and that of other nations. Charles Dibdin in his *Complete History of the English Stage* (ca. 1797-1800) does this on a very large scale indeed. And in French drama he pays most attention to Molière, whose great Paris phase he also distinguishes by according it a chapter of its own,[73] which represents the longest and most detailed treatment of Molière (outside the collected translation prefaces) which I have seen in the entire period. Like the "Lives" prefixed to the translated *Works*, he proceeds from play to play, without adding anything particularly novel. However, it is interesting to note how the argumentation of Bourdaloue against *Tartuffe*, from which he quotes only to dismiss it (364-65), later on seems to gain with him, so that he practically approaches the stance of *The Lounger*, No. L. Nevertheless, Dibdin's main position is quite firm. Molière ranks highest, even if he did not, impeded by unfavorable circumstances, attain a still higher standard (which remains unspecified but is easily guessed). As portions of Dibdin's summary echo and combine several arguments concerning Molière which were presented

---

[70] Ed. Hooker, II, 249.

[71] As opposed, e.g., to Horace Walpole, "Thoughts on Comedy" (1775–76), publ. in the *Works*, II (1798), 315–22, recently repr. by F. W. Bateson in *EIC*, 15 (1965), 162–70 ("Exhumations"). Walpole's references to Molière are not infrequent, but diffuse and fairly superficial.

[72] The others mentioned are Cibber, Jonson, Shadwell, Dryden, and of course Congreve. *Miscellaneous Pieces in Prose* by J. and A. L. Aikin (probably written earlier than 1773), 1–26.

[73] Five Vols., divided into 10 Books, of which nearly three are devoted to the theaters of other nations. Molière is dealt with in a wider framework in Book II, Chapters XI–XIII, of which the last is solely about him (Vol. II, 355–77).

earlier on, it may suitably stand near the close of this study, even as it stands near the end of our period and its concern with Molière:

> The rank *Moliere* held in literature has been long estimated and decided. We have nothing to do but to compare his works with whatever we know of, perfect and admirable, in the ancients, and we shall find him in every point of view rising greatly superior to them all. He has all the pointed severity of *Aristophanes*, without his wickedness and his malignity; he has to the beauty, the fidelity, the portraiture of *Menander*, added higher and more finished graces of his own; he has the nerve and strength of *Plautus* without his grossness and his obscenity; and he has a thousand times more elegance from nature and genius, assisted by philosophic observation, than *Terence*.
>
> Nature, and the absurdities of the age in which he lived, supplied him with an inexhaustible source of materials. Comedy took a new form in his hands, and became a scourge for the vices and follies of all ranks, to the truth of which all were implicitly obliged to subscribe; and there can be but little doubt, if he could have written independantly, and have been independantly attended, but he would have carried comedy, true comedy as correct as it can be defined, to a higher degree of perfection than any author has done either before or since. (374–75)

It has become evident, I hope, that Schmidt's statement, which formed the point of departure, cannot be said to correspond to the facts. On the contrary, it may be asserted that basically all the prominent features of Molière criticism in the nineteenth century have been anticipated: We have seen ample evidence of enthusiasm matching that of Scott; samples of reasoned appreciation foreshadowing that of later, admittedly more detailed studies; and one instance at least of Molière's constantly and quite naturally coming to mind in a loosely systematic treatise on the comic and on comedy, as happens later with Meredith (and of course Bergson). On the other hand the widely spread indifference to Molière, noted in the absence of references to him both in private communications and in writings dealing with comedy, cannot be disregarded and appreciably qualifies, along with the various objections raised against Molière's plays, Dibdin's Olympian phrase "The rank *Moliere* held in literature has been long estimated and decided." However, on the whole one may say that his importance, after a considerable period of neglect, was realised more and more from 1700 onwards. The phase of least limited approval seems, on balance, to be the first half of the eighteenth century. But continued—if often differently motivated—opposition and relegation to strictly limited significance notwithstanding, his status never relapsed into that of the pre-1700 stage.

However, everything revolves around one essential point. Generally

Molière's impact on actual critical principles remained relatively slight. There is little evidence of the traditional rules being placed second to a "goût naturel" (Spence) or of Molière's plays having become, as the writer of the seventh of the "Original Letters" asserted, "the surest standards to judge of Comedy." This point is not even reached in the *Select Comedies* "Preface" in spite of Molière's presentation as a model, although this text gets as close to such a stance as was perhaps possible. Molière is constantly judged by rules established independently of his art, and raised or blamed as he happens to conform to, or depart from, the individual's interpretation of these rules. Even if one could not easily trace the standard objections, or at any rate some of them, to French critics, notably to Boileau and Rapin, it would not be difficult to show that the rules are largely governed by a neoclassical concept of comedy, as Dibdin puts it, "true comedy as correct as it can be defined." And in spite of the fact that some of Molière's plays, still regarded as his greatest, pass muster with the earlier critics, one feels a little relieved that Molière did have to write under the circumstances so often deplored and was thus prevented from writing this unutterably correct kind of Comedy Dibdin and numerous others envisaged.

The selection of material for this short study has, albeit that breadth was certainly intended, not been evenly balanced, the first criterion having been the likelihood of finding commentary on Molière. It would be interesting to approach the question of his role in the critical thought of the seventeenth and eighteenth centuries from quite different angles, of which some have already partially emerged here: The Collier controversy, for example, or the Sentimental movement, or pre-Romanticism and Romanticism. In another direction one could, complementing the many studies of Molière's influence on individual writers which were disregarded here, study the reactions to Molière, both those I have discussed (quite consciously) as on the same footing, and others I may have overlooked, from the point of view of their relative literary and critical importance. And also the investigation of the individual plays' critical fortunes might valuably contribute to our knowledge of Molière's place in comic theory and, as all the other aspects mentioned, through this enhance our understanding of the age's concepts of comedy.

MOLIÈRE AND WRITERS
OF THE ENGLISH ROMANTIC ERA,
ESPECIALLY BYRON

Abraham Avni

It seems obvious that the great English Romantics, in their lyrical poetry of the despairing individual or physical nature, would have little use for Molière, his dramatic matter (action, characters) or form. In spite of this, they could, of course, have known his comedies, having either read or seen them performed and thus been influenced by the spirit of his ethical satire, his view of human nature or attitude towards life and people. Furthermore, English Romantic writing is not made of one cloth. In addition to lyrical and narrative poetry, it includes criticism, essays on different questions, and satire and thus leaves more scope for an interest in and influence by Molière.[1] I should like to examine the question of this influence, on which we have been given only odds and ends of information until now. It will not be possible to distinguish with certainty sources from analogues so that in some cases the discovered resemblance will not be a discovery of derivation but of parallels in kindred spirits.

First, the English Romantics' knowledge of Molière: it could have been derived from the viewing of his comedies which in this time (1790-1830) seem to have been performed in London theaters. It is hard to tell, in spite of the titles, which of the plays were pure Molière, which free adaptations and which others' plays with mere insertions of scenes from Molière.[2] I found no evidence that the English Romantics did see his comedies, although for most of them it was physically possible because they either lived in London at the time or made occasional visits. Unlike viewing, reading is more easily attested, explicitly or implicitly, either by library holdings or by testimony of the writers themselves. Keats owned a three-volume edition of Molière's work preserved in the Keats House in London. Peacock possessed two different editions of the comic dramatist,

---

[1] Romantic plays are not treated in this essay, nor is the critical reception accorded to the performance of Molière's comedies on the English stage in 1780–1830.

[2] John Genest, ed. *The English Stage from the Restoration in* 1660–1830 (1832; rpt. New York: Franklin, n.d.), IV, 425–441; X, (index) 1–140.

according to the sale's catalogue of his library.[3] Mary Shelley makes four
entries in her journal which give two dates for her reading of Molière's
work (in French) in general and two separate dates for *George Dandin*.[4]
This comedy seems to be the only one read by her husband-poet.[5] Why
this popularity of *George Dandin*? The reason may be that George Dandin
is not really a comic, but rather a tragic figure and that, in view of Shelley's
own love affairs, the play attracted him because it is the only one where
adultery is involved. A more diligent reader of Molière was another
member of the Shelley circle, Claire Clairmont, who was romantically
involved with both Shelley and Byron and bore the latter a daughter. Her
journal notes the reading of eight different plays of Molière in four days.
Her entry for these days includes a quotation of several lines from *Tartuffe*
"descriptive of the doctrines of Christianity."[6] Henry Crabb Robinson,
a critic and friend of the great Romantics, records in his diary a reading
of Voltaire's "life of Molière."[7] Southey does more than that as he gives
a detailed account of his reading of Molière in the French edition of
Didot (1790–91) in his commonplace book. He comments on the linguistic
aspects of the plays, e.g. neologisms, the circumstances of the first performance, and also quotes Boileau, who criticized Molière because he
made rustics in his plays speak their own language. Finally, he deals with
the theatrical aspect of *L'Amour médecin*, remarking that the play cannot
be really appreciated unless seen acted on the stage.[8] Southey is raising
here a question of concern to his Romantic contemporaries, the proper
diction for poetry or drama and the stage presentation vs. reading of
dramas.

We can also offer some instances of allusions to Molière's characters
and quotations. In a polemical essay "Political Economy, The Standard

[3] Allen N. Munby, ed. *Sale Catalogues of Libraries of Eminent Persons* (London: Mansell, 1971), I, 192. Among these catalogues is also Byron's.

[4] Mary Shelley, *Mary Shelley's Journals*, ed. Frederick L. Jones (Norman: Univ. of Oklahoma Press, 1947), 86, 90, 96, 114.

[5] Adolphe Droop, *Die Belesenheit Percy Bysshe Shelleys* as quoted by James A. Noto-poulos, *The Platonism of Shelley*, (1949; rpt. New York: Octagon, 1969), 132.

[6] Claire Clairmont, *The Journals of Claire Clairmont*, ed. Marion K. Stocking (Cambridge, Mass; Harvard Univ. Press, 1968), 89–90. The lines quoted from I, vi, are spoken by Orgon: "Qui suit bien ses [Tartuffe's] leçons goûte une paix profonde/Et comme du fumier regarde tout le monde/Oui, je deviens tout autre avec son entretien. . ."

[7] Henry Crabb Robinson, *Diary, Reminiscences and Correspondence* (Boston: Fields, Os-good, 1870), I, 380. Robinson describes the short "Vie de Molière," included as preface in the Garnier edition of the playwright (1946) as "amusing enough."

[8] Robert Southey, *Southey's Common Place Book*, ed. John W. Warter (London: Long-man, 1850), 296–98.

and the Edinburgh Saturday Post," published in *The Quarterly Review* of November 10, 1827, De Quincey deals with the demand that more of Britain's land be brought under cultivation lest Britain be dependent for its subsistence upon foreigners. He remarks that "to the demand we answer like Thomas Diafoirus, by distinguishing . . . ." He continues that the distinction should be made depending on whether the viewpoint is political economy or "larger considerations of general political prudence."[9] To a present-day reader not familiar with the particular passage in *Le Malade imaginaire* (II, vii), De Quincey's allusion will certainly appear far-fetched. Mary Shelley's allusion in her letter to Leigh Hunt of March 7, 1817, will sound more appropriate. In it she reproaches her correspondent for being unable to pronounce and spell correctly the text of the "marseillaise" and concludes, "When I see you, you must either learn that [French] or Italian that we may not always shock one another with our vernacular tongue. A thing Molière's philosopher would not endure."[10] Byron includes, in a letter to *Blackwood's Edinburgh Magazine*, the following critical comment on Wordsworth, which is a near quotation from *Le Bourgeois gentilhomme* (II, vi): "Wordsworth is the reverse of Molière's gentleman who had been 'talking prose all his life without knowing it' for he thinks that he has been all his life writing both prose and verse and neither of what he conceives to be such can be properly said to be either one or the other." Also in his correspondence, in a letter to his half-sister Augusta, Byron alludes to the main character in *L'Avare*: "Can't you drive this cousin of ours [Colonel Leigh, her future husband] out of your pretty head? Or if you are so far gone, why don't you give old L'Harpagon (I mean the General [Colonel Leigh's father]) the slip and take a trip . . . ?"[11] In his short-lived newspaper *The Watchman*, Coleridge criticizes a speech in Parliament by Mr. Wyndham, the then Secretary of War, because he justified the erection of controversial military barracks by the need "to secure the attachment of the soldiers to the government." And the poet drives his point home by freely quoting Sganarelle's words in *Le Médecin malgré lui* (III, iv): "When Sedition and Treason were daily and nightly disseminated he [Wyndham] would say to the soldiers in the

[9] Thomas De Quincey, *New Essays by DeQuincey*, ed. Stuart M. Tave (Princeton: Princeton Univ. Press, 1966), 175.

[10] Mary Shelley, *The Letters of Mary Shelley*, ed. Frederick L. Jones (Norman: Oklahoma Univ. Press, 1946), I, 22.

[11] Lord Byron, *The Works of Lord Byron, Letters and Journals*, ed. Rowland E. Prothero (1898–1901; rpt. New York: Octagon, 1966), I, 35–36.

words of the French comedian 'If I cannot make them dumb, I will make you deaf.'"[12] I cannot discover a particular pattern in these allusions and quotations of the Romantics, but they all come in polemical or quarrel-some writing of political or literary nature and certainly add to the argument presented a humorous, vivid, and cogent quality, particularly if the reader knows a bit of Molière.

The critical attention paid to Molière by English Romantics is also worthy of note (Southey's entry in his *Commonplace Book* came close to criticism) although much of it consisted of general praise. Hazlitt, who offered a relative wealth of critical comments on Molière, should be considered in a separate article. Coleridge mentions Molière as one of the few Frenchmen whom he appreciates, although he explains the ob-stacle to a deeper or more intimate evaluation: "O that I could find a France for my love! But spite of Pascal, Madame Guyon and Molière, France is my Babylon, the mother of whoredoms in morality, philosophy, taste. The French themselves feel a foreignness in these writers. How indeed is it possible at once to love Pascal and Voltaire?"[13] Coleridge values Molière because he considers him a Platonist for whom he feels a spiritual affinity as he does for Dante, Shakespeare, Milton, Pascal, and Madame Guyon, whereas for writers whom he considers Aristoteleans, like Dryden, Pope, Johnson, and Voltaire, he shows indifference if not disdain. This distinction between Platonists and Aristotelians became for Coleridge synonymous with a distinction between writers of genius and those of mere talent, writers of imagination and writers of mere fancy.[14] Also in *The Friend* Coleridge deals briefly with Molière's eccentric types of the hypochondriac, hypocrite, and miser. He admits their "excess and ludi-crous quality," but their eccentricity as presented by the dramatist appears to him as "a natural growth of the human mind and as such can apply to my own heart or at least to whole classes of my fellow creatures . . . " In the same periodical he included Molière in his "brief list of the Goths, those whose Gothic blood had not been adulterated with Celtic."[15] Yet

[12] *The Watchman* appeared from 1 Mar. to 13 May 1796. Samuel Taylor Coleridge, *The Watchman*, ed. Lewis Patton, vol. II of *Collected Works of Samuel Taylor Coleridge* (Prince-ton: Princeton Univ. Press, 1970) 259.
[13] Samuel Taylor Coleridge, *The Notebooks of Samuel Taylor Coleridge*, ed. Cathleen Koburn (New York: Pantheon Books, 1961), II, Note 2598.
[14] Paul Deschamps, *La Formation de la pensée de Coleridge* 1772–1804 (Paris: Didier, 1964), 375.
[15] Samuel Taylor Coleridge, *The Friend*, ed. Barbara Rooke, vol. IV of *Collected Works of Samuel Taylor Coleridge* (Princeton: Princeton Univ. Press, 1969), II, 217, 217n. Coleridge

little that Coleridge had to say on Molière has survived, and that is of a rather general nature. Applying his distinction between a poem whose immediate object is pleasure and other kinds of literature whose immediate object is truth, would he have considered Molière to be primarily a moralist who has fulfilled his didactic function of relating art to society or rather, first and foremost, the amusing artist and satirist?

The praise of Walter S. Landor, the Romantic poet of old age, is couched in even more general terms but in poetical form. He extols, for example, Molière's dialogue for its true comic art as opposed to the bitter humor of Swift, "Is nothing good at home?/Yes . . . but I look in vain /For a Molière or La Fontaine./Swift in his humour was as strong/But there was gall upon his tongue/Bitters and acids may excite/Yet satisfy not appetite"; and as opposed to the mere "banter" of Lucian. In another epigram Landor praises the wisdom of Molière's elderly women, none of whom he finds in his country, "We have old women and to spare/None fit to judge like thine Molière . . . ."[16]

The references to Molière in Byron's work, in addition to the above allusions, are not numerous, but they are more meaningful and useful for consideration of possible influences.[17] Molière's *Dom Juan* is named once in a conversation between Byron and Mrs. Guiccioli, with whom the poet lived for about four years in Italy. In it the two discuss a previous conversation with Medwin, a member of their circle, in which the latter praised the constancy of women while Byron took the opposite view in order to punish Medwin for his vanity. Byron did so at the risk, as he now admits to Guiccioli, of the world's thinking him "a real Don Juan . . . Molière's Don Juan."[18] A second mention of Molière is found in an entry in Byron's diary for January 21, 1821. Here he first quotes Baron Grimm that comedy writers were not happy or gay persons in real life, and he adds

---

concludes the praise, "In the comedy of Shakespeare and Molière the more accurate my knowledge or the more profoundly I think the greater the satisfaction that mingles with my laughter."

[16] Walter S. Landor, *The Complete Works of Walter Savage Landor*, ed. Stephen Wheeler (London: Chapman, 1933), XIV, 250n; XV, 209.

[17] The works of Molière are not included either in the sale's catalogue of Byron's library (see note 3) or in the catalogue of books the poet claimed to have read in his youth and which are listed in Moore's *Life* of Byron as quoted by Clement T. Good, *Byron as a Critic* (Weimar: Wagner, 1923), 34–37. However, Byron remarked, "I have omitted several from my catalogue." *Ibid*, 37n. Also, a poet's posthumous library catalogue does not give a fully reliable clue to his readings or borrowings.

[18] Peter Quennell, ed. *Byron: A Self-Portrait. Letters and Diaries 1798–1824* (London: Murray, 1950), II, 570. To make my references clearer, I shall always call Molière's work *Dom Juan* as he did in the original.

that at this moment "I feel as bilious as the best comic writer of them all, . . . Molière, who has written some of the best comedies in any language and who is supposed to have committed suicide."[19] Byron not only gives recognition to Molière's greatness but also shows knowledge of his personality and the mysterious circumstances of his death which gave rise to rumors that he took his own life. Third, Byron names Molière in his *Don Juan*, "If all these seemed a heterogeneous mass/To be assembled at a country seat . . ./The days of Comedy are gone alas!/When Congreve's fool could vie with Molière's *bête*/Society is smoothed to that excess/That manners hardly differ more than dress" (XIII, 94). By assembling a great array of characters at the banquet in Norman Abbey and then actually forgetting all of them except four and Don Juan, who are given a full portrayal, Byron intends to "do homage to Congreve, and in corollary, to analyse and rebuke that contemporary uniformity of 'manners' and 'dress' which he goes on to prove unnatural and untrustworthy."[20] This may be so. But the above line also acknowledges Byron's debt to Molière's comedy of manners. The satire of *Don Juan* being ethical makes, I think, Byron's poem closer to Molière than to Restoration comedy.

Indeed Byron's satire, *Don Juan*, reflects the influence of Molière in several ways, particularly of *Dom Juan*. True, Byron shaped his *Don Juan* in such an original manner that he hardly seems indebted to any previous adaptations of the Don Juan myth: he completely changed his hero from huntsman to prey and omitted most other traditional characters. If there is any noticeable debt, critics tend to ascribe it to Tirso de Molina's, Goldoni's, or Da Ponte's versions or other adaptations of the myth, for example the shipwreck and subsequent rescue of Don Juan.[21] Yet there are other elements in Byron's *Don Juan* which make his work more similar to Molière's than we were led to believe till now. What speaks, in my view, for Molière's influence rather than that of the other authors of the Don Juan plays is, first, the references to Molière described above and unequalled by comparable references to these other authors; and, second, specific points of similarity which link *Dom Juan* to Byron's satire.

First, the episodic nature of Molière's comedy, the series of disconti-

---

[19] Ernest J. Lovell, ed. *His Very Self and Voice: Collected Conversations of Lord Byron* (New York: MacMillan, 1954), 278. In yet another reference Byron describes Molière as "saturnine." See Prothero, V, 578.

[20] M. G. Cooke, *The Blind Man Traces the Circle: On the Patterns and Philosophy of Byron's Poetry* (Princeton: Princeton Univ. Press, 1969), 133.

[21] For details and reasons of these descriptions, see Leo Weinstein, *The Metamorphoses of Don Juan*, Stanford Studies in Lang. and Lit., No. 18 (Stanford Univ. Press, 1959), 79n.

nuous, barely connected events, is reminiscent of Byron's open-ended satire of a similar nature. Second, there are comparable incidents or elements in the plot of the two works in addition to the shipwreck: Thus Dom Juan lures Elmire out of a convent, but by his outrageous conduct he makes her return to her convent (IV, vi), just as Don Juan's amatory entanglement with Julia causes her to be sent to a convent for life (I, 111). Dom Juan, examining Charlotte's teeth and eyes as if she were a slave up for auction (II, ii), does to her as slave traders on behalf of the sultana do to Don Juan in the slave market of Constantinople (V, 24). Third, it has been pointed out that Byron's innovation is to have completely done away with Don Juan's valet, who elsewhere serves as his companion and foil. This is not completely true even if we discount as such a companion the tutor Pedro, whose role is short and ineffectual (e.g. II, 56). Byron has given Don Juan a real companion in the harem and war cantos (V-VIII) in the person of John Johnson, who is an English soldier of fortune, a character of good sense and sang-froid, a foil to the more sensitive and somewhat passive character of Don Juan. By his remarks and practical counsel, Johnson sustains Don Juan in many critical situations.

In addition, the role of Sganarelle is comparable to that of Byron as a persona, as the ironic commentator in all cantos of *Don Juan*. Whereas the valets in the other versions of *Don Juan* remain mere buffoons, Sganarelle is not only a Sancho Panza-like foil to his master but also such a commentator. His healthy and natural humor equips him for his role of ironic commentator, in which he applies both moral reproach and ridicule to Dom Juan's base actions and to the noble sentiments in which he cloaks them.[22] Byron adopts a comparable role vis-à-vis Don Juan with a temporary and partial help from John Johnson. As a commentator he similarly interposes between the reader and the public, clarifying the real nature and motives of Don Juan, although his comment, subtler and broader and beyond Don Juan, is more concerned with mankind in general.

What also makes the role of Sganarelle comparable to the role of Byron the ironic commentator is digression. There is a digression in the very first passage of Molière's play. It is an amusing, trivial discourse on the merit of tobacco, but it inserts a little piece of topical interest. In *Don Juan*, Byron of course makes many more topical comments, be they on champagne, food, the contemporary political situation, or literary scene. And

---

[22] Francis Lawrence, "The Ironic Commentator in Molière's *Don Juan*," *Studi Francesi*, 12 (1968), 201–07.

in his "Island" (II, 19) he addresses an apostrophe to "Sublime tobacco!" reminiscent of Sganarelle's praise that "there is nothing to equal tobacco" (I, ii).

Yet another comparison of the two works involves infidelity. Since a defense of inconstancy was unsuitable to Byron's young hero, the author presents it as one of his own reflections. Drawing the comparison we find Byron using similar arguments in such a defense as does Dom Juan.[23] Dom Juan's words, "Constancy is only suitable for fools. All beautiful women have the right to attract us. I use my eyes to observe the value of all women, and to each one I pay that homage and tribute which nature demands from us," (I,ii),[24] are echoed in Byron's lines, ". . . inconstancy is nothing more/Than admiration due where Nature's rich/Profusion with young beauty covers o'er/Some favoured object . . ./In short, it is the use of our own eyes/With one or two small senses added, just/To hint that flesh is form'd of fiery dust" (II, 211–12). Finally, we may compare the language of Sganarelle and of Byron the ironic commentator, even though Molière wrote in prose. Sganarelle's language is one of easy colloquialism, appealing to everyday experience which, for example, at the beginning of the play, stands out against the high language of Gusman, Elvira's squire. Similarly, Byron the ironic commentator, who often speaks in the last two or three lines of the ottava rima, uses a very direct, colloquial language in contrast to the more ornate diction of Byron the narrator. We could also mention the many farces which enliven or cheapen the action of both *Dom Juan* and *Don Juan*.[25]

We can now broaden and strengthen our limited comparison by noting common, recurrent themes which bind together Byron's satires and Molière's comedies. Such a common theme is, first, hypocrisy. In Molière, the theme of the more serious comedies is the exposure of hypocrisy and affectations in all their different forms. It is, for example, the religious hypocrisy of a Tartuffe, who perseveres in it, and of Dom Juan, for whom it is a last resort, a vaunted stratagem, which is laid bare. In other plays social hypocrisy in court, the falsities of convention, and repression as a way to develop virtue—all are humorously revealed or satirically lashed.

---

[23] The similarity was noted by Willis Pratt. See *Byron's Don Juan*, ed. Truman G. Steffan and Willis W. Pratt (Austin: Univ. of Texas Press, 1957), IV, 80–81.

[24] My quotation is from Molière, *Don Juan. The Statue at the Banquet*, trans. Wallace Fowlie (Great Neck, N.Y.: Barron, 1964), 16.

[25] The often noted contribution of Don Juan to the elements of crime, egoism and pride in Manfred's character is not our concern in this paper.

Hypocrisy is similarly a dominant theme, or at least a secondary theme, in three of Byron's principal satires: "Beppo," "Vision of Judgment," and *Don Juan*. In "Beppo" the pretense of English marital "fidelity" maintained at the cost of secret extramarital affairs is held up satirically against the openness, honesty, and even nonchalance with which such an affair is treated in Italy, and religious hypocrisy (e.g. in connection with Lent) is also lashed. "Vision of Judgement" is an exposure of the religious and literary hypocrisies in Southey's "Vision of Judgment," which was written as an apotheosis of George III on his death and which Byron's "Vision" parodies. The kinds of hypocrisy exposed in *Don Juan* cover a broad range, including the hypocrisy of Platonic love; the prevalence of cant in religion, politics and education; the pretense and boredom of English society. Although both authors exhibit and denounce this common vice humorously or satirically, they also do not simply extol uncompromising frankness and honesty, because they admit extenuating or complicating circumstances. In *Misanthrope* Molière is obviously not on the side of Alceste, who is blindly attacking the perfidies and flatteries of society and whose honesty almost becomes a monomania or pose, but on the side of his friend Philinte, an intelligent man who admits the corruption of society yet prefers to accept its rules and make the best of them. In *Tartuffe* Elmire accepts compromises to avoid clashes and preserve her family, and she is certainly presented by the author as a sympathetic character. She is in a sense comparable to Byron's more complicated Adeline in *Don Juan*. Adeline is a chief exponent of English hypocrisy, but she has to show coldly polished manners and self-discipline to maintain her position as the wife of the lord of the manor and the hostess at his frequent banquets. By suppressing her emotions beneath a layer of ice, she is also sublimating or refining them (XIII, 36-39). Byron has therefore an ambivalent attitude towards her if not as favorable as Molière seems to have towards Elmire. The two writers seem to be recognizing the complex origin of hypocritical social conduct at the very time they are attacking hypocrisy.

Another theme common to Byron and Molière is the bluestocking. The attack on the bluestocking can, however, be linked to the attack on hypocrisy, because Molière and Byron, I think, see in the bluestocking an artificial being who covers up or distorts its true human or female nature as the hypocrites do. Also, Byron's interest in and dislike for literary, pedantic women was strengthened if not inspired by his wife Annabella Milbanke, whom he considered to be true to the type. Beside *Les Précieuses ridicules* and *Les Femmes savantes* we can thus place some comparable treatment of the type by Byron. He described the absurdity of "ladies intellectual" in the person of the learned Donna Inez in *Don Juan* (I); he included a short satire on the English learned ladies, "literary coxcombs," in "Beppo" (St. 75); and he devoted a whole satire, "Blues," to bluestockings. The poet calls the "Blues" an eclogue, but it is actually a closet drama consisting of two dialogues, in the first of which Messrs. Tracy and Inkel ridicule the critic Scamp, but they also talk about Miss Lilac ("a poet, chymist, mathematician") whom Tracy is wooing and intending to marry, although he is warned by his interlocutor that she is a rabid bluestocking. Then comes a short soliloquy of a bluestocking's husband, Sir Richard Bluebottle, complaining of his wretched life that is completely dominated if not smothered by the cultural interests and pre-occupations of his wife. This is followed by the second dialogue involving three bluestockings defending the writers Scamp (Hazlitt), Mouthy (Southey) and Wordswords (Wordsworth) against Inkel's satiric thrusts. Byron is here doing to writers scorned by him what Molière does in *Les Femmes savantes*, when in the persons of Trissotin and Vadius, admired by the *femmes savantes* of the comedy, he treats derisively the Abbé Cotin and Ménage respectively, both writers of some reputation in his time. But it is the bluestockings who are the main butt of the satire in both works, as the titles indicate, and Sir Bluebottle is comparable to Molière's sub-missive and timid Chrysale. Finally, there are many gibes at doctors in Byron's satires and letters, which is certainly much less than four or five different plays of Molière which turn directly on the ridicule of the medical profession.

Another writer of the Romantic period who invites comparison with Molière's plots and characters is Thomas Love Peacock. As does Byron's, a considerable part of his writing displays unromantic features and pre-sents antiromantic attitudes and criticism. This is the valuable part of his writing, not his romantic poetry, and to it belong his novels of talk, a type of narrative comedy for which models or analogues can be found in a variety of earlier literature. To these analogues belongs the comedy of Molière because of similar tone, conception of character interrelation-ships and some details of plot. One may associate Peacock's work with that of Molière "who has a related interest in forms of anti-social mono-mania and who finds his common-sense antidote as much in beautiful women as in *honnêtes hommes*."[26] These women, generally devoted to

---

[26] Carl Dawson, *His Fine Wit: A Study of Thomas Love Peacock* (Berkeley: Univ. of California Press, 1970), 172–73.

books, are in a sense the central characters in Peacock's conversation novels. There is a formula for these novels of little plot: a host collects a party of eccentric and amusing guests and engages them in long discussion on different subjects. Sometimes the assembled group travels and courtships develop. The female characters in Peacock's novels recall similar and related heroines in comedies of Molière, for example Célimène or Elmire. They are not *femmes fatales* or women of too ardent feelings. They smooth discord, speak with sense and sensibility, but sometimes they are *femmes savantes*. For example, Anthelia Melincourt, in *Melincourt*, is at once an independent heiress, a child of the mountains, and an authority on the five great poets of Italy. But it is in particular in *Crotchet Castle* that we are reminded of Molière. Like Célimène in *Misanthrope* (II, iv), who, when confronted with three of her admirers, gives a thumb-nail sketch of each of them and other courtiers, so Clarinda, one of the invited at squire Crotchet's courthouse, comments for her lover on the assembled guests (chap. V, "Characters").[27] Her depiction, flavored with the ingredients of a true satirist, draws an expressive portrait of each character. Some similarity may also be noted between the eccentric young gentleman Algernon Falconer in *Gryll Grange* and Molière's Alceste, although Falconer has little self-knowledge. He lives a solitary meditative life in a tower viewing as the highest good of life complete tranquility.[28]

There is another novelist of the English Romantic period whose methods of characterization recall Molière: Jane Austen. She is a novelist who in the high years of the major English Romantic poets rejected the Romantic cult of the personality and sentimentalism. As her novelistic method is derived from the tradition of the comedy of manners, a similarity to Molière, whether or not due to a debt, is not surprising. It is a similarity which is dependent on her comic art combined with an insight into the relation between social convention and individual temperament. Certainly worthy of a Molière and reminiscent of him is her comic characterization of Mr. Bennet in *Pride and Prejudice*, which delineation reveals a marital situation that, if fully explored, would show its tragic aspects. In the same novel, the relation of Darcy, the ideal English gentleman as comedy sees that type, to Elizabeth Bennet is roughly that of Alceste to Célimène. Also in *Pride and Prejudice*, Jane Austen draws in Lady Catherine and Charlotte Lucas characters of the sort "which Molière and

[27] Dawson, 187, 260.
[28] *Ibid.*, 287.

Congreve would have adapted to the glare of the theatre—that is to say she excludes all points but the point of highest relief."[29] It is therefore the economy of her characterization which is reminiscent of that of Molière, so that we may also compare the descriptions of the jealous relationship of Emma to Harriet, in *Emma*, and of Célimène and Arsinoé, in *Le Misanthrope*. *Emma* is more obviously comic than Jane Austen's other novels; the heroine is as greatly concerned to make a good match for her protégée Harriet as she is blind to the plain facts of human nature, including her own emotions. Her self-deception causes her blunders which are the unifying principle of the book, just as Lélie's are of *L'Etourdi*, but they do not have the symmetry and ordered neatness of Lélie's blunders. Considering the didactic purpose of the two authors, one may parallel, for example, *Tartuffe*, which exposes the hypocrite not in order to reform him but to open the eyes of the dupes, with *Pride and Prejudice*, where the object is not to put virtue into immoral Wickham, but sense into thoughtless Lydia.[30] In general, first, Miss Austen's best characterization (drawing on dialogue, behavior and comic gaiety) has the quality of poignant characterization found in a comedy like Molière's. Second, the peculiarly comic nature of her art recalling Molière resides in the structure of her novels which like a comedy consists "of a contrived pattern of the interrelations between character and event devised to obstruct the course which should lead direct to the happy ending."[31]

Thus we have, on the one hand, English Romantics who knew Molière or about him and did no more than show interest or express their general admiration for him. This admiration led to Coleridge's brief comments on Molière's realism and imagination and to Hazlitt's more detailed critical considerations. On the other hand, we have to associate the work of Molière with Byron and Peacock, who in their satirical writing stand apart from English Romantics and turn against it. It is in their satirical writings that character types, incidents, modes of characterization and views of human nature are often reminiscent of Molière. This may be a matter of debt or of spiritual affinity, although the English writers used more the sharp lash of satire than the soft stick of comedy. And in the same era the completely unromantic Austen also recalls Molière by the pro-

[29] Oscar W. Firkins, *Jane Austen* (1920; rpt. N.Y.: Russell, 1965), 45–46.
[30] Firkins, 99, 202.
[31] Rachel Trickett, "Jane Austen's Comedy and the Nineteenth Century" in *Critical Essays on Jane Austen*, ed. B. C. Southham (London: Routledge, 1968), 168–170. Miss Trickett quotes from George H. Lewes, who was the first to compare Austen to Molière.

fundity and economy of her character delineation, the structure of her novels, and her moralistic intent. Over these three writers the spirit of Molière hovers in this period of English literary history more than over the few and weak comedy writers for the English theater, then in such a sorry state.

The year 1864 saw the publication of that worrisome tome, Holberg considéré comme imitateur de Molière. *Needless to say, the attitude expressed in the title constitutes an item against which subsequent critics have had to react, and the topic is, like that of Molière and the literature of the English Restoration, one that has been cultivated in scholarly gardens. Anne S. Lundquist's essay incorporates an attempt to bring the problem to a reasonable solution. Anne E. Jensen establishes perspective on the problem through her description of Molière and the Danish theater of the eighteenth century. The last essay of this section takes up the relationship between Strindberg and Molière, a relationship of probable debt and inspiration complicated by Strinberg's disavowal of any admiration for the French playwright.*

LUDVIG HOLBERG AND MOLIÈRE: IMITATION OR CONSTRUCTIVE EMULATION?

Anne S. Lundquist

When Molière and the Béjarts formed L'Illustre Théâtre in 1643, stage conditions were still primitive in France. Similarly, in Denmark, when Ludvig Holberg first presented his comedies in 1723, drama had practically no traditions at all. Holberg went on to lay the foundation to a form of theater and a brand of satire distinctly Danish, and in the process he exposed all of Scandinavia to the influences of great foreign productions. He especially read and emulated Molière.[1]

It is unfortunate that one of Holberg's major international biographies, Legrelle's work of 1864 *Holberg considéré comme imitateur de Molière,*

---

[1] The following is listed as a brief bibliography pertinent to this study:

Brix, Hans. *Ludvig Holbergs Komedier.* Copenhagen, 1942.
Campbell, Oscar James, Jr. *The Comedies of Ludvig Holberg.* Cambridge, 1914.
Holberg, Ludvig. *Komedier.* Copenhagen, 1922.
Hoogland, Claes. *Den satiriske Holberg.* Stockholm, 1963.
Legrelle, A. *Holberg considéré comme imitateur de Molière.* Paris, 1864.

by its very title reduced and limited the scope of Holberg's talents even more severely than the minor language he wrote in. While Holberg unquestioningly modelled himself after the French dramatist, he was also an original and skillful writer with a style all his own. We need to fill in his background and analyze his abilities before we can place him and his comic plays in the proper relationship to Molière.

Ludvig Holberg was born in the Norwegian seaport of Bergen, where the sons of prosperous tradesmen usually went abroad to travel and to be educated. Before he graduated from the University of Copenhagen in 1704, he had visited Holland, France, Germany, Italy, and England. From Italy he brought back the techniques of the *commedia dell' arte*. In England, he was impressed by Addison and Swift, and he allowed their satire to temper his own. He read Locke; he was familiar with Bayle's philosophy, with Montaigne and Montesquieu, as well as Grotius. Precisely because he shared so many of the intellectual prejudices of his time, he found his own insular little country provocative to satire, ignorant as it was of the ideas current in the international centers of culture. He wrote to force his provincial countrymen to examine themselves in the light of progressive European thought. While his early and continuing interests were history and philosophy, his first permanent appointment as a professor was in metaphysics in Copenhagen in 1717. Two years later, he became Professor of Latin. In the autumn of 1719, he published under the pseudonym of Hans Mikkelsen a mock-heroic poem he called *Peder Paars*. It is a parody of the classical epic, a thinly disguised *Aeneid*. It is also a satire on Danish life as Holberg saw it, less polished and more acid than his later works.

The repertoire of the Danish theaters up until then had consisted mostly of comedies by Molière, Dancourt, and Legrand; of farces from Gherardi's *Théâtre Italien*; and of a few tragedies by Corneille and Racine. There was a need for drama in the vernacular which could be of interest to a sophisticated audience. When *Peder Paars* appeared, Holberg was encouraged to try writing for the stage. He presented his first comedies in 1723, and by 1728 he had composed as many as fifteen major plays. He learned from Molière in regard to timing his entrances and exits, balancing his groups, and developing his characters. The figures themselves and the plots they were involved in were patterned on the *commedia dell' arte*. His approach was descriptive rather than analytic. The characters were motivated by the Jonsonian "humours" rather than by psychological truths. The object of Holberg's satire was the manners of men, not their morals.

The dimension of believability was added by the little touches, by the mannerisms of his characters, details so acutely personal and yet so humanly general that his audiences were convinced they were watching caricatures of definite contemporary personages. Holberg did not appreciate this kind of interpretation. He had already said of *Peder Paars* that if his work had been translated into Persian, many of the Persians would swear that the satire was directed against them.

Unlike Molière, who wished to depict the follies and foibles of mankind, Holberg was intent on bringing out the elements of ridicule in what was particularly and parochially Danish. *Jeppe paa Bjerget* (*Jeppe of the Hill*) treats of a drunkard, but he is not just any drunkard: he is a Danish peasant drunkard who sleeps in a dung heap and smells foul. *Den politiske Kandestøber* (*The Political Tinker*) is a parody on a very Scandinavian kind of grandiloquence. In fact, the noun *kandestøberi* has gone into their languages to describe a way of speaking most importantly about politics without understanding the least of it.

The closing of the Danish national theatre by King Christian VI's pietistic revoking of the licensed theaters' right to operate more or less coincided with Holberg's own loss of interest in frenetic playwriting around 1730. The theaters remained closed until Christian died in 1746, and during these years Holberg turned with serious application to the writing of, among other things, a comprehensive history of Denmark, and a collection of moral reflections, based on his Latin epigrams, some serious, some humorous. Also, he published at Leipzig—perhaps to evade the Danish censors—the first Latin version of his novel about Niels Klim. It is a satire modelled on Jonathan Swift's Gulliver. The book proved that Holberg could still write up a storm and cause a furor, and the following year after having found its way back into Denmark anyway, it came out in Danish. That the satirical Holberg was still as intrinsically Danish as some of his own unsubtle characters is shown perhaps by his choice of name for one of the locations of the novel: Potu, a state whose name should quite obviously be read backwards.

Like Molière, Holberg lived to enjoy both his riches and his fame. But both were troubled with lingering ill health toward the end. Holberg died in his seventieth year, still a bachelor, and was elevated to the rank of baron —ironically, not because of the literary treasures he had bequeathed his country, but because of the financial assets he had willed it.

Holberg's comic spirit remained unaffectedly Danish and although modified by his wide ranging tastes in literature, it was never anything but the original, refined. He admired and studied Molière, but only so that he might enhance his own techniques. What he borrowed in the construction of his pieces, such as bits of comic detail or even an entire plot or two, he deftly incorporated into his own style. The core of Holberg's satire evolved from the construction of his characters. In his earliest comedies these characters were constructed à la Molière, around a flaw in their moral fibre. Holberg took the patterns of miserliness from *L'Avare*, for instance, and applied it in the form of some different weakness to a central character of his own. A good example of this would be Master Gert Westphaler, from the play by the same name. Master Gert's shortcoming is one that he shares with many a compulsive talker and story teller: in the excitement of hearing his own voice, he forgets what he was intending to say. He feels that he has important tidings to relate, but he loses his audience before he gets to the point. Thus he attempts three times to propose to his beloved, gets sidetracked by his own verbosity, and loses the girl.

In *Erasmus Montanus*, which Holberg finished a few years later, we can see how he departed from the original pattern by lightening the consequences of these moral flaws to suit his own comic purposes. Erasmus Montanus, born Rasmus Berg, is merely pompous, and he gets his just deserts. He has been to the university, and he is about to prove it to the folks back home. The satire builds on the real differences between learning and wisdom, and the kind of academic snobbery that a true education does away with. Per Degn, who in the play is an older *academicus*, has been asked by Erasmus's father to help him read one of his son's letters home, liberally sprinkled with Latin. The awed father wants to know if Per can read Greek as well:

> Per—Ach jeg har kunnet for tyve Aar siden staae paa een Fod og laese det hele Litanie paa Graesk. Jeg kan endnu komme ihu, at det sidste Ord hedder Amen.

> Ah, twenty years ago I could have stood on one foot and read the entire Litany in Greek. I can still remember that the last word is "Amen."

This kind of character exposition is very Holbergian. In another play, *Jakob von Tyboe*, Tyboe cannot quite manage to keep his German and his everyday Danish apart. His liberties with the use of the German language are exercised with the same restraint as his modesty in the employment of military strategy, where he as a pretend-General defends the rear. Tyboe's Latin presentations ("Hej, Pedantus, Pedanta, Pedantum"), by the way, are almost straight out of Molière's *Le Malade imaginaire*: "Ignorantus, ignoranta, ignorantum."

Holberg had learned the techniques of utilizing *types* as characters in his study of the *commedia dell' arte*. These masques (rather than characters) were without moralizing intent, in this sense not at all related to the complex Pirandellian ones of today. In *Henrich og Pernille* (*Henrich and Pernille*), 1731, Holberg made an effort to create a comedy of intrigue, using the character *types* of servants in disguise. This blending of two techniques was used by Holberg in several of his comedies. The generation of Frenchmen who preceded Molière had been exposed to the kind of farce which would best be described as domestic situation comedy, or even burlesque. Classical comedy, like tragedy, grew strictly out of character. Character shaped destiny. Holberg's comedies are, in this sense, entirely unclassical, whereas Molière's are not. However, like the Greeks, Holberg saw comedy as meaning drama that often interspersed beautiful lyrics and rigid construction with obscenity and broad vernacular humor. This, as in Aristophanes, added up to penetrating social satire. As Aristotle pointed out, there is a very fine line of distinction between great comedy and great tragedy, and where Holberg at times writes brilliant comedy, Molière's comedies verge on tragedy. Both Molière and Holberg accomplish their aims partially by their accurate descriptions of the social scene, depicting manners rather than morals. To this extent, both Holberg and Molière differ in their respective treatment of the comedy of manners from, for instance, Congreve and other authors of the English Restoration. Here the plot is often unrealistic, and the characters (although perhaps no more highly individualized) are witty and less stylized. Still, they do take precedence over their own particular social background; the settings are not of the same integral importance as in either Holberg or Molière: one fan being pretty much like another fan, one silk screen interchangeable with another. Thus a dimension of realism is lost on the English stage of this period.

The immediate atmosphere of the household—family members and servants—is important in both Holberg and Molière. The unifying figure here is quite often the mother. She sets the tone and moderates policy. She functions as wife, mother and mother-in-law, and more often than not as a domestic tyrant with, of course, a lifetime appointment. When she is not center stage, it is usually to make room for the bourgeois father. Both Holberg and Molière make him bear the brunt of the satire on parental tyranny. Fathers object to their daughters' lovers-fiancés either because the man is not the first financial choice of a prudent family (as in *L'Avare*), or because of political malpractice (*Den politiske Kandestøber*), or for some other chosen reason.

In the plays of both authors, there is a figure whose main dramatic duty it is to act either as an exponent of common sense or as the alter ego of the playwright. This is the *raisonneur*. He, of course, can be traced back to the chorus in the drama of antiquity, or as the paripatetic member of a group —an uncle or a neighbor—of Roman comedy (Plautus, Terence). He is often found in Molière (for example, Philinte in *Le Misanthrope*) and in the drama of the *Deuxième Empire* in general, in *la pièce bien faite* (Scribe), and somewhat later as the teaching moralist in Dumas *fils*. It is in the latter (in *L'Etrangère*, 1876) that we first encounter the doctor-*raisonneur* that was used by Ibsen in *Vildanden* (*The Wild Duck*: Dr. Relling) and by Strindberg in *Fadren* (*The Father*: Dr. Östermark). Thus, from Molière (Philinte, as well as Ariste in *Les Femmes savantes*) by way of Holberg (the poet Philemon in *Det lykkelige Skibbrud, The Fortunate Shipwreck*; Ovidius in *Uden Hoved og Hale, Without Head or Tail*) a major literary invention entered Scandinavia. The two lovers and the inevitable intriguing servant are figures too common to stagecraft of all ages to attempt even to trace them from Molière to Holberg.

In the list of *dramatis personae*, then, we have finally narrowed ourselves down to a comparison of the main character, the principal comic figure. Holberg has wisely taken a page directly out of Molière, who delayed the entrance of the comic hero until his nature and personality had been thoroughly described and established by the other players for at least the full first act. In *Tartuffe* the hypocrite does not appear until the beginning of the third act. In *Erasmus Montanus* Holberg staves off the appearance of his hero until the early part of the second act. This is a difficult device to handle, but when used correctly it is very effective. Few playwrights have undertaken it.

Like a painter or a musician, having adopted and mastered the techniques he found useful in the work of others—and in Holberg's case, especially of Molière—the playwright sifted them through his own particular philosophy and experience. In merely translating continental concepts into written Danish, Holberg made a veritable storehouse of resources available to other artists of his generation in Scandinavia. Not only did Ludvig Holberg have his own indisputable gift for comedy, but he also had the talent to choose well and prudently among the inspirations of others.

Holberg's first aim as a writer was to entertain and at the same time to wave a didactic finger at the social ineptitudes of his provincial contemporaries. They need not so much to change drastically at the very roots of their personalities as simply to be admonished and lectured in the use of common sense and manners.

This, simply stated, was Holberg's basic approach to satire. Molière's involvement, also, was largely dispassionate. In spite of nearly fifteen years in the French provinces with a troupe of actors, Molière wrote chiefly for audiences with an instinctive sense of form and style. His figures, then, came to *reflect* the standards of his audience, as Holberg tried to *inflict* them upon his. It was not thus only the mirrors, but the spectators that differed. The Danes were not the French. At a first glance, the outlines overlap; the patterns confuse. And why not? The stuff of comedy is everywhere.

MOLIÈRE IN DENMARK
IN THE 18TH CENTURY
Anne E. Jensen

Around the year 1700 the Dual Monarchy, Denmark-Norway, had a population of approximately one and a half million, the greater part of which were farmers. In the towns the inhabitants lived mostly as tradesmen and artisans and the only big city was the capital, Copenhagen, with 70,000 inhabitants. Copenhagen was the seat of the Court, the Goverment and of the only university in the Monarchy. Since 1660 the kings of Denmark had been absolute rulers, and several foreign visitors to Denmark had criticized this autocracy, e.g. the British ambassador to the Court of Denmark, Robert Molesworth, in his book *Account of Denmark, as it was in the year 1692*, published in London in 1694.

Since the Reformation in 1536 the Lutheran Church had been the state church and all other religious communities were absolutely forbidden. The Lutheran Church was opposed to most worldly pleasures and the only theater accepted by it was the so-called "school plays" authorized by Luther and Melanchthon. These were either Latin plays, especially those of Terence, German plays translated into Danish, or original Danish plays plays composed by schoolmasters. They were performed by the pupils at the grammer schools or by the students at the university, and their sole purpose was the education of the young actors and the audiences. Terence was favored because of his moral attitude and his noble style; the German and Danish plays were mostly dramatized incidents from the Old Testament, wherein the authors attempted to twist the stories of Solomon, Nabal, Susanna and others to fit into orthodox Lutheran instruction.

From the time of the Reformation and until the middle of the seventeenth century, the school plays were performed with great success in the larger towns, in Copenhagen, and at Court. But then new theatrical forms came to the country in defiance of the church. Dutch and German wandering troupes performed their *Haupt- und Staatsaktionen* in the larger towns and in Copenhagen, either indoors or in the open air. The Dutch and German languages were more or less understood by the Danish population, and, as the larger troupes excelled in splendid scenery, brilliant costumes, music, dancing, and acrobatics, it was of less importance that the dialogues were only partly grasped. For some years the wandering troupes were also much favored by the Danish Court, but from about 1680 the King of Denmark, Christian V, wished to imitate the court of Versailles, which he had visited in his youth, and so he called in a French troupe to act permanently at his court. We know very little of King Christian's troupe, but must assume that it performed a French classical repertory of the same kind as that of many provincial troupes in France.

Owing to a critical financial situation, the king had to dismiss his French troupe in 1694, and its members left for France with the exception of one of the leading actors, René Montaigu, who tried to earn his living as a teacher of languages in Copenhagen. Montaigu was born about 1661 in France, a son of the dramatist Jean Magnon, whose plays had been acted by Molière and his troupe. It has been postulated that René Magnon de Montaigu was trained in the art of acting by Molière, but no evidence to support the theory has been established. In fact we know nothing of Montaigu's life before 1686, when he was engaged as a member of the court troupe of Christian V. When King Frederik IV succeeded his father on the throne, he asked Montaigu to establish a new French troupe and to be its leading actor and director. The new troupe consisted of eight actors, five actresses, four dancers, a ballet master and some musicians. We have little information about the repertory of the troupe, which played at the Court from 1701 to 1721, but we know for certain that it included Molière's *L'Avare, Amphitryon* and *Dom Juan*. Supported by the king, Montaigu visited Paris four times in order to keep himself informed about new plays at the Parisian theaters, and these travels indicate that the king wished his troupe to maintain a repertory *à la mode*. Only members of the royal household and the Danish aristocracy, together with high officials, were admitted to the French performances at the Court. The great French classical drama of the seventeenth century was unknown outside the Court, with the exception of some very small bourgeois literary circles, who were well versed in the French language and so able to read Corneille Racine, and Molière.

In 1721 the king tired of his French troupe, dismissed it, and engaged instead a German opera company. All the French actors and actresses left Copenhagen, but Montaigu stayed on once more, this time together with his young wife and three children. He had married a young actress in his troupe, Marie Magdalene de la Croix, born in Copenhagen of French parents. Montaigu had obtained a small pension from the king, but it was too small for a family of five, and Montaigu was not inclined to give up his profession. He asked, and was granted, royal permission to established a Danish theater in the center of Copenhagen, and during the summer of 1722 he succeeded in gathering a company of amateurs, seven students and three young ladies, one of them his own wife, who was destined to be the primadonna of the troupe. Montaigu himself was not able to act in the Danish language, but understood it well enough to perform the task of leader and director.

Montaigu's greatest problem was to provide his company with a Danish repertory. He got some young civil servants to translate comedies by Molière, Regnard, Thomas Corneille, Boindin, Desmares, Palaprat and Hauteroche. And as a piece of good fortune for Danish literature, he encouraged Ludvig Holberg to write comedies for the new theater. At that time Holberg was an ambitious professor at the University of Copenhagen, but from 1719 to 1722 he had published a long epic poem and five satires, inspired by the French classical writers, especially Boileau.

Montaigu opened his theatre in the street named "Lille Grönnegade" on the 23rd of September 1722—a memorable day in the history of the Danish theater, for that night he founded the national theater now existing under the name of The Royal Theater, and for the opening night he chose Molière's *L'Avare*. On the second night the company presented Holberg's first comedy *The Political Tinker*, and during the following six years Molière and Holberg dominated the repertory. We have knowledge of approximately one-third of the repertory, mainly through playbills luckily handed down to us. They show that at least sixteen comedies of Molière were performed.

These performances of Molière's comedies became most important for the Danish theater in the eighteenth century. First of all, Molière's plays were made familiar to a bourgeois audience who had not known them before and whose dramatic taste was thereby greatly improved. In the second place the young amateur company was trained in the art of acting by Montaigu, who was conversant with acting in the style of Molière, which he had been taught in his youth in France. Holberg complained that the comedies of Molière were better acted than his own plays just because of Montaigu's particular skill in the technique of acting Molière. Montaigu must have studied this technique in France around 1680 and must certainly have practiced it himself in the two troupes at the Danish Court between 1686 and 1721, where he undoubtedly acted many leading parts in Molière's plays. We are therefore justified in saying that the bourgeois audiences in Copenhagen in the 1720's have had the unique chance of seeing Molière's comedies acted in a style very close to the style of Molière's own company. And thanks to the special conditions in the Danish theater in the eighteenth century, this traditional style of Molière was allowed to continue until the end of the century.

Literary critics inside and outside Denmark have heatedly discussed whether Holberg was only an imitator of Molière or an original playwright who found inspiration and material in many different types of plays, in Molière and Regnard, in the Roman comedy (especially Plautus), in the *commedia dell'arte*, in the Théâtre Italien, and the Théâtre de la Foire. A. Legrelle and R. Prutz had a bitter fight over the connection between Molière and Holberg. The title of Legrelle's book of 1864, *Holberg considéré comme imitateur de Molière*, states clearly his main theory, whereas Robert Prutz found the influence of Molière on the comedies of Holberg to be of minor importance and instead characterized Holberg as a true disciple of the *commedia dell'arte*, (*Ludwig Holberg, sein Leben und seine Schriften nebst einer Auswahl seiner Komödien*, 1857). O. J. Campbell in his study on Holberg, *The Comedies of Holberg* (1914), tried to draw attention to the influence of English literature on Holberg, and he found Legrelle's thesis "too one-sided to be just," (135). Campbell admitted that "Holberg's knowledge of Molière influenced fundamentally his dramatic ideas. It formed his general conception of a comedy of character. It supplied him with much of the action assigned to the similar members of similarly constituted families" (116). But Campbell thought that "the works of the two writers undeniably produce radically different total impressions" and that Holberg "into each one of his borrowed forms . . . introduced much of his own independent comic spirit" (117).

Molière and Holberg wrote for rather different audiences, and this has certainly affected the distinct structures of their characters and their dialogues. Although some members of the Danish aristocracy attended the productions of the theater in Lille Grönnegade, the greater part of the public was bourgeois, and this public wanted realistic comedies with well-known characters and milieu. Holberg, knowing this, let his comedies take place in typical Danish surroundings, and his dialogues have more of the somewhat coarse comic spirit of Plautus than of Molière. Incidentally it is interesting to realize that Holberg's comedies have never been a success in France and that a contemporary French critic, Professor A. Jolivet, although admiring Holberg's comic spirit, his "festivitas," feels that Molière is a far greater psychologist than Holberg (*Théâtre de Holberg I–II*, 1955, translated by Judith and Gilles Gérard-Arlberg).

It is understandable that so many have been occupied in studying the influence of Molière on Holberg, but in my view it is just as interesting to study Molière's importance to the Danish theater on the whole. In this short study I am confining myself to discussing some main points concerning Molière's position in the Danish theater in the eighteenth century and so have to leave out much interesting material from the nineteenth and twentieth centuries.

Owing to the great fire of Copenhagen in 1728, the theater in Lille Grönnegade had to cease its productions, and shortly after King Christian VI came to the throne in 1730, he was imbued with German pietism and tried to impress his own austere religion on the whole population. No theatrical performances were allowed during his reign (1730–46); the theater in Lille Grönnegade was demolished. The actors gained poor livelihoods as minor civil servants and Montaigu and his wife died in the most deplorable misery. Only Holberg managed to survive; he reached a high position at the university. But only a few months after the king's death his worldly minded son, Frederik V, planned a restoration of theatrical life in Copenhagen. Without any hesitation, he gave his permission to re-establish the Danish theater and gave financial support to the building of a beautiful theater in the center of Copenhagen on the Royal Square. At the same time he engaged a French troupe to act at Court and an Italian opera company to give performances at the theater alternately with the Danish theatrical company.

In many ways the new Danish theater resumed the traditions of the old one in Lille Grönnegade, helped by two persons who had known the old theater thoroughly: Holberg, now an elderly and most respected professor and historian, and one of the former leading actors, Frederik Pilloy. The new company had no difficulty in procuring a repertory, as twenty-five of Holberg's comedies were printed, and so were several of the old translations of Molière and Regnard. The new company had more French plays translated, and although the number of French authors acted by this company is rather impressive, Molière was, next to Holberg, the dramatist whose plays were most frequently on the playbill. In the period between 1747 and 1800 no less than twenty-one of Molière's comedies were performed, some of them being the most popular plays in the repertory, e.g. *Dom Juan, L'Avare, Le Malade imaginaire, Le Dépit amoureux,*

L'Ecole des Maris, Les Précieuses ridicules, Tartuffe and *Le Mariage forcé*.

Although the theater in Lille Grönnegade had only been in existence for six years, it had created a special repertory dominated by Molière, Holberg, and Regnard. Only a few English plays were performed and these with no success; no German or Italian plays were acted and only a few tragedies. All verse comedies were translated into Danish prose, and the French milieu was often given Danish local color. The strained financial situation of the theater allowed only a modest amount of scenery, music and dance, and Molière's *ballets* were acted as prose comedies with small musical *divertimenti* and some dances by the actors themselves, as no *corps de ballet* was available.

In the new theater, built in 1747, and since 1770 called the Royal Danish Theater, the repertory was influenced for a long period by the traditions of the old theater. French comedy from the seventeenth and early eighteenth centuries predominated, together with Holberg's comedies, and the repertory was changed only very slowly. As some of the audience in the 1760's were in favor of the sentimental plays by Destouches and De la Chaussée, the management tried, not very successfully, in the 1770's to introduce French tragedies; but not until the arrival in the 1780's of the French *opéra comique* and of the German bourgeois domestic drama did the repertory change perceptibly.

Nevertheless, in spite of all the modern trends in the repertory, it still maintained a certain conservative stamp, owing to the leading actors of the company. They had begun their career in 1747 and had been trained by Pilloy to act Molière and Holberg. A considerable number of the theatergoers in Copenhagen preferred to see their favorites in the "old" comedies, and there is no doubt that the Danish actors really achieved their greatest successes in the comedies of Molière and Holberg. We know this thanks to a young critic by the name of Peder Rosenstand-Goiske, who in 1771 started *The Dramatic Journal*, a Danish magazine on the lines of Lessing's *Hamburgische Dramaturgie*. The Royal Theater gave performances two or three times weekly and for one and a half years Rosenstand-Goiske attended every one of them, making penetrating analyses of the acting. From his detailed descriptions of the actors' achievements in Molière's comedies, it is clearly seen that the acting style René Montaigu had brought to the Danish theater in 1722 was still a valuable inspiration.

During the years that Rosenstand-Goiske studied the Danish actors, a French troupe at the court of Christian VII performed a repertory *à la mode* consisting of *opéra comique*, sentimental French comedies, and a vast number of Voltaire's tragedies, whereas Molière was seldom on the playbill. It is a rather interesting situation: a French modern troupe that almost neglected their great classical comedian and a modest Danish theater still paying homage to him. I doubt whether any theater outside France has been more faithful to Molière than the Danish theater in the eighteenth century.

STRINDBERG AND MOLIÈRE:
PARALLELS, INFLUENCE, IMAGE

Barbara Lide

Few scholars of the drama would accept without question the idea that August Strindberg might have been influenced by Molière during his naturalistic period—or at any other time. Some who have read the plays of both dramatists might even doubt whether the names Molière and Strindberg could be linked together, and if we are willing to believe Strindberg's last recorded statement on Molière, "Molière has his admirers, although I have never liked him,"[1] there would probably be no basis for discussing a connection between the two writers.

The above negative judgment of Molière was expressed in a memorandum to the Intimate Theater, a small theater established in Stockholm in 1907 by the Swedish actor, August Falck. The purpose of the Intimate Theater was to produce Strindberg's plays, and his correspondence with Falck was, therefore, extensive. In that memorandum, Strindberg adds: "the Germans have resurrected Kleist and Hebbel, but for me they remain fossils," yet in a separate note to Falck, written around the same time, he suggests no less than six plays by Hebbel for the Intimate Theater's repertoire.[2] In the same vein, it is puzzling to read in Strindberg's diary the entry of 25 April 1899, in which he states that Shakespeare has always been repulsive to him,[3] when there are so many instances in which Strindberg expresses his admiration for Shakespeare, particularly in his essays on *Hamlet* and *Julius Caesar*.[4] Such contradictions invite a challenge to the

---

[1] *Öppna brev till Intima Teatern*, in *Strindbergs samlade skrifter*, ed. John Landquist (Stockholm, 1912–1921), L, 40. *Open Letters to the Intimate Theatre*, trsl. Walter Johnson (Seattle, 1966).

[2] See August Falck, Fem år med Strindberg, Stockholm, 1935, p. 31. In this letter, written in 1907 but undated, Strindberg suggests several plays from both the classical and modern repertoire which he thought might be performed by Falck's actors. He later changed his mind and insisted that the Intimate Theatre repertoire be limited to his plays only. Falck includes a list of plays performed at the Intimate Theatre during its years of operation from 1907 to 1910. Walter Johnson includes this list in his introduction to *Open Letters to the Intimate Theatre*, 12f.

[3] *Okkulta dagbok*, entry No. 85, Foliokartong No. 11, Carlheim-Gyllenskjöld samling, deposited in Kungliga Biblioteket, Sthlm.

[4] *Samlade skrifter*, L, 49–157.

accuracy of Strindberg's flat statement that he never liked Molière. There is, moreover, evidence in Strindberg's dramas, essays, and letters, which indicates that there were certain aspects of Molière's work which he did admire, and that Molière, while he cannot be considered a principal guiding figure in Strindberg's artistic development, did indeed have some influence on him, both in the writing and staging of some of his dramas.

Strindberg's preface to *Miss Julie* offers an explanation as to why he may have professed to have a low regard for Molière. As a representative of the late nineteenth century, Strindberg had a deep interest in character development and psychological motivation. Although in *Miss Julie* it is Jean's power of suggestion that finally forces Julie to take her own life, Strindberg provides her with a complex of circumstances which motivate her suicide. He discusses his play as a modern psychological drama and his Julie as a modern character, and he prides himself on being abreast of the times by giving Julie such diverse motives for her actions.[5] Strindberg does not even want to call the personae in his play "characters" because he feels the word has come to mean someone who is "fixed and finished, who invariably appears on the scene as drunk, jocular, or sorrowful, . . . for characterization it was necessary only to add a little physical defect, a clubfoot, a wooden leg, a red nose, or to have the character repeat an expression such as: 'That's capital!'"[6] Strindberg criticizes Molière for having what he considers to be a simplistic view of human character, and he cites *L'Avare* to illustrate his point: "Harpagon is merely a miser, although Harpagon could have been both a miser and an excellent financier, a fine father, and a good man of the community, and what is worse, his 'defect' is most advantageous for his son-in-law and daughter, who are his heirs and therefore ought not blame him."[7]

Although he finds fault with Molière for presenting his principal characters as fixed and static, a practice which any naturalistic writer would find unacceptable, Strindberg did find in Molière's writings a certain modernity which he admired. As he was developing the technique of writing naturalistic plays, Strindberg tried to follow the guidelines set by Zola, and, probably taking his cue from Zola, he began to look toward the French classical drama which, he found, "sought to sustain interest in psychological development, not using machinery and props in order to

---

[5] Preface to *Fröken Julie* in *Samlade skrifter*, XXIII, 103.
[6] *Ibid.*
[7] *Ibid.*, 103 f.

analyze the intellectual and emotional lives of the characters."[8] Zola traces his naturalistic formula to the source of the French national stage, the classical formula. In Corneille's tragedies and Molière's comedies, Zola finds that plot is secondary to "the continuous analysis of character" which he considers so necessary. Zola proposes combining the classical formula, with its adherence to the unities of time, place, and action, with the scientific method of analyzing the characters in terms of all the physical and social causes which make them what they are.[9] Strindberg accepts Zola's formula, but he finds that Molière, in spite of some of the static characters he created, comes closer to following that formula than does Zola himself. In his essay, "On Modern Drama and Modern Theater," Strindberg welcomes Zola's *Thérèse Raquin* as a new departure, a play with "grand style and deep probing of the human soul," but he sees in it imperfections in form that arise from its being an adaptation of the novel. He cannot accept, for example, the time lapse of a whole year between the first and second acts. On the other hand, he condemns the stage adaptation of Zola's novel, *Renée*, as a "return to the form of traditional Parisian comedy," and as a play in which "psychology is neglected and characterization diluted."[10]

In the same essay, Strindberg praises Molière for the concentration of form which he feels is lacking in Zola: "With Molière," he writes, "the French drama entered into a stage in which all trappings are left out, and the psychological nuances become the most important element, so that Tartuffe's marvelous vivisection takes place in one room furnished with two taborets. The number of characters is reduced and the major interest is strictly limited to a few primary characters." Strindberg feels that, with this play, Molière anticipates the style of modern comedy.[11] The "vivisection" Strindberg refers to occurs in the scene between Elmire and Tartuffe at the end of Act IV, and by calling it "Tartuffe's vivisection," he uses one of his favorite terms of that period. In April of 1887, Strindberg began writing a series of character sketches entitled *Vivisections*. These sketches reflect his keen interest in the psychological research which was currently attracting attention in France, particularly that of Charcot and Bernheim of the Nancy school. Probing into the human psyche

---

[8] "Utveckling," in *Likt och olikt, Samlade skrifter*, XVII, 257f.
[9] Emile Zola, "Le Naturalisme au théâtre" in *Le Roman expérimental, Oeuvres completes*, Vol. X, Paris, 1968, 1254.
[10] *Likt och olikt*, in *Samlade skrifter*, XVII, 287f.
[11] *Ibid*, 285.

fascinated Strindberg, and the technique he uses in *Vivisections* is one of gradually stripping away the facade of his characters in order to expose them as they really are. In Strindbergian terms, this is essentially what Elmire does to Tartuffe.

It may be, then, that Strindberg praises Molière's treatment of Tartuffe merely because it is similar to what he admires in his own works. Martin Lamm, however, suggests that Strindberg may have had the simplicity of the vivisection of Tartuffe in mind when he wrote *Miss Julie*, in which "he allows the whole drama to be played in one setting, in order to have the characters 'develop in their milieu.'" Lamm adds that, "although . . . [Strindberg's] outline shows that he had originally planned an act division, 'as an experiment' he had the whole piece played without a curtain fall."[12]

It is even more likely, however, that the scene between Elmire and Tartuffe was the model for a similar scene in the tragicomedy, *Creditors* (*Fordringsägare*), a play which Strindberg considered to be "even better than *Miss Julie*, with three persons, one table, and two chairs . . . !"[13] Strindberg finished *Creditors* in August of 1888, shortly after he wrote *Miss Julie*, and about six months before he finished his essay, "On Modern Drama and Modern Theater."

From a brief outline of Strindberg's play, it can be seen that, thematically, *Creditors* is worlds apart from *Tartuffe*. It depicts the revenge of a deceived husband, Gustav. Some years after he has divorced his wife, Tekla, he visits the resort hotel where she and her present husband are spending their summer vacation. Gustav arrives just after Tekla has left to attend a meeting, and the play opens on the day she is to return. Gustav has been at the hotel for a week under an assumed name, and he has made the acquaintance of Adolf, the husband, and gained his confidence. Tekla, the woman in Strindberg's unusual triangle, is one of several vampires who appear in Strindberg's dramas. These are characters who are intellectually and spiritually empty and therefore must derive strength and substance from others, in Tekla's case, her two husbands. Gustav, who, in Tekla's words, had taught her to think, and from whom she took her vocabulary and her mannerisms during their marriage, has long since recuperated from his experience as Tekla's husband. Adolf, on the other hand, has given of himself until there is nothing more for Tekla to take. He has descended to a point at which he is so weak, both physically and

---

[12] Martin Lamm, *August Strindberg*, (Aldusserien) (Stockholm, 1948), 184. Trsl. and ed. by Henry C. Carlson (New York, 1971).

[13] Letter to K. O. Bonnier, 21 August 1888. In *August Strindbergs brev*, ed. Torsten Eklund (Stockholm, 1948–1969), VII, 105.

emotionally, that he has no resistance against the power of suggestion as exercised by either Gustav or Tekla, and he allows himself to be destroyed by them. Little by little, Gustav opens Adolf's eyes so that he sees what has happened to him as a result of his life with Tekla. Finally, Gustav suggests that he have a conversation with Tekla which Adolf can observe unseen. From his hiding place, Adolf not only learns Gustav's identity, but he watches as Gustav reveals how selfish and vain Tekla really is, and as Gustav flatters Tekla until he persuades her to accept him as her lover that evening. The weakened Adolf dies of an epileptic attack, but he is actually the victim of psychic murder, one of Strindberg's favorite themes during his naturalistic period.

The synopsis gives the impression that *Creditors* is a very grim play, but in fact it is not. A mere plot summary cannot include the genuinely comic elements and the witty dialogue in the play, which Strindberg himself regarded as one of his best, "... modern throughout, humane, amiable, with all three characters sympathetic and interesting from beginning to end."[14] Strindberg wrote to the actor who first performed the role of Gustav, telling him he wanted that role performed in a "playfully good-natured" manner—and indeed much of the dialogue supports such an interpretation. Gustav was to have the attitude of a "cat playing with a rat before he bites it, never angry, never moralizing, never preaching."[15]

Obviously, it is not primarily in the subject matter that the similarities between *Tartuffe* and *Creditors* lie. Nevertheless, certain parallels are evident, and these exist mainly between the Elmire-Tartuffe scene which Strindberg mentions in his essay on modern drama and the scene between Gustav and Tekla. Molière's Elmire wants to reveal to Orgon that Tartuffe is a parasite in an effort to save him and the household they share. Strindberg's Gustav wants Adolf to witness the unmasking of Tekla as part of his plan to ruin them both. Yet, although they act for totally different reasons, Elmire and Gustav proceed in very much the same manner.

Before comparing the two scenes, let us first consider the similarities in the relationships between Tartuffe and Orgon and between Tekla and Adolf, both of which can be regarded as parasite-host relationships. In both cases the host is a most willing one. Orgon has not only taken Tartuffe into his home, but his blind esteem for Tartuffe has completely erased from his mind all concern for his own family's happiness. In the first act of

[14] Letter to Joseph Seligmann, 16 October 1888, in *August Strindbergs brev*, VII, 145.
[15] Letter to Hans Riber Hunderup, 3 March 1889, in *August Strindbergs brev*, VII, 259.

Tartuffe, Dorine repeatedly tries to tell Orgon that his wife has been ill. He does not listen to what Dorine says about Elmire, but asks again and again: "Et Tartuffe?" Orgon intends to sign over his entire estate to Tartuffe. He is also prepared to force his daughter to become Tartuffe's wife against her will, and, at the end of the third act, when his son, Damis, reveals to Orgon the fact that Tartuffe has attempted to make love to Elmire, Orgon defends Tartuffe and orders Damis to leave his house. Orgon sums up his feelings as he tells his brother-in-law, Cléante:

> Oui, je deviens tout autre avec son entretien;
> Il m'enseigne à n'avoir affection pour rien,
> De toutes amities il détache mon âme;
> Et je verrais mourir frère, enfants, mère, et femme
> Que je m'en soucierais autant que de cela.

(Act I, Scene VI)

Just as Moliere's Orgon delights in giving all that he has to Tartuffe, Strindberg's Adolf is happy to give Tekla all that he has to offer her. He believes that he somehow elevates her by doing so, and that, consequently, his love and respect for her increase. As he explains to Gustav, "I want to respect her more than myself, want her to be my better self . . . I enjoy being always a little worse than she is." Adolf goes on to explain the process by which he manages to become "a little worse than she is:" ". . . for example, I taught her to swim and now I enjoy having her boast that she is a more skillful and bolder swimmer than I. First I pretended to be inferior and afraid in order to give her strength, but as it went on, one fine day I was the more inferior and cowardly one. It seems to me as if she actually took my courage from me!"[16] Adolf, a talented and successful painter, prompted Tekla to become a writer, even when he thought her writing abominable. He introduced her into literary circles and kept the critics from dealing harshly with her. He tells Gustav: "When my artistic success was about to overshadow her—and her name—I tried to instill courage in her by belittling myself and making my art subordinate to hers. I talked so much about the unimportance of the role of painting as compared to that of the other arts, that I finally convinced myself of its insignificance."[17] In contrast to Orgon, who appears to be hypnotized by Tartuffe, Adolf is not completely unaware that he is the unfortunate victim of a parasite. Yet, he is no less helpless than Orgon. At first he accepts and even enjoys

---

[16] *Samlade skrifter*, XXIII, 209.
[17] *Ibid*, 211.

his situation, but later, after Tekla has sapped him of most of his strength, he is too weak to resist her power over him.

In *Tartuffe*, the crucial scene between Tartuffe and Elmire occurs when Elmire finally decides that she must prove to Orgon that Tartuffe does not love him and is not his friend. She arranges a meeting with Tartuffe and persuades Orgon to hide under the table so that he might observe what takes place. She cautions Orgon:

> Au moins, je vais toucher une étrange matière,
> Ne vous scandalisez en aucune manière.

(Act IV, Scene IV)

In the corresponding scene in *Creditors* Gustav instructs Adolf to hide in the adjoining room while he talks to Tekla, warning him, "But don't become alarmed when you see how I dissect a human soul and lay the insides here on the table."[18]

In both plays, what follows is a scene in which two combatants are involved in a cat and mouse game until the victim is trapped. Both Elmire and Gustav succeed in penetrating beneath the merely superficial and stripping away the respective facades of Tartuffe and Tekla. Orgon and Adolf, both forewarned, one hidden under the table, the other in an adjoining room, must observe the proceedings, which in both cases appear to be leading to their being cuckolded. In the case of Orgon, not only must he watch as Tartuffe is revealed as a hypocrite who would pose as his friend while he married his daughter and seduced his wife; he is also forced to listen to Tartuffe say about him:

> C'est un homme, entre nous, à mener par le nez.
> De tous nos entretiens il est pour faire gloire,
> Et je l'ai mis au point de voir tout sans rien croire.

(Act IV, Scene IV)

In Strindberg's play, Adolf finds himself watching Gustav perform his psychic vivisection on Tekla. Tekla, like Tartuffe, allows herself to be taken in by flattery. Adolf observes her as she playfully responds to Gustav's compliments. He sees her in Gustav's embrace, and he listens as she arranges a rendezvous with Gustav for later that evening. He is forced to hear her as she tells Gustav that she does not care what her husband might say about her behavior, and, when Gustav suggests that her attitude might make her husband look ridiculous, Adolf learns from her reply that she already considers him to be so.

---

[18] *Ibid*, 223.

In both *Creditors* and *Tartuffe*, it appears that these crucial scenes result in ruin for Adolf and for Orgon. Adolf's experience precipitates his fatal epileptic attack, and Orgon is faced with bankruptcy and imprisonment. Molière's play reaches the brink of tragedy, since it appears certain that Tartuffe will indeed take over Orgon's estate and have him sent to prison. It is only in the final moments that the king intervenes and saves Orgon from disaster, thereby making possible the traditional happy ending.

The above noted parallels are supported by the external evidence. In the first place, *Creditors* was written at the end of August, 1888, and the essay, "On Modern Drama and Modern Theater," in which Strindberg praises *Tartuffe*, was completed in February, 1889, no more than six months later. These facts indicate that both *Creditors* and *Tartuffe* occupied Strindberg's thoughts at roughly the same time. Second, Strindberg writes about "Tartuffe's vivisection" and has Gustav refer to his treatment of Tekla as the "dissection of a human soul." Third, he commends Molière for presenting Tartuffe's vivisection "in one room furnished with two taboretes," and boasts that *Creditors* has only "three persons, one table, and two chairs." Together with the obvious and convincing parallels in the two works themselves, this external evidence argues strongly that Strindberg had Molière's comedy in mind when he wrote *Creditors*.

The impact of *Tartuffe* upon Strindberg extends beyond the naturalistic period and is evident in the historical drama, *Gustav Vasa* (1899) in the technique Strindberg uses to portray the king. Gustav Vasa's presence is felt, if not seen, throughout the play. Although he does not appear on stage in the first act, set in a miner's cottage in the Dalecarlian region of Sweden, he is represented by two paintings on the walls which depict his activities in Dalecarlia. The other characters on stage are awaiting the king's arrival in Dalecarlia, and they do not seem to forget him for a moment. As the play progresses, Gustav Vasa is seen through the eyes of all the principal characters, one of whom describes the king's omnipresence as "always this giant hand, which one never can see, only feel."[19] Although the figure of the king is perceivable in every scene, Strindberg does not actually bring him onto the stage until the third act, after which, onstage or off, he is the center of attention. It is known that Strindberg "weighed and considered many means of presenting Gustav Vasa,"[20] and that he discussed with a friend Molière's device, employed in *Tartuffe*,

---

[19] *Gustav Vasa* in *Samlade skrifter*, XXXVIII, 195.
[20] See Walter Johnson, *Strindberg and the Historical Drama* (Seattle, 1963), 96.

of not having the principal character appear until the third act, after the other characters have described him from their several points of view and shown how he has affected their lives.[21] Strindberg scholars generally agree that Gustav Vasa's third act appearance was inspired by *Tartuffe*.[22]

Mention must also be made of what Strindberg called the Intimate Theater's Molière stage. By the time the Intimate Theater opened in 1907, Strindberg had long since ceased to write concentrated one-act naturalistic dramas that required only one simple stage set. He had written several expressionistic dramas and historical plays which called for many scene changes and, in some cases, complex scenic effects. Both the physical size and the budget of the Intimate Theater, however, demanded extreme simplicity of stage design. Strindberg found in Molière the solution to some of the staging problems. First he notes that "Molière's comedies were played in one and the same room."[23] Then, in a letter to August Falck, he suggests that his play, *Queen Christina*, might be played on a Molière stage, and adds that he has condensed his historical drama, *Gustav III*, into a chamber play, which could be played on the same stage. He advises Falck to "see Ring's Theater Book," in order to find a model for the Molière stage.[24] The book Strindberg refers to is Herman Ring's *History of the Theater*, which includes a picture of what Ring calls a "Molière stage."[25] The picture, probably a sketch of the stage at the Petit-Bourbon, or rather what Ring believed to be a sketch of it, shows a typical stage of the French classical theater, with a strictly symmetrical set designed to give the stage an illusion of depth. There is a balustrade on either side of the proscenium, extending about one-quarter of the distance toward center stage. The picture in Ring's book is very similar to Strindberg's sketch for the set of *A Dream Play*.[26] The balustrades are missing in Strindberg's sketch, but he did intend to use them. In a letter to the Intimate Theater concerning the staging of *A Dream Play*, he writes: "On

---

[21] See Martin Lamm, 279.

[22] See Gunnar Ollén, *Strindbergs Dramatik* (Stockholm, 1961), 270; Brita Mortensen and Brian W. Downs, *Strindberg: An Introduction to his Life and Work* (Cambridge, 1949), 125; Walter Johnson, *Strindberg and the Historical Drama*, 100; and Martin Lamm, 279.

[23] From Strindberg's notes on the theater in Foliokartong No. 13, Carlheim-Gyllenskjöld samling, Kungliga Biblioteket, Stockholm.

[24] Letter of 22 February 1908, in *Strindberg och Teater. Bref till Medlemmar af Gamla Intima Teatern från August Strindberg*, med en inledning samt kommentar af August Falck (Stockholm, 1918), 3. The condensed version of *Gustav III* was never produced at the Intimate Theater. See also Falck, *Fem år med Strindberg*, 139.

[25] Herman Ring, *Teaterns Historia* (Stockholm, 1898), 222.

[26] Reproduced in Falck, *Fem år med Strindberg*, 273, and in Johnson, *Open Letters to the Intimate Theatre*, 147.

the railing we have borrowed from the Molière stage, we had intended to set up allegorical properties, indicating in a visual image the locale in which the scene could be thought to take place."[27]

The versatility of the Molière stage and that of another set, the so-called drapery stage, which combines a few props and the balustrades from the Molière stage against a drapery background, allowed the Intimate Theater to produce twenty-four of Strindberg's plays, using a minimum of scenic design.

It has been mentioned that Strindberg thought his drama about Queen Christina of Sweden was especially suitable for the Molière stage. He noted that Christina was a contemporary of Molière, [28] and saw in her personality a tinge of the *precieuse ridicule*.[29] Not only did Strindberg want *Queen Christina* to be played on the Molière stage, but he also wanted the drama performed with a certain elegance reminiscent of Molière's theater. The main reason was to save his play from being attacked by the critics. As Martin Lamm expresses it: "In *Queen Christina*, . . . the figures are handled so presumptuously that the play has the flavor of a scandalous historical masquerade."[30] Fearing the conservative critics, Strindberg wrote to Falck: "Keep it on a higher level than I did. Elevate the historical personages! And try to evoke a little grandeur and the so-called times (historical). A little stiffness in the playing, which the costumes necessitate; a bit of elegance (Molière), otherwise it will be a ridiculous farce."[31]

Strindberg's references to Molière in connection with his *Queen Christina*, though brief, are revealing. The very name Molière is for Strindberg a form of shorthand for a polished and elegant style of acting and theatrical production. More generally, Molière represents seventeenth century courtliness, and he epitomizes for Strindberg the French classical theater, one of the unique theatrical idioms in the history of Western drama, which Strindberg chose as a model to follow in his naturalistic period, and to which he returned from time to time throughout his career.

[27] *Samlade skrifter*, L, 289.
[28] Letter of 1 April 1908, in *Strindberg och Teater*.
[29] *En blå bok II*, in *Samlade skrifter*, XXXXVII, 546.
[30] Martin Lamm, 293.
[31] Falck, *Fem år med Strindberg*, 138.

Molière, Austria, and Germany

Of the great nations participating in the literary history of Europe, the Germanic countries have perhaps been the most receptive to the contributions of foreign lands. Boccaccio, the commedia dell'arte, Lope de Vega, Calderón, French Classicism, Shakespeare, Marlowe, Milton, Rousseau, Byron, Zola, Tolstoy, Dostoevsky, Ibsen and Strindberg— all of these, among other writers and events, have played essential roles in the history of literature written in the German language. Historians have felt the need to talk much about influences, and the critics of literature, whenever they wrote, have tended to keep a watchful eye on non-German literature. Indeed, the great literary disputes have sometimes resembled ghostly battles between the vassals of foreign giants from past times. The eighteenth century in Germany witnessed a spectral confrontation between Corneille, Racine, and Molière on the one hand and Shakespeare and Milton on the other. To be sure, these unwitting antagonists would probably have had more to admire and less to disparage in each other's works than was discovered and marshalled up by Gottsched, Bodmer, Breitinger, Lessing, and the German Romantics. In the midst of the disputes, Molière was admired even by those who opposed French Classicism in favor of other sources of inspiration. Unlike Corneille, Molière was not seriously taken as the negative point of departure for literary or critical polemics.

That Gottsched and his influential wife embraced the tenets and expressions of French Classicism, the works of Molière included, is an established fact. The following essays begin with a discussion of one of the first significant reactions to Gottsched's argument, namely the critical position of Lessing. Others take up key points in the chronicle of literature in German, points when the impact of Molière's comedies was keenly felt.

LESSING AND MOLIÈRE
Wolfgang F. Michael

We are accustomed to view Lessing as the sharp critic of French classical drama. At a time when German literature began to grope for its own paths, when German men of letters started to groan under the long-endured harness of classical rules, when they were about to consider them more as a hindrance than as guidance, Lessing more than anyone else struggled to free the Germans from the supposed yoke of French suppression. Yet even in the greatest of his literary battles, Lessing never became indiscriminate. To be sure, he held up the banner of English literature, especially of Shakespeare, and condemned French literature in general and the frenchifying Germans in particular. But he made significant exceptions. Lessing always admired the concepts and ideas of Diderot, for instance. Lessing's criticism is aimed most often at French tragedy, and even here Racine remains on the whole unchallenged. Lessing's attacks are directed chiefly at Corneille, who he seemed to think was the epitome of French classical tragedians, and at Voltaire, Lessing's own former master. Years before, Lessing had carelessly taken along one of Voltaire's manuscripts and became suspected of literary piracy. Perhaps this unhappy occurrence —one that ended all relations between the two men—contributed to the bitterness of Lessing's attacks, but we would like to believe that Lessing was above such personal animosities.

We have to look at the development of Lessing's attitudes. Having received an outstanding classical education at the famous Fürstenschule in Meissen, the seventeen-year-old student arrived in Leipzig in 1746 and began to work completely in the world of the traditional French classical literature. In Leipzig, perhaps the cultural center of Germany at the time, lived university professor Johann Christoph Gottsched, who, with a rule-book of critical aesthetics in his hand, reformed and purified German literature, most of all German theater, and led it from the extremes of lasciviousness and extravaganza, of improvisation, of blood and thunder, and of simple bawdiness into a somewhat boring, but respectable instrument for his ideals and his coterie. French drama was the admired model

271

that Gottsched used. By no means blind to the German past, Gottsched was the first to point to medieval German drama and to acknowledge the charm of Hans Sachs. But in the literary development of his day, his strong advocacy of French drama, especially French tragedy, remained far more significant. The six-stress line of the Alexandrine, ill-adapted to the highly accentuated German, the three unities, great heroes and princes as the protagonists and antagonists in tragedy, and common folk as the main figures in comedy—these were Gottsched's not very original prescriptions. With them Gottsched ruled the field.

Young Lessing had, it seems, no personal contact with Gottsched, but his first little comedy, *Der junge Gelehrte*, was very successfully performed by the Leipzig theater group of Madame Neuber, which at the time worked under the personal tutelage of our professorial dictator. Lessing's early utterances seem to echo Gottsched's concepts. Already in 1747 he attacked in a rather clumsy youthful poem "Männer, die die Sitten lehren,/Und dich, Molier [sic], nicht ehren."[1] He still showed his admiration for French drama in general when a few years later he moved from Gottsched's Leipzig to the more liberal Berlin of Frederick the Great. Here, he was active as a journalist for the newly established *Berlinische priviligierte Zeitung* (that was to dominate journalistic tradition as the *Vossische Zeitung* until almost two centuries later when Hitler killed it). In 1751 he praised La Fontaine, Molière, Racine, Regnard and other French authors as the best writers (IV, 457). A little further in the same essay he claimed Corneille and Molière had raised the French theater to the greatness which was supported by Racine and Regnard and which still continued in the works of Crébillon, Voltaire, des Touches, la Chaussée, and Boissy. We can assume that until the late fifties Lessing's viewpoint remained the same. But in 1758 he translated large excerpts of Dryden's *Essay on Dramatic Poesie*. This treatise is arranged in dialogues between literary friends. At first French tragedy with its strict classical form is favorably contrasted with the supposedly formless English dramas. But later Shakespeare and his compatriots Ben Jonson, Beaumont, and Fletcher are considered far superior to the French.

> What is easier than writing a regular French play? And what is more difficult than writing irregular English ones like those of Fletcher or Shakespeare? If

[1] Gotthold Ephraim Lessing, *Sämtliche Schriften*, ed. Karl Lachman ("dritte aufs neue durchgesehene und vermehrte Auflage besorgt durch Franz Muncker"), 23 vols., (Stuttgart, 1895–1924; photomechanic reprint, 1968), I, 106. All further references to this edition, including citations translated, are given in the text with volume and page number.

we, like Corneille, concentrate on a single bare intrigue whose outcome like that of a poor puzzle we foresee before it is half demonstrated, we can just as easily be regular. But if you want to create a rich piece with manifold complications as some have tryed since Corneille's authority has faded, they write just as irregularly as we. For our plays in regard to structure have more variety and in execution far more wit and ideas. . . . In most irregular plays of Shakespeare and Fletcher a more manly imagination, more wisdom and wit are manifest than in any French play. (VI, 286–7)

Lessing's acquaintance with this essay marks the turning point in his attitude toward French literature. Some of his most striking later attacks seem to be supplied and supported by the armory of Dryden's thoughts. "Name the play of the great Corneille which I could not do better. What do you bet? But I want to add: reliably I will do better and still not be a Corneille and still not have done a masterpiece, I won't have done anything but what anybody can do who believes as strongly in Aristotle as I do" (X, 216). This outburst in his *Hamburgische Dramaturgie* (1768) is reminiscent of Dryden's "What is easier than writing a regular French play?"

Lessing began his great campaign against French literature in his famous 17th letter concerning modern literature (1759). This was only a short time after his Dryden excerpts had appeared. It was a two-pronged attack against Gottsched and, through him, against the French. Gottsched should not have used the French as his model; Shakespeare, Jonson, Beaumont, and Fletcher he neglected. (These are the same four dramatists that appear in Dryden's essay. Marlowe and Kyd are not mentioned by Lessing or by Dryden, nor did I find any reference to them in later works of Lessing.)

"Even following the models of antiquity Shakespeare is a far greater dramatic poet than Corneille. Corneille comes closer to antiquity in mere mechanics, Shakespeare in the essentials" (VIII, 43). Dryden's thought still seems to echo in these statements. Ten years later, in his *Hamburgische Dramaturgie*, Lessing's criticism becomes far more detailed. In analyzing various plays he goes far beyond Dryden's more general treatment. In the heat of battle he is out to kill, and his analysis of Corneille's *Rodogune* is his most devastating criticism. Lessing starts out calm enough to talk about the masterpiece of this great man. The phrase "the great Corneille" is repeated throughout, but it sounds more and more like mere sarcasm; it seems a clever device to arouse the reader's opposition. Lessing's criticism of *Rodogune* is as much a masterpiece of critical attack as it is at the same time completely unfair to the work criticized.

Corneille is the main victim of Lessing's sharp blows; however, other

Frenchmen, notably Voltaire, share Corneille's fate. But, all the more significant, Lessing never records an unkind word about Molière. In the *Hamburgische Dramaturgie* Molière is mentioned a number of times; he is never attacked; on the contrary, he is defended against the criticism of others. Obviously to the very end Lessing considered Molière as unquestionably the great comedy writer even as he considered Shakespeare the great genius of tragedy. In 1778, a few years before his death, in the middle of a theological battle, Lessing states somewhat as an aside, "Who could doubt that Molière and Shakespeare would have made splendid sermons and delivered them if they had chosen the pulpit instead of the stage" (XIII, 151).

What separates Lessing from Corneille and brings him closer to Shakespeare and Molière? In the *Hamburgische Dramaturgie* Molière appears still clearly as the outstanding comedy writer when Lessing remarks about a play by Quinault: "There is really much in it that is good and comic and of which a Molière need not have been ashamed" (IX, 242). But in other passages Lessing becomes more specific. For example, of *L'Ecole des femmes* Voltaire had claimed that everything is only narration although it seems to be action (X, 6). Not so, says Lessing; everything is action although everything seems to be narration, for it is not the events narrated that are decisive but the reactions of the deceived old man. Mere narration would indeed be unfit for the stage.

Lessing states here his fundamental concept of drama. The Aristotelian sees action or plot as the core of all theatre. But this does not completely explain Lessing's attitude. Another issue seems more important in this respect: the question of characterization. A discussion of a play by Gellert (IX, 273) shows one aspect of Lessing's view. Gellert's play, Lessing thinks, portrays the characters as they are in real life: "Every spectator believes to recognize a cousin, a brother-in-law, an aunt." But these characters remain too trivial, too flat: "We only see one side; that one side soon becomes boring." Lessing seems to indicate, although only implicity, that we need characters, not types. This same question is treated in a lengthy discussion of the general and the particular in comedy and tragedy as Diderot, the English commentator Hurd, and Aristotle interpret it (X, 140–88). Hurd, best remembered for his discussions of Horace, and Diderot seem to say that tragedy uses particular characters; comedy, general characters. But here both authors appear to contradict Aristotle, who claimed that all characters must be general. Lessing seeks a way out in giving the word "general" two meanings. A general character can bring together all traits noticed in real life: that would be an "overloaded" character. Or the character can reflect an average of the traits of various models. At this decisive point Lessing breaks off. Since supposedly he never intended to give a systematic treatment of drama, he can just as well leave this question unanswered. The lengthy quotations from Hurd show that he was deeply interested in the complex question, but the abrupt way in which he breaks off shows that he was not sure of his own position.

Lessing's attitude toward comic characters is perhaps most clear in his defense of Molière's *Misanthrope*. He quotes a passage from Rousseau: "Molière makes us laugh at the Misanthrope and yet the Misanthrope is the good man of the play. Molière shows himself then as an enemy of virtue in making the virtuous contemptible." Not so, Lessing states, "the Misanthrope does not become contemptible, he remains what he is, and the laughter does not in the least take away our esteem. We laugh about him but do we therefore despise him?" (Lessing distinguishes here between simple "lachen," to laugh, and "verlachen," to laugh at, to deride.) "We esteem his good qualities." Without these good qualities the character would be disgusting, repulsive, rather than comic.

"Comedy would reform by laughter not derision. . . . It's true, general benefit lies in laughter itself" (IX, 303). This passage is basic to Lessing's interpretation of Molière. What he here claimed for *Le Misanthrope*, he could have applied to his own great comedy, *Minna von Barnhelm*. We should laugh about, not laugh at its hero, Tellheim. This sympathetic laughter is rarely understood by critics who want to divide the figures in comedy, as in tragedy, into good and bad, serious and laughable, while the mixed characters seem much more interesting, more true to life, and more artistic.

In Lessing's concept of tragedy, *Mitleiden* (empathy) was central. Therefore he attacked Corneille. The middle-class dramatist had no taste for what he considered the strutting heroes of French tragedy. They were meant for a theater under the impact of a courtly society. Yet the same courtly society could have its fun with the everyday people as Molière depicted them, good or bad and good and bad. With these, Lessing could be empathetic.

INTIMATIONS OF MOLIÈRE
IN GOETHE'S LEIPZIG COMEDIES

Carl Hammer, Jr.

The boy Goethe first saw plays by the great classical dramatists of France at the French theater in Frankfurt during the occupation of 1759 to 1763. As soon as he had learned enough of the language, he read their works.[1] His lasting admiration for Racine is well known, while his regard for Corneille was often underestimated, as I have endeavored to show elsewhere.[2] Molière is one of the writers most consistently praised by Goethe, in whose perennial esteem he stands beside Shakespeare. As a student at Leipzig, called in *Faust* "ein klein Paris," he saw further French dramas performed, among them *Tartuffe*. Many diary entries attest to Goethe's continued interest in Molière; for instance, on March 14, 1778, he read *Le Médecin malgré lui* at one sitting. The following October he played the role of Lucas in a performance at Ettersburg. He produced *L'Avare* (in Zschokke's translation) on the Weimar stage in 1805 and 1806. On July 1, 1813, he noted in his diary: "Molières *George Dandin*." August Wilhelm Schlegel's charge that Molière was just a writer of farces for the amusement of his royal master, Louis XIV, drew from Goethe a belated though spirited defense of the French playwright. This is but one of his old-age references which reveal an almost reverential attitude toward Molière. He told Eckermann (May 13, 1825) that he read some of the plays every year. In another conversation with Eckermann (March 28, 1827) Goethe made it clear that he admired Molière not only for his perfection as an artist, but also for his amiable nature. On that occasion he extolled the dramatic power evidenced by *Le Malade imaginaire*.

Resemblances to *Tartuffe* have been claimed for the satirical pieces, *Pater Brey* and *Satyros*, as well as for *Der Großkophta*, a drama born of Goethe's reaction to the Cagliostro imposture. *Les Fourberies de Scapin* lent the name of the leading figure in *Scherz, List und Rache*. Likenesses

---

[1] Johann Wolfgang von Goethe, *Werke*, "Weimarer Ausgabe," (Weimar, 1887–1919), Series I (literary works), 26:171; cited as W.A.I with volume and page numbers. Only dates are given for letters and conversations.

[2] Carl Hammer, Jr., "Re-examining Goethe's Views of Corneille," *The Germanic Review*, XXXI (1954), 260–68.

exist between *Le Misanthrope* (especially prized by Goethe) and *Torquato Tasso*; e.g., neither Alceste nor Tasso can rule his tongue, and both feel disillusioned by the artificiality prevailing in court circles. Similarities between *Don Juan* and *Faust* have likewise been noted.[3] Reminders of Molière are particularly striking in *Die Laune des Verliebten*, written in Leipzig, and *Die Mitschuldigen*, which (contrary to Goethe's implication in *Dichtung und Wahrheit*[4]) took shape only after his return to Frankfurt. Still, he undoubtedly received the initial inspiration during his Leipzig sojourn; hence the title of this study of his earliest extant completed plays in relation to the pristine enthusiasm of Goethe for Molière's works. Limitations of space necessitate a suggestive rather than an exhaustive comparison.

Whether or not Goethe thought of *Les Précieuses ridicules* when he wrote his sister Cornelia (October 12, 1767) that he had all but given up Constanze Breitkopf as hopeless because she had read too much, he was experiencing an analogous situation in real life. Similarly, his stormy love affair with Käthchen Schönkopf formed a realistic background for his "Schäferspiel in Versen und einem Akte," *Die Laune des Verliebten*,[5] with which, as Ernst Beutler remarks, a two-thousand-year development of pastoral poetry ends.[6] Signalizing Goethe's success with the "Formtypus" of that genre, Wolfgang Kayser regards this work as the last representative of its kind to live on in literature.[7] Despite retention of the pastoral form, numerous technical details, and the customary alexandrine, indicative of firm adherence to tradition, Heinz Kindermann points out that the author frequently transcends the bounds of rococo style.[8] Whatever connection may obtain between Goethe's pastoral and the plays of such predecessors

---

[3] Cf. Auguste Ehrhard, *Les Comédies de Molière en Allemagne* (Paris, 1888), 310–13; 328–29; 350–61; also, Bertram Barnes, *Goethe's Knowledge of French Literature* (Oxford, 1937), 12–17.

[4] W.A.I, 27:144. See Goethe's letter of November 24, 1768, to Ernst Theodor Langer (not discovered until 1922), *Der junge Goethe*. Neubearbeitete Ausgabe in 5 Bänden, hrsg. von Hanna Fischer-Lamberg (Berlin, 1963–), I, 261. Both Fischer-Lamberg (*Ibid.*, 506–507) and Kayser (*vide* note 7) allude to some of the correspondences with Molière mentioned in this article.

[5] Cf. Julius Vogel, *Käthchen Schönkopf. Eine Frauengestalt aus Goethes Jugendzeit* (Leipzig, 1920), 62–63.

[6] Ernst Beutler, "Einführung" to *Goethes Werke*, "Gedenkausgabe" (Zürich, 1948–54), 4:1001.

[7] *Goethes Werke*, "Hamburger Ausgabe," (Hamburg, 1948–64), 4:471. This edition is the source of all quotations from *Die Laune des Verliebten* and *Die Mitschuldigen* (indicated parenthetically in the text by verse numbers).

[8] Heinz Kindermann, *Der Rokoko-Goethe* ("Deutsche Literatur in Entwicklungsreihen. Reihe Irrationalismus," Bd. 2 [Leipzig, 1932]), 35.

as Favart and Gellert, *Die Laune des Verliebten* bespeaks kinship with Molière's comedies in the treatment of the theme of the jealous lovers. Here we encounter, as repeatedly in Molière, a lovers' quarrel resting on superficial misunderstandings. The shepherd Eridon tyrannizes his faithful Amine, while Lamon and Egle love each other without distrust. Eridon offers analogies with a number of Molière's jealous men, for example, the Prince in *Don Garcie de Navarre*.

Egle tells Amine that Eridon's supposed love for her is actually his satisfaction in having someone to command (26–28). Amine insists that it is not obstinacy, but a moody vexation that plagues him (40–41). In like manner, Done Elvire complains of seeing the Prince so carried away by jealousy as to lose the respect that love inspires in true lovers. Thereupon Élise contends that love's intensity is thus expressed all the better; that the more jealous he is, the more he should be loved.[9] Amine's concluding words:

> Und doch vergnüg ich mich, da, wenn er mich nur sieht,
> Wenn er mein Schmeicheln hört, bald seine Laune flieht (43–44),

may be compared to these lines of Élise:

> Mais tout ce qu'un amant nous peut montrer d'alarmes
> Doit, lorsque nous l'aimons, avoir pour nous des charmes. (I. i)

Admitting that she is surrounded by languishing suitors, Amine asks Eridon what more he wants, since he alone has her heart. Could he not allow the poor fellows to look at her? Eridon answers that he knows she is his, but what worries him is that one of them may think he is being made happy in the same way, and

> Schaut in das Auge dir und glaubt dich schon zu küssen
> Und triumphiert wohl gar, daß er dich mir entrissen. (289–90)

In reply to Done Elvire's reproaches, Don Garcie acknowledges that, in spite of his efforts, a little jealousy steals into his heart, because of the fear of a rival and the ever-present belief that she longs for the other man,

> Et que, malgré mes soins, vos soupirs amoureux
> Vont trouver à tous coups ce rival trop heureux. (I. iii)

Eridon, fond of solitude and impatient at Amine's being the center of male attention, shares this tendency with the hero of *Le Misanthrope*, for

---

[9] *OEuvres complètes de Molière*, éd. par Louis Moland (Paris, 1880–85), 3:384–85; quoted, with one exception, for all plays concerned, with number of volume (in first reference), act, and/or scene, in the text.

Alceste is driven to fury by Célimène's delight in the society of courtiers. By contrast, Lamon and Egle are like Philinte and Éliante in their tolerance of harmless flirtations. When Eridon chides Amine for being unwilling to offend other admirers, she asks whether love bids us forsake humanity, adding that a heart that loves *one* cannot hate any person (317–18). According to Eridon, she ought to hate her luckless wooers *because* they love her (312–13). In similar fashion, Alceste accuses Célimène of being obsessed with the homage of too many beaux, whereupon she inquires whether she can prevent their finding her lovable and whether she should respond to their efforts by chasing them out with a stick (vol. 7; act II, scene i). Both impetuous lovers demand exclusive love in return. Eridon tells Amine:

> Ich dank den Göttern, die mir dieses Glücke gaben,
> Doch ich verlang's allein, kein andrer soll es haben. (309–10)

Alceste expresses a corresponding attitude:

> Vous avez trop d'amants qu'on voit vous obséder,
> Et mon cœur de cela ne peut s'accommoder. (II. i)

Finally, each is alarmed by the number of his rivals, whose company his inamorata enjoys so much. To Amine Eridon exclaims:

> Wie schön verteidigst du
> Des zärtlichen Geschlechts hochmütiges Vergnügen,
> Wenn zwanzig Toren knien, die zwanzig zu betrügen! (320–22)

As Célimène objects to Alceste's complaint:

> Mais de tout l'univers vous devenez jaloux,

he counters with:

> C'est que tout l'univers est bien reçu de vous. (II. i)

Amine confides to Egle that she rejoices at seeing Eridon envy the whole world the sight of her. She continues:

> Ich seh an diesem Neid, wie mich mein Liebster schätzt,
> Und meinem kleinen Stolz wird alle Qual ersetzt. (67–68)

Her defense of Eridon is in the spirit of the reply given by Éraste, in *Le Dépit amoureux*, to Lucile's plea that one in love treats the beloved otherwise:

> Quand on aime les gens, on peut, de jalousie,
> Sur beaucoup d'apparence, avoir l'âme saisie.

Lucile then assures him:

> La pure jalousie est plus respectueuse,

whereupon Éraste rejoins:

> On voit d'œil plus doux une offense amoureuse. (vol. 2; IV. iii)

Amine's excuses for Eridon also bear resemblance to the comment of Éliante (in *Le Misanthrope*) that love is usually little adapted to prescribed laws, and that lovers always vaunt their choice. She further observes:

> Jamais leur passion n'y voit rien de blâmable,
> Et dans l'objet aimé tout leur devient aimable;
> Ils comptent les défauts pour des perfections,
> Et savent y donner de favorables noms. (II. v)

The opposite couples, Eridon and Amine, continually in "dépit amoureux," and Lamon and Egle, happy in a love free from jealousy, exemplify the maxim enunciated by the Éraste of *Les Fâcheux* as judge of a debate between Orante and Climène. Whereas Orante holds that a lover is more pleasing if he is not jealous, Climène declares:

> Et c'est mon sentiment que qui s'attache à nous
> Nous aime d'autant plus qu'il se montre jaloux. (vol. 4; II. iv)

Éraste's verdict aims at satisfying both sides:

> Et pour ne point blâmer ce qui plaît à vos yeux,
> Le jaloux aime plus, et l'autre aime bien mieux. (*Ibid.*)

Egle warns Eridon that when embitterment prevails, and where freedom is lacking, every joy perishes. Let him bear this in mind regarding Amine:

> Wenn du ihr Freiheit läßt, so wird sie dich nicht lassen;
> Doch, machst du's ihr zu arg, gib acht, sie wird dich hassen. (422–23)

Her advice coincides with the moral of *L'École des maris.* Sganarelle quotes approvingly the admonition of his brother, Ariste, against being too strict, since one wins people's minds through gentleness. He concludes:

> Et les soins défiants, les verrous et les grilles
> Ne font pas la vertu des femmes ni des filles;
> Nous les portons au mal par tant d'austérité.
> Et leur sexe demande un peu de liberté. (vol. 4; III. vi)

At the end of Goethe's pastoral the hitherto jealous Eridon gives positive indication of taking this lesson to heart.

In the *Tag- und Jahreshefte* for 1765–1769 (written more than half a century afterward) Goethe claims that a careful reading of *Die Mitschuldigen* cannot fail to reveal the author's study of Molière's world.[10] Hippolyte Loiseau questions that latter-day assertion, believing that the clearness of plan, liveliness of action, and rapid, natural dialog could have been inspired more readily by Lessing's *Minna von Barnhelm*, which Goethe had greeted with enthusiasm upon its then recent appearance.[11] Nevertheless, Loiseau agrees with Ehrhard concerning similarities of character and situation in Molière.

Sganarelle ou le Cocu imaginaire has been aptly described as "a highly intellectual comedy of errors," in which all the characters become ever more deeply involved through pursuing an intrinsically coherent reasoning based on mistaken premises.[12] The same is largely true of *Die Mitschuldigen*, where equally false perceptions cause the persons of the drama to accuse one another erroneously, as in Molière's comedy. In both cases the victims of an initial misapprehension see that perception confirmed by each subsequent happening.

Of the characters in Goethe's three-act play (the first version has one act), the one most suggestive of Molière is the deceived husband, of whom Ehrhard says: "Il y a l'étoffe de plusieurs Sganarelles et d'un George Dandin."[13] If, as Hubert maintains, Dandin is the "least noble" character among Molière's creations,[14] he has a true literary descendant in Goethe's Söller. The neglected wife, for instance, Martine in *Le Médecin malgré lui*, is reincarnated in Sophie, the innkeeper's daughter. Of course, the name Alcest did not have to be derived from Molière, but it is all the more reminiscent of the latter's misanthropic protagonist in that Sophie's returned erstwhile lover exhibits, like the earlier Alceste, a disdainful attitude and tactless frankness. The host himself is endowed with a curiosity equal to that of the "Wirt" in Lessing's *Minna*.

In the opening scene the innkeeper upbraids his son-in-law, accusing him of ingratitude toward his benefactor:

> Er sieht nicht, was er ist, er denkt nicht, was er war,
> Nicht an den povern Stand, aus dem ich ihn gerissen,
> An seine Schulden nicht; davon will er nichts wissen. (22–24)

[10] W.A.I, 35:4.
[11] Hippolyte Loiseau, *Goethe et la France, ce qu'il en a connu, pensé et dit* (Paris, 1930), 321–23.
[12] J. D. Hubert, *Molière and the Comedy of Intellect* (New York, 1962), 24.
[13] Ehrhard, *Les Comédies de Molière*, 312.
[14] Hubert, *Molière*, 195.

Although this refers to material benefits, one recalls that in *George Dandin ou le Mari confondu* the parents-in-law of Dandin, M. and Mme de Sotenville, tirelessly remind him of the advantages he derived from marrying into an aristocratic family. Söller sings during the reproachful speech of his father-in-law. The Sotenvilles are no less indifferent to Dandin's retort that it was *they* who profited—financially—from that union (vol. 9; I. iv).

Upon finding nothing important in Alcest's letter and hearing that the latter's money has been stolen, the innkeeper engages in a tirade after the manner of Harpagon in *L'Avare*. He first grasps his wig, then runs about the stage, brandishing a cane, and finally beats his easy chair with it, in the same sort of blind rage that causes Molière's miser to seize his own arm as if he had hold of the "coquin" who has robbed him. Both are boundlessly committed to vengeance; the innkeeper shouts:

> O wär ich doch ein Wind mit ein paar hundert Flügeln,
> Ich möcht' die ganze Welt, Sonn, Mond und Sterne prügeln. (763–64)

Harpagon threatens to have his entire household put to the torture. After calling for all agents of law enforcement, he resolves:

> Je veux faire pendre tout le monde; et si je ne retrouve
> mon argent, je me pendrai moi-même après. (vol. 9; IV. vii)

Like her father, Sophie complains about Söller's heedless extravagance (after they have argued about who profited from their marriage):

> Es wankt das ganze Haus;
> Du nimmst allein nichts ein, und gibst allein fast aus.
> Du lebst in Tag hinein; fehlt dir's, so machst du Schulden,
> Und wenn die Frau was braucht, so hat sie keinen Gulden. (121–24)

The Sganarelle of *Le Médecin malgré lui* and his wife, Martine, have a similar dispute. When Sganarelle says she was very lucky to find him (even as Söller tells Sophie regarding himself), she retorts:

> Qu'appelles-tu bien heureuse de te trouver? Un homme qui me
> réduit à l'hôpital, un dèbauchè, un traître, qui me mange
> tout ce que j'ai! (vol. 8; I. i)

When Sophie admonishes Söller:

> Willst du ein braves Weib, so sei ein rechter Mann. (126)

one remembers Angélique's answer to Dandin's question about a husband's role:

> Le personnage d'un honnête homme, qui est bien aise de voir
> sa femme considérée. (II. iv)

Söller implies that Alcest is lengthening his stay because of Sophie
(104). Likewise, Dandin tells Angélique, referring to Clitandre:

> Le voilà qui vient rôder autour de vous. (II. iv)

When thus confronted, both wives inquire what they are expected to do
about it.

Concerning Alcest, Söller asks Sophie:

> Wenn er dich liebte, he! gäbst du ihm wohl Gehör? (109)

The wife of Sganarelle (the "cocu") displays an inclination like that attributed to Sophie. On finding a miniature of Lélie, she says to herself:

> Avouons qu'on doit être ravie
> Quand d'un homme ainsi fait on se peut voir servie,
> Et que, s'il en contoit avec attention,
> Le penchant seroit grand à la tentation. (vi)

As Sophie awaits Alcest's nocturnal visit, she muses:

> Das Schicksal trennt uns bald, und ach! für meine Sünden
> Mußt ich mich—welch ein Muß—mit einem Vieh verbinden. (403–04)

In a kindred frame of mind Sganarelle's wife sighs with regret that she
cannot lawfully change husbands the way she changes her chemise. Later,
as she looks at Lélie's picture, she laments:

> Ah! que n'ai-je un mari d'une aussi bonne mine!
> Au lieu de mon pelé, de mon rustre . . . (vi)

Both Söller and Sganarelle bemoan their cuckoldry and allude to the
horns that symbolize it. Witnessing from his hiding place the clandestine
meeting of Sophie and Alcest in the latter's room, Söller mutters:

> Was fang ich an! Ich bin ein Hahnrei! (494)

Under similar circumstances Sganarelle says to himself:

> Sganarelle est un nom qu'on ne me dira plus,
> Et l'on va m'appeler seigneur Cornelius. (vi)

Each thinks that living as a cuckold is preferable to execution; in Söller's
words:

> Als Hahnrei kann man sich ehals am Galgen trösten. (500)

Sganarelle reflects:

> Et.quant à moi, je trouve, ayant tout compassé,
> Qu'il vaut mieux être encor cocu que trépassé. (xvii)

Söller's exclamation about saving himself:

> Gib deine Stirne preis! Parier nur deinen Rücken! (784)

brings to mind Sganarelle's utterance in a parallel case:

> Il pourroit bien, mettant affront dessus affront,
> Charger de bois mon dos, comme il a fait mon front. (xvii)

Retreating before Alcest's rapier, Söller inwardly curses his cowardice:

> Geh, Memme, Bösewicht! Warum erschrickst du so? (790)

In a like predicament Sganarelle reviles himself, in an aside:

> Ah! poltron! dont j'enrage;
> Lâche! vrai cœur de poule! (xxi)

Söller characterizes Alcest in the following terms:

> Es steht ihm an der Stirn: Hirschapotheksproviser. (872)

and Sganarelle comments similarly on Lélie:

> Cet étrange propos me rend aussi confus
> Que s'il m'étoit venu des cornes à la tête! (xvi)

Both Söller and Dandin are unwilling witnesses as their wives hold nocturnal trysts, each with a "gentleman." Söller, hidden in the alcove of Alcest's room, peers through the curtains at the lovers. Dandin, suspecting Angélique of engaging in an amorous adventure, conceals himself in the dark and listens to the affectionate dialog. Söller despairs of Sophie's virtue:

> Wenn's schon bergunter geht! Wer gibt mir einen Dreier
> Für ihre Tugend? (472–73),

while Dandin, no less enraged at Angélique's slurring remarks about certain husbands, observes (in still another aside):

> Voilà nos carognes de femmes! (III. v)

Alcest, condoling Sophie in her marital misfortune, relegates Söller to the great order of deceived horned spouses, and Clitandre assures Angélique that she has a husband unworthy of the honor.

Thinking that Söller really went to the ball, Alcest rebukes him:

> . . . und es ist gar nicht fein,
> Er läßt der jungen Frau das kalte Bett allein. (893–94)

Angélique's parents wrongfully accuse Dandin of staying out late drinking, and Claudine, the maid, taunts him thus:

> Cela est-il beau d'aller ivrogner toute la nuit, et de laisser
> ainsi toute seule une pauvre jeune femme dans la maison? (III, xi)

When Söller protests:

> Herr! Freund von Frauenzimmern!
> Sie ist nun meine Frau, und Sie kann's nichts bekümmern,
> . . . .
> Mein Herd ist doch mein Herd!
> Trotz jedem fremden Koch! (903–904; 909–910),

he follows the pattern of Sganarelle's appeal to Lélie:

> Mais votre conscience et le soin de votre âme
> Vous devroient mettre aux yeux que ma femme est ma femme. (xxi)

On hearing Alcest laud Sophie's virtue, Söller answers:

> Ja, sie hat mir ziemlich warm gemacht. (990)

Under like circumstances Sganarelle exclaims:

> Mon front l'a, sur mon âme, eu bien chaude pourtant. (xxii)

Both married couples are partly reconciled in the final scene. At Alcest's insistence, Sophie shakes hands with her husband. Sganarelle, although mistaken about Lélie, claims to run more risk than his wife, whom he begs to accept his suggestions for harmony. She replies:

> Soit. Mais gare le bois, si j'apprends quelque chose! (xxii)

Alcest gives Söller a parting admonition about future behavior (just as the Sotenvilles warn Dandin). Seeing his rival's gesture, Söller groans:

> Nein, das wär zu viel—ein Hahnrei und gehangen! (1008)

In a like vein of despair, Sganarelle finally asks:

> A-t-on mieux cru jamais être cocu que moi? (xxiv)

And George Dandin opines that the only thing left for a "mari confondu" is to throw himself into the river, headfirst (III, xv).

The foregoing comparisons of passages suggest an affinity with Molière, even granted that similar comic scenes by other dramatists were known to the youthful Goethe. How far he may have been aware of these apparent reminiscences while writing *Die Laune des Verliebten* and *Die Mitschuldigen* cannot be determined with certainty. Yet these seem to be unmistakable early instances of Goethe's lifelong wont to glean from multifarious sources whatever met his artistic demands and then proceed along his own creative way.

DOM JUAN AND DON GIOVANNI
Adèle Bloch

Fascination with the Don Juan myth has never waned, and now more ink is flowing as modern dramatic reincarnations are created and volumes of criticism keep the myth's controversial nature alive. One may wonder at the perennial youth of a figure which has haunted us for the past three centuries. The key may well be inherent in the myth's basic ambiguity and ambivalence, which has intrigued readers and theatrical audiences, as well as music lovers, for so many years. The very durability of the archetype may be grounded on its basic attributes: prestige coupled with scandal.

The myth does not date back to pre-Christian times. In order to achieve shock value and to violate a deep taboo, Don Juan needed a Christian setting extolling the virtues of monogamy and the repression of vagabond instincts. The legend unfurled shortly after the Renaissance and attained its initial peak in Spain, although it was by no means limited to that country. Don Juan offers a striking contrast to Don Quixote, as his persiflage demolishes antiquated codes of courtly love to which the Castillian knight clings.[1] Already in these early stages two main aspects of the character can be distinguished: profligacy and blasphemy.[2]

The first literary and theatrical incarnation of the legendary hero must be ascribed to the Spanish monk Tirso de Molina, whose original subtitle, "El Burlador de Sevilla," needs clarification. The word *Burlador*, it should be emphasized, actually means "trickster," a Panurge-like picaresque character, who likes to play, rather than "deceiver." Tirso's hero, whose prototypes may have been the Duke of Villamediana or even King Philip IV himself, is presented as a vain braggart who keeps postponing the moment of repentance until death surprises him with a tragic accident. The moral is evident in the churchman's didactic play: repent in time! As far as the structure of the drama is concerned, most elements are already present, although in a somewhat disjointed form. There are two noble ladies, Isabella and Anna, who fall prey to Don Juan's seduction.

[1] Michel Berveiller, *L'Eternel Don Juan* (Paris: Hachette, 1961), 17.
[2] Edward J. Dent, *Mozart's Operas* (London: Chatto and Windus, 1913), 193.

The former, daughter of the Viceroy in Naples, is the victim of rape by the Andalusian hidalgo, who gains access to her quarters by impersonating her fiancé. Catalinon, the ever-present valet, is already an indispensable appendage. Also the peasants are present, but in a poeticized form, as is the extra character, the fisher-girl Tisbea, who attempts suicide after being abandoned by the hero. There is one scene of cynical disrespect towards the father; there is the murder of the Commendatore; the scene with the statue, and the final banquet and fall into Hell's fire.

In the ensuing thirty years' interim, the theme was appropriated by the Italian theater and transformed by slapstick humor, while the religious and moral overtone vanished. The valet became more comical and began to resemble Arlecchino in the *commedia dell'arte*. Cicognini was the dramatic author who exerted the most influence on Molière, though the latter was to omit the scene of the Commendatore in the hope of presenting a less objectionable hero. The valet had become "Passarino" in the midst of farcical "lazzis," which were to be revived by Mozart but abolished by Molière—the switch of clothes between master and servant, for example, the "catalogue" of female conquests, and the lackey's aping of his master's lechery. On the other hand, the servant's final scream for wages on which the play ends was to be appropriated by Molière but mitigated by Mozart. Although Cicognini's play was a source to be exploited successfully at a later date, this Italian playwright had stripped Don Juan's figure of its verve. Yet more and more versions of the drama proliferated. Gags multiplied while the action grew less complicated.[3]

In French versions, Dorimon in 1659 and Villiers in 1660 presented in turn their own *Festin de pierre*, both of which lacked finesse and showed the Don as a cruel and cowardly rapist. The other protagonists were treated as pastoral stereotypes and given names such as Brunetta, Rosalba and Amarante, which hardly fitted peasant girls.[4] To the delight of a public avid of supernatural phantasmagoria, hellfires, talking statues and in general of elaborate stage machinery, the predictably melodramatic elements of the play became emphasized.

Molière, at that time, had suffered from opposition to his *Tartuffe*. While he was already working on his *Misanthrope*, financial necessity

---

[3] Alfons Rosenberg, *Don Giovanni, Mozarts Oper und Don Juans Gestalt* (Munich: Prestel, 1968), 56.

[4] Daniel Mornet, *Molière* (Paris: Hatier Boivin, 1943), 99.

prompted him to produce a play sure to draw big audiences. In his mind, a play on the theme of Don Juan was certain to succeed. Since 1658, three plays on this same subject had been given in Paris.[5]

Molière's contribution, then, was hardly the construction of an original plot. The merit of his play lies in his judgment in reducing the supernatural episodes and in his genius in creating a hero very much alive, paradoxically attractive yet repulsive. When he composed the play he hardly had time to polish it nor couch it in rhymed alexandrines. He also gingerly dispensed with classical unities and verisimilitude, while he added his own elements to the drama, such as ridiculing doctors, noblemen, and the devout (Jouanny, 710). He is responsible for changing its primitive humor into a more social satire, although he had hoped to avoid the renewed censorship of pious groups. Molière must have realized the sketchy nature of his play, which was to be performed only fifteen times from February 15, 1665, until Easter of the same year, and which he never bothered to print.

Now the question of Molière's real intent still lingers on, as well as the enigma of his sympathy or antipathy for the libertine lord he created. We cannot be sure of his true convictions, nor can we state with certainty that the author was a materialist or an Epicurean disciple of Gassendi.[6] Daniel Mornet alleges that Molière cannot be proven to have been an atheist. More likely, he might have been a sceptic or just a lukewarm Christian. In his time, when the pendulum was swinging between atheism and Jansenism, Molière's tendency towards moderation presumably placed him as an exponent of the middle road (Fernandez, 138). Nor is it plausible to assume, as some critics do, that Dom Juan is his creator's mouthpiece, since his character displays some loathsome and extreme facets which an "honnête homme" could never condone. However, the protagonist does exude charm and bravery, and Molière might well have endowed him with a juxtaposition of vice and virtue reminiscent of the Chevalier de Lorraine, de Guiche, Vardes, and Lauzun, all aristocrats whose verve might have dazzled the dramatist despite himself (Mornet, 105). Molière did in fact frequent sceptic circles, and his cynical hero might have borrowed some traits from friends like Le Vayer and Chapelle. Dom Juan is actually depicted as the typical freethinker who solely believes in nature and in

[5] Robert Jouanny, Notes to *Oeuvres complètes de Molière* (Paris: Garnier, 1962), 707.
[6] Ramon Fernandez, *Molière, the Man seen through his Plays*, trans. Wilson Follett (New York: Hill & Wang, 1958), 136.

mathematical certainty: "Je crois que deux et deux sont quatre, et quatre et quatre sont huit" (act III, scene i). Otherwise he believes in nothing.[7]

This "grand seigneur méchant homme," as he is so aptly designated by his valet in the very first scene of the drama, owes little to his Spanish and Italian predecessors. He is purely French in temperament and never bestial in love. Elegance graces even his vice, which displays a cerebral quality and on occasions elicits the flourishes of preciosity (Mornet, 105). Like some of his real-life courtier prototypes, he excites a mixture of admiration and distaste; yet unlike his theatrical forebears, he never stoops to rape, nor is he particularly concerned with the act of love. Seduction becomes his main sport, while sensualism moves to the background. It is significant to note that he enjoys pitting one farm girl against another rather than seizing an easy conquest. This ice-cold hero is bent on reducing others to his will. We soon come to realize that we are not confronted by a banal womanizer, but a "parieur contre Dieu" (Jouanny, 712), whose commands he flouts with egomaniacal relish. His intelligence is evident at all times, as are his irony and wit. He uses sound psychological insight on his interlocutors when it suits him; at other times his approach is sarcastic, alternatingly playful or manipulative of others' foibles. Cartesian logic is the main weapon in his struggle to reduce the world around him to the state of an object to subjugate, enjoy and ultimately cast away. Sex is by no means the power which motivates him, and his appetite appears jaded rather than lusty, foreshadowing later libertine heroes like Valmont or Lovelace. Molière's Dom Juan takes ample time to woo the recalcitrant prey Elvire, whom he had to tear from a cloister. Here, God is his ultimate rival.[8] For him the spice of attraction lies in the infringement on other people's property. Nothing goads him like a couple's happiness, for his will can tolerate no competition. In his desire to overpower every obstacle in his path, the prize which eludes him obsesses him. After Elvire escapes from his bondage by sublimating her love for him, he very untypically desires her afresh. Mere possession is not his goal, for a subject reduced to the state of an object immediately loses its interest for him. Actually, he seems endowed far more with the intellectual faculties of reasoning and calculating than with the capacity for passion or even emotion.

To sum up, the question arises as to whether Molière's protagonist

---

[7] Molière may have borrowed this line from the last words attributed to the Prince of Orange who rebuffed his confessor exhorting him to a deathbed act of repentance.

[8] Lionel Gossman, *Men and Masks, A Study of Molière* (Baltimore: Johns Hopkins, 1963), 43–44.

pursues women because he is an atheist or whether his hedonistic life-style is eroding his faith. Furthermore, Dom Juan delights in confusing the public (both on and off stage) by his posturing and by his alternately flouting and denying the aristocratic values to which it adheres. A certain sadistic element appears in his relations with men, whom he dumbfounds, as well as with women. Maybe Dom Juan is featured as the last scion[9] of a caste which has lived according to feudal standards that are beginning to become obsolete. In him the warlike instincts might have been perverted into petticoat strategy and ultimate hypocrisy, the only available outlets for his repressed energies.

Molière includes the controversial pauper's episode in his play, thereby adding another perennial question mark. Some modern critics see in Dom Juan, who gives alms to Francisque "in the name of humanity," a prefiguration of eighteenth-century deists and "philosophers" endowed with a social conscience. Such sentimental interpretations, however, may be far-fetched and anachronistic. It would seem more logical to consider the scene within the light of its own epoch and according to the general characterization of the Dom Juan. He likes to dazzle and to bewilder his audience of onlookers. He is thus just as likely to amuse himself by humiliating the poor hermit as by mystifying and crushing with his superior intellect the pious morons who preach endless platitudes. We should be wary of ascribing our own post-Romantic interpretations to Molière, who probably saw no tragic or pathetic elements in situations he conceived within the context of his day and world, where a crueller sense of the comic prevailed.[10]

A few years after the play faltered, partly due to the denunciations of the devout, Molière's widow, who was hard pressed for money, asked Thomas Corneille for an adaption in verse. The expurgated and anodyne version which ensued was to be the one the public knew for one hundred and seventy-four years. Yet its theme was revived in various forms and in different places. Shadwell's *Libertine*, which appeared in London in 1675, acquired some features from English Restoration lords like Rochester. In this case, the libertine hero was shown under a disgusting and despicable light. The Venetian Goldoni gave his own version, *Il Dissoluto*, which displayed only mediocre merit. In Paris Le Tellier composed the first opera

---

[9] It is significant that Dom Juan in Molière's play as well as in any other drama on the subject, is presented as barren, as separate from a procreative role.

[10] Gaston Hall, "A Comic Don Juan," in *Molière, A Collection of Critical Essays*, ed. Jacques Guicharnaud (Englewood Cliffs: Prentice-Hall, 1964), 106.

on the subject in 1713, and Gluck a ballet in 1761, whereas the Italians Vincenzo Righini and Giuseppe Gazzaniga continued the musical trend by each composing an opera which was performed by the former in Prague in 1776 and by the latter in Venice in January, 1781.

Molière's influence also continued to survive in the theater of Beaumarchais. Mozart had composed his immensely successful *Marriage of Figaro* just one year prior to *Don Giovanni*, which may be viewed as the only worthwhile Don Juan play to succeed Molière's drama in a span of one hundred and twenty-two years. In the case of both Mozartian comic operas, Lorenzo Da Ponte was the librettist, and if we are to believe the *Memoirs* of this adventurer and poet, the idea for the latter opera originated with him, since he had already embarked on the text with no particular composer in mind,[11] even though Mozart had originally approached him with the plan for *The Marriage of Figaro*. However, we must be wary of accepting Da Ponte's allegations. He was born in Venice, as was another famed libertine, Giacomo Casanova, his senior by some twenty years and his lifelong model, friend and, ultimately, collaborator of sorts in the *Don Giovanni* text and score. Casanova may have lent some of his traits to the operatic hero, and his valet served as a model for Leporello, the Don's servant. Casanova is seriously believed to have contributed not only sketches, but an actual piece of recitative and the aria "Ah! pieta, Signori miei" for Mozart, while Da Ponte had to be temporarily absent from Prague. He is also supposed to have revamped a bit of the score he thought too tame.[12] This theory is reinforced by the knowledge that Casanova attended the opera's premiere, and that the text for a new sextett was posthumously found amidst his effects (Rosenberg, 185–86).

Basically, Da Ponte was not a great poet. His exploits, if we are to believe them as reflected in his *Memoirs*, seem to be weak copies of his envied idol's, Casanova's, yet more colorful and baroque than his verse. His end was rather staid: having moved to America, he became a professor in Columbia University (Kings College at the time), and lived to an extremely old age. In 1823 he was instrumental in introducing the opera *Don Giovanni* to New York audiences. Although he lacked originality, Da Ponte recognized genius whenever he encountered it, and he did much

---

[11] Lorenzo Da Ponte, *Memoirs*, trans. Elizabeth Abbot (New York: Dover, 1967), 174.

[12] Paul Nettl, "Don Giovanni und Casanova," *Mozart Jahrbuch* (Salzburg, 1958), 108–15.

to publicize Mozart beyond the status of such acclaimed colleagues as Salieri and Martini in the Prague and Vienna of his day.[13]

Da Ponte was a courtier who had succeeded in currying imperial favor. He was chiefly known for the libretto of *The Marriage of Figaro*, a polished jewel which enjoyed far greater popularity in Vienna than *Don Giovanni*. Wishing to profit by the favorable climate created by *Figaro*, he launched on the next libretto, which he claims to have written simultaneously with two other operatic works, keeping several possible composers in mind. Since the finished product indicates an amazing degree of collaboration between script-writer and composer, we might take his allegation of unilateral effort with a grain of salt, while we may accept his claim to having written the work in a matter of days.

Don Giovanni was first performed in Prague on October 29th, 1787, with great success, and next in Vienna on May 7th, 1788. The author of its libretto, far from displaying qualities of originality, would according to modern standards be accused of plagiarism. In fact, following a practice common in his day, he borrowed his material from the Venetian Bertati, who with Gazzaniga had produced a very popular opera in his Adriatic hometown as late as the spring of 1787.

Bertati must be credited with knowing where to find his sources. Through the mouth of his impresario, he admits his play is based on Tirso and on Molière, although he takes pride in having added his own details (*Dent*, 203). When Da Ponte, who envied him after losing his post as court poet to him, had to pay Bertati his first mandatory call, he spied on top of his desk the tome of Molière's *Comédies* from which he originally and admittedly had drawn his material (Da Ponte, 227). Although Da Ponte calls him a windbag and a charlatan, he himself did not flinch from drawing heavily, in turn, from this Venetian colleague.

Bertati, a man endowed with meager talent, had written a popular one-act opera buffa for a small company with limited means. His libretto has some merit, as he frees *Don Giovanni* from the rampant rationalism of his epoch (Rosenberg, 175). In his own plot he retains some of Molière's features, such as the peasant couple and the quid-pro-quo scene between two women, wherein Don Giovanni tells each that the other is demented; yet he adds a few extraneous elements. He includes a Donna

---

[13] R. B. Moberly, trans., *Three Mozart Operas : Figaro, Don Giovanni and the Magic Flute* (London : Victor Gollancz Ltd., 1967), 155–57.

Ximena (reminiscent of the Cornelian heroine Chimène) and a fiancé, Don Octavio, and he inserts a funny scene after the hellfire episode at the end. In this operetta the valet (named here Pasquariello) also undergoes some regression as he is depicted with Arlecchino-like levity.

This rather unpolished model was transformed by Da Ponte into an elegant, witty, fairly well-constructed work, which could dispense with superfluous elements, such as the character Ximena (Dent, 208). Furthermore the plot was stretched so as to form two acts, the first subdivided into five scenes, the second into six.

The opera opens with the murder of the Commendatore, who duels with Don Giovanni as he tries to flee from the scene of the attempted rape of Donna Anna. Her fiancé, Don Ottavio, swears to avenge the crime. The noble girl, like Chimène, will postpone her wedding until the masked assailant is identified and caught. In the second scene Donna Elvira, who has been seduced and deserted by Don Giovanni, but has neither been abducted by him from a convent nor married to him, swears to pursue her errant lover. She is pointedly reminded of his true character by the servant Leporello, who in scurrilous fashion enumerates to her in the famous "Catalogo" aria (based on Bertati) his master's amorous conquests. In the third scene we see a peasant wedding. Da Ponte has limited the number of characters to just one couple of main protagonists: Zerlina and her groom, the bumpkin Masetto. The Don muscles in on the festivities and is ready to decoy the bride when Elvira intervenes and identifies the culprit, who manages to escape. The rest of the act is taken up by reconciliation and preparation for the ballroom scene, a gala where the protagonist proposes to lure Zerlina and other country girls. In the midst of the music and hubbub, he tries to attack Zerlina, who is now more wary of his wiles and is rescued just in time.

The second act opens with Don Giovanni's praise of womanizing, followed by an exchange of dress with his valet, whom he wishes to impersonate so as to woo Elvira's (unseen) maid by a serenade. Masetto, seeking revenge, gets a beating while Leporello, dressed in his master's clothes, is pursued and unmasked but flees. In the third scene, which shifts to a mausoleum, the Don extends a dinner invitation to the Commendatore's statue, after his servant flinches at the order. Then there is one more Cornelian scene between Anna and her betrothed, whose hand she still refuses while vengeance is yet to be taken. The fifth scene culminates in the banquet. Elvira (and no longer Molière's "Specter of Time") issues a last warning to her unrepentant lover. The statue appears and, after one vain admonishment, carries the hero to Hell. The sixth and last scene, which Mozart omitted in the Vienna performance, brings the opera to the happy conclusion required by Baroque tradition. Singing in gay ensemble, all characters voice their plans: the engaged couples can finally marry—although Anna asks for one year's delay—Elvira will retire to a convent; and Leporello is free to seek a better employer.

The opera is more compact than the play by Molière. The action is less diffuse and more concentrated, as can be seen in such instances as the single supper scene, which almost immediately follows the provocation of the statue. The supernatural element is also considerably reduced, for the admonishing phantom has been replaced by the warning voice of a live, concerned mistress. There are fewer characters, diversions, and digressions, so that the overall effect may appear to be the result of standards more classical than the ones prevailing in Molière's play. However, the quality which makes *Don Giovanni* a masterpiece and not just one more drama begotten by the Don Juan theme is Mozart's.

Mozart's music is far more tender and profound than the often platitudinous words being metamorphosed by its magic. It has moments of sombreness contrasting with ebullient spirit and sunshine. Mozart added a polyphony of characters, which enabled him to run the gamut from the fervid "Champagne Aria" through the folk sound of the "Serenade," with its guitar accompaniment, to the stately "Minuet" that climaxes the ballroom scene and contrasts with the gloom of the sepulchral episodes. Although some critics do see a predominating tragic element in this music, we would be misled in exaggerating the composer's forebodings of death. Mozart did in fact write an *opera giocosa*; hence the pathos had to be tempered by gaiety. Although he himself was no libertine like Da Ponte, it would be just as anachronistic for us to see his work in a perspective of Romantic despair as if we viewed Molière's *Dom Juan* from a purely tragic slant. In this *opera giocosa* a balance is maintained between contrasting tragic and comic elements. Furthermore, Mozart did not repudiate the lusty realism of his century, which permitted a more licentious tone than Molière's century, a time still bound by *bienséances* or decorum.

According to reliable music critics like Moberly (195), bawdy humor permeates the opera, and Mozart indulges in some ribald musical jokes by associating horns with cuckoldry, as for example in the scenes of Zerlina's overt and covert seduction. Since in Molière's play vulgar sexualism might have conflicted with courtly taste, his hero never actually indulges in physical conquests, but only reminisces or schemes, whereas Mozart's rake remains unfettered by such conventional restraints. He never ceases to amaze us by his love of life, his prodigious energy, sleepless activity, and his appetite not only for sex but for food, wine, and music. He enjoys fun for its own sake and never strikes us as odious, hypocritical or denatured. In some respects he appears more sympathetic than his French predecessor, also more boyish, impulsive, and even helpless on occasions. On the other hand, he is less aristocratic, less intelligent, and he has to stoop to physical violence and subterfuge to gain the submission of some female victims. Mozart's protagonist does, however, come close to showing signs of a conscience. He hates to kill an old man in a duel, and he even reveals traces of sentiment on rare occasions. Like Molière, Mozart must have felt a degree of sympathy for his creation.

Offending God is certainly not this hero's main concern, possibly because he is the scion of a Godless age and not particularly interested in blasphemy. He has a passion for collecting people. He even seduces the old and the ugly in order to include them in his list. He professes that the reason he deceives them all is "because I love them all! To be faithful to one alone would be cruel to others. I . . . wish well to every one of them! But as the women cannot count beyond one, they call my good and natural power deception" (Moberly trans., 196). In this respect he almost paraphrases the French Dom Juan's tirades. Like his forerunner, the Italianized Don Giovanni is a barren wastrel and delights in manipulating others at will, regardless of their sex. Furthermore, he never assumes the role of a Tartuffe while feigning conversion, and he never marries any of his victims. In short, Don Giovanni appears much earthier and healthier than his more elegant French counterpart.

One more difference must be brought out here: the Mozart-Da Ponte team did revive two characters that preceded Molière's work, Donna Anna (merely alluded to in the French comedy) and her conventional lover, Don Ottavio. In the peasant couple, Zerlina and Masetto, however, Mozart and Da Ponte are within the Molièresque tradition. These two are almost carbon copies not only of the Picardy country folk who appear in *Dom Juan* but of farmers in other plays, such as *Georges Dandin*.

Donna Elvira, the second female lead, appears on the surface to be an exact replica of Molière's heroine except for her inability to repress her love for the unfaithful Don Giovanni. Yet she lacks the aura of dignity with which Molière imbues her. In the opera she appears simply as a thwarted woman who professes hate in a Racinian fashion, whereas Molière assigned a more Cornelian role to her. It is interesting to note that in the opera the Cornelian part is shifted to Donna Anna, who resolutely sticks to the code of avenging honor. Yet early nineteenth century critics, like the Romantic poet E. T. A. Hoffmann, think she has repressed feelings for the protagonist whom they see as her secret seducer. Such an interpretation does seem a bit farfetched when we consider Mozart and Da Ponte in the light of their traditions which would seem to preclude such veiled insinuations.

The valet Leporello also has undergone considerable changes. Sgnarelle, his counterpart, was typically French and belonged to the species of *cocus* in medieval Gallic farces, a species which also includes Orgon, Arnolphe, and Dandin.[14] Leporello, although he shares his French colleague's cowardice, weakness, and selfishness, lacks his long-winded rationalism. Far from being a *raisonneur*, he lacks even the slightest pretentions to intellect. On the negative side, Leporello also lacks Sganarelle's sense of right and wrong, and he is more submissive and envious. Whereas Sganarelle reproves his young lord for his excesses and his impieties, Leporello covets his master's amorous conquests and his easy life. He voices social criticism that seems to echo Figaro's complaints, but he is not the only one who loudly protests abuse. The mistreated farmer Masetto also expresses his bitterness against the privileges of caste. In Molière's day it would have been less likely for a peasant or a lackey overtly to criticize an aristocrat or to conceive of a social order wherein the menial would be his employer's equal.

In both the play and the libretto the valet plays a crucial role: he is the very opposite of his master, and although the domestic is dependent for economic reasons, the lord is dependent on his servant's constant attendance, on his services and admiration. Don Giovanni, as well as Dom Juan, needs a perpetual audience in order to strike his theatrical poses. Shocking a valet whom he yet despises for his proletarian grossness is indispensable for him. Actually the stupidly pious Sganarelle is a foil for the lucidly atheistic Dom Juan, just as the envious and lecherous Leporello is the unsuccessful shadow of his charming young master. Both servants are condemned to a slavish social role and are the butt of ridicule for a parasitic and corrupt upper caste. It is significant to note that neither valet, despite a long association, weeps at the untimely death of his employer.

Critics continue to write contradictory statements about *Dom Juan* and

---

[14] Gustave Lanson, "Molière and Farce," trans. Ruby Cohen, in *Molière, A Collection of Critical Essays*, ed. Jacques Guicharnaud (Englewood Cliffs: Prentice-Hall, 1964), 26.

Don Giovanni. The Romanticists deified the hero and saw in him the prototype of revolt or a Promethean dark angel of death. Modern scholars interpret the ambiguities both in the drama and in the music according to their own school of thought, be it Freudian, Jungian, or Marxist (to name but a few recent ones). A reliable musicologist like Rosenberg, for example, sees Don Giovanni as an archetypal father-killer presaging the parricide and regicide of the French Revolution. The ending of the opera for such a critic means the epiphany of the father, since order must ultimately return (Rosenberg, 292). To some other interpreters and dramatists, Don Juan could represent either a superhero, an insurgent against a decaying order (Fernandez, 140), or on the contrary a hollow scion clinging effetely to a crumbling and degenerating feudal code (Gossman, 65). Some have gone so far as to attribute homosexual tendencies to a hero who would run from woman to woman in a vain effort to satisfy some unquenched needs.[15]

The character continues to fascinate students of literature, psychologists, and poets alike. Its mysteries and ambiguities can still be revised and interpreted in diverse and often drastically opposite ways, so that even today the subject is alive. Yet only two creative geniuses were instrumental in imbuing a rather banal legend with an aura of charm and dismay: Molière, who first salvaged it from Limbo, and Mozart, whose music perpetuated its precarious balance between sympathy and antipathy, hybris and human frailty, Eros and Thanatos.

---

[15] See Lenormand's play: *L'Homme et ses Fantômes.*

Among the writers of comic drama in the land of Goethe, one author before all others, comes forward to be presented as the leading candidate for the honor of the designation "serious comedian." He is Heinrich von Kleist, a man whose life, like Molière's, was not set in a mood of continual joviality. When one considers Molière's patrimony to the German-speaking countries, one thinks almost immediately of Kleist, more specifically of his Amphitryon, *which he subtitled* Nach Molière. *The following three essays take up the subject of Molière and Kleist, each with a different point to make. In addition to these three, the reader will find, in another section, Professor Wittkowski's more general treatment of the Amphitryon myth, a treatment which naturally includes further discussion of Heinrich von Kleist.*

MOLIÈRE UND DIE KLEISTISCHE KOMÖDIE: VERSUCH EINER DEUTUNG

Carl Steiner

Es ist unsere These, daß die Forschung in ihren vielgestaltigen Untersuchungen über die literarischen Beziehungen zwischen Kleist und Molière bisher zwei wichtige Erwägungen weitgehend unberücksichtigt gelassen hat. Unbeantwortet blieb erstens, was den jungen deutschen Dramatiker Kleist überhaupt zu dem französischen Komödiendichter Molière hingezogen haben mag, und nicht geklärt ist zweitens, ob und inwieweit Kleists literarischer Kontakt mit Molière sich fruchtbringend auf sein entstehendes dramatisches Werk ausgewirkt hat.

Bereits die erste dieser beiden Fragen bedarf einer gründlichen Untersuchung, denn auf den ersten Blick haben beide Dichter nur wenig miteinander gemein, und dieser Mangel an offensichtlichen Gemeinsamkeiten erstreckt sich nicht nur auf die verschiedenen Kulturen, Sprachbereiche und Zeitalter, denen sie angehörten. Der Sohn bürgerlicher Eltern Jean Baptiste Poquelin, genannt Molière, hatte bekanntlich von frühester Jugend an den Ehrgeiz, Schauspieler zu werden. Nach dem frühen Tod der Mutter ließ ihm der Vater in dem von Jesuiten geleiteten

Collège de Clermont eine für die damalige Zeit erstklassige Erziehung
angedeihen, sich der Hoffnung hingebend, daß der Sohn, seinem Beispiel
folgend, ebenfalls in den Dienst des Königs treten würde. Aber dieser
brach mit aller Tradition und gründete als Einundzwanzigjähriger mit
der Schauspielerin Madeleine Béjart eine Schauspielgruppe, mußte aber
bald wegen Geldschwierigkeiten Paris verlassen und sich als Leiter einer
Wandertruppe in der Provinz recht und schlecht durchschlagen. So war
zwar Molières innigster Wunsch erfüllt, den damals noch recht anrüchigen
Beruf eines Schauspielers zu ergreifen. Doch sollte er von Enttäuschungen
nicht verschont bleiben. Es war nicht nur der dauernde Geldmangel, der
sich ihm auch später trotz der sich einstellenden königlichen Gunst zäh
an die Fersen heftete. In erster Linie war es die große Enttäuschung, die
er fühlte, durch Wuchs und Auftreten gezwungen zu sein, nicht Tragöde,
sondern Komödiant zu werden. Aber gerade diesen Umständen verdanken
wir seine weltberühmten Komödien. Bemerkenswerterweise schrieb er sie
weder aus weltanschaulichen Gründen noch aus tiefgehenden literarischen
Erwägungen heraus. Er hat sich auch nur sehr selten theoretisch über sein
Werk geäußert. Er schrieb seine Komödien, in deren Hauptrollen er selber
auftrat, für seine Bühne und nicht für den Druck und hat sich auch Zeit
seines Lebens nie ernsthaft mit dem Gedanken getragen, sie als Dichtungen
in gesammelter und gedruckter Form herausgeben zu wollen. Dennoch
aber hat Molière sowohl stofflich als auch dramaturgisch aus der gesamten
europäischen Überlieferung der Komödie geschöpft, so daß sein Werk,
trotz einer bewußten Zeitbezogenheit in seiner Darstellung sozialer und
kultureller Mißstände, zeitlose menschliche Schwächen bloßlegt, geißelt
und, was noch wichtiger ist, für alle Zeiten lächerlich macht. Der Tod
raffte ihn beinahe wortwörtlich von der Bühne weg, und er starb nach einer
Aufführung seines letzten Stückes, *Le Malade imaginaire*, im zweiund-
fünfzigsten Lebensjahr.

Heinrich von Kleist war im Gegensatz der Nachfahre eines alten preu-
ßischen Adelsgeschlechts. Obwohl ein Onkel in seiner Familie, Ewald
Christian von Kleist, sich innerhalb seiner Epoche literarisch hervorragend betätigt und als Dichter anakreontischer Poesie nationale Anerkennung gefunden hatte, schien der junge Heinrich von Kleist von vornherein
für eine Offizierslaufbahn vorbestimmt. Tatsächlich schlug er diese auch
als Fünfzehnjähriger ein. Wie die Tradition es forderte, trat er in das 2.
Potsdamer Gardebataillon als Gefreiter und nahm zwei Jahre später—
man zählte das Jahr 1793—am Rheinfeldzug teil. Überraschenderweise
gab er einige Jahre danach, mittlerweile zum Leutnant avanciert, seine

militärische Laufbahn auf und wandte sich darauf einem gleichfalls zu keiner Befriedigung führenden Studium zu. Man hat immer wieder auf die schwere Krise hingewiesen, die das Studium des Kantischen Kritizismus in dem sich geistig entwickelnden Dreiundzwanzigjährigen hervorgerufen hat. Seiner selbst und der Welt ungewiß begab sich Kleist 1801 auf eine Reise, die ihn über Dresden, Mainz und Straßburg vorübergehend nach Paris führte. Ein Jahr später finden wir ihn in der Schweiz, wo er unter dem Einfluß des Rousseauismus seiner Zeit den Versuch unternimmt, Landwirt zu werden. Von da zieht es ihn in die "große Welt" nach Weimar. Sein Traum: die Griechen, Shakespeare und Goethe, Schicksals- und Charaktertragödie miteinander und in sich zu vereinigen, führt zu einem tragischen Ringen mit dem "Guiskard"-Stoff. Anschließend macht er eine zweite Reise nach Paris, diesmal zu Fuß, und trägt sich, von Selbstmordvisionen gepeinigt, mit dem Gedanken, dem Invasionskorps Napoleons gegen England beizutreten. Nach dem zu erwartenden geistigen und körperlichen Zusammenbruch kehrt er in seine preußische Heimat zurück, wo er jahrelang zu einem äußerst aktiven Franzosengegner wird. Nach vergeblichem Ringen mit Geschick und Epoche, die ihm zu seinen Lebzeiten beides, Dichterruhm und Anerkennung verweigert haben, scheidet er, im fünfunddreißigsten Lebensjahr stehend, mit der ihm befreundeten Henriette Vogel freiwillig aus dem Leben.

Es war Kleists Schicksal, außerhalb der zeitgenössischen deutschen Kunst- und Lebenshaltung, außerhalb von Klassik, Romantik und philosophischem Idealismus stehen zu müssen und dennoch Elemente dieser Geistesrichtungen in seiner Dichtung enthalten zu sehen. Er ist Dramatiker und Erzähler. Als ersterer schreckt er seine Zeitgenossen durch die Kühnheit seiner Bildsprache und die Unmittelbarkeit seiner Dialogführung ab, als letzterer distanziert er sich bewußt von dem mit großer Dynamik berichteten Geschehen. Gegensätzlichkeit auch hier. Nach seinem Tode kam es zu einer ständig anwachsenden Anerkennung seines dichterischen Ruhms, an welcher der sich für ihn entschieden einsetzende Ludwig Tieck hervorragenden Anteil hatte. Aber erst im 20. Jahrhundert wurde man sich der wahren Bedeutung von Kleists eigenwilligem Genius voll bewußt. Nacheinander haben ihn mit teilweiser Berechtigung die literarischen Vertreter der expressionistischen, nationalistischen und existentialistischen Schule als einen der ihren erkannt und gefeiert. Heute gilt er in Deutschland sowohl als in Frankreich nicht nur als ein Dichter, der die weltanschauliche Problematik sowie die literarische Thematik der Moderne vorausgeahnt und in Leben und Werk mit dieser

Erkenntnis gerungen hat, sondern überhaupt als der genialste deutsche Dramatiker.

Eine auch noch so oberflächliche Betrachtung der Lebensläufe der beiden Autoren zeigt aber, daß trotz gewaltiger persönlicher Gegensätze, die auf zeit- und milieubedingte sowie gesellschaftliche Zustände und Umstände zurückzuführen sind, sich dennoch gewisse natürliche Anknüpfungspunkte abzuzeichnen beginnen. Die gemeinsame Grundlage ihrer verschieden gestalteten Persönlichkeit ist zweifellos das sie anleitende und antreibende dichterische Genie. Molière, der zur Zeit—als Kleist plante, ein großer, wenn nicht der größte Dichter zu werden—schon etwa 130 Jahre tot war, hatte damals bereits als Theatergenie und als Komödiendichter den ersten und erhabensten Platz unter den literarischen Größen seiner unmittelbaren Heimat eingenommen und galt darüber hinaus auch bereits im benachbarten Deutschland als ein für alle Mal arriviert. Daß gerade zu dieser Zeit alle Produkte des französischen Geistes vergangener oder zeitgenössischer Orientierung in Deutschland besonders diskutabel waren, ist eine bekannte Tatsache. Von besonderem Interesse wäre es aber jetzt, Kleists Einstellung zu Frankreich einer genaueren Untersuchung zu unterziehen. Claude David hat in einem aufschlußreichen Essay Kleists Verhältnis zu Frankreich näher untersucht. Ihm zufolge ist die allgemein verbreitete These, Kleist sei grundlegend als kein Freund Frankreichs zu betrachten, nicht mehr haltbar. David weist darauf hin, daß es—mit Ausnahme von Heine—kaum je einen zweiten deutschen Dichter gegeben habe, "dessen ganzes Leben und Wirken so eng auf Frankreich bezogen schien, wie gerade Heinrich von Kleist".[1] Seine gründlichen Französisch-Kenntnisse, die—den Berichten von Zeitgenossen nach—eine Zeitlang seine Deutsch-Kenntnisse überflügelt haben sollen, seine trotz allem oberflächlichen Wissen begeisterte Aufnahme Rousseauistischen Gedankenguts, seine persönlichen Kontakte mit Frankreich—die Pariser Reise von 1801 und die Frankreichfahrt des Jahres 1803—, all dies spricht für eine über das allgemeine Interesse seiner Zeit hinausgehende Bereitwilligkeit, sich der französischen Mentalität zu nähern und zu öffnen. Andererseits aber ist er von Paris enttäuscht, das er—einen C. F. Meyer und einen Rilke vorwegnehmend—als Stadt der Sünde und des Verfalls darstellt, stoßen ihn während seines Schweizer Aufenthalts die französischen Truppen so ab, daß er sein Projekt aufgibt, sich dort anzukaufen. Nach der Niederlage bei Jena und seinem zwangs-

---

[1] "Kleist und Frankreich", in: *Kleist und Frankreich*, 10.

weisen Aufenthalt als Staatsgefangener im Fort Joux scheint sich eine radikale Wendung in seiner Einstellung zu Frankreich vorzubereiten. Doch ist er noch 1808 bereit, "eine Zusammenarbeit mit Frankreich, eine Unterstützung durch Frankreich anzunehmen".[2] Kurz darauf veröffentlicht er, seine Zwiespältigkeit unterstreichend, bekanntlich das literarische Hauptdokument seines Frankreichhasses: *Die Hermannsschlacht*. Aber erst in den drei letzten Jahren seines Lebens steht er eindeutig auf Seiten der nationalen Sache gegen Frankreich.

Folglich wäre es ein Fehlurteil, Kleist einfach als "un romantique ennemi de la France"[3] zu bezeichnen. Seine Einstellung zu Frankreich ist trotz aller manchmal bis an den Wahnwitz grenzenden Feindseligkeit ambivalenter Natur und spiegelt nach außen hin fatale, den persönlichen Untergang vorausdeutende psychologische Schwierigkeiten seines Inneren. Sie ist am besten mit dem uns Modernen nur allzu bekannten Begriff der Haß-Liebe charakterisiert. Symbolisch dafür ist sein geplantes Meisterwerk "Robert Guiskard, Herzog der Normänner", das er in Paris in einem Wahnsinnsanfall zerriß. Benno von Wiese faßt die Problematik dieser Entwicklung so zusammen: "Die Großstadt Paris wird ihm zum Inbegriff des Scheußlichen und Lasterhaften, die Seine zu einem abscheulichen, häßlichen Fluß, sehr unterschieden von seiner poetischen Verklärung der Elbe und des Rheins. Dennoch hat er eine uneingestandene Liebe zu Frankreich. Das Ambivalente in diesem Verhältnis zu Frankreich behielt er sein Leben lang, etwas von Haß-Liebe scheint stets dabei mitzuschwingen, selbst noch in den Übertreibungen der *Hermannsschlacht*."[4]

Die auf die "Guiskard"-Krise folgenden Jahre gelten bekanntlich als die schrecklichsten seines Lebens, gleichzeitig aber als seine fruchtbarsten. Es sind dies auch die Jahre des intensiven literarischen Kontakts mit Molière. Nach dem geistigen und körperlichen Zusammenbruch, den sein tragisches Ringen mit dem "Guiskard"-Stoff hervorgerufen hatte, sah sich Kleist außerstande, neue Dichtungen zu entwerfen. In Königsberg, wo er sich von Mai 1805 bis Ende des darauffolgenden Jahres vorübergehend niedergelassen hatte, beschäftigte er sich eingehend mit der französischen Literatur und übersetzte jetzt neben La Fontaines Fabel von den zwei Tauben, die einige Jahre später in dem von ihm und Adam

---

[2] Ebd., 20.
[3] Vgl. René Laurets Artikel "Un romantique ennemi de la France: Henri de Kleist" in der Zeitschrift *Les marches de l'est* (1912). Siehe auch *Kleist und Frankreich*, 24.
[4] Benno von Wiese, "Heinrich von Kleist", in: *Deutsche Dichter der Romantik: Ihr Leben und Werk* (Berlin, 1971), 231.

Müller besorgten Journal *Phöbus* herauskommen sollte, auch Molières *Amphitryon*.[5] Allem Anschein nach hatte Kleist vorübergehend den Glauben an sein dichterisches Genie verloren und begab sich—wie es zu dieser Zeit auch allgemein üblich war—in die Schule des Übersetzers, um sich wiederzufinden. So stark war aber damals noch sein dichterischer Eigenwille, daß es auch hier nicht beim bloßen Übersetzen blieb.[6] Obwohl Kleist sein entstehendes Stück "Ein Lustspiel nach Molière" nennen sollte—eine offenbar bescheidene Unterordnung seines literarischen Unterfangens, welche Annahme er aber in einem Brief an den Dichter Wieland wieder widerlegt[7]—, handelt es sich, wie viele bekannte Studien und Auslegungen im Anklang an diesen Brief nachgewiesen haben, um eine beachtliche dichterische Umgestaltung eines vorliegenden Originals. Zugegebenermaßen sind die Dokumente und Belege aus diesen Jahren ziemlich spärlich, und David hat sicher nicht unrecht, wenn er in diesem Zusammenhang feststellt: "Und nirgends in seinem Briefwechsel oder in seinen Gesprächen wird erwähnt, daß er [Kleist] diese Übertragung des Molièreschen Lustspiels als diese Konfrontierung des deutschen Wesens mit dem französischen Geist aufgefaßt hätte, die viele Zeitgenossen nachträglich aus ihr herauslesen wollten."[8] Es läßt sich jedoch nicht

---

[5] Interessanterweise läßt sich der Name "Phöbus", das homerische Beiwort des Apollo, in Molières *Amphitryon* nachweisen. Vgl. Acte I, Scène 2:

> Cette nuit, en longueur me semble sans pareille:
> Il faut, depuis le temps que je suis en chemin,
> Ou que mon maître ait pris le soir pour le matin,
> Ou que trop tard au lit le blond *Phébus* sommeille,
> Pour avoir trop pris de son vin.

Bei Kleist erscheint diese Stelle folgendermaßen:

> Fünf Stunden nach der Sonnenuhr von Theben,
> Will ich stückweise sie vom Turme schießen.
> Entweder hat in Trunkenheit des Siegs
> Mein Herr den Abend für den Morgen angesehn,
> Oder der lockre *Phöbus* schlummert noch,
> Weil er zu tief ins Fläschchen gestern guckte.

(Der Kursivdruck ist von mir.)

[6] Vgl. John C. Blankenagel, *The Dramas of Heinrich von Kleist: A Biographical and Critical Study* (Chapel Hill, 1931), 81.

[7] In einem Brief an seine Schwester Ulrike vom 17. September 1807 berichtet Kleist von seiner erfolgreichen "Übersetzung" des Molièreschen *Amphitryon*, den er auch bei verschiedenen Gelegenheiten in Dresden vorgelesen habe. Am 17. Dezember desselben Jahres aber spricht er in dem Brief an Wieland von einer "Umarbeitung" des Molièreschen Stückes. Kleist schreibt hier: "Der Gegenstand meines Briefes war, wenn ich nicht irre, der Amphitryon, eine Umarbeitung des Molièrischen, die Ihnen vielleicht jetzt durch den Druck bekannt sein wird, und von der Ihnen damals das Manuskript, zur gültigen Empfehlung an einen Buchhändler, zugeschickt werden sollte." (Abgedruckt in: *Dichter über ihre Dichtungen: Heinrich von Kleist*, hrsg. v. Helmut Sembdner [o. J.], 34.)

[8] David, "Kleist und Frankreich", 18.

leugnen, daß trotz Mangels an persönlichen Kommentaren seitens des Dichters über dieses Werk—die übrigens, soweit sie vorhanden sind, mit Ausnahme des Briefes an Wieland, über geschäftliche Mitteilungen nicht hinausgehen—der Kontakt mit Molière sich fruchtbringend auf das dichterische Schaffen Kleists ausgewirkt hat und innerhalb seines Frankreich-Komplexes einen durchaus positiven Platz einnimmt.

Die neuere Forschung hat darauf aufmerksam gemacht, daß die erste Anregung zur Übersetzung und Umgestaltung des Molièreschen *Amphitryon*—eine Arbeit, die, wie wir wissen, erst später 1806 in Königsberg zur vollen Reife gelangte—bereits während seines Schweizer Aufenthaltes im Jahre 1802 erfolgt sein mag.[9] Zu jener Zeit in der Schweiz stand Kleist nämlich in einem freundschaftlichen Verkehr mit dem Schriftsteller Heinrich Zschokke, der sich gerade daran machte, eine Molière-Übersetzung herauszubringen. Es liegt also nahe anzunehmen, daß sich die beiden Freunde des näheren über diese Pläne und den französischen Meister selbst unterhalten haben. Die Tatsache, daß in Zschokkes Molière-Übersetzung aus dem Jahre 1805 der "Amphitryon" fehlt, führt zu der Vermutung, Kleist sei beauftragt gewesen, dieses Stück zu übertragen oder habe sich selbst mit dieser Absicht getragen und sie Zschokke gegenüber erwähnt. Auf jeden Fall ist der Name Zschokke auch für die Konzipierung von Kleists Meisterkomödie *Der zerbrochene Krug* von großer Bedeutung.[10] Inwieweit sich ihr Zustandekommen mit dem des *Amphitryon* verquickt, wird noch zu untersuchen sein.

Wie wir gesehen haben, läßt sich also die Frage, warum Kleist eine Amphitryon-Komödie nach Molières Vorlage geschrieben hat, nicht ohne

---

[9] Siehe dazu Günter Blöcker, *Heinrich von Kleist oder das absolute Ich* (Berlin, 1960), 299, und Hans Joachim Kreutzer, *Die dichterische Entwicklung Heinrichs von Kleist: Untersuchungen zu seinen Briefen und zur Chronologie und Aufbau seiner Werke* (Berlin, 1968), 157 und 162.

[10] Kleists Aufenthalt in der Schweiz ist deshalb so wichtig für unser Verständnis seiner Entwicklung, weil in dieser Zeit sein geistiger Durchbruch zum Dichter erfolgte. Hier lernte er nämlich eine ihn ansprechende Gruppe von jungen Literaten kennen, mit denen er sich befreundete. Zu diesen zählte neben dem geborenen Preußen Heinrich Zschokke, der sich im Schweizer politischen Leben hervorragend betätigt hatte und ein Freund des berühmten Schweizer Pädagogen Pestalozzi war, Ludwig Wieland, der etwas mißratene Sohn des Dichters Christoph Martin Wieland, und der Schweizer Herausgeber Heinrich Geßner, der Sohn des bekannten Schweizer Schriftstellers Salomon Geßner. Hier konzipierte Kleist neben anderen Frühwerken auch das Lustspiel *Der zerbrochene Krug*, dessen Anlaß bekanntlich der französische Kupferstich *Le juge ou la cruche cassée* von Le Veau war nach dem Original von P. L. Debucourt. Wie uns Zschokke später mitteilt, habe die Ansicht des Bildes die drei Freunde so belustigt, daß sie im Scherz einen Wettstreit eingegangen seien und gelobt hätten, über die im Bilde dargestellte Szene eines Rechtsspruchs eine Dichtung anzufertigen. Wieland habe eine Satire, Kleist ein Lustspiel und er selber eine Erzählung versprochen. (Vgl. hierzu Jakob Otto Kehrli, *Wie 'Der zerbrochene Krug' von Heinrich von Kleist entstanden ist* [Bern, 1957].)

weiteres beantworten. Ausschlaggebend für Kleists Wahl war wohl die schon zu seiner Zeit erkennbare allgemeine Beliebtheit des Amphitryon-Stoffes; haben wir es doch, wie auf der Hand liegt, mit einem der meist behandelten Bühnenstoffe der Weltliteratur zu tun. Und gerade mit diesem Stoff und seiner Molièreschen Vorlage wollte Kleist sich messen, dessen literarischer Ehrgeiz es war, das Talent eines Shakespeare und eines Sophokles zu vereinen und Goethe den Lorbeerkranz vom Dichterhaupt zu reißen. Mit dieser Absicht spricht er aber nicht nur dem Stoff seine Anerkennung aus, sondern unverkennbar auch dem Autor seiner Vorlage.

Das Lustspiel Molières ist keineswegs die erste französische Behandlung des Amphitryon-Stoffes. Diese stammt bekanntlich von Jean de Rotrou, der ihn 1638 in seiner Farce *Les Sosies* verarbeitete. Doch behält Molière inhaltlich, von Einzelheiten abgesehen—wie zum Beispiel der Einführung der Cléanthis als Ehepartnerin für Sosie—, den Stoff des antiken Vorbildes bei. Wohl wird die Geburt des Herkules nur angekündigt, während sie bei Plautus innerhalb des Handlungsablaufs stattgefunden hat. Wohl weicht die "Göttliche Komödie" der Antike einer modernen und lebensfreudigen Urbanität. Es kommt sozusagen zur Entmythologisierung der Legende. Das zentrale, die Komik des Ganzen tragende Doppelgängermotiv wird jedoch beibehalten. Was aber dieses Werk von allen seinen Vorgängern— Plautus mit einbezogen—unterscheidet, ist vor allem die Eleganz seiner Form und seiner Sprache. Das läßt sich schon am Prolog erkennen, der in seiner Phantasiefreudigkeit überdies äußerst bühnenwirksam ist. In brillant verfaßten *vers libres*, die mit ihrem blendenden Witz den genialen Dichter und Darsteller der Komödie verraten, eröffnet sich uns eine formale Eleganz, die bis auf den heutigen Tag von ihrem Scharm nichts eingebüßt hat. Ein kurzer Auszug aus dem Vorspiel, wo Mercure im Gespräch mit La Nuit und mit Hinweis auf Jupiter die Handlung zusammenfassend vorausdeutet, muß genügen, den Reichtum und das sprühende Leben dieses Stils zu enthüllen:

> Que vos chevaux, par vous au petit pas réduits,
> Pour satisfaire aux voeux de son âme amoureuse,
>   D'une nuit si délicieuse,
>   Fassent la plus longue des nuits;
> Qu'à ses transports vous donniez plus d'espace,
>   Et retardiez la naissance du jour,
>   Qui doit avancer le retour
>   De celui dont il tient la place.[11]

[11] Jean Baptiste Poquelin Molière, *Oeuvres complètes*, hrsg. v. Maurice Rat (Paris, 1959), II, 224–25.

Es ist hier am Platz, den folgenden Kommentar von Costa über Molières dichterisches Können in seinem *Amphitryon* zu zitieren: "In reading the play one has to remind oneself, in the midst of its elegance and sophistication, that it is about adultery and a cruel trick played by an Olympian god: a good example of the treatment of a work of art transcending its subject-matter."[12] Ist es da zu verwundern, daß Kleist von dieser Schön- und Scharfgeistigkeit angesprochen und fasziniert vor allen Werken Molières gerade diesem den Vorzug gibt und seine Vorlage dem eigenen Empfindungsvermögen anzugleichen versucht?

Wenn Kleist beim Zustandekommen seines *Amphitryon* auch andere Vorbilder herangezogen haben mag—wie neuerdings Helmut Sembdner nachzuweisen versuchte, der Johann Daniel Falks *Amphitruon* als eine Quelle zum Verständnis der Kleistischen Dichtung vorschlägt[13]—, so würde das der primären Stellung, die die Molièresche Vorlage bei seiner Bearbeitung des Amphitryon-Stoffes einnimmt, keinerlei Abbruch tun. Sie ist von Kleist selbst und der Forschung gründlichst dokumentiert und bedarf keiner eigentlichen Beweise mehr. In der Tat hat sich Kleists Stück so sehr an Molière gehalten, daß es lange als eine freie Übersetzung des französischen Modells galt. Schließlich hat Kleist ja eigentlich nur den Prolog gestrichen, zwei eigne Szenen hinzugefügt, zwei andere umgeändert und ansonsten, was den Inhalt anbelangt, nur geringfügige Veränderungen durchgeführt. Daß dabei, vor allem was Ton, Sprache und Form anbetrifft, ein ganz neuartiges Spiel entstanden ist, das von den meisten Interpreten dem Tragischen näher als dem Komischen gerückt worden ist, bedarf auch keiner ausführlicheren Auseinandersetzung mehr. Überdies hat sich auch schon Molières Stück im Vergleich zu seinen Vorgängern in diese Richtung hin bewegt.

Die gesamte und sehr umfangreiche Kleistforschung hat sich so ausführlich mit der Auslegung seines *Amphitryon* befaßt, daß ein weiterer in die Länge und Breite führender Versuch wenig fruchtbringend wäre. Es ist auch nicht das Ziel unserer Arbeit, erneut zu beweisen, wie selbständig und genial Kleist letzten Endes sein "Lustspiel nach Molière" verfaßt hat. Was wir aber in unserer Diskussion über den Kleistischen Beitrag zur Entwicklung des Amphitryon-Stoffes noch besonders hervorheben wollen, ist die unverkennbare Tatsache, daß bei ihm—und darin besteht

---

[12] Costa, "The Amphitryo Theme", 99.
[13] *Johann Daniel Falks Bearbeitung des Amphitryonstoffes: Ein Beitrag zur Kleistforschung* (Jahresgabe der Heinrich-von-Kleist-Gesellschaft, 1969–70).

vielleicht der größte innere Gegensatz zu der Molièreschen Vorlage—die von Molière meisterhaft durchgeführte Entmythologisierung der antiken Legende wieder aufgehoben wird. Es ist unserer Meinung nach aber nicht ein christlicher Mythos bzw. eine romantische Erneuerung des Marienkults, die Kleist hier anstrebt. Vielmehr will er bei seiner Umarbeitung im geraden Gegensatz dazu die Verkörperung des antik-heidnischen Ethos in der Gestalt der Alkmene feiern, trägt er sich doch—ein typisches Merkmal seines dichterischen Entwicklungsvorganges—um die selbe Zeit bereits gedanklich mit einer Art Gegenstück zu dem antiken Mythos im Amphitryon- bzw. Alkmene-Stoff, das seinen geistigen Niederschlag in der *Penthesilea* finden wird. Hier steht dann dem hehren Thema der Liebe und Treue der ergebenen Frau das düstere Motiv der abwegigen, sich bis zur Raserei steigernden weiblichen Leidenschaft gegenüber. Das Bild des apollinischen Griechenland weicht so schon früh dem des dionysischen.

Wir wollen aber diese Ramifikationen nicht weiter verfolgen, sondern vielmehr zu unserer eigentlichen Problemstellung zurückkehren. Was das literarische Schaffen Kleists dieser Jahre anbelangt, so lassen sich vom Standpunkt der Chronologie aus keine eindeutigen Daten für das Zustandekommen seiner Komödien ermitteln. Man hat seit langem den *Zerbrochenen Krug*, der als eines der bedeutendsten Lustspiele der deutschen Literatur gilt, chronologisch vor den *Amphitryon* gesetzt. Dieser Ansicht haben einige bedeutende Forschungen der letzten Jahre insofern widersprochen, als sie darauf hinwiesen, daß die Arbeit an beiden Werken sich zeitweilig überschnitt. So schreibt Hans Joachim Kreutzer: "Der 'Amphitryon' wurde [als Manuskript] vor dem 'Krug' abgesandt. Sollte das bedeuten, daß er auch früher vollendet wurde, so könnte das die Zeugniskraft des Datums vom 23. April 1805 für die Vollendung des 'Krugs' entwerten."[14] Kreutzer weist darauf hin, daß nicht nur diese beiden Stücke, sondern auch Kleists *Familie Schroffenstein* und sein "Guiskard" sich auf gemeinsame Anfänge aus der Zeit seines Schweizer Aufenthaltes zurückverfolgen lassen und die "enge Verflochtenheit seines dramatischen Schaffens"[15] deutlich mache. "'Amphitryon' und 'Krug' sind selbständige Metamorphosen großer Vorbilder. Sie fallen in eine Zeit bewußten Lernens nach dem Zusammenbruch über den 'Guiskard'."[16] Es liegt aber nun nahe, anzunehmen, daß die Molièresche Komödie als

[14] Kreutzer, 163.
[15] Ebd., 220.
[16] Ebd., 221.

solche auch das "große Vorbild" zu Kleists *Zerbrochenem Krug* abgab und nicht allein der *Ödipus* des Sophokles, als dessen tragisches Gegenstück Friedrich Braig den *Krug* in seinem Kleistbuch erblicken zu dürfen glaubte.[17]

Von allen Werken Molières scheint seine Meisterkomödie *Tartuffe* am besten geeignet, als mögliches Vorbild zu Kleists *Krug* herangezogen zu werden. Auf die Charakterverwandtschaft von Dorfrichter Adam und Tartuffe spielt indirekt schon Günter Blöcker in seinem Buch *Heinrich von Kleist oder das absolute Ich* an, in dem er in einer prägnanten Charakterisierung der Kleistischen Lustspielfigur betont: ". . . und Dorfrichter Adam ist—sehr im Gegensatz zu seinem Urbild Tartuff—ein in all seiner Ungeschlachtheit beinahe graziöser Lump, dessen Finten und Volten wir mit innigem Behagen verfolgen".[18] Bei allen Unterschieden von Zeit, Ort und Handlung finden wir aber gerade in der Charakterzeichnung der beiden Hauptpersonen auch wieder Gemeinsamkeiten, die wir näher untersuchen wollen. Folgerichtig ist der Dorfrichter Adam, seiner ländlichen Umgebung angepaßt, ein viel primitiverer Typ als der gesellschaftlich versierte Tartuffe. Dieser ist ein Heuchler, der sich klettenartig bei einer ehrlichen gutbürgerlichen Familie einnistet, den Sohn aus dem Haus treiben und die Tochter heiraten will sowie die Frau verführen und den Hausherrn ins Verderben stürzen möchte. All dies gelingt ihm beinahe. Wie die etymologische Wurzel seines aus dem Italienischen stammenden Namens andeutet, ist er im Grunde ein pilzartiges, parasitisches Wesen.[19] Der Name Adam weist auf den Ursprung bzw. den ersten Sündenfall

---

[17] Braig beruft sich in seiner Annahme auf Kleists "Vorrede" zum *Zerbrochenen Krug*, die einen Hinweis auf den "Ödip" enthält, führt aber im Kern seines Arguments an: "König Ödipus muß über sich selbst zu Gericht sitzen und das furchtbare Urteil fällen, unwissend, daß er selbst der Gerichtete ist, Adam aber ist der bewußte Sünder, der sich richtend verurteilen soll und der sich doch gleichzeitig diesem Gerichte und Urteile entziehen will." (*Heinrich von Kleist* [München, 1925], 169.) Damit hat Braig jedoch gleichzeitig auch, von andersgeartetem Genre ganz zu schweigen, auf die grundlegenden Unterschiede zwischen Sophokles' *Ödipus* und Kleists Komödie hingewiesen. Obwohl der Richter in beiden Stücken schuldig ist, wird er sich bei Sophokles seiner Schuld erst gegen Ende bewußt, bei Kleist aber weiß er sich von vornherein schuldig. Darüber hinaus will Ödipus auch unbedingt der Wahrheit auf den Grund gehen, Adam jedoch versucht, diese von allem Anfang an zu verheimlichen.

[18] *Günter Blöcker, Heinrich von Kleist oder das absolute Ich* (Berlin, 1960), 279.

[19] Der Name "Tartuffe", den Molière der *commedia dell'arte* entnommen hat, entspricht dem Italienischen "tartufo", was wörtlich "Trüffel" bedeutet, im übertragenen Sinn aber "Heuchler". Der Name ist im Französischen erstmalig im Jahre 1609 belegt und begann sich zur Zeit, als Molière sein Stück schrieb, in Frankreich als Familienname einzubürgern. Ende des Jahrhunderts wurde er von der Akademie offiziell im Sinne von "Heuchler" eingeführt. Später entwickelten sich daraus die Abstrakta "tartufferie" und "tartuffiage".

zurück. Nur ist dieses Modell eines korrupten Dorfrichters nicht das ursprünglich weiße, unbeschriebene Blatt, als das sein biblisches Vorbild gelten mag. Statt als tugendhafter Beschützer des Gesetzes aufzutreten, nützt er es aus und versucht, es zu seinen Gunsten zu biegen. Die Tatsache, daß er einen Klumpfuß hat, weist auf das Diabolische in seinem Charakter hin, das ihn trotz aller Unbeholfenheit dominiert. So wird er zum Verführer und Erpresser und zu guter Letzt durch Zwang der Umstände zum Verteidiger seiner eigenen Untaten, deren Dingsymbol der zerbrochene Krug ist. Eve, die Tochter des verstorbenen Freundes, ist dem entsprechend auch nicht die sinnliche, mannbetörende Verführerin des weiblichen Urbildes, sondern soll ähnlich wie Elmire in Molières Stück den Lustgegenstand männlicher Begierden abgeben. In beiden Fällen mißlingt aber die Intrige des Bösen und das Gute triumphiert am Ende.

In beiden Komödien handelt es sich also um die Entlarvung eines Heuchlers, der seine geistigen Gaben und seine Position dazu ausgenützt hat, sich schadlos zu halten sowie seine Mitmenschen rücksichtslos hinters Licht zu führen und auszunützen. Sowohl Tartuffe wie auch Adam sind im Grunde ihres Wesens und trotz allem komischen Anstrich Verbrechertypen, die sich an die Unwissenden und Gutgläubigen halten und sie auszubeuten verstehen. Bei Molière hat sich Tartuffe in das Vertrauen seines naiven, zur Frömmigkeit neigenden Gastgebers eingeschlichen, bei Kleist erringt Adam auf ähnliche heuchlerische Weise die Achtung der einfachen Dorfleute. Was das fromme Gebaren für den einen ist, bedeutet das Richteramt für den anderen: eine bequeme Maske, hinter der man den wahren Charakter anstandslos verbergen kann. In beiden Fällen geht der Krug—den volkstümlichen Charakter der werkimmanenten Moral hervorhebend—so lange zum Brunnen, bis er bricht. Unkraut verdirbt doch, denn wer nicht Treu' und Redlichkeit übt und von Gottes und der Menschlichkeit Wegen abweicht, muß kurz oder lang von den ewig mahlenden Mühlen der Gerechtigkeit zermalmt werden. Beide Heuchler schwindeln so lange, bis man ihnen auf ihre Schliche kommt und ihnen das leidige Handwerk legt. Molière faßt diese Moral in den Worten des das Heuchlertum bekämpfenden Schwagers Cléante zusammen:

> Vous voyez votre erreur, et vous avez connu
> Que par un zèle feint vous étiez prévenu;
> Mais pour vous corriger, quelle raison demande
> Que vous alliez passer dans une erreur plus grande,
> Et qu'avecque le coeur d'un perfide vaurien

Vous confondiez les coeurs de tous les gens de bien?
Quoi! parce qu'un fripon vous dupe avec audace
Sous le pompeux éclat d'une austère grimace,
Vous voulez que partout on soit fait comme lui,
Et qu'aucun vrai dévot ne se trouve aujourd'hui?
Laissez aux libertins ces sottes conséquences;
Démêlez la vertu d'avec ses apparences,
Ne hasardez jamais votre estime trop tôt,
Et soyez pour cela dans le milieu qu'il faut.[20]

Die Exposition der beiden Charaktere wird jedoch von zwei entgegengesetzten Ausgangspunkten in Angriff genommen. Bei Molière wird Tartuffe—*nomen est omen*—beinahe von Anfang an als gefährlicher Bursche bloßgestellt. Nach einer einführenden Lobrede der Madame Pernelle, die ihn als Mutter des zur Zeit abwesenden Hausherrn vor Familie und Bedienten hoch in den Himmel hebt, kommt es zu aufklärenden kritischen Worten über Tartuffe seitens des Schwagers Cléante und der getreuen Zofe Dorine. Der erstere stellt ihn uns als frommen Heuchler vor:

Il est de faux dévots ainsi que de faux braves;
Et, comme on ne voit pas qu'où l'honneur les conduits
Les vrais braves soient ceux qui font beaucoup de bruit,
Les bons et vrais dévots, qu'on doit suivre à la trace,
Ne sont pas ceux aussi qui font tant de grimace.
Hé quoi! vous ne ferez nulle distinction
Entre l'hypocrisie et la dévotion?
. . . .
Aucune chose au monde et plus noble et plus belle
Que la sainte faveur d'un véritable zèle,
Aussi ne vois-je rien qui soit plus odieux,
Que le dehors plâtré d'un zèle spécieux,
Que ces francs charlatans, que ces dévots de place,
De qui la sacrilège et trompeuse grimace
Abuse impunément et se joue à leur gré
De ce qu'ont les mortels de plus saint et sacré
. . . .
Ces gens, dis-je, qu'on voit d'une ardeur non commune
Par le chemin du Ciel courir à leur fortune,
Qui, brûlants et priants, demandent chaque jour,
Et prêchent la retraite au milieu de la cour,
Qui savent ajuster leur zèle avec leurs vices,
Sont prompts, vindicatifs, sans foi, pleins d'artifices,
Et pour perdre quelqu'un couvrent insolemment
De l'intérêt du Ciel leur fier ressentiment;[21]

---

[20] Molière, *Oeuvres*, I, 753.
[21] Ebd., 698–99.

Die Zofe will den Hausherrn Orgon gleichfalls über den schlechten Charakter Tartuffes aufklären. Auf seine Versicherung, daß dieser ein Edelmann aus dem vornehmsten Geschlecht sei, erwidert sie:

> Qui, c'est lui qui le dit, et cette vanité,
> Monsieur, ne sied pas bien avec la piété.
> Qui d'une sainte vie embrasse l'innocence
> Ne doit point tant prôner son nom et sa naissance,
> Et l'humble procédé de la dévotion
> Souffre mal les éclats de cette ambition.
> A quoi bon cet orgueil?... Mais ce discours vous blesse:
> Parlons de sa personne, et laissons sa noblesse.[22]

Erst im 3. Aufzug der fünfaktigen Komödie tritt der so eingeführte Scheinheilige selbst auf und bestätigt uns das negativ angezeigte Charakterbild, indem er Elmire, der Gattin des Gastgebers, ein Geständnis seiner Leidenschaft macht und sie unter möglicher Beschwichtigung ihres Gewissens zu verführen sucht. Am Höhepunkt dieses Unterfangens läßt er sich zu dem Geständnis hinreißen:

> Ah! pour être dévot, je n'en suis pas moins homme;
> Et lorsqu'on vient à voir vos célestes appas,
> Un coeur se laisse prendre, et ne raisonne pas.
> Je sais qu'un tel discours de moi paraît étrange;
> Mais, Madame, après tout, je ne suis pas un ange,
> ....
> Mais les gens comme nous brûlent d'un feu discret,
> Avec qui pour toujours on est sûr du secret.
> Le soin que nous prenons de notre renommée
> Répond de toute chose à la personne aimée,
> Et c'est en nous qu'on trouve, acceptant notre coeur,
> De l'amour sans scandale et du plaisir sans peur.[23]

Von jetzt ab haben wir ihn und seine Absichten völlig durchschaut. Daß er im 4. Akt noch stürmischer um Elmire wirbt, überrascht uns nicht im geringsten. Geschickt versteht Molière es jedoch, unser Interesse am Handlungsablauf durch eine Variation des retardierenden Moments zu steigern. Tartuffe, jetzt auch dem Gatten in seiner Gemeinheit bekannt und durch Elmire bloßgestellt, zeigt sich durch seine diabolische Gewandtheit dennoch als Meister seiner anscheinend fatalen Lage, indem er den Spieß schleunigst umdreht und sich als Herrn aufspielt. Am Ende kann ihn der Arm der Gerechtigkeit nur noch durch Eingreifen der höchsten Instanz, des Königs selber, erreichen und so seinem verbre-

---

[22] Ebd., 706.
[23] Ebd., 729–30.

cherischen Unwesen ein für alle Mal Einhalt gebieten. Zu Unrecht hat
man dieses Eingreifen des Königs als Technik des *deus ex machina* kritisiert, denn wir haben es in Tartuffe mit einem diabolischen Schwindler
ersten Ranges zu tun, mit einem Giganten des Betrugs, dem nur durch
die allerhöchste Behörde das Handwerk gelegt werden kann.

Wie behandelt Kleist das Thema des ertappten und überführten Böse-
wichts? Im *Zerbrochenen Krug* wird uns der Übeltäter gleich am Anfang
des dramatischen Geschehens vorgeführt, nur daß er sich uns eigentlich
als solcher erst im fortschreitenden Ablauf der Handlung mehr und mehr
zu erkennen gibt. Wir haben es bei Kleist mit einer sich im Spiel und aus
dem Spiel selbst entfaltenden Charakterstudie zu tun. Eingangs wirkt
der Richter Adam eher komisch als betrügerisch. Aber bald gibt auch
er sich als Heuchler zu erkennen. Vor allem lügt er wie gedruckt. Zuerst
belügt er den Gerichtsdiener Licht über den zerschundenen Zustand, in
dem er uns vor Augen tritt, und über seine verloren gegangene Perücke.
Dann versucht er den Gerichtsrat Walter, der seinen Gerichtshof inspiziert
und symbolisch die Gerechtigkeit verkörpert, hinters Licht zu führen,
indem er über die Art der Rechtsprechung in der niederländischen
Gemeinde Huisum, dem Ort der Handlung, falschen Bescheid gibt:

> Wir haben hier, mit Euerer Erlaubnis,
> Statuten, eigentümliche, in Huisum,
> Nicht aufgeschriebene, muß ich gestehn, doch durch
> Bewährte Tradition uns überliefert.
> Von dieser Form, getrau ich mir zu hoffen,
> Bin ich noch heut kein Jota abgewichen.[24]

Wie Tartuffe versucht Adam, seine Mitmenschen zu korrumpieren.
Zuerst tut er dem Gerichtsdiener Licht schön, der als symbolische Figur
durch geschickte Fragen das Dunkel seiner Existenz zu erhellen sucht
und den er sich vor dem Kommen des gefürchteten Gerichtsrats gefügig
machen will:

> Zu Mittag! Gut, Gevatter! Jetzt gilts Freundschaft.
> Ihr wißt, wie sich zwei Hände waschen können.
> Ihr wollt auch gern, ich weiß, Dorfrichter werden,
> Und Ihr verdients, bei Gott, so gut wie einer.
> Doch heut ist noch nicht die Gelegenheit,
> Heut laßt Ihr noch den Kelch vorübergehn.[25]

Dann versucht Adam sein Glück bei Walter selbst, der als handelnde

---

[24] Heinrich von Kleist, *Sämtliche Werke und Briefe*, hrsg. v. Helmut Sembdner, 2. Auflage
(München, 1961), I, 199.
[25] Ebd., 181.

Person und auch symbolisch Verwalter der Gerechtigkeit ist und in diesem Sinn dem König in Molières *Tartuffe* gleichzusetzen wäre. Als Adam aber mit Servilität und gespielter Gastfreundschaft nicht den gewünschten Eindruck macht, verlegt er sich auf taktische Manöver, die darauf abzielen, den vor den kritischen Augen des Gerichtsrats ablaufenden Prozeß in die Länge zu ziehen und womöglich auf einen Termin nach dessen Abreise zu vertagen. Doch verstrickt sich Adam angesichts der Wachsamkeit und des wachsenden Argwohns seines strengen Vorgesetzten immer mehr in ein Lügengewebe, aus dem ein Entrinnen nicht mehr möglich ist. Vor Walters Ethos, das dieser in der Mahnung zusammenfaßt, "Was recht und gut und treu ist, Richter Adam!"[26], kann Adam ganz einfach nicht bestehen. Zu guter Letzt steht er vor dem der Wahrheit auf den Grund gehenden Gerichtsbeamten als Übeltäter da. Wie sich herausstellt, hat er nicht nur den Krug der Witwe Marthe zerschlagen, sondern auch ihre Tochter Eve durch erpresserische Mittel seinem Willen gefügig machen wollen. Der Krug seiner fragwürdigen Moralität war so lange zum sprichwörtlichen Brunnen der Gesetzlichkeit gegangen, bis er brach. Zerbrochen und zerschlagen ist auch sein Richteramt, entblößt und hilflos windet er sich, einem Wurm gleich, vor den richtenden und verurteilenden Augen seiner Mitmenschen.

Wieder einmal siegt auch bei Kleist in dem ewig währenden Kampf zwischen Gut und Böse das Recht über das Unrecht. So gesehen, sind beide Figuren, Molières scheinheiliger Parasit Tartuffe und Kleists parasitenhafter Heuchler Adam, zwei Manifestationen des Unwürdigen, Schädlichen und Verderblichen im Menschen. Beide Autoren stellen aber diese menschlichen Schädlinge in ihrer Charakterunwürdigkeit nicht mit erhobenem Zeigefinger und didaktischer Miene dar, sondern zeigen sie—zum Teil humorvoll lächelnd, teilweise mit unverkennbarer Ironie—in ihrer Schwäche und Lächerlichkeit. Aber gerade so wirken diese Gestalten heute noch überzeugend und belehrend. (Wäre es fehl am Platz, hier eine Antizipierung bzw. frühe Vorwegnahme der Problematik der modernen Bühne erkennen zu wollen, wie sie zum Beispiel in Dürrenmatts *Besuch der alten Dame* oder in Max Frischs *Biedermann* uns vor Augen tritt?)

Auch bezüglich ihrer weltimmanenten und, wenn auch nicht antireligiösen, so doch areligiösen Weltanschauung weisen beide Komödien einen bemerkenswerten Parallelismus auf. Religiöse Kreise haben vor allem Molières Komödie—bekanntlich schon seit der Uraufführung der

---

[26] Ebd., 229.

ersten Version im Jahre 1664[27]—als blasphemische antireligiöse Schmäh-
schrift hingestellt. Einige Literarhistoriker haben behauptet, daß es
Molières Absicht gewesen sei, mit diesem Stück das Jansenisten- und
Jesuitentum anzugreifen und anzuprangern. Molière selbst, der sich nur
sehr selten theoretisch über sein Werk geäußert hat, verwahrt sich in
seinem Vorwort zur dritten Ausgabe des Stückes gegen diese Anschuldi-
gungen, aber entkräftigt damit durchaus nicht die Innerweltlichkeit
seiner Schau. Eine ähnliche weltimmanente Einstellung legt Kleist im
Krug an den Tag, als er den Gerichtsrat Walter, sein moralisches Sprach-
rohr, auf die Beteuerungen der als Kronzeugin fungierenden Frau Brigitte
hin: ein Teufel habe hier sein Unwesen getrieben, ungeduldig sagen läßt:

> Frau, obs der Teufel war, will ich nicht untersuchen,
> Ihn aber, ihn denunziiert man nicht,
> Kann Sie von einem andern melden, gut:
> Doch mit dem Sünder, da verschont Sie uns.[28]

Eine weitere Frage ist noch zu beantworten. Was macht diese beiden
Typen, Molières Tartuffe und Kleists Adam, überhaupt komisch? Curt
Hohoff gibt in bezug auf den Kleistischen Übeltäter die folgende formel-
hafte Antwort: "Adam wird komisch, indem er die Umkehrung der Alkmene ist, indem er nicht seinem harmonischen Gefühl gemäß lebt."[29]
Bedingt könnte dieses Urteil wohl auch auf Molières Heuchlerfigur übertragen werden. Auch er ist das Gegenteil des Ehrenmannes, als der er
sich nach außen hin zur Schau stellt. Daß er im Inneren verkommen ist,
reizt aber kaum zum Lachen. Vielmehr ließe es sich eher als einen
zynischen Kommentar auf die menschliche Natur überhaupt ausdeuten.
Durchaus komisch mutet jedoch die Tatsache an, daß ein sich nach außen
hin äußerst würdig und fromm gebärdender Mensch, indem er seine
inneren natürlichen Triebe zu verdecken sucht, letzten Endes doch unter
ihre Knute gezwungen wird, nur daß er sich dabei nicht wie ein Sieger,
sondern wie ein Besiegter, nicht wie ein Ehrenmann, sondern wie ein
süchtiger, am Gängelband seiner leidenschaftlichen inneren Natur tan-
zender Narr benehmen muß und sich dann ertappt mit rotem Kopf dem
kritischen Licht einer ihn verurteilenden Öffentlichkeit ausgesetzt sieht.
Jacques Guicharnaud definiert das Komische dieses Charaktertyps im
Rahmen der Molièreschen Komödie auf diese Art: "Nothing is funnier

---

[27] Die uns überlieferte dritte Version von *Tartuffe* wurde 1669 von Ludwig XIV. der Bühne
trotz des Protests der Geistlichkeit zugänglich gemacht.
[28] Kleist, *Werke*, I, 234.
[29] *Komik und Humor bei Heinrich von Kleist* (Berlin, 1937), 39.

than a character in Molière who says 'I want . . .' with all the ardor of a
Cartesian 'généreux,' whereas it is not *he* who wants but *something* in
him, something the opposite of his freedom. This misunderstanding with
oneself is the source of a drama which goes round in circles—the drama
of mania; but such maniacs are quite simply caricatures of ourselves to
the extent that we live according to our passions."[30] Aber mit dieser
Beobachtung haben wir auch die innerliche Problematik und Fragwür-
digkeit des Dorfrichters Adam aufgedeckt. Wie Tartuffe ist er ein treibend
Getriebener, der letzten Endes seiner amtlichen Kleidung und Würden
beraubt, nackt und glatzköpfig vor uns steht und in seiner würdelosen
Tolpatschigkeit, aller unserer Sympathien verlustig, nur noch unsere
Lachmuskeln anregen kann.

Beide Dichter haben mit dieser Aufdeckung und Ausdeutung mensch-
licher Unzulänglichkeiten, die uns zu guter Letzt zwingen, über die
menschlichen Schwächen in uns selbst zu lachen, einen Höhepunkt ihrer
dramatischen Schaffenskunst erreicht, der von ihrer Nachwelt auch trotz
ursprünglicher kritischer Stellungnahme bei den ersten Vorführungen auf
der Bühne anerkannt worden ist. Was Gustave Lanson allgemein mit
Bezug auf die frühe kritische Aufnahme von Molières Stil sagt, läßt sich
ohne weiteres auch im besonderen auf Kleist übertragen: "On lui a
reproché du barbarisme et du jargon, des phrases forcées, des entassements
de métaphores, du galimatias, des impropriétés, des incorrections, des
chevilles, des répétitions fatigantes, un style *inorganique* . . . Le style
intense, chargé, emporté de Molière, est merveilleusement efficace. Les
qualités qu'il a négligées, ou sont inutiles, ou sont des défauts à la scène.
Son vers et sa prose sont faits pour être dits, et non pour être lus."[31]
Lansons geistreiche Apologie der Molièreschen Dichtkunst umreißt auch
Kleists dichterischen Ausdruck, vor allem wie er sich uns im *Zerbrochenen
Krug* darbietet.

Auf die Anfeindungen, denen Molières *Tartuffe* nach seinem Erscheinen
auf der Bühne ausgesetzt war, ist schon hingewiesen worden. Ähnliche
Schwierigkeiten sind auch Kleists *Zerbrochenem Krug* widerfahren. Die
Uraufführung des Lustspiels auf der Weimarer Bühne war bekanntlich
ein Fiasko. Goethe, der dem *Zerbrochenen Krug* keineswegs einen gewissen
Geist und Humor absprach, glaubte dennoch nicht an die Bühnenfähigkeit

---

[30] *Molière: A Collection of Critical Essays* (Englewood Cliffs, 1964), 8.
[31] *Histoire de la littérature française* (Paris, o. J.), 516–17.

des Stückes. Dieser Ansicht schrieb er auch den unter seiner Leitung erfolgten Durchfall der Komödie bei der Uraufführung zu.[32] Kleists dichterisches Streben, seine tragische Weiterentwicklung als Mensch und als Dichter, persönliche Frustrierungen, das Unverständnis seiner Mitmenschen dem eigenen dichterischen Wollen gegenüber sowie der innere Dämon[33] haben es ihm verwehrt, sich mit Ausnahme des im *Phöbus* erschienenen farcenhaften Fragments "Der Schrecken im Bade"[34] weiter auf dem befreienden Boden der Komödie zu betätigen. Doch hat sich sein von uns dargestellter Kontakt mit Molière, der dem des französischen mit dem deutschen dichterischen Genie gleichkommt, fruchtbringend auf die Weiterentwicklung der deutschen Komödie ausgewirkt. Dieser Kontakt ist um so bemerkenswerter, als er—wie wir heute erkennen—zwischen den zwei genialsten Bühnendichtern der beiden benachbarten Kulturen stattgefunden hat.

Obwohl Molières unmittelbarer Einfluß auf das deutsche Lustspiel—wenn wir von Gutzkows komischem, auf die Tagespolitik abzielendem Spiel *Das Urbild des Tartuffe* absehen wollen—sich sonst nur in der Komödie von Hugo von Hofmannsthal einwandfrei nachweisen läßt, deutet der Weg von Kleists Lustspiel zu den großen komischen Bühnenschöpfungen der Moderne, die über Einzelleistungen von Gustav Freytag und Gerhart Hauptmann zu Sternheim[35] und Zuckmayer weisen und gegenwärtig in Dürrenmatts Tragikomödien neue Triumphe auf der Bühne feiern. Trotz mancher Rückschläge hat das 20. Jahrhundert die Erringung des höchsten menschlichen Ideals—die Erzielung der Menschwerdung des Menschen—nicht aufgegeben. Der Schritt zum idealen Menschentum muß aber durch das befreiende Lachen der menschlichen Selbsterkenntnis führen. Ein berühmtes Wort von La Rochefoucauld besagt: "Les grandes âmes ne sont celles qui ont moins de passions et

---

[32] Da das Regiebuch verloren gegangen ist, wissen wir nur wenig über eine etwaige Bearbeitung des Lustspiels von Goethes Seite her. Fest steht jedoch, daß es in drei Aufzügen statt der von Kleist selbst so gewollten dreizehn Szenen aufgeführt worden war. Aus diesem Umstand heraus sowie aus dem für das klassisch geschulte Weimarer Publikum ungewohnten Stil und Milieu des Stückes, das eine neue realistische Epoche vorausahnen läßt, hat die Kritik den Mißerfolg des *Zerbrochenen Krugs* bei seiner Erstaufführung erklärt.

[33] Vgl. zu diesem Thema Stefan Zweig, *Baumeister der Welt: Der Kampf mit dem Dämon* (Wien, 1936), 265 ff.

[34] Erster Jahrgang, Elftes und Zwölftes Stück (November und Dezember 1808), 30–35. (Siehe Nachdruck der Originalausgabe [Stuttgart, 1961].)

[35] Sternheim sah sich selber als "deutscher Molière". Die Forschung hat sich jedoch mit Bezug auf diesen Ehrentitel bisher im großen und ganzen sehr zurückhaltend verhalten.

plus de vertu que les âmes communes, mais celles seulement qui ont de plus grands desseins."[36] Sowohl Molière als auch Kleist haben uns den Weg gewiesen.

---

[36] *Maximes supprimées*, No. 602.

MOLIÈRE AS A SOURCE
OF GERMAN COMEDY
John Theodore Krumpelmann

The third decade of the present century marks a renewal if not the discovery in France of Heinrich von Kleist criticism, for "from this period dates the true annexation of Kleist by the French." The production in 1929 of Giraudoux's *Amphitryon 38* caused the publication in the Parisian journal *Comedia* (March 15, 1930) of Jean Travel's article on Kleist. But it was Roger Ayrault's lengthy study, *Heinrich von Kleist*, and his *La Légende de Heinrich von Kleist: Un poète devant la critique* (both Paris, 1934) that supplied the French critics with abundant material to attract attention to the German author, and an opportunity to extend the appreciation of his works. Richardson writes: "Ayrault sees as Kleist's key work *Amphitryon*;" and "he sees the essentials of *Krug* (i.e., the figure of Adam) as having been drawn from Molière's *Tartuffe*."[1]

As early as 1948 Jean Jacques Ansett's article "J. Giraudoux et H. von Kleist. A propos d'Amphitryon 38" indicates basic similarities in form in these two comedies. He "finds the essential theme of the two plays to be the same, the confrontation of the divine and the human," assuming that Giraudoux knew Kleist's drama, since Giraudoux had studied German from 1906 until 1911.[2]

Kleist's *Prinz Friedrich von Homburg* was presented for the first time in France at Avignon in August, 1951, and in Paris in February, 1952. Thus did this spark of comedy, enkindled in that metropolis a century and a half earlier (1801), return to the cradle of Jean Baptiste Poquelin to record the two hundred and nineteenth birthday of Molière. Prompted by the success of the presentations of the *Prinz*, the French producers undertook the presentation of Kleist's *Penthesilea* and the *Krug*, with questionable success, the latter having been staged earlier in Paris in 1904. Despite the varying success of these attempts, Richardson concludes: "By 1951, the French stage was clearly ready for Kleist . . . to anyone aware of the development in Kleist criticism of the previous twenty years, a very well

---

[1] F. C. Richardson, *Kleist in France* (Chapel Hill, N. C., 1962), 91, 108, 114.
[2] *Ibid.*, 133–35, 200.

prepared surprise." This is after having asserted: "More than a century after Kleist's first appearance in France, the only one of his major works yet in any sense to be discovered remained his version of the Amphitryon legend."[3]

When Kleist left Berlin in April, 1801, he fled the society of Prussia, which he thought he could no longer endure. On February 5, 1801, he had written to his sister Ulrike: "Ich passe mich nicht unter die Menschen, es ist eine traurige Wahrheit, aber eine Wahrheit; . . . froh kann ich nur in meiner eignen Gesellschaft sein." On March 23rd: "Mein einziges und höchstes Ziel ist gesunken, ich habe keines mehr. . . . Ich laufe auf Caffee-häuser und Tabagien, in Concerte und Schauspiele." Already, as early as November 13, 1800, he had proposed a plan of escape to Wilhelmine, his betrothed. "Wir hielten uns irgendwo in Frankreich auf, etwa in dem südlichen Theile, in der französichen Schweiz . . . und zwar aus diesem Grunde, um Unterricht dort in der deutschen Sprache zu geben." As further motivation for this move he indicates: "und drittens, welches der Hauptgrund ist, weil ich mir da recht die französische Sprache aneignen könnte, welches zu der Verpflanzung der neuesten Philosophie in dieses Land, wo man gar nichts davon weisz, notwendig ist."[4]

Actually Kleist did begin his residence in Paris in time to witness the celebration of Bastille Day there in 1801. He was not favorably impressed by the country ("reifer zum Untergange als irgend eine andere europäische Nation" [Brief, 15. Aug. 1801]), but he did experience the life and activities of the community, including attendance at the theaters. Nowhere, however, does he mention Molière, with whose *Amphitryon* he must have become acquainted, and with the translation of which he was soon to busy himself, and thus produce what he chose to designate "ein Lustspiel nach Molière."

Not without justification have Wilhelm Herzog and Walter Silz introduced the comedy-compositions of Kleist by treating his *Amphitryon* before *Der zerbrochene Krug*.[5] Neither of these critics attempts to disclose

---

[3] *Ibid.*, 140–43; chapter XI, esp. 150–51; 154, 175, 186.

[4] One must assume that this former officer in the Prussia of Frederick the Great and this admirer of Rousseau (cf. Brief, d. 3. Juni, 1801) had become acquainted with the French idiom while still a youth.

[5] Cf. E. L. Stahl, *Heinrich von Kleist's Dramas* (Oxford, 1948), 141. Chronological Table of Kleist's Life and Works: 1801 Visit to Paris. Beginnings of *Robert Guiskard* (published 1808) and of *Die Familie Schroffenstein* (published 1803). 1801–2 Visit to Switzerland. Beginnings of *Der Zerbrochene Krug* (completed 1808, published 1811). 1806 *Amphitryon* (published 1807).

the actual source of Kleist's devotion to dramatic comedy and his assumption of a leading, if not the leading, place in this not overcrowded field of German literature. More modern, contemporary investigation seems to indicate that Kleist's residence in Paris and his acquaintance with Molière's comedies served as the source of the inspiration, or challenge, that resulted in this new direction, culminating in Kleist's present reputation in Germany, France, and America as a master in the field in which Molière has long been universally recognized as world-master.

In attempting to translate Molière's "leichtes Lustspiel—mehr, und Tieferes wollte er nicht geben—Kleist, . . . verführt durch das Problem, schob . . . die Grenzen des Lustspiels weit hinaus. . . . Er schuf auf einer Seite ein bewegtes niederländisches Gemälde voll derben und kräftigen Humors [the Sosias element, cf. also *Der zerbrochene Krug*], Szenen, so urwüchsig und drastisch, daß sie an Shakespeares beste Lustspiele erinnern, und auf der andern: [Amphitryon-Alkmene] ein weihvolles Mysterium, erhaben–feierliche Liebeslyrik eines eifersüchtigen Gottes, die in einem tiefgefühlten Pantheismus abgründige psychologische Probleme zu entschleiern sucht. . . ."[6] Thus Kleist saw the dual nature of the human comedy, the earthly (or earthy) component, a handful of dust; and the divine, the spirit breathed into the humus (human) by the Divine Creator, making it a divine comedy.

Kleist admired and imitated his master, Molière, who created these human characters, but he also endeavored to eliminate the "humus" and preserve the divine (the spirit). Hence Kleist revamped one part of the action and transformed the lecherous, earth-walking Jupiter into a more divine character.

Kleist perceived that even as God had originally created man in his own image, so now man, in his turn, had created God, just as the Parisian master of comedy had created his Theban Jupiter in the human image of the playboy of Gallic society. Kleist, as a student of Kantian philosophy, was probably morally concerned about the divine nature of gods and of man, but, intrigued by the practical philosophy of the European master of literary comedy, he quietly learned from him how to compose in this genre and became able to create some of the best comedies known to German literature.

Although Kleist's *Amphitryon* was not published until 1807, it is evident he had been interested in such an undertaking ever since his arrival in

---

[6] Wilhelm Herzog, *Heinrich von Kleist* (München, 1911), 318.

Paris in 1801. The "Konzeption von Amphitryon" has been assigned to 1805–1806.[7] In spite of this and of E. L. Stahl's statement that Kleist "probably began his work not earlier than 1806,"[8] more recent criticism indicates that the concrete results of Kleist's French sojourn began to manifest themselves earlier. Helmut Sembdner asserts: "*Amphitryon* und *Zerbrochener Krug*, sie verdanken beide ihre Entstehung dem Dresdener Sommer von 1803. Ja, es läßt sich sogar Nachweis führen, daß die *Amphitryon*-Bearbeitung, deren Entstehung man bisher in Kleists Königsberger Zeit gelegt hat, noch vor dem *Zerbrochenen Krug* in Angriff genommen wurde." He substantiates this conclusion with excerpts from the respective dramas and further concludes: "Überhaupt ist die sprachliche Verwandtschaft beider Stücke erstaunlich eng."[9]

The Sembdner article likewise disagrees with Stahl's surmise that "it is unlikely that Kleist was influenced by J. D. Falk's version of Plautus' *Amphitrus*" (1804), for Sembdner states: "Mit dem *Zerbrochenen Krug* führt Kleist zudem ein Motiv weiter, das ihm in Falks *Amphitruon* begegnet war [i.e., Falk IV, 3, 4]" "Adams nächtliches Rendezvous mit Eve." Sembdner concludes: "Von hier aus wird eine innere Beziehung des *Amphitryon* zum *Zerbrochenen Krug* deutlich."[10]

Hence the composition of Kleist's other early comedy, *Der zerbrochene Krug* (winter 1802), would be practically coeval with his *Amphitryon* translation. This time the stimulant was a French copper engraving by Jean Jacques LeVeau, "Le juge ou la cruche cassée," of a painting by Louis Philibert Debucourt that Kleist had seen in the chamber of Zschokke in Switzerland. Now Kleist locates the action in "einem niederländischen Dorfe" instead of "vor dem Schlosze in Theban." The protagonist is "Adam," the supreme representative of the law in the community. "Eve," a peasant maiden of the village, is the target of Adam's lustful intrigue. So here one has, instead of a divine comedy, a village (rustic) seduction. Father ("Dorfrichter") Adam flees the scene of his dual role, but Gerichtsrat Walter pardons the judical Verführer, last seen as he "Berg auf, Berg ab, . . . Das aufgepflügte Winterfeld durchstampft" (1955 f.) saying: "Zur Desertion ihn zwingen will ich nicht" (1966). Eve has been spared Alkmene's fate. Pater Jupiter, having promised Alkmene a

---

[7] Cf. Friedrich Koch, *Heinrich von Kleist* (Stuttgart, 1958), 325.

[8] Stahl, *Kleist's Dramas*, 59.

[9] Helmut Sembdner, *Jahrbuch der deutschen Schillergesellschaft*, 13. Jahrgang, Körner Verlag (Stuttgart, 1939), 392, 393.

[10] Stahl, *Kleist's Dramas*, 59; Sembdner, *Jahrbuch des deutschen Schillergesellschaft*, 393–94.

Heracles, "verliert sich in den Wolken," instead of, as the clubfooted Pater Adam, stomping his way, "up hill, down hill," through the wintry, flat terrain of Holland.[11]

Although *Amphitryon* and *Der zerbrochene Krug* are the only two of Kleist's comedies that have been awarded wide, and even international, attention, the comic elements initiated in them recur in subsequent dramas. His first drama, *Die Familie Schroffenstein* (1802), and his last, *Penthesilea* (1807), which Kleist himself refers to facetiously as a "Hundekömodie" (*Epigramme* 2, 5), may be said to be void of comic elements, but every other drama is interspersed with comedy. An article, "Fear and Farce in Fehrbellin,"[12] sets forth the basis for regarding Kleist's *Prinz Friedrich von Homburg, Ein Schauspiel* (1810)[13] to be one of his three comedies which have features characteristic of Molière.

Our author, who experienced much tragedy in his own short life, came to realize that the human being, though made of mud, possesses also an immortal spirit, breathed into him by his maker at creation. When the earthy man fails, i.e., the Prinz von Homburg, "als ein Nachtwandler, im Schlaf sich träumend, [vom] Mondschein gelockt, den prächt'gen Kranz des Ruhmes einwindet" (24–28), is challenged by his dual superior, "Kurfürst" and uncle, he nevertheless demonstrates that he too, a Prussian, can confront his commander and become the victor. The poetic prince had to confront his imperious Kurfürst and sentimental uncle by demonstrating that even underlings are children of the immortal spirit and, as such, have a right to enter the Garden of Eden, even though they must make "die Reise um die Welt, und sehen, ob es vielleicht hinten irgendwo offen ist" (*Marionettentheater*). In other words, even though a straight line is the shortest distance between two points, the goal may be attainable by devious ways.[14] One must not forget that Kleist was philosopher as well as mathematician.

---

[11] *N.B.:* In our divine comedy, Jupiter (Zeus-pater), in the *Krug*, Dorfrichter, Chief-Official of the community and, in *Käthchen von Heilbronn* (1808), the heroine, the natural daughter (Bänkeltochter) of the Emperor, conceived as "der Jupiter ging eben mit seinem funkelnden Licht im Osten auf" (V, ii, ll)! Does it require more than this to suggest that Molière's *Amphitryon* induced Kleist to resort, in these comedies, to the use of high dignitaries as seducers of women espoused to other men?

[12] *Studies in German Literature of the Nineteenth and Twentieth Centuries. Festschrift for Frederic Coenen* (Chapel Hill, University of North Carolina Press, 1970), 24–34.

[13] The drama might be called "*The Rape of the Glove*" (Z. 70[+], 77[+], 105, 139[+], 218[+], 286, 291[+] ff.) *N.B.*, "erhaschen," 184 ff., "gerissen," 107.

[14] Cf. Lawrence Ryan, *Kleist und Frankreich* (Berlin, 1968): "Amphitryon—doch ein Lustspielstoff!" (83–121). S. 92: "Zu den Regeln eines solchen Spieles gehört es aber, daß der

As in Shakespeare, so too in Kleist one finds much comic relief even in the more serious dramas. But Kleist, as in his *Prinz von Homburg*, tends to be most generous with the relief elements in the final act in order to create a grand finale.

In *Käthchen von Heilbronn* (1808) the climax begins with the "Gottesgericht." The ancient Theobald, cuckold father of Käthchen, Bänkeltochter of the Emperor (2212), clad in "voller Rüstung," is to engage in mortal combat with the youthful Graf vom Strahl, who exclaims in knightly language, "jene graue Scheitel dort, Flach schmettr' ich sie, wie einen Schweizerkäse" (2180 ff.).

In the *Hermannschlacht, Ein Drama* (1808) the comic elements are contained, for the most part, in the Hermann and Thusnelda scenes (II, iii, 511–701; III, 999 ff.) which might justify calling the play *The Rape of the Lock*.[15] "Hier ist die Locke wieder, schau', Die er dir jüngst vom Scheitel abgelöst" (1743 f.).

The comic element also extends to a play on words with placenames, e.g. "_____kon" (926, 1120, 1644, 1860 ff., 1876–1915). "Helakon," "Pfiffi-Iphikon," coined placenames, remind of the "H_____," "Hackel _____" compounds in the *Prinz von Homburg* drama (comedy),[16] similar to the post–World War II jest of the Allied delegates to the "Yalta" conference who called it "Malta" instead.

Kleist's eager play with words in all his dramas seems to tie in with his essay "Über die allmählige Verfertigung der Gedanken beim Reden" (1805–1806), written about the time of the "Konzeption" of his *Amphitryon* and replete with echoes from the French, e.g., "Der Franzose sagt, l'appetit vient en mangeant, und dieser Erfahrungsatz bleibt wahr, wenn

---

Mensch nicht etwa nur Spielball einer autoritativen Macht ist, sondern in seiner Freiheit anerkannt wird—was auch besagt, daß der Gott nicht befehlen kann, sondern überreden muß und zudem noch das Risiko eingeht, abgewiesen zu werden. . . . Einen Augenblick lang, als Alkmene sich seinen Argumenten unzugänglich zeigt, glaubt Jupiter, dieser Gefahr erlegen zu sein: 'Verflucht der Wahn, der mich hieher gelockt!' (V. 1512). Ganz ähnlich wird der Kurfürst 'betroffen' (V. 1147), 'verwirrt' (V. 1175), er befindet sich 'im äuß ersten Erstaunen' (V. 1156), als er die unerwartete Nachricht von der Todesfurcht Homburgs erhält. Beiden gelingt es allerdings—dem Zeus und dem 'Kurfürsten, mit der Stirn des Zeus' (V. 158)—, der Gefahr zu begegnen und das Spiel zu Ende zu führen," [so daß] "durch das Mitspielen von Gott und Mensch das 'letzte Kapitel von der Geschichte der Welt' andeutungsweise vorweggenommen wird."

[15] Cf. Verses 1780, 1791. "Locke(n)" occurs in the text not less than twenty times, as do numerous other references to the purloining of the lock.

[16] Cf. *Der Prinz von Homburg*, especially verses 223 to 683.

[17] Walter Silz, *Heinrich von Kleist. Studies in his Works and Literary Character* (Philadelphia, 1961), 45f.

man ihn parodiert, und sagt, l'idée vient en parlant." Examples cited are from the sayings of French authors only, viz., Molière, Mirabeau, La Fontaine; Bacon, a thinker, not a French comedian, says in essence the same in his phrase "Conference maketh a ready man" (*Of Studies*, 1624).

Silz aptly asserts: "Kleist grafted upon a gay and piquant French comedy a deep and metaphysical German tragedy," and suspects that "*diese geistig reizende Oszillation und Doppeldeutigkeit* . . . particularly endeared the play to Thomas Mann,"[18] thus noting the duality, not only in Kleist's dramas, but in the playwright himself.

It is not a "puzzling question" of "how a man with such ability to laugh at life could so soon have found it unbearable."[19] The fact is that Kleist had also learned to question, "Oh death—where is thy sting?" His embracing of death, it would seem, might have been not because he loved life less but that he loved death more. He wrote to Ulrike von Kleist ("am Morgen meines Todes"), "zufrieden und heiter, wie ich bin, mit der ganzen Welt . . . möge dir der Himmel einen Tod schencken nur halb an Freude und unaussprechlicher Heiterkeit, dem meinigen gleich."[20]

He had suffered so much misfortune in his routine life and discovered so much joy in his fictitious existence (his writings) that he had learned to know earthly life in all its oscillations and duplications. He found Jupiter, the supreme deity and seducer of the wife of a noble husband; Adam, a village justice and lecherous rustic; and Prince Friedrich Arthur of Homburg, General of Cavalry, a winder of wreaths, a sleep-walker, a suppliant on bended knee before the Kurfürst, when unnerved at the sight of the grave, open to receive his corpse on the morrow, who, having been convicted by a court martial, continued to behave as a "miles gloriosus," and to enjoy the fragrance of "Nachtviolen," "Levkoien" and "Nelken," and even as he is proclaimed "Sieger in der Schlacht bei Fehrbellin," awakening from his faint, asking: "Ist es ein Traum?" (1856). Verily, "La Vida es sueño." Kleist had learned, as the Bavarian says: "Das Leben ist ein Kasperlspiel." He was acquainted with Schiller's "Spieltrieb." He could well subscribe to the philosophy of Schnitzler's lines in *Paracelsus*:

> Es [das Leben] war ein Spiel! Was sollt'es anders sein?
> Was ist nicht Spiel, was wir auf Erden treiben,
> Und schien es doch so tief, so ernst zu sein!

[18] See Thomas Mann, *Gesammelte Werke* (Fischer Verlag; Frankfurt, 1960), IX, 208.
[19] Silz, *Kleist*, 46.
[20] Cf. *Briefe*. Also "An Marie von Kleist," 12. Nov. 1811.

Man is, forsooth, ein Mittelding zwischen Gott und Kot. Created with a dual nature, man, be he "homo" (*humus*) or "vir" (*vis*), can run the gamut from Amphitryon to Zeus, or from *Amphitryon* to the *Zerbrochene Krug*, or from "A" to Izzard.

Goethe's two youthful comedies, *Die Laune der Verliebten* and *Die Mitschuldigen*, written in verse in the French manner, never earned for him a reputation, even in his own land, whereas Kleist's two comedies, the result of his residence in Paris and his study of Molière, served to make their author perhaps the leading writer of comedy in Germany. Despite the fact that the *Krug* was broken, but not "zerbrochen," when Goethe staged it in Weimar, it has experienced probably more translations and performances and has won more fame than either of Goethe's youthful comedies.

KLEIST'S VERSION OF MOLIÈRE'S
AMPHITRYON:
OLYMPIAN CUCKOLDING AND UNIO MYSTICA

James M. McGlathery

Thomas Mann, whose 1927 interpretation remains one of the best of the many studies of Heinrich von Kleist's complex and puzzling Amphitryon drama, declared it to be "the world's most profound and beautiful theater play."[1] What particularly impressed him was Kleist's dramatic genius in retaining the satirical spirit of the French comedy while providing a "metaphysical background" both worthy of the tradition of German Idealistic philosophy and characteristic of Kleist's interest in the subconscious. Making the point that Goethe was unfair in condemning Kleist's preoccupation with mental pathology, since Goethe himself had pioneered in such portrayals, Mann reaffirms Goethe's judgment that the play depicts a "confusing of emotions."[2] It is Mann's own view that Kleist's intent is the portrayal of identity crisis and schizophrenia. This interpretation is convincing for the tragicomic role of Amphitryon, where Kleist more closely follows Molière, but not for Kleist's tragic conception of Alkmene, which represents also to Mann the German poet's main contribution. The present study argues that Kleist's pushing of husband and wife to the brink of despair is subordinate to his romantic portrayal of erotic love as inseparable from a subconscious transcendent longing.

In adapting Molière's *Amphitryon* to the bent of his own poetic genius, Kleist shifted the psychological interest from Amphitryon's reaction at being cuckolded to Alkmene's realization that she has been seduced.[3] Even more radical is Kleist's exploring whether Alkmene's heart belongs to her seducer or to her husband. Molière largely avoids this offense

---

[1] "Kleists Amphitryon. Eine Wiedereroberung," in Mann, *Schriften und Reden zur Literatur, Kunst und Philosophie*, 1. Bd. (Frankfurt u. Hamburg), 282. The most recent and reliable scholarly edition of the play is that by Helmut Sembdner, *Heinrich von Kleist. Sämtliche Werke und Briefe*, 1. Bd., 3. vermehrte u. revidierte Aufl. (München, 1964).

[2] "Verwirrung des Gefühls," in Goethe's diary entry for July 13, 1807.

[3] Among the more useful and accessible comparative commentaries on the Kleist and Molière plays are those by William H. McClain, "Kleist and Molière as Comic Writers," *Germanic Review*, 24 (1949), 21–33; the chapters on Kleist's *Amphitryon* in Heinrich Meyer-Benfey, *Das Drama Heinrich von Kleists*, 1. Bd. (Göttingen, 1911); and John C. Blankenagel, *The Dramas of Heinrich von Kleist* (Chapel Hill, 1931).

against decorum and sensibility by excluding Alcmène from the play's last act.[4] Kleist's emphasis on Alkmene's reaction to the seventeen-hour night of lovemaking with Jupiter is important, however, for his investigation of how the chaste, pious young wife is affected by the realization that she has unknowingly had sexual intercourse with a god.

Piety would demand that Alkmene rejoice at this revelation. Her failure to do so may imply only resentment at Jupiter's imposture as her husband, leaving open the possibility that under other circumstances she might have been willing to accept the Olympian as lover in fulfillment of a religious obligation. Yet Alkmene consistently maintains that the thought of making love to anyone other than her husband is abhorrent to her. Because Alkmene extends society's prohibition against adultery to include intercourse with the gods, her chastity seems more than conventional virtue. A quite personal humility prevents her from imagining herself as the object of Olympian desire. In the end she finds herself forced to accept not only the fact of her seduction by a god but also her sexual preference for Jupiter over Amphitryon, with the implication that her chaste love for Amphitryon has proven inseparable, because indistinguishable, from a subconscious lusting after gods. Alkmene's tragedy consists in the shattering of her illusion about the nature of her conjugal love.

The intermingling of sexual passion and mystical yearning in Alkmene —not to mention its mirrorings in Jupiter's emotional need to seduce her—has been almost universally neglected in the criticism of Kleist's play. The critics generally have addressed themselves to moral or philosophical issues rather than to the psychological portrayal. Most of the discussion is devoted to an assessment of Alkmene's fidelity and to criticism of Jupiter's justification of the imposture.[5] Alkmene's tragic dignity

[4] McClain, "Kleist and Molière," 32, argues unconvincingly that Molière was concerned that "In the presence of his wife he [Amphitryon] would have had to make a greater display of anger."

[5] A moralizing condemnation of Jupiter's deceit is common to some American critics, including Blankenagel, *The Dramas of H. v. K.*, 96; Walter Silz, *Heinrich von Kleist, Studies in His Works and Literary Character* (Philadelphia, 1961), 62–63; and John Gearey, *Heinrich von Kleist: A Study in Tragedy and Anxiety* (Philadelphia, 1968), 38. This schoolmasterly censoring of the Olympian's imposture is softened through reference to the comic tradition of punishing seducers in the most detailed study of the play by an American scholar: H. W. Nordmeyers, "Kleists Amphitryon. Zur Deutung der Komödie," *Monatshefte*, 38 (1946), 1–19, 165–76, 268–83, 349–59, and 38 (1947), 89–125; see esp. 38 (1946), 19. German scholars generally have concentrated on exonerating Alkmene from all suspicion of guilt and infidelity, usually by resort to a Platonic interpretation of Alkmene's sexual preference for Jupiter. Among the proponents of the Platonic view are Meyer-Benfey, *Das Drama H. v. K.s*, 355–56; Hermann August Korff, *Geist der Goethezeit*, IV. Teil, 5. unveränderte Aufl. (Leipzig, 1962), 63, and Günter Blöcker, *Heinrich von Kleist oder Das absolute Ich*, 2. Aufl. (Berlin, 1962), 166. Benno von Wiese attempts to distinguish between the Platonic explanation and his own

is viewed as resting on her unyielding virtue in the face of Jupiter's appeals to her vanity, while Jupiter is seen as a jealous god bent on punishing Alkmene's idolatrous worship of her husband.[6] Aside from Richard March's unsupported assertion that "Kleist touches on a mystical element in erotic experience on which in fact the whole love relationship in its profounder aspect turns,"[7] Thomas Mann apparently is the only other critic who hints at the possibility that Alkmene's sexual attraction to Jupiter implies subconscious mystical yearning, and therefore also constitutes spiritual infidelity.[8]

It has been pointed out by some critics that Kleist's Jupiter, unlike Molière's, desires not only a night of lovemaking with Alkmene but also the satisfaction of having her guess his identity.[9] This is reason enough for his appearing to Alkmene incognito; that he must impersonate Amphitryon is dictated, of course, by Alkmene's chasteness. In Kleist's play, though, Jupiter seems also to relish the imposture as a chance to prove his superiority over the husband. Jupiter's hope of being recognized is disappointed by Alkmene, who fails time and again to seize upon the god's increasingly obvious hints at his identity. Her suppression of awareness regarding Jupiter's identity suggests a subconscious horror at the thought that her idolization of Amphitryon has led her to violate the tabu against lusting after gods.

Jupiter's achievement of his related aim—Alkmene's sexual preference of himself over Amphitryon—is far more significant for Alkmene's tragic role in Kleist's play than is the triumph of her virtue in failing to guess his identity. As protagonist, she clings desperately to the belief that she has remained faithful to her husband and that the enhancement of their love is attributable to Amphitryon's elation over returning from battle as a

---

existentialist interpretation, *Die deutsche Tragödie von Lessing bis Hebbel*, 2. Aufl. (Hamburg, 1952), 308–309.

[6] Walter Müller-Seidel adopts the extreme view that as supreme god Jupiter is obliged to punish Alkmene's blasphemy, *Versehen und Erkennen. Eine Studie über Heinrich von Kleist* (Köln u. Graz, 1961), 132: "Es handelt sich dabei zum wenigsten um den 'Egoismus' des in den Menschen verwandelten Gottes."

[7] Richard March, *Heinrich von Kleist* (New Haven, 1954), 28.

[8] Mann, "Kleists Amphitryon," 296: ". . . sie bittet noch, ihr 'die Regung nicht zu mißdeuten'! Den sie empfing, war Amphitryon. Da es aber der Gott war, so war es Amphitryon voller, stärker, vollkommener als sonst, und so war dennoch, im letzten Grunde, das unsägliche Glück dieser Nacht ein wenig schuldhaft?"

[9] Mann, "Kleists Amphitryon," 290–91, 297–98, and Nordmeyer, "Kleists Amphitryon," *Monatshefte*, 38 (1946), 277, among others. This contrast with Molière's Jupiter is noted by Blankenagel, *The Dramas of H. v. K.*, 94; McClain, "Kleist and Molière," 24–25, and especially by Friedrich Koch, *Heinrich von Kleist* (Stuttgart, 1958), 112.

conquering hero and to her increased appeal as a result of his prolonged absence. Jupiter, the antagonist, is bent on forcing her to recognize that the intensification of her love for Amphitryon owes itself to her instinctive preference for the ruler of the gods.

Because Alkmene's struggle takes place in the subconscious, it is revealed largely by the progress of Jupiter's efforts at winning her recognition of his identity. As he prepares to depart following their night of love, Jupiter urges Alkmene to distinguish between Amphitryon the lover and Amphitryon the husband. Though he hardly can expect her to have guessed the truth from this and other frequent hints, Alkmene does remark to her maid, Charis, that her lover that night was as though descended from the heavens (II, iii, 1197–1200). Next, Jupiter uses his supernatural powers to transform the initial on the diadem he gave Alkmene from "A" to "J," but neither the magical nature of the change nor the implication of the Olympian's initial leads her to guess correctly. When, instead, the discovery fills her with despair at the thought of unwitting infidelity, Jupiter returns, still disguised as Amphitryon, to calm her and to take advantage of her dawning awareness that her lover was not Amphitryon. Although he now succeeds in gaining her admission that, hypothetically, she would not refuse Jupiter as lover, she balks at the suggestion that she might be capable of preferring a god over her husband. Jupiter must settle for her admission that she prefers the "Amphitryon" who is with her now (whom she believes is her husband) to any other "Amphitryon" who might subsequently appear to her.

Is Jupiter, as he at least pretends, satisfied with Alkmene's declaration that her love belongs to him, even though she continues to ignore his persistent hints of his divine identity? If what Jupiter seeks is proof of his appeal for Alkmene,[10] his identity is important only for securing Alkmene's admission that her love no longer belongs to her husband. He is determined, of course, that Alkmene must eventually discover that the "man" she loves is Jupiter, but first she must confirm her sexual preference by choosing between the two "Amphitryons." At the end of the first act he has secured her admission that the Amphitryon who made love to her

---

[10] Jupiter's sexual interest in winning Alkmene's favor has been commented upon by several critics, none of whom have touched upon the extent to which it is the Olympian's male pride which is at stake, as distinguished from his sense of his divinity; see particularly Blankenagel, *The Dramas of H. v. K.*, 96, 97–98; Gerhard Fricke, *Gefühl und Schicksal bei Heinrich von Kleist* (Berlin, 1929), 91, and Nordmeyer, "Kleists Amphitryon," *Monatshefte*, 38 (1946), 168–69.

that night has outdone himself. In act two he has won her confession that, if there are two Amphitryons, she prefers the one who is at her side. Thus, Jupiter's subsequent order for the feast which provides the setting for act three aims at confirming Alkmene's preference through an actual test of that hypothetical condition.

Before he can confidently confront Alkmene with both Amphitryons, Jupiter apparently feels he must remove a final obstacle. At the end of their dialogue in act two, scene five, Alkmene made the qualification that if a second Amphitryon appeared, she would wish that he were Jupiter and that the Amphitryon she is with were her husband, as she believes him to be. She is willing to accept the proposition that, if she has been deceived, it must have been by a god,[11] for, although lusting after gods is tabu, there is nothing dishonorable or humiliating about having been tricked by a god. In act three Jupiter announces to Alkmene (offstage) that a second, "mortal" Amphitryon has appeared at her doorstep, with the result that she reacts with extreme rage when she is forced to admit to herself that her lover was a man posing as Amphitryon, and, therefore, that she has been guilty of adultery in the ordinary sense. In her rage, she is blind to the implication that the "Amphitryon" to whom she ardently clings at that moment is Jupiter, i.e., that the hypothetical situation she had been led to imagine has been realized in reverse. Indeed, the suppression of this dreaded admission may help explain the vehemence of her scorn for the "impostor."[12] Her outburst of righteous indignation represents a triumph for Jupiter, since he views it as testifying to Alkmene's sexual preference for himself and, more importantly, as reflecting her subconscious admission of his divine identity.

His own triumph confirmed, Jupiter gallantly proceeds to insure the vindication of Alkmene's honor before revealing his identity.[13] He compels Amphitryon to decide, considering Alkmene's preference, who the impostor is. Only after the husband had testified to his absolute faith in

---

[11] At least two critics believe that Alkmene already has accepted completely the explanation that she was visited by Jupiter: Meyer-Benfey, *Das Drama H. v. K.s*, 339, and Fricke, *Gefühl und Schicksal*, 94.

[12] Meyer-Benfey, *Das Drama H. v. K.s*, 341, gives yet another interpretation of Alkmene's rage: "Man hat die Ma losigkeit ihrer Schmähungen beanstandet. Aber der Grund ist deutlich: Da er nun für sie der Betrüger ist, so muß sie ihn ja für das, was sie gelitten hat und leidet, verantwortlich machen."

[13] Hermann J. Weigand, "Das Motiv des Vertrauens im Drama Heinrichs von Kleist," *Monatshefte*, 30 (1938), 233–45, 238–39, and Nordmeyer, "Kleists Amphitryon," *Monatshefte*, 38 (1946), 271, argue that Jupiter's test of Alkmene in act three is aimed primarily, or even solely, at her vindication.

the chasteness of his wife's love does Jupiter reveal himself. Amphitryon's orthodox piety spares him any feelings of jealousy—or at least any expression of them, for he acknowledges the god's right of property over everything, including a man's wife. Nor has Amphitryon lost respect for Alkmene because of her seduction by Jupiter; on the contrary, he rejoices at Jupiter's granting of his wish that the god shall have sired a son by her. Not for a moment does Amphitryon consider Alkmene capable of an unnatural lusting after gods. Whatever subconscious jealousy or revulsion he might feel is suppressed by his male pride as soldier and husband. His religion offers him a rationalization of such threats to his honor, and he instinctively seizes upon it.

The concluding scene of act two, however, has informed us of the view of the matter likely to be held by the servant class and common folk, and this perspective, as is so often the case in Western literature, may hint at the author's own assessment. Having overheard talk that it was Jupiter who visited Alkmene, Charis, her maid servant, eagerly concludes that Apollo (or at least Mercury, or perhaps only Ganymed) must have accompanied him and paid a visit to her posing as her husband Sosias. Although Alkmene appears devoid of this vanity attributed to her sex in literature and the popular imagination, she subconsciously may indeed be susceptible to such dreams of exaltation, however Platonic or mystical their expression on the conscious level. Similarly, while Alkmene may be too pious to share Sosias' view that sexual intercourse between gods and men is unnatural, like crossbreeding, by the same token her piety involves the subconscious fear that such intercourse has proved appealing to her.

To what extent then has Jupiter succeeded in winning Alkmene's heart? In the end she is forced to admit to herself that she bestowed her preference on the god. When Jupiter reveals his identity, she faints in her husband's arms. On the conscious level the revelation comes as a complete surprise; but her faint also results from the dreaded confirmation of intimations which she struggled throughout to suppress. In idolizing her husband she has succumbed to the seductions of a god incarnate. For a woman whose piety and humility involve feelings of awe engendered by sexual and spiritual tabus, this self-admission must sever the ties which bound her to life. It is Alkmene's personal mysticism which now leaves her equally unable to find happiness in life or to escape into dreams of immortality. Jupiter's triumph has destroyed her self-image by revealing the secret nature of her love for Amphitryon, which has proven to be "unnatural" from Sosias' viewpoint and tabu in terms of Alkmene's own piety. [14] She has been guilty of the sort of vanity she would condemn in her maid servant while following what she proudly believed were the dictates of a chaste heart.

As he is about to return to Olympus, Jupiter warns Amphitryon that if he wants Alkmene to "remain his" he must "leave her alone." Here, and throughout the concluding act, Jupiter speaks as triumphant lover rather than as lord of creation. Possibly his enigmatic remark is intended as a threat that he will take Alkmene from Amphitryon if he insists on his rights as a husband; or perhaps Jupiter is merely warning Amphitryon of the consequences for Alkmene's mental state if he should try to resume his role as husband in the full sense. It is also possible that Jupiter means only that Amphitryon should not awaken Alkmene until he has gone, [15] because he imagines that she would die of a broken heart at being left behind—not an unlikely ending in a work by Kleist. [16] In any case, Jupiter clearly wishes to believe that Alkmene's faint is the ultimate assurance that he has won her heart.

Alkmene's sigh at the play's end may express a feeling of relief, but certainly not without a note of despair. [17] Her tragic self-revelation poses the question often asked by German Romantics from Tieck to Eichendorff, whether erotic love is not expressive of a subconscious, transcendent yearning for immortality. [18] As Kleist's Herr C. . . insists in the dialogue, "Uber das Marionettentheater," the story of the Fall is basic to an understanding of man and history.

---

[14] Although they do not entertain the possibility that Alkmene's idolization involves a subconscious dream of mystical union, the following critics implicitly judge her capable of a preference for gods over men: Hanna Hellmann, *Heinrich von Kleist. Darstellung des Problems* (Heidelberg, 1911), 31; Meyer-Benfey, *Das Drama H. v. K.s*, 351, and E. L. Stahl, *Heinrich von Kleist's Dramas* (Oxford, 1948), 64–65.

[15] August Sauer, "Zu Kleists Amphitryon," *Euphorion*, 20 (1913), 93–104, 94, insists that "Ruhn lassen" is meant by Jupiter in the Biblical sense of "nicht erkennen."

[16] That Alkmene may harbor an unadmitted desire to follow Jupiter to Olympus is argued by Hanna Hellmann, "Kleists Amphitryon," *Euphorion*, 25 (1924), 241–51.

[17] The interpretation of Alkmene's "Ach!" as a sigh of relief from torment is given by, among others, Meyer-Benfey, *Das Drama H. v. K.s*, 343, and Fricke, *Gefühl und Schicksal*, 96.

[18] Meyer-Benfey, *Das Drama H. v. K.s*, S. 358, is persuaded that "Es ist durchaus verkehrt und dem Sinn der Dichtung zuwider, wenn man darin die romantische Lehre von der *Einheit der Liebe und der Religion* [italics are Meyer-Benfey's] ausgedrückt findet," but Friedrich Gundolf, *Heinrich von Kleist* (Berlin, 1922), 88, provides an interesting formulation of the relationship between sexual lust and mystical longing, which has been the subject of the present study: "Liebe freilich ist nicht das rechte Wort für die Kleistische Wallung, wenn man unter Liebe das Gefühl versteht, welches durch ein ersehntes Wesen sich erlöst und erfüllt. . . . Aus den Finsternissen des Blutes steigen . . . die Träume dieses wilden [schwülen] Triebs, seine Götzen und Opfer jenseits aller Wirklichkeit."

Literary movements in Germany during the second half of the nine-teenth century seem to contradict that bias of taste which would make Molière an influential figure. And yet the comedian's patrimony con-tinued, almost as a counterculture, despite the tendencies of Realism and Naturalism to dispense with highly conventionalized theater and literature. In the next essay, there is a description of Molière's status in Germany during this period.

In Austria, Realism and Naturalism never achieved quite the impact that they did in Immermann's and Hauptmann's Germany. The tradition of comic theater had been maintained with the works of Raimund and Nestroy, and early in the twentieth century the inspiration of Molière reasserted itself through the literary efforts of Hugo von Hofmannsthal, an author particularly open to the riches of world literature.

THE DRAMATIC DIOSCURI: MOLIÈRE'S GERMAN RECEPTION IN THE LATE NINETEENTH CENTURY

Siegfried Mews

Molière und Shakespeare—schöner Doppelstern
Am Bühnenhimmel,—hohe Dioskuren—
So nah einander und zugleich so fern,
Verwandt und doch verschiedene Naturen—
Noch richtet sich nach Euch der Lootse gern
Und lenkt sein Steu'r in Euren lichten Spuren,
Den Leitstern segnend auf dem weiten Meere
Dramat'scher Dichtung—Shakespeare und Molière!
. . . .
— — —Sein Tempel ist die Welt,
Der trotzt dem Alter und Barbarenhieben.
So lange noch Natur und Witz gefällt,
So lange Menschen lachen, leiden, lieben,
So lang die letzte Bretterbude hält,
So lang lebt er und das, was er geschrieben.

Der Stern, der einst nur Frankreich leuchten konnte,
Glänzt jetzt und stets am Menschheits-Horizonte.[1]

This poetic tribute to Molière by Franz von Dingelstedt, writer, translator of Shakespeare, and director of the famous Vienna Burgtheater in the eighteen seventies, might lead one to believe that Shakespeare and Molière occupied a position of equal importance in the German realm of letters in general and on the stages of the German-speaking countries in particular during the period from approximately 1865 to 1900. But even the most ardent admirer of Molière will be forced to admit in the face of overwhelming factual evidence that the impact of Shakespeare's drama upon Germany was far greater than that of Molière's comedies.[2] Molière's impact on the German literary scene was not, however, at all negligible. The publication of a respectable number of Molière's works in both the original and in translation, the fact that historians of literature and critics alike sought to promote Molière's acceptance by the German reading public and theatergoers, and the critical acclaim that was accorded Molière in the influential periodicals of the period—all attest to the solidity of the French dramatist's reputation on German soil.

Specifically, it is the goal of this essay to shed some new light on the factual evidence of Molière's reception in Germany during a comparatively limited period. I intend to follow an "extrinsic" approach, relying on verifiable external factors such as book production and critical appraisals in journals rather than indulging in equally valid, but often arbitrary influence studies that seek to establish one or several writers' dependence on another.

Any assessment of the degree of popularity a literary figure enjoys in a foreign land will have to take into account the availability and quality of translations as the main vehicles for transmitting an author's work abroad. The following table, which lists the frequency and years of publication of individual translated works by Molière (including both new translations and reissues or new editions of older translations), shows clearly that Molière's work attracted a sufficiently great reading public to justify repeated publication of his plays.

---

[1] Franz von Dingelstedt, in Ferdinand Lotheissen, *Molière. Sein Leben und seine Werke* (Frankfurt, 1880), 400.

[2] It is not the place here to delve into the many facets of Shakespeare's German reception; rather, see my brief account of Shakespeare's extraordinary place in the annals of German literature: "The Reception of 'Weltliteratur' in Germany, 1871–1890: A Study in Literary Taste," (Diss., University of Illinois, 1967), 77 ff., and *passim*.

Molière's Works in German Translation, c. 1865–1900[3]

Title	Year of Publication		Number of
	First	Last	Translations
L'Avare	1868	c.1888	5
Le Bourgeois gentilhomme	1878	1896	2
L'Ecole des femmes	c.1875		1
Les Fâcheux	c.1875	1895	2
Les Femmes savantes	c.1868	1888	5
George Dandin	c.1875		1
Le Malade imaginaire	1868	1899	9
Le Misanthrope	1867	c.1888	5
Monsieur de Pourceaugnac	1899		1
Les Petits Savoyards	1899		1
Les Précieuses ridicules	c.1874	1878	2
Sganarelle	c.1880		1
Le Tartuffe	c.1869	1891	5

Although such a statistical tabulation as the one above cannot provide information as to the quality of the translations in question or as to the precise impact of Molière's works on the German reading public, the table does clearly demonstrate that practically all of Molière's major works were available on the book market and were presumably read fairly widely. Perhaps even more telling evidence for Molière's acceptance is offered by the several editions of his entire or selected works that were published in the late nineteenth century:

1) *Lustspiele.* 4 vols. Transl. W. Graf Baudissin. Leipzig, 1865–1867.

2) *Charakter-Komödien.* 3 vols. Transl. A. Laun. Hildburghausen, 1865. (New ed., c. 1880; another ed., 1 vol., Leipzig, 1886.)

3) *Sämmtliche Werke.* 2 vols. Ed. E. Schröder, Intro. H. Th. Rötscher. Leipzig, 1871.

4) *Ausgewählte Lustspiele.* Transl. A. Laun. Leipzig, 1881.

5) *Ausgewählte Werke.* 3 vols. Transl. F.S. Bierling, Intro. P. Lindau. Stuttgart, 1883. (Reissue of a translation which appeared first in 1752!)

6) *Meisterwerke.* Transl. L. Fulda. Stuttgart, 1892. (2nd enlarged ed., 1896; 4th enlarged ed., 2 vols., 1905; 5th enlarged ed., 2 vols., 1911.)

Among the translations listed above, those by Baudissin (1), Laun (2) and Fulda (6) should be singled out as successful attempts to acquaint the German reading public with Molière. Both Baudissin's and Fulda's translations were reissued in part or as a whole after World War II—no

---

[3] The data were compiled on the basis of Kayser's *Vollständiges Bücher-Lexikon* and Hans Fromm, *Bibliographie deutscher Übersetzungen aus dem Französischen* 1700–1948, IV (Baden-Baden, 1951).

small sign of recognition. Apart from the commercial success attested to by the publication of new editions, the minor controversy involving the renderings into German of Molière's works by the scholar Adolf Laun served to focus the attention of the *literati* on the problems inherent in any Molière translation and forced them to reconsider their presuppositions. The controversy began when Paul Lindau, influential francophile critic and author of minor literary works, launched an attack on Adolf Laun's translation of *Le Tartuffe* "in fünffüßigen paarweis gereimten Jamben" (Berlin, 1872) in his newly founded journal *Die Gegenwart* (3 [1873], 23–25). Lindau charged that Laun had violated both spirit and form of the play by presenting it in the "unnatural" medium of iambic pentameter. Even Paul Lindau, who a few years earlier had paid tribute to the French dramatist in his monograph *Molière* (Leipzig, 1871), assumed that it would be impossible to ever produce a Molière translation which would approximate the artistic quality of the Schlegel-Tieck Shakespeare rendering. Yet, he preferred the German versions of both Wolf Graf Baudissin (1), who, incidentally, had been a collaborator on the Schlegel-Tieck Shakespeare translation, and Emilie Schröder (3) to those of Laun. Although Laun attempted to refute Lindau's criticism by implying that *Le Tartuffe* constituted an improvement over his previous 1865 translation (1) written in alexandrines and by referring to favorable critics in support of his point of view, Paul Lindau's opinion was upheld by the French scholar Auguste Ehrhard. Ehrhard praised Baudissin: "Sa traduction est un chef-d'oeuvre de fidélité, de précision et d'élégance. Son style a une aisance telle, qu'on croirait lire une oeuvre originale."[4] But he had less flattering things to say about Laun's version: "Les alexandrins de Laun . . . sont de véritables tours de force."[5] In contrast to Laun, the dramatist and translator Ludwig Fulda (6) fared much better at the hands of the critics—despite the fact that he employed rhymed iambic pentameter like Laun. In his assessment one reviewer echoed a familiar sentiment when he pointed out that only Shakespeare had succeeded in becoming fully germanized by means of a congenial and superior translation which was still lacking—if it could be achieved at all—in the case of Molière.[6] At any rate, Fulda's new trans-

---

[4] Auguste Ehrhard, *Les Comédies de Molière en Allemagne. Le Théâtre et la critique* (Paris, 1888), 530–31.

[5] *Ibid.*, 531.

[6] Paul Schlenther, in *Das Magazin für Litteratur* (1893), 237. This periodical was also published under slightly different titles. It will henceforth be cited as *Magazin*. See also my article, "Information and Propagation: A German Mediator of 'Weltliteratur' in the Late Nineteenth Century," *Revue de Littérature Comparée*, 42 (1968), 50–75.

lations were credited with contributing to the success of performances of Molière's play in the Berlin theaters in the nineties.[7]

Molière's greatest impact was felt, of course, with the performance of his plays; the collective experience of the theatergoers was, by its very nature, designed to have more far-reaching and profound effects than the individual reader's encounter with Molière's translated texts without the benefit of acting, staging, etc. Regrettably, precise data are somewhat hard to come by. Yet it can be assumed with a considerable degree of certainty that Molière's plays, in particular *Le Misanthrope* and *Le Tartuffe*, belonged to the standard fare of the German theaters. Kürschner's *Jahrbuch für das deutsche Theater* (2 vols.; Leipzig, 1879–1880) provides a clear indication that Molière's plays were indeed performed in Germany, and the famous theatrical company, the "Meininger," innovators in acting and staging techniques, included some of Molière's plays in their repertory—as is evidenced by the publication of *Les Femmes savantes* and *Le Malade imaginaire* (both 1879) in the "Repertoir" of the Meining Hoftheater. In concluding his cursory survey of Molière performances in the seventies and eighties, Auguste Ehrhard bestows the ultimate accolade on Molière's theatrical propagation in a foreign land: "Ce nombre de représentations qu'obtient Molière en une seule année [1878] dans les diverses villes d'Allemagne n'est-il pas imposant? Notre poète parait-il beaucoup plus souvent sur nos scènes françaises?"[8]

Any account of Molière's reception would be incomplete without passing mention of the editions in the original French—which, to be sure, found a far more limited reading public than those in German. It is no mean achievement of scholars, editors, and publishers that there were at least four separate editions of Molière's complete or selected works:

1) *Sämmtliche Werke.* 14 vols. (Commentary, etc. in German.) Ed. A. Laun, continued by W. Knörich. Leipzig, 1873 ff.

2) *Ausgewählte Lustspiele.* 6 vols. Ed. K. Brunnemann. Berlin, 1876–1877.

3) *Ausgewählte Lustspiele.* 7 vols. Ed. H. Fritsche. Berlin, 1877 ff. (Superseded the inferior Brunnemann ed.)[9]

4) *Oeuvres Complètes.* 1 vol. (no more published?) Leipzig, 1885.

---

[7] Eugen Zabel, "Molièresche Dramen auf deutschen Bühnen," *Zur modernen Dramaturgie* (Oldenburg, 1900), 144–67.

[8] Ehrhard, *Les Comédies de Molière*, 530.

[9] Cf. Richard Mahrenholtz, *Molière's Leben und Werke vom Standpunkt der heutigen Forschung* (Heilbronn, 1883), 232.

These collected works were supplemented by a veritable host of single-play editions which, for the most part, were destined to be used as texts in schools. Despite the avowed pedagogical purpose—and, hence, limited appeal—of many of these books, some of them seemed to achieve a resounding success. Even if one takes into consideration that the entries in Kayser's *Vollständiges Bücherlexikon* may not be entirely accurate, an average of almost one edition per year over a period of approximately twenty years for the *Théâtre français* volume (only *one* of several *L'Avare* versions available on the book market) is quite astounding.

But the most significant contribution to furthering Molière in Germany was, without doubt, Laun's collection (1). Apart from the fact that several of the volumes were reprinted, the critics took a favorable view of Laun's enterprise. With explicit reference to Shakespeare, one anonymous reviewer recommended Laun's edition: "Wie Shakespeare für die Tragödie und das große historische Drama, so ist Molière das Muster treuer Sittenschilderung und feiner Charakterzeichnung geworden."[10]

The same reviewer, however, could not refrain from making disparaging remarks about the French national character—especially the desire to be the center of attention even under unflattering circumstances. Precisely such outbursts of anti-French sentiments, which were not infrequently encountered after the Franco-Prussian War of 1870–1871, threatened occasionally to overcome the German critics' traditional receptiveness towards foreign literature. After all, no less a figure than Goethe had propounded the concept of "Weltliteratur"—a concept to which most of the critics in the nineteenth century still subscribed. Moreover, Molière as an established classic was far less affected by outbreaks of hostility motivated by national pride than the French dramatists Eugène Scribe, Emile Augier, Eugène Labiche, Alexandre Dumas *fils*, Victorien Sardou, who indeed posed a serious threat to struggling German playwrights by providing an extraordinarily large share of the theatrical fare in the German-speaking countries.

To see things in their proper perspective, some of the several monographs on Molière that were published during the period should be mentioned here. They ranged from detailed scholarly studies to books with an avowed partisan and propagandistic purpose. The activities of scholars, literary critics, and translators alike prompted one reviewer to observe: "Molière ist bekanntlich in neuester Zeit zur Losung einer Partei

---

[10] *Magazin*, 83 (1873), 186.

geworden, welche ihn gegenüber Shakspeare [sic] auf den Schild heben möchte."[11] Indeed, the efforts of the Molière partisans to make their dramatist a universally recognized "Weltdichter" deserve full recognition —a recognition which was implicitly extended by the French scholar Ehrhard.[12]

The high hopes the propagators of Molière cherished are, to some extent, expressed by Paul Lindau. In his biographically oriented study, he cited the almost mandatory comparison of the "dioscuri": "Unter den dramatischen Dichtern von Bedeutung ist Molière der subjectivste und Shakespeare der objectivste." [13] Works of a more academic and scholarly nature, which could hardly be expected to have a broad appeal, were occasionally also issued in a popularized version. This happened in the case of Richard Mahrenholtz' *Molière* (Heilbronn, 1883), which made the results of his intensive Molière studies (Stettin, 1881) palatable for the general reading public. Ferdinand Lotheissen's "leicht und flüssig wie ein Roman geschriebenes Buch" (*Molière* [Frankfurt am Main, 1880]) gave rise to the reviewer's expectation that Molière's plays might never disappear from the German stage.[14]

The general studies of Molière's life and works were supplemented by specialized treatises. In fact, some of the German *Moliéristes* exhibited the same traits of "fanatisme intolérant" of their counterparts, the French "savants de profession."[15] Regrettably, the efforts of the German Molière enthusiasts were not always met with the goodwill and encouragement they deserved. Thus a minor scholarly feud developed when A. Baluffe sought to refute H. Fritsche's etymological derivation of the word "Sganarelle" in his *Molière et les Allemands* (Paris, 1884).[16]

The efforts of Molière's promoters in Germany continued undaunted, however. The periodical *Molière-Museum* (1879 ff.), a "Sammelwerk zur Förderung des Studiums des Dramatikers in Deutschland," served as a rallying point for the pro-Molière forces. It was founded by the medical doctor and longtime Paris resident Heinrich Schweitzer and counted among its collaborators and contributors such eminent Molière scholars

---

[11] *Blätter für literarische Unterhaltung* (Nov., 1871), 751.
[12] Ehrhard, *Les Comédies de Molière*, 533–34.
[13] Paul Lindau, *Molière. Eine Ergänzung der Biographie des Dichters aus seinen Werken* (Leipzig, 1871), 1.
[14] *Die Gegenwart*, 22 (1882), 79.
[15] Ehrhard, *Les Comédies de Molière*, 534.
[16] *Ibid.*, 535.

as A. Laun and H. Fritsche. Despite its positive reception by the critics —some of whom in somewhat self-congratulatory fashion pointed out the lack of anti-French sentiments evidenced by the publication of the periodical[17]—*Molière-Museum* neither achieved the eminence nor longevity of its rival, *Jahrbuch der deutschen Shakespeare-Gesellschaft* (1864 ff.), which survived World War II and now reflects the political division of Germany by being issued separately in the FDR and GDR.

Precisely the claim that Molière was Shakespeare's equal motivated many Molière enthusiasts in their efforts to achieve for their dramatist the kind of public awareness and recognition which the British playwright enjoyed. Perhaps no single man propounded the equality theory more arduously then C. Humbert. In 1869 his *Molière, Shakespeare und die deutsche Kritik* appeared. This book was followed by the programmatically entitled *Englands Urteil über Molière, den einzigen Nebenbuhler Shakespeares und den größten Komiker aller Zeiten* (Bielefeld, 1878; 2nd ed. Weimar, 1884) and by two other works.[18] Humbert discarded the argument of the differing tastes of the Germanic peoples on the one hand and of the Romanic peoples on the other by pointing out that Shakespeare, though kindred in spirit, was not fully accepted or understood until Lessing, the poets of the Storm and Stress Movement and the Romantics, among whom A. W. Schlegel most derisively attacked Molière, made Shakespeare a household word. Moreover, Humbert asked rhetorically, if not totally convincingly, which right do Germans have to place Shakespeare above Molière when the British themselves compare the latter favorably to the former.[19]

Admirable as Humbert's commitment to Molière's cause might be, he failed to convince all the critics of the justice of his claim. Actually, the ardent promotion of the French dramatist caused some minor backlash, as can be seen from the publication of O. W. Stichling's pamphlet, *Molière und kein Ende. Ein Mahnwort an Deutschlands Molièreisten* (Berlin, 1887). Ironically, Goethe had voiced his apprehension about the Shakespeare cult in Germany in his essay in 1815, "Shakespeare und kein Ende," in a similar fashion.

Ultimately, the role of periodicals in contributing to a better understanding of the French dramatist must be considered more effective than

---

[17] *Magazin*, 96 (1879), 642–43.
[18] C. Humbert, *Deutschlands Urteil über Molière* (Oppeln, 1883); *Schiller, Lessing, Goethe, Molière und Herr Dr. Paul Lindau* (Bielefeld, 1885).
[19] Humbert, *Englands Urteil über Molière*, 120.

that of books. After all, periodicals in general reached a significant number of readers in various socioeconomic strata. Hence, the cumulative effect of prolonged dissemination of information about or propagation of one specific author could be fairly impressive. In addition, as periodicals tend to be a comparatively accurate mirror of the preoccupations and predilections of the times, a perusal of periodicals can offer insights into the general intellectual-cultural atmosphere which may directly or indirectly have a bearing on the reception of an individual foreign author or an entire national literature. Thus, Molière's reception in Germany was, to some extent, dependent on the attitude towards French literature in general. This attitude was not entirely positive, particularly in the years following the Franco-Prussian War of 1870–1871 when the German unification raised high hopes for a rejuvenation and flourishing of German literature, which was to result in the native products' assuming a larger share of the book market and their becoming a more substantial part of theatrical fare. Alas, these hopes remained largely unfulfilled. Despite the deplorable lack of reciprocity in France concerning the reception of German letters and despite the anguished warnings against the German mania of translating foreign works indiscriminately, both the established and newly founded periodicals were, in general, well disposed towards the notion of cultural cross-fertilization, if a somewhat one-sided one in the case of France.

Among the reputable literary reviews *Magazin*[20] provided the most extensive coverage of the various facets of the efforts to secure Molière a firm place in the realm of German letters. *Magazin* functioned primarily as a review organ of translations, secondary literature, and the like. Yet, the series of articles entitled "Die neuesten Forschungen über Molières Leben"[21] is indicative of the scope of *Magazin*'s coverage and the intellectual demands it made on its readers.

The weekly *Die Gegenwart*, founded in 1872 by Paul Lindau, also accorded Molière considerable space in its pages. The versatile Paul Lindau, clearly an important mediator because of his decided preference for French literature, contributed the bulk of articles on Molière—mostly reviews of performances of Molière's plays. Another important and well-established literary review, *Blätter für literarische Unterhaltung*, likewise opened its pages to Molière by printing reviews of the important German

[20] See n. 6, above.
[21] *Magazin*, 91 (1877), 5–7, 37–39, 78–80, 134–36.

and some non-German scholarly literature on the French dramatist. The controversy which was incited by the famous figures of literary history was limited to scholarly circles and mild compared to the battle that raged around the French Naturalists, Zola in particular, in the seventies and eighties. Therefore, statements which expressed the familiar lament about the callous disregard of German letters in France could not significantly damage the position Molière had attained in Germany.

It is true that, as R. Mahrenholtz wrote in 1890, "in Deutschland die Tage der Molière-Begeisterung längst vorübergegangen [sind]."[22] But it is equally true that Molière was far from forgotten and attracted the attention of the intellectually inclined and sophisticated to whom the literary reviews catered. Even such an important journal as Julius Rodenberg's *Deutsche Rundschau*, which was to become the representative review of the newly founded German Empire and its emerging cultural and political center, Berlin, did not entirely ignore Molière, despite the fact that it heavily favored contemporary literature. Other journals of repute, like the once-renowned *Die Grenzboten* and the less significant *Im Neuen Reich* took sides in the debate of whether Molière should be accorded equal status with Shakespeare; both cast their votes for the latter and against the former. Molière's markedly French characteristics and his limited range as indicated by his exclusive employment of the comic genre made him an ill-suited candidate for a comparison with Shakespeare, one reviewer opined.[23]

An examination of the periodical literature of the seventies and eighties reveals that Molière was essentially an author of the establishment in that his life, his works, and the hardly negligible scholarly output about him were discussed in a somewhat detached fashion in the great reviews which hewed to a fairly conservative aesthetic course. Curiously, Molière also was to be found, if only temporarily, in the camp of the literary opposition, i.e., in the camp of younger writers who were often dedicated to the cause of Naturalism and sought to change the literary scene. Among the first attempts to revolutionize literature and to alter the reading public's taste were those of the brothers Julius and Heinrich Hart, who, in one of their many short-lived ventures in the realm of periodical publishing, elevated Molière, along with Shakespeare, Milton, Goethe, and others, to the lofty

---

[22] *Blätter für literarische Unterhaltung* (Feb., 1890), 83.
[23] *Die Grenzboten*, 40/4 (1881), 459–69.

position of an inspirational model for the literature of the future—a literature which would shun both the excesses of sordid milieu realism and poetic idealization of life.[24]

One surely should not overrate the Harts' reference to Molière as a model to be emulated. Yet this slight gesture of approval and admiration, if seen in connection with the products of the scholars', translators', critics', and theater directors' enthusiasm and diligence, somewhat unexpectedly attests to the basic validity of Franz von Dingelstedt's poetic effusion: "Der Stern, der einst nur Frankreich leuchten konnte,/Glänzt jetzt am Menschheits-Horizonte." As the foregoing discussion has shown, there was little reason to fear that Molière would ever fall into oblivion.

[24] *Berliner Monatshefte*, 1 (1885), 66.

MOLIÈRE AND HOFMANNSTHAL

Hanna B. Lewis

Molière's continuing universality as a comic dramatist is probably best demonstrated, not by the scores of revivals, translations and adaptations of his plays on the modern stage, but in the transmutation of his plots and characters in modern comedies that seem to have no direct connection with him. The development of Hugo von Hofmannsthal (1874–1929) as writer of comedies shows this transmutation in its most characteristic form.

Hofmannsthal began as an adolescent prodigy, writing some of the greatest modern German poetry before the age of twenty-five, and producing a series of essays (under the pseudonym of Loris), short stories, and lyric dramas that can hold their place with those of the most prominent European writers of his day. Like many brilliant young lyricists, he found his ability to express the world in instinctive language lessening as he grew older. He began to search for other genres to make possible his change from, which in Friedrich Schiller's terms would be, the naïve to the sentimental writer.

In his quest, he used many other writers' works as points of departure. At first, it was basically the Elizabethans. Having used a letter by a fictitious Lord Philip Chandos to Sir Francis Bacon as the vehicle for stating the universal problem of the poet's inability to express objects and actions by language in "Ein Brief" (1901), he continued by trying to write an Elizabethan drama of his own. Several unfinished attempts were followed by his successful adaptation of Thomas Otway's *Venice Preserved*, *Das gerettete Venedig* (1905), which added Shakespearean and Neo-Romantic elements to the Restoration original. Simultaneously, he also experimented with Greek drama, especially with the plays of Sophocles. The German adaptation of *Electra* was not only successful as a verse drama, but the opera produced from it by the collaboration of Hofmannsthal and Richard Strauss is still a standard part of the repertoire.

Although he never abandoned serious drama, Hofmannsthal began to turn to comedy in the middle of the first decade of this century. Here his models were to be French, Spanish, and Italian, rather than English or

Greek. He was particularly well suited to working with French literature. He grew up in a Francophile Vienna. One has only to read any literary work of his day to realize how the French language had invaded the speech of the cultural elite. He studied French literature at the University of Vienna, receiving his doctorate in 1899 with a dissertation entitled "Das Sprachgebrauch bei den Dichtern der Plejade." He had intended to become a professor of "Romanistik" and wrote a "Habilitationsschrift" on the literary development of Victor Hugo, but decided to become a professional writer instead.

As a schoolboy of eighteen, he adapted his first French play, Maurice Maeterlinck's *Les Aveugles*, for a presentation by the Wiener Freie Bühne.[1] Other early adaptations for the stage included that of Jules Renar's *Poil de Carrote* (*Fuchs* in its German version). With Molière also, Hofmannsthal began with translations and adaptations. Max Reinhardt requested an adaptation of *Le Mariage forcé* (*Die Heirat wider Willen*) for his Kammerspiele des Deutschen Theaters, which was successfully presented in the 1910/1911 season.[2] At this time, Hofmannsthal and his friend, the dramatist Carl Sternheim, were tentatively planning a new German edition of Molière's works, since both writers were now actively engaged in writing comedies after Molière's models. (Sternheim was working on *George Dandin*).[3] Certain differences in their concept of the role Molière should play in the modern theater made this collaboration unsatisfactory. Sternheim wanted to show the "historisch-gesellschaftliche Aktualität" he saw in the "aufklärische" manner Molière had employed. Hofmannsthal, on the other hand, admired Molière as a playwright who used some of the traditions of the Jonsonian masque (especially in the early plays like *Le Mariage forcé*) and whose techniques and materials presented an excellent point of departure for his own dramatic endeavors.[4] Their views were not totally irreconcilable, since the main purpose for both seemed to be that of producing stageable versions of the French plays for Reinhardt, rather than exact translations. However, the unexpected publication of another German Molière edition (by Georg Müller), as well as the demands of other literary projects upon each of them, dealt the death blow to this plan.

---

[1] Werner Volke, *Hofmannsthal* (Reinbeck bei Hamburg, 1967), 37.

[2] Carl Sternheim—Hugo von Hofmannsthal, "Briefe," *Hofmannsthal Blätter*, 4 (Spring, 1970), 251.

[3] Leonhard M. Fiedler, "Eine Molière-Ausgabe von Hofmannsthal und Sternheim," *Hofmannsthal Blätter*, 4(Spring,1970), 258.

[4] *Ibid.*

Hofmannsthal's interest in Molière had already begun to show in works not translated or adapted. *Monsieur de Pourceaugnac* plays an important part in the development of plot and character in *Der Rosenkavalier*. The latter was the play on which Hofmannsthal was working when he and Sternheim were planning the Molière edition. (Two earlier comedies, *Sylvia im "Stern"* [unfinished] and *Cristinas Heimreise* had not been very successful.) Hofmannsthal's original draft for the play not only gave Baron Ochs a far more important role than he was to have later, but even kept the name of Pourceaugnac. Later the "little piglet" changes into an "ox." In the final version, the Marschallin becomes the center of the action, but she is a far more original creation than Ochs.[5]

The similarities between Pourceaugnac and Ochs are quite striking. Both are country squires who come to the big, sophisticated city (home to the courts of the Roi Soleil and Maria Theresa respectively) to seek a bride. Although Ochs is more worldly wise than Pourceaugnac (after all, he is of the nobility), his sophistication is only a veneer over a basic crudeness inherited from his peasant ancestors. Och's savoir faire shows itself mainly in his multitudinous earlier love affairs with inferiors, which make him a little less susceptible to trickery than his French original, and in a certain miserliness, so that he can never quite be duped financially in the manner Pourceaugnac is by Sbrigani. Under the skin, the country bumpkins are alike.

Plot technique is an even more important similarity, for, as Hofmannsthal later wrote, "Auch die Molièrsche Komödie ruht nicht so sehr auf den Charakteren selbst als auf der Relation der sehr oft typischen Figuren

---

[5] There are several excellent studies already about the influence of Molière on Hofmannsthal. Far more facts about individual aspects than the present brief article can present are given in them. Particularly recommended are Hilde Burger, "Hofmannsthal's Debt to Molière," *Modern Languages*, 39 (1958), 56–61, which deals with the influence of *Monsieur de Pourceaugnac* on *Der Rosenkavalier*; and Victor A. Oswald, "Hofmannsthal's Collaboration with Molière," *Germanic Review*, XXIX, 1 (1954), 18–30, which covers all the known influences. Other articles include Julius Bab, "Molière und Hofmannsthal," *New Yorker Staatszeitung* (Dec. 18, 1949); and Helmut Wocke, "Hofmannsthal und Molière," *Neuphilologische Zeitschrift*, II, 2 (1950), 127–37, which limits itself to a general survey of French influence on Hofmannsthal, and the plays adapted or translated directly from Molière. Another brief mention of the Hofmannsthal-Molière relationship is in F. H. Oppenheim, "Der Einfluß der französischen Literatur auf die deutsche," *Aufriß*, III (1963), 89–90. Further comments may be found in articles dealing with *Der Rosenkavalier* und *Ariadne auf Naxos*. But the best record of Molière's influence on Hofmannsthal, and one that everyone who is interested in this subject uses as his main source, is the correspondence between Hofmannsthal and Strauss, Richard Strauss and Hugo von Hofmannsthal, *Briefwechsel* (2nd ed., Zürich, 1955). For those readers not fluent in German, an excellent English translation is available by Hanns Hammelmann and Ewald Oser under the title of *A Working Friendship* (New York, 1961).

zueinander."[6] *Der Rosenkavalier* is a "Komödie für Musik" and the use of music and dance is an essential element in promoting plot and character development, more interwoven but not so totally different to the songs and ballets that heighten the comic elements in *Monsieur de Pourceaugnac*. In addition, the denouement in both plays is even caused by the same type of incident: the appearance of a wife (or wives), complete with squalling offspring yelling "Papa, Papa, Papa" (in German) and "Mon papa! Mon papa! Mon papa!" (in French), who accuse the "villain" of bigamy and bring him to justice.

Le Bourgeois gentilhomme is undoubtedly the play whose influence is most pervasive in Hofmannsthal's comic development. The features of Monsieur Jourdain can already be seen to some extent in the character-ization of *Der Rosenkavalier*'s Faninal, in his desire to marry his daughter to a nobleman and then gain entrance to a higher level of society. But Hofmannsthal was to decide to utilize *Le Bourgeois gentilhomme* to a greater extent. He wrote to Richard Strauss in May, 1911,[7] that this play would be perfect as a framework for their planned operatic *divertissement*, *Ariadne auf Naxos*. The five acts were to be condensed to two, and *Ariadne* could be performed after dinner in the presence of Jourdain and his guests. The prose scene before the *divertissement* was to show the composer and the music teacher and dancing master, each with a performance to direct: the composer and music teacher to produce a serious opera, the dancing master, an afterpiece for the Italian comedians. Suddenly Jourdain would order the combination of both pieces. Everyone would be in despair until Zerbinetta, the soubrette, promised to manage as well as she could; she thought Ariadne an idiot anyway and could not take the opera seriously.

Hofmannsthal felt that this combination of the comic and tragic in a comic framework was the true interpretation of the spirit of Molière:

> Die ganze Sache ist ja aus den beiden theatralischen Elementen der Mo-lièrschen Zeit förmlich herausdestilliert, aus der mythologischen Oper und aus den "maschere," den tanzenden und singenden Komödiantenfiguren. Lully könnte das vertont, Callot es entworfen haben. Auf den ersten Blick—wäre man ja nicht einmal überrascht, dieses ganze Divertissement dem Text, dem authentischen Text, unserer comédie-ballet "Bürger als Edelmann" beige-druckt zu sehen.[8]

Unfortunately, Hofmannsthal's enthusiasm was greater than that of his audience. The scissors-and-paste method of condensation did nothing for

---

[6] Hugo von Hofmannsthal, *Der Rosenkavalier*, zum Geleit N. R. (1949).
[7] Strauss-Hofmannsthal, *Briefwechsed*, 98–99.
[8] *Ibid.*, 123.

the Molière play. *Ariadne*, with its modern music, its carefully developed contrast between the idealist and the pragmatist, as represented by Ariadne and Zerbinetta, and the "Verwandlung" of Ariadne into a human being, capable of facing life as it is rather than surrendering to a noble death, had great possibilities alone.

Hofmannsthal was distressed about the poor reception of his work, blaming it partly on the inability of his audience to comprehend the "komplette Gestalt" of *Ariadne*, partly on lack of appreciation of a genius as lucid and radiant as Molière, and partly on the lack of true comic actors in Germany. (An opera, with music by Wolf-Ferrari and Richard Batka, *Der Liebhaber als Arzt*, based on *Le Médecin malgré lui*, presented in Dresden in December, 1913, on the other hand, received great critical and popular acclaim, much to the discomfiture of Strauss and Hofmannsthal). Apparently, in eliminating many of Molière's comic scenes (the Turkish ceremony, the love intrigue) and characters (Lucile, Cléonte, and Co-vielle), Hofmannsthal had also eliminated the attention of the audience, who were bored with the play and wanted to get on to the opera.

The second version of *Ariadne* had little of Molière left. Only the music master and composer were left in the prologue, which introduced the real opera with a musical prelude. *Der Bürger als Edelmann* was subjected to complete revision. In this one, most of Molière's plots and characters are reinstated, although somewhat changed. Jourdain is, of course, the center of action. The minor characters are grouped according to what they can hope to gain from him: the hirelings, the philosopher, fencing master, dacing master, music teacher, and tailor, who can get extra pay; Mascarille, Nerine, and Lucette, who are somewhat more sophisticated con artists; Dorante, who uses Jourdain to get Dorimene; and Cléonte and Lucile, who only want to get married. Actually, Lucile has a far larger role in Hofmannsthal's play, since his innate sympathy with female characters (the women in his plays are frequently the only ones with common sense and are the salvation of more idealistic, more confused male characters) makes him develop her into a mediatrix between her father and her lover with all the attendant conflict of loyalties this entails. The adaptation was presented anonymously (as was that of *Die Lästigen*, *Les Fâcheux*, performed in 1916) by request of Hofmannsthal, who felt " . . . daß ein lebender Dichter es für richtig findet, das Werk eines Klassikers frei zu bearbeiten, ist ein ganz singulärer Fall: die Verantwortlichkeit trage ich vor mir selber; die Anonymität ist die Form, welche Respekt und Takt mir vorschreiben."[9]

[9] *Ibid.*, 326.

Unfortunately, perhaps, Hofmannsthal had still interfered too much. Although he protested to Strauss that his main purpose in the adaptation had been to provide a setting for Strauss's music from the original framework for *Ariadne*, which would otherwise had to have been scrapped, and some additional musical pieces in the same style, which Strauss would have to write, Hofmannsthal really felt he had created a new genre, neither "Singspiel" nor operetta, but "ein Genre für sich, das aber in den schon bestehenden eineinhalb Akten klar und deutlich vorgezeichnet ist."[10] But Hofmannsthal's vision of comedy was basically serious, and his comic heroes are really tragic clowns. Anything Hofmannsthal considered in bad taste was removed. Thus we lose the quarrel between the Philosopher and the other masters, and the spelling scene, and all that might be deemed "niedrig-komisch" or "läppisch,"[11] such as Jourdain's song of the kitten. At any rate, the play was a failure, which Hofmannsthal blamed on the interference of the music in the plot—rather curiously, since Lully's music had always been there, and he had written the new adaptation largely as a vehicle for Strauss's music.

The previously mentioned adaptation of *Les Fâcheux*, *Die Lästigen*, which had already been presented by Reinhardt before the new version of *Le Bourgeois gentilhomme*, is primarily interesting in its influence on Hofmannsthal greatest comedy, *Der Schwierige*. *Die Lästigen* owes as much to *Le Misanthrope* as to its true original. Even the lover's name is Alcest, and other characters are derived from the more important play. Orphise, in her relationship to Alcest (Eraste, originally) is a progenitrix of Helene Altenwyl in *Der Schwierige*. At the conclusion of *Die Lästigen*, she assumes the responsibility of guiding the future life of her lover, although he is "schwierig."

It is in *Der Schwierige*, then, that the influence of Molière, of the type originally stated in this article, can be clearly seen. *Der Schwierige* is drawing-room comedy, portraying the Austrian aristocracy after World War I, and its hero is not only characteristic of the artistic type per se, but has many of the facets of Hofmannsthal's own personality. Kari Bühl is charming, witty, brave and trustworthy, but he cannot adapt to society, cannot assume his responsibilities to his class and his country. He sees himself as a clown, like one Furlani, whose performance he admires:

Es spielt seine Rolle: er ist der, der alle begreifen, der allen helfen möchte und dabei alles in die größte Konfusion bringt. Er macht die dümmsten Lazzi,

[10] *Ibid.*, 318.
[11] *Ibid.*, 336.

die Galerie kugelt sich vor Lachen, und dabei behält er eine élégance, eine Diskretion, man merkt, daß er sich selbst und alles, was auf der Welt ist, respektiert. Er bringt alles durcheinander, wie Kraut und Rüben; wo er hingeht, geht alles drunter und drüber, und dabei möchte man rufen: "Er hat ja recht."[12]

Everyone sees a different mask of Kari's: the mask that fits his need. Only Helene, the understanding woman, can remove the mask, the clown's makeup, and bring out the real man behind it.

Only few traces of Molière are left in this comedy; some of the minor characters, for example, Neuhoff, show characteristics reminiscent of the French dramatist. But this is a great comedy, as representative of the Vienna of its day, socially, historically, and psychologically, as *Le Misanthrope* was characteristic of the France of its time. Although there is no direct influence of Molière on *Der Schwierige*, the pattern of Hofmannsthal's development as a comic writer shows it would not have been the same play without the apprenticeship he had served, translating, adapting, and finally transmuting Molière's works. Hofmannsthal was a great writer in a way very different from that of Molière. The social and educational background of both men and their personalities were diametrically opposed (to say nothing of their actual physical environments). This made successful translation or adaptation very difficult; it is almost impossible for one artist to completely subordinate his talent to that of another. But before working with Molière, Hofmannsthal could not write first-rate comedy; afterwards, he could and did. He had learned much.

Hofmannsthal wrote, in his "Worte zum Gedächtnis Molières" (1922), which was to be spoken by an actress, dressed as Toinette, as a prologue to *Le Malade imaginaire*, that what he particularly admired was Molière's "Verstehen der Menschen, nicht so, wie einer bloß mit dem Kopfe versteht, sondern mit dem ganzen Ich und allen Eingeweiden, daß er im Verstehen sich mit meinte, und sich selber mit verspottete, denn er hielt es, was des Verhalten im Leben anlagt, für das Richtige, daß jeder mit Anstand seinem Geschäfte nachgehe, und das seinige war nun einmal, die Leute lachen zu machen."[13] It is the humanity of Molière and his ability to make people laugh, not his greatness or spiritual values, that Hofmannsthal admired, and these are the qualities that could and can influence the writers of our century in their development in the comic theater.

---

[12] Hugo von Hofmannsthal, *Gesammelte Werke in Einzelausgaben: Lustspiele II* (Stockholm, 1948), 343.

[13] *Ibid., Prosa IV* (Frankfurt am Main, 1966), 82–83.

Molière, Central
and Eastern Europe

The penetration of Molière into those regions beyond the borders of the antique Roman state represents an historical reoccurence of the cultural diffusion that created the Romania—that union of classic and barbarian whence issued modern occidental culture and literature. That Moscow has been named a third Rome lends support to the supposition that Molière would have been well received in Russia. If we conceive Molière as one epitome of the classic and, by extension, French spirit, then it becomes evident that his role in the enlightenments of Poland and Hungary is no more than a repetition climaxing tendencies of cosmopolitanism already present in those countries.

The essay on Molière in Hungary provides the reader with a survey of the dramatist's fortunes, bringing the story to its logical conclusion by describing the patrimony as it has been received by Marxist critics. In the second article, C. S. Durer delineates Molière's reception in Poland, where native writers seem to have been especially quick to accept the inspiration of the Frenchman. The Russian Griboiedov is the topic of the last essay; its author is less sympathetic toward the view of Marxist critics than is Professor Katona, author of the first essay in the section.

MOLIÈRE IN HUNGARY: HIS REPUTATION

Anna Katona

The discovery of Molière in Hungary coincided with the twenty-three years' bloom of the Hungarian Enlightenment.[1] The whole movement was inspired by an increasing resistance against the colonial state of the country under Hapsburg rule and a growing insistence on the use of the Hungarian language instead of German among the aristocracy. The year 1772 marks the beginning of the Hungarian Enlightenment when György Bessenyei, the most important of the writers inspired by the new ideas of the French, entered the literary scene. In 1795 a progressive political conspiracy led by Ignác Martinovics came to be uncovered, and most of the radical Hungarian intellectuals were either executed or imprisoned. A glorious period came to a tragic and rapid end.

Besides political aims there were two main, closely interwoven objectives in the minds of the leaders of the Enlightenment in Hungary: the development of the language, and the creation of theater. As the periodical *Magyar Kurir* stated in 1790, "in order to make the language more flexible and more widely used, play-acting should be employed as a skating exercise for the language." Considering the entire lack of original works, it is no wonder that translating became one of the main tasks of the writers of Enlightenment in Hungary. Ferenc Kazinczy, one of the leading minds of the country, made it plain in his recollections: "In my lifetime it was perhaps best to translate well, and better than that, if possible, the goal was to give an example in creative work as well as in speech, and through both to ennoble literary taste."

Molière enjoyed great popularity with the learned of the country, and György Szerdahelyi, a university professor, explained in 1784 in his *Poesis dramatica*: "In Misanthropo et Eruditis Mulieribus, et alibi frequentius pictor, ac philosophus est admirabilis."

The first translations close to the original were the works of protestant

---

[1] It is the author's aim to condense the material and to concentrate on the main issues rather than all details.

college students in Nagyenyed. Their Hungarian versions of *Le Mariage forcé* and *Le Médecin malgré lui* of 1791 appeared in print the following year in the so-called *Próba* (*Experiment*). The preface testifies to the patriotic zeal of the students: "We aspire to no praise, nor are we inspired by a mean desire for any recompense: we performed our work out of love for our dear mother tongue and wanted to follow the example set by our elders."[2] The *Médecin malgré lui* was first performed in Debrecen in 1799 and has remained one of the most popular Molière plays in this country.

Two additional accurate translations of the late eighteenth century are to be mentioned: that of the *Fourberies de Scapin* in 1793 and of *Amphitryon*, which did not appear in print, in 1794. Much more important, however, and much more typical are the free adaptations of the time. Important because they prepared the way for original Hungarian writing and typical because many a Molière play came to be produced in the twentieth century on the Hungarian stage with rather close translation but free interpretation. School dramas prepared by priests paved the way for play-acting in Hungary. Molière became popular in the eighteenth century among Hungarian Jesuits and other teaching orders, and the free adaptations of some of his plays derive from this fact.

Kristóf Simai produced in 1792 a Hungarian version of *L'Avare*. The scene is set in Rév-Komárom, Simai's birthplace; the time is that of Emperor Leopold I; and the family is dispersed because of Thököly's and Rákóczi's War of Independence. In the same year Simai published a free version of *Sganarelle ou le cocu imaginaire*. Hungarian names and circumstances misled literary critics, and it took a century before the play was proved to be an adaptation.[3] The performances had great success in Debrecen, Buda, and Kolozsvár. Simai's principle served the needs of the time. His Hungarized versions of Molière, with their sometimes rude and vulgar language, provided the first theater groups with amusing plays which caught the interest of the first Hungarian theater audiences.

The Jesuit Péter Illei followed in the same line. He revived the first Molière play ever performed in Hungary, *Le Bourgeois gentilhomme*. An adaptation of this comedy was produced in Eger in 1769 as a school performance in which there was no love plot and no female roles. Jourdain appeared as a "labanc," a name given to those traitors who, in Rákóczi's War of Independence against the Hapsburgs, fought on the Austrian

---

[2] For a detailed analysis of the two translations see Leo Weiner, *Az első magyar Molière-forditások* (Budapest: Fritz Armin, 1917).
[3] In 1893 by István Ernyei.

side. In his 1798 version Illei called Jourdain "Péter Tornyos." The nickname "tornyos" ("having a tower") was given at that time to rich people whose towered homes bore witness to their wealth. In Illei's adaptation the play strongly criticised contemporary social circumstances in Hungary.

The few Molière plays translated or freely adapted in the late eighteenth century enjoyed enormous popularity and were performed all over the country by wandering troupes. It is worth mentioning that Mihály Csokonai, the greatest poet of the Hungarian Enlightenment, translated a scene from *Le Malade imaginaire* under the title of *Doctorandus*. We know of a 1792 performance of *Le Malade imaginaire*. The name of the translator is uncertain; he might have been László Kelemen, who established the first short-lived but continuing (1790–1796) theater in the Hungarian capital. The uncovering of the Martinovics plot put an end to the literary bloom of the Hungarian Enlightenment, to Kelemen's theater, and in consequence of all this, to Molière's first triumph on the Hungarian stage.

Ferenc Kazinczy continued his translating activity during the hard years of his imprisonment, but his rather free versions of *Le Médecin malgré lui* and *Le Mariage forcé* came to be printed only in the 1830's in the series *Foreign Stage*. Kazinczy, the great modernizer of the Hungarian language who came under heavy attacks for his rather refined and sophisticated speech, gave in these translations irrefutable evidence of his ability to use highly popular language. He did so out of love for the Hungarian tongue. During his imprisonment he confessed: "Sie ist meine Freude, sie ist mein Idol, in das ich verliebt bin." The early twenties witnessed the appearance of a new Hungarian *L'Avare*, the work of Gábor Döbrentei, an adaptation rather than translation with notes and a brief survey of Molière's life and career. Most probably inspired by Rousseau's criticism, Döbrentei objected to the moral tendency of the play and even omitted some scenes he considered indecent. Ferenc Kölcsey, the great Romantic poet who enjoyed Molière when he was sixteen and never ceased to admire his genius, objected to *Tartuffe*, because, as he put it, "moral weakness can be exposed in a comedy but never evil."

These few instances of criticism were chosen to illustrate that the Romantic Age in Hungary was rather unfavorable to Molière in its basic tendency. It should be emphasized, however, that the Romantic writer József Bajza, the first director of the National Theater, duly appreciated French drama, and Molière's career on the stage of the National Theater was initiated by him. There was, however, a great obstacle to performing

Molière. Though Kazinczy's two adaptations are still the standard Hungarian translations in Gyula Illyés's artistic revision, they were and are the exceptions. The Hungarian language developed so rapidly in the early nineteenth century due to the cultural and literary revival of the Reform Age in the thirties that late eighteenth-century translations became entirely obsolete and irrelevant. One of the greatest tasks performed by the literary society called Kisfaludy Társaság in the second half of the century was the production of an entire Hungarian Molière edition, the work of twenty years (1863–83) and many poets. The Kisfaludy translation is close to the original in form, also; the eighteenth century had disregarded form entirely, and prose prevailed in all plays.

János Arany, a great poet and translator of Shakespeare, was one of the masterminds behind the Molière program. And yet critics and writers in Hungary were of a rather divided mind about Molière in the second half of the nineteenth century. Literary criticism was conditioned by the political atmosphere during the years of oppression in the fifties and sixties after the defeat of the War of Independence of 1848/49. A kind of "poetical" realism emerged with a strong moral bias, in which social forces were replaced by moral ones, and which required the final triumph of the moral order. Another important feature of that "poetical" realism was its strong emphasis on ideals. The defeated nation that lost its illusions after the catastrophe of 1849 badly needed ideals that would keep hope and patriotic feeling alive.

It is rewarding to consider how contradictory reactions to Molière fitted into the above described pattern of the idea of a literature that should be morally and nationally conditioned. Imre Vahot conceded in 1853 in *Magyar Thália*, a short story of the world stage, that in contrast to tragedy, French comedy shows a healthy tendency to display national character. Yet Molière, who played for the king at court, seemed repulsive to him. The most important critical mind of the time, Pál Gyulai, objected strongly to Corneille and Racine for turning their backs on national subjects. He stated, "Only the French comedy took its subject matter from French life, since being obliged to deal with character, it could not possibly forgo dealing with the nation. In consequence, the French classical comedy is much more national in its character than the tragedy, if only because of its subject." And Tamás Szana, who in 1878 published the first book on Molière in Hungary, praised *L'Avare* for its moral teaching and appreciated *Tartuffe* as a skillful union of the real with the ideal, a play in which the moral order comes to be restored in the end. With the first performance of *Le Misanthrope* in the National Theater in 1869, one of the most important contemporary periodicals, *Fővárosi Lapok*, described Molière as the supreme patriotic poet of his age. And since wandering theater groups performed a patriotic task in Hungary, bringing culture to far-off places and keeping up the national spirit, it is no wonder that actors should have admired the French playwright-actor as their ideal in 1860 (*Magyar Szinházi Lapok*).

Pál Gyulai not only pointed to the national character of French classical comedy but he also vehemently defended Molière against Rousseau's moral attacks, because, as Gyulai put it, "no comedy can be written about virtuous characters," and the tendency of the play should be judged by different means. Gyulai strongly refuted Schlegel's artistic objections to the French playwright as unjust; according to the Hungarian critic, Schlegel simply did not understand Harpagon's character.

In the late nineteenth century, academic French studies made an important step forward in Hungary. The well known writer and critic Zsolt Beöthy wrote about Molière; Agoston Greguss lectured at the University of Budapest on him; and Gyula Haraszti, a great pioneer of French studies, published a two volume work on Molière in 1897. Haraszti still insisted on the necessity of the moral bias and emphasized that Molière aspired to more than the role of entertainer; he wished to pass moral judgment on his characters. Haraszti also praised Molière for accommodating both the national and universal human in his plays.

The eighties and nineties of the last century witnessed a growth in the popularity of Molière's plays.[4] His fame came to be established on the stage of the National Theater under Ede Szigligeti who in 1874 produced *Le Mariage forcé*, *Sganarelle*, *Les Femmes savantes* and *L'Ecole des femmes*. Szigligeti was convinced that an experiment to introduce French tragedy on the Hungarian stage was doomed to fail. "We should prefer to learn the masterpieces of Shakespeare and Molière—there are still enough enough of them!" he said. Ede Paulay followed the path of his predecessor, adding to the list *Le Misanthrope*, *L'Avare*, *L'Ecole des maris*, *Le Bourgeois gentilhomme*, *George Dandin*, *La Critique de l'Ecole des femmes*.

About twelve Molière plays were on the repertory of the National Theater by the end of the century, and Károly Szász's enthusiastic view was shared by the best minds of the country: "In Molière more than in any other writer of the world we can follow up the whole development of an

---

[4] Péter Nagy, *A francia klasszikus dráma fogadtatása Magyarországon* (Budapest, 1943).

entire literary form from its starting point to its perfection. Molière's comedies comprise in themselves the whole history of the comedy, all the stages of its rise."

Most of the great poets and writers of the early twentieth century in this country had a great reverance for Molière. Endre Ady, who modernized Hungarian lyrical poetry, greeted the performance of *George Dandin* in 1905 with the following words: "Dear National Theater, well, we are no cannibals. We are overjoyed to greet a Hungarian genius if there is any. But in the interest of great playwrights to come, please, do perform Molière." In 1912 the poet Árpád Tóth was pleasantly surprised to see the bust of the French writer at the opening of the theater in his native Debrecen. The great novelist Zsigmond Móricz translated *L'Avare* himself, reviewed several performances, and planned to translate the entire Molière into enjoyable Hungarian so that provincial theaters would start playing him on a large scale. His plan was never realized.

During the short months of the first Hungarian Communist Republic in 1919, Molière was among the playwrights produced with inexpensive entrance fees for the masses. But in the years of political reaction to follow, in the early twenties, the decisive voice was that of a Kálmán Harsányi, who protested against the performance of *Tartuffe* and who deliberately emphasized a certain "air of coolness" surrounding Molière performances in Hungary. In 1943 the evenings that *Tartuffe* was on the stage were marked as a sort of political demonstration against all the hypocrites who supported fascist rule.[5]

There is a strange paradox in Molière's reputation in Hungary. His name, as we have seen, was closely connected with the emergence of theater life and the reform of the Hungarian language. He has always been a permanent figure on the stage of the National Theater, and the important literary society, the Kisfaludy Társaság, dedicated a great deal of work and energy to the translation of his *oeuvre*. And yet Molière's popularity lagged far behind that of Shakespeare, who, ever since Arany's *Hamlet* and *Midsummer's Night's Dream* in the nineteenth century, has been considered a Hungarian classic. Géza Laczkó meditated upon Molière's checkered career in 1922 in the literary periodical *Nyugat* on the occasion of the three hundredth anniversary of his birth. He found the answer to the enigma in historical circumstances. Molière was, after all, a playwright of the French court; his whole activity was inseparable from the favor

---

[5] Gábor Mihályi: *Molière* (Budapest: Müvelt Nép Könyvkiadó, 1954).

and disfavor of the king. His plays are about the teeming aristocracy at court and the emerging bourgeoisie. Due to historical circumstances Hungary came to be governed from Vienna. Consequently, there was no royal court in the Hungarian capital, and the whole way of life connected with such a court was unfamiliar and uninteresting to the people. The Hungarian aristocracy rushed to Vienna, and the German-speaking life they led was in a way strangely severed from that of the people.

Laczkó also complained about the quality of the available translations and described them as second rate as compared to the Hungarian Shakespeare, the work of our most talented writers and poets. His remarks was truly justified, but the fact should not be overlooked that in the first half of the century there were many new initiatives in this field. Special mention should be made here of Gyula Hevesi, the producer, playwright, and translator, who excelled both in translating several plays of Molière into up-to-date Hungarian and in producing them on the stage in an entirely new conception, with a great emphasis on theatrical means, in which the deliberate strain for effect was easily recognized. These performances, however, no longer used the Kisfaludy translations. Instead the two volumes of *Molière remekei* (*Masterpieces of Molière*, 1901–08) provided the text. Five plays were translated by Hevesi himself, and *L'Etourdi*, by the poet Dezső Kosztolányi, should be singled out as an outstanding achievement.

In criticism, besides the writings of the leading figure in French studies, Sándor Eckhardt, the voice of two excellent writers and sophisticated critics must not be overlooked even in this short survey. Mihály Babits's *Az európai irodalom története* (*The History of European Literature*) and Antal Szerb's *A világirodalom története* (*The History of World Literature*) were standard reference books in the hands of progressive intellectuals. Babits described Molière as the representative of the rational mind of the people and praised him for being national and contemporary at the same time. Szerb also emphasized his rationality, conceived of him as a forerunner of the Enlightenment. To him Molière's comedies were more shattering than the great French tragedies. Molière also entered *belles-lettres*. In 1938 Imre Balassa published his novel *Molière*, ending with the description of the funeral in secret. Sándor Góth's *Ha Molière naplót irt volna* (*If Molière had Written a Diary*) appeared in 1943, calling the French playwright the martyr of love and stage.

Two Molière performances before World War II are of a special interest because of their free interpretation which prepared the way for a new image of Molière after 1945 in Hungary. The radically minded *Kulturfront*, invited by the Théâtre du Peuple, performed *George Dandin* in Paris in 1937 and presented in the hero a revolting peasant who broke his bonds, and thus suggested resistance to the audience. In 1941 the same play came to be performed in the open by Communist actors for the masses in Budapest. It presented in the title-hero a true Hungarian peasant. However, performances were soon banned for political reasons.

After World War II there came an era of new Molière translations, new performances with an entirely new voice in criticism as well. The first Molière play produced after the war was *George Dandin*, acted in 1945 with workers as amateur performers in the Jókai Szinkör. Early performances of *L'Avare* in the Madách Theater and *George Dandin* and *Les Femmes savantes* in the National Theater show the struggle between two different conceptions of producing Molière for a mass audience in Hungary. Harpagon appeared in Hungarian cloth and spoke a robust, vulgar, popular Hungarian in order to gain easy access to the audience. In the National Theater the plays remained on French soil in seventeenth century France and proved to be of eternal value in their unchanged form. Yet the temptation prevailed to adapt, if not the text, at least the message. The most recent productions by Tamás Major, who was instrumental in the abortive *George Dandin* performance of 1941, suggest that Molière is relevant to the Hungary of the seventies. Major, the best Hungarian Tartuffe ever, chose for the National Theater's 1972 program *Amphitryon* and *Les Femmes savantes*. In *Amphitryon* Major discovered a valid instrument for mocking the irrationality of fashionable absurd plays and at the same time an opportunity for striking at those who, in any society, attempt to create and live by their own laws. In the performance of *Les Femmes savantes* Major wanted to hit at the growing number of false geniuses in Hungarian cultural life.

Between 1945 and 1972 Molière editions appeared in several inexpensive paperbacks. Yet the most important achievement in publishing the French playwright was the two-volume edition of his *oeuvre* in 1965, with notes and an entirely new, artistic translation. Among those who participated, the names of some notable poets should be mentioned: Gyula Illyés, István Vas, Lőrinc Szabó, László Kálnoky, and Gábor Devecseri.

Molière continued to survive in *belles-lettres* as well. Miklós Rónaszegi published in 1965 a novel entitled *Keserü komédia* (*Bitter Comedy*). Like that of Balassa it ends with the funeral, but the tone is entirely different. Rónaszegi emphasizes the sympathy of the people for Molière.

In criticism we must concentrate on the intensive effort to find a Marxist interpretation to Molière's *oeuvre*. The start was made by Gyula Illyés, a French-educated Hungarian poet with a poor peasant background. In his interpretation of *L'Avare* in *Válasz* (1949), Illyés pointed out that Molière's characters do not change, and that Molière wanted to change society rather than individuals. The true *monstre* was not Harpagon but society and the values which it contributed to the shaping of the hero's character. György Somlyó reviewed the 1949 performance of *Tartuffe* in *Fórum* at the time when the Mindszenty conspiracy was on everyone's mind. The anticlerical aspect of the play came to be overemphasized and even distorted. In his final conclusion Somlyó considered the play a deliberate blow at the entire moral and material structure of feudal society. István Vas described the play later (*Évek és Művek*, 1958) as antireligious, rational, and enlightened. Károly Szalay analyzed the difference between humor and satire in *Valóság* (1960). He ranged Molière among the satirists who, according to his view, differed from the humorists through their more conscious ideology, by which they condemn the behavior of a certain social class. Marcell Benedek discovered something of the adolescent attitude in *Le Misanthrope* because of its unforgiving bitterness (*Hajnaltól alkonyig*, 1966). In an analysis of several plays in *Ingyen lakoma* (1964), Illyés comes to the conclusion that Molière was a revolutionary who wanted to change the social structure, and who played to the king with the interest of the charwoman in his mind.

Gábor Mihályi's *Molière* (1954) is the only monograph of the postwar years. It.brings a fresh approach to many problems, yet the effort to make Molière a plebeian sort of writer is unmistakable. In the author's view Molière has at last become part of the cultural heritage of the Hungarian people and at the same time a valid weapon in the class struggle helping to unmask the enemy. It is interesting to read Mihályi's 1967 review of a new performance of *L'Avare* in *Nagyvilág*. He seems to have lost his former enthusiasm for the French playwright who is now undeservedly ranked with assigned readings.

This brief reference to Mihályi has a certain relevance to our topic, i.e. Molière's highly ambiguous reputation in Hungary. The discovery of Molière in this country was closely connected with the pioneering of Hungarian theater, in a way a political issue in the fight for cultural independence. In the late nineteenth century the Hungarian National Theater was second only to the Comédie-Française in the number of Molière plays in its repertory. There are three different Hungarian versions of his *oeuvre*, one from the nineteenth century, one from the early twentieth, and the best

from the sixties, György Kósa composed an opera from *Tartuffe*; Aurél
Kern wrote music to *L'Amour médecin* in 1907, and György Ránki to *Don
Juan* in 1957. In all centuries Molière was used as an easy reference among
writers. To give a few examples, the eighteenth-century letter writer
Kelemen Mikes used phrases from *Les Femmes savantes* in one of his
writings, and the nineteenth-century poet László Tompa angrily quoted
from *George Dandin* in a letter. In 1912 Árpád Tóth compared the lack of
medical care for the people to the practices of Molière's false doctors.
After 1945 Molière came to be used as an agent in the class struggle and
was produced by wandering theater groups to village audiences. In spite
of all this, or perhaps because of it, there is a disturbing element in
Molière's reputation in Hungary. In a country where Corneille and Racine
have never been acceptable, their great contemporary, Molière, has
become an attractive but rather strange phenomenon. He has never
achieved the popularity of Shakespeare. Perhaps his serving rather too
often as a political tool prevented him from becoming a cultural asset
with the status of Shakespeare.

MOLIÈRE AND POLISH COMEDY

C. S. Durer

Before addressing myself to the vast subject of the relation of Polish comedy to Molière, which within the limits of this essay I can only discuss in its
most essential aspects, I should like to make two broad statements in order
to clarify the reasons for the extraordinary impact which Molière had in
Poland. First, ever since the seventeenth century France has been the
country with which Polish writers felt a particularly close affinity, and in
the following centuries the cultural links between the two countries grew
to be even stronger and more diverse. French literature of the eighteenth
and nineteenth centuries exerted a powerful influence on Polish literature
of the same period and French ideas quickly found their way to Poland.
This receptivity to French letters, and the generally good reception which
was accorded to them, explain in part the vogue of Molière in Poland,
particularly in the eighteenth century, and his quick and ready acceptance
by Polish playwrights and theatrical public alike. Secondly, we should be
aware of the relatively late beginnings of drama, tragedy as well as comedy,
in Polish literature, a literature which otherwise follows the same historical
course and is responsive to the same movements and trends as the main
Western-European literatures. The paucity of Polish comedy in the first
half of the eighteenth century, for instance, and the absence of a strong
native comic tradition at this time are responsible in the next half of the
century for numerous borrowings by Polish playwrights from foreign authors. Molière occupies an important place among them and finds many
Polish imitators.

This history of the crucial relationship of Polish comedy to Molière
comprises two distinct phases: (1) the latter part of the eighteenth century
when a number of Polish playwrights were reforming the Polish stage and
founding a new Polish comedy, often using Molière as a model. We are
confronted in this instance by numerous translations, adaptations, and imitations of Molière, showing the strong and direct influence of the French
master; although towards the end of the eighteenth century, as Polish
comedy becomes less dependent on foreign models, plots and themes from
Molière's plays are being reworked in a new, more original manner. (2)

In the first part of the nineteenth century, a different aspect of this relationship can be seen in the comedies of the greatest Polish comedy writer, Aleksander Fredro (1793–1876). Molière's influence on Fredro is often secondhand, through Goldoni and Beaumarchais, and in the mature work of the Polish dramatist manifests itself in numerous analogies and affinities with Molière, often amounting to a reproduction and transformation of Molière's comic elements and the resetting of them into an otherwise original comedy of manners and character.

Molière came late to Poland. The first recorded production, that of *Le Bourgeois gentilhomme*, performed probably in the original, took place in 1687 in the country house of a Polish nobleman, Rafal Leszczynski. From that date on, plays of Molière were performed in the houses of the nobility, but these productions were infrequent, and in any case relatively unimportant for the development of the Polish comedy. It is only around the middle of the eighteenth century that numerous plays of Molière began to be translated and adapted to the Polish stage, and this new trend was initiated by an adaptation of *Les Amants magnifiques* (1749) by Urszula Radziwill. The same translator adapted several other plays of Molière, among them *Le Médecin malgré lui*, which was produced in 1753, and Polish versions of Molière's plays followed in great numbers.

In November 1765, a year after the coronation of King Stanislaw August Poniatowski, the Polish National Theatre was founded in Warsaw, and the first play produced on its boards, *The Obtruders* (*Natręci*) by Józef Bielawski, was modeled on Molière's *Les Fâcheux*. The Stanislavian period, 1764–95, was also the period of the Polish Enlightenment, and it marked a new intense interest in the drama. The king, a patron of the arts and a *philosophe*, in touch with Western intellectual movements, had taken part in theatrical productions in his youth, and throughout his life showed a keen interest in the stage. At his initiative the National Theater was founded, and foreign troupes, mostly French and Italian, were brought to Warsaw, while the king's special ambition was to promote a new indigenous Polish comedy.

In fact, the new Polish comedy was born during these Stanislavian years, and the translations and adaptations of Molière played a very significant part in its birth. As in the rest of Europe at this time, so in Poland, it is often difficult to distinguish between the imitations and adaptations of Molière's works on the one hand, and the translations of them on the other, since the Stanislavian "translators" shared in the general contemporary European trend of adapting foreign plays to suit the taste and the dramatic requirements of their country. Eighteenth-century Polish pronouncements about translating Molière are of interest since they tell us how free the translating practices of these devotees of foreign drama were. The first Polish theoretician of drama, Adam Kazimierz Czartoryski, whose views have much in common with those of J.-B. Dubos, and who was a dramatist in his own right, wrote in the preface to his play *The Marriageable Maiden* (*Panna na Wydaniu*, 1774) about the advisability of adapting foreign plays to suit particular national conditions, adding that Molière's Harpagon could not appeal vividly to Polish audiences unless he had been "polonized" and unless the model had been taken "from our usurer dealing with contracts." In the same spirit, Jan Baudouin (1735–1822), adapter of numerous French, English, and German plays, wrote in the preface to his translation-adaptation of *Le Tartuffe*, begun in 1775 and finished in the following year:

> I have been taken to task by some people that in my translation I departed too far from the original. How could I have adapted this comedy to our customs and our national taste, had I not made substantial changes in it? The manners and customs of the previous age, when this comedy was written, are not in the least compatible with those of Frenchmen, let alone with those of the Poles of today. Because the first two acts struck me as being a little cold, I supplied Fanatycki [Orgon in the original] with a servant who by his waggish manner of speaking brightens up those scenes which are in need of it. The bailiff who takes possession of the house—which does not figure in the original [*sic*]—was a great favorite with the audience, and especially with the esteemed members of the legal profession who told me that I had created him well. Hence I do not regret the labor spent on this play, because its success went far beyond my expectations.[1]

In the same confident manner Wojciech Boguslawski (1757–1829), a famous actor, one of the directors of the Polish National Theater, and author of over eighty plays—most of them adaptations from the French and Italian—justified the changes which he made in his version of *L'École des femmes*. Boguslawski supplied Agnès with a maid and Horace with a man-servant in order to give this play "a greater sense of movement" and to resolve, as he says, a "great contradiction in Molière's play."[2]

Similarly, other eighteenth-century Polish translators of Molière added or cut out characters from his plays, and took other liberties with the text.

---

[1] My translation; Jan Baudouin, *Utwory Dramatyczne*, ed. Maria Wielanier (Warsaw, 1966), 50–51.
[2] Wojciech Boguslawski, "Uwagi nad Komedją *Szkola Kobiet*" (Comments about the Comedy *School for Wives*), in the collective volume *Teatr Narodowy 1765–1794*, ed. Janina Pawlowiczowa (Warsaw, 1967), 301–02.

Generally, Molière was polonized—the characters and the settings were Polish—and often farce was more important than in the original. In Baudouin's *Tartuffe*, for example, the added character of the man-servant intensifies the element of farce—the servant Trefnicki sets upon the bailiff in the fifth act and pushes him out-of-doors, to the accompaniment of much verbal abuse—the situation which in Molière is treated more discreetly. Baudouin's translation is in prose, and it is a very free translation indeed, from which large portions of the original have been eliminated, or else have been so rewritten that the verbal affinity with the original disappears. By our standards today it is not a good translation, though it was well received at the time and was important for the development of Polish comedy. Instead of the gracefulness and vigor of the French dialogue, we encounter in Baudouin's adaptation stilted language, frequently broken up, it is true, by brisk exchanges, but hardly conveying the comic qualities of the original. In the process characterization has been weakened, the tone of the play reduced to that of wrangles and altercations, with the effect that the Polish version is a new play, cruder and less witty than the French. Yet *Le Tartuffe* was offered in "Polish dress" and in a version for which Polish audiences could well be expected to show empathy; the plot has been transposed into Stanislavian times, allusions to contemporary political events in Poland have been added, and the flattery of the popular King Poniatowski surpassed that of Louis XIV.

Baudouin's adaptation of *Tartuffe*, imperfect as it was, had another significance. It was the very first in Poland, and it helped to create new interest in Molière, this time in his great comedies of character rather than in his farces and early comedies, which had been in vogue before. It is, in all probability, not an accident that in the 1780's the National Theater in Warsaw put on no less than thirteen comedies of Molière, among them *L'Avare* and *Dom Juan*.[3] The pendulum swung the other way, and a new facet of Molière's genius was displayed to the Polish audience.

Baudouin, Boguslawski, and to a lesser extent Czartoryski, were important as middlemen offering to the Polish public some of the treasures of the French dramatist. But to see a more concentrated impact of Molière in a situation which touches the very pulse of nascent Polish comedy, and which incidentally shows us another aspect of the eighteenth-century art of imitation and adaptation, we have to go to the comedies of Franciszek

---

[3] Jan Baudouin, *Utwory Dramatyczne*, ed. Maria Wielanier (Warsaw, 1966), Zbigniew Raszewski "Introduction," 19.

Bohomolec (1720–84), the most important dramatist of the Polish Enlightenment, and justly called the father of Polish comedy.

Bohomolec was a Jesuit priest, for many years professor of rhetoric in Warsaw, editor of the journal *Monitor*, which was one of the most influential organs of the Polish Enlightenment, and, in addition, a publicist and a historian. Between 1755 and 1760, twenty-five of his comedies appeared in print, and many of these were either modeled on the early farces and comedies of Molière, or else were straight adaptations of Molière's plays. These early pieces were written expressly for college productions, and they form part of the writer's extensive activity as educator and teacher of rhetoric. After the foundation of the Polish National Theater Bohomolec began to write plays to strengthen the repertoire of the new stage. The later comedies, eight in number, were published beginning in 1767. Bohomolec wrote exclusively comedies and farces, and while the influence of Molière can be seen clearly in his entire dramatic work, the early "college" comedies show a more direct indebtedness to the French master.

Men of fashion (*Kawalerowie Modni*), for instance, is an adaptation of *Les Precieuses ridicules*, and *The Polish Parisian* (*Paryżanin Polski*) is also heavily indebted to this early comedy of Molière. *Les Fourberies de Scapin* served as a model for several plays of Bohomolec in which the central character is Figlacki, a rogue and opportunist whose genealogy comes from Scapin, Muscarille and also from Arlecchino of the *commedia dell'arte*. The Figlacki comedies constitute the development and polonization of the character of Scapin, who in the Polish plays is not only a servant but becomes in turn a tutor, a man of fashion, and a politician. Bohomolec employs the figure of a rogue to suit his own pedagogical and didactic ends; he places his rogue in high places and through him appraises and satirizes contemporary society. Bohomolec's plan for comedy was conceived in the spirit of the Enlightenment, and was stated by him in the *Preface* to the 1755 edition of his works, where he says "the goal of comedy and its essential purpose is, after all, to correct bad customs by making them subject to laughter."

Faithful to this plan Bohomolec's numerous plays flay affectation, religious hypocrisy, opportunism, grossness, snobbery, superstition, and other vices—more explicitly, to be sure, and with a greater sense of a pedagogical mission than is the habit of Molière. But, on the satirical level, the parallel between the two dramatists is a close one, and some of the celebrated targets of Molière's attack—affectation in *Les Précieuses ri-*

dicules and *Les Femmes savantes*, hypocrisy in *Le Tartuffe*, miserliness in *L'Avare*, opportunism in *Le Bourgeois gentilhomme*, ridiculous provincial manners in *La Comtesse d'Escarbagnas*, are similar to the ones in which Bohomolec buries his satirical shafts.

Female roles are absent from Bohomolec's "college" plays, and any form of eroticism is scrupulously avoided. In adapting foreign comedies the formidable professor of rhetoric substituted male for female roles, and instead of amorous adventures provided other temptations—usually gambling, excessive eating, or self-adulation.

In *Men of Fashion* the characters of Magdelon and Cathos have been taken by two young male *précieux*, Tomasz and Jan. Affected in their speech, the two are also excessively attentive to their clothes and hairstyles, which they wear *à la pigeonne*, in accordance with the latest fashion. The play follows the French model closely, utilizing the disguise of the two servants as nobles, the whole farcical plot and the final chastisement of the two principals, adding only one new character, the tutor Martinier, who gives himself extraordinary airs, parades his slight knowledge of French, and is exposed in the end as a former stable boy and a thief. In *Men of Fashion* Bohomolec attacks French fashions, effeminacy in young men, their infatuation with foreign countries, and his play, produced for the first time probably in 1756, held the stage well and was frequently produced during the author's lifetime.

In order to see how Bohomolec adapts Molière to his own uses, it might be worth our while to examine corresponding portions of the two plays. Du Croisy and La Grange, and their Polish counterparts, Kleont and Dorant, have just left the house of their *précieux* friends, and they now review their reception. The opening situation is identical in both plays, and this is how the well known French dialogue runs:

Du croisy. Seigneur La Grange. . . .
La grange. Quoi?
D C. Regardez-moi un peu sans rire.
L G. Eh bien?
D C. Que dites-vous de notre visite? en êtes-vous fort satisfait?
L G. A votre avis, avons-nous sujet de l'être tous deux?
D C. Pas tout à fait, à dire vrai.
L C. Pour moi, je vous avoue que j'en suis tout scandalisé. A-t-on jamais vu, dites-moi, deux pecques provinciales faire plus les renchéries que celles-là, et deux hommes traités avec plus de mépris que nous? A peine ont-elles pu se résoudre à nous faire donner des sièges. Je n'ai jamais vu tant parler à l'oreille qu'elles ont fait entre elles, tant bâiller, tant se frotter les yeux, et demander tant de fois: «Quelle heure est-il?» Ont-elles répondu que oui et non à tout ce que

nous avons pu leur dire? Et ne m'avouerez-vous pas enfin que, quand nous aurions été les dernières personnes du monde, on ne pouvait nous faire pis qu'elles ont fait?

D C. Il me semble que vous prenez la chose fort à coeur.

L G. Sans doute, je l'y prends, et de telle façon, que je veux me venger de cette impertinence. Je connais ce qui nous a fait mépriser. L'air précieux n'a pas seulement infecté Paris, il s'est aussi répandu dans les provinces, et nos donzelles ridicules en ont humé leur bonne part. En un mot, c'est un ambigu de précieuse et de coquette que leur personne. Je vois ce qu'il faut être pour en être bien reçu; et si vous m'en croyez, nous leur jouerons tous deux une pièce qui leur fera voir leur sottise, et pourra leur apprendre à connaître un peu mieux leur monde.

As we remember, in his next speech La Grange will announce that he will send his servant, dressed as a nobleman, to the house of Gorgibus and in this way the trap will be set for the two *précieuses*. Let us look now at the corresponding portion of the first scene in Bohomolec' *Men of Fashion*, which I am translating as literally as possible.

KLEON. Well, Dorant, are you pleased with our visit?

DORANT. Let those yokels go and fry their eggs; I've never seen such conceited or stupid young men.

K. Conceit is always the result of foolishness. The more sensible and rational one is, the more humble and pleasant one is too.

D. All their talk was about fashions, about manners, about learning, and they know absolutely nothing about these things.

K. What surprises me most is that they've never been to Paris, and yet they want to do everything in the Parisian way.

D. It isn't only that they have never been to Paris, but they haven't even set foot in a large town before. This is the very first time that they have seen Warsaw, and yet they are ready to find fault with and criticize those who saw a good part of the world.

K. One could forgive them everything, except that being born in Poland, and owing her both life and worldly success, they can't bear their native country, and they scarcely count fellow Poles as members of the human race.

D. I wouldn't have gone to see them in the first place, had Anselm, their father, not asked me to do it.

K. The old man's on the lookout for other young men as refined as his sons, and he'd like to widen the circle of their acquaintances; but behaving as they do, they frighten everyone away.[4]

In this vein the conversation continues a little longer until Dorant announces the same intention as La Grange.

Clearly, Bohomolec has a copy of *Les Précieuses ridicules* by his elbow while writing *Men of Fashion*, and he adapts the French play to suit his educational purposes. The brief portion quoted here is a typical example of his technique of adaptation, and stress is laid in it, as we can see, on moral

---

[4] Franciszek Bohomolec, *Komedie Konwiktowe*, ed. Jan Kott (Warsaw, 1959), 427–28.

and patriotic values, and not merely on ridiculous affected manners, which are the main subject of conversation in the French play. *Men of Fashion* is, in fact, a *pièce a thèse* calling for a return to native customs and advocating rationality and decorum. The Polish excerpt is, we notice at once, didactic in tone, while the French is not, and this vein of didacticism will continue to the very end. Differently constructed also in the two plays is the dialogue, which, in the Polish passage quoted above as well as in the rest of the play, consists of short speeches very rarely exceeding three or, at the most, four short sentences, thus contrasting with the occasionally longer expository speeches of Cathos and Magdelon. While this stylistic pattern gives the play a certain sense of quick movement, gone are the spontaneity, and indeed much of the energy and humor of *Les Précieuses ridicules*, the last of which is sustained both by longer passages, serving as examples of affectation, and also by farce and surprise. The language of *Men of Fashion*, vivid and colloquial as it is at times, resembles that of a rhetorical exercise, and is subordinated to the author's didactic program.

Like the other Stanislavian comedy writers, Bohomolec utilized to the full the resources of Molière's farce, and his plays often employ the burlesque and exaggeration. In *The Polish Parisian* much of the humor derives from the foppish behavior of the main character, who strikes ridiculous poses, speaks French to people who do not understand that language, and is an accomplished master of yawning and sneezing *à la Parisienne*. Satirist and reformer that he is, adapting Molière's satire to indigenous Polish subjects, Bohomolec ridicules the faults of the contemporary Polish society; and instead of the universal pronouncements of *honnêtes hommes* found in Molière, of the common-sensical advice of a Philinte or a Cléante, the Polish plays urge a return to native manners and customs. A representative of the Enlightenment (the Polish writer's cultural program has much in common with that of Joseph Addison and Gotthold Ephraim Lessing), Bohomolec narrows and nationalizes the scope of Molière's satire, while presenting much of his comic mechanism.

A different aspect of Molière's influence appears in the work of one of the most talented playwrights of the Stanislavian period, Franciszek Zablocki (1754–1821), who like many of his fellow dramatists, began his career by translating and adapting foreign plays, mostly French and Italian. In the course of his intense activity Zablocki supplied the Polish stage with many adaptations of Corneille, Beaumarchais and other well known dramatists, in addition to Molière. His fragment of *Le Misanthrope* appeared in 1774, *Le Médecin malgré lui* in 1782, and the much praised and frequently performed *Amphitryon* in 1783. All in all, Zablocki left behind him over seventy plays—most of them free translations or adaptations. Important as this facet of his work is for the later generations of Polish playwrights, it need not occupy us any longer here, since Zablocki's translations are similar to those of Baudouin and Bohomolec, though they generally lack the latter's didactic bias.

However, Zablocki is also the author of *The Fop Suitor* (*Fircyk w Zalotach*, 1781), still today the best known comedy of the Polish Enlightenment and artistically far superior to other Polish comedies of the period. There is no doubt that in the author of *The Fop Suitor* the sense of artistic independence was stronger than in his dramatic contemporaries, and, while examining the foreign sources and models which contributed to the creation of this delightful comedy, we face a situation similar to the one we face in discussing the Italian sources of early Shakespearian comedy, or, for that matter, Molière's own use of the *commedia dell' arte*. In *The Fop Suitor* foreign plots and situations are employed, but they have been given a new comic dimension, and the play, though indebted to Molière and to other dramatists, is in its comic vision fundamentally original.

The tightly controlled action of Zablocki's comedy occupies one day and is impelled by the courtship of the Fop, a young man of pleasure, and Podstolina, an attractive and wealthy widow. The Fop pays a social call on Aryst, Podstolina's brother, at his country estate, and the courtship takes place there. It is marred by suspicions and misunderstandings—the Fop imagines that Podstolina loves another man, while in reality she secretly loves him, and she in turn is led to believe that her brother's guest is secretly paying court to a rich countess living in the neighborhood—until just before the play ends, all the misunderstandings and false imputations are dispelled, and the two principals declare their love for each other and are about to marry.

The Fop Suitor is based on Romagnesi's play *Le Petit maître amoureux*, but artistically exceeds it by far. In addition it shows marked affinities with several of Molière's plays, *Sganarelle ou le Cocu imaginaire*, *Le Dépit amoureux*, and *Le Misanthrope*, in particular. In both *Le Cocu imaginaire* and the Polish play, jealousy takes hold of the main characters, and the monologues of Sganarelle and of his wife, in which they inveigh against each other's treachery—imaginary as it turns out—are paralleled by the monologues of the Fop and of Podstolina, who also imagine that they have been deceived. Similarly, the amorous misunderstandings of Eraste and Lucille in *Le Dépit amoureux*, especially the former's complaints about his beloved's fickleness and addressed to his valet Gros-Rèné, show resemblance to the speeches of the Fop. There are other analogies, too, between Molière and *The Fop Suitor*. Dom Juan's ringing declaration of his libertinism and his view of the world as being fundamentally amoral are echoed, in a lower key, by the Fop's cynical judgment of humanity seen as a mixed bag of cheats and gamblers. Still another sign of Zablocki's indebtedness to Molière can be seen in the two resourceful servants of *The Fop Suitor*, Emptyhead and Whistlehead, who are often more clearheaded than their masters and are conceived in the tradition of Molière's Scapin and Sganarelle.

In the annals of Polish comedy, *The Fop Suitor* shows a new, heretofore unknown, affiliation with Molière. It borrows farcical elements from both Molière and, of course, from Romagnesi and transforms them into more mature comic ones, providing an excellent characterization of the main figures and probing more deeply than either *Le Cocu imaginaire* or *Le Dépit amoureux* does into the psychology of people in love and who as a result of this love are prone to inexplicable fits of jealousy and anger. It is, in essence, the psychology of *The Fop Suitor* no less than its careful and brilliant characterization that brings this eighteenth-century Polish comedy close to Molière's great comedies of character—paradoxically so, since its plot, based on misconceptions and misunderstandings, resembles Molière's farce and early comedy. After Zablocki no important Polish comedy will be a mere adaptation of Molière, no matter how skillful or innovative. From now on the influence of the French dramatist will be subtler and less direct, and will constitute an integral part of the already well developed tradition of Polish comedy, which in its early stages of existence Molière helped so much to enrich and develop. This influence, moreover, will relate far less than before to plot construction and individual situations, and much more to the art of characterization and the complexities of Molière's comic spirit. These considerations take us straight to the work of Aleksander Fredro (1793–1876).

Fredro was born in Galicia, Southern Poland, and in 1809 he joined the Polish Legion, which fought on the side of Napoleon. As a cavalry officer he saw service in the *Grande Armée* and, after Napoleon's retreat from Moscow, he accompanied the remnants of Napoleon's army back to Paris, where he stayed for several months. In the French capital Fredro came to know the French theater intimately, especially comedy, since he showed himself indifferent to tragedy, as being too stilted and declamatory. The Polish comedy writer knew the work of Molière well, which together with that of Goldoni exerted a varied and strong influence upon him. Fredro, it should be remembered, is an anomaly in Polish and, to a lesser extent, in European comedy. His most important creative period, 1822–35, coincides with the triumph of Polish Romanticism and with the Romantic Movement in other European countries, but his great comedies have little in common with romantic ideology. Practically all of Fredro's plays contain love themes, but these are subjected to an ironic scrutiny, and are, for the most part, set in masterly constructed plots. His best plays are marked by a delicate balance between characterization and intrigue, so that neither dominates the other, and although several of them show marked similarities to the plays of Molière, they are wholly original. Tender and even sentimental as some of these comedies are, at least in part, they are also analytic and full of detachment. Fredro's comic vision often shows an affinity to that of Jane Austen, another great humorist whose work defied the spirit of the age. The relationship between this acknowledged master of Polish comedy and Molière has occupied numerous Polish literary historians and critics, among them the greatest Polish translator of French literature, Tadeusz Boy-Żelenski, and quite recently Harold B. Segel in the introduction to his translation of selected plays of Fredro took up this matter again.[5] The recent view, contradicting earlier nineteenth-century judgments of Fredro, according to which he was "a Polish Molière," and seeing in him the creator of an entirely new form of comedy, is certainly closer to the truth.

We have to distinguish between the early and the mature Fredro. During the period of his dramatic apprenticeship the influence of Molière is profound and direct (it is reminiscent of that exerted on the Stanislavian playwrights), and so, for instance, *Mister Moneybags* (*Pan Geldhab*, 1818) bears considerable resemblance to both *Le Bourgeois gentilhomme* and to *Les Précieuses ridicules*, its principal character, a snob and social climber, being similar to Monsieur Jourdain, while his daughter Flora shows a likeness to Magdalen and Cathos.

Once we look at Fredro's mature comedies, we see this mimetic relation to Molière drastically changed. We can see how intricate it has now become when we look jointly at *The Life Annuity* (*Dożywocie*, 1835), one of Fredro's acknowledged masterpieces, and *L'Avare*, of which it was

---

[5] Tadeusz Zelenski (Boy), *Obrachunki Fredrowski, Pisma* (*Settling Accounts with Fredro, Collected Works*), Vol. V (Warsaw). See also Harold B. Segel, *The Major Comedies of Alexander Fredro* (Princeton University Press: 1969), 45–54, 345–50.

once believed the Polish play was an adaptation and with which it has often been compared. The plot of *The Life Annuity* is briefly as follows: a money lender, Patch, purchases the life annuity of Leon Birbancki from a third party without Leon's knowledge. The fixed income will accrue to Patch so long as Leon lives, but to his amazement Patch discovers that Leon's way of life is such as to send him to an early grave. Leon is a heavy drinker, a gambler, and spends most of his nights at parties and in amorous escapades. Patch feels that he has to protect Leon against himself, and the major action of the play concerns Patch's frantic attempts to "prolong" Leon's life. A subplot involves a young woman Rose with whom Leon is in love, but whose father is heavily indebted to Patch, and who has reconciled herself to the prospect of marrying Patch. Having discovered at last who Patch really is, and what his designs are, Leon tricks the money lender by announcing that he will kill himself unless he marries Rose; thus he succeeds in winning her for himself, and incidentally in regaining the possession of his life annuity.

Much of the comic force of this witty comedy stems from the Patch-Leon relationship in which a callous money lender perforce becomes an oversolicitous guardian angel to his "investment." Important also are the scenes where Patch, having convinced himself that Leon will not live long, tries to sell the annuity to a fellow money lender Hardcoin, who is, however, too shrewd and knowing. Miserliness, which dominates the French play through the figure of Harpagon, is also present in the Polish one, not only in Patch, but also in Hardcoin, and to a lesser extent in Orgon, Rose's father. Yet, *The Life Annuity* is devoid, as are most of Fredro's comedies, of the somber or indeed tragic elements which figure so prominently in *L'Avare*. As a comedy it is playful and gay. It does not portray a revolt against reason and the "natural" course of human conduct, as *L'Avare* does, and its treatment of the family has nothing to do with the lacerating relationship between father and son which in the French play threatens the very existence of the family. Furthermore, the staple techniques in Molière's great comedies of intermingling sad and somber scenes with farce, and the particular comic method employed in *L'Avare*—the successive confrontation of Harpagon with a variety of characters so that the enormity of his mania and the different aspects of his personality may be made clear to us—are not found in *The Life Annuity*. The Polish comedy is not dominated by a single character. In contrast to the French it presents to us several people, all of whom are fully drawn and are engaged in intrigues infinitely more subtle and complicated than those in Molière's play.

If the humor of *The Life Annuity* is richer than that of *L'Avare*, since it springs from a greater variety of comic situations, there are, nevertheless, important points of contact between the two plays. Apart from several lesser similarities—the figures of Marianne and Rose in relation to Harpagon and Cléante, and Patch and Leon respectively is one of them— the French and the Polish dramatists are closest in creating comic exaggerations and in portraying a miser's disturbed psychology, leading ultimately to a sort of absurd comic association whereby money is identified with abstract qualities or with one's life. In the famous monologue (Act IV, Scene 7) Harpagon laments the loss of the money box, addressing it as if it were his dearest friend, and then declaring that he is dying of a broken heart. Upon hearing that Leon is about to shoot himself, Patch, in a scene which is a great *coup de théâtre* in the tradition of Molière, hurls himself on the table where the pistols are lying, covers them with his own body and exclaims:

> ... But no ... no ... I know what I will do—I'll take you to court ... I bought your life and it's mine now. No one's got any right to it, and whoever makes threats at it, is a killer, a traitor, a swindler. He's a robber, he's a — murderer! Help me! Help me! —He's a murderer! Yes! I'll fall before the judges, I'll tell them about your foul thoughts, I'll tell them about your intention, and the kind court, the considerate court, will hand down a ten-year sentence—not counting all the expenses of the trial.[6]

Another well known play of Fredro, *Husband and Wife* (*Mąż i Żona*, 1822), which analyzes the love relations of two men and two women— Count Vatslav, his wife Elvira, the maid Justinia, who is Vatslav's mistress as well as the mistress of Elvira's lover Alfred—reveals a similarity to several plays of Molière, to *Le Misanthrope* and *George Dandin* most of all. Analogies and affinities between other plays of Fredro and Molière are legion. We know that the Polish dramatist admired Molière and ranked him very highly, and his particular debt to the Frenchman appears to lie both in the range of his comic *oeuvre* and in what might be called the *potential comic elements*, derived from Molière, which Fredro transforms and recreates into highly original creations of his own.

No comic talent equal to Fredro's appeared in Poland in the nineteenth century, although Fredro had numerous disciples and followers. Among

---

[6] *The Major Comedies of Alexander Fredro*, ibid, 399.

these Józef Bliziński (1827–93) and Michal Balucki (1837–1901) were the most important, but Molière's influence on them is often elusive, since it operated through Fredro, and, moreover, it clashed with that of the recent and contemporary European dramatists. After Molière, Goldoni, and Beaumarchais, Polish comic writers of the nineteenth century turned, with ever increasing interest, to the works of Scribe and Labiche, and later to those of Augier and Sardou. Before the middle of the nineteenth century Molière was accepted in Poland as a *classic*, and while universally recognized as one of the world's greatest comic writers, he ceased to influence greatly the succeeding generations of Polish playwrights. In this he shared the lot of other *classics*, whose reputation often exceeds their impact.

Yet, in the relatively short span of eighty years or so, from the early comedies of Bohomolec written in the 1750's through the great period of Fredro's mature works of the 1820's and '30's, Molière's role as a comic model, a repository of motifs and plots, and a source of inspiration from which Polish playwrights drew at will was very great indeed. Without him comedy in Poland might well have been different, and certainly poorer. He gave it a new direction and supplied it with novel subject matter and new techniques.

The uniqueness of Molière hardly needs any defenders today, and his power as a theatrical illusionist, his superb imagination, his vitality, inventiveness, and universality found fervent admirers in Poland, no less than in other countries. Polish comedy of the eighteenth century felt his greatness, but it rarely rose to his level; or rather it took one aspect of his work, profited from it and made it, as it were, its own point of departure. In an age bent on social and political reform and determined to sharpen its intellect, Molière became the master satirist. His farces and early comedies, more than his later works, were a powerful stimulant. The realism of the highly satirical theater of the Polish Enlightenment was in itself an adaptation of Molière's realism in a new age; while the new complexities of plot and intrigue observable in Fredro constituted the next stage in the development of that European comedy of which Molière was the greatest modern craftsman. He found followers in Poland who from the richness of his genius extracted what they needed most, and what "the age demanded." Being well aware of what his own age demanded, he probably would not have minded.

MOLIÈRE AND GRIBOIEDOV

Yvette Louria

The year 1672 is generally considered the official beginning of the Russian theater. The first play to be performed was *The Comedy of Artaxerxes* by Johann Gottfried Gregorii, an Esther play written at the behest of Tsar Alexei, who had a theater built in Moscow especially for this performance. Subsequently, in addition to the original Russian plays, both German and Italian comedies and tragedies found their way to the Moscow stage. After a while its repertory included also several of Molière's plays: *Amphitryon*, *Le Médecin malgré lui*, and *Les Précieuses ridicules*. Somewhat later, in 1782, Fonvizin's famous comedy, *The Minor* (*Nedorosl'*, 1781), in which Molière's influence is discernible, was presented.

It was at the beginning of the nineteenth century that Alexandr Sergeevich Griboiedov wrote what has been since considered the greatest Russian comedy of all times: *Gore ot Uma* (1823), translated into English as *Woe from Wit*, *Wit Works Woe*, *The Mischief of Being Clever*, and *'Tis Folly to be Wise*. The title *Woe from Wit* seems to be the nearest to its Russian original both in its brevity and its meaning.

A. S. Griboiedov's family belonged to ancient Russian aristocracy. He received an excellent education and knew several foreign languages, among them French. Born in 1795, Griboiedov was so gifted that he entered the university in 1808 at the age of thirteen. By that time he was not only thoroughly familiar with the greatest works of European literature but also accomplished in music. He received his law degree at sixteen, but remained at the university to study natural sciences. Later, he owed his reputation as one of the best educated men of his time in Russia to his knowledge of the most important European languages, as well as Latin, Persian, and Sanskrit. His great love of literature did not prevent him from joining the Foreign Office and following a brilliant diplomatic career, during which he was made Russian Minister to Persia. Before going to Teheran in 1828, Griboiedov married the lovely sixteen-year-old Georgian Princess Nina Chavchavadze. She stayed in Tabriz while he went to negotiate directly with the Persian Shah. The members of the Russian legation in Teheran—Griboiedov among them—were savagely killed by

379

an irate crowd which misunderstood certain of their proposals, and his widow is said to have remained faithful to Griboiedov's memory until her death thirty years later.

Although critics justly consider Griboiedov a *homo unius libri*, he also wrote poetry, essays, and a dozen or so other plays. All these are but inferior literary endeavours compared to *Woe from Wit*. Upon reading his *magnum opus* without any preconceived notions, one is immediately struck with the similarity that exists between Griboiedov's comedy and Molière's *Le Misanthrope*. Chatsky, the hero of *Woe from Wit*, is a Russian Alceste, deploring the hypocrisy that surrounds him, antagonizing everybody, and adoring a woman who does not reciprocate his love. This second *atrabiliaire amoureux* is accused by the woman he loves of being always "ready to pour his bile on anyone" whom he encounters.[1] One could, of course, space permitting, introduce innumerable examples of the affinity between the major characters and the plots of Griboiedov's and Molière's plays, for it has already been proven conclusively that Chatsky was patterned upon Alceste and that Griboiedov's debt to Molière is evident. What is surprising, therefore, is the paucity of references to Molière in the critical essays dealing with *Woe from Wit*, both by Griboiedov's contemporaries and the Soviet critics. As a matter of fact, one gains the impression of a conspiracy of silence, so much the more so astonishing since *Woe from Wit* is likened to *Don Quixote* (V. Belinsky, 1840), to *Faust* and *Hamlet* (S. M. Petrov, 1950), and referred to as being similar in its impact on the public to Beaumarchais' *The Marriage of Figaro* (O. I. Senkovsky, 1834).

While the correspondences between Chatsky and Alceste are mostly ignored, a momentous controversy has raged since the play's appearance in manuscript form and continues until today. Scholars debate whether Chatsky is a "positive hero" or a so-called "superfluous man," whether he can be considered a predecessor of the "Decembrists" or simply an unhappy lover, whether he is a clever man himself or only a puppet in the hands of a clever writer. In his famous essay "A Thousand Tortures" ("Milion Terzany," 1871) I. A. Goncharov, the author of *Oblomov*, suggests that Chatsky is not a "positive hero," but an extremely intelligent man whose *bon sens* (*zdravy um*) has deserted him; yet even Goncharov does not refer to Molière.

Veselovsky, on the other hand, is one of the rare critics who suggests

---

[1]   Act III, scene 1. The translation is mine.

that those journalists and writers whose reaction to *Woe from Wit* was favorable were afraid that Griboiedov's originality would be doubted were *Le Misanthrope* to be mentioned. Be that as it may, in his *Etiudy i Kharakteristiki* (1903), Veselovsky asserts that a simple derogatory sketch of the Moscow society which Griboiedov had contemplated writing underwent a thorough change due, not only to the writer's maturing, but also to his discovery of a prototype in Molière's hero, with whom he could completely sympathize.[2]

One would have hoped that contemporary scholarship in Soviet Russia, in view of the unchallenged position that *Woe from Wit* has held and still is holding in Russian literature and theater, would not hesitate to acknowledge Griboiedov's debt to Molière. This, however, is not the case: in one of the latest scholarly editions of the comedy (1969), N. K. Piksanov, in a lengthy essay, vaguely states that "*Woe from Wit* represents a dialectic unity of several elements and energies. One can feel in it the beginning of classicism, Molièrism [*sic*,], which can be seen in a multitude of monologues, in the traditional character traits of Lisa [the *soubrette*], in the dynamic development of action . . ." (p. 260). And then he hastens to add that Griboiedov had written "the first Russian comedy which was in no way imitative" (277).[3] It is mostly twentieth-century non-Soviet scholars, among them the Russian émigrés Mirsky and Slonim, the American Harkins, and the Dane Stender-Petersen, who firmly acknowledge Molière's *Le Misanthrope* as the source of Griboiedov's *Woe from Wit*.

Two curious facts surrounding Molière and Griboiedov might be briefly mentioned: first, that just as there seems to be a strong affinity between Molière's work and that of the French fable writer La Fontaine, it is generally considered that Griboiedov's work has a strong affinity with that of Krylov (the Russian fable writer whose emulation of La Fontaine is generally recognized); and second, that just as the part of Alceste is one of the greatest opportunities for a French actor, so is that of Chatsky sought after by the Russian actor. Thus one of the great triumphs of the Moscow Art Theater was the 1906 staging of *Woe from Wit* by Nemirovich-Danchenko, in which the famous actor Kachalov played Chatsky.

Nemirovich-Danchenko (the originator, with Stanislavsky, of the Moscow Art Theater) suggests in an article on *Woe from Wit* in 1910 that it

---

[2] For an excellent translation of Alexei Veselovsky's essay comparing in detail both plays, see Andrew Field, *The Complection of Russian Literature* (New York, 1971).

[3] A. S. Griboiedov, *Gore ot Uma*, ed. N. K. Piksanov (Moscow, 1969). The translation is mine.

was a tremendous mistake in former productions of the comedy to transfer "the center of the play" from the intimate relationship between Sofya, Chatsky, Famusov (Sofya's father) and Molchalin (the man Sofya loves) to a gallery of types which have only a social significance and to commentaries which may carry political implications. In this way, Nemirovich-Danchenko indicates that the literary critics in their conception of *Woe from Wit* as a socially-conscious and quasi-revolutionary work, had influenced the directors producing it: even before the Soviets, the Russian "intellectual élite" had always sought to discover the political message in great works of art. It is this particular attitude which could have induced the critics not to acknowledge Molière's influence upon Griboiedov. The Misanthrope, in his forthrightness, may deplore the ways of the world but he is by no means a revolutionary. If Alceste were accepted as the *Vorbild*, the prototype, of Chatsky, then the opposition of Alceste as a "negative" hero to Philinte the "positive" character would become cumbersome to critics desirous of discerning a revolutionary note in *Woe from Wit*. It is this political concern which may well be the reason for the paucity of acknowledgement by Russian scholars of Griboiedov's debt to Molière.

Molière and the New World

One discovers with pleasure that theater in French Canada was almost founded on the plays of Molière. Marjorie A. Fitzpatrick describes Molière's role in Montreal and Quebec during the years 1790 to 1840, a role which testified to "the good judgment of those pioneering amateurs." Regarding the fate of the playwright's patrimony in the United States, the reader will find considerable information in the bibliographical section of this volume and, in this section, a brief outline of the reception of Molière's plays in New York, especially since World War One. A note on two recent theatrical productions in Brazil indicates the topicality of Le Bourgeois gentilhomme *and* Les Femmes savantes, *showing us once again the infinite adaptability of that universal quality embedded in the lines of the great Frenchman.*

MOLIÈRE AND THE EARLY YEARS
OF FRENCH-CANADIAN THEATER
Marjorie A. Fitzpatrick

Although there were sporadic dramatic performances in New France as early as the first half of the seventeenth century, theater as a fairly regular form of public entertainment in French Canada dates only from around 1790. A subscription series given by an amateur troupe in Montreal during the winter of 1789–90 and a similar venture undertaken in Quebec the following winter were the first real theatrical "seasons" in the history of the colony. Thereafter, theater in the accepted sense could truly be said to exist in French Canada. From then until 1840 the single feature which most stands out in the theatrical development of French Canada's two major cities was the prominence of Molière comedies.[1]

The situation was particularly ironic, since the long delay before theater was finally established in the colony was itself the result of an abortive attempt to present *Tartuffe* a century before. In 1694 Mgr de Saint-Vallier, the strait-laced second bishop of Quebec, paid the cynical Governor General Frontenac the substantial sum of one hundred *pistoles* not to carry through his plan to present Molière's controversial comedy at the Château Saint-Louis. The *mandement* issued by the bishop at the time contained a stinging denunciation of all theater and called *Tartuffe* a prime example of the "comédies impies, ou impures, ou injurieuses au prochain" which Saint-Vallier saw as a particular moral danger.[2] It was the bishop's stringent condemnation of *la comédie*, reinforced by later ecclesiastics, which effectively kept theater from gaining a firm foothold in French Canada until a century later, three decades after the conquest of the territory by Great Britain.

Molière's name again came into the *petite histoire* of both Montreal and Quebec, however, before regular theater became a reality there. The first

---

[1] For fuller details see Marjorie A. Fitzpatrick, "The Fortunes of Molière in French Canada," unpublished Ph.D. dissertation (University of Toronto, 1968).

[2] H. Têtu and C.-O. Gagnon, éd., *Mandements, lettres pastorales et circulaires des évêques de Québec* (Quebec, 1887–88), I, 303. See also the accounts of the *affaire 'Tartuffe'* in Herman Prins Salomon, *Tartuffe devant l'opinion française* (Paris, 1962), and William John Eccles, *Canada under Louis XIV, 1663–1701* (Toronto, 1964).

known public performance of a French comedy in Quebec after Saint-Vallier's ban was *Le Festin de Pierre*, Thomas Corneille's adaptation of Molière's *Dom Juan*, in 1765. According to an announcement in the *Quebec Gazette* of April 11, a Pierre Chartier and his troupe were to give the play on the 15th "A la Basse Ville, à l'Enseigne du Québec, chez le Sieur *Jean Roi*." In Montreal also the first documented programs were Molière comedies.[3] E.-Z. Massicotte first brought to light the curious papers found in the Château de Ramezay which seemed to indicate that English soldiers garrisoned in Montreal gave four performances of *Le Bourgeois gentil-homme* and two of *Le Médecin malgré lui* in 1774. Massicotte also published two petitions from the garrison amateurs to their military commander for permission to use the old Jesuit quarters for a presentation of *Les Fourberies de Scapin* in early 1781.[4] A year later the protonotary Joseph-François Perrault mentioned in a letter that plans were being laid in Montreal to present "la comédie de Grégoire & des fourberies de Scapin" during the forthcoming *Carnaval*. Perrault noted that all the women's roles had been eliminated from the play, presumably to avert the displeasure of the Church.[5]

As noted, however, the history of the French-Canadian stage really began only a decade or so from the end of the eighteenth century with the founding of the first lasting amateur troupes in Quebec and Montreal. Much of what we know about the Quebec troupe is due to the Church's stern disapproval of its activities. An anonymous letter in the *Quebec Gazette* of January 20, 1791, revealed that a group called the Messieurs Canadiens had apparently aroused the wrath of the ecclesiastical authorities by presenting a program of light comedies, identified in another letter on the 27th as *Le Malade imaginaire* and possibly *L'Avare*.[6] The

---

[3] A comedy of unknown identity was apparently presented there in 1749. Madame Élisabeth Bégon wrote to her son-in-law on February 14, 1749, that several of her friends might not be permitted to receive their Easter Communion, "surtout ceux qui iront à la comédie qui doit se jouer les 3 derniers jours gras." (Published in the *Rapports de l'Archiviste de la Province de Québec* [hereafter *RAPQ*], 1935–36, 203.) Diligent efforts by several researchers have failed to establish what comedy was given, or by whom.

[4] *Bulletin des recherches historiques* (hereafter *BRH*), XLIII, 12 (December, 1917), 373–74, and "Recherches historiques sur les spectacles à Montréal, de 1760 à 1800," *Mémoires de la Société Royale du Canada*, 3e série, XXVI (1932), 113–22.

[5] Marine Leland, "Joseph-François Perrault: Années de jeunesse—1753–1783," extrait de la *Revue de l'Université Laval*, XIII, 2–3 (octobre–novembre, 1958), and 5–9 (janvier–mai, 1959).

[6] The ambiguity arises from the following passage in the letter of January 27: "L'Aimable Comédie de l'inimitable Molière . . . a été bien accueillie par un nombre de personnes respectables de cette ville, et aux acteurs a mérité des applaudissemens. *Le Malade imaginaire, le Harpagon* ont surtout excellé."

author of the earlier letter professed surprise that "on se recrierait contre un amusement décent et honête" like the performance of the Messieurs Canadiens: "On voudroit persuader que le théâtre est dangereux pour la jeunesse qui le fréquente; mais cela n'est point du tout vraisemblable; au contraire, un peu de réflexion nous convaincra que les acteurs et les spectateurs mêmes pouroient employer le tems qu'ils donnent à ces spectacles dans des amusemens beaucoup moins décens, beaucoup plus préjudiciables aux bonnes moeurs, à leurs intérêts, à leur santé et à l'édification du prochain."[7]

Further letters and editorials in the *Gazette* over the next several weeks proved that the objections had indeed emanated from clerical sources. The Messieurs Canadiens were so little intimidated, however, that they gave a second performance of *Le Malade imaginaire* on February 26, 1791, this time with *Le Barbier de Séville*, and another performance of the latter before their brief but significant season came to a close in March. Despite their make-shift sets and inadequate hall (mentioned in the March 10 *Gazette*), they had at least contributed to Quebec theater the previously lacking element of continuity. With *Le Malade imaginaire* they inaugurated the series of programs which at long last made theater a reality in Quebec.

The following winter the troupe, now called the Jeunes Messieurs Canadiens, devoted all its efforts to preparing *La Comtesse d'Escarbagnas* and *Le Médecin malgré lui* for the gala reopening of the renovated Théâtre du marché à foin on February 18, 1792. The visiting Duke of Kent and Lieutenant Governors Clarke and Simcoe were among the distinguished guests in the audience at the well-attended performance.[8] On December 27 of that year the players again turned to Molière, giving *L'Avare* and *Les Précieuses ridicules* as part of a subscription series. According to the *Gazette* they presented six additional plays during the busy 1792–93 season, of which three (*George Dandin*, *Le Bourgeois gentilhomme* and *Monsieur de Pourceaugnac*) were by Molière. The paper used the heading "Théâtre canadien" in its advertisements for six more French plays presented two seasons later, including *Le Festin de Pierre* on November 26, 1795, and *Le Bourgeois gentilhomme* on January 28, 1796.

During roughly those same years of the early 1790's, French theater also

---

[7] In this and all succeeding quotations obvious misprints in the original are corrected. Antiquated spellings, however, are retained.

[8] *Gazette*, February 16, 1792, and *BRH*, XLIII, 2, 35.

made its first sustained appearance in Montreal. Under the title "Théâtre de Société" the *Montreal Gazette* of November 19, 1789, announced that a Regnard-Florian program was to be given on the 24th "à la Salle de Spectacle, chez M. Dulongpré." Here, too, there was consternation among the clergy at the news, the more so because it was learned that the project involved a subscription series intended to last all winter. In response to several anxious letters then and later from Gabriel-Jean Brassier, the Montreal vicar general, Bishop Hubert of Quebec approved the refusal of absolution to anyone abetting the theatrical activities but counseled discretion and especially recommended avoiding direct public confrontation with any of the prominent Montrealers involved.[9] In spite of all this, the series went forward as planned; ten works were performed by the amateurs during the winter of 1790–91. The lone Molière comedy among them was *Le Médecin malgré lui* on January 14.

The choice of Molière was lauded in a letter in the *Montreal Gazette* on the day of the performance by an English-speaking correspondent using the pseudonym "Senex," who wrote:

> French comedy is a school of manners, while ours [English comedy] has been too often that of vice. —In the display of peculiar character the French excel. All Molière's best pieces are of this kind: his *Avare*, for instance, his *Misanthrope*, his *Tartuffe*. —Besides Molière France has produced several other eminent comic writers, such as Regnard, Dufresny and Marivaux, whose compositions are strongly marked with chastity and decency; —but the Writer whom they celebrate most, and most justly, is Molière. For Comic Powers, in all the distinguished reign of Louis the 14th, he was the most distinguished. —For, even according to Voltaire, he has reached the summit of comic perfection.

"Senex"'s invoking of Voltaire shows an admiration for the French eighteenth century which was much more marked at the time in Montreal than in Quebec. The twenty works of known identity presented by the Théâtre de Société until the group apparently ceased operations in 1797 were all by eighteenth-century authors except *Le Médecin malgré lui* (given again on December 28, 1795) and Hauteroche's Moliéresque farce, *Crispin médecin*. In Quebec, by contrast, the Jeunes Messieurs Canadiens presented Molière eleven times (including nine different comedies) among their twenty-one known programs between 1790 and 1796.

No more performances, English or French, were mentioned in the press

[9] Archives de la Chancellerie du Diocèse de Montréal, No. 901.012—Carton 2; Archives de l'Archevêché de Québec, Régistre des lettres 2, pp. 240–41; Ivanhoë Caron, "Inventaire de la correspondance de Mgr Hubert," *RAPQ*, 1930–31; 223, 324. The assistance of Father François Beaudin in Montreal and Father Armand Gagné in Quebec is gratefully acknowledged.

of either city until 1804. The first notice of a French play in the *Montreal Gazette* after the long lapse was for "Le FESTIN DE PIERRE, Comédie en cinq actes, par Monsr. De Molière," to be given with Bruey's *Avocat Pathelin* at the Hamilton Hotel on November 29 under the auspices of the Théâtre de Société. Two of the six other works presented that winter in Montreal were also by Molière: *Le Médecin malgré lui* on December 28 and *L'Avare* on February 22. The following passage from an anonymous letter published in the *Gazette* of December 2, after the performance of *Le Festin de Pierre*, illustrates the vague phraseology and undiscriminating praise which were all too representative of the letters of that era: "Les caractères se sont soutenus d'une manière si admirable, que leur mérite surpasse tous les éloges. Il suffit de dire que l'attention vigilante et la satisfaction avec laquelle la pièce a été entendue d'une assemblée respectable, confirment la haute idée que l'on s'étoit formée de tous les acteurs, de l'exécution de cette comédie dans tous ses détails & de la régularité & de l'éclat de toutes les représentations."

The clear suggestion in the last sentence that there were earlier performances by the troupe is not substantiated by any record in the newspapers. This kind of discrepancy is a useful reminder that the press, our principal and often only lead to the theatrical activities of the period, was not an infallible guide. One fact we do know, however, is that during that one winter of 1804–05, the only active season of French theater in Montreal between 1796 and 1815, Molière's works were given greater prominence than at any previous time. Three of the eight works known to have been presented that season were Molière comedies.

That same winter also saw the return of French theater to Quebec for the first time since 1796, and Molière's continuing popularity there was evident from the programs advertised in the *Quebec Gazette*. The first, given by the Messieurs Canadiens at the Patagonian Theater on October 24, consisted of *Le Mariage forcé* and *Les Plaideurs*. A month later they gave an all-Molière program, *Les Fourberies de Scapin* and *Le Médecin malgré lui*. There was even enough enthusiasm for theater in the city for the *Gazette* to launch a drive to raise funds for a new hall, which opened on the site of the old Théâtre du marché à foin in January, 1806. Various issues of the *Gazette* and an article on this "Théâtre nouveau" in the *BRH* (XLIII, 3, 65 *ss.*) document eleven performances in French given there over the next three seasons, including seven of Molière comedies: *Le Malade imaginaire*, *Le Mariage forcé* and *L'Avare*, each given twice, and *Les Précieuses ridicules*.

That was apparently the end of French theater in Quebec until late 1814, and in Montreal until 1815. In a sense, then, the activities of the Montreal amateurs from 1789 through 1805 and of the Quebec troupes from 1790 through 1808 form a unit, the first real page of French Canada's theatrical history. A brief review of the statistics for those years underlines once more the prominence of Molière comedies, particularly in Quebec, where they accounted for over half of all known performances in French (twenty-two of thirty-eight). The impressive list of Molière repertory played there included eleven different works—*L'Avare*, *Le Malade imaginaire*, *La Comtesse d'Escarbagnas*, *Le Médecin malgré lui*, *Les Précieuses ridicules*, *George Dandin*, *Le Bourgeois gentilhomme*, *Monsieur de Pourceaugnac*, *Dom Juan* (as modified by Thomas Corneille), *Le Mariage forcé*, and *Les Fourberies de Scapin*. While the Montreal amateurs devoted much less attention to Molière than their Quebec counterparts before 1796, the proportion rose considerably in their 1804–05 season. Throughout the whole period they gave five Molière programs among their twenty-eight productions, including performances of *Le Festin de Pierre*, *Le Médecin malgré lui* and *L'Avare*. Without question, Molière's name was already firmly established in the annals of the French-Canadian stage.

Another of the periodic spurts which characterized the early development of theater occurred between the end of 1814 and 1818. According to an advertisement in the *Quebec Gazette* of December 29, a new troupe calling itself the "Société de Jeunes Messieurs Canadiens" made its debut in Quebec on the last day of 1814 in *Les Fourberies de Scapin* and *L'Avocat Pathelin*. A review in the *Gazette* on January 5 said that the players, all novices to the stage, had never even seen a public performance, yet their roles had been rendered with grace and realism and "Scapin et quelques autres caractères de marque auroient figurés avantageusement sur Théâtres Européens." [*sic*] A second performance of the two plays was given on January 7.

The Jeunes Artistes, a different group, were introduced in an article written by their manager for the *Quebec Gazette* of May 11, 1815, as "Plusieurs Jeunes Étrangers," although their nationality was not specified. The newspapers recorded five programs of two plays each given by the Jeunes Artistes in Quebec between May 17 and June 24. On four of the five occasions Molière was on the bill (*Le Médecin malgré lui* on May 17 and June 10, *Monsieur de Pourceaugnac* on June 6 and 24). Subsequently the players moved on to Montreal, where they gave *Monsieur de Pourceaugnac* on August 11 and *Les Fourberies de Scapin* on October 14, the only generally well known plays among their repertory. The Jeunes Artistes faded from sight at that point, but other amateur troupes sprang up in their wake in both cities.

A group known simply as the "Amateurs" gave twenty performances in Quebec over three seasons beginning in January, 1816. Among its productions (documented in the *Gazette* and in a history of the Théâtre du marché à foin in *BRH*, XLIII, 4, 97) were three presentations of *Le Mariage forcé* and one of *Les Fourberies de Scapin*. In Montreal, meanwhile, the *Spectateur canadien* carried notices throughout the winter of 1815–16 about the activities of a new troupe whose first program, *L'Amour médecin* and Voltaire's *Mort de César*, was followed by six more plays including *L'Avare*. In a letter signed "Un Amateur" in the *Spectateur canadien* of December 25, 1815, one theater-lover wrote that he hoped the amateurs' efforts would inspire many such ventures, so that at long last a great *lacune* in French Canada's cultural life would be filled: "Alors on ne dira plus par manière de reproche, qu'avec deux villes riches et peuplées, les Canadiens connoissent à peine les représentations théâtrales. A la vérité, ce ne sera pas la première fois qu'on aura donné ici des Comédies, mais la chose arrive si rarement, à Montréal surtout, que quand on y joue une pièce, à peine se souvient-on qu'on y en a joué d'autres auparavant."

The letter continued with a long, passionate defense of theater and a pointed reference to Pope Leo X's love of the dramatic arts. An even stronger letter from one "Argus" appeared in the *Spectateur canadien* on January 13, 1817, two days after *Le Malade imaginaire* was presented at the Hotel Tesseyman. The performance must have provoked a stern sermon against theater, judging from Argus's vitriolic point-by-point rebuttal:

Passe encore si comme les Cottin du siècle de Louis XIV ils [the clergy] se contentoient d'endormir leur auditoire, ou de vouloir être éloquents en dépit du bon goût, et de la saine raison, mais non, ce genre n'est plus à la mode; il faut maintenant du véhément, des invectives, des épithètes dont on ne connaît nullement la force, il faut prêter aux gens des motifs qui ne leur sont jamais entrés dans la pensée, et dont ils se croiroient déshonorés; il faut citer au peuple les *Chinois* et les *Romains*, pour lui inspirer l'horreur pour la Comédie, et pour ses partisans; . . . l'on dit au peuple que l'on prive des sacrements les personnes qui vont voir jouer des pièces très morales sur le Théâtre de Société de Montréal, mais on a grand soin de lui cacher que sa Majesté très Chrétienne qui assiste tous les soirs, soit à la Comédie, ou à l'Opéra, qui y voit souvent représenter des pièces sinon obscènes, au moins très libres, fait régulièrement ses Pâques, que sous le règne de Louis XIV les plus grands personnages et le Roi lui-même ont figuré dans les pièces de Molière, cependant ils n'étaient point censés exercer un *Métier infame*; de plus, que le Théâtre était, dit-on, sous la surveillance de l'Archevêque de Paris qui permit qu'on y jouât le *Médecin malgré lui* et qui s'opposa à la production du *Tartuffe*, ce qui, dit-on aussi, lui valut un congé très poli, et lui fit perdre sa place de *Directeur du Théâtre* de son souverain *bien aimé.*

Among the eight other performances which also took place that winter at the Tesseyman was *La Comtesse d'Escarbagnas* (February 14). All were advertised in the *Spectateur canadien* under the heading "Théâtre de Société." Nevertheless, the Church's unrelenting war against all theater effectively prevented the development of any strong, uninterrupted tradition.

After 1818 there was a decline in Molière's popularity, even during the occasional periods when theatrical troupes were relatively active. The change was particularly noticeable in Quebec, where Molière's share of all programs given had previously been so high. Between 1818 and 1838 only three public presentations of Molière took place on the Quebec stage. *Le Mariage forcé* was the first, given with Destouches's *Tambour nocturne* by the Amateurs Canadiens on January 30, 1824, to raise money for charity. In an enthusiastic review in the *Canadien* of February 4, a spectator especially praised the unnamed actor who had played Sganarelle in the Molière play and Monsieur Pince in the other. He also ventured his opinion that "Molière dont le mérite ne saura jamais être trop apprécié a converti par ses comédies, un plus grand nombre de personnes à la bonne morale, que les Bossuet et les Bourdaloue n'en n' ont par leurs sermons converti à l'église."

The second of the three was an unreviewed performance on April 21, 1824, of *Les Fourberies de Scapin*, the last known program of the Amateurs Canadiens. The last was a full fourteen years later, on October 25, 1838, when another group, also called the Amateurs Canadiens, presented *Scapin* once more. During the '20's and '30's the Molière programs which had previously enjoyed such favor in Quebec were replaced chiefly by *vaudevilles* and *boulevard* pieces, first popularized by French professional actors of very uneven talents on their sporadic tours. There were still a few amateur projects from time to time, but in general the vigor which had characterized the theatrical activities of a few decades earlier seemed to have disappeared.

There was, however, one very interesting experiment under private auspices—the presentation of *Les Fourberies de Scapin* on January 27, 1837, at Castel-Coucy, Louis Panet's country estate in Petite-Rivière near Quebec. The editor of the *Canadien* reported on January 30 that over a hundred people had attended this latter-day *fête champêtre*, and the affair's success gave him an idea. Why not fill the theatrical void in the city, he wrote, by following the example of French high society on summer holiday and of Panet himself and organize "des représentations bourgeoises ou de société" in various "cercles de fréquentation"? He admitted the deficiencies of the Castel-Coucy production—the use of men in the women's roles and the inexperience of the players—but felt that on balance the project had been well worthwhile: "Nous croyons pouvoir dire . . . que la pièce qui a été représentée est une des plus difficiles du genre que renferme le répertoire français, les acteurs étaient de jeunes et novices amateurs, et que malgré cela de nombreux applaudissemens ont acqueilli leurs efforts dans une tâche qu'on aurait pu croire téméraire."

He wished Panet well in the latter's announced intention of fitting out his country theater in style and holding productions in it regularly in the future. Two days later the *Canadien* published a letter from "Un Amateur" warmly seconding the editor's suggestion and decrying "le malheureux et funeste préjugé, entretenu et fomenté dans la société canadienne contre les spectacles publics." He wrote that this prejudice seemed, happily, to be on the wane, and repeated the long list of reasons usually adduced to prove the worth of theater as an institution. In his second paragraph he raised and disposed of several "objections spécieuses" brought by theater's detractors and even defended English theater, in terms reminiscent of Molière himself: "Le théâtre français ne blesse presque jamais les convenances, et le théâtre anglais, auquel on a longtemps reproché l' obscénité, s'est considérablement réformé et sait ménager aujourd'hui les plus châtouilleuses délicatesses: du reste il faut avoir l'imagination étrangement vive pour découvrir à travers la masses [*sic*] des décorations les cajoleries du Green room; si toutefois cajoleries il y a." One intriguing new argument he presented for encouraging *théâtre en société* on the Panet model was the value of drama practice for correcting "les expressions impropres qui gâtent le langage des canadiens." With all the controversy surrounding that very sensitive subject in later years it would be of great interest to know precisely what the writer meant by "expressions impropres" in the context of the 1830's.

Despite all the apparent enthusiasm at the time, nothing further was heard of Panet's plan or the editor's suggestion. The next French theater recorded in the Quebec press took place over a year later when a group called the Amateurs Canadiens gave one program in March, 1838, and *Les Fourberies de Scapin* the following October (see *supra*). The latter performance, although of little intrinsic importance, marked an important date in French-Canadian theatrical history. As the last public presentation of a Molière comedy in Quebec that we have been able to document until nearly the end of the century, it brought to a close the first clearly defined chapter of theater in French Canada, the half century during which Molière's name had dominated Quebec's dramatic world.

The story in Montreal was much the same as in Quebec. After 1818 amateur theater declined, and with it the frequency of Molière performances. As Marcel Trudel noted in his *Influence de Voltaire au Canada* (Montreal, 1945, I, 121), a French professional actor named Artiguenave announced in 1819 that he would give public recitations from some of the French masterpieces, but no record exists that he gave any *déclamations* from Molière's works. The next documented performance in French in Montreal was on February 9, 1824, when Messieurs les Amateurs Canadiens presented *Le Mariage forcé* and *Crispin médecin*. The following winter four more plays, none of them by Molière, were advertised in the *Spectateur canadien*, after which there was another lull until 1829. In a letter to the *Canadian Spectator* (not to be confused with the *Spectateur canadien*) of August 2, 1826, an anonymous French-Canadian deplored the misguided religious prejudices which caused his compatriots to shun theater, with the result that "ce pays est le seul sur le globe où il y a peu ou point de théâtres et où ils sont si peu fréquentés." A series of routine *comédies-vaudevilles* and the like, given in the city by a mediocre French professional troupe in early 1827, did nothing to advance the cause of worthwhile theater.

The first several months of 1829, however, were for reasons unknown very rich in amateur theater generally and Molière performances in particular. On January 26 Messieurs les Amateurs Canadiens gave *Le Tambour nocturne* and *Le Mariage forcé*, the first of a series of performances by the troupe at the Theater Royal and the subject of a warm review in the Montreal daily *Le Minerve* on January 29. An unprecedented situation arose in April when two different troupes, the Amateurs Canadiens and Messieurs les Amateurs de Montréal, both scheduled Molière performances for charity within the same week. In several issues the *Minerve* urged its readers to attend both programs and take advantage of this rare chance to compare the merits of competing troupes.

First to perform were the Amateurs Canadiens, who gave *Le Malade imaginaire* and Dhell's *Gilles Ravisseur* on the 24th. Most of the long review in the *Minerve* of April 27 dealt with the Molière play, though in general terms rather than critical detail. One fact which did emerge was that the roles of Béline, Toinette and Louison had been taken by young boys. (Angélique, according to another article in the *Minerve* of April 30, had been played by a girl.) Three days after that performance Messieurs les Amateurs de Montréal gave *L'Avare*. The *Minerve* reviewer praised the amateurs on their competent production of such a difficult play and had special plaudits for "Harpagon," of whom he wrote: "Il a excellé surtout dans le fameux Monologue dont les acteurs de profession ne se chargent qu'avec crainte." In this case also all the women's roles were performed by boys.

The reviewer did mention two reservations in his article on *Le Malade imaginaire* and *Gilles Ravisseur*. He expressed regret that the Amateurs Canadiens had not chosen a less familiar program, since many people had stayed away from the amateurs' performance "parce qu'ils avaient déjà donné ces deux comédies." Also, he wrote, the program had been marred by "quelques expressions que l'on pardonnerait dans un autre pays, et que nos habitudes réprouvent ainsi que le bon goût." He mentioned pointedly that these criticisms did not apply to *L'Avare*, due to be given that evening (April 27) by the other troupe: "Nous n'avons besoin de dire que *l'AVARE* est la première pièce de tous les Théâtres; c'est le chef-d'oeuvre du père de la comédie française . . . . Il y a très longtemps qu'elle a été représentée [*sic*] en cette ville. Elle ne contient rien qui puisse offenser les oreilles les plus délicates . . . ."

He stressed the same two points in his account of *L'Avare* on April 30, noting that it had not been played in Montreal since 1816 and adding: "Ils ont montré beaucoup de goût et ils ont le mérite d'avoir bien joué le chef d'oeuvre de Molière que son génie a rendu le concitoyen de toutes les nations." We can only guess that he may have been referring to some of the more pungent lines of *Le Malade imaginaire* in his remarks about language, but his other criticism remains puzzling. While *L'Avare* had indeed not been played in Montreal since 1816, there is no record that *Le Malade imaginaire* had been given there either since 1817. In contrasting the two programs the reviewer was perhaps thinking of the other play on the bill of the 24th, *Gilles Ravisseur*, which had in fact been given rather frequently, most recently by the Amateurs Canadiens themselves the preceding February. There could, of course, have been a more recent but unrecorded performance of *Le Malade imaginaire*, or the reviewer may even have been simply trying to stimulate the public's curiosity to assure a large audience for *L'Avare*. His article of April 30 revealed that the attendance at both programs had been disappointingly small.

It would be a mistake to suppose that all the amateur activities in 1829 signaled any softening of the Church's position on theater. Mgr J.-J. Lartigue, the suffragan bishop of Montreal, was so obdurate on the subject that in 1830 he even denounced his fellow prelate, Vicar General William MacDonald of Kingston, for publicly approving similar ventures there. Letters from Lartigue calling MacDonald's behavior scandalous were sent to Bishop Panet of Quebec, to Panet's co-adjutor, and to Alexander McDonell, the bishop of Kingston.[10] During that year not a single performance in French took place in Montreal. The *Minerve* noted on April 26, after an isolated performance by some English-speaking amateurs: "Les amusemens de notre ville sont si peu nombreux, qu'une représentation dramatique fait sensation parmi nous."

A short-lived attempt to establish a viable amateur troupe the following year began with the announcement in the *Minerve* of January 3 that "les Messieurs formant la Compagnie du *Théâtre de Société de Montréal"* would give their first program, *Les Fourberies de Scapin* and Pigault-Lebrun's *Orpheline*, later that month. The *Minerve* reported on February 7 that the performance, finally given two days before, had been well attended and that in light of this initial success the amateurs planned a second dramatic evening featuring "quelques pièces de nos grands-maîtres." Despite the promising start, however, there was apparently no sequel to the performance of February 5.

In December, 1831, a French professional actor named Prud'homme gave a series of public *déclamations* in Montreal which included excerpts from *Athalie, Phèdre, Cinna* and *Tartuffe.* Surprisingly, there is no record of any adverse reaction to this first presentation in French Canada of any part of Molière's controversial comedy. At the end of the month Prud'homme and Messieurs les Amateurs Canadiens collaborated to present three plays, one of which was *George Dandin.* The long review in the *Minerve* of December 29, however, virtually ignored the Molière play, dismissing it in one sentence: "Après la comédie de George Dandin qui a été jouée à la perfection et qui a fait rire les assistans depuis le commencement jusqu'à la fin, et a été applaudie comme elle devait l'être, a été représenté Napoléon à Ste-Hélène [an historical drama written by Prud'homme]." Prud'homme and the Amateurs intended to give Ducis's *Othello* and *L'Amour médecin* in February, 1833, according to a notice

---

[10] Archives de l'Archevéché de Québec, Lettres reçues III, f 211; Archives de la Chancellerie du Diocèse de Montréal, RLL 5, 216–20.

in the January 17 *Minerve*, but there is no record that the performance actually took place. While Prud'homme continued to appear at intervals in Montreal and Quebec until 1839, none of his other known programs included Molière.

The rest of 1833 and all 1834 passed without any French theater in Montreal. Then on February 24, 1835, a group called Messieurs les Amateurs Canadiens (novices to the stage, according to a review in the March 5 *Minerve*) gave a benefit program of two Molière farces, *Les Fourberies de Scapin* and *Le Médecin malgré lui*. The modestly worded review implied that the reporter himself had perhaps been a member of the cast. "Les Amateurs Canadiens," he wrote, "comptaient beaucoup plus sur l'indulgence des spectateurs que sur leurs propres moyens," and the public "a daigné se montrer envers eux d'une bonté on ne peut plus encourageante." Their charitable purpose fulfilled, this group then disbanded.

The fashion among more sustained troupes, meanwhile, was shifting decidedly away from Molière and the seventeenth century. The Société des Amateurs Canadiens did give *Les Plaideurs* in 1836, but its other known productions as recorded in the *Ami du peuple* over a three-year period were an obscure melodrama, works by Lesage and Scribe and a one-act comedy called *Valentine ou la Nina canadienne* by Montreal journalist H. Leblanc de Marconnay. As in Quebec, Molière's popularity in Montreal was succeeded in the late 1830's by a passion for nineteenth-century *boulevard* and, increasingly, for plays written by French-Canadians themselves.[11] All branches of native creativity were given a strong impetus by the provocative statement in Lord Durham's famous *Report*, published in 1839, to the effect that the French-Canadians were "a people with no history and no literature."[12]

This evolution in French-Canadian theatrical history, however, in no way detracted from the extraordinary importance of Molière's role in the preceding fifty years. From 1789 through 1840 one play of every five given in Montreal was a Molière comedy (one in four, if the performances of the garrison amateurs from 1774 to 1781 are included). In Quebec Molière works accounted for over a third of all known performances from the

---

[11] Six years after Marconnay's play was given in Montreal the Amateurs Typographes of Quebec presented *La Donation*, the first of several comedies written for the troupe by Quebec playwright Pierre Petitclair. (See the *Canadien*, 1842, *passim*.)

[12] John George, Earl of Durham, *Lord Durham's Report on the Affairs of British North America*, Sir C. P. Lucas, ed. (Oxford, 1912; orig. pub. House of Commons, 1839), II, 294–95.

Conquest to 1840. Although the proportion of Molière comedies was at first much greater in Quebec than in Montreal the pattern was later reversed, and by 1840 eleven different works had been given in each city.

Ten of the eleven, covering a broad range of comic genres, were played in both places: *Le Bourgeois gentilhomme, Les Fourberies de Scapin, Dom Juan* (in Corneille's version), *L'Avare, Monsieur de Pourceaugnac, Le Malade imaginaire, La Comtesse d'Escarbagnas, Le Médecin malgré lui, Le Mariage forcé* and *George Dandin.* (*Les Précieuses ridicules* was also given in Quebec, and *L'Amour médecin* in Montreal.) Plays like *Le Bourgeois gentilhomme* which require lavish spectacle apparently did not intimidate the performers, but they did confine themselves to those written in prose, with the probable exception of Corneille's version of *Dom Juan.* Perhaps predictably, the most popular works were those with broad farcical content. The Molière comedy most often given between 1789 and 1840 was *Le Mariage forcé,* followed closely by *Le Médecin malgré lui* and *Les Fourberies de Scapin.* It is unfortunate that so little is known about the nature of the many Molière performances—in most cases we can establish only the title and date—but the occasional comments we do have from letters in the newspaper and other sources show the esteem in which his works were held. Despite the Church's disapproval, advocates of theater pointed repeatedly to the moral and cultural benefits of the institution and often cited Molière comedies as examples.

Molière was also an eminently reasonable choice for the amateurs themselves. The lively *jeu* and strong visual humor of his comedies could be exploited even by troupes without formal training or elaborate sets. His penetrating view of the foibles of human nature was as valid in the New World of the early nineteenth century as at the elegant court of Louis XIV. Moreover, Molière's acknowledged universality had a special richness for French-Canadians, as proudly conscious of their Gallic heritage as they were of their own unique North American culture.

This affinity was stressed in later years by many prominent French-Canadians, both in and out of the theatrical world. No less a nationalist than the Abbé Lionel Groulx declared in 1912 that nothing could be more "canadienne" than the literature of seventeenth-century France.[13] When Father Émile Legault and his Compagnons de Saint-Laurent began their radical rejuvenation of French-Canadian theater in the 1940's, Molière

[13] *Premier congrès de la langue française au Canada, Québec 24–30 juin 1912: Mémoires* (Quebec, 1913–14), I, 264.

was the author to whom they turned most often in their effort to unite theater of the highest quality with entertainment having broad audience appeal. Still later, his works became the mainstay in the repertory of Montreal's renowned professional troupe, the Théâtre du Nouveau Monde. Thus, the good judgment of those pioneering amateurs who made Molière the dominant figure of the first fifty years of French-Canadian theater has been confirmed. Once again, as the *Minerve* critic wrote in 1824, he has been shown to be "le concitoyen de toutes les nations."

MOLIÈRE IN NEW YORK
L. Clark Keating

Despite more than a century and a quarter of traditional friendship between France and the United States, American production of Molière's plays had to await the era of the First World War. It was then that all things French enjoyed a sudden and understandable vogue. New York department stores advertised their merchandise as "dernières nouveautés," "objets de ménage," and the like. Culture with a capital C was swept in along with a current of sympathy for French resistance to the Kaiser's hordes in gray. The American decision to enter the war, after the *Lusitania* incident, strengthened the popularity of France, and the New York theater began the active production of French plays. As with other importations three categories may be distinguished. Molière was played in the original, he was translated, or he was adapted, the last sort of production being the least successful.

The Molière début of those days occurred in 1917 with *The Imaginary Invalid*, in English, and the performance was enthusiastically headlined in the *Herald*; "as interesting as when he wrote it 234 years ago." The tone of the review was set by these words, and cast and stage business were equally praised. Mention was also made of Molière's death at the conclusion of the play. The company was headed by the well known team of Charles Coburn and wife. The *Times* was similarly pleased and called the spectacle "an old French play that could amuse anyone." The review then went on to praise the cast individually and collectively, and said that "the ancient and salutary diversion of teasing doctors never found another practitioner half so deft until Mr. Shaw came along 200 years later."

After this brilliant beginning in English, the war years were to see seven of Molière's plays produced, one in English, the rest in French. All of them were an almost unqualified success, as the reviews plainly indicate. First of the wartime plays was *Sganarelle*, done by the Washington Square players and received with modest praise. Much credit for the success of the remainder was due to Jacques Copeau's decision to move his Théâtre du Vieux Colombier to New York lock, stock and barrel for the duration. Copeau took parts himself, and his company included such young stalwarts as

Charles Dullin and Louis Jouvet. Reviews indicate that his women players were only slightly less skillful, but none of them ever attained the fame of Dullin and Jouvet. The titles of the Copeau successes were: *Les Fourberies de Scapin*, *La Jalousie de Barbouille*, *L'Amour médecin*, *L'Avare*, *Le Médecin malgré lui* and, finally in 1919 after the end of the war but belonging to the same general period, *Le Misanthrope*. One wonders at this choice of titles, for with the exception of *Le Médecin malgré lui*, *L'Avare* and *Le Misanthrope*, the rest are farces seldom seen in these days even by Molière specialists. If one may guess at the reason for the choice of plays, a guess which has some basis in the kind of reviews that greeted the French versions of the plays, it is that Copeau shrewdly decided that a foreign language would be far less of a barrier in a slapstick comedy than in tragedy or some other form of serious play. This was especially true of Molière, whose use of pratfalls, beatings, grimaces, and the like does much to carry the burden of his plots. As Marshall McLuhan would say "the medium is the message." Still the fact that Copeau ended what may be called his wartime series with *L'Avare* and *Le Misanthrope* makes it look as if he had been asking himself whether during his years in New York he had trained his audiences well enough in French theater to enable them to appreciate some truly quintessential Molière plays, in which stage business is at a minimum, and subtleties of meaning are many and complicated. Reviews in the *Times* and *Herald* respectively show two reactions. The reviewer of the latter damns *Le Misanthrope* with faint praise, saying: "M. Jacques Copeau last night played the title role, and he put into his lines the proper touch of cynicism. A misanthrope not yet quite sure of himself, Alceste is a most interesting dramatic figure. . . ." The *Times* man was apparently more at home with the play, and referred to the performance as "a burst of brilliance," adding that "scarcely once last night—and this is as it should be—was the bitter and pitiless hater and scourge of mankind lost to the pitying favor of the audience, even in his final debacle. . . ." New York, it seems, had passed this final examination of its course in French theater with mixed success.

Outside the Molière tradition proper, but highly suggestive of the interest that the playwright's works had aroused, was the performance of a play called *Molière*, which dealt with the comedian's life. Its author was Philip Moeller, who had done the translation of *Sganarelle* used by the Washington Square players. His new play had its premiere on March 17, 1919. He seems to have been lucky in his cast, for reviews make clear that Molière, as played by an actor named Henry Miller; Louis XIV, played by the noted Holbrook Blinn; and Mme de Montespan, played by Blanche Bates, did a great deal to keep the play from being an out-and-out failure. Critics said that it was talky, slow, and sketchy as to plot. Still the fact that such a theme was attempted at all shows to what extent Molière had captivated the heart of the city.

Just a week later John Corbin, of the *Times*, did his best in a long article to pull the props out from under Mr. Moeller's drama. He thought that its plot travestied history, that its characterization was weak, and its situations were impossible. He concluded ironically that on the very same evening *Molière* had its premiere Copeau did far greater honor to the playwright by putting on his greatest play, *Le Misanthrope*. His discussion, which is erudite as well as good-humored, does a rather complete job of demolishing Mr. Moeller's well meant dramatic tribute to Molière.

If John Corbin was a scholar sufficiently well informed to attack pretentious Molière worship, the new generation of *Times* critics, which included Alexander Woolcott and Wolcott Gibbs, were scholars with senses of humor and sharp tongues. The postwar era was, in a sense, opened up by a piece of Mr. Woolcott on French plays, seventeen of which hit New York in the 1922 season. It happens that no comedy by Molière is mentioned by him, but his remarks are addressed to the horrible English that passes for translation of the French. Of this Molière, of course, had been a victim at times. Woolcott was by turns indignant and amused by the atrocious gallicisms that afflicted the Broadway theater.

It was in this same year (1922) that the Coburns revived their version of *Le Malade imaginaire*, first seen in 1917. This time they used the Columbia University gymnasium for their performance and employed many amateurs in their cast. The occasion was the three hundredth anniversary of Molière's birth. Once again the public was amused beyond its wildest dreams. Those who came because they thought they should, wrote the *Times* reviewer, remained to have a rollicking good time.

The next season saw the first of what was to be a long series of visits by French touring companies. The Comédie-Française was first, and chose for its vehicle the time-tested *Le Misanthrope*, for which Copeau had prepared the way six years before. Corbin spoke of it as "enshrined among the supreme achievements of French genius," while another *Times* writer gave it a rave review (Nov. 22, 1922). For their second play they chose *Tartuffe*, and one wonders why it took so long for this play to reach New York. The audiences were delighted with it, if the *Times* reaction is typical. The satire, irony, and downright villainy of the principal character had, the critic said, a visceral effect on the spectator. The year 1924 saw the importation of *L'Avare* again, and most of the plaudits went to the veteran actor Féraudy for his understanding and delightful interpretation of Harpagon. In the course of his review the critic noted the reputation of the Comédie-Française for freezing the spirit of her actors into a mold, but he thought that Féraudy had completely escaped this pitfall.

The official French company of the year was that of the Odéon, playing *Le Bourgeois gentilhomme*. The performance seems to have been anything but academic, and the reviewer was pleased to see the actors performing all over the theater. Nowhere, incidentally, in any of these reviews, appeared a hint of linguistic chauvinism to the effect that English would be a better vehicle even for so French a playwright as Molière. All seemed to agree tacitly that Molière plays should be in French. Apropos of this, George Middleton, in the *Times*, commenting on the perils of the translator, said "it is always a problem how much one must keep French in handling a French play of French character, but sometimes literal interpretation destroys in us the reaction desired" (Oct.4, 1925).

It was with the opening of *Le Misanthrope* with the Comédie-Française company in 1925 that the first notes of doubt and skepticism are heard amidst the chorus of adulation of Molière. In contrast to the usual praise of the play this is what one reviewer had to say: "Certainly, of his plays, *Le Misanthrope* is one of the least entertaining to a modern audience. Only friendship for France and unquestioning acceptance of the excellence of French acting could induce a New York audience to endure yards and yards of monotonous, if clever, rhyming and rhetoric." And he adds petulantly a "less polite audience might have yawned." A couple of years later, in 1928, the redoubtable Brooks Atkinson took on a Molière play himself. The adaptation he chose to comment on was of *Le Bourgeois gentilhomme*, called *The Would-be Gentleman*, and played by one of his favorite actresses, Eva LeGallienne. But Mr. Atkinson was not amused. He alluded to a previous French version, which he thought far superior to the version provided by the veteran British translator, F. Anstey. His discussion, incidentally, reveals as always his complete mastery of his subject. He correctly placed the play for his readers in a moment at the court of Versailles when King Louis wished to punish a Turkish ambassador for his lack of reverence toward the French court.

A few years passed before New York was to see Molière again, in 1936. This time the Louis Jouvet company appeared in *L'Ecole des femmes*. Jouvet was, of course, quite unfettered by the Comédie-Française tradition, and so he allowed himself considerable leeway in his interpretation. The *Times* reviewer was favorably impressed by this fact: "Best of all he has frankly taken it as a comic piece written by a comedian, which Molière was, for himself to act." It is perhaps of passing interest to note that during this same year Molière received the ultimate acceptance implied by a performance of one of his plays by a federal theater project.

In 1937 the Compagnie des quatre saisons came to New York. Among its presentations were two plays that had already been given during the war years, *Le Médecin malgré lui* and *La Jalousie de Barbouille*. In this venture the company revealed a charming contempt for tradition, and when it returned a year later with *Les Fourberies de Scapin* and *Les Précieuses ridicules*, it continued in the same vein. What the critics liked especially about this troupe was its youth and iconoclasm, and audiences were delighted also.

It was nearly ten years later when Molière returned to the metropolis, this time in an off-Broadway production of the *Bourgeois gentilhomme* in English. One wonders, of course, why the same plays were always chosen. Since Molière was in the public domain, why did not some company attempt a play that had not been tried before? Unfortunately innovations were rare. Even Louis Jouvet succumbed to the temptation to repeat himself, and when he returned in 1951 it was with *L'Ecole des femmes*. Once again an irreverent note is heard in one of the reviews. The *Times* man said of the play: "it has a simple, symmetrical plot with a pat solution that Molière would have to be censured for if he were not already revered in the liberal arts colleges. He could be as bad as Shakespeare when he wanted to pull down the curtain and go home. But since Molière is a classic, he must not be criticised, especially overseas, and the student of French can sit happily in the Anta Playhouse, reassured by hearing the words *femme*, *coeur* and *infidélité* popping cheerfully out of the dialogue." One wonders if the same jaded reviewer was sent by the *Times* in 1952 to cover the opening of the Madeleine Renaud-Louis Barrault Company in their performance of *Amphitryon*. If so, he was a changed man. This time he called the troupe "the finest that any student of the theater, regardless of the condition of his French, could care to see," and the remainder of the review is couched in similarly ecstatic terms. No praise was too high. The actors were "masters of make-believe," "they revel in the pleasure of playing theater." Molière evidently rode in on his actors' coattails, for the reviewers even praised *Les Fourberies de Scapin*, which followed.

Before another French company could win such plaudits, there was a disastrous attempt, so Mr. Atkinson thought, at redoing *L'Avare* in a miserable adaptation. In his view, the principal of the company, Maurice

Schwartz, reduced Molière to the level of a Second Avenue stock company production. Obviously he was gravely displeased, one might almost say offended.

The 1955 season saw another visit of the Comédie-Française, and Herbert Matthews hailed it, mistakenly, as their first. His reverence for the master was typically "liberal arts college," to borrow a phrase from a reviewer previously cited. Molière for him was *the great*. It is "all laughter," he said. "It was a happy stroke of genius to choose this gay and witty play" (*Le Bourgeois gentilhomme*).

In 1956 *Dom Juan* was offered for the first time to a New York audience. The *Times* reviewer was Louis Calta, who was as much of an idol smasher as Mr. Matthews was a worshipper at the shrine. He said of the performance at the Downtown Theater: "Was this trip necessary?" He blamed much of the play's failure on the dullness of the performance, but though he tried to be fair to Molière, he seems hardly to have been yearning to see any more of his plays performed. During that same year *Le Misanthrope* was also attempted in English, and again Mr. Calta registered his disapproval. Although he conceded the play to be Molière's greatest, it appeared to him to be "prolix and fluffy." In effect he praised the performance but could hardly stand the play. A year later, continuing a series of apparently unrelated revivals of Molière in English, *The Doctor in Spite of Himself* appeared. Its reviewer, at opposite poles from Calta, thought it "imperishable." The same year *The School for Wives* was put on, but any relation between this production and previous Molière adaptations was purely coincidental. Molière's comedy was transferred to the early days of New Orleans, mixed up with Mardi Gras, and otherwise reworked beyond recognition. All this might have been to the good in the right hands, but it was instead simply awful. In 1967 *Mod Molière* was an equally unsuccessful try at updating seventeenth-century comedy, but those who played Molière straight enjoyed real success. In October of 1956 *Tartuffe* hit the boards, also in English. This too was a bad production, the blame for which, said the reviewer, was not to be laid at Molière's door.

With these English versions of Molière a not too successful epoch seems to close, for the next Molière production was a French version of *Le Malade imaginaire* in the excellent and classic tradition. "If there was a doctor in the house" said the reviewer, "he certainly enjoyed himself." A month later a Canadian troupe presented three Molière farces in English, including for the first time *Le Mariage forcé*. With all three they scored a notable success. *Dom Juan* was performed for the second time that fall by the troupe of the Paris Théâtre National populaire, with but moderate success.

As we approach our own era, New York productions of Molière continue unabated. The great plays are repeated, in English or French, as suits the producer. Unfortunately the Brooks Atkinsons and the Alexander Woolcotts are gone. In their place we sometimes have men "who know not Molière." But this is not inevitably bad. Pompous pseudo-respect for Molière, such as his plays sometimes elicited, never did him any good. Sensible praise is something else again. One likes to recall Atkinson's remarks on *Le Misanthrope*: "Some think Molière wrote *Le Misanthrope* because he was fighting with his wife, and, in addition, was having stomachaches. Others believe that Molière had reached the stage at which nearly all great playwrights arrive: he had a *Hamlet* in his system and had to get it out. M. Dumesnil's Alceste resembled Hamlet only in that he was a great brooding figure surrounded by so called practical and reasonable people who just could not believe that anyone could be so difficult about life" (Feb. 1961). At about this same time *L'Impromptu de Versailles* had its New York premiere with the Comédie-Française company.

What of the future? Unless the atmosphere changes radically we shall continue to look forward to annual or semi-annual visits to our shores of the great French troupes, and among the classics they will certainly give us Molière. But henceforth not merely New York, as the theatrical capital, but also small towns and villages in the rest of the country will become accustomed to hearing Molière in French. This we have recently observed as the traveling companies have included universities in their circuit.

Molière is undoubtedly at his best when played in French, for as will be noticed among the reviews of his plays, English versions have almost always fared worst. This is perhaps due to the fact that humor, like poetry, translates poorly. Modern American slang, the medium used to render some of his best quips, is ill suited to its purpose. With translation much of Molière's charm, as well as his greatness as an observer of human nature, is lost. When New York was felt to be the only place willing to admire Molière, the occasional use of English seemed justified. Now that fifty or a hundred college campuses have been host to his plays, the need to translate is lessened. Henceforth, happily, Molière will not be confined to New York, which for most of this century has been a home away from home. It may even be significant that a few years ago when I went to the theater in San Francisco, the current dramatic offering was *Tartuffe*.

RECENT BRAZILIAN PRODUCTIONS
OF *LE BOURGEOIS GENTILHOMME* AND
LES FEMMES SAVANTES
Winifred Kera Stevens

It seems fitting that in 1970 Air France awarded their prize for outstanding performance in the theater (appropriately called "Prémio Molière") to one of Brazil's leading actors and producers, Paulo Autran. Just two years before, he had taken the title role in a very successful production of *Le Bourgeois gentilhomme* (*O Burguês Fidalgo*, 1968), and the year after, he appeared in a completely contrasting part as the long-suffering husband in *Les Femmes savantes* (*As Sabichonas*, 1971). The productions were not only put on in Rio de Janeiro and São Paulo but also in other centers[1] so that many Brazilians in different parts of the country were able to enjoy them. I would like to make a few brief observations on these Brazilian versions of two of Molière's most famous plays.

In *O Burguês Fidalgo* (*fidalgo* with its echoes of Portuguese nobility long banished from Brazil), Paulo Autran, his usually slender figure well cushioned and wearing his *peruca* as to the manner born, brought a simple *joie de vivre* to every situation, and the same spirit of fun imbued the whole play. It was very different from the classic interpretation of the Comédie-Française, where the fun seemed more spiked with malice. The theme of the efforts of the *nouveau riche* is not at all an unusual one in São Paulo, and many of the Paulista audience would sympathize with his trials; centuries-old tradition would not prevent them from laughing both *with* and *at* him. The finale with the Turkish marriage scene came across in particularly hilarious style. To this the modernized language of the translation by Stanislaw Ponte Preta contributed considerably. Madame Jourdain's comment on entering, " . . . . qu'est-ce que c'est que ceci?" became the typically Brazilian "Que bagunça é essa?" and her threat that she would strangle her daughter if "elle avait fait un coup comme celui-là" became the very colloquial "se ela se meter a dar o golpe do bau." To give one more

---

[1] The production of *O Burguês Fidalgo* was sponsored by the Parana State government and was put on first in Curitiba, then the Federal Capital, Brasilia and in Belo Horizonte, capital of Minas Gerais, before opening in São Paulo. It was later taken on tour again.

example, her French exclamation on learning that Cléonte was pretending
to be the son of the Grand Turk was simply "Ah, Ah," while her Brazilian
counterpart naturally says "Virgem Maria! ! !"[2]

As Sabichonas, a title which at once gives the impression of women
showing off their "knowledge" (different from a *dona sábia*), appeared in
the entertainment columns as *As Sabichonas ou: Betty Friedan nao é
Pioneira*. Women's Lib, as such, is not so popular here, where the patriar-
chal tradition has been strong, as it has been in the United States. Nevertheless, recent years have seen considerable changes in the position of
women. Many more are attending the university and working, even after
marriage, and becoming, one hopes, *donas sábias* rather than *sabichonas*.
Again, the play was very well received, much helped by the translation of
Millor Fernandes, who has many translations of plays and plays of his own
to his credit. He made no attempt to reproduce Molière's classic rhyming
couplets in Portuguese, although this is a language to which they are
particularly suited, but turned them into a convincing light and modern
prose, with occasional internal rhymes. The text might be called more of
an adaptation than a translation, since Millor Fernandes, like Ponte Preta,
lost no opportunity of making it as real to his public as possible. He was
particularly fortunate in the way in which (unlike Ponte Preta) he adapted
the names, so that, for example, Trissotin became the very Brazilian-
sounding Tremembó; Vadius became Vadio (still common usage for
"lazy" and "good-for-nothing") and Philaminte became Filomena. Once
again Paulo Autran brought his presence and splendid diction to a classic
role[3] and created a husband very different from M. Jourdain, one who was
a perfect foil for the gallery of women in the play. The play was cut, and the
producer, Silnei Siqueira, speeded the tempo (more than was strictly necessary, for Molière's own tempo is usually quite swift), as if accompanying
the rhythm of the bustling city of six million outside the theater. Once
again Molière's words in Portuguese made an audience rock with laughter,
and, while they watched, probably few remembered where the comedy

---

[2] Molière, *O Burguês Fidalgo*, trans. by Stanislaw Ponte Preta, Rio, Cia,. Editora Fon-
Fon e Seleta, 1968. (*golpe do bau*—Brazilian colloquial expression describing some successful, if not always honest, way of acquiring riches, etc.)

[3] "Um dos aspectos que o classico tem é que êle é bom por isso é classico e continuará
sempre sendo bom" (*Journal do Brasil*, April 3, 1970). Paulo Autran declares his belief in
the continuing excellence of the classic work of art. He has appeared in plays by, among
others, Sophocles, Pirandello, Gorki, Anouilh, Sartre, Beckett, Goldoni and Shakespeare,
where he found the role considered by many his best—Othello.

had originated. It seemed very much at home and touched with *graça brasileira*.

Thus, centuries later, south of the equator, Molière's characters speak out as clearly as ever in two modern colloquial texts, while the public enjoys the triumph of good sense in situations as topical as when they were first described. One might adapt Sacha Guitry's famous answer to the country gentleman newly arrived in Paris. "Ce qu'il y a de nouveau à São Paulo, mon ami? . . . Molière!"

Molière
and the Older Tradition

No one would seriously deny that Molière possessed a large measure of creativity; thus there is no reason to slight his immense receptivity to the literary tradition extant at the time he wrote. His contributing significantly to the spirit of the Commonwealth of Letters subsequent to his epoch involved more than a spinning out of hermetic personal impulses. He variously accepted, assimilated, rejected, cultivated, refined, and exploited ideas from the wealth of classical, medieval, and Renaissance literature, and he established himself as a master of practical erudition.

Behind Roman drama, whence came much of Molière's inspiration, lies Greek New Comedy, exemplified in Menander. The first essay of this section may dispel the enthusiasm of those who would spring to the task of tracing influence from the Greek to the Frenchman, for the connection seems indeed tenuous, and yet there are points of valid, positive comparison. Much more accepted in the liturgy of Molière criticism is the linking of the French playwright with Terence. Professor Stambler pursues this topic in the second essay, establishing the basis for such a comparison while at the same time attaching specific qualifications to the notion that the two are similar.

MENANDER AND MOLIÈRE

Warren Anderson

Julius Caesar referred to the Roman playwright Terence as a "half-Menander (*dimidiatus Menander*)";[1] Molière has long been known as the French Terence. The difficulty is that of finding a relationship between the historical extremes in this sequence. It might seem that use of the middle term could provide the solution. In fact, the argument has been advanced that one should use Plautus and Terence, taken with the fragments of the original Greek, to gain some idea of the masters of Greek New Comedy—principally Diphilus and Philemon in addition to Menander (*ca.* 342-293/89 B.C.)—whose works were, in different ways and in varying degrees, refashioned for Roman audiences.[2]

It is certain, at all events, that during his six years at the Jesuit Collège de Clermont the young Molière would have had no opportunity to come to know his Greek predecessors directly. Aside from scattered listings of phrases or lines in the lexicons, no writer of New Comedy except Menander had a place, however insignificant, in seventeenth-century European thought. Not even he had achieved real recognition as a dramatist, for his plays were misrepresented by a collection of more than eight hundred moralizing single lines, the *Monostichs*, of which only a few are actually attributable to him. In the course of the centuries these generalities figured serviceably in a variety of sources, including the letters of St. Paul; unfortunately they could give no proper idea of the power and refinement of Menander's writing. Molière, it would appear, never encountered them. His biographers testify to the thoroughness with which he learned Latin, and likewise to his neglect of the Greek authors in the syllabus. Latin was the classroom language at the Collège de Clermont, where plays by Plautus, Terence, and Seneca were regularly performed; but to go back to the sources of the Roman playwrights—meaning Menander above all others—was not possible.

Such was the situation, not only in the seventeenth century but through-

---

[1] Caesar, quoted by Suetonius, *Vita Terenti.*

[2] Wolfgang Salzmann, *Molière und die lateinische Komödie* (Heidelberg, 1969), 14-18, esp. 15.

out the two centuries that followed. It underwent a radical change with the discovery of papyrus fragments which yielded sizeable portions of the text of several plays by Menander. To these finds, made around the turn of the century, others have now been added by various means. Perhaps the greatest amount of attention was roused in the late 1950's by a manuscript which had long been mislaid in a private European collection. It proved to contain an almost complete text of the *Dyscolus*, sometimes translated as "The Ill-Tempered Man." Although discoveries have continued, for Diphilus and Philemon and for many lesser dramatists of the period, we still have nothing substantial. It is around the leading figure of Menander that the evidence has been gathering, and he must serve here as the representative of his age.

For Athens, which engrossed him completely throughout his life, that age was not uneventful. Although the city's military strength and political vitality had proved to be no match for the power of Macedon, the stability of long-established democratic forms of government remained as a counter against unrest under the generals who inherited Alexander's empire. It was, among other things, a time of intense commercial activity and of expansion into undeveloped territories. With these larger aspects and events, however, Menander was not concerned, for the social criticism of Aristophanic Old Comedy was no longer possible. The great world intrudes upon the smaller world of his plays less frequently than is the case with Molière. With the latter, one is unlikely to forget for very long the presence of a powerful monarch in the background; and there are veiled allusions, for example, to the Fronde. In Molière's world, the king stands at the summit of an extensive and elaborate social hierarchy, a scheme of which the author and his characters are keenly conscious, though often in unlike ways. By contrast, the leisured upper middle-class figures created by Menander—like the "character" sketched by Theophrastus in the same period—have no such worries, although they possess comparable social standing.

To be sure, Athenian New Comedy had its world of intrigue, made eminently possible by the device of the subplot or double. This had not been a part of tragedy; now it was used with great repetitiousness. The plays invariably dealt with romantic complications and often with the case of a young woman whose status as a freeborn citizen seemed in peril, or who was about to give birth with no father clearly accounted for. Terentian comedy has familiarized us with such situations. On the other hand, it gives us no idea of the delicacy with which Menander could portray the feelings of a marriageable but lonely and shy girl, as he did in the *Dyscolus*.

Besides showing that the author felt free to use plot as a means rather than an end, this same play exemplifies in Cnemon, the unsociable old man himself, a combination of comic and tragic qualities that many have found also in Molière. In fact, some readers may find the Athenian misanthrope more sympathetic than Alceste. The French writer's work, however, has been thought to deal typically with some deviation from the normal standards of society, or occasionally with the task of exposing its pretenses. Neither approach characterizes Menander, although his world has its clearly defined standards of behavior; the second, as seen in the two versions of *Les Femmes savantes*, calls to mind rather the social satire of Aristophanes. Like Old Comedy, the New Comedy of Menander can include the boisterous singing and dancing that takes up so much of the final portion of *Le Bourgeois gentilhomme*. One would hardly have suspected this from the plays of Terence, nor is it an evident part of Plautus' heavier-handed fun.

While the plays of Menander are peopled by stock types and subtypes, it has long been recognized as his great achievement that he gave them individuality. Terence at his best, as in his version of Menander's *Adelphoi* (*The Brothers*), was able to do this surpassingly well; and it was of course from Terence that Molière learned. Yet the degree of individuation to be found in Menander goes beyond what one might have expected, extending at times to very minor roles. A similar delicacy of treatment may be seen in Molière, who could not often use profitably the knockabout slave humor of the Roman comic poets.

A final link is the presence of a strongly aphoristic element in both writers. Both, as it happened, encountered Epicurus: Menander as actual friend and admirer of the philosopher, Molière as, for a time, a disciple of the devoutly Epicurean Gassendi. It is doubtful whether any Epicurean doctrine can be found in Menander's surviving works, where the aphorism has dramatic and often ironic functions; concerning Molière no qualified opinion can be offered here. As for the *sententiae* themselves, both playwrights belonged to periods of marked intellectual activity and literary creative energy. In this respect Plautus and Terence are less comparable as predecessors, despite the latter's high attainments.

Undeniably, there are many differences separating the two remarkable writers who have been briefly and inadequately considered here. Molière has rightly been thought the more abstract and formal. He displays also, in a celebrated degree, that quality which we call wit and for which there is very little indeed by way of classical counterpart. His best works are held together by an interplay of intellectual forces hard to match except in the dialogue of certain Greek and Shakespearean tragedies. Yet for humanity, for depth and balance of perception in the portrayal of character, some readers may find the more thoughtful note in the writings of Menander. As a fine scholar of classical literature has pointed out, he was not "witty in the manner of Restoration comedy and of Oscar Wilde. He was himself, and that is sufficient; and his province was the same as Molière's."[3]

---

[3] Arnold W. Gomme, *Essays in Greek History and Literature* (Oxford, 1937), 294.

TERENCE AND MOLIÈRE
Bernard Stambler

Linking of Terence and Molière began early and continued enthusiastically.[1] Terence had been the only ancient dramatist whose canon and position remained unchanged from his own day through the "Dark" and "Middle" Ages well into the seventeenth century. The indexes to the hundreds of volumes of Migne's Latin Patrology indicate that the Latin Fathers and their immediate successors read Terence with the attention, avidity, and approval that they gave, among the pagans, to only two others —Virgil and Cicero. With the coming of the Renaissance it was, for the dramatists, Terence who was at hand for translation and imitation—both in the Latin of school plays and in the various vernaculars of Europe. More than any other writer, Terence helped establish whatever formality and regularity the European dramatists chose to employ after the fourteenth century.

In addition, Terence traveled always in the company of a powerful adjuvant: Donatus. Donatus, teacher of St. Jerome (and so in a sense the mentor of the Latinity of the Vulgate), was equally known as the authoritative commentator on Terence (his commentaries on five of the six plays survived) and as the author of an elementary Latin grammar[2] used throughout Europe, with or without modification, for fifteen hundred years—well into the twentieth century, "donat" was the word in most European languages for *any* Latin grammar. And Donatus had freely mined Terence for paradigmatic usages.

In the Renaissance, then, one's Latinity is acquired via Donatus-cum-Terence. The young playwright has a double reason for using Terence

[1] A study of the direct relations between Terence and Molière is embodied in Katherine E. Wheatley's *Molière and Terence, A Study in Molière's Realism* (Austin, Texas; 1931). Dr. Wheatley's work (originally a University of Chicago dissertation) has three major sections: (1) a detailed study of the relationships between the *Phormio* and *Les Fourberies de Scapin*, with tables of parallel passages; (2) a similar task for the *Adelphoe* and *L'Ecole des maris*; (3) a study of "Donatus and Molière's Theory of Drama." I have made some use of this third section in the later pages of this paper: Dr. Wheatley names her chapter correctly, since Donatus's theory of comedy (ostensibly being followed by Molière) probably owes more to Horace and to other theorists in poetics or rhetoric than it does to Terence.

[2] Donatus's *Ars Minor*; his more advanced work in the same field, the *Ars Maior*, found somewhat less use.

as the source of his techniques of regular drama. But what precisely was this Terence so prominently available to the sixteenth-century dramatist? The lineaments of this portrait, or interpretation, of Terence are easily located, but are so many, so extended, and so interwoven in the cultures of the preceding twelve hundred years that I can do no more than name them and then give a sample of the fabric.

Donatus's commentary offered detail after detail in which Terence held a mirror up to life, and it then proceeded to allegorical extensions of these details. Subsequently the medieval energy which had been expended on squeezing the tiniest drop of allegorical significance from scriptural texts was diverted, during the early Renaissance, with increased depth and breadth of flow, into select pagan channels. The most accessible instance of this is the allegoresis of *Ovide moralisé*, with the new resources of pagan and Eastern wisdom—bestiaries, astrologies, and psycho-physiological medical lore.

For application of all this to Terence I may most economically borrow from Edwin W. Robbins.[3] We learn that the characters of Terence are to be differentiated (by the Humors out of Donatus) by their names. Thus, Simo = flat-nosed (and flat-nosed people are irascible); Chremes gets his name from his constant hawking, a senile habit; Pamphilus = all-loving; Philumena = persevering in love. . . . (This kind of analysis unfortunately ignores Terence's habit of repeating names from play to play, presumably with the same etymologies and humors but often with different personalities.)

I borrow, again from Robbins, two extended instances which can bring before us two centuries of schoolmasters' texts and teachings—of the kind that Molière himself met during his years at a Jesuit college. Willichius, in his widely used Zürich edition of 1550, analyzes the Terentian plays scene by scene for their moral content. Speaking of *Andria*, I. 1, he informs us (Robbins, 30):

1. In Sosia is the duty of slaves.
2. In Pamphilus are the manners and interests of youth.
3. In Chrysis are the degrees whereby lives proceed from goodness to baseness.
4. In Glycerium is the respect of a sister at a funeral and in youthful love.
5. In Simo is the concern of parents that their sons be called away from love of courtesans into matrimony.

Each character, thus, is a type of moral behavior in each scene. Adding

---

[3] Edwin W. Robbins, *Dramatic Characterization in Terence, 1473–1600* (Illinois Studies in Language and Literature, v. XXXV, no. 4, 1951).

these together, Willichius arrives at these summary propositions for the import of the whole play:

1. Matrimony is the very best cure for those in love.
2. Slaves' ways are completely pernicious, for such guardianship is more pestilent than the plague.
3. There is a fitting penalty for wicked, disobedient slaves.
4. The indulgence of parents is to be condemned. For always it is the duty of the father to discipline his son with the rod; so that there would be no need for the labor of slaves to guarantee that sons return to the right way.

(What can one say to this wisdom? Perhaps: Sound man, that Terence. Or: After reading Willichius I abjure forever the use of critical pen and paper.) Willichius might be of use for a schoolboy, but how could such a Terence as this be seriously linked with Molière, a link that Molière himself avowed, a link that had unanimous critical endorsement at least through the end of the century? Let us first see a few instances.

In 1663, in his *Nouvelles nouvelles*, Donneau de Visé affirmed that the author of *L'Ecole des femmes* "peut passer pour le Térence de son siècle." Ph. de la Croix, in his *Guerre comique*, presents a dispute between the partisans and the enemies of Molière before the tribunal of Apollo. After the arguments the god pronounces sentence in favor of the *nouveau Térence*: when the accounting has been completed, one must reckon Molière for *Térence ressuscité*.

Within a decade this linking has become a commonplace and so remains until the end of the century. Two questions arise: why did Molière accept, even welcome, this link? The second question, and its answer, are the beginning of my response to the first: what was meant by this linking, what was being thus said about the quality of either poet? Boileau, in his *Stances de l'Ecole des femmes*, written about the same time as the *Nouvelles nouvelles*, thus praises Molière:

> Que tu ris agréablement!
> Que tu badines savamment!
> Celui qui sut vaincre Numance,
> Que mit Carthage sous sa loi,
> Jadis, sous le nom de Térence,
> Sut-il mieux badiner que toi?

(As with Shakespeare, critics have found it easier to admire the writings of the low-born playwright by believing him merely a mask for a nobleman unwilling to stoop to the theater in his own name.) For the seventeenth century, Terence was the *savant badineur* of antiquity among dramatists: Menander's works were not at hand; no one would dare to imitate Aristophanes; Plautus bore the heavy weight of his buffooneries, of his jargon, of his lapses into bad taste—or, as Racine put it, of his liberty. Terence was set alongside Virgil by the French seventeenth century and admired for the same qualities: good sense, naturalness, taste, *bienséance*.[4]

Here, then, is the notion of both Terence and Molière. Molière's contemporaries called him *le Peintre*: an observer, conscientious and exact, of reality. The seventeenth century, with its own definition of realism, found both Terence and Molière prime realists: one then looked at an *adulescens* or *senex* of Terence, or at Molière's hypocrite or hypochondriac, and was compelled to say, "Yes, there is the *adulescens* or the hypocrite to the life." Here is where we should make our first demurral to this linking. There are many types of comedy: Terence wrote in one only; Molière wrote in many, but none of these can be precisely equated with Terence's.

Terentian comedy (plus much of Plautus, of Greek New Comedy, of the *commedia dell'arte*) utilizes an aggregation of "stock" characters: the *senex*, the *leno*, etc. (or *arlecchino*, pantaloon, etc.), of whom all or nearly all appear, in character, in play after play. In Terence the differences between one *senex* and another are more than clear—they are of the essence of his drama. And that he was fully aware of this is to be seen from the regularity with which he pairs, within a given play, *senex* with *senex*, or *adulescens* with *adulescens*. (For perhaps the most skillful and meaningful instances, look at the *senes* of *Heautontimoroumenos* or at the *adulescentes* of *Adelphoe*.) Now take another type of comedy. Imagine a human trait—hypochondria, for instance—put into a culture-bath and there grown into the semblance of a man: such, by Theophrastus's characters out of Aristotle's notions of universal human traits, is very nearly the lineage of the persons of the Comedy of Manners.

The "Terentian" and the mannered existed side by side in New Comedy: *L'Avare*, based on a Plautine comedy, is instance enough. Yet the difference in types is there. Although in form and emphasis Molière's plays are rich in variety, there can be no doubt about which of these two types he leaned towards. (His reasons, political, moral, and artistic, are of tremendous importance, but I shall be able to mention them only tangentially.) Where Molière has not in the name of a play told us which manner or humor he is projecting into persons (*l'avare*, *les précieuses*, etc.) he has attained the same end by his dominance over the language. Is not Tartuffe

---

[4] I owe these instances to René Bray, *Molière Homme de Théâtre* (Paris, 1954) 331–32.

a common, abstract noun? Terence's art, then, is to individualize the members of a broad category of humanity; Molière's, to humanize an abstracted trait or quirk.

In another aspect of their work Terence and Molière come together: both aimed at creating what, in today's jargons, might be called a para-cosmos—an aim shared by only a handful of writers. Menander may well have been the first (with the quality seen in him by Aristophanes of Byzantium when he said, "O Menander, O Life, which of you imitated the other?"), then Dante, Shakespeare, Balzac, perhaps Proust. Few others leap to mind as having even attempted to construct, in a series or sequence of works, an interdependent whole view of a created world. With other, not necessarily lesser, writers, one work may cast helpful light on another; with these writers, each work is a sector without which the wheel of their art cannot revolve—as though the total opus had been planned and to each work its non-duplicated function assigned. More simply stated, the paracosmos reflects a writer's interest in examining a (generally) rather small number of persons, or types of persons, in a variety of circumstances and relationships: he has marked out a portion of the world as his own and works upon it to make it his.

These paracosmoi are of writers who, however strong in convictions, are not directly interested in presenting those convictions in their works. Shakespeare, Terence, and even Balzac and Molière are in a certain sense invisible and inaudible in their writings, but only because these writers are focussed, hypersensitively, upon the fictional life within their works. Shakespeare shows this most clearly, in a way almost unique among dramatists, in the intensity with which his persons listen to, and respond to, each other—an intensity almost unreal when one sees that most con-versations, actual or fictional, are only a polite semblance of listening while one is preparing the next thing to say. All that is lacking in most dialogue are Swift's flappers.

Another statement of this same thing appears in one of the early critiques of Molière (cited by Bray, 278–79):

> Guéret le remarquait en 1669: quand Molière fixe son texte sur le papier, il traduit une vue scénique de la comédie à laquelle il rêve, vue qui comporte la totalité de l'interprétation, c'est-à-dire non seulement la mise en scène, mais les acteurs dans leurs particularités, avec leurs dons propres, leurs possibilités et leurs limites, leur allure, leur costume, leurs traits. Le spectateur est tellement frappé de la correspondance entre le comédien et le personnage que, renversant le processus, il croit le premier fait pour le second et non le second pour le pre-mier. Une confusion s'établit entre deux êtres, dont l'un relève de la vie

commune et l'autre de la vie poétique. Cette illusion a pour fondement la profession de Molière: l'imagination du poète comédien s'inscrit directement dans l'espace fictif de la scène hanté par les fantômes des interprètes.

Molière like Terence is a precise and meticulous painter: both merge realism with a sort of pointillism, though each approaches this merger from his own side. Terence paints ever a different facet of, say, old-manness, until the *senex* of Greek and Roman comedy (or, possibly, society) comes complete and full before us; Molière dabs away at the miserliness, the rascality, the pretentiousness in men, deliberately confusing the representation with the things represented, until all these add together to give us society as it was in seventeenth-century France.

But here we are at another divergence of the two playwrights, perhaps the most important of all. Both are painters, careful and accurate, of that which "realistically" lies before them. But where can we find identity, or even much similarity, in that which lay before them? Only by swallowing an Aristotelian or German-Romantic notion of "universality" could we do this. (Perhaps the greatest unattempted essential task of literary historico-sociology is the close examination of the eras and the men passionately devoted to varying concepts and functions of "universality.") But the large question of artistic influence is inseparable from the great paradox of "universality": stated most simple-mindedly, if there were not certain universal traits, why would an artist be impelled to adapt a work from the past to his own time? But if these traits were really universal, why would major efforts of a creative artist be required for such adaptation? I shall touch upon this question later. As an approach, however, to the general issue of influence, I may use the particular question of Terence and *contaminatio*.

This question of *contaminatio*, although in most ways a petty literary squabble resolved two thousand years ago, may still provoke profitable explorations into Terence's artistry, into considerations of what a society may demand of its artists, and of the problems of what one artist can acquire (or borrow) from another. *Contaminatio*, for Terence, rears its head in the prologue to his first play, the *Andria*. Here Terence says that a malevolent old poet (identified by commentators as Luscus Lanuvinus) finds him at fault for having taken, for use in the *Andria*, certain passages from another play of Menander, the *Perinthia*, since (l. 16): . . . *contaminari non decere fabulas.* . . . This may be translated, has been translated, either as "two plays ought not thus to be combined into one" (Sargeaunt), or as "plays should not thus be contaminated" (Duckworth).

Let me try to explain. An etymological dictionary would tell us that *contamino* is derived from *con* + (obs) *tamino* or (obs) *tago*, or -*tango* or -*tingo*—all of which amount to the same thing: to touch together, to mix or cause to mix together. However, this etymology does not help much.

Contaminare (like *commiscere* and *confundere*, all of them neutral enough in origin) seems to have been used *only* pejoratively from as far back as its literary usage can be traced. From equivalent pejorations in the languages of Iran and India, of Greece and other areas of Europe, one begins to suspect an identity of "mixing" and "polluting," in sacral and bloodline areas of life, as part of the general Great Migration ideology. According to Ernont and Meillet's *Dictionnaire étymologique de la Langue Latine*, Donatus's gloss on *contamino* is *contaminare contingere est*. But we are immediately told that this sense is rare: "le verbe ayant pris un sens pejoratif 'souiller par contact.'" And then, "Dans la langue littéraire [with the only citation from Terence] a le sens spécial de 'rendre méconnaissable en mélangeant.'" Other lexicons provide the same data, adding citations from Cicero, Seneca, Tacitus, Livy, Petronius, Horace, Martial, Caesar, and Terence himself (at *Eun.* 3.5.4) in which *contaminare* is invariably glossed as one of the following: *foedare, polluere, commaculare, corrumpere*, and the like.

In the prologue to the *Andria*, Terence further tells us that his predecessors, particularly Plautus, were also guilty of this practice, and that (at l. 20) he would rather follow the *neclegentia* of these great writers than the *obscuram diligentiam* of his detractors. Returning to these accusers in the prologue to the *Heaut.* (16 ff) he makes it clear that the charge is that he has "contaminated" many Greek plays while writing a few in Latin.

A rich field for scholarship in the nineteenth century was opened for examining Plautus' *contaminationes*. Since the originals were lacking, the scholars (mostly German) had to work with the heady and stimulating stuffs of internal and stylistic criteria, involving hundreds of critics in more hermeneutic circles than August Boeckh had ever dreamed on. The net value of this scholarship is approximately zero.[5]

Terence is another matter. Whether or not he is lying about the earlier Roman poets' use of *contaminatio*[6] is not really much to the point. Terence

---

[5] A bibliographical survey of these Plautine explorations is to be found in George E. Duckworth, *The Nature of Roman Comedy* (Princeton University Press, 1952), 205–08.

[6] William Beare, in *The Roman Stage* (London, 1964), believes, 96, that Terence is telling an outright lie about Plautus's use of *contaminatio*. Also, 92, " . . . from what has just been

is using *contaminatio*, acknowledges that he is, and promises to continue doing so. His repeated asseverations on this matter (in the prologues to five of the plays) show that at least some critics and some in the audience objected to this practice. His only reason for continuing must have been his belief that with *contaminatio* he was turning out a better play than the current form of Hellenophilia would allow him to write in a "pure" translation or adaptation. This very Hellenophilia would bar him from saying so directly; the prologues, however, particularly those to the *Andria* and the *Eunuchus*, come as close as need be to such a statement. The opening ten or twelve lines of both these prologues present an unmistakable self-portrait of a conscious, proud, and inner-directed artist. It may be more than accident that it was Donatus, that sub-ego of Terence, who uttered the eternal motto of the artist who calls down malediction on the previous sayers of *his* thoughts: *Damnati sunt qui ante nos nostra* [*verba*] *dixerunt.*

Why does a writer borrow from a predecessor or a contemporary? A tabulation of some of the possible motives may help us at this point.

1. He may admire, or be struck by, a motif (a phrase, a character, an episode, or even a form or structure) and want to see how it looks or works or sounds in *his* new context for it.

2. He may simply want to save himself trouble—perhaps less in the actual labor of inventing a plot (or the like) than in the matter of starting from something that *will* work because it *has* worked, and in the writings of a great man.

3. Not only artistic caution, as just above, but political caution may be his motive. A chancy sentiment, a dangerous or suspect plot-action may become safe when wrapped in the holy mantle of an esteemed predecessor.

4. Some of the great borrowers intend to transfer a significant "statement" to the greatly different data of their own times. Thus Milton promulgated, in *Paradise Lost*, his belief in individualism, in freedom of conscience, as a deliberate alternative to the "general good" which Virgil (perhaps necessarily or only apparently) put forth in the *Aeneid*. Similar to this is a great list of works deriving from the belief early adopted by Christianity that the Old Testament dispensation and also (starting from

---

said, it should be clear (1) that there never was in Latin literary history a recognized method of composition by fusion of originals, (2) that the term *contaminatio*, 'spoiling,' could not possibly be used as a technical term for any literary method whatever."

Augustine's *City of God*) the works of the good pagans were but shadow
and promise to the fulfillment and light of the Christian dispensation.

5. An old work, or theme, may challenge an artist to do better.

6. A story (or myth or play) may stimulate an author in one of these
ways:

a. To reverse the import of it, tragic to comic or comic to tragic;
burlesque, parody, pastiche are special instances of this.

b. To flout or mock the standards or values of the generation which
educated him.

c. To discover and expose in an adaptation a hidden, or forgotten,
sense intended by the original writer.

Behind all these lie a pair of important questions: what *can* be borrowed? What kind of thing can *not* be borrowed.[7] These questions may lead
us into the concluding sections of this paper. First a look at the materials
used by Terence, with some consideration of their utility for Molière.

Terence operates all his plays with four or five major characters and
a half dozen of lesser importance: indispensable in each play are the
senex, the *adulescens* (more helpless than in Molière's day), the *servus*
(more essential to the action than in Molière's day), the *virgo* (although
in only one of Terence's plays does she have a speaking role); of lesser
importance are three female roles (*matrona, ancilla, meretrix*) and a few
functional male roles (*leno, parasitus, cocus*, etc.). Of these lesser roles
Terence does not make such rich or frequent use as had Plautus (and,
presumably, New Comedy); however, Terence almost invariably uses
pairs of the major roles, and from the interplay among these pairings gets
his subtlest and deepest effects. Then think of the tremendous range of
Molière's persons (especially of the lively and outspoken young women),
and of the infrequency with which one play repeats a major character
type from another. Was Terence's society less rich in varieties of human
behavior than Molière's? The range of Plautus's persons supplies a flat
answer: no.

Every Terentian play is constructed on variations of tightly knit threads
of a specific social system. It is a system centering in a city of commerce,
with some farming in the suburbs; in which young, or youngish, men must
voyage to friendly trading countries over stormy and pirate-infested seas;

[7] That the entire "renaissance" is to be seen as a special, extended instance of influence,
or *Fortleben*, is implicit in the name of the era. These two questions, however, are rarely faced,
or balanced, by historians; an exception is Erwin Panofsky in his *Renaissance and Rena-
scences in Western Art* (Harper Torchbooks, 1969), particularly 1–54 and 177–210.

in which kidnapped or otherwise lost children are a staple of family life; in which girl infants may be exposed, or else sold into one sort or another of slavery (and when grown, identified as citizens' daughters by a ring or bracelet); in which one may be a slave by birth, by poverty, by conquest, but rarely by temperament; in which the citizen of the city alone has full rights (except for a few fringe issues, such as power to contract a legal marriage with a non-citizen); in which certain citizens, without patrimony and without occupation befitting a citizen, must live by clever and improvised sponging on other citizens; in which no one seems to have any civic or political functions. This is the world of Athens during the time New Comedy was written, with some schematic exaggerations, and with the same omission of the higher levels of society that we may note among Chaucer's Canterbury pilgrims.

This Athenian world of New Comedy bears some, but not much, resemblance to the Rome of Terence. His solution of the culture-gap was simple: he made no effort to change the venue, either overtly or covertly, from Athens to Rome. And for any resemblance to Molière's Paris, or France, we would look in vain.

In the conditions of performance, there are at least two essential differences between the age of Terence and that of Molière. First is the theater itself. The theaters of France varied greatly in size and resources, but never did Molière use one of the meagerness of Terence's: a simple, temporary structure whose stage had painted flats (representing, usually two or three houses separated by a street). There was no possibility of indoor scenes, with the uses Molière found for them in intimacy or psychological exploration. For Terence's stage, action and conversation could be of only three kinds: (1) most frequently, meetings of two or three people in front of one of the houses; (2) a lurking *servus* or *senex* secretly listening in on such a conversation, or sometimes on a soliloquy; (3) infrequently, orders, or brief conversations, shouted back into the house by someone standing at the door.

The second difference lies in the audience. In Terence's day, plays were presented at certain annual festivals and at a few other occasions, such as funeral games: a Roman might thus, if he were an assiduous playgoer, have about fifteen (never more than twenty-five) opportunities during the year to see a play. Molière's audience had, or could have, the greater involvement and sophistication that come from frequent attendance at plays. The very nature of the plays is affected by this. The infrequency of performance in Rome permitted, or even encouraged, the repetition of character and plot that we have noted in Terence. The variety of Molière's forms and styles is encouraged, if not mandated, by the greater play-consumption of the Parisians.

Let me, finally, sum up each of these playwrights. Terence was a lapidary artist. Working with an incredibly small set of building stones—in characters, plot formulas, stage settings, stage conventions—he seems to have remained artistically content within these limits. His one departure, that of *contaminatio*, is a wish to perfect these means rather than an effort to increase their number: his goal is to write plays *sine vitiis* (*Heaut.*, prologue 30). What his life contained beyond the polishing of his verses and of his characterizations is not even fruitful for speculation. One has a choice of legends and slanders about that life, but one's choice (except for the slander that other men wrote his plays) does not much matter. In the content and tone of the plays, a gentle decency and understanding mark his treatment of each character. Some critics have perceived an unusual kindliness shown to the courtesans and slaves, a reflection of his own life as slave. One can only wonder whether this perception came before or after the critic learned the (presumed) fact of Terence's slavery.

Contrast Terence as artistic personality with Molière. One might begin by saying that no part of the above description of Terence would have significant application to Molière. In the matter of dramatic forms and characters, it would be difficult to find a writer more impatient with anything he has already done and triumphed over. While no two critics agree on the precise nature, or value, of Molière's philosophical, moral, or religious convictions, few deny that he had such convictions, and that his concept of his art demanded that he express them somehow within the structures and strictures of his time. At some time early in his career, Molière became dissatisfied with the prevailing modes of comedy—farcical, built on intrigue and bubbling activity. Even the earlier formula, "To hold a mirror up to Nature," which Molière was later to echo, was not enough. The tag, "Castigat ridendo mores" (which he was to use later in his 1664 defense of *Tartuffe* as: "Le devoir de la comédie est de corriger les hommes en les divertissant"), would have been closer, but neither he nor those he wrote for were ready for such a creed. To write this kind of play, in the critical world of the 1640's and 1650's, required proof, by way of precedent and authority, that such plays could be written.

Such an authority was at hand in Donatus, with the extra benefit of a dramatist, Terence, whom Molière was to call in a 1682 preface, "the best of models." How much of this was a true admiration of Terence;

how much was the accident of his early adaptation of a lively Terence-based Italian comedy; how much was conscious expedient in his desire to write comedies that could rival tragedy in respectability, seriousness, and obedience to rules? Probably Molière himself could not have made the proper apportionments among these motives. The fiction of his likeness to Terence was pleasant and in some measure useful, both to himself and to critics in search of a handhold.

All this had happened before. Around Terence, first of all, had been built the Renaissance mythology fleshing out the bones of Aristotle's *Poetics*: the unities, at first only embryonic, of time, place, and action; the division into five acts and definite scenes. It mattered to no one then, and perhaps to few today, that Terence's plays were written for continuous performance, that Aristotle's prescriptions (useless as they may be in general to a practicing playwright) at least have the virtue of not mandating the three unities. In any case, this use of Terence in the early Renaissance was as much crypto-political as it was an aesthetic search for new artistic worlds; in the fifteenth and sixteenth centuries we would have been concerned with the *use* of Terence rather than with the validity, or even possibility, of such use. So too, possibly, with Terence and Molière.

If we were interested in increasing the list of literary categories, we might venture to speak of a Comedy of Reality, wherein we might locate Terence as well as Molière, and perhaps G. B. Shaw and a few others. In Molière's terms, this comedy would represent not a total movement away from farcical and other exaggerated/unreal elements but rather a proper proportioning of them, along with a measure of satirical and of mannered elements. In his own day, for all the talk of Molière as the Painter, there was little agreement that all this painting was "from nature." Both friends and enemies recognized that the natural persons in his plays were greatly outnumbered by the conventional—those that could never be thought of as having originated in "an observed reality," but only as having born in a Terentian or Plautine, mannered or humored world.

Our final question is a simple one. How much light, what kind of light, is cast on Molière by reading Terence? More simply yet, must one know Terence to understand what Molière is driving at? To the latter form of the question, a flat no. To the first form, a number of scholarly responses are possible.

First come the collectors' items. Molière *did*, directly or through an intermediary play, derive such-and-such lines, phrases, and episodes from Terence. Next would come a more or less elaborate comparison, within the old and the new contexts, of these shared ingredients. With another pair of writers, such comparison might lead into discovery of real affinities; with Terence and Molière one is led to the unsurprising discovery that two good cooks can make unrelated dishes from the same ingredients.

The final stage is the one I am suggesting. After looking at the real and numerous borrowings by Molière, one moves to the statements, by Molière and a host of his contemporaries, of the deep resemblances between the two. Not finding such, but curious about the reasons for the insistence on the resemblances, one is led into the avenues I have been traversing in this paper. If one cannot learn from the past the art of the possible, one should at least see the possibilities of art.

The diversity of Molière's sources is obvious in the next two essays. In the first, the question is not so much one of influence as it is of determining genres and the effect of the types of farce, *both on Molière's plays and in general. Professor Wadsworth's article deals with the* commedia erudita, *specifically with a play by Lorenzino de' Medici,* L'Aridosia, *which may well have been a significant source for* L'Ecole des maris.

FROM *FARCE* IN THE *ÂGE BOURGEOIS* (1440–1500) TO *FARCE MOLIÉRESQUE:* THE STRUCTURE OF GENERIC CHANGE

Lewis A. M. Sumberg

In his *Sentimental Journey* (1768), the English philosopher and novelist Sterne notes: "If the French have a fault, they are too serious," an appraisal to be echoed some two centuries later by the French philosopher and novelist Saint-Exupéry (*Le Petit Prince*). While no argument can be mustered which would *a priori* preclude absolutely the eventual proving of such an assessment (considering the number and diligence of modern quantifiers), there are at the same time to be reckoned with certain facts, both historical and cultural, as they articulate themselves in an art constantly confronted by human experience. I am referring to the vast fund of comic literature and specifically to one category thereof, the *farce*, whose geneology would seem to extend at least as far back as the Middle Ages, and whose progeny continues to be seemingly without limit. I so qualify this genre at this point, taking as a main premise that from medieval *farce* to *farce moliéresque* there is an identifiable continuum, although one which may not be equicontinuous. It is with the essential components of *farce* (variables, invariables, constants) as they come together to effect generic change, that the present essay will concern itself.

The question as to whether *farce* can indeed be called an autonomous genre, has already been answered: while its form might be said to be man-made, that form has been authenticated by a long tradition and we note that (most of) the works designated as *farce* lend themselves to the usual criteria of literature (mimetic, symbolic, thematic plausibility; work functions as an esthetic object; uses all of the devices particular to it to enhance its meaning; etc.). As we examine the conditions and underlying principles of generic change as they pertain to *farce*, an archetypal approach, with its multiplying of distinctions, would seem from the beginning to impose itself because, already in the mind of the medieval people, *farce* was quite distinct from the other modes and registers of secular drama, each with its own *méthode d'invention*, themes, mechanics, conventions. This is abundantly attested to not only by the formal designations (occasionally erroneous) given specific works, but also by the fact of the various *confréries* each having by the fifteenth century staked out claims as to its speciality or specialities. Since the purpose of criticism by genres is to clarify such traditions and affinities,[1] it will be useful to the discussion following, to resume the principal characteristics of the major comic genres.

a) *sotie* (15th–16th cent.) —Short comic genre (300–500 octosyll.). So named because of the *Sots* or *Fous*, who in fool's costume and with suggestive names, celebrated at Shrovetide their rite of burlesque solemnities akin to the *mascarade* (*Fête des Fous*; *Fête de l'Ane*). As we know from an allusion of *Mère folle* in the farce *Les Chroniqueurs* (1515): " . . . nous sommes les folz croniqueurs," it has as its intention political or social satire. Loosely structured, lacking in symmetry and in dramatic movement, it is more dependent on the verbal and physical skills of the actor than on a plot well-wrought. Like the OFr. *serventois*, its arguments are *ad hominem*: it seeks to injure and to ridicule, as in Pierre Gringoire's *Le Jeu* (= *sotie*) *du prince des sots* (1512), comprising a *cri* (summons to the people), *sotie, moralité* (q.v.), of which the second component (*sotie*) exposes to ridicule Pope Julius II who had betrayed Louis XII. At the end of the play, Mère Sotte having been stripped of her clothes, we see that she is in fact Holy Church. Another work of the same period holds up to ridicule the Maréchal de Rohan who had had a quarrel with Queen Anne: the blacksmith (named Maréchal) receives a violent kick from the *âne* he is trying to shoe. In yet another, *Le Nouveau Monde* (1508; attrib. A. de la Vigne), a satire of the University against the abolition of the

---

[1] See Northrop Frye, *Anatomy of Criticism*, "Fourth Essay: Rhetorical Criticism: Theory of Genres" (Princeton, 1971), 247.

Pragmatic Sanction by Louis XI, *Quelqu'un* (= Louis XII) is petitioned to send back to Rome *Père saint* (= the Pope), *Légat*, and *Provision apostolique*.

 b) *moralité* (14th–16th cent.) —Of two principal types: *moralité courte* (300–500 verses, 4–5 characters); *moralité longue* (1,000 verses or more; 12 or more characters). Preoccupied like the *sotie* with political, social or religious questions, but didactic, of a fairly sophisticated nature, and often ambitious in scope (*Bien avisé, Mal avisé*, ca. 1396; 8,000 verses, 59 characters; performed at Rennes in 1439), its intention is to instruct in a moral lesson (*moraliser*), usually by means of allegory and of personnified abstractions. While its intention is rarely comical (as in the *sermon joyeux*, q.v.), its means (satire, verbal fantasies, burlesque) and its effect often attain the hilarious, as in Andrieu de la Vigne's *L'Aveugle et le boiteux*, 1496. It attacks the vices of the time, such as the excesses of gourmandise: in the *Condamnation de Banquet* (1507) by Nicholas de La Chesnaye, *Banquet*—having been taken prisoner by *Secours*, *Diette*, *Remede*, *Saignée*, *Pillule* and *Clistere* and condemned to be hanged—confesses his sins, avows that he has never served anyone but the physicians, and asks that the latter pray for him. Elsewhere, the subject is chicanery (E. Deschamps's *Maître Trubert et Antroignart*, late 14th cent.). Some, like the *moralité joyeuse* of Benoet du Lac (Claude Bonet) *Carême prenant* (1595), despite a prologue promising a play "plus grave que grasse" and an edifying ending, are of a grossness in detail that would have made Rabelais blush. A real bitterness pervades the bourgeois *moralité satirique* entitled *Eglise, Noblesse et Pauvreté qui fait la lessive* performed by the Conards de Rouen in 1541: *Eglise* and *Noblesse* make *Pauvreté* wash their dirty linen and when the job is done, load it on her back. Later, the Reform will make extensive use of this genre, as in the Protestant *moralité* entitled *Le Pape malade* (1561), a violent diatribe against the Pope, succored by *Prêtrise*, *Moinerie* and *Satan*. The same author characterizes thus the genre: " . . . c'est le natural des comedies d'avoir commencement fascheux et issue joyeuse."

 c) *sermon joyeux* (16th cent.) —Parody of the *sermon* and of the *Vie de saint*, this short genre (200 verses)—performed by a *Fou* disguised as a preacher at the *Fête des Fous*—irreverently recounts the supposed martyrdom of a new legion of saints: *Monsieur Saint Hareng*; *Monseigneur Saint Jambon et Madame Andouille*; *Saint Ognon*; *Les grands et merveilleux faits de Nemo*, ca. 1540, attrib. Jean d'Abondance; *Les maux du mariage*; etc. Several extant examples parody the Latin of preachers and lawyers, as in the satirical *Le Quartier de mouton*. Occasionally, the genre reduces an identical theme treated in the *farce*, as for example in the *Ramoneur* (*de cheminées*).

d) *monologue dramatique* (15th–ca. 1600) —Taking its inspiration from the earlier tradition of the *dit* (13th cent.) and making abundant use of burlesque, this *farce à un personnage* puts on stage a single character who with utter naivety acts out a personal virtue or vice: monologue of the pusillanimous bourgeois militiaman, the *Franc Archier de Bagnolet*,[2] 1468; monologue of a lover: *Monologue de la Botte de foin ou monologue Coquillart*, 1460.

The fate of the aforementioned genres is well known. The *sermon joyeux* will cease to exist autonomously after the early seventeenth century; the Renaissance (esp. Rabelais) will draw abundantly on the *sotie* as a source of its political and social comedy; the *moralité* will aliment the seventeenth-century comedy of manners and of characters; the *monologue dramatique* will find new expression in the soliloquies of the comedy of character of both the sixteenth and seventeenth centuries.

e) *farce* (1389?; 15th–20th cent.; < Lat. *farcire* = fill up, stuff, combine; 12th cent. pop. Lat. *farsa* [< *farsus*, p.p. of *farcire*] = spiced, chopped meat used for stuffing fowl, a meat pasty, etc.). Of the medieval comic genres, *farce* is by far the most important not only by reason of its art and its vitality, but also of the number of its practitioners, judging by the extant examples (more than 150 plays for the period 1440–1560).[3] Having an average length of 300–400 verses, with 3–5 characters designating social roles—husband, wife, wag, valet, lover—it almost always has a plot, however rudimentary,[4] with the principal mainsprings being *sottise* and *ruse*.

Because the resources of *farce*[5] are as large as life itself, the genre is not

---

[2] An analogous theme is found in a *farce à quatre personnages*: *Trois galants et Philipot*. See L. Petit de Julleville, *Répertoire du Théâtre comique en France au moyen-âge* (Paris, 1886), 141.

[3] E. K. Chambers (*The Mediaeval Stage*, 5th ed. [London, 1963], II, 197) notes that England has nothing comparable for this same period.

[4] *Messieurs de Mallepaye et de Baillevent* is one of a small number of exceptions to this general rule.

[5] An extensive treatment in Barbara C. Bowen, *Les caractéristiques essentielles de la farce française et leur survivance dans les années 1550–1620* (Urbana, 1964).

easily defined, its range encompassing works as well wrought as the *Deux Amoureux récréatifs et joyeux* (1541) of Clément Marot, as sly as *L'Abesse et les soeurs* (ca. 1540) and as clumsy as *Un Aveugle, son valet et une tripière.* Some *farces* are pure divertissement while others, including the most indecent ones, end with a moral lesson, or with verse in which the author excuses himself for his coarseness. Still and all, it can be said that *farce* is "what happens" between the *point du départ de l'intrigue* and its *actualisation.* Viewed as "recipe," it might be said that, like the stuffing in my wife's Thanksgiving turkey—chestnuts, onions, mushrooms and apples (as nearly as I have been able to determine, at any rate)—farce is the situation stuffed with a variety of constituent units (functioning as increments or decrements, because no two recipes and no two cooks are exactly alike) and which we might might term *farsemes*, akin to the *narremes* of narrative structure in Romance Epic.[6]

Sometimes (as in the kitchen) the unexpected happens, as during a performance of the *Miracle de Saint-Martin* at Seurre in 1496, when, emerging from his subterranean exit, Satan caught fire at the back of his robe. Fortunately, it was promptly extinguished and the play was able to continue. At the beginning of the next day's performance, Satan wittily alluded to his close call, saying to Lucifer: "Malle mort te puisse avorter/ Paillart, fils de putain cognu/ Pour à mal faire t'enorter/ Je me suis tout brulé le cul."

Obviously all of the aforementioned genres fall within the larger context of "Laughter," although a laughter more unbridled than thoughtful. All have root in a common soil, that nourishing what we might call the bourgeois value system, with its stress on *astuce*, and from which come legumes as varied and as complementary as the *fabliau, sotte chanson, jeu, nouvelle.* A typical program of comic entertainment would comprise (usually in this order) *sotie, monologue dramatique* or *sermon joyeux, moralité, farce.*[7] It is not surprising, therefore, that despite efforts to maintain the generic distinctions, there will be some contamination: we have works designated as *farces morales* (P. Gringoire's *Peuple françois, Peuple italique, l'Homme obstiné, Punition divine, Simonie et Hypocrisie,* 1512) and others as *moralités farcies*; still others (*Mars et Justice,* 1566) divide into two acts, the first of which is a *moralité*, the second, a *sotie.*[8]

Products with rare exception are of the *collectivité anonyme*, the vast

---

[6] See Eugene Dorfman, *The Narreme in the Medieval Romance Epic: An Introduction to Narrative Structures* (Toronto, 1969), 223.

[7] Still, even when played as comic *intermède* in the *mystère*, it did not occupy a fixed place. See Julleville, *Répertoire*, 117.

[8] *Ibid.*, 81–83, 97–98.

repertory performed by elements of the middle classes—bourgeois, students, clerks of the *Parlement*—grouped together in both loose association and in more permanent *confréries joyeuses* (the *basochiens* and their "*roi*"), with the *Enfants-sans-souci* doing its recruiting mostly among the indigent families. That the comic genres have in common a constant—they are *res publicae*[9] and are born of the same *esprit gaulois*—is shown by the fact that comparable troupes are found in any number of cities of the period: the *Cornards* (or *Conards*) at Rouen, the *Coqueluchiers* at Evreux, the *Suppôts de la Mère Folle* at Dijon, the *Confrérie du Prévost des Etourdis* at Douai, that of the *Prince d'Amour* at Lille; others flourish (until the suppression of the theater of the Basoche in 1582) in Grenoble, Bordeaux, Toulouse, Aix-en-Provence, Poitiers, etc.

To what considerable extent the social climate may generate and fecundate popular theater is illustrated by the fact that in France the heyday of *farce* coincides almost exactly with the expulsion of the English and the emancipation of the towns from the last vestiges of feudal domination (Louis XI, Charles VIII, Louis XII). The relative peace and freedom (social, political) of this period will contribute to the self-expression of the masses, a phenomenon possibly not without precedent in Antiquity: old Attic comedy, with its extravagant farcical elements of which many are borrowed from the rural districts, dates from the complete establishment of democracy by Pericles. Conversely, the overthrow of the democracy (411), followed by the eventual restoration of liberty (404), will have an extraordinarily sobering effect on comedy, which will henceforth preoccupy itself primarily with literary and social themes. In like manner, the heyday of Roman *farce* as exemplified by the Fescinnine verse, the *Atillanae* and *Tabernariae*, coincides with periods of freedom, which in this instance is often freedom from all moral restraint. Fundamentally, then, it would seem that a freedom of sorts is one of the conditions most propitious to popular *farce*.

Sixteenth Century —The attitude of the young generation of playwrights ca. 1550 toward *farce* is summarized in the prefatory remarks of Jean de la Taille to his play *Les Corrivaux* (1562): "Oui, une comédie, pour certain, vous y verrez; non point une farse, ni une moralité; nous ne nous amusons point en chose ni si basse, ni si sotte, et qui ne monstre qu'une pure ignorance de nos vieux François."[10] Add to this the difficult situation of the

[9] Cf. the earlier *puys*, such as that of Arras.
[10] L. Petit de Julleville, *La Comédie et les Moeurs en France au moyen âge* (Paris, 1886), Slatkine Repr. (Genève, 1968), 335.

farceurs (given the recurrent ban on public assemblies) always under strict surveillance, the eventual banning of the theater of the *Basoche* in 1582, and the sobering effect of the religious conflict, and one would be tempted to say that *farce* was doomed.

Not so. In the first place, it is doubtful whether a comic mode whose spirit (*l'esprit gaulois*), whose principal *ressorts* (*le bouffon* and *l'imprévu*), and whose comic rhythm belong in a real sense to folk art,[11] could die in a century so free as we would judge it by its remarkable satire (Rabelais, Bauchet, du Fail, des Périers, Truquet, etc.). Secondly, the deprecatory remarks of the *Pléiade* bent on imitating Italian models notwithstanding, many of the most salient features of *farce* will in fact be absorbed by the new comedy, while oftentimes the farcical elements will have sufficient dimension and coherence to function as *intermède* or as play within the play. A case in point is Jodelle's *Eugène* (1552), which, despite its classical pretentions, trods a *sentier battu* known both to the *fabliau* and to the medieval conjugal *farce*: impudent wife; inadequate, naive husband; deceitful ecclesiastic. A small number of other comedies of the second half of the century will readapt familiar themes and personages of the medieval *farce*: Grévin's *La Trésorière* (1558) and *Les Esbahis* (1561); Belleau's *La Reconnue* (1577; theme of the inadequate husband); the Italian-born Larivey's *Les Esprits* (1579) whose miser, while consciously modeled on Lorenzo de' Medici's *Aridosio*, unconsciously reflects the medieval French farcical tradition, while at the same time announcing both Molière's *Avare* and the *Ec. des Maris*, and Regnard's *Le Retour imprévu*.

A third factor having direct influence on the generic structure of *farce* in the sixteenth century is the presence in France of the *commedia dell'arte*, heir to the Latin *Atillanae*.[12] At the time of their arrival in France (ca. 1574), the prestige of Italian letters is such that they can address themselves both to the masses with their love of buffoonery, and to an elite capable of following the dialogue in the native idiom. Taking fixed roles (costume and mask), names, and in predetermined relationships, these professionals improvise comedy (*commedia a soggetto*)[13] based on a skeletal, written *scenario*, whose performance is punctuated by clowning, burlesque and grossness, and with the dénouement always the expected one; that is to say, a *farce* of convention, "du mécanique plaqué sur le vivant" (Bergson,

---

[11] Suzanne K. Langer, *Feeling and Form. A Theory of Art* (New York, 1953), 346.

[12] Maurice Sand, *The History of the Harlequinade*, B. Blom (New York, 1968), I, 32.

[13] See R. C. D. Perman, "The Influence of the *Commedia dell'arte* on the French Theatre Before 1640," *FS*, IX (Oct. 1955), 293–303.

Le Rire). By Molière's time, however, the delicate balance between the personages will have been disrupted, due to the language barrier, to the effect that the dialogue will be a hodgepodge of Italian and French (cf. the macaronic language of the *sermon joyeux* and of *Pathelin*), or will disappear altogether, with the masks, reducing the comedy to *farce*.

17th Century —In the first quarter of the century, *farce* is represented chiefly by Gros-Guillaume, Gaultier-Gargouille, Turlupin, Bruscambille, and Tabarin (variously Philippe and Antoine Girard), all of whom are strongly influenced by the Italians of the Hôtel de Bourgogne (their *imbroglios* and character types: capricious wife, jealous husband, lover speaking French and Italian, dull-witted servant) and by Rabelais (himself indebted to Falengo and Pulci) from whom Tabarin will borrow his enumerative procedures and often entire expressions. The eternal subject is cuckoldry and in the specific case of Tabarin, who distinguishes three categories of *cocus*, sympathies are all with the unfortunate husband. The works of this theater—like that of the medieval *farce*—are intended for oral presentation, not for reading, while their audience is that of the *peuple*: artisans, merchants, students, all living close to the realities of life. Still, that *farce* as a genre is held in lowest esteem can be seen from the remarks of Bruscambille at the beginning of the century, when he feels obliged to spring to its defense and justification.[14]

The condition of the *farceur*, humanly and professionally, is that of the pariah, as it has been since Tertullian; and despite the famous declaration of Louis XII wherein he endeavors to rehabilitate the comedians, careful distinctions are made between "good" and "bad" theater (G. Scudéry, *Apologie du théâtre*, 1639; abbé d'Aubignac, *Dissertation sur la condamnation des théâtres* [1666], who recommends censorship). Add to this the rampant Jansenism of the mid-century, and one perceives the difficult but not impossible conditions under which the *farceurs* must operate. After all, it is during this same period that the *commedia dell'arte* returns to Paris, while the satirical and pithy spirit of the indigenous *farce* finds expression in other genres and modes of bourgeois inspiration: the *parodie burlesque* (mixture of *finesse* and *grossièreté*), *peinture réaliste*, and *grotesque* (ca. 1640–60) as exemplified by works of Sorel (*Le Berger extravagant* [1627] known in later editions as *L'Anti-Roman*; *L'Histoire comique de Francion*, 1622), Boileau (*Dialogue des héros de roman*, 1665), Scarron (*Le Virgile travesti*, 1648; *Le Typhon ou La Gigantomachie*, 1644; *Le Roman comique*,

---

[14] See Bowen, *op. cit.* 175–76.

1651–57), Saint-Amant (*Rome ridicule*, 1643), Furetière (*Le Roman bourgeois*, 1666), d'Assouci (*Ovide en belle humeur*, 1650), etc.

Molière —What were the bourgeois Molière's contributions to the evolving structure of *farce*? We must first determine what in the main he owes to his predecessors and to his contemporaries. Only by stretching the imagination, could one qualify even as "high" *farce* Scarron's *Jodelet* (1645), *Jodelet souffleté* (1646), *Don Japhet d'Arménie* (1652), all of which reflect too much verve and irony, while lacking extravagant caricature, to be called anything other than comedies. As for Corneille's *l'Illusion comique* (1636), its *féérie* and *pathétique* clearly place it outside the dimensions of farce, while its Matamore bears some close resemblance to the *soldat fanfaron* type of a *monologue dramatique*. We likewise reject his *Mélite* (1629), it having none of the stock characters of *farce*.

By his own admission, Molière seems to have attached himself to no single period nor source ("Je prends mon bien où je le trouve"). At the same time, we know that the influence of the *commedia dell'arte* on Molière was at least as great as that on other playwrights of the era, including Shakespeare and Lope de Vega. We should suppose that the *contemplateur*, ever on the lookout for new material, had ample opportunity to study the art of the Italian comedians during his several sojourns in Lyons, where a sizeable Italian colony flourished since the fifteenth century, and through which the *commedianti* often passed en route to Paris. It would appear that Molière's schooling in the art of *improvisation* (the selection and ordering of the sequences of individual episodes for a given performance)—a mighty step forward for French *farce*—dates from this period.[15]

The consumate skill shown by the author-director-actor Molière in "lifting" an entire scene from one of his earliest *farces*, the *Jalousie du Barbouillé*, to incorporate it into his *George Dandin*, will be demonstrated time and again: the "urine scene" of the *Médecin volant* will be reutilized in *L'Amour médecin* and in the *Médecin malgré lui*, the latter drawing at the same time on an earlier *parade farcesque*, *Le Fagotier*, or *Médecin par force*. This composing by *tiroirs* will enable the playwright to draw at will from a fund supplying either increment or decrement, a device which Molière will bring to an even finer perfection during the years 1659–1662, when he will share with the Italians facilities at the Petit-Bourbon and at the Palais-Royal.

---

[15] See Winifred Smith, *The Commedia dell'arte* (New York, 1964), 158–65.

The Italian influence is manifestly present not only in Molière's *comédies*, but in many of his *farces* and *farce comédies*. *La Jalousie du Barbouillé* (1645) is based on a *scenario*, itself based on a tale of Boccaccio. *Le Médecin volant* (1645) is based on a *scenario* of Scaramouche's *Il Medico volante*. The plot of the *Fourberies de Scapin* (1671) is drawn from a *scenario* based on Groto's *Emilia*. Dr. Diafoirus of the *Malade imaginaire* (1673) has as his model the *Il Dottore* (Graziano) of the *commedia*, although the *farce* itself is drawn from Molière's own bitter experiences with the medical profession. *L'Etourdi ou les Contretemps* (1653, Lyons) is a slavish imitation of Nicolo Barbieri's *L'Inavertito, overo Scapino disturbato e Mezzetino travagliato*, first performed as improvisation, but later committed to writing. *Le Dépit amoureux* (1656) is drawn from Nicolo Secchi's *L'Interesse* (1595), while the *Ecole des femmes* (1662) has as its Italian antecedent the *Astuta simplicita di Angiolo*. *Monsieur de Pourceaugnac* (1669) betrays more than a detail or two borrowed from the *Policinella pazzo per forza* and the *Policinella burlato*, while functioning as a "frame" for the musical and dancing interludes so loved by the King. Finally, we might note that reminiscences of the Italian style are found in all of Molière's plays in which Sganarelle plays a leading role, whether as servant (*Dom Juan*), father (*L'Amour médecin*), fiancé (*Le Mariage forcé*), husband *(L'Ecole des maris*; *Le Médecin malgré lui*; *Le Cocu imaginaire*). If the arbiter of good taste Boileau did not appreciate the *farces*, thinking them to be beneath the playwright's talent, there is every reason to believe that their author did. Written in his declining years, *Pourceaugnac, Le B. gentilhomme*, and *Scapin* may well have provided him with his sole relief from his tribulations, and it is possible that they may uniquely qualify as *farce personnelle*.

Another entirely new increment in the generic structure of *farce* is Molière's use of *portrait à clef*, which was still one of the great divertissements of the salons of the time. He was certainly not the first playwright in the seventeenth century to use it: Corneille's *Le Menteur* was invariably associated with the famous actor Bellerose, whose reputation as a *galant* was notorious. Nor will Molière be the last to use the device: in de Chalussay's *Elomire hypocondre ou les Médecins vengés* (1670), it is Molière who is slandered, while the other members of his troupe are ridiculed.

Still, in sheer output of such nasty portraits both in *farce* and *farce comedy*, he has no equal. In the *Femmes savantes*, he has Trissotin caricaturize the abbé Cotin, reading two poems from his *Oeuvres galantes*, while in the same play, Vadius is a caricature of Ménage; both renew the character type of the ludicrous pedant, the mediocre mind abhorred by all honest men. In the *Amour médecin* (*Les Médecin* in the *Régistre* of La Grange), five well-known physicians of the day serve as models for as many portraits: d'Aquin, de Fougerais, Guénaut, Esprit, Yvelin, are respectively physicians of the King, the municipality, the Queen, Monsieur, Madame. For sources closer to home he appears to have modeled Béline (*Le Mal. imag.*) after his cantankerous stepmother, Catherine Fleurette.

In the *Misanthrope*, the portraits have been identified as follows: Alceste is Boileau, Montausier, or Molière; Philinte is Chapelle; Oronte is Saint-Aignan; Acaste is Guiche; Clitandre is Richelieu; Célimène is Mlle Molière. The chief protagonist of the *Comtesse d'Escarbagnas* is Sarah de Pérusse, a noble lady of Angoulême (fortunately deceased before the play was performed). In the *Impromptu de Versailles*, Molière parodies his rivals of the Hôtel de Bourgogne, particularly the manner of Beauchâteau (François Châtelet) against whom he harbored a grudge, and indulges himself in caustic comments on the acting abilities of B.'s wife. In the *Crit. de l'Ec. des femmes*, the idiotic marquis is a caricature of the courtier de la Feuillade.

Obviously, the tone and intention of these portraits with their arguments *ad hominem*, recall the manner of the *sotie*. A notable exception is *L'Avare*, wherein Harpagon (played by Molière) says of La Flèche (played by his brother-in-law Louis Béjart): "Voilà un pendard de valet qui m'incommode fort, et je ne me plais point à voir ce chien de boiteux-là" (I. iv)—a dig which provoked peals of laughter from the audience well aware of the accident of some years before in which Béjart had received his infirmity and also of the great affection in which he was held by Molière. We should also cite the portrait of the *B. gentilhomme*, this one somewhat less damning than might have been the case, were M. Jourdain not an eclectic representation of certain would-be "gentlemen": Thomas Corneille (M. de l'Isle); Molière's father, *tapissier ordinaire du Roi*; and the author himself (J. B. Poquelin de Molière).

Besides his plays which are clearly *farces*, are there others which, while so designated, may in fact belong to another genre? We have numerous examples of such misnomers in the comic theater, of which the most striking example might be the so-called *Farce de maître Pathelin*, which, while having farcical elements, is clearly a *comedy* and a very good one. It has been shown that our own misinterpretation of gesture in *Tartuffe* (III, iii) or more exactly, our neglecting to assess its meaning within the context of the dialogue and the iconography of Italian *farce*, may mislead us into reading into that play meanings which are not at all there.[16] Anyone who has seen the productions of Molière in translation and adaptation as played by most university drama schools would have to agree that few authors' works lend themselves as readily to "hamming it up."

Obviously, *Le Tartuffe*, *Le Misanthrope*, *Dom Juan*, *Les Fâcheux*, *L'Ec. des maris*, *L'Ec. des femmes*, *L'Avare*, deal with serious matters, and despite their farcical elements, they seem much closer to the *moralité* in their preoccupation with things religious, social and political and in their personification of abstractions (hypocrite, misanthrope, unbeliever, etc.).[17] True, these "heroes" are unrepentant and at the end of the play remain unchanged, but that may in fact be part of the "message" ("man does not change"), rather than an indifference to the moral issues raised or the inability to resolve the questions plausibly, as some have claimed (the *deus ex machina* ending of *Tartuffe*, for example).

To continue with matters generic. The soliloquy of the miser who has lost his beloved *cassette* (*L'Avare*) should be seen for what it really is, and already was at the time of Larivey: a *monologue dramatique*. Those works dating from the author's years riding theater circuit in the provinces and developing his art of improvisation are authentic *farces*, *Le Docteur amoureux*, *Gros René écolier*, *Les Trois Docteurs*, *Le fin Lourdaud*, *Le Fagotier*; plus doubtless many more which have not survived. Some of the one-act plays, to look at their formal criteria, qualify as *farces*: *La Jal. du Barbouillé*, *Le Médecin volant*, *Sganarelle ou Le Cocu imaginaire*, *La Comtesse d'Escarbagnas*, *Les Précieuses ridicules*. *Le Méd. malgré lui* is a *farce*, being a triple reworking of other materials: the author's old farce *le Fagotier*, the *fabliau Le Vilain mire*, a medieval *farce* recounted by Rabelais (*La farce de celui qui avait une femme mute*). Likewise *George Dandin ou Le Mari confondu*, based on the fifteenth-century *farce Georges le Veau*. The *Fourberies* draws not only on Groto's *scenario*, but is as well an updating of a plot already used in *Gorgibus dans le Sac* (1661).

As for the ensemble of plays which qualify *grosso modo* as *comédie-ballets*, at least five are clearly *farces*. Despite an intention to confer *titres nobiliaires* on the latter through a felicitous fusion of theater, music, and dance for Court divertissement in the sumptuous settings of the Louvre, Palais-Royal, Chambord, the plays remain easily identifiable for what they

---

[16] See Jacques Guicharnaud, *Molière, une aventure théâtrale* (Paris, 1963), 152.
[17] On embryonic germ of comedy in tragedy vs. tragic germ in comedy, see Frye, *op. cit.*, "Third Essay: Archetypal Criticism: Theory of Myths," 218.

are, except that they are also, of course, frame plays. *M. de Pourceaugnac*, an attempt to make a silk purse out of a sow's ear by calling it a *farce à danser*, is nonetheless a *farce*, as was its Italian model; likewise the *Comtesse d'Escarbagnas* (*farce à danser*) and the comedy ballets *Le Bourg. gentilhomme, Le Mariage forcé* (drawn from farcical subjects in Rabelais and Sorel as well as from Giordano Bruno), *Le Mal. imaginaire* (very close in Béline's role and in its theme to Jean d'Abondance's medieval *farce* of the *Cornette*). A sixth might also qualify, *L'Amour médecin* being essentially a musical adaptation of the author's earlier *farce, Le Méd. volant*. Of course, the affective and rhetorical components provided by such musical spectacle do enhance the generic structure by giving it relief, but without fundamentally altering it. Like that excellent dish called *miroton* (1691) which about this same time makes its formal appearance on the culinary scene, the musical *farces* are as *restes accomodés avec une sauce vinaigrette*.

To conclude, the growth of French *farce* is greatest at the two points I have taken respectively as *terminus a quo* and *ad quem* for this study, and were we to view them as focii of a single and same phenomenon, its graphic representation would take the form of an ellipse. However, considered from a qualitative standpoint, it is the unique contribution of Molière in a century resplendent with literary talent to have been the first to have sensed, measured, and exploited the possibilities inherent in the genetic structure of *farce*, to have cracked Nature's mold: " . . . *destructuration* de structurations anciennes et *structuration* de totalités nouvelles aptes à crèer des équilibres qui sauraient satisfaire aux nouvelles exigences des groupes sociaux qui les élaborent."[18] Fertile inventer of strategies calculated to disturb the equilibrium of all human relationships, he renews joyously and for our great joy the dynamics of the timeless universal contest.[19]

[18] Lucien Goldmann, "Le Structuralisme génétique en histoire de la littérature," *MLN*, LXXIX, No. 3 (May 1964), 226.
[19] For possibilities by "simple choices" and "complex strategies" by twos and threes (combinations at the base of much of our drama), see Kenneth E. Boulding's provocative study: *Conflict and Defense. A General Theory*, ch. 3: "The Contribution of Game Theory" (New York, 1963), 41–57.

FROM THE *COMMEDIA ERUDITA* TO MOLIÈRE

Philip A. Wadsworth

Molière was every inch a man of the theater, but we must not forget that he was also an inveterate reader; he admired and often imitated the literature of the past. Coming to the French stage at a time when comedy was only beginning to assert its rights as a major genre, he and some of his contemporaries inevitably sought to exploit the rich though rather bookish heritage of Latin and Italian drama. He was of course well acquainted with every form of stage performance, both in Paris and the provinces, including the accomplishments of Corneille and other playwrights, the old-fashioned farces which still survived here and there, and the buffoonery of various *commedia dell'arte* troupes which made so many triumphant visits to France. But he had a distinct predilection for Italian literature and, early in his career, he found in the *commedia erudita* the inspiration for his most ambitious dramatic efforts: his first three five-act plays in verse. *L'Etourdi*, staged at Lyons in 1655 and in Paris three years later, is a fairly close imitation of *L'Inavvertito* by Niccolò Barbieri, first published in Turin in 1629. *Le Dépit amoureux* (Béziers, 1656, then Paris at the end of 1658) is adapted from an older Italian comedy, *L'Interesse* by Niccolò Secchi, composed around 1550. These two ventures, both highly successful, were followed in a few years by Molière's worst failure, *Dom Garcie de Navarre* (1661), an ill-conceived revision of *Le Gelosie fortunate del principe Rodrigo* by Giacinto Andrea Cicognini (Perugia, 1654). Rather than studying here these three Italian texts,[1] I shall attempt to provide a brief and generalized description of the *commedia erudita* and then to focus on a single comedy which is fairly characteristic of the movement as a whole. The play, Lorenzino de' Medici's *L'Aridosia*, illustrates particularly well the assimilation of Latin themes and traditions in the

---

[1] I am much indebted to the Folger Shakespeare Library, where I held a resident fellowship in 1971 for research on Molière and the Italian theater. Some studies are in progress and one article has appeared: "The Italian Source of Molière's *L'Etourdi*," *Kentucky Romance Quarterly*, 18 (1971), 319–31.

Italian theater and their further transmission to France and, in one way
or another, to Molière.

The renaissance of the theater in Italy began in the latter half of the
fifteenth century, when the works of Plautus and Terence were discovered,
diffused, imitated in Latin, and translated into Italian, and it stayed vigorously alive for over a hundred years. Throughout the sixteenth century a
multitude of Italian playwrights wrote works for the stage, and literary
theorists wrote treatises on drama. The magnitude of this movement may
be judged by the number of published plays which have survived in European libraries or which, more surprisingly, have found their way into
collections in North America. Recent bibliographical surveys, covering
the period 1500–1700, have listed the titles of more than five hundred
Italian plays in the library of the University of Toronto, some six hundred
at the University of Illinois, and about nine hundred at the Folger Shakespeare Library.[2] Various genres including sacred drama, tragedy, and pastoral were cultivated, but comedy outweighed the others by far, not only
in the number and quality of the plays but in the influence which they
exerted outside of Italy. The comic art of Molière, or of Shakespeare for
that matter, cannot be understood without some knowledge of the Italian
traditions which nourished it.

It is important to distinguish between two theatrical manifestations
or movements which eventually drew closer together and frequently
borrowed from one another: the literary (i.e. published) plays comprising
the *commedia erudita* and those of the *commedia dell'arte*, which were far
more popular but remained unpublished. (The *commedia dell'arte* erupted
rather suddenly, toward the middle of the sixteenth century, when professional actors organized themselves in troupes and began making tours. It
is known of course for its handwritten scenarios, its improvised dialogue,
its use of masked players, and its comic types with their *lazzi* or exaggerated clowning.) Erudite or learned comedy is so named because it was
launched by humanistic writers who composed imitations or adaptations
of plays by Plautus and Terence. It may be designated also as *commedia
regolare*, since it accepted the rules of Aristotle as interpreted by a number
of Italian commentators and theorists. Another term often used is *commedia sostenuta*, either because these plays were always structured to fill

---

[2] Beatrice Corrigan, *Catalogue of Italian Plays, 1500–1700, in the Library of the University
of Toronto* (Toronto: Univ. of Toronto Press, 1961); Marvin T. Herrick, *Italian Plays, 1500–
1700, in the University of Illinois Library* (Urbana and London: Univ. of Illinois Press, 1966);
and Louise G. Clubb, *Italian Plays (1500–1700) in the Folger Library* (Florence: L.S.
Olschki, 1968).

five acts or else because their style, whether in prose or in verse, was generally sustained at a high level to please an aristocratic audience. Most of these comedies, whether written by amateurs or by men-of-letters, did not reach a wide theatrical audience; they were performed primarily as entertainments for various Italian academies and princely courts.

There must have been at least a thousand plays of the sixteenth century, many of them mediocre, which can be classified as *commedia erudita*. No scholar has attempted to study them all, but many of the better ones have been singled out and are rather well known today. The most extensive modern survey of the field, Irenio Sanesi's long chapter in *La Commedia*, provides useful information on about ninety comedies. Herrick discusses some of them in more detail in his book on Italian Renaissance comedy. A recent work by Radcliff-Umstead deals with neo-Latin plays and also with a score of Italian ones which followed in their wake, giving an overall view of comedy's literary development in the early Renaissance. The major playwrights have of course attracted considerable attention: Ariosto and Machiavelli, who were prominent near the beginning of the sixteenth century; Aretino a little later; and Giordano Bruno toward the end of it. It is also worthy of mention that Giambattista Della Porta, a very prolific and influential writer of comedies, has finally received (from Mrs. Louise Clubb) the recognition which he deserves.[3]

Throughout most of the sixteenth century the basic Latin pattern of learned comedy remained monotonously strong and more or less intact, i.e. five-act comedies of intrigue in which ardent young men seek to gain possession of the girls they love, girls who seldom appear on the stage. The heroes must maneuver against their fathers, usually stern and miserly old men, but they are aided by crafty slaves or servants. Disguise, eavesdropping, impersonation, schemes for obtaining money, and other forms of trickery are important elements in the plot. In many cases false identities or questions of birth are suddenly resolved; obstacles must disappear so that the young lovers can marry at the end of the play. All this takes place in a conventional setting, a street or square in front of two or three houses equipped with doors and windows, and within a span of twelve to twenty-four hours.

By the middle of the sixteenth century more and more native materials

[3] Ireneo Sanesi, *La Commedia*, 2nd ed., 2 vols. (Milan: F. Vallardi, 1954); Marvin T. Herrick, *Italian Comedy in the Renaissance* (Urbana: Univ. of Illinois Press, 1960); Douglas Radcliff-Umstead, *The Birth of Modern Comedy in Renaissance Italy* (Chicago and London: Univ. of Chicago Press, 1969); and Louise G. Clubb, *Giambattista Della Porta Dramatist* (Princeton: Princeton Univ. Press, 1965).

from Italian life and literature were filling the classical framework. The Latin parasite began to disappear, the boastful soldier took on more modern, often Spanish features, the slave girls and courtesans became daughters or wives in middle-class families (with important roles to play, as in the *commedia dell'arte*), and the *senex* of ancient times was more likely to be portrayed as a prosperous merchant or a garrulous *dottore*. The stock characters were joined by a crowd of new ones: corrupt friars and priests, innkeepers, university students, magicians and witches, peasants, a variety of pimps and bawds, and a vast gallery of servants ranging from the most stupid to the most astute. New themes and situations were introduced, coming primarily from the *novella*: adultery and cuckolding, girls disguised as boys, mixups in darkened rooms, magic potions, strange trances and the like. Literary style also assumed greater importance, becoming more realistic in satirical passages and, with a strong influence from Petrarch, more artificial and figurative in the language used by young lovers. Later in the century, under the sway of the Counter-Reformation, dramatists tended to avoid licentious and anti-clerical themes and began to write more serious comedies exploring emotional and moral problems. But they still clung to classical structure, to complex and ingenious plots, and to many of the conventional situations and characters inherited from the Roman stage.

Without passing judgment on the faults and merits of the *commedia erudita* one must acknowledge its importance as a theatrical movement. It discovered and seized upon a rich vein in Latin literature which it imitated, modernized, and multiplied on a very large scale. It returned to ancient but undying comic themes, archetypal themes, and gave them new vitality and prestige. At the same time it accepted and imposed some useful rules or conventions which spread to other countries and which have helped to shape comic structure down to the present day. There are obviously many contacts and resemblances between the comedies of sixteenth-century Italy and those of Molière, as well as those of all his contemporaries and followers.

It is not easy to sort out ancient and Renaissance elements in Italian comedy or to trace and define their influence upon Molière. I should like to discuss a *commedia erudita* which—whether or not it was one of his sources—will point up the complexity of the problem. *L'Aridosia*, a play in prose by Lorenzino de' Medici, was written and performed in 1536, first published in 1548 at Lucca and Bologna, and reprinted in four or five other editions in the late sixteenth century. Several scholars have studied it briefly, notably Herrick (104–05) and Sanesi (I, 336–39), and the latter has made it available in a good modern edition.[4]

The prologue to *L'Aridosia* announces that old things are better than new ones and that this comedy presents some characters who have stood the test of time: young people in love, a miserly old man who stands in the way of their happiness, and an unscrupulous servant who finds ways to help them. All this is true; in fact Lorenzino drew much of his material from three well-known Latin plays, which in their turn may have been descended from Greek ancestors. His method of contamination was quite common among humanistic dramatists. Terence's *Adelphi* contributed the two brothers (Erminio and Tiberio) raised in accordance with contrasting theories of education, a challenging theme which Molière revived when he invented the sisters and their guardians in *L'Ecole des maris*. Erminio has been brought up by his soft-hearted uncle (Marcantonio) and Tiberio by his severe and niggardly father, Aridosio, who resembles Terence's Demea. Aridosio is also partially modeled after Euclio, the miser in Plautus's *Aulularia*, and undergoes a series of similar misadventures involving a purse full of money which he hides underground, which is then stolen, and which he finally recovers at the end of the play. Finally, Aridosio is credulous and superstitious, traits inherited from Theopropides in Plautus's *Mostellaria*. When he wants to enter his house (where, as it happens, Tiberio and a slave girl are enjoying themselves in bed) the clever servant Lucido, like Plautus's Tranio, frightens him and keeps him outside by demonstrating that the house is haunted. Thus Aridosio has an unusually complex personality, but I think not to the point of being inconsistent and implausible, as Sanesi has argued. (The same criticism is sometimes directed at another descendant of Euclio, Molière's Harpagon.)

Aridosio has not only two sons but a daughter, and their various love affairs, patterned mainly after those in the *Adelphi*, go to form the central plot and its complications. The daughter's suitor is the one who steals Aridosio's money, returning it finally when the old man consents to their marriage. Tiberio lacks money too, but his seductive slave turns out to be a girl of good family; her long-lost father arrives and is glad to provide her with a generous dowry. As for Erminio, he has been making love to Fiammetta, a girl brought up in a convent and supposedly about to take the veil. But she is now in an advanced state of pregnancy and in fact their baby is born before the play is over. Erminio's ever-indulgent uncle makes

---

[4] Ireneo Sanesi, ed., *Commedie del cinquecento*, 2 vols. (Bari: Laterza, 1912), II, 125–203. An early edition (Lucca, 1549), with the title *Aridosio*, is located at the Folger Library.

the best of a bad situation, arranging for the girl to be released from the convent so that she can marry his nephew. With the three love plots, in addition to the haunted house and the stolen purse, the play may seem too tangled or too crowded with sentimental characters. The emotional situations tend to be rather simple and one-sided, however, since only one of the three young women (the slave) appears on the stage, and in a very minor role. (The anachronistic slave and her ludicrous slave dealer, Ruffo, were commonplace types who can be found in other learned comedies of the period.) Also, Lorenzino simplified his task by paying little attention to verisimilitude; he made frequent use of monologues, asides, chance meetings, and overheard conversations. If we accept these dramatic conventions, as we should, we shall find that the comedy progresses quite smoothly and swiftly, provoking many hearty laughs along the way.

Although inspired by ancient texts, *L'Aridosia* was conceived as an up-to-date play giving an ironic view of life in sixteenth-century Italy. Various allusions indicate that the action takes place on a street in the city of Lucca; the stage requirements consist of two houses, belonging to Marcantonio and Aridosio, and also the entrance to a convent. The author introduced a remarkably strong dose of anticlerical satire. Erminio has an accomplice among the nuns, Sister Marietta, who appears at the door of the convent and reports to him on Fiammetta's condition and the problems of concealing the imminent arrival of her baby. A vicious priest, Ser Iacopo, has a more important role to play, since he is hired by Lucido to hoodwink Aridosio. He offers to exorcise the evil spirits who are haunting Aridosio's house, terrifies the old man with his mumbo jumbo and magical trappings, intimidates him mercilessly, and helps Lucido to steal a ruby ring from him. The portrait of this laughable but sinister priest stands out as the most original feature of Lorenzino de' Medici's comedy.

L'Aridosia found wide favor and enjoyed a long posterity. It served as a source for at least one Italian play, *La Spiritata* by Grazzini, and it reached France in a version by Pierre de Larivey, with the title *Les Esprits*. Larivey published *Les Esprits* in 1579 in his *Six premières comédies facétieuses* . . . which, like his other three surviving plays, are all translations or close adaptations of works by Italian dramatists.[5] The success of the *Six premières comédies facétieuses* is attested by four further printings in the years 1597–1611. Although Larivey has never been studied adequate-

---

[5] The nine plays by Larivey are reprinted in vols. 5–7 of *Ancien Théâtre François*, ed. Viollet-le-Duc (Paris: P. Jannet, 1854–57); for *Les Esprits* see V, 199–291.

ly, Brian Jeffery's recent book on Renaissance comedy contains some useful information on his literary career and provides a summary of *Les Esprits*; it also reminds us that this play has come to life again within the past thirty years. Albert Camus composed a very free adaptation of *Les Esprits* which was performed in Algeria in 1946 and, with further modifications, at Angers in 1953.[6]

Larivey was of Italian parentage and knew the language well; he had the ability to convey in idiomatic French the stylistic qualities of the original texts. He was basically a translator, but in the independent Renaissance manner. While keeping the traditional characters and the main features of plot and structure, he undertook to locate the action in France, using French names and French historical details. He tended to simplify his models, omitting some minor characters or episodic situations, but he was also capable of lengthening certain scenes or introducing new materials. It should be added that Larivey was a well-meaning priest and that he occasionally tried to emphasize moral teachings.

With this approach to his subject, Larivey composed a play which often reproduces *L'Aridosia* quite literally scene by scene or even line by line, but sometimes departs from it in striking ways. The events of *Les Esprits* take place in Paris, the miser is now called Séverin, and his sons are Urbain and Fortuné. The latter has been raised by his permissive uncle Hilaire. The love affairs follow the same pattern as in *L'Aridosia*, but all three girls are kept offstage; the one seduced by Urbain is said to be of good family, but she has fallen into the hands of a *maquereau* with the name of Ruffin. The role of the mischievous servant (Frontin) remains virtually unchanged, but several small ones have been suppressed including that of the conniving nun. Fortuné's mistress lives in a convent and has her baby there, but Larivey makes it clear that she was placed there against her will by her cruel father, thus relieving the nuns of any blame. The vicious priest has been transformed into a sorcerer, Maître Joss, so that nothing in the play can be considered irreligious or anticlerical. To arrive at the dénouement it is necessary for the father of Urbain's fiancée to reappear suddenly after an absence of some years. Larivey had the idea of making the father a Protestant victim of the religious wars who had been forced to flee from Paris and take refuge at La Rochelle, returning home when the situation has become less dangerous. While making all

---

[6] Brian Jeffery, *French Renaissance Comedy*, 1552–1630 (Oxford: Clarendon Press, 1969). The 1953 version of *Les Esprits* by Albert Camus has been republished in a collection of his works: *Théâtre, Récits, Nouvelles*, Bibliothèque de la Pléiade (Paris: Gallimard, 1962).

these changes Larivey still retained the best comic situations of *L'Aridosia*
—the noisy haunted house and the hidden money which is stolen—and
he succeded in writing a play which is better constructed than the original.
And in spite of its foreign themes it is thoroughly French.

Les Esprits and some of Larivey's other plays may have been acted from
time to time, although they were not specifically written for performance
on the stage. But they apparently reached many readers and they helped
immeasurably to domesticate in France the theatrical traditions stemming
from ancient and Italian comedy. Molière had first-hand knowledge of
these traditions, of course, and he was also acquainted with Larivey's
treatment of them. Molière's editors have found reminiscences of Larivey
in several of his plays, but they appear as incidental details rather than
as major themes. After his early imitations of Italian works—in which
Molière's method of composition was not far removed from that of
Lorenzino and Larivey—his art became increasingly complex and took
advantage of readings, theatrical performance, anecdotes, personal experiences, and observations of the world around him. In the mysterious
process of inspiration and creation, the importance of his "sources" is
extremely hard to assess, and, indeed, many of them cannot even be clearly
identified. *Les Esprits* and *L'Aridosia*, a mixture of several Latin streams,
flow into other currents and almost vanish from sight.

A brief glance at Molière scholarship will suffice to show that there is
much disagreement on the genesis of his comedies. *L'Ecole des maris* has
often been said to reflect or even to grow out of the situation dramatized
in Terence's *Adelphi* (two elderly brothers, two adolescents whom they
have raised, two theories of education, two love affairs) with the example
of Larivey possibly stimulating Molière to make a new exploration of these
themes while at the same time incorporating material from several other
sources. This view, approximately, can be found in the Despois-Mesnard
edition (Grands Ecrivains de la France), in the study by Michaut (*Les
Débuts de Molière à Paris*), and in Jasinski's recent book on the playwright's life and works. Other investigators have been more inclined to
stress close parallels between *L'Ecole des maris* and a Spanish play by
Mendoza, *El marido hace mujer*, or certain resemblances to a comedy
by Dorimond (and its source in Boccaccio), or current discussions of
marriage and the proper education for women, or Molière's own prospective matrimonial venture with Armande Béjart. H. C. Lancaster has
argued against the influence of Terence, except for a few details not available elsewhere, and he found "no sound evidence to prove that Molière

used Larivey's *Esprits.*" Lancaster's judgment is shared, in most respects, by Antoine Adam and by Georges Couton in his important new edition, but they do not refer to Larivey. None of these scholars mentions *L'Aridosia* as a possible source for *L'Ecole des maris.*[7]

All these commentaries have much to recommend them, and they bear witness to the vast store of knowledge and ideas which Molière had at his command; they also raise doubts about the possibility of identifying precise sources. I am more inclined to agree with the critics who give greater weight to the vitality of the classical heritage in seventeenth-century France. Educated people were well acquainted with Terence, whose works were school texts, and they undoubtedly relished the *Adelphi* with its striking contrasts and ageless themes. This rich vein of comedy, which possessed so many possibilities for variation and modernization, was a major source of inspiration for Lorenzino, Larivey, Mendoza, and certainly Molière. Numerous other elements, some of them quite personal, may have entered into the composition of *L'Ecole des maris,* but it seems likely that *L'Aridosia,* perhaps by way of *Les Esprits,* had a certain amount of influence.

Traces of the same Italian influence emerged again in *L'Avare,* seven years later. *L'Avare* is a more serious work, tinged with harshness and bitterness, but like *L'Ecole des maris* it reaches back to the Roman stage and also makes use of recent Italian and French materials. Plautus, whom Molière had already imitated in *Amphitryon,* is said by some scholars to be the central and essential source of *L'Avare*; certainly the role of Euclio in the *Aulularia* provided many features and even certain speeches for Molière's Harpagon. Mesnard emphasizes this influence, in the Grands Ecrivains edition, while also calling attention to numerous minor sources (VII, 14–33), and similar views are expressed by Jasinski (192–93) and Couton (II, 508–10). Lancaster, on the other hand (III, 714–16) minimizes the importance of Plautus and claims that *L'Avare* is derived primarily from other French plays, by Boisrobert and Chappuzeau, and Adam reaches the same general conclusion (III, 371–73). Chappuzeau seems insignificant to me, but it is undoubtedly true that Molière was strongly

---

[7] Among the standard authorities, see the Despois-Mesnard edition, II, 339–45; Gustave Michaut, *Les Débuts de Molière à Paris,* 118–21; H.C. Lancaster, *A History of French Dramatic Literature . . .,* Part III, 234–36 (refuting Katherine Wheatley's *Molière and Terence,* 1931); Antoine Adam, *Histoire de la littérature française au XVIIe siècle,* III, 273–74; and more recently René Jasinski, *Molière* (Paris: Hatier, 1969), 76; and Georges Couton's edition of Molière, *Oeuvres complètes,* 2 vols., Bibliothèque de la Pléiade (Paris: Gallimard, 1971), I, 412–13.

impressed by the comedy by Boisrobert, *La Belle Plaideuse*, which presents a crooked business man and usurer, Amidor, who lends money at outrageous rates and discovers that his victim is his spendthrift son. This situation and several others recur in *L'Avare*. *La Belle Plaideuse* is a hard-hitting play about dishonest characters in a sordid, almost criminal world, and Molière seems to share this vision of a corrupt society. If we leave aside minor influences and borrowed details, I think we can say that Molière's conception of his subject was supported mainly by two earlier works, *La Belle Plaideuse* and the *Aulularia*.

But Plautus had many descendants among writers of *commedie erudite*, in this instance Lorenzino de' Medici. Mesnard dwells on all the direct points of contact between *L'Avare* and the *Aulularia*, but he does not overlook Lorenzino and Larivey: "Il n'est pas douteux que Molière ne connût fort bien l'imitateur français et sans doute aussi l'auteur italien" (VII, 22). Plautus's hoarder, who buries his gold and watches over it so nervously, is copied closely, with a few embellishments, in *L'Aridosia* and *Les Esprits*, and he survives in both plays as an intensely comic yet formidable creature. Anyone interested in the metamorphoses of Euclio-Harpagon, or in the tangled maze of Molière sources, might wish to check some of the scenes which have been repeated over the centuries, perhaps the miser's frenzied monologue upon discovering that his treasure has been stolen. This famous speech recurs with small variations in all four comedies: *Aulularia*, IV, 9; *L'Aridosia*, III, 6; *Les Esprits*, III, 6; and *L'Avare*, IV, 7. A confrontation of texts would show that Molière adopted many features from the scene by Plautus while making Harpagon more obsessive and more ridiculous than Euclio in the Latin model. Also, Lancaster has stated (III, 715) that Molière introduced certain details which he could have found only in Larivey. The fact is that these same details appear in Lorenzino. The reading of one of these sixteenth-century predecessors, or of both, made a lasting impression on Molière's mind.

L'Avare reflects many other literary memories which cannot always be positively identified. Among those discussed by Mesnard are *La Veuve* by Larivey (again an adaptation of an Italian play), *La Sporta* by Gelli (which is based on Plautus), and, more tangibly because of some lines which are virtually translated, a scene from Ariosto's famous comedy, *I Suppositi*. Thus, three more texts of the *commedia erudita* which seem to have been more or less familiar to Molière. The evidence is suggestive and rather surprising, particularly in the case of a late play such as *L'Avare*, a mature work where Molière's independence and creative powers are so manifest.

His interest in Italian drama was not merely the dominant influence in his early comedies; apparently it remained quite active during his whole theatrical career.

The origins of Molière's art, the influences which he underwent, the specific sources which he utilized—all these matters offer inexhaustible but very risky subjects for investigation. What we have said about *L'Avare* and *L'Ecole des maris* merely touches the surface of these plays to bring out their possible relationship to an Italian learned comedy based on Plautus and Terence. The characters and the structure of *L'Aridosia*, or their prolongation in *Les Esprits*, somehow worked upon the imagination of Molière, as did many other subtle forces. He was an incomparable innovator, but, more than is generally realized, he was also a custodian of Latin and Italian traditions.

The Plays

Prolonged consideration of what it is that Molière has bequeathed to this or that political, cultural, or linguistic body leads one ultimately back to the most facinating of all questions: what is the nature of the the stuff the man wrote, and how did the playwright achieve his peculiar effect? The following set of essays represents a series of attempts to extract meaning from the oeuvre or to formulate truths about its nature. While none of the authors of this section is particularly concerned about Molière's patrimony, as it is treated in other sections of this collection, the varied backgrounds of the essayists provide an interesting backdrop for their radically different approaches.

CÉLIMÈNE AS ANTI-INGENUE: MOLIÈRE AND THE TRANSFORMATION OF COMIC TYPES

Norma Louise Hutman

A Midsummer Night's Dream concludes with a celebration; *The Misanthrope* finishes unfinished. And thereby hangs a tale. Both our experience and Northrop Frye's critical categories envision resolution as the fit end of comedy: obstacles overcome, the old society is replaced by a new order, blocking characters are driven out or assimilated into the harmonious group, lovers with their proper lovers live—as observes the cliché—happily ever after. Or so they had done until a vision of universal absurdity which predicates that no superior order is possible has shaped comedy in this image of the absurd. This, no less than tragedy and epic, is a world in which "things fall apart; the center cannot hold." In the comedies of Pirandello and Beckett, of Genet and Pinter, resolution is by definition impossible.

But the world of miscast characters who undo their own fortune is already present in Moliére's category-defying comedies. We recognize easily enough that Alceste plays both potential hero and blocking character in *The Misanthrope*. But his critical role reversal is duplicated to an equally radical degree in the figure of Célimène, who is both ingenue and obstacle to the birth of the new society and the anticipated resolution.

The archetypal comic society tends to include in its conclusion as many people as possible,[1] the unworthy no less frequently than the worthy. "The tendency of the comic society to include rather than exclude is the reason for the traditional importance of the parasite, who has no business to be at the final festival but is nevertheless there."[2] The blocking character, no less than the parasite, may find a place at the banquet. Sebastian and Antonio are among the accepted participants in the new society with which *The Tempest* ends. Hermia's father—who has been perfectly willing to have his daughter slain for disobedience—is reconciled to the union of lovers in *A Midsummer Night's Dream*. On occasion, as in *The Merchant*

---

[1] Northrop Frye. *Anatomy of Criticism* (New York: Atheneum, 1965), 165.
[2] Frye, 166.

of Venice, the human obstacle to union and happiness is literally and even cruelly removed. But this sacrifice purchases the birth of the new order (Jewess and Christian wed; Antonio's life spared; financial difficulties overcome). In these examples a critical agent in the transforming of the social order has been the ingenue, functioning in different guises. Miranda is a classic innocent who knows not evil and envisions as completely pure her "brave new world," but she nevertheless speaks her mind, declares her favoring of Ferdinand and opposes her father's apparent will (though rather fulfilling in fact his expectations) to confess her love. Hermia makes bold to speak her mind to Theseus and is described as decisive both when beloved of Lysander and Demetrius and, though the characterization becomes more shrewish, when rejected by both. Portia literally and vigorously brings about the vanquishing of the enemy and, even when teasing and tricking her husband, the effecting of the new order with its appropriate pairs of lovers.

Against the example of these damsels, Célimène's actions are altogether inappropriate for the classic ingenue. If we examine each of the aspects of classical comedy in the light of the ingenue's role, we shall find Célimène at work undoing simultaneously her own function and the play's archetypal ground.

Structurally comedy works from randomness to order. The Shakespearean comedy with its disguises, mismatched lovers, and altered affections is a model for the form. Restoration comedy proceeds along similar lines, settling conflicts and pairing off potential partners with the intervention of fate, finance, and occasionally catalytic characters. *The Beaux' Strategem*, for example, gives us instances of all these elements with a heroine who works to undo her marriage, wed her true beloved, and provide a similar happy fate for her friend in the manner of enterprising heroines and proper ingenues of the traditional stamp. Even Oscar Wilde's parody of the form brings pairs out of confusion and effects a traditional conclusion.

Not so Molière; not so Célimène. The structure of Molière's work is much more dependent upon Célimène's volitional control than upon that of Alceste. To save Alceste from his self-elected alienation, to effect unions where potential unions suggest themselves, Célimène needs make a choice. But so enmeshed in her own lies is our ingenue that any choice threatens to reveal the fabric of her deceit. Each suitor has epistles which will reveal Célimène's negative opinion of the others. Only Alceste, presumably, is willing to forgive this duplicity, charge it up to the age's evil influence, and marry her, lies notwithstanding. In the face of this potential resolution, Célimène simply says no, succeeding finally in disillusioning an Alceste who has through five acts resisted disillusionment. Thus, instead of toppling the old order where frivolity is king and effecting a new society into which the criticizing Alceste can be integrated, she freezes society in its ancient state, opting for frivolity—she is, she says, too young to flee the world—and severing Alceste's last commitment to the structure of society.

We are accustomed to recognize that Alceste is a misanthrope by choice or at least by predisposition. He is scarcely on stage before he announces to Philinte: "I choose to be rude, Sir."[3] He disdains holding the same opinion as everyone else (I, i); pronounces à propos his fellow man that "all are corrupt" (I, i); scores contemporary society on every occasion; and seems to see evil as much endemic to human nature as to a particular age, for he informs Philinte in the second act, "Men, Sir, are always wrong, and that's the reason/ That righteous anger's never out of season" (II, v). He is, in brief, precisely what he chooses to be and is described as rigid, stiff, unbending and inflexible. His rigidity denies society sufficient flexibility to transform itself.

But Célimène is and elects to be exactly the opposite while leading to the same disintegrating effect. She is described as frivolous, brittle and coquettish; Eliante, her cousin, opines that Célimène herself does not know when she is telling the truth; "her heart's a stranger to its own emotion" (IV, i). She encourages everyone and deceives everyone. To him who is present she is attentive; about the absent friend, malicious. If, therefore, Alceste is rigidity personified, Célimène is total fluidity and denies from her perspective, no less than Alceste from his, the possibility of social transformation. Alceste demands a single absolute structure, his own. Célimène tries to embrace all possible structures and allows each to escape her. Because she toys with every possible pairing, she fails in the ingenue's role of agent of the new order to effect any pairing at all, save for the second-hand and second-best liaison between Philinte and Eliante at the fifth act's conclusion.

In this final union we see Molière's kinship with Beckett's and Pinter's splintered societies. Prospero does not reform Sebastian and Antonio,

---

[3] Quotations from *The Misanthrope* refer to Richard Wilbur's translation (New York: Harcourt, Brace and World; 1954) and will hereafter be identified by act and scene in the text. I, i.

but the brave new world of Miranda's vision includes them. There is nothing so little like the dawn discovery of Ferdinand and Miranda as the better-than-nothing acceptance whereby Philinte and Eliante are united. This new world consists not of dreams realized but of the philosophy of making do.

Célimène will not make do. She accepts nothing. Indeed, refusal and disruption consistently characterize her influence. She will not tell Orante and Alceste which she favors because she wants both (as well as everyone else) still dangling from her string. But she teases them into believing that she knows perfectly well which she prefers (V, ii). Of such tender messages are duels rather than transformed societies made. Her words are treacherous and her letters treasonable. She plays at disowning her missives, but, caught finally in her falsehood, puts the whole matter by as nothing of consequence. This attitude brings the end we would suppose: each of the suitors deserts Célimène in turn, leaving her to Alceste whose condition of retreat from society she rejects. Having driven off the dozens, she dismisses the one loyal suitor. Philinte suggests to Alceste that his honesty will undo the fabric of society, but Célimène's duplicity (which might better be styled multiplicity) shreds society even more successfully.

Ultimately both Alceste and Célimène by their opposite actions are trapped in the old society: the former because he rejects its mores categorically and can therefore find no continuity to lead out of the old order and into a new; the latter because she is altogether the tool of social norms, evidencing no capacity to live by her own decisions and shape her own context.

Célimène in the same manner fails to pass those judgments which are required for the reordering processes. Such judgments must arise from social rather than ethical considerations, allowing the unworthy no less than the worthy a seat at the final festivities. But the only judgments which prevail in Molière's play are ethical: Alceste rejects and Philinte accepts. The latter urges a philosophic view of the shortcomings of the age which allows opportunities for the practice of virtue. Alceste admits the cleverness but not the validity of the argument. Since Philinte will not serve to realign society, some other social ethic must be posited against the moral ethic of the protagonist. This role too Célimène refuses. Célimène embodies the old society's moral vacuum, but at the same time she plays it false. She would have all the suitors and a faithful suitor; she would be judged on her word alone but constantly demonstrates that she cannot be trusted.

Since the characters of comedy are functions of the structure,[4] Célimène's loss of potential identity in the mores of the old order renders impossible the conception of the new. That purgation of sympathy and ridiculousness which corresponds to the Aristotelian purgations proper
to tragedy cannot, therefore, be realized. For neither Alceste nor Célimène has merited our sympathies—each appearing responsible for his
own ultimate alienation—nor appeared, in their manifest ridiculousness,
as mutually redeeming. Because Célimène cannot accept Alceste's condition of retirement from society and because Alceste cannot accept her refusal for the marriage she does offer, each operates to undo the potential
resolution in which, as presumptive heirs of the aborted new society, they
might have been united.

Molière's use of the comic characters effects, then, a particularly modern
fate: the isolation of Alceste by choice and Célimène by having overplayed
the coquette. Philinte and Eliante are moved to pity and promise to better
the situation; what they do not promise is hope. "The tendency of comedy" writes Frye, "is to include as many people as possible in its final society." But Molière tears society apart to reveal, as do his contemporary
counterparts, how hero and heroine can become, through the conventions
of comedy, the agents of their own undoing. Anticipating the bitch-god-
dess of modern theater, Célimène redefines the possibilities of a type and
so with Alceste begins to redefine the limits of comedy.

DE L'UNITÉ DE *DOM JUAN*
Takuzô Obase

Il est presque unanimement reconnu que parmi toutes les pièces de Molière, *Dom Juan* est une oeuvre exceptionnelle. Il n'y a là ni unité de temps, ni unité de lieu. Quelques-uns prétendent même que l'unité d'action y est équivoque. Francis Sarcey, le plus virulent à cet égard, dit : "Y eut-il jamais comédie plus mal faite que celle de *Dom Juan*? Les scènes tombent les unes par-dessus les autres, sans qu'aucun lien les rattache l'une à l'autre. Les personnages passent comme des héros de lanterne magique ; ils disent leur mot, et disparaissent : on ne les revoit plus. Ils étaient inutiles à l'action. De l'action, il n'y en a pas ombre" (*Quarante ans de théâtre, Molière et la comédie classique*, 1900,82).

On explique ce manque d'unité par le fait que, *Le Tartuffe* ayant été interdit, Molière dût écrire à la hâte une pièce nouvelle. Maurice Donnay écrit par exemple :

> Si cette pièce n'a pas d'unité de lieu, ni de temps, ni d'action, ni de genre, c'est qu'elle est chargée d'imitations, c'est que Molière a été influencé par tout ce qui a été fait antérieurement sur le même sujet, par *El Burlador* espagnol, de Tirso de Molina ; par deux *Il convitato di pietra* italiens, de Cicognini et de Giliberto ; par les deux *Festins de Pierre* français de Dorimon et de Villiers, et même par une *commedia dell'arte* que les Italiens jouent à Paris sur une scénario de Biancolelli. . . . Molière est pressé ; il n'a pas le temps. Alors, il emprunte à tous ; il ne s'attache pas à chercher des combinaisons originales. Mais ce qui complique encore le mélange, c'est que, à ces imitations, Molière ajoute ses observations, ses rancunes et ses haines. (*Molière*, 1922, 176–77).

Il est indéniable qu'il lui fallut une pièce nouvelle pour combler le vide dû à l'interdiction du *Tartuffe*. Mais par rapport aux oeuvres de ses prédécesseurs, Molière a rejeté sans regret plusieurs scènes vraiment comiques. Il a abandonné par exemple la scène bouffonne du scénario où Arlequin, lançant vers le parterre une longue liste de noms de femmes séduites et délaissées par son maître, demande si quelqu'un n'y reconnait pas le nom de son épouse ; ou cette autre scène comique où Fighetto, qui soupçonne Dom Juan d'être le meutrier du Commandeur, tente d'acheter Passarino, valet de Dom Juan, pour 100,000 écus ; celui-ci feint d'abord d'accepter, mais déclare au dernier moment : "C'est Fighetto !"

Certains placent l'unité d'action de la pièce de Molière dans la damnation du héros, mais si l'on compare son *Dom Juan* à ceux de ses prédécesseurs, on s'apperçoit que Molière a sensiblement abrégé les scènes surnaturelles où apparaît la Statue du Commandeur : le premier banquet ne dure qu'une minute chez Molière tandis que chez Villiers la même scène compte cent cinquante vers et chez Dorimon cent huit. Dans cette scène il développe ni sermon de la Statue ni lazzi du valet ; il substitue au long sermon de ses prédécesseurs cette courte phrase éloquente et laconique : "On n'a pas besoin de lumière, quand on est conduit par le Ciel" (Acte IV, scène 8). Molière a supprimé complètement le second banquet où, dans les pièces de ses devanciers, la Statue se régale de serpents et de scorpions. Dans Molière la Statue réapparaît et prend tout de suite la main de Dom Juan.

D'ailleurs il faut tenir compte du fait que, ami de Cyrano, de Chapelle, de d'Assoucy et de La Mothe Le Vayer, Molière ne paraît pas croire en un Dieu vengeur et rémunérateur. S'il fait tomber son héros en enfer ce n'est que pour suivre la légende. Il faut donc conclure que la damnation n'est point l'action de la pièce.

Emile Faguet a placé le sujet de la pièce dans le goût du mal de Dom Juan. Il s'y précipite à toutes les occasions : il trompe Elvire, essaie d'enlever la jeune fiancée d'un autre, séduit à la fois Charlotte et Mathurine, tente de faire jurer le Pauvre, se moque de la Statue, bafoue M. Dimanche, dupe son père, abuse Dom Carlos. Ainsi notre héros est, d'après Faguet, le disciple de Nietzsche ou plutôt Néron transporté de la tragédie dans la comédie. (Cf. *En lisant Molière*, 1914, 184 et sq.) De là l'incohérence de la pièce. Dom Juan fait le mal pour le mal : il y a là unité de caractère, mais pas unité d'action.

Molière dût écrire la pièce en hâte, il est vrai. Il faut remarquer cependant qu'il ne suit l'intrigue d'aucun de ses prédécesseurs. Inventer une intrigue tout à fait différente est évidemment un travail plus pénible qu'inventer de nouvelles scènes en suivant une intrigue toute faite. Il faut ainsi conclure que Molière, malgré le manque de temps, n'a pas bâclé sa pièce en empruntant des scènes ici et là. Mais pourquoi invente-t-il une intrigue toute différente ? Pour répondre à cette question il faut chercher le véritable sujet de *Dom Juan* : Molière l'a présenté très clairement au début du Ier acte selon la règle du théâtre classique. Sganarelle, le valet, dit : "Le grand seigneur méchant homme est une terrible chose" (Acte I, scène 1). Sous le masque d'une légende étrangère, Molière a voulu peindre un tableau des grands de Versailles et y a parfaitement réussi.

En France au XVIIe siècle, il y avait force Dom Juan et Tartuffe, car

Dom Juan et Tartuffe ne sont que les figures nées de la noblesse française de ce temps. A la suite de la politique absolutiste de Richelieu et de Mazarin, notamment à la suite de la défaite de la Fronde, la noblesse d'épée, ainsi que la noblesse de robe, ont perdu le droit d'intervenir dans la politique. Les droits féodaux ont cependant été maintenus avec le revenu foncier (le cens s'élevait à la moitié de la récolte). Mais une vie de luxe et de débauches engloutissait leurs revenus; c'est pourquoi les nobles bénéficiaient d'autres revenus provenant des charges de la cour ainsi que de biens ecclésiastiques qui leur étaient alloués en commande. Ils jouissaient également de pensions accordées par le Roi. Louis XIV, pour les éloigner de la politique, choisit des ministres sortis de la bourgeoisie tels Colbert et Louvois. Le pouvoir central une fois affermi, les guerres civiles cessèrent, les seigneurs étaient libérés ainsi de leur devoir de protection envers leurs serfs. La fonction de la noblesse d'épée se réduit désormais à la présence à la cour pour rendre plus éclatante la gloire du Roi Soleil; ils y menaient une vie oisive et dispendieuse. Dans son *"Sermon sur l'oisiveté"* Louis Bourdaloue dit:

> Il est un nombre infini de personnes, qui sont, à ce qui paraît, sur la terre (voyez si j'en conçois une idée juste) que pour y recevoir les tributs du travail d'autrui, sans jamais payer du leur; qui n'ont point d'autre emploi dans leur condition que de jouir des aises et des douceurs de la vie; dont le plus grand soin et la plus grande affaire est de couler le temps; qui se divertissent toujours ou qui, plutôt, à force de se divertir, ne se divertissent plus; il semble, à les voir, que la loi ne soit pas pour eux et qu'ils ne soient pas compris dans la masse commune du genre humain. . . . Ce jeune homme de qualité passe ses premières années dans les divertissements et les plaisirs; comment acquerra-t-il les connaissances qui sont le fondement nécessaire, sur lequel il doit bâtir ce qu'il sera un jour? . . . Commencera-t-il à s'intruire, losqu'il sera question de juger et de décider? Fera-t-il l'apprentissage de son ignorance aux dépens d'autrui? Justifiera-t-il ses fautes et ses erreurs par l'oisiveté de sa jeunesse?

Bien que les moeurs brutales et grossières de l'époque de la guerre de religion aient été polies par la vie sociale, seule la surface avait changé. Cette classe privilégiée traite les vilains en bêtes brutes; son arrogance et son égoïsme n'étaient point adoucis. Ainsi le gracieux Hôtel de Rambouillet et la splendide cour de Versailles sont devenus le magnifique manteau qui couvre la laideur dévoilée par les mémoires du duc de Saint-Simon, de la princesse Palatine, de Primi Visconti, etc. Si ce Dom Juan, très galant au premier abord, très intelligent et spirituel en apparence, si richement habillé que Charlotte et Mathurine sont éblouies, qui n'emploie jamais la violence pour attraper les femmes, si ce Dom Juan galant homme a en réalité une âme cruelle, égoïste, même cynique, c'est que Molière a peint en lui la grande noblesse de cour dans son apparence et dans sa réalité. Il n'y a rien d'étonnant à ce que, très haut placés dans la hiérarchie sociale et tout à fait oisifs, ayant hérité des moeurs grossières du siècle précédent, ces nobles privilégiés se débauchassent dans les luxes de parure et de la table, dans le jeu et surtout dans le plaisir des conquêtes féminines. Citons quelques exemples historiques:

Henri de Lorraine, duc de Guise, nommé archevêque de Reims à quinze ans, mena une vie dissolue avec ses cousines Anne et Bénédicte de Gonzague dans le couvent d'Avenay; il eut une liaison avec Bénédicte et épousa Anne en secret. En abandonnant celle-ci, il épousa derechef la comtesse de Bossu et se remaria avec Mademoiselle de Pons. Pendant ce temps, il devint l'amant de dames de la haute noblesse telle Madame de Cannuel; en même temps il se divertissait avec des courtisanes telle la célèbre Nina Barcarole. D'après la liste établie par lui-même, le nombre de femmes avec lesquelles il eut rapport s'élève à mille et trois. Le comte de Guiche courtisa Mademoiselle de La Vallière, favorite du roi, ainsi qu'Henriette d'Angleterre, épouse de Monsieur. Il séduisit d'innombrables dames et demoiselles dont, selon *La Fameuse Comédienne*, le méchant libelle contre Molière, Armande Béjart (ce qui n'a jamais été confirmé). Primi Visconti dit: "le comte faisait grand ravage parmi les femmes, malgré sa réputation d'impuissance" (*Mémoires sur la cour de Louis XIV*, tr. par Jean Lemoine, s.d., 4).

Le comte de Lauzun, célèbre par sa liaison avec la Grande Mademoiselle, conservait et étiquetait les souvenirs de ses victoires galantes. Madame de Sévigné en parle ainsi dans la lettre du 23 décembre 1671: "On a trouvé, dit-on, mille belles merveilles dans les cassettes de M. de Lauzun, des portraits sans compte et sans nombre, une sans tête, une autre les yeux crevés, des cheveux grands et petits, des étiquettes pour éviter la confusion: à l'un grison d'une telle, à l'autre mousse de la mère, à l'autre blondin pris en bon lieu, ainsi mille gentillesses; mais je n'en voudrais pas jurer, car vous savez comme on invente dans ces occasions." Visconti écrit de lui: "Je ne pouvais comprendre comment Lauzun avait pu être en vogue parmi les femmes, car il était tout petit, laid de visage, à moitié chauve, graisseux, sale et difforme . . . . Lauzun avait grande audace en faisant à tous de grandes promesses, presque toutes les femmes le voulaient pour montrer qu'elles gouvernaient le favori du Roi" (*Op. cit.*, 14).

Le prince de Conti fut amoureux de sa propre soeur, la duchesse de Longueville; il mena une vie déréglée au château de La Grange en Languedoc avec sa concubine Mademoiselle Calvimont, femme légitime de l'avocat au Parlement de Bordeaux. Il épousa cependant une des nièces de Mazarin, mariage tout à fait machiavélique.

Bien que Louis XIV n'ait embastillé que rarement les nobles débauchés, le marquis de Vardes fut enfermé derrière ces murs et comme il n'amendait pas sa conduite, il fut déporté dans la marécageuse Aigues-Mortes. Et le comte de Bussy-Rabutin eut des liaisons avec d'innombrables femmes, dont une qu'il enleva, à main armée, dans le Bois de Boulogne. Chacun sait qu'il consigna ses souvenirs et les affaires galantes des autres dans *l'Histoire amoureuse des Gaules*.

Louis XIV lui-même n'était-il pas un Dom Juan? Marie-Thérèse, son épouse légitime venue d'Espagne, n'est célèbre que par l'oraison funèbre de Bossuet. Elle était une figure moins brillante que Mademoiselle de La Vallière qui avait été fille d'honneur de la duchesse d'Orléans, que Madame de Maintenon, veuve de Scarron, qui avait été d'abord la gouvernante des enfants illégitimes de Louis et de Montespan, mais qui remplaça celle-ci. En outre parmi les femmes aimées ou courtisées par Louis, on trouve les noms de Catherine de Beauvais, première femme de chambre de la reine; de Marie Mancini, nièce de Mazarin; d'Henriette d'Angleterre, sa belle soeur; de Mlle d'Elbeuf, d'une branche cadette de la maison de Lorraine; de Mlle Touchy, fille de la maréchale de La Mothe et alors gouvernante du Dauphin; de la princesse de Soubise, fille de la duchesse de Rohan et du duc de Rohan-Chabot; de la princesse de Monaco, fille de feu maréchal de Grammont et femme du prince de Monaco; de Mlle de Fontange, fille du comte de Rousille et fille d'honneur de Madame; de la comtesse de Ludres, chanoinesse, et de mesdemoiselles de Théobon, de La Mothe, etc., etc. De Louis XIV la princesse Palatine a écrit sans gêne: " . . . tout lui était bon, pourvu que ce fussent des femmes, les paysannes, les filles de jardiniers, les femmes de chambre, les dames de qualité; elles n'avaient qu'à faire semblant d'être amoureuses de lui" (*Mémoires de la Palatine*, I, cité par F. Gaiffe dans *L'Envers du Grand Siècle*, 1924, 19). Le ton de la Palatine est fort semblable à celui de Sganarelle qui parle de son maître: "Dame, demoiselle, bourgeoise, paysanne, il ne trouve rien de trop chaud, ni de trop froid pour lui" (Acte I, scène 1).

La plupart de ces nobles dépravés étaient athées comme Dom Juan. Le père Mersenne avait écrit dès 1623 qu'il y avait à Paris cinquante mille libertins; le nombre ne paraît pas avoir diminué à l'époque de Molière. Mais le libertinage de ces nobles est bien différent de celui des philosophes tels Gassendi et La Mothe Le Vayer. Pour ces libertins érudits il s'agissait du matérialisme permettant de s'affranchir du dogme médiéval. Par contre pour les soi-disant libertins de la noblesse versaillaise, il s'agissait de justifier leur manière de vivre éhontée en dénigrant la religion qui était le fondement de la morale; en d'autres termes ils cherchaient à s'enfoncer dans la débouche en se libérant de toute conscience morale. Leur connaissance philosophique ou théologique était par conséquent très superficielle et restait au niveau de la culture de M. Jourdain qui engage des maîtres de danse, d'escrime et de grammaire. Mais comme le pédant ignorant crie à haute voix, leurs actes blasphématoires étaient d'autant plus bruyants. Pour ne citer que quelques exemples, la princesse Palatine, avant sa conversion, tentait de brûler un morceau de la vraie croix en compagnie du grand Condé et du médecin Bourdelot. Guiche, Bussy-Rabutin, Manicamp, etc. faisaient des orgies le jour même du vendredi saint. Retz, Matha, Fontrailles et leurs amis chargèrent dans la rue, l'épée à la main, contre un crucifix en criant "Voilà l'ennemi!" Le duc de Nevers faisait baptiser un cochon et le chevalier de Roquelaure un chien. Madame Deshoulières faisait baptiser son chien et ne faisait pas baptiser sa fille qui ne le fut qu'à vingt-neuf ans. Le chevalier de Roquelaure, ayant rencontré dans la rue un pauvre maudissant Dieu, lui donna cinq sols en le louant et il l'incita à proférer davantage de malédictions; c'est ainsi qu'il lui donna cinq sols trois fois de suite.

L'histoire de Bussy-Rabutin lors du siège de Lérida (*Mémoires*, éd. Ludovic Lalane, 1857, I, 147) est plus diabolique:

> Le chevalier de la Vallière, maréchal de camp de jour à la tranchée du maréchal de Gramont, me sachant de garde à la tranchée du prince, m'envoya prier de grand matin à dîner, me mandant que Barbantane, lieutenant des gendarmes d'Enghien, et Jumeaux, maréchal de bataille, deux de mes meilleurs amis, s'y trouvaient. J'acceptai le parti, et je me rendis sur les sept heures à l'ouverture de la tranchée du maréchal, qui était dans les masures d'une vieille église ruinée. Je ne fus pas arrivé qu'on nous fit déjeuner; nous avions les petits violons du prince; pendant qu'ils jouaient, Barbantane ne sachant à quoi s'amuser, lève le dessus d'une tombe et trouve dedans un corps tout entier, sur lequel était encore le linge dont il avait été enseveli. Il nous apporte le cadavre, et la Bretêche, guidon des gandarmes d'Enghien, l'ayant pris de l'autre main, ils se mettent à le faire danser entre eux deux; cela me fit horreur, et je leur témoignai tant de fois trouver ce plaisir-là ridicule, qu'ils reportèrent le cadavre dans son cercueil.

Après avoir lu ces lignes, ne serait-on pas tenté de s'écrier avec Sganarelle que c'est "un enragé, un chien, un diable, un Turc, un hérétique, qui ne croit ni Ciel, ni Enfer, ni loup-garou" (Acte I, scène 2)?

Leurs actes blasphématoires ne sont qu'effets d'un cynisme qui se plait à fouler aux pieds ce qui est sacré et objet de vénération; c'est pur enfantillage sans aucun rapport avec la philosophie. Par contre Gassendi, La Mothe Le Vayer et d'autres libertins érudits menaient une vie austère en vrai chrétiens.

A première vue, ils étaient des rationalistes qui croyaient que "deux et deux font quatre" (Acte III, scène 1). Mais il est fort douteux qu'ils le croyaient après une méditation plus ou moins profonde. Cette parole, rendue célèbre par la bouche de Dom Juan, est ce qu'avait dit Maurice de Nassau à son lit de mort et qui était fort répandue parmi les libertins débauchés. C'est donc que Dom Juan la répète. L'exemple le plus convaincant de la minceur de leurs connaissances philosophiques se manifeste dans leur croyance aux sciences occultes en dépit de leur soi-disant rationalisme. Le duc de Nevers, le duc de Brissac, pour ne citer qu'un exemple, cherchaient à évoquer le diable en étudiant la sorcellerie. Primi Visconti dit d'eux: "Je me rendis à plusieurs entretiens avec eux; une fois, on en vint à parler de sciences occultes: Agrippa, Paracelse, Cardan, la clavicule de Solomon et autres choses semblables. Tous les deux se disaient désireux de voir le diable, lequel, malgré leurs longues recherches, leurs imprécations et dépenses, n'avait jamais satisfait leur curiosité" (*Op. cit.* 20). A l'Hôtel de Soissons où plusieurs libertins privilégiés se réunissaient, on discutait vivement d'astrologie et s'enthousiasmait pour une drogue qui ferait prévoir l'avenir par l'intermédiaire du diable. Il faut donc penser que dans leur âme ténébreuse coéxistaient le rationalisme de ceux qui affirme que deux et deux font quatre et l'irrationalisme de ceux qui croient à l'existence du diable.

Devenus vieux ou leurs conditions d'existence ayant changé, ces nobles athées se convertissaient et devenaient des dévots qui étalaient leur foi aussi bruyamment qu'ils avaient blasphémé dans le passé. Henri de Lorraine devint marguillier de sa paroisse et s'enrôla dans la confrérie de Saint-Roch. Le prince de Conti se fit membre acharné de la Compagnie du Saint-Sacrement de l'Autel. Tous les moriéristes savent qu'il persécutait le théâtre qu'il avait protégé autrefois. Les conversions du grand Condé et du cardinal Retz étaient aussi bruyantes. Louis XIV qui avait protégé Molière contre la cabale des dévots devint bigot au cours des dernières années sous l'influence de Madame de Maintenon et en révoquant l'Edit de Nantes, il persécutait les protestants. La princesse Palatine écrit de lui: "On avait fait au roi tellement peur de l'enfer, qu'il croyait que tous ceux qui n'avaient pas été instruits par les jésuites étaient damnés, et qu'il craignait d'être damné aussi en les fréquentant. Quand on voulait perdre quelqu'un, il suffisait de dire: il est huguenot ou janséniste: alors son affaire est faite" (*Mémoires*, tome I, cité par F. Gaiffe dans *L'Envers du Grand Siècle*, 15–16). Depuis qu'il était devenu dévot, les nobles libertins se hâtaient de se convertir. La Bruyère écrit ironiquement : "Le courtisan autrefois avait ses cheveux, était en chausses et en pourpoint, portant de larges canons, et il était libertin. Cela ne sied plus : il porte une perruque, l'habit serré, le bas uni, et il est dévot : tout se règle par la mode" (*Les Caractères*, chap. XIII).

Pour ces nouveaux convertis la foi n'était qu'un grand manteau pour se débaucher sans scandale et s'abandonner dans les plaisirs scabreux sans avoir aucun poids sur la conscience. Le libertinage et la foi, Dom Juan et Tartuffe ne sont pas contradictoires ; ils se complètent l'un l'autre.

De l'arrogance exorbitante de la noblesse d'épée de Versailles, il parait inutile de donner des exemples réels. Contentons-nous donc de citer le témoignage de Bourdaloue :

> Ce qui nous indispose à l'égard des grands, dit-il, et ce qui nous porte le plus souvent, contre eux aux murmures et aux mépris, ce sont leurs hauteurs et leurs fiertés, ce sont leurs airs dédaigneux et méprisants, ce sont leurs façons de parler, leurs termes, leurs gestes, leurs regards, toutes leurs manières, ou brusques ou rebutantes, ou trop impérieuses et trop dominantes ; ce sont encore bien plus leurs tyrannies et leurs duretés, quand, par l'abus du plus énorme pouvoir dont ils ont été revêtus, ils tiennent dans l'oppression des hommes comme eux, et leur font sentir sans ménagement tout le poids de leur grandeur ; quand par l'indifférence la plus mortelle, uniquement attentifs à ce qui les touche, et renonçant à tous les sentiments de la charité, ils voient d'un oeil tranquille, et sans nulle compassion, des misères dont assez ordinairement ils sont eux-mêmes auteurs ; quand par une monstrueuse ingratitude, ils laissent sans récompense les services les plus importants et oublient des gens qui se sont immolés et qui s'immolent sans cesse pour leur intérêt ; ce sont leurs injustices, leurs violences, leurs concussions, et si je puis user ce terme, leurs brigandages. (*Pensées. De la vraie et de la fausse dévotion*, cité par F. Gaiffe dans *l'Envers de Grand Siècle*, 89–90.)

Se moquant de l'intérêt public et social, ne visant que la vie de luxure, ils gaspillaient l'argent et devenaient esclaves de leurs dettes malgré d'immenses revenus et aussi une rente énorme accordée par le roi. Primi Visconti a écrit dans ses *Mémoires* : "Je m'étonne pourtant de la manière dont se font les mariages. Tout le monde veut de l'argent, souvent ils se trompent entre eux, et par suite il ne faut pas s'étonner si les séparations sont aussi nombreuses. . . . Il y a à Paris plus de vingt mille gentilshommes qui n'ont pas un sou et qui subsistent pourtant par le jeu et les femmes, ou qui vivent d'industrie" (*op. cit.*, 251-52).

Mais se piquant de leur qualité de noblesse et méprisant les bourgeois et les paysans, ils ne payaient guère leurs dettes. Bourdaloue, dans son

Sermon sur l'aumône dit "le commencement de la charité est de payer des dettes à des valets et à des marchands." Il lança dans le *Sermon sur la Restitution* une violente critique contre "la peine que témoignent certains riches et certains grands du monde quand il s'agit d'acquitter des dettes légitimement contractées; et la violence qu'ils se font, ou plutôt qu'il leur faut faire pour arracher d'eux un payement dont ils conviennent les premiers qu'ils ne peuvent se défendre. Par combien de paroles et de vaines promesses n'éludent-ils pas les poursuites d'un créancier? Combien de rebuts ne l'obligent-ils pas à essuyer? De combien de retardements de remises ne fatiguent-ils pas sa patience; et cela, sans prendre garde aux effets terribles et aux engagements de conscience dont une semblable dureté est nécessairement suivie?" Même le doux Fénelon écrit que "le dernier de leurs devoirs est celui de payer ses dettes. Les predicateurs n'osent plus parler pour les pauvres, à la vue d'une foule de créanciers dont les clameurs montent jusqu'au ciel" (*Sermon pour la fête de l'Epiphanie*).

Mais je ne puis résister à la tentation de reproduire ici un épisode du duc de la Feuillarde qui est l'original du ridicule marquis de *La Tarte à la crème* de la *Critique de l'Ecole des femmes* et qui, pour se venger de la satire de Molière, a meurtri à Versailles le visage de notre grand comique en le frottant contre les boutons et les broderies d'or de son habit. C'est l'anecdote que Boursalut raconte dans une lettre à l'eveque de Langres:

Du temps qu'il était garçon, comme M. de la Feuillarde était de toutes les fêtes de la cour, où il faisait une figure considérable, sa dépense excédait de beaucoup son revenu. On se piquait alors d'être bien monté, et M. de la Feuillarde était un de ceux qui l'étaient toujours le mieux, aux dépens de qui il appartiendrait. Gaveau, marchand de chevaux, dont Molière a immortalisé le nom en le mettant dans la comédie des *Fâcheux*, étant, un matin au lever de M. de la Feuillarde, pour deux cents louis d'or qu'il lui devait, M. de la Feuillarde commanda à un valet de chambre de lui aller chercher six papillons morts, qui étaient dans un tiroir de son cabinet. —Votre Grandeur se souvient, ajoute Boursault, que pendant un an ou deux, on fut, à la cour et à Paris même, dans un engouement pour les papillons, qui était une espèce de manie. On était, si j'ose me servir de ce mot, enthousiasmé de la beauté de leurs ailes, et ceux qui n'en avaient point de peint dans leurs cabinets ne paraissaient point pour les gens de bon goût.

M. de la Feuillarde, qui enchérissait toujours sur les modes, ayant fait apporter ses papillons, demanda à Gaveau ce qu'il en pensait:—Ah! Monsieur, s'écria Gaveau, la belle chose! L'arc-en-ciel n'a pas de si agréables couleurs, et j'aimerais mieux une aile de vos papillons que tous les queues de paons qui sont en France.—Eh! que l'imagines-tu que cela vaille? lui dit M. de la Feuillarde. —Ma foi! Monsieur, répondit Gaveau, cela est trop beau, pour n'être pas cher. Je crois qu'ils valent tout au moins mille écus.—Tu as raison de dire tout au moins, repartit M. de la Feuillarde, ils valent davantage ; mais je n'ai pas d'argent présentement, prends-les, je te les donne, pour les deux coureurs que je te dois. —Oh ! parbleu ! Monsieur, répliqua Gaveau, je vous remercie ; mon négoce est de chevaux, et non pas de papillons, et quand je vais en Espagne ou en Danemark acheter les plus beaux chevaux de ces pays-là, si je ne portais que des papillons, je ne ramenerais guère de marchandise.

M. de la Feuillarde, voyant que ceux-là ne l'accomodaient pas, en fit apporter six autres : —"Hé ! de ceux-ci, mon ami Gaveau, qu'en dis-tu ? De quel prix crois-tu qu'ils soient ?" Gaveau qui les trouva imcomparablement plus beaux que les premiers, en fut charmé, et dit que, si on les donnait à deux mille écus, c'était pour rien. —"Eh bien ! reprit M. de la Feuillarde, je te les donne, et rends-moi mon billet. Avec qui gagneras-tu, si ce n'est avec un grand seigneur comme moi ? (*Lettres nouvelles*, 1703, II, 229–31, cité par Ed. Fournier dans ses *Etudes sur la vie et les oeuvres de Molière*, 1885, 107–09.)

C'est vraiment une scène molièresque ; mais telle était l'attitude générale des nobles endettés envers leurs créanciers. Bussy-Rabutin, habile à courtiser les femmes, était aussi habile à payer ses créanciers en monnaie de singe. On sait que Saint-Simon, l'orgueuilleux et fier duc et pair pour qui le siècle de Louis XIV ne fut qu'un long règne de la bourgeoisie, est mort comme un bourgeois d'un coin de rue en devant de l'argent à ses valets, à ses marchands et à son apothicaire.

Si on examine ainsi les moeurs et le mode de vie de la noblesse française sous Louis XIV, on se convaincra facilement que les visées de Molière dans *Dom Juan* n'étaient pas de peindre un simple chasseur de femmes. Molière n'a pas accordé d'importance à Dom Juan suborneur du sexe féminin, ce qui est prouvé par le fait que les paroles le concernant ne dépassent pas un quart de la pièce toute entière. Non, ce qu'a entrepris notre grand comique dans cette oeuvre était de donner un tableau complet de la noblesse versaillaise qui gaspillait temps et argent dans toutes sortes de débauches. Il est tout à fait naturel que ce héros espagnol s'habille tout comme les courtisans de Versailles. (Voir la description du costume de Dom Juan au IIe acte.) La légende de Don Juan ne fournit à Molière que le cadre pour donner un magnifique tableau de la noblesse française. Dom Juan de Molière, gracieux et même courtois à la différence du Don Juan italien pour ne pas remonter au Don Juan espagnol que Molière ne paraît pas consulter, n'emploie jamais la violence vis-à-vis des femmes. Très élégant, spiritual et assez courageux pour se battre sur un point d'honneur, d'ailleurs jeune et beau garçon, il est muni de toutes les qualités suffisantes pour charmer les femmes. Mais ce qui est caché sous son manteau d'or et d'argent, sous cette apparence éblouissante, c'est la fierté, l'arrogance, la rudesse de coeur, le cynisme très près du sadisme, l'égoïsme sans pareil, le désir du conquérant à la Nietzsche, l'hypocrisie: en un mot tous les vices de la noblesse de l'époque se sont incarnés en lui. S'il y a un vice que Molière n'a pas osé peindre chez son héros, ce n'est que l'homosexualité assez répandue parmi eux. En ce sens Dom Juan est le symbole des grands seigneurs sous Louis XIV.

Si le but de Molière est de donner ce portrait, l'intrigue qu'il a suivie est très logique: la poursuite du plaisir, l'épicurisme pour justifier sa conduite contre les reproches venant de toutes parts, le blasphème pour obtenir un alibi de ses actes scandaleux en niant Dieu qui était le fondement de la morale, et finalement l'hypocrisie qui couvre tous les actes inhumains— tel était le processus général parcouru par la plupart des représentants de la noblesse dépravée. Molière développe le caractère de son héros selon ce processus: aux Ier et IIe actes, Dom Juan est avant tout un séducteur; pour cet épicurien insatiable la terre est trop étroite et il souhaite comme Alexandre qu' "il y eût d'autres mondes pour y pouvoir étendre (mes) conquêtes" (Acte I, scène 2). Dom Juan ayant un goût affiné par la politesse mondaine ne se contente pas de satisfactions charnelles; il trouve aussi une volupté pour ainsi dire spirituelle à dépraver les femmes, ce qui est un trait que l'on ne trouve pas dans le Don Juan italien: "On goûte, dit-il, une douceur extrême à réduire, par cent hommages, le coeur d'une beauté, à voir de jour en jour les petits progrès qu'on y fait, à combattre par des transports, par des larmes et des soupirs, l'innocente pudeur d'une âme qui a peine à rendre les armes, à forcer pied-à-pied toutes les petites résistances qu'elle nous oppose, à vaincre les scrupules dont elle se fait un honneur et à la mener doucement où nous avons envie de la faire venir" (Acte I, scène 2). Pour ce libertinage du corps et de l'esprit, il ne craint pas Dieu (son athéisme n'apparaît pas encore, il reste sceptique), ne s'effraie pas de devenir meutrier (il a tué le Commandeur), ne se soucie point d'autrui (il tente par jalousie d'enlever la fiancée à l'amant; il ne peut supporter le bonheur d'autrui), piétine son bienfaiteur (il frappe Pierrot qui lui a sauvé la vie). Le IIIe acte commence par un ridicule débat théologique entre Dom Juan et Sganarelle; ensuite vient la scène du Pauvre que notre héros tente de faire blasphémer; et l'acte se termine par l'invitation faite à la Statue. Cet acte est donc destiné à montrer Dom Juan athée. Une scène d'une autre nature est intercalée: Dom Juan, voyant un homme attaqué par trois autres, va à son secours et le sauve. Mais songez que Condé était un illustre général, que Henri de Lorraine était un capitaine intrépide et que Bussy-Rabutin était un excellent duelliste. Alors vous vous convaincrez que la scène n'est pas déplacée. Dans le IVe

acte Dom Juan berne son créancier; homme insensible, il fait fi de tout lien familial: fils impie, mari dissolu, il est mis au ban de la famille et de la société. Au Ve acte, Molière parachève le grand tableau de Dom Juan en le rendant hypocrite; il est au sommet de sa dépravation: il trompe Dom Carlos, éconduit Dom Louis sous le manteau de la religion et déclare que "sous cet abri favorable, je veux me sauver, et mettre en sûreté mes affaires. ... Enfin c'est là le vrai moyen de faire impunément tout ce que je voudrai" (Acte V, scène 2).

Interprété ainsi, *Dom Juan*, quelque irrégulier qu'il paraisse, est très logique et conséquent: le développement de la pièce correspond parfaitement au progrès de la dépravation des nobles de la cour de Versailles, ses modèles. Voilà la raison pour laquelle cette pièce, qui pourrait au premier abord passer pour décousue, donne une impression d'unité et de réalité.

C'est la manière habituelle de Molière de peindre un vice frappant de l'époque en le concentrant dans un personnage: Arnolphe est un bourgeois aux idées démodées en matière d'amour et de mariage qui continue à accorder de l'importance à la fortune et à l'honneur; Tartuffe personnifie le haut clergé (la plupart de ses membres étaient les fils d'une noblesse de vieille souche; les titres d'évêque, d'archevêque et d'abbé leur étaient accordés par le roi; jouissant ainsi d'un revenu considérable fourni par les domaines et les paroisses, ils menaient une vie de galanteries à la cour de Versailles); Célimène est la personnification de la vie mondaine, frivole et oisive; Philaminte est la cristallisation de l'engouement pour les sciences, très à la mode parmi les dames du monde.

Dans cette personnification des vices de l'époque, Molière a, avant *Le Misanthrope*, utilisé, comme noyau de cristallisation, des personnages de la comédie italienne ou espagnole: Arnolphe descend de Pantalon de la *commedia dell'arte* et du *gracioso* de la comédie espagnole par l'intermédiaire de Sganarelle du *Cocu imaginaire*; le prototype du Tartuffe est le parasite de la comédie italienne, notamment l'*Hypocrito* de l'Arétin. *Le Festin de pierre* n'est point un cas exceptionnel: le héros était traité, comme chacun le sait, dans les pièces de Cicognini, de Giliberto et dans le scénario de Domenico Biancolelli.

Le Dom Juan de Molière cependant, comparé au héros italien, présente des différences assez frappantes. Don Juan au delà des Alpes est un garçon impétueux qui agit d'instinct, et la chaleur de son désir ne lui permet pas d'attendre la jouissance du plaisir; il emploie ainsi la violence assez souvent; il ne fait aucun cas de la société et de la loi. Nous trouvons là un épigone de la philosophie naturaliste de la Renaissance italienne. Le Don

Juan des auteurs transalpins reflète certainement les moeurs de l'époque décadante de la Renaissance ; mais le caractère une fois saisi, les écrivains italiens s'attachaient peu à donner une peinture fidèle des moeurs de l'époque et se consacraient à la recherche d'effets comiques au moyen de ce personnage légendaire et son valet, ce qui apparaît à l'évidence dans le scénario où Arlequin est le véritable personnage principal. Cicognini et Giliberto (connu par la pièce de Dorimon, notamment par celle de Villiers, car le texte de Giliberto est perdu), eux aussi, ne laissaient échapper aucune chance de faire rire les spectateurs ; on trouve chez eux force lazzi et Dom Juan y est mis au même niveau que son valet.

Le but que Molière s'imposa est tout à fait différent. En utilisant ce personnage légendaire, d'ailleurs étranger, pour échapper à la censure, il a cherché à donner une peinture très réaliste et complète des grands de la cour de Versailles. Il y a aussi parfaitement réussi comme nous l'avons vu que dans *le Tartuffe* et dans *le Misanthrope*. Voilà le vrai génie de Molière.

Il faut donc conclure que *Dom Juan*, loin d'être une oeuvre exceptionnelle, décousue, ou "une méchante comédie" comme dit F. Sarcey, est tout à fait dans la règle de la dramaturgie moliéresque et un incomparable chef-d'oeuvre de réalisme.

AMPHITRYON: DIE KUNST, AUTORITÄTSKRITIK DURCH KOMÖDIE ZU VERSCHLEIERN

Wolfgang Wittkowski

Was hat so viele Schriftsteller gereizt, das Amphitryon-Thema über die Jahrhunderte hinweg wetteifernd immer wieder neu zu gestalten? Als erster beschreibt die Fabel um 700 v.Z. der Mitschöpfer der griechischen Götterlehre, Hesiod. Er legt alles Gewicht auf die Zeugung des Herkules, des Retters und Beschützers der Menschen. Zeus besucht Alkmene um jenes hohen Zweckes willen—zugleich aber auch, um die Leidenschaft zu stillen, die das Muster aller Frauen in ihm weckte. Wir erfahren nur, daß er bei Nacht erscheint; noch nicht, ob er dabei Amphitryons Gestalt annimmt. Dieser kehrt in derselben Nacht von einem Kriegszug heim und zeugt den Ipikles. Alkmene bringt beide Söhne als Zwillinge zur Welt. Welchen Eindruck die zwei Besuche während ein und derselben Nacht auf ihre Seele machten, bleibt im Dunkeln. Die fromme Andacht kennt noch keinerlei psychisches oder ethisch-metaphysisches Problem.

Das muß sich spätestens geändert haben, als Aischylos, nach mehreren anderen Dichtern, den Stoff als Tragödie gestaltete (die ebensowenig wie die anderen antiken Amphitryon- bzw. Alkmene-Tragödien erhalten ist). Der Schöpfer des *Prometheus* ist der erste, von dem wir wissen, daß er über den Zwiespalt zwischen göttlichem Walten und ewiger Ordnung nachgrübelte.[1] Stehen gut und böse unverrückbar fest? Sollen wir Gottes Handeln nur dann gut nennen, wenn es gut ist? Oder sollen wir alles und nur das als gut bezeichnen, was Gott und weil Gott es für gut erklärt bzw. selber tut? Im vorliegenden Fall hieße das: Ist der Besuch des Gottes wirklich, wie die Religion will, Wohltat, Gnade, Auszeichnung? Oder ist er Beleidigung der Menschen und Mißbrauch der göttlichen Übermacht? Oder schärfer zugespitzt: Hört darum, weil es ein Gott war, die erschlichene Umarmung auf, Betrug und Ehebruch zu sein? Kann der Rang des Gottes den Namen des Verbrechens auslöschen und in Segen umwandeln? Natürlich kann er es, gemäß den Lehren der Religion, und

---

[1] Bruno Snell, *Die Entdeckung des Geistes* (Hamburg, 1946).

475

zumal wenn eine hierarchisch gegliederte Gesellschaft sich die Religion als Institution und Konvention zueigen macht. In vorchristlicher wie in christlicher Zeit war der Amphitryon-Stoff das gegebene Feld, auf welchem Prometheus im Namen der ewigen Ordnung, der autonomen Ethik, gegen die Umwertung der Werte, gegen die Bevormundung durch die Autorität von Religion und Konvention protestierte.

Bei Aischylos hatte Alkmene vielleicht die prometheische Kraft, Zeus' Werben zurückzuweisen, so daß er sich gezwungen sah, die Gestalt des einzig geliebten Gatten anzunehmen. Trotzdem dürfte sein Drama ein mythisch-religiöses Weihespiel gewesen sein, ebenso das des Sophokles und auch das des Euripides[2]—wenigstens äußerlich. Eine Vasenzeichnung überliefert, daß seine Alkmene schon auf dem Scheiterhaufen steht, als Zeus erscheint und ihre Schande in Triumph verwandelt. Man mag sich fragen, ob der *deus ex machina* die allerhöchste Regelung nicht doch als eine willkürliche Umwertung der Werte bloßstellte, die konventionelle Lösung also *ad absurdum* führte. Freilich geschähe es verhüllt und ließe dem Publikum samt seinen Priestern die Möglichkeit, das Stück als Weihespiel zu nehmen. Wie dem auch sei, man sieht, der Amphitryon-Stoff bietet grundsätzlich Gelegenheit nicht nur zum prometheischen Protest, sondern zugleich zu dessen Verhüllung. Darauf hat man bisher nicht geachtet. Uns interessiert im folgenden, ob ein Dramatiker jene beiden Möglichkeiten nutzte und was ihn dazu bewog. Die Überlieferung verweist uns von nun an zwar auf die Komödie. Alkmenes und auch Amphitryons Schicksal konnten dennoch in tragischem Licht erscheinen und den ernsten Kern des Problems andeuten, zumal der Mythos und noch mehr eben die Komödie genug Deckung boten—genug, um Jupiter (und was immer er repräsentieren sollte) zur Zielscheibe der Satire zu machen.

Der *Amphitruo* des Plautus (um 200 v.Z.) bildet den Anfang der Reihe und zugleich das Muster, dem die Epigonen und insbesondere die Meister Molière und Kleist unbedenklich folgten. Im puritanischen Rom des 2. Punischen Kriegs galt Griechenland als Paradebeispiel jedes sittlichen Verfalls. In griechischem Gewand konnte man die römische Wertordnung

---

[2] Zu den antiken Gestaltungen des Themas vgl. Franz Stoessl, „Amphitryon. Wachstum und Wandlung eines poetischen Stoffes", *Trivium* 2 (1944), 93–117; zur Plautus-Nachfolge Karl v. Reinhardstoettner, *Plautus. Spätere Bearbeitungen plautinischer Lustspiele* (1886); eine Gesamtgeschichte des Motivs bietet Örjan Lindberger, *The Transformations of Amphitryon* (1956). Weitere Literatur, insbesondere zu Molière und Kleist, in meinem Artikel „The New Prometheus. Molière's and Kleist's *Amphitryon*", *Comparative Literature Studies*, (1971), 109–24.

auf den Kopf stellen, und damit hatte Plautus ungeheuren Erfolg.[3]
Lediglich im *Amphitruo*, soviel ich weiß, verfuhr er etwas anders. Die
patriotische, treu-liebevolle Alcumena steht in seinem komischen Gesamt-
werk einzig da und gehört samt einigen ihrer Nachfolgerinnen zu den
edelsten Frauengestalten der Weltliteratur. Aber warum erscheint sie
hier? Und warum behandelt Plautus den Mythos, mit dem er sich
gleichfalls allein in diesem Stück beschäftigt, nicht ganz ohne Ehrerbietung
(insbesondere die Epiphanie Jupiters)? Mußte er das? Immerhin treten
Roms Götter auf! Aber auch, wenn er keine Zensur zu fürchten hatte,
verliehen jene ernsten Elemente dem Stück erst das Gewicht, ohne welches
die Satire rettungslos zur Posse verflacht wäre.

Das scheint nun allerdings weitgehend doch der Fall zu sein. Vor allem
ist hier wichtig, daß nicht nur Jupiter die Gestalt Amphitryons, sondern
auch Merkur die des Sklaven Sosias annehmen. So kommt es zu den
komischen Verwechslungen and Verwirrungen, die zwei Jahrtausende
lang als unübertrefflich empfunden und im wesentlichen unverändert
übernommen wurden. Aber später sind es die aufsässigen Witze des Sosias,
die vom herkömmlichen Respekt vor der göttlichen Autorität befreien.
Hier dagegen verteidigt Merkur Jupiters und sein eigenes Treiben auf
eine Weise, die zynisch durchblicken läßt: das Tun der Götter ist nicht
zu rechtfertigen. Es bedarf dessen jedoch nicht; denn sie haben die Macht.
Daher gilt alles, was sie tun, als gut. Diese höhnisch unverhüllte Ironie
erheitert und erbittert. Besonders provozierend wirkte die ernsthafte
Versicherung:

> . . . nemo id probro
> profecto ducet Alcumenae; nam deum
> non par videtur facere, delictum suom
> suamque ut culpam expetere in mortalem ut sint. (v. 492ff.)

> . . . und keiner soll
> Alkmenes Gattentreue je bezweifeln!
> Denn eines Gottes kühner Übergriff
> Kann nie verletzen eines Menschen Ehre.

So hat man die Stelle übertragen,[4] nicht ganz wortgetreu. Aber hier wird
in der Tat vorausgesetzt, daß das Vergehen, weil angetan von einem Gott,
den Menschen nicht beleidigt, sondern ehrt. Amphitryon, noch bei Kleist
offiziell der Hauptbetroffene, bedankt sich denn auch überschwänglich

---

[3] Vgl. Erich Segal, *Roman Laughter*, (1968).
[4] *Amphitryon: Plautus, Molière, Dryden, Kleist, Giraudoux, Kaiser*, Hrsg. J. Schondorff
(1964), 50.

für die Ehre, mit Jupiter,, des Hauses Glück" teilen zu dürfen. Die fromme
Pointe bildet die Achse fast aller späteren Bearbeitungen. Auch hier wird
sie festlich gesteigert durch Jupiters Epiphanie und die Verkündigung der
Ruhmestaten des Herkules. Dann freilich schließt Merkur als Theater-
herold mit der Aufforderung:

> Und nun, ihr lieben Hörer, rührt zu Ehren
> Des höchsten Gottes kräftig eure Hände!

Das ernüchtert auf lächerliche Weise. Nicht bloß, weil man dem Gott so
profan huldigt, sondern vielmehr, weil Merkur schon im Prolog den Gott
mit seinem Darsteller gleichsetzte: er habe Lampenfieber und dürfe nach
leidlicher Aufführug erwarten, daß man ihn beklatscht. Dergleichen
erhöht natürlich den befreienden Spielcharakter der Komödie. Aber es
erinnert auch daran, daß beide Götter im Stück herabgesetzt werden—
oder soll es gerade davon ablenken? Jedenfalls nimmt Plautus die Umwertung der Werte durch die höchste, hier die religiöse, Autorität bissig
aufs Korn. Er erstreckt sie sogar auf die Definition der Gattung. Merkur
kündigt die Fabel des Trauerspiels an, unterbricht sich aber: „Ihr runzelt
eure Stirnen?" „Ich bin ein Gott, ich kann es ändern." „Ich mache sofort
ein Lustspiel aus dem Trauerspiel, und ohne einen einz'gen Vers zu
streichen!" Endlich entscheidet er jedoch für „Tragikomödie", und zwar
wegen der mitwirkenden Helden und Götter. Die Begründung könnte
kaum konventioneller und fadenscheiniger sein. Offenbar verweist der
Vorgang gleichfalls auf den ideologischen Charakter der von der obersten
Autorität willkürlich aufgezwungenen Wertordnung. Das geschieht hier
aber immer scherzhaft, scheinbar harmlos und verhüllt damit den prometheischen Protest, der sich in jenen Hinweisen Luft macht.

Dieser triumphale Einsatz der Amphitryon-Komödien blieb während
der Antike unerreicht. Im christlichen Mittelalter lebte er als kümmerliche
Posse fort (Vitalis von Blois, Anfang 12. Jh.). Plautus selbst wurde
vergessen, bis Nicolaus Cusanus 1427 zwölf seiner Komödien, darunter
Amphitruo in Deutschland neu entdeckte. Eine Lücke im IV. Akt füllte
der Humanist Kardinal Hermolaus Barbarus mit derb possenhaften
Szenen. Diese Fassung bearbeitete man mehrfach zu möglichst obszöner
Unterhaltung, aber auch zu frommer Erbauung. Noch fast im Stil der
Moralitäten schrieb der Geistliche Herr Johannes Burmeister seine *Sacri
Mater Virgo* (1621). Er setzte Herkules mit Jesus gleich und die drei Haupt-
figuren mit Maria, Joseph und dem Engel Gabriel, das Ganze also, biblisch
gesprochen, mit der „Überschattung" Marias durch den Heiligen Geist.

Die Möglichkeit, den Stoff in diesem Sinne auszudeuten, war nun immer gegenwärtig und forderte die Renaissance dazu heraus, seine prometheische Potenz wieder zu beleben. Die italienische Version des Pandolfo Collenuccio (15. Jh.) dehnt zwar—um dem Haus d'Este zu huldigen— den Bericht über die Geburt des Herkules gewaltig aus; am Schluß aber meint Amphitryon, zum Publikum gewandt, Jupiter hätte ihm seine Gunst ebensogut und besser auch auf andre Weise zeigen können.[5] Der Portugiese Luís de Camões läßt ihn (zwischen 1540 und 1550) sogar ähnlich reagieren wie dann Molière: als Jupiter ihm sagt, er dürfe sich geehrt fühlen, antwortet er mit einem Schweigen, das eine beredte Sprache spricht. Vorher nämlich beklagte er den Verlust von Glück und Ehre mit echten Herzenstönen. Jupiter wird etwas herabgesetzt: erst als schon beschlossen ist, daß er Alkmene genießen will, bläst ihm Merkur die mythisch so wichtige Geburt des Herkules als opportunen Rechtfertigungsgrund ein.

Noch eindeutiger geht es bei Juan Timoneda (1559) zu.[6] Jupiter hat sich herabgelassen, Alkmenes Körper ,,auszuleihen", Amphitryons ,,Dinge" (*cosas*) zu gebrauchen. Sosias drückt sich noch deftiger aus. Überhaupt kommt nun seine Rolle zur Entfaltung. Er protestiert gegen Jupiters Tun, beschimpft ihn und Merkur und beklagt die ganze Bescherung endlich etwa so: ,,Ich weiß wirklich nicht, was ich von euch Göttern denken soll. Der Vater ein Ehebrecher, der Sohn ein Mörder (bezieht sich auf den nächsten Punkt), Sosias geprügelt, Alkmene entehrt, Amphitryon gehörnt." Die Parallelität der Beleidigungen ist bedeutsam. Sosias spricht auch von einer Handlungsparallele, von einem Besuch Merkurs bei der Dienerin. Doch erst Molière wird das ausführen, und zwar als Kontrast zu Jupiters galanter Werbung. Und vollends erst wieder bei Kleist würde die Dienerin, im Kontrast zu Alkmene, den Besuch wie hier als Ehrung ansehen, Sosias dagegen als Hurerei. Seine Frechheiten gipfeln dennoch in dem Verlangen, zur Kompensation für die Schwängerung Alkmenes solle Jupiter den Menschenmännern ein paar Göttinnen zur Verfügung stellen. Der Feldherr wird mehrfach aufgefordert, den Schlingel zum Schweigen zu bringen. Einmal tut er es mit der vielsagenden Begründung: ,,Göttern gegenüber äußert man seine Meinung nicht so ungeschminkt!" Ein andermal weigert er sich: Jupiter habe ihn so beglückt, daß er niemand böse sein könne, schon gar nicht jenem Einfaltspinsel. Das nimmt einiges

---

[5] Lindberger, *op. cit.*, 46, 50.
[6] Meine Ausführungen über Camões und Timoneda stützen sich hauptsächlich auf Informationen, die ich meinem Kollegen Professor Aristobulo Prado zu danken habe.

vorweg von der boshaften Ironie, mit der Molières Sosias am Schluß brilliert. So hat vielleicht niemand die Möglichkeiten, die dem Stoffe innewohnen, vielseitiger und kräftiger weiter entwickelt als Timoneda. Mag auch sein, daß er bei den göttlichen Übergriffen an die Anmaßungen weltlicher und geistlicher Instanzen dachte. Das wäre allerdings aus großer, unverbindlicher Distanz geschehen. Wir sehen zwar, wie sehr man sich gekränkt fühlen könnte; doch wir sehen nicht, daß wirklich jemand leidet. Und diese antiken Götter können wir durchaus nicht ernst nehmen. Die Posse breitet sich um der Posse willen aus; sie raubt der Autoritätskritik jeden Ernst und damit den Charakter eines Wagnisses, das der Verschleierung bedürfte.

Der Spiegel vom 25. 12.72 meldete, daß ein Dramaturg und Übersetzer *The Birth of Hercules* (etwa 1590) Shakespeare zuschreibt. Hoffentlich gelingt der Nachweis nie schlüssig. Das anonym erschienene Prosastück ist eine gelehrt-trockene Bearbeitung des Plautus. Um die possenhaften Partien wenigstens zu vermehren, gab man dem Sosias einen Dienerkollegen, den Dromio, der sich allerdings nebst einigen *Amphitruon*-Motiven in der gleichzeitigen *Comedy of Errors* findet. Dafür ist alles weggelassen, was bei Plautus an das problematische Verhältnis zwischen Göttern und Menschen, Hoch- und Niedriggestellten mahnt. Erregten jene Elemente in einflußreichen Kreisen von einiger Bildung so viel Ärgernis, daß man sich bemüßigt fand, das römische Muster restlos zu verdünnen und um seine satirische Substanz zu bringen?

Jean Rotrou spielt in der Literaturgeschichte stets die undankbare Rolle des Molière-Vorläufers. Gegenwärtig findet indessen seine ironisch verhüllte Sozialkritik wachsendes Interesse.[7] Das verdient auch seine Komödie *Les Sosies* (1636), die zudem einen langanhaltenden Erfolg hatte, noch neben dem Stück Molières. Sie gehört den frühen Werken an, mit denen der Dichter Anschluß an die klassizistische Strömung suchte. Daher lehnte er sich wieder enger an Plautus an, dämpfte jedoch die Diener-Possen und hob die Würde der Götter. Ausfälle gegen sie gewannen durch die pompösen Alexandriner einerseits Gewicht, andererseits wirkten sie ohnmächtig und absurd. Im Prolog kündigt Juno die Leiden des Herkules an: ihre Rache für Jupiters Untreue. Vor Eifersucht vermag sie, wie Merkur meldet, nicht der Hauptleidenschaft der Olympier

---

[7] Z. B. Jacques Morel, *Jean Rotrou. Dramaturgie de l'ambiguité* (Paris, 1968); Harold C. Knutsen, *The Ironic Game: A Study of Rotrou's Comic Theatre* (Berkeley, 1966); Robert J. Nelson, *Immanence and Transcendence: The Theater of Jean Rotrou* (1969).

zu frönen, dem Genuß des Nektars. Solche Satire bleibt innerhalb der
Götterwelt und geht die Menschen wenig an.

Anders dagegen im einleitenden Monolog Merkurs. Der Mond soll
Jupiters Abenteuer unterstützen durch Verlängerung der Nacht. Mora-
lische Bedenken werden aus dem Weg geräumt durch Hinweis auf die
Vorrechte der Götter. Molière wird daran anschließen, es aber schärfer
akzentuieren, und ebenso die bittere Resignation, mit der Amphitryon
schon hier göttliche Nebenbuhlerschaft zur Kenntnis nimmt:

> Je plaindrois mon honneur d'un affront glorieux,
> D'avoir eu pour rival de monarque des dieux!
> Ma couche est partagée, Alcmène est infidèle,
> Mais l'affront en est doux, et la honte en est belle,
> L'outrage est obligeant; le rang du suborneuer
> Avecque mon injure accorde mon honneur.
> Alcmène [. . .]
> Peut entre ses honneurs conter un adultère;
> Son crime la relève, il accroît son renom . . .

Ein Hauptmann sagt zu Amphitryon: "Vous partagez des biens avecque
Jupiter." Doch Sosias ist skeptisch:

> Cet honneur, ce me semble, est un triste avantage:
> On appelle cela lui sucrer le breuvage.

Der höfische Stil setzt die Stände-Hierarchie voraus; sie verlangt hier,
daß die Menschen genasführt und dem Gelächter preisgegeben werden.
Rotrou aber ist der erste Dichter, der die Menschen dafür rächt, indem
er die Götter gleichfalls genasführt und lächerlich erscheinen läßt. Allen
voran den Göttervater. Das fällt um so schwerer ins Gewicht, als Jupiter
das höfische Heldenideal am vollkommensten verkörpert. Und dennoch:
um Alkmene zu genießen, besucht er sie in Amphitryons Gestalt; dann
aber merkt er enttäuscht, daß ihre Zärtlichkeit nicht ihm galt, sondern
dem, für welchen sie ihn hielt. Nachträglich versucht er, seine Identität
durch allerlei Anspielungen kenntlich zu machen. Alkmene bemerkt auch
überrascht, welche Jugendlichkeit seine Haut bewahrte und wie unge-
wöhnlich unter Eheleuten die galante Liebeserklärung ist, mit der er ihren
Zwist beilegt. Dergleichen heißt indessen nur, daß sie trotz aller Anzeichen
Jupiter nicht erkennt und ihn für ihren Gatten hält: daß der Gott also die
Rolle dessen spielen muß, den er zum Hahnrei machte. Der Spieß kehrt
sich gegen ihn selber um; er fing sich in der eigenen Schlinge. Viel Wesens
wird damit freilich nicht gemacht. Es ergibt sich mehr als Folgerung. Wie

denn überhaupt die ironische Verhüllung der Autoritätskritik zum guten
Teil dadurch geleistet wird, daß das Motiv nur gelegentlich anklingt.

Ganz anders Molière. Er macht seinen *Amphitryon* zu einem Meisterwerk unter anderem dadurch, daß er alle Teile von einer thematischen
Mitte her gestaltet, und das ist die Autoritätskritik. Sie hängt engstens
zusammen mit seiner komischen Kunst überhaupt. Sie hat es weniger auf
das bloß Lächerliche abgesehen, als auf die absurden Paradoxien, die
das Verhältnis des Menschen zur Gesellschaft beherrschen. Genügt er
nämlich ihren Konventionen, so verstößt er damit nur allzu häufig gegen
die Forderungen von Vernunft und Natur.[8] Das tut er indessen auch,
wenn er sich den Diktaten der Institutionen offen widersetzt;[9] denn so
gibt es kein Überleben in dieser Welt. Er ist deren Gefangener, wohin er
sich auch wendet. Heute würde man das vermutlich tragisch nennen.
Molière betrachtet es von seinem kühleren Standort aus als komisch. Als
einzigen befriedigenden Ausweg zeigt er den Kompromiß: äußerlich sich
mit der Gesellschaft arrangieren, innerlich aber sich über ihre Konventionen und die eigene Unterlegenheit ironisch erheben.

Amphitryon und Sosias wissen, daß sie Söhne eines philosophischen
Jahrhunderts sind. Den Herrn plagt daher nicht bloß seine Schande,
sondern außerdem die Angst vor der Blamage, angesichts der mysteriösen
Ähnlichkeit des Betrügers—an thessalische Hexen glauben zu müssen.
Sosias dagegen fühlt sich verpflichtet, Merkurs Logik zu glauben, derzufolge jener ebenfalls Sosias ist. Viele Forscher, die dem Diener an philo-
sophischer Beschlagenheit nicht nachzustehen wünschen, nehmen ernsthaft an, er (wie auch sein Herr) verlöre sein Identitätsbewußtsein. Das
geschieht indessen nicht. Dadurch fühlt der Zuschauer sich befriedigt von
dem Druck befreit, den die Konvention der Philosophiemode und mittels
ihrer die Götter üben. Dazu verhilft Sosias uns immer wieder. Im Schutze
seiner Obskurität huldigt er immer wieder dem, was in der Gesellschaft
Ansehen genießt—und nicht zuletzt sind das die Götter—auf ostentativ
äußerliche Weise oder kehrt ihm gar mit offener Respektlosigkeit den
Rücken, etwa um sich so unzweideutigen Werten zuzuwenden wie dem
Sattwerden, Keine-Prügel-Kriegen und Am-Leben-Bleiben. Darüber hin-

---

[8] James Doolittle, „Human Nature and Institutions in Molière's Plots", *Studies in Seventeenth-Century French Literature*, ed. J. J. Demorest (1962), 153–64.
[9] W. G. Moore, „Molière's Theory of Comedy", *L'Esprit Createur*, VI, 3 (1966) 137–44.
Vgl. auch unter 2 genannte Studie sowie meine ausführlichere Untersuchung: „Der
neue Prometheus: Kleists Amphitryon zwischen Molière und Giraudoux", *Kleist und
Frankreich* (1969), 27–82.

aus enthüllt er unbefangen die Absurdität der Konvention, die den Übergriff der Götter rechtfertigt. Es ist die doppelte Moral, derzufolge ein Höhergestellter sich erlauben darf, was ein Niedriggestellter sich verbieten muß. Als Sosias seinem Herrn berichtet, wie ein anderer Sosias ihn verprügelte, und das heißt nach der geltenden Logik, wie er selber sich verprügelte—da will Amphitryon ihm das begreiflicherweise nicht glauben. Darauf Sosias, in Kleists kongenialer Übersetzung:

> So ist's. Weil es aus meinem Munde kommt,
> Ist's albern Zeug, nicht wert, daß man es höre.
> Doch hätte sich ein Großer selbst zerwalkt,
> So würde man Mirakel schrein.

Das gilt für Herren und Diener. Und es gilt für Götter und Menschen. Daß dies Molières Thema ist, verdeutlicht Merkur gleich im Prolog. Er erweitert die anzügliche Randbemerkung bei Rotrou zu einer ausführlichen Diskussion des göttlichen Dekorums. Sie gipfelt in der Definition jener doppelten Moral. Die Nacht soll Jupiter zuliebe länger bleiben. Als sie, mit mäßigem Unbehagen, einwendet, Kupplerdienst gelte nicht als ehrbar, belehrt sie Merkur:

> Un tel Employ n'est bassesse,
> Que chez les petites Gens.
> Lors que dans un haut Rang on a l'heur de paroistre,
> Tout ce qu'on fait est toujours bel, et bon;
> Et suivant ce qu'on peut estre,
> Les choses changent de nom. (124–31)

Die Verwechslungskomödie bestätigt das. Solange die Götter sich nicht zu erkennen geben, erregt ihr Tun Empörung. Am Ende soll sich das mit einem Schlage umkehren. Sosias soll die empfangenen Götterprügel als ehrende Auszeichnung betrachten, und ebenso Amphitryon—nun in strenger Parallelität—Jupiters Ehebruch mit seiner Frau. *Le Seigneur Jupiter sait dorer la pilule*, bemerkt Sosias ähnlich wie bei Rotrou; sein Herr aber schweigt, wie bei Camões. Eine ohnmächtige Gebärde des Protests. Wie ohnmächtig aber und daher wie bitter sie ist, das enthüllt und verhüllt zugleich das ironische Schlußwort des Dieners.

Die hektischen Glückwünsche, die man dem Pflegevater des Herkules darbringt, seien unangebracht; sie drückten nicht annähernd aus, welche Ehre dem Haus Amphitryon widerfuhr. Sosias versucht sich jedoch selbst in solchen Floskeln und—bricht ab mit der unvermittelten Erklärung, in solchen Fällen halte man besser den Mund. Warum? Die konventionellen Redensarten zeigen es. Sie drücken den Enthusiasmus über die göttliche

Auszeichnung so erbärmlich klappernd aus, daß hier weniger die Ausdrucksgrenzen der konventionellen Sprache deutlich werden als vielmehr die Grenzen eben jenes vorgeschriebenen frommen Enthusiasmus. Das könnte verräterisch sein. Amphitryons unhöfliches Schweigen ist es allerdings nicht weniger. So oder so ist er gefangen. So oder so aber hält er sich auch innerhalb des Bereichs, in dem die Gesellschaft und Jupiter seinen Protest tolerieren können. Es hat etwas Tragikomisches an sich, wie er das Äußerste, den offenen Zusammenstoß, vernünftig-klug vermeidet und wie die so kräftig unterminierte Überlegenheit Jupiters dennoch unangefochten weiter gilt.

Diese letzte Ambivalenz bekräftigt der Gott selber mit dem Eingeständnis, er sei in Wahrheit der Verlierer. Er denkt dabei freilich nicht an seine Verurteilung durch ein sittliches Empfinden, das sich an Natur und Vernunft orientiert. Statt dessen wurmt ihn wie bei Rotrou, daß Alkmenes Zärtlichkeit nicht ihm galt, sondern Amphitryon, den er nur in dessen eigener Gestalt hintergehen konnte. Seine Behauptung, er habe sie nicht einmal in seines Ruhmes Glanz betören können, geht also spöttisch-ironisch über die Gegebenheiten des Stücks hinaus. Er hat sie ja gerade nicht vor die Wahl zwischen Mensch und Gott stellen können (die dann bei Kleist im Zentrum steht). Das entwertet spöttisch-ironisch ihre Treue-Leistung, verdeckt aber auch ihre wahre; und es verdeckt zugleich Jupiters wahres Ansinnen und dessen Scheitern, was beides weit kläglicher ausfällt, als die offizielle Version ahnen läßt. Er forderte ja nur, sie solle unterscheiden zwischen dem Gemahl und dem Geliebten. Da er als Amphitryon auftritt, erscheint sein Verlangen abwegig und wird ernst, sogar unter Berufung auf ihn selbst, den Schirmherr der Ehe, abgewiesen. Diese hochkomische Szene I,3, die Molière erfunden hat, zeigt Jupiters blamables Scheitern erst in vollem Umfang: es gelingt ihm nicht, sich aus der eigenen Schlinge zu befreien, die er schürzte und in die er sich verwickelte, indem er die Gestalt Amphitryons annahm.

Der größeren Blamage entspricht dialektisch der größere Aufwand, sie zu verhüllen und den unangefochten Überlegenen zu spielen. Damit hat Jupiter hier überall Erfolg, nur nicht bei Alkmene (die deshalb am Ende nicht gegenwärtig sein darf). In der großen Auseinandersetzung mit ihr (II, 6) sieht er zwar gleichfalls überlegen aus. Er sieht sich hier genötigt, sie mit ihrem Gatten zu versöhnen, den er mit ihr betrog und dessen Rolle er jetzt spielen muß. Er schafft es endlich wie bei Rotrou mit Hilfe einer zwischen Eheleuten durchaus nicht üblichen theatralischen Liebeserklärung. Er zitiert dabei längere Partien aus Molières älterem Stück *Don*

Garcie de Navarre, was das Publikum natürlich auf Kosten Alkmenes belächelte. Jupiter demonstriert damit ferner, mit welch automatischer Verläßlichkeit die literatur-gewordene galante Konvention funktioniert; zugleich ironisiert er aber auch—freiwillig oder nicht—sich selbst, der auf sie angewiesen ist und also ihr Gefangener ist, wie er in der Schlinge der Amphitryon-Rolle gefangen bleibt.

Darüber hinaus aber steht er im Zeichen einer weiteren Ironie, von der er sicher nichts bemerkt. Alkmene läßt sich nämlich weder von seinem pompösen Kabinettstück erweichen noch von Sosias und Cleanthis, die auf den Knien um Gnade für den scheinbaren Amphitryon bitten und Jupiter damit eine wenig imposante Hilfestellung leisten. Schon bei Plautus siegte der Gott nicht eigentlich dadurch, daß er—bei Jupiter— sich selber fluchte, falls seine Liebesschwüre unaufrichtig wären. Alkmene gibt hier wie dann bei Molière mit einer Plötzlichkeit nach, die in sich selber komisch wirkt, zugleich aber als das wahre Motiv ihre Liebe zu Amphitryon enthüllt. Bei Molière fühlt sie noch immer, daß der Ehren- kodex der Gesellschaft ihr verbietet, dem Verdächtiger ihrer Reinheit zu verzeihen. Doch ihr Versuch, getreu solcher Konvention Amphitryon zu hassen, scheitert einfach an ihrer Liebe. Es ist ein Triumph dessen, was natürlich und vernünftig ist, über die gesellschaftliche Konvention. Und es bezeugt, am Maßstab von Natur und Vernunft gemessen, die Über- legenheit des Menschen über das, was hier als institutionalisierte Autorität der Religion auftritt. Deshalb gewinnt Alkmene, die noch Rotrou in ziemlich inferiorem Lichte zeigt, bei Molière die weibliche Vollkommen- heit zurück, die Plautus ihr verlieh; nur ist ihre Würde nun um charmante Natürlichkeit bereichert.

Die Konvention der doppelten Moral wird auch auf der Dienerebene kritisiert. Auch Cleanthis spricht sich gegen außereheliche Abenteuer aus. Im Kontrast zu Alkmene begründet sie das zwar mit einem ganz äußerlichen Respekt vor der Konvention der Ehrbarkeit, des guten Rufs. Der Ehebruch—nicht bloss der mit Göttern—gehört indessen ebenfalls zur Konvention, wie Merkur im Prolog bemerkt. Die Dienerin wählt die Konvention der Treue also aus natürlicher Treue oder wenigstens aus feigem, schwächlichem Unvermögen zur Untreue. Selbst dann aber kommt das immer noch einem Sieg dessen gleich, was Natur und Vernunft fordern; es steht zuletzt besser da als Merkurs zynische Ermunterung zum Ehebruch mit einem dritten—diese Parallele zu den Empfehlungen, die Jupiter, gleichfalls in der Maske des Ehemannes, erteilt, nur daß er hofft, selbst der Nutznießer zu sein. Nur an der Oberfläche wird hier der betrogene Ehemann lächerlich gemacht. Molière verteidigt, wenn nicht die Ehe als Institution, so doch die eheliche Liebe und Treue.[10] Er verteidigt sie als hohe Werte, die der Mensch im Namen von Natur und Vernunft heilig halten sollte—selbst gegen die unsittlichen Forderungen der religiösen Autoritäten.

Der elegant laszive Ton der Komödie verschleierte diese satirische Tendenz. An einer Stelle aber, soviel ich sehe, läßt der Dichter die aktuelle Anzüglichkeit des Stückes, wenn auch wieder nur verhüllt, durchblicken. Alkmene nennt den verkappten Jupiter mehrmals ein *monstre*. Als das war Molière in dem Pamphlet eines Geistlichen beschimpft worden, ferner als Teufel in Menschengestalt, der den Glauben an Gott und die Kirche untergrabe; Augustus habe einen Jokulator hinrichten lassen, weil er über Jupiter scherzte.[11] Möglich, daß Molière auch daran dachte, als er sich für den Stoff entschied, und daß er damit Ludwig XIV. ironisch provozierte. Er befand sich nämlich in recht prekärer Lage zwischen der Kirche und dem König, seinem Gönner. 1664 brach er mit der Tradition, die Kirche von der Satire auszunehmen; er entlarvte im *Tartuffe* die klerikale Heuchelei. Der für seine Sittenlosigkeit berüchtigte Pariser Erzbischof und die geheime Compagnie du Saint-Sacrament zwangen Ludwig, das Stück zu verbieten. Im nächsten Jahr wiederholte sich das gleiche mit dem *Dom Juan*. Der Held läßt seine Sünden in der Heuchelei gipfeln, der Sünde des Tartuffe. Prompt drohte der Erzbischof jeden zu exkommunizieren, der—den *Tartuffe* las. Das richtete sich besonders gegen Ludwig, der das Kursieren von Manuskripten ebenso duldete wie Privatlesungen. 1669 kam *Tartuffe* wieder auf die Bühne und trat nun seinen einzigartigen Siegeslauf an. Das Werk sprach dem Jahrhundert aus der Seele. Im selben Jahr erschien es als Buch mit einer Vorrede.

Inzwischen waren die ersten Meisterwerke entstanden: neben *Dom Juan* noch *Le Misanthrope* (1665) und *Amphitryon* (1668). In all diesen Werken und in den Bittschriften (Plazets) um Wiederaufführung des *Tartuffe* praktiziert Molière die Lehre, die er aus dem Streit um die Heuchler-Komödie ziehen konnte: er heuchelt mit, läßt es jedoch ironisch durchblicken und erhebt sich damit—resigniert-schmerzlich, zornig und spöttisch-überlegen lachend über die Gesellschaft, über sich selber und die Welt. Die Plazets

---

[10] Ganz ähnlich tut er es in *Les Femmes savantes*. Armande trägt bezeichnenderweise den Namen Madame Molières und wurde wohl auch von ihr gespielt. Sie will lieber einen Verehrer als einen Gatten. Damit ist sie negative Kontrastfigur zu Henriette, die den geliebten Mann zum Gatten, nicht zum Liebhaber will.

[11] John Palmer, *Molière* (1933), 384.

und das Vorwort feiern den König als Quelle aller Macht und Autorität— obwohl Ludwig in dieser Sache jahrelang nichts gegen die religiöse Autorität ausrichten konnte. Der Bittsteller hat sogar die Stirn, sich auf den Beifall des päpstlichen Legaten zu berufen, der einer der verpönten Lesungen in Versailles beiwohnen und sich selbst der Autorität des königlichen Urteils unterwerfen mußte. Daneben spricht er freilich ganz offen: Die Komödie straft das Laster. Die Kirche hat keinen Anspruch, davon ausgenommen zu werden oder Angriffe gegen sie als Angriffe gegen Gott hinzustellen. Solche Äußerungen, zusammen mit dem Kampf um den *Tartuffe*, mit Werken wie *Dom Juan* und *Amphitryon* machen Molières Kritik an der institutionalisierten Autorität der Religion zu einer einzigartigen Erscheinung des Jahrhunderts.[12]

Nirgends zwar vereinte der Dichter so viel Satire mit so viel ironischem Versteckspiel wie in *Amphitryon*, dessen Aufführung denn auch m. W. auf keine Schwierigkeiten stieß. Doch die Kirche wußte, mit wem sie zu tun hatte, und vergaß es nicht. Als der todkranke Mime bei einer Aufführung des *Malade imaginaire* 1673 zusammenbrach und man nach einem Priester rief, damit Molière, wie es üblich war, die Sünde des Schauspielens widerrufen und die Sakramente erhalten konnte, da ließ die Geistlichkeit es nicht zu dieser ihrer letzten ironisch heuchelnden Verhöhnung kommen. Zwei Priester weigerten sich, der dritte traf zu spät ein. Nicht einmal der König konnte durchsetzen, daß Frankreichs größter Dichter ein christliches Begräbnis erhielt.

Daß in verwandter Zeitlage ein bohrender und des Ärgernisses fähiger Geist die Komödie Molières durchaus verstehen konnte—eben als ironisch verhüllte Autoritätskritik—beweist John Dryden. Sein *Amphitryon* (1690) kehrt allerdings, so scheint es auf den ersten Blick, die Satire übermäßig klar und derb, zu eindeutig hervor. Da ist gleich die Eingangsszene. Merkur nennt Jupiters Abenteuer unumwunden Ehebruch, ja Hurerei. Phöbus nimmt in Gedanken Anstoß an dem Kontrast zwischen dem äußerlichen Dekorum der Heiligkeit und dem heimlichen Frevel. Jupiter gibt zu, wegen all der Frommen müßten Könige und Priester die Tugendhaften mimen. Seine Schöpfer-Allmacht gebe ihm das Recht, über seine Kreaturen zu verfügen, wie ein absoluter Fürst über seine Untertanen. Der Kommentar der Untergötter: Die Allmacht, einem Manne Hörner aufzusetzen und ihn trotzdem nicht zu verunzieren, heiße, Recht und Unrecht nach dem Dekorum des gesellschaftlichen Ranges zu unterschei-

---

[12] Percy Addison Chapman, *The Spirit of Molière. An Interpretation* (1940), 222.

den, in Wahrheit also nicht zu unterscheiden. Das sei Despotie; der Schwache halte aber lieber den Mund.

Am Ende wird das wieder aufgenommen. Was Jupiter genießt, wird eben dadurch rein und heilig. „What Jupiter enjoys, he sanctifies from vice." Die Ehrung ist bei Licht besehen jedoch nur die Versüßung einer bittren Pille, ein kniffliger Punkt, über den man besser schweige, was Amphitryon auch tut. So bleibt Jupiters Dekorum der obersten Autorität gewahrt; und er darf zugeben, daß er besiegt wurde von dem Ehepaar (das deutet auf Giraudoux voraus). Denn alle Zärtlichkeit, die er der schönen Frau entlockte, galt ihrem Mann. Andere Autoren werden Dryden darin folgen, daß Alkmene zwischen den beiden Amphitryonen wählen muß und den Gott wählt—was Irrtum und beileibe keine Entscheidung für das Göttliche bedeutet—und daß sie bei der Epiphanie zugegen ist. Auch sie hüllt sich auf Jupiters Erklärung hin in Schweigen. Im Kontext der angeführten Kommentare kann das nur bekräftigen, was sie unmittelbar vor der Offenbarung sagte:

> I know not what to hope, nor what to fear.
> A simple error is a real crime,
> And unconsenting innocence is lost.

Das sind Worte schwerster Niedergeschlagenheit. Zusammen mit Amphitryons Verzweiflungsausbrüchen geben sie dem Protest gegen die Umwertung der Werte durch die gesellschaftlich anerkannte religiöse Autorität zusätzlich menschlich-sittliches Gewicht. Aber so deutlich und überdeutlich das alles hervorzutreten scheint, Dryden hat die Tendenz des Stückes andererseits vielfältig verhüllt—und sie doch wieder durchblicken lassen. Die Satire maskiert sich erstens gewissermaßen durch sich selbst, nämlich durch ihre völlig hemmungslose Unverschämtheit. Dergleichen konnte einfach nicht auf gegenwärtig herrschende Verhältnisse anspielen. Um so näher lag vielmehr zweitens die Beziehung auf Charles Stuart II., der dem Theater, insbesondere den Schauspielerinnen, große Gunst erwiesen und damit dem ganzen Hof ein Beispiel gesetzt hatte.

Dem Thema der Erotik ist der Epilog gewidmet. Aber gerade er verwandelt die Verdammung der Vergangenheit in Lob. Er endet mit dem Sehnsuchtsruf der Frauen, Jupiters Galanterie und die Vitalität seiner Mitgötter möchten wiederkehren im nächsten Zeitalter. Das gegenwärtige nämlich, das dem ersten Reich der Olympier folgte, fordere eine strenge (sprich: puritanische) Lebensauffassung. Mit solcher *severity of life* ende man zwar ohnehin, sobald man nicht mehr imstande sei zu sündigen; bis dahin aber sei sie doch zu trostlos.

Die Frivolität dient offenkundig als Vehikel für das andere Thema: Wie rasch wechseln die Epochen und ihre Wertsysteme! Zwei Jahre nach der glorreichen Revolution von 1688 war das hochaktuell. Die Widmung spricht das unumwunden aus. Sie wendet sich an eine einflußreiche Persönlichkeit der Revolution, an jemand, der den Autor seine Treue zur vergangenen Epoche nicht entgelten lasse. Eine Wendung wie *in this ruin of my small fortune* enthüllt die Ironie der Phrase *this wonderful Revolution*. Schließlich hatte Dryden seine einträglichen Posten als Hofhistoriograph und Poeta laureatus der Stuarts eingebüßt. Walter Scott wies auf solche Ausfälle gegen das derzeitige Regime hin.[13] Später indessen erklärte man das Stück für eine reaktionäre, sehnsüchtige Rechtfertigung der guten alten Zeit—ohne satirische Spitze gegen die jetzige.[14] Wendet Dryden sich doch schon im Prolog dem Thema Erotik zu, nachdem er einleitend sich verbreitet darüber, daß die Satire ohne echten Zorn weder provoziere noch gefalle. Eine schillernde Behauptung. Mag sein, daß man sie verstehen sollte als Erklärung, die Satire, die den Autor einst berühmt machte, sei ihm jetzt nicht mehr erlaubt.[15] Dem Wortlaut nach handelt es sich aber eher um die Ankündigung einer Satire. Das Stück ist eine solche jedenfalls. Und die Bemerkungen in Prolog und Epilog lassen keinen Zweifel: die Umwertung aller Werte durch die oberste, die religiöse Autorität, geißelt nicht bloß Charles II. erotische Extravaganzen, sondern ebenso die allerhöchste Regelung, daß, was gestern gut hieß (das Katholische), heute schlecht sei. Das mußte den Dichter schwer treffen. In *Religio Laici or A Layman's Faith* (1682) hatte er die Autorität von Kirche, Bibel und Vernunft mit skeptischen Vorbehalten diskutiert. Nach seiner Konversion feierte er in *The Hind and the Panther* (1685/6) die Autorität der katholischen Religion. 1693 erschien sein letztes Werk, eine ganze Sammlung lateinischer Satiren in Übersetzung. Sein *Amphitryon* von 1690 wurde ein großer Bühnenerfolg. Spürte und genoß das Publikum, daß sich hinter der Kritik am Vergangenen und dem mythischen Allotria eine Satire auf das neue Regime verbarg? Oder genoß es,

---

[13] Walter Scott, *The Life of John Dryden* (1805); Neudruck (1963), 306.
[14] Ned. B. Allen, *The Sources of John Dryden's Comedies* (1935), 234, 236; Lindberger, *op. cit.*, 98f.
[15] Kenneth Young, *John Dryden: A Critical Biography* (1954), 166.

weil die Provokation so gut verborgen war, unbefangen nur die derb-saftige Unterhaltung? Bedenkt man, wie gutgläubig die „Kritik" die Dinge sieht, möchte man letzteres annehmen. Doch das Verständnis für die zweideutige Sprache des verborgenen Protests verliert sich eben oft fast unmittelbar mit der jeweiligen politisch-gesellschaftlichen Situation. Ja, immer wieder erstaunt man, wie wenig die Autoritäten davon merken, daß sie angegriffen werden.

Da ist z. B. das Opernlibretto *Anfitriao* des António José da Silva. Es lehnt sich offenbar mehr an Rotrou an, jedoch im Geist Molières. Hier übertreffen Juno und Jupiter nämlich alles, was wir bisher von der Grausamkeit der Götter hörten. Jupiter läßt Amphitryon zum Tod durch den Strang verurteilen. Aus Eifersucht betört und besticht Juno den macht-gierigen Priester-Richter Teiresias, daß er Alkmene wegen Ehebruchs und Sosias wegen seiner Dienste für den nur angeblich falschen Am-phitryon im Tempel opfert. Teiresias weiß, daß Alkmene subjektiv un-schuldig ist, schlägt seine Gewissensbisse aber in den Wind. Jupiter verhindert das äußerste, entschädigt das Paar zu dessen dankbarer Zufriedenheit mit dem göttlichen Nachkommen Herkules und entschul-digt Alkmene: sie mußte einem Trick erliegen, der einem göttlichen Impuls entsprang, der Liebe. Der Schlußchor wundert sich, welch hohen Flug die Religion der Liebe nehmen kann.[16]

Da Silva hatte und erhielt traurige Ursache genug, darüber zu er-staunen. Als portugiesischer Jude (1705–39) wurde er von der Inquisition ständig verfolgt, mehrfach gefoltert und endlich gehängt, nachdem seine Frau und seine Eltern dieses Schicksal vor ihm erleiden mußten. Sein Stück aber wurde ebenso wie seine anderen in Lissabon vielfach aufge-führt, von der Inquisition nicht verboten und 1759 zum viertenmale aufgelegt.

Noch bevor da Silva geboren wurde, erschien die vielgelesene *Unpar-teyische Kirchen- und Ketzergeschichte* (1700) des Pfarrers Gottfried Arnold. Sie versicherte, der Ketzer sei der bessere, der wahre Christ. Thomas Paine erklärte in *The Age of Reason* (1794/95), alle historischen Religionen seien Erfindungen zum Zweck der Unterdrückung von Wis-senschaft und Freiheit. Das Buch wurde gleich nach Erscheinen ins Deutsche übersetzt (1796). Verleger und Übersetzer wahrten allerdings

---

[16] Professor Prado, dem ich auch hier Dank für seine Hilfe schulde, hält es für möglich, daß Jupiters Eröffnung und der fromme Dank des Paares an Mariä Verkündigung an-klingen. Das ist bei Kleist ganz offenbar der Fall. Doch bei da Silva könnte es sich um einen sehr ernstgemeinten Angriff gegen das Christentum handeln.
tryon-Stoffes (1971) und die äußeren Beziehungen zu Kleist untersucht im *fahrbuch der deutschen Schillergesellschaft*; 13 (1969), 361–96.

die Anonymität. Und die umfangreichen Erläuterungen griffen den Verfasser scheinbar wegen seiner Unchristlichkeit an, in Wahrheit aber wegen seiner allzugroßen Nachsicht gegen Kirche und Bibel. Das ist der verhüllte Aufstand des Prometheus. Auch die berühmteste Gestaltung des Motivs erschien zuerst anonym, ohne Wissen des Verfassers, in einer Schrift, die den sogenannten Pantheismusstreit zwischen Lessing und Mendelssohn auslöste.[17] Es ging um den Pantheismus des Spinoza, und damals hieß das: Atheismus. Das Werk aber war Goethes Ode *Prometheus*. Und Goethe schrieb scherzend, er komme „bey dieser Gelegenheit mit Lessing auf einen Scheiterhaufen zu sitzen.''[18] Später reihte er rückblickend den Prometheus seiner Ode den Titanen an, die damals seine „Heiligen'' waren, „Glieder einer ungeheuren Opposition im Hintergrunde meiner Iphigenie.''[19] Gleichwohl rettete er in jenem Drama das Bild der Götter durch einen guten Ausgang. Und das tat auch sein Verehrer Johann Daniel Falk in zwei Gestaltungen des Amphitryonstoffs.

In dem umfangreichen, antikisierenden Lustspiel *Amphitruon* von 1804 verzichtet Jupiter dem Geist Goethescher Humanität gemäß darauf, Alkmene zu besuchen. Im selben Jahr erholte sich Falk gleichsam von seinen feierlichen Anstrengungen mit der Posse *Das Ich und das Nicht-Ich, oder die lustige Hahnreischaft*: Alkmene ist eine Gewohnheits-Ehebrecherin, die selbst einen Jupiter nicht länger als vier Wochen zum Liebhaber möchte. Der Gatte gibt sich mit einer finanziellen Abfindung zufrieden.[20] Molière liefert hier nur die Verwechslungskomödie. Im übrigen wird er korrigiert: Falk verspottet die Götter, wo sie nur Karikaturen, also gar nicht getroffen sind; und er rettet ihr sittliches Bild, wo sie mit herkömmlicher Würde auftreten. Was die höchste, die religiöse Autorität angeht, so vermeidet Falk jeden Affront, ja, jede riskante Zweideutigkeit. So forderten es die klassizistische Ästhetik der Gattungsreinheit und die europäische Reaktion auf den Königs- und Religionssturz durch die Französische Revolution.

Heinrich von Kleist, der preußische Protestant, war ebensowenig ein grundsätzlicher Feind weltlicher und religiöser Autorität. Im Gegenteil, er erwartete alles Heil von dort. Doch gerade darum legte er den höchsten

---

[17] Friedrich Heinrich Jacobi, *Über die Lehre des Spinoza in Briefen an Herrn Moses Mendelssohn* (1785).
[18] 11. September 1785 an Jacobi.
[19] *Dichtung und Wahrheit*, 17. Buch.
[20] H. Sembdner hat beide Stücke neu herausgegeben (*J. D. Falks Bearbeitung des Amphi-*

Maßstab an ihre positiven Erscheinungsformen; und das hieß: er unterzog
sie einer ebenso leidenschaftlichen wie raffiniert verhüllenden Kritik.
Von seinem ersten Drama bis zu seiner letzten Erzählung wies er—in
zunehmend versteckter Form—auf die Gefahren hin, die sich aus der
Selbstgerechtigkeit weltlicher Autorität und aus der handgreiflichen
religiösen Lebens-Interpretation ergeben können. Das Göttliche ließ er,
gut romantisch, in parapsychischen Nachtseiten der Naturvorgänge und,
gut idealistisch, im Menschen der sittlichen Vollendung gelten.[21] Kleists
Amphitryon (1807) hat man nur selten als Autoritätssatire und überwiegend als hohes Lied auf die pantheistische Einung des Menschen mit
dem Göttlichen im Medium der Liebe ausgelegt. Pantheismus gibt es
tatsächlich im Munde Jupiters, an einer Stelle deutlich nach dem Vorbild
Falks und Goethes, dessen *Faust* seit 1790 als Fragment vorlag. Und wie
Fausts pantheistisches Credo zur Verführungsrede für Gretchen werden
soll, so ist es auch die Frage, ob Kleists Jupiter Alkmene belehren oder
verführen will. Er wirft ihr vor, daß sie ihn nicht in der Natur wahrnimmt
und statt dessen in Amphitryon anbetet. Er, der in Gestalt Amphitryons
erschien und von Alkmene für letzteren gehalten wird, will hier doch gar
nichts von pantheistischer Identität mit Amphitryon wissen, sondern von
ihm unterschieden werden. Alkmene verspricht es—und verwechselt
beide doch im selben Atemzug. Jupiters Ansinnen scheitert, und seine
pantheistische Argumentation entlarvt sich als sophistisches Vehikel
seines eifersüchtigen Werbens. Er lügt auch, als sie ihn einmal fragt, ob er,
Amphitryon, oder ein anderer sie besuchte: ,,Warst du's, warst du es
nicht?'' Er kann ehrlich antworten: ,,Ich wars.'' Für sie aber heißt das, es
war Amphitryon; und von dem will er ja unterschieden werden. So fährt
er fort:

> Sei's wer es wolle. Sei—sei ruhig.
> Was du gesehn, gefühlt, gedacht, empfunden,
> War ich: wer wäre außer mir, Geliebte?

Da Alkmene ihren Partner für ihren Gatten hält, erkennt sie dieses
Pantheismus-Philosophem gar nicht und hält es für eine Fortsetzung

---

[21] Weiteres hierzu in Aufsätzen des Vf., ,,Skepsis, Noblesse, Ironie: Formen des Als-ob in
Kleists *Erdbeben*'', *Euphorion* (1969), 249–83; ,,*Die heilige Cäcilie* und *Der Zweikampf*:
Kleists Legenden und die romantische Ironie'', *Coloquia Germanica* (1972), 17–58; ,,Weltdia-
lektik und Weltüberwindung: Zur Dramaturgie Kleists'', *Deutsche Dramentheorien*, hrsg.
R. Grimm (1972), 270–92. Zu *Amphitryon* vgl. meine unter 2 und 9 genannten Untersu-
chungen.

des maßlos übertreibenden Arguments, das ihre subjektive Schuldlosigkeit bestätigen soll und uns Jupiters nagende Eifersucht verrät: „Alles, was sich dir nahet, ist Amphitryon." Es ist komisch, daß Jupiter mit seiner Sophisterei hier nichts erreicht. Und es ist ebenso komisch, daß er damit Erfolg hat, wo die Absurdität deutlich sein sollte. Am Ende bereitet er seine Epiphanie vor mit der Erklärung, er sei nicht nur Amphitryon, sondern auch Argatiphontidas, der lächerliche *miles gloriosus*, ja selbst

> Die Kadmusburg und Griechenland,
> Das Licht, der Äther, und das Flüssige,
> Das, was da war, was ist, und was sein wird.

Erhabenes mischt sich da mit Lächerlichem. So ist es verständlich und zugleich doch wieder komisch, daß niemand Jupiter als Allgottheit nimmt —weder jetzt, wo niemand ihn auf Grund solcher theologischen Indizien erkennt (einzig Alkmene, die eben katechisiert wurde, ahnt etwas); noch später, nach der Offenbarung, wo der Gott seine panentheistische Identität mit Amphitryon so formuliert:

> Was du, in mir, dir selbst getan, wird dir
> Bei mir, dem, was ich ewig bin, nicht schaden.

Er behauptet also: Was an ihm selbst Amphitryon ist, das hat sich selbst betrogen; und was an Amphitryon Gott ist, nimmt es nicht übel. Dann könnte er ebensogut auch sagen, er sei, als er Alkmene besuchte, mit sich selbst zu Bett gegangen. Tatsächlich macht er aber gar kein Hehl daraus, daß er sich in Amphitryons Haus gefiel, dort also weilte, während der Gatte abwesend war. Wie denn im ganzen Stück Amphitryon und Jupiter niemals identisch, sondern zwei verschiedene Individuen sind. Der Gott fragt denn auch Alkmene abschließend noch ein letztes Mal, ob sie meine, Amphitryon sei ihr erschienen, Er erwartet die Antwort „Nein, ich weiß nun, es war Jupiter, und ich bin einverstanden" oder ähnlich. Statt dessen fleht sie ihn an, er möge sie in dem Glauben lassen, es sei Amphitryon gewesen. Sie lehnt seinen Besuch auch diesmal ab.

Seine Komik hat sich also gegenüber Molière intensiviert. Er ist zwar Gott, aber nicht gemäß den theologischen Kategorien, die er beansprucht. Und er selbst wird ausdrücklich von Alkmene abgewiesen. Sie erkennt frühzeitig, daß vielleicht ein Fremder sie besuchte, und wäre, obwohl er etwas Göttliches an sich hatte, verzweifelt. Jupiter ist überzeugt, daß sie seinen Besuch nicht als Unglück ansieht, wenn sie ihn erst erkennt, sondern als „Triumph." Er sagt ihr daher, in der Gestalt Amphitryons, die Wahrheit—und muß erfahren, daß sie trotzdem unglücklich bleibt. Er will es nicht wahrhaben, und dringt mit komischer Dickköpfigkeit immer wieder in sie, ob sie ihn nicht lieben könne, mehr als den Gatten, oder wenigstens ebenso wie ihn. Am Schluß dieses großen Versöhnungs- oder Versuchungsgespräches fragt er sie, abermals Unterscheidung fordernd:

> Wenn ich, der Gott, dich hier umschlungen hielte,
> Und jetzo dein Amphitryon sich zeigte,
> Wie würd' dein Herz sich wohl erklären?

Sie antwortet:

> Ja—dann so traurig würd' ich sein, und wünschen,
> Daß er der Gott mir wäre, und daß du
> Amphitryon mir bliebst, wie du es bist.

Das heißt: falls Jupiter-Amphitryon sie im Arm hält und Amphitryon sich daneben zeigt, ist sie traurig und will, daß der, den sie für Amphitryon hält, sie im Arm hält, der Gott in Amphitryons Gestalt aber daneben steht. Daß es sich um einen Korb handelt, geht schon daraus hervor, daß Jupiter in immer neuen Variationen die gleiche Frage stellt, also niemals befriedigende Antwort erhielt. Außerdem verflucht er in der Mitte und am Ende seinen Besuch, ja sogar die Seligkeit, die er genoß. Niemals aber gibt er offen zu, was ihn so quält, nämlich daß Alkmenes Zärtlichkeit nicht ihm galt, sondern dem geliebten Gatten. Auf ihre Absagen reagiert er verdutzt, gereizt—oder er tut, als sei er zufrieden, und macht gute Miene zu bösem Spiel. Das hat die Kritik derart verwirrt, daß sie überwiegend annahm, Jupiter gewinne Alkmenes Zustimmung doch, womit Sinn und Komik des Dramas auf den Kopf gestellt werden.

Vor allem führte es irre, daß Alkmene in der Schlußszene zwischen beiden Amphitryonen wählen soll und sich für Jupiter entscheidet. Da bevorzuge sie doch deutlich den Gott oder wenigstens den Jupiter-Amphitryon, hat man gemeint. Das ist aber gerade nicht der Fall. Sie glaubt jetzt, auf ein Wort Jupiters hin, den sie für Amphitryon hält, auch der Betrüger sei ein Sterblicher. Zwischen beiden kann sie lange nicht entscheiden, da sie einander wie zwei Wassertropfen gleichen. Endlich entscheidet sie, mehr um ihre „bitterste der Lebensstunden" zu beenden, für den, der eben als ihr Gatte bei ihr weilte. Ihn, Jupiter also, läßt sie nahezu unbeachtet als den Gatten stehen, von dem sie sich nun trennen muß. Und ihr ganzer Schmerz und Zorn ergießt sich über den, den sie für den Betrüger nicht eigentlich hält, sondern nur erklärte. Und nun behauptet sie sogar, er sei häßlich. Daß er ihr damals gottgleich erschien, hat sie vergessen. So kann sie eine wahre Schimpfkanonade loslassen—die Jupiter auf sich beziehen muß, was außer ihm nur der Zuschauer erkennt. So wird dem Gott eine durch ihre Komik vernichtende Niederlage bereitet; doch sie wird zugleich halbwegs verhüllt durch all die Mißverständnisse, die die Verwechslungskomödie mit sich bringt; durch die Umständlichkeit der Erörterung im Modus des Möglichen; endlich durch die geistesgegenwärtige Geschicklichkeit Jupiters, aber auch durch seine wahrhaft hinreißende Rhetorik.

Und noch etwas. Wie in einigen der früheren Stücke, im Gegensatz jedoch zu Molière und auch zu der ohnmächtig zusammenbrechenden Alkmene hier, nimmt Amphitryon die Ehrung dankbar an. Viele Interpreten haben ihn für diese Hochschätzung des Göttlichen gelobt. Kleist aber hat ihn dafür kritisiert, und zwar durch die Art, wie er die Dienerhandlung ausgestaltete. Nachdem der scheinbare Gemahl Alkmene davon überzeugte, daß Jupiter sie besuchte, hält Charis nun den richtigen Sosias für Apollo. Eine Szene von umwerfender Komik. Und während die Herrin den Ehebruch ablehnt, auch wenn es mit einem Gott sein soll, wäre die auf ihre Reputation bedachte Dienerin in solch heiligem Falle zu jedem Seitensprung bereit. Amphitryon denkt grundsätzlich ebenso und wird durch die Analogie zu Charis verhöhnt. Alkmenes Denkweise dagegen wird parallelisiert durch Sosias, der die Ehre der Götterprügel undankbar ablehnt. Ehebruch mit dem Gott, Götterprügel—eine weitere Parallele ist der Versuch der Götter, Herrn und Diener um das Gefühl der Identität zu bringen, was wie bei Molière mißlingt. Mokierte der Franzose sich dabei über die Umständlichkeit der cartesianischen Philosophie, so Kleist über die der Fichteschen. Darin folgte er Falk, ebenso in der ethischen Erhöhung des Ehepaares und der offenen Konfrontierung Alkmenes mit der Frage, ob sie Jupiter lieben könne. Doch im Gegensatz zu Falk—und Goethe—rettet er das Bild der Götter nicht. Darin folgte er Molière; mit innerster Berechtigung nannte er sein Werk *Ein Lustspiel nach Molière.*

Natürlich war das schon äußerlich berechtigt. Keiner hat sich so sehr an Molières Text angelehnt wie Kleist. Bis in den II. Akt hinein handelt es sich um eine Übersetzung. Aber so vollkommen, wie dieser Teil in Kleists Sprache umgegossen ist, so echt Kleistisch ist die Um- und Weiterbildung von da an. Sie erfolgt im Geist Molières. Die Ironie der Kritik, die halb verhüllte Komik Jupiters, die Symmetrie der Figuren und ihrer Positionen: all das ist—wie die weitere Geschichte des Stoffes zeigt—bis zu einem Grade fortgeführt, der nicht mehr übertroffen werden konnte. Zu den Möglichkeiten, die 150 Jahre vorher einfach noch nicht gegeben waren, gehört die menschliche Verinnerlichung Alkmenes und Amphitryons, selbst Jupiters. Typisch Kleistisch ist aber auch ein Zug, den man Molière gegenüber als Mangel bezeichnen kann. Es ist das, was Goethe am *Zerbrochnen Krug*, der seinerseits nicht ohne *Tartuffe* zu denken wäre, mißbilligend die „stationäre Prozeßform" nannte. Es ist hier das stufenweise fortschreitende und doch eigenwillig hartnäckige Insistieren auf ein und derselben, ständig wiederkehrenden „Gretchen-Frage": Gott oder Mensch? Es intensiviert, spitzt das Problem zu echt kleistischer Radikalität zu—aber es ermüdet auch. Was die Gefälligkeit, Verständlichkeit und insbesondere die Theaterwirksamkeit angeht, so triumphiert Molières Kunst noch über den größten Dichter, der—bei grundsätzlich gleicher Gesinnung und in tiefster Ehrerbietung—mit ihm wetteiferte.

Die Gestaltungen des Amphitryon-Themas haben damit ihren Höhepunkt überschritten. Eine Ursache des nun einsetzenden Niederganges ist die berufsmäßige Literaturkritik, die sich jetzt breit entwickelt. Sie tat Molières Stück als frivole Gesellschaftskomödie ab und feierte Kleists Werk als Exempel für die mystische Vereinigung des Menschen mit dem Göttlichen.[22] Daher läßt sich manchmal schwer sagen, ob die späteren Amphitryon-Autoren mit oder gegen Molière und Kleist schreiben wollten. Wilhelm Henzen ließ sein Stück (1905) als Bühnenbearbeitung Kleists erscheinen. Neben stilistischen Schlimmbesserungen baute er eine gröbere Version der Falkschen Lösung ein: es kommt nicht zum Besuch Jupiters; und zwar scheucht Alkmene den Gott geradezu davon, indem sie sich auf die eheliche Treue beruft. Das ist sehr prometheisch gemeint. Aber ein Gott, der sich vom Zetern einer Frau in die Flucht schlagen läßt, ist nicht mehr Gegenstand eines ernsthaften Wagnisses.

Das ist auch der wunde Punkt an Jean Giraudouxs *Amphitryon 38*

---

[22] Vgl. meine Übersicht über das Schicksal des Kleistschen *Amphitryon* in der Kritik: „Die Verschleierung der Wahrheit in und über Kleists *Amphitryon*", *Wahrheit und Sprache*. Festschrift Bert Nagel (1972).

(1929). Jupiter wird hier am Schluß der Schutzpatron des Ehepaars; er erlaubt ihm, das Ideal ehelicher Liebe und Treue zu erfüllen. Andererseits hat er Alkmene doch besucht und Herkules gezeugt, wie es der Mythos und Jupiters Verlangen forderten. Der Gott verzichtet lediglich auf einen weiteren, den offiziellen Besuch; und er läßt das Paar auf dessen Bitte hin den Tag einfach vergessen—eine wohltätige Aufhebung der Tragödie, wie Kleists Alkmene sie vergebens erfleht. Er gibt in dieser Weise nach, weil Alkmene sich eher das Leben nähme, als ihm zu Willen zu sein, und weil ihm ihre selbstgenügsame Beschränkung auf die Werte des menschlichen Daseins imponiert. Es ist komisch und zugleich herzbewegend, wie der Allmächtige sein Hauptziel nicht erreicht—daß Alkmene ihn ihrem Gatten vorzieht—und wie der Allwissende einsehen lernt, daß es unter den Menschen eine prometheische Eigenständigkeit gibt, vor deren Tugenden der Sanftmut, Treue, Hingabe der Machtanspruch der Götter jämmerlich zuschanden wird. Darum ist Alkmene nach seinem Wort „le vrai Prométhée" (II,3).

Freilich gibt es daneben die offizielle mythische Ideologie, derzufolge das Göttliche dem Menschlichen in jeder Hinsicht überlegen ist und ein Ehebruch mit Gott ehrenvolle Auszeichnung bedeutet. Doch in prometheischem Geist verneint das vorbildliche Paar die Autorität jener Konvention selbstverständlich und gelassen. Der Protest erfolgt, wenigstens für den Zuschauer, völlig unverhüllt; und er wird von Jupiter gebilligt. Dadurch aber hört der Gott auf, der ganz andere, Furchtbare zu sein, und der Aufstand gegen ihn hat nur sehr wenig von einem prometheischen Wagnis an sich. Die Ironie, die sich hauptsächlich gegen die Masse und die Götter richtet, ist eindeutig, also um ihr bestes Salz gebracht. Die kommentierende Dienerhandlung—seit Plautus das komische Glanzstück aller Bearbeitungen—fällt fort wie überall nach Kleist. Alkmene, die die erfahrene Leda für sich einspringen lassen will, wird trotzdem von Jupiter getäuscht. Leda empfängt Amphitryon im Glauben, es sei Jupiter; und jener hält sie für Alkmene. Ein blasser und wenig amüsanter Ersatz für die kunstvoll-komischen Kontraste und Analogien, für den derben Übermut der aufgegebenen Verwechslungspartien.

Sie fehlen auch in Georg Kaisers *Zweimal Amphitryon* (1943). Der aus Nazi-Deutschland emigrierte Dichter vergröberte den Stoff zu einem Antikriegsstück und einer Werbeschrift für Religion. Die salbungsvolle religiöse Exzentrik echot die deutschen akademischen Kleistvorlesungen von 1920 bis 1960. Ähnlich wie bei Hesiod führt Amphitryon Krieg um des Krieges willen und vernachlässigt darüber seine Frau. Diese besteht die Liebesprobe, der der Gott sie unterzieht. Ihr Sohn Herkules soll die Menschheit erlösen—durch Gründung der olympischen Spiele. Alkmene aber trauert dem entschwundenen Gott nach. Das schwerfällig versifizierte Bildungsdrama präsentiert die herkömmliche Rangordnung zwischen Göttlichem und Menschlichem. Die Ironie und Komik der Dienerhandlung und der Verwechslungen sind—wie nun immer—ersetzt durch Raisonnement.

Die Alkmene des klassischen Philologen Eckart Peterich (*Alkmene*, 1959) verweigert sich Jupiter. Um einem unpopulären Moralismus vorzubeugen, heißt es, sie handle so aus Liebe, nicht aus Tugend. Plautus, Molière und Kleist ließen beides zusammenfallen. Die „fromme Legende von der Heiligkeit der Ehe" (Nachwort) versittlicht den Mythos in humanistischem Geist. Jupiter verschont Alkmene wirklich. Und am Ende trauert er, der zurückgewiesene, schuldige Gott. Eine Lösung, die tiefsinnig und zugleich lustig sein soll, was man dem Text selbst freilich nicht anmerkt.

Der derzeit letzte *Amphitryon*, von dem in der DDR lebenden Peter Hacks (1969), wehrt sich offenbar gegen den feierlichen Tiefsinn der konservativen Kleistkritik und -nachfolge. Glaubt er zu Molière zurückzukehren? Das Stück ist ebenfalls in Blankversen, doch es geht derb und herzhaft zu. Jupiter kommt voll auf seine Kosten, sogar zu einer zweiten Umarmung, zu der Alkmene den erkannten Gott auffordert. Die Folgen sind weder mythisch (Herkules) noch seelisch für einen der Beteiligten belangreich. Protestiert die amoralish unverbindliche Burleske mit ihrer fleischlichen Freigeisterei gegen die puritanische Sittenverwaltung der Obrigkeit? Dann handelte es sich noch einmal um Autoritätskritik, die sich mit Komödie maskierte. Mit Geist und Kunst Molières und Kleists hat sie sonst nichts zu tun. Indessen, es empfiehlt sich kaum, hierzu ein letztes Wort zu sagen. Denn wie schwer es ist, die Sprache des verhüllten Widerstandes zu verstehen, daran hat dieser Überblick vielleicht erinnern können.

MOLIÈRE'S DIALECTICS OF THE GROTESQUE AND THE STRUGGLE FOR NATURAL ORDER

Miroslav J. Hanak

It was Molière's ungrateful task to provide the grotesque commentary on the compromise between French grandeur and reality's seamier side which was being tried out with varying degrees of enthusiasm by the exponents of Realpolitik among the Sun King's policy makers. Molière's masterful grasp of empirical reality fashioned flesh-and-blood beings rather than moralizing concepts. The grotesqueness of his larger-than-life archetypes of human frailty is carefully balanced with sharply observed individual quirks. Such grotesqueness results neither from diseased aestheticism, nor from a radically decayed frame of reference. Molière undertook the task of preserving the viable elements of the France of Henri IV with the same eagerness he displayed in ridiculing and chastising all that became corrupt in that heritage.

His creatures are unbalanced with the intention to reform rather than to shock and destroy what is beyond recovery. Molière was ever mindful of the purpose of his art: to correct, to save, and to preserve. A genuine admirer of Louis, he deplored, rather than attacked, the tragedy of abortive grandeur which began spreading from the king to the nation in the second decade of his reign. Even at the onset of the reign of the Sun King, the ascendancy of false appearance over truth was in evidence; increasing in tempo and viciousness, the will to impress began to corrode the moral and economic reality of the prosperous bourgeois and of the penniless courtier. Those of Molière's plays that have achieved classical measure owe it to a systematic exposure of behavioral extremes which tend to negate the positive core inherent in every social attitude. Cathos of *Les Précieuses ridicules* embodies a perverted emphasis on erudition; catering to vanity, she contents herself with appearance and conformity to ruling opinion at the expense of truth: "j'aurais toutes les hontes du monde s'il fallait qu'on vînt à me demander si j'aurais vu quelque chose de nouveau que je n'aurais pas vu" (Scene 9). Arnolphe, the male chauvinist of *L'Ecole des femmes*, adopts for the same reason what seems to him a genteel and dignifying surname of M. de la Souche. He spares no effort to maintain his ward Agnes in total ignorance concerning cultural and social matters in order to mold her behavior according to the ideal obsequious wife, the only kind unlikely to cuckhold him.

> Et celle que j' épouse a toute l'innocence
> Qui peut sauver mon front de maligne influence. (I.i)

Arnolphe demonstrates the viciousness of the opposite extreme of the *Précieuses ridicules*. A man who equates feminine virtue with ignorance ostensibly fears the refinements of the spirit out of the feeling of sexual inadequacy:

> Je ne veux point d'un esprit qui soit haut
> Et femme qui compose en sait plus qu'il ne faut. (*Ibid.*)

Such treatment would reduce any woman to a state of imbecility, conducive to answering any question with "tarte à la crème." Arnolphe's plan of education which allows a woman "De savoir prier Dieu, m'aimer, coudre et filer" (*Ibid.*) is a view of reality as partial and false as the pedant's preciosity which seeks an absolute sublimation of material existence just for the show of the effort. The dialectic quest for the behavioral mean keeps Molière's characters, in spite of their grotesqueness, from reaching the dimension of dehumanized or superhuman abstractions.

The hypocrisy of Tartuffe tends to alienate the family of Orgon from reality through a burlesque travesty of truth, but does not succeed in blotting out the common sense of the servant girl Dorine, or in triumphing over the love of the young people, Marianne and Valère. Long before Tartuffe's unmasking, Dorine attempts to show to her master the inauthenticity of the hypocrite's teachings and the danger they hold for the family's moral health. Orgon's slavish imitation of Tartuffe's poses further aggravates the grotesque alienation from truth which begins to envelop the household, a living proof for the persuasiveness of the genius of evil. Dorine's terse comment on her master's freshly acquired and badly imitated art of dissimulation demonstrates the contagious quality of self-deception: "Ah! vous êtes dévot, et vous vous emportez!" (II. ii). Molière's secret which lends his grotesque archetypes their dramatic spark lies in the dialectic mastery of playing personal quirks and follies against a few eternal verities, which are barely suggested in the background with a light but firm hand. Gradually, this background becomes tacitly manifest to every rational creature as an immutable norm of behavior, transcending social and national boundaries. At the same time, it throws into relief all that is true, noble and real in French existence, especially in the healthy bourgeoisie and in unspoiled country folk. Tartuffe demonstrates primarily the false reality of the *via contemplativa* professed by a mock ascetic:

> Qui suit bien ses leçons, goûte une paix profonde,
> Et comme du fumier regarde tout le monde. (*Tartuffe*, I. v)

The play threatens to turn into a grotesque farce when Tartuffe, who has earlier confided to Orgon's wife that "for all his devout behavior he is not less a man" (III. iii), tries to seduce her while the husband is hiding under the table (IV. v). But the measure of a sober and lively *étude de moeurs* quickly recovers the balance of no-nonsense reality, in which tragic elements seldom lack. The king's providential vigilance intervenes just in time to prevent the triumph of evil. The authentic love of the young triumphs, the antics of the Tartuffes and Arnolphes notwithstanding: a stern but forgiving order is reestablished by the *rex ex machina*, who watches constantly over the best interests of his subjects, remembering their services and condoning their pecadillos.

> Nous vivons sous un Prince ennemi de la fraude,
> Un prince dont les yeux se font jour dans les coeurs,
> Et que ne peut tromper tout l'art des imposteurs. (V. 7)

Molière recast Tirso's *Burlador de Sevilla* as an atheist Don Juan, a "grand-seigneur méchant homme," who fully exploits the fascinating attraction of the fallen angel and who delights in spreading woe to everything he touches. Careful providence, this time not merely royal but transcendent, intervenes once more in the moment of highest need on behalf of earthly justice when man-made laws fail to shake the libertine's cynical nihilism, which has become unassailable thanks to his stance beyond good and evil. Molière's seducer answers his servant's observation that "one must believe in something in this world" with a declaration of faith in the self-evident and therefore, undebatable principles of mathematics: "Je crois que deux et deux sont quatre, Sganarelle, et que quatre et quatre sont huit" (III. i.). Unlike the "mille e tre" pragmatism of Mozart's *Don Giovanni*, preached by a fascinating rogue whose very voluptuousness tends to excuse him, Molière's seducer does not enumerate his conquests in a geographical catalogue of handy female graces, but reduces reality to an abstract formula. Not even the reckless villainy of Tirso's don Juan emptied life so radically of its warmth. Mathematical precision is the ultimate in satanism: it proclaims the law of absolute alienation of human affects, degrading them below even lechery and homicidal neurosis. Molière's version of donjuanism is a matter of dispassionate planning, not an unbridled passion to possess for the sake of sampling, nor the crude joy of crushing what is most precious in a surrendering woman, her ingenuous bewilderment over her behavior.

In his *enjôleur* Molière created a monster of that perverse rationalism which leads to false enlightenment. The idea anticipates Hegels's critique of the French Revolution as "absolute freedom" which, caught in its own abstraction, can act only in "its self-destructive sphere," without achieving "the subject's essential freedom."[1] Molière's play is an attack against the radical *esprits forts* who would excuse libertinage and fraud as long as they can be expressed in logically verifiable propositions. This "mathematical justice" calls "just" anything that adds up logically.

Dom Juan is Molière's thrust against the opposite pole of false devotion, the vice of self-destructive agnosticism. Faithful to his thesis that universal order is always preserved, the author calls forth an act of God when man's justice proves impotent before dehumanized logic. The drama follows the pattern of a momentary lapse into the grotesque in order to accentuate the need for a prompt and violent restitution of balance and sanity.

In the scene with the pauper whom the grand seigneur tries to induce to blaspheme in exchange for a louis d'or (III. ii), the libertine suffers a setback from two simple minds. Sganarelle's horse sense rebels against his master's gratuitous tempting of providence; with cold detachment, he analyzes the blessings of education. "Il faut avouer que [l' arithmétique . . . met] d'étranges folies dans la tête des hommes, et que, pour avoir bien étudié, on est bien moins sage le plus souvant" (III. i). Mimicking his master's cynicism, Sganarelle drives mathematical amoralism to its absurd conclusion. He exhorts the pauper to blaspheme, for it "adds up" to do it for profit, since science has proved that there is no reality besides conceptual abstractions; least of all, there exists a difference between good and

---

[1] Georg Wilhelm Friedrich Hegel, *The Phenomenology of the Spirit*, trans. J. J. B. Bailey (London: Macmillan, 1910), I, 604.

evil. "Va, va, jure un peu, il n'y a pas de mal" (III. ii). Not all of Molière's peasants are blessed with common sense nor his princes polarized between guardians and scoffers of justice. The woodcutter Sganarelle quickly learns in his involuntary role of "physician in spite of himself" that what the world wants is dissimulation on a grand scale. He begins to enjoy conforming to false opinion. Insistence on truth earns Sganerelle a beating, conformity to the lie, prestige and money, thanks to the blindness of a father who tries to force the standards of his reality on his daughter. He learns to imitate the quack's learned gibberish to confirm public opinion in its ignorance. But the very ambiguity of the world which prefers appearance to essential truth catches up with the adaptable woodcutter: by catering to the grotesque representation that men entertain in their minds about medicine, Sganarelle tastes both the reward of deceit and the wrath of the disillusioned. Having learned too well the worship of universal folly, he comes close to paying with his head for its exploitation. In the end, it is doubtful that he has learned anything, aside from self-deceit. The play ends with Sganarelle's advice to his wife, which is only half ironic: "prépare-toi désormais à vivre dans un grand respect avec un homme de ma conséquence et songe que la colère d'un médecin est plus à craindre qu'on ne peut croire" (III. xi). To keep his dialectic impartial, apart from false healers, Molière attacks the hypochondriacs who allow themselves to be duped by unscrupulous swindlers. *Le Malade imaginaire* questions the reputation of medicine as an exact science. The only reliable revelation that the hypochondriac may expect from his doctors is that he has been spectacularly wrong about assessing the feelings that his family entertains about him. As soon as his exaggerated faith in the miraculous virtues of medical science is dispelled, he recovers his common sense and with it, his health.

The alienation of man from reality due to an exaggerated confidence in everything except nature is the essence of Molière's social and moral comment. "Unnatural" is the worship of arts and sciences by the cloddish Monsieur Jourdain, who is nonplussed that, "unbeknowest to him, he has been practicing prose for more than forty years" (*Le Bourgeois gentil-homme*, II. iv). He exemplifies the vice of self-overreaching which turns a basically decent human being into an insufferable bore and, gradually, into an unjust tyrant.

The obsession with wealth, rather than social graces and learning out of proportion to individual capacity is the vice of Harpagon, the miser.

The ambition to acquire learning, elegance, and culture, which are the sterling qualities of the bourgeois, become virtue grotesquely distorted when the bourgeois seeks to be what by nature he is not.

Finally, even the sincere insistence on truth at any cost causes alienation from human existence. Demanding absolute truth of man leads necessarily to misanthropy as a radical rejection of the human species. Alceste the misanthrope is cursed with the passion for uncompromising sincerity that makes absolutely no allowance for human imperfection. He not only demands truth at any cost, but once he has ascertained what he thinks is true, he feels honor-bound to publicize it with a cavalier disregard for the sensibilities of the world around him. After losing his last friends, the misanthrope withdraws into his "desert," which means both retirement from Paris to the country and a total withdrawal into the inner self. Alceste's radical isolation demonstrates that absolute truth is neither of nor for this world. Insisting on its possession leads to a distortion of reality every bit as grotesque as the false appearances affected by the two "petits marquis," Acaste and Clitandre, and as perverse as the egoism of the spoiled "society widow" Célimène. Molière's own discontent with France under Louis XIV avoids the pitfall of hybris so tempting to the radical reformer. He agreed with his misanthrope that the French court had corrupted sincere admiration through exaggerated flattery: "c'est n'estimer rien qu'estimer tout le monde" (I. i), but he also argues with Alceste's friend Philinte that civility is the highest virtue in intercourse between men.

> Mais quand on est du monde, il faut bien que l'on rende
> Quelques dehors civils que l'usage demande. (*Ibid.*)

The only other alternative in the face of Alceste's dismal view of existence as "lâche flatterie . . . injustice, intérêt, trahison, fourberie" (*Ibid.*) is a physical and spiritual emigration from humanity.

> . . . chercher sur la terre un endroit écarté
> Ou d'être homme d'honneur on ait la liberté. (V.iv)

Molière never wavers in his conviction that man's imperfect nature is perfectible, although by virtue of its imperfection, it resists absolutist panaceas. This is why Molière's grotesque epilogue to the ethos of Corneille's *gloire* and the pathos of Racine's *passion* does not reach the infra-human dimensions of Quevedo's nightmares. Though painfully aware of the vainglorious tendencies of his countrymen, Molière doesn't attack worldly glory per se, out of respect for his beloved king to whom it was a most precious asset. What he does attack mercilessly is appearance masquerading as truth in a vast panorama of existential situations which give an all-human significance to his dramaturgy.

The political philosopher Eric Voegelin's analysis of Plato's *Republic* distinguishes seven levels in Plato's critique of progressive social corruption. On the first level, the citizen in an as yet uncorrupt society "accepts the historically grown standards of justice and injustice" without "pretending that the one is the other." As the corruption deepens and broadens, "just action [comes to] conflict with the external standards of law, customs and mores of a society." Next, corruption reaches the point when "just conduct by social standards becomes *appearance* in relation to *true* justice." In the next stage, society lays claim to power over individual conscience: "Whether the individual conduct be *truly* just or unjust, the fate of the individual will on the whole depend on his conformity with the standards that are socially recognized." On the fifth level "the consciousness in the now wholly corrupt society becomes permanently split." The split between appearance and reality of justice is recognized by the members of the corrupt society, but the power of society is on the side of appearance. The last two steps follow necessarily, hastening the process of society's total alienation from truth: first, "the accent of reality shifts from truth to the socially overpowering appearance"; second, "*doxa*, or belief [rather than certain knowledge] becomes *aletheia*, truth. . . . The accent of reality has shifted so far that *truth*, in the sense of conformity of man with himself, is achieved by the will to be unjust in order to harmonize with society."[2]

It is evident that Molière's campaign for the reversal of the trend from certain knowledge of man's self to a false belief sets in at the fifth level, when apparent justice in all judgments is beginning to be preferred over real justice, while the split between the two is still recognized by "the members of the corrupt society."

It is not an idle speculation to state that France had never reached, except for brief spasms of collective insanity to which all nations are exposed at one time or another, the total and definitive inversion of truth into belief through an overt "will to be unjust." Unlike post-classical Athens and Spain, France exercised continuous hegemony throughout

---

[2] Eric Voegelin, *Plato* (Baton Rouge: Louisiana University Press, 1966), 79.

the formative years of modern Europe, much of the time in politics, and always in culture. In support of the thesis that the lion share of this accomplishment is due to Molière, a hypothetical question should be asked: would France have been able to harness the demon of her restless and inventive spirit into productive channels most of the time between 1660 and 1870 without the cynically wise dramatic *pointes* bequeathed to her by her noble gadfly, reminding her constantly of the danger that the corruption of the best is the worst.

The grotesque "excesses" of farce and slapstick fun which bothered many a devotee of classical measure must be revalued in the light of Molière's existential, moral, and perhaps most importantly, of his aesthetic concerns. In order to achieve the maximum faithfulness in the recreation of human nature in the dramatic medium, he "exaggerates with measure," allowing abysmal vice and stupidity an almost geometrically calculated "something extra," to produce the optimum effect of an aesthetically graduated reality. Molière's grotesqueness represents a carefully administered dose of super and infra-reality to make the truth of everyday existence more piquant and amenable to self-examination. His grotesque reality is more than an existential fact; it is an aesthetic stimulus and an ethical weapon.

Molière died mercifully before Louis XIV's fading splendor made a Moloch of military glory and a desert of the French countryside. While Bossuet endeavored to demonstrate God's justice to man by empirical induction, citing as paradigms of a divine order in all things the exemplary Christian deaths of noted figures of the French court, the real funeral orations announcing the sunset of Louis's Golden Age were pronounced in a far less dogmatic and a more subtle fashion on the stage of the Palais Royal, decades before French decadence became a self-evident truth.

MOLIÈRE AND THE TRADITION
OF THE GROTESQUE
Edith Kern

"We usually speak of Molière with such awe, we listen so respect-
fully to his most foolish jests as if they were matters profound and filled
with serious meaning, that, when one of his contemporaries, such as
Somaize, tells us that he was 'first among French writers of farce,' or, such
as Monfleury, that he was the successor of Scaramouche, such scant praise
seems to us like an insult."[1] With these words Lanson started his perceptive essay on Molière and the farce, which he published in 1901 and which
initiated a new era in Molière criticism. Lanson's study corrected an historical imbalance by recognizing the world of both Italian and French
farce as essential elements in Molière's art, elements that could not be
ignored by the objective literary historian. The essay also clearly revealed
that the beginnings of the playwright-actor's career coincided with a transition in the taste of Parisian audiences from a preference for French farce
to one for the Italian, the *commedia dell'arte* with its stress on the romanesque. Molière's early experiences in the theater—his travels in the provinces
with his troupe and the sharing of the Petit Bourbon theater with the Italian players in Paris—had exposed him to both traditions, and his genius
was nourished by both. But though he acknowledged the presence of such
influences in Molière's work, Lanson felt called upon to defend its originality rather than explore the nature of those "foolish jests." The critic was,
after all, a man of his time, which still adhered to classical tastes and, like
Boileau, would have assigned first place in comedy to Molière, if

> Il n'eût pas fait souvent grimacer ses figures,
> Quitté pour le bouffon l'agréable et le fin,
> Et sans honte à Térence allié Tabarin.[2]

Like Boileau, Lanson and his contemporaries decidely preferred *Le Misanthrope*, the least farcical of Molière's plays, to *Les Fourberies de Scapin*,
one of his most exuberantly grotesque later comedies. Their reactions

---

[1] Gustave Lanson, "Molière et la Farce," in *Essais de Méthode de Critique et d'Histoire Littéraire*, ed. Henri Peyre. Paris: Hachette, 1965, 189. The translation is my own.
[2] Quoted by Lanson, *ibid.*, 190.

at the Comédie-Française were glacial, Lanson noted, "when, on Tuesdays, blows, beatings and kicks hail down on the faces, the backs, and other parts of the Sganarelles and Gérontes, when imperative syringes are in pursuit of bewildered victims, when grotesque speeches are delivered, spiked with vulgar expressions that seem to have been 'picked up in the gutters of Les Halles'!"[3] Lanson could only go as far as to condone such farce, and it is only more recent scholarship that has given us a deeper understanding of popular farce and enabled us to look at Molière's "foolish jests" in a different light. Less tinged by classicism, this light makes them appear, I think, as matters truly profound. For it makes us see them as part of the tradition of the grotesque.

When Lanson designated as grotesque some elements in Molière's comedies, he most likely used the word in the vague and generally accepted meaning that it has had since the seventeenth century. French dictionaries of the time consider it the equivalent of "silly," "bizarre," "extravagant," or even "pleasantly ridiculous."[4] They record it as synonymous of *ridicule*, *comique*, or *burlesque*. Yet—and Lanson may have been aware of this— even as a specific term of art criticism, the word was early associated with farce. The etchings of Jacques Callot (1592–1635), for instance, his whimsical chronicles of *commedia dell'arte* types, were as early as 1620 considered perfect examples of grotesque art,[5] and even outside of France, critics continued to associate the term with this type of theater.[6]

It was Wolfgang Kayser who, in his seminal work, *The Grotesque in Art and Literature*,[7] traced the history of the word as a critical concept. French *grotesque* (the English word has clearly been adopted from French), although seemingly related to Old French *crot*, was derived from Italian *grottesco*, designating something that had its origin in a *grotto* (cave). It came to describe, in the late fifteenth century, a particular style of paintings that had been found in a *grotto* as it were: the murals of Titus' Baths which had been excavated at that time. Their ancient style was one that had been unknown previous to the excavations and was remarkable because it defied all verisimilitude, not unlike the manner of dreams. It combined human forms with those of animals and plants and the inani-

---

[3] *Ibid.*, 190. The translation is my own.

[4] Wolfgang Kayser, *The Grotesque in Art and Literature*, trans. Ulrich Weisstein (Bloomington: Indiana University Press, 1963), 26–27.

[5] *Ibid.*, 27.

[6] *Ibid.*, 29, 37–38.

[7] The original version of this work appeared in 1957 and was entitled *Das Groteske: seine Gestalt in Malerei und Dichtung* (Oldenburg: Gerhard Stalling Verlag).

mate with the animate. Already at the time of Augustus, they had been criticized by the Roman architect Vitruvius for the monstrous forms they portrayed and which resembled nothing that had ever existed or ever could exist. He had declared them to be without rhyme or reason. The reactions of those who saw them upon their excavation was similar. They criticized them for subverting the natural order of things, for their lack of proper proportion, and for the bastard forms and the topsy-turvy world they depicted. Yet the grotesque style of these paintings seems to have left its mark on Renaissance painters as different as Raphael and Brueghel. In Raphael's paintings the grotesque assumes the form of playfully fantastic ornaments; in those of Brueghel it combines a playful with a monstrous and threatening aspect, conveying a world in the process of dissolution. Kayser, as if hypnotized by this threatening aspect of the grotesque, sees it as the predominant trait everywhere. Like E. T. A. Hoffmann, who was to admire Callot's sketches of *commedia dell'arte* figures, Kayser recognizes in their grotesque combination of human and animal mask mainly "the irony which . . . mocks man and all his trifling activities."[8] It is not difficult to see why the concept, almost from the start, was made to include not only artistic but also literary form and content. Kayser credits Montaigne with having been the first to apply the term to the architecture of his work. Fully conscious of his having fused in his essays different realms of the intellect and of their lack of organization and proportion, Montaigne referred to them as "grotesque and monstrous bodies, pieced together of the most diverse members, without distinct form, in which order and proportion are left to chance."[9] It may be worth mentioning here that this description does not vary essentially from one made by Lanson of the structure of most of Molière's comedies. He considers them as lacking in plot and consisting rather of a series of loosely connected scenes.[10] Yet it is not here that Molière's link with the tradition of the grotesque truly resides. Nor does Kayser's definition of the grotesque suffice in establishing this link. To make it apparent, we have to turn to Mikhail Bakhtin's brilliant *Rabelais and His World.*[11]

In defining the grotesque, the Russian scholar's perspective is wider and therefore more inclusive than Kayser's. While he accepts Kayser's

[8] Kayser, 39–40.
[9] *Ibid.*, 24.
[10] Cf. Lanson, 202.
[11] Mikhail Bakhtin, *Rabelais and His World*, trans. Helene Iwolsky (Cambridge, Mass.: The M.I.T. Press, 1968). The original was published in 1965.

history of the term and considers his study "the first . . . serious work on
the theory of the grotesque," he believes the phenomenon to be more
ancient and finds its frightening aspect mainly restricted to the Romantics—especially if seen through modern eyes. To Bakhtin it represents,
above all, folk humor of a carnivalesque nature and origin that was at its
height during the Middle Ages and the Renaissance and was akin to that
of the Roman Saturnalia. As such, it disclosed the potentiality of a world
different from the ordinary, "of another order, another way of life. It leads
men out of the confines of the apparent (false) unity, of the indisputable
and stable. Born of folk humor, it always represents in one form or another,
. . . the return of Saturn's golden age to earth."[12] Bakhtin considers
the laughter of grotesque folk humor as festive and ambivalent. Instead
of the totally negative laughter of more recent satire, whose perpetrators
consider themselves alienated from the world they mock, it stressed the
ubiquity of what is droll in the world and saw itself as part of it. Carnival
laughter was, therefore, a laughter of all the people, not merely their reaction to a specific comic event and, being directed at all and everyone,
was both benign and cruel, asserting and denying. "Carnival," Bakhtin
maintains, "celebrated temporary liberation from the prevailing truth
and from the established order; it marked the suspension of all hierarchical
rank, privileges, norms, and prohibitions. Carnival was the true feast
of time, the feast of becoming, change, and renewal. It was hostile to all
that was immortalized and completed."[13] Man was not seen as the individual but as partaking of that great cycle of Nature which consisted of birth,
maturity, old age, and death.[14] In support of his own conception of the
grotesque as the opposite of the stability and precise delimitation of form
required by a classicism based on the rational *cogito* of the individual,
Bakhtin quotes a fellow scholar: "In the grotesque, life passes through
all the degrees from the lowest, inert and primitive, to the highest, most
mobile, and spiritualized; this garland of various forms bears witness to
their oneness, brings together that which is removed, combines elements
which exclude each other, contradicts all current conceptions. Grotesque
in art is related to the paradox in logic. At first glance, the grotesque is
merely witty and amusing, but it contains great potentialities."[15] In the
grotesque spirit of carnival laughter, all that is powerful is degraded: the

---

[12] *Ibid.*, 48.
[13] *Ibid.*, 10.
[14] *Ibid.*, 29.
[15] *Ibid.*, 32, n.12.

fool becomes king, and the end of his rule, rather than being tragic, may be celebrated in a mock funeral. For carnival, in Bakhtin's view, liberated man not only from external censorship but also from fears he had developed during centuries: "fear of the sacred, of prohibitions, of the past, of power," of death. Emboldened by the carnival spirit, man laughed at all and everything with impunity. According to Bakhtin, all of Rabelais's work is imbued with this carnival spirit, which must be understood if the work's depth is to be appreciated. But the classical spirit was as hostile to it (and La Bruyère's harsh judgment of Rabelais gives vivid evidence of this[16]) as it was to be to the farcical elements in Molière's work which are vestiges of it.[17] What Bakhtin observed with regard to Rabelais, holds therefore to a smaller extent for Molière: one cannot do full justice to his art without reacquainting oneself with that irreverently grotesque carnival laughter which classic concepts of rationality and *bienséance* had repressed and condemned to an oblivion the more total the more it had depended on oral tradition.

Three of Molière's comedies, chosen quite at random, might serve here to illustrate this point: *La Jalouisie du Barbouillé*, a farce; *L'Ecole des femmes*; and *Le Tartuffe*. In each of these plays—as in most of his comedies —Molière adhered more or less to the basic character constellations found in the *commedia dell'arte* and before that in Greek (after Aristophanes) and Latin comedy. Mauron enumerates them as follows: "a rich father (and his avatars), an amorous son without money, knavish servants, courtisans (women servants), and young women, often accompanied by a string of grotesque and more ancient characters, the parasite, the cook, the braggard soldier, the peasant, etc."[18] Compared to the average *commedia dell'arte* scenario, the romanesque is reduced in Molière's comedies. But the fundamental division into two or more generic groups is maintained, and it is on this visual division rather than on psychological conflicts that the drama rests.[19] The groups that oppose—or in a comic manner parallel each other—are: two or even four old men, on the one hand, and, on the other, two young men (and possibly a captain) and two young women, aided and abetted by a number of *zanni* (usually servants), and a maid-in-waiting.

---

[16] *Ibid.*, 94.
[17] *Ibid.*, 34.
[18] Charles Mauron, *Psychocritique du genre comique* (Paris: José Corti, 1964), 80.
[19] Gustave Attinger, *L'Esprit de la commedia dell'arte dans le théâtre français* (Geneva: Slatkine Reprints, 1969), 43.

In *La Jalousie du Barbouillé*, whose title seems to link it to French farce (where actors daubed their faces, while *commedia dell'arte* actors wore masks), the two opposing groups are formed by Angélique, the young wife of the Barbouillé, her lover Valère, and her maid Cathau on the one hand; the Barbouillé and the *Docteur*, falling in the category of "old men," on the other. In *L'Ecole des femmes*, Agnès and Horace represent the group of young and rather innocent lovers, abetted by the Old Woman and the peasants Alain and Georgette, while Arnolphe is the rich old man outwitted. The constellation of characters in *Le Tartuffe*, though of greater complexity, also consists of two opposing groups clearly defined in the opening scene of the comedy, when Madame Pernelle, playing the judge supreme, verbally separates what seem to her the sinners from the just. She herself (and it is not without interest that her part was first played by a man, the old Béjart), together with Orgon and Tartuffe, is in the camp of the "old men," whereas Elmire, Orgon's young second wife, his son, his daughter, and her lover as well as her *suivante*, are in that of the young whose love is thwarted by the old. What complicates the character pattern of this play is the figure of Tartuffe, who not only has amorous notions of his own but also adds to the romanesque conflict overtones of a religious nature.

In the tradition of such comedy, the conflict is resolved with the victory of the young, and many of Molière's plays adhere to this tradition. Examining, for instance, *L'Ecole des femmes*, Mauron found it to conform to the following universal pattern: greenhorn outwits greybeard.[20]

son (greenhorn)——woman	Horace——Agnès
↓	↓
father (greybeard)	Arnolphe

Realizing the fundamentally oedipal relationships it represents, Mauron also recognized that it had within it the germ of tragedy. Indeed, Voltaire had already been aware of the essential resemblance between the plot of Molière's *L'Avare* and Racine's *Mithridate*, which both reflect this pattern.[21] What accounts for the difference in their genres is, according to a study by Ludwig Jekel, the distribution of guilt. In tragedy it is the son who is guilty in the amorous rivalry with his father, whereas in comedy it is the older man, the father, who is the intruder. While the guilty son is tragically punished, the guilty father is merely outwitted,[22] allowing for

[20] Mauron, 57–60.
[21] *Ibid.*, 69.
[22] *Ibid.*, 69.

laughter as a fantasy of triumph (in a manner in which both Bergson and Freud had allowed for it).[23] But Mauron's oedipal pattern would prove to be a strait jacket if we tried to press all of Molière's vibrant imagination into it. In his subtle and penetrating study, Gutwirth has shown, for instance, how greatly the figures of fathers and their relationships to the members of their families vary in the work of the playwright. Not even the lines between youth and old age are always clearly drawn by Molière. In *L'Ecole des maris*, for instance, it is the older of the two brothers who is the wiser and more successful in love.[24]

While the notion of moliéresque comedy as a fantasy of triumph seems valid, it also seems to ally itself more easily with Bakhtin's triumphant carnival laughter than with the narrow oedipal pattern which Mauron's psychocritique suggests. Molière seemed to be capable of such laughter even in his own life: a laughter that equally defied death and suffering, youth and old age, ignorance and learnedness, religion and the lack thereof. Like a participant in a carnival, he must have been uniquely capable of making a fool of himself and laughing at himself. In his comedies it was usually he who took the part of the character who was outwitted—even when he was at his cleverest as Scapin in *Les Fourberies*. It must be considered a fantasy of triumph that the deadly ill playwright could laugh at himself as the imaginary invalid, could play at being dead, and even fancy himself magnificently to become his own doctor by donning doctoral garbs. As in carnival, life has become play; play, life. It is in the same spirit of triumphant carnival laughter and fantasy that the ignorant Agnès becomes clever; the rich Arnolphe is, with his own full consent, kicked out of his house by his servants; and the Bourgeois gentilhomme is made a *Mamamouchi* in the manner in which, in Sorel's *Francion*, Hortensius is made King of Poland. For, as Bakhtin reminds us, in this carnival spirit, "victory over fear is not its abstract elimination; it is a simultaneous uncrowning and renewal, a gay transformation."[25]

In the farce *La Jalousie du Barbouillé*, such grotesque carnival laughter prevails as a matter of course. What draws Angélique to her lover Valère is not even presented as love, but is merely one of the elements that contrive to make the old man, her husband, appear ridiculous as he is outwitted by youth. His rigid views on marriage and a married woman's obligations

---

[23] *Ibid.*, 57.
[24] Marcel Gutwirth, *Molière ou l'Invention comique: la métamorphose des thèmes, la création des types* (Paris: Lettres Modernes, 1966), especially ch. IV.
[25] Bakhtin, 91.

are triumphed over in a manner that is both fantastic and visually powerful. By means of her ruse, Angélique is virtually enabled to take his place up at the window, while he is reduced to taking hers down on the street and to plead with her to let him back into the house. What was up has come down, what was down has gone up. The role of the *Docteur* would be totally gratuitous in any rational plot. But in this farce he serves to some extent to counterbalance the defeat of the *Barbouillé*. For it is the *Barbouillé* who, in his turn, pulls the *Docteur* to the ground in good time. As both old men are defeated in this impersonal manner, we can laugh at them in the same way in which we can laugh at the cruelties undergone by the Dandins and Pourceaugnacs: their defeat was destined by the very cycle of the seasons that makes old age give way to youth.

The *Docteur*'s use of language is grotesque. He piles up synonyms in the manner of Rabelais. In his etymologies he turns logic upside down, explaining, for instance, that *bonnet* is derived from Latin *bonum est*, which in French becomes *bon est*. He concludes from this that the bonnet is good because it protects people against head colds.[26] Like carnivalesque gamboilers, words seem to play with each other and establish new relationships with each other.[27] In this same carnivalesque spirit, the pedant translates Angélique's amorous behavior into grammatical terms; thereby turning her to ridicule:

> *Docteur*: Tu es docteur quand tu veux, mais je pense que tu es un plaisant Docteur. Tu as la mine de suivre fort ton caprice: des parties d'oraison, tu n'aimes que la conjonction; des genres, le masculin; des declinaisons, le génitif; de la syntaxe, *mobile cum fixo*; et enfin, de la quantité, tu n'aimes que le dactyle, *quia constat ex una longa et duabus brevibus*. . . . [28]

With this speech, the *Docteur* places himself squarely in a grotesque tradition that, according to Bakhtin, was very popular in the Middle Ages. He reminds us of the *Vergilius Maro Grammaticus* that abounded in grammatical instructions of this kind as well as of the comic dialogues between Solomon and Morolf, wherein it was the part of the latter to bring the conversation down to "a strongly emphasized bodily level of food, drink, digestion, and sexual life."[29] "Not only parody in its narrow sense," Bakhtin states, "but all the other forms of grotesque realism degrade, bring down to earth, turn their subject into flesh. . . . Laughter degrades

---

[26] Molière, *Oeuvres complètes*, ed. Maurice Rat (Paris: Gallimard, 1947), I, 26.
[27] Bakhtin, 423.
[28] Molière, 27.
[29] Bakhtin, 20, 21.

and materializes."[30] It is dramatically significant that in Molière's farce the *Docteur* himself is degraded and brought down to earth at the end of his speech, as he is tripped by the Barbouillé. He is pulled off the stage in the most grotesque manner, but at the end of the farce is seen again up at his window complaining about the noise his neighbors make. Thus Molière presents us visually with a perpetual changing of places, a cycle with its perpetual up-and-down movement, allowing for moments when all is topsy-turvy and fantasy triumphs.

Arnolphe at the end of *L'Ecole des femmes* might equally be looked at in the light of this carnivalesque tradition. Seen outside this tradition, he might appear to be a decent average bourgeois, quite selfish, somewhat vain, and almost deadly afraid of being cuckolded. As such he is almost a tragic figure deserving of pity and fear. When we see the wealthy old man, quite capable of being a good friend, go off alone at the conclusion of the play, while all others have reason to rejoice, we are reminded of Chaplin at the end of his movies. Arnolphe's desire to know the truth (although the truth is limited to Agnès's faithfulness or the lack thereof), is not unlike that of Oedipus, and finding it is equally painful:

> O fâcheux examen d'un mystère fatal,
> Où l'examinateur souffre seul tout le mal![31]

His final lot seems to be the punishment for his crime of having kept Agnès isolated and deprived of an education, for it is of a crime that Horace accuses him, without knowing his identity with M. de la Souche. As in tragedy, pride also adds to his tragic flaw. Fancying himself a Pygmalion, he had considered Agnès to be but wax in his hands for him to shape— only to find that love had done the shaping for him in a manner contrary to his desires: "l'amour est un grand maître!" A situation that had only held promise of happiness for him has turned into its opposite: unhappiness of the very kind that he had spent a lifetime avoiding.

But such tragic overtones are diminished as soon as we recognize Arnolphe as a representative of the "Gallic tradition" of cuckoldry that so preoccupied Panurge. This tradition meant, as Bakhtin explains, "the uncrowning of the old husband and a new act of procreation with the young husband. In this system of images the cuckolded husband assumes the role of uncrowned old age, of the old year, and the receding winter. He is stripped of his robes, mocked, and beaten"—all in the spirit of carnival

---

[30] *Ibid.*, 20.
[31] Molière, I, 469.

laughter.[32] Arnolphe's insistence on an outdated marriage code further contributes to his stature as a comic carnival figure. For those became also the butt of mockery and uncrowning during carnival who were men of prominence and did not recognize "the comic nature of their pretentions to eternity and immutability," coming "to the end of their role still serious, although their spectators have been laughing for a long time. . . . Time has transformed old truth and authority into a Mardi Gras dummy, a comic monster that the laughing crowd rends to pieces in the market place."[33] Arnolphe is presented in Molière's comedy as what Rabelais called an *agelast*, someone "who does not know how to laugh and who is hostile to laughter"[34] and therefore punishable in the spirit of the grotesque.

Molière skillfully draws the dignified Arnolphe into this farcical realm by having the zanni/peasants Alain and Georgette include him in their *lazzi*. When he wants to enter Agnès's house after his absence, they quarrel as to who should open the door, instead of opening it for him. When his impatience mounts and he threatens to punish whoever does not open, each tries to keep the other from getting there first, thus still preventing him from entering. But when the door finally is opened, the blows they exchange hit him. They exuberantly insult him when he has them practice on him how to be rude to Horace, should he try to bribe his way into the house. They call him "un sot," "un nigaud," "un fripon," and rudely throw him out of the house.[35]

The manner in which these peasant/zanni express themselves is grotesque and belongs to the world of farce and carnival. As such it could not but offend the growing sensitivity of the *honnêtes gens* who were beginning to be far removed from this popular festive spirit, which often expressed the abstract in terms of food and thereby degraded and ridiculed it. This is why they objected to Alain's explanation of jealousy and to his image of a wife as her husband's "*potage*" into which he might not wish to let other famished men "tremper leurs doigts." This form of grotesque degradation is akin to another, which may be found everywhere in farce and in Molière's work and which I have designated elsewhere as "concretization of metaphor."[36] An example of it can be found in Agnès's

---

[32] Bakhtin, 241.
[33] *Ibid.*, 213.
[34] *Ibid.*, 267.
[35] Molière, I, 491–92.
[36] Edith Kern, "Concretization of Metaphor in the Commedia dell'Arte and the Modern

dutiful account to Arnolphe of her conversation with the Old Woman:

> *Agnès*: Moi, j'ai blessé quelqu'un! fis-je tout étonnée.
> – Oui, dit-elle, blessé, mais blessé tout de bon;
> Et c'est l'homme qu'hier vous vîtes du balcon.
> – Hélas! qui pourrait, dis-je, en avoir été cause?
> Sur lui, sans y penser, fis-je choir quelque chose?
> – Non, dit-elle, vos yeux ont fait ce coup fatal,
>
> . . .
>
> Hé! mon Dieu! ma surprise est, fis-je sans seconde:
> Mes yeux ont-ils du mal pour en donner au monde?
> – Oui, fit-elle, vos yeux pour causer le trépas,
> Ma fille, ont un venin que vous ne savez pas.[37]

Agnès's naive ignorance of the metaphorical meaning of *blesser* or *coup fatal* or of the eyes as Love's instrument both for the wounding and healing of the lover; her touching simplicity in assuming that she might have hurt the young man by having let some object fall on him as he passed her balcony—all these shift our attention from the abstract realm of love to the physical and concrete. The world has been grotesquely turned upside down, for the direction of metaphor is usually from the concrete to the abstract. "Once our attention is fixed on the material aspect of a metaphor, the idea expressed becomes comic," Bergson observed.[38]

Agnès's naiveté, which brings about this farcical concretization of metaphor adds ironic perspective to the play and permits Molière to mock all and everything. His laughter is not the negative laughter of outright satire but the ambivalent laughter of carnival. In this carnival spirit Molière can make us laugh here at Arnolphe who is defeated by the very lack of sophistication in Agnès that he had cherished, and, later, at the *Femmes savantes* who are defeated by their excess of sophistication.

Such ambivalent carnival laughter permeates even *Le Tartuffe*, if we look at the play against the background of the tradition of the grotesque. It, too, as is well known, was severely attacked by the playwright's contemporaries who no longer knew or wanted to know the language of this tradition. It was often considered to be a drama rather than a comedy, indeed, without its *deus-ex-machina* ending it might well give the impression of a tragedy, but it loses this character as soon as we hear the farcical laughter behind and in some of its scenes.

Theatre," in *Proceedings of the IVth Congress of the International Comparative Literature Association*, ed. François Jost (The Hague: Mouton, 1966), 1232–42.
[37] Molière, I, 467.
[38] Quoted by Edith Kern, *op. cit.*, 1232.

Many attempts have been made to explain the origin of the play's name. None has been completely convincing. The two most likely explanations that have been offered are that it was derived from Italian *tartufo* (evil person) or from German *Teufel* (devil). If the latter meaning was at all intended by Molière, the character would clearly correspond to the grotesque devils of medieval stage and carnival. It appears that the famous *commedia dell'arte* Harlequin mask derived its name from these devils, that is, from the Flemish word Hellekin (little hell). For they issued, in medieval theater, from the stage which was considered to be the Mouth of Hell, a notion long preserved in the designation of the front of the stage as "le manteau d'Harlequin."[39] Some recent performances, notably one at the San Francisco Workshop presented Tartuffe, indeed, as such a grotesquely comical figure of farce. Molière's text itself seems to support this conception. For Tartuffe is depicted as well fed and rosy cheeked, while his preachings are those of the devout ascete.

But even if we disregard all theories about his name and merely look at his role, we find that his speech and behavior place him in the comic category of the medieval monk who travesties clerical terms in order to seduce the wife of another man, preferably his host. We encounter this grotesque figure in much of medieval Latin and vernacular literature. "In Latin recreational literature of the twelfth and thirteenth centuries," Bakhtin tells us, "banquet images as well as those linked with procreative force are usually centered around the figure of a monk, portrayed as a drunkard, glutton, and lecher. . . . First, as a devotee of material bodily life he sharply contradicts the ascetic ideal that he serves. Second, his gluttony represents the parasitism of a sluggard. But, third, he also expresses the positive, shrove principles of food, drink, procreative force, and merriment. The authors offer these three aspects concurrently, and it is difficult to say where praise ends and where condemnation starts. . . . We hear the voice of the democratic cleric who tries to eulogize the material bodily values while remaining within the confines of the ecclesiastical system of philosophy." While in these medieval stories the authors' sympathies are usually extended to the monk caught by the husband in amorous embrace, Molière's sympathies are hardly with Tartuffe. Yet Elmire's admirer uses language as ambiguously religious as that of his medieval forbears (he is, after all, almost a monk). He assures her, for instance that

---

[39] Cf., for instance, Bakhtin, 349.

L'Amour qui nous attache aux beautés éternelles
N'étouffe pas en nous l'amour des temporelles.
Nos sens facilement peuvent être charmés
Des ouvrages parfaits que le Ciel a formés.[40]

As he uses elevated language with religious overtones to express his sensuous and illicit desire for her, he degrades such language in the same manner in which medieval authors degraded sacred texts by travestying them. When Bakhtin reminds us that Rabelais followed a tradition when he turned "Christ's last words on the cross, *sitio* (I thirst) and *consummatum est* (it is consummated) . . . into terms of eating and over-indulgence,"[41] we realize that Tartuffe is not altogether removed from this same tradition and that he is as farcical as Orgon hidden underneath the table. What he loses in threatening individuality, he gains in grotesque comedy the ambivalent laughter of which justifies irreverence and here mocks both the simple-minded husband and the clever old seducer, while youth (Elmire) remains triumphant—and all are temporarily liberated from prevailing and established "truth" and its censorship.

Alceste is most comic at moments like the sonnet scene with Oronte (I. 2), when his sincerity clashes frontally with social illusion. He cannot accept that society exists by means of illusion, and that very fact transforms illusion into reality. He will not praise, or even tolerate, Oronte's sonnet; he will not pay compliments to Célimène, he refuses to curry favor with the judges at his trial; he will not do what must be done in order to survive in a social context. It is this attitude which leads to his conflicts and to his eventual failure to cope with reality. His solution is to flee all manifestations of reality, to withdraw in to a *désert* empty of any human contact. At the end, there are no illusions left, and the play ends on a somber note. Despite the union of Philinte and Eliante, there is little joy at the conclusion of this comedy; the deceits of Célimène have been discovered; her acid relationship with Arsinoé has become an open enmity; Oronte and the little marquis are unmasked as witless fools; and Alceste's illusion of his right to judge the world has been revealed as vain pretension bordering on hypocrisy.

Molière's real contribution to the paradox of illusion and reality may be found in words he himself recited in the role of *Amphitryon*'s Sosie. The valet has tried to explain to his irritated and uncomprehending master that his double (Mercure) is in residence at the general's home:

[40] *Ibid.*, 294.
[41] Molière, I, 728.

> *Amphitryon*
> D'où peut procéder, je te prie,
> Ce galimatias maudit?
> Est-ce songe? est-ce ivrognerie?
> Aliénation d'esprit?
> Ou méchante plaisanterie?
> . . . .
> Au mystère nouveau que tu me viens conter
> Est-il quelque ombre d'apparence?
> *Sosie*
> Non; vous avez raison, et la chose à chacun
> Hors de créance doit paraître.
> C'est un fait à n'y rien connaître,
> Un conte extravagant, ridicule, importun;
> Cela choque le sens commun;
> Mais cela ne laisse pas d'être. (II. 1)

Reality is ridiculous, indistinguishable from illusion. Life can be borne only by those who, like the philosophical Philinte or the farcical Sganarelle of *Le Médecin malgré lui*, like "mamamouchi" Jourdain or "Doctor" Argan, ally illusion with reality, creating a new reality, genuine and viable, because it functions with the least harm and most joy. Those who fail at life, Alceste and Orgon, Arnolphe and Harpagon, however noble or ignominious their motives or character, are doomed by their inability to play at life. Molière, man of the theater par excellence, spent his life in the no man's land between illusion and reality; his ability to fuse the two in his theater, and to make that fusion carry a part of his *Weltanschauung*, paved the way for complexities undreamed of in earlier days: Marivaux and Beaumarchais, Anouilh and Pirandello (and how many others!)— all owe some small part of their sophisticated use of the paradox of illusion and reality to the genius of Molière.

ILLUSION AND REALITY;
A NEW RESOLUTION OF AN OLD PARADOX
William A. Mould.

Je ne sais si cela se peut, mais
je sais bien que cela est.
—Lisette in *L'Amour Médecin* (II.2)

Molière is the first French dramatist to use the paradox of illusion and reality to express a sophisticated world view. His work transformed a dramatic device into a powerful statement of belief in man's ability to create his own universe. The distinction between illusion and reality forms the basis of theatrical experience, implicit in all drama, and explicit at certain moments in dramatic history. The earliest Greek plays used masks and other visible exaggerations partially to emphasize the nonreality of the spectacle; Plautus and Terence often had one character disguise himself to deceive another. Early French drama and the *commedia dell'arte* also offered on occasion primitive plays within plays, and the baroque theater of Rotrou's *Saint Genest* (1646) and Corneille's *Illusion comique* (1636) shows a renewed interest in the device. Although Rotrou had employed the play within a play to blur the distinction between tragic reality and the illusion of tragedy on stage, and although Corneille had used the device to excellent comic effect while enhancing the aesthetic impact of his comedy, it was Molière who used the play within a play to create a new perception of reality. "Corneille's subject is not the theatricality of life but the theatricality of the theater. . . . Sure of his values, the artist does not confuse appearance and reality except to the extent that he deliberately does so in order to please."[1]

The seventeenth century had a real passion for the theater, perhaps because everyday life was itself so theatrical. The tribunes of Gothic and Renaissance cathedrals became the theater loges of the Jesuit-style church of Saint Paul-Saint Louis. Extraordinary etiquette and polite circumlocutions veiled genuine feelings. High titles and great offices were costly, empty charges. Versailles was a gigantic theater, the monarch, its chief actor, the Hall of Mirrors its symbolic deception. People from all walks of life went often to the theater, and in real life frequently acted as if they

---

[1] Robert J. Nelson, *Play within a Play* (New Haven: Yale University Press, 1958), 56, 61.

were playing roles. The reality of this theatrical illusion was prevalent in human activities and is mirrored in Molière's theater. His audience liked to recognize on stage representations of characters and situations familiar to their daily life, yet they wished the theater to be far enough removed from the reality they knew to be comic. Molière's theater created a link between the reality of illusion in life and the illusion of reality in the theater. His plays are often very realistic in their portrayal of characters and social mores; the illusion closely resembles the reality of daily existence. It was, of course, precisely this realism which so delighted and infuriated Molière's contemporaries.

The comic universe is based in part on the ironic disparity between illusion and reality. Molière invents doctors who do not cure, a sick man who is not ill, a misanthrope in love with a coquette, and, for *Tartuffe*, a Monsieur Loyal who "porte un air bien déloyal."[2] Eventually, the comic spectacle created through interaction among the characters will be generally superceded by the comedy of illusion resulting from self-deception. The Mascarille of *L'Etourdi* is the prototype for Scapin, adding ruse to plot, but always maintaining a clear distinction between the real and the imaginary world. The Mascarille of *Les Précieuses ridicules* refuses to leave his fantasy world where he is a cultivated marquis, just as Monsieur Jourdain remains convinced at the end of *Le Bourgeois gentilhomme* that he is a true "mamamouchi." The hypocrisy practised by Tartuffe, with its creation of sinister illusions, is another form of Molière's investigation of the problem of illusion and reality. Finally, the process finds its culmination in *Le Misanthrope* where Alceste, the iconoclast, is so self-deceived that his concept of reality is itself an illusion.

Molière has several approaches to the paradox of illusion and reality, and these approaches become more sophisticated as he matures. At first, like his predecessors, Molière uses it principally as a theatrical device to amuse, with only accidental deeper import. The play within a play is the principal manifestation of this early approach, and it first appears in *L'Etourdi* (1658). Mascarille (his name means, appropriately, "little mask") is a valet serving the love of his master Lélie for the beautiful Célie. The servant piles playlet upon playlet, creating illusions almost more quickly than they can be dispelled. Like a medieval *meneur du jeu*, Mascarille tries to induce others to play roles, but he is continually foiled by

---

[2] Maurice Rat, ed., *Molière: Oeuvres complètes* (Paris: Gallimard, 1962), I, 765. All quotations of Molière are taken from this two volume edition, and will be indicated in the text by act and scene number (e.g., *Taruffe*, V. 4).

the honest naiveté of his master. Lélie, like Pridamant in *L'Illusion comique*, is always the spectator, so the audience is never completely deluded by Mascarille's playlets. Lélie tries time after time to join in his valet's illusions, but he is incapable of it; he has an indirect role, and rather than acting in Mascarille's spectacles, he reacts to them from outside. This helps the spectator to remain very certain as to the line between illusion and reality. That clarity occurs frequently in Molière's theater: Toinette in *Le Malade imaginaire* (III. 8 and 10) is obviously in disguise as a doctor; the same is true of Clitandre in *L'Amour médecin*. Only the fools Argan and Géronte are deceived in the latter play, just as only old Argante and Géronte are fooled by the *fourberies* of Scapin. In the end, Lélie wins Célie, not through any of the increasingly theatrical machinations of Mascarille, but by virtue of his honesty and inability to feign. All of Mascarille's schemes are pointless; the goal is reached without him. Lélie, completely open and truly incapable of deception, cannot function in a world of illusion, but triumphs with the weapon of truth. If the later Scapin wins out through trickery more malicious than Mascarille's, it is perhaps due to the progressive darkening of Molière's attitudes. Despite the possible significance of the victory of naiveté in *L'Etourdi*, the real function of these playlets is dramatic and not ethical. A play within a play renders the main drama more "real," because the spectator's awareness of illusion is transferred to the second play. In later comedies such as *Tartuffe* and *Le Malade imaginaire*, the play within a play presents an illusion which leads to the truth. Elmire, pretending affection for Tartuffe, convinces her husband of the hypocrite's treacherous nature. Argan, feigning death, learns the true sentiments his wife and his daughter hold for him. In both cases, an illusion has been constructed in order to clarify reality.

When Molière approaches illusion on a more significant level, his attitude is often highly critical. In *Tartuffe* we are no longer dealing with light-hearted machinations designed to serve young love, but with vicious hypocrisy whose goal is self-advancement and universal destruction. In the hands of Tartuffe, truth is twisted into lies; he convinces Orgon that his own son, Damis, has falsely accused the hypocrite:

> Vous fiez-vous, mon frère, à mon extérieur?
> Et, pour tout ce qu'on voit, me croyez-vous meilleur?
> Non, non, vous vous laissez tromper à l'apparence,
> . . . .
> Mais la vérité pure est que je ne vaux rien. (III. 6)

Only Tartuffe is dishonest; the other characters could say, with Mme Pernelle, "Je vous parle un peu franc, mais c'est là mon humeur" (I. 1). Gradually, the construction of appearances which forms Tartuffe's existence leads even the honest Orgon to equivocate. The casuistry of Tartuffe causes Orgon first to lie to his brother-in-law Cléante about Mariane's marriage, and then to 'faire des serments contre la vérité' (V. 1), swearing that he does not have papers which, for all practical purposes, he does possess. Tartuffe's world of deception leads others, especially Orgon, to be incapable of distinguishing appearance from reality. Orgon believes that he, too, can create a world by the sheer effort of his will: 'Mais je veux que cela soit une vérité' (II. 1). His attempt to fuse illusion and reality is doomed, for the fusion would be based on transforming his daughter's affection for Valère into distaste, and her loathing for Tartuffe into love. Mythopoesis can function only when the new universe corresponds to the desires of its participants; that is, the illusion created by Tartuffe for Orgon and Mme Pernelle is acceptable to them because they wish to find a person of his sort of piety. It matters little that Cléante is able 'du faux avec le vrai faire la différence' (I. 5); the world built by Tartuffe can be destroyed only by the suspension of belief on the part of Orgon.

The dénouement of *Tartuffe*, like the endings of so many of Molière's plays, has often been attacked for its lack of verisimilitude. It is, indeed, fantastic that the King's justice should descend on all, condemning Tartuffe and pardoning Orgon. Such extravagant scenes, which mark the endings not only of *Tartuffe*, but of *L'Ecole des femmes*, *L'Avare*, *Les Fourberies de Scapin* and *L'Etourdi*, are sometimes thought to be due to the impoverished imagination of their author. Mascarille may well say:

C'est qu'en fait d'aventure il est très-ordinaire
De voir gens pris sur mer par quelque Turc consaire,
Puis être à leur famille à point nommé rendus,
Après quinze ou vingt ans qu'on les a crus perdus.

(L'Etourdi, IV. 1)

There is nothing at all ordinary about such adventures. In each of these dénouements Molière has created a new illusion. Such extravagance underlines with heavy irony the very impossibility of happiness and balance in a universe dominated by monomania and hypocrisy; a huge and improbable illusion is constructed in the final scene, so that the comedy may end happily. These dénouements, springing from recognition scenes, are dependent on events beyond the control of the characters, but the final scenes of *Le Bourgeois gentilhomme* and *Le Malade imaginaire* rise out of the obsessions of the major characters. Monsieur Jourdain will live forever in the belief that he has attained the noble rank of "mamamouchi"; Argan is convinced of the validity of his farcical initiation into the medical fraternity. In both cases, happiness for the other characters, especially the young lovers, can be attained only by acceding to the illusions of the monomaniac and by constructing a final, everlasting illusion around him. Illusion becomes the only way to bear the horror of a reality which would dictate that Jourdain's daughter marry an unknown nobleman she cannot love, and that Argan's Angélique be wedded to the atrocious Thomas Diafoirus. The men who give themselves over to these illusions have departed from a reality which rejects their foibles. Fortunately for them, both Monsieur Jourdain and Argan are in a position to create their own reality; it suffices that each believe his obsession to be satisfied, for all of the results to occur as if that illusion were true. Such, of course, is not the case with the valet Mascarille of *Les Précieuses ridicules*, described by his master as "un extravagant qui s'est mis dans la tête de vouloir faire l'homme de condition" (I. 1). In this first play (1659) where Molière shows a fusion between illusion and reality, the servant enters so well into his role of foppish marquis, that the blows and insults heaped on him at the end of the play do not really seem to disabuse him. He is so taken with his role that he confuses illusion and reality, and refuses to abandon his assumed identity: "Je vois bien qu'on n'aime ici que la vaine apparence, et qu'on ne considère point la vertu toute nue" (sc. 16). Nonetheless, valet or master, mamamouchi or doctor, Molière's men will often insist on living in a world where they have fused their illusions with reality in order to create a bearable existence.

In some of his most sophisticated plays, the dramatist Molière joins his characters in operating a fusion between illusion and reality. Now, there is no one left on stage who does not deal with nonreality to considerable extent. *Amphitryon* (1668) is the story of a complicated illusion created by Jupiter to seduce the faithful Alcmène. Jupiter disguised as Amphitryon, and Mercure as the valet Sosie, play their roles perfectly. Until the very end, neither god does anything to break the illusion they have created; unlike Tartuffe, Mascarille (*Les Précieuses ridicules*), or Sganarelle (badly disguised as a doctor in *Le Médecin malgré lui*), they remain quite in character. The gods have created a new reality, accepted by all the characters save Amphitryon. The general's inability to accept the new reality leads to his ridiculous posture in the scenes forming the second half of Act III. It is Jupiter himself, the master illusion maker, who tries to re-establish the boundaries between the old reality and the new. In his attempt to appropriate some of Alcmène's love, he tries to force her to distinguish between her husband (Amphitryon) and her lover (Jupiter). But Jupiter's illusion is perfect, and Alcmène refuses to make a distinction which seems to her unrelated to any needs her husband might have. Jupiter, in the unusual role of both magician and iconoclast, is unable to re-establish a reality which he has definitively altered by the injection of imperceptible illusion.

It is, unsurprisingly, in *Le Misanthrope* that the fusion between illusion and reality is most complete. Like Amphitryon, Alceste is ridiculous because he refuses to accept illusion as reality. Here, the illusion is much more universal, for it includes the very foundations of human society. As Philinte says: "Tout marche par cabale et par pur intérêt;/Ce n'est plus que la ruse aujourd'hui qui l'emporte" (V. 2). Philinte also suggests the necessity of accepting illusion and hypocrisy as a reality forming the basis for social existence:

> Lorsqu'un homme vous vient embrasser avec joie,
> Il faut bien le payer de la même monnoie,
> Répondre, comme on peut, à ses empressements,
> Et rendre offre pour offre et serments pour serments. (I. 1)

MOLIÈRE AND THE COMICAL TEUTON

F. W. Vogler

Molière's readers will recall that his first major original play, *L'Etourdi*, had the good fortune not only to please its initial audience in Lyons in the mid-1650's but also to succeed well enough later in Paris to become a repertory staple for Molière's company during its early years there. As was to be customary in the composition of most of his later comedies, Molière was indebted to a number of other contemporary or near-contemporary authors—in this case, Italian, Spanish, and French—for elements of plot and character used in *L'Etourdi*. However, one device that does not appear to have been borrowed is the valet Mascarille's disguise as a Swiss innkeeper in one of his frustrated attempts to advance his master's campaign to win a beautiful young slave girl away from her presumptive owner; Lancaster notes the significance of this novelty: "It is in his rôle that Molière first makes use of a foreigner's French, disguising Mascarille as an innkeeper from German-speaking Switzerland. In doing so he was probably imitating the accent of Swiss he had encountered at Lyons. *L'Etourdi* is the first seventeenth-century play of any importance in which this comic device is employed, though dialectic and Latinized French had been used before."[1]

In this scene, it is not Mascarille's dress or gestures that are comical, nor is it really the substance of what he has to say; rather, it is how he says it, as indicated by Molière's phonetic transcription of grammatically defective French spoken with a heavy Germanic accent, with particular emphasis given to mispronounced consonants:[2]

ANDRÈS
Seigneur suisse, êtes-vous de ce logis le maître?
MASCARILLE
Moi, pour serfir à fous.
ANDRÈS
Pourrons-nous y bien être?

---

[1] Henry Carrington Lancaster, *A History of French Dramatic Literature in the Seventeenth Century. Part III: The Period of Molière, 1652–1672* (Baltimore: The Johns Hopkins University Press, 1936), I, 108.

[2] The following passage and all subsequent passages from Molière are taken from the R. Jouanny edition of the *Oeuvres complètes* (Paris: Garnier, 1962).

MASCARILLE

Oui, moi pour d'estrancher chappon champre garni;
Mais ché non point locher te gent te méchant vi.

ANDRÈS

Je crois votre maison franche de tout ombrage.

MASCARILLE

Fous nouviau dant sti fil, moi foir à la fissage. (V. iii)

In later plays, Molière would mock provincial accents and dialects in this same way, but, oddly enough, he did not choose to have real or feigned *non-Germanic* foreign characters speak faulty French with a distinctive accent, whether Spanish, Italian, Greek, or Turkish. However, bad French spoken with some sort of Germanic accent seems to have been recognized by Molière as having a special comic value worthy of exploitation. In *Les Fâcheux* (1661), he provides a fleeting glimpse of what seems to have already become a source of derisive amusement to the French: the stereotype of the excessively thorough German tourist who examines and records anything that appears to be informative along his path. The pedant Caritidès, "François de nation, Grec de profession," reads aloud a petition he intends to present to the King, requesting that he be made royal overseer of public signs, heretofore so shamefully lacking in attention to spelling and literary merit: " . . . au grand scandale de la république des lettres, et de la nation françoise, qui se décrie et déshonore par lesdits abus et fautes grossières envers les étrangers, et notamment envers les Allemands, curieux lecteurs et inspectateurs desdites inscriptions . . . " (III. ii).

In 1669 Molière again used the foreigner's-French device, this time in the mouths of two characters disguised as Swiss tourists in *Monsieur de Pourceaugnac*. As in Mascarille's case in *L'Etourdi*, these pseudo-Swiss are made comical by their use of bad grammar and thick accent:

PREMIER SUISSE

Allons, dépeschons, camerade, ly faut allair tous deux nous à la Crève pour regarter un peu choustcier sti Monsiu de Porcegnac, qui l'a esté contané par ortonnance à l'estre pendu par son cou.

SECOND SUISSE

Ly faut nous loër un fenestre pour foir sti choustice.   (III. iii)

But a new comic element is now introduced, for these "tourists" are shown to be barbarous in manners as well as in speech. As foreigners "on the town," they display an outrageous impropriety in their remarks to the protagonist, here disguised as a woman:

PREMIER SUISSE

Ly est là un petit teton qui l'est drole.

MONSIEUR DE POURCEAUGNAC

Tout beau.

PREMIER SUISSE

Mon foy! moy couchair pien avec fous.

MONSIEUR DE POURCEAUGNAC

Ah! c'en est trop, et ces sortes d'ordures-là ne se disent point à une femme de ma condition.

SECOND SUISSE

Laisse, toy; l'est moy qui le veut couchair avec elle.

Bienséance could be safely disregarded by Molière in this instance, for his Court or Parisian audience would recognize such language as being typical of unrefined foreign visitors, of whom no better could be expected.

Earlier in the same play, the "homme d'intrigue" Sbrigani had appeared disguised as a Flemish merchant in a trick intended to make Monsieur de Pourceaugnac appear to be a poor credit risk in the eyes of his prospective father-in-law. As it happens, this pseudo-Fleming sounds very much like Molière's pseudo-Swiss, with perhaps the exception of a few *v*-sounds which are not transformed into *f*'s; all this device required for Molière's purposes was the use of bad grammar and a Germanic accent of more or less indeterminate national origin:

SBRIGANI

Et sti Montsir de Pourcegnac, Montsir, l'est un homme que doivre beaucoup grandement à dix ou douze marchanne Flamane qui estre venu ici.

ORONTE

Ce Monsieur de Pourceaugnac doit beaucoup à dix ou douze marchands?

SBRIGANI

Oui, Montsir; et depuis huit mois, nous avoir obtenir un petit sentence contre lui, et lui à remettre à payer tou ce créanciers de sti mariage que sti Montsir Oronte donne pour son fille.

(II. iii)

A year later, Molière included a Swiss character in the "Ballet des Nations" at the conclusion of *Le Bourgeois gentilhomme*; unlike the Spaniards and Italians who also figure in this ballet and who sing in their own languages, the Swiss once again cuts a ridiculous figure—as does a Gascon character—by speaking defective and accented French:

LE SUISSE

Mon'-sieur le donneur de papieir,
Que veul dir sty façon de fifre?
Moy l'écorchair tout mon gosieir
A crieir,
Sans que je pouvre afoir ein lifre:
Pardy, mon foy! Mon'-sieur, je pense fous l'estre ifre.

(*Première entrée*)

In 1671, Molière's comical Teuton appeared for the last time in *Les Fourberies de Scapin.* As the hapless Géronte is being thrashed in his sack, his tormentor Scapin conducts imaginary dialogues with various bellicose strangers with whom he pretends to struggle; one of these is identified only as having "la mine d'un étranger," but his speech is that distinctive Germanic *baragouin* already used by Molière in three earlier plays:

> SCAPIN
> "Dites-moi un peu fous, Monsir l'homme, s'il ve plaist, fous savoir point où l'est stil Gironte que moi cherchair?" Non, Monsieur, je ne sais point où est Géronte. "Dites-moi-le vous frenchemente, moi li fouloir pas grande chose à lui. L'est seulement pour li donnair un petite régale sur le dos d'un douzaine de coups de bastonne, et de trois ou quatre petites coups d'épée au trafers de son poitrine."   (III. ii)

Although Molière's Germanic foreigners—"Swiss" and "Flemish"— were actually impostors in every case except for that of the Swiss in the "Ballet des Nations" of *Le Bourgeois gentilhomme*, the entertainment that their speech afforded seventeenth-century audiences and all subsequent ones reflects what seems to be a cultural reaction on the part of native Frenchmen from regions other than Alsace or Flanders. Anyone who has been unable to overcome a foreign accent is likely to attract unfavorable attention to himself when he speaks, a situation by no means limited to France and the French language; but it does appear that a Germanic accent in French is almost guaranteed to reduce the speaker to a comic rôle of linguistic inferiority, no matter what his position or attainments. In our own century, an excellent example of this comic-reduction reaction can be found in the works of no less a social observer than Proust in *Le Côté de Guermantes*. For some time the narrator had been aware of the presence in Paris of a prominent German aristocrat, the Prince de Faffenheim-Munsterburg-Weiningen. In addition to being a Rhinegrave and an Elector Palatine, the Prince had enjoyed a distinguished career as an ambassador and as Foreign Minister; at this point in his life, the honor he coveted most was election to the French *Académie des Sciences morales et politiques* as a corresponding member, an ambition which seemed reasonable enough to the narrator, considering the unquestioned eminence and culture of the candidate. But this admirable German visitor to Paris had a shortcoming which would demolish his image in the first four words that the narrator heard him utter; Proust's description of that event is memorable:

C'est ainsi que le prince de Faffenheim avait été amené à venir voir Mme de

Villeparisis. Ma profonde désillusion eut lieu quand il parla. Je n'avais pas songé que, si une époque a des traits particuliers et généraux plus forts qu'une nationalité, de sorte que, dans un dictionnaire illustré où l'on donne jusqu'au portrait authentique de Minerve, Leibniz avec sa perruque et sa fraise diffère peu de Marivaux ou de Samuel Bernard, une nationalité a des traits particuliers plus forts que sa caste. Or ils se traduisirent devant moi, non par un discours où je croyais d'avance que j'entendrais le frôlement des elfes et la danse des Kobolds, mais par une transposition qui ne certifiait pas moins cette poétique origine: le fait qu'en s'inclinant, petit, rouge et ventru, devant Mme de Ville-parisis, le Rhingrave lui dit: "Ponchour, Matame la marquise" avec le même accent qu'un concierge alsacien.[3]

Here Proust has swiftly achieved his effect by using the transcription device that Molière had shown to be so reliable for the same purpose.

Other German visitors in modern French literature have lost their dignity as swiftly as did Proust's Rhinegrave, although in different circumstances. For example, in Jean Eparvier's *A Paris sous la botte des Nazis*[4], two unnumbered pages are devoted to surreptitious photographs of German officers and men of the Occupation garrison seeking feminine companionship during off-duty hours. In the accompanying text, the difficulty of their quest is acerbically described: "Nombreuses, jolies, fines, vraies Parisiennes, en un mot il y avait celles qui ne tournaient jamais la tête. Rares, vulgaires, épaisses, il y avait celles qui acceptaient la *bedide bromenade.* . . . " Not only were these soldiers unattractive in appearance and manners, but even their attempts to speak French were dismissed as clumsily Teutonic.

It is not surprising to find Germans held up to ridicule in such a book as *A Paris sous la botte des Nazis*, published as it was only three months after the liberation of Paris. What is significant, however, is Eparvier's use of the phonetic-transcription device to mock their accent in spoken French. The invader and occupier is swiftly cut down to size and shown to be inferior to his victims in that he has been unable to master their language and must appear comical with nearly every word that he utters. Eparvier's woman-hunting German soldiers elicit much the same reaction as did Molière's pseudo-Swiss tourists who so crudely importuned an earlier "Frenchwoman," Léonard de Pourceaugnac.

With the departure of the Wehrmacht and other groups of involuntary but no less unwelcome German visitors at the end of World War II, the French were once again able to receive authentic foreign tourists whose

[3] *A la recherche du temps perdu* (Paris: Gallimard, 1949), VII, 105.
[4] Paris: Editions Raymond Schall, 1944.

activities could now be viewed with amused detachment rather than with concern and resentment. By the nineteen-fifties, touring buses jammed with chattering, camera-clutching foreigners were a familiar part of the Paris scene, with Germans making up a sizeable part of the number, as they always had in time of peace. In fact, the stereotype of the curious German tourist noted by Molière in *Les Fâcheux* could be vivid enough to cause other foreign types to be assimilated to it in the eyes and ears of uncosmopolitan Parisians; witness Queneau's Zazie and her associates at the foot of the Eiffel Tower:

> Des voyageurs faisaient le cercle autour de [Gabriel] l'ayant pris pour un guide complémentaire. Ils tournèrent la tête dans la direction de son regard.
> —Et que voyez-vous? demanda l'un d'eux particulièrement versé dans la langue française.
> —Oui, approuva un autre, qu'y a-t-il à voir?
> —En effet, ajoute un troisième, que devons-nous voir?
> —Kouavouar? demanda un quatrième, kouavouar? kouavouar? kouavouar?
> —Kouavouar? répondit Gabriel, mais (grand geste) Zazie, Zazie ma nièce qui sort de la pile et s'en vient vers nous.
> Les caméras crépitent, puis on laisse passer l'enfant. Qui ricane.[5]

As the scene continues, several of the more enterprising foreigners offer comments and questions in English. But as far as their French bus driver-guide is concerned, these culture-avid but inarticulate tourists are all to be herded about as Germans: "—Allons grouillons! qu'il se mit à gueuler. Schnell! Schnell! remontons dans le car et que ça saute!"[6]

Although three hundred years separate Molière from Queneau, Mascarille from Zazie, the comic value of a foreigner's spoken French—phonetically transcribed in literature—remains undiminished, especially when the accent is assumed to be a Germanic one of some sort. Here again is evidence of Molière's ability to discern and to use that which has proved to be permanently, unfailingly amusing to Frenchmen of any century. As a successful dramatist, he was the first to exploit this particular comic element for the benefit of a significantly large audience, the theater-going public of his day. And, in view of the minuscule size of the French *reading* public before the nineteenth century, it appears certain that Molière's use of this device in four successfully staged plays was surely more influential than similar satire could possibly have been in the works of non-dramatic French authors before the Revolution.

---

[5] Raymond Queneau, *Zazie dans le métro* (Paris: Gallimard, 1959), 121.
[6] *Ibid.*, 123.

SONGS AND SONNETS:
PATTERNS OF CHARACTERIZATION
Peter V. Conroy, Jr.

At one time or another just about every editor, critic and reader of Molière has noticed scattered throughout his plays certain poems and songs which the personages sing or recite as an integral part of their role and dramatic characterization. Yet no one has tried to understand these poems as one bloc of material, to explain what function they serve or to discover how they operate. Some logic does seem to govern them because, in at least four separate instances,[1] Molière uses them to construct a situation which clearly delineates the comic nature of the characters involved and which offers a small replica of his total comic vision.

The basic and most simple situation depends upon one single poem. As the center of the pattern, the poem provokes in those who hear it reactions which clearly characterize and define them. To the extent that the poem is itself comic or ridiculous, those who praise it suffer the necessary demeaning consequences. Most importantly, this process of definition is both active and internal. Molière does not impose a characterization upon the personage from the outside; rather by his own reaction to the stimulus offered, the latter seeks out and wins his own identity for himself. Similarly, the spectator is not given once and for all a formulated definition of those on stage. He too must make an individual effort to understand the total pattern and each character's particular role in it. Here then is a fine example of the "cool" which McLuhan reserves exclusively for modern media.[2]

Molière first employed this pattern in the *Précieuses ridicules*. Amidst a string of other foolish words and deeds, Mascarille announces an impromptu which he proceeds to recite to Magdelon and Cathos:

> *Oh! oh! je n'y prenois pas garde:*
> *Tandis que, sans songer à mal, je vous regarde,*
> *Votre oeil en tapinois me dérobe mon coeur.*
> *Au voleur, au voleur, au voleur, au voleur!*[3]

[1] For an enumeration of all Molière's singing roles, see René Bray, *Molière homme de théâtre* (Paris: Mercure de France, 1954), 159.

[2] Marshall MuLuhan, "Media Hot and Cold," in his *Understanding Media* (New York: McGraw Hill, 1964), 22–32.

[3] Molière, *Oeuvres Complètes*, Robert Jouanny ed. (Paris: Garnier, 1962), I, 207. All subsequent references will be indicated in the text.

Both *précieuses* are enchanted. As they lavish undue praise on every artless detail of the impromptu, they reveal themselves to be in fact very *ridicules*:

CATHOS

Ah! mon Dieu! voilà qui est poussé dans le dernier galant.

MAGDELON

Oui, je trouve ce *oh, oh!* admirable . . . j'aimerois mieux avoir fait ce *oh, oh!* qu'un poème épique. (Scene ix) (p. 207)

Mascarille himself joins in the accolades, thereby damning himself doubly, once for composing the impromptu, the second time for admiring it:

Mais n'admirez-vous pas aussi *je n'y prenois pas garde? Je n'y prenois pas garde,* je ne m'apercevois pas de cela: façon de parler naturelle: *je n'y prenois pas garde* . . . *Au voleur, au voleur, au voleur, au voleur!* Ne diriez-vous pas que c'est un homme qui crie et court après un voleur, pour le faire arrêter? *Au voleur, au voleur, au voleur, au voleur.*   (Scene ix)

In *Les Femmes savantes*, Molière repeats precisely this same pattern. Trissotin, in only a slightly more sophisticated *salon précieux*, recites his *Sonnet à la Princesse Uranie sur sa fièvre.* Unlike Mascarille's impromptu,[4] this sonnet was not composed by Molière. On the contrary, he lifted it whole, with only a slight change in the title, from the Abbé Cotin's *Oeuvres galantes.* An amplification but not an improvement of Mascarille's style and sentiments, Trissotin's sonnet establishes the first link between these two scenes. Then the comments made by Trissotin's listeners sound just like the extravagant praises of the *précieuses*:

BELISE

Ah! le joli début!

ARMANDE

Qu'il a le tour galant!

ARMANDE

A *prudence endormie* il faut rendre les armes.

BELISE

Loger son ennemie est pour moi plein de charmes

. . . .

ARMANDE

De *quoi qu'on die* aussi mon coeur est amoureux.

BELISE

Je suis de votre avis, *quoi qu'on die* est heureux.

ARMANDE

Je voudrois l'avoir fait. (III. ii)

---

[4] It is possible that for this impromptu Molière borrowed from or imitated some then current poem. See *Les Précieuses ridicules*, ed. Jean Balcou (Paris: Nouveaux Classiques Larousse, n.d.), 46, note.

In both *Les Précieuses ridicules* and *Les Femmes savantes*, therefore, the central poem itself functions as a critical lodestone which identifies the nature and quality of those around it. The pattern in both cases is identical, each character showing her ridiculousness by her enthusiastic praise of the poem. Cathos and Armande both enjoy opening lines that are *galant*, a modish and very in-term no doubt, while Magdelon and Armande give the ultimate compliment: they wish that they had written it. All these women (and Mascarille too) are painted with the same comic brush because they voice the same meaningless platitudes in praise of two singularly poor examples of poetry.

This basic pattern becomes more complex when one element in the structure changes. In *Le Bourgeois gentilhomme*, a pair of contrasting songs rather than one central poem operates as the defining force of the comic situation. After hearing the music teacher sing

> *Je languis nuit et jour, et mon mal est extrême,*
> *Depuis qu'à vos rigueurs vos beaux yeux m'ont soumis;*
> *Si vous traitez ainsi, belle Iris, qui vous aime,*
> *Hélas! que pourriez-vous faire à vos ennemis?* (I. ii)

M. Jourdain counters with his own version of what a good *chanson* really is:

> *Je croyois Janneton*
> *Aussi douce que belle,*
> *Je croyois Janneton*
> *Plus douce qu'un mouton:*
> *Hélas! hélas! elle est cent fois,*
> *Mille fois plus cruelle,*
> *Que n'est le tigre aux bois.* (I. ii)

Participants here characterize themselves not by agreeing, as in the previous examples, but by disagreeing. Like Mascarille and Trissotin, the music teacher presents a stilted and pretentious poem which illustrates very well the overwrought and mannered style of the worst *préciosité*: its exhaustive use of certain conceits, like the eyes, its hyperbolic vocabulary (e.g. "ennemi") and the absence of any warmth or emotion. We should guard here against being misled by Lulli's charming musical setting of this song, which only obscures the utter vacuousness of the lyrics and Molière's ultimate intention. Nonetheless, due to their obvious literary similarities, Molière forges a comic chain linking these three poets and their poems.

In contrast to this sophisticated *préciosité*, M. Jourdain's song is coarse and vulgar. To see in such a *chanson* an old-fashioned ideal or a past golden age which Molière would prefer to contemporary decadence is to misread the pattern. With its meaningless repetitions, its rhythmic breakdown, and its animal metaphor (the woman as sheep and tiger) standing in burlesque conjunction with a precious term like "cruelle," his song can only be ludicrous. Staging also dictates a farcical treatment. Molière played M. Jourdain himself: with his broken, unharmonious and overly nasal voice, which rendered him unsuitable for serious roles and which was a distinctive mark of his acting technique, he could only have sung out of key, comically.[5] Thus two equally comic songs confront each other here.

Heretofore the pattern was comic because various personages acquiesced in a demeaning situation, namely praising an unworthy poem. Now the pattern becomes a confrontation, opposing to one ridiculous extreme an equally ridiculous alternative. Always the pattern retains its inclusive scope: both Trissotin and the *femmes savantes* are foolish; both M. Jourdain and his music teacher are ridiculous.

Having once seen these latter two in such a comic situation, we are more attuned to the satiric implications of their subsequent actions. For example, the music teacher's statement "Il n'y a rien qui soit si utile dans un Etat que la musique" (I. ii), often taken too seriously,[6] falls into its proper perspective when we know him to be a fool, just as M. Jourdain's ascension to the aristocratic state does. In the play if not also in fact (such seditious thoughts could easily justify the innocuous veneer that Lulli's music provides), the essence of being noble is but Mamamouchi, that is sham and Turkish ceremonies, which are not a far cry from royal ballets and divertissements, as Molière well knew.

Finally *Le Misanthrope* gives to this pattern its most complex expression by combining elements from the two forms we have already seen.

Authority to place these four scenes in relation to one another, to seek out a unifying pattern comes not only from the (by now hopefully) self-evident similarities among them but also from a specific invitation to see such relationships which Molière[7] made in the "Lettre sur la comédie de *L'Imposteur*" (1667):

> nostre imagination qui est le receptacle du ridicule, selon sa maniere ordinaire d'agir, en attache si fortement le caractere au materiel dans quoi elle voit,

---

[5] Bray, *op. cit.*, 159–160.

[6] Jouanny, *op. cit.*, II, 882, note 1512.

[7] On the question of Molière's authorship of the "Lettre," see René Robert, "Des commentaires de première main sur les chefs-d'oeuvres les plus discutés de Molière," *RSH*, no. 81 (1956), 19–53.

comme sont ici les paroles et les manieres de Panulphe, qu' *en quelqu'autre lieu*
quoique plus decent, que nous trouvions ces mesmes manieres, nous sommes
d'abord frappez d'un souvenir de cette premiere fois, si elle a fait une impression
extraordinaire, lequel se mêlant mal à propos avec l'occasion presente, et parta-
geant l'âme à force de plaisir qu'il luy donne, confond les deux occasions en une
et transporte dans la derniere tout ce qui nous a charmez et nous a donné de la
joie dans la premiere; ce qui n'est autre que le ridicule de cette premiere. . . .
[l'âme] a une *repugnance naturelle à cesser de considerer comme ridicule, ce
qu'elle a une fois consideré comme tel*: et c'est peut-estre pour cette raison que,
comme il arrive souvent, nous ne saurions traiter serieusement de certaines
choses, pour les avoir d'abord envisagées de quelque côté ou ridicule ou seulement qui a rapport à quelque idée de ridicule que nous avions, et qui nous
l'a rafraichie.[8]

Molière would therefore approve our effort to understand Alceste in the
light of other characters who share with him the same manners, albeit in
a less proper way.

Desiring Alceste's critical evaluation of his sonnet, Oronte recites the
poem and thereby initiates the comic pattern with which we are now
familiar:

> *L'espoir, il est vrai, nous soulage,*
> *Et nous berce un temps notre ennui;*
> *Mais, Philis, le triste avantage,*
> *Lorsque rien ne marche après lui!*
>
> *Vous eûtes de la complaisance;*
> *Mais vous en deviez moins avoir,*
> *Et ne vous pas mettre en dépense*
> *Pour ne me donner que l'espoir.*
>
> *S'il faut qu'une attente éternelle*
> *Pousse à bout l'ardeur de mon zèle,*
> *Le trépas sera mon recours.*
>
> *Vos soins ne m'en peuvent distraire:*
> *Belle Philis, on désespère,*
> *Alors qu'on espère toujours.*   (I. ii)

In its overly rhetorical and mannered expression, its repetition of the
same hackneyed clichés, and its use of wit at the expense of emotion, this
sonnet echoes Trissotin's, and exemplifies the type of *préciosité* which
Molière detested and constantly denigrated. Using their poems as a basis
of comparison, we see Oronte as a more sophisticated music teacher, a
Trissotin outside his feminist salon. Still, all three belong in the comic
center of the pattern.

---

[8] Molière, *Lettre sur la comédie de l'Imposteur* (Genève: Slatkine Reprints, 1969), 64–65;
67–68. My italics.

At first there is agreement and convergence of opinion. Philinte is often interpreted as the ideal of moderation and tact, the exemplar of those social virtues which Alceste so sorely lacks and as the *porte-parole* of Molière himself.[9] But here he prattles on, praising Oronte's poem in the same terms that the *précieuses* and the *femmes savantes* used: "Ah! qu'en termes galants ces choses-là sont mises" and "La chute en est jolie, amoureuse, admirable" (I. ii). By making such similarities evident, the pattern places Oronte and Philinte in the comic perspective which alone can explain them.

Now the pattern changes to the opposition of equivalent poems, as in *Le Bourgeois gentilhomme*. After his initial hesitancy and unwillingness to pronounce a judgment, Alceste finally admits that he dislikes the poem. He goes on to contrast it with a "vieille chanson" in which "la passion parle . . . toute pure" (I. iii):

> *Si le Roi m'avoit donné*
> *Paris sa grand'ville,*
> *Et qu'il me fallût quitter*
> *L'amour de ma mie,*
> *Je dirois au roi Henri:*
> *« Reprenez votre Paris:*
> *J'aime mieux ma mie, au gué!*
> *J'aime mieux ma mie. »*   (I. iii)

Although few critics are willing to draw the inescapable conclusion from this pattern,[10] it seems evident that Alceste's reaction is identical, even in the style of song chosen, to M. Jourdain's. They are, in a most subtle yet perfectly obvious manner, brothers under the skin.

One difficulty in equating these two scenes stems apparently from the contention that the poems in the *Misanthrope* are better than those in the *Bourgeois gentilhomme*. Molière's own listeners, according to Donneau de Visé in his *Lettre sur le Misanthrope* (1667), "crièrent que le sonnet était bon avant que le Misanthrope en fît la critique et demeurèrent ensuite

---

[9] For this interpretation of Philante, see especially René Jasinski, *Molière et le Misanthrope* (Paris: Colin, 1951), 202, and G. Michaut, *Les Luttes de Molière* (Paris: Hachette, 1925), 228.

[10] John Cairncross, *Molière Bourgeois et Libertin* (Paris: Nizet, 1956), 76: "De plus, Alceste n'est nullement ridicule en louant la chanson populaire." And especially Jouanny, *op. cit.*, I, 937, note 1013: "Le sonnet d'Oronte n'est pas du tout du ton de l'impromptu de Mascarille, et inversement la chanson du roi Henri n'est pas davantage dans la note de la chanson de M. Jourdain: 'Je croyais Janneton …' Ici nous sommes dans la haute comédie et non dans la farce."

tout confus."[11] Since then Jules Lemaitre[12] and most recently Jacques Guicharnaud have defended Oronte: " . . . le sonnet n'est pas mauvais. Il n'est en tout cas pas pire que certains passages des divertissements écrits par Molière lui-même."[13] Such misunderstandings (to which may be added Lulli's music which unfortunately redeemed what should be the music teacher's mediocre song) derive precisely from the failure to perceive the total structure into which the sonnet fits and the general pattern which orients and connects these scenes. To move from the farce of the *Bourgeois gentilhomme* to the high comedy of the *Misanthrope*, while it might change the tone of the poems involved, in no way alters the structure or diminishes the import of the pattern.

Indeed one could even justify the use of better poems here. By making Oronte's sonnet a reasonably good one, Molière heightens the intensity and complexity of the scene. To the extent that the audience at first likes his sonnet, just as many contemporaries doubtless enjoyed the Abbé Cotin's poetry or the light verse lampooned in Mascarille's impromptu, Alceste's ultimate criticism becomes more surprising and unexpected. Such a reversal leads us to believe that Alceste's counter proposal, his *chanson*, will be excellent. His reluctance to judge the sonnet, his politely reiterated "Je ne dis pas cela" (I. ii), his efforts not to offend Oronte directly all reinforce this expectation, which is quickly shown to be completely unfounded. Alceste's homely and artless song—Molière playing Alceste could sing no better here than in the *Bourgeois gentilhomme*—not only is no better than Oronte's sonnet, but also it definitely and outrageously connects the serious Alceste with the smiling clown Jourdain.

To make a case for the seriousness of this ditty, Antoine Adam has pointed to the then current vogue of such folk music.[14] What this explanation ignores, however, is that the Abbé Cotin was also very fashionable at that time, a social distinction which did not save him from Molière's sharp satire but which more probably provoked it.

---

[11] Quoted in Pierre Mélèse, *Un Homme de lettres au temps du grand roi. Donneau de Visé* (Paris: Droz, 1936), 62.

[12] Jules Lemaitre, *Impressions de théâtre* (Paris: Lecène et Oudin, 1888), première série, 41–42: "Je suis sûr que, lu d'un certaine façon, avec une certaine voix, par Mme Sarah Bernhardt si vous voulez, le sonnet d'Oronte nous charmerait, éveillerait sur nos lèvres un sourire délicat. La chanson du roi Henri vaut mieux. Mais, en un sens, la chanson du roi Henri vaut mieux que tout, vaut mieux même que le *Misanthrope*."

[13] Jacques Guicharnaud, *Molière, une aventure théâtrale* (Paris: Gallimard, 1963), 380.

[14] Antoine Adam, *Histoire de la littérature française au XVIIième siècle* (Paris: del Duca, 1962), III, 344–45.

Although they belong to different genres then, neither poem can be judged better than the other. Both are bad, and through them, Alceste and Oronte define themselves as comic equals: " . . . Oronte au cours de son sketch est l'égal comique d'Alceste."[15] When, later in the play, Oronte and Alceste confront each other over Célimène,[16] they will repeat this same pattern, which equates in comic terms their mutually exclusive and contradictory actions and personalities.

Taken together, these songs and sonnets offer us the rare occasion to see on a common terrain several of Molière's highly disparate and seemingly unrelated characters. Taken separately, each of these four scenes is comic in and of itself; connected by similar words and actions —repetitions in a sense, or at least echoes—they acquire another deeper and more disconcerting comic dimension. In the pattern of convergence as well as that of opposition, Molière's comic vision remains radical. Like a double-edged sword, it cuts in two directions at once. Everyone involved, even as respectable a figure as Philinte, is forced to show his unflattering and ridiculous side. In not one of these situations does Molière present an ideal to emulate. Rather he offers the two extremes, the Sylla and Charybdis one should avoid in seeking the correct way to act.[17] This explains why Molière remains so funny and so healthy, why he can consistently avoid any taint of preaching or of being morally didactic, why W. G. Moore calls him "the most unintellectual of dramatists . . . who concealed his own views so successfully behind his dramatic creations that the critics determined to discover doctrine have only succeeded in extracting the dullest and flattest of principles from comedy that is never dull and never flat."[18] Only when we regard a character like Philinte as a *raisonneur* or a *porte-parole* does he turn dull and lifeless. How much more interesting is he, how much more complex the play, if we see him as a *précieux!*[19] By depicting only abuses, by bringing on stage only those who deserve to be mocked and ridiculed, Molière lightens his comedy and makes it more effective.

---

[15] Guicharnaud, *op. cit.*, 388.

[16] Frank W. Lindsay, "Alceste and the Sonnet," *FR*, no. 18 (April 1955), 395–402 studies the sonnet, its theme of "l'espoir" and its function as an indication of the fundamental conflict between Oronte and Alceste.

[17] Lionel Gossman, *Men and Masks. A Study of Molière* (Baltimore: Johns Hopkins Press, 1963), 215.

[18] W. G. Moore, *Molière. A New Criticism* (Oxford: Clarendon Press, 1949), 115–16.

[19] Guicharnaud, *op. cit.*, 359, does not go quite far enough when he describes Philinte as a "frémissement mondain."

In these scenes we see, too, at the most basic level and in its most elementary form, the internal coherence of Molière's work. As is true for the French classical tradition as a whole, there is here a poverty, or better an economy of means: Molière does not hesitate to return to the same situation, to use the same pattern again and again. With the momentum gathered from these repetitions, he creates groups or families of comic figures who resemble each other in strange and startling ways. In Alceste we notice some of M. Jourdain's outright foolishness, just as Jourdain possesses some of Alceste's ultimate seriousness, his confrontation with the cant and hypocrisy of the world. Any attempt therefore, like Jean-Jacques Rousseau's, which tries to understand Alceste without taking into account this close affinity with M. Jourdain, is foredoomed to failure. Without sacrificing Alceste's tragic dimension, we may still observe his ridiculous side: "Of course Alceste is a fundamentally sympathetic and even admirable character: yet good as his qualities are, they are manifested under circumstances that cannot but draw a smile. Tragic as his situation has often appeared to those who have drawn the deepest satisfaction from the play, his predicament is invariably presented in a comic light."[20]

All of these songs and sonnets, then, whether borrowed or original, are at bottom pretentious: either they pretend to be first-rate when in fact they are but mediocre, or they pretend to be superior to some other poem. In this blindness, in this unawareness of their own nature, they reflect the principal figures of Molière's theater like Orgon, Alceste, and Dom Juan, who are blind to themselves. Thus the songs and sonnets studied here function not only as a fixed pattern for revealing the ever present comic element in all men, but also as a replication *in petto* of the basic theme of ignorance towards self which is fundamental to Molière's work as a whole.

---

[20] Percy Addison Chapman, *The Spirit of Molière* (New York: Russell and Russell, 1965), 142.

TRAGIKER MOLIÈRE
Christa Reinig

Manch gewissenhafter Zuschauer hat schon gemurrt, wenn sich am Schluß
des *Bourgeois gentilhomme* die Handlung rund um Herrn Jourdain in eine
Wolke von Tanz und Musik auflöst. Er fühlt sich um den Schluß geprellt.
Das Stück müßte doch ein richtiges Ende haben, meint er. Wie soll das
Ende beschaffen sein? Nun gut, probieren wir es!
    Zum Beispiel könnte ein Kommissar des Königs in die Handlung ein-
treten. Herr Jourdain wird durch königliche Gnade in den Adelsstand
erhoben und ist am Ziel seiner Wünsche. Er tut sich den Mummenschanz
ab und bringt seine verworrenen Familienangelegenheiten in Ordnung.
Aber das wäre doch ein elender Schluß. Wenn man die Handlung so
enden ließe, würde einem bewußt werden, wie wenig es äußere Umstände
sind, die Herrn Jourdain in diese erbärmliche Lage gebracht haben: Als
Untertan eines christlichen Königs steht er mit einem Türkenturban auf
dem Kopf da, will Palestina beschützen und den Sohn des Großtürken
zum Schwiegersohn bekommen. Wenn Herr Jourdain unter seinem Turban aus seiner Verblendung erwachte, müßte er sich zu Tode schämen.
Es wäre aber keineswegs lustig, wenn ein solcher Charakter sich vor un-
seren Augen so tief demütigen müßte. Es wäre keine Komödie mehr.
Der gewissenhafte Zuschauer mag selbst urteilen, ob er Herrn Jourdain
in dieser Situation vorfinden möchte und noch den Mut hätte, über ihn
zu lachen. Im Grunde hat er am Anfang des Stücks selten Gelegenheit
gehabt, über diesen Mann zu lachen. Gewiß, er steht im Mittelpunkt eines
Lustspiels. Um ihn herum ist das übliche Gerüst einer Komödienhandlung
aufgebaut: verliebte junge Leute, eine eifersüchtige Ehefrau, eine Mai-
tresse, die sich mit einem anderen abgibt, begriffsstutzige Dienstboten,
alles, was dem Zuschauer Vergnügen macht. Was ist nun an Herrn
Jourdain so vergnüglich?
    Er ist kein Geizhals, kein Angsthase, kein Blödian. Er läßt sich zwar
durch den Apparat der Künste und Wissenschaften gehörig beeindrucken.
Aber er behauptet gegen die Philosophie sein gutes Recht, zornig sein zu
dürfen, wenn ihm danach zumute ist. Den Brief, den er an seine Geliebte
zu schreiben wünscht, kann auch der Lehrer nicht besser schreiben. Der

Text bleibt nach einigen Versuchen so, wie ihn der Schüler aufgesetzt hat.
Der einzige, der ihn verblüffen kann, ist der Schneider. Er kann ihm die
Borte, die oben hingehört, nach unten schwatzen, wo sie fälschlich hin-
geraten ist. Aber das ist Schneiders Beruf und besser und billiger als wie-
derauftrennen und neu zusammennähen müssen.

Insgesamt ist Herr Jourdain ein ganzer Mann und das eben ist sein
Fehler. Wenn der Titel des Edelmanns dem Würdigen von selbst zufiele,
dann wäre er ein Edelmann mit allem moralischen Recht auf diesen Titel.
Ich will aus dem Stück nicht irgend ein Geheimnis herauslesen oder phi-
lologische Betrachtungen über den Begriff „Le Bourgeois gentilhomme"
anstellen. Es scheint mir aber, als ob die Wirkung dieses Stücks gerade
darin liegt, daß Herr Jourdain ein „bürgerlicher Edelmann" ist, oder ein
Bürger-Edelmann im allerwörtlichsten Sinn. Und das ist's, was ihn wurmt,
daß doch er der bessere Mann ist im Vergleich zu denen, die nach dem
Herkommen die Höchsten im Lande sind. Es wäre aber sinnlos, wenn
Herr Jourdain sich dagegen auflehnen würde. Ein Bürger, der in seiner
Situation gegen den herkömmlichen Adelsstand anzurennen versuchte,
wäre verrückt. Herr Jourdain tut das normalste, was in seiner Lage
möglich ist. Er versucht Stufe für Stufe nach oben zu kommen. Was er
nicht schaffen wird, das wird einst seinem Enkel gelingen oder dem Enkel
seines Enkels. Irgend ein Jourdain wird einst König sein. Bis dahin ver-
bringt Herr Jourdain seine Zeit damit, alles anzuhimmeln, was mit Aris-
tokratie zu tun hat. Dadurch gerät er in Widerspruch zu seiner bürgerlichen Umwelt, die sich beschieden hat. Er kann sich nicht bescheiden. Er
darf mit seinem Ehrgeiz, der für ihn und die Seinen zum Schaden ist, die
Worte in Anspruch nehmen, die Ödipus auf Kolonos spricht: „Zwar bin
ich schuldig, doch ich bin im Recht." Sein falsches Tun ist nur dem Schein
nach falsch. Der Aberwitz der menschlichen Gesellschaft zwingt ihn, so
und nicht anders zu handeln.

Damit kommen wir zum Schuldkonto des Mannes, der anderen Leuten
aus ihren Schulden so großzügig heraushelfen kann. Nun wird ihm selbst
die Rechnung präsentiert: Er geht allen Ernstes darauf aus, seine Frau
zu betrügen und seine Tochter um ihr Lebensglück zu bringen. Nun finden
die Geschädigten sich zusammen und machen einen Narren aus ihm. Am
Ende wird er seine Geliebte nicht bekommen, dafür aber einen Schwiegersohn, einen bürgerlichen, wie er ihn nicht wollte. Für alle geht das Spiel
gut aus. Nur ein Posten steht noch offen. Was tut Herr Jourdain, wenn
ihm klargeworden ist, daß er sich zum Narren gemacht hat? Da er ja nach
seinem Stande ein Bürger ist, findet er sich drein. Wenn er aber kein Bürger

ist? Was tut ein Edelmann, wenn er sich mit Schimpf und Schande bedeckt vorfindet und feststellen muß, daß er zum Gelächter der Welt geworden ist?

Im Grunde bin ich froh darüber, daß Molière, statt die Legion der guten Tragödien auf ein weiteres Dutzend anzureichern, sich entschlossen hat, die kümmerliche Zahl der echten Komödien zu vermehren und einige dazuzustellen, die nicht ihresgleichen haben. Ich verzichte gern darauf, an der Leiche Herrn Jourdains in Katharsis zu verfallen. Mir ist das Schlußballett lieber, wenn plötzlich alle Völker durcheinandertanzen und die Probleme Herrn Jourdains gleichsam auf höherer Ebene gelöst werden, da, wo es nicht Stufen und Stufen sondern Menschen und Menschen gibt: „Die Götter haben nichts schöneres gesehn." Diese Erhebung ist wohl eine Katharsis wert.

Aber dann, wenn das Stück aus ist, wenn ich die Welt Herrn Jourdains verlassen habe und darüber nachdenken muß, wie es wohl weitergehen könnte, dann weiß ich, was der Dichter ja nicht wissen konnte: wie die Handlung seines Stückes über ihn hinweggeht. Sie verläßt das Theater, geht auf die Straße, tritt ein in die Historie und findet dort ihr angemessenes Ende, ein blutiges, ein tragisches Ende.

Molière Celebrated

Those who wish to pay direct homage to figures of historical importance are normally limited to activities such as naming buildings, dams, and the like after them; erecting statues or other physical memorials; writing books; and, especially in the case of dramatists and composers, organizing festivals. The first of the following essays describes the activities surrounding the first centenary of Molière's death, a sort of festival, but one that seems to tell us more about changing—perhaps deteriorating—tastes in 1773 than anything else. The second article outlines and describes a form of celebration that is relatively peculiar and not always positive, the establishment of Molière as hero in biographical plays. The very existence of such pieces, created as they were by those who deigned to be colleagues of the master, probably constitutes evidence of Molière's extraordinarily powerful influence on the shape of comedy after 1673. At least one can assume that authors who wrote plays with Molière in them knew and were to a degree occupied with the man's art. Fortunately such plays are not the only testimony we have concerning playwrights' knowledge of the author of Tartuffe, *but they do make a highly interesting and sometimes acutely revealing portrait of Molière's legacy.*

THE FIRST CENTENARY
OF MOLIÈRE'S DEATH

Francis W. Gravit

The first centenary of the death of Molière was celebrated at the Comédie-Française, at that time, since 1770, in the "Salle des machines" of the Palais des Tuileries[1] on February 17 and 18, 1773. Each night there was a performance of a Molière play, followed by a one-act playlet (an *à-propos*), which paid homage to the master. The Molière offering of January 17 was *Tartuffe*, ~~and for February 18 there was~~ *Le Misanthrope*[2]. The first *à-propos* was *L'Assemblée*[3] by the abbé Augustin-Théodore-Vincent Le Beau de Schosne, certainly a minor author in his time and unknown today. The title page of *L'Assemblée* indicates that he was a member of the Académie de Nîmes and the Société des Sciences et Belles-Lettres of Auxerre. Grente says he was born in Paris, but gives no date. He further notes that Le Beau collaborated on the *Mercure* and that, in addition to *L'Assemblée*, he is the author of some five published *poèmes*, of *Féroud*, (no date); of *Thalie* (1752), both one-act plays, and of *Mélézinde* (1758), a three-act play in verse. There is also a *Lettre à M. Crébillon sur les spectacles de Paris* (1761), about the projected union of the Comédie-Italienne and the Opéra-Comique[4]. If Cioranescu is correct in assigning to him a play called *L'Astrologue favorable*, *comédie en un acte et en vers* (1785), he probably lived at least until then[5], but I have no more accurate information. Fréron, in the *Année littéraire*, has reviewed (unfavorably) *Mélézinde*, but says of the author "Il est jeune; il a du talent."[6]

---

[1] Max Aghion, *Le Théâtre à Paris au dix-huitième siècle.* (Paris: Librairie de France, n. d.), 114.

[2] Grimm, Diderot, et. al., *Correspondance littéraire*, Maurice Tourneur, ed. (Paris: Garnier, 1877–81), X, 188. Hereafter called Grimm.

[3] *L'Assemblée, comédie en un acte et en vers, avec l'Apothéose de Molière, Ballet Héroïque; Représentés pour la première fois par les Comédiens François Ordinaires du Roi, le 17 février 1773; par M. l'Abbé de Schosne, de l'Académie Royale de Nismes et de la Société des Sciences et Belles-Lettres d'Auxerre.* (Paris, Chez L. Cellot, rue Dauphine, 1773). Another edition (the one I have been able to consult) has an identical title page, but bears the imprint: Avignon, chez Louis Chambeaux, Imprimeur-Libraire, près le Collège, 1773.

[4] Cardinal Georges Grente, comp. *Dictionnaire des lettres françaises. Dix-huitième siècle.* (Paris: Fayard, 1960), art. Le Beau de Schosne.

[5] Alexandre Cioranescu, *Bibliographie de la littérature française du 18ᵉ siècle* (Paris: C.N.R.S., 1969), art. Le Beau de Schosne.

[6] *Année littéraire* (1759), IV, 251–259. Hereafter called *AnLit*.

We have two rather extended accounts of *L'Assemblée*, one by Grimm[7], the other by Fréron[8]. Grimm's is the more lively, Fréron's the more thorough. Between them they give as good an idea of it as I could and I shall quote them at length. The *Assemblée* is exactly that—a general meeting of the Sociétaires of the Comédie-Française to hear the reading of a new play. The beginning is filled with "comic" portrayal of life behind the scenes. Grimm (X, 183) says, "Le semainier s'ennuie de ne pas voir arriver ses camarades, il apprend qu'ils sont tous allés voir chez Pigalle la statue de Voltaire. Il s'entretient successivement avec un garçon du théâtre et avec la concierge de la comédie qui lui disent des choses bien plates. . . ." Finally all are present and we are treated to some of the "petits travers des comédiens" (*AnLit*, 1773, III, 82)—a quarrel over holidays, a quarrel between Mme Vestris and Mlle Saint-Val *aînée*, over who will play the chief rôle in a new tragedy. Their language becomes somewhat sharp at times:

> *Mlle Saint-Val*
> Si l'on dit un seul mot,
> Je vais, Messieurs, quitter la Comédie.
> *Mme Vestris*
> A vous permis si telle est votre envie.
> *Mlle Saint-Val*
> Vous avez bien de la vivacité.
> *Mme Vestris*
> On voit bien chez vous la plus vaine fierté.
> *Mlle Saint-Val*
> Vous m'insultez, je crois, Mademoiselle.

Both Grimm and Fréron are in agreement that the actors refused to use any of this material, although Le Beau put it in the published version. They did, however, use some scenes satirizing the *poète* or author[9], a *gagiste* named Robert who had been a voice in a marionette show, and more recently, a "moucheur de chandelles" in a theater, but, as he says

> Je n'ai pas là borné mon talent;
> Ce que j'ai fait est presque un phénomène.
> ...Monsieur, une même semaine
> M'a vû Moucheur, Contrôleur, Receveur,
> Décorateur, Afficheur et Souffleur.

---

[7] Vol X, 183–88.
[8] *AnLit* (1773), III, 73–85, dated 24 April.
[9] *AnLit* (1773), III, 78–81.

Later he played minor parts, then kings, but

> Je n'eus pourtant du Parterre indocile
> Que des sifflets. Je vins en cette ville,
> Où, renonçant à la grandeur des Rois,
> J'entrai gagiste au Théâtre-François.

The *gagiste* now proposes his play, which is to honor Molière, but it is only a *canevas* which the actors are to fill in. They protest at first—this is done only by the *comédiens italiens*—but they finally agree and the author gives the outline. "Une Magicienne évoquera l'ombre de *Molière* qui s'offrira aux yeux de l'Assemblée; les Comédiens lui rendront leurs hommages. L'un d'eux vient se plaindre à lui des funestes révolutions arrivées sur la scène depuis sa mort, de ce qu'on ne rit plus en France, de ce que le théâtre a perdu sa gaîté. Molière demande[ra] des détails . . . on lui joue[ra] les meilleures scènes des Comédies modernes: Il y trouve[ra] de l'éclat, de la légèreté, mais point de vérité, de peinture des passions, de vrai comique." Then Molière will say he once possessed the glass with which Terence observed the human heart: he hopes soon to send this to the Comédie-Française.[10] At this point a whistle blows (Grimm, X, 184) and the bust of Molière appears on a pedestal in a magnificent peristyle surrounded by a laurel woods.[11]

Now the actors become priests and priestesses of Apollo. "Le Grand-Prêtre et les autres Prêtres et Prêtresses *d'Apollon* forment une marche au son des instruments et prononcent chacun une strophe d'une espèce d'Hymne en l'honneur du grand homme qu'on célèbre."[12] The High Priestess crowns the bust of Molière. Another Priestess, Mlle Raucourt, who had been with the Comédie only since September 1772, recites an *Ode au Temps* which Fréron says "est très peu lyrique et qu'on auroit bien fait de supprimer." Grimm is in agreement: "La plus triste des odes fut assez mal récitée; mais la prêtresse était belle comme l'Amour."[13] Except for the ballet at the end, which was "fort long, fort héroïque et fort ennuyeux," Le Beau's effort was, according to Grimm, rather well received because of the occasion (X, 184). *L'Assemblée* was played five times at the Comédie-Française[14] and once at Bordeaux.[15]

---

[10] *AnLit* (1773), III, 75.

[11] *AnLit, loc. cit.*

[12] *AnLit* (1773), III, 76.

[13] Françoise Clairien, known as Mlle Raucourt (1753–1815), had made a very successful début. Later she lost favor somewhat as the result of scandals. She had a most adventurous life. See Hoeffer, *Nouvelle biographie générale* (Paris: Didot, 1857–66), art. Raucourt.

[14] See A. Joannidès, *La Comédie-Française de 1680 à 1900* (Paris: Plon, 1901), year 1773.

[15] Paul Lacroix, *Bibliographie moliéresque* (Paris: Fontaine, 1875), No. 1278.

The celebration on February 18 featured *La [sic] Centenaire de Molière* by Jean-Baptiste Artaud as the *à-propos*.[16] Artaud was born in Montpellier in 1732 and died in Paris in 1796. He is the author of three plays and an *opéra-comique* which apparently were neither produced nor published.[17] His published work begins with *La Petite Poste dévalisée* (Amsterdam, Paris, 1767), a comic series (Grente, art. Artaud, uses the term *essais comiques*), based on the idea of divulging the contents of some purloined letters. Fréron has the best account.

> "De jeunes fous, dans une suite de débauche, entrent dans une guinguette; l'un d'eux, sous une table inondée de vin, aperçoit un paquet; il le ramasse ...et voilà une quantité de lettres sur la nappe . . . Elles ont amusé; elles peuvent en amuser d'autres. Oui, dit l'un de nos extravagans, il faut les faire imprimer. Vous voyez, Monsieur, l'idée générale de ces lettres; . . . c'est un rendez-vous donné; c'est de l'argent qu'on demande à un usurier . . . c'est une jeune personne qui consent à quitter ses parents pour s'abandonner à son amant . . . "[18]

Fréron did not think highly of the results and Grimm is even more unfavorable (VII, 311). Artaud is also the author of *Taconet, ou Mémoires historiques pour servir à l'histoire de cet homme célèbre. Article oublié dans le "Nécrologe" de 1775*. (Amsterdam, Paris, n.d.). I cannot agree with Grente (art. Artaud) that this is a parody using an imaginary character. Toussaint-Gaspard Taconet did, indeed, exist. He was an *acteur de la foire et des boulevards*, author of eighty-three vaudevilles, etc., and a drunk.[19] A later work by Artaud—*Taconet resuscité voyageant à Paris et en Province*, (1790)—is imaginary, however.

Artaud, in 1773, was secretary to the Duc de Duras,[20] one of the *premiers gentilshommes de la chambre* who administered the Comédie-Française. According to Bachaumont he was dismissed by Duras (he is now called a *bibliothécaire*) in 1774 because "on a découvert qu'il avoit

---

[16] *La Centenaire de Molière, comédie en un acte, en vers et en prose ; Suivie d'un Divertissement relatif à l'Apothéose de Molière. Représentée pour la première fois par les Comédiens François Ordinaires du Roi, à Paris le Jeudi 18 Février 1773.Et à Versailles devant Sa Majesté, le Mardi 2 Mars 1773.* (Paris, chez la Veuve Duchesne, rue Saint-Jacques, 1773), 70 pp.

[17] See J.-M. Quérard, *La France littéraire* (Paris: Firmin-Didot, 1827–1839), I, 101. The titles are: *L'Echange raisonnable* (3 acts), *l'Heureuse Entrevue* (1 act, in verse), *Sophie* (5 acts, in verse), and *Le Troc, opéra-commique.*

[18] *AnLit* (1767), III, 311–12.

[19] Grente, in the article on Taconet, which seems to be unaware of the Artaud entry, cites Artaud as a source. Cf. also *Grande Encyclopédie*, (Paris: Societé Anonyme de la Grande Encyclopédie, n. d.) art. Taconet. Fréron has a good review of the book in *AnLit* (1775), III, 118–24.

[20] Emmanuel-Félicité Durfort, duc de Duras (1715–1789). See *Grande Encyclopédie*, art. Durfort.

vendu plusieurs livres de la bibliothèque."[21] Bachaumont says that he was a candidate to write an *à-propos* for the centenary of Corneille's death.[22] Artaud was also, about 1773, *censeur royal.* According to the *Grande Encyclopédie* he received a grant of 1500 *livres* from the Convention Nationale in 1795. Quérard (I, 101) says he published the *Courrier d'Avignon* starting in 1775.

Despite certain reservations on the part of Grimm and Fréron, *La Centenaire* is a fairly amusing playlet. It is no imitation of *L'Assemblée,* although both efforts have one ultimate aim in common—to get the statue of Molière on stage for the final curtain. The play begins with a scene between Thalie, the goddess of comedy, disguised as Night, and Momus, the god of satire, disguised as a physician. This permits some rather moderate satire of medecine. Jupiter has sent them exactly one hundred years after Molière's death because he is anxious "De sçavoir si toujours Molière/Plaît ici bas comme il charme les Dieux." They are also to look for some new and original character who may once more amuse the king of the gods. Momus, the physician, knows how to attract everyone to his door—handbills passed out on the Pont-Neuf, in the cafés, on the promenades, promising

<blockquote>
Consultations
Blanc éternel, vrais cosmétiques,
Essences, préparations,
Secrets inconnus, alchymiques,
Et pour mieux appeler les Grands et les Petits
J'ai mis un mot divin.
Thalie
Et ce mot, c'est?
Momus
Gratis.
</blockquote>

This is the bait to bring a flood of visitors, but, as Grimm says (X, 185), "pour nous prouver que Molière a tout épuisé et n'a rien laissé à faire à ses successeurs, les originaux que le grand poète a mis sur la scène viennent à l'audience de Momus l'un après l'autre, et au milieu de tant de monde, pas un caractère nouveau." One by one they appear—Amphitryon's valet Sosie, Mme Pernelle, Lélie the Etourdi, Tartuffe, Harpagon, Trissotin, Alceste, George Dandin, Angélique his wife, Clitandre her lover, and Claudine the servant, and finally, M. Jourdain, in a *chaise* and *robe de*

---

[21] Louis Petit de Bachaumont, *Mémoires secrets* (London: John Adamson, 1777–1789), VII, 254 (28 October 1774).
[22] Vol. XXVI, 292.

chambre, exclaiming, "Un homme de qualité. Qui est-ce qui parle de moi, là?"

As in the case of M. Jourdain the characters are introduced by a well-known characteristic or a well-known key line. "Allons, Phlipotte, allons" (Mme Pernelle). Sosie makes various allusions to the beating he receives from Mercury. Lélie obviously makes a social faux-pas in talking to Thalie (a widow since the death of Molière). Tartuffe's entrance line is "Que le Ciel à jamais par sa toute bonté/ Et de l'âme et du corps vous donne la santé." Trissotin is the argumentative literary critic. Alceste, the obvious misogynist, announces his entrance thus, "Point de cérémonie/Supprimez avec moi les façons, je vous prie." Angélique enters with an admonition to Claudine to watch the door and warn "si vous voyez arriver mon bourgeois de mari." Dandin exclaims at one point "Ah! pauvre George Dandin! Tu l'as voulu."

Grimm says (X, 185) that Artaud "est véhémentement soupçonné d'avoir voulu remettre sur la scène M. Fréron sous le nom de M. Trissotin; le public a appliqué à Jean Fréron toute la scène de Trissotin, et cela n'a pas nui à son succès." This idea probably rests on Trissotin's lines

> Jamais la justice et le goût
> N'ont d'un si grand éclat brillé dans la critique,
> Et tout homme occupé de la chose publique,
> Poète, Médecin, Artiste, Bel-Esprit,
> Ne peut être estimé qu'autant que je l'ai dit.

I suspect that Fréron also thought he was the target, for the second portion of his review of the play is a severe criticism of what he considers its lack of truth (there *have* been characters developed since Molière) and logical development, its poor style, its exaggerations.[23]

All this ends in a grand finale with the bust of Molière center stage, all the comedy actors in Molière costumes on the right and the tragedy actors on the left. The actor Brizard, as Augustus, places his crown on the statue. A choir sings "Vivat, vivat, cent fois vivat/Solus actor qui tam bene parlat." There is music and a grand march (Marche des Apothécaires from the *Malade imaginaire*, alternating with a march from a tragic play). Comedy is led by Préville (Sosie), Tragedy by Lekain. "On va saluer la statue de Molière deux à deux; et quand Thalie et Momus sont auprès de la statue, ils attachent au piedestal, l'un sa marotte, l'autre son masque, et Sosie place sa lanterne dans l'attitude de Diogène." Next is a ballet made up

---

[23] *AnLit* (1773), III, 145–63.

of various "divertissements de Molière," followed by a "vaudeville" for which the introductory music is given and in which the Molière characters in the play all join.

Grimm thinks the *Centenaire* a feeble work, but he says "Elle a eu beaucoup de succès . . . . Les acteurs et les spectateurs, mieux disposés qu'à l'ordinaire, ne formaient pour ainsi dire qu'un même divertissement." (X, 185). *La Centenaire* was given sixteen times in all (three in 1774), including the production at Versailles indicated on the title page.[24] I do not know what plays accompanied it after the first performance, but this is certainly evidence of its momentary attraction. Grimm (X, 180) says that general opinion was that it greatly resembled *L'Ombre de Molière* of Brécourt,[25] a tribute given a few days after Molière's death. In a sense this is true. Molière appears before Pluto to be judged and is assailed by characters who have a grudge against him—a Précieuse, Mascarille, the Cocu imaginaire, Nicole from the *Bourgeois gentilhomme*, Pourceaugnac, Mme Jourdain, and four doctors. But the emphasis is on a lengthy condemnation of medicine, and I personally find less sparkle in Brécourt than in Artaud.

An *Avis du libraire* at the end of the printed version of *La Centenaire* says "M. Bret, Auteur du nouveau Commentaire des *Oeuvres* de Molière, dont l'édition va paraître incessament ayant paru désirer que cette pièce fût imprimée dans le même format, on s'est empressé de satisfaire à son désir." Antoine Bret's edition of Molière[26] seems, indeed, to have been part of the centenary celebration. Fréron, who reviewed the work in October 1773,[27] is most elogious: "Si c'est faire honneur à la mémoire d'un écrivain que de réimprimer ses Oeuvres avec le pompeux du Commentaire et de la gravure, qui méritoit mieux cet hommage que l'immortel Molière? . . . L'homme de Lettres qu'on a choisi pour présider à la superbe édition que je vous annonce, Monsieur, est lui-même un auteur distingué . . . Il était digne sur-tout de ce choix, par l'espèce de vénération dont il semble pénétré pour Molière," and he is ecstatic over the engravings based on drawings or paintings by J.-M. Moreau le jeune,

---

[24] Joannidès, *La Comédie-Française de 1680 à 1900*, years 1773 and 1774.

[25] Guillaume Marcoureau de Brécourt, *L'Ombre de Molière* (1673). *Comédie en un acte et en prose*. Avec une notice par le Bibliophile Jacob (Paris: Librairie des Bibliophiles, 1880).

[26] *Oeuvres de Molière, avec des Remarques grammaticales, des Avertissements et des Observations sur chaque pièce*. (Paris, Par la Compagnie des libraires associés, 1773). 6 vols, in 8°. Bret (1717–1792) was a fecund but minor *littérateur*. The *Molière* is about all that has survived. See Grente, art. Bret.

[27] *AnLit* (1773), IV, 145–73.

and executed by "les meilleurs graveurs."[28] Grimm (X, 267), while admitting the beauty of the plates and typography (which I find superb), is very unenthusiastic about Bret as an editor. Nonetheless, this edition, which also contained the *Vie de Molière* of Voltaire, plus a *Supplément* by Bret, *a fait époque*. It was republished in whole or in part some thirteen times up to 1821, at least four times with some or all of the plates.[29] In addition the engravings were reproduced separately in various ways until 1869.[30]

A further tribute to Molière, duly chronicled by Fréron, was a large engraving by J.-F. Beauvarlet (1731–1797), of a portrait by Sébastien Bourdon, the so-called "Molière sans moustaches," or "Molière des gentilshommes de la chambre," since it was dedicated to them.[31] It was to be had from Maille, Quai de l'Ecole. But let Fréron describe it: "De tous les portraits de *Molière* qu'on connaît en gravure, il n'est aucun, Monsieur, qui soit aussi satisfaisant à tous égards que celui que je vous annonce . . . Molière est ici représenté assis devant une table, et paroît méditer sur la composition d'un de ces chefs d'oeuvre qui feront à jamais la gloire et le triomphe de la scène française."[32]

There is at least a reasonable doubt as to whether this Bourdon painting really represents Molière. Lacroix says "le type du portrait diffère notablement du type généralement accepté," but concludes that the "gentilshommes de la chambre" must have accepted it as genuine.[33]

Finally, there was a bust of Molière by Jean-Antoine Houdon. According to Grimm (X, 184), and according to Le Beau de Schosne's preface, when *L'Assemblée* was announced, "On lisait sur l'affiche que le produit de la recette de cette soirée était destinée par les comédiens à l'érection de la statue de Molière dans la nouvelle salle de la Comédie dont la construction n'est pas encore décidée." (This is today the Odéon.) "Malgré tout cela, je ne crois pas que la recette ait produit beaucoup au delà de mille

---

[28] There were thirty-three plates and eleven engravers involved, plus L.-J. Cathelin, who reproduced a portrait by Mignard. See Paul Lacroix, *Iconographie moliéresque*, 2e éd. (Paris: Fontaine, 1876), No. 587.

[29] Lacroix, *Bibliographie moliéresque*, 2e éd. (Paris: Fontaine, 1875). See Nos. 347, 349, 350, 356, 360, 364, 367, 370, 371, 372, 378, 383, 385.

[30] Lacroix, *Iconographie*, Nos. 587, 589, 590, 609, 610, 616.

[31] Du Monceau, "Bibliographie moliéresque," *Le Moliériste*, 1880, 271.

[32] *AnLit* 1773, 4, 263–64.

[33] *Iconographie*, No. 19. As intimated by Lacroix, however, H.-A. Soleirol, who had studied at great length the portraits and engravings of Molière and his actors, was convinced that the painting was a likeness of Molière as of 1646. See Henri-Augustin Soleirol, *Molière et sa troupe*. (Paris: chez l'auteur, 1858), 45 and 47.

écus, et ce n'est pas assez pour faire la statue de Molière." The result was that Lekain moved to reduce the project to a bust only.[34] According to Grimm (letter of May, 1778; XII, 103), "M. Houdon . . . vient de finir deux ouvrages . . c'est le buste de Molière et celui de Voltaire; le premier a été fait d'après une copie assez médiocre qui appartient à la Comédie-Française. . . . Ce n'est qu'après l'avoir, pour ainsi dire, achevé, qu'il a découvert l'original de la copie sur laquelle il avait été obligé de travailler. Cet original est de Mignard."[35] Actually, Houdon made two marble busts at the same time. One was presented to the French Academy by D'Alembert in 1778 and is still there. The other, apparently the one in question, Houdon "avait donné aux Comédiens, en échange de ses entrées au théâtre."[36] It is possible that the statue was in part paid for by a pass to the theater. I can find no further information about this. The work is now in the public foyer of the Théâtre Français. I do not know the date of delivery.

Two *à-propos*, one presented six times, the other sixteen (in two years), one well illustrated edition, one engraving and one marble bust—this does not seem to be a very impressive memorial, especially when compared to the one hundred and twenty-three performances of Molière during the birth-centenary year and the one hundred and forty-eight performances in 1873,[37] nor does it seem impressive in the light of the elaborate ceremonies and celebrations of 1922. At that time the Comédie-Française gave some one hundred and eighty-nine performances of Molière plays, plus a number of *à-propos* and special ceremonies.[38] I believe the explanation lies in a decreasing popularity of Molière in the period 1750–1800. Starting in 1750, the total annual number of performances certainly drops sharply, from one thousand and four in 1740-49 to five hundred and eighty-four in the decade which concerns us, with only forty-six Molière performances in all of the centennial year—the all time low except for 1754 when Molière was performed only forty-two times.[39] Otis Fellows shows that Molière was produced in the decade 1789–99, but it should be noted that the five

[34] Charles H. Hart and Edward Biddle, *Jean-Antoine Houdon* (Philadelphia: Printed for the Authors, 1911), 110.
[35] Apparently all Mignard portraits of Molière are only "attribués." See Lacroix, *Iconographie*, Nos. 10, 12, 13, 21. I have not been able to identify the portrait used by Houdon.
[36] Lacroix, *Iconographie*, Nos. 195, 196.
[37] See for these figures Joannidès, *La Comédie-Française de 1680 à 1900*, years 1722, 1773, 1873.
[38] See *Revue d'histoire littéraire de la France*, 28 (1921), 626–27. Cf. Joannidès, *La Comédie-Française, 1er Janvier 1920–31 Décembre 1925* (Paris: Plon, 1926), 87–88; 150–63.
[39] See Joannidès, *La Comédie-Française de 1680 à 1900* for the years in question.

hundred performances he suggests (still less than the five hundred and eighty-four in 1770–79) represent *all* Parisian theaters.[40] The public was becoming more interested in "social" plays—the comedies of Destouches, Regnard, Dancourt hold their place, while newer writers such as Beaumarchais, Collet, Diderot (certainly not overplayed in this decade), Dorat, Ducis, Dudoyer, Rochon de Chabannes, Sedaine, and, of course, Voltaire tend to take an important place at the Théâtre Français. It is also obvious from the list given by Gaiffe[41] that the opera and melodrama were increasingly popular.

It is significant that *L'Assemblée* did not produce the anticipated funds for the statue, but I believe this statement of Grimm (X, 188) even more significant: "j'ai été peu surpris, mais édifié, de remarquer que la moitié du spectacle et les trois quarts des petites loges n'arrivèrent qu'après la grande pièce, pour éviter l'ennui de voir les chefs d'oeuvre de Molière, que cependant on adore, et pour ne voir que les pièces de ses deux rivaux, de Schosne et d'Artaud. Cette attention m'a paru au moins aussi éloquente que l'apothéose."

---

[40] "Molière à la fin du siècle des Lumières," in *The Age of Enlightenment: Studies Presented to Theodore Besterman*, eds. W. H. Barber *et al.* (Edinburgh: Oliver and Boyd, 1967), 346.
[41] Félix Gaiffe, *Le Drame en France au XVIIIe siècle*. (1910; rpt. Paris: Colin, 1971), 558–77.

THE PLAYWRIGHT AS HERO:
BIOGRAPHICAL PLAYS WITH MOLIÈRE
AS PROTAGONIST: 1673–1972
W. D. Howarth.

One thing that can be predicted with some certainty about the Molière tercentenary is that it will add to the stock of biographical plays, based on episodes from the playwright's life, of which there already exist well over a hundred and fifty. Auguste Vitu was no doubt exaggerating when he wrote that "le nombre des pièces de théâtre dont Molière a été le héros, le sujet ou le prétexte est cent fois plus considérable que celui de ses chefs-d'oeuvre . . . On en ferait une bibliothèque, qui comprendrait certaine-ment plus de mille compositions diverses" (Preface to E. d'Hervilly, *Cinq Anniversaires de Molière*, Paris, 1887)—and in any case he was including, alongside plays featuring Molière as a living character, those belonging to other, quite separate genres: conversation-pieces of the *dialogue des morts* type between Molière and, say, Aristophanes in the Elysian Fields, or sketches in which the ghost of Molière visits his successors. In compiling the following list, we have rigorously excluded all those plays, starting with Brécourt's *Ombre de Molière* (1674), which portray, not the living Molière, but his reappearance in ghostly form; we have, in fact, followed the distinction established by E. H. Kadler in his *Literary Figures in French Drama, 1784–1834* (The Hague, 1969). It is clear from this work that in the period studied Molière far outstrips other literary figures as a popular subject for biographical plays; Kadler's observation, however, that these fifty years constitute "the only period in which this particular genre really flourished" (125) does not apply at all to Molière, and even if his comment, that "this type of play was mostly written in the form of a one-act comedy" (126) is true on a purely statistical basis in the case of those dealing with Molière, the author of *Tartuffe* has also inspired a considerable number of more substantial plays, including some by dramatists of note.

The vast majority, nevertheless, are slight, ephemeral and of little literary or theatrical value; though the very profusion of titles over such a long period makes the biographical play a phenomenon of some signifi-cance in the secondary literature of Molière studies. The changes in approach and emphasis provide a not uninteresting reflection of the way in which critical attitudes towards the dramatist have developed since the eighteenth century. Molière's popularity as a subject seems to be due to three complementary causes: the esteem and affection his personality evidently inspired in contemporaries—a notable contrast with the case of certain other prominent men of letters; the relative wealth of anecdotal material (whether factual or apocryphal) about his life; and the unique veneration accorded to him in the French theater since his death. For a large part of the last three hundred years, the Théâtre-Français and the Odéon both maintained the tradition of celebrating the poet's birthday on January 15th every year with an appropriate *hommage*, which often took the form of a one-act play. Although biographical plays have always formed a minority among such tributes, there are certain topics which have never ceased to exercise a fascination for the aspiring playwright: the young Poquelin breaking with his family background to go on the stage; the dramatist submitting his dialogue to his servant La Forêt for her approval; Grimarest's anecdote about the supper party at Auteuil, when Molière saved Chapelle and other friends from suicide by drowning; the appeal to the King to reverse the ban on *Tartuffe*; and, of course, the final performance of *Le Malade imaginaire* closely followed by Molière's death.

More generally, the well-documented accounts of friction between Molière and his wife have inspired a wide range of imaginative attempts to solve the enigma of their relationship; while the theme of the philosopher-poet, hiding his private sorrows under the comic actor's mask, and sublimating the disappointments of his personal life in the creation of his masterpieces, evidently had a strong appeal, particularly during the Romantic period. Although Grimarest, as one would expect, is the most frequently traceable source of biographical material, various other anecdotes dating from Molière's lifetime are also exploited (for instance, the playwright's friendship with Ninon de l'Enclos forms the subject of at least five plays); while a considerable number of plays (approximately one-eighth of those listed) are based on the accounts of Molière's provincial wanderings, and his traditional association with a particular locality. Finally, authors seldom seem to have been inhibited from supplementing the bare outlines provided by biographical fact with a generous addition of invented detail, for instance as regards Molière's relations with the *dévots* and the doctors.

It would hardly be realistic to suppose that the following list is complete, though it is certainly fuller than any that has been compiled hitherto[1]. Wherever possible, ambiguous or insufficiently informative titles have been checked, and some titles appearing in earlier lists have been eliminated because the works concerned have been found to fall outside our category of biographical play. Plays are recorded in chronological order according to the year of their first appearance, whether this took the form of publication or of performance (in the few cases of unpublished manuscripts that can be dated, the year is that of composition). Where first performance took place in Paris, the theater is given; otherwise, the town. The following abbreviations are used: c. = *comédie*; d. = *drame*; p. = *pièce*; vaud. = *vaudeville*; hist. = *historique*; a-pr. = *à-propos*; prol. = *prologue*; a. = *acte (s)*; pr. = *prose*; v. = *verse*; perf. = *performed*; pub. = *published*; C.-F. = *Comédie-Française*; Th. = *Théâtre*; ca. = *circa*; anon. = *anonymous*; MS Rondel = manuscript in Rondel collection, Bibliothèque de l'Arsenal, Paris[2].

1. C. Goldoni, *Il Molière*, c. 5 a., v. Perf. Turin 1751; pub. Venice 1751.
2. P. Chiari, *Molière marito geloso*, c. 5 a., v. Perf. Verona 1753; pub. Bologna 1759.
3. L.-S. Mercier, *Molière, imité de Goldoni, ou Supplément aux oeuvres de Molière*, d. 5 a., pr. Pub. Amsterdam 1776.
4. L.-S. Mercier, *La Maison de Molière, ou la Journée de Tartuffe*, c. 4 a., pr. Perf. C.-F. 1787; pub. Paris 1824. (Same as no. 3, reduced to 4 a.).
5. H. Pellet-Desbarreaux, *Molière à Toulouse*, c. 1 a., v. Perf. Toulouse 1787; pub. Toulouse 1787.
6. F.-J. Willemain d'Abancourt, *La Convalescence de Molière*, c. Perf. 1788.
7. O. de Gouges, *Molière chez Ninon, ou le Siècle des grands hommes*, p. épisodique 5 a., pr. Pub. Paris 1788.
8. M. Cubières-Palmezeaux, *La Mort de Molière*, p. 3 a., v. Pub. Paris 1788; perf. C.-F. 1789.
9. M****, *La Matinée de Molière*, c. 1 a., pr. Perf. Th. de Monsieur 1789.
10. C.-L. Cadet de Gassicourt, *Le Souper de Molière, ou la Soirée d'Auteuil*, fait hist., 1 a., pr. Perf. Vaudeville 1795; pub. Paris 1795.
11. J.-M. Deschamps, Segur aîné and Desprez, *Molière à Lyon*, vaud. 1 a. Perf. Vaudeville 1799.

[1] For the secondary literature on the subject, see: P. Peisert, *Molières Leben in Bühnenarbeitung* (Halle, 1905); V. Klemperer, "Die Gestalt Molières auf der Bühne," *Bühne und Welt*, VIII (2), 1906, 668–73, 719–24, 792; M. J. Moses, "Dramatising the Life of Molière," *The Bellman*, XXVI, 1919, 375–8; E. Déborde de Montcorin, "Les Centenaires de Molière dans l'histoire," *Revue des études historiques*, LXXXVIII, 1922, 151–60; C. Levi, "Molière dramatis persona dans le théâtre italien," *Nouvelle Revue d'Italie*, XIX (2), 1922, 1–28; R. Fenzl, "J. Anouilhs Molièrebild," *Neueren Sprachen*, neue Folge, IX, 1960, 242–7; E. H. Kadler, *Literary Figures in French Drama*, The Hague, 1969, ch. ii ("Molière") 28–45.
[2] For help in compiling this list, my thanks are due to Mme Sylvie Chevalley, Archiviste-Bibliothécaire of the Comédie-Française; to the staff of the Bibliothèque de l'Arsenal; to Miss Alison Adams; and to Dr. H. Gaston Hall.

12. M****, *La Servante de Molière*, c.-vaud. 1 a. Perf. Gaîté 1799.

13. A. Creuzé de Lesser, *Ninon de l'Enclos, ou l'Epicuréisme*, c.-vaud. 1 a., pr. Perf. Troubadours 1800; pub. Paris 1800.

14. Anon. (T.-M. Dumersan?) *Molière jaloux*. Perf. Th. de la Cité 1801.

15. A.-F. Rigault and J.-A. Jacquelin, *Molière avec ses amis, ou le Souper d'Auteuil*, c. hist. 2 a., pr. + vaud. Perf. Jeunes-Artistes 1801; pub. Paris 1801.

16. Anon., *La Jalousie de Molière*, com. anecdotique. Perf. Th. Mareux, 1802.

17. R.-A. de Chazet, *Molière chez Ninon, ou la Lecture de Tartuffe*, c. 1 a., v. Perf. Th. Louvois 1802; pub. Paris 1802.

18. M. Cubières-Palmezeaux, *La Mort de Molière*, p. hist. 4 a., v. Perf. Th. des Jeunes-Elèves 1802; pub. Paris 1802. (Same as no. 8, with addition of a 4th-act "Apothéose").

19. P.-Y. Barré, Radet and Desfontaines, *La Chambre de Molière*, divertissement 1 a. Perf. Vaudeville 1803.

20. G.-S. Andrieux, *Molière avec ses amis, ou la Soirée d'Auteuil*, c. 1 a., v. Perf. C.-F. 1804; pub. Paris 1804.

21. Alteyrac, *Molière avec ses amis, ou la Soirée d'Auteuil arrangée pour un divertissement de jeunes gens*. Perf. Cambrai 1805 (?); pub. Cambrai 1805. (Adaptation of no. 20).

22. Desfontaines and H. Dupin, *Le Voyage de Chambord, ou la Veille de la première représentation du Bourgeois gentilhomme*, c. 1 a., mêlée de vaud. Perf, Vaudeville 1808; pub. Paris 1808.

23. H. Simon, *Ninon, Molière et Tartuffe*, c.-vaud. 1 a., v. Perf. Vaudeville 1815; pub. Paris 1815.

24. T.-M. Dumersan, *L'Original de Pourceaugnac, ou Molière et les médecins*, c. 1 a., mêlée de vaud. Perf. Vaudeville 1816; pub. Paris 1816.

25. E. de Pradel, *Un Trait de Molière, prologue du Tartuffe*, prol. 1 a., v. Perf. Th. de la rue Chantereine 1821; pub. Paris 1821.

26. J. Gensoul and A. Naudet, *Le Ménage de Molière*, c. 1 a., v. + prol. Perf. C.-F. 1822; pub. Paris 1822.

27. J.-F.-A. Bayard and A. Romieu, *Molière au théâtre*, c. 1 a., v. libres. Perf. Odéon 1824; pub. Paris 1824.

28. B.-A. Brûleboeuf-Letournan, *Racine chez Corneille, ou la Lecture de Psyché*, c. 1 a, v. Perf. Rouen 1825; pub. Paris 1825.

29. J.-I. Samson, *La Fête de Molière*, c. épisodique 1 a., v. Perf. Odéon 1825; pub. Paris 1825.

30. A. Du Laurent, *Ninon à la campagne*, c 1 a., pr. Pub. Lyon 1826.

31. F. Garnier, *Le Mariage de Molière, ou le Manteau de Tartuffe*, c. 3 a., v. Pub. Paris 1828.

32. Ludovic, *La Première Représentation à Nantes, ou une Page de la vie d'un grand homme*, scène hist., 1 a. Pub. Nantes 1829.

33. E. de Pradel, *Molière et Mignard à Avignon*, c.-vaud. 1 a. Perf. Avignon 1829; pub. Avignon 1829.

34. P. Roger de Bruges, *Baron chez Molière*, c. 1 a., pr. Perf. Brussels 1829.

35. Anon., *Molière in famiglia*, c. 3 a. Pub. Livorno 1830.

36. T.-M. Dumersan, *La Mort de Molière*, d. 3 a., pr. Perf. Odéon 1830, pub. Paris 1830.

37. C.-D. Dupeuty and E. Arago, *La Vie de Molière*, c. 3 a., pr. mêlée de couplets. Perf. Vaudeville 1832; pub. Paris 1832.

38. P.F. Camus (*dit* Merville) and A. Martin, *Molière, ou la Première Représentation de Tartuffe*, c. 2 a., pr. Perf. Nouveau Th. Molière 1832.
39. Anon, *Molière*. Perf. Ambigu-Comique 1833.
40. E. Moreau and W. Addison, *Molière*, d. hist. 1a., pr. Perf. Gymnase Enfantin 1833.
41. J.-A. Ancelot and J. Arago, *Les Papillotes*, c. 1 a., mêlée de chants. Perf. Vaudeville 1834; pub. Paris 1834.
42. C. Mellinet, *Souvenirs du pays, Molière à Nantes*, projet d'une scène dramatique. Pub. Nantes 1838.
43. T. Pernot (*dit* Colomb), *Un Amour de Molière*, c.-vaud. 2 a. Perf. Ambigu-Comique 1838; pub. Paris 1838.
44. A.F.Dercy, *Molière et son Tartuffe*, étude en trois époques, v. Pub. Paris 1839.
45. F. Vallet, *Molière apprentif tapissier*, c. 1 a., pr. mêlée de chants. Perf. Gymnase Enfantin 1840.
46. C. Desnoyers and E. Labat, *La Vie d'un comédien*, c. 4 a., pr. Perf. Odéon 1841; pub. Paris 1842.
47. A. Desportes, *Molière à Chambord*, c. 4 a., v. Perf. Odéon 1843; pub. Paris 1843.
48. Adolphe Dumas, *Mlle de la Vallière*, d 5 a., v. Perf. Porte-Saint-Martin 1843; pub. Paris 1843.
49. K.F. Gutzkow, *Das Urbild des Tartuffe*, c. 5 a., pr. Perf. Oldenburg 1844; pub. Leipzig 1847.
50. J. Méry, *Le Quinze janvier, ou comédiens et parrains*, c. 1 a., v. Perf. Odéon 1847; pub. Paris 1847.
51. J. P. F. Lesguillon and E. Déaddé (*dit* Saint-Yves), *Le Protégé de Molière*, c. 1 a., v. Perf. Odéon 1848; pub. Paris 1848.
52. G. de Nerval, *Tartuffe chez Molière*. (Neither published nor performed, nor is the MS extant. Dated ca. 1850 by Gautier).
53. F. Ponsard, *Molière à Vienne*, c. 2 a., pr. Perf. Vienne 1851; pub. Vienne 1851.
54. G. Sand, *Molière*, d. 4 a., pr. Perf. Gaîté 1851; pub. Paris 1851.
55. R. Brucker, *Le Carême du Roi*, c. 3 a., v. Pub. Paris 1853.
56. Alexandre Dumas *père*, *La Jeunesse de Louis XIV*, c. 5 a., pr. Perf. Brussels 1854; pub. Paris 1856.
57. A. Jannet, *Molière en ménage*, c. 1 a. Perf. Angoulême 1855; pub. Angoulême 1856.
58. M. Pillon, *Molière à Pézenas*, a-pr. 1 a., v. Pub. Paris 1855.
59. E. Vierne, *Molière enfant*, c. 1 a., v. Perf. Odéon 1855; pub. Paris 1855.
60. H. Minier, *Le Songe de Molière*, épisode. Perf. Bordeaux 1857; pub. Bordeaux 1857.
61. L. Fréville, *Molière et Benserade*, anecdote dramatique. Pub. Paris 1859.
62. A. Martin, *La Fête de Molière*, c. 1 a., v. Perf. Odéon 1860; pub. Paris 1860.
63. A Carcassonne, *La Fête de Molière*, c.-a-pr. 1 a. Perf. Marseille 1863; pub. Marseille 1863.
64. E. Fournier, *La Fille de Molière*, c. 1 a., v. Perf. Odéon 1863; pub. Paris 1863.
65. Marcel-Briol, *Molière à Nantes*, a-pr. hist., v. Perf. Nantes 1863; pub. Nantes 1863.

66. H. Minier, *Molière à Bordeaux*, c. épisodique 2 a., v. Perf. Bordeaux 1865; pub. Bordeaux 1865.
67. A. Pagès, *Molière à Pézenas*, prol. 1 a., v. Perf. Odéon 1866; pub. Paris 1866.
68. E. Fournier, *La Valise de Molière*, c. 1 a., pr. Perf. C.-F. 1868; pub. Paris 1868.
69. E. Morand, *Les Amis de Poquelin*, 1 a., v. (Unperformed and unpublished; MS Rondel 159, dated 1869).
70. X. Aubryet, *Le Docteur Molière*, c. 1 a., v. Perf. Odéon 1873; pub. Paris 1873.
71. M. Pinchon, *La Mort de Molière*, d. 4 a. (& 6 tableaux), v. Perf. Th. Italien 1873; pub. Paris 1873.
72. L. Bigot, *L'Ange du poète*, c.-étude 1 a., v. Pub. Paris 1874.
73. Alexandre Dumas *père*, *La Jeunesse de Louis XIV* (no. 56, revised by A. Dumas *fils*), d. 5 a., pr. Perf. Odéon 1874; pub. Paris 1874.
74. E. d'Hervilly, *Le Docteur sans pareil*, 1 a., v. Perf. Odéon 1875; pub. Paris 1887.
75. P. Barbier, *Le Roi chez Molière*, intermède, v. Perf. Gaîté 1876; pub. Paris 1876.
76. E. Blémont and L. Valade, *Molière à Auteuil*, c. 1 a., v. Perf. Odéon 1876; pub. Paris 1898.
77. E. Blémont and L. Valade, *Le Barbier de Pézenas*, c. 1 a., v. Pub. Paris 1877; perf. C.-F. 1898.
78. E. d'Hervilly, *Le Magister*, 1 a., v. Perf. C.-F. 1877; pub. Paris 1877.
79. P. de Mussy, *L'Amour poète, ou Corneille chez Molière*, c.-idylle 1 a., v. Pub. Rouen 1878.
80. A. Roger, *Le Médecin de Molière*. Perf. Odéon 1878; pub. Paris 1878.
81. A. Belotti, *Molière*, d. 4 a. Pub. Bergamo 1879.
82. E. Bondroit, *Molière chez lui*, c. 1 a., Pub. Liége 1879.
83. F. Fabié, *Molière et Montespan*, c. 1 a., v. Perf. Troisième Th. Français 1879; pub. Toulon 1882.
84. C. Hugues, *Une Nuit de Molière*, c. 1 a., v. Perf. Marseille 1879; pub. Marseille 1879.
85. G. Longhaye, S. J., *Le Souper d'Auteuil*, c. 1 a., v. Pub. Tours 1879.
86. A. Nancey, *Un Souper chez Molière*, scène en vers. Pub. Troyes 1879.
87. B. Pifteau, *Molière en voyage*, c. 1 a., v. Pub. Paris 1879.
88. E. d.Hervilly, *Poquelin père et fils*, c. 1 a., v. Perf. Odéon 1881; pub. Paris 1887.
89. J.-B. and P. Pujol, *L'Oeuvre de Molière*. Perf. Toulouse and Béziers 1881; pub. Paris 1881.
90. F. Fabié, *Placet au Roi*, c. 1 a., v. Perf. Odéon 1884; pub. Paris 1884.
91. E. Billard, *La Vocation de Molière*, saynète en vers. Pub. Paris 1885.
92. A. Ephraïm and A. Aderer, *La Première du Misanthrope*, c. 1 a., pr. Perf. Odéon 1886; pub. Paris 1886.
93. E. d'Hervilly, *Molière en prison*, c. 1 a., v. Perf. C.-F. 1886; pub. Paris 1887.
94. A. Copin, *Molière chez Conti*, c. 1 a., v. Perf. Odéon 1887; pub. Paris 1887.
95. G. Monnier de la Motte, *Molière au berceau*, saynète 1 a., v. Pub. Paris 1887.
96. E. des Essarts, *Molière à Limoges, ou si l'on veut, la Jeunesse de Pourceaugnac*, 1 a., v. (Unperformed und unpublished; offered to Odéon 1888. MS Rondel 160).

97. E. Godin, *La Lyre de Cahors*, a-pr. comique, 1 a., v. Pub. Paris 1888.
98. A. Lambert, *Une Collaboration*, c. 1 a., v. Perf. Odéon 1888; pub. Paris 1888.
99. A. Bernède, *La Vocation de Poquelin; ou, Molière à vingt ans*, c. 1 a., avec chants et musique. Pub. Paris 1891; perf. Saint-Pons 1912.
100. H. Chantavoine, *Les Médecins de Molière*, 1 a., v. Perf. Odéon 1891; pub. Paris 1891.
101. G. Calvino, *Molière*, c. 4 a. Pub. Avellino 1892.
102. M. Fiorentino, *Armande Béjart*, p. 1 a., v. Perf. Odéon 1892; pub. Paris 1901.
103. L. Augé de Lassus, *La Saint-Jean*, c. 1 a., v. Perf. Odéon 1893; pub. Paris 1893.
104. G. Bois, *Racine à Chevreuse*, c. 1 a., v. Pub. Paris 1893.
105. E. Legentil, *La Revanche de Sganarelle*. (Unperformed and unpublished; rejected by Odéon 1893. MS Rondel 170).
106. J. Noury, *Molière à Rouen, juin 1658*, lever de rideau hist., v. Pub. Rouen 1893.
107. L. Claretie and H. Potez, *Le Prêcheur converti*, a-pr. 1 a., v. Pub. Paris 1896.
108. E. Blémont (and L. Valade?), *Molière en bonne fortune*, c. 1a., v. Pub. Paris 1897.
109. J. Griselin, *Alliance*, a-pr. 1 a., v. Perf. Odéon 1897; pub. Paris 1897.
110. E. Blémont (and L. Valade?), *Au Bât d'argent*, c. 1 a., v. Pub. Paris 1898.
111. L. Marsolleau, *Le Dernier Madrigal*, c. 1 a., v. Perf. C.-F. 1898; pub. Paris 1898.
112. G. Jubin, *Molière et Cyrano*, c. 1 a., v. Perf. Odéon 1899; pub. Paris 1899.
113. A. Laroche, *La Permission du Roi*, a-pr. 1 a., v. Pub. Paris 1899.
114. E. des Essarts, *L'Illustre Théâtre*, c. 1 a., v. Perf. Odéon 1900; pub. Moulins 1900.
115. S. Henriquet, *La Voix du rêve*, a-pr. 1 a., v. Perf. C.-F. 1900; pub. Paris 1900.
116. L. Tiercelin, *Le Secret de Molière*, c. 1 a., v. Perf. Odéon 1901; pub. Paris 1901.
117. G. Janelli, *La Fin de Molière*, 1 a. Perf. Turin 1902.
118. L. Muratori, *Il Precettore di Molière*, c. 1 a. Perf. Rome 1902; pub. Bari 1902.
119. L. Leloir and P. Gravollet, *Molière et Scaramouche*, c. 1 a., v. Pub. Paris 1903; perf. C.-F. 1904.
120. M. Millot, *Molière et sa servante*. Perf. C.-F. 1903; pub. Paris 1903.
121. L. Victor-Meunier, *Le Rire*, a-pr. 1 a., v. Perf. Odéon 1903; pub. Paris 1903.
122. G. Montoya, *Le Frisson de la gloire*, p. 1 a., v. Perf. Odéon 1904; pub. Paris 1904.
123. P. Lafenestre, *La Farce du médecin*, c. 1 a., v. Perf. Odéon 1905; pub. Paris 1905.
124. Anon., *Les Médecins de Molière*, c. 1 a., v. Pub. 1906.
125. M. Allou, *Molière en province*, c. 1 a., v. Perf. Odéon 1906; pub. Paris 1906.
126. A Crémieux, *Madame Molière (1666)*, c. 1 a., v. Perf. Th. Molière 1906; pub. Paris 1906.

127. F. Dellevaux, *Le Grand Corneille chez Molière*, a-pr. 1 a., v. Pub. Paris 1906.
128. R. Trébor, *L'Impromptu du barbier*, c. 1 a. Perf. C.-F. 1907; pub. Paris 1907.
129. J.-C. Moulié, *Le Pauvre Homme!*, c.-a-pr. 1 a., v. (Unperformed and unpublished. MS Rondel 162 dated 1909).
130. M. Pottecher, *Molière et sa femme*, c. 1 a., v. Perf. Odéon 1909; pub. Paris 1909.
131. G. G. Rovetta, *Molière e sua moglie*, c. 3 a. Perf. Rome 1909; pub. Rome 1910.
132. H. Allorge, *Les Ailes de l'âme*, p. 1 a., v. Pub. Paris 1910.
133. L. Leloir and G. Nigond, *Mademoiselle Molière*, p. 4 a. Perf. Odéon 1910.
134. G. Montoya, *Monsieur Purgon*, c. 1 a., v. Perf. C.-F. 1911; pub. Paris 1911.
135. M. Donnay, *Le Ménage de Molière*, c. 5 a. & 6 tableaux, v. Perf. C.-F. 1912; pub. Paris 1912.
136. R. Givelet, *Le Songe de Molière*, c. 1 a., v. (Unperformed and unpublished. MS Rondel 169 dated 1912).
137. J. F. Lucas, *Les Médecins de Molière*, c. 1 a. avec prol. Pub. Paris 1912.
138. L. Rénard, *La Revanche de Molière*, c. 1 a., v. Perf. Collège Stanislas 1912; pub. Paris 1913.
139. V. Ménagé, *Les Deux Psychés, ou l'Ecole des vieillards*, c. dramatique, 3 a., v. Pub. Paris 1913.
140. Anon., *Le Dernier Soir de Molière*, 1 a., v. Pub. Paris 1914.
141. P. Moeller, *Molière: a romantic play in three acts*. Perf. Baltimore 1919; pub. New York 1919.
142. R.-C. Frogé, *L'Exil de Molière*, 1 a., v. Perf. Odéon 1921; pub. Paris 1921.
143. E. Denarié, *Le Maître à l'école*, a-pr. Pub. Paris 1922.
144. J.-J. Frappa and H. Dupuy-Mazuel, *Molière*, p. 4 a. & 6 tableaux. Perf. Odéon 1922; pub. Paris 1922.
145. M. Lange, *Un Rêve de Molière*, c. 1 a., v. Pub. Strasbourg 1922.
146. C. Martel, *L'Illustre Théâtre, épisode de la jeunesse de Molière*, 1 a., v. Pub. Paris 1922.
147. J. Richepin, *Molière et son ombre*, 1 a. Perf. Renaissance 1922; pub. Paris 1922.
148. M. Rostand, *La Mort de Molière*, poème dramatique 1 a. Perf. Th. Sarah-Bernhardt 1922; pub. Paris 1922.
149. F. Le Guyader, *Molière vainqueur*, c. 4 a., v. Pub. Quimper 1924.
150. A. Crémieux, *Molière et son coeur*. Pub. 1932.
151. M. Bulgakov, *Kabala sviatosh (La Cabale des dévots)*, 4 a., pr. Perf. Moscow 1936; pub. Moscow 1962; (French translation) Paris 1972.
152. F. Bovesse, *Molière*, 3 a., v. Perf. Brussels 1938; pub. Liége 1938.
153. G. Loiseau, *L'Appel de la gloire*, c. 1 a. Pub. Paris 1938.
154. W. Bodnicki, *Komediant*, tragicomedy. Pub. Warsaw 1946.
155. J. Chabannes, *Monsieur et Madame Molière*, c. Pub. Paris 1948; perf. Th. des Hauts-de-Seine 1967.
156. Rochemay-Gordios, *Molière et sa servante, ou Simplicité du génie: tableau intime de la vie de Molière*, 1 a., pr. + prol. & epilogue in v. Pub. Paris 1954.
157. S. d'Arverne, *Molière, ou le Comédien*, p. 1 a. Pub. Paris 1957.
158. Anon., *Une Soirée chez Molière*, c. 1 a., v. Pub. Halle 1958 (from much earlier undated MS in Bibliothèque du Louvre).

Goldoni's *Il Molière*, the first of his comedies in verse, is a self-consciously moral comedy, in which the defeat and conversion of the Tartuffe-like Pirlone is accompanied by the edifying portrait of Molière the *philosophe*. Genius has imposed its burden on Goldoni's hero, who himself proclaims:

> Un uom che ha il peso grave di dar piacere altrui,
> Non può si lietamente passare i giorni sui. (I. i)

Not only is he beset in public life by knaves and fools, but his private affairs too produce their difficulties, as his friend Valerio observes:

> Filosofia non vale contro il poter d'amore;
> E gli uomini più dotti non han di selce il core. (III. ii)

It cannot be said that the play tells us much about the real Molière. Liberties have been taken with the chronology, so that Molière's marriage to Armande (which took place in 1662) can coincide with the performance of *Tartuffe* in 1667; the central plot dealing with Pirlone, the "original" of Tartuffe, is completely invented, for this character is taken, with a slight change in his name, from the *Don Pilone* of Gigli; while the hostility between Madeleine and Armande which runs through the whole play, if not equally fanciful, has as its source Grimarest's very biased account of Molière's domestic relationships, based on the assumption that Armande was Madeleine's daughter. Of the subsidiary characters, one, the Conte Lasca, is a copy of Molière's own *marquis*, while the others, although somewhat distorted to serve the ends of the plot, have a basis in fact: Foresta is the servant La Forêt, Valerio is Baron, and Leandro represents Chapelle.

However, documentary accuracy was obviously not Goldoni's concern. He is said to have seen himself in his hero, and to that extent the portrait of Molière can be said to have an allegorical purpose. But more generally,

159. J. Anouilh, *La Petite Molière*, scénario. Perf. Bordeaux 1959; pub. Paris 1959.
160. J. C. Marrey, *Les Neuf Images de Molière*. Perf. Strasbourg (1970?)

The following titles remain undated:
161. Anon., *Un Souper chez Molière*, c. 2 a. + epilogue, v. (MS Rondel 164).
162. L. Gaulard, *Vers la gloire*, a-pr. 1 a., v. (MS Rondel 167).
163. C. Gille, *Le Barbier de Pézenas*, 1 a., v. (MS Rondel 168).
164. G. Lemoine and P. Quillard, *Molière*, a-pr. 1 a., v. (MS Rondel 171).
165. V. L'Ostiak, *La Paix de Molière*, 1 a., v. (MS Rondel 172).
166. J. Pons, *Le Coeur de Molière*, a-pr. 1 a., v. (MS Rondel 163).
167. P. Richard. *Une Heure chez Molière*, 1 a., v. (MS Rondel 174).

Il Molière is a representative example of that edifying, didactic genre which was the uninspired eighteenth-century version of Molière's own *haute comédie*. It is a comedy with a message, and that message is expressed in a nutshell by Leandro, when he says:

> Molière è un uomo saggio, Molière è un uomo tale,
> Di cui la Francia nostra non ha, non ebbe eguale;
> Ed esser non potrebbe in scena autor valente,
> S'egli non fosse in casa filosofo eccellente. (IV. ix)

Not that one would want to quarrel with these sentiments; but the portrait on which they are based in Goldoni's play is a highly idealized one, and it is evident that even in the first of this long series of biographical plays, the tendency towards hagiography is already very strong.

In his *Du Théâtre*, which had appeared in 1773, Mercier's admiration of Molière had stopped a long way short of adulation; but in adapting Goldoni's play for the French stage in 1776 he eagerly seized the opportunity to enroll Molière in the illustrious company of sages whose exemplary lives could provide the subject-matter for a new kind of theater (cf. his *Maison de Socrate, Fénelon dans son diocèse*, and *Montesquieu à Marseille*). This new genre was to be didactic, and at the same time true to life:

> Le talent du poète s'exerce trop souvent sur un caractère idéal, et le mensonge perce nécessairement, parce qu'il a fallu créer en entier un personnage non-existant. Pourquoi le poète ne s'attacherait-il pas aujourd'hui à ces figures animées, pleines de noblesse et de vie, qui sont, pour ainsi dire, de notre société, puisque leurs noms, leurs ouvrages, et les traits de leur caractère sont nécessairement mêlés à nos entretiens journaliers? (Preface to *Montesquieu à Marseille*, Lausanne, 1784)

It might be thought that the change from Goldoni's verse to Mercier's prose would be a distinct step towards realism; but Mercier's prose is the over-emphatic medium of so many contemporary *drames*. The play opens with a series of scenes not in Goldoni, based on Grimarest's anecdote about Molière destroying the manuscript of his translation of Lucretius in a fit of temper, when his valet had taken some pages to use as curling-papers; but from this point onwards the main lines of the play are fairly closely modelled on Goldoni's text, though Mercier pads out his dialogue with much additional material of an anecdotal and allusive character, to an extent which made the play quite unactable in this form. The very anecdotal additions which were intended to give greater documentary precision and credibility, unfortunately reduce the play to the level of a rather feeble academic exercise.

The five-act version remained unplayed, and it was only when it had been reduced to four acts that Mercier's adaptation was accepted for performance at the Comédie-Française in 1787 under the title *La Maison de Molière*. Having been pruned of some of the sententious verbiage, this revision certainly appears to make his play more stageworthy; it is clear from the preface to an edition published in Paris in 1788, however, that the cuts had not all been made with the author's approval: this edition restores the five-act division, and forms an intermediate stage between the original text and the acting version reproduced in the *Oeuvres choisies* of 1824—though even here, the sententiousness is only attenuated, not eliminated. "Quels propos d'un moliérisme douteux!" writes Félix Gaiffe of this dialogue (*Le Drame en France au xviiie siècle*, Paris, 1910, 427). For what Mercier has written is a *pièce à thèse*: he has used Molière as a mouthpiece not only for the humanitarian ideas of the Enlightenment, but also for the literary ideals of the *drame bourgeois*.

It is with the generation following Mercier that the spate of slight anecdotal one-acters begins. Several of our authors in this period occupy a position of worthy mediocrity among the active dramatists of the time (Cubières, Desfontaines, Mme de Gouges); while later, in the heyday of the *boulevard* theaters, one recognises the names of some of the most prolific *vaudevillistes* of the early nineteenth century. During the latter period, of course, there began to develop, largely outside the professional theater, the much more sober documentary genre of the *scène historique*, which can be seen illustrated not only in item no. 32, which bears this label, but also, in the middle years of the century, in such examples as nos. 42, 61, 65, 66. At the same time, more substantial plays on Molière were contributed by some of the leading figures of the Romantic generation; and if we can do no more than regret the disappearance of Nerval's text, those of George Sand and Dumas *père* remain, to present a notable contrast in aims and achievements.

Before we reach 1851, however, Gutzkow's *Das Urbild des Tartuffe* represents an interesting halfway stage between Goldoni's *comédie de caractère* and Dumas's *drame historique*. While some of the liberties taken with historical fact have their source in Goldoni's play—Molière's marriage coinciding in date with the performance of *Tartuffe*, Molière playing the role of the hypocrite himself, and wearing the clothes of a real-life Tartuffe, obtained for him by a clever trick—the more absurd features are of the German playwright's own invention. Thus in *Das Urbild*, which purports to present events of 1667, Madeleine Béjart is shown as an aspiring young actress freshly arrived from the provinces, while Armande is already "die erste Künstlerin des Jahrhunderts"; Chapelle is a disappointed playwright and jealous rival of Molière's; and the King has for some time been a frustrated admirer of Armande Béjart. Goldoni's conventional stage villain Pirlone here receives a historical identity as the Président La Roquette, often named as a likely "original" of Tartuffe, but here shown as having played a similar role in the family of which Armande and Madeleine are the two surviving members. In short, there is hardly a character or a situation in the play which has not been considerably adapted to suit the needs of the romanesque plot—but paradoxically, amongst all its absurdities Gutzkow's play manages to convey better than Goldoni's or Mercier's some measure of the task Molière was faced with in seeking a showdown with the powerful *cabale des dévots*.

George Sand's *Molière* was written with the declared purpose of portraying "la rigidité et la douleur de Molière honnête homme; la jalousie, la passion, la faiblesse et la force de Molière amoureux; la miséricorde, la tendresse, la douceur de Molière généreux et bon"—and as a corollary of this, "Armande y est entière aussi avec sa froideur, sa moquerie, sa vanité, son ingratitude, sa sagesse même" (*Préface*). The portrait is a thoroughly Romantic one, as much of its age as Musset's celebrated couplet about *Le Misanthrope*. It presents Molière as the victim of the indifference and heartlessness of others, and the tone of the play is summed up in the dying hero's curtain-line: "Mais, mon Dieu! qu'un homme souffre avant de pouvoir mourir!" The five acts span virtually the whole of Molière's career, beginning with the provincial wanderings. Coincidental reappearances of characters such as the Prince de Condé prevent the structure being too episodic; and although the author has exercised to the full her right to impose a personal interpretation where factual evidence gives insufficient guidance—in the case of the central relationship between Molière and his wife—on the whole her play impresses the reader by its combination of a responsible attitude towards history, typical of the *scène historique*, and a dramatic impact which that over-academic genre usually lacks.

Dedicating her play to Dumas *père*, George Sand suggested that it would make a "contraste marqué avec les vivantes et brillantes compositions dont vous avez illustré la scène moderne." The play (no. 56) which Dumas brought out three years later is typical of his historical dramas in the comprehensiveness of its subject matter and the lively way in which this is treated: the plot abounds in characteristic disguises, impersonations and quidproquos. As the title suggests, the play is primarily concerned with Louis XIV: his assumption of power, his emancipation from the control of Anne of Austria and Mazarin, his statesmanlike pardon of Condé, and his renunciation of Marie Mancini—but all through, Molière's fortunes are interwoven with those of the King, from the first scene, in which Poquelin *père* petitions Mazarin for a *lettre de cachet* against his son to stop him going on stage, to the last, in which the King relieves Molière of his functions as *valet de chambre* and invites him to sit at table with him. A particularly important center-piece in the third act shows Louis consulting Molière about his policy towards the *frondeurs*, and it is the playwright's advice that brings about the King's act of clemency. Needless to say, there is little enough historical fact in all this; and if *La Jeunesse de Louis XIV* makes a welcome change from the constant preoccupation of biographers with the intimate details of the dramatist's conjugal life, it must be admitted that his transformation into a secret agent takes us a good deal further from the real Molière even than did the Enlightenment sage favored by Goldoni and Mercier.[3]

The second half of the nineteenth century, through to 1914, represents the heyday of the anecdotal play about Molière. The full-scale five-act drama gives way almost entirely during this period to the one-act "lever de rideau" of the *scène historique* type, and from a sampling of these it is possible to say with some confidence that the attitude of pious veneration has now largely been replaced by a much more objective and scholarly approach to the subject. Among those who became specialists in the genre we may note the names of E. d'Hervilly, E. Blémont and Léon Valade, three minor poets who belonged to the group round Verlaine and Rimbaud. D'Hervilly's anecdotal plays (nos. 74, 78, 88, 93) form part of his *Cinq Anniversaires de Molière*, published in 1887, while those written in collaboration by Blémont and Valade (nos. 76, 77, 108, 110) were published in the former's *Théâtre moliéresque et cornélien* of 1898. One full-length play of this time by a dramatist of note, which shows considerable qualities of historical scholarship, is Maurice Donnay's *Le Ménage de Molière* (no. 135). Like George Sand's play, this covers a fair span of time, from 1661 to 1672; chronology is respected, and the twenty-odd pages of notes attached to the text are evidence of scrupulous documentation. But the whole is rather labored: the author is too self-conscious with his

---

[3] The effect of the 1874 revision of the play by Dumas *fils* for the Odéon (no. 73) was to make the action more economical, and incidentally to reduce somewhat the role of Molière.

allusions, too erudite, too reluctant to impose a decisive character on Molière and the other protagonists, so that there remains something very secondhand and derivative about the play. Structure is weak, and the ending is particularly feeble; altogether the play lacks impact. These are the faults of the *scène historique* writ large; but they did not prevent Donnay's play achieving a run of thirty-three performances at the Comédie-Française.

Attached to the MS of the unpublished *Songe de Molière* (no. 136) is a letter from André Antoine to the author, dated August 1912: "Je ne vois rien à en faire à l'Odéon, malgré l'ingéniosité de cet acte; je cultive de moins en moins l'à-propos, dont le public se désintéresse beaucoup." Indeed, although the two national theaters continued to provide a regular outlet for the anecdotal one-acter until the 1914 war, there was little life left in the tradition by now, and apart from a temporary fillip provided by the 1922 tercentenary of Molière's birth, the flow of plays had almost ceased by the time we reach the period between the two wars. It is true that the last half-century may have seen the performance or publication of more Molière plays than the dozen we have been able to trace, but it is unlikely that this figure is far out: fashions have changed, so that this now looks like a very outmoded genre. And yet, among the examples produced during this period are two that might well in the long run prove to be the outstanding plays of the whole series.

To appreciate Bulgakov's play (no. 151), it is necessary to adopt quite different criteria from those used so far. Considered purely as a biographical essay, it is just as careless of historical accuracy as Gutzkow's, and Bulgakov mixes fact and fiction just as readily as Dumas. This is the least idealized of all these portraits of Molière: he is shown betrayed by wife and colleagues, exploited by King and courtiers, and hounded to his death by the *cabale des dévots*. But this is not merely, or not primarily, a historical portrait: Bulgakov's Molière is the Artist, doomed to be the victim of society—and though ostensibly the play is an attack on capitalist society, its power derives from the inevitable application of this attack to the regime under which it was written. For Bulgakov had experienced just such a confrontation with Stalin; and his play, after four years' deliberate delays in production at the Moscow Art Theater, was to be killed off by savage attacks in the party newspapers. This is a far cry from the biographical plays of the nineteenth century: the academic flavor of the *scènes historiques*, with their rather self-conscious use of documentary sources, has given way to a much freer, highly imaginative treatment of the milieux of theater and Court. Though the liberties taken are such as to irritate any knowledgeable *moliériste*, the result is a highly original play, which gains remarkable unity and dramatic force from the author's *a priori* thesis—a thesis which, if exaggerated for polemical purposes, is nevertheless acceptable as legitimate comment on Molière and his age.

Anouilh's *La Petite Molière* is equally impressive, but for the opposite reason. Instead of putting Molière and the other characters into the mould of an *a priori* thesis, Anouilh allows the spectator gradually to build up their portraits from evidence presented piecemeal—an inductive process which is helped by the structure of the play: originally a film scenario, it is extremely disjointed by normal dramaturgical standards, but we do receive a convincing impression of the complex interplay of cause and effect. To anyone who knows Anouilh's early theater, this is really surprising: it is not difficult to imagine the sort of Molière and Armande he might have created ten years earlier, on the lines of the husband-wife relationship in *Colombe*, for instance. Instead, he has given us what is probably the most balanced of all the full-length biographical portraits: we see Molière "warts and all," and the character that emerges is more rounded, more credible, more human, than any of the others we have examined.

On the other hand, one of the reasons for the success of *La Petite Molière* is undoubtedly the fact that Anouilh has not abdicated his characteristic style of writing. The play is a blend of *brillant* and *grinçant* in which Molière is portrayed as engaged, like the heroes of *La Valse des toréadors* or *L'Hurluberlu*, in one more phase of the perennial battle of the sexes. With all this, Anouilh's is one of the most genuine of these tributes to the Master. It is not dictated by conventional piety or uncritical adulation, but is inspired by real understanding of, and affection for, Molière as a man of flesh and blood: a man of weaknesses and faults as well as the unmistakable mark of greatness.[4]

"C'est assez insignifiant et vide; écrit en vers de qualité ordinaire": so runs the Odéon's report on the MS of no. 96. *Mutatis mutandis*, this comment could be applied only too well to the great majority of these plays, those in prose as well as the verse ones. Few of them break away from the sententious, over-literary diction common to this genre; and when a writer like Anouilh does succeed in avoiding this fault, it is by going

---

[4] For a fuller analysis of this play, see my article "Anouilh and Molière" in *Molière: Stage and Study. Essays in honour of W. G. Moore*, ed. W. D. Howarth and Merlin Thomas (Oxford, 1973), 273–88.

to the other extreme, and using a language that is splendidly theatrical, but is too much of the twentieth century to be convincing as a version of Molière's own. After three centuries, there still remains only one text which provides a realistic record of Molière and his troupe as they spoke, moved, and behaved in real life: nobody since Molière has managed to capture the flavor of the inimitable *Impromptu de Versailles*.

Molière Staged

To a large extent, Louis Jouvet dedicated his life and his finest energies to acting and producing Molière plays. This section, which includes essays dealing with problems (and some history) of production, begins with Jouvet's own comments concerning the staging of Dom Juan. *As Charlotte Delbo relates in her introductory remarks, the* mise en scène *was transcribed by her in 1945. It is through the good offices of Mme Delbo and Cynthia Haft that Jouvet's plans are here recorded.*

The second and third items are essays on Molière productions by modern theatrical giants, André Antoine and Max Reinhardt, each of whom received the patrimony of the master and molded it according to his own lights and educated sensitivity.

MISE EN SCÈNE
DE *DOM JUAN*
PAR LOUIS JOUVET

(transcribed by) Charlotte Delbo
(edited by) Cynthia Haft

Louis Jouvet (1887–1951) n'a pas été seulement le découvreur de Jules Romains (*Knock*, 1924), de Jean Giraudoux (*Siegfried*, 1928) et de Jean Genêt (*Les Bonnes*, 1947), on peut dire de lui qu'il a été le re-découvreur de Molière.

En effet, jusqu'à *L'Ecole des femmes*, montée en 1936 au théâtre de l'Athénée, rares étaient les gens qui ne considéraient pas Molière comme un auteur ennuyeux, vieilli, voué aux matinées classiques de la Comédie-Française et à l'éducation des collégiens, sauf lorsque Madame Cécile Sorel faisait de Célimène le rôle unique d'une pièce où un certain Alceste lui donnait la réplique.

Molière, étouffé par la tradition, surchargé des traditions que chaque interprète célèbre y avait ajouté au cours des ans, n'amusait plus et sa devise: "Plaire" était bien oubliée. Restait un monument historique que tout Français se devait d'avoir vu, sans oser avouer que le monument était démodé et ne le touchait plus guère.

Avec Jouvet, *L'Ecole des femmes*, dépoussiérée, retrouvait ses couleurs originales, sa fraîcheur, sa vivacité, son intrigue, son langage que tout le monde s'étonnait d'entendre sonner si moderne, si juste, si gai. Car Jouvet a mis la pièce en scène à partir de l'intrigue, lui rendant sa vie, son mouvement, son ressort dramatique (alors qu'on en était arrivé à jouer la pièce à partir d'un seul rôle, Arnolphe, et au bénéfice du comédien qui l'interprétait, le reste étant tout à fait secondaire). Avec Jouvet, *L'Ecole des femmes* était une course, une aventure, un ballet, une fête. Et depuis lors, Molière est un auteur jeune dont les personnages nous sont proches parce qu'ils parlent notre langue et vivent de nos passions.

Le miracle s'est reproduit pour *Dom Juan*, pièce réputée malchanceuse, qui avait eu moins de cent représentations entre sa création par Molière et sa re-création par Jouvet en 1947. Depuis que Jouvet a prouvé qu'elle était jouable et même qu'elle pouvait avoir un grand succès, elle a été souvent reprise. *Dom Juan* a été une des grandes réussites de Jean Vilar au Théâtre National Populaire.

Le texte qui suit est une note que m'a dictée Louis Jouvet le 29 décembre 1945, dans sa loge, au Théâtre de l'Athénée. Cette note, venue d'une longue méditation sur la pièce était destinée à Christian Bérard que Jouvet avait chargé de faire les décors de *Dom Juan.*

Louis Jouvet est mort en 1951 après avoir monté *Tartuffe*, sans avoir eu le temps de monter *le Misanthrope* auquel il avait pensé toute sa vie.

Charlotte Delbo

Dans toutes les conceptions d'exécution de «Dom Juan», dans la recherche de cette mise en scène—où les préoccupations de machinerie, à cause des changements de tableaux successifs, qui sont si importants et qui doivent être liés, sont grandes—il reste un problème très difficile, à notre époque où le spectateur est habitué au cinéma et à une facilité que le théâtre ne peut lui donner—de sorte que j'en viens presque à une conception plus simple, moins prétentieuse, que je dois à Baudelaire.

On pourrait jouer «Dom Juan» dans des décors extrêmement simples à condition qu'ils s'enchaînent les uns aux autres dans une continuité voulue et bien affirmée.

Il y a sept décors pour les 5 actes. Les quatre premiers vont jusqu'à la scène du tombeau du Commandeur. Puis il y a le patio de Dom Juan et cette espèce de jardin dans lequel se termine le 5ème acte avec la perspective des statues à l'infini, où il meurt, et le 7ème décor—que j'invente—qui est une nécropole où se trouve le mausolée de Dom Juan pour le dernier propos de Sganarelle.

Par tous les biais où on peut prendre la pièce, il y a cette idée qui m'est venue de Baudelaire, que toute la pièce pourrait se jouer presque en noir et blanc, c'est-à-dire des décors sans couleurs proprement dites, où seul compterait pour la couleur, le *ciel*—et quand j'entends le ciel, ce n'est pas seulement la toile de fond, c'est tout le cadre de scène, les trois côtés de la scène, avec une absence de frise, afin que le décor n'ait pas de limites, que le ciel soit infini dans sa hauteur (ce qui compte au théâtre: la hauteur).

Je verrais par exemple, pour le Ier acte qui montre un palais: quelques colonnes suffisent pour évoquer ce palais, des colonnes qui n'ont pas besoin d'être coiffées, mais qui sont déjà *ornées* de figures, c'est-à-dire de masques, de signes et de visages, ce qui prépare au mausolée de la fin, à la nécropole des statues. Ceci est noir et blanc. C'est le ciel tout alentour que je ne vois pas, mais que j'imagine d'un rose faux et cruel comme la pièce et comme le personnage, comme la scène qui va se jouer avec Done Elvire, où Dom Juan est avec elle d'une cruauté effroyable, un rose qui est aussi le rose de cette volupté qui préoccupe Dom Juan. Il y a un petit bateau qu'on voit au fond du décor, et qui participe déjà à cette coloration du ciel avec ses voiles de couleur—ce petit bateau est le seul élément colorié qu'il y ait là. Il faut aussi que les costumes restent dans la teinte de ce noir et blanc. On peut les faire dans des tons non violents qui participent de ce camaïeu en noir et blanc où dominent les teintes foncées, de manière qu'il n'y ait pas de teintes éclatantes du tout.

Le 2ème acte se passe au bord de la mer. Ce sont simplement des rochers verticaux, couronnés d'une espèce de verdure. Ce qu'il y a de plus important, c'est la plage et la mer.

Tout est également gris, comme les rochers. Toute la scène est grise, comme sont gris les galets, les rochers, sauf quelques pousses de verdure, qui préparent déjà le vert de la forêt du 3ème acte. Il y a la mer qui est verte et qui laisse subsister sur son horizon le rose faux du premier acte, qui est un rose de fin de tempête, le reste du ciel étant bleu, d'un bleu faux et sombre.

Le changement se fait pour le 3ème acte et on arrive dans la forêt. Là le gris s'accentue au noir dans les arbres et les feuillages (qui étaient déjà annoncés par la verdure du 2ème acte). Maintenant le ciel est presque invisible parce que la forêt recouvre le ciel, qu'on doit voir simplement par éclaircies en hauteur avec d'étranges taches blanches. Là, la couleur menace d'envahir le décor. C'est le moment où la scène pourrait se colorer, s'animer. Dans ce vert sombre de la forêt, il y a des éclaircies pâles, presque bleues, des éclaircies très pâles à travers les arbres. Ces éclaircies vont s'assombrir dans un indigo profond qui est l'approche de la nuit, du crépuscule qui va présider au 4ème acte.

Le décor de la forêt, après l'assombrissement de la chute du jour (la scène de Don Carlos et Don Alonso se joue presque à la nuit), change brusquement pour le 4ème décor.

(Tous ces décors jusqu'à la forêt nous ont menés à la nuit, à la scène du Pauvre. Toutes ces scènes se passent dans une sorte de crépuscule et, sous la voûte sombre que fait la forêt, il y a une ou deux lueurs qui passent, vagues lueurs qui éclairent la place où se tiennent les personnages. C'est déjà crépusculaire et macabre comme certains crépuscules et certaines tombées de jour).

Et brusquement, dans ces presque ténèbres, le changement de décor du tombeau. Ça vient presque dans la nuit et c'est un décor de nuit. C'est un décor de nuit où, par une astuce de l'éclairagiste, on redonne un peu de lumière dans cette nuit, qui fait surgir sous les yeux des spectateurs comme sous les yeux de Dom Juan et de Sganarelle, des couleurs sourdes, comme de vitrail; dans cette architecture de marbres presque noirs, surgissent quelques couleurs sourdes comme s'il y avait dans certains endroits des incrustations de marbres de couleurs qui luisent dans l'épaisseur du marbre noir, comme s'il y avait deux ou trois vitraux qui s'éclairent un peu par des effets de lune, et, au milieu de ce marbre noir, la statue du Commandeur—grise d'abord—qui petit à petit, par un effet diffus de lune, va blanchir au fur et à mesure de la scène, jusqu'au moment où Dom Juan, devant la statue, l'invite à dîner. A ce moment, la Statue a une sorte de recrudescence dans le blanc. Le blanc s'accuse, devient éclatant sous un effet de lumière fugitif, et une branche d'arbre (par exemple) balaie la statue, semble la faire se mouvoir un peu.

Nous atteignons, à la fin de cette première partie, à un moment d'intensité noire et blanche, qui est le thème de la symphonie, de cette décoration en noir et blanc, car de tous temps, depuis que le monde célèbre la mort, il la célèbre en noir et blanc et en violet (nous trouverons le violet à la fin).

Nous arrivons au 4ème acte. C'est la nuit—5ème décor: c'est le patio de Dom Juan: immense table en marbre noir et blanc, colonnes. Il y a le ciel, d'un bleu très profond, presque noir. Toute la scène se passe à la clarté des flambeaux (bougies ou torches), et tout le 4ème acte se joue dans un décor assez mortuaire, puisque nous sommes dans le blanc et noir, jusqu'au moment où Dom Juan, qui durant tout cet acte donne l'impression d'un homme qui n'agit pas beaucoup—sauf dans la scène avec M. Dimanche, où il essaie de se changer les idées. Il ne donne pas l'impression d'un homme qui réagit parce qu'il ne répond pas, ni à son père, ni à Done Elvire. Il donne l'impression d'un homme qui est saisi par une idée: l'idée de l'incident qui s'est produit à l'acte du tombeau. Incident d'autant plus notable que, dès le début de l'acte, on a la première réplique à Sganarelle: «Si tu me parles encore de cette statue, je te fais donner des coups de nerf de boeuf par mes gens.» Tout à coup l'obsession est telle en lui qu'au moment où il essaie de se divertir en faisant des plaisanteries avec Sganarelle, où il veut lui ouvrir la joue avec une lancette, où il lui fait enlever son assiette et son verre, à ce moment, brusquement, il entend frapper. Lui seul entend frapper. C'est un saisissement intérieur que Dom Juan éprouve à retardement après la scène du tombeau. Il y a une sorte de distraction profonde en lui à ce moment—ça dure l'espace de deux secondes, la scène doit durer deux minutes, mais il faut donner au public l'impression que c'est un phénomène intérieur à Dom Juan—, et brusquement, Dom Juan, au milieu de ses plaisanteries un peu grosses, s'arrête, suspendu. Il suspend son geste et dit: «Qui frappe de la sorte?» Tout le monde s'arrête, puisqu'il est le maître. Tous se regardent avec étonnement. Personne n'a entendu frapper, mais puisque le maître a entendu frapper, les autres entendent aussi frapper. Dom Juan va à la porte. C'est à ce moment que la fantasmagorie recommence, que la distraction profonde, le vrai miracle se produisent. Dom Juan s'imagine, croit voir entrer la Statue. Ça dure ce que dure la scène, deux minutes, mais c'est en réalité un phénomène d'une brièveté intense, et il faut qu'on puisse l'expliquer, c'est-à-dire le faire ressentir au public pour traduire l'état dans lequel est Dom Juan: cette espèce d'embrasement intérieur qui le saisit à cause de cette imagination. On peut peut-être le donner dans le décor par une transparence des matériaux, une illumination des objets, c'est-à-dire que dans tout ce marbre noir et blanc, le noir s'abolit brusquement. Tout le décor devient blanc, les veines noires de la table, des colonnes, disparaissent et tout devient blanc, blanc et un peu incandescent, comme un état de conscience, comme cet état de conscience physiologique que j'essaie de traduire par cette impression lumineuse. C'est par là que je traduis pour le spectateur l'état de Dom Juan, que j'essaie de donner au spectateur un état équivalent. C'est la première phase, le premier moment de la mort de Dom Juan. C'est le premier état physique, c'est la première phase de l'état dans lequel Dom Juan va entrer à l'acte suivant quand il va mourir. Un homme ressent les atteintes de sa mort sans s'en douter, parfois. Il les ressent physiquement en lui. Là, Dom Juan les subit. Est-ce de cet état qu'il meurt, est-ce de cet état physique qu'il va mourir? Métaphysiquement, pour l'intérêt de la pièce, il meurt de son doute, il meurt du fait que l'état d'imagination dans lequel il est entré n'a rien fécondé en lui. C'est parce que cet état d'imagination n'a rien produit en lui: c'est l'état dans lequel se joue la scène, où tous les personnages doivent parler comme en rêve et où, quand la Statue s'en va, tout le décor reprend son volume et sa couleur (le décor était devenu translucide et un peu irradié, ce qui annonce déjà une espèce de phosphorescence que je voudrais réaliser au dernier acte, au moment de la mort—une phosphorescence comme celle des cadrans lumineux (on rallume et on retrouve le cadran noir et blanc, comme avant); là, on retrouve les personnages dans le geste exact qu'ils avaient au moment où a eu lieu le choc chez Dom Juan, au moment où il a entendu frapper.

Là, il faut nécessairement un temps. Il y a un changement de décor pour entrer dans le dernier acte de la pièce. 1^0- il faut laisser aux machinistes le temps d'arranger les deux derniers décors; et 2^0- il ne faut pas enchaîner tout de suite pour laisser le spectateur sous l'impression qu'il vient de ressentir. Comment fera-t-on? Je n'en sais rien, peut-être prolonger cette fin par un effet musical, mais il faut obtenir cela sans faire vraiment un entr'acte.

Le rêve fini, le rideau tombe sans qu'il y ait rien d'autre, pas de mot de la fin. Les acteurs restent dans cet état de suspens. Il faut que cette suspension dure à la fois pour l'acteur et pour le spectateur. Cette suspension va nous mener au début du 5ème acte dont le décor—comme à l'époque de Molière—représente une perspective de statues à l'infini—qui doit être telle qu'on enchaîne avec l'impression que le spectateur a eue au 4ème acte, sorte d'impression quasi métaphysique, sur un ciel dont je ne vois pas la couleur, mais qui doit avoir à la fois le violet de l'éclair et le soufre du lointain derrière la statue. Le ciel a des reflets soufre avec des fulgurances violacées que prend l'éclair dans cette perspective de statues. Tout cela doit donner cette sensation métaphysique qu'on cherche à donner quand on parle de l'élysée.

On retrouve Dom Juan discutant avec une hypocrisie furieuse, d'abord avec son père, puis avec Don Carlos et même avec Sganarelle, et quand il est au point le plus haut de cet endurcissement, de cette calosité d'âme, brusquement il y a l'apparition de la dame voilée. C'est certainement Elvire, qui vient et qui parle, non pas de sa voix propre, mais d'une voix que seul Dom Juan entend; c'est la conscience de Dom Juan qui entend. A ce moment, c'est le dernier avertissement du ciel (si tant est que la pièce puisse être considérée comme une série d'avertissements), c'est le dernier avertissement qu'entend Dom Juan, contre lequel il s'endurcit encore. A ce moment, nous avons toujours les deux théories; la théorie physiologique médicale: Dom Juan va mourir, physiquement il va mourir. Il a dans la tête la musique de ceux qui vont mourir. Il y a parallèlement la théorie métaphysique: c'est la chute dans l'infini de Dom Juan.

Et la fantasmagorie recommence, car Dom Juan voit la mort qui s'approche de lui: la dame à la faux, le temps avec une faux: c'est la mort. Il y a à ce moment la fantasmagorie de la Mort. La dame à la faux, c'est la mort que se représente tout le monde, c'est-à-dire un squelette (comme elle est représentée dans tous les Holbein et les peintres du Moyen-Age). La Mort s'approche de Dom Juan et le frappe. A partir de ce moment, il y a sur scène une espèce de nuit. En entrant dans cette obscurité qui, à la fois, traduit l'état physique dans lequel est l'homme qui meurt et l'homme qui perd la conscience, et qui donne au public l'impression de l'ensevelissement.

A ce moment, tout ce qui est autour de Dom Juan, comme tout ce qui est autour d'un mourant, se meut. Les statues semblent se déplacer comme des larves. Derrière Dom Juan, il y a une statue à laquelle il est presque adossé, qui devient, par l'apparition brusque de linéaments, phospho-rescente (la statue a tout à coup des veines qu'elle n'avait pas avant, des filets, des ramures). Elle devient une espèce de personnage qui évoque la Statue du Commandeur, et c'est cette sorte d'apparition phosphorescente derrière Dom Juan, qui lui parle et lui dit les dernières paroles: «Dom Juan l'endurcissement.......» Dom Juan, petit à petit, prend une sorte de phosphorescence qui semble être un reflet de la phosphorescence de la statue et c'est tout ce qui reste sur la scène. Dans le noir de la scène, il ne subsiste plus que deux espèces de stèles phosphorescentes dont l'une est le Commandeur et l'autre Dom Juan, qui petit à petit s'amenuisent, s'effacent, et tout à la fin, il n'y a plus sur la scène qu'une sorte de feu-follet verdâtre. Et c'est le noir total.

Et brusquement, la musique relie cet état final de décomposition et d'anéantissement absolu (le tableau et le décor le plus saisissant de la pièce, et qui doit justifier tous les autres décors, les résumer) avec le décor qu'on doit attendre et qui doit surprendre néanmoins (c'est-à-dire qu'on ne l'attend pas parce qu'on n'a pas l'habitude de voir Dom Juan dans ces décors), c'est le décor—si possible avec les mêmes statues qu'auparavant —d'une nécropole à l'infini avec les tombeaux alignés et leurs statues en noir et blanc (garder ce même principe du noir et blanc) avec au centre, à l'endroit où Dom Juan a disparu, le mausolée de Dom Juan. C'est sur un ciel parfaitement clair, d'un bleu très pur et ensoleillé par places, avec cette poésie qu'il y a dans les cimetières par un bel après-midi d'automne, devant lequel l'esprit en général est parfaitement fermé aux conceptions métaphysiques, ou au contraire saisi par une nostalgie et une tristesse qui sont dans le caractère de tous les hommes depuis qu'ils vivent entre cette interrogation vers une fin qu'on ne connaît pas et cet attachement persistant à la vie, cette dualité dans laquelle nous sommes.

Les signes et les figures, les masques dans le décor du Ier acte (du palais) on peut les trouver aussi dans les rochers, dans les arbres de la forêt aussi. Il y en a dans les statues à l'infini.

Tout, autour de Dom Juan, fait des signes. Et tout se termine dans ce peuple de morts statufiés où Dom Juan vient prendre sa place à son tour.

LE TARTUFFE D'ANTOINE (1907): ESSAI DE MISE EN SCÈNE RATIONNELLE

James B. Sanders

Dans une importante «Causerie sur la mise en scène» de 1903,[1] André Antoine, alors directeur du Théâtre Antoine, prévoyant son éventuel avènement à l'Odéon, préconisait la représentation des pièces de Corneille et de Racine avec les habits de cour et les décors simples du XVIIe siècle, quelque anachronique et invraisemblable que pût paraître le résultat. Il déclarait que toute recherche de couleur locale ou de vérité historique lui semblait vaine pour de tels chefs-d'oeuvre. «Je crois fermement» disait-il en outre, «que c'est altérer la signification de ces merveilleuses tragédies que de les ‹situer› sinon dans le pays ou le temps où elles sont nées.» Antoine n'ignorait pas qu'Edouard Thierry, qui prit la direction de la Comédie-Française en 1859, avait démontré, sans le vouloir, combien de tels projets étaient chimériques et voués à l'échec. Thierry demanda à ses décorateurs de reconstituer pour *Esther* de Racine l'antique Assyrie. Le résultat fut une merveille d'exactitude archéologique qui enchanta Théophile Gautier, mais plus d'un critique en éprouva un sentiment de malaise.[2] Les décors authentiques qui encadraient la tragédie, les costumes fidèlement copiés sur des bas-reliefs, détonnèrent puisque les personnages n'avaient en fait d'assyrien que leurs noms. Antoine se borna donc durant son septennat à l'Odéon (1906–14) à reconstituer avec exactitude, voire minutie, les *premières* représentations du *Cid* ou d'*Andromaque*, faisant ce que Denis Bablet appela fort justement du «naturalisme au deuxième degré».[3]

Par contre, lorsqu'il s'agit de se mesurer avec le «Contemplateur», le fondateur du premier théâtre libre européen (1887), disciple de Zola,[4] avait un tout autre dessein, relevant en bonne partie de l'esthétique naturaliste: renouveler le théâtre de Molière en commençant par le dehors (le décor)

---

[1] *La Revue de Paris*, X (1er avril, 1903), 596–612.

[2] Voir la chronique de Sarcey dans *Le Temps* le 20 août 1883.

[3] Bablet, *Esthétique générale du décor de théâtre de 1870 à 1914*, (Paris: Editions du Centre national de la recherche scientifique, 1965), 136.

[4] «Vous êtes mon général et vous portez le drapeau.» Lettre d'Antoine à Zola du 4 septembre 1901, Bibliothèque nationale, Mss, nouv. acq. fr. ≠24.510.

avec l'espoir de lui faire revêtir finalement son caractère véritable. Antoine parla même de rendre au théâtre de Molière ses couleurs primitives, expression fort ambiguë au premier abord.[5] A tort ou à raison, il demeurait en effet convaincu que si Molière n'avait pas été soumis à la règle de l'unité de lieu, si, en outre, il avait pu disposer de moyens techniques plus perfectionnés, il aurait envisagé autre chose que le décor omnibus. Selon Antoine, le texte de Molière, contrairement à celui de Corneille et de Racine, contient en puissance tous les éléments d'une mise en scène complète et authentique. Il importait de repenser tout le théâtre de Molière en s'inspirant de la logique et du bon sens, ainsi que des indications du texte, des placets, préfaces et dédicaces et de ne jamais, sous peine d'échec, aller à l'encontre de ce texte.

La première grande expérience rénovatrice fut tentée à l'Odéon le 31 octobre 1907 en matinée du jeudi lorsque l'Odéon présenta *Tartuffe*. Antoine avait alors un collaborateur de premier ordre, Jacques Arnavon (né en 1877), secrétaire d'ambassade mais aussi grand amateur de théâtre qui vouait un culte particulier à Molière. Arnavon lui proposa ses services et lui envoya en septembre le manuscrit de son *Tartuffe, la mise en scène rationnelle et la tradition*, que devait publier Ollendorff en 1909, accompagné de nombreuses «Notes complémentaires». Tout comme Antoine, Arnavon veilla à ce que *Tartuffe* fût joué *in extenso*, car tous deux préconisaient l'intégralité, et à ce que la mise en scène épousât la pièce jusqu'aux moindres contours.

Disons tout de suite que la nouveauté de la représentation de *Tartuffe* à l'Odéon dut peu à l'interprétation, seulement moyenne, et encore moins au vedettisme car Antoine exécrait la virtuosité pure. A l'exception d'Emilienne Dux, qui incarna à la perfection Elmire et reçut une véritable ovation de la salle entière au quatrième acte, les acteurs ne furent pas particulièrement brillants. Charles Mosnier (Orgon), peu familiarisé avec les pièces en vers, tendait à déclamer avec emphase et à rendre mélodramatique la première scène du cinquième acte, celle de la cassette d'Argas. Philippe Garnier (Cléante) disait juste mais déplut par l'expression uniformément sombre qu'il prêtait au visage du *raisonneur*. Malgré ses dons considérables de comédien, Maxime Desjardins ne conféra aucune dimension nouvelle au rôle de l'Imposteur dont il fit une sorte de mousquetaire dévot fort élégant. Il eut au moins le mérite d'avoir évité de faire de Tartuffe le personnage huileux de la tradition, suant l'hypocrisie.

---

[5] Voir sa lettre à Charles Morice, reproduite dans *Paris-Journal* le 6 novembre 1908.

Quelques jeux de scène ingénieux furent pourtant introduits dont voici peut-être le meilleur exemple. Dans les représentations traditionnelles de la pièce, le public éprouvait souvent une impression de gêne durant la dernière scène du cinquième acte du fait que Tartuffe, revenu de sa surprise, a l'air d'attendre patiemment qu'on l'emmène en prison. Arnavon et Antoine y remédièrent: sitôt après avoir dit: «Ce n'est pas vous à qui j'en veux rendre raison», l'exempt fait un geste impérieux aux soldats qui aussitôt saisissent le fourbe et l'expédient dans le couloir. Tartuffe, dont la présence est désormais inutile, est ainsi arraché à la vue du public.[6]

Il est intéressant de noter qu'Antoine et Arnavon avaient d'ailleurs des opinions fort différentes sur le véritable caractère de *Tartuffe*. Alors que l'un prétendait y voir surtout le tableau d'une famille charmante, aux jolis caractères et aux passions généreuses—son appréciation n'était sans doute pas exempte d'ironie—l'autre croyait y discerner «l'effort d'un esprit libre contre le joug intolérable et cruel d'une Eglise qui torturait ou brûlait selon les cas les indépendants». Antoine aurait même insisté devant son jeune conseiller sur le caractère suranné de l'hypocrisie et de la vraie dévotion de *Tartuffe*; celui-ci, par contre, voulait mettre en relief les belles tirades de Cléante, «libre-penseur, au beau sens du mot».[7] L'anti-cléricalisme d'Arnavon ne prévalut pas. Mais si ses idées et celles d'Antoine ne se rencontrèrent pas à ce propos, s'il ne parvint pas à convaincre Antoine de pousser à la charge afin de secouer le joug ecclésiastique, qui d'ailleurs en 1907 n'existait plus, il le persuada sans difficulté de réagir énergiquement contre celui de l'unité de lieu. Ce joug rendait quasi impossible toute recherche de mise en scène et aboutissait d'ordinaire à de pauvres réalisations théâtrales. Car, à l'exemple de Zola, Antoine croyait fermement à l'importance du milieu scénique et de la nature ambiante. Tout jeune, il avait en partie tiré son inspiration des articles dans lesquels le «maître» répétait inlassablement que le décor faisait partie intégrante du drame, participait à l'action, l'expliquait, déterminait les personnages.[8] Sandoz, porte-parole de Zola dans *L'Oeuvre* (1886), n'avait-il pas proclamé le rôle tout-puissant rendu aux milieux?[9] Nous ne sommes plus paralysés,

[6] Voir une lettre d'Arnavon à Antoine du 3 novembre 1907, fonds Rondel de la Bibliothèque de l'Arsenal.

[7] Arnavon résuma leurs opinions à l'égard de *Tartuffe* dans une longue lettre du 18 septembre 1907 qu'il adressa à Antoine et conservée à l'Arsenal. D'après Arnavon, Antoine lui aurait même avoué son peu de goût pour la comédie qu'il connaissait pourtant par coeur!

[8] Zola, «Le Décor et les Accessoires», dans *Le Naturalisme au théâtre, Oeuvres complètes*, éd. H. Mitterand, (Paris: Cercle du livre précieux, 1966–70), XI, 339.

[9] *Ibid.*, V, 590.

dit encore Antoine dans sa «Causerie», par les réminiscences classiques, de sorte que nous n'en sommes plus aux éternelles dispositions symétriques et à l'unique table de *Tartuffe*.

C'est donc dans un décor conçu selon les principes naturalistes, décor ruisselant de vie et de mouvement, qu'il faut chercher la raison pour laquelle Georges Gaulis intitula son article du *Journal de Genève* du 13 novembre 1907, «La Résurrection de *Tartuffe*». Un décor qui, dans les représentations traditionnelles de *Tartuffe*, sous la pression des événements et de certains personnages trépignants, donne un peu l'impression de vouloir éclater, [10] éclata pour de vrai en octobre-novembre 1907 au second Théâtre Français. Et cependant, Antoine essaya sagement d'atténuer le côté révolutionnaire d'un projet qui lui tenait fort au coeur depuis la fin de 1904: «On a beaucoup parlé et beaucoup écrit sur les projets de M. Antoine au sujet de cette mise en scène», écrivit le chroniqueur de *Comoedia* le 8 octobre. «On lui prête l'intention de bouleverser toutes les traditions. Pensons plutôt que son effort portera sur la vérité de certains détails.» Alors que Molière situait l'action de *Tartuffe* dans une pièce de la maison d'Orgon à Paris—ce qui donnait invariablement lieu à un insipide décor vague et composite qui ne figurait ni un salon, ni une salle à manger, ni un vestibule—Antoine imagina des décors réels et variés pour chaque acte. Le décorateur Paul Paquereau brossa des tableaux très riches en couleur. Antoine se garda pourtant du *réalisme plaqué* qu'avait imaginé à l'Odéon quelques décennies plus tôt Charles Albert Fechter.

Une confidence faite par Antoine à Ibels en dit long sur ses intentions:

> *Tartuffe*, mon vieux [. . .], c'est une comédie qui restera toujours moderne. Elle pourrait être jouée en habit, nous ferons mieux, nous allons la situer dans son véritable milieu. D'abord le jardin, pour la rentrée d'Orgon, et la sortie de Mme Pernelle. Puis le salon paré, avec la découverte du grand escalier, par lequel descendra Tartuffe au troisième acte. Hein! cette entrée de Tartuffe, si admirablement préparée par Molière pendant deux actes, comme elle va encore se trouver accentuée par la descente du faux dévot, dont on voit d'abord les pieds, puis le corps, puis la tête [. . .]. [11]

Nous voyons ici Antoine préoccupé par la scène à effet, tout autant que par le désir de faire vrai et exact. Faire descendre Tartuffe par un escalier véritable! Il se livra donc à des recherches de mise en scène fort poussées. A la place du décor pauvre et ridicule, du cadre uniforme, du salon entièrement vide avec sa grande table, quatre décors constituant le cadre

---

[10] Voir Jacques Scherer, *Structures de Tartuffe*, (Paris: Sedes, 1966), 173.
[11] Ibels, «La Carrière d'Antoine» dans *Je Sais tout*, 25 mai, 1914.

approprié à la vie de la riche bourgeoisie du milieu du dix-septième siècle :

– le jardin du premier acte
– le salon ou parloir du rez-de-chaussée du deuxième et troisième actes
– le petit salon-boudoir du quatrième acte.
– le vestibule ou la galerie du cinquième acte

La totalité de cette décoration occupe toute la profondeur du théâtre. Le jardin est de style Louis XIII restauré dans le style Louis XIV, l'ameublement également un composé de ces deux styles mais la maison a un décor Louis XIV pur. Cinéaste avant la lettre, Antoine détermina même l'angle sous lequel ces différents endroits devaient être vus (prise de vue).

Le premier acte, fort mouvementé, ne devait pas, selon Arnavon, se jouer dans un intérieur. «Allons, Flipote, allons, que d'eux je me délivre.» Jusqu'alors, Mme Pernelle disait le premier vers en se dirigeant vers le trou du souffleur. Dans le nouveau *Tartuffe* de l'Odéon, elle va sortir dans le jardin afin de rejoindre son domicile particulier. Les membres de la famille engagent une conversation sous un vieil arbre. On voit Orgon arriver dans une chaise à porteurs et Cléante s'entretient avec lui sur le perron même de la maison[12] dont la décoration et les accessoires dégagent une impression de vie réelle, de vie vécue. Il y a, par exemple, des sièges confortables où l'on ne craint pas de s'asseoir, un escalier qui a une fonction, tout un jeu de portes dont on se sert. Il y a des objets rangés ou qui traînent car, comme le dit Antoine, toujours dans sa «Causerie» de 1903, dans des décorations d'intérieur, il ne faut jamais craindre la profusion et la diversité des menus objets. (Les meubles et les bibelots de *Tartuffe* coûtèrent à Antoine plus de dix mille francs!) On dépouilla par contre l'oeuvre des accessoires peints qui attiraient et gênaient le regard du spectateur, aussi bien que de «cet affligeant cortège d'accessoires sordides, fauteuils usés, tapisseries banales et passées, où se profilent en nuées cigognes, canards et autres gibiers, décors sans vérité, sans vie, sans gaieté».[13]

Au lieu d'adresser à Elmire sa brûlante déclaration dans l'endroit même où Damis l'a surpris ou, selon la tradition, dans quelque vague lieu de

---

[12] «Le théâtre représentera [. . .] un grand jardin très profond précédant l'hôtel d'Orgon. Cet hôtel borde une rue des faubourgs de Paris [. . .].'' Arnavon, *op. cit.*, 27. Ce point de vue fut contesté par Mme Dussane qui, reproduisant dans son édition de *Tartuffe*, publiée par Didier-Privat en 1932, une photographie de cette première scène du *Tartuffe* de l'Odéon, conclut : «Remarquez comme il serait bizarre que Cléante eût avec Orgon une conversation aussi importante que celle de la cinquième scène du premier acte sur le perron de sa maison, ce qui arrivera nécessairement dans la mise en scène ci-dessus.»

[13] Arnavon, *Op. cit.*, 107.

passage, Tartuffe, soupçonneux, se retrouve avec elle dans une sorte de salon intime contenant de lourdes tentures et un divan discret. Là, il espère pouvoir recevoir enfin les «réelles faveurs» dont il est question.

Quel fut l'accueil réservé à cet essai? Antoine avait prévu des objections car on ne peut pas bouleverser une mise en scène en balayant les invraisemblances sans provoquer des cris de protestation. Lors de la présentation de *Tartuffe* à l'Odéon, on put en effet remarquer une certaine polarisation de la critique. D'abord, la réaction inévitable des traditionalistes, des «irréductibles» au dire d'Antoine. Le ministre Paul-Boncour fit un rapport dans lequel il reprochait à Antoine d'avoir modifié la mise en scène de *Tartuffe*. Adolphe Brisson goûta fort peu la scène du jardin du premier acte, la splendeur des robes de Marianne et d'Elmire et le décolletage de «ces dames» qu'il aurait préféré voir dans les habits «décents et convenables» qui seyaient à leur condition bourgeoise.[14] Il y revint un mois plus tard dans une autre chronique pour dire qu'il avait trouvé *Tartuffe* «gêné» dans le nouvel habit dont Antoine l'avait doté, sauf au deuxième et au troisième actes où il estimait l'innovation heureuse.[15] «A tout cela, vous devinez l'objection, n'est-ce pas?» s'exclama Edmond Stoullig: «Molière n'y a jamais pensé!» Ce chroniqueur, écrivant le 31 octobre dans *Les Annales du théâtre*, tout en parlant d'un succès triomphal, soutenait avec quelque justification que le fond de décors réaliste avait le désavantage de faire ressortir le caractère factice de certains personnages: Dorine, par exemple, en tant que servante moralisante et sermonneuse. Enfin, un certain Jean Delon, plus royaliste que le roi, écrivit à Emile Faguet, «Il faut défendre la tradition. Jouer *Tartuffe* dans un décor pittoresque, c'est situer quelque part des caractères qui sont partout; c'est faire du particulier avec du général. On sait bien que Molière est un réaliste; mais on sait bien aussi que son réalisme est dans le tracé des caractères et non pas dans les choses, dans le détail, dans le décor.»[16]

Par contre, auprès de critiques plus libéraux, le *Tartuffe* de l'Odéon eut un légitime succès. Nozière (Fernand Weil) applaudit à «l'entorse faite à la tradition»[17] et Serge Basset à une «tentative [. . .] aussi féconde que

---

[14] *Le Temps*, 11 novembre 1907.

[15] *Ibid.*, 16 décembre. L'attitude de Brisson différait peu de celle de son beau-père, Francisque Sarcey, qui déclara dans *Le Temps*, le 4 juin 1888: «Une restitution absolument exacte du passé, si elle était possible, dérouterait et contrarierait le spectateur plus qu'elle ne lui serait agréable.»

[16] *Le Journal des débats*, 2 décembre 1907.

[17] *Gil Blas*, 5 novembre 1907.

hardie».[18] Jules Renard, écrivant le 8 novembre dans *Messidor*, parla d'une «minute rare au théâtre» qu'il avait vécu grâce à une nouvelle et heureuse mise en scène. Même Brisson avoua que jamais le chef-d'oeuvre ne lui avait paru aussi jeune[19] et Faguet, qui n'approuvait pas sans réserves les changements de lieu, dit confesser que *Tartuffe* à l'Odéon «a fait beaucoup de plaisir».[20] Il ajouta: «Quant à jouer la comédie du dix-septième siècle dans des appartements du dix-septième siècle et dans des meubles du dix-septième siècle, on sait que cela a toujours été mon avis, pour la bonne raison que c'est évidemment ce qu'aurait fait Molière s'il avait pu le faire.» Faguet convenait aussi qu'en voulant trop «délocaliser» Molière, on le rendait plus abstrait, donc moins vivant.[21]

Bref, au lieu d'étouffer dans une mise en scène étriquée, *Tartuffe* s'épanouit sur les planches de l'Odéon. Cette mise en scène nouvelle n'eut toutefois rien d'excessif car, d'après la théorie d'Arnavon mise en pratique par Antoine, elle devait servir seulement à rehausser le tableau sans pour cela sortir de son rôle. Le jeune Arnavon jubila et vit le triomphe imminent de sa réforme. «L'essentiel, dit-il, était que cette barrière barbare fût brisée et qu'on abordât les grandes comédies du maître dans un esprit d'indépendance et de raison.»[22]

Cinq ans après la première de *Tartuffe* à l'Odéon, Roll déclara le 6 décembre dans *Comoedia*: «Aujourd' hui la tentative de M. Antoine ne rencontre plus guère de détracteurs et, pour ma part, je supporte avec peine l'idée d'un recul possible en arrière. *Tartuffe* ne peut plus désormais se jouer—à l'Odéon—dans un seul décor.»

Certes, de toutes les reconstitutions tentées par Antoine, celles des comédies de Molière furent à la fois les plus nombreuses et les plus contestées. En général, celles qui firent le plus de bruit rencontrèrent le plus de succès réel. Il y avait sans aucun doute une certaine affinité entre Antoine et Molière. «Plus j'étudie Molière, écrivit Arnavon à Antoine le 6 décembre 1912, plus je me réjouis de voir comme vos doctrines sont en puissance en lui.»[23] Après *Tartuffe*, restitution-type, comédie reprise périodiquement par Antoine durant son septennat, vint toute une série de comédies de Molière. A vrai dire, Antoine fut le premier metteur en

[18] *Le Figaro*, 4 octobre 1907.
[19] *Le Temps*, 11 novembre 1907.
[20] *Le Journal des débats*, 11 novembre 1907.
[21] *Ibid.*, 2 décembre 1907.
[22] Lettre à Antoine du 6 octobre 1907, Arsenal.
[23] Arsenal.

scène à entreprendre systématiquement de tels essais. Sans encombrer les classiques de réalités dégradantes, il parvint à les restituer, comme le dit Bernard Dort «non sous le signe d'une fallacieuse éternité, mais inscrits dans une société précise, compris à travers l'histoire de leur temps telle que nous pouvons l'imaginer aujourd'hui».[24]

---

[24] Dort, «Antoine le patron» dans *Théâtre public*, 1953–66, (Paris: Seuil, 1967), 300.

MOLIÈRE ON
MAX REINHARDT'S STAGE

Leonhard M. Fiedler

When Max Reinhardt died in exile in New York on October 31, 1943, he was nearly forgotten after almost four decades in which he had been honored and praised as well as heavily attacked.[1] Few friends had survived, most of them emigrants like himself, One of them, Heinrich Mann, expressed his admiration for the great director in his memorial address:

> Man weiß, er hat das Theater revolutioniert. . . . Ich müßte nicht wissen, daß er auf unseren Schiller, den jungen, revolutionären Schiller, immer wieder zurückgegriffen hat. Ich könnte die große Entdeckung Reinhardts vergessen, den längst vergessenen Revolutionär Büchner. . . . Die bürgerlichen Komödien von Sternheim—der sozial gerichtete Brahm hätte sie wahrscheinlich noch verworfen; sie zeigen von dem Aufstand gegen eine Klasse das neuere Gesicht. Wer Sternheim wagte, war Reinhardt. Dies alles sind Ergebnisse.[2]

Mann's statement is true, but it is not the only truth. A closer investigation of Reinhardt's work reveals that Reinhardt was not an heir of the Enlightenment like Heinrich Mann, that he *did* perform—very convincingly—emancipatory plays, but it also reveals that this tendency was not the center of his interest. This can be clearly seen in Reinhardt's relationship to Molière, who has often been interpreted as an early "enlightened" critic of his time. After all, it is almost impossible to say that Reinhardt was the representative of just *one* style or *one* tendency like other reformers of the theater—Brahm, Piscator, Stanislavski, or Antoine. Herbert Ihering, a critic who did not always agree with Reinhardt, said about his production: "Es gab keine Tradition, keine festen Grundlagen mehr. Jedes Werk wurde von sich aus inszeniert. Mit jeder neuen Einstudierung wurde die Theaterkunst von vorn angefangen."[3]

[1] Shortened version of a lecture delivered in Spring 1972 at the State University of New York at Binghamton; Indiana University, Bloomington; Colgate University, Hamilton, N. Y.; McMaster University, Hamilton, Ontario; University of Pennsylvania, Philadelphia; Washington University, St. Louis, Missouri; and the University of Toronto. I should like to express my thanks to Mrs. Rosemarie Altenhofer, M.A., for helping me with the translation into English of this essay. See also the author's study: *Max Reinhardt und Molière. Text-und Bilddokumentation* (Salzburg, Otto Müller Verlag), 1972.
[2] Heinrich Mann, *Essays III* (Berlin, 1962), 520 f.; and: Leonard M. Fiedler, *Hofmannsthals Molière-Bearbeitungen*. Die Erneuerung der comédie-ballet auf Max Reinhardts Bühnen (Darmstadt, Agora Verlag), 1974.
[3] Herbert Ihering, *Regie* (Berlin, 1943), 12.

"A new beginning of theatrical art," in this case, means going back to the origin of every play and every theatrical genre, but also starting immediately from the text and discussing it without regard to any convention. This attitude towards tradition enabled Reinhardt, as the first stage director, to overcome with his productions of classical plays the obsolete style practiced by the court theaters. It is no accident that Shakespeare played a main part in this revival, because he was at the same time a playwright, a stage manager, and an actor. Reinhardt, too, wanted to achieve this synthesis, and he succeeded in combining different artistic activities with different artistic media.

In order to compare Heinrich Mann's description with Reinhardt's own view, I would like to quote from a programmatic statement by Reinhardt from the year 1940, which will illustrate his concern: "Zu allen Zeiten haben dramatische Dichter für das Bedürfnis bestimmter Theater ältere Werke adaptiert. . . . Shakespeare, Molière, Raimund, Nestroy und viele andere haben im engsten Umkreis ihrer Truppen gelebt und den Schauspielern die Rollen auf den Leib geschrieben. Und die meisten guten französischen Theaterstücke sind hinter den Kulissen und in den Garderoben der Schauspieler concipiert worden."[4] This statement clearly shows a main concern of Reinhardt. It also shows his special interest in Molière.

I shall now try to illustrate the manner in which this much admired form of theatrical production was realized in Reinhardt's Molière productions. The basis for these observations is a series of little known facts and new sources, which for the first time permit examination of this very complex problem and thus show the continuity of Reinhardt's activity. Reinhardt was fortunate enough to find contemporary playwrights who helped him to translate Molière's plays and to adapt them to the needs of his own theater. These playwrights—Frank Wedekind, Carl Sternheim, Carl Vollmoeller, and above all Hugo von Hofmannsthal—were perfectly familiar with the demands of the theater and the possibilities of the stage. They cooperated with Reinhardt in such an intimate way that it is often impossible to differentiate between the role of the director and the role of the author or the adaptor.

Molière's *Tartuffe*, however, when it had been first produced by Reinhardt in 1906 in the Deutsches Theater of Berlin, was treated in a different way. Reinhardt used the translation of Ludwig Fulda, who was still under

---

[4] Max Reinhardt, *Ausgewählte Briefe, Reden, Schriften, und Szenen aus Regiebüchern.* Ed. Franz Hadamowsky (Wien, 1963), 114

the influence of nineteenth-century conventions, which influence means that he had a certain, but not precisely defined, ideal of the art of translation, but no concern about whether the script was performable in that form. Reinhardt's initiative in this production was obviously restricted to collaboration with the actors and the effort of transforming an author into an actor: Frank Wedekind, who normally appeared on stage only in his own plays, took the part of Tartuffe. The experiment failed; the performance was unsuccessful.

The essential revival of Molière began some years later, in 1910, when Hugo von Hofmannsthal wrote his first Molière adaptation for Max Reinhardt. The special choice made among Molière's comedies and the integration of ballet, pantomime, and music into the play—which resulted from Hofmannsthal's and Reinhardt's choices—characterize the revival. Hofmannsthal once wrote, quoting Diderot: "Si l'on croit qu'il y ait beaucoup plus d'hommes capables de faire *Pourceaugnac* que le *Misanthrope*, on se trompe."[5] In other words, the shorter, less known, and rarely performed comedies of Molière are not his worst ones. It is especially to these shorter plays—except for the *Bourgeois gentilhomme*—that Hofmannsthal turned. It is not by accident that he did not adapt *L'Avare*, *Le Misanthrope*, or *Dom Juan*; it is the logical consequence of his close connection with theater. All the plays Hofmannsthal adapted belonged to a type calling for a realization on the stage—far more than the famous character comedies— because their peculiarity consists in their magnificent optical and acoustical effects. The genre I speak of is Molière's *comédie-ballet*, a comedy containing dances and music. Fourteen of Molière's plays, almost half of his work, are *comédies-ballets,* a fact which had been until today generally disregarded by many scholars, as well as men of the theater. Most of the *comédies-ballets* have scarcely been produced, only six or seven of the classical comedies are to be found in the repertory of the theaters. The reason for this unfortunate abstinence is not to be found in their minor value, but rather in the specific character of the *comédie-ballet* itself, which, on the one hand, cannot simply be given as a literary text, and which, on the other hand, calls for technical equipment only few theaters are able or willing to provide.

The *comédie-ballet* originated in the baroque festival, brought to an apex in Saint Germain and the Versailles of Louis XIV. All the arts and armies of artists collaborated in a magnificent joint work of art which represented

[5] Hugo von Hofmannsthal, *Aufzeichnungen* (Frankfurt a.M., 1959), 181.

the power of the monarch. The king himself and the members of the court appeared on stage as actors, especially in the ballet, which was Louis's favorite art. This court is the origin of the *comédie-ballet*. Having been commissioned by the king to write comedies for the court festivals and to perform them with his company, Molière combined the long-isolated arts, drama, music, and ballet, by transforming the mythological and allegorical figures of the traditional *ballet de cour* into pantomimic action and by connecting them with the dialogue-scenes of the play. Jean-Baptiste Lully, who later transformed the genre into the *opera comique*, usually composed the music. *Monsieur de Pourceaugnac* or the *Bourgeois gentilhomme* could almost be called comical operas. (The relationship between Molière and Lully is, in several respects, comparable to the collaboration of Hofmannsthal and Richard Strauss). Outside of the courtly festival tradition, the *comédie-ballet* lost its original shape, the interludes being reduced or eliminated. The reason for this was that no repertory theater was able to afford the technical equipment necessary for the performance of the original version. In addition, a presentation of the original would have taken far too many hours, and the main social motive—the self-presentation of the court in the ballet–did not exist for other theaters. Molière regretted these restrictions, which he had to accept himself when his plays were performed *à la ville*. In the preface to his *comédie-ballet*, *L'Amour médecin* —by the way, it is one of the few personal statements by Molière of which we know—Molière stressed the importance of the playful elements in the comedy, especially the connection of ballet and music:

> On sait bien que les comédies ne sont faites que pour être jouées; et je ne conseille de lire celle-ci qu'aux personnes qui ont des yeux pour découvrir dans la lecture tout le jeu du theâtre. Ce que je vous dirai, c'est qu'il seroit à souhaiter que ces sortes d'ouvrages pussent toujours se montrer à vous avec les ornements qui les accompagnent chez le Roi. Vous les verriez dans un état beaucoup plus supportable; et les airs et les symphonies de l'incomparable Monsieur Lully, mêlés à la beauté des voix et à l'adresse des danseurs, leur donnent sans doute des grâces dont ils ont toutes les peines du monde à se passer.[6]

This is the common starting point for Hofmannsthal and Reinhardt. Both of them tried to overcome the traditional spoken play by means of pantomime and music. Of course it was not their intention simply to restore the *comédie-ballet*, which was impossible anyway. Performances in the theater were no longer festivals; the festival of Louis XIV could at best

---

[6] Molière, *Oeuvres*. Ed. Eugène Despois, Paul Mesnard. (Paris, 1873–93), Les Grands Écrivains de la France. VIII, 30.

be transformed into festive drama. Hofmannsthal and Reinhardt, however, found a way to preserve as much as possible of the original character and included the festival in the performance as part of the plot.

I want to give an example of this: the first, a rather insignificant Molière adaptation by Hofmannsthal, *Die Heirat wider Willen*. Molière's *Le Mariage forcé* was originally divided into three acts, connected or interrupted by pantomimic scenes and by a series of *entrées de ballet*: Sganarelle's misgivings—he is the fiancé who is deceived even before he gets married—are illustrated in various dances by allegorical figures like Jealousy, Sorrow, and Suspicion; magicians and gipsy women are questioned in pantomime, and at the end colorfully dressed figures sing and dance at Sganarelle's wedding. Hofmannsthal did not make use of the numerous intermezzi. He first translated—rather accurately—the one-act version (the play had been reduced to one act after the performance at the court) into a slightly archaic language which was supposed to give the audience the impression of a certain historical authenticity. With regard to Reinhardt's production he closed his adaptation with a pantomime:

> Musikanten spielen auf. Es treten auf Lykast und hinter ihm noch sechs hübsche junge vornehme Leute seinesgleichen. Sganarell reicht seiner Zukünftigen die Hand zum Tanz, diese gerät aber sogleich an den Lykast, von diesem an den nächsten jungen Herrn und so fort. Zugleich sind die beiden Zigeunerinnen abermals aufgetreten, haben Sganarell tanzend und singend nach der anderen Seite hinübergezogen. Er will herüber zu seiner Frau, aber die beiden Philosophen, die mit wilden Sprüngen hereingetanzt kommen, nehmen ihn in ihre Mitte. Indem alle gleichzeitig singen und tanzen und Sganarell von den Zigeunerinnen und den Philosophen abwechselnd hergenommen wird, fällt der Vorhang.[7]

This final pantomime, developing a motif Molière had only hinted, repeatedly reflects the plot of the comedy and predicts Sganarelle's coming fate. It is an ironic point that this pantomime is supposed to be a wedding, the celebration of the forced blessed marriage. Reinhardt stressed the festive character of the play within the play in his production: a servant lit the candles and lifted the curtain, the musicians wore historical costumes and sat on the stage as a kind of frame. The success of this production encouraged Reinhardt.

During the same season the world premiere of *Der Rosenkavalier* took place in Dresden. New, similar projects followed. Inspired by Molière's *comédie-ballet*, Hofmannsthal and Richard Strauss concentrated on musi-

---

[7] Hugo von Hofmannsthal, *Lustspiele II* (Frankfurt a.M., 1965), 94.

cal comedy—*Komödie für Musik* is the subtitle of the *Rose Bearer*—and they planned, in yet closer connection with Molière, another comic opera. We know today that *Ariadne auf Naxos* was planned immediately before the first performance of *Der Rosenkavalier*. Because Reinhardt had helped anonymously in the production of *Der Rosenkavalier*, Hofmannsthal wanted to thank him by translating Molière's *comédie-ballet, La Comtesse d'Escarbagnas*, for a performance in Reinhardt's theater. It was supposed to be a sort of frame to *Ariadne auf Naxos*. This Molière adaptation, unknown thus far, has now been found. Unlike the *Bourgeois gentilhomme*, which Hofmannsthal finally destined to be the frame to *Ariadne*, the original of this comedy was already thought by Molière to be the framework to other plays. It was written as the introduction of the play within the play, when Louis XIV intended to perform a series of ballets. Without an interlude following it, the plot of the comedy is incomplete. Reinhardt never produced the *Countess of Escarbagnas*; we do not know when it was written. It was only known that in 1916 and in 1918 performances were planned.

A further project, recently discovered, was planned immediately after the premiere of the *Rosenkavalier*. Although never realized, it was an indirect contribution to the revival of Molière's work. In February 1911, Hofmannsthal and Carl Sternheim met at Reinhardt's home and decided to translate Molière's plays, obviously for productions made by Reinhardt. Recently discovered letters show that the question was discussed of how to distribute the work of Molière between the two authors.[8] Sternheim began to translate *George Dandin*, which suggested itself, because the first of his bourgeois comedies, *Die Hose*, which definitely is influenced by *George Dandin*, had just had its premiere at Reinhardt's stage. Sternheim did not finish his translation. Instead, Carl Vollmoeller, whose pantomime *The Miracle*, produced by Reinhardt and performed in London, had just been Reinhardt's first great international success, translated *George Dandin*, maintaining Molière's interludes. For centuries *George Dandin* had been performed as a tragic farce, now it again obtained its original form as a *comédie-ballet*: dancing and singing shepherds, choruses of fishermen and bacchants interrupted the spoken scenes—just as in the time of Louis XIV—and dissolved the tragic elements in festive play. It

---

[8] Cf. Carl Sternheim und Hugo von Hofmannsthal, *Briefe*. Ed. Leonhard M. Fiedler. in: *Hofmannsthal-Blätter*, Heft 4., 1970, 243–54. See also: Leonhard M. Fiedler, *Eine Molière-Ausgabe von Hofmannsthal und Sternheim. Begegnungen und gemeinsame Pläne. Ibid.*, 255–63.

was a development inaugurated with *Die Heirat wider Willen*, when actors like Alexander Moissi and Josef Dannegger also appeared as dancers and singers. The combination of tragedy and farce renewed in this way reminds one also very closely of the first version of *Ariadne auf Naxos*, which was performed for the first time in Stuttgart by Reinhardt's company in October 1912, half a year after the premiere of *George Dandin*. This very complex work of art—Hofmannsthal, Reinhardt, and Strauss were the main initiators—can perhaps be called the culminating point in the revival of the *comédie-ballet*. Here the idea of festival and the technique of the play within the play were brought to a climax, and Reinhardt provided equipment which was nearly equal to that of the courtly performances: an *opera buffa* and an *opera seria* company, dancers, an actor's company, an orchestra to play the music by Richard Strauss, and the fantastic baroque scene designs by Ernst Stern. In the original version the play within the play was far more developed than in the revised version of the opera, which is being played now. Hofmannsthal, who according to his former practice translated Molière's *Bourgeois gentilhomme* in an archaic language (using in this case the eighteenth-century translation by Samuel Bierling) retained some of the interludes, which are especially numerous in this *comédie-ballet* (in contemporary performances little is left of these interludes), and varied them. With his dramaturgical changes, Hofmannsthal succeeded in emphasizing the framework character of Molière's text. This was achieved by cutting scenes and by introducing numerous hints into the spoken part which prepared the audience for the opera following the play. A little scene, which as a kind of interlude takes place in the world of the actors, anticipates in a playful manner the plot of the opera. In an ironic way this scene gives the pragmatic motivation for the symbolic confrontation of Ariadne-Zerbinetta attributing it to Jourdain's "sudden order" to perform dance-masquerade and drama at the same time. This ironical element, and with it the accentuation of the festival character, was carried through to the end. Jourdain and his guests on the stage remained visible in the wings as the audience of the opera; from time to time the *bourgeois* gave his comments on the performance (this was mostly done in pantomimic gestures), and Jourdain's last monologue after the opera again accentuated the frame of the play.

This festival within the play can be traced back not only to the tradition of real court festivals, but also to Molière's *comédie-ballet* itself, which at times reproduced such festivals on stage. In addition to that, the *Ariadne* opera itself is akin in style to the Molière adaptations, because the plot could be put together from fragments of Molière. Without Reinhardt the genesis of the *Gesamtkunstwerk—Bürger als Edelmann-Ariadne auf Naxos* —would not have taken place. Every detail of the text and the scenic presentation was discussed with Reinhardt and Ernst Stern, and Hofmannsthal tried to convince Richard Strauss that this work could only be produced by Reinhardt. "Nicht zehn Pferde bringen mich dazu," he wrote to Strauss, "die Adaptierung des Molière und die Einleitungsszene auch nur zu *machen*, wenn es nicht Reinhardt sein sollte, der es herausbrächte. Dies nicht aus sentimentalen Gründen, sondern weil dieses bizarre Ganze nur in Reinhardts Atmosphäre bestehen kann, auf die es berechnet ist."[9] He was right, considering the failure of later performances, which finally led to a new version.

In 1918, as in 1911–12, Hofmannsthal defended Reinhardt against Strauss when they talked about his second, three-act adaptation of *Le Bourgeois gentilhomme*. This problematic adaptation is completely adjusted to Reinhardt's particular way of producing and to Reinhardt's company. For some of the interludes, Strauss used the original music by Lully.

In Hofmannsthal's comedy *Die Lästigen*, this kind of authenticity has been achieved in a very sophisticated way. The masterpiece, which has generally not been appreciated adequately, also owes very much to Reinhardt. Being one of Hofmannsthal's most accomplished plays, it was performed by Reinhardt as a comedy by Molière. A few years after the performance at the Deutsches Theater, when Hofmannsthal sent the play to a friend, he commented as follows: "ein einaktiges Lustspiel, das mit dem gleichnamigen Molières nur Titel und vagste Grundidee gemein hat, eine völlige Improvisation, nach einem Gespräch mit Reinhardt über Gesellschaftscomödie (dessen Gespräche mir immer äusserst anregend sind) in vier oder fünf Tagen hingeschrieben, dann von Reinhardt unter dem Namen Molière gespielt und von der ganzen breitmäuligen Presse, mit einer einzigen Ausnahme, als solcher hingenommen."[10] As a matter of fact *Die Lästigen* has little in common with Moliere's *Les Fâcheux*. There is no passage in Hofmannsthal's play which can be considered to be a

---

[9] Richard Strauss und Hugo von Hofmannsthal, *Briefwechsel*. Ed. Willi Schuh (Zürich, 1964), 148. (Letter of November 4, 1911).
[10] "Aus Hofmannsthals Briefen an Rudolf Pannwitz" in: *Mesa* 5 (1955), 28 (Letter of January 16, 1918).

translation of Molière's text, especially since Hofmannsthal presents a completely different picture of a modern society. It is no longer an individual troublesome person who is being exposed to ridicule and excluded from society in the name of established social standards. Now it is society itself with all its conventions and vanities which is considered as troublesome and annoying. Hofmannsthal tried to veil this actualization and modernization of Molière's theme under many historically authentic reminiscences of and allusions to Molière's time and surroundings. In fact none of Molière's own comedies contains so many local and historical allusions to Paris and the court to Louis XIV as Hofmannsthal's *Die Lästigen*. To give a few examples, Hofmannsthal's play names the Elysée, the rue Royale, the Faubourg Saint-Honoré, Vigarani and Torelli, Le Nôtre and Beauchamps, Lully and La Fontaine. Most of these allusions refer directly to the courtly festivals and the *comédie-ballet*.

Whereas Molière's comedy is supposed to take place at the end of a theater performance, Hofmannsthal shifted the whole action to the foyer of the theater hall belonging to a private palace, where people expect the beginning of a ballet-festival. Norbert Altenhofer has pointed out that the festival which the figures in Hofmannsthal's comedy are going to celebrate is exactly the one at which *Les Fâcheux* (which by the way was Molière's first *comédie-ballet*) was being performed for the very first time.[11] In Hofmannsthal's play this festival is the main topic of conversation, the comedy is the frame and the prelude to the ensuing ballet. The synthesis of Hofmannsthal's comedy with ballet is carried out on different levels—similar to the first version of *Ariadne*. On the one hand, the ballet—it is *Die grüne Flöte*—symbollically reflects the plot of the comedy; on the other hand, there is a metaphorical connection between comedy and ballet, since society itself is understood to be a ballet. In addition, we find, as an introduction to the play within the play, a little song of the program seller, which gives an ironical, rather trivial explanation of the content of the ballet.

Die grüne Flöte was a tremendous success, but *Die Lästigen* seemed neither remarkable nor new, because it was performed without naming the adaptor (the real author) and was considered to be a mere translation of Molière. Later, Reinhardt transferred *Die grüne Flöte* to the Berlin Wintergarten, which was a large show hall, and Hofmannsthal wrote a new

---

[11] Norbert Altenhofer, "Frei nach dem Molière. Zu Hofmannsthals Gesellschaftskomödie 'Die Lästigen'" in: *Festschrift für Bernhard Blume.* Ed. Egon Schwarz (and others) (Göttingen, 1967), 218–37.

prelude, which has been preserved among his literary remains. Thus the fate of *Die Lästigen* and *Die grüne Flöte* was similar to that of *Der Bürger als Edelmann* and the first version of *Ariadne*. Reinhardt's audience seems to have had a special liking for the playful, revue-like spectacle, just as did the audience of the court festivals.

As a result of this revival, in 1917, Carl Sternheim also resumed his interest in Molière. This time he finished his adaptation of *L'Avare*. In 1911 after the premiere of Sternheim's *Die Kassette*, some critics had compared the play with Molière's *Miser*, a parallel which almost suggested itself. Sternheim adapted Molière's comedy now in accordance with the style of his own bourgeois comedies. This is to be seen in the language as well as in his technique of characterizing the figures of the play. Sternheim's Harpagon is a much more pleasant bourgeois than the original Harpagon; his avarice is made understandable by stressing the extravagance of his son Cleanthe, which is only hinted at in Molière's play. The accentuation of Cleanthe's part also gave an opportunity to change Molière's comedy (which originally was not a *comédie-ballet*) into a *comédie-ballet*. Cleanthe organizes a festival. A pantomime is being performed, which ironically alludes to Harpagon's seeking young Marianne's hand, and Harpagon is present at this pantomime. Sternheim's adaptation was made for a Reinhardt production, but surprisingly enough, it was played without the pantomime. Possibly it was censored because of its erotic content. This is no mere supposition when you consider the way censorship was usually exercised by the police. In the copy of the *Miser*, which had to be sent to the censor, Sternheim's stage directions—"Ein schönes junges Mädchen kommt aus der Bettnische, nimmt Hut und Mantille vom Stuhl, knixt tief vor Cleanthe, der ihr groß und gönnerhaft zuwinkt, exit" (on page 48)— were crossed out with the commentary: "Kann bleiben, falls das Mädchen aus dem Speisezimmer kommt." This anecdote is of some importance because it gives an idea of the conditions under which authors and producers had to work before the abolition of censorship.

Reinhardt's most successful and most played Molière production was *Der eingebildete Kranke*, first produced by him in the spring of 1916. Reinhardt used Ludwig Fulda's translation, but again he had Hugo von Hofmannsthal's help: he translated one of the most charming scenes, which Fulda had suppressed, and Reinhardt wanted a ballet of Hofmannsthal's, *Die Schäferinnen*, to be performed at the end of the play. The missing text of this ballet has also been found recently. Hofmannsthal had invented it as an interlude to *Die Gräfin von Escarbagnas* after *Der Bürger als Edelmann* had become the framework to *Ariadne*:

> Im Tal Tempe, dem Sitz des Frohsinns und der Anmut, leben zwei Schäferinnen und freuen sich ihrer Jugend. Die Nymphe des Tales wacht über ihren Spielen. Den reizenden Mädchen nahen sich zwei sehnsüchtige Hirten. Ihre Werbungen weden mit zarter Freude aufgenommen. Unmittelbar nach ihnen betreten zwei Seeräuber das stille Tal. Auch ihre, weit stürmischeren Huldigungen finden freundliche Aufnahme, und als zuletzt zwei Wilde sich annähern, so gewinnen die Schäferinnen auch diesen Beteuerungen huldigender Liebe Geschmack ab. Ein Wink der stets wohlwollenden Nymphe ruft zum Schluss alle Partner des kleinen Spieles zusammen, und jede der freundlichen Siegerinnen tanzt mit den drei so verschieden Gearteten, die es zu bezähmen wußte, einen Reigen.[12]

This little ballet very clearly reflects the themes and style of the pastoral scenes which were inserted in Molière's various *comédies-ballets*, but without using a definite work by Molière as a model.

The success of Reinhardt's various productions of *Le Malade imaginaire* was also due to the genius of Max Pallenberg, whom Reinhardt thought to be the only actor able to improvise. In 1923, with Pallenberg playing Argan, Reinhardt reproduced in a very light, yet realistic way, what in his former Molière productions had always been an indirect dramaturgical reconstruction: a real courtly festival. Max Reinhardt invited friends and guests from all over the world and performed the *Imaginary Invalid* during a real festival in his own baroque castle of Leopoldskron near Salzburg. Just as at the court festivals of Louis XIV, life and theater were confronted. At the reception, Pallenberg, dressed as Argan, welcomed the guests in front of the house with a special greeting for each of them—partly improvised, partly prepared by Reinhardt—but he never acted out of his character, the *malade imaginaire*. Servants in livery with full-bottomed wigs led the guests to the marble hall where the actress who played the part of Toinette served tea. Argan's armchair stood in front of the fireplace, and there were more chairs for the other actors. In the gallery musicians dressed in historical costumes played Lully's music, arranged by Einar Nilson. Reinhardt did not, of course, neglect dance and pantomime in this performance. Instead of Molière's interludes—partly pastoral scenes, partly satirical doctor's ceremonies—he introduced pantomimic intermezzi taken from the *commedia dell' arte* with the masks of Colombine, Arlequin, Polichinelle, Scaramouche, Dottore, and Zerbinetta. Obviously, it was Reinhardt himself who invented these interludes, which are pre-

[12] Unpublished autograph by Hugo von Hofmannsthal.

served in his prompt-book. Between the first and second act it says: "Polichinelle und Colombine treffen sich zu einem zärtlichen Tänzchen. Arlequin und Scaramouche treten von zwei Seiten auf. Sie betten Polichinelle
zur Ruhe und flößen ihm etwas ein. Er brummt, schnarcht und summt im
Schlaf. Inzwischen tanzt Colombine abwechselnd mit den beiden und
läuft dann mit ihnen ab. Polichinelle steht auf, summt und tanzt."[13]

Reinhardt's pantomimes allude to the actual plot of the play; the connection with it, however, is rather loose—which is perfectly in harmony
with the tradition of court festivals.

On the occasion of the performance at Leopoldskron, Raoul Auern-
heimer wrote the following:

> Was Max Reinhardt auf so weit auseinanderliegenden Wegen immer wieder
> anstrebt, ist das ihm vorschwebende Ideal, das Theater von aller Gewerbsmä-
> ßigkeit zu befreien, ihm gleichsam seine erste Unschuld wiederzugeben. Und er
> tut dies, indem er es auf seinen Ursprung zurückführt. Der Ursprung des Thea-
> ters ist, das vergessen die zünftigen Bühnenleiter zuweilen, nicht das Schau-
> spielhaus, sondern das Leben. Daran auf geistreiche Weise immer wieder zu
> erinnern, ist vielleicht die Sendung und sicher das Verdienst Reinhardts. . . .
> Es ist vor allem das auch künstlerisch zu rechtfertigende Verlangen, das thea-
> tralische Kunstwerk aus seinen lebendigen Voraussetzungen abzuleiten.[14]

Perhaps the festival of Leopoldskron had been the most perfect realization of Reinhardt's longing. To us this may seem an anachronism. If we
accept the category of play, however, in its original sense as a set value,
Reinhardt's play is legitimate too, especially through its affinity with the
great model, Molière, who by the way is no longer being interpreted even
in literary criticism as a mere social critic of his time.

---

[13] See: *Max Reinhardt und die Welt der commedia dell'arte. Text-und Bilddokumentation.*
Ed. Edda Leisler and Gisela Prossnitz (Salzburg, 1970).
[14] Neue Freie Presse, No. 21179, Wien, August 26, 1923. (Also in: Günther Rühle, *Theater
für die Republik* (Frankfurt a.M., 1967), 468 f.

Whenever a play is staged, a sort of translation takes place, for the words on some page must be rendered into a different mode and made to move through the air and affect the ear, while spectacle or arrangement impresses the eye. To take the original composition, however, and render it into a living event in another language is a task of such magnitude that one must pause to wonder that Molière or any writer has ever successfully been made over into another language and culture. It is the translators who shoulder much of the burden of bringing the plays of Molière to the world, and the next two essays treat some of the problems—relating successes and failures—of translating the great French comedies.

PROBLEMS AND SUGGESTED SOLUTIONS IN TRANSLATING MOLIÈRE
Samuel Solomon

Of the thirty-three plays in Molière's theater, about half, including most of his greatest, like *Le Misanthrope, Tartuffe, Les Femmes savantes,* and *L'Ecole des femmes,* are in verse, for the most part being in the classic French meter of the Alexandrine couplet.

The first problem therefore that a translator of Molière must face is how he is to render in English Molière's verse. Until fairly recently there would have been little question, with the successful examples of Dryden's and Pope's satire before us, that the best way to catch the satiric and comic inflexion of Molière's Alexandrine couplets in English would be to render them in the heroic couplets of Dryden's satire. Thus when Dryden, in his "Mac Flecknoe," wished to crush his adversary Shadwell, and the poetasters in his coterie, he annihilated them with:

The rest [i.e. Shadwell's literary friends] to some faint meaning make pretence,
But *Sh*—— never deviates into sense.[1]

Nor had the rhyming couplet fallen into disuse, even in twentieth century

---

[1] "Mac Flecknoe" appeared in London in *Miscellany Poems,* in 1684, with Shadwell's name abbreviated to Sh——. The cited text is as appears in *The Poems and Fables of John Dryden* (London: Oxford University Press, 1962).

satire. For instance in *The Saint and Satan*,[2] a satire on Gandhi, the Mahatma is found accusing the "Satanic" British government of the disorder that again ensued on his second civil disobedience movement, after he had repented in fasting of the "Himalayan miscalculation," resulting in violence, of his first:

> And yet though heads were daily broken, battered,
> My faith unshaken still remained unshattered,
> The while I kept on calmly spinning, spinning—
> If only Government had ceased its sinning!
> But no! with power Satanic, violence-tainted
> They really were much worse than I have painted,
> Requited force of Soul with Force of muscle
> And blamed, of all men, me, for all the tussle,
> As though a Saint had not diviner notions
> Of when to start and when to cease commotions!

and ending with:

> be thine the curse, O Britain,
> Tainted with blood and close allied with Satan!

to which Satan replies:

> "Enough!" cried Satan, "You have spun enough!
> It is high time for me to call your bluff.
> On Taint you harp, but I'm expert on Taint,
> A saint, twice sorry, is a sorry saint."

But with the reaction against rhyme, made unfamiliar by its scant use in modern verse, the rendering of Molière into English rhymed couplets has latterly aroused fierce controversy. Thus Richard Wilbur's rhymed *Tartuffe*, when performed at the National Theatre, London, in November 1967 was dubbed by W. A. Darlington,[3] the dramatic critic of the *Daily Telegraph*, an "uninspired jog-trot translation" recalling Victorian pantomimic "doggerel," as though a poet as distinguished as Wilbur could at all descend to doggerel, or the National Theatre be so blind as not to notice it! True, Wilbur's rhymed *Tartuffe* has delighted audiences all over America, where an eminent American scholar of English,[4] noted for his writings on Shakespeare and on tragedy, told me that Molière in English

---

[2] Melusa Moolson (London: India Publications, 1930).

[3] London, the *Daily Telegraph*, 22nd November 1967. Critics in New York, like Clive Barnes and John Simon, have expressed quite other views of Wilbur's rhymed Molière, views endorsed by the enthusiasm of American audiences.

[4] Robert B. Heilman, author of *Tragedy and Melodrama* etc. (Seattle and London: University of Washington Press, 1968).

had at last come alive to him in the Wilbur version. All this however did not deter Sean Day-Lewis, son of the late Poet Laureate, in his review of the B.B.C. Television braodcast of Wilbur's *Tartuffe*, on November 28, 1971, from complaining in the *Daily Telegraph* (London) the following morning, in amusing doggerel, that he wanted "lines not chimes." I had viewed the broadcast myself and decided to make an impromptu survey of other viewers' reactions to the rhymes. Of seven persons consulted, six had found the production wholly delightful, rhymes and all; only one (a B.B.C. specialist) had been disconcerted. It is clear therefore that in actual practice the great majority of contemporary audiences, whether in Seattle or London, can take in their stride a rhymed Molière translation in a competent performance, however acute the discomfort of a critical few, who may console themselves with the thought that half of Molière's theater, being in prose, must be translated into prose.

So much for generalization. Let us examine in particular how modern Molière translators have themselves tackled this problem of rendering Molière's verse plays.

John Wood,[5] in the introduction to his prose translation of *Le Misanthrope and Other Plays*, observes with discernment: "In the verse plays Molière uses metre and rhyme to accentuate the rhythmical and musical qualities of the speech, to give the effect of brilliance appropriate to the scene, as in *The Misanthrope*, and to provide a witty, ironic, or comic counterpoint to the sentiments expressed. Much of this is inevitably lost in a prose translation."

How evident this loss is can be plainly seen by putting into prose Dryden's couplet quoted above: "The rest pretend to some faint meaning, but Shadwell never deviates into sense." Here, though the superb second line with the key word "deviates" remains intact, the effect is clearly muted. Despite the inversion, and the somewhat devious "make pretence" of the first line, the assonance of "faint" and "make" in the verse line, culminating in the rhyme, is immeasurably superior to the prose. It is therefore manifest that to translate Molière's verse plays into prose is to castrate them. Nor, in comedy, is it much more virile to use unrhymed verse, where although some striking lines may be achieved here and there, the general effect remains limp. Morris Bishop, whose translations of some of Molière's prose plays achieve a high competence, is less successful in the verse plays where he uses the unrhymed pentameter. Let us illustrate our conclusion

[5] (Harmondsworth, Middlesex: Penguin Books, 1963)—covering all references to Wood.

from one of the most beautiful couplets in *Le Misanthrope*, where Molière
is, as often at his best, writing on two levels, here the comic and the lyric.
Alceste, nauseated by the flattery the foppish Marquises have been shower-
ing on the backbiting Célimène, bursts out:

> Plus on aime quelqu'un, moins il faut qu'on le flatte:
> A ne rien pardonner le pur amour éclate.''
>
> (II. iv)

At first sight the couplet seems merely comic, showing Alceste as just
perverse, but a closer examination discloses, in the lyric cry of the perfect
second line with its subtle alliteration in 'r' and 'p' climaxing on the
illuminating *éclate*, the depth of Alceste's love that longs to find faultless
the object of his passion. John Wood's prose translation reads: "The
greater one's love for a person the less room for flattery. The proof of true
love is to be unsparing in criticism." Morris Bishop's[6] unrhymed verse
runs: "The more you love, the less you ought to flatter;/And true love is
incapable of pardon." Richard Wilbur[7] has: "The more one loves, the
more one should object/To every blemish, every least defect." Donald
Frame,[8] in a more recent version, translates: "Loving and flattery are
worlds apart./ The least forgiving is the truest heart." Both Wood and
Bishop seem prosaic. Wilbur has completely ignored the beauty of the
second, superior line. Frame comes nearer to the spirit but is perhaps a
little too free.

To keep as near as possible to the original, while trying at the same time
to recapture something of the superb lyricism of the second line, I would
suggest:

> The greatest love to flattery least inclines;
> In pardoning nothing love that's purest shines.

apologizing for the fact that the exigences of English verse and my desire
to reproduce the key word "pur" have compelled me to opt for the super-
lative, rather than the comparative of the first line of the original, the literal
rendering of which has been further subordinated to the paramount
necessity of bringing out the beauty of the perfect second line.

The most recent rendering of *Le Misanthrope* is Tony Harrison's adap-

---

[6] (New York: the Modern Library, Random House; 1957)—covering all references to
Bishop.

[7] *The Misanthrope* (London: Faber, 1958); *Tartuffe* (1964).

[8] *Tartuffe and Other Plays* (New York: New American Library, 1967), including *The
School for Wives*, later cited. Ditto *The Misanthrope and Other Plays* (1968).

tation, which the National Theatre, London, commissioned for its Molière tercentenary production, presented to popular acclaim in February, 1973. Although this version, set in de Gaulle's Paris of 1966, is unfaithful to Molière in many more important respects, it faithfully and successfully retains the rhymed couplet.

One of the most important problems facing any translator is how far he may presume to deviate from an exact rendering of the original. In a verse translation it is sometimes necessary to exercise a little freedom, and such deviation from the letter may be permissible when the requirements of English verse demand it, provided it is not against the spirit of the original. Any deviation from the spirit is traducing and not translating, and is to be condemned.

In one of the most moving scenes of *Le Misanthrope*, Alceste, made desperate with jealousy by the terms of a letter in Célimène's handwriting, which Arsinoë, in her malice, has thrust on him, begs Célimène in the most urgent tones to prove her innocence:

> Rendez-moi, s'il se peut, ce billet innocent:
> A vous prêter les mains ma tendresse consent;
> Efforcez-vous ici de paraître fidèle,
> Et je m'efforcerai, moi, de vous croire telle.
> (IV. iii)

The key line here is the second, betraying the extreme anxiety of Alceste to be able to find Célimène guiltless, and this anxiety is emphasized by the repetition of "s'efforcer"—to try one's best—in the third and fourth lines. Bishop translates:

> Prove if you can this letter innocent;
> My love will even struggle to assist you.
> If you endeavour only to seem true,
> I shall endeavour to believe you so.

Wilbur's version runs:

> Defend this letter and your innocence
> And I, poor fool, will aid in your defense.
> Pretend, pretend that you are just and true
> And I shall make myself believe in you.

Frame translates:

> Show me the innocence of what you wrote;
> My fond heart will forget about the note.
> Just try your best to seem faithful, and know
> That I will try my best to think you so.

While Bishop and Frame have not betrayed Molière's meaning, Wilbur, by adding "poor fool" and mistranslating "Pretend, pretend," may possibly achieve an impermissible laugh, but only at the expense of violating Molière's intention of enhancing the audience's sympathy for Alceste in his near-tragic predicament, which should not fail to leave a tear in their souls[9] at the end of any successful performance of the play. I would suggest the following translation to evoke as much as possible the sympathy for Alceste at which Molière is clearly aiming in this scene, containing, as we should not forget, whole passages lifted from *Dom Garcie de Navarre*, Molière's noncomic play:

> Prove, if you can, this letter innocent:
> My love, to help you do so, will consent:
> Do try your best to show me you are true,
> And I shall try my best to think it too.

The temptation to achieve a laugh in contravention of the spirit of Molière's text must be resisted. I myself was very tempted to do so in translating a passage in the prose play, *Le Mariage forcé*, where the ageing Sganarelle looks lasciviously at the luscious young Dorimène he is about to marry:

> "You are going to be mine, from head to foot", he dribbles, "and I shall be lord of everything; of your lively little eyes, of your naughty little nose, of your luscious lips, of your chewable ears, and your pretty little chin, of your plump little tits, of your . . . .; in short, all your person will be at my own sweet will, and I shall be in a position to caress you as much as I like. Aren't you delighted to marry me, my sweet baby?"

For "delighted to marry me" ("bien aise de ce mariage"), I was sorely tempted to mistranslate, "delighted at the prospect" and so to make sure of a laugh, but desisted, as Dorimène on answering, "Most delighted," makes clear at once that it is not Sganarelle's caresses she seeks, but his name in marriage, under cover of which she means to find younger caresses elsewhere!

One must also be careful to be precise in translating when Molière, to achieve the utmost comic effect, is deliberately being ambiguous. A famous example occurs in Act IV, Scene V of *Tartuffe*, where Elmire, with her husband Orgon hidden under the table, is frantically trying to cut short

---

[9] I have used the expression "a tear in their souls" in antithesis to Donneau de Visé's fine insight in his "Lettre écrite sur La comédie du Misanthrope," included in the first edition of the play in 1667, that *Le Misanthrope*, is one of those comedies that "font continuellment rire dans l'âme."

Tartuffe's furious pawing of her by spurring Orgon to emerge. When all her frenzied coughing fails to make her husband budge, Elmire proceeds in her apparent tête-à-tête with Tartuffe:

> Enfin je vois qu'il faut se résoudre à céder,
> Qu'il faut que je consente à vous tout accorder,
> Et qu'à moins de cela je ne dois point prétendre
> Qu'on puisse être content et qu'on veuille se rendre.
> Sans doute il est fâcheux d'en venir jusque-là,
> Et c'est bien malgré moi que je franchis cela;
> Mais puisque l'on s'obstine à m'y vouloir réduire,
> Puisqu'on ne veut point croire à tout ce qu'on peut dire,
> Et qu'on veut des témoins qui soient plus convaincants,
> Il faut bien s'y résoudre et contenter les gens.
>
> (IV. v)

In this important passage Elmire shifts from "vous" (denoting Tartuffe) to the indefinite "on" which, as wielded by seventeenth-century writers, could flexibly refer to a pronoun of any person, first, second, or third, depending on the context. Here it is employed by Molière as a masterly *double entendre*, so that while Tartuffe laps it all up as referring to him, her remarks are in fact being directed at her husband under the table. It is therefore essential not to translate "on" as "you," which could only refer to Tartuffe, but more vaguely in the third person, so that it could refer both to Tartuffe and to Orgon. While Wood and Bishop have brought this point over correctly, both Wilbur and Frame, with imprecise precision, have fallen for "you." I would suggest translating as follows:

> I see I must agree to everything
> And let you, after all, enjoy your fling;
> And that, with less than this, I cannot claim
> To satisfy the man at whom I aim.
> Doubtless it is not nice to go so far,
> And it's against the grain I cross the bar;
> But, since he still insists, I bow my head,
> As else he'll not believe a word that's said,
> And since he wants the evidence of facts,
> I'll satisfy my man now by my acts.

We have seen how necessary it is to translate exactly where the artistic interests of the original so demand, and in translations of the prose plays there is no reason why we should not be exact throughout within the freedom necessitated by the different syntaxes and linguistics of the two languages.

We have also noted, how, in translating into verse a greater freedom, within narrow limits, is permissible, but this freedom may only be exercised in the same direction as the author was going. A border line case may perhaps be cited from my translation of *Dom Garcie de Navarre*, Molière's "heroic" play, where the neurotic young hero Dom Garcie, who unlike Alceste in *Le Misanthrope*, is jealous without cause, is finally forgiven at the end of the play by the long-suffering Elvire, whom he loves and has repeatedly been wrongly suspecting of loving another. In his final happiness Dom Garcie bursts out:

> Ciel, dans l'excès des biens que cet aveu m'octroie,
> Rends capable mon coeur de supporter sa joie!
> (V. vi)

I have here deliberately translated somewhat freely:

> In the surpassing bliss she now confers,
> Heaven, make my bursting heart worthy of hers!

The addition, through "worthy of hers," of a grateful tribute to Elvire's moral superiority over him enhances the sympathy of the audience (or the reader, for the play, alas, is hardly performed) for Dom Garcie, whose insufficient hold on one's sympathy is the main cause for the failure of the play.

Although the couplet cited above from my translation of *Dom Garcie* rhymes, the work, being a "heroic" play, is rendered mostly in unrhymed verse according to the principles I have advocated in dealing with French classical tragedy and comedy in my forewords to my Racine and Corneille translations[10]—which need not be repeated here. In the two plays, *Amphitryon* and *Psyché* (the latter written in collaboration with Corneille and Quinault), where Molière has adopted a freely rhymed verse pattern, there is no good reason not to follow the rhyme pattern of the original. As an example may be cited a few lines from the prologue to *Amphitryon*, where Mercury cynically comments on Jupiter's success in seducing Alcmène in the form of her absent husband:

> Son stratagème ici se trouve salutaire;
> Mais, près de maint objet chéri,
> Pareil déguisement serait pour ne rien faire,
> Et ce n'est pas partout un bon moyen de plaire
> Que la figure d'un mari.

---

[10] *The Complete Plays of Jean Racine* (New York: Random House, 1967); *Pierre Corneille, Seven Plays* (1969).

This I would render:

> His stratagem has been successful here;
> And yet, in many another case,
> Such a disguise would really get nowhere;
> Not every woman is impressed, I fear,
> By a husband's humdrum face.

Here, the addition of "humdrum," necessitated by the metrical exigences of English verse, merely makes comically explicit what is clearly implied in the original.

The translator of Molière is faced with a number of problems when tackling the peculiarities and eccentricities of speech of his comic characters. There are difficulties of dialect, as in *Dom Juan*, of interjections, incorrect speech, alien speech. The difficulty of dialect is frankly insoluble, when we remember that Molière is played in English from San Francisco, through London to Sydney, and dialects notoriously vary from region to region. Therefore, instead of wearying the reader with a possibly unintelligible jargon on the printed page, it would perhaps be best to translate more or less straightforwardly with a footnote denoting that the character is using a provincial dialect, so that, in performance, the actor may be able to affect a dialect intelligible to the particular audience he is addressing. Interjections offer a problem only a little less difficult. While for the most part they cannot be ignored because they add a distinct flavour to the character speaking, they too vary from country to country—if not from region to region—and from age to age. Thus a liberal use of the contemporary "Egad" or "Begad" for "Morbleu" or "Parbleu" would be insufferable in a modern version, and might perhaps only be permitted a rare inclusion in a play like *Le Misanthrope*, to bring out the period atmosphere of courtly elegance. This, moreover, is an area where there is sometimes a marked difference between American and English usage. Thus, "my," as an interjection, used by some American translators, perfectly acceptable in polite society in America, might raise eyebrows in London. Other differences, not very numerous, between American and British usage are best resolved by the translator at the draft stage, in consultation with a colleague of the other nationality.

In the case of incorrect speech, as in that of the kitchen-maid, Martine, in *Les Femmes savantes*, it would be necessary to reproduce it in translation as the action of the play requires it. Similarly, some attempt should be made to reproduce alien speech, as for instance in *L'Etourdi*, where in

Act V, Scene iii, Mascarille disguises himself as a Swiss guard and apes a heavy German accent. And when, as in Act V, Scene v, of the play, Mascarille continues the charade even after he is recognized by his master, and says he is an honest man and no "Maquerille," it would be quite in order to render this with an equivalent malapropism: "I be no Mackerel, but honest man." All these matters of detail pose pitfalls which the Molière translator must attempt to negotiate to the best of his ability, and for the most part can hope to surmount more or less successfully.

What, however, is of far greater importance is that the translator should be fully alive to the lyric and the near tragic element in many of Molière's comedies, including his finest, which endow them with a complexity and richness that make Molière, at his best, almost certainly the greatest writer of comedy the world has seen. Too many translators of Molière, bewitched by his luxuriantly comic Wood, fail to notice the trees, rooted in lyric and near tragic feeling, that add stature and grace to his theater, and their translations, in consequence, are much impoverished by the absence of these elements subtly infusing the original. Let us cite some examples.

In Act V, Scene iv of *L'Ecole des femmes*, Arnolphe sees falling into ruin all his plans to marry Agnès, an innocent girl, whom he has carefully brought up ignorant of the facts of life, in the hope of thus ensuring her chastity in marriage. Agnès, however, by chance has seen and fallen in love with a young man, Horace, with whom she means to elope, despite all Arnolphe's precautions. Arnolphe upbraids Agnès, whom he himself now truly loves with:

> Malgré tous mes bienfaits former un tel dessein!
> Petit serpent que j'ai réchauffé dans mon sein,
> Et qui, dès qu'il se sent, par une humeur ingrate,
> Cherche à faire du mal à celui qui le flatte!

I would suggest:

> In spite of all my care, to play this part!
> Ah, little snake, I've warmed beside my heart,
> That, consciousness regained, in thankless fit,
> Is out to sting the hand that's fondling it!

The key word here is "petit" in the second line, in which Arnolphe's love for Agnès willy-nilly wells up. Both Bishop and Frame have failed to bring out this important point. Instead of "little snake," Bishop has: "Serpent, whom I have cherished in my bosom" and Frame: "You serpent, whom

I fostered at my breast." Wilbur,[11] moreover, by changing the "serpent" from the second to the third person, with: "Oh, I have warmed a serpent at my breast" is perhaps even remoter from the lyricism that Molière has infused into Arnolphe's "Petit serpent," though very near to the ungrateful snake of Aesop's fable, which Arnolphe doubtless had in mind.

Further on in the scene, in a desperately comic passage, where the distraught Arnolphe tries to win over Agnès with the most passionate pleas, he suddenly touches the brink of tragedy when he broadly hints in contradiction to all the philosophy of wifely fidelity he has been propounding throughout the play, that if only Agnès will marry him, he will turn a blind eye on anything she may do with Horace:

> Sans cesse, nuit et jour, je te caresserai,
> Je te bouchonnerai, baiserai, mangerai.
> Tout comme tu voudras, tu pourras te conduire;
> Je ne m'explique point, et cela, c'est tout dire.

which I would render:

> All night and day I'll pet you without stop,
> I'll kiss you, cuddle you and eat you up;
> You may do anything you like at all:
> I'll go no further; that is saying all.

It is essential here to repeat the "all," like "tout" in the original, even if the English rhyme leaves something to be desired. In comedy, and especially satire, as Byron has shown in *Don Juan*, an occasional ingenious or exiguous rhyme scarcely jars.

In Act II of the delightful *Mélicerte*, performed as a fragment at Court, but left unfinished by Molière, there is a most moving scene between the shepherd Lycarsis and his teenage son, Myrtil. The boy wants to marry Mélicerte, whom he loves, but his father favors two rich shepherdesses, both of whom dote on Myrtil. Lycarsis has just found his son on his knees before Mélicerte, kissing her hands, and scolds him. Myrtil passionately begs his father to relent:

> Le jour est un présent que j'ai reçu de vous;
> Mais de quoi vous serai-je aujourd'hui redevable,
> Si vous me l'allez rendre, hélas! insupportable?
> Il est, sans Mélicerte, un supplice à mes yeux;
> Sans ses divins appas rien ne m'est précieux;
> Ils font tout mon bonheur et toute mon envie;
> Et si vous me l'ôtez, vous m'arrachez la vie.

---

[11] *The School for Wives* (New York: Harcourt Brace Jovanovich, 1971).

LYCARSIS *à part*

> Aux douleurs de son âme il me fait prendre part!
> Qui l'aurait jamais cru de ce petit pendard?
>
> (II. v)

The great charm of this scene lies in the intense lyricism of Myrtil's appeal, which completely wins over Lycarsis, whose paternal tenderness gushes out in the expression, "ce petit pendard."
In translation I would offer:

> Life is a present you have given me;
> But how to thank you for my days that pass,
> If you'll make them unbearable, alas?
> Without my Melicerte, my life's bereft:
> Without her charms divine there's nothing left;
> They constitute my whole bliss, my whole strife;
> And if you take her, you will take my life.

Lycarsis (aside)

> His anguish melts my heart and will be heard.
> Who could have dreamt . . . .? My little gallows-bird!

So much for the lyric element in Molière. The near tragic element, which gives a further dimension to his comedy, needs one or two more examples to illumine the profundity of Molière's art. At the end of Act III, Scene iv of *Amphitryon*, Amphitryon decides to get to the bottom of the mystery that has haunted his house in his absence, making his wife believe that he whom she had admitted to her bed was her husband. This state of affairs had made Amphitryon clutch the hope that she had gone out of her mind, and he poses his dilemma in these words:

> Voyons quelle fortune en ce jour peut m'attendre.
> Débrouillons ce mystère, et sachons notre sort.
> Hélas! je brûle de l'apprendre,
> Et je le crains plus que la mort.

> Let's see today what fate's apportioned me,
> Unravel this imbroglio, learn my plight.
> I long to know what it may be,
> Yet dread it more than death's dark night.

and immediately brings home to the audience that what has been merely a delicious prank for Jupiter is for Amphitryon mortal pain.

Another fine example of the comedy, indeed the farce spilling over into near tragedy is afforded by the monologue of Act IV, Scene vii of *L'Avare*, where the miser, Harpagon, finding his treasure stolen, is literally out of his senses. Aware that his cries of ruin evoke laughter, Harpagon, in a supreme theatrical stroke, is made by Molière to turn in his desperation to the audience: "De grâce, si l'on sait des nouvelles de mon voleur, je supplie que l'on m'en dise. N'est-il point caché là parmi vous? Ils me regardent tous, et se mettent à rire." Here the curmudgeonly Harpagon becomes, for a moment, an object of true tragic pity. There are, of course, no difficulties of translation in this straightforward prose passage, which may run: "Please, if you have news of my thief, I entreat you to let me know. Is he not perhaps hiding there among you? They are all staring at me and bursting out laughing."

Finally, as we began our Molière quotations with a beautiful example of lyricism from *Le Misanthrope*, let us end them with an example of tragic feeling from the same incomparable play. Alceste, suspecting Célimène, not without good reason as it later transpires, of having let him down despite her asseverations of her love, is beside himself:

> Percé d'un coup mortel dont vous m'assassinez,
> Mes sens par la raison ne sont plus gouvernés,
> Je cède aux mouvements d'une juste colère,
> Et je ne reponds pas de ce que je puis faire.
>
> (IV. iii)

Although the verb "assassiner" is sometimes used in comedy preciously, as we use "killing," it is clear that, in this context, it must be given its full tragic force. Any watering down in translation would be betraying Molière at one of his greatest moments. Alceste, at this precise point in the scene, is no longer the comic character he was when the scene began, but a near tragic figure who is fully justified in detesting the flippancy with which Célimène has been treating his tragic passion for her—tragic, because he, like Phèdre, loves against his will, without, however, any cause for guilt like Phèdre.

Bishop translates:

> Since you have struck me with a mortal blow,
> My senses are no longer ruled by reason.
> I yield to the impulses of my anger;
> I'm not responsible for what I do.

Wilbur has:

> Shocked by the knowledge of your double dealings,
> My reason can't restrain my savage feelings;
> A righteous wrath deprives me of my senses
> And I won't answer for the consequences.

Frame's version is:

> Pierced by the mortal blow with which you slay me,
> My reason cannot make my sense obey me;
> Ruled by the anger that I feel for you,
> I cannot answer for what I may do.

Wilbur's very free paraphrase of the first line, in which the key word, *assassinez*, is hopelessly lost, needlessly spoils what might have been a very good translation. My own version is:

> Pierced by your mortal blow that's murdering me,
> My passions from my reason's grip spring free;
> I yield to my just anger against you
> And am not answerable for what I'll do.

It is clear, even from these few pages, how wide a field Molière's theater covers, from low farce,[12] through satire and comedy and lyrical interludes to the brink of tragedy, and it is the duty of the translator of Molière to bring out fully and faithfully all these aspects of his genius, unsurpassed in its richness and depth by any comic playwright in the world.

---

[12] Molière did not eschew the lowest farce in his early days. Even in the generally delightful *L'Etourdi*—his first verse play, and Victor Hugo's favourite comedy—chamberpots are a conspicuous feature, and the first act ends in spectacular permissiveness with Lelio (Lélie) answering the cascade of abuse, in which he has just been inundated for his repeated bunglings, by his valet Mascarille, with: "Il nous le faut mener en quelque hôtellerie,/ Et faire sur les pots décharger sa furie." which I have permissibly rendered: "I'll have to take him to some inn, the spout,/Where he may privily piss his fury out."

MOLIÈRE EN AFRIKAANS
Pierre Haffter

Cet article a pour but d'esquisser l'accueil réservé à notre immortel homme de théâtre par la plus jeune des langues européennes, l'afrikaans. Cette langue est parlée par les descendants des marins et pionniers d'origine hollandaise qui s'étaient établis aux environs du Cap de Bonne-Espérance et qui s'étaient lentement aventurés à l'intérieur du continent africain au courant des XVIIIe et XIXe siècles. Grossie par des immigrants hugenots, que la révocation de l'Edit de Nantes avait chassés de France et fait échouer au Cap, renforcée plus tard par un important élément d'origine allemande et de confession luthérienne, cette population paysanne se distinguait, et se distingue encore, par une religiosité intense et par un amour de la terre. Leur langue parlée, comparée par les administrateurs anglais à un «hollandais de cuisine», s'était émancipée de 1920 à 1930 de la tutelle du néerlandais, la langue officielle et aussi la langue dans laquelle ces pionniers et fermiers lisaient la Bible, et la nouvelle langue fut appelée *afrikaans*, pour bien montrer que ces pionniers avaient trouvé sur le sol africain leur vraie patrie. Eloignée de sa langue génératrice dont elle conserve de nombreux traits linguistiques propres aux dialectes néerlandais du XVIIe siècle, modifiée—ou «créolisée», d'après quelques-uns—au contact des populations hottentotes du Cap, cette jeune langue est avant tout marquée par sa structure verbale où les substantifs abstraits sont bien moins nombreux que dans les autres langues européennes ainsi que par son lexique paysan où abondent les mots concrets et les métaphores dues à un contact étroit avec la terre, le labour et les animaux.

Lexique où la stricte observance du calvinisme a érigé de nombreux tabous, en bannissant par exemple les mots pour *foudre* ou *tonnerre*, car ces deux météores sont définis par l'Ancien Testament comme des attributs sacrés du Seigneur. Hostile à l'art et aux jeux de toute sorte, le calvinisme avait supprimé en grande partie le vocabulaire relatif à ces deux champs sémantiques.

Enfin, s'étant divisé les immenses territoires vides où ils régnaient en maîtres absolus, chacun bien pour soi, ces colons perdaient toute notion de stratification sociale. Après avoir arraché à l'afrikaans le statut de langue officielle, les Afrikaanders se sentirent obligés d'*illustrer* (dans le sens que Du Bellay aurait donné au mot) leur langue par des oeuvres originales et par la traduction en afrikaans d'un certain nombre d'oeuvres occidentales. A l'encontre de leurs compatriotes de langue anglaise, les Afrikaanders ne pouvaient pas librement puiser dans un fonds culturel mis à leur disposition par une lointaine métropole, mais avaient à constituer par eux-memes un patrimoine littéraire et artistique. Bien sûr, la conquête des républiques boers aux mains de l'Angleterre victorienne donna un immense avantage à la littérature anglaise qui par conséquent fournit aux traducteurs afrikaans les premiers points de départ. Quand la deuxième guerre mondiale creusa un fossé entre la population d'origine anglaise et celle afrikaans, cette dernière étant opposée à tout effort militaire susceptible de consolider l'Empire britannique, les littérateurs afrikaans se tournèrent délibérément vers d'autres littératures, vers la littérature française surtout.

L'école afrikaans, cependant, avait donné une place de choix à la seule langue étrangère qu'elle admettait, à l'allemand, le français étant traditionnellement enseigné dans les seules écoles de langue anglaise. Ainsi, l'ouverture vers la littérature française était contrebalancée par un manque total de préparation scolaire. Le public afrikaans—n'en déplaise à Mr. Guicharnaud—n'est justement pas ce «public érudit qui assiste à la représentation d'une oeuvre célèbre du passé»,[1] il n'est pas «prévenu par les impératifs scolaires français»; une mise en scène du *Tartuffe* est «la découverte d'un astre nouveau suspendu dans le vide de l'espace». Telle est donc la situation que rencontraient les premières traductions d'oeuvres rédigées trois siècles auparavant par l'auteur que nous commémorons cette année. Je dis bien, «premières traductions», car au cours des vingt dernières années cette situation s'est quelque peu modifiée.

[1] Le but de cet article n'étant pas polémique, je limite mes renvois à quelques points de départ indispensables et bien connus des critiques moliéresques. Les titres des ouvrages dont proviennent mes citations sont: Jacques Guicharnaud, *Molière: Une aventure théâtrale* (Gallimard, 1963); Jill Dorothy Daugherty, *Le Tartuffe afrikaans: Un examen de deux adaptations afrikaans du «Tartuffe» de Molière*, Thèse, M. A. (Univ. de Prétoria, 1970); J. Vinay et B. Darbelnet, *Stylistique comparée de l'anglais et du français* (Didier, 1968); Jacques Schérer, *Structures de Tartuffe* (Paris, 1966); et Guy Michaud, *Les Luttes de Molière* (Genève: Slatkine, 1968, réimpression.)

Table des traductions afrikaans publiées jusqu'en 1968

Titre original	Traducteur	Titre de la traduction*	Présen-tation**	Date
Le Malade imaginaire	?	Die ingebeelde sieke (Le malade imaginaire)	Radio	1943
Le Malade imaginaire	A. F. H. van Dijk	Die Ieperkonders (Les hypocondriaques)	Théâtre	1950
Le Bourgeois gentilhomme	?	Die adellike burger (Le bourgeois noble)	Radio	1944
Le Médecin malgré lui	F. P. van der Merwe	Dokter teen wil en dank (Médecin contre son gré)	Radio	1944
Le Médecin malgré lui	U. Krige	Dokter teen wil en dank (Médecin contre son gré)	Théâtre	1966
Les Précieuses ridicules	?	Die aanstellerige dames (Les dames "chichiteuses")	Radio	1945, 1962
L'Avare	A. F. H. van Dijk	Die Vrek*** (L'avare)	Théâtre	1952
L'Avare	F. P. van der Merwe	Die Gierigaard*** (L'avare)	Radio	1953
Tartuffe	J. Olivier	Die Huigelaar (L'hypocrite)	Radio	1953
Tartuffe	J. Brink	Tartuffe	Théâtre	1956
Tartuffe	G. Beukes	Tartuffe	Théâtre	1967, 1968
Dom Juan	?	Don Juan	Radio	1957
Les Fourberies de Scapin	B. Smit	Die jakkalstreke van Scapino (Les tours de Scapin)	Théâtre	1958, 1967
L'Ecole des femmes	L. van der Merwe	Die Bruidskool (L'école des épouses)	Théâtre	1962
Sganarelle	N. Ferreira	Sganarelle	Théâtre	1964

* Les re-traductions en français se veulent aussi fidèles que possible au titre de la version afrikaans, pour que le lecteur puisse apprécier les modifications que le titre original a subies.

** Par «radio», on entend la section afrikaans de la South African Broadcasting Corporation; sous «théâtre» sont comprises les représentations données par des troupes d'amateurs et par des professionnels.

*** Ces deux mots sont des synonymes, dont le premier, *vrek*, est plus usuel, mais considéré comme trop rustre par le second traducteur en raison du voisinage phonétique avec *vrek* (= crever!). On voit que ce premier titre propose au public non-averti un climat particulier.

Cette table est révélatrice à plus d'un égard. D'abord, elle documente l'importance de la radio afrikaans qui, devant le manque de troupes professionnelles désireuses de présenter à leur public des textes d'origine étrangère, se chargea du rôle de pionnier. A partir de 1962, la scène prédomine nettement, car c'est au cours de cette année que les agences de spectacles (Performing Arts Council) généreusement subventionnées par l'Etat virent le jour. Les conditions propres à la diffusion radiophonique imposèrent aux premiers traducteurs des modifications notables, ce qui poussa les troupes à faire appel à de nouvelles traductions pour leurs représentations scéniques. Ensuite, on notera l'absence des spectacles de cour (*La Princesse d'Elide*), d'*Amphitryon* et du *Misanthrope*, c'est-à-dire de ces oeuvres qui forment le pôle opposé de la farce. Il n'est pas étonnant que les traducteurs les plus connus, Uys Krige et Bartho Smit, aient mis leur talent au service de deux farces, *Le Médecin malgré lui* (Krige) et les *Fourberies de Scapin* (Smit). Trop conscients des difficultés que les grandes comédies opposent à leur langue si fortement empreinte par une tradition paysanne, les deux traducteurs, qui sont aussi des écrivains de renom bien au diapason de la culture française, partagent cette tendance moderne à faire confiance plutôt au déchaînement scénique qu'au raffinement linguistique des dialogues entre Alceste et Philinte. Enfin, les titres donnés aux versions afrikaans de *Tartuffe* sont significatifs: le premier titre qui explicite soigneusement un des traits de caractère fondamentaux du protagoniste permet à ses successeurs de reprendre le titre original. Le public sortait de son «état de virginité» (Guicharnaud) et s'apprêtait à considérer la pièce comme un phénomène historique. Comme nous le verrons, le troisième traducteur de *Tartuffe* soumettra à ses spectateurs une version solidement ancrée dans le XVIIe siècle.

En outre, enthousiasmés par la première mise en scène de *Die vrek* (*L'Avare*) en 1951, les Afrikaanders se plaisaient à rapprocher de ce spectacle inoubliable les mises en scène qui allaient suivre, au risque de perdre en ingénuité ce qu'ils gagnaient en érudition. L'intérêt particulier réservé à *Tartuffe* nous invite à examiner plus en détail les versions afrikaans de cette pièce. A toutes fins utiles, laissons de côté l'adaptation radiophonique où trop est sacrifié aux exigences techniques qu'impose la radiodiffusion et concentrons-nous sur les deux versions scéniques dont la comparaison a d'ailleurs fait le sujet de la très utile thèse de maîtrise de J.D. Daugherty. Comme toutes les autres traductions d'oeuvres moliéresques en vers, les deux versions du *Tartuffe* sont en prose; ni Madame Brink ni Mr. Beukes n'ont tenté d'émuler les alexandrins du traducteur allemand Rudolf Alexander Schroeder. Suivant en ceci la plupart de leurs devanciers et collègues, nos deux traducteurs ont assez sévèrement manipulé les répliques originales, en abrégeant les discours originaux et en répartissant parfois les éléments du raisonnement sur plusieurs répliques. Ecoutons Elmire se justifier (IV.3) :

> Est-ce qu'au simple aveu d'un amoureux transport
> Il faut que notre honneur se gendarme si fort?
> [Et ne peut-on répondre à tout ce qui le touche
> Que le feu dans les yeux et l'injure à la bouche?]
> Pour moi, de tes propos je me ris simplement,
> Et l'éclat là-dessus ne me plaît nullement.

Brink

> Une femme rangée n'a aucunement besoin de faire le policier quand on lui chuchote à l'oreille quelques belles paroles. D'ailleurs, je me fâche beaucoup à entendre les gens vous débiter de ces vieilles balivernes.[2]

Les deux vers entre crochets ne sont pas rendus en afrikaans, parce que la traductrice les considère sans doute comme répétitifs. Le tour impersonnel et abstrait «il faut que notre honneur . . .» est concrétisé en afrikaans vers «une femme rangée . . .» où la traductrice compense (dans le sens que Vinay-Darbelnet donnent au terme) la perte de l'abstrait par la généralisation, procédé astucieux dans une langue peu douée pour l'abstraction. A l'interrogatif rhétorique de l'original se substitue une affirmative qui ne feint plus d'attendre une réponse connue d'avance. Notons aussi la concrétisation du verbe *se gendarmer* par *faire le policier*. Difficile à retraduire est l'idiome afrikaans *ou kooie uit die sloot haal*, littéralement *aller chercher de vieilles vaches dans le ravin*, qui transpose au figuré cette expérience des paysans afrikaans qui se seraient bien gardés de toucher aux charognes abandonnées aux vautours dans un ravin.

Ces quelques observations dues à l'examen détaillé d'une seule réplique permettent assez bien de cerner les problèmes auxquels les traducteurs afrikaans doivent faire face. Ils relèvent en premier lieu de la théorie de la traduction. Beaucoup de ces différences qui d'après Vinay-Darbelnet distinguent le français de l'anglais s'appliquent dans une plus large mesure à la stylistique comparée du français et de l'afrikaans, le dernier préférant de loin le concret à l'abstrait; les idiomes sont encore fortement attachés à des expériences concrètes qui restent présentes à l'esprit du sujet parlant,

---

[2] Dis glad nie vir 'n ordentlike vrou nodig om polisieman te speel as iemand 'n paar mooi woorde in haar oor fluister nie. Buitendien vererg ek my sommer as mense sulke ou kooie uit die sloot haal.

même s'il vit en ville. Non moins problématique se révèle l'usage des pronoms personnels dans les formules de politesse. L'afrikaans utilisait, jusqu'à une date assez récente, pour la deuxième personne le pronom *jy*, sans faire de distinction entre les personnes de respect et les amis intimes, sans distinguer donc entre *tu* et *vous*. Bien entendu, cette langue connaissait un pronom *u* (vous), mais celui-ci était réservé à Dieu. Avec l'effritement de la culture paysanne au sillage d'une urbanisation accélérée, la distinction entre une formule marquant l'intimité et une autre marquant le respect devenait inévitable: l'ancien pronom *u* a dû céder une partie de son royaume. Cette transformation «microscopique» est documentée dans l'exemple suivant où un écart de onze ans sépare les deux versions afrikaans (Dorine à Marianne, II.2):

> Allez, ne croyez point à Monsieur votre père.
> Il raille.

> *Brink* (1956)
> Ne crois pas ton papa; c'est encore une de ses bourdes.[3]

> *Beukes* (1967)

> Ne vous effrayez pas, mademoiselle, votre père n'a fait qu'une blague.[4]

Les deux impératifs de la retraduction remontent au même impératif négatif afrikaans (*moenie*: tu ne dois pas . . .) dont le second est placé sur le niveau du respect par l'addition de *juffrou* (mademoiselle); la traduction postérieure utilise aussi le possessif poli *u vader* où la traduction antérieure s'était encore contentée du possessif moyen *jou pa*. La même tendance vers une langue cultivée se reconnaît dans la traduction postérieure où *vader* (père) remplace le quotidien *pa* (papa).

Aux nombreux problèmes suscités par le génie si différent des deux langues s'ajoutent les différences d'ordre social et religieux, sensibles avant tout dans une pièce dont le protagoniste est un imposteur religieux. Tartuffe, actif dans une époque définie et dans un pays catholique, exige un grand nombre d'adaptations (de nouveau dans le sens que Vinay-Darbelent donnent à ce terme), si son imposture est à rendre tangible pour des spectateurs calvinistes. Nos deux traducteurs se sont-ils efforcés de rapprocher le personnage de leur public? Voici comment ils adaptent le célèbre récit d'Orgon à la situation religieuse locale (I. 5):

---

[3] Moenie jou pa glo nie; dis sommer weer een van sy kaskenades.
[4] Moenie ontsteld wees nie, Juffrou, u vader het maar net 'n grap gemaak.

Chaque jour à l'église il venait d'un air doux
Tout vis-à-vis de moi se mettre à deux genoux
Il attirait les yeux de l'assemblée entière
Par l'ardeur dont au ciel il poussait sa prière ;
[Il faisait des soupirs, de grands élancements,
Et baisait humblement la terre à tous moments ;]
Et lorsque je sortais, il me dévançait vite
Pour m'aller à la porte offrir de l'eau bénite.

Brink

Il venait régulièrement à l'église, en baissant profondément sa tête avec la plus grande dévotion, juste devant moi. Jamais je n'ai entendu des prières aussi ferventes au cours d'une heure de prières. A la porte de l'église, il me saluait toujours avec humilité.[5]

Beukes

A chaque culte, il venait s'agenouiller humblement à mes côtés, et par la sincérité et l'abandon de ses prières il attirait les yeux de toute la communauté. Mais ce n'était pas tout : dans son humilité, il savait toujours se mettre à la porte de l'église pour m'offrir un peu d'eau sainte.[6]

Déjà la première lecture met en lumière les différences entre les deux versions qui toutes les deux omettent les éléments des vers entre crochets. Joan Brink situe les gestes de l'imposteur délibérément dans le rituel calviniste, alors que Beukes aspire à faire participer ses spectateurs aux coutumes catholiques. Quel Sud-Africain ne connaîtrait pas ces têtes, baissées pendant les prières ? Un public qui ne s'agenouille pas au temple considère au mieux le récit donné par Beukes comme un enrichissement de son bagage culturel, tout comme «l'eau bénite» que Beukes doit rendre par *heilige water* (eau sainte), l'afrikaans étant dépourvu de l'équivalent direct du terme catholique. Quelle conviction de nouveau, dans le texte de Mme Brink : le dimanche sous les porches de leurs temples, tout comme les farmers américains, les Afrikaanders ont coutume de tenir parfois de longues conversations, qui représentent pour ces fermiers vivant éloignés les uns des autres un événement social important. Le salut humble, encore «transporté» par la ferveur religieuse, du Tartuffe afrikaans est parfaite-

---

[5] Hy het gereeld kerk toe gekom en met die grootste ootmoed reg voor my sy kop diep gebuig. Nog nooit het ek sulke gloeiende gebede tydens 'n biduur gehoor nie. By die kerkdeur het hy my altyd nederig gegroet.
[6] Elke diens het hy nederig langs my kom kniel, en deur die erns en oorgawe van sy gebede het hy die oë van die hele gemeente op hom gevestig. Maar dit was nie al nie : met groot nederigheid het hy altyd gesorg dat hy by die uitgang van die kerk gereed staan met 'n bietjie heilige water om my aan te bied.

ment conforme à la réalité. Le même souci de l'actualité est présent dans les premières paroles de Tartuffe (III.2):

> Laurent, serrez ma haire avec ma discipline.

Brink

> Laurent, va mettre mon livre de psaumes dans ma chambre.[7]

Beukes

> Voici ma verge, mets-la dans ma chambre.[8]

Certes, l'autoflagellation et le port de la haire, si importants pour situer l'hypocrite dans sa carnalité, ne sont pas mentionnés par Brink, alors que Beukes se permet la concentration sur la seule verge comme instrument de pénitence, mais ce renvoi aux mortifications physiques—feintes d'ailleurs—fait simplement appel au bagage culturel de spectateurs qui ont banni la flagellation de leurs habitudes religieuses. Brink lui substitue un objet de dévotion bien protestante, le livre de psaumes, ancré lui aussi, comme le salut dévot à la sortie du temple, dans la vivante réalité du culte calviniste. Ce livre que le Tartuffe de Madame Brink mentionne avec onction est visible le dimanche soir à la main de tous les pratiquants, qu'ils descendent de leurs voitures étincelantes ou qu'ils se pavanent endimanchés et chapeautés. Pour *jeûnes*, autre methode soi-disant pratiquée par le Tartuffe original, nos traducteurs recourent à *selfkastyding* (mortification) et ôtent ainsi à la punition le côté corporel. Le «ciel» que Tartuffe invoque avec prédilection apparaît dans nos textes sous forme de *Genadige Alwetende* (Brink—l'omniscient plein de miséricorde) et *Algenade* (Beukes —grâce suprême), deux termes préférés par les calvinistes parce qu'ils évitent de parler de Dieu à travers ses attributs météorologiques et aussi parce que *genade* (grâce) joue dans la doctrine calviniste un rôle essentiel. Parfois, nos traducteurs emploient *Skepper* (Créateur) ou *Hoër Hand* (une main supérieure), deux circonlocutions bien connues de leurs spectateurs. L'afrikaans est si sensible à ce commandement qui défend aux fidèles de nommer Dieu mal à propos que les traducteurs sont obligés de modifier des locutions parfaitement anodines aux oreilles du spectateur français. Si la colère arrache à Damis (III. 1)—«Que la foudre sur l'heure achève mon destin!»—le jeune homme enfreint ce même commandement, car la foudre est une des manifestations de Dieu et ne peut être mentionnée

---

[7] Laurent, neem asseblief my gesangboek op kamer toe.

[8] Hier, neem my géselroede, gaan bêre dit in my kamer.

qu'avec crainte. Aussi Joan Brink se tire-t-elle d'affaire par «Que les montagnes tombent sur moi!»[9], idiome afrikaans sémantiquement semblable à l'original mais heureusement libre de mots tabous. Autre adaptation notable: inconnus des Calvinistes, les saints n'ont pas domicile en afrikaans, ce qui invite nos traducteurs à utiliser «prophète» à leur place, les prophètes de l'Ancien Testament jouissant parmi les Calvinistes d'une réputation presque aussi considérable que celle accordée aux saints par les peuples catholiques.

Après tout ceci, il faut se féliciter du fait que la famille d'Orgon soit «vue hors de son histoire» (Guicharnaud). Des allusions historiques trop nombreuses auraient infiniment compliqué la tâche de nos deux traducteurs. Retenons que les «galants de cour» (III.2) auxquels Tartuffe se sent supérieur représentent une difficulté majeure pour cette langue qui n'a jamais connu ni princes ni comtes. Brink compense astucieusement l'élément de «cour» par celui de «jeunesse» et corrige «galant» par «élégant»: les rivaux inoffensifs de Tartuffe sont chez elle des *swierige jongkerels* (jeunes gens élégants) que rien n'emprisonne dans une période historique particulière. Que les déclarations de Tartuffe (III. 3) utilisent en partie un vocabulaire démodé au moment de la création, Elmire l'a déjà dit en se justifiant devant sa famille par l'images des «vieilles vaches». Joan Brink réussit admirablement à exposer ce décalage lexical en recourant à des termes bibliques et des tournures hollandaises vieillies; sa déclaration afrikaans est sans aucun doute cette «savoureuse mosaïque de dévotion et de galanterie» dont parle Jacques Schérer, quoique sa mosaique présente des couleurs entièrement différentes. Mais que faire du Prince et de tout le dénouement si âprement discuté par les spécialistes? Examinons le début du discours de l'Exempt (V.7):

> Nous vivons sous un prince ennemi de la fraude,
> Un prince dont les yeux se font jour dans les coeurs
> Et que ne peut tromper tout l'art des imposteurs.

Brink

Nous l'avons à l'oeil depuis longtemps.[10]

Beukes

Notre roi a percé son masque mensonger.[11]

---

[9] Maar ek sê jou, berge kan op my val!
[10] Ons het lankal 'n ogie op hom.
[11] Ons koning het deur sy leuenmasker gesien.

Fidèle à son concept, Brink élimine délibérément le prince; chez elle, l'autorité qui veille sur la tranquillité de la famille est la police au nom de laquelle parle l'officier.

Qui est choqué par ce radicalisme a intérêt à relire le passage où Guicharnaud rappelle que le Prince «est en plus chef de la police». Beukes conserve le roi et sa perspicacité supérieure; il le fait même apparaître en personne au finale qui rappelle de loin le dernier tableau de la mise en scène de Louis Jouvet. Cette apparition personnelle de roi chez Beukes nous laisse songeurs. Serait-elle à mettre au même compte que les nombreuses autres additions rencontrées dès l'acte premier? La comparaison des deux traductions avec l'original montre que des répliques entières ont été ajoutées, que des jeux de scène ont été développés à l'extrême et que de nombreux calembours ont été plaqués sur le dialogue original. Ces additions sont toujours communes à Brink et à Beukes: elles semblent provenir d'une source extérieure. Cette source est l'adaptation anglaise de Miles Malleson qui a fourni à nos deux traducteurs leur point de départ. Les nombreuses simplifications du texte, que cet article a passées sous silence pour mieux mettre en relief la problématique linguistique et extra-littéraire, ne sont pas le fruit d'une vision personnelle sud-africaine, mais bien l'héritage d'une réadaptation du *Tartuffe* vu à travers le prisme anglais, avec tous les dangers que cela comporte. Cette situation est sans aucun doute à déplorer, car elle amoindrit les mérites des deux traducteurs. Ces mérites sont incontestables. Dans ce pays marqué par la forte influence de l'église protestante, qui d'ailleurs a réussi jusqu'ici à bannir de la scène des pièces jugées «athées» comme *Putsonderwater* du traducteur du *Médecin malgré lui*, Bartho Smit, Joan Brink a eu le courage de camper son Tartuffe solidement dans la réalité du spectateur et de faire de son texte une savoureuse satire de la bigoterie calviniste. Sa traduction engage le public à chaque pas et fait courir sur le dos du spectateur quelques-uns de ces frissons qu'ont pu sentir les honnêtes gens du XVIIe siècle. A travers le travail de Brink, l'historien de la littérature française reconnaît avec stupeur combien le texte moliéresque était *engagé* et voit se dresser l'ombre de la Confrérie du Saint Sacrement dans certains compte-rendus publiés lors de la représentation de 1956.

En tant qu'actrice professionnelle et animatrice de renom, chargée de mettre en scène sa propre traduction, la traductrice fait une contribution valable à cette discussion qui porte sur la manière de faire revivre les oeuvres du passé. Gerhard Beukes, écrivain et lettré, n'a pas essayé d'imiter l'entreprise hardie de sa devancière. Commanditée par l'agence des spectacles de la Province du Cap, sa traduction se veut historique et s'efforce à grand-peine de préserver l'ambiance de l'époque ainsi que les allusions au rituel catholique. Ses efforts sont contrecarrés par la nature même de la langue afrikaans qui lui impose souvent des idiomes rustiques et une syntaxe lapidaire mal appropriés au climat urbain de l'original. C'est à coup sûr une traduction plus fidèle, mais une traduction qui fait songer à l'aveu de Guy Michaud : «Je l'avouerai, ce comique de Tartuffe le plus souvent m'échappe». Beukes a sans doute fourni un texte qui remplit d'admiration le Sud-Africain reçu à l'examen de B.A., mais laisse sur leur faim ces amis de Molière qui voudraient rendre au grand comédien l'emprise directe sur le public contemporain.

The task is always before us, to continue validly, sensitively, and imaginatively to stage the comedies of Molière. There follow two essays which attack the problem directly. Opinions vary, but the debates and expressed attitudes of those who actually participate in the live preservation of Molière's plays are not what are called outside academic circles "academic questions." They are vital and significant. The last essay of this section describes the fate of Molière on French television, a medium that has absorbed much of traditional theater and created a sort of drama all its own.

ON STAGING MOLIÈRE TODAY
Frédéric O'Brady

Not very long ago a student at Princeton declared that no play written before 1900 should ever be performed again. We must refrain from arguing with such a compact statement on the grounds that it is somewhat too peremptory to be quite mature, and perhaps founded on too scanty information about plays, acting and the theater in general. Besides, in matters of taste, nobody has ever persuaded, converted, or even shaken anybody. It would be also pointless to remind the student that very few plays—if any—written between, say, 1900 and 1925 are worth reviving. Thus the suggested repertory would merely consist of the highly interesting but numerically poor and in many instances wildly overestimated theater of the absurd, with a sprinkling of Shaw, O'Neill, Williams and Giraudoux—the latter being often quite touchingly misunderstood by Americans, by the way (but that is another story). Whom else can we think of? Maeterlinck? Schnitzler? Bernstein? Anouilh? Albee? Miller? The first victims of such a holocaust would be, of course, the classics. Or rather those who might enjoy them still. However, we have lately seen performances of Elizabethan and French "Louisian" plays that made us wonder whether they had not better be left alone. Theatrically speaking, our times are just as confused as seen from other points of view; and staging Molière's plays, for example, brings clarity as to what the Occidental theater used to mean at its best. Moreover, it seems to be the most efficient way to train actors, even if they will never play a classic again during their whole career. Supposing I were to discuss the student's sweeping verdict, I fancy this would be my first argument, irrelevant as it might seem to him.

It would be senseless and about impossible to produce and direct a classic today, either *Tartuffe* or *Othello, Bérénice* or *The Tempest*, as a historical retrospective, trying to "recapture" the atmosphere of the times. The simplest and maybe the best way to do justice to those works is to perform what is written, but felt, shown and seen through our present-day theatrical intelligence—such as it is—and new, enhanced possibilities, both technically and mentally. Let us remember that the intellectual actor appeared later than the electric light. Both achieved one of those rare revolutions that really brought about some improvement.

We will discard the childish "innovation" attempts to stage Molière in twentieth-century dress, along with some supposedly witty business using cigarettes, television, and rock 'n roll records, but otherwise "respecting" the text. We are neither shocked nor even startled at this, and we are aware of the candid argument that even Racine's and Corneille's Greek or Roman heroes appeared in Versailles court apparel at the time those plays were new. Should we then dismiss the idea of visually modernizing Molière on the grounds that our image of history has changed since Louis XIV? We would rather object to the experiment because today the shifting of fashions centuries ahead looks like an innocent joke and no more, whereas it was sheer convention in the seventeenth-century. When Armande, in the first scene of *Les Femmes savantes*, is doing yoga exercises during her long speech about marriage, we feel like telling her that uttering those lines in breathless staccato slices is not Molière and is not the play. We all know, of course, that there is a distinct and unfortunate tendency afoot nowadays to perform a play different from the one mentioned in the program.

The trouble with such conception is that mid-twentieth-century disguise cannot stop there. A performance is based on rhythm; and modern dress simply does not allow us to deliver lines, to move about, to sit and rise, trying to do justice to Molière. Sprawling over streamlined Danish armchairs, pouring whisky into Dunhill glassware just will not match

> Vous en voulez beaucoup à cette pauvre cour,
> Et son malheur est grand de voir que chaque jour
> Vous autres beaux esprits vous déclamiez contre elle,
> Que de tous vos chagrins vous lui fassiez querelle . . . .
> (*Les Femmes savantes.* IV. iii)

In today's atmosphere we would massacre such words—no gesture made in modern clothes could make sense accompanying them. Besides, what court is Clitandre, wearing a double-breasted suit *de chez Cardin*, alluding to? De Gaulle's?

While we are trying to establish what the staging of a Molière comedy should *not* be, we might as well reflect on another tendency of which Molière is far from being the only victim. Since our era has no playwright of a statue commensurate with its preoccupations (which are gigantic indeed), this generation of directors is prone to reassess, reinterpret, and even rewrite the classics. This is a penchant parallel to a paranoiac trend in modern literary criticism: namely, the assumption a) that writers do not say all they ought to say; b) that they do not know what they have said until the critic kindly explains it to them; c) that whatever they managed to express without such guidance is too obscure for the common reader; and d) that fiction, poetry, and drama are full of subconscious involuntary symbolism, waiting to be detected by the critic. Thus we saw a Célimène ogling for audience complicity during her quarrel with Alceste in the fourth act of *Le Misanthrope*, and some awkward business between Tartuffe and Orgon to "prove" homosexual undercurrents in the latter's attachment to the imposter. Nothing in Molière even allusively suggests these attitudes.

No doubt we are able today to play Molière with infinitely more efficient timing and subtlety than he and his company ever dreamed of. Timing, the very essence of comedy acting as we see it now, was hardly thinkable on a stage where members of the audience could come and go and converse loudly, engage in fights, while actors politely waited till the disturbance was over (see Eraste's speech in the first scene of *Les Fâcheux*); and there was no room for delicate insinuation by tone and stage business or facial expression to audiences that were practically never quiet, let alone respectful, in theaters where you had to hurl each line over candle footlights, and then step back into gloom to let your partner do his bit in turn. There was of course no director in our sense of the word, and if Molière—and his contemporaries—did not think it worthwhile to sprinkle *didaskalia* between their lines, e.g., *A pause—He goes to the window—She opens her fan—He throws his hat at the valet*, etc., the reason for such omissions was not their implicit trust in actors, but the obvious uselessness of precision. Nor was it necessary or imaginable to explain "psychological motivations" to actors and waste precious rehearsal time with such empty talk, as it is customary today. For in Molière's time, people who fancied themselves intellectuals did not dream of playing in a theater, as they often do now. Actors in Molière's day relied on their instinct and imagination as real actors still do. But gifted actors have always been as rare as good painters or composers, notwithstanding the widespread modern myth that play-acting can be taught to anybody. And notwithstanding the trend to write and produce plays that are just raw material for self-appointed directors, and that, in their subjective arbitrariness, can neither prove nor disprove playacting competence. The only recognizable style in most of these plays is a naive pretension to impart various feelings of discomfort to the audience—hundreds of such plays might have been written by the same little shortsighted and unkempt but enthusiastic coed, and supervised by the same assistant professor of creative writing, who also believed in spontaneity and latent expressive power in everyone.

This brings us to a rather flat and authoritative statement: nothing can prove acting ability more convincingly than a bit of Molière. For the audition of an actress, Armande's first speech in *Les Femmes savantes* would show talent—or its absence—without the shadow of a doubt; as a young man could satisfy any director's curiosity by acting out Alceste's defeat in the fourth act of *Le Misanthrope* (lines 1371 to 1390): "Ciel! rien de plus cruel peut-il être inventé?" or Tartuffe's declaration to Elmire: "L'amour qui nous attache aux beautés éternelles" (III. 3) etc, precisely because there are no stage directions in the text.

Molière, an actor himself, never wrote a useless line. The shortest parts in his plays, such as the tailor's apprentice in *Le Bourgeois gentilhomme* or DuBois in *Le Misanthrope*, are all highly rewarding for a young actor. The acting value of Molière's texts lies in their density, their style depends on delivery. The virtues of sincerity and spontaneity are singularly in-sufficient for a proper Molière reading. Actors nowadays are sometimes encouraged not to read the whole play in which they are supposed to act, so as to safeguard their spontaneity. Any nonsense is conceivable in drama teaching. A New York production of *The Misanthrope*, in Richard Wilbur's virtuoso version, a few years ago, had Alceste expostulate quietly with Philinte in the first act, and shout angrily in the fifth; whereas Molière obviously wanted the contrary (I. i. verses 162–172; V. i. verses 1517–1524); it showed Alceste jealous of an elderly fool who looked like a Greenwich Village antique dealer, in spite of what is said of Oronte (Philinte's first speech in the fourth act); and both Arsinoé and Célimène *sat* through their bitchy dialogue in the third act, heedless not only of Molière's contrary indication (verses 877–878), but of simple theatrical sensitivity as well. Blunders arise through faulty information, too. Some American directors consider *Marquis* a title only middle-aged men can claim, and thus we see portly, sedate and deadpan Acastes and Clitandres, instead of exuberant and overdressed boys of seventeen. Or, although it is likely that a seventeenth-century French bourgeois made himself comfortable on entering his house, it is in unnecessary bad taste to have Tartuffe's Orgon doff his wig in the presence of his wife and daughter, displaying a twentieth-century vision of baldness. It is a different kind of comic situation, not Molière's.

But since modern literature and the movies have probed human behavior to hitherto unsuspected psychoanalytical depths, and shown us terrifying enlargements of it, we may use these discoveries in staging Molière without "betraying" his intentions, on the contrary, improving on a traditional, all too slick, delivery of his alexandrins, handed down from the times when silence of more than three seconds were unthinkable onstage. Acting has—or ought to have—gained subtleness during the last hundred years.

The third scene of the fourth act in *Le Misanthrope* teaches one of the best lessons in acting and directing with its quasi-inexhaustible possibilities. It is the famous scene dealing with Célimène's letter—supposedly addressed to Oronte.

The real danger here, for a sensitive director, is to overpolish interpretation at the expense of verse, while he is trying to convey those changing states of mind in both protagonists, and to make them plausible. Molière's verse is no great poetry (there are some pretty awkward lines in *Tartuffe*, especially), but remarkably effective and to the point, an incomparable vehicle for the actor. The balance must be found here between glib readings of a—to French audiences—very familiar text, and too many "motivation" pauses. But the verse must be manifest: half the fun is lost if the rhymes are discreetly glided over. Rhyme presents a different problem in Wilbur's version (I hope *The Misanthrope* in English will never again be played in any other) because of the English frequency of monosyllabic rhymes and the fact that they fall faster than in French (two syllables less in each line), not to mention the fundamental difference between French and English prosody: *écoute le vent* rhymes with *dit-il en s'arretant*, for example; but *this is my ring* does not with *he is going*). Our idea of acting today has not only changed owing to a more civilized behavior of audiences in general, but because we got used to cinematographic close-ups and meaningful silences. It would be no daring innovation to let Célimène enter humming and stopping short when she notices Alceste. His reaction may bring a laugh before he wonders, aside, whether he can be *maître* of his *transports*. That line of his stands isolated between two short pauses, his eyes catching Célimène's and then looking away.

The position is, let us say

$$C \qquad \qquad A$$

and if the proscenium allows it, Alceste leans to the stage frame with his left hand. Célimène advances diagonally downstage to say her three lines that follow. Now Alceste turns to her and pronounces "Que toutes les horreurs . . . ." gaining speed.

$$C \searrow A \qquad \qquad C \vec{A}$$

Célimène crosses to stage left during her line "Voilà certainement des douceurs que j'admire," stops and turns round to listen to Alceste's long speech. On "Oui, oui . . . .," Alceste advances and hurls the last six lines to her face.

$$\overset{\nearrow C}{A}$$

According to temperament, the last line may be accompanied by a gesture as if he meant to hit her. He stops there, inhibited, for a count of two; then Célimène, an octave lower: "D'où vient donc, je vous prie, un tel emportement?/Avez-vous, dites-moi, perdu le jugement?" Then Alceste, hoarsely: "Oui, oui, je l'ai perdu . . ."

oui, je l'ai perdu . . . ."

As he finishes his four lines, Célimène nods as if to say "you poor fool," and crosses back behind him with quick steps

$$C \overset{\leftarrow}{A} C$$

There she stops, counts one, and says "De quelle trahison pouvez-vous donc vous plaindre?"

The text gives the intonation as clearly as music. It would be ludicrous to wonder whether Célimène is sincere or not. No insinuation in tone is necessary, nor is there room for profound analysis of who Célimène really is. She is simply being sincere at every moment, but her impulses change fast. For the actress this is irrelevant; in the rhythm of a comedy in verse the very density of verbal expression carries the meaning if only one understands the words one is saying. And those words have to be pronounced clearly—*perlé*—: actors and actresses should not underplay rhyme in order to be realistic.

Molière's characters are not complex, from the purely theatrical point of view. Undertones are made evident by choice of words and syntax. Artists at the Comédie-Française remember their saturation with *explica-*

tions de texte when they were at the *lycée*, and they need not delve into deeper meanings beyond the written lines. For a relatively short period there was a tendency in France to "deepen" Alceste's personality, and actors were tempted to hamletize the Misanthrope. But Copeau showed that Alceste's plight was rooted in comedy: throughout the play, until the final showdown, he strives in vain to clarify the apparent contradiction between Célimène's superficiality and his infatuation with her, but that crucial dialogue never comes off; there is always an unwelcome intrusion, from the entrance of the two Marquis in the second act to DuBois's farcical appearance in the fourth act. Nobody questions today the fact that Molière intended Alceste to be a comic figure, in spite of the actor's task to portray the contrast between his fierce indignation in the beginning and the tone of defeat in the fifth act. Barrault himself, in 1938, played the last act as a tragic broken man, although among the many Alcestes I have seen he was the only one to get a laugh on the line "Pour n'avoir pas trouvé que son sonnet fût bon!" because of a genial flash imitating suddenly Oronte's voice on the word *sonnet*.

Let us return now to Célimène and Alceste whom we had left at the most dramatic moment of the play. The places I am suggesting here are by no means from the traditional staging at the Comédie, but I think they may help to demonstrate a necessary balance between the two characters. Alceste, then, stands center downstage, with Célimène at his right, about two steps further upstage, almost behind him. As he turns sharply round— "Ah! que ce coeur est double et sait bien l'art de feindre!"—we are getting to an intriguing problem a director has to solve here, and which I have never seen dealt with to my full satisfaction, although I have often watched the play, and even stage-managed it more than a hundred times in Paris. A stage manager, of course, has no right to interfere with direction.

I believe that psychological explanations of these all too obvious characters in a classic comedy would be superfluous and puerile. A director's preoccupations ought to be centered on the mechanics of action. To my mind, the problem here is the letter. What exactly happens to that letter? Where does Alceste take it from and where does it go after DuBois enters? Or does it disappear somehow before Célimène says "Voici Monsieur DuBois plaisamment figuré—?" Molière leaves the matter entirely to us. That letter is one of the rare props Molière uses, ever. Directors, as a rule, resort to makeshifts, and spectators simply forget the object as the scene progresses. Actors leave it on chairs, tables, on the floor, and even put it back into their pockets (the high cuffs of those period coats provide convenient substitutes for pockets). Which is a "psychological" error? Why should Alceste want to keep it? Though he may pull it out of his cuff on "J'ai des moyens tout prêts."

One night, thirty-four years ago, as I was on duty in the wings of the Théâtre des Ambassadeurs in Paris, and Henri Rollan played Alceste, I thought I had found an optically valid solution to that letter problem. If my memory does not fail me, Rollan used to leave the letter on a table, and nothing more was done about it. I felt somehow that it was a decisive object in that scene, one of the most exciting comedy moments ever conceived; but I had to wait another thirty years before I was allowed to direct *Le Misanthrope*.

This is how it worked: Alceste, holding the letter before him, pats it with the back of his hand, saying "Ce billet découvert suffit pour vous confondre/Et contre ce témoin on n'a rien à répondre." There is a pause for the count of three, during which Célimène steps forward to verify the letter over Alceste's shoulder before she retorts "Voilà donc le sujet qui vous trouble l'esprit?" Let the actress keep the interrogative tone, for if she deflects the cadence on *trouble l'esprit*, it would sound like "So this is what bothers you," which is slightly out of character. Wilbur translates: "Is this what sent you into such a fit?" She leaves Alceste and goes upstage —the line "Oronte! Qui vous dit que la lettre est pour lui?" is said with her back to the audience, her head turned to the right. With her next cue she comes downstage again. But Alceste has a double-take (glance at Célimène —at the letter—back at Célimène) when she says ". . .et qu'a-t-il de coupable?" He utters a short, bitter laugh.

It is strange that Wilbur misinterprets Alceste's third line "Et me voilà, par là, convaincu tout à fait," the intention of which is clearly ironical, by rendering it with "Your guilt is clear. I need no more persuasion." (Wilbur's only "mistake"). Alceste then lowers his tone to angry reproach in "Osez-vous recourir à ces ruses grossières?", rising to domination at the end of the speech to mark the contrast with his imminent defeat. According to tradition, Alceste throws in his apologetic "Non, non, sans s'emporter . . ." right after Célimène's line, but I venture to suggest he should underline his first surrender. Thus Célimène ought to cross to stage left in front of him, on a curtly pronounced "Il ne me plaît pas, moi," striking the paper with her fan so that it drops to the floor. She has her back turned to him as she finishes ". . . ce que vous m'osez dire." (Advice to prop men: with tape, stick a penny onto the letter, so that the paper does not flutter away but drops straight.)

Count of five. Then, slowly, Alceste stoops to pick up the letter and goes on, much subdued: "Non, non, sans s'emporter . . ." But Célimène walks upstage and crosses again to the right behind him, so that Alceste's soliloquy is delivered in diagonal opposition, Célimène upstage right, Alceste downstage left, at the proscenium again, with a special spotlight on him. He still holds the letter.

Célimène descends on his "Ah! que vous savez bien . . ."; he goes towards her with "Défendez-vous . . .," and he is on his knees by "Et je m'efforcerai . . . ," his head bent in humiliation. Long pause. And, very softly, Célimène: "Allons, vous êtes fou dans vos transports jaloux," as realistically sincere as she can make it.

And now for the letter. Alceste, kneeling in profile, facing stage right, holds it visibly in his left hand. Célimène, on " . . . aux bassesses de feindre," reaches down, gets the paper, and by the time she is saying "Quoi? de mes sentiments . . . ," it is already torn up and thrown away, behind her, behind a desk or a chest of drawers. Oddly enough, it is a fortunate alliteration in Wilbur's text, " . . . inform you of it, simply and sincerely," which points out the right moment to tear the letter up, "simply" (one tear) "and sincerely" (second tear). She makes him rise on "Et n'est-il pas coupable en ne s'assurant pas/ A ce qu'on ne dit point qu'aprés de grands combats?" DuBois should enter from upstage left, so that Célimène must see him first.

Such mechanical indications, or their equivalent in other possible conceptions, are certainly far more helpful to actors than hours of psychological exegesis. Neither Tartuffe, nor Alceste, nor Monsieur Jourdain, let alone Harpagon, could bear motivational direction with idle talk about what goes on under the surface. There is nothing left unsaid in these plays. That is precisely why, in their verbal strictness, classic comedies in verse ought to be primary material in the training of actors. And there is total expression in what a Molière character says.

The identity of the American theater, established since O'Neill, is largely psychological and realistic. Unfortunately, many American directors believe that every kind of acting is based on "motivation problems." I do not believe anything is. If nothing else in Molière, the unsurpassed theatrical efficiency of, say, Alceste's dialogue with Oronte in the first act certainly proves how right the late Louis Jouvet was when he warned young actors not to "build up novels" about what a character was likely to have done before the play began. (Who killed the plucked fowl hanging in Velasquez's picture?) A character just does not exist before entering the stage. Drama classes and rehearsals should neither be literature courses nor psychedelic séances. They ought to display, impart and apply technique instead, whatever the individual actor tries to do intellectually with his role when he is alone. His meditations are wholly irrelevant to acting, anyhow. Nobody cares whether the difficult, convulsive laughter scenes of Nicole (*Le Bourgeois*) or Zerbinette (*Scapin*) succeed through the actress concentrating on her vibrating diaphragm or working herself up to hysteria: if she cannot play those cascades properly, she ought to withdraw from the stage and have children, even get married if she chooses. In any case, she has not learned how to laugh—which is technique, and quite unintellectual.

It would not make much sense to stage these comedies in arbitrary fantasy as has been so successfully done, with *A Midsummer Night's Dream*, for instance. All Molière has written belongs to style, manner and epoch. His greatness is not in what he said, but in how he said it; it is extrovert, flamboyant expression; and it would be an embarrassing compliment indeed to call him a poet and a philosopher.

A director staging a Molière play should remember first that none of these dialogues calls for the slightest intimacy in attitude: those costumes were silk and velvet fortresses, and people spoke to one another at a distance. Some believe that such airy aloofness in conversation was due to the fact that at the time hygiene was at its lowest ebb in European history: nobody ever got washed properly, and people did not smell nice. Whatever their reason might have been, twentieth-century gesticulation, e.g., with elbows welded to the body, is incongruous and awkward in those dresses, and Molière's gentlemen—let alone ladies—never wore the intellectual stoop and the sagging shoulder. Costumes are half the fun and a priceless lesson to young actors, even if they have to play nothing but detergent commercials and Israel Horowitz ever after. What would a tuxedoed Oronte do while he says "Je suis votre valet, Monsieur, de tout mon coeur . . . " if there is no business with a hat? Fancy Miller's Salesman in medieval armor, asking for a sandwich.

Men's wigs are part of the fortress-costume. But today even the Comédie-Française relents, and in Bourseiller's *Dom Juan*, with stylized, shiny plastic costumes and a nowhere-décor, there were no wigs: Jacques Charon, as Sganarelle, had almost a crewcut. Planchon's exquisite *Tartuffe* in the sixties kept dresses in style, but hairdressing was only allusive and sketchy, probably because long hair for men has come to mean something else for us during the last decade. Orgon even wore a George V beard. The point is that for French audiences any unorthodox staging of Molière "would do," because they mentally re-establish the conventional manner, remember and compare collectively: they have "terms of reference," whereas in America one should keep as closely as possible to the French seventeenth-century style, since no fancy transportation can overcome the double estrangement of epoch and language.

DOM JUAN, A REASSESSMENT
IN VIEW OF MODERN EXISTENTIALISM

Jytte Wiingaard

Nous ne sommes pas libres. Et le ciel peut encore nous tomber sur la tête. Et le théâtre est fait pour nous apprendre d'abord cela (Artaud).

Absurd drama is on the way out—absurd tradition on the way in. Remembering our own modern state of existentialistic anxiety, the absurd tradition makes us regard the world of drama in an existentialistic way. We want to comprehend the universal theme—want to recognize ourselves in the drama—and to see our own age mirrored in the play. Thus the English are re-interpretating Shakespeare in new ways: Edward Bond even dares call his horror drama *Lear*. And the French, nurtured as they are on existentialism, do the same to their classics. According to Ionesco, the greatest authors have always been absurd. Is Ionesco right? Or are we in our manipulations and searches for universal truth in the great dramas actually destroying the classics and losing the author's real intention in interpretations which emphasize cruelty and destruction? Or have we, really, wrested the deepest secret from the drama?

Molière's *Dom Juan* is traditionally performed as a gay comedy with a ridiculous Sganarelle strengthening the farcical aspect, and an end where the charming seducer, Dom Juan, is unmasked as a depraved mocker who is punished by divine justice for his profligate way of living.

But the absurd tradition sees Dom Juan as a man who is fighting supernatural powers—a lonely and helpless existentialist on earth. His rational self and his feelings for human beings cannot help him against the metaphysical in a realm of anxiety. In a world of madness, which looks for divine assistance, Dom Juan is the only one to know that life must be lived here and now. Perhaps one should view *Dom Juan* as a moral farcical comedy, a view which can be supported by the text, contemporary stage conventions, and some of the background of the play.

The Dom Juan theme had been treated in literature before Molière used it in 1665. Tirso de Molina was the first to do so in *El Burlador de Sevilla* in the beginning of the seventeenth century. The Spanish comedy formed the raw material for a commedia dell'arte, where Arlecchino was the Spanish nobleman's servant. This *commedia* was performed with great success in Paris in 1657. In 1658 and 1659, French companies which wanted to cash in on the Italians' success made two new versions, both titled *Le Festin de Pierre ou Le fils criminel*. Molière took what he needed for his comedy from these two companies, notably from the commedia dell'arte, one which alternated with his own before he took charge of the Palais-Royal, a rich baroque theater fully equipped with up-to-date stage machinery and mechanical devices evolved from Torelli's innovations. As in the earlier versions, Molière exploits scene changes in *Dom Juan*: each act has a different setting and moves from palace to country scene, from forest to a room, and finally to another country scene. Theatrical machines—which were so popular in the Baroque—were used extensively in Molière's play: a grave opens; a statue nods; a ghost enters the stage and changes into Death with the scythe in full view of the audience; and near the end, there is great rumbling and Bengal light and flames are shown while the earth opens and swallows Dom Juan.

La Grange, the *jeune premier*, played Dom Juan. In contrast with the Spanish aristocrat (wearing a Spanish costume) in the other plays, he was dressed as a French nobleman, a young demoralized dandy, a familiar type in contemporary France.

Already at the beginning of the play, Molière shows us the seducer of women who is too much of a coward to tell Donna Elvira the truth (I. iii).[1] When passions are rising, Dom Juan is revealed even more: he sneaks away from the two peasant girls after his plans have failed (II. iv). He uses rough tricks not to pay his merchant (IV. iii), and feels no commiseration for his old father whom he treats outrageously (IV. iv and V. i). The comedy of moral culminates at the end of the play where Heaven, symbolized by the statue, metes out divine justice to the unprincipled nobleman.

Molière himself had Sganarelle's part. This character, appearing in several of Molière's plays, is based on two commedia dell'arte figures, Brighella, a sly venomous bandit, and Scaramouche, a ridiculous braggart. Tiberio Fiorelli, who came to Paris in 1645, had made Scaramouche a famous figure of the stage. His powers of mimicry exerted so much influence on Molière that the age considered him Fiorelli's pupil.

Molière, a master at reciting monologue, opened the comedy in the

---

[1] Molière, *Dom Juan, ou le festin de Pierre*. (Edition's du Seuil, Paris, 1962). Further citations are from this text and are indicated parenthetically. I am indebted to Mr. Cay Dollerup for assistance in expressing this essay in English.

farcical manner. The audience observed an actor playing clown who—like Scaramouche—made the most of his mimicry to rouse laughter. It is obvious from the text, i.e. the lazzi scene where Sganarelle gets the slap intended for Pierrot (II. iii), the scenes with the statue (III. v, IV. vii, V. vi) and the specter (V. iv, v), that Molière meant to allow full scope for the farcical actor's mimics and gestures. Nobody would pity this ludicrous character at the end of the play, and the monologue after Dom Juan's fall is intended to rehabilitate everybody except this stupid person.

The very choice of the noble La Grange for the lead points to an interpretation of his role as that of a charming scoundrel who, albeit opposing social and moral conventions, gets his desserts in the end. The fact that Molière, the brilliant actor of clownish parts, had Sganarelle's part gave special emphasis to the notion that this was a gay comedy, and the extensive use of stage machinery increased the air of mirth and catered to the taste of the contemporary audience.

The above would be a fair summary of the accepted views on *Dom Juan* in the eyes of critics and scholars in the history of drama. But it seems to me that by applying some of the ideas of modern absurd tradition—as has already been done by stage directors—in our reading of the text, we could profitably view the drama in a radically different manner. And, what is more, it seems to me that there is not only textual authority for doing this, but also several pointers in what we could call the historical background in the broadest sense: absurd tradition may thus help us, not to read what we would like to into the play, but once again to add, see, and comprehend a dimension which is sometimes overlooked. And in so doing, let us reconsider the play: Dom Juan still the protagonist, Sganarelle the antagonist.

Sganarelle opens the play with a characterization of Dom Juan: "mais par précaution, je t'apprends, *inter nos*, que tu vois en dom Juan mon maître, le plus grand scélérat que la terre ait jamais porté, un enragé, un chien, un diable, un Turck, un hérétique, qui ne croit ni ciel, ni enfer, ni loup-garou; qui passe cette vie en véritable bête brute; un pourceau d'Epicure, en vrai Sardanapale, qui ferme l'oreille à toutes les remontrances chrétiennes, qu'on lui peut faire, et traite de billevesées tout ce que nous croyons" (I. i). Quite an introduction. Dom Juan is not only a seducer of women, but an atheist to boot. This must be a highly disparaging view of the protagonist in the mouth of a timid antagonist—whereas it must show a higher level of awareness from the viewpoint of an existentialistic protagonist.

The second act is consistently farcical. Two silly peasant girls trust a man they do not know at all and his promises of marriage. The farcical situation arises from the absurd fact that, by way of gratitude to Pierrot for having saved him from drowning, Dom Juan turns the head of Pierrot's fiancée. Contrasted with Dom Juan's world of irony, the peasant girls represent a world of a lower order of mental consciousness with creatures devoid of intelligence and common sense.

In the third act we are presented with Dom Juan's credo: "Je crois que deux et deux sont quatre, Sganarelle; et que quatre et quatre son huit" (III. i). Initially professing to believe "Le moine bourru," Sganarelle's defense against Dom Juan's rationalism is singularly unconvincing. Sganarelle tries to prove God's existence by pointing out what is admirable in the human being, and which no scientist can explain: "Je veux frapper des mains, hausser le bras, lever les yeux au ciel, baisser la tête, remuer les pieds, aller à droite, à gauche, en avant, en arrière, tourner . . ." (III. i). In his attempt to demonstrate how the body is guided by willpower, Sganarelle tumbles, and in so doing his argument must—according to his supposition—also fall apart. In the same act there is a dialogue between Dom Juan and a poor man.

Dom Juan
Quelle est ton occupation parmi ces arbres?
Le Pauvre
De prier le Ciel tout le jour pour la prospérité des gens de bien qui me donnent quelque chose.
Dom Juan
Il ne se peut donc pas que tu ne sois bien à ton aise?
Le Pauvre
Hélas! Monsieur, je suis dans la plus grande nécessité du monde.
Dom Juan
Tu te moques: un homme qui prie le Ciel tout le jour ne peut pas manquer d'être bien dans ses affaires. . . . Ah! ah! je m'en vais te donner un louis d'or tout à l'heure, pourvu que tu veuilles jurer.
Le Pauvre
Ah! Monsieur, voudriez-vous que je commisse un tel péché?
Dom Juan
Tu n'as qu'a voir si tu veux gagner un louis d'or ou non. En voici un que je te donne, si tu jures; tiens, il faut jurer . . .
Le Pauvre
Non, monsieur, j'aime mieux mourir de faim.
Dom Juan
Va, va. Je te le donne pour l'amour de l'humanite. (III. ii)

Faith and trust in God and charity have not helped the poor man in his penury. On the other hand he receives some small assistance from another man. Opposed to the empty cliché "Pour l'amour de Dieu," Dom Juan's words "pour l'amour de l'humanité" are poignant with meaning as he gives the poor man a louis d'or.

Dom Juan gives further proof of his magnanimity in saving Don Carlos' life (III. iii), in his behaviour towards Donna Elvira (IV. vi), and by keeping his promise to the statue (V. vi). In these cases he then shows generosity in his actions, and his father's reply must accordingly be interpreted as ironical: "Apprenez enfin qu'un gentilhomme qui vit mal est un monstre dans la nature; que la vertu est le premier titre de noblesse; que je regarde bien moins au nom qu'un signe, qu'aux actions qu'on fait, et que je ferais plus d'état du fils d'un crocheteur qui serait honnête homme, que du fils d'un monarque qui vivrait comme vous" (IV. iv).

In the third scene of the fourth act and in the first and third scenes of the fifth act Dom Juan plays the hypocrite, and is found immensely attractive by the others; the truth, however, is that hyprocrisy was a common vogue at the time: "Il n'y a plus de honte maintenant à cela, l'hypocrisie est un vice à la mode, et tous les vices à la mode passent pour vertus. Le personnage d'homme de bien est le meilleur de tous les personnages qu'on puisse jouer aujourd'hui, et la profession d'hypocrite a de merveilleux avantages. C'est un art de qui l'imposture est toujours respectée; et, quoiqu'on la découvre, on n'ose rien dire contre elle . . ." (V. ii).

From an existentialistic point of view, the last scene must be interpreted as follows: a fearless man tries to provoke the supernatural but is vanquished by the invincible. From an existentialistic life, from jubilant enjoyment, Dom Juan passes on to anxious awareness in the place where the metaphysical world, in all its inevitability, metes out horror and cruelty to life on earth. Sganarelle goes no further than thinking of his lost salary. His stupidity limits him to unfeeling selfishness.

Tartuffe was performed at Versaille on the twelfth of May, 1664. The comedy pleased Louis XIV, whereas the clergy prohibited further performances (although one took place at Palais-Royal on the fifth of August, 1667), because they interpreted *Tartuffe* as an attack, not only on hypocondriacs, but on the church itself. Molière was deeply hurt, and in spite of several *placets* he was not allowed to perform the comedy again until 1669. It was in this period—when he attempted to perform *Tartuffe* and was exposed to attacks—that Molière wrote *Dom Juan, ou le festin de Pierre*, which had its first appearance at the Palais-Royal on the fifteenth of February, 1665. At the time, many were sceptical of religion, and people were questioning God's existence. One would have to content oneself with faith alone, since one could not adduce convincing arguments from rationalism, from knowledge, or from science. This is what makes it very likely that Molière, highly perceptive and widely read, wanted to comment on one of the most burning questions of his age.

As we have seen, religion is viewed in a more cruel and searching light in *Dom Juan* than in *Tartuffe*. Nevertheless the play was approved by the ecclesiastical censorship, because Molière, taught by bitter experience, camouflaged his real intention. For coverage he used a well-known tale about an ungodly nobleman who is punished for his sins. He used machine effects, normal in his *comédie-ballets*, but certainly not in his character comedies. He pleased his audience by following the vogue for fascinating changes of scene. From the popular commedia dell'arte he took comic *jeux du théâtre* and *lazzi*, and from the modern *comédie romanesque* the fanciful action and a fairy-tale of love, transferred to an exotic country.

In his stage directions, in selecting La Grange for the part of the charming Dom Juan, and in playing Sganarelle himself, Molière consciously hid the play's subversive tendency. "C'est ainsi qu'il faut profiter des faiblesses des hommes, et qu'un sage esprit s'accommode aux vices de son siècle," says Dom Juan (V. ii). And this is exactly what Molière tried to do in avoiding censorship by giving the comedy a conventional dress.

In Dom Juan, the protagonist, Molière shows us an existentialistic man, who refuses to believe in God, because this is in conflict with his rational outlook. In addition, he shows us Dom Juan as a man with some of the very best qualities: truthfulness, intelligence, consciousness of his own mental life and generosity, one who gives himself up to metaphysical destruction. For the characters on a lower level of awareness in the comedy, the statue is a symbol of God and maintenace of world order—for Dom Juan, in his life of freedom and responsibility, the statue symbolized meaningless death and metaphysical cruelty.

With this in mind, and noting that he used contemporary theatrical conventions to camouflage his true intention, it seems as if we will be nearer the truth if we perform *Dom Juan* more as an existentialistic play than as a gay comedy.

MOLIÈRE
AND FRENCH TELEVISION

Norman R. Savoie

Molière est mort! Vive Molière! It has often been said that one of the great signs of a creator's genius is the ability of that person's works to live on through time, able to withstand the decaying effects of decade after decade of rediscovery and reevaluation by succeeding generations. Along with the great technical strides of the twentieth century have come new tests of strength for the reputation of past and present-day geniuses, notably the cinema and television. Molière, who naturally found intense delight and satisfaction in seeing his works presented before select audiences, most assuredly never dreamed of the complex means future technology would produce in order to present works such as his to larger, less select audiences. The author, who it would seem was not lacking in self-esteem and self-confidence, would probably have looked forward to this ultimate test, assured of victory. This, of course, is supposition. Nonetheless, Molière's conclusion would have been correct.

Before examining Molière's fate on French television, it might be useful to present a few salient facts concerning the O.R.T.F. (l'Office de la radio-diffusion-télévision française) and dramatic productions of the O.R.T.F.[1] The first experimental French television studio was set up in 1930 in Montrouge, a suburb of Paris. Beginning in 1938, regular presentations were broadcast approximately three hours daily, but about half of these broadcasts were simply motion pictures.[2] Regular broadcasting, though still not as we think of it today, began in 1949. The O.R.T.F. was to remain for many years a very small organization.[3] Its great period of development began in the mid-1950's.

[1] For an in-depth study of the question and references to numerous sources, one might consult my unpublished dissertation (Indiana Univ., 1971), "French Television and Dramatic Literature."

[2] Television receivers were not sold commercially until 1945. The three hundred or so sets which were privately owned in France before the war seem to have belonged mostly to individuals involved in the technical or artistic development of the new medium.

[3] Until 1953, in fact, the O.R.T.F. would cease all operations during the month of August in order to grant its employees a few weeks of vacation.

645

By 1964, after twelve years of expensive preparation, all of France was able to receive television programs direct from Paris. The same year, a second channel, the *Deuxième Chaîne*, began regular broadcasting and a third channel went on the air on December 31, 1972.[4] All channels are state-controlled and there are no private television enterprises in France. Color telecasting began in 1967, on the *Deuxième Chaîne* only. The third station is designed for color telecasts also. In 1950, there were less than four thousand privately-owned sets in the country; that number had grown to nearly one million by 1958 and has continued to grow by approximately one million per year since, with nearly twelve million sets today, of which, incidentally, only six hundred thousand are capable of receiving color programs.[5]

The production part of the O.R.T.F.—as opposed to the administrative part—is divided into separate departments or sections called *services*. From 1945 to the mid-1950's these were all located at 15, rue Cognacq-Jay, in the seventh arrondissement of Paris, where the Germans had equipped a television studio in 1943. But the growth of the new medium soon forced several of the departments to find larger facilities elsewhere. For that reason, the O.R.T.F. now has offices and studios scattered throughout the city of Paris, as well as in its suburbs.[6] The seven major *services* are News, Sports, Cinema, Children's Programs, Documentaries, Variety Programs, and Drama. The offices and studios of the last two departments, *Le Service des variétés* and *Le Service des émissions dramatiques*, are located at the Centre René Barthélemy, 36, rue des Alouettes, in the nineteenth arrondissement. Since this center is near the large Parc des Buttes-Chaumont, it is often referred to as Les Buttes or Les Buttes-Chaumont.[7]

In the history of the *Service des émissions dramatiques*, 1956 is a key

---

[4] The *Deuxième Chaîne*, it would seem, was to telecast programs of a "serious" nature. For this reason, it is often referred to as *la chaîne culturelle*. If this difference between the programming philosophy of the two channels did exist for a time, it no longer does. The two channels are now competitive and both offer the same types of programs. The third channel is also competitive.

[5] "French 3d Web to bow Dec. 31, '72" (anon.), *Variety*, Jan. 5, 1972, 108.

[6] The well-known Maison Ronde at 116, avenue du Président Kennedy houses French radio facilities and is the administrative center of the O.R.T.F. The only televising done here is for programs—usually concerts—necessitating the use of one of the building's three large auditoriums.

[7] The main part of the Buttes-Chaumont building, previously occupied by the Gaumont Film Company, was purchased by the O.R.T.F. in the early 1950's. Since then, the structure has been enlarged several times. According to two directors at the O.R.T.F., the building is now larger than the château de Versailles, if one compares the number of square feet of floor space.

date. That year, it moved from rue Cognacq-Jay to the Buttes-Chaumont
where it found more adequate space and better working conditions. More
important, André Frank was named as its head. Frank, born in Paris in
1909, was a man of the theater. As former secretary-general of the Renaud-
Barrault acting company from 1935 to 1956, he arrived at the O.R.T.F.
with both administrative and literary abilities, which he quickly put to
work. Along with Jean d'Arcy, then *Directeur de la Télévision Française*,
he realized that as far as dramatic productions were concerned, French
television was not being used to its full potential. With the support
of d'Arcy, Frank's department soon became an experimental center,
working to set up rules concerning television's proper approach to
literature. During the next ten years, from 1956 to 1966, the Buttes-
Chaumont became important and respected. It greatly influenced the
shaping of similar centers in the television systems of other countries,
especially those of England and West Germany. It is for this reason that the
name *Ecole des Buttes-Chaumont* has been given to this ten-year period of
the *Service des émissions dramatiques*.

The *Ecole des Buttes-Chaumont* does not concern us too much here,
since its experiments dealt primarily, although not solely, with the creation
of original works written for television as well as with the adaptation of
novels and short stories for the medium. These types of productions
became much more common after 1957, whereas they had been scarce
before that time. Dramatic presentations on French television before 1957
consisted almost entirely of works taken from the repertory of the theater.
Until then, the medium simply served as a means of transmitting to the
general public theatrical works such as they would have been seen on any
stage. By the mid-1950's, the number of dramatic productions had risen
to about sixty per year, an impressive figure if one takes into consideration
the lack of working space and of material means in the studios of rue
Cognacq-Jay, and especially the fact that most programs were still being
presented live. Such conditions greatly reduced, if not completely eliminated, the possibilities of experimentation. Not until 1958 were any
dramatic productions filmed in their entirety. Before this date, certain
short inserts were occasionally filmed, but nothing more. Only in 1960
did the kinescope process become used regularly, and only after the mid-
1960's was video-tape commonly used.[8]

[8] Roger Andrey, "Les Dramatiques," *La Technique. L'Exploitation cinématographique*
(Paris: Editions Astéria), No. 295 (April 1968), 88–89. [I might add here that filming a pro-

After 1957, the number of annual dramatic productions rose constantly, from eighty-four in 1958 to one hundred sixty-one in 1967.[9] Although more and more adaptations and original works were presented each year, the greatest percentage of the works produced for television was still taken from the repertory of the theater—from forty to fifty percent annually.

Whether one looks at statistics of dramatic productions produced for French television between 1950 and 1970 or from 1957 to 1970, whether or not one includes all genres of works or limits oneself to those taken from the repertory of the theater, the number of productions based on Molière's works outnumbers by far those of any other author, French or foreign, with one exception, Eugène Labiche.[10]

From January 1950 to December 1969, works by Molière were aired forty-two times on French television. Twenty-two of the author's thirty-three works have been produced; eleven of these have been produced at least twice, and six of these have been produced three times each. Thus thirty-nine different productions.[11] In addition, three productions have been aired twice. Listed here are the twenty-two works with their dates of broadcast. The plays are listed in the chronological order of their first showing. (An asterisk indicates that the play was performed by the Comédie-Française.)

1–*Les Précieuses ridicules*	1950		
2–*Le Mariage forcé*	1950	1964	
3–*Le Malade imaginaire*	1950	1959*	1966*
4–*Le Bourgeois gentilhomme*	1951	1952	1968
5–*L'Ecole des maris*	1952	1955*	1958*
6–*Tartuffe*	1952*	1955	1960*
7–*Le Médecin malgré lui*	1952*	1961	1964 (repeated in 1965)
8–*L'Avare*	1952	1964	1966
9–*Dépit amoureux*	1953		
10–*George Dandin*	1953		

duction is about three times as expensive as video-taping it, but much more beneficial since film can be used directly on any television system throughout the world, whereas video-tapes have to be "translated" from one picture definition to another, should this last not be the same.]

[9] Andrey, Nos. 293–302 (Feb.–Dec. 1968).

[10] I have made a lengthy compilation of dramatic productions of the O.R.T.F. from January 1950 to December 1969, with date of broadcast, name of director, adaptor, etc. Many different sources were used for this study, and the complete results are in an appendix of my dissertation.

[11] There have been likewise thirty-nine different productions of Labiche's works, dealing with thirty-six different plays. In addition, two of these productions were broadcast twice. Works by Labiche, therefore, have been aired a total of forty-one times, one short of Molière.

11–*Le Misanthrope*	1954	1959
12–*Le Sicilien ou l'Amour peintre*	1955	
13–*Monsieur de Pourceaugnac*	1958	
14–*Les Fourberies de Scapin*	1958	1965
15–*L'Ecole des femmes*	1959	
16–*Les Femmes savantes*	1959*	1966*
17–*Amphitryon*	1960	1967*
18–*La Jalousie du Barbouillé*	1960 (repeated in 1961)	
19–*Le Médecin volant*	1961	
20–*Les Fâcheux*	1962	
21–*L'Amour médecin*	1964	
22–*Dom Juan*	1965 (repeated in 1969)	

It would be difficult to state positively any obviously discernible pattern in the order of presentation of these plays. As for the frequency of the broadcasts over the twenty-year period, with such small figures and over so short a period of time, it might be misleading to try to read too much out of the information. One fact which can be assumed is that the fifteen productions presented before 1958 were aired live, with, perhaps, a few filmed inserts. It was doubtlessly because of this added need for accuracy and perfection that a good many of these early productions were performed by professional acting companies, especially by the Comédie-Française.[12] The Oiseaux sur la Branche Company presented the first version of *Le Mariage forcé* (1950), the Renaud-Barrault Company offered *Le Misanthrope* (1954) and *Amphitryon* (1960), and *Le Sicilien ou l'Amour peintre* (1955) was acted out by the Lionel Baylac Company. Students of the Conservatoire National d'Art Dramatique performed in *Les Précieuses ridicules* (1950).

It is not difficult to understand why Molière ranks as the most "popular" author when it comes to O.R.T.F. dramatic productions: he is an author whose important works are widely-known and studied in school and who promises to have something delightful and witty to say; his works are often fairly simple to stage for television and can be masterfully presented by well-known acting companies. These are but a few of the reasons which somewhat assure the O.R.T.F. administration of a broadcast's probable

[12] Since the early 1950's, the O.R.T.F. and the Comédie-Française have worked together on approximately eighty occasions. For many years, the Comédie-Française would perform one work for television every other month. The financial remuneration offered by the O.R.T.F. was for the use of the actors and their costumes, as well as for the production rights to one broadcast. The play was performed in the O.R.T.F. studios. It is interesting to note that the Comédie-Française, which has a total annual audience of slightly over one half million, had a potential audience of six million viewers for its one televised performance of *Tartuffe* in 1960.

success. The same reasons would explain the high number of broadcasts based on the works of other authors: Labiche (forty-one), Marivaux (thirty-three), Courteline (twenty-six). Even Chekhov (twenty-three) and Shakespeare (nineteen) have fared well.

Besides assuring themselves of success vis-à-vis the audience, O.R.T.F. administrators probably feel also that they are accomplishing their primary goals when broadcasting Molière's works. The French National Assembly describes the O.R.T.F. as "un établissement public de l'Etat ... [créé] en vue de satisfaire les besoins d'information, de culture, d'éducation et de distraction du public."[13] Who could deny that productions based on Molière's works do not fulfill at least three of these goals: "culture," "éducation," and "distraction"—with an added dose of culture when the play is being performed by a well-known acting company, especially the Comédie-Française?

If during the early years of the O.R.T.F. French television simply served as a means of transmitting live theatrical works as they would have been seen on any stage, this approach slowly changed as the technical abilities of television became more refined (introduction of film, video-tape, etc.), as the directors became more aware of the possibilities offered them by this new medium, and as budgets and facilities were increased. Television allowed certain approaches impossible on stage, perhaps because the medium allows technical achievements virtually impossible or very difficult to reproduce on stage, such as close-up camera shots, superimpositions, split-shots, and flashbacks; or perhaps simply because a camera is a mobile object, and certain scenes can be filmed outdoors where they supposedly occur. This mobility of the camera has allowed some of Molière's works to take on a new freshness. For example, François Gir's production of *Le Médecin malgré lui*, broadcast in 1964, acquired a new dimension simply because the entire work was filmed outdoors in one of the most scenic areas of France, Provence, next to the Fontaine de Vaucluse. Pierre Badel's 1968 production of *Le Bourgeois gentilhomme* had many exterior scenes filmed on the grounds of the château de Courances and the château de Nandy. Contrary to what occurs in stage productions of Molière's works, television directors have often opted to have different scenes of one play occur in different settings. In Badel's work, just mentioned, the interior scenes take the viewer to many parts of the château de Nandy, from its vestibule to its attic. Claude Dagues' *Tartuffe* (1960) sees the

---

[13] *Journal officiel de l'Assemblée nationale*, No. 150 (June 28, 1964), 5636.

action move about from Mariane's room, to Orgon's drawing room, his waiting room, and the corridor between these last two rooms. Also, because of the smaller mobile cameras already available in 1960, Dagues attempted a completely different camera shot in *Tartuffe*, and with great success. Every reader of Molière is familiar with the fifth scene of the fifth act: Orgon hiding under a table, watching Tartuffe and Elmire. Dagues placed a small mobile camera under the table and allowed the viewer to see the scene as Orgon himself would see it. Obviously, such a subjective view would be wholly impossible to create in an ordinary stage production.

One of the greater advantages the technical side of television offers is the possibility of seeing close-up shots of the actors and their reactions. Director Jean Kerchbron has often used this advantage to give a completely different interpretation to a work, as he did in 1965 with *Les Fourberies de Scapin*. "Dans sa mise en scène pour la télévision, Jean Kerchbron a volontairement sacrifié le style ballet de la comédie à l'opposition psychologique des personnages, à la mise en valeur des visages; la bouffonnerie s'efface devant l'étude des caractères."[14] With his repeated and well-timed close-up shots of the actors' faces and reactions, Kerchbron creates an *intimité* between the actors and the spectator which is impossible to create in an ordinary stage production.

Kerchbron had used this special approach well before his 1965 production of *Les Fourberies de Scapin*. During most of the 1950's, very few attempts had been made to televise any of the tragedies of Corneille or Racine. These seemed to be "off-limits" for television. It was only at the very end of 1958 that someone dared produce a tragedy in this unconventional manner. "Ce fut le coup du 2 décembre 1958. Jean Kerchbron, un jeune réalisateur, tentait l'expérience avec . . . *Bajazet*."[15] Kerchbron, faithful to Racine's text and to the three classic unities, avoided the traditional dynamic atmosphere of the tragedy presented on stage, and gave the play an air of intimacy, creating a *tête-à-tête* between the viewer and the actors. By using good close-up shots of the actors' faces to show their expressions, and by having them say their alexandrines in a relatively natural manner—rather than majestically declaiming them at the top of their voices—Kerchbron was better able to display the characters' most secret passions. The young director's new approach was highly praised.

[14] This quotation as well as most of the examples referred to in these pages are found in the catalogue *Emissions et films de télévision* (Paris: Imprimeries de l'O.R.T.F., 1967), 6.

[15] André Brincourt, *La Télévision et ses promesses* (Paris: La Table Ronde, 1960), 197.

One of the more striking aspects of Kerchbron's productions was his *décor*. He was convinced that it should be as simple as possible, that anything unnecessary would simply distract the viewer and perhaps break this special tie he held at that moment with the actors. The director therefore chose a *décor* based on the concept of *stylisation*, stressing as complete an abstraction of scenery as possible, for example, seven or eight steps leading to a dais on which stands a throne. The viewer is aware that the action is taking place in a palace. Nothing else is necessary.

Kerchbron employed the same technique and basically the same *décor* with later productions, *Britannicus* and *Bérénice* (both in 1959), and *Horace* (1963) and *Cinna* (1964). These were all unqualified successes. He attempted the same approach with Molière's *Le Misanthrope* in 1959, but many television critics reacted unfavorably. The entire play was presented in one room with a black cyclorama as a background, and the only furnishings— a few armchairs—obviously placed the action in the seventeenth century, and yet did not emphasize this fact. What critics reacted against was the floor: large white and black tiles representing an enormous checker-board. One had this to say about Kerchbron's staging:

> En montant le *Misanthrope*, il fut victime d'une trop bonne idée. Celle de l'échiquier. Il était tentant de souligner par un sol en damiers noirs et blancs le caractère dépouillé et mathématique de la démonstration. La suppression du décor sortait les personnages du temps et de l'espace, les "chargeait d'éternité," mieux encore : notre intérêt tout entier se reportait sur le jeu des visages et par là même donnait à l'expérience son juste prix. Grave erreur, mais celle-là fut profitable : l'échiquier n'avait en fait pas d'existence pour le spectateur. Et cette absence de lieu, pour une pièce essentiellement enfermée dans un salon d'époque, donnait le vertige. Nous n'étions nulle part, notre regard s'égarait, surpris chaque fois de constater que les personnages perdus eux-mêmes dans cet infini et comme "trop libres" pour jouer ce jeu infernal ne pouvaient, au vrai, ni entrer ni sortir. Le décor simplifié à l'excès compliqua tout. Le son prenait une résonance désagréable ; ces gens parlaient dans une cathédrale ; les ombres et les bruits révélaient autour des acteurs d'insupportables présences.[16]

Even if many critics felt that Kerchbron had made a serious error in his choice of *décor* for this one production, most were in agreement that he had used the camera very well and that the numerous close-up shots had allowed the viewer to see the play in an interesting new manner which no stage production could ever duplicate.

Despite the unfavorable reaction to this production of *Le Misanthrope*, television critics were nevertheless intrigued by Kerchbron's work with

[16] Brincourt, 199–200.

the classical tragedies, and awarded him the coveted Prix de la Critique
for the year 1959. With his three productions, *Bajazet, Britannicus,* and
Bérénice—all presented within one year—Kerchbron toppled the growing
legend that it was impossible to present successfully the French classic
theater on television. Not only did he present it successfully, but he let
millions of viewers see these plays in an unprecedented manner, "car il
appartenait et pour la première fois à des tragédiens, de nous 'faire
entendre des regards' qui jusqu'alors restaient muets."[17]

But in later years not all directors would treat classical works with the
same respect that Kerchbron had shown. *Le Bourgeois gentilhomme* has
been produced twice recently—by Pierre Badel in 1968, and by Pierre
Sabbagh, for the series *Au théâtre ce soir*, in 1970. Badel's production
treated the play in a cavalier manner—although there were many interesting ideas present in the staging. Sabbagh's production was pure
slapstick, and of the worst kind.

Badel attempted to film (in color) a super-production. He not only
modernized the text at certain points (for example, in the fifth scene of
the second act, *en enbas* and *en enhaut* becoming *en bas* and *en haut*[18]),
but also changed it occasionally: Monsieur Jourdain's song (in the second
scene of the first act) no longer ends with the words "Elle est cent fois, mille
fois plus cruelle/ Que n'est le tigre aux bois," but with ". . . / Que n'est le
tigre aux abois," an unnecessary and questionable modification.[19] Badel
also changed the opening of the play to indicate that Monsieur Jourdain is
in the process of moving into his newly acquired château. This makes no
sense in a later scene when we hear:

Madame Jourdain
        . . . Je ne sais plus ce que c'est que notre maison. On dirait qu'il est
céans carême-prenant tous les jours; et dès le matin, de peur d'y manquer, on y
entend des vacarmes de violons ou de chanteurs dont tout le voisinage se trouve
incommodé.
Nicole
Madame parle bien. Je ne saurais plus voir mon ménage propre avec cet attirail
de gens que vous faites venir chez vous. Ils ont des pieds qui vont chercher de la
boue dans tous les quartiers de la ville pour l'apporter ici; et la pauvre Françoise
est presque sur les dents à frotter les planchers que vos biaux maîtres viennent
crotter régulièrement tous les jours.

(III. iii)

[17] Brincourt, 199.

[18] But how accurate are these changes? For example, in Act III, Scene 3, Madame Jourdain
says "Çamon vraiment!" This is changed in the script to "Ça non, vraiment!" which is incorrect, since *çamon* means *certainement*.

[19] The observations presented here are based on the original text found in Molière, *Oeuvres
complètes*, ed. Robert Jouanny, 2 vols. (Paris: Garnier, 1962).

These words would make no sense if Monsieur Jourdain and his family had just moved into the château (*céans, tous les jours, régulièrement*, etc.). Furthermore, would Madame Jourdain have cause to worry about disturbing *le voisinage*?

Some scenes of the play are filmed in the gardens of the château de Courances, and others inside and outside the château de Nandy. (We are, supposedly, at the same château.) Although this violates the unity of place which Molière had incorporated in the play, it creates movement and allows interesting changes in the traditional staging. The first act, for example, takes place in the gardens in front of the château de Nandy, where a small stage has been set up for the presentation of a play. The fight between the teachers, at the beginning of the second act, occurs in the attic of the château. The confrontation between Monsieur Jourdain and Nicole, in the second scene of the third act, comes about behind the palace, where the former cloth salesman keeps a mini-zoo: several cages with different species of birds, and one cage with a monkey—wearing an outfit remarkably similar to its master's. The scenes with Cléonte, Covielle, Lucille, and Nicole at the end of the same act are filmed in the gardens of Courances, with their beautiful ponds and alleys bordered by trees. Most of the remaining scenes take place inside the château de Nandy, showing its vestibule, imposing stairway, sumptuous drawing room and dining room.

Some of the stunts used by Badel to add humor to Molière's comedy are highly questionable. During the last scene filmed on the stage set up outside the palace, one of the dancers, imitating Monsieur Jourdain's attempt to learn the proper method of executing a curtsy, falls off the side of the stage. During the fight between the teachers, feathers, plates, and chairs can be seen flying about the attic. The philosophy teacher is then thrown down a flight of stairs, complains that one of his teeth was knocked loose during the skirmish, and finally pulls it out. Later, during the *turquerie*, Monsieur Jourdain puts a sword in his mouth and accidentally bites off the tip.

From the point of view of technical quality, Badel uses many good close-up shots, although there is an obvious lack of reaction shots at times. There are several excellent subjective camera shots (actors speaking to the camera as if it were the person being addressed). *Plongée* and *contre-plongée* angles (subjective camera looking down or looking up at someone) are used very well—but perhaps too often—especially in scenes where one actor is in the vestibule and another in the stairway. Some very excellent special effects are employed, especially in the scene where Monsieur Jourdain is being dressed in his new clothes. We see a quick series of still pictures, each showing him wearing an additional piece of clothing. The close of the film is quite extraordinary: the names of the cast members and the production credits are shown as part of a spectacular shower of fireworks in front of the château de Nandy. This was accomplished by filming the actual fireworks, and then superimposing the special effect letters over them.

The choreography all too often lacks precision, especially during the *turquerie* where too many dancers are involved. It becomes evident at times that many of these scenes are filmed inserts. It is obvious (by the different quality in sound) that most of the songs heard during the production were first pre-recorded, and then presented in play-back during the filming. This is especially noticeable when the Mufti sings during the *turquerie*. The music is that of Jean-Baptiste Lulli, performed by the O.R.T.F. symphony orchestra.

Two scenes from *Le Bourgeois gentilhomme* which always appear unnatural on stage seem quite natural in the television production. The first is in the sixth scene of the third act when Monsieur Jourdain and Dorante are secretly discussing preparations for the banquet in honor of the Marquise. Madame Jourdain and Nicole are present on stage at the same time, but supposedly out of hearing distance of the two men. On stage, the would-be lover and his friend must speak loudly enough for the audience to hear. Madame Jourdain and Nicole must do the same. This seems unrealistic on a stage, but, through theatrical convention, the situation is acceptable. In a television production, on the other hand, the two couples can whisper, and, using close-up camera shots, the scene appears perfectly normal. A similar problem occurs in the seventh scene of the fifth act. Covielle has moved aside with Madame Jourdain to explain to her that the son of the Grand Turk is, in fact, Cléonte and that the entire masquerade has been acted out to trick her husband. The new Mamamouchi is also present on stage and, of course, must not overhear the two speaking. Again, contrary to what occurs on stage, the couples may speak softly for the television production.

Less than eighteen months after Badel's production, Molière's same play was reproduced, this time by Pierre Sabbagh for his series *Au théâtre ce soir*—a series which normally chooses plays in the *théâtre de Boulevard* genre and presents them once only before a live audience at the Théâtre Marigny near the Champs-Elysées. This production is video-taped for future broadcast. Obviously, such a method greatly restricts the possibilities of camera movement and the use of special effects such as super-impositions and split-screens. The actors have to act primarily for the audience in the theater. The resulting gestures and the need to speak the roles loudly are the exact opposite of what creates the intimacy of television. For this reason, most critics and directors oppose such a use of the medium and refer to it as *anti-télévision*.[20] Although many serious critics rarely praise *Au théâtre ce soir* productions, most avoid criticizing the series too vehemently, perhaps because the programs are among the most popular with the viewers.

Le Bourgeois gentilhomme was produced for the series in 1970 and treated in a grotesque manner. The text was not respected. Neither were the author's stage directions. The camera cutting was almost as badly-timed as the choreography. Characters chase each other around the stage, up and down a staircase, around bushes, and along the cement wall surrounding a water fountain. In another scene, the philosophy teacher bites and tears his hat when he becomes angry, and is thrown into the water fountain by the other teachers. Later, he drinks hard liquor from a bottle, gets drunk, and finally accidentally spits on Monsieur Jourdain. These are but a few examples of the bad taste demonstrated in the production. One critic, Jacques Siclier, hardly restrained himself when he described the production of *Le Bourgeois gentilhomme* in his newspaper column.

"Au théâtre ce soir" sacrifie à la culture. Voici qu'on y monte Molière avec un luxe inhabituel . . . . On pourrait faire remarquer que cette entreprise n'était pas nécessaire puisqu'il existe un *Bourgeois gentilhomme* réalisé . . . pour la télévision par Pierre Badel, en décors naturels . . . . Oui, mais Molière . . . c'est avant tout le théâtre. Et ne faut-il pas féliciter Pierre Sabbagh de son ambition? On le pourrait peut-être si le spectacle avait d'autres qualités que ses décors et sa machinerie. Mais, hélas! dans la mise en scène de Jean Le Poulain, le *Bourgeois gentilhomme* devient une caricature outrancière. Si la conception de Pierre Badel appelait quelques réserves, elle avait du moins le mérite de l'origi-nalité et du bon goût. Jean Le Poulain joue M. Jourdain comme le vice-roi de la *Périchole*, son grand succès de cet hiver: en pantalonnade. Son Jourdain est un fantoche que seul explique le cabotinage. Il cligne de l'oeil au public, sautille, fait des mines, jette ses chaussures à travers la scène.

Le texte de Molière est prétexte à effects burlesques qui, loin de lui donner un nouvel éclairage, le ramènent au ras des planches. Nicole ne se contente pas d'éclater de rire en voyant l'habit ridicule de son maître, elle tombe les quatre fers en l'air, et Jourdain l'enfouit en trépignant sous un paquet de linge.[21]

---

[20] Andrey, No. 295, 85.
[21] "*Le Bourgeois gentilhomme* dans la mise en scène de Jean Le Poulain," *Le Monde*, May 9, 1970, 15.

When watching one of Molière's greatest works treated so unfortunately, one is reminded of Dorante's words in *La Critique de l'Ecole des femmes*: "C'est une étrange entreprise que celle dè faire rire les honnêtes gens."

By contrast, one of the greatest dramatic presentations ever to come out of the Buttes-Chaumont is Marcel Bluwal's black and white production of Molière's *Dom Juan*, broadcast on November 6, 1965, on the occasion of the play's three-hundredth anniversary. Feeling that Dom Juan was a character of all centuries, and not only of Molière's time, Bluwal used the camera to film the work in a timeless atmosphere. Several scenes take place on the streets and quais of Paris, for example, but nothing concrete is seen which would allow one to situate the action in any one period. The same is true for scenes filmed in the Parc de Versailles, in the royal salina of Arc-et-Senans, in the stables of Chantilly, in the Saint Sulpice Church, and in the large banquet rooms of the Trianon-Palace. Even the costumes are timeless. Many of the characters are attired in simple riding gear which would seem appropriate for the twentieth century, as well as for the seventeenth, eighteenth, or nineteenth centuries. Although most of the scenes take place in large rooms or outdoors, Bluwal respected the intimate quality of television with close-up shots and by focusing the activity on small groups. This intimacy is especially striking when one listens to the characters speaking. The soft-spoken tone of the voices makes us forget that we are in large spaces, and allows us to penetrate more deeply into the fictional world. One television critic suggested that this intimacy had been pushed too far and had ruined the true spirit of Molière's play.

> Bluwal a cinégraphié *Dom Juan*: du coup, il l'a rendu maussade. Arrachés au plateau, ce tremplin, et aux conventions scéniques, le gentil Pierrot n'est plus qu'un péquenaud inintelligible et Sganarelle un lourdaud bavard . . . . Il y a pire: la chute du ton, la transmutation de *Dom Juan* en spectacle "ordinaire." Les acteurs n'y peuvent rien: Piccoli [Dom Juan] est bien le séducteur qu'on dit, mais pour films de Vadim; Anouk Ferjac [Elvire] est toujours belle et sensible, mais la technique du gros plan [close-up shot] supprime la démarche et le geste qui *sont* Elvire autant que ses répliques. On joue vrai, c'est-à-dire quotidien, on remplace le mystère par l'imprévu, le lyrisme par le baroque. *Dom Juan* devient Dom Juan, mon ami, et, par instants, Dom Juan, mon pote. Et, finalement, on se demande à quoi sert une entreprise qui, malgré une telle dépense de talent, n'aboutit qu'à tuer l'âme d'un chef-d'oeuvre.[22]

Despite the harshness of this commentary, Bluwal's production is still considered by most experts as a masterpiece. Several scenes are of an incomparable beauty and, once viewed, can never be forgotten. For

---

[22] Morvan Lebesque, "La Tragédie des dramatiques," *L'Express*, November 8, 1965, 68.

example, when the statue of the Commandeur walks into Dom Juan's apartment to invite him for dinner, we witness *plongée* and *contre-plongée* camera shots. Since the statue of the Commandeur is approximately fifteen feet high, we look down at Dom Juan when the Commandeur is speaking to him, and we look up at the statue when Dom Juan is answering. The effect is quite striking. In a later scene, when Dom Juan is going to visit the Commandeur, he encounters a specter disguised as a woman, but speaking in a man's voice, who warns him of his impending doom if he does not repent. The specter's face suddenly takes on the appearance of a skull, and Dom Juan, angered, tries to pierce the apparition with his sword. But the specter literally fades away—something technically possible on television, but highly impracticable on stage.

Dom Juan was one of Molière's least known plays until Bluwal produced it for television and presented it to millions of viewers who were awed by the magnificence and contemporary relevance of this seventeenth-century work. Bluwal spent ten years preparing his film, and his name will, for a long time, remain synonymous with this production destined to become one of the great classics of French television.

It would be impossible in these few pages to treat in detail every production that French television has made of Molière's works. With a few exceptions, it can be said that the seventeenth-century author has been treated well, and, quite often, with imagination and respect.

A very limited number of Molière productions have also been used on French instructional television, *Télévision scolaire*. This organization is not part of the O.R.T.F. but is under the direction of the Institut Pédagogique National—a branch of the Ministère de l'Education Nationale—which, in fact, has its own offices and television studios in Montrouge, a suburb of Paris, and employs a complete staff of its own. The section concerned with the theater has, however, usually found it more advantageous to rent dramatic productions from the Buttes-Chaumont. It is more economical to do this than to produce a completely new version of a play. It also assures better quality, since the budget of *Télévision scolaire* is far inferior to that of the Buttes-Chaumont. A dramatic production could be presented in its entirely, but this would be too time consuming. Normally, therefore, only excerpts from one or more rented works are used for one program, or, more commonly, for a series of programs.

These excerpts do not constitute the main part of the televised lessons, but are used to illustrate vividly a central theme or topic presented to the students in several manners: a simulated classroom discussion, an interview with a director or an actor, or, more simply, one person lecturing before the camera.[23]

Many series concerning the theater have been produced by *Télévision scolaire* during the past decade: *Molière pour vous, Connaissance du Théâtre*, and *Théâtre, qui es-tu?* being but a few titles. A more recent series is *Théâtre de tous les temps*,[24] created in 1966 and designed for high school students. Seven productions were completed before 1970. These study various aspects of *Macbeth, Cinna, L'Ecole des femmes* and *Le Misanthrope, Les Fausses Confidences*, Goldoni's *Les Amoureux*, and Chekhov's *Les Trois Soeurs*. Each of these productions, about three hours in length, consists of two parts: two hours of excerpts, followed by a one-hour *Postface*. At the rate of one hour of television time per week, it therefore requires three weeks to broadcast one production. Selections are shown from both cinematographic and television versions of the same work, if both exist. Dramatic productions were rented from the Buttes-Chaumont for five of the series. The Institut Pédagogique National filmed its own excerpts for *L'Ecole des femmes* and *Les Fausses Confidences*, but this procedure proved too costly. The plan of a *Postface* varies from one series to the next. It can consist of discussions between students and teachers, or interviews with directors and actors, or both these approaches, but it is always well illustrated with television or cinema excerpts, some of which have already been seen during the first part of the program.

Several of the Buttes-Chaumont productions of Molière's works, therefore, have been used for two different purposes. But whether broadcast for general purposes or included in an instructional series, they no doubt have added joy to the education of students and to the continuing education of their older countrymen.

One final aspect of Molière and French television is worthy of examination. It deals not with the broadcast of one of his works, but with the production of an original work written for the O.R.T.F., Pierre-Aimé Touchard's *Il y a trois cents ans ce soir*, a ninety-minute program directed by Roger Iglésis, broadcast on October 24, 1958, to commemorate the three-hundredth anniversary of Molière's first performance before King

---

[23] See M. Egly, "Les Médecins. Molière aux sources," *First Seminar for Producers and Directors of School Television* (Basel: European Broadcasting Union Press, February 1962), 42.

[24] I am grateful to the producer of the series, Raymond Laubreaux, for the following information.

Louis XIV. Touchard's work, presented live, was summed up in the magazine *Mon programme* as follows:

> En 1646, Molière et sa troupe ont subi un échec à Paris et ils sont repartis pour la province. En 1658, ils revinrent à Paris et, le 24 octobre, ils jouèrent au Louvre, pour la première fois, devant Louis XIV. Représentation décisive: de l'accueil du Roi dépend le sort de l'Illustre Théâtre. Au programme: *Nicomède*. C'est Molière lui-même qui a choisi la tragédie de Corneille pour faire sa rentrée. Le comédien nommé Molière n'est pas un bon tragédien et son spectacle ennuie le Roi et la Cour. Cela se présente mal! Ecoutant la suggestion d'une de ses artistes, le chef de troupe décide de jouer une farce de sa façon: *Le Docteur amoureux*. On la joue, le Roi se déride, les courtisans n'oublient pas d'en faire autant. On rit. L'affaire est dans le sac: Jean-Baptiste Poquelin a gagné son match: l'avenir s'ouvre devant lui.[25]

Touchard's play was preceded by a ten-minute prologue, during which he and Pierre Dumayet discussed the historical background of Molière and L'Illustre Théâtre, as well as the Parisian theater at the time: the near monopoly of the Hôtel de Bourgogne and the Théâtre du Marais, the prestige of such actors as Montfleury, Floridor, and Mlle Beauchâteau. Numerous pictures and drawings are shown to illustrate the discussion. The importance of the performance before Louis XIV is well explained: Molière has secretly obtained the protection of the King's brother, Monsieur, and through the efforts of this man, Molière has received permission to present a play in the Salle des Cariatides, in the Louvre, with the King himself present. The success or failure of the performance will decide Molière's fate and that of his company. Among the King's invited guests are Montfleury and Floridor, who are certainly not anxious to see a third acting company receive royal protection. The prologue ends with two comments on Touchard's play. First, the language is that of the mid-1950's. Touchard felt that to use the French spoken at the time of Molière would have been too distracting and would have made the play seem, in fact, less realistic. Finally, it is explained that, in reality, Molière chose the farce *Le Docteur amoureux* to follow *Nicomède*, but since the text of this farce is lost today, another of the author's farces was substituted for it in the television production: *Le Médecin volant*.

One of the interesting aspects of this dramatic presentation is the utilization of different points of view. Although most of the action occurs backstage—in the wings or in Molière's dressing room—the action on the stage and the reactions of the King and his guests are also shown, as seen

[25] (Anon.), No. 1016 (October 18, 1958), 35.

from backstage. (The audience can be seen through a peephole.) Likewise, the stage is shown as viewed from the audience, and vice versa. Such complicated camera maneuvering is extremely hazardous in a live program, but director Roger Iglésis handled the problem masterfully.

As *Il y a trois cents ans ce soir* opens, the performance of *Nicomède* is nearing the end of the third act. The atmosphere backstage is one of disappointment, since the audience—especially the King—seems completely uninterested. The actors begin speaking frankly among themselves and accuse Molière of putting the entire fate of the company at stake with this one performance. They feel he should have followed Madeleine Béjart's plan, which was to perform their plays before less important audiences at the Jeu de Paume, before attempting a performance in the presence of Louis XIV. During the intermission of *Nicomède*, Monsieur comes backstage, and Molière obtains his permission to present a farce after the completion of the first play. As Molière later explains to Du Parc: "C'est un peu risqué, parce qu'on n'a jamais encore présenté quelque chose d'aussi cru à la Cour."[26] A little later, still during intermission, there comes about a complete misunderstanding between Molière and the other actors. They accuse him, to his face, of wanting to take over complete control of the company from Madeleine Béjart, of showing favoritism towards the younger actresses, and of reserving the best male roles for himself. Molière defends himself—more or less well—and manages to reunite the company and to get it to agree to go on with the evening's performance.

The King and most of his guests react very favorably to *Le Médecin volant*, the last scenes of which are shown as seen by the audience in the Louvre. After the performance, Monsieur again comes backstage to congratulate the actors, and to inform them that the King has granted them permission to perform regularly in the theater of the Petit-Bourbon.

Although this dramatic production has not become one of the classics of the Buttes-Chaumont, it remains important as an example of an original work based on a literary topic. Besides being delightful and enjoyable, it is factual and offers the interested viewer many new insights into the life and times of one of the world's greatest literary figures. What could have been more appropriate on the anniversary of Molière's first triumph before the Sun King and his Court?

During 1973, the anniversary year of Molière's death, many scholars have shown in their own way how Molière was a genius and how the years

---

[26] *Il y a trois cents ans ce soir* (Paris: Imprimeries de l'O.R.T.F., 1958), 26.

that separate us from the time of his death have proven this. The author's reputation has withstood the test of time. It has also withstood the tests of modern technology. The cinema and especially television have done much, in France at least, to further solidify the reputation of one of literature's best-known and best-loved authors. Television has brought to life, more than ever, Molière's characters and, indeed, Molière himself. Molière est mort! Vive Molière!

Bibliography
and the State of Criticism

*When the matter of art encounters some recipient, when it is observed
or perused and absorbed by its audience, whenever the process of dissemination and exposure takes place—then an inexorable change
follows in both the matter and the audience. Indeed there can be only
one fixed point in the study and performance of Molière's plays, and
that is the plays themselves; yet even the texts are established only
painstakingly and through a process of drawn-out dialectics, established in a manner of speaking, for the process is by no means finished.
Thus, to delineate the integration of Molière with our own sensibilities
at any given point in time is a calculus of astounding complexity. What
we know of the original matter has been filtered through a civilization
it helped to shape. The reaction of this or that director, critic, or historian may have modified the world's view of, for example, the culpa-
bility of a Dom Juan. Opinions have given rise to enforcing and counter
opinions, and throughout it all the fictional being himself has accommo-
dated the sometimes outrageous vacillations of politics, morality, and
esthetic values.*

*Those who have come to know Molière and have found an ear to
attend their analyses have participated in the vital process of maintaining
and passing on the patrimony of the playwright. Molière criticism, and
thus our knowledge and appreciation of Molière, could not, for example,
be the same after W. G. Moore's* Molière: A New Criticism *as it was
before. Those who catalogue and order the analyses likewise participate
in the vital act of preservation and modification: while Paul Saintonge
would be the first to claim that the great Molière has meant much to
him, it should not be forgotten that the good professor has returned the
favor. To make sense of the quick threads binding the expression of
Molière to the axioms of our own age is one (always incomplete) task*

663

of this section. Here the reader will encounter both material for further research and the product of research.

Hannelore Wierschin provides a list of seventeenth and eighteenth century Molière editions now located in North American libraries, thus establishing information of particular relevance to scholars of those countries. Erich Albrecht presents his checklist of translations. From these two lists one understands that there is yet much to learn of Molière. Laurence Romero centers his essay around a fundamental and recurring topic of Molière criticism, the relationship between the plays (or Molière himself) and morality.

A LIST OF MOLIÈRE EDITIONS
OF THE SEVENTEENTH
AND EIGHTEENTH CENTURIES
IN NORTH AMERICAN LIBRARIES

Hannelore Wierschin

The following list of Molière editions is primarily based on the hitherto unpublished Molière file of the National Union Catalog in Washington (*The National Union Catalog. Pre –1956 Imprints*. vol. 1– London, 1968–). To complete the information supplied by the participating libraries or to identify certain editions, additional bibliographical sources have been consulted and these are listed in parentheses before the symbols designating the libraries where the specific editions can be found. In most cases these bibliographical sources as well as the National Union Catalog supply more information than can be included here, e.g. contents for multivolume editions, type of binding, type of paper, relationship to earlier or later editions of the same work, illustrations, etc.

This list does not claim to be absolutely complete. Though the libraries which can be expected to have major holdings of Molière editions (Harvard University Library, Yale University Library, the Library of Congress, and the New York Public Library) have made a conscientious effort to report every cataloged item to the National Union Catalog, other libraries have reported only selectively from their collections.

Multivolume sets of collected works are listed under collections only. The frequent practice of the Library of Congress of listing collected works under the collective titles and also under the individual titles of the single volumes has not been followed. In cases where a library cataloged an edition of collected works under the individual titles only, I gathered them under the collective title.

Versions of Molière's plays in other languages which can be regarded as adaptations rather than as translations are included only if the National Union Catalog also lists the work under Molière rather than under the adaptor. The format (in centimeters) is included whenever this information was supplied by the individual libraries. Bilingual editions are interfiled with the translations, whereas polyglot editions (in three or more languages) are listed after the corresponding titles of the original (i.e. before the translations). The heading "Collections" includes complete and selective editions of Molière's works.

Abbreviations and Symbols

AU	University of Alabama, University, Ala.
Banerji	Banerji, H. K. *Henry Fielding*. New York, 1962.
BM	*British Museum. General Catalogue of Printed Books. Photolithographic Ed. to 1955*. London, 1965–66.
BN	*Catalogue général des livres imprimés de la Bibliothèque Nationale*. Paris, 1897–
CLSU	University of Southern California, Los Angeles, Calif.
CLU	University of California, Los Angeles
CLU*	*University of California, Los Angeles. Dictionary Catalog of the University Library, 1919–1962*. Boston, 1963.
CLU-C	University of California, Los Angeles. William Andrews Clark Memorial Library
Copinger	Copinger, H. B. *The Elzevier Press*. London, 1927.
CSmH	Henry E. Huntington Library, San Marino, Calif.
CtY	Yale University, New Haven, Conn.
CU	University of California, Berkeley, Calif.
CU*	*University of California, Berkeley. Library. Author-Title Catalog*. Boston, 1963.
CU-S	University of California, San Diego, La Jolla, Calif.
CU-S*	*University of California, San Diego, La Jolla, Calif. Central University Library. Card Catalog.*
DFo	Folger Shakespeare Library, Washington, D. C.
DLC	U.S. Library of Congress, Washington, D. C.
DSI	Smithsonian Institution Libraries, Washington, D. C.
FMF	Flager Memorial Library, Miami, Fla.
Fromm	Fromm, H. *Bibliographie deutscher Übersetzungen aus dem Französischen, 1700–1948*. Baden-Baden, 1950–53.
FU	University of Florida, Gainesville, Fla.
Gale	*Library of Congress and National Union Catalog Author Lists, 1942–1962: A Master Cumulation*. Detroit, Gale Research Co., 1969–71.
ICN	Newberry Library, Chicago, Ill.
ICRL	Center for Research Libraries, Chicago, Ill.
ICRL*	*The Center for Research Libraries [Chicago]. Catalog. Monographs*. Chicago, 1969–70.
ICU	University of Chicago, Chicago, Ill.
IEN	Northwestern University, Evanston, Ill.
InU	Indiana University, Bloomington, Ind.
IU	University of Illinois, Urbana, Ill.
Lacroix	Lacroix, P. *Bibliographie moliéresque. 2. éd*. Paris, 1875.
LU	Louisiana State University, Baton Rouge, La.
MB	Boston Public Library, Boston, Mass.
MdBG	Goucher College, Baltimore, Md.

MdBP	Peabody Institute, Baltimore, Md.
MeB	Bowdoin College, Brunswick, Maine
MH	Harvard University, Cambridge, Mass.
MH*	*Catalogue of the Molière Collection in Harvard College Library.* Cambridge, Mass., 1906. In: Library of Harvard University. Bibliographical Contributions, no. 57.
MiU	University of Michigan, Ann Arbor, Mich.
MnU	University of Minnesota, Minneapolis, Minn.
MoU	University of Missouri, Columbia, Mo.
MWA	American Antiquarian Society, Worcester, Mass.
MWelC	Wellesley College, Wellesley, Mass.
MWiW-C	Williams College, Williamstown, Mass. Chapin Library
NcD	Duke University Library, Durham, N.C.
NcU	University of North Carolina, Chapel Hill, N.C.
NdU	University of North Dakota Library, Grand Forks, N.D.
NIC	Cornell University, Ithaca, N.Y.
NjN	Newark Public Library, N.J.
NjP	Princeton University, Princeton, N.J.
NjR	Rutgers, The State University, New Brunswick, N.J.
NL	Newberry Library, Chicago, N.Y.
NN	New York Public Library, N.Y.
NNC	Columbia University, N.Y.
NNU-W	New York University Libraries, N.Y. Washington Square Library
NPV	Vassar College, Poughkeepsie, N.Y. Library
NPV*	*Vassar College, Poughkeepsie, N.Y. Library, Card Catalog*
NRU	University of Rochester, Rochester, N.Y.
NUC	*The National Union Catalog. Pre –1956 Imprints.* London, Mansell, 1968–
OCl	Cleveland Public Library, Ohio
OClStM	Saint Mary's Seminary, Cleveland, Ohio
OClU	Cleveland State University, Cleveland, Ohio (formerly Fenn College)
OCU	University of Cincinnati, Cincinnati, Ohio
OO	Oberlin College, Oberlin, Ohio
OU	Ohio State University, Columbus, Ohio
PBm	Bryn Mawr College, Bryn Mawr, Pa.
PP	Free Library of Philadelphia, Philadelphia, Pa.
PPAmP	American Philosophical Society, Philadelphia, Pa.
PPL	Library Company of Philadelphia, Philadelphia, Pa.
PPL-R	Library Company of Philadelphia, Ridgeway Branch, Pa.
PPM	Mercantile Library, Philadelphia, Pa.
PPRF	Rosenbach Foundation, Philadelphia, Pa.
PU	University of Pennsylvania, Philadelphia, Pa.
PV	Villanova College, Villanova, Pa.
PWW	Washington & Jefferson College, Washington, Pa.
Quérard	Quérard, J. M. *La France littéraire.* Paris, 1827–64.
ScU	University of South Carolina, Columbia, S.C.
Tchemerzine	Tchemerzine, A. *Bibliographie d'éditions originales et rares d'auteurs français des XVe, XVIe, XVIIe et XVIIIe siècles . . .* Paris, 1927–33.
TxU	University of Texas, Austin, Tex.
ViU	University of Virginia, Charlottesville, Va.

ViWC   Colonial Williamsburg, Williamsburg, Va.
Willems   Willems, A.C.J. *Les Elzevier*. Bruxelles, 1880.
WU   University of Wisconsin, Madison, Wis.

Collections—French

Les Oeuvres de Monsieur Molière. Paris, J. Guignard fils, 1666. 2 vols. (NUC, MH*
    1) MH.
Oeuvres de Monsieur de Molière. Paris, D. Thierry et C. Barbin, 1674–75. 7 vols.
    (Lacroix 269, NUC, MH* 2) MH.
Les Oeuvres de Monsieur Molière. Amsterdam, Chez Jacques le Jeune [i.e. D.
    Elzevier] 1675. 5 vols. 13 cm. Made up of remainders of separate plays printed
    at Amsterdam with the imprint "Suivant la copie imprimée à Paris" dated 1673–75;
    with general title pages. For vol. 6 see under *Les Oeuvres posthumes*. Amsterdam,
    1689. (Lacroix 271, NUC, MH* 3) DLC MH MWiW-C: vol. 1 only, cataloged
    individually. NcU: vol. 4 only, cataloged individually.
Les Oeuvres de Monsieur Molière. Amsterdam, Chez Jacques le Jeune [i.e. D.
    Elzevier] 1679. 5 vols. 13 cm. Made up of remainders of separate plays and some
    newly printed plays printed at Amsterdam with the imprint "Suivant la copie
    imprimée à Paris" (except Le Malade imaginaire, which reads "Suivant qu'elle
    a esté représentée à Paris") dated 1674–81; with general title pages. (Lacroix 272,
    NUC, MH* 4) DLC MH MnU: vol. 1 only, cataloged individually.
Les Oeuvres de Monsieur de Molière. Paris, D. Thierry, C. Barbin et P. Trabouillet,
    1681. 5 vols. 15½ cm. (Lacroix 273, NUC, MH* 5, 6) CLU-C MH.
*Les Oeuvres de Monsieur de Molière. Revuës, corrigées & augmentées. Enrichies de
    figures en taille-douce*. Paris, D. Thierry, C. Barbin et P. Trabouillet, 1682. 8 vols.
    16¼ cm. Vols. 7–8 have title: *Les Oeuvres posthumes de Molière*. (Lacroix 277,
    NUC, MH* 7) CLU-C CU MWiW-C MB MH NN.
*Les Oeuvres de Monsieur Molière. Edition nouvelle, enrichie de figures en taille-douce ;
    & augmentée des oeuvres posthumes*. Amsterdam, Chez Jacques le Jeune [i.e.
    H.Wetstein] 1684. 5 vols. 13½ cm. Made up of remainders of separate plays, some
    newly printed plays, general title pages, with recuttings of Brissart's engr. plates.
    For vol. 6 see *Les Oeuvres posthumes*. Amsterdam, 1684. (Lacroix 279, NUC,
    MH* 8) CtY: vol. 5 only, cataloged individually. DLC: copy 1, vol. 1–5; copy 2,
    vol. 5. InU: vol. 1 only. MH MnU: vol. 1 only cataloged individually.
Les Oeuvres posthumes de Monsieur de Molière. Enrichies de figures en taille-douce.
    Amsterdam, Chez Jacques le Jeune [i.e. H. Wetstein] 1684. 5 pts. in 1 vol. 13 cm.
    (Lacroix 70, NUC, MH* 8) DLC MH.
Les Oeuvres posthumes de Monsieur de Molière. Enrichies de figures en taille-douce.
    Amsterdam, Chez Guillaume le Jeune [i.e. H. Wetstein [1689. 5 pts. in 1 vol. 13½]
    cm. (Lacroix 70, NUC, MH* 9) DLC MH.
*Les Oeuvres de Monsieur Molière. Edition nouvelle, enrichie de figures en taille-
    douce; & augmentée des oeuvres posthumes*. Amsterdam, H. Wetstein, 1691. 6 vols.
    14 cm. (NUC) ICU.
*Les Oeuvres de Monsieur de Molière, revues, corrigées et augmentées du Médecin
    vangé et des Epitaphes les plus curieuses sur sa mort. Enrichies de figures en taille-
    douce à chaque pièce*. Lyon, J. Lyons, 1692. 8 vols. (Lacroix 283, NUC) DLC.
*Les Oeuvres de Monsieur de Molière. Nouvelle édition, corrigée & augmentée des
    oeuvres posthumes*. Brusselles, G. de Backer, 1694. 4 vols. (Lacroix 284, NUC,
    MH* 10) MH.

Les Comédies de Monsieur de Molière. Edition nouvelle. Nuremberg, J. D. Tauber, 1694. 3 vols. in 1. Evidently the French portion of the German and French ed. published by Tauber in this year. (NUC, MH* 11) MH.

Les Oeuvres posthumes. Lyon, J. Lions, 1696. 2 vols. (NUC) InU: vol. 2 only.

Les Oeuvres de Monsieur de Molière. Revues, corrigées & augmentées . . . Paris, D. Thierry, C. Barbin et P. Trabouillet, 1697. 8 vols. $17\frac{1}{2}$ cm. Vols. 7–8 have title: *Les Oeuvres posthumes de Molière.* (NUC, MH* 12) ICU MH MiU ViWC.

Les Oeuvres de Monsieur Molière. Amsterdam, H. Wetstein, 1698. 4 vols. (Lacroix 289, NUC, MH* 13) CLU-C MH.

Oeuvres de M. de Molière. Revues, corrigées et augmentées, enrichies de figures en taille-douce. Toulouse, J. F. Caranove, 1699. 8 vols. See also under *Oeuvres.* Toulouse [1710?]. (Lacroix 290, NUC) CtY: vol. 1 only. InU: vol. 8 only. MH: vols. 1–8 (vol. 1, "Nouvelle et dernière édition"; 2–8, "Revues, corrigées & augmentées"; 8 has imprint: Toulouse, J. Dupuy [etc.] 1697) NL: vol. 8 only.

Les Oeuvres de Molière. Berlin, R. Roger, imprimeur & libraire de S. S. Electorale, 1700. 4 vols. 16 cm. (Lacroix 291, NUC) CtY.

Les Oeuvres de Monsieur Molière. Nouvelle édition, revue & corrigée. Amsterdam, H. Desbordes, 1704. 4 vols. (Lacroix 295, NUC) IU.

Oeuvres. Nouvelle édition. Liége, J. F. Broncart, 1706. 4 vols. 15 cm. (Lacroix 296, NUC) LU: vol. 4, pp. 333–404 = Les Amans magnifiques, cataloged individually.

Les Oeuvres. Nouvelle édition, revuë, corrigée & augmentée. Paris, La veuve G. Huart, 1710. 8 vols. (MH* 15) MH.

Oeuvres. Tome 1. Toulouse, J. F. Caranove, 1699 [1710?]. A pirated and antedated ed. based on the Paris 1710 ed. (NUC; The Nation, New York, March 26, 1914; Le Moliériste, Paris, vol. 8, 1886, p. 213) MH.

Oeuvres. Nouvelle édition, revue, corrigée et augmentée (avec la Vie de l'auteur), enrichie de figures en taille-douce. Amsterdam, 1713. 4 vols. (Lacroix 302, NUC) MH PPL-R.

Oeuvres. Nouvelle édition, revue, corrigée et augmentée. Amsterdam, J. F. Bernard, 1716. 8 vols. (Lacroix 304, NPV*) NPV: vol. 2 only.

Les Oeuvres. Nouvelle édition, revue, corrigée & augmentée. Paris, Compagnie des libraires, 1718. 8 vols. (Lacroix 307, NUC, BN, MH* 16) MH.

Les Oeuvres. Nouvelle édition, revue, corrigée & augmentée d'une nouvelle Vie de l'auteur & de la Princesse d'Elide, toute en vers, telle qu'elle se joue à présent, imprimée pour la première fois. Amsterdam, 1725. 4 vols. (Lacroix 309, NUC, MH* 17) CLU-C MH MWA NPV: vol. 4 only. PPL-R.

Oeuvres de Molière. Enrichies de jolies figures en taille-douce. Paris, Compagnie des libraires, 1730. 8 vols. (Lacroix 312, NUC, MH* 18) InU MH PPL-R.

Oeuvres. Nouvelle édition revue, corrigée & augmentée. Rotterdam, B. Arnoul, 1732. 8 vols. in 4. (Lacroix 313, NUC, MH* 19) MH.

Oeuvres. Paris, H. Charpentier, 1733. 6 vols. (Lacroix 314, NUC) CtY: vol. 5 only.

Oeuvres de Molière. Nouvelle édition. Paris [De l'imprimerie de P. Prault] 1734. 6 vols. 30 cm. Contains 33 plates by François Boucher, engr. by Laurent Cars. See also following entry. (Lacroix 316, NUC, MH* 20) CLU-C CtY MH NN PBm.

Les Oeuvres de Molière. Inventées & dessinées par F. Boucher & sculptées par L. Cars. [Paris? 1734?] 33 plates. Title page in ms. Being plates from ed. Lacroix 316? See also preceding entry. (NUC) NN.

Les Oeuvres de Monsieur de Molière. Nouvelle édition, revue, corrigée & augmentée d'une nouvelle Vie de l'auteur & de la Princesse d'Elide, toute en vers, telle qu'elle se joue à présent, imprimée pour la première fois. Enrichie de figures en taille-douce.

Amsterdam, H. Uytwerf, 1735. 4 vols. (Lacroix 317, NUC, MH* 21) MH.

The same. Amsterdam, Wetstein & Smith, 1735. 4 vols. 14 cm. (Lacroix 317, NUC, MH* 21).

The same. La Haye, J. M. Husson, 1735. 4 vols. 16 cm. (Lacroix 317, NUC) WU: vols. 1–2 only.

Oeuvres. Nouvelle édition. Paris, David l'aîné, 1739. 8 vols. Edited by A. F. Jolly. (MH* 22) MH OCU.

Les Oeuvres de Monsieur de Molière. Nouvelle édition. Amsterdam, Arkstée et Merkus, 1744. 4 vols. (Lacroix 325, NUC) DLC.

Les Oeuvres de Monsieur de Molière. Nouvelle édition, revue & corrigée. Tubingue, C. G. Cotta, 1747. 6 vols. in 3. (Lacroix 327, NUC) DLC OCl.

Oeuvres. Nouvelle édition [éditée par François Antoine Jolly, illustrée par François Boucher]. Paris, Damonneville, 1749. 8 vols. 14 cm. (NUC) MH PU ViU.

Oeuvres. Nouvelle édition. Paris, Prault fils [and Durand] 1749. 8 vols. Vol. 1 published by Prault fils; 2–8 by Durand. A reprint of Jolly's 1739 ed. (MH* 24) MH.

Oeuvres de Molière. Nouvelle édition. Amsterdam [etc.] 1750. 4 vols. $14\frac{1}{2}$ cm. (NUC) CtY.

Oeuvres. Nouvelle édition. Paris, Bordelet, 1753. 8 vols. A reprint of Jolly's 1739 ed. (MH* 25) MH: vol. 1 only.

Oeuvres. Nouvelle édition. Paris, Ganeau, 1753. 8 vols. A reprint of Jolly's 1739 ed. (NUC) MH.

Oeuvres. Nouvelle édition. Paris, Le Clerc, 1753. 8 vols. $14\frac{1}{2}$ cm. A reprint of Jolly's 1739 ed. (Lacroix 335, NUC) CtY: vols. 4–8 only.

Pièces choisies. Edinburgh, 1754. 431 pp. (NUC) OO.

Oeuvres de Molière. Nouvelle édition. Paris, Mouchet, Ganeau, 1758. 8 vols. 15 cm. (NUC, Quérard) DLC: vol. 5 only.

Les Oeuvres de Monsieur de Molière. Nouvelle édition, revuë, corrigée & augmentée d'une nouvelle Vie de l'auteur & de La Princesse d'Elide. Enrichie de figures en taille-douce. Basle, E. Tourneisen, 1760. 4 vols. 14 cm. (NUC, MH* 26) MH NcD.

Oeuvres de Molière. Nouvelle édition. Paris, Aumont, 1760. 8 vols. $14\frac{1}{2}$ cm. (NUC) ViU.

Oeuvres de Molière. Nouvelle édition. Paris, Brocas, 1760. 8 vols. (NUC) MH PPM.

Oeuvres de Molière. Nouvelle édition. Paris, Davitz, 1760. 6 vols. (NUC) OCl.

Les Oeuvres. Nouvelle édition, revue, corrigée et augmentée de l'explication des mots et des phrases les plus difficiles [par H. F. Roux et Herold]. Jène, P. Fickelscherr, 1761. 3 vols. (NUC, MH* 27) MH.

Oeuvres. Nouvelle édition, augmentée de la Vie de l'auteur & des remarques historiques et critiques, par M. de Voltaire. Amsterdam et Leipzig, Arkstée & Merkus, 1765. 6 vols. (NUC, MH* 28) DLC MB: vols. 1–2 only. MH NN: vols. 1–3, 5–6.

Oeuvres. Nouvelle édition. Paris, La veuve David, 1768. 8 vols. (MH* 29) MH.

Chef-d'oeuvres. Liége, 1770. 2 vols. (NUC, MH* 30) MH.

Oeuvres de Molière. Nouvelle édition. Paris, Bailly, 1770. 8 vols. 15 cm. (NUC, CU-S*) CU-S MH: vol. 4 only.

Oeuvres de Molière. Avec des remarques grammaticales, des avertissemens et des observations sur chaque pièce, par M. Bret. Paris, Compagnie des libraires associés, 1773. 6 vols. 20 cm. (NUC, MH* 31) CtY DLC MeB MH NN.

Oeuvres de Molière. Avec des remarques grammaticales, des avertissemens et des observations sur chaque pièce, par M. Bret. Edition augmentée . . . Neuchâtel, Société typographique, 1775. 6 vols. $18\frac{1}{2}$ cm. (NUC) CtY.

L'Esprit de Molière, ou Choix de maximes, pensées, caractères, portraits & réflexions tirés de ses ouvrages. Avec un abrégé de sa vie, un catalogue de ses pièces, le temps de leurs premières représentations, et des anecdotes relatives à ces pièces. Londres, Paris, Lacombe, 1777. 2 vols. 17 cm. Compiled by L. F. Beffara. (NUC, MH* 120) CtY ICN InU IU MH.

Oeuvres de Molière. Avec des remarques grammaticales, des avertissements et des observations sur chaque pièce. Par M. Bret. Paris, Aux dépens des Libraires associés, 1778. 8 vols. $14\frac{1}{2}$ cm. (NUC) NNC.

La Petite Thalie, ou Morceaux quintessenciés des plus belles pièces de Molière, suivis de remarques grammaticales et autres, utiles à l'instruction de la jeunesse qui s'applique à l'étude du françois. Berlin, Weber, 1780. 253 pp. (CU*) CU.

Oeuvres de Molière. Nouvelle édition. Londres et Paris, Valade, 1784. 7 vols. 12 cm. (Lacroix 353, NUC, MH* 32) MH NjP.

Oeuvres de Molière. Avec des remarques grammaticales, des avertissements et des observations sur chaque pièce, par M. Bret. Paris, Aux dépens des Libraires associés, 1786. 8 vols. 15 cm. (NUC, MH* 33) CtY MH: vols. 1–6, 8.

Chef-d'oeuvres de Molière. Paris, Bélin [etc.] 1787. 94, x, 132, vi, 114 pp. $13\frac{1}{2}$ cm. In: Petite bibliothèque des théâtres [vol. 44] Théâtre françois, comédies, t. 13. (NUC) MiU.

Chefs d'oeuvres [sic] *de Molière.* Rouen, J. Racine, 1787. 2 vols. (NUC, Quérard) NjP PPL.

Oeuvres de Molière. Avec des remarques grammaticales, des avertissemens et des observations sur chaque pièce, par. M. Bret. Paris, Compagnie des libraires associés, 1788. 6 vols. $20\frac{1}{2}$ cm. (NUC, MH* 34) DLC MB MH NN PPL-R.

Oeuvres. Avec la Vie de l'auteur par M. de Voltaire. Berlin, F. Maurer, 1788–91. 12 vols. in 6. (NUC) MH.

Les Oeuvres de Monsieur de Molière. Nouvelle édition, revue, corrigée & augmentée d'une nouvelle Vie de l'auteur & de La Princesse d'Elide, toute en vers, telle qu'elle se joue à présent. Enrichie de figures en taille-douce. Basle, E. & J. R. Thourneisen, 1791. 4 vols. 13 cm. (NUC) CtY: vol. 4 only.

Chefs-d'oeuvre [sic] *dramatiques.* Paris, Bélin, 1791. 10 vols. (Lacroix 363, NUC) NN.

Oeuvres de J. B. Poquelin de Molière. Paris, P. Didot l'aîné, 1791–94. 6 vols. $31\frac{1}{2}$ cm. In: Collection des auteurs classiques françois et latins. (NUC, MH* 35) DLC MH NjN PV.

Oeuvres choisies de Molière, en deux volumes. Avec des remarques grammaticales et les observations de M. Bret sur chaque pièce. Oxford, J. Cooke, et Hanwell et Parker [etc.] 1799. 2 vols. $12\frac{1}{2}$ cm. (NUC, MH* 36) CtY MH.

Oeuvres. Edition stéréotype, d'après le procédé de Firmin Didot. Paris, P. Didot l'aîné et F. Didot, 1799. 8 vols. (NUC, BN, Gale, MH* 37 Quérard) DLC DSI-Watts de P. Coll. FMF: vols. 1–2 only. MdBP MH: vol. 6 only. NN OClStM PPM ScU.

Collections—Polyglot

Dialogues français, anglais et italiens sur divers sujets aussi intéressants qu'agréables, extraits des comédies de Molière [par L. Chambaud]. Paris, Vergani, an VII [1799] iv, 122 p. 22 cm. For edition in French and English (Dialogues French and English . . . London, 1767) see under section *Collections—English.* (Lacroix 238, NUC, MH* 121) MH ViU.

Collections—English

Molière's Plays. Translated by John Ozell. London, 1714. 6 vols. See under *Don Garcia of Navarre; or, The Jealous Prince,* London, 1714.

The Works of Monsieur de Molière. London, Printed for B. Lintott, 1714. 6 vols. Translated by John Ozell. (NUC, MH* 131) CLU-C CSmH CtY ICU LU MB MH PV TxU.

Select Comedies of Mr. de Molière, French and English. In eight Volumes. With a Frontispiece to each Comedy. To which is prefix'd a Curious Print of the Author, with his Life in French and English. London, Printed for J. Watts, 1732. 8 vols. 17½ cm. Probably translated by Henry Baker, Martin Clare, and James Miller. (NUC, MH* 132) CtY LU: each title cataloged individually. MdBG MH MWelC NjP NjR: each title cataloged individually. PWW TxU.

The Works of Molière, French and English. London, J. Watts, 1739. 10 vols. Translated by Henry Baker and James Miller. (Lacroix 644, NUC, MH* 133) MH OCU PPL-R TxU.

The Works of Molière, French and English. A New Edition. London, Printed for D. Browne and A. Millar, 1739–55. 10 vols. 17 cm. Translated by Henry Baker and James Miller. (NUC) CtY NN.

The Works of Molière, French and English. London, Printed by and for J. Watts, 1748. 10 vols. 17 cm. Translated by Henry Baker and James Miller. (NUC, MH* 134) CLSU DLC: vols. 1, 3–10. MH PPL-R PV ViU.

The Works of Molière. Glasgow, Printed by R. Urie and sold by J. Gilmour, 1751. 5 vols. Translated by Henry Baker and James Miller. (NUC) CtY ICN MH: copy 1, vols. 1–5; copy 2, vol. 5, with autograph of Ellis Cornelia Knight and ms. notes in Lady Hamilton's hand. PPL-R.

The Works of Molière, French and English. London, Printed for D. Browne and A. Millar, 1755. 10 vols. 17 cm. Translated by Henry Baker and James Miller. (NUC, MH* 135) DLC MdBP MH MoU: Microprint, each volume cataloged individually. OClU ViU.

Dialogues French and English, upon the Most Entertaining and Humorous Subjects. Extracted out of the Comedies of Molière, and Containing the Idiom of the Conversation of Courtiers, Citizens, Merchants [etc.]. By Lewis Chambaud. 3^d Ed. London, G. Keith, 1767. 168 pp. For ed. in French, English, and Italian (*Dialogues français, anglais et italiens.* Paris, 1799) see under section *Collections —Polyglot.* (NUC, BM) MH.

The Works of Molière. A New Translation. Berwick, Printed for R. Taylor, 1771. 6 vols. 18 cm. Translation variously attributed to John Ozell, Henry Baker, James Miller, and Charles J. Johnson. (NUC, MH* 136) AU CLU-C CtY MH MnU.

Plays. Berwick, Printed for R. Taylor, 1771. 92 pp. 17½ cm. (NUC) CtY.

The Works of Monsieur de Molière. London, B. Lintott, 1784. 6 vols. (NUC) PV.

Collections—German

Derer Comödien des Herrn von Molière . . . Erster [-dritter] Theil . . . Der Jugend aber, welche der frantzösischen Sprach begierig seyn mag . . . in das Teutsche übersetzet durch J [ohanna] E [leonore] P [etersen]. Mit schönen Kupffern gezieret und das erstemal also gedruckt. Nürnberg, D. Tauber, 1694. 3 vols. 16 cm. (NUC, Fromm) CtY MH.

Histrio gallicus comico-satyrus sine exemplo: Oder Die überaus anmuthigen und lustigen Comödien des . . . Herrn von Molière, wieder aufs Neue . . . in das reine Teutsche übersetzt. Nürnberg, J. D. Tauber, 1695. 3 vols. 16 cm. (NUC) AU CtY ICU.

Sämmtliche Lustspiele. Nach einer freyen und sorgfältigen Uebersetzung von F. S. Bierling. Hamburg, Herold, 1752. 4 vols. (CU*, NUC, MH* 143, Fromm) CU MH.

Sämmtliche Lustspiele. Nach einer sorgfältigen Uebersetzung [von F. S. Bierling]. 2. verbesserte Ausg. Hamburg, C. Herold's W [ittwe] 1769. 4 vols. (NUC, MH* 144) MH.

Collections—Italian

Le opere. Tradotte da Nic. di Castelli. Lipsia, Gleditsch, 1698. 4 vols. (NUC, MH* 157) CLU-C CU: vols. 1–3. MH: copy 1, vol. 1–4; copy 2, vol. 2–4.

LES AMANTS MAGNIFIQUES

Les Amans magnifiques. Comédie meslée de musique, & d'entrées de balet. Par J. B. de Molière. Amsterdam, Chez Jacques le Jeune [i.e. H. Wetstein]. 1684. 72 pp. 15 cm. (NUC) DLC MH.

L'AMOUR MEDECIN

L'Amour médecin. Comédie par J. B. P. Molière. Paris, Th. Girard, 1666. 59 [i.e. 95] pp. 15 cm. (Lacroix 11, NUC) CLU-C.

L'Amour médecin, Paris, J. Corneille, 1710. 54 pp. $12\frac{1}{2}$ cm. (NUC) DLC.

L'Amour médecin. Comédie-ballet, en trois actes, en prose, avec un prologue, en vers, et des intermèdes, mêlés de chants et de danses, par Molière. Paris, Bélin [etc.] 1788. xiv, 53 pp. $13\frac{1}{3}$ cm. In: Petite bibliothèque des théâtres [vol. 51] Théâtre françois, comédies, t. 18. (NUC) MiU NN.

De spyt der verliefden. Blyspel. Amsteldam, Erfgen van J. Lescailje, 1708. 96 pp. 17 cm. Translated by D. Kroon. (NUC) ICU.

AMPHITRYON

Amphitryon. Comédie par J. B. P. de Molière. Paris, J. Ribou, 1668. 88 pp. 15 cm. (Lacroix 16, NUC) CLU-C.

Amphitryon. Comédie par I. B. P. Molière. Suivant la copie imprimée a Paris. [Amsterdam, D. Elzevier] 1675. 84 pp. 13 cm. (NUC) NNC.

Amphitrion. Comédie. Représentée pour le divertissement du Roi. Par J. B. P. de Molière. Brusselles, G. de Backer, 1694. 80 pp. $16\frac{1}{2}$ cm. (NUC) CtY.

Amphitryon. Comédie. Représentée pour le divertissement du Roi. Par J. B. P. de Molière. Suivant la copie imprimée à Paris. [Holland?] 1698. 84 pp. $15\frac{1}{2}$ cm. (NUC) CtY.

Amphitryon. Comédie en trois actes. Vienna, Van Ghelen, 1752. 94 pp. (ICRL*) ICRL: Microcard ed.

Amphitryon. Comédie . . . Nouvelle édition. Paris, 1775. 63 pp. (NUC) MeB.

Amphitryon. Comédie en trois actes, par Monsieur de Molière. Nouvelle édition. Paris, 1778. 64 pp. $19\frac{1}{2}$ cm. (NUC) CtY: Incomplete copy, lacks all after page 64.

Amphitryon. Comédie en trois actes, en vers libres, avec un prologue, de Molière. Paris, Bélin [etc.] 1788. xiv, 107 pp. 13 cm. In: Petite bibliothèque des théâtres [v. 53] Théâtre françois, comédies, t. 20. (NUC) DLC MiU NN.

Jupiter en Amphitrion, of De twee gelyke Sosiaas. Blyspel. Amsteldam, D. Ruarus, 1730. 76 pp. 17 cm. Translated by H. Koning. (Lacroix 701, NUC) ICU MH.

Amphitrion. Comédie par Monsieur de Molière. Amphitryon. A Comedy from the French of Molière. London, Printed for J. Watts, 1732. 167 pp. 17 cm. French and English on opposite pages. Probably part of the *Select Comedies of Mr. de Molière*, in French and English, 1732. (NUC) LU.

L'AVARE

L'Avare. Comédie par I. B. P. Molière. Paris, I. Ribov, 1669. 150 pp. 14½ cm. (Lacroix 17, NUC) CLU-C DLC MH MWiW-C.

L'Avare. Comédie par J. B. P. de Molière. Suivant la copie imprimée à Paris. [Amsterdam? Elzevier?] 1693. 108 pp. 13½ cm. (NUC) CLU-C.

L'Avare. Comédie. [Paris? 17—]. [157]–274 pp. 17 cm. In: Bibliothèque des théâtres. [1. sér.] t.3. Extracted from an unidentified work. (NUC) MiU.

L'Avare. Comédie de Molière, avec des remarques, où l'on explique ce qu'il y a de particulier dans l'idiome et la prononciation, et où l'on rapporte des sons tirés de mots anglois semblables à ceux de certaines syllables en françois . . . Et un discours sur la prononciation françoise, par M. L. B. Paris, C. Leclerc; London, J. Nourse, 1751. xxxii, 138, 17 pp. (Lacroix 158, NUC, BM, BN, MH* 176) MH.

L'Avare. Comédie en cinq actes. La Haye, Aux dépens des Associés, 1755. 99 pp. 20 cm. In: [Pièces de théâtre, vol. 14, no. 3] (NUC) OCU.

L'Avare. Comédie en prose, et en cinq actes . . . Nouvelle édition. Paris, Compagnie des libraires, 1760. 100 pp. 19½ cm. (NUC) CtY.

L'Avare. Comédie en prose . . . Nouvelle édition. Paris, 1767. 84 pp. (NUC) PU.

L'Avare. Comédie de Molière, en cinq actes, mise en vers, avec des changemens, par M. Mailhol. Bouillon, Impr. de la Société typographique, 1775. vii, 142 pp. (NUC, Quérard) CU.

L'Avare. Comédie en cinq actes, en prose, de Molière. Paris, Bélin [etc.] 1788. xxvi, 143 pp. 13½ cm. In: Petite bibliothèque des théâtres [v. 51] Théâtre françois, comédies, t.18. (NUC) MiU NN.

De vrék. Blyspél, uit het Fransch van Monsr. Molliere [sic]. Amsterdam, A. Magnus, 1685. 111 pp. 16½ cm. Translated by Joan Pluimer. (NUC) CtY DLC.

L'Avare. Comédie par Mons. de Molière. The Miser. Comedy. New done into English from the French of Molière. By Mr. Ozell. With the Original French opposite to the English; and Both more correctly printed than any that have yet appear'd. Highly Useful and Entertaining for the Learners of either Language. London, Printed for B. Lintot, and sold by H. Lintot, 1732. xiv, 139 pp. 16 cm. (NUC) CLU-C InU.

The Miser. Act I. Translated from the French. In: Hughes, John. Poems, 1735, pp. 219–244. (MH* 213) MH

El avaro. Comedia en prosa en cinco actos. Escrita por el señor Molier [sic]. *Traducida al castellano por Orchard-Old.* Barcelona, J. F. Piferrer, [176–?] 36 pp. 21 cm. (NUC) MnU.

L'Avare, eller Den Girige. Comoedia uti fem Acter af den namnkunnige Molliere [sic], *på den Fransöska Theatren aldraförst föreställd, och nu af Fransöskan förswenskad.* Stockholm, H. Gercken, 1731. 112 pp. Translated by Magnus Lagerström. (Lacroix 820, NUC) CtY.

BALLET DES BALLETS

Ballet des ballets, dansé devant Sa Majesté en son chasteau de S. Germain en Laye au mois de décembre 1671. Paris, R. Ballard, 1671. 64 pp. 23 cm. (NUC) DLC MH.

LE BOURGEOIS GENTILHOMME

Le Bourgeois gentilhomme. Comédie-ballet. Paris, 1685. 108 pp. (ICRL*) ICRL: Microcard ed.

Le Bourgeois gentilhomme. Comédie-ballet . . . [Paris? 17—] 159 pp. 17 cm. In: Bibliothèque des théâtres [l. sér.] t.6 (NUC) MiU.

Le Bourgeois gentilhomme. Comédie-ballet, en cinq actes . . . *Nouvelle édition.* Paris, Compagnie des libraires, 1761. 111 p. 19 $\frac{1}{2}$ cm. (NUC, MH* 219) CtY MH.

Le Bourgeois gentilhomme. Comédie-ballet, en cinq actes, en prose, avec des intermèdes, mêlés de chants et de danses, par Molière, musique de Lully. Paris, Bélin [etc.] 1788. xii, 159 p. 13 $\frac{1}{2}$ cm. In: Petite bibliothèque des théâtres [v. 54] Théâtre françois, comédies, t.21. (NUC) MiU NN.

De burgerlyke edelman. Blyspel. Uit het Fransch van de Heer Molière. Amsteldam, J. Lescailje, 1700. 64 pp. (NUC) NN.

De burgerlyke edelman. Blyspel. Uit het Fransch van den Heer Molière. Amsteldam, Erfgen van J. Lescailje en D. Rank, 1728. 63 pp. 16 $\frac{1}{2}$ cm. (NUC) DLC.

Le Bourgeois gentilhomme. Comédie-ballet. The Cit turned Gentleman. London, J. Watts, 1732. 29 pp. French and English on opposite pages.—Translated by Henry Baker and James Miller.—Probably part of the *Select Comedies of Mr. de Molière,* in French and English, 1732. (NUC) NN.

Der adelsüchtige Bürger. Eine Posse. Mit Tanz untermischt. Nach dem Molière [*von Friederike Helene Unger*]. Berlin, Unger, 1788. 100 pp. 15 $\frac{1}{2}$ cm. (CLU*, Fromm) CLU.

Il cittadino gentilhuomo. Comedia di G. B. P. Molière, tradotta da Nic. di Castelli. Lipsia, A spese dell' autore & appresso G. L. Gleditsch, 1697. 134 pp. 14 $\frac{1}{2}$ cm. (NUC) CtY.

Il cittadino gentiluomo. Commedia. [Venezia, 1756]. 88 pp. Detached portion of Gaspare Gozzi's translation of the *Opere,* Venice, 1756, which appeared in vol. 4. (NUC, MH* 244) MH.

O peão fidalgo. Comedia traduzida em vulgar pelo capitão Manuel de Sousa, para se 1769. 183 pp. (Lacroix 625, NUC) CtY.

Comedia nova: O saloyo cidadão. [Lisboa, S. T. Ferreira, 1773]. 40 pp. (NUC) NN.

LA COMTESSE D'ESCARBAGNAS

La Comtesse d'Escarbagnas. Comédie . . . [Paris? 17—] 40 pp. 17 cm. In: Bibliothèque des théâtres [l. sér.] t.9. (NUC) MiU.

La Comtesse d'Escarbagnas. Comédie, en un acte, en prose, de Molière. Paris, Bélin [etc.] 1788. vi. 44 pp. 13 $\frac{1}{2}$ cm. In: Petite bibliothèque des théâtres [v. 54] Théâtre françois, comédies, t.21. (NUC) MiU NN.

La Comtesse d'Escarbagnas. Comédie, en un acte, en prose, de Molière. Paris, 1788. vi, 42 pp. In: Petite bibliothèque des théâtres [1788, vol. 6]. (NUC) NN: Incomplete copy, lacks all after p. 42.

LA CRITIQUE DE L'ECOLE DES FEMMES

La Critique de l'Escole des femmes. Comédie. Par I. B. P. Molière. Suivant la copie imprimée à Paris. [Amsterdam, L. and D. Elzevier] 1663. 68 pp. 13 $\frac{1}{2}$ cm. (Lacroix 44, NUC) DLC MH.

La Critiqve de l'Escole des femmes. Comédie. Par I. B. P. Molière. Paris, G. Qvinet, 1663. 117 pp. 14 cm. (Lacroix 8, NUC, MH* 246) CLU-C CtY DLC MH.

La Critique de l'Escole des femmes. Comédie. Par J. B. P. Molière. Suivant la copie imprimée à Paris. [Amsterdam, D. Elzevier] 1680. 48 pp. 15 cm. (NUC, MH* 247) DLC MH.

LE DEPIT AMOUREUX

Dépit amoureux. Comédie représentée sur le théâtre du Palais royal. Par J. B. P. Molière. Suivant la copie imprimée à Paris. Amsterdam, Chez Jacques le Jeune [i.e. H. Wetstein] 1683. 84 pp. 13 cm. (NUC) DLC MnU.
Le Dépit amoureux. Comédie en cinq actes et en vers. Vienna, Van Ghelen, 1754. 112 pp. (ICRL*) ICRL: Microcard ed.
Le Dépit amoureux. Comédie en cinq actes . . . retouchée & mise en deux actes par Mr. Valville. Marseille, J. Mossy, 1773. 28 pp. 20 cm. (NUC) MiU.
Le Dépit amoureux. Comédie en cinq actes, en vers, de Molière. Paris, 1787. vi, 114 pp. In: Petite bibliothèque des théâtres [1787, vol. 8]. (NUC) NN.
Der Ehemann aus Irrthum. Ein Lustspiel in fünf Aufzügen, nach dem Dépit amoureux des Molière frey bearb. von R********r [Rundschmer]. Für das Kais. Kön. National-Hoftheater. Wien, F. A. Hartmann, 1786. 135 pp. 20 cm. (NUC) CLSU DLC. DLC.

DOM GARCIE DE NAVARRE

De school voor de jaloerschen. Blyspel uit het Fransch. Amsterdam, Erfgen van J. Lescailje, 1691. Translated by Joan Pluimer. 63 pp. (Lacroix 675, NUC) NN.
Don Garcia of Navarre; or, The Jealous Prince. A Comedy. [Translated by J. Ozell]. [n.p.] 1714. pp. 149–197. In: "Plays", 487. Probably part of *Molière's Plays, translated by John Ozell.* London, 1714. (NUC) CtY.

L'ECOLE DES FEMMES

L'Escole des femmes. Comédie par J. B. P. Molière. Paris, C. Barbin, 1663. 95 pp. $16\frac{1}{2}$ cm. (Lacroix 6B, NUC) CLU-C.
L'Escole des femmes. Comédie par I. B. P. Molière. Paris, E. Loyson, 1663. 95 pp. 14 cm. (Lacroix 6B, NUC) DLC MH.
L'Escole des femmes. Comédie par J. B. P. Molière. Amsterdam, Chez Jacques le Jeune [i.e. H. Wetstein] 1684. 84 pp. 15 cm. (NUC, MH* 263) DLC MH.
L'Ecole des femmes. Comédie, en cinq actes, en vers, de Molière. Paris, Bélin [etc.] 1787. xxiv, 107 pp. $13\frac{1}{2}$ cm. In: Petite bibliothèque des théâtres [v. 46] Théâtre françois, comédies, t.15. (NUC) MiU NN.
Het school voor de vrouwen. Blyspel, uit het Fransch, van den Heer Molliere [sic], *vertaald door T. Arendsz.* Amsteldam, I. Duim, 1753. 88 pp. $16\frac{1}{2}$ cm. (NUC) DLC.
L'Ecole des femmes. Comédie . . . The School for Wives. A Comedy. From the French of Molière. London, Printed for J. Watts, 1732. 165 pp. French and English on opposite pages.—Probably part of the *Select Comedies of Mr. de Molière,* in French and English, 1732. (NUC) IU.
A escola das mulheres. Traduzida, e posta ao gosto portuguez . . . Lisboa, F. Borges de Sousa, 1782. 39 pp. (NUC) NN.

L'ECOLE DES MARIS

L'Escole des maris. Comédie de J. B. P. Molière. Représentée sur le théâtre du Palais royal. Paris, C. Barbin, 1661. 65, [5] pp. $15\frac{1}{2}$ cm. (Lacroix 5, NUC) CLU-C.
L'Escole des maris. Comédie de J.B.P. Molière. Représentée sur le théâtre du Palais

royal. Amsterdam, Chez Jacques le Jeune [i.e. H. Wetstein] 1684. 60 pp. 15 cm. (NUC, MH* 275) CLU-C DLC MH.

L'Ecole des maris. Comédie, en trois actes, en vers. Représentée par les comédiens français, le 24 juin 1661. Par. Mr. Molière. Paris, La veuve Duchesne, 1775. 54 pp. 21½ cm. (NUC) CtY.

L'Ecole des maris. Traduction de l'anglois. Amsterdam, Changuion [etc.] 1776. xvi, 288, 291 p. 16 (NUC) MH.

L'Ecole des maris. Comédie, en trois actes, en vers, de Molière. Paris, Bélin [etc.] 1787. xxii, 74 pp. 13½ cm. In: Petite bibliothèque des théâtres [v. 46] Théâtre françois, comédies, t.15. (NUC) MiU NN.

Steiloorige Egbert, of De twee ongelijke broeders. Blyspel door K. Verlove. Amsterdam, G. de Groot, 1690. 56 pp. (Lacroix 676, NUC) MH.

Het school van de mannen. Vertaelt door A. V[an] B[ulderen]. 's Gravenhage, W. Eyckmans [1716]. Unpaged. 16½ cm. (Lacroix 678, NUC, MH* 281) MH.

De listige vryster, of De verschalkte voogd. Blyspel. In vaerzen aan byzondere maat noch rym gebonden. Amsteldam, Kunstgenootschap Nil Volentibus Arduum, 1730. 63 pp. (NUC) NN.

L'ETOURDI

L'Estovrdy, ov Les contre-temps. Comédie. Représentée svr le théâtre du Palais royal. Par I. B. P. Molière. Paris, G. Qvinet, 1663. 117 pp. 14½ cm. (NUC) DLC MH MWiW-C.

L'Estourdy, ou Les contretemps. Comédie par J. B. P. Molière. Suivant la copie imprimée à Paris. [Amsterdam, Chez Jacques le Jeune] 1683. 96 pp. 13 cm. Apparently detached from *Les Oeuvres de Monsieur Molière. Ed. nouv. . . . A Amsterdam, Chez Jacques le Jeune,* 1684 (t.1) published by H. Wetstein. Cf. Rahir, Cat. d. vols. impr. par les Elzevier, no. 2801. (NUC) DLC MH MnU.

L'Etourdi, ou Les contretems. Comédie en cinq actes. Nouvelle édition. Paris, Compagnie des libraires, 1760. 91 pp. (MH* 285) MH.

L'Etourdi, ou Les contre-tems. Comédie de Molière. Paris, 1787. x, 132 pp. In: Petite bibliothèque des théâtres [1787, vol. 8]. (NUC) NN.

L'Etourdi, ou Les contre-tems. Comédie par Monsieur de Molière. The Blunderer; or, The Counter-Plots. A Comedy. From the French of Molière. London, Printed for J. Watts, 1732. 203 pp. 15½ cm. French and English on opposite pages. Probably part of the *Select Comedies of Mr. de Molière,* in French and English, 1732. (NUC) DLC.

The Blunderer. In: The Comic Theatre . . . a Translation of all the Best French Comedies. By Samuel Foote, Esq. and others . . . London, 1762. 20 cm. vol. 4, p. [1]–103. (NUC) DLC: 2 copies.

LES FACHEUX

Les Fâcheux. Comédie de J. B. P. Molière. Représentée sur le théâtre du Palais royal. Paris, J. Guignard le fils, 1662. 76 pp. 14½ cm. (Lacroix 7, NUC) CLU-C.

Les Faschevx. Comédie de I. B. P. Molière. Représentée svr le théâtre du Palais royal. Paris, C. de Sercy, 1663. 82 pp. 15 cm. (NUC) CtY.

Les Fascheux. Comédie de J. B. P. Molière. Représentée sur le théâtre du Palais royal. Amsterdam, Chez Jacques le Jeune [i.e. H. Wetstein] 1684. 60 pp. 13 cm. (NUC) DLC MnU.

De quel-geesten. Blyspel, nagevolgd uyt het Frans. Amsterdam, H. Bosch; Leide, G. Knotter [ca. 1730]. 48 pp. 16 cm. (Lacroix 679, NUC) NjP.

LES FEMMES SAVANTES

Les Femmes sçavantes. Comédie par I. B. P. Molière. Et se vend pour l'autheur. Paris, & chez P. Promé, 1673. 92 pp. 15 cm. (Lacroix 23, NUC) CtY DLC MH NN.
Les Femmes sçavantes. Comédie. Brusselles, 1694. 80 pp. 17 cm. (NUC) CtY.
Les Femmes savantes. Comédie. [Paris? 17—]. pp. [191]–280. 17 cm. In: Bibliothèque des théâtres [1. ser.] t.18. Extracted from vol. 7 of an unidentified set. (NUC) MiU.
Les Femmes savantes. Comédie, en vers et en cinq actes . . . Nouvelle édition. Paris, La veuve Duchesne, 1773. 83 pp. $19\frac{1}{2}$ cm. (NUC) CtY.
Les Femmes sçavantes. Comédie en vers et cinq actes. Par Molière. Nouvelle édition. Paris, La veuve Duchesne, 1776. 80 pp. $19\frac{1}{2}$ cm. (NUC) NcD.
Les Femmes savantes. Comédie, en cinq actes, en vers, de Molière. Paris, 1788. xvi, 111 pp. In: Petite bibliothèque des théâtres [1788, vol. 7]. (NUC) MiU NN.
De geleerde vrouwen. Bly-spel. Uyt het Frans nagevolgt. Thiel, Gedrukt by G. van Leeuwen, 1713. 109 pp. $15\frac{1}{2}$ cm. Translated by Pieter Burman. (NUC) ICU.
De geleerde vrouwen. Blÿspel. Nagevolgt uÿt het Frans. Utrecht, H. Schouten, 1723. 111 pp. Translated by Pieter Burman. (NUC) NN.

LES FÊTES DE L'AMOUR ET DE BACCHUS

Les Festes de l'amour et de Bacchus. Pastorale. Représentée par l'Académie royale de musique. Suivant la copie imprimée à Paris. [Amsterdam] 1686. 45 pp. 21 cm. (NUC) NL NRU.

LES FOURBERIES DE SCAPIN

Les Fourberies de Scapin. Comédie par J. B. P. Molière. Et se vend pour l'autheur. Paris, chez P. Le Monnier, 1671. 123 pp. $15\frac{1}{2}$ cm. (Lacroix 22, NUC) CLU-C InU MWiW-C.
Les Fourberies de Scapin. Comédie . . . [Paris? 17—]. 107 pp. 17 cm. In: Bibliothèque des théâtres [1. sér.] t. 19. (NUC) MiU.
Les Fourberies de Scapin. Comédie en trois actes. Nouvelle édition. Paris, Campagnie des libraires, 1760. 75 pp. (MH* 327) MH.
Les Fourberies de Scapin. Comédie en 3 actes. Nouvelle édition. Paris, Compagnie des libraires, 1775. 75 pp. 20 cm. (NUC) CtY.
Les Fourberies de Scapin. Comédie, en trois actes, en prose, de Molière. Paris, 1788. vi, 105 pp. In: Petite bibliothèque des théâtres [1788, vol. 6]. (NUC) MiU NN.
Scapins Skalkestykker. Komoedie i tre Akter. Oversat efter Molières franske Original. In: Skuespil til Brug for den Danske Skueplads. Kiøbenhavn, Gyldendal, 1787. 17 cm. vol. 11, pp. [143]–234. Translated by Barthold Johan Lodde. (NUC, Bibliotheca Danica, 1902, vol. 4, col. 292) IU.
Schapyn. Bly-spel, vertoont op de Amsterdamse schouburg. Amsterdam, Gedruckt by B. O. Smient, 1680. 52 pp. 17 cm. Translated by Abraham Peys. (NUC) ICU.
The Cheats of Scapin. Dublin, Printed by T. Wilkinson [17—?]. 36 pp. $17\frac{1}{2}$ cm. Translated by Thomas Otway. (NUC) MH.
The Cheats of Scapin. A Farce, taken from the Manager's Book, at the Theatre Royal, Covent-Garden. London, Butters [17—?] 24 pp. (NUC) NcD PPM.
The Cheats of Scapin. A Comedy of three Acts. As it is acted at the Theatre Royal by His Majesty's Servants. London, Printed for the Proprietors [17—?]. 36 pp. 16 cm. Translated by Thomas Otway. (NUC) CtY.

The Cheats of Scapin. A Farce. London, Printed for the Proprietors, 1787. 28 pp. 18 cm. (NUC) MH.

The Comedy of The Cheats of Scapin. In three Acts. As performed at the Theatre-Royal, Smoke-Alley. [Dublin] The Booksellers, 1792. 48 pp. 16 cm. Translated by Thomas Otway. (NUC) CtY DLC NN.

The Comedy of the Cheats of Scapin. In three Acts. [London? 1792]. 48 pp. 15 cm. (NUC) MH.

Le nuove furberie del servitore Scappino. Ridotta alla regolar purità dello stile toscano-romano moderno da Mattia Cramero. In: Kramer, M. Del Molière redivivo. Norimberga, 1723, i. (MH* 338) MH.

Pseudoli fallaciae, Molieri comoedia. Fourberies de Scapin gallice dicta, quam . . . latine vertit J. D. A. Münster. Cellis, typis Schulzianis, 1778. 66 pp. (Lacroix 591, NUC, MH* 339) MH.

As astucias de Escapim. Traducçaõ do insigne Molière . . . [Lisboa, Officina Luisiana, 1778]. 46 pp. (NUC) NN.

GEORGE DANDIN

George Dandin, ou Le mary confondu, Comédie par I. B. P. de Molière. Suivant la copie imprimée à Paris. [Amsterdam, D. Elzevier] 1669. 60 pp. 13½ cm. (NUC, MH* 340) DLC MH.

George Dandin, ou Le mary confondu. Comédie par J. B. P. de Molière. Paris, J. Ribou, 1669. 155 pp. 14 cm. (Lacroix 18, NUC) CLU-C MWiW-C.

George Dandin, ou Le mari confondu. Comédie . . . [Paris? 17—]. 85 pp. 17 cm. In: Bibliothèque des théâtres [1. sér.] t.21. (NUC) MiU.

George Dandin, ou Le mari confondu. Comédie, en trois actes, en prose, de Molière. Paris, 1788. xii, 86 pp. In: Petite bibliothèque des théâtres [1788, vol. 5]. (NUC) DLC MiU NN.

Lubbert Lubbertze, of De geadelde boer. Blyspel. Uit het Fransch van Hr. Mollière [sic]. Amsterdam, A. Magnus, 1686. 77 pp. Translation variously attributed to M. van Breda and P. de la Croix. (Lacroix 702, NUC) NN.

Lubbert Lubbertze, of De geadelde boer. Blyspel. Amsterdam, A. Bastiaansz, 1721. 79 pp. 16 cm. Translation variously attributed to M. van Breda and P. de la Croix. (Lacroix 702, NUC) ICU NN.

Lubbert Lubbertze, of De geadelde boer. Blyspel. Uit het Fransch van Mr. Molliere [sic]. Amsteldam, I. Duim, 1753. 79 pp. 17½ cm. Translation variously attributed to M. van Breda and P. de la Croix. (Lacroix 702, NUC, MH* p. 29) ICU MH.

LA GLOIRE DU VAL-DE-GRACE

La Gloire du Val-de-Grâce. In: Mazière de Monville, La Vie de Pierre Mignard. Paris, 1730, pp. 191–203. (NUC) MB.

La Gloire du Val de Grâce. In: Mazière de Monville, La Vie de Pierre Mignard. Paris, 1731, pp. 158–170. (MH* 160) MH.

LE MALADE IMAGINAIRE

Le Malade imaginaire. Comédie, meslée de musique et de dance. Par M. de Molière. Cologne, J. Sambix, 1674. 130 pp. 15 cm. (Lacroix 27, NUC) CtY.

Le Malade imaginaire. Comédie meslée de musique, de chansons & de dances. Par M^r. de Molière. Suivant qu'elle a esté représentée à Paris. [n.p.] 1683. (NUC) DLC MH.

Le Malade imaginaire. Comédie meslée de musique, de chansons & de dances. Par
M^r*. de Molière. Suivant qu'elle a esté représentée à Paris, 1683.* Amsterdam, Jacques
le Jeune [i.e. H. Wetstein] 1690. 92 pp. (Lacroix 68, NUC) CtY DLC ICRL:
Microcard ed.

Le Malade imaginaire. Comédie-ballet, en trois actes, avec le prologue & les intermèdes
... Nouvelle édition. Paris, Compagnie des libraires, 1761. 110 pp. 20 cm. (NUC,
MH* 349) CtY MH NjP.

Le Malade imaginaire. Comédie-ballet, en trois actes, avec le prologue & les intermèdes.
Nouvelle édition. Paris, 1782. 84 pp. (NUC) PPAmP.

Le Malade imaginaire. Comédie-ballet, en trois actes, en prose avec deux prologues
et des intermèdes, en vers libres, mêlés de chants et de danses, par Molière, musique
de Charpentier. Paris, Bélin [etc.] 1788. xiv, 166 pp. 13 cm. In: Petite bibliothèque
des théâtres [v. 56] Théâtre françois, comédies, t.22. (NUC) MiU NN.

De ingebeelde zieke. Blÿspél. Amsterdam, P. Rotterdam, 1715. 85 pp. Translated
by Pieter de la Croix. (NUC) NN.

Doctor Last in His Chariot. A Comedy as it is performed at the Theatre Royal in the
Hay-Market. Translated by Isaac Bickerstaffe. London, Printed for W. Griffin,
1769. iv, 70 p. (NUC) CU DLC IU.

Doctor Last in His Chariot. A Comedy . . . London, W. Griffin 1773. iv, 70 pp. Translated by I. Bickerstaffe. (NUC) NN.

Dr. Last in His Chariot. A Comedy, in Three Acts. Translated by Isaac Bickerstaffe,
and Some New Scenes by Samuel Foote. London, J. Jarvis, 1794. 76 pp. (NUC)
MH.

Dr. Last in His Chariot. A Comedy, in Three Acts, Translated by Isaac Bickerstaffe,
and Some New Scenes by Samuel Foote, as Performed at the Theatre-Royal, Hay-
Market . . . London, J. Parsons, 1794. 76 pp. In: The Minor Theatre. 1794, vol.
6 [no. 3]. (NUC, BM) CU MH NL.

O doente imaginativo. Comedia de monsieur Molière. Lisboa, M. Antonio, 1774.
44 pp. 20$\frac{1}{2}$ cm. (NUC) MH.

LE MARIAGE FORCE

Le Mariage forcé. Comédie par J. B. P. de Molière. Paris, J. Ribou, 1668. 91 pp. 15
cm. (Lacroix 10, NUC) CLU-C MWiW-C.

Le Mariage forcé. Comédie par J. B. P. Molière. Suivant la copie imprimée à Paris.
[Amsterdam, Chez Jacques le Jeune (i.e. H. Wetstein)] 1683. 36 pp. 13 cm. (Lacroix
48, NUC) DLC.

Le Mariage forcé. Paris, J. Corneille, 1710. 48 pp. 12$\frac{1}{2}$ cm. (NUC) DLC.

Het gedwongene huuwelÿk. Blyspel. In vaerzen aan bezondre maat noch rijm gebonden.
Amsterdam, Kunstgenootschap Nil Volentibus Arduum, 1710. 52 pp. (NUC)
ICU NN.

Het gedwongene huuwelyk. Blyspel. In vaerzen aan bezondre maat noch rym gebonden.
Amsteldam, I. Duim, 1747. 52 pp. 16 cm. (NUC) ICU MH.

Le Mariage forcé. Comédie par Monsieur de Molière. The Forced Marriage. A Comedy
from the French of Molière. London, Printed for J. Watts, 1732. iv, 75 pp. 17 cm.
French and English on opposite pages. Probably part of the *Select Comedies of*
Mr. de Molière, in French and English, 1732. (NUC) LU MoU NjR TxU.

El casamiento por fuerza. Comedia en tres actos. Madrid, R. Ruiz, 1795. [Louisville,
Ky., Falls City Press, 19] 61. 2 cards. 7 × 12 cm. Microprint copy. Collation of
the original: 94 pp. 16 cm. (NUC) FU ICRL MoU.

El casamiento por fuerza. Comedia en tres actos. [n.p., P. Nadal, 1797]. 28 pp. 21 cm.

In: Teatro antiguo Borrás, vol. 2, no. 8. (NUC) NcU.
Entremez do Esganarelo, ou O cazamento por força. [Lisboa, A. Gomes, 1794]. 15 pp. (NUC) NN.

LE MEDECIN MALGRE LUI

Le Médecin malgré-lvy. Comédie par I. B. P. de Molière. Paris, I. Ribov, 1667. 152 pp. 15 cm. (Lacroix 13, (NUC) DLC MH.
De Médecin malgré lvy. Comédie par I. B. P. Molière. Et se vend pour la veuve de l'autheur. Paris, Chez H. Loyson, 1673. 87 pp. 14½ cm. (Lacroix 128, NUC) DLC MH.
Le Médecin malgré-luy. Comédie par J. B. P. Molière. Suivant la copie imprimée à Paris. [Amsterdam, D. Elzevier] 1674. 60 pp. 13½ cm. (NUC) CLU-C.
Le Médecin malgré-luy. Comédie. [Amsterdam, D. Elzevier] 1679. 60 pp. (NUC, Copinger 3192, Willems 1382) PU.
Le Médecin malgré lui. Comédie en trois actes. Nouvelle édition. Paris, Compagnie des libraires, 1760. 58 pp. (MH* 374) MH.
Le Médecin malgré lui. Comédie . . . Paris, 1778. 47 pp. (NUC) MeB.
Le Médecin malgré lui. Comédie, en trois actes, en prose, de Molière. Paris, 1788. xiv, 77 pp. In: Petite bibliothèque des théâtres. [1788, vol. 3]. (NUC) MiU NN.
Le Médecin malgré lui. Comédie en trois actes et en prose. Troyes, Gobelet, 1799. 52 pp. (NUC) PU.
The Mock Doctor; or, The Dumb Lady Cur'd. A Farce. Taken from the Manager's Book, at the Theatre Royal, Drury-Lane. London, Printed for H. D. Symonds [etc., 17—?] 24 pp. 17½ cm. H. Fielding's adaptation. (NUC) CtY.
The Mock Doctor; or, The Dumb Lady Cur'd. A Comedy. Done from Molière. As It Is Acted at the Theatre-Royal in Drury-Lane. By His Majesty's Servants. With the Musick Prefix'd to Each Song. London, Printed for J. Watts, 1732. 32 pp. 19½ cm. H. Fielding's adaptation. (NUC, Banerji 281, BM) CLU-C CtY MoU: Microprint TxU.
The Mock Doctor; or, The Dumb Lady Cur'd. A Comedy. Done from Molière. As It Is Acted at the Theatre-Royal in Drury-Lane. By His Majesty's Servants. London, Printed for J. Watts, 1732. 29 pp. H. Fielding's adaptation. (NUC) MH.
The Mock Doctor; or, The Dumb Lady Cur'd. A Comedy. Done from Molière. As It Is Acted at the Theatre-Royal in Drury-Lane. By His Majesty's Servants. London, Printed for W. James [1732?]. 24 pp. 20 cm. H. Fielding's adaptation. (NUC) CtY.
The Mock Doctor; or, The Dumb Lady Cur'd. A Comedy. As It Is Acted at the Theatre-Royal in Drury-Lane. By His Majesty's Servants. Done from Molière. With Songs to Each Act. London, Printed; and, Dublin, Reprinted by F. Faulkner, 1732. 36 pp. 16½ cm. H. Fielding's adaptation. (NUC) MdBG.
Le Médecin malgré lui. Comédie par Monsieur de Molière. A Doctor and No Doctor. A Comedy. From the French of Molière. London, J. Watts, 1732. 129 pp. 17 cm. French and English on opposite pages. Translated by Henry Baker and James Miller. Probably part of the *Select Comedies of Mr. de Molière,* in French and English, 1732. (NUC) CLU-C DLC NN.
The Mock Doctor; or, The Dumb Lady Cur'd. A Comedy. Done from Molière. As It Is Acted at the Theatre-Royal in Drury-Lane. By His Majesty's Servants. With the Musick Prefix'd to Each Song. The 2d Ed., with Additional Songs and Alterations. London, Printed for J. Watts, 1732. 34 pp. 21 cm. H. Fielding's adaptation. (NUC) CLU-C CSmH CtY DLC MH NjP TxU.

The Mock Doctor; or, The Dumb Lady Cur'd. A Comedy. Done from Molière. With the Musick Prefix'd to Each Song. 3d Ed., with Additional Songs and Alterations. London, J. Watts, 1742. 33 pp. H. Fielding's adaptation. (NUC) MH.

The Mock Doctor; or, The Dumb Lady Cur'd. A Comedy. Done from Moilère. The 5th Ed., with Additional Songs and Alterations. Oxford, Printed by R. Walker and W. Jackson, 1747. 36 pp. H. Fielding's adaptation. (NUC) DFO.

The Mock Doctor; or, The Dumb Lady Cur'd. A Comedy. As It Is Acted at the Theatre-Royal in Drury-Lane. By His Majesty's Servants. Done from Molière. With Songs in Each Act. Dublin, Printed by G. Faulkner, 1752. 30 pp. $16\frac{1}{2}$ cm. H. Fielding's adaptation. (NUC) DFo MB.

The Mock Doctor; or, The Dumb Lady Cur'd. A Comedy. Done from Molière. As It Is Acted at the Theatre-Royal in Drury-Lane. By His Majesty's Servants. With the Musick Prefix'd to Each Song. The 4th Ed., with Additional Songs and Alterations. London, Printed for J. Watts, 1753. 33 pp. 21 cm. H. Fielding's adaptation. (NUC) CtY IU MB MH NNC.

The same. In: The Dramatic Works of Henry Fielding. London, 1765. [vol. 2, no. 4]. (NUC) InU PPRF.

The Mock Doctor; or, The Dumb Lady Cur'd. A Comedy. Done from Molière. As It Was Acted at the Theatre-Royal in Drury-Lane. By His Majesty's Servants. With Additional Songs and Alterations. By Henry Fielding, Esq. London, 1760. 32 pp. 16 cm. (NUC) CtY.

The Mock Doctor; or, The Dumb Lady Cur'd. A Comedy. Done from Molière. As It Is Acted at the Theatre-Royal in Drury-Lane. By His Majesty's Servants. With the Musick Prefix'd to Each Song. A New Ed. With Additional Songs and Alterations. London, A. Millar, 1761. 33 pp. 20 cm. H. Fielding's adaptation. (NUC) DLC.

The Faggot-Binder; or, The Mock Doctor. In: The Comic Theatre, Being a Free Translation of All the Best French Comedies, by S. Foote and Others. London, 1762. 20 cm. vol. 5, pp. [89]–153. (NUC) DLC.

The Mock Doctor; or, The Dumb Lady Cur'd. A Comedy. As It Is Acted at the Theatre-Royal in Drury-Lane. By His Majesty's Servants. Done from Volière [sic]. *With Songs in Each Act.* Belfast, Printed and Sold by J. Magee, 1763. 30 pp. 17 cm. H. Fielding's adaptation. (NUC) CtY MH.

The Mock Doctor; or, The Dumb Lady Cur'd. A Comedy. Done from Molière. As It Is Acted at the Theatre-Royal in Drury-Lane. By His Majesty's Servants. With the Musick Prefix'd to Each Song. A New Ed. With Additional Songs and Alterations. London, Printed for T. Caslon [etc.] 1771. 33 pp. 21 cm. H. Fielding's adaptation. (NUC) CLU-C CtY MH MiU PU.

The Mock Doctor . . . [London? 1779?]. 8 pp. 22 cm. In: Theatrical Magazine, vol. 3. H. Fielding's adaptation. (NUC) CtY DFo NN TxU.

The Mock Doctor; or, The Dumb Lady Cur'd. A Comedy. As It Is Acted at the Theatre-Royal in Drury-Lane. By His Majesty's Servants. Done from Molière. With Songs in Each Act. 6th Ed. Belfast, Printed by J. Magee, 1781. 31 pp. $16\frac{1}{2}$ cm. H. Fielding's adaptation. (NUC) MB MH.

The Mock Doctor; or, The Dumb Lady Cur'd. In two Acts, by Henry Fielding. In: [Bell, John] Supplement to Bell's British Theatre: . . . Farces . . . London, 1784. 18 cm. vol. 1, pp. [135]–136 [i.e. 161]. Page 161 wrongly numbered 136. (NUC) MH NIC.

The Mock Doctor; or, The Dumb Lady Cur'd. In Two Acts, by Henry Fielding. In: A Collection of the Most Esteemed Farces and Entertainments Performed on the British Stage . . . A New Ed. Edinburgh, 1786. 20 cm. vol. 1, pp. [135]–136 [i.e. 161]. Page 161 wrongly numbered 136. (NUC) CtY: 2 copies, 1 in ser., 1 detached.

The Mock Doctor; or, The Dumb Lady Cur'd. In Two Acts, by Henry Fielding. In: A Collection of the Most Esteemed Farces and Entertainments, Performed on the British Stage. Edinburgh, 1792. vol. 1, [no.] 4, pp. [135]–161. (NUC) CtY.

The Mock Doctor; or, The Dumb Lady Cured. A Ballad Farce, in Two Acts, Written by Henry Fielding. As Performed at the Theatres-Royal, Covent-Garden and Hay-Market . . . In: The Minor Theatre. London, 1794. vol. 4, [no.] 4. (NUC) MH NL.

LE MISANTROPE

Le Misantrope. Comédie par I. B. P. de Molière. Paris, I. Ribov, 1667. 84 pp. 14½ cm. (NUC, MH* 392) DLC MH MWiW-C NN.

Le Misantrope. Comédie par J. B. P. de Molière. Paris, D. Thierry et C. Barbin, 1675. 84 pp. 15 cm. (NUC, MH* 393) DLC MH.

Le Misantrope. Comédie par J. B. P. de Molière. Amsterdam, Chez Jacques le Jeune [i.e. H. Wetstein] 1684. 62 [i.e. 96] pp. 13 cm. Page 96 wrongly numbered 62. (NUC) DLC.

Le Misantrope. Comédie, en cinq actes, et en vers. Par Monsieur Molière. Représentée pour la première fois, par les comédiens ordinaires du Roi. Nouvelle édition. Paris, Ruault, 1778. 58 pp. 19½ cm. (NUC) CtY.

Le Misantrope. Comédie, en cinq actes, en vers, de Molière. Paris, 1788. xxiv, 102 pp. In: Petite bibliothèque des théâtres. [1788, vol. 1]. (NUC) MiU NN.

Le Misantrope. Comédie, en cinq actes, et en vers. Par Monsieur Molière. Nouvelle édition. Paris, Didot l'aîné, 1790. 56 pp. 22 cm. (NUC) NNU-W PU.

The Misanthrope. A Comedy. From the French of Monsieur de Molière . . . London, 1709. 86 pp. 16½ cm. In: The Monthly Amusement, no. 2, 1709, May. Translated by John Hughes. (NUC) CtY.

The Man-Hater [or, Le Misantrope. Translated by] James Miller and H. Baker. London, 1740. 143 pp. French and English on opposite pages. (NUC) MoU: Microprint. NN.

Der Menschenfeind. Ein Lustspiel aus dem Französischen. Wien, 1774. 83 pp. (NUC) MH.

Il misantropo a caso maritato, o sia L'orgoglio punito. Commedia. Bologna, L. dalla Volpe, 1748. 112 pp. 18½ pp. Adaptation by Luisa Bergalli, afterwards Contessa Gozzi. First ed., 1745, published under title: *Il misantropo. Commedia tratta da Molière.* (NUC) IU MH.

Il misantropo. Commedia del sig. Molier [sic]. Tradotta dal francese in versi toscani dall' abate Enrico Girolami. Firenze, G. P. Giovannelli, 1749. 140 pp. (Lacroix 603, NUC) CLU IU.

Comedia nueva: El misantropo. [Madrid, 1780?]. 36 pp. Translated by José Lopez de Sedano. (NUC, BM) NN.

MONSIEUR DE POURCEAUGNAC

Monsievr de Povrceavgnac. Comédie. Faite à Chambord pour le diuertissement du Roy. Par I. B. P. Molière. Paris, I. Ribov, 1670. 78 pp. 14 cm. (NUC, MH* 438) DLC MH.

Monsieur de Pourceaugnac. Comédie. Faite à Chambord, pour le divertissement du Roy. Par I. B. P. Molière. Suivant la copie imprimée à Paris. [Amsterdam, D. Elzevier] 1674. 72 pp. 13 cm. (NUC) NNC.

*Monsieur de Pourceaugnac. Comédie-ballet . . . représentée . . . pour la première fois
. . . 1669 . . . [Paris? 17—]. 96 pp. 17 cm. In: Bibliothèque des théâtres [1. sér.] t.35.
(NUC) MiU.*

Monsieur de Pourceaugnac. Nouvelle édition. Paris, Compagnie des libraires, 1762.
69 pp. (MH* 439) MH.

*Monsieur de Pourceaugnac. Comédie-ballet, en trois actes, en prose, avec des intermèdes,
mêlés de chants et de danses, par Molière.* Paris, 1788. vi, 100 pp. In: Petite bibliothèque des théâtres [1788, vol. 5]. (NUC) DLC MiU NN.

*Monsieur de Pourceaugnac; or, Squire Trelooby. Acted at the Subscription Musick
at the Theatre Royal in Lincoln's-Inn-Fields. March 30,* 1704. *By Select Comedians
from Both Houses. Done into English from a Comedy of Molière's . . .* London,
Printed for W. Davis [etc.] 1704. 55 pp. 22 cm. Translated by John Ozell. (NUC,
MH* 443) CLU-C CSmH CtY DLC InU MH NjP OO OU TxU.

*The Cornish Squire. A Comedy. As It Is Acted at the Theatre-Royal in Drury-Lane,
by His Majesty's Servants. Done from the French by the Late Sir John Vanbrugh.*
London, J. Watts, 1734. 66 pp. 19 cm. In: [Longe, F. Collection of Plays, vol. 56,
no. 6]. (NUC) CtY DFo DLC ICU NjP TxU.

LES PRECIEUSES RIDICULES

Les Précievses ridicvles. Comédie. Représentée au Petit Bourbon. Paris, G. de Luyne,
1663. 87 pp. 15½ cm. "Traduction en vers . . . par le sieur de Somaise." Cf. Lacroix
3, note. (Lacroix 3, NUC) CtY.

Les Précieuses ridicules. Comédie, en un acte, en prose . . . représentée . . . 1659.
[Paris? 17—] 48 pp. 17 cm. In: Bibliothèque des théâtres [1. sér.] t.35. (NUC) MiU.

*Les Précieuses ridicules. Comédie, en un acte, en prose, par M. Molière. Représentée
pour la première fois à Paris sur le Théâtre du petit Bourbon, le 18 novembre 1659.*
[Amsterdam? Elzevier? 1674? or 1679?] 48 pp. 19 cm. (Lacroix 39?, NUC) MH.

Les Précieuses ridicules. Comédie, en un acte, en prose . . . Nouvelle édition. Paris,
N. B. Duchesne, 1777. 28 pp. 19½ cm. (NUC) CtY.

*Les Précieuses ridicules. Comédie, en un acte et en prose, de Molière. Nouvelle édition
. . .* Paris, Duchesne, 1786. 28 pp. (CU*) CU.

Les Précieuses ridicules. Comédie, en un acte et en prose, de Molière. Paris, 1787. xxiv,
51 pp. In: Petite bibliothèque des théâtres [1787, vol. 5]. (NUC) MiU NN.

Les Précieuses ridicules. Comédie, en un acte et en prose, de Molière. Nouvelle édition.
Avignon, A. Berenguier, an VIII [1799]. 52 [i.e. 25] pp. (NUC) ICU.

*Les Précieuses ridicules. Comédie. Par Monsieur Molière. The Conceited Ladies. A
Comedy. From the French of Molière.* London, Printed for J. Watts, 1732. 89 pp.
15½ cm. French and English on opposite pages. Translated by Henry Baker and
James Miller. Probably part of the *Select Comedies of Mr. de Molière*, in French
and English, 1732. (NUC) DLC LU.

Le pretiose ridicole. Comedia di G. B. P. di Molière, tradotta da Nic. di Castelli . . .
Lipsia, A spese dell' autore & appresso G. L. Gleditsch, 1697. 44 pp. 14½ cm.
(NUC) CtY.

LA PRINCESSE D'ELIDE

*Les Plaisirs de l'Isle enchantée. Course de bague; collation ornée de machines; comédie,
meslée de danse et de musique; ballet du palais d'Alcine; feu d'artifice: et autres
feste galantes et magnifiques, faites par le Roy à Versailles, le VII may MDCLXIV
et continuées plusieurs autres jours.* Paris, Imprimerie royale, 1673 [i.e. 1674]. 91
pp. 43 cm. "Comédie meslée de danse et de musique" (Molière's La Princesse

d'Elide) on pp. 21–80. (NUC, MH* 471) DLC MH.

La Princesse d'Elide. Comédie du sieur Molière. Ensemble Les Plaisirs de l'Isle enchantée. Course de bague; collation ornée de machines, meslée de danse & de musique; ballet du palais d'Alcine; feu d'artifice; et autres festes galantes de Versailles. Suivant la copie imprimée à Paris. [Amsterdam, D. Elzevier] 1674. 108 pp. 13½ cm. (Lacroix 45, NUC) CLU-C.

La Princesse d'Elide. Comédie du sieur Mollière. Ensemble Les plaisirs de l'Isle enchantée. Course de bague; collation ornée de machines, meslée de danse & de musique; ballet du palais d'Alcine; feu d'artifice: et autres festes galantes de Versailles. Suivant la copie imprimée à Paris. [Amsterdam, H. Wetstein] 1684. 108 pp. 13 cm. (Lacroix 45, NUC, MH* 472) DLC MH.

PSYCHE

Psiché. Tragédie-ballet . . . Suivant la copie imprimée à Paris. [Amsterdam, Elzevier] 1671. 82 pp. (Lacroix 62, NUC) ICN NL.

Psiché. Tragi-comédie et ballet. Dansé devant Sa Majesté au mois de ianvier 1671. Paris, R. Ballard, 1671. 48 pp. 22 cm. (NUC) DLC MH.

Psiché. Tragédie-ballet par J. B. P. Molière. Suivant la copie imprimée à Paris. [Amsterdam, Elzevier] 1680. 84 pp. 14 cm. (Lacroix 62, NUC) NcU.

Psiché. Tragédie-ballet représentée pour le divertissement du Roi . . . Paris, G. de Luyne, 1700. 84 pp. 16 cm. (NUC) NjP.

SGANARELLE, OU LE COCU IMAGINAIRE

Sganarelle, ou Le cocu imaginaire. Comédie. Avec les arguments de chaque scène. Paris, G. de Luyne, 1662. 59 pp. 15 cm. Arguments by Neuf-Villenaine. (NUC, Tchemerzine, vol. 8, p. 298 ‹b›) CLU-C MWiW-C.

Sganarelle, ov Le cocv imaginaire. Comédie. Avec les argvmens de chaque scéne. Paris, G. de Lvyne, 1665. 59 pp. 15 cm. Arguments by Neuf-Villenaine. (NUC, MH* 478) DLC MH.

De verwarde jalouzy. Kluchtspel. Amsteldam, D. Ruarus, 1730. 32 pp.

Os amantes zelozos. Entremez, traduzido por . . . [Lisboa, J. da Silva Nazareth, 1771]. 16 pp. (NUC) NN.

Sganarel'; ili, Myslenno-rogatyĭ. Komedïïa v 3 dïeĭstvïĭakh. [Perevod] R. G. Moskva, V Univ. tip., u N. Novikova, 1788. 47 pp. 20 cm. (Gale) DLC.

LE SICILIEN, OU L'AMOUR PEINTRE

Le Sicilien, ou L'Amour peintre. Comédie par J. B. P. de Molière. Paris, J. Ribou, 1668. 81 pp. 15 cm. (Lacroix 14, NUC) CLU-C.

Le Sicilien, ou L'Amour peintre. Comédie en un acte mêlée d'ariettes. [Paroles arrangées par M. Le Vasseur, musique de M. d'Auvergne. Paris] P. R. C. Ballard [1780]. 5, [2], 44 pp. and 20 pp. of music. (MH* 485) MH.

Le Sicilien, ou L'Amour peintre. Comédie-ballet, en un acte et en prose, mêlée de chants et de danses, de Molière. Paris, Bélin [etc.] 1788. x, 44 pp. 13½ cm. In: Petite bibliothèque des théâtres [vol. 51] Théâtre françois, comédies, t.18 (NUC) MiU NN.

Le Sicilien, ou L'Amour peintre. Comédie par Monsieur de Molière. The Sicilian; or, Love Makes a Painter. A Comedy. From the French of Molière. London, Printed for J. Watts, 1732. 63 pp. 16½ cm. French and English on opposite pages. Probably part of the *Select Comedies of Mr. de Molière,* in French and English, 1732. (NUC) MoU TxU.

LE TARTUFFE

L'Imposteur, ov Le Tartvffe. Comédie par I. B. P. de Molière. Sur l'imprimé aux despens de l'autheur. Paris, I. Ribov, 1669. 96 pp. 14 cm. (NUC, MH* 490) DLC MH.

Le Tartvffe, ov L'Impostevr. Comédie par I. B. P. de Molière. Paris, I. Ribov, 1669 [Repr. Paris, Editions des bibliothèques nationales de France, 1934]. 96 pp. 15 cm. (NUC) DLC ICU IEN NjP NN.

Tartuffe, ou L'Imposteur. Comédie . . . Nouvelle édition. Paris, Compagnie des libraires, 1773. 71 pp. 19 ½ cm. (NUC) CtY.

Le Tartuffe. Comédie en vers et en cinq actes, de Molière. Nouvelle édition . . . Paris, La veuve Duchesne, 1774. 92 pp. 19 cm. (NUC) DLC PPL-R.

Tartuffe, ou L'Imposteur. Comédie, en cinq actes, en vers, de Molière. Paris, Bélin [etc.] 1788. liv, 114 pp. 13 ½ cm. In : Petite bibliothèque des théâtres [vol. 49] Théâtre françois, comédies, t.17. (NUC) MiU NN.

Tartuffe, eller Den Skinhellige. Comoidie i 5 Acter, forestillet paa den Danske Skueplads. Kjøbenhavn, J. J. Høpffner, 1724 [Repr. in : Nystrøm, E. Skuespiltekster fra Komediehuset i Lille Grønnegade. København, 1921. Bind 2, pp. 195–291]. Translation ascribed to Diderich Seckman. (NUC) NN.

Steyl-oor, of De schijnheylige bedrieger. Waer in is nagevolgt de Tartuffe, van den Heer J. B. P. de Molière. Desen 2. druck van verscheyde fouten gesuyvert. Amsterdam, A. van Blancken, 1677. 78 pp. 15 ½ cm. Translated by Pieter Schaak. (NUC) ICU.

De huigchelaar. Blyspel. Naar den Tartuffe van Molière. Door J. Nomsz. Amsteldam, J. Helders en A. Mars, 1789. 95 pp. 16 ½ cm. (NUC) ICU MB MH NN.

Tartuffe ; or, The French Puritan. A Comedy, Lately Acted at the Theatre Royal. Written in French by Molière ; and Rendered into English with Much Addition and Advantage, by M. Medbourne . . . London, Printed by H. L. and R. B. for James Magnus, 1670. 66 pp. 21 ½ cm. In : [Longe, F. Collection of Plays, vol. 5, no. 5]. (NUC) CLU-C CSmH CU DLC MH MWiW-C NIC OCU PU ViU : 2 microfilms.

Tartuffe ; or, The French Puritan. A Comedy, Acted at the Theatre-Royal. Written in French by Molière, and Render'd into English, with Much Addition and Advantage, by M. Medbourne . . . London, Printed for R. Wellington, 1707. 65 pp. 22 cm. (NUC, MH* 521) CLU-C CSmH CU DLC MH MiU NjP TxU.

Der Mucker, oder Molierens Scheinheiliger Betrüger Tartüffe. Breslau, Pietsch, 1748. 119 pp. (NUC) CLU-C.

Der Gleissner, oder Scheinheilige Betrüger. Ein Lustspiel des Herrn Molière in Versen und fünf Aufzügen. Wien, Krauss, 1763. 111 S. In : Neue Sammlung von Schauspielen, welche auf der K. K. privil. deutschen Schaubühne zu Wien aufgeführet worden, Bd. 6 [Nr. 4]. (NUC, Fromm) PU.

Il don Pilone, ovvero Il bacchettone falso. Commedia tratta nuovamente dal franzese da Girolamo Gigli . . . Lucca, Marescandoli, 1711. 6 p.l., 124 pp. 17 cm. Another ed. with same imprint collates 7 p.l., 135 pp. (Lacroix 605, NUC) CU DLC: 2 copies. MH.

Il don Pilone, ovvero Il bacchettone falso. Commedia. Si aggiunge La sorellina di don Pilone. Commedia. [Lucca? 1712?] xiv, 278 pp: (NUC) CtY CU MH.

Il don Pilone, ovvero Il bacchettone falso. Commedia tratta nuovamente dal franzese da Girolamo Gigli . . . Lucca, Marescandoli, 1715. 147 pp. 16 cm. (NUC) DLC NjP NN.

Il don Pilone, ovvero Il bacchettone falso. Commedia nuovamente tradotta dal francese da Girolamo Gigli. Bologna, Longhi, 1717. 139 pp. (NUC) NjP.

Il don Pilone, ovvero Il bacchettone falso. Si aggiunge La sorellina di don Pilone. [Firenze? 177–?] xvi, 278 pp. (NUC) ICU.

MOLIÈRE'S PLAYS
IN RECENT TRANSLATION:
A CHECKLIST

Erich A. Albrecht

Since the appearance of Professor Paul Saintonge's *Fifty Years of Molière Studies*, which contains a valuable bibliography of translations of the plays and other writings of Molière up to the Second World War, and since the publication of Professor Fernand Baldensperger's and W. P. Friedrich's *Bibliography of Comparative Literature* in 1960, it might safely be said that Molière has ceased to be the more or less exclusive concern of European scholars and translators and has become a world figure. This is clearly shown by the nearly 500 translations listed below which have been gleaned from the bibliographies of 43 countries and unions of countries. Considering the latter, i.e., the Soviet Union, India, and some others, the number of languages into which Molière's plays have been translated is considerably larger.

Although the actual and proposed studies of Molière in countries other than Europe and the Middle East have constantly risen since 1948, the appearance of the vastly greater number of translations of Molière's plays listed below calls for a host of additional studies.

The most obvious are, of course, the "Molière and —" and the "Molière in ——." Next, considering the fact that this is a list of translations, an examination of the new translations against the French originals will have to be done. Often the particular translation of the title of the play alone amounts to an interpretation of the play.

As far as non-European countries are concerned, the cultural anthropologists, the social scientists, and the psychologists will be especially interested in plays that in translation have titles such as: *Jakkalstreke von Scapino* (Afrikaans), *The School of Women*, *The Beardless Ones* (Turkey), *Truth also Falsehood* (Telegu, India) and others. Those who love Molière and his plays will, of course, see numerous additional problems worthy of scholarly concern.

In almost all cases the second item in the individual listings will be the name of the translator. The method of giving rather brief information in each case was adopted to save space, as it is done by the *Index Transla-tionum*, a major source for this and many other bibliographical studies.

Single Works

LES AMANTS MAGNIFIQUES

Sanli âşiklar. Oktay Rifat. Istanbul. Millî Eğitim Basimevi. 1965. 71 p. Turkey.

L'AMOUR MEDECIN

Ha-Rofe Ha Medhav. Eliyahu Hazan and Jozef Anay. Tel-Aviv. Merkaz Le-Tarbut. 1951. 27 p. Israel.
Die Liebe als Arzt. Ludwig Hoffmann. Leipzig. VEB Hofmeister. 1959. 27 p. Germany.

AMPHITRYON

Amphitryon. Traduit en vers par G. Politis. Athènes. Institut Français d'Athènes. 1948. 101 p. Greece.
Amphitryon. Arthur Luther. Stuttgart. Reclam. 1962. Germany.
Amifitrüon. [Est.] A. Sang. Tallin. Estgosizdat III. 1962. Estonian S.S.R.
Amphitryon. Ali Teoman. Istanbul. Millî Egitim. 1965. Basmevi. 72 p. Turkey.

L'AVARE

Povananchen Taplen. [Marathi-Konkani] Shanai Gonybab. Bombay. K.S. Nayak. 1948. 72 p. India (from the English translation).
L'Avare. Lustspiel in 5 Akten. Hrsg. Josef Zwerenz. Wien. Hölder-Pichler-Temsky. Österr. Bundesverlag. 1949. 128 p. Austria.
L'avaro. A cura di massimo bontempelli. Milano. Universale Economica. 1950. 144 p. Italy.
D'r Gitzhals. Robert Sauer. Mulhouse. Editions Salvator. 1950. (2e ed.). 56 p. Alsace.
The Miser. Adapted by Miles Malleson. London. Samuel French. 1950. 74 p. England.
Den Girige. Bearb. för Amatörteatern av Torsten Friedlander. Göteborg, Elanders Bocktryckeri. (Stockholm, Seelig and Co.). 1950. 64 p. Sweden.
L'avaro. Ugo Déttore. Milano. Rizzoli. 1951. 93 p. Italy.
De Giizhals. [Schweizerdeutsch] Hans Bader. Aarau. Sauerländer. 1951. 92 p. Switzerland.
The Miser in a new adaptation. B. Hewitt. Urbana. University of Illinois. 1951. 59 p. U.S.A.
Lakomec. František Kalina. Martin. Matica Slovenská. 1952. 113 p. Czechoslovakia.
Der Geizige. Wolf Graf Baudissin. Leipzig. Reclam. 1952. 80 p. Also: Reinbeck, Rowohlt. 1964, 1965. Germany.
Der Geizige. Walter Widmer. Stuttgart. Reclam. 1952. 95 p. Germany.
[L'Avare] Lubdan. M.P. Paul. Kottayam. National Book Stall. 1953. XIV. 191 p.
Der Geizhals. Übers. von Georg Goyert. Nachwort von Walter Widmer. Stuttgart. Reclam. 1954. 85 p. Germany.
Skąpiec. Tadeusz Żeleński-Boy. Wroclaw, Zakl. im Ossolińskich. (Wyd. 6 Przejrz-ane). XXXII–136, 1954. (CWYD 7) XXXII, 138, 1956. WYD 8, 1961, 1962, 1966, 1967. Poland.

Tvrdica. Branislav Miljković. Beograd, Znanje. 1954. 98 p. Also: Beograd. Nolit, 1956 and 1962. Yugoslavia.

Der Geizhals. Georg Goyert. Stuttgart. Reclam. 1954, 1962, 1963, 1966, 1968. (Nachdruck) 85 p. Germany.

L'Avare. S. M. A. Djamâl-Zâdeh. Tehrān. B.T.N.K. 1957. 188 p. Iran.

Si Bachil. Noor Sutan Iskandar. Djakarta, Balai Pustaka. 1957. 108 p. Indonesia.

Chien Lin Jên. Taipei. The Ch'i Ming Book Co. III. 1958. 130 p. China.

O Filargyros. G. Simiriotis. Ath., Marís. 1958. 112 p. Greece.

Karumi. Trsl. from English by C.R. Myleru, Madras. Umadevan Co. 1959. VIII. 112 p. India.

Kañgus. R. M. Dogara. Delhi. Sahitya sansthan. 1959. 88 p. India.

Ha-Kamtsan. Natan Alterman. Tel Aviv. Ha-Kibbuz Ha-Meuhad. 1958/59. 105 p. Israel.

Lakomec. E.A. Saudek. Praha. Orbis. 1959. 92 p. Czechoslovakia.

Kopraci. E. Fico. Tiranë. Ministria e Arësimit dhe Kulturës. 1960. 63 p. Albania.

El Avaro. José López Rubio. Madrid. Alfil. 1960. 80 p. Spain.

A Fösvény. [Mag.]. Illyés Gyula. Bukarest. Állami Irodalmi és Müvészeti Kiadó. 1960. 124 p. Romania.

Tvradica. Midhat Šamić. Sarajevo. Svjetlost. 1961. 98 p. Yugoslavia.

Cimri. Yaşar Nabi Nayir. İstanbul. Varlik Yayinevi. 1961. 96 p. Turkey.

Cimri. Beş perdelik komedya. 2 bsl. Çeviren. Sabahattin. Istanbul. 1963 and 1968. Turkey.

Den Girige. Hjalmar Gullberg. Lund. Gleerup (4 uppl.). 1963. 103 p. Sweden.

Kopraci. E. Fico. Tiranë. Drejt. Bot. Shkollore. 67 p. (1964). 1966. (Bot. i. 3-të), 71 p. Albania.

A Fösveny. Gyula Illyes. Budapest. Szépirodalmi Kiadó. 1964, 1965. 96 p. Hungary.

The Miser. Wallace Fowlie. Great Neck, New York. Barron's Ed. Series, 1964, XIII, 96 p. U.S.A.

Saituri. Lauri Hirvensalo. Porvoo; Helsinki. Werner Söderström. (1965) 140 p.; (1965) (2ed., 139 p.); (1967). (3 ed., 139 p.) Finland.

Der Geizige. Walter Widmer. Reinbeck. Rowohlt, 1965. 151 p. Germany.

Kamnanh Krau Damra. Chan Mom Phavy. Phnôm-Penh. Librairie Séng-Nguon Huot. 1965. 191 p. Cambodia.

Der Geizige. Hans Weigel. Zürich. Diogenes Verlag. 1965. 103 p. Switzerland.

Den girige. Gunnar Tilander. Stockholm. Wahlström and Widstrand. 1966. 98 p. Sweden.

Al-Bakhīl. Yusuf Muḥammed Riḍā and Khalil Charaf al-Din. Beyrouth. Dār al-Kitāb al-Lubnānī. Librairie de l'École. 1967. 242 p. Lebanon.

Sjon Pichiri. Adaptá na papiamentu pa May Henriquez for di "L'Avare" di Molière. In: Antilliaanse cahiers. Jaarg 5. no. 4; 65–153 pp. 1967. West Indian.

Lakomec. František Kalina. Bratislava. Diliza. 1967. 78 p. Czechoslovakia.

Der Geizige. Bearbeitet von Walter Teich. Frankfurt am Main. M. Diesterweg. 1967. Germany.

The Miser. H. van Laun. A bilingual ed. New York. French and European Publications. 1969. 210 p. U.S.A.

LE BOURGEOIS GENTILHOMME

Mchuuzi mwungwana . . . Uliotungwa na A. Morrison. Uchezwe na watu wa Afrika. Dar-es-Salaam. Edinburgh printed. 1948. viii, 56 p. Swahili.

Úrhatnám polgár. Komédia. Tibor Hegedüs. Budapest. Budapest Irod. Int. 1949. 152 p. Hungary.

Mieszczanin szlachcicem. Czeslaw Jastrzebiec-Kozlowski. Kraków, Wydawn. M. Kot. 1951. 105 p. Poland.

Az úrhatnám polgár. Dezsö Mészöly. Budapest. Szépirod. Kiadó. 1951. 94 p. Hungary.

Meštiak šl'achticom. Zlatan Sýkora. Turč. Sv. Martin. Matica Slovenská. 1951. 90 p. Czechoslovakia.

The prodigious snob. (Adaptation) by Miles Malleson. London. Samuel French. 1952. England.

Il borghese gentiluomo. Piero Jahier. Torino, Einaudi. 1953. 109 p. Italy.

Il borghese gentiluomo. Corrado Pavolini. Milano, Rizzoli. 1954. 148 p. Italy.

Il borghese gentiluomo. Cesare Levi. Firenze, Sansoni. 1954. 200 p. Italy.

Burgezul boerit. [Mol.] R. Portnoj. Kišinev. Škoala Sovetikė. 1954. U.S.S.R.

The Middle-Class Gentleman. Herma Briffault. Great Neck, New York. Barron's Educational Series. 111 p. 1957. U.S.A.

The Proper Gentleman. Trsl. and adapt. by Henry S. Taylor. London. Ginn. (c. 1959). VIII, 87 p. England.

Tru'ở'ng già hoc làm sang. Lu'u-Bàng. Saigon. Loai Sách Song Ngđ'. 1959. 119 p. Vietnam.

Meštiak šl'achticom. Blahoslav Hečko. Bratislavia. SVKL. 1961. 208 p. Czechoslovakia.

Ricachon en la corte. E. Espasa. Calpe. Madrid, Spain.

Meščanin vo dvorjanstve. N. Ljubimov and Argo. Moskva. Det. lit. 96 p. Also: Moskva: İskusstvo. 1964 and 1965. 104 p. U.S.S.R.

Neak mean khlean yos. Phnôm-Penh. Librairie Phnôm-Penh. 1965. 219 p. Cambodia.

Le Bourgeois gentilhomme. Trsl. and adapt. by Henry S. Taylor. In: Saffron (Robert) Great Farces. Edited by R. Saffron. 1966. 65–120 pp.

Građanin plemić. Mladen Škiljan. Zagreb. Hrvatsko narodno kazalište. 1966. 62 p. Yugoslavia.

Al-muthrī al-nabil. Yusuf Muḥammad Riḍā. Beyrouth. Dār al-Kitāb al-Lubnānī. Librairie de l'École. 1967. 238 p. Lebanon.

Assayyed al bourgeoizy. Youssef Mohamed Reda. Beirut. Dār al-Kitāb al-Lubnānī. 1968. 187 p. Lebanon.

Ne oldum delisi. Istanbul. Remzi Kitabevi. 1968. 48 p. Turkey.

Der Bürger als Edelmann. Arthur Luther. Stuttgart. Reclam. 1969. 85 p. Germany.

LA CRITIQUE DE L'ECOLE DES FEMMES

Kadinlar mektebinin tenkidi. Delimize çeriren. Sabahattin Eyüboğ-lu. Istanbul. Millî Eğitim Basimevi. 1965. 37 p. Turkey.

DOM GARCIE DE NAVARRE

Yahut, Kiskanc prens. Reşat Nuri Darago. Istanbul. Millî Eğitim Basmeri. 1949. II. 62 p. Turkey.

DOM JUAN

Don Giovanni o il convitato di pietra. C. Vico Lodovici. Torino. Il Dramma. 1948 and 1966. 83 p. Italy.

Don Giovanni o il convitato di pietra. Eugenio Levi. Firenze, Sansoni. 1949. XX. 178 p. Italy.

Don Juan. Li, Chian-Wu. Shêng-hai. K'ai-Ming shu chü. 1949. VIII. 90 p. China.

Don Juan. Rikie Suzuki. Tôkyô. Iwanami shoten. 1952. 119 p. Japan.

Don Juan. Bearbeitung von Bertolt Brecht. Stücke XII. Frankfurt/M. Suhrkamp. 1952.

Don Juan of de stenen gast. M.J. Premsela. Amsterdam. Wereldbibliotheek. 1954. 95 p. Also: Antwerpen. 1954. Netherlands.

Don Giovanni o il concitato di pietra. Fernanda Turvisi. Bologna. Capelli. 1957. 108 p. Italy.

Don Zhuani, ose Mysafiri i Gurtë. Sotir Caci. Tiranë: Shtetërore E Botimeve. 1958. 78 p. Albania.

Don Juan. Jozef Štefánik. Bratislava. Diliza. 1959. 74 p. Czechoslovakia.

Don Juan. Karel Kraus. Praha. Dilia. 1960. 68 p. Czechoslovakia.

Dūn Juwān. Idward Mikhā'īl. al Qāhirah. Lajna al-Ta'lif wal Tarjamar wal Nashr. 16, 149 p. 1962. United Arab Republic.

Don John; or, The Libertine. A comedy. 1665. Trsl. by John Ozell. Revised and augmented by Oscar Mandel. IN: Mandel (Oscar) The Theatre of Don Juan, etc. 1963. pp. 118–63.

Don Juan. [Est] Ott Ojamaa. Tallin. Èstgosizdat. 1964. 94 p. U.S.S.R.

Don Juan; or, The Statue at the Banquet. Wallace Fowlie. Great Neck, New York. Barron's Ed. Series. 1964. 83 p. U.S.A.

Don Juan. Eugen Neresheimer. Frankfurt/M. Ullstein. 1965. 206 p. Germany.

Don Juan. N. Alterman. Tel-Aviv. Hakibbutz Hameuchad. 1965. 81 p. Israel.

Don Juan. Arthur Luther. Stuttgart. Reclam. 1966, 1969. 64 p. Germany.

Don Juan eller Stengästen. Komedi i fem akter. Tor Hedberg. Sthlm. Sveriges dramatikerförb. Seelig. 1967. 63 p. Sweden.

Don Juan. Yusuf Moḥammad Riḍā. Beyrouth. Dār al-Kitāb al Lubnānī.

L'ECOLE DES FEMMES

[L'école des femmes]. Stéf. Morfis. Athènes. Ed. Govostis. 1948. 76 p. Greece.

Škola žien. Vojtech Mihálek and Jozef Štefanik. (Liptovský Sv. Mikuláš). Tranoscius. 1948. Czechoslovakia.

Škola žien. Josef Štefánik and Vojtech Michálik. Bratislava. N [árodni] D [ivadlo] 1948. 21 p. Czechoslovakia.

The School for Wives. Earl of Longford. Dublin. Hodges Figgis. 1948. 56 p. Ireland.

La scuola delle mogli. La critica alla scoula delle mogli. Paola Ojetti. Milano. Rizzoli. 1951. 134 p. Italy.

School voor vrouwen. (Blijspel) Bert Voeten. Amsterdam. C.P.J. Van Der Peet. 1953. 82 p. Netherlands.

The School for Wives. Miles Malleson. London. S. French. 1956. 102 p. [French's Acting Ed.] Same: Free Version by M. Malleson in: Plays of the Year. Vol. 10, 1954. Same: Free Version by M. Malleson. London. Elek Books. 1960 (c. 1954). England.

Nök iskolája. Lörinc Szabó. Budapest. Uj Magyar Kiadó. 1956. 83 p. Hungary.

Naiste kool. [Est] A. Sang. Tallin. Èstgosizdat. 1961. 111 p. U.S.S.R.

Die Schule der Frauen. Hans Weigel. Zürich. Diogenes Verlag. 1964. 132 p. Switzerland.

Die Schule der Frauen. Rudolf Alexander Schröder. Stuttgart, Reclam. 1964. (Nachdruck 1967?) 72 p. Germany.
The School for Wives. Miles Malleson. Chester Springs, Pa. Dufour. 1964. 116 p. U.S.A.
Kocalar okulu. Vahdi Hatay. Istanbul. Millî Eğitim Basimevi (2 bs.) 1965. 55 p. Turkey.
Bet sefer le-našim. L. Goldberg. Jerusalem. Mosad Bialik. 1966. 111 p. Israel.
The School for Wives. Richard Wilbur. (1st ed.) New York. Harcourt Brace Jovanovich. 1971. XIV. 146 p. U.S.A.

L'ECOLE DES MARIS

El avo y la escuela de los maridos. — Madrid. Diana. 1949. 23 p. Spain.
A escola dos maridos. Artur Azevedo. Rio de Janeiro. M.E.C. Serv. de Documentação. 1957. 111 p. Brazil.
Madrasat al-arwāj. Yusuf Muhammad Ridā. Beyrouth. Dar al-Kitāb al Lubnāni. Librairie de l'École. 1967. 142 p. Lebanon.
Madrasat al-azwaj. Youssef Mohamed Reda. Beirut. Dar al-Kitāb al-Lubnani. 1968. 103 p. Lebanon.

L'ETOURDI

Şaskin. 2 bsl. B. Enver Koryak. M.E.B. Istanbul. Millî Eğitim Basimev. 1964 and 1966. 87 p. Turkey.

LES FACHEUX

Münasebetsizler. Yaşar Nabi Nayir. Istanbul. Millî Eğitim Basimevi (2 bsl.) V. 1965. 39 p. Turkey.

LES FEMMES SAVANTES

Onna Gakusha. Seiichi Yashiro. Tôkyô. Kawade Shobô. 1953. 127 p. Japan.
The learned ladies. Renée Waldinger. Great Neck, New York. Barron's Educational Series. 1957. 87 p. U.S.A.
Učene Ženy. Vojtech Mihálik and Jozef Štefánik. Bratislava. SVKL. 1959. 127 p. Czechoslovakia.
Die gelehrten Frauen. Arthur Luther. Stuttgart. Reclam. 1960, 1966, 1969. 72 p. Germany.
Las mujeres sabias. ed bilingue, trad. Mujica Láinez, Manuel. 1964. 242 p. Sudamericana.
Die gelehrten Frauen. Hans Weigel. Zürich. Diogenes. 1965. 108 p. Switzerland.
The Learned Ladies. Joachim Neugroschel. New York. American R.D.M. 1966. 104 p. U.S.A.
La mujeres sabias. — Madrid. Escelicer. 1968. 72 p. Spain.
Las mujeres sabias. Enrique Llovet. Madrid. Ediciones Alfil. 1967, 1968. 122 p. Spain.
Las mujeres sabias. — Nacional. 1967–1968. 102 p. Spain.
The Learned Ladies. Henri Van Laun. New York. French and European Publications. 1969. 165 p. U.S.A.

LES FOURBERIES DE SCAPIN

Les furberies de Scapino. V. Boni. Milano. Ancora. 1948. 52 p. Italy.
Scapin no warudakumi. Rikie Suzuki. Tôkyô. Iwanami Shoten. 1953. 116 p. Japan.

Scapins Schelmenstreiche. Margret Wilmsen-Marx. Kassel. Bärenreiter-Verl. 1954. 78 p. Germany.

Die Streiche des Scapin. Lustspiel in 3 Akten. Übers. u. bearb. Lothar Ehrlich. Berlin. Henschel. 1954. 50 p. Germany.

As velhacarias de Scapin. Leopoldo de Araójo. Lisboa. Contraponto, S.C. 1956. Portugal.

Skapinova šibalství. Svatopluk Kadlec. Praha. Orbis. 1956. 74 p. Czechoslovakia.

Artimanhas de Scapino. Carlos D. de Andrade. Rio de Janeiro. Ministério da Educacão e Cultura. Serviso de Documentação, 1962. 91 p. Brazil.

Jakkalsstreke van Scapino. uit die Frans vertaal deur Bartho Smit. Johannesburg. Dagbreek-boekhandel. 1962. 65 p. South Africa.

Ayyar Hamza. Mehmet Âli. Istanbul. Remzi Kitabevi. 1955. (2 bs.) 117 p. 1968 (3 bs.) 121 p. Turkey.

The Rogueries of Scapin. Henri van Laun. New York. French and European Publications. 1968. 157 p. U.S.A.

Scapins Streiche. Arthur Luther. Stuttgart. Reclam. 1968. 64 p. Germany.

Dem luussert seng Spichten. René Weimerskirch. Gasperich. 1962. Luxembourg.

GEORGE DANDIN.

Duda Gyuri Vígjáték. Ferenc Hont and Tamás Major. Budapest. Franklin. 1949. 50 p. Hungary.

Dandin György. [Mag.] — Noviszád. 3 Tesvériség-Egység. 1950. 47 p. Yugoslavia.

George Dandin. Für d. dt. Bühne übertr. u. eingerichtet von Gerhard Neumann. Unverkäufl. Berlin. Henschel. 1952. 35 p. Germany.

Dandin Görgy. [Mag.] Daniel Imre. Bratislava. SDLZ. 1956. 58 p. Czechoslavakia.

Dandin György. Vagy a megcsufolt férj. Gyula Illyés. Budapest. Müvelt Nep. 1955. 69 p. Hungary.

Jíra danda aneb chudák manžel. E.A. Saudek. Praha. Orbis (2 ed.) 1960. 56 p. Czechoslovakia.

George Dandin. Tr. 1964, 1965, 1966. 64 p. Lib. Gongora. Spain. Also: George Dandin. Edit Herrero. Mexico.

Oklamaný Manžel. Blahoslar Hečko. Bratislava. DILIZA. 1965. 45 p. Czechoslovakia.

George Dandin oder Der betrogene Ehemann. Ludwig Wolde. Stuttgart. Reclam. 1966. 56 p. Germany.

George Dandin oder Der genasführte Ehemann. Hans Carl Artman. Wien. Universal Ed. 1969. 98 p. Austria.

LA JALOUSIE DU BARBOUILLE

A féltékeny Maszatos. László Pödör. Budapest. Terra. 1959. 41 p. Hungary.

LE MALADE IMAGINAIRE

Der eingebildete Kranke. Wolf Graf Baudissin. Berlin. Cornelsen. 1948. 147 p. Also: Reclam. 1950, 1951, 1960. 80 p. Germany.

Le Malade Imaginaire. René Pierre Louis Ledésert and Wilson. London. Harrap. 1949. 119 p. England.

The Would-be Invalid. Trsl. and edit. by Morris Bishop. New York. Appleton Century Crofts. 1950. lx, 79 p. U.S.A.

De ingebeelde Zieke. J.A. Brouwer. Baarn, Hollandia. 1950. 83 p. Netherlands.

D'r ingebèld krank. Robert Sauer. Mulhouse, Editions Salvator. 1950 (2ᵉ ed). 48 p. France: Alsace.

The Imaginary Invalid. Henri van Laun. Adapted by C. Fenton. Sydney. Whitehall Productions. 1950. 30 p. Australia.

De Grochsi. Es Lustspiel. 3 Akte. [Schweizerdeutsch] Hans Bader. Aarau, Sauerländer. 1951 (3 Aufl.) 90 p. Switzerland.

Zdravý Nemocný. Komedie-Balet o 3 Dejstvích. Svatopluk Kadlec. Praha, Osvěta. 1952. 96 p. Czechoslovakia.

Der eingebildete Kranke. Johannes von Guenther. Stuttgart. Reclam. 1954, 1956, 1962, 1964, 1966. Nachdruck, 1968. 80 p. Germany.

D'r inbildungs krank. 1960. [Alsacien]. Claus Reinbolt. Woerth. Sutter. 1959. 93 p. France: Alsace.

The Hypochondriac. — Greenwich, Connecticut. Fawcett Publications. 1961. U.S.A.

The Hypochondriac. H. Baker and J. Miller. In: Loggins (Vernon) 3 Great French Plays. 1961. 111 p.

Den hèr schrobildgen. René Weimerskirch. Gasperich. 1961. 46 p. Luxembourg.

Ha-Hole Ha-medume. Natan Alterman. Tel Aviv. Ha-Kibbuẓ Ha-Meuḥad. 1958/ 1959. 1961. 117 p. Israel.

Doctor's Delight; A Farce. Milton Levine. New York. L. Hayward Agency. U.S.A.

Il malato imaginario. Ugo Dettore. Milano. Rizzoli. 1962. 144 p. Italy.

The Imaginary Invalid. [In Plays of the Year, V. 19] Miles Mallison. London. Elek Books. 1960. 111 p. England.

Hastalik Hastasi (2 bs.) Dilimize çeviren. İsmail Hâmi Danişment, [Turkiye Cumhuriyetti]. Istanbul. Millî Eğitim Basimevi. 1962. 94 p. Turkey.

Der eingebildete Kranke. Walter Widmer. Reinbek. Rowohlt. 1962. 158 p. Germany.

Hastalik Hastasi. İsmail Hâmi Danişment. Istanbul. Türkiye Cumburiyeti Millî Eğitim Bakanliği (2 ed.) 1962. 94 p. Turkey.

Al-marīd al-wahmī. Yusuf Muḥammad Riḍā. Beyrouth. Dār al-Kitāb al-Lubnānī, Librairie de l'École. 1967. 216 p. Lebanon.

The Imaginary Invalid. Bert Briscoe. Birmingham. C. Combridge. 1967. 69 p. England.

The Imaginary Invalid. Bert Briscoe. C. Combridge. Birmingham. (Schools edition with plates). 1967. 69 p. England.

LE MARIAGE FORCE

Zor mikâh. [Adapte eden] Ahmet Vefik Paşa. Tertibeden. Mustafa Nihat Özön. Istanbul. 1950. Remzi Kitabevi. XVI. 80 p. Turkey.

Brak ponevole. N. Ljubimov. Moskva. Iskusstvo. 1956. 47 p. U.S.S.R.

Die erzwungene Heirat. Adapt. by Ludwig Hoffman. Leipzig. VEB Hofmeister. 1958. 27 p. Germany.

Zorla evlenme. Afif Obay. Istanbul. Millî Eğitim Basimevi (2 bsl.) 1965. 35 p. Turkey.

LE MEDECIN MALGRE LUI

Dokter tegen wil en dank. H. van der Loos, Jr. Baarn. Hollandia. 1950. 3e dr. 53 p. Netherlands.

A botcsinálta doktor [Mag]—Noviszád. Testvériség-Egység. 1950. 38 p. Yugoslavia.

Ha-rofe bal korkho. D.A. Tel Aviv. Ha-merkaz Le-tarbut. 1950. 41 p. Israel.

Der Arzt wider Willen. Clotilde Schenck zu Schweinsberg. München. Höfling. 1956. 86 p. Germany.

El médico a la fuerza. Julio Gómez de la Serna. Lima. Servicio de Difusión de la Escuela Nacional de Arte Escénico. 1957. 37 p. Peru.

Der Arzt wider Willen. Adapt. by Ludwig Hoffmann. Leipzig. VEB Hofmeister. 1958. 35 p. Germany.

Zoraki Hekim. Sabiha Omay. İstanbul. Maarif Basimevi. 1958. (2 ed.) 52 p. Turkey.

Dokter uit-en-aan. Martin J. Premsela. Amst. Strengholt. 1959. 20 p. Netherlands.

Yasa wedaya. Newton Pinto. Colombo. M.D. Gunasena and Co. Ltd. 1960. 128 p. Ceylon.

The Unwilling Doctor. Adapted and trsl. by Lisl Beer. Boston. Bruce Humphries. 1961. 22 p. (The Silver Series of Puppet Plays.) U.S.A.

Iyaiga nagara isha ni sare. Rikie Suzuki. Tokio Iwanami Shoten. 1964. 109 p. Japan.

Zoraki Meslek. Istanbul: Remzi Kitaberi. 1968. 31 p. Turkey.

The Reluctant Doctor. W. Hannan. London. Heinemann Educational Books, XIV. 1965. 31 p. England.

Kroupét veasna laâ. Chan Mom Phavy. Phnôm-Penh. Librâirie Phnôm-Penh. 1965. Cambodia.

The Doctor in spite of himself. — Port-of-Spain. University of the West Indies, Extra Mural Dept. 1966. (The N.U. Catal. 1970. Vol. 9) West Indies.

Al-Tabīb Raghman 'Anhu. Yusuf Muḥammad Riḍā. Beyrouth. Dār al-Kitāb al-Lubnānī. Librairie de l'Ecole. 1967. 99. Lebanon.

Dokter tegen wil en dank. E. Dobbneberg. Baarn. Hollandia (4ᵉ dr.) 1969. 53 p. Netherlands.

Molière's "Le Médecin malgre lui" in Afrikaans. Krige, Uys. Theoria 34:1–19. [Ind. trsl.] 1970. South Africa.

Dokter teen-wil-en-dank; vry verwerk na Molière se Le Médecin malgré lui [deur] Uys Krige. Pretoria. Van Schaik. South African Natl. Bibl. 1971. 85 p. South Africa.

LE MEDECIN VOLANT

Arzt in Liebessachen. Walter Klefisch. Weinheim. Deutscher Laienspiel-Verlag. 1956. Germany.

Dokter uit-en-aan. Martin J. Premsela. Amsterdam. Strengholt. 1959. 20 p. Netherlands.

LE MISANTHROPE

Misantrop. Svatopluk Kadlek. Praha. Ceskoslovenský Kompas. 1948. 105 p. Czechoslovakia.

Der Misanthrop. Wolf Graf Baudissin. Leipzig. Reclam. Neudruck. 1948, 63 p. Germany.

Der Menschenfeind. Arthur Luther. Wiesbaden. Insel Verlag. 1949. 88 p. Germany.

Der Misanthrop. Emilie Schröder. Freiburg. Herder. 1949. X. 149 p. Germany.

El misantropo. [Cat.] Joan Oliver. Barcelona. Aymá. 1950. Spain.

Mizantrop. Tadeusz Żeliński-Boy. Wrocław, Wydawn. Zakl. Narod. im. Ossoliń-skich. 1951. (Wyd. 3 przejrzane) XLII. 109 p. Poland.

Ningen Girai. Arô Naitô. Tôkyô. Shinchôsha. 1952. 108 p. Japan.

Kokyaku. Yutaka Tatsuno. Tôkyô. Hakusui-Sha. 1953. 170 p. Japan.

Der Menschenfeind. Paul Mochmann. Berlin. Henschel. 1954, 1955. 66 p. Germany.

The Misanthrope. (In English verse). Richard Wilbur. New York. Harcourt, Brace. 1955. XII. 140 p. U.S.A. Also: 1958. England.

Misantrop. J. Z. Novák. Praha. ĈDLJ. 59. 1955. Czechoslovakia.
Embergyülölö. Lörinc Szabó. Budapest. Uj Magyar Kiadó. 1956. 82 p. Hungary.
Misantropen. André Bjerke. Oslo. Aschenoug. 1957. 93 p. Norway.
Le Misanthrope, in a new adaptation. The Slave of Truth, by Miles Malleson. London.
    French. 1957. 65 p. England.
Adamčil. Bu eser Ali Süha Delilbasĭ tarajĭndan tercüme edilmiştir. 2 baskĭ. Istanbul.
    Maarif Basimevi. 1958. IX. 109 p. Turkey.
Mizantrop. Stefan Petrov. Sofija. Nar. Kultura. 1959. 110 p. Bulgaria.
Der Menschenfeind. Arthur Luther. Stuttgart. Reclam, 1959. 74 p. (1966, Nachdruck)
    1968. Germany.
Hên shih chê. Wu Yen-p'ing and Chêng Ching-chad. Taipei. Hsieh Chin Industrial
    Development Association. 1959. I. 62 p. China.
The Misanthrope. Bernard D. N. Grebanier. Great Neck, New York. Barron's
    Educational Series. 1959. 76 p. U.S.A.
The Slave of Truth. New English version. New York. Coward-McCann. 1960. U.S.A.
Misantroop. [Est.] A. S'ang. Talli Éstgosizdat. 1961. 103 p. Estonian S.S.R.
Mizantrop. Vladimir Gerić. Zagreb. Zagrebačko Dramsko Kazalište. 1961. 87 p.
    Yugoslavia.
Misantropen. Scapinos Skälmstycken. Viveka Heyman. Sthlm. Tiden. 1961. 149 p.
    Sweden.
Misantropen. Peter Hansen. Kǿbenhavn. Gyldendal. 1962. 175 p. Denmark.
Der Menschenfeind. Hans Weigel. Zürich. Diogenes Verlag. 1965. 100 p. Switzerland.
The Misanthrope. Joachim Neugroschel. New York. 1966. U.S.A.
The Misanthrope. Trsl. into verse by Richard Wilbur, Methuen and Co. London.
    1967. 84 p. England.
Kāreh Al-Bashar. Yusuf Muḥammad Riḍā. Beyrouth. Dār al-Kitāb al Lubnānī.
    Librairie de l'École. 1967. 224 p. Lebanon.
'Aduww al-Bashar. Muhammad Ghunimi Hilāl. s.I., s.n., 1967. United Arab
    Republic.
Mizantrop. Jan Kott. Wwa. Czytelnik, 1967. 117 p. Poland.
Mizantrop. (Wolny przeklad proza Jana Kotta. O wspólczesnościach Moliera
    napisal Jan Kott.) Warszawa. 1967. 117 p. Poland.
Misantropen. (I svensk tolkning av Allan Bergstrand.) Stockholm. Svenska Rikstea-
    tern. 1968. Sweden.

MONSIEUR DE POURCEAUGNAC

Der Edelmann als Freier. Posse mit Gesang u. Tanz in 3 Akten. Paul Mochmann.
    Berlin. Henschel. 1951. 46 p. Germany.
Der Herr aus der Provinz. Hans Weigel. Zürich. Diogenes Verlag. 1964. 74 p.
    Switzerland.

LES PRECIEUSES RIDICULES

Les Precieuses ridicules. Chien Wu Lee. Shanghai. Kai-Ming Bookstore. 1949. 41 p.
    China.
El-Mutahaslikaat. Mohamed Badran and M. Abdel Hafiz Mo'awad. Cairo.
    Maktabat El-Nahda Al-Misria. 1950. 102 p. Egypt.
De Belachelijke "Précieuses". M.J. Premsela. Baarn. Hollandia. 2e dr. 1950. 37 p.
    Netherland.
A kényeskedök [Mag.]. — Noviszád, Bratsztvo-Jedinsztvo. 1950. 26 p. Hungary.

Pocieszne wykwintnisie. Komedia. Tadeusz Boy-Żeleński. Wrocław, Wydawn. Zaki Narod. im. Ossolińskich (Wyd. 2) XXX−48. 1950. Poland.
Le preziose ridicole [Fr., It.]. Francesco Picco. Firenze, Sansoni. 1953. 139 p. Italy.
Smehotvornye žemannicy. N. Jakovleva. Moskva. Iskusstvo. 1956. 47 p. U.S.S.R.
La Mokindaj Preciozulinoj [Esperanto]. André Ribot. Den Haag. Internacia Esperanto-Instituto. 1957. Netherlands.
The Pretentious Young Ladies. Herma Briffault. Great Neck, New York. Barron's Barron's Educational Series. 1959. 38 p. U.S.A.
Al-mutahzliqāt al-sakhīfāt. Yusuf Muḥammad Riḍā. Beyrouth. Dār al-Kitāb al-Lubnānī. Librairie de l'École. 1967. 95 p. Lebanon.
De ziirlige Damer. Poul Reumert. Herning. Poul Kristensen. (Ny udg) 1967. 117 p. Denmark.

SGANARELLE, OU LE COCU IMAGINAIRE.

Sganarel, ili mnimyj rogonosec. A. Onoškovič-Jacyna. Moskva. Iskusstvo. 1956. U.S.S.R.
Sgaranelle. Free English version by Miles Malleson. London. Samuel French. 1955. p. 34. [Same] In: Plays of the Year. Vol. II, 377–378. England.
Sganarelle. Rolf Thieme. Leipzig. VEB Hofmeister. 1958. 38 p. Germany.
Le Cocu imaginaire [Kannada] [Pratyakṣa pramana]. Trsl. by P. Narasingarav. 1961. 24 p. India.

TARTUFFE

Tartüff. Wolf Graf Baudissin. Leipzig. Reklam. 1948, Neudr. 1951, 1952. 68 p. Germany.
Tartüff. Ludwig Fulda. Berlin. Cornelsen. 1948. 104 p. 1949, 103 p. Germany.
Tartuf. Asen Razcvetnikov. Sofia, Nar Prosv. 1949. 133 p. Also: Sofia, Nar Kultura (7 izd.) 1959, 1960, 1962, 1964, 1966, 1967, (14 izd.) 1969. 148 p. Bulgaria. .
Tartüff. Neufassung im Versmass des Orig. Ernst Leopold Stahl. Frei nach Adolf Laun. Offenburg-Baden. Lehrmittel-Verl. 1949. 95 p. Germany.
Tartufo. Eugenio Levi. Milano, Univ. Econ., 1949, 102 p. 1952, 105 p. Italy.
Świetoszek. (Tartuf). Czesław Jastrzębiec-Kozlowski. Kraków, Wydawn. M. Kot, 1949. 106 p. 1950, 100 p. Poland.
Le Tartuffe. René Pierre Louis Ledésert. London. Harrap. 1949. New Ed., 106 p. England.
Tartuffe, or The imposter; Freely adapted . . . with a prologue taken from "L'impromptu de Versailles". Miles Malleson. London. Samuel French. [c. 1950]. v–78 p. London. Elek Books, 1960. 103 p. England.
Tartufo; Don Juan o el convidado de piedra. Carlos M. Princivalle and A. Cebrián. Buenos Aires, Espasa-Calpe. 1950. 163 p. Argentina.
Tartufe, czyli Świetoszek. Tadeusz Zeleński-Boy. Warszawa, Nakł. Gebethnera Wolffa. 1951. 88 p. Poland.
Świętoszck. Tadeusz Boy-Żeleński. Wroslaw, Wydawn. Zakl. Narod. im. Ossolinskich, 1951 (Wyd. 2, przejrzane) XXXIV, 136 p. (Wyd. 3, 1953, 152 p.); same: 1958; same, 1961; same 1964; same: 1968. Warszawa, Czytelnik, 1955. Poland.
Tartuffe. István Vas. Budapest. Uj Magyar Kiadó. 1951 (1956). 91 p. Same: Budapest. Szépirodalmi Kiadó. 1956. 120 p. Hungary.
Tartuffe. Arthur Luther. Leipzig. Insel Verlag. 1951, 95 p. Same: Wiesbaden, Insel Verlag. 1954, 95 p. Same: Stuttgart, Reclam. 1966 (Nachdruck). 74 p. Germany.

Tartufo. Tradução Livre em Dodecassílabos com um prólogo. Guilherme Figueiredo. Rio de Janeiro. Dept. de Imprensa Nacional, 1952. Same: Rio de Janeiro, Civilição Brasileira, 1959. 135 p. Brazil.

Tartuffe. Svatopluk Kadlec. Praha. Osvěta. 1952. 116 p. Czechoslovakia.

Tartuffe. Tor Hedberg. Stockholm, Svenska Bokförlaget, 1953. 80 p. Bonnier (1956); (1959) (1960). Sweden.

O Tartoufos. G. Simiriotis. Athinai. Anagnostidis, s.d. 1954. 94 p. Greece.

Tartuffe. Reinhard Koester. Stuttgart, Reclam. 1954, 1960, 1964, 1967, 1969. 80 p. Germany.

Tartuffe. Ferenc Jankovich. Budapest, Müvelt Nép. 1954. 91 p. Hungary.

Świętoszek. Tadeusz Boy-Żeleński. Wrocław. Zakład im Ossolińskich. (Wyd. 4 Przejrzane) XLII, 1956. 166 p. Poland.

Tartuffe. Rikie Suzuki. Tokyo. Iwanami Shoten. 1956. 121 p. Same: Tokyo, Chikuma shobó. 1969. 497 p. Japan.

Tartjuf, or' Ynšelétoryl. [Mol.] Konstantin Kondrja. Kišinev. Škoala sovetikė. 1956. IX, 104 p. U.S.S.R.

Tartuffe. [Slovène] Oton Župančić. Ljubljana. Mladinska Knjiga. 1956. 1967. 82 p. (2 neizm izd.) Yugoslavia.

Tartuffe, avagy a képmutató. István Vas. Budapest. Corvina. 1957. 287 p. Hungary.

L'impostore ovvero il tartufo. Ugo Dèttore. Milano. Rizzoli. 1957. 89 p. Italy.

Tartufi. Sotir Caci. Tiranë. Ndërmarrja Shtetërore e Botimeve. 1958. 138 p. Albania.

Tartufo. Commedia. Salvatore Quasimodo. Milano. Bompiani. 1958, 121 p. 1966, 2ᵃ ed., 216 p. Italy.

Tartuffe. Haskell M. Block. New York. Appleton-Century-Crofts. 1958. 81 p. U.S.A.

Tartuffe. The Hypocrite. Renée Waldinger. Great Neck, New York. Barron's Educational Series. 1959. 97 p. U.S.A.

Tartufo. Il malato immaginario. Giorgio Dandino. Mario Bonfantini. Torino. U.T.E.T. 1959 (2ᵃ ed.) 302 p. Italy.

Tartuffe. István Vas. Budapest. Szépirodalmi Kiadó. 1960, 1962. 119 p. Hungary.

Tartuffe, or The Hypocrite. Curtis Hidden Page. (In Continental Drama.) New York, 1961, 1968, (The Harvard Classics, v. 26. 197–296.) U.S.A.

Tartuffe, ehk Petis. [Est.] A Sang. Tallin. Ėstgosizdat, 1961. 120 p. Estonian S.S.R.

Upadešiyar. [Malayalam] K. Sukumaran. Kozhikode. P.K. Bros. 1961. 141 p. India.

Tartufi. [Alb] Gertruda Panda. Beograd. Botim e treksteve e Republikës Popullore të Serbis. 1962. 1963. 148 p. Yugoslavia.

Tartuffe (Verse tr.) James L. Rosenberg. San Francisco. Chandler, 1962, 62 p. U.S.A.

Tartyuph [Ben] Lokenath Bhattacharya. New Dehli. Sahitya Akademi. 1963. XIV. 69 p. India.

Tartuffe (Verse tr.) Richard Wilbur. New York. Harcourt, Brace and World. 1963. XII, 106 p. U.S.A.

Tartuffe. Cevdet Perin. Istanbul. Remzi Kitabvri. 1963. 78 p. Turkey.

Tartuffe eller den skinnhellige. André Bjerke. Oslo. Aschehoug. 1963. 97 p. Norway.

Tartufo o el imposter. 5.00 E. Rev. Literaria. Madrid. 1963? Spain.

Tartuffe. R. Wilbur. London. Faber, 1964. XII. 106 p. England.

Tartufi ose Mashtronjësi. S. Çaçi. Tiranë. Inst. i. Studimeve dhe Bot. Shkollore (Bot. i. 2. -të) 1965. 112 p. Albania.

Tartufo. — Mediterráneo. 30 E. 1965. 132 p. Spain.

Tartif. [Mak] Lazo Karovski. Skopje. Kočo Racin. 1966. 121 p. Yugoslavia.

Tartuffe. Robert W. Hartle. Indianapolis. Bobbs, Merrill, 1965 and 1966, XXIV, 84 p. U.S.A.

Tartuffe. Miles Malleson. Chester Springs, Pa. : DuFour. 1966. 103 p. U.S.A.

Tartuffe. Vojtech Mihàlik and Fedor Ballo. Bratislava. Tatran. 1966. 493 p. Czechoslovakia.

Tartuffee oder der Betrüger. Hans Weigel. Zürich. Diogenes Verlag. 1967. 111 p. Switzerland.

Tartūf. Yusuf Muhammad Ridā. Beyrouth. Dār al-Kitāb al-Lubnānī. Librairie de l'École. 1967. 186 p. Lebanon.

Tartuffe [Fr., Eng.] Henry van Laun. New York. French & European Publications. 1968. 169 p. U.S.A.

El tartufo. Enrique Llovet. Madrid, Edit. Escelicer. 1970. 96 p. Spain.

Two or More Works in one Volume.

Argentina

El Avaro; Tartufo. Buenos Aires. Tor. 1950. 192 p.

Tartufo; Don Juan, o El Convidado De Piedra. Carlos M. Princivalle and A. Cebrián. Buenos Aires. Espasa-Calpe. 1950. 176 p.

Teatro Clásico Francés. Miguel Pérez Ferrero. Maria Alfaro, et al. Buenos Aires, "El Ateneo". 1952. 1019 p.

El Médico A Palos. El Misántropo. José Olivares Larrondo. Buenos Aires. Sopena. 1956. 157 p.

El Tartufo. Las Preciosas Ridículas. José Olivares Larrondo. Buenos Aires. Sopena. 1956. 158 p.

Brazil

As preciosas ridiculas e Sganarello (o côrno imaginario). Miécio Táti. Rio de Janeiro. Ed. Civ. Brasileria. 1957. 107 p.

As Sabichonas. Escola de Mulheres. Jenny Klabin Segall. S. Paulo Martins. 1963. 201 p. [Les Femmes savantes. L'École des femmes].

Comédias. Omar P. Lannes. Guanabara. M. Peixoto. 1965. 254 p.

Czechoslovakia

Lakomec; Komedie o pěti dějstvích. Přel. Svatopluk Kadlec. I. vyd V. Praze. Uměni, 1949. 156 p.

Hry (Sv. 2.) Tartuffe; Don Juan; Misantrop; Amfitryon. Svatopluk Kadlec. Praha. Snklhu. 397 p. Oeuvres complètes. 1954. Hry, (3 Sv.) 1955, 390 p.

Hry (Sv. 4.) Skapinova Šibalství; Hraběnka z Nouzova; Učené Ženy; Zdravý Nemocný. Svatopluk Kadlec. Praha. Snklhu. 363 p. 1956. Les Fourberies de Scapin, La Contesse d'Escarbagnas; Les Femmes savantes; Le Malade imaginaire.

Lakomec, Misantrop, Tartuffe. E.A. Saudek, J.Z. Novak and František Vrba. Praha. Mladá Fronta. 1966. 284 p.

Komédie (1:) Smiešne preciózky. Škola žien. Kritika školy žien. Versailleská improvizácia. Tartuffe. Vojtech Mihálik, Fedor Ballo and Jozef Štefánik. Bratislava: Tatran. 1967. 376 p.

Denmark

Molières Digte. Marinus Børup Tegninger. Leo Estrad. København, Korch, 1948.

Komedier. (1:) Don Juan. Misantropen. Tartuffe. Chr. Ludvigsen, P. Hansen, A. Flinch. København. Borgen. 1964. 255 p.

England

The Burgher in Purple. Scapin the Scamp. (Two Comedies). George Graveley. St. Albans (Herts.), Cartmel. 1952. 942 p.

Five Plays: The Would-be Gentleman; That Scoundrel Scapin; The Miser; Love's the Best Doctor; Don Juan, or the Statue at the Feast. John Wood. London, Penguin Books, 1953, XXVIII, 252 p. 1958, XXVII, 251 p.

The Miser. Coxcombs in Petticoats. (Two Comedies). George Graveley. St. Albans, (Herts.), Cartmel and Sons, 1953, 109 p.

Don Juan, Forced to be a Doctor: Two Comedies. George Graveley. St. Albans, (Herts.), Cartmel. 1954. 111 p.

The Misanthrope and other plays. John Wood. London. Penguin Books. 1959. 282 p.

The School for Husbands; with, The Flying Doctor, The Uneasy Husband, Love is the Best Remedy; Four Short Farces. Trsl. and adapted by Allan Clayson. London. Heinemann Educational. 1969. 125 p.

Finland

Komedioja (I–II). Otto and Sulevi Manninen. Tyyni Tuulio *et al.* Porvod. Helsinki. Werner Söderström. 1959.

Germany

Sämtliche Werke. M. Beutler *et al.* Mit einer Einführung von Wilhelm Friedmann. Hrsg. von Eugen Neresheimer. Berlin. Propyläenverlag. n.d.

Dramen, 3 Bde. 1. Tartüff. Der Misanthrop. Der Geizige. 2. Die gelehrten Frauen. Der eingebildete Kranke. Der Zwist der Verliebten. 3. Der bürgerliche Edelmann. Amphitryon. Die Lästigen. Sganarell. Ludwig Fulda. Urach, Port. 1947–1948.

Sämtliche Werke, 3 Bde. 1. Die Komödien der Jahre 1656–1664; 2. Die Komödien der Jahre 1664–1668; 3. Die Komödien der Jahre 1669–1673. Dr. Roland Seffrin and Ernst Preusse. Hamburg, Eckardt and Messtorff. 1948. 382 p.; 349 p.; 409 p.

Komödien. (Teils.) Wolf Graf Baudissin. Hrsg. u. eingel. von Victor Klemperer. Leipzig, Dieterich. 1950. LIV–328 p.

Werke. Arthur Luther, Rudolf Alexander Schröder and Ludwig Wolde. Wiesbaden. Insel Verl. 1954, 1079 p. Deutsche Buchgemeinschaft, 1959, 1083 p. 1968, (2. Auflage) 1117 p.

Vier Lustspiele. Walter Widmer. Berlin. Aufbau-Verl. 1957. 314 p.

Tartuffe. Amphitryon. Der eingebildete Kranke. München. Goldmann. 1959. 190 p.

Der Misanthrop. Der Bürger als Edelmann. Rudolf Alexander Schröder. Hugo von Hofmannsthal. Frankfurt. Hamburg. Fischer Bücherei. 1960. 151 p.

Werke. Arthur Luther *et al.* Stuttgart. Europäischer Buchklub, Europäische Buchgemeinschaft. 1097 p. Nur für Mitglieder. 1968.

Der Menschenfeind. Der Geizige, Die gelehrten Frauen [Teilsamml., dt.] Übers. von Gustav Fabricius. München. Goldmann 1969. 191 p.

Komedien. Aus d. Franz. übertr. von Gustav Fabricius u. Walter Widmer. München. Winkler. 1970. 1069 p.

Greece

Me to zori pantreia; O tartouphos; Oi katergaries tou Skapinou. Th. Stauros. Athēnai. G. Papadēmētrios. 1951. [Le Mariage forcé] [Tartuffe; Scapin].

Hungary

Válogatott Vigjátékai. Gyula Illyes and Ferenc Karinthy, etc. Budapest, Szépirodalmi Könyvkiadó. [Comedies choisies.] 1954. 1038 p.
Tartuffe; A fösvény; A képzelt beteg. István Vas, Gyula Illyés. Budapest. Uj Magyar Kiadó. [Le Tartuffe ou l'Imposteur; L'Avare; Le Malade imaginaire.] 1956. 294 p.
A fösvény. Kényeskedök. Gyula Illyés. Budapest. Szépirodalmi Kiadó. [L'Avare; Les Précieuses ridicules]. 1965. 125 p.
Összes szinmüvei. 2 v. Gabor Deveccséri, Endre Illés et al. Budapest. Magyar Helikon. [Collected Works.] 1966. 250 p.
A fösvény, Kényeskedök. Gyula Illyés and Istrán Vas. Budapest. Európa Kiadó. 371 p. [L'Avare, Les Précieuses ridicules.] 1966, 1967 (2 ed.) 370 p.

India

Moliēr dē dō nātak. Gurbakhaś Singh. Delhi, Navyug. Publ., May 1958. 183 p. [Tartuffe and Le Bourgeois gentilhomme].
Eradu nātakagula. Trsl. from English by A.N. Murtirav. Mysore. Kavayalaya. 1959. XXIII, 193 p. [Tartuffe and Le Bourgeois gentilhomme.]
Natako. Hamśā Maheta. New Delhi. Sahitya Akademi. 1959. 166 p. [Tartuffe and Le Bourgeois gentilhomme.]
Iru Natakankal. [Tam] K.S. Venkatarāman. Madras. New Century Book House. 1959. XXVIII. 139 p. [Tartuffe; Le Bourgeois gentilhomme].
Rantu Molière Natakannal. [Malayalam] S. Gyptan Nāyar. Kottayam. Sahitya Pravathaka C.S. 1962. 351 p. [Tartuffe, Le Bourgeois gentilhomme].
Do Natak [Hindi]. Brajanāth Mādhav Vajpeyī. New Delhi. Sahitya Akademi. 1964. II. p. 169. [Tartuffe, Le Bourgeois gentilhomme.]
Kuppan pittalāṭṭankal. Śri Sri. Ācārya. Madras. Amuda nilayam. 1958. 91 p.

Italy

Capolavori del grande attore-scrittore. — Torino, S.E.T., 1949. LXXXVI. 672 p.
Il misantropo, Sganarello. Ugo Dettore. Milano, Rizzoli. 1952. 95 p.
Teatro (I–II). Corrado Tumiati, Alfredo Bartoli. Firenze. Sansoni. 1952.
Il convitato di pietra. Il borghese gentiluomo. Nicoletta Neri. Torino. 1953. 293 p. [Dom Juan ou le Festin de pierre; Le Bourgeois gentilhomme.]
Commedie Scelte. (Le preziose ridicole. Tartuffo. Il misantropo. L'avaro. Il borghese gentiluomo). Silvio Pons. Roma. Cremonese. XXVIII. 1955. 482 p.
Il tartufo. Il malato immaginario. Mario Bonfantini. Milano. Mondadori. 1956. 205 p.
Commedie. Le preziose ridicole. Il misantropo. L'avaro. Tartufo. Il borghese gentiluomo. Le trappolerie di Scarpino. Antonio Masini. Firenze, Salani. 1958. 479 p.
Il teatro (Vol. I–II). Alcibiade Moretti and Franco A. Rigano. Roma. Editr. Italiana di Cultura. 1958; A. Moretti, 2 v. 18 Tarr. 1961. Complessivamente.
Commedie. (Le preziose ridicole. La scuola delle mogli. Don Giovanni. Il misantropo. Il tartufo. L'avaro). Alfredo Bartoli. Corrado Tumiati. Mario Bonfantini. Milano. Mondadori. 1960. 339 p.
Tartufo. Il misantropo. Corrado Tumiati. Padova : Rebellaro Ed. 1960. 191 p. Italy.

Teatro. Il convitato di pietra, Il borghese gentiluomo, Le mariuolerie di Scapino. Nicoletta Neri. Torino. U.T.E.T. 1962. (nuóva ed.) 406 p.

Japan

Meisaku-shû: Sokotsu-mono; Teishu gakkô; Nyôbô gakkô; Tartuffe; Don Juan; Kokyaku; Shusendo; Jogakusha; Ki de yamu otoko. Rikie Suzuki, Takuzô Obase, *et al.* Tôkyô. Hakusui-sha. 1951. 652 p. [L'Étourdi; L'École des maris; L'École des femmes; Tartuffe; Don Juan; Le Misanthrope; L'Avare; Les Femmes savantes; Le Malade imaginaire.
Sekai Bungaku Zenshû. (II–11:) Tartuffe; Don Juan; Kokuhaku; Shusen-do; (Jogakusha.) Atsushi Kawaguchi; Rikie Suzuki, *et al.* Tokyo, Kawade shobô, 1951. 305 p. [Tartuffe; Don Juan; Le Misanthrope; L'Avare; Les Femmes savantes.]
Onna-gakusha: Ki de yamu otoko. Arô Naitô. Tôkyô. Shinchô-sha. 1952. 222 p. [Les Femmes savantes; Le Malade imaginaire.]
Nyôbô Gakkô. Yutaka Tatsuno; Rikie Suzuki. Tôkyô. Iwanami Shoten. 1957. 198 p. [L'École des femmes; La Critiaue de l'École des femmes; L'Impromptu de Versailles.]
Tartuffe. Ningengirai. Shusendo. (Beaumarchais:) Seville no rihatsushi. Figaro no kekkon. (Sekai Bungaku Zenshû, III–3). Yutaka Tatsuno, *et al.* Tôkyô. Kawade Shobo Shinsha. 1958. 362 p. [Tartuffe; Le Misanthrope; L'Avare.]
Moliere Shogekishu. Hiroto Arinaga. Tôkyô. Hakusui-Sha. 1959. 327 p. [Comedies.]
Ningen-girai; Tartuffe; Shusendo (Furansu Bungaku Zenshû, 2). Senriki Shirakawa. Tôkyô. Tôzai Gogatsu-sha. 1960. 454 p. [Le Misanthrope; Tartuffe; L'Avare.]
Tartuffe. Don Juan. Okorippoi koibito. Shusendo. Yamai wa kikara. Nyôbô gakko (Sekai bungaku zenshû, III–5). Suzuki Rikie, Imura Jun'ichi and Kanagawa Mitsuo. Tôkyô. Kawade, shobô shinsha, 1965. 454 p. [Tartuffe; Don Juan; Le Misanthrope; L'Avare; Le Malade imaginaire; L'Ecole des femmes].

Israel

Ha-Kamẓan. Ha-Ḥole Ha-Medume. Natan Alterman. Tel Aviv. Ha-Kibbuz Ha Meuḥad. 1955. 226 p. [Tartuffe, Le Malade imaginaire.]
Qomedyot. N. Alterman. Tel Aviv. Hakibbutz Hameuchad. 3 v. [12 comedies] 1967.

Pakistan

Panchti Natak. [Ben] Shawket Osman. Dacca. Bengali Academy. 319 p. [Le Médecin malgré lui; Tartuffe; Les Fourberies de Scapin; L'Amour médecin; Le Misanthrope.] 1965.

Poland

Dzieła. (T 1–6). Tadeusz Żelenski-Boy. Warszawa. Ksiażka i Wiedza. 1952.

Portugal

O Tartufo. O médico ã Força. O avarento. Mário Augusto de Almeida Braga. Porto. Civilizaçao. [Tartuffe; Le Médecin malgré lui; L'Avare]. 1966. 285 p.

Romania

Opere. (1:) Nechibzuitul sau boroboaţete. Dragoste cu toane. Pretioasele ridicole. Sganarel sau încornoratul închipuit. Şcoala bărbaţilor. Pisălogii. (2:) Şcoala nevestelor. Critica şoclii nevestelor. Improvizaţia de la Versailles. Căsătoria cu de-asila. Tartuffe sau impostorul. Amorul medic. Adrian Maniu. Al. Kiriţescu. Bucureşti, E.S.P. L.A. 2 vols. 1955.

Opere. (2, 3). (2:) Şcoala nevestelor. Critica şcolii neveşţelor. Improvizatia de la Versailles. Căsătoria cu de-a sila. Tartuffe sau impostorul. Don Juan sau Ospăţul de piatră. Amorul medic. (3:) Mizantropul. Doctorul fără voie. Sıcilianul sau amorul zugrav. Amphitryon. George Dandin sau soţul păcălit. George F. Gesticone; Nina Cassian *et al.* Bucuresti. E.S.P.L.A. 2 vols., 1956.

Opere. (4). Alexandru Kiriţescu; Tudor Arghezi *et al.* Bucureşti. E.S.P.L.A. 1958. 735 p.

Comedii. Mizantropul. George Dandin sau soţul păcălit. Avarul. Domnul de Pourceaugnac. Tudor Arghezi. Bucureşti. Editura pentru literatura. XLIII. 412 p. [Le Misanthrope, George Dandin, L'Avare, Monsieur de Pourceaugnac.] 1964.

Tartüffe. Avarul. A. Toma; Alexandru Kiriţescu. Bucureşti. Editura pentru literatură universală. (Ed. a 2–a) 232 p.

Spain

El avo y la Escuela de los maridos. — Nadrud, Diana. 1949. 23 p.

Obras completas. Julio Gomez de la Serna. Madrid, Aguilar. 1951 (2ª ed.) 1060 p. 1963 (7ª ed.) 1154 p.

Selección de obras. Carlos Barral. Barcelona, Montaner y Simón. 1952. XVIII. 393 p.

Extractos. Mario Grande Ramos. Barcelona, Labor. 1952.

El Atolondrado, o Los contratiempos. Las trapacerías de Scapin. Julio Gomez de la Serna. Barcelona. Sopena. 1960. 184 p.

Tartufo o el impostor. El despecho amoroso. Julio Gómez de la Serna. Barcelona. Sopena. 1960. 176 p.

El amor médico. El enfermo imaginario. (Comedia con bailables). Julio Gómez de la Serna. Barcelona Sopena. 1960, 1964. 175 p.

Comedias. 2 v. — Iberia.

Comedias. — Barcelona. Maucci. 1962. 604 p.

Comedias. — 606 p. Augusta.

La escuela de los maridos y El hypócrita. — 2 t. Atlas. Madrid. 208 p.

El Avaro y Medico a la Fuerza. Ramón Sopena. Barcelona.

Tartufo. Don Juan. — Madrid. Espasa-Calpe. (3ª ed.) 1963. 159 p.

El Avaro y Tartufo y La preciosas redículas. tr. y ed. de Julio Gómez de la Serna. 4ª ed. Aguilar, 1963. 482 p.

El Ricachón en la corte. El enfermo de aprensión. J.J. Alberti. Madrid. Espasa-Calpe. (6ª ed.) 1963, 1967. 166 p.

Las preciosas ridículas. Don García de Navarra. Enrique Azcoaga. Madrid. E.D.A.F. 1967.

Obras. Enrique Azcoaga. Madrid. E.D.A.F. (3ª ed.) 1968. 588 p.

Tartufo. Don Juan, el convidado de piedra. Carlos M. Princivalle *et al.* Madrid. Espasa-Calpe. 1968.

Las preciosas ridículas. Don Garcia de Navarra. La escuela de los maridos. La escuela de las mujeres. etc. — Madrid. E.D.A.F. 1968. 1628 p.

El enfermo imaginario. El médico a palos. Barcelona. Salvat. 1969. 186 p.

Swahili

Mchuuzi mwungwana . . . Uliotungwa na A. Morrison. Uchezwe na watu wa Afrika. Dar-es-Salaam; Edinburgh printed, 1948. VIII, 56 p.

Sweden

Komedien. Allan Bergstrang. Malmö. Allhem. 5 vols. 1965.
Misantropen. Scapinos skälmstycken. Viveka Heyman. Sthlm. Tiden. 1965. 149 p.

U.S.A.

Plays. — New York, Modern Library. 1950. 364 p.
Five Plays. John Wood. Baltimore. Penguin Books. 1953. 1958, 1960. 251 p.
Six Prose Comedies. (Coxcombs in Petticoats; Don Juan; The Reluctant Doctor;
    The Miser; The Self-made Gentleman; Scapin the Scamp). George Graveley.
    New York. Oxford. 1956. 1968. VII. 378 p.
Eight Plays. Morris Bishop. New York. Random House. 1957. 399 p.
The Slave of Truth. Tartuffe. The Imaginary Invalid. Miles Malleson. New York.
    Coward-McCann, 1960. VIII. 269 p.
Three Great French Plays. (Corneille:) Polyeucte. (Racine:) Phedre. (Molière:)
    The Hypochondriac. T. Constable, R.B. Boswell *et al*. Greenwich, Conn. Fawcett.
    1961. 256 p.
Tartuffe, The Would-be Gentleman. H. Baker and J. Miller. New York. Limited
    Editions-Club. 1963. XVI. 197 p. Also: Heritage, 1964.
One-act Comedies of Molière. Albert Bermel. Cleveland. World Publishing Co.
    1964. 177 p.
The Misanthrope. Tartuffe (verse tr.). Richard Wilbur. New York. Harcourt, Brace
    and World. 1965. 326 p.
The Works. 6 v. in 3. — New York. B. Blom. 1967.
Tartuffe and Other Plays. (The Ridiculous Precieuses. The School for Husbands.
    The School for Wives. The Critique of the School for Wives. The Versailles
    Impromptu. Don Juan). Donald M. Frame. New York. New American Library.
    1967, iv, 384 p.
The Misanthrope, and Other Plays. Donald Frame. New York, New American
    Library. 1968. VX, 512 p. (Content: The Misanthrope. The Doctor-in-Spite of
    Himself. The Miser. The Would-Be Gentleman. The Mischievous Machinations
    of Scapin. The Learned Women. The Imaginary Invalid.)

U.S.S.R.

Komedii. — Moskva, Iskusstvo (Izd. 2e). 1954. 560 p.
Sobranie Sočinenii. 2 v. Moskva. Goslitizdat. 1957.
Komedii. Kyiv, Derzh, vyd-vo-khudozh. lit. ry. 1958.
Komediji. [Ukr.] Iryna Stešenko *et al*. Kiev. Goslitizdat. Okrainy. 1958. 775 p.
Polnoe sobranie sočinenij. V 4t (T. 1). E. Polonskaja *et al*. Moskva. Iskusstvo. 1965.
    671 p. [Collected Works.]
Polnoe sobranie sočinenij. V. 4t (T. 2). N. Ljubimov *et al*. Moskva. Iskusstvo. 1966.
    531 p.
Polnoe sobranie sočinenij. V 4t (T. 3). Valerij Brjusov *et al*. Moskva. Iskusstvo. 1966.
    543 p. [Complete collected works.].
Polnoe sobranie sočinenij. V 4t (T. 4). N. Daruzes *et al*. Moskva. Iskusstvo. 1967.
    419 p.
"Tartiufas" ir kitos komedijos. [Lith]. Aleksys Churginas *et al*. Vilnjus. Vaga, 1967.
    481 p.

Yugoslavia

Don Juan. Škrtac. Radovan Ivšić. Zagreb "Zora". [Don Juan, L'Avare] 1950. 206 p.

Izabrane komedije. (Prva knjiga) [Ser-Cr.] Sima Pandurović, Radmila Miljanić-Nikolić, *et al.* Beograd, Prosveta. 1950. 559 p.

Izabrana djela (Svezak Prvi). [Ser-Cr.] Ivo Hergešić and Slavko Ježić. Zagreb, Matica Hrvatska. 1951. 399 p.

Izabrane komedije. Druga knjiga, [Ser-Cr.]. Dušan Z. Milaćić, Milan Predić, *et al.* Beograd, Prosveta. 1951. 594 p. [L'Avare, George Dandin, L'École des femmes, Le Malade imaginaire, Les Precieuses ridicules.]

Izbrano delo. (II kniga:) Sganarel ali namišljeni rogonosec; Šola za može; Kritika šole za žene; Improvizacija v Versaillesu; Izsiljena ženitev; Don Juan ali kameniti gost; Zdravnik po sili; George Dandin. Slovenije. Josip Vidmar. Ljubljana. Državna Založba Slovenije. 1956. 724 p.

Priložnostni zdravnik. (Anouilh:) Cecilija ali šola za očete. [Slovène] Draga Ahačič; Davorin Bažec. Ljubljana. Prosvetni Servis. 1959. [Le Médecin volant; Cécile, ou l'École des pères.]

Smešne precioze. Gradjanin plemić. Raško Dimitrijević. Beograd. Nolit. 144. [Les Précieuses ridicules; Le Bourgeois gentilhomme.] 1960.

Tartif. Don Žuan. Sima Pandurović and Mladen Leskovac. Beograd. Rad. 213. 1960; 1963.

Tvrdica. Tartif. Branislav Miljković. Beograd. Nolit. [L'Avare; Tartuffe] 1966. 184 p.

MOLIÈRE'S *MORALE*:
DEBATES IN CRITICISM

Laurence Romero

There has long been a strain in moliéresque criticism concerned with establishing a relationship between Molière's comedies and a coherent philosophical, moralistic world-view. This is in keeping with things, for traditionally the essence of comedy has been interpreted as being essentially satirical, designed as it were to ridicule mores and attitudes, and thereby to correct: "castigat ridendo mores" has often been considered comedy's primary function for the "vis comica" is, in this view, nature's best balm. This is more true for comedy than for tragedy, especially in their classical forms. Tragedy deals with the unfathomable, the dark inevitabilities, the god-sent pains, a profound and unswervable destiny which is immutable and incorrigible. Thus tragedy can only be a hopeless cry of despair after the fact; its only lesson is to beware of the gods while we remain impotent against them. In this sense tragedy is merely factual, and so essentially amoral. Comedy, on the other hand, seems to deal more with what is correctible: foibles, illusions, fantasies. Against these moral excentricities, good common sense is proffered as an antidote: it is a simple matter of being *pied-sur-terre*, of coming to grips with and controlling reality. Thus the would-be lesson of the play is constantly sought. In Molière's case this attitude was fostered from the beginning. LaGrange, the comic poet's faithful friend and fellow player, called Molière a "fort bon humaniste et encore plus grand philosophe." He maintained further that the comedies had as an end "d'obliger les hommes à se corriger de leurs défauts." Often, however, the lesson emanating from the staged works was considered less than edifying, indeed dangerous to the common good, particularly as defined in religious dogma. So it was that during and immediately after the poet's time, his work came under sharp attack. The jansenist Baillet believed that Molière was "un des plus dangereux ennemis que le siècle ou le monde ait suscités à l'Eglise de Jésus-Christ"; Rouillé exclaimed that he was "un démon vêtu de chair et habillé en homme"; Bossuet and Bourdaloue were hardly more generous. The antagonism was often severe, for it was designed to discredit the playwright-

706

player (who was already excommunicated by mere virtue of his profession —no pun intended). At the same time, it was part of a larger attempt by *Mater Eglesia* to stem the unhealthy tide of popularity the theater was enjoying. Similar tirades aimed especially at diminishing the prestige of Molière and his troupe at the Sun King's court. Of these, the most dastard was from Mondory, a rival player at the Hôtel de Bourgogne. In a note to the King, he charged that Molière had contracted an incestuous marriage, apparently hoping to ostracize the director of the Troupe du Roi and thereby gain the advantage for his own company. With Racine's help however, the accusation was discredited, and it had no repercussions at the Court. Other wild thrusts more often than not missed their marks. Even the interminable polemics around *L'Ecole des femmes* remained superficial and limited because they were, in the main, the workings of vicious and fanatical minds. The eighteenth century reoriented some of these questions but usually in order to incorporate them into the prevailing ideological dialogues. Voltaire and the *philosophes*, for example, dissolved a good dose of propaganda into their commentaries on the comedies, but there was no concerted effort to establish a substantial *philosophie de Molière*.

The focusing on specific moralistic content in the comedies really began in the nineteenth century. From the modest suppositions of Soulié, to the rigor of Brunetière, Molière-the-libertine first took form. This is what Paul Bénichou had in mind when he noted that "Agnès n'a été trouvée inquiétante qu'au XIXe siècle." This line of inquiry continued into our time and resulted in a preoccupation that sometimes verged on mania. In every play, the vaguest allusion of a philosophical, moralistic or religious nature was microscopically scruntinized: the "maximes du mariage" in *L'Ecole des femmes*, the kings in *Psyché* and *Dom Juan* as blasphemers, Tartuffe as "libertin et faux dévot," duplicituous love in *Amphitryon* and *Les Amants magnifiques*, the questionable morality of *Le Misanthrope*. The ground was fertile, some thought, and it did not go untilled. Albert Thibaudet referred to this aspect of moliéresque criticism as "la phase religieuse," in which "le génie de Molière semble s'opposer au génie du christianisme." Daniel Mornet alluded to the academic and pedagogic tradition which made of Molière "un 'penseur', un 'philosophe', à la fois profond et mystérieux dont il fallait sans cesse sonder les dessins hardis et cachés." This essay will attempt to sketch the general lines of thinking on the subject in French and Anglo-American criticism, from the late nineteenth century to the present, with emphasis on the recent period. For convenience and contrast, these questions will be dealt with in two unequal parts: from Brunetière to Guicharnaud (from the latter half of the previous century to 1963), and then the last ten years. This will mark more clearly both continuance and change in critical appreciation of the last decade.

In the history of Molière criticism, the nineteenth century distinguished itself by the sheer bulk of its contribution. With the exception of Sainte-Beuve, it was a period marked by minute research, heavy documentation and lengthy tracts covering nearly all aspects of Molière's (mostly private) life. Nonetheless, scholars like Taschereau, Bazin, Monval, Soulié, Despois, and Mesnard rightfully earned a place among eminent "moliéristes." During the Second Empire, these men were at the center of the first generation of serious scholars who launched "la grande critique" in Molière studies, a tradition which continued into the early years of the twentieth century. *Tartuffe* was the play around which most of the research and speculation centered at this time. Heavily documented essays and books probed into the "cabale," the "Société du Saint Sacrement," seeking possible models for the false zealot; apparently this activity assumed that the light of history would elucidate the mysteries of *Tartuffe*. It was in part from this source that a fairly unanimous consensus of opinion was formed among professional and academic critics on the comic poet's ethic: it was believed that Molière was a willful, undeceived libertine, and for some, an active revolutionary in the sphere of ideas. In *La Morale de Molière*, C.-J. Jeannel concluded that the comedies were indeed suspect and that there was a certain "joyeuse et séduisante immoralité dans l'ensemble des tableaux."[1] Brunetière, one of the most imposing critics of his time, placed Molière in the honored gallic tradition of "libre penseur," synonymous here with *libertinage* and a certain robust paganism. For this critic, the comic poet was the only important link in the seventeenth century between the great predecessors, Rabelais and Montaigne, and then Voltaire and Diderot in the following age. In forceful prose, Brunetière argued that since conditions at Louis's court were essentially immoral, there was no profit for anyone pretending religious fervor, nothing to be gained from acting the "faux dévot." Thus, the true object of Molière's sharpest attacks was not the false zealots; "les ennemis ou les adversaires de Molière [furent] les vrais dévots, non pas les faux. . . . ceux dont l'imagination et le crédit menaçaient ou pouvaient menacer la liberté de son art. . . . c'est

---

[1] C. -J. Jeannel, *La Morale de Molière* (E. Thorin, 1867), 257.

au profit de la nature qu'il a voulu détruire la religion de l'effort de la contrainte morale."[2] Following the same line of argumentation was L. Veuillot in his *Molière et Bourdaloue*. In this book, the conservative Catholic critic juxtaposed texts showing what he considered to be Bourdaloue's eloquent orthodoxy and Molière's immoral bantering, intending thereby to expose the moral shabbyness of the comedies.[3] F.-T. Perrins' *Les Libertins en France au 17ème siècle* placed Molière resolutely in the libertine camp: "Molière, lui est libertin jusqu'aux moelles."[4] From his interpretations of *Tartuffe* and *Dom Juan*, the historian can only conclude that the poet attacked the clergy and religion and that along with La Fontaine, he was "la gloire du libertinage." Some time later the journalist Paul Souday wrote that Molière was surely "avec Dom Juan."[5]

In part, some of these attitudes have persisted into more recent criticism, albeit with more nuance. In a note appended to his long study of "le libertinage érudit," René Pintard aligned Molière with the free-thinking group of "Chapelle et ses amis,"[6] while Georges Mongrédien associated the dramatist with Ninon's epicurean côterie.[7] The implications suggest, however, that part of the guilt is by association only, and that Molière was probably influenced by the prevailing ideologies of the time, much as his contemporaries had been. One exception to this more flexible approach is John Cairncross's *Molière Bourgeois et libertin*, in which the author proclaims boldly that "Molière est bien libertin et non-conformiste."[8] His

---

[2] F. Brunetière, *Etudes critiques* (Hachette, 1898), 4th series, 202 and 209. E. Faguet expresses a similar view in his *En lisant Molière* (Hachette, 1914).

[3] Louis Veuillot, *Molière et Bourdaloue* (Palme, 1877). Mme. Dussane provides an interesting counterargument when she states that Bourdaloue could have been misled by the "dévots" on questions concerning Molière and, as a result, had over-reacted in his condemnation of *Tartuffe*. She suggests that the cleric and the dramatist had in fact shared a common aversion for hypocrisy and other vices. "Eternellement l'orthodoxie de Bourdaloue et le libre jugement de Molière diront les mêmes choses dans un langage différent et sans pouvoir se résoudre à un accord." (In *La Revue universelle*, 38, 641–56; essentials of this article are reprinted in her edition of *Tartuffe*, 1932, 239–51.)

[4] F. -T. Perrins, *Les Libertins en France au XVIIe siècle* (Calman Lévy, 1899), 342.

[5] In *Temps*, 15 février, 1917; also quoted by Jacques Arnavon in his *Le Dom Juan de Molière* (Copenhagen: Gyldendel, 1947), 60. Arnavon also published a rather ambiguous *Morale de Molière* (Editions universelles, 1945) which seems to perceive in the comedies a kind of philosophical "accommodement."

[6] René Pintard, *Le Libertinage érudit dans la première moitié du 17e siècle* (Boivin, 1943), 2, 624.

[7] Georges Mongrédien, *La Vie privée de Molière* (Hachette, 1950), 148. The author thinks that Ninon's côterie was one of the primary sources for Molière's epicureanism. See also Mongrédien's contribution in *Pierre Gassendi, Sa Vie et son oeuvre 1592–1655* (A. Michel, 1955).

[8] John Cairncross, *Molière bourgeois et libertin* (Nizet, 1963); see particularly chapters 3 and 5.

main thesis is that Dom Juan was conceived as an ideal and that whenever he was made to appear ridiculous or repugnant, it was merely to serve the mythic convention and to prepare for the inevitable end. The play is discussed in an historical perspective, and much is made of certain attitudes which supposedly concern the battle for *Tartuffe*. Everywhere there are libertine overtones, including in *Le Misanthrope*. Cairncross hypothesises that the first and second acts of that work were written around 1661, at the time Molière is believed to have been working on the Lucretius translation. The method of this book is rigorously historical, but many of the conclusions remain tenuous.

Inevitably, in the larger context of such questioning, historians have speculated on what *la religion de Molière* might have been. Antoine Adam associates the poet with the *libre pensée* circles which gravitated around La Mothe Le Vayer and Bernier, and he opines that "Molère fut un chrétien moins que tiède."[9] Quoting the well-known passage from *La Lettre sur l'Imposture* (of which the authorship is disputed), "la religion n'est que raison plus parfaite," Adam comments: "Elle est la grande puissance d'ordre, d'harmonie, de solidarité qui maintient la société civile. La raison, ayant une valuer universelle, est présente chez les hommes de tous les climats et de toutes les époques. Et par conséquent la religion, expression de la raison, peut s'enseigner hors des églises, elle condamne l'esprit de secte et de cabale, elle unit les hommes au lieu de les opposer les uns aux autres."[10] The implications here are clear: Molière is reaffirming the humanistic values of Erasmus and the Renaissance which conform with the ideals of other contemporaries (Gassendi and La Mothe Le Vayer), and which become principles for the Enlightenment. In fact, Molière's religion is akin to "la religion des philosophes." We shall see that this attitude still persists in recent criticism, especially from England.

For Jean Calvet there was never in Molière's case a break with orthodoxy but a more subtle "séparation de la vie et de la religion," in which religion is reduced to "un rite traditionnel, un décorum social, une hygiène personnelle."[11] The result is less a religion than a "doctrine mondaine," and M. Calvet thinks of Molière as a "législateur des convenances." (Some forty years earlier Emile Faguet had proposed a similar title for the comic dramatist.) With this attitude, it follows that Molière remained ignorant

---

[9] A. Adam, *Histoire de la littérature française au XVIIe siècle* (Del Duca, 1962), 3, 310.
[10] *Ibid.*, 311–12.
[11] Msgr. J. Calvet, *La Littérature religieuse de François de Sales à Fénélon* (J. de Gigord, 1938), 5, 548.

of much of the letter and spirit of religion and of the religious reform doctrines of the 1660's. He saw only the excesses of the overly zealous, and he sometimes tended to overreact. His *Tartuffe*, for example, contains " . . . certains mots de colère, certains traits . . . grossis par le parti pris ou déformés pour la polémique"; it is a "déposition sincère d'un mondain sur un problème qui ne relève peut-être pas de la comédie."[12] Nevertheless, the poet was not a defamer of the faith. According to M. Calvet, *Dom Juan* clearly exposes the blasphemer to ridicule. Sganarelle, le Pauvre, Elvire, and Dom Louis, all represent in subtle ways the triumph of morality and religion over the don's elegant waywardness. Hence, the poet's stance was essentially ambivalent. "Il a l'instinct religieux qui croit une religion nécessaire; il n'a pas le sens religieux qui comprend ce qu'est une religion."[13] Molière's religion was finally a kind of "déisme de bon ton" and what was lacking, according to M. Calvet, was a profound feeling for the potential greatness of true devotion. "Il est l'homme pour qui la sainteté n'a pas de sens."[14]

Henri Busson's excellent *La Religion des classiques* situates Molière's *morale* within a broad philosophical ambiance in a state of flux at the time, and which came to a crisis of the spirit in France between 1660 and 1685. This crisis was marked by the loss of credit for the final vestiges of peripatetic philosophy and scholasticism, a weakening of the prestige of stoicism and the rising prominence of a new and more progressive scientific ideology, intellectual libertinism. Molière was an advocate of this new creed. The historian's main arguments are founded on his reading of two unlikely plays, *Les Amants magnifiques* and *Psyché*. Busson contends that the rational free-thinkers of the time were highly skeptical about the value of oracles and did much to discredit this outdated notion while at the same time attacking the Church. He relates this tactic to the strategy of the false oracle in *Les Amants magnifiques*. The idea here is that the false oracle in the play is actually "une imposture sacerdotale," and "précisement c'est là une thèse soutenue par tous les libertins quand il s'agit des oracles anciens. Molière rejoint ici Vanini et il annonce Voltaire."[15] Thus Eriphile and Sostrate are related in spirit to Dom Juan. In a similar

---

[12] Msgr. J. Calvet, *Molière, est-il chrétien?* (F. Lanore, 1954), 60.

[13] *Ibid.*, 96. See also Msgr. Calvet's interesting but contestable interpretation of "la scène du pauvre," 99–110.

[14] *Ibid.*, 73.

[15] Henri Busson, *La Religion des classiques* (P.U.F., 1948), 262. On oracles and the like, see a curious article by E. Bouvier, "La Croyance au merveilleux à l'époque classique" in *Mélanges . . . offerts à Daniel Mornet* (Nizet, 1951), 99–108.

vein, *Psyché* represents a final break with stoicism at precisely the time (1660–70) of its sharp decline in France. In Molière's play it comes in the form of a categorical refusal of "toute consolation," which Busson claims was a central tenet of "la philosophie du Portique." In the moment of crisis in the second act, while Psyché is brave, her father the King is defiantly blasphemous against the gods who demand his daughter in sacrifice because her unique beauty is an affront to Venus. Busson believes that Molière identifies with the King.[16] The author also detects a crisis in Molière's private life around 1670 in which stoicism was found "insuffisant pour la vie." This represented a major shift in the dramatist's thinking, for his stoic attitude had informed and animated many of his greatest stage creations, including Alceste and Dona Elvire. Like the Rev. Calvet, Busson concludes that "Molière n'est peut-être pas irréligieux; mais tenu hors de l'église par sa profession, il n'a vu la religion que de l'extérieur et elle ne l'intéresse que pour son comportement social."[17]

Parallel to this effort at meshing a moliéresque ethic into the philosophical and religious fabric of the Classical Age, there have been propositions linking Molière's *Weltanschauung* to a specific philosopher, and Gassendi and La Mothe Le Vayer are the two most illustrious alleged "maîtres à philosopher." In a series of lectures before the Collège de France (1904–05), Abel LeFranc stated categorically that Molière had been a student and friend of Gassendi in Paris around 1641, and that the mathematician was "maître de Molière, celui qui a exercé probablement l'action la plus profonde sur le développement de sa pensée. L'influence de Gassendi sur Molière ne saurait être contestée."[18] Some twenty years later, Gustave Michaut discredicted LeFranc's contention that there had been personal contact between Molière and Gassendi,[19] while the larger question concerning "le gassendisme" in the comedies remained open. Georges Poulet made an interesting effort at linking intellectually Molière with Gassendi. The critic detects in Molière's work "un univers des passions . . . où l'on est dans une tension incessante, dans une agitation sans trêve, dans un recommencement perpétuel des mêmes désirs." He then interprets this cyclical, ever-renewing temporality as a central axiom

---

[16] *Ibid.*, 239–45.

[17] *Ibid.*, 271. See also Busson's useful synthesis of the various points of view on these questions, 229–70.

[18] A. LeFranc, "La Vie et les ouvrages de Molière" in *Revue des cours et conférences*, II/2 (1906), 506–08.

[19] G. Michaut, *La Jeunesse de Molière* (Hachette, 1922), 67–77.

in Gassendi ("maître de Molière"). This phenomenon is linked with the essentially nominalistic fashion in which Molière develops his characters: "répétition constante des traits essentiels."[20] Unfortunately, Poulet's essay is very abstract, refers only obliquely to a few minor plays and is founded in large part on a disputed text, *La Lettre sur la comédie de l'Imposteur*. The results are necessarily inconclusive, a fact which the author himself has admitted.[21]

The other philosopher who looms large in speculation on Molière's spiritual development was the pyrrhonist, erudit skeptic, La Mothe Le Vayer. In 1933, A.L. Sells's long article concentrated on the importance of Le Vayer's *La Prose chagrine* (1661), especially for *Le Misanthrope*. A number of themes common to both works were adumbrated: the general abuses and disorders of the age, a questionable educational system which produced an inordinate number of pedants and fools, and an untenable ethic which hardly distinguished vice from virtue.[22] But it was René Jasinski who offered the most substantial contribution on the subject. In the chapter "La Leçon du Misanthrope," in his impressive *Molière et le Misanthrope*, Jasinski stated that although Molière was surely familiar and sympathetic with Gassendi's epicureanism, he did not align himself with it. The Gassendist system was too detached, contemplative, hedonistic. By temperament Molière was more attracted to Le Vayer's brand of Christian skepticism and, in fact, "d'étroites affinités de pensée relient Molière au vieux philosophe."[23] A close reading of the works of the philosopher and the dramatist leads Jasinski to broaden his argument and to posit a far-reaching but debatable conclusion:

Toute conduite morale, à plus forte raison méditée, implique une conception générale de l'homme et de l'univers; il [Molière] s'accordait là aussi avec Le Vayer et les initiés ne pouvaient s'y tromper. On saisit maintenant l'originalité suprême du *Misanthrope*. Par une tentative sans précédent, Molière ne porte pas seulement à la scène une allégorie philosophique: sans rompre avec la vie, bien plus, en créant des types immortels, il illustre, en l'affermissant, un système, et pose, au sens le plus élevé du mot, les principes d'une philosophie.[24]

This view is not applicable for *Le Misanthrope* alone, but rather it repre-

---

[20] G. Poulet, *Etudes sur le temps humain* (Plon, 1966), 85 sq. See also L. Goldmann, *Sciences humaines et philosophie* (Gonthier, 1966), 114.

[21] See M. Poulet's letter to René Wellek on the limits of his Molière essay, in S. Lawall, *The Critics of Consciousness* (Cambridge: Harvard University Press, 1968), 92.

[22] A.L. Sells, "Molière and La Mothe Le Vayer" in *Modern Language Review*, 28 (1933), 352 sq.

[23] René Jasinski, *Molière et le Misanthrope* (A. Colin, 1951), 260.

[24] *Ibid.*, 267.

sents a morality which is "celle de Molière dans sa plus haute expression." This is, in fact, the comic poet's life philosophy, and it has much in common with Le Vayer's: their pyrrhonism is pessimistic, it considers humanity corrupt and it has no faith in providence or established religion. "Molière aboutit à une morale toute humaine, libertine certes, mais au sens le plus élevé du mot. Elle ne heurt pas ouvertement le dogme ni la foi. Mais elle s'en passe. Elle s'édifie en dehors d'eux. Elle trouve en elle-même ses moyens et ses fins."[25]

Jasinski's endeavor to relate Molière to a single thinker and to create a systematic philosophical view of human nature represents the most penetrating recent argument for a "philosophie de Molière" by a literary critic. In 1960 J.S. Spink offered somewhat of a synthesis of the major currents of opinion on the subject. In his own view, Molière was in touch both with Gassendi's epicureanism and Le Vayer's skepticism, while tending toward the former. "Both the old intellectualism and the new intellectualism seem to be out of favor in Molière's eyes. Does that mean that the old (Aristotelian) naturalism and the new (epicurean) naturalism were given a positive preference? That Molière's doubting unbelief caused him not to hold the balance between a naturalistic and an intellectualized view of man's estate? That indeed is the answer which best accounts for the facts."[26] Spink believes that Molière reflects an attitude, "the re-habilitation of Epicurus," which took on new impetus after the Fronde and had its *aboutissement* in the elegant writings of Saint-Evremont. This is not to say that Spink understands Molière in the same way as Brunetière and LeFranc had. One of the main points of distinction he makes for the new epicureanism is that it is highly tinged with cartesian rationalism ("rational skepticism"), which closely combines naturalism and pure skepticism. The end result is an intermediary ethical position. "The criterion which Molière seems to have had was a conception of a coherent and coordinated life, governed by its own inner principal, spontaneous and therefore natural, ordered and therefore rational."[27] What is interesting

---

[25] *Ibid.*, 274. Molière as libertine in *Dom Juan* ("pièce de philosophie") is also André Villiers's view. Here, however, the libertine *élan vital* is understood as a humanistic element as it was debated in the heyday of existentialism just after the last War. Given the time of its publication, this book is a remarkable contribution to studies on *Dom Juan* and much of it is still pertinent today. *Le Dom Juan de Molière: Un problème de mise en scène* (Masques, 1947).

[26] J.S. Spink, *French Free Thought from Gassendi to Voltaire* (London: Athlone Press, 1960), 148.

[27] *Ibid.*, 149.

here is that Spink's inquiry into a possible Molière philosophy has as its outcome an attitude which is much less a systematic ideology than a well-tempered life, an equilibrium. This coincides with yet another line of thinking which views Molière as partisan of solid bourgeois, common-sense morality.

At the turn of the century when this notion was just beginning to establish itself, no one was more convinced of its validity than George Meredith. In the *Essay on Comedy*, he sees Molière as a satirical moralist above all else: "Never did man wield so shrieking a scourge against vice."[28] The long and arduous struggle against barbarism has been won, says Meredith, mostly by the efforts of the most civilized social class, the bourgeois, employing its most formidable weapon, "common sense." Here briefly is the situation: "In all countries the middle class represents the public which, fighting the world, and with a good footing in the fight, knows the world best. . . . Cultivated men and women who do not skim the cream of life, and are attached to duties, yet escape the harsher blows, make acute and balanced observers. Molière is their poet."[29]

In French academic criticism, Gustave Lanson is generally considered among the earliest advocates of the *bon sens* view and there is little doubt that the pages on the subject in his classic *Histoire* . . . did much to disseminate this concept in France. Refuting Brunetière, Lanson suggested that Molière was on the side of *la nature* in the tradition of Rabelais and Montaigne, without being an enemy of religion. In fact, a combination of reason and nature makes the comic poet a moderate: "Molière ajoute la raison à la nature . . . qui fixe à la nature, à l'instinct, leur mesure et leurs bornes."[30] Lanson's student, Daniel Mornet, believed that a broad view of skepticism was the best approach to Molière, for this path "nous débarassera le plus sûrement des hypothèses aventureuses . . . et nous permettra de rester dans ce riche milieu."[31] In this perspective, Mornet refuses to read *L'Ecole des femmes* as a frontal attack against either orthodoxy or libertinsim, but rather as a position "entre les deux piétés" which eschews the excesses of both. This is Mornet's Molière "prudent

[28] George Meredith, "An Essay on Comedy" in *Comedy*, ed. by W. Sypher (New York: Doubleday, 1956), 17.

[29] *Ibid.*, 13. Similar ideas are expressed in Martin Turnell, *The Classical Moment* (London: Hamish Hamilton, 1957) and in Albert Cook, *The Dark Voyage and the Golden Mean* (New York: Norton, 1966).

[30] G. Lanson, *Histoire de la littérature française* (Hachette, 1938), 18th edition, 527.

[31] Daniel Mornet, *Molière* (Boivin, 1943): see especially the author's introduction and the chapter "La Philosophie de Molière."

et clair" which, along with the Lanson interpretation, became part of the fixed (and often oversimplified) view of Molière as the bourgeois moderate. Even some of the most recent criticism reaffirms this position. "Le bon sens et la sagesse nous conduisent ensemble à une vérité qu'il faut accepter . . . un message de bonheur fondé sur la connaissance de la nature et sur la raison";[32] and, "Le théâtre de Molière revendique en faveur de la sage raison et du bon sens."[33] Pierre-Henri Simon wrote that a close study of the literature of Louis' high reign reveals a general demise of the epic and romanesque styles, "l'effondrement du lyrisme" and a debasing of the idea of the hero. The emerging tone is rather one of "prudence bourgeoise," and among others, Molière is "le type de l'écrivain bourgeois, animé par une conception réaliste de la vie, de la morale et de l'art."[34] But as we shall see, another book had already made this kind of thinking obsolete.

Into the elaboration of the case for making Molière the high-priest of bourgeois morality comes the inevitable question of the "raisonneurs": do these characters really have a special moralistic function, standing apart or slightly aside from the main line of action and proposing a clear, common-sensical solution to the dilemma of the story? This is perhaps one of the oldest debates in Molière criticism, and in the first quarter of the century, Gustave Michaut strongly reaffirmed this concept of the "raisonneurs." But in 1949 and 1954, two books impressively refuted Michaut and radicalized thinking on this question, as on almost all other aspects of Molière studies. W.G. Moore understood the comedies as being structured around loosely linked scenes which build a "vision not of a person, nor of a plot but of a choice of attitudes." In this light, he considers the rôle of the reasoners: theirs is not to reason why, writes Moore, their main purpose is esthetic. "They ensure symmetry and roundness of comic presentation. Excess is more distinguishable if its opposite is exhibited at the same time. Sense shows up nonsense, sobriety offsets bad temper."[35] René Bray reaffirms the Englishman's view and takes the case further:

[32] G. Milhaud, "Les Farces philosophiques" in *Europe*, 385–86 (mai-juin 1961), 97.

[33] J. Guillerme, "Bon sens et scepticisme chez Molière" in *Europe*, 441–42 (janvier-février 1966), 128. See also for a similar view, A.J. Kreilsheimer, *Studies in Self-Interest* (Oxford: Clarendon Press, 1962).

[34] Pierre-Henri Simon, *Le Domaine héroïque des lettres françaises* (A. Colin, 1963), 208. See also the interesting citation from the Goncourt journals on the same page.

[35] W.G. Moore, *Molière: A New Criticism* (Oxford: Clarendon Press, 1964), 74. For another more recent formalist view, see the elegant essay by Octave Nadal, "Molière et le sens de la vie" in *A Mesure haute* (Mercure de France, 1964), 91–108.

"Il n'y a pas de raisonneurs dans le théâtre de Molière. Chaque personnage est exigé par sa fonction dramatique, non par une prétendue fonction morale inventée par la critique. . . . l'intention de Molière, la pensée qui donne à son oeuvre la force et l'unité, ce n'est pas une pensée de moraliste, c'est une intention d'artiste. . . . La comédie n'a pas sa fin hors d'elle même, dans une moralisation par le rire à laquelle personne ne peut ajouter foi. . . . Elle est une création autonome qui se justifie par sa seule existence, par la force avec laquelle elle s'impose au spectateur."[36] In this sharp departure from the main line of thinking on the subject, there is no message, moral or philosophical, and the characters who supposedly express the wisdom of the comedies have instead an esthetic, dramatic function. But this formalist view did not convince everyone. Recently, some well-known commentators have returned to the pre-Moore attitude and attempted to find the reason behind the reasoners. For Jacques Morel, these characters represent the *juste milieu* which he defines as the *honnêteté* ethic of the comic poet's time. From this perspective, Morel argues that Molière castigates "les ridicules," those who sin against the three basic *morales d'honnêteté*: "le naturel ou l'acceptation de ce qu'on est, le réalisme ou l'acceptation de la société et de l'événement, la raison, enfin, ou la capacité de discerner le masque et le visage."[37] Lionel Gossman defines the major conflict in the comedies as one between "men and masks," i.e., between being and appearing, illusion and authenticity. It is the comic character in each play who is entrapped in this futile game, "in their being for others and in their obsessive preoccupation with their image." Against the mask-players, Gossman perceives the reasoners as the only authentic personnages in the comedies and their genuineness affords them the self-confidence and inner strength which in turn is the source of their equilibrated well-being. They are finally a model of good sense, the primal virtue for leading the right life. Thus Molière's message, conveyed through the reasoners, is clear and Gossman's book is one of the most substantial reaffirmations in recent years that there is such a message at all.[38]

One readily observes that the common ground to these widely diverging theses is indeed large. So large in fact, that it would be an overstatement

---

[36] René Bray, *Molière, Homme de théâtre* (Mercure de France, 1954), 28 and 31–32.

[37] J. Morel. "Molière ou la dramaturgie de l'honnêteté" in *L'Information littéraire*, 15 (nov-déc. 1963), 189.

[38] Lionel Gossman, *Men and Masks: A Study of Molière* (Baltimore: *The Johns Hopkins Press*, 1963).

to speak of a revolution as such on the question. Nonetheless, there has been sharp bifurcation in the debate on the comic poet's world-view, beginning with Moore and Bray. Their premise is one of the elements in the new orientation since 1950: that the *philosophie de Molière* is in fact a non-ethic, a poetic statement, and a necessary dramaturgical device. Other new ideas on the subject include the proposition that Molière's comedies represent an anti-bourgeois aristocratic ethic rooted in the structure of Louis's court, and finally, that the poet's world-view is an intensely personal apprehension which is never explicitly stated or formulated as an end in itself.

Paul Bénichou's *Morales du grand siècle* is essentially historical. The term *morales* has a special connotation here: it represents the ideals and aspirations of a certain humanism inherent in the broad historical movement of the period and in the writings of the major authors. In such wise, the term is analogous to the concept of *ideology* in marxist usage, although the author carefully eschews such immoderate terminology. In one of many reconsiderations on classical literature, Bénichou takes issue with the long standing contention that Molière was the representative of bourgeois morality. The critic argues effectively that, logically, because of the poe.'s success at both "la cour et la ville," the opposite would appear nearer the truth. Bénichou holds that in the comedies, "le bourgeois est presque toujours médiocre ou ridicule," and that Molière's ideal is hardly Chrysale's view ("prosaïque et risible"), but the more elegant attitude of a Clitandre.[39] The critic detects a paradox between "Molière galant," defender of the aristocratic ethic, and "un Molière libre et naturel" who is plebian in spirit. What is pertinent here is that there is no intermediary bourgeois stance. The original, unreconciled "ton moliéresque" is "le mélange de l'agrément noble avec la raillerie populaire . . . un accord de la galanterie noble et de la franchise ou de l'humour plébéien et cet accord se fait en sautant par dessus les régions de l'honorabilité bourgeoise."[40] The paradox is resolved in the crucial years 1664–1666, when the dramatist firmly establishes himself as the promoter and defender of the aristocratic ethic, of the elite, noble "honnête homme," and this Molière is the opposite of a bourgeois, moderate poet. From this point on, the great plays propound the ethical standards of Louis's galant court where any

[39] Paul Bénichou, *Morales du grand siècle* (Gallimard, 1948), 172.
[40] *Ibid.*, 195.

attempt at constraint other than what is innate in the *générosité* of the *honnête homme* is unacceptable. Thus *Tartuffe* is not specifically directed against a religious group but against "tout ce qui dans le christianisme pouvait permettre de censurer, persécuter, envahir,"[41] But this aristocratic liberalism can be threatened by others than the "dévots." Alceste incarnates "l'idéalisme réformateur" and is no less a threat. It follows that Molière must treat him harshly and not allow him to triumph. Thus Alceste's "droiture" is portrayed as the result of weaknesses and shortcomings in his character, operating as a sort of ego-counterpoise in lieu of a disinterested virtue. Therein lies his failure. As a result, the person who could have threatened the "moeurs dociles et adroites . . . l'ouvrage et le soutient du pouvoir absolu" is exiled and the aristocratic status-quo is maintained. This clearly illustrates Molière's conformity and his special morality: "Toute la morale de Molière consiste à savoir s'incliner devant un certain nombre de faits. La force des usages défie autant chez lui la justice que la force des désirs défie la bienséance. . . . tout au moins a-t-il réduit la morale à n'être que l'accompagnement le plus discret possible de la vie."[42]

Obviously Bénichou does not attach negative value to this *morale mondaine*, quite the contrary. Corneille's heroism, Pascal's stringent morality, and Molière's flexible ethic are all part of the "révalorisation de l'humain" which takes on special impetus in the seventeenth century and continues through to the Revolution. In this light, the seventeenth and eighteenth centuries are complimentary, involved as they were in a common effort, "par la valeur qu'ils attribuent, dans l'ensemble, à la qualité d'homme, à l'équilibre de la lucidité et de l'instinct, par la façon dont ils allient tous deux, le beau et le naturel, dont ils dessinent le caractère et les exigences de la véritable humanité."[43] Molière's work, his "morale," are part of this humanistic impetus.

Erich Auerbach's view of Molière is similar to Bénichou's. In *Mimesis*, the critic contended that Molière's course was essentially in the middle, and in a later essay he specified more clearly what this middle consisted of: an amalgam of status-seeking "grande bourgeoisie de robe" (*la ville*), and disenfranchised "noblesse" (*la cour*). In the course of the seventeenth

---

[41] *Ibid.*, 206. Raymond Fernandez had expressed similar opinions in his excellent *Vie de Molière* (N.R.F., 1929).
[42] *Ibid.*, 214.
[43] *Ibid.*, 222.

century, these two elements were fused into a "common cultural ideal . . . self-contained homogeneous society."[44] This formed the bulk of Molière's Parisian public, and it was their interest he served. In essence, Auerbach's "homogeneous society" and Bénichou's aristocratic public share the same ethic. Others since have associated Molière's morals with the prevailing social structure. Recently, an editor suggested that much in Molière "ne peut s'expliquer que si l'on se réfère à la 'fonction sociale' de l'auteur comique, telle que la concevait Molière."[45]

What then was the state of affairs in the early 1960's? The Moore-Bray proposition had considerably changed the picture. The outright rejection of a moralistic message, and the placing of a key element of this theory— the reasoners—within the actual functioning of the play, as one of the internal working parts, was new and original. While it did not go un-contested (Gossman for one called it "hiding behind esthetics"), it did have broad impact on the general orientation of Molière exegesis. Disavowing the message had cast the medium into an entirely new light. In effect, the "new criticism" reaffirmed the play itself in its total freedom as a work of art, an independent and self-contained whole, without a mediatory predetermined world-view. After Moore and Bray, those who persisted in seeking the elements of a definable morality began dealing more speci-fically with the comic matrix of Molière's total *oeuvre*. But this method is also tenuous, for how does one proceed with confidence to extract a coherent moral attitude from the labyrinth of capricious comic poetry? Judd Hubert alluded to this problem when he pointed out that "One of the axioms in these comedies is that no amount of 'raisonnement' can ever persuade a person to change the impertinence of his conduct." And the would-be reasoners do not help a wit. They are often "the most frustrated of characters who, though rarely ridiculous in themselves, provoke laugh-ter by the inextricable situations in which they find themselves—and by the inevitability of their failure."[46] No single character tells all, no one rôle directs the consciousness of the complex whole play. If there is a moral

---

[44] Erich Auerbach, *Mimesis* (New York: Doubleday, n.d.), 322; and "La Cour et la Ville" in *Scenes from the Drama of European Literature* (New York: Meridian Books, 1959), 133–79. Within a similar context of inquiry, see an excellent but apparently little-known article by the eminent German scholar Werner Krauss: "Molière und das Problem des Verstehens in der Welt des 17. Jahrhunderts" in *Sinn und Form*, 4 (1952), 87–118. Professor Krauss defines Molière's special "Einvernehmen" (essentially against any form of ideology) and elaborates its double function, literary and political.

[45] Molière, *Le Misanthrope*, edited by E. Lop and A. Sauvage (Editions sociales, 1963), 10.

[46] J.D. Hubert, *Molière and the Comedy of Intellect* (Berkeley: University of California Press, 1962), 118.

sense in the comedies, it seems to take the form of *tâtonnements*, gropings, which do not seem to be directed toward a predetermined grand scheme of universal axioms. On the contrary, there was a growing feeling in criticism that if there was a spiritual voyage in Molière's works, it was directed less toward society at large than toward the poet's own inner imperatives. Robert Jouanny wrote that *Le Misanthrope* projects "la trajectoire sauvage d'une destinée que Molière dessine pour lui, parce qu'il a besoin d'y voir clair."[47] In the great plays at least, Molière seems less concerned with moralisms of general edification than with seeking himself, with "seeing clear" in his own destiny.

Jacques Guicharnaud's conception of Molière's *aventure théâtrale* is germane to this idea. In the three plays at the apex of Molière's career, Professor Guicharnaud plots a movement toward an impasse which is finally manifested in *Le Misanthrope*. This impasse is double: dramaturgical, in that it reaches the ultimate limits of comedy and veers towards the darker domain of "le drame," and profoundly personal, for it rests on an implicit conception of the human condition. In the masterpiece of 1666, Guicharnaud suggests that Molière reached the zero degree of conflict revealed in the irreducibility of human nature, the total impossibility of beings to relate unselfishly to each other and to share intimately a common destiny. The root *défaut irréductible* is the cardinal sin which all classical moralists warned against, *l'amour de soi*. Accordingly, in terms of its resolution, the play opens not onto a harmonious world, but one ultimately defined by "la confrontation des exigences qui se solde . . . par l'affirmation d'une permanence du désaccord . . . la dispersion des êtres. Le monde n'est plus fait du conflit de la tyrannie et du consentement, mais du jeu sans solution des résistances mutuelles."[48] But there is no strategy or scheme on the poet's part, no deliberate intention of purpose. On the contrary, Guicharnaud deals deftly with what he thinks Poquelin's most intimate intuitions might have been in terms of his art only, without regard to biography or possible ideology. From Brunetière to Guicharnaud, "la philosophie de Molière" evolved from a conscious, systematic engagement, to a subtle, poetic and more private impression.

That was ten years ago. Since then, debate has continued and diversity of opinion still prevails over consensus. In some cases old questions resurfaced. For example, recent criticism on *Dom Juan* and *Tartuffe* has

---

[47] *Molière: Oeuvres complètes*, edited by Robert Jouanny, (Classiques Garnier, 1962), I, 813–14.

[48] Guicharnaud, *Molière, Une Aventure théâtrale* (Gallimard, 1963), 533.

asked again, "Molière, fut-il impie?" The responses of course have been markedly less peremptory of late than in the days of Jeannel, Veuillot, and Perrins. Nonetheless, the general feeling persists that to a greater or lesser degree, the playwright did express an attitude which was essentially irreligious. For Richard Coe, Molière might indeed have been impious but he was "not an atheist." Dom Juan is struck down for his intellectual arrogance ("immense, almost transcendental self-confidence"); his sin is wanting "to argue with God on God's own level, God being the only form of mind that can make the argument worth while."[49] Raymond Picard nuanced the case by suggesting that the play was *impie* only to the extent that "pour les docteurs et les prédicateurs," it represented "une satire diabolique de la vraie religion."[50] But for members of Louis's court, Molière's most important constituency, *Tartuffe* was almost certainly not considered offensive because in their view, "la religion devant de toute nécessité—il faut s'y résigner—être adaptée au monde."[51] For this group at least, Molière could hardly have been considered *impie*. Jacques Scherer argued that an unprejudiced reading of *Tartuffe* reveals that Molière was more or less indifferent to religion. And yet this indifference (with, perhaps, a dash of prudence added) was sufficient to keep him in the mainstream of his contemporaries, as is suggested by his attitude in *Dom Juan*. Here Professor Scherer sees Molière taking a clear stand against one of the more dangerous elements of the libertine creed: "la leçon manifeste de la pièce qui est si claire . . [et] aisée à formuler: l'athéisme, racine des vices et des crimes de Dom Juan, appelle une punition exemplaire et spectaculaire par le Ciel. . . . La pièce est contre l'athéisme, ce qui est parfaitement admissible pour le public de Molière."[52] Philip Butler's reading of *Tartuffe* gives the play more specificity and insists more on the author's intent. He

[49] R. N. Coe, "The Ambiguity of Dom Juan" in *Australian Journal of French Studies*, 1 (1964), 34. These remarks seem to have been inspired by Jean Vilar's famous production of *Dom Juan* at the T.N.P. (1953). For an opposite view of the same Vilar production, see R. Barthes' "Le Silence de Dom Juan" in *Les Lettres Nouvelles* (1954). Here the "silence" Vilar projected in the title role is a blatant expression of atheism, brandished at a bourgeois public for the first time in recent history. See also R. Grimsley, "The Dom Juan Theme in Molière and Kierkegaard" in *Comparative Literature*, 6 (1954), 316–34.

[50] R. Picard, "*Tartuffe*, production impie?" in *Mélanges . . . offerts à Raymond Lebègue* (Nizet, 1969), 239. In *Le Malade imaginaire*, C. François thinks Molière went much further in attacking religion: "Médicine et religion chez Molière, deux facettes d'une même absurdité" in *The French Review*, 42, 665–72. See also Peter Nurse's good edition of *Le Malade imaginaire* (Oxford: The University Press, 1965) and his discussion of these problems.

[51] *Ibid.* Georges Couton brings some noteworthy clarifications of an historical nature on the connotations of *hypocrisie* and *imposteur* and shows how *hypocrisie* could actually be used in service to dogma instead of being a sin against it. "*Tartuffe* et le péché d'hypocrisie, cas réservé" in *Revue d'Histoire littéraire*, mai-août 1969, 404–13.

[52] Jacques Scherer, *Sur le Dom Juan de Molière* (Sedes, 1967), 79.

argues (as Michelet had) that Molière's play is directed especially against the insidious authority of the *directeur de conscience*. To this end, the dramatist's resolve is deliberate: "la position prise par l'auteur et ses intentions polémiques sont parfaitement nettes: ce qu'il raille et discrédite, ce n'est pas simplement le mauvais directeur . . . c'est le principe de la direction telle que l'a conçue la Contre-Réforme."[53]

These bids at specifying a religious attitude in moliéresque comedy are perhaps a less recurring preoccupation in criticism than the desire to situate the comic poet in a philosophical or ethical tradition. Here too, since 1963, virtually all views have been restated. A recent study interprets *Dom Juan* in light of a determined libertine philosophy. Its conclusion may seem outdated when asking, "Molière, dont less malheurs de sa vie ont dû accentuer la gravité naturelle de son esprit, n'était-il pas Dom Juan? N'a-t-il pas éprouvé les mêmes craintes que lui, partagé les mêmes préoccupations?"[54] Another decided opinion views Alceste's drama as an internal conflict between stoicism and epicureanism. Originally a neo-stoic in matters of love, the hero is tempted and almost compromised by Célimène's forceful epicureanism. In the end, however, Alceste recognizes the futility of such a pact and arrives at the only possible solution: "il ira s'enfermer dans la retraite . . . il va devenir un stoicien renforcé."[55]

These attitudes are not typical however. The more common efforts of the past decade on this question have avoided untenable theories associating the playwright with a single, well-defined dogma. There remains nonetheless a strong feeling that the total *oeuvre* does reflect an attitude of mind on certain moral issues of the poet's time. "Après tout [says Raymond Picard], il n'est pas interdit à un homme de théâtre d'avoir des idées." The real problem as it now exists for the objective commentator was summed up recently by an English academic: "The difficulty is not to find social, ethical and religious statements in Molière's plays, but to establish which one of them, if any, he stood by."[56]

---

[53] Philip Butler, "*Tartuffe* et la direction spirituelle au 17e siècle" in *Modern Miscellany presented to Eugene Vinaver* (Manchester: Manchester University Press, 1969), 61. See also Butler's companion piece to this article, "Orgon le dirigé" in *Gallica* (Cardiff: University of Wales Press, 1969), 103–19. Michelet's vigorous contribution to the subject is in his *Du Prêtre, de la Femme, de la Famille* (Comptoir des imprimeurs, 1845); see especially Part 1, chapter 6.

[54] Jean-Marie Teyssier, *Réflexions sur Dom Juan de Molière* (Nizet, 1970), 185. For another uninspired contribution which insists on perceiving "la foi religieuse" in all of Molière's works, see A. Garreau, *Inquisitions* (Editions du Cèdre, 1970).

[55] L. Hippeau, *Essai sur la morale de La Rochefoucauld* (Nizet, 1967), 180.

[56] R. Fargher, "Molière and his Reasoners" in *Studies in French Literature Presented to H.W. Lawton* (Manchester: Manchester University Press, 1968), 114.

In line with this opinion, the same critic, R. Fargher, opines that Molière was in fact a moralist, that his reasoners do function as mouthpieces expressing a kind of proto-voltarian rationalism. "It seems to me abundantly clear that the Molière who mocked Holy Scripture, who created the sceptic Béralde, who poured scorn on the obscurantist opponents of modern science, was something less than 'bien pensant' and that his plays do manifest an attitude of mind which in the following century, informed another comic genius, Voltaire."[57] For Peter Nurse, Molière's characteristic voice in his scepticism: "The final impression that emerges from Molière's work . . . is one which was formulated by the Sceptic Montaigne." Thus Molière's attitude is "the traditional Sceptic-Epicurean view of the 'human comedy'; one of its earliest formulations is in Lucretius' *De Natura rerum* while it is also found in La Mothe le Vayer."[58] The humanistic impulse in Molière's work is all the more remarkable in that it flourished at the center of Louis XIV's court, and it is easy to imagine the instincts of a more common soul going in another direction. But even in this alien environment, "jamais Molière . . . ne s'est trahi comme dramaturge humaniste, héritier de la tradition d'Erasme et de Montaigne."[59] Since Antoine Adam's influential *Histoire de la littérature française au XVIIᵉ siècle*, this view has become an accepted idea in most academic criticism on Molière today, and it seems to recur most regularly in the writings of British commentators. It should be reiterated that this view considers the humanistic thrust in Molière's work more as an inherent, instinctive impulse rather than as the agressive persuasion of an established philosophical dogma. It is one thing to place Molière within the tradition of Erasmus and Montaigne, and quite another to see him as a disciple of Gassendi or La Mothe Le Vayer.

One of the most impressive reconsiderations of Molière's *morale* was

---

[57] *Ibid.*, 116. For an opposing view, see the excellent essay by F.L. Lawrence, *Molière and the Comedy of Unreason* (New Orleans: Tulane Studies in Romance Languages and Literatures, 1968).

[58] Peter Nurse, *Classical Voices* (London: Harrop, 1971), 178 and 184. From the same author, see also: "Le Rire et la morale dans l'oeuvre de Molière" in *XVIIᵉSiècle*, v. 52 (1951); "Essai de définition du comique moliéresque" in *Revue des Sciences humaines* (1964), 9–24; "Molière and Satire" in *The University of Toronto Quarterly* (1967), 113–128. A similar and interesting view is in G.S. Burgess, "Molière and the Pursuit of Criteria" in *Symposium*, (Spring 1969), 5–15.

[59] Marc Fumaroli, "Microcosme comique et macrocosme solaire" in *Revue des Sciences humaines*, 145 (1972), 114. In the same number of *RSH*, Bernard Magné writes about the humanistic element implied in Agnès' "conquête de la parole": "L'Ecole des femmes ou la conquête de la parole", 125–4p. This fine piece is one of the first two substantial structural analyses of Molière's works.

advanced recently in two complementary articles by Professor Jules Brody. In his "Esthétique et Société chez Molière," the author begins with Bénichou's well-known contention that Molière's work promoted an aristocratic ethic; Professor Brody suggests instead that Molière supported an aristocratic esthetic. Since, in the dramatist's eyes, society seemed so insensitive to the most basic values and so vulnerable to the excesses of tyrants and maniacs, one's best defense was esthetic beauty. Hence, if the bourgeois characters in Molière's comedies always seem to come out second best, it is because they are incapable of attaining *cette vraie noblesse*, the absolute esthetic of elegance and natural grace; and regardless of their material wealth, they are incapable of buying this quality. In this view therefore, the main conflict in the comedies is not between morality or immorality, but between grace and gaucherie.[60] Thus, M. Jourdain's fault is "une insuffisance esthétique plutôt qu'une tare morale" and, although morally right, George Dandin is "esthétiquement dans son tort."[61] Brody's conclusions to this first part has implication for all of Molière's work: "Le rôle comique est toujours réservé à ceux qui ne savent trouver, malgré la justice de leur cause, ni motif impérieux ni stratégie harmonieuse qui leur permettent d'ajuster leur contenance selon les pressions et les vicissitudes de l'existence sociale."[62]

In a second essay in English, Professor Brody focuses on Dom Juan's "deft histrionics" and Célimène's "imperturable grace," both outstanding examples of the "esthetics of individualism." Departing from Moore's view of a Dom Juan dashed by the limits of his humanity, and comic because of his blindness to those limits, Brody thinks that the don's imposing individuality keeps him immune to the leveling effects of comedy, as though he were "exempt from the laws governing the common destiny of mankind."[63] Dom Juan's incomparable, sublime egocentricity remains beyond human check, allowing him "to exercise indeterminate freedom." That this is possible, is proof that the protagonist inhabits "a rotten world falling apart at the seams, ruled by vanity, self-interest, hypocrisy and indifference; a world in decline . . . ."[64]

[60] Jules Brody, "Esthétique et Société chez Molière" in *Dramaturgie et Société au 16 è et au 17è siècles* (C.R.N.S., 1968), 316–317.

[61] *Ibid.*, 318, 322.

[62] *Ibid.*, 323. The extended conclusion, insisting on the permanence of "corruption" and "mal" in Molière's works, seems to parallel Guicharnaud's thinking at the end of his book.

[63] Jules Brody, "*Dom Juan* and *Le Misanthrope*, or The Esthetics of Individualism in Molière" in *P.M.L.A.*, 84 (May 1969), 559.

[64] *Ibid.*, 568.

The don's counterpart is Célimène. More insightful than Alceste, she has realized that in their tarnished world there are no absolutes and no perfection. For her, happiness is "the result of the same conscious, energetic enterprise on which the viability of social life itself depends: the harmonization of a multitude of warring elements, the disarming of hostility, the reconciliation of rivalries, the persistent imposition of decorum, the constant assertion of form."[65] Taking issue with J. Guicharnaud, Brody contends that in the resolution of *Le Misanthrope*, Molière did not intend Célimène to suffer defeat; Alceste's ultimatum merely provokes a "*déconvenue* . . . a momentary reversal, a pause in her progress toward elegant felicity."[66] In the final analysis, Dom Juan and Célimène's individuality are projected beyond mere crass and valueless egomania. Their attitudes are part of a "noble esthetic" designed to assure "a modicum of levity, style and beauty in a world that would otherwise be devoured by folly, ugliness and mediocrity."[67]

Now one could say that Professor Brody's contributions represent just one more viewpoint on the question of Molière's *morale*. And yet the original and pertinent manner in which he incorporates and renews some of the best criticism on the subject since Bénichou ranks his two articles among the best contributions to Molière studies in the last decade.

But questions persist and responses remain provisional, for Molière criticism continues apace. Although no definitive conclusions are possible, there are a few discernable tendencies. In terms of definable dogma, no specific religious or philosophical credo emerges clearly from Molière's comedies. Even the attempt at organizing ideas and determining the nature of their meaning seems a most perilous task. In truth, efforts to particularize anything concerning ideas, philosophy, or religion in the thirty-odd comedies have remained hypothetical and debatable. This accounts for the reorientation in criticism recently, from specificity to generality; instead of relating Molière to a particular philosopher, the trend is to view the comic poet more generally in the long tradition of humanism. The fact of the matter is that Molière's comic structures function too efficiently on the various levels of fantasy, irony, and those qualities of the imagination which are most ethereal. As one critic pointed out years ago, the sum total of Molière's work represents "une oeuvre de dislocation" wherein

[65] *Ibid.*, 573.
[66] *Ibid.*, 575. M. Guicharnaud has a different idea: see his *Aventure*, 488 sqq.
[67] *Ibid.*, 576.

necessarily, "la pensée hésite sur les conséquences à tirer."[68] In the arguments and counter-arguments on Molière's *morale*, at least one idea seems to have been permanently dashed, the conception of Molière as a revolutionary thinker. In fact, that idea has been reduced to a laughing matter: "La belle plaisanterie pourtant: Molière ne s'est pas dit un beau matin, comme pourrait le faire quelque personnage humouristique d'un film de René Clair: 'Je m'en vais déblayer le chemin pour l'Encyclopédia, souffler des apostrophes célèbres à Beaumarchais et préparer la Révolution Française!'"[69]

It seems finally, that the Moore-Bray "estheticism" steered opinion away from the excesses of the "Molière penseur" school. Bénichou's work also rendered virtually untenable, for most critics at least, the view of Molière as propagandist of the prudent "bon bourgeois" ethic. And while Professor Guicharnaud does not address himself directly to these questions, his study clearly suggests that Molière's real *aventure* was deeply personal, quasi-existential. The sum of these shifts of focus toward more suppleness is reflected in this recent characterization of "la philosophie de Molière": "Elle ne se réduit pas aux théories simplistes professées par Ariste, Cléante, Philinte et autres adeptes de la raison: accepter la vie comme elle est, agir avec prudence, fuir toute extrémité. Elle est dans l'atmosphère de son théâtre, plus facile à sentir qu'à formuler. Elle s'exprime sous forme de suggestions discrètes et non de conseils impérieux."[70]

But all is not yet said. For surely Alfred Simon's dictum was prophetic: "On risque de disputer encore longtemps sur la leçon qui émane des comédies de Molière."[71]

---

[68] A. Villiers, "Dom Juan ou le libertin de l'esprit" in *La Revue théâtrale*, 4 (January–March, 1947), 33.

[69] *Ibid.*

[70] P. Salomon, *Précis d'histoire de la littérature française* (Masson, 1964), 158.

[71] A. Simon, "Puissance de l'illusion comique" in *Cahiers Renaud-Barrault*, 26 (May 1959), 13.

The crown of this work consists of companion pieces, Gaston Hall's eloquent sketch of the present state of Molière studies and Paul Saintonge's continuation of the famous Fifty Years. *The latter is followed by its own index, which precedes the volume index. "Thirty Years of Molière Criticism" has sections and entries that are partially duplicated in at least two other articles in this book. Differences of organization, scope, and treatment, however, make each valuable in its own right.*

THE PRESENT STATE OF MOLIÈRE STUDIES

H. Gaston Hall

To Albert G. Sanders

"Il y a un fait certain," Paul Hazard declared in commemorating the first Molière tercentennial in 1922: "Molière occupe non seulement dans notre histoire littéraire, mais dans toute notre vie intellectuelle, un rang sans égal."[1] Approaching the tercentennial of Molière's death half a century later, one may doubt that he still maintains such a grip upon the minds and hearts of Frenchmen. Nor indeed, though Messrs Heath and Barber have done as much as anyone since 1066 to bring Britain closer to France, can one readily imagine a Prime Minister rewarding a Chancellor of the Exchequer with a folio edition of Molière's works, the form taken by Gladstone's gratitude to the Earl of Rosebery following the Midlothian campaigns of 1879–80.[2] Yet it is equally clear that Molière continues to exert a powerful attraction in the theater world, to cite only the twelve Molière plays to be performed in the 1972–3 season at the Comédie-Française. Molière would also appear to be the only playwright three of whose plays were concurrently performed in separate public theaters in New York in the spring of 1972.

Molière scholarship presents the same mixed picture. While two

---

[1] Paul Hazard, "Ce que Molière représente pour la France," in Maurice Mignon, ed., *Molière*, Rome, Editions de la Nouvelle Revue Italienne, 2nd ed., 1931 [1922], 91. The place of publication is Paris unless otherwise stated.

[2] Eva Rosebery, "The Library at Barnbougle Castle," reprinted from *The Book Collector*, Spring 1962, 9.

periodicals are devoted to Racine, and many a lesser writer can claim a specialist journal, no one now remembers the demise of the short-lived *Moliériste* in 1889. Academic writing on Molière is abundant and some of high quality, but it hardly rivals the literary industries based on Shakespeare, Balzac, or Voltaire. This is not merely because we have no Molière drafts, proofs, or correspondence to lead us to—and sometimes from—the author's published word. The example of Shakespeare shows that. The less developed French bibliographical tradition, the recent fashionableness of violence and revolution in preference to humour and conciliation, and the persistent prejudice that comedy is less real and earnest than tragedy or self-expression doubtless play a part. But much in the present state of Molière studies can be explained by the unwarranted assumption, widespread among students and even among colleagues who should know better, that the important work on this writer has been done. Whence a certain amount of complacent gleaning in fields largely left to go fallow, while other areas are left almost entirely uncultivated because the richness of the harvest available to more developed scholarly techniques is hardly suspected. The hard fact is that the Molière industry is now directed largely toward school children, as the brightly illustrated current French editions of separate comedies suggest: a corollary to Pierre Dux's observation that school children now constitute eighty per cent of the audience for Molière in France.[3]

Molière, as Paul Hazard recognized, is far too significant to be left at that; and recent years have witnessed new editions and research tools that should considerably advance Molière studies. At the same time the critical trend that in the 1950's tended to reduce Molière to a mindless entertainer, as if laughter were incompatible with thought and dramatic quality depended upon moral insignificance, has been firmly checked if not totally discredited.[4] The trend was queried by Raymond Picard in his "Etat présent des études moliéresques" (*L'Information littéraire*, vol. 10, 1958), the last such general survey. Five years later Professor Jacques Morel demonstrated in the same periodical that the satirical attacks in Molière's comedies on misers, fops, misanthropists, pedants, *précieuses*, etc. outline the sort of character these all are not: "la caricature présente comme le

[3] Pierre Dux, "Molière parmi nous," in *Les Annales*, no. 165, 1964, 5–24.
[4] Vivian Mercier: "*Le Misanthrope* is one of the purest examples of the drama of ideas, a member of that very small group of plays which tease the mind long after one has left the theater" ("From Myth to Ideas—and Back," in John Gassner, ed., *Ideas in the Drama*, New York, Columbia University Press, 1964, 63).

moule en creux de l'honnête homme," so that the negative satirical outline represents a positive moralist conception: *honnêteté* (*IL*, 15, 1963, p. 187). This ideal includes both integrity and comeliness, but is specifically concerned with social deportment and the attitudes conducive to harmony. It specifically excludes bringing discomfort to immediate neighbors in the name of the distant benefits of a cherished reform or of some better world to come, which is why the satirical treatment of Orgon scandalized the religious bigots of Molière's day and Alceste appeals even through the satire to Marxists and terrorists prepared to cause unlimited immediate suffering in the name of the millenium promised by their mythology.[5] Critical trends, however, will be briefly reviewed only after significant new editions, and research tools, and biography.

Editions

The new Pléiade *Oeuvres complètes* in two volumes edited by Georges Couton (Gallimard, 1971) deserves pride of place. It goes some way toward fulfilling the editor's intention to provide "une édition aisément lisible, commode, mais qui enregistrât également nos connaissances actuelles sur Molière et constituât un apport" (I. xi). I have been impressed in the soundings taken with the quality of the introduction, *notices* to individual plays, and notes. Doubtless there are points to query, but Molière scholarship to about 1969 is effectively used to elucidate the text

---

[5] Tartuffe's doctrine with its heavenly orientation allows Orgon to regard everyone else he meets in this life as dung (ll. 273 ff.) just as in *Le Misanthrope* the "vertus des vieux âges" (l. 153) allow Alceste to despise everyone "dans le siècle où nous sommes" (l. 117), forming the theoretical justification of his rudeness to whomever he encounters and of his attempt totally to dominate Célimène. Compare George F. Kennon's 1946 telegram from Moscow to the effect that Marxism "with its basic altruism of purpose" furnished the Soviet government with justification for their "fear of [the] outside world . . . . In the name of Marxism they sacrificed every single ethical value in their methods and tactics" (quoted in Dean Acheson, *Present at the Creation*, New York, Norton, 1969, 151); and Mircea Eliade: "Marx reprend et prolonge un des grands mythes escatologiques du monde asiano-méditerranéen, à savoir: le rôle rédempteur du Juste (l'"élu," l'"oint," l'"innocent," le "messager"; de nos jours, le prolétariat), dont les souffrances sont appelées à changer le statut ontologique du monde. En effet, la société sans classes de Marx et la disparition conséquente des tensions historiques trouvent leur plus exact précédent dans le mythe de l'Age d'Or qui, suivant des traditions multiples, caractérise le commencement et la fin de l'Histoire" (*Le Sacré et le profane*, Gallimard, coll. "Idées," 1965, 175). It is often conveniently forgotten—in forcing Alceste into the archtypal Just—that part of Alceste's discontent springs from infringement of class privileges (cf. ll. 129, 1074), that his insistence "qu'on me distingue" (l. 63) is as remote as possible from egalitarianism, and that he has no workable plan for social reform but simply advocates (but in the play does not practice) retreat to a country estate (his "désert") supported by unearned income. However, it is the psychological affinity of Orgon and Alceste to the tyrant and the terrorist that prompts these tendentious remarks.

"en le replaçant dans le mouvement des idées et le contexte historique" (I. xii). The textual criticism, however, seems a little naïve. If M. Couton rightly prefers the texts of the first editions, it seems wrong to lump these witnesses of very different qualities so much together; and he too lightly imposes on the best of them arbitrarily the fashion in punctuation now current in France. The resultant textual apparatus is less satisfactory in some respects than that of the Despois and Mesnard edition.

This shortcoming is compensated by a more sophisticated level of literary criticism, the cream of twentieth-century scholarship, and generous appendices containing complementary texts—sources, polemics, contemporary criticism, indeed most of the valuable documentation from both the large Moland and the Despois and Mesnard editions except the glossaries.

As far as the corpus of Molière's writings is concerned, M. Couton supports his inclusion of *Le Médecin volant* and *La Jalousie du Barbouillé* by adding actorly considerations to Austin Gill's literary analyses in "The Doctor in the farce and Molière" (*French Studies*, II, 1948). But he omits *Le Docteur amoureux*, the one-act farce in prose published by A. J. Guibert ("Textes Littéraires Français," 91, 1960), mainly on the grounds that this play was written for Jodelet. Since Jodelet is assumed not to have entered Molière's troupe before Easter 1659, it would follow that this was not the farce performed for the king with *Nicomède* 24 October 1658 (I, 6–7). The flaw in this argument is the first premise. The document attesting Jodelet's transfer, Loret's *Gazette* for 26 April 1659, implies that Jodelet had already performed with Molière's troupe on a temporary basis, as Gill points out in his review of the Guibert edition: "Jodelet a changé de troupe, Et s'en va jouer, *pour de bon*, Dezormais au Palais-Bourbon" (quoted in *French Studies*, XIV, 1961, 57). Surely Gill is right therefore to conclude that the new *Docteur amoureux*, adapted from Gillet de la Tessonnerie's *Le Desniasé*, "is a promising claimant to the honour of being acknowledged the most famous of the 'petites comédies'" (57). Its omission in the Pléiade and other recent editions of Molière's works is regrettable.

More lavishly produced and boosted by the editor is the *Oeuvres complètes* edited "avec une vie de l'auteur, un examen de chaque pièce, des études sur les personnages et des notes inédites" by Jean Meyer (Gonon, 10 vols., 1968–71). It is a beautifully printed set with many attractive illustrations, new and old. The claim to offer "une iconographie incomparable . . . plus de cinquante documents inédits" is more nearly honored than the claim to present "un texte . . . collationné à la fois sur les éditions originales, sur l'édition de 1674–5 préparée par Molière lui-même . . . , enfin sur l'édition définitive de 1682 . . . de VIVOT et de LA GRANGE (I, 11–12). For there is scant evidence of collation, variants are scarce, and the notes are summary, even when the text of the early editions is altered, as in the attribution of "Oui" to Chrysale in line 1655 of *Les Femmes savantes*, whereas the substitution of Chrysale for Trissotin at this point was first made in 1734. Readers of M. Meyer's *Molière* (Perrin, 1963) will not perhaps be surprised to meet literary analyses fairly represented by the following passage: "Il est hors de doute que le Maître Simon de *l'Avare* est juif et il y a de fortes probabilités que Monsieur Dimanche dans *Dom Juan* le soit aussi," and possibly M. Jourdain as well (VIII, 254). But few scholars will agree that this will be the twentieth-century counterpart to the Despois and Mesnard edition, as the editor proposes (I, 12). My gratitude to M. Meyer is for the many hours of pleasure he has given me in the role of Sganarelle in *Le Médecin malgré lui* and as probably the best producer of *Le Bourgeois gentilhomme* since Molière.

What I have seen of the *Edition pour le tricentenaire de la mort de Molière* (Michel de l'Ormeraie, vol. 7, 1970) is a beautifully produced fascimile reprint of the 1734 edition, which however was in six volumes.

Separate editions continue to appear in series generally well known and of more pedagogical than scholarly interest. Generally these are distinctly better than their counterparts of a decade ago in terms of paper, print, presentation, and particularly illustration, whether one thinks of the Classiques de la civilisation française (Didier), the Classiques illustrés Hatier, or the Nouveaux Classiques Larousse, the appendices to which are now labeled *documentation thématique*. The Petits Classiques Bordas, which in the early sixties helped bring about the change, do not appear to have evolved as far as Molière editions are concerned and now look relatively less attractive. But it is salutory to reflect that as recently as 1965 the old Classiques Larousse still distributed a bowdlerized version of *Le Médecin malgré lui* destined to protect the young from Sganarelle's more sexually adventurous ploys. Editions in the Classiques illustrés Hachette (e.g. *Les Femmes savantes*, ed. H. Carrier, 1968) aim a little lower than the Nouveaux Classiques Larousse and should not be confused with the same publisher's Classiques du théâtre, an attractive series of editions with minimal verbal presentation, but with photographs and stage directions from the same recent production on every verso, notably *Le Bourgeois gentilhomme* in Meyer's production at the Comédie-Française, edited by G. Sandier, 1965.

The only series of separate editions in France now pursuing a scholarly revaluation of Molière's plays is Les Classiques du peuple (Editions sociales), with the political bias to be expected from a Communist press, but stimulating discussion and often a striking *éclairage*. *Le Misanthrope* (ed. E. Lop and A. Sauvage, 1963) is now—with Gustave Rudler's edition in the Blackwell's French Texts (Oxford, Blackwell, 1947)—is now undoubtedly the most serious separate edition. The Classiques du peuple *Tartuffe* (1958) and *L'Ecole des femmes* (1964), both edited by Suzanne Rossat-Mignod, *Dom Juan* (ed. G. Leclerc, 1960), and *Les Femmes savantes* (ed. Jean Cazalbou and Denise Sévely, 1971) are also well worth consulting. This new *Femmes savantes* in particular should help rescue the comedy from the critical aberration of the 1950's by which M. Antoine Adam, for instance, could write that Henriette is "une fille haïssable . . . une petite vipère."[6] Though the expession seems strange concerning a century in which books were published also with the titles *L'Honnête femme* (by Du Bosc, 3 vols., 1632–6) and even *L'Honnête fille* (by François de Grenaille, 3 vols., 1639–40), the editiors are surely right to see Henriette as "le véritable *honnête homme* de la pièce. . . . Un beau caractère . . . et qui . . . montre à quel point Molière apprécie l'esprit et la culture chez une jeune fille" (53).

It is a sad fact that the only serious textual criticism has been undertaken for editions published in England. The two reasons why, in the absence of manuscripts, the early editions should be re-examined in the full light of the most alert bibliographical techniques are (1) that they represent our nearest approach to Molière's dramatic imagination and (2) that, being witnesses of widely differing qualities, they deserve separate treatment according to the degree of authority they represent. The absence of absolute certainty in such matters is no sufficient reason to neglect judgments on the basis of the reliable textual evidence readily available to the proper bibliographical techniques.[7] No editor can compete with a photographer in physically reproducing a copy of an early edition "warts and all", but he should have more judgment than a camera.

---

[6] Antoine Adam, *Histoire de littérature française au XVIIe siècle*, 5 vols., Domat, 1949–56, vol. III, 1952, 392.
[7] Compare Wallace Kirsop, *Bibliographie matérielle et critique textuelle* ("Biblio notes", 1), Lettres modernes, 1970.

When dealing with obviously careless editions, this judgment requires the courage to make sensible alterations, though it is always helpful to specialists to have a photographic facsimile like M. Guibert's *Docteur amoureux*. But judgment ought also to caution against the imposition of alien criteria. Far more alterations are required in the exceptional case of *Dom Juan* than in any of the late comedies which were published by Molière himself (inscribed "et se vend pour l'auteur" on the title page) and probably supervised by him as well. *Dom Juan* was first published in the Vivot-La Grange edition of 1682 and censored in the press, but a separate edition was carelessly pirated from what appears to have been a superior manuscript (Amsterdam, 1683). It is the latter that serves as the basis of Professor W. D. Howarth's edition (Blackwell's French Texts, 1958), since despite the typographical shortcomings which have discredited it with other editors, it "comes nearest to reproducing Molière's original text" (xxxvii).[8] When, as here, the witness is so obviously faulty, the editor may have good reason for bringing punctuation "into line with modern practice": that is, to substitute his own reading for the original printer's, but without the latter's access to the manuscript.

The case for altering punctuation—the common practice in current editions—is clearly weaker when the first edition is coherently punctuated by the criteria of Molière's time. Editors have been too ready to ascribe to the capriciousness of printers what in many cases are seventeenth-century conventions not properly understood and which could be better approached as a code not fully cracked. The great majority of the exclamation points (!) that punctuate Molière's comedies in current editions were not introduced until 1734, at the height of the fashion for *comédie larmoyante*. But exclamation points were used, and it is surprising to find sometimes a query (?) where one might be expected or vice versa. When such signs are interchanged, as in many editions of *Le Bourgeois gentilhomme*, in the third scene of the fourth act, the best guide to the intended tone—and thus characterization—is lost. Three considerations guide my attitude to this question: (1) sound, as opposed to sight, was still a relatively more prestigious sense in the seventeenth century than now;[9] (2)

---

[8] M. Couton declares that "le texte hollandais a l'immense mérite d'être aussi près que possible de la version jouée en 1665" (Molière, *Oeuvres complètes*, II, 1291), but prints a hybrid text based on the uncancelled state of the Paris edition of 1682 with insertions from the Amsterdam edition in the conviction that the Paris edition reflects revisions to the text made by Molière himself not recorded on the MS. that found its way to Amsterdam.

[9] Compare Robert Mandrou on sixteenth-century sensibility: "Le grand pourvoyeur de

texts of any sort were generally punctuated more for the voice and the ear
than for the eye and the mind (for being read aloud or with moving lips,
not silently); and (3) these considerations apply particularly to dramatic
texts, destined in the first instance to be spoken by actors and in the second
to recall performances, which does not of course exclude a wider public
not reached by the performances. The argument is that the latter is better
helped in its *dramatic* imagination to Molière's *dramatic* thought by
respecting such interpretative clues as we have in the comedies where
these seem to be reliable.

In many cases individual points may hardly matter; and sometimes a
conventional comma at the caesura of an alexandrine may seem fussy or
superfluous, a convention which Molière seems careful not to abuse. But
note what happens rhythmically to an ordinary line of *Les Femmes
savantes* (l. 305). The first edition reading, "La figure est adroite, et pour
n'en point sortir," gets another comma in the Despois and Mesnard
edition: "La figure est adroite, et, pour n'en point sortir." It is then the
second, "logical," comma which is retained, while the first one disappears
in the Nouveaux Classiques Larousse edition: "La figure est adroite et,
pour n'en point sortir." Independently of the personal inflection that
any actress must bring to the role, the rhythm of the line has been drastically altered.

Or consider Chrysale's complaint in the same play, which in the first
edition reads: "Il faut que je l'appelle, et mon coeur, et ma mie" (1.676).
Despois and Mesnard prefer: "Il faut que je l'appell et "mon coeur" et
"ma mie." It may be that the quotation marks suggest the idea of comic
mimicry just as well as the original commas, but they do not get the timing;
and they are dropped—without restoration of the commas—in the

---

leur imagination, c'est l'ouïe, bien plus que la vue; c'est le toucher également, plus que la vue,
toujours . . . " (*Introduction à la France moderne. Essai de psychologie historique*, 1500–1640,
A. Michel, 1961, 69, quoted in Henriette Lucius, *La Littérature "visionnaire" en France du
début du XVIe au début du XVIe siècle*, Bienne, Schüler, 1970, 29). Orgon's lines:

> Je l'ai vu, dis-je, vu, de mes propres yeux vu,
> Ce qu'on appelle vu : faut-il vous le rebattre
> Aux oreilles cent fois, et crier comme quatre?
> (*Tartuffe*, ll. 1676–8)

reflect a change in sensibility which can almost certainly be linked to the rising prestige of
sight among the growing number of spiritual heirs to Humanism whose values would soon be
expressed in the visual image *Enlightenment*. Hence too Bossuet's preoccupation with
concupiscence des yeux in his *Maximes et réflections sur la comédie* of 1694.

Nouveaux Classiques Larousse edition. This seems to me not so much to help the modern reader as to deprive him of a clue to the sort of emphasis that gives Chrysale his dramatic vitality and *Les Femmes savantes* its comic verve. Conversely, when Despois and Mesnard and after them Les Nouveaux Classiques Larousse etc. change Henriette's line 113: "Il me le dit, ma soeur, et pour moi je le croi," to: "Il me le dit, ma soeur, et, pour moi, je le croi," they add an emphasis entirely absent in the original and leading directly to the sort of characterization by which Henriette can be mistakenly interpreted as a *petite vipère*.

The question is no less serious in the late prose comedies, as an example from *Le Bourgeois gentilhomme*, in the third scene of the third act, will show: M. Jourdain's reply to his wife's question concerning his desire to show off his new clothes, "et avez-vous envie qu'on se raille partout de vous?", which nearly all current editions (including the new Pléiade) print after Despois and Mesnard as follows: "Il n'y a que des sots et des sottes, ma femme, qui se railleront de moi." But the first edition has another, most important comma: "Il n'y a que des sots, et des sottes, ma femme, qui se railleront de moi." The phrase "et des sottes" adds nothing logically to the reply, but a great deal dramatically. To omit this comma is not so much to "modernize" as to miss the comic point, which the implied pause prepares, inviting emphasis and some accusing glance or gesture or raised finger to accompany the words "des sottes" which Molière's stagecraft has written into the line and which editors have been too ready to take out. There is, of course, no absolute certainty concerning the relation of Molière's lost manuscript to the first edition. But the relative rarity of pauses in the lines of the Maître à danser, and their abundance in those of the Maître de philosophie, are more likely to indicate a stylistic differentiation between the masters than the caprice of an otherwise careful printer, a differentiation lost in any of the "modernized" editions.

It does not follow that because we cannot totally revive the first performances, which in any case must have varied much as modern productions do, that this aspect of Molière's art should be obscured by an inexpert editorial tradition. The more exact editions required cannot convey all the information that might be desirable, but they could give a far clearer idea of the relation of Molière's texts—of certain texts—to his stagecraft. Happily there are signs of change. The example from *Le Bourgeois gentilhomme* is taken from my own edition in the *Textes français classiques et modernes* series (University of London Press, 1966); and it is gratifying to see the same principles adopted for J. T. Stoker's edition of *Les*

Fourberies de Scapin in the same series (1971), with the observation that "punctuation of the original edition can be regarded as the actors' speaking text and differs in many instances from recently published texts" (19). At least the punctuation preserved by the Stoker edition is nearer than anything else we have to the speaking texts, and he is undoubtedly right that occasionally "commas have been put in by Molière in order to show breath-groups." It is encouraging too that Professor Howarth, skeptical of this editorial approach in reviewing the ULP *Bourgeois gentilhomme* (*French Studies*, XXII, 1968), has now accepted an edition of *Les Femmes savantes* prepared on the same principles for his own *Clarendon French Series* (Oxford University Press), which already contains the most useful separate edition of *Le Malade imaginaire* (ed. P. H. Nurse, 1965).

Research tools and biography

The 1960's brought the best harvest in this area for many years. M. A. J. Guibert's *Bibliographie des oeuvres de Molière publiées au XVIIᵉ siècle* (C.N.R.S., 2 vols., 1961, supplément, 1965) is now familiar to specialists, though D. C. Potts was certainly right to remark that "the techniques of description will seem crude to those brought up on Bowers or McKerrow."[10] This *Bibliographie* is complemented by Georges Mongrédien's *Recueil des textes et des documents du XVIIᵉ siècle relatifs à Molière* (C.N.R.S., 2 vols., 1965), a most helpful reference set which would be more so if it listed not only performances of Molière's own plays, but those of other playwrights performed by his company. For we are reminded by Pierre Gaxotte that "sur les 95 pièces montées par la troupe de 1658 à 1673. le tiers seulement . . . sont de lui."[11] Naturally there are omissions, such as the crucial passage in Loret's *Gazette* for 26 April 1659 cited above.

The most obvious addendum is the document discovered in the Minutier Central by G. E. Reed proving that 15 April 1673 Barbin and Thierry bought two-thirds of Molière's privileges and two-thirds of the stocks of his works from Anne David (Mme Ribou).[12] The *Bibliographie de la littérature française du dix-septième siècle* by Alexandre Cioranescu (C.N.R.S., 3 vols., 1965–6) with two thousand nine hundred and eighty-two Molière items to 1960–1 in volume II is invaluable, as is Mongrédien's *Dictionnaire biographique des comédiens français du XVIIᵉ siècle* (C.N.R.S., 1961). The latter has a full system of references allowing control of the

---

[10] D. C. Potts, in *The Year's Work in Modern Language Studies*, XXIV (1962), 1963, 91.
[11] Pierre Gaxotte, *Molière, fameux comédien*, Hachette, 1971, 28–29.
[12] G. E. Reed, "Molière's Privilege of 18 March 1671," in *The Library*, XX, 1965.

sources, which vary in reliability. Mongrédien himself has put meat on these bones in *La Vie quotidienne des comédiens au temps de Molière* (Hachette, 1966). Full discussion of background books would take us far beyond our brief, but mention could be made here also of François Mille-pierres, *La Vie quotidienne des médecins au temps de Molière* (Hachette, 1964), and of Roger Lathuillère, *La Préciosité* (Geneva, Droz, 1966).

As far as Molière and his own troupe are concerned, by far the most important book in the past decade is M. Jurgens and E. Maxfield-Miller, *Cent Ans de recherches sur Molière, sur sa famille, et sur les comédiens de sa troupe* (Imprimerie Nationale, 1963). The editors have collected in one large volume all the most important Molière documents, including many previously unpublished, increasing—mainly through the Minutier Central—the known Molière documents by about fifty per cent and the number of documents concerning his own and the Béjart families some-thing like fourfold. New documents show that Molière did not break with his father, Jean Pocquelin, who helped his son through early difficulties, paid his debts, provided a legal address for his return to Paris along with furniture for home and for stage use, and was helped in turn by Molière during his last illness. One gets a far clearer idea than available before of how favorable to the theater the bourgeois milieu in which Molière grew up was. The dean of the Confrères de la Passion, owners of the Hôtel de Bourgogne, was indeed a personal friend to both Molière's father and grandfather.

Other documents in the volume help directly in the interpretation of individual plays, notably the agreement signed 3 December 1664 for the stage sets of *Dom Juan*. This shows of course that the play must have been nearly complete at that date and not composed in great haste thereafter. It also indicates that stage machinery must have been in use throughout the play, especially after the third act, and is not therefore arbitrarily brought in at the last moment for the dénouement. This new information helps René Pintard to show the extent to which, a legend to the contrary notwithstanding, Molière observes a relative unity of time (36 hours) and of place by the use of flats depicting various scenes within easy reach of each other in his play, though widely scattered in the Don Juan legend.[13]

Further biographical documentation is provided by Madame Suzanne Dulait's *Inventaire raisonné des autographes de Molière avec fac-similés*

---

[13] René Pintard, "Temps et lieux dans le *Dom Juan* de Molière", in *Studi in onore di Italo Siciliano*, Florence, Olschki, 1966, II.

de tous les autographes dont on possède encore l'original ou la reproduction figurée (1643–1967) (Geneva, Droz, 1967), complementary to *Cent Ans de recherches* . . . . Only one hundred Molière autographs have ever been seriously proposed. Of these, thirteen are more or less seriously disputed, twenty-three (dated or undated, whether authentic or not) have entirely disappeared, and eight others exist now only in facsimile after loss or destruction of the originals. A handful of signatures on notarized acts is really about all we have directly from the hand of the master. The Pézenas receipts (with a few manuscript lines) are disputed, the third *Placet de Tartuffe* is a manifest forgery, and the words inscribed on a parchment on the back of one of Sébastian Bourdon's paintings—along with the signatures, marginalia, and manuscript corrections in various books proposed as Molière autographs—are all either extremely dubious or useless, since insufficient examples of Molière's handwriting (which in any case varies enormously in the authentic signatures) have been discovered to establish their authenticity. It is salutory to be reminded that, although Molière is known to have left a library of around eight hundred books, uncatalogued, not one of these has ever been positively traced to him.

In a masterly article on "l'état civil d'Armande Béjart," M. Couton historicizes the calumny which, supposing Armande to be the daughter and not the sister of Madeleine, accuses Molière of having married his mistress's daughter (in its extreme form, his own daughter by Madeleine).[14] New documents in *Cent Ans de recherches* . . . prove that Joseph Béjart, Armande's legal father, died in the summer of 1641: that is, late enough to be the father of Armande, probably born that year. Mmes Jurgens and Maxfield-Miller also publish Marie Hervé's *acte de baptême* (1 August 1593), indicating an age for her at the time of forty-eight, an age not incompatible with bearing an eleventh child (130–1). M. Couton proceeds with further research and impeccable logic to demonstrate step by step how the calumny was fostered by hostility and scandal without the slightest concrete evidence and often on the basis of erroneous suppositions (e.g., that Marie Hervé was well past fifty at the time of Armande's birth) firmly belied by the new documents.

Cent Ans de recherches . . . is used by Georges Bordonove, Molière's most recent biographer.[15] But the same information in fewer words,

---

[14] Georges Couton, "L'Etat civil d'Armande Béjart, femme de Molière, ou l'historique d'une légende," in *Revue des sciences humaines*, no. 115, 1964.

[15] Georges Bordonove, *Molière génial et familier*, Laffont, 1967.

and with more ideas, is available in René Jasinski's *Molière, l'homme et l'oeuvre* (Hatier, 1969), which replaces the book with the same title by Daniel Mornet in the *Connaissance des lettres* series. Students may be put off by the very density of the information crammed into two hundred and eighty-eight pages; and critics may wince at the occasional biographical or historical interpretation pushed beyond the evidence, but not often and not nearly so much as in Jasinski's books on Racine and La Fontaine. At the same time he has provided the most compendious all-round approach to Molière, not only because it contains more information than other books of comparable size, but because so many of the critical insights are sensitive and stimulating. Hallam Walker's *Molière* (New York, Twayne, 1971) aims a great deal lower, but will be more useful to English-speaking students approaching Molière for the first time.

Though we are now well into the no man's land between research tools, teaching aids, and criticism, mention could be made here of *Les Grands Rôles du théâtre de Molière*, by Maurice Descotes (Presses universitaires de France, 1960), which is not to deny that it contains some of the finest pages of Molière criticism. This history of the great roles and of the plays in which they occur at the Comédie-Française is an indispensable guide to the different Molières presented to the Paris theater public and (with Descotes's companion volumes on Corneille and Racine) to dramatic sensibility over the past three centuries. It is particularly helpful in the consequences to other characters in a play when the interpretation of any important role is altered, as in *Le Misanthrope*:

le public se trouve en face d'un ensemble et le visage d'Alceste reçoit l'éclairage des autres protagonistes de la comédie. Que l'actrice fasse de Célimène une coquette vraiment cruelle, insensible, et Alceste paraît une victime digne de compassion. Si au contraire Célimène est une très jeune femme, tête légère, peu consciente du mal qu'elle provoque, Alceste devient moins émouvant . . . (96).

Around 1882 Mirecourt interpreted Oronte as an elegant nobleman with only the amusing fault of reading out a mediocre sonnet. But Coquelin turned the role upside down so that Oronte "bavard, outrageusement fat et plein de lui, justifiait par là même l'aigreur d'Alceste" (96). It is not difficult to see that such different productions arise from and propagate different conceptions of Molière's idea of *Le Misanthrope*.

The importance of such data for evaluating literary influence can best be shown by a fresh look at the Tartuffe taken as the model of Stendhal's Julien Sorel in *Le Rouge et le noir*. For Stendhal must have been guided by the two Tartuffes he had seen on stage: Fleury in 1804, and Firmin in 1822, neither much concerned with comedy or laughter. The dominant interpretation was that of Molé, whose Tartuffe "n'avait rien de commun avec le rustre déchaîné," for Molé played the role as a seductive and vivacious aristocrat (160–1): "La noblesse et le bon ton étaient . . . tellement incrustés dans son jeu et dans toute sa personne, qu'il ne put jamais descendre à la bassesse du personnage."[16] Fleury appears to have aimed at essentially the same effects, but with somewhat more flexibility and plausibility. Similarly Firmin, whom Stendhal saw as Tartuffe to Mlle Mars's Elmire, was no impostor, but "fait pour jouer les amoureux passionnés" (160–1). He later became the brilliant creator of Hernani precisely in early 1830; but the foregoing remarks suggest the extent to which certain classical roles—and in particular Tartuffe—had been romanticized before many of the most romantic roles were written. Such in any case is the background to the otherwise strange process by which Julien Sorel comes to quote "son maître Tartufe, dont il savait le rôle par coeur" amidst Stendhal's recollections of such elevated company as the bishop of Beauvais, Mephistopheles, and Cardinal Gravelle (*Le Rouge et le noir*, II, chap. 13). It is the wealth of such concrete information that makes Descotes's *Grands Rôles* . . . more helpful, to me at least, than other books that might be mentioned on the literary fortune of Molière.[17]

Criticism

One of the most striking shifts in Molière studies in the past fifteen years has been the great interest in *Dom Juan*, which did not precisely begin with W. G. Moore's article "*Dom Juan* Reconsidered" (*Modern Language Review*, vol. 52, 1957) but has certainly made such headway since as to make it difficult to imagine how a play of such quality was neglected by the Comédie-Française until 1847 in favour of Thomas Corneille's verse version. Not only does it figure with *Tartuffe* and *Le Misanthrope* in the books mentioned below by Cairncross, Gossman, and Guicharnaud, but is the only individual play to which three essays are devoted by Jacques Guicharnaud in *Molière, a Collection of Critical Essays* in the *Twentieth Century Views* series (Englewood Cliffs, N.J., Prentice-Hall, 1964). Eight

---

[16] *Journal de Paris*, 12 October 1812, quoted by M. Descotes, *Grands Rôles*, 160.

[17] These include M. Descotes' *Molière et sa fortune littéraire*, Bordeaux, Ducros, 1970, in the series with the misleading title *Tels qu'en eux-mêmes*, since the information published by M. Descotes abundantly proves that a major author's reputation is not transmuted into its essential being by death and eternity, but remains quite as subject to the historical fluctuation of outlooks and tastes as that of living authors.

of twenty articles in *Molière combattant* (*Europe*, nos. 441–2, 1966) are devoted to *Dom Juan*, far more than to *Tartuffe* or *Le Misanthrope*, also commemorated.[18] However, neither of the separate studies of the play makes efficient use of recent scholarship.[19] There is also some confusion in interpretations put forward. In *Men and Masks, a Study of Molière*, Lionel Gossman suggests that "the very structure of the comedy bears the imprint of the Dom's passivity" (Baltimore, Johns Hopkins University Press, 1963, 37). For Gossman Dom Juan is not even a sensualist since he bungles his only attempt in the play at seduction (44).

Yet Richard Coe interprets Dom Juan as an incarnation of the will.[20] And now J.-M. Teyssier is positive that Dom Juan is passive but considers him sensual as well, if that is what he means in declaring that in the first two acts of *Dom Juan* " . . . l'intention de Molière ne peut être que celle de nous montrer en Dom Juan un homme sensible aux beautés de ce monde, sans doute, mais surtout un homme faible qui cache sa faiblesse sous des dehors de Matamore . . ." (*Reflections . . .*, 75–76). It is generally neglected that the double seduction scene closely follows a parallel scene in Dorimond's *L'Inconstance punie*, which is a firm link with the comic stage tradition of the inconstant Hylas emanating from d'Urfé's *L'Astrée*. Many of the difficulties encountered by the sort of contradictory interpretations of *Dom Juan* could be avoided simply by allowing that the play is—in the generic sense—a *comédie* as designated by Molière and that Dom Juan is intended mainly as a comic character, as argued most recently by Roger Laufer.[21]

Of the significant critical studies on Molière published in the past decade, several of the most important have come from American universities and deal mainly with aesthetic questions, though none of these really replaces W. G. Moore's *Molière, a New Criticism* (Oxford University Press, 1949). Professor J. D. Hubert's *Molière and the Comedy of Intellect*

---

[18] This was not the case, however, with the Molière day at the Association internationale des études françaises in 1963 (*CAIEF*, no. 16, 1964) or the Molière number of *L'Esprit créateur*, no. 3, 1966, in which aspects of farce, poetry, and style in Molière are discussed.

[19] Jacques Scherer, *Sur le Dom Juan de Molière* (SEDES, 1967) and Jean-Marie Teyssier, *Réflexions sur "Dom Juan" de Molière* (Nizet, 1970).

[20] R. N. C. Coe, "The Ambiguity of Dom Juan," in *Australian Journal of French Studies*, I, 1964.

[21] Roger Laufer, "Le Comique du personnage de Dom Juan de Molière," in *Modern Language Review*, LVIII, 1963. It is none the less true, however, that, as Couton observes concerning the first editions: "Une étude comparée des trois textes, qui ne se bornerait pas à enregistrer les modifications, mais tâcherait de les expliquer serait à faire" (Molière, *Oeuvres complètes*, II, 29).

(Berkeley and Los Angeles, University of California Press, 1962) explores not only Molière's satire of intellectuals and the appeal that his comedies make to the mind, but a number of crucial stylistic questions connected with all the major plays chapter by chapter. In *Molière, une aventure théâtrale* (Gallimard, 1963) Professor Guicharnaud concentrates on three plays only—*Tartuffe, Dom Juan,* and *Le Misanthrope*—from the point of view of the ideal spectator to an ideal performance, with suggestive remarks on dramatic—though too seldom on comic—aspects of these plays, concluding that Molière ". . . n'a jamais sombré dans l'esthétisme formel, comme il ne s'est jamais romantiquement confessé, comme il n'a jamais non plus 'philosophé'. Dans son oeuvre, il n'y a pas de forme sans signification, comme il n'y a pas de signification en dehors de la forme" (519–20). Yet it is difficult to accept that Molière's comedy abuts on a determinist conception of man deprived of freedom, that the "essentialism" of his characterization implies a pitiless prison, or that comedy is an illusory genre which evaporates into nothingness after Célimène and Alceste exeunt in the fifth act of *Le Misanthrope* (532).

In the first place, it is not true that Molière's characters are all rigid. Orgon in particular, though constant in his enthusiasm and tendency toward violent solutions, does significantly alter his outlook in the last act of *Tartuffe,* a change interpreted by E. S. Chill as a rally to the courtly ethic embraced by the young king evoked in the last lines of the play and radically opposed precisely to the Jansenist currents to which Guicharnaud would assimilate the implications of Molière's comedy.[22] Many will prefer Marcel Gutwirth's premise that laughter is "la conscience joyeuse de notre finitude."[23] Even for the Jansenists human freedom, none the less real for being limited, miraculously co-existed with the omnipotence of God. Gutwirth's *Molière* contains an abundance of subtle literary analysis that can be read by specialist or beginner with equal profit, but readers curious about the psychological implications of comic themes and characterization are referred also to the late Charles Mauron's studies.[24] I should add that Mauron's approach suits *L'Avare* better than *Le Misanthrope*

[22] E. S. Chill, "*Tartuffe,* Religion, and Courtly Culture", in *French Historical Studies,* III, 1964. In an important review of Guicharnaud's *Molière, une aventure théâtrale,* Lionel Gossman undermines his assumption that "comedy rests on optimism and confidence concerning human nature and the order of things" (*French Review,* XXXVIII, 1965).

[23] Marcel Gutwirth, *Molière ou l'invention comique,* Minard, 1966, 10.

[24] Charles Mauron, "L'Evolution créatrice de Molière," in Id., *Des Métaphores obsédantes au mythe personnel, introduction à la psychocritique,* Corti, 1963, and *Psychocritique du genre comique,* Corti, 1964.

and shares the weakness of all criticism that attempts to reduce to some general principle complex works to which the critic is drawn precisely because they are unique.

Attempts to situate Molière's theater historically or ideologically include John Cairncross's *Molière bourgeois et libertin* (Nizet, 1963), which is a somewhat forced attempt to see *Tartuffe, Dom Juan*, and *Le Misanthrope* as expressions of bourgeois attitudes and of French free thought. Though in some ways a useful corrective to the overassimilation of Molière's outlook to courtly values advocated most lucidly by Paul Bénichou in *Morales du grand siècle* (Gallimard, 1948), the scholarship is too often careless. *Dom Juan* and *Le Misanthrope* were never in Molière's lifetime performed at Court, but *Tartuffe*, written for a *fête galante*, satirizes the puritanical values of a bourgeois "opposition." Nor does it follow that, because a courtly circle is satirized in *Le Misanthrope*, Molière's angle of vision is bourgeois, since some of the polemical portraits through which the satire is expressed are adapted from epigrams current in thoroughly aristocratic salons and Célimène's behavior can be related to advice sympathetically offered to an aristocratic lady a few months before the play's premiere.[25]

New information concerning the religious background of *Tartuffe* is available in H. P. Salomon's *Tartuffe devant l'opinion française* (Presses Universitaires de France, 1962) and in Rachmiel Brandwajn's *Twarz i Maska—Rzece o "Swietoszku" Moliera* (Warsaw, Wiedsa Powszechna, 1965), the main points of which are available in French in Jacques Birnberg's detailed review in *Studi francesi*, no. 41, 1970. Jacques Scherer, *Structures de Tartuffe* (SEDES, 1965) presents more rounded information and perhaps a better balanced view of the play with a faint structuralist glow refracted through the Sorbonne.

Lionel Gossman's *Men and Masks, a Study of Molière* (Baltimore, Johns Hopkins University Press, 1963) examines *Tartuffe, Amphitryon, Dom Juan, Le Misanthrope*, and *George Dandin* in an attempt to isolate what he sees as their common elements of structure in terms of contemporary experience and ideas. Though deliberately neglecting Molière's personal development as an artist, this approach opens a number of exciting perspectives on the works considered, though it must be added

---

[25] Compare H. G. Hall, "The Literary Context of Molière's *Le Misanthrope*," in *Studi Francesi*, no. 40, 1970, and "Molière's *Le Misanthrope* in the Light of d'Aubignac's *Conseils d'Ariste à Célimène*," in *Kentucky Romance Quarterly*, XIX, 1972.

that the penetration of seventeenth-century background is not always deep and that there is too little concern with specifically dramatic considerations for all the insights and analyses to ring quite true. Two recent papers by Jules Brody seem more helpful in relating esthetic questions to social and moral issues.[26]

As nearly as my inexpert German allows me to judge, Wolfgang Salzmann, *Molière und die lateinische Komödie. Ein Stil- und Struktur-vergleich* (Heidelberg, Winter, 1969) is now the most thorough discussion of the community of inspiration between Molière, Plautus, and Terence. The structural comparison, like the stylistic, is esthetic and does not refer to the different social and dramatic traditions in which the playwrights worked. I am skeptical of recent Italian efforts to place Molière in the continuity of French poetic and free-thought traditions, ignored by Salzmann. Though published in Spanish in Chile, these most notably include Daniela Dalla Valle's *De Théophile a Molière, aspectos de una continuidad* (Santiago, El Espejo de papel, 2 vols., 1968), which suffers from a tendency to assume that the speeches of characters (especially Dom Juan) straightforwardly represent the views of the playwright and a failure to note that where, in *Le Misanthrope*, Molière does indeed adapt a passage from Lucretius, it is also adapted to values radically opposed to Epicurean ideology.

In conclusion, there remains great scope in Molière studies not only for more exact editions, but for reconsidering his work in the light of much wider samples of contemporary literary and moralist activity than those normally taken, especially the minor poetic genres, contemporary translations, and the long neglected moralist dialogue.[27] This is not urged as a hunt for sources, though these may facilitate stylistic analysis of Molière's finished lines in something of the way the drafts or variants of other poets do. It is urged in order to deepen our perception of how Molière received a rich cultural heritage at an exciting time of new developments in French sensibility at once captured and transcended in his unique achievements. There is a no less urgent need to relate aspects of Molière's texts, correctly

[26] Jules Brody, "Esthétique et société chez Molière," in Jean Jacquot, ed., *Dramaturgie et société*, CNRS, 1968, 2 vols., I, and "*Don Juan* and *Le Misanthrope*, or the Esthetics of Individualism in Molière", in *PMLA*, LXXXIV, 1969.
[27] Little has ever been made of the fact that the plays of Samuel Chappuzeau performed and pillaged by Molière derive in part from the *Colloquies* of Erasmus, which Chappuzeau translated. But the changes dramatized by the Frenchmen in the continuity of the Erasmian tradition can certainly help particularize their solutions to traditional European problems.

printed, to his dramatic imagination in its entirety. [28] This is partly a matter of textual criticism, partly of theater archeology, but mainly a question of bringing to critical study of the plays those "yeux pour découvrir dans la lecture tout le jeu du théâtre" that Molière demands of the reader of *L'Amour médecin* and a willingness to allow that such play may be symbolic and meaningful.

[28] Q. M. Hope, "Molière's Curtain Lines" (*French Studies*, XXVI, 1972) evidences a most promising approach to this problem, and I have ventured my own approach in "Comedy and Romance in Molière's 'dépits amoureux'" (*Australian Journal of French Studies*, VIII, 1971).

THIRTY YEARS
OF MOLIÈRE STUDIES:
A BIBLIOGRAPHY, 1942–1971
Paul Saintonge

TABLE OF CONTENTS

PREFACE

"Thirty Years of Molière Studies, A Bibliography, 1942–1971," continues my *Fifty Years of Molière Studies, A Bibliography, 1892–1941*, published in 1942 by The Johns Hopkins Press, and "Additions and Omissions" which appeared in *Modern Language Notes* 59: 282–5, 1944. Titles which had escaped my notice, particularly for the late 1930's, have been included here as well as reprints of previous important Molière studies which have been appearing within the last few years. In 1961 I prepared the section on Molière for *A Critical Bibliography of French Literature*, volume 3, *The Seventeenth Century*, edited by Nathan Edelman and published by The Syracuse University Press. I have included such items which appeared between 1942 and 1959 but have not given complete bibliographical data. I refer to the entry number as follows: See CrB, no.——, so that readers may have the pertinent information about these items.

In the last thirty years I have collected, read or had résuméd all material published in this period. When Professor Roger Johnson, Jr., of the University of Southern Mississippi kindly offered to publish this Molière bibliography as part of the Molière Festschrift, I had intended to conclude my research with the year 1969. But at the request of Professor H. Gaston Hall of the University of Warwick, England, I have carried the listings through 1971. The findings are not complete, however, for some material which appeared in 1971 has undoubtedly escaped my notice, particularly items which appeared in periodicals difficult to find in the United States. I do believe that all French, English, German, and American books and articles have been covered. Professor Hall has kindly furnished me with all his findings. I am also deeply indebted to Professor Otto Klapp, editor and publisher of the *Bibliographie der französischen Literaturwissenschaft*, for a copy of his findings on Molière for the tenth volume of his bibliography, which has just recently appeared but which will not reach me in time to consult. He also very kindly shared with me the listings he has for 1971, which will be published in his eleventh volume in 1973. I take this occasion to express my gratitude for his kindness and to compliment him on the thoroughness of his bibliographical research of the last ten years.

At this time I wish to express my sincerest thanks to several colleagues for their help in locating many titles and especially to three in particular: Nancy M. Devine and Elizabeth F. Christe of the Mount Holyoke College Library and Mary D. McFeely of the Amherst College Library.

Two substantial grants made much of the research in libraries in Europe and in the United States possible for me during the last few years. One, in 1966, from the Services Culturels de l'Ambassade de France à New York and the other, in 1968, from Mount Holyoke College, permitted me to consult materials in libraries in France, England, Italy and the United States. Colleagues at the Bibliothèque Nationale, the Arsenal, the Mazarine in Paris, and at the Taylorian at Oxford, particularly Professor Will G. Moore, facilitated my work in these institutions. I have also been extremely fortunate in having the cooperation of our four college libraries: Amherst, Mount Holyoke, Smith and the University of Massachusetts, which together have holdings that made possible the research of the last few months.

The material included is classified according to content, and cross-references are given when the material comes under two or more headings. All biographical material is given in one section and no attempt has been made to break it down as I did in my first bibliography. Under the heading Critical Studies, questions of language, style, technique, psychology, comedy, ideas, sources, influences, and reputation have been lumped together without a breakdown into individual categories as the titles themselves are indicative of the category. Nor have I made critical evaluations of this material, but have given, instead, references to reviews by outstanding Molière scholars and critics. The user can therefore have at hand one or several points of view about the book or the article. Professor Hall in his contribution to this volume will give critical comments on the most important Molière studies of the sixties and seventies.

A special section on individual plays, listed chronologically and not alphabetically, includes the most important editions published during the last thirty years. Complete bibliographical information on these editions has been omitted; only editor, place, publisher and number of pages have been given. Reviews of interpretations and performances in France are also included in this group as well as all critical studies of the individual plays.

In all sections of this bibliography any main entry which contains studies by various authors gives the author, title and page reference, and the later cross-references mention only the author and the number of the entry.

The section on translations is not intended to be complete, and here again, the bibliographical information has been reduced to the translator, place, publisher, year, and number of pages. Nor have foreign titles been given: the plays are listed chronologically under their French titles. The list of these translations in various foreign languages, though not exhaustive, gives the user of this bibliography an understanding of the efforts made within the last twenty years to give foreign audiences a sense of Molière's eternal appeal to all theater-goers. Some extraordinarily good translations have been made and are in themselves works of art, and it is gratifying to the Moliériste that the plays have been translated or adapted for East African audiences, Chinese and South Indian readers and Turkish Moliéristes.

I have employed the form of entry used in the *Critical Bibliography*. The abbreviation M. is used throughout for Molière, and when the place of publication is omitted, Paris is understood. I have altered in some cases the form of entry whenever I thought that the information given was made clearer than if I had adhered to the form used by the editors of the *Critical Bibliography*.

I regret that the bibliography can not include material appearing in 1972, though I have cited a few which I have read during the last few months. The year 1973, the tercentenary of Molière's death, will certainly produce many valuable books and articles, and my hope is that I can publish an "Additions and Ommissions" in 1974 which will list all these materials.

I am greatly indebted for my enthusiasm for Molière to students in my Molière course at Mount Holyoke College during forty years of teaching. As I wrote in 1942: "Generations of Mount Holyoke College students in the course on Molière have made contributions to this work." This is even truer now than then. I wish to express my sincerest thanks to one in particular, Madeleine Carusone, whose research and clerical assistance have been invaluable.

And I should like to dedicate this bibliography to my wife, Constance Meadnis Saintonge of Mount Holyoke College, who has stood by me for over forty years as an indefatigable research, editorial, and stylistic assistant. She is the Moliériste par excellence.

September, 1972.

LIST OF ABBREVIATIONS

AbES	Abstract of English studies (Champagne, Ill.)
ABou	Annales de Bourgogne (Dijon)
Aevum	Rassegna di scienze, storiche, linguistiche e filologiche (Milan)
AIFZa	Annales de l'Institut de Zagreb (Zagreb)
AIOc	Annales de l'Institut d'études occidentales (Paris)
AkZD	Akzente, Zeitschrift für Dichtung (Munich)
ALASH	Acta litteraria academiae scientiarum hungaricae (Budapest)
AlB	Almanach de Brioude (Brioude)
Alib	Amor di libro (Florence)
Anh	Anhembi (São Paolo, Brazil)
ANice	Annales de la Faculté de lettres et de sciences humaines de Nice (Nice)
ANor	Annales de Normandie (Caen)
APro	Année propédeutique (Paris)
Arch	Archiv für das Studium der neueren Sprachen und Literaturen (Braunschweig)
ASBe	Académie des sciences, belles-lettres et arts de Besançon (Besançon)
ASc	Avant-scène du théâtre (Paris)
ASLH	American Society of the Legion of Honor Magazine (New York)
AtL	Comptes-rendus de l'Athénée louisianais (New Orleans)
ATou	Annales de l'Université de Toulouse—Le Mirail (Toulouse)
AuL	L'Auvergne littéraire, artistique et historique (Clermont-Ferrand)
AUMLA	Journal of the Australasian Universities language and literature Association (Christchurch, New Zealand)
AUP	Annales de l'Université de Paris (Paris)
BALB	Bulletin de l'Académie royale de langue et de littérature française (Bruxelles)

BARB	Bulletin de l'Académie royale de Belgique (Bruxelles)
BAV	Bulletin de l'Académie du Var (Toulon)
BBB	Bulletin du bibliophile et du bibliothécaire (Paris)
BBFr	Bulletin des bibliothèques de France (Paris)
BC	Book collector (London)
BCLi	Bulletin critique du livre français (Paris)
BECh	Bibliothèque de l'Ecole des Chartres (Paris)
Bel	Belfagor, Rassegna di varia umantità (Messina, Florence)
BFol	Bulletin folklorique de l'Ile de France (Paris)
BGB	Bulletin de l'Association Guillaume Budé (Paris)
BHis	Bulletin hispanique—Annales de la Faculté des Lettres de Bordeaux (Bordeaux)
BIfr	Bulletin de l'Institut français de Copenhague (Copenhagen)
BILAL	Bulletin d'information du laboratoire d'analyse lexicologique (Paris)
BNan	Bulletin de la Société historique et archéologique de Nantes (Nantes)
BouF	Le Bouquiniste français (Paris)
BSAl	Bulletin de la Société historique et archéologique de l'Orne (Alençon)
BSAM	Bulletin de la Société des amis de Montaigne (Poitiers, Paris)
BSAube	Bulletin mensuel de la Société académique, d'agriculture. . . . du département de l'Aube (Troyes)
BSFl	Bulletin de la Société des amis de Flaubert (Rouen)
BSGuy	Bulletin de la Société des bibliophiles de Guyenne (Bordeaux)
BSIV	Bulletin et mémoires de la Société archéologique du département d'Ille-et-Vilaine (Rennes)
BSMo	Bulletin de la Société polymathique du Morbihan (Vannes)
BSOr	Bulletin de la Société archéologique et historique de l'Orléanais (Orléans)
BSPā	Bulletin de l'Université de São Paolo (São Paolo, Brazil)
BSPI	Bulletin de la Société de l'histoire de Paris et de l'Ile de France (Paris)
BucR	Bucknell Review (Lewisburg, Pa.)
CaAt	Cahiers d'analyse textuelle (Paris)
CaCh	Les Cahiers du chemin (Paris)
CaErom	Cahiers des étudiants romanistes (Leiden)
CAIEF	Cahiers de l'Association internationale des études françaises (Paris)
Car	Carrefour (Paris)
CasMF	Casopsis pro moderni filologii (Prague)
CB	Congrès Budé (Paris)
CBy	Cahiers archéologiques et historiques du Berry (Bourges)
CC	Chercheurs et curieux (Paris)
CCRB	Cahiers de la Compagnie Madeleine Renaud-Jean Louis Barrault (Paris)
CDr	Cahiers drômois (Tournon)
CDU	Centre de documentation universitaire (Paris)
CESCh	Centre d'enseignement supérieur (Chambéry)
CFr	Culture française. Rassegna di lingua, letteratura e civiltà francese (Bari)
CG	Colloquia germanica (Lexington, Ky.)
ChGL	Chroniques des gens de lettres (Paris)
CivM	Civiltà moderna (Florence)
CL	Comparative literature (Eugene, Ore.)

Clex	Cahiers de lexicologie (Besançon)
CLS	Comparative literature studies (Urbana, Ill.)
CNRS	Centre national de recherches scientifiques (Paris)
Conf	Annales-Conferencia (Paris)
Cped	Cahiers pédagogiques (Paris)
Crat	Cahiers rationalistes (Paris)
CrB	A critical bibliography of French literature, v. 3, The seventeenth century (Syracuse, N.Y.)
Crit	Critique (Paris)
CSai	Cahiers des saisons (Paris)
CSH	Colloques des sciences humaines—dramaturgie et société (Paris, 1968)
CSMar	Cahiers de Saint Martin (Pontoise)
Csu	Cahiers du sud (Marseilles)
Cult	Culture (Québec)
CVo	Le cerf volant (Paris)
D	Drama (London)
Diss abs	Dissertation abstracts (Ann Arbor, Mich.)
DrS	Drama survey (Minneapolis, Minn.)
DS	Diderot studies (Geneva)
DSS	Bulletin de la société des études du dix-septième siècle (Paris)
DT	Dialog Teateridskrift (Stockholm)
DurJ	Durham University journal (Durham, England)
Ec	Ecole. Classes du second cycle; enseignement littéraire (Paris)
EcoL	L'école des lettres (Paris)
Echo	L'Echo d'Auxerre (Auxerre)
Echoj	Echos juridiques girondins (Bordeaux)
ECl	Etudes classiques (Namur)
EcP	Ecrits de Paris (Paris)
Edda	Edda (Oslo)
EDMac	Essays in English literature of the classical period presented to Dougald Macmillan (Chapel Hill, N. C., 1967)
EdN	Education nationale (Paris)
EEPS	Epistèmonikè Epetèris tès Philosophikès Scholès tou Panepistimiou (Athens)
EF	Etudes françaises (Paris)
EGer	Etudes germaniques (Paris)
EJHT	Essays presented to John Haywood Thomas (Cardiffe, Wales, 1969)
EL	Etudes littéraires (Québec)
ELLF	Etudes de langue et de littérature françaises (Tokyo)
ELN	English language notes (Boulder, Colo.)
Eph	Etudes philosophiques (Paris)
EsCr	L'esprit créateur (Lawrence, Kansas)
ESov	Etudes soviétiques (Paris)
Et	Etudes [Pères de la Compagnie de Jésus] (Paris)
EtFr	Etudes françaises (Montreal)
ETJ	Educational theatre journal (Columbia, Mo.)
EtJE	De l'Encyclopédie à la Contrerévolution: Marmontel; études réunies et présentées par J. Ehrard (Clermont-Ferrand, 1970)

EUQ	Emory University quarterly (Decatur, Ga.)
Eur	Europe (Paris)
FestBB	Festschrift für Bernhard Blume (Göttingen, 1967)
FestEH	Festschrift für Ernst Howald (Erlenbach-Zurich, 1947)
FestKU	Festschrift udg. af Københavns Universitet (Copenhagen, 1964)
FestVK	Festschrift für Victor Klemperer (Halle, 1958)
FHS	French historical studies (Raleigh, N. C.)
Fig	Figura (Stockholm)
FL	Le Figaro littéraire (Paris)
Fl	Le Flambeau (Bruxelles)
FMLS	Forum for modern language studies (St. Andrews, Scotland)
FMod	Le français moderne (Paris)
FR	French studies (Oxford)
FTBG	Das französiche Theater vom Barock bis zur Gegenwart (Düsseldorf, 1969)
Git	Giornale italiano di filologia (Naples)
GMonat	Germanisch-romanische Monatsschrift (Heidelberg)
GR	Germanic review (New York)
Gua	Guadernos hispanoamericanos (Madrid)
HCL	Les humanités. Classes de lettres, section classique (Paris)
HFB	Het Franseboek (Amsterdam)
Hist	Historia (Paris)
HM	Hommes et monde (Paris)
Hmed	Histoire de la médecine (Paris)
HMo	Heute und Morgen (Schwerin)
Hmod	Les humanités. Classes de lettres, section moderne (Paris)
HomEC	Hommages au Doyen Etienne Cros (Cap, 1959)
HomEM	Hommages à Ernest Martinenche (Paris, 1939)
HomJB	Hommages à Jean Boyet (Bruxelles, 1964)
HSTh	High School Thespians (Cincinnati, Ohio)
HudR	Hudson review (New York)
Hum	Les humanités. Cycle d'observation (Paris)
ICLA	Proceedings of the 4th congress of the international comparative literary association (The Hague, 1966), v. 2.
Il	Informations littéraires (Paris)
IT	Illustre théâtre (Paris)
Ital	Italica (Evanston, Ill.)
ItS	Italian studies (Manchester, England)
JS	Journal des savants (Paris)
JSchil	Jahrbuch der deutschen Schillergesellschaft (Marbach)
KFLQ	Kentucky foreign language quarterly or Kentucky romance quarterly (Lexington, Ky.)
KKGe	Kölner Jahrbuch für Vor- und Frühgeschichte (Otto Doppelfeld zum Geburtstag) (Berlin)
KKSt	Književne-Kasalisne studije (Zagreb)
KN	Kwartalnik Neofilologiczny (Warsaw)
KR	Kenyon review (Gambier, Ohio)
KsStP	Ksiega pamiat kowa zu czei St Pigonia (Krakow, 1961)
LevT	Levende Talen (Groningen)
LFr	Les lettres françaises (Paris)

LHR	Lock Haven review (Lock Haven, Pa.)
Lib	The Library (Oxford)
LinAnt	Linguistica antwerpiensa (Antwerp)
LM	Lettres du monde (Paris)
Lmod	Les lettres modernes (Paris)
LN	Les lettres nouvelles (Paris)
LQ	Language quarterly, University of Southern Florida (Tampa, Fla.)
LRo	Les lettres romanes (Louvain)
Lst	Lingue straniere (Rome)
M.	Moliére
MCLB	Modern and classical language bulletin (Edmonton, Alberta)
MedF	Médecine de France (Paris)
MelDM	Mélanges Daniel Mornet (Paris, 1951)
MelKom	Mélanges de la Faculté des lettres de l'Université Komazawa (Tokyo)
MelMB	Mélanges de littérature comparée et de philologie offerts à Mieczyslaw Brahmer (Warsaw, 1967)
MelPJ	Mélanges d'histoire et de critique littéraire offerts à Pierre Jourda (Paris, 1970)
MelRL	Mélanges d'histoire littéraire offerts à Raymond Lebègue (Paris, 1969)
MF	Mercure de France (Paris)
MHis	Miroir de l'histoire (Paris)
MirH	Miroir historique (Paris)
MK	Maske und Kothurn (Graz-Köln)
MKS	Memoriam Karl Sandfield (Copenhagen, 1943)
ML	Modern languages (London)
MLEL	Modern languages, études littéraires (Montreal)
MLN	Modern language notes (Baltimore, Md.)
MLQ	Modern language quarterly (Seattle, Was.)
MLR	Modern language review (Cambridge, Mass.)
MMEV	Modern miscellany presented to Eugene Vinaver (Manchester, England, 1969)
Mon	Le Monde (Paris)
Monat	Der Monat (Berlin)
MP	Modern philology (Chicago)
Mro	Marche romane (Liège)
MSCr	Mémoire de la Société des sciences naturelles et archéologiques de la Creuse (Guéret)
MSprak	Moderna Sprak (Saltsjô-Duvnäs, Yugoslavia)
MSRC	Mémoire de la Société royale du Canada (Toronto)
Ncr	La nouvelle critique (Paris)
Neo	Neophilologus (Gröningen)
NL	Les nouvelles littéraires (Paris)
NMit	Neusprachliche Mitteilungen (Helsinski)
NRF	La nouvelle revue française (Paris)
NRI	Nouvelle revue d'Italie (Rome)
NRped	Nouvelle revue pédagogique de Paris (Paris)
NS	Die neueren Sprachen (Frankfort /M)
NTid	Nordisk Tidskrift för Vetenskap, Konst och Industri (Stockholm)
Op	Opéra, hebdomadaire du théâtre, du cinéma, des lettres et des arts (Paris)

OrL	Orbis litterarum (Copenhagen)
OsRom	L'Osservatore romano (Rome)
Palc	Palcoscenico (Milan)
PC	La pensée catholique (Paris)
Pen	La pensée (Paris)
PerF	Permanente franceze (Bucharest)
PhQ	Philological quarterly (Iowa Citty, Iowa)
PMed	La presse médicale (Paris)
PMLA	Publications of the Modern Language Association (New York)
Pre	Preuves (Paris)
PrMed	Progrès médical (Paris)
QL	La quinzaine littéraire (Paris)
RBG	Revue historique de Bordeaux et du département de la Gironde (Bordeaux)
RBP	Revue belge de philologie et d'histoire (Bruxelles)
RbPoi	Revue du Bas-Poitou (Fontenay-le-Comte)
RDDM	Revue des deux mondes (Paris)
Reflets	Reflets (Paris)
RenWLW	Renaissance and other studies in honor of William Leon Wiley (Chapel Hill, N. C., 1968)
REsth	Revue d'esthétique (Paris)
RestT	Restauration and 18th century theater (Chicago)
RevES	Revista Estudios (Madrid)
RFor	Romanische Forschungen (Frankfort /M)
RFr	Revue française (Paris)
RGB	Revue générale belge (Bruxelles)
RGen	Revue générale (Paris)
RHis	Revue historique (Paris)
RHLF	Revue de l'histoire littéraire de la France (Paris)
RHPh	Revue d'histoire de la pharmacie (Paris)
RHT	Revue de l'histoire du théâtre (Paris)
RJ	Romanistiches Jahrbuch (Hamburg)
RLau	Revue de l'Université laurentienne (Sudbury, Ontario)
RLav	Revue de l'Université de Laval (Québec)
RLC	Revue de littérature comparée (Paris)
RLM	Revue des lettres modernes (Paris)
RLMC	Rivista di letteratura moderne e comparate (Florence)
RLV	Revue des langues vivantes (Bruxelles)
RMa	Revue du département de la Manche (St. Lô)
RMed	Revue de la Méditerranée (Algiers)
RMM	Revue de métaphysique et de morale (Paris)
RN	Romance notes (Chapel Hill, N. C.)
RNat	La revue nationale (Bruxelles)
RNCut	Revista nacional del cultura (Caracas)
Rnou	Revue nouvelle (Tournai-Paris)
ROtt	Revue de l'Université d'Ottawa (Ottawa)
RP	Revue de Paris (Paris)
RPol	Review of politics (Notre Dame, Ind.)
RR	Romanic review (New York)
Rrat	Revue rationaliste (Paris)
RRom	Revue romane (Copenhagen)

WZFSU   Wissenschaftliche Zeitschrift der Friedrich Schiller Universität (Jena)
WZH   Wissenschaftliche Zeitschrift der Humboldt Universität (Berlin)
YFS   Yale French studies (New Haven, Conn.)
ZFSL   Zeitschrift für fransösische Sprache und Literatur (Wiesbaden)

I   BIBLIOGRAPHIES

1. Debauve, J. L. Notes sur les éditions de M. de la bibliothèque publique de Vannes. BSMo: 8–12, July, 1966.

2. Guibert, Albert-Jean. Bibliographie des oeuvres de M. publiées au XVIIIe siècle. CNRS, 1961. 2 v. Supplément, 1965. 40p.
   rev. L. Chancerel *in* RHT 14: 68–9, 1962; G. Mongrédien *in* DSS 56: 82–3, 1962. G. Rouzet *in* RN 34: 339–40, 1962.

3. Hall, H. Gaston. Quelques ouvrages récents sur M. StF 29: 299–302, 1966.

4. Mélèse, Pierre. Activités moliéresques, 1940–1948. RHT 1 : 25–32, 1948.

5. Moore, Will G. M. studies: present position. FS 1: 291–301, 1947. *See* CrB 2127.

6. Morel, Jacques. Quelques publications récentes relatifs à M. JS 65: 250–2, 1967.

7. Picard, Raymond. Etats présents des études moliéresques. IL 10 : 53–6, 1958.

8. Saintonge, Paul & Robert W. Christ. Fifty years of M. studies, a bibliography, 1892–1941. Baltimore, Johns Hopkins Press, 1942. 313 p. *See* CrB 2129.

9. ———. Omissions and additions to *Fifty years of M. studies.* MLN 59: 282–5, 1944.

10. ———. M. *in* A critical bibliography of French literature, v. 3: The seventeenth century, ed. by Nathan Edelman (Syracuse, N.Y., Syracuse Univ. Press, 1961): 226–43.

II   AUTOGRAPHS AND MANUSCRIPTS

11. Contades, Comte Gérard de. Une enquête moliéresque. BSAI 5 : 342–4, 1950.

12. Courville, Luce. Une nouvelle signature de M. (Nantes, 1648). RHT 60: 313–5, 1960.

13. Dulait, Suzanne. Inventaire raisonné des autographes de M., avec facsimiles de tous les autographes dont on possède encore l'original ou la reproduction figurée (1643–1967). Geneva, Droz, 1967. 112 p.
    rev. H. G. Hall *in* StF 35: 357–8, 1968; G. Mongrédien *in* RHLF 69: 690–1, 1969; P. Saintonge *in* FR 42: 626, 1969; W. D. Howarth *in* FS 24: 290, 1970.

14. Gobillot, René. La venue et les manuscrits de M. au Château de la Ferrière. RHT 4: 413–4, 1951.

15. Lenôtre, Georges. Les papiers de M. Hist 270: 74–5, 1969.

16. Levron, Jacques. Armande Béjart, Feucherolles et les papiers de M. MF 338: 161–6, 1951.

17. Maxfield-Miller, Elizabeth & Madeleine Jurgens. Etat actuel des autographes de M. RHT 19: 371–6, 1967.

18. Robert, J. Un inédit du maître d'écriture de M. (George Pinel). RHT 19: 377–82, 1967.
    rev. H. G. Hall *in* StF 36: 551, 1968.

III   ICONOGRAPHY

19. Barrault, Jean-Louis. Portrait de M. CCRB 49: 3–55, 1965.
20. Bjurström. Per. Les illustrations de Boucher pour M. Fig., n.s.1: 138–52, 1959.
21. Coèle, René T. Le M. en habit de théâtre du Musée Cantini à Marseilles. RHT 8: 45–7, 1956.
22. ———. Madeleine Béjart et M., modèles des peintres, Nicolas Mignard et Pierre Mignard, Avignon, 1657. RHT 9: 276–90, 1957.
23. Descotes, Maurice. M., apologiste de Mignard. EEPS 12: 248–65, 1962.
24. Hammelmann, H. A. A cancel in the Boucher M., 1734. BC 14: 367, 1965.
25. Köllmann, Erich. M.-Boucher-Berlin. KJGe 9: 177–80, 1967/8.
26. Tieghen, Philippe van. Die Geburt des Dramas aus dem Geist des Theaters; zur Umwertung des M.-Bildes. MK 2: 269–73, 1956.

IV   EDITIONS OF COMPLETE WORKS

27. Oeuvres complètes. *Ed. by* René Bray. Belles Lettres, 1935–52. 8 v. *See* CrB 2137.
28. Oeuvres complètes. *Ed. by* Maurice Rat. Gallimard (BibP), 1947, 1951, 1956. 2 v. *See* CrB 2138.
29. Oeuvres complètes. *Ed. by* Gustave Michaut. Imp. Nationale, 1949. 11 v. *See* CrB 2138.
30. Oeuvres complètes. Ed. établie, présentée et annotée par René Bray et Jacques Scherer. Club du meilleur livre, 1955–6. 3 v.
31. Théâtre. Ed. annotée par Pierre-Aimé Touchard. Club des libraires de France, 1956. 4 v.
    rev. L. Chancerel *in* RHT 11: 232–3, 1959.
32. Oeuvres complètes. Oxford, Univ. Press, 1959. 659 p. (Reprint of the 1900 first edition; the Despois & Mesnard text.)
33. Oeuvres complètes. Texte établi, avec préface, chronologie de la vie de M., bibliographie, notices, notes . . . par Robert Jouanny. Garnier, 1960, 1962, 1965. 961 p.
34. Théâtre. Préface de Henry A. Parys. Documentation photographique. (Bibliothèque de la Comédie-Française) Ambassade du livre, 1961.
35. Oeuvres complètes. Préface de Pierre-Aimé Touchard. Ed. du Seuil, 1962. 667 p. (Collection l'Intégrale) *Also* N. Y., Macmillan, 1962, 1963. 675 p.
36. Théâtre complet. Préface et notes de Jean Vagne. Lausanne, Ed. Rencontre, 1962. 5 v.
37. Oeuvres complètes. Chronologie, introduction et notice par Georges Mongrédien, Garnier-Flammarion, 1964–5. 3 v.
38. Théâtre. Présenté et annoté par Alfred Simon. Club du livre, 1965. 1 v.
39. Théâtre complet. Présenté par Marcel Jouhandeau. Notes par Maurice Rat. Hachette, 1963–7. 4 v. (Livre de poche)
40. Théâtre complet. Ed. réalisée et annotée par Pierre-Aimé Touchard. Levallois-Périer, Cercle du bibliophile, 1968. 6 v.
41. Oeuvres complètes, avec une vie de l'auteur, un examen de chaque pièce, des études sur les personnages et des notes inédites par Jean Meyer. M. Gonon, 1967–70. 6 v.

42. Théâtre. Introduction par Marcel Achard. Club des classiques, 1969. 2 v.
43. Oeuvres. Ed. pour le tricentenaire de la mort de M. (Reproduction de l'édition de 1735, illustrée par Boucher.) De l'Ormeraie, 1970–3, 9 v.
44. Oeuvres complètes. Ed. et établies par Georges Couton, avec notes, chronologie, bibliographie, variantes . . . . Gallimard (BibP), 1971. 2 v.
    rev. G. Mongrédien *in* NL 2326: 12, 1972.

SELECTED PLAYS

45. Théâtre choisi. Texte intégrale établi sur l'édition collective de 1682, avec introduction . . . . par Maurice Rat. Garnier, 1954, 1958, 1962. 701 p.
46. Théâtre choisi. Texte établi et présenté par Georges Mongrédien. Presses universitaires, 1960. 288 p.
47. Théâtre choisi. Ed. publiée conformément au texte de l'édition des Grands Ecrivains de la France avec des notices et des notes par Ernest Thirton. Hachette, 1960. 1890 p.
48. Théâtre. Tallandier, 1967. 2 v. (collection le Trésor des lettres françaises).
49. Comédies-ballets. *Ed. by* Jacques Copeau. (Lyon), I.A.C., 1944. 2 v. *See* CrB 2140.
49a. Raeders, Georges. M. Montreal, Ed. de l'Arbre. 1944. 2 v.
    Contains: Les Précieuses ridicules, l'Ecole des maris, l'Ecole des femmes, Don Juan, le Misanthrope, le Médecin malgré lui, l'Avare, le Tartuffe, le Bourgeois gentilhomme, les Fourberies de Scapin, les Femmes savantes, le Malade imaginaire.

V BIOGRAPHIES AND BIOGRAPHICAL MATERIAL

50. Allainval, l'abbé. Mémoires sur M. et sur Madame Guérin, sa veuve, suivis des Mémoires sur Baron et sur Mlle. Lecouvreur (Ponthieu, 1822). *Reprint,* Geneva, Slatkine, 1968. 348 p.
51. Alliès, Albert Paul. Une ville d'Etats, Pézenas au XVIe et XVIIe siècle. M. à Pézenas. Préf. de M. le Duc de Castries, illus. de Georges Maury. 3e éd. Montpellier, Causse et Castelnau, 1963. 389 p.
52. Bäckvall, H. Comment M. prononçait-il "Monsieur"? MSprak 62: 156–61, 1968.
53. Baldner, R. W. M. and his daughter. MLN 72: 505–6, 1957. *See no.* 125.
54. Berlioz, Jean. Les comédiens du Duc de Savoie à Lyon en 1672. VP: 206–7, Jan. 1965.
55. Bordonove, Georges. M., génial et famillier. Robert Laffont, 1967. 541 p.
    rev. G. Mongrédien *in* NL 45: 7, 1967; L. Losito *in* Cult 15: 13–4, 1968; R. Pouilliart *in* LR 23: 182–3, 1969.
56. Boudin, Mme. Histoire des intrigues amoureuses de M. et de sa femme. Frankfort, Arnaud, 1967. 96 p.
57. Boulet-Sautel, Marguerite. M., Orléans et le droit. BSOr n.s.3: 61–73, 1964.
58. Bouvet, M. La maison où habita M., rue des Jardins. RHT 3: 415, 1951.
59. Bray, René. Le répertoire de la troupe de M. (1659–73). MélDM: 91–8, 1951. *See* CrB 2146.
60. ——. Le mariage de M. et le *Régistre* de La Grange. RHT 3: 179–81, 1951.
61. ——. M., homme de théâtre. Mercure de France, 1954. 398 p. *See* CrB 2190.
62. Brett, Vladimir. M., herec, režisér, dramaturg. CasMF 42: 209–17, 1960.

[Continuation of his prefaces and comments for the Czech edition of *Pièces choisies* (Prague, Hry, 1953/6, 4 v.)]

63.   ——. M. Prague, Orbis, 1967. 260 p.
       rev. F. Götz *in* CasMF 50: 247-8, 1968.

64.   Brisson, Pierre. M., sa vie dans ses oeuvres. Gallimard, 1943. 316 p.
       See CrB 2147.

65.   Bulgakov, Michail Afanas' evic. Zhisn' gospodina de Mol'era. Moscow, Molodaya Gvardiya, 1963. 237 p.

66.   ——. La vita del signor di M. Intro. di Veņjamín Kavérin; trad. di Emilia Piersigilli. Milan, Mondadori, 1969. 240 p.
       rev. A. Rigoni *in* OsRom: 10–1, Nov. 5, 1969.

67.   ——. Das Leben des Herrn de M. *Ausg. von* Thomas Reschke. Berlin, Volk und Welt, 1970. 240 p. *Also* Neuwied, Luchterhand, 1971. 170 p.

68.   ——. The life of Monsieur de M. *Tr. by* Mirra Ginsberg. N. Y., Funk & Wagnalls, 1970. 259 p. *Also in* The early plays of Mikhail Bulgakov, *tr. by* Carl R. Proffer and Ellendea Proffer. Indianapolis, Indiana Univ. Press, 1972 *which also contains his* Cabal of hypocrits.

69.   ——. Le roman de Monsieur de M., suivi de La cabale des dévots. *Tr. par* Paul Kalinine. Champs libre, 1972. 336 p.

70.   Cairncross, John. M., bourgeois et libertin. Nizet, 1963. 192 p.
       rev. J. C. Tournaud *in* RHLF 65: 298–9, 1965; J. P. Chauveau *in* RSH 122–3: 311–4, 1966.

71.   Caza, Marcel. M. à Toulouse. L'Auta 263: 50–6; 264: 70–1, 1957.

72.   Chabannes, Jacques. Mademoiselle M. Fayard, 1961. 199 p.

73.   Chancerel, Léon. M. Presses littéraires de France, 1953. 73 p. *See* CrB 2149.

74.   ——. M., chef de troupe et metteur en scène. Entretiens avec Louis Jouvet, Pierre Bertin, Dominique Blanchar. CCRB 26 bis: 8–27, 1959.

75.   ——. Les années d'apprentissage ou de Paris à Paris (1622–58). *See no. 220.*

76.   Charpentier, John. M. Tallandier, 1942. 346 p. *Reprinted* 1948. *See* CrB 2150.

77.   Chevalley, Sylvie. M. La Comédie Française, 1963. 64 p.
       rev. H. G. Hall *in* StF 24: 552, 1964.

78.   Cingria, H. M. en Languedoc. LF: 9, May 9, 1957.

79.   Copeau, Jacques. La voix de M. CCRB 15: 2–9, 1956. *Reprint of his 1922 article.*

80.   Coulaudon, Aimé. De Royat à M. AuL 33: 26–8, 1956.

81.   ——. Par sa grand-mère, M. était auvergnat. RSCl 14: 15, 1963.

82.   Courville, Luce. M. à Nantes. RBP 71: 121–2, 1960.

83.   Couton, Georges. L'état civil d'Armande Béjart, femme de M., ou historique d'une légende. RSH 115: 311–51, 1964.
       rev. D. Dalla Valle *in* StF 24: 553, 1964.

84.   ——. La jeunesse de M., ou M. "rive-gauche." LF 1427: 7–8, 1972.

85.   Deflandre, Maurice. En marge d'un 350e anniversaire de naissance. Les gagne-petits de la rue au temps de M. RNat 44: 121–2, 1972.

86.   Deierkauf-Holsboer, S. Wilma. La famille de la mère de M. DSS 28: 221–30, 1955.

87.   Descaves, Pierre. Monsieur M. Bruxelles, Brepols, 1958. 134 p.

88.   Doménech, Ricardo. M. Gua 72: 420–8, 1968.

89.   Donnay, Maurice. Le curieux ménage de M. Hist 119: 243–9, 1956.

90.   Dorman, Menachem. Môlyer. Tel Aviv, Hakibutz Hamenchad, 1956. 66 p.

91.   Dussane, Béatrix. Un comédien nommé M. Plon, 1956. 284 p. *See* CrB 2152.

92. ———. Il y a trois cents ans, le mariage de M. Conf 140: 24–33, 1962.

93. Elmquist, Carl Johan. M. Copenhagen, Gads Forlag, 1966. 96 p.

94. Escofet, José. M., su vida y su obra. Mexico, Editora nacional, 1957. 208 p.

95. Farnoux-Reynaud, Lucien. L'aventure comique ou M. sans littérature. Lyon, Imp. du salut public, 1944. 176 p.

96. Fau, Guy. L'énigme de la mort de M. CDr 3: 27–33, 1965.

97. Forestier, Henri. Les costumes de scène de M. Echo 53: 3–4, 1964.

98. Fornairon, Ernest. Une plaisante aventure de Mademoiselle M. Hist 168: 569–73, 1960.

99. Frank, André. M. à Bordeaux et à Cadillac. CCRB 26: 17–8. 1959. *See no.* 167.
    rev. L. Derla *in* StF 16: 153, 1962.

100. Galt, Tom. Appel aux Moliéristes. DSS 48: 74–5, 1960.
    [Information about Jean Lescuyer, M.'s great-grandfather.]

101. Gaxotte, Pierre. M., fameux comédien. Hachette, 1971. 133 p.
    rev. G. Sanvoisin *in* RDDM 24: 503–5, 1971.

102. Góth, Sándor. Wenn M. ein Tagebuch geführt hätte. Budapest, Corvina, 1955. 204 p. *Edited by* Lázló Püdör, *tran. by* Géza Engl.

103. Graves, Geneviève. Double naissance de Mlle M. MHis 102: 710–16, 1958.

104. Grimarest, Jean Léonor le Gallois de. La vie de Monsieur de M., éd. par Georges Mongrédien. Brient, 1955. 174 p. *See* CrB 2154.

105. Guillot, Michel. La famille de M. à Suresnes. Ssu 5: 228–32, 1965.

106. Guirec, Jean. Tricentenaire de l'arrivée de M. à la Grange des Prés et son départ du Languedoc. ChGL 92: 26–8, 1957.

107. Henry, Hélène. Armande Béjart, femme de M., était-elle sa fille? SMB 26: 1538–40, 1549–52, 1964.

108. Jenny, J. Où M. fut-il reçu licencié en droit? CBy 15: 8–9, 1968.

109. Jurgens, Madeleine. Deux logis inconnus de M., Place du Palais Royal. DSS 48: 16–27, 1960.
    rev. F. Simone *in* StF 16: 153, 1962.

110. ——— & M. A. Fleury. Documents du Minutier central concernant l'histoire littéraire (1650–1700), analysés par . . . Presses Universitaires de France, 1960. 510 p.
    rev. F. Simone *in* StF 18: 548, 1962.

111. ——— & Elizabeth Maxfield-Miller. Cent ans de recherches sur M., sur sa famille et sur les comédiens de sa troupe. Préface d'A. Chamson. Imprimerie nationale, 1963. 855 p.
    rev. W. G. Moore *in* MLR 59:476–8, 1964; Y. Landers *in* Rhist 232: 291–2, 1964; H. G. Hall *in* StF 24: 553, 1964; G. Mongrédien *in* RDDM 17: 397–405, 1964, *and in* RHT 17: 195–7, 1965; R. J. Nelson *in* FR 38: 803–4, 1965; P. Saintonge *in* MLN 80: 417–9, 1965; P. Mélèse *in* DSS 75: 85, 1967; R. Lanbreaux *in* Cped 70: 59–60, 1967.

112. Kohn, Richard. La vie catholique et la mort de M. Bref: 98, 1966.

113. Kubokawa, Eisui. Autour de M., sur les relations entre Madeleine et Armande Béjart. MélKom 20, 1962.

114. LaForce, le Duc de. M. s'est-il assis à la table de Louis XIV? Hist 98: 55–8, 1955.

115. LaGrange, Charles Varlet, sieur de. Le *Régistre* de LaGrange . . . *ed. by* Bert E. & Grace P. Young. Droz, 1947. 2 v. *See* CrB 2158.

116. Larnac, Jean. Molière ou Mulier? CSu 35: 99–105, 1952.

117. Laulan, Robert. Le départ de M. de la Grange des Prés. MF 331: 707–8, 1957.

118. Levron, Jacques. Une fille de M. MF 335: 348–51, 1959.

119. Lima, Cristiano. M. *in his* A vida amorosa dos homens celebres. Lisbon, Editorial enciclopédia, 1946. 337 p.

120. Loiselet, Jean-Louis. De quoi vivait M.? Ed. des deux rives, 1950. 129 p. *See* CrB 2160.

121. Magne, Emile. M. et la maison des Pilliers des Halles. DSS 23: 522–71, 1954.

122. Mander, Gertrud. Jean-Baptiste M. Hannover, Friedrich, 1967. 163 p.

123. Maxfield-Miller, Elizabeth. A document of April 12, 1672, signed by M. RR 47: 166–78, 1956.

124. ———. La famille de la mère de M. DSS 40: 258–72, 1958.

125. ———. M. and his homonym Louis de Mollier. MLN 74: 612–21, 1959.
    rev. L. Derla *in* StF 11: 347, 1960; P. Mélèse *in* RHT 12: 150, 1960. *See no.* 53.

126. ———. M.'s tercentenaries 1959–1973. FR 34: 389–92, 1960.

127. ———. Les Poqueline, grands-parents de M. d'après quelques documents inédits. Appendice: quelques tableaux généologiques de la famille M. RHT 14: 29–60, 1962.
    rev. M. Richter *in* StF 19: 154–5, 1963.

128. ———. New findings on M. and his first patron in southern France: Bernard de Nogaret, duc d'Epernon. RN 10: 94–102, 1968.
    rev. W. Leiner *in* StF 40: 157, 1970.

129. Mélèse, Pierre. Les demeures parisiennes de M. MF 329: 260–95, 1957.
    rev. F. Simone *in* StF 6: 495, 1958.

130. Meyer, Jean. M. Perrin, 1963. 315 p.
    rev. H. G. Hall *in* StF 24: 553, 1964.

131. Michaut, Gustave. *Reprint of his* La jeunesse de M. (1922), Les débuts de M. à Paris (1923) & Les luttes de M. (1925). Geneva, Slatkine, 1970.

132. Moliériste, le. *Reprint.* Geneva, Slatkine, 1969.

133. Mongrédien, Georges. La vie privée de M. Hachette, 1950. 246 p. *See* CrB 2172.

134. ———. Les biographies de M. au XVIIIe siècle. RHT 8: 342–54, 1956.

135. ———. Connaissance de la vie parisienne de M. BSPI 89: 42–3, 1963.

136. ———. Recueil des textes et des documents du XVIIIe siècle relatifs à M. CNRS, 1965. 2 v.
    rev. F. Simone *in* StF 28: 149, 1966; R. Guichemerre *in* RHLF 67: 625–6, 1967: B. Beugnot *in* EF 3: 105–11, 1967; J. Lough *in* Erasmus 23: 801–4, 1971.

137. ———. Le dernier jour de M. NL: 2095, 1967.

138. Moore, Will G. M.'s last word. StJO: 188–97, 1953.

139. Moudouès, Rose-Marie. Chronologie de la vie de M. Eur. 385–6: 148–55, 1961. *See no.* 220.

140. Neveux, G. Il y a trois cents ans . . . M. (retour à Paris). IT 4: 8–13, 1958.

141. Nicolet, André. Grimarest's M.-biografi. MKS: 158–63, 1943.

142. Noël, André. M., Armande Béjart à St. Germain, Marly et Feucherolles. Le Vieux Marly 3: 3–7, s.d.

143. Obase, Takuzo. A propos de quelques créances de Poquelin père. ELLF 8: 1–2, 1966.

144. Origine du surnom J-B Poquelin. CC 5(54): 542-4, 1955.

145. Ormesson, Comte Wladimir d'. Tricentenaire du départ de M. de la cour

du Prince de Conti et du théâtre des Etats de Languedoc. RDDM 10: 716–24, 1957. *Also* Firmin-Didot, 1957. 12 p.

146. Perrat, Charles, *éd.* Araspe, histoire véritable écrite par une dame de la cour. Texte établi sur l'unique édition de 1672. Avignon, 1959. 104 p. (*Attributed to Madeleine Béjart*)

147. Person, Maurice de. M. à Grenoble. Miroir de l'histoire 51: 420, 1954.

148. Pocquet du Haut-Jussé, B-A. Sur les pas de M. à Rennes, rue Saint Michel. BSIV 74: 65–8, 1964.

149. Rat, Maurice. Inconnues dans la vie de M. IT 7: 33–5, 1956.

150. ——. Quatre gloires d'un grand lycée (Louis-le-Grand). FL: 8, May 18, 1963.

151. Reed, Gervais E. M.'s privilege of 18 March 1671. Lib 20: 57–63. 1965.
    rev. H. G. Hall *in* StF 27: 546, 1965.

152. Rochemay-Gordios, G. M. M. et sa servante, ou simplicité du génie, tableau intime de la vie de M. Billaudot, 1954. 18 p.

153. Rousin, A. M. à Dijon. ABou 29: 181–9, 1957.
    rev. F. Simone *in* StF 6: 496, 1958.

154. Scherer, Jacques. Réflexions sur Armande Béjart. RHLF 69: 393–403, 1969.

155. Servat, Pierre. M., juriste orléanais. Orléans, Imp. du Bourdon-Blanc, 1964. 20 p.

156. Simon, Alfred. M. par lui-même. Ed. du Seuil, 1957. 191 p.
    rev. P. Mélèse in RHT 10: 52–3, 1958; *See* CrB 2246; *also* no. 223.

157. Thoorens, Léon. La vie passionnée de M. Viviers, Gérard & Cie., 1959. 341 p.
    rev. G. Sion *in* RGB 94: 137–40, 1958; N. Houssa *in* VW 32: 295–6, 1958.

158. ——. *tr. as* The king's player *by* Alice Brown. London, Elek, 1960, 287 p.

159. ——. M. à vif. RGB 94: 84–97, 1958.

160. ——. Le dossier M. Viviers, Gérard & Cie., 1964. 317 p.
    rev. A. Sorelli *in* VW 38: 204–5, 1964; H. G. Hall *in* StF 29: 299–302, 1966; *also contains* S. W. Deierkauf-Holsboer. Les difficultés d'une jeune compagnie au XVIIe siècle, 39–46 *and* Jean Anouilh. La mort de M., 171–88.

161. ——. La fin de M. fut-elle naturelle? RGB 105: 55–66, 1968.

162. Tombe commune de M. et de LaFontaine. CC 9: 638–41, 1959.

163. Touchard, Pierre-Aimé. Le 24 octobre, 1658. CCRB 26: 8–12, 1959.
    rev. L. Derla *in* StF 16: 153, 1962.

164. Toudouze, Georges G. M., bourgeois de Paris et tapissier du roi. Floury, 1946. 186 p. *See* CrB 2177.

165. Tricentenaire du séjour de M. à Lyon. Lyon, 112, quai Pierre Scize, 1953. 66 p. *Also in* Reflets, Feb.-Mar., 1953.

166. Vaultier, Robert. M. et le droit. Vj 598: 6–7, 1957.

167. d'Welles, J. M. en Guyenne, à Cadillac et à Bordeaux. RGB 4: 273–94, 1955. *Also* Bordeaux, Bière, 1955. 23 p.
    rev. R. T. Coèle *in* RHT 9: 321–2, 1957.

168. Y. N. M. et la Normandie: des coïncidences réelles ou imaginaires mais pas de conclusion positive. RMa 9: 159–60, 1967.

VI L'ILLUSTRE THÉÂTRE, LA TROUPE DE MONSIEUR, LA TROUPE DU ROI, MOLIÈRE AND HIS CONTEMPORARIES

169. Abdella, Christine von Hülphershausen. Donneau de Visé and M. (Thesis, Rice University, 1969) 218 p. Diss abs A 30: 1974, 1969/70.

170. Anatole, Charles. Conti, M. et quelques autres. AIOc 2: 259–70, 1966.
      rev. S. Crotto *in* StF 36: 550, 1968.
171. Beer, Jean de. M. et les débuts de Jean Racine. IT 5: 52–6, 1956.
171a. Berraud, H. M. et Lulli étaient-ils contemporains? IT 5: 49–50, 1956.
172. Bowers, Alice T. Allusions to the private life of Louis XIV in the dramatic
      literature of the seventeenth century. (Thesis, Univ. of Missouri, 1968)
      222 p. Diss abs A 29: 2701, 1968/9.
173. Busson, Henri. La pension de Louis Béjart. RHT 4: 250, 1952.
174. Chagny, André. Une grande comédienne lyonnaise: Marquise. Lyon, Le
      Crocodile, 1940. Non-paginé.
175. Chancerel, Léon. Le comédien M. et ses camarades italiens. IT 4: 11–40,
      1945. *See* CrB 2148.
176. ——. Architecture et décorations. 2ᵉ cahier, XVIIᵉ siècle. Lyon, Ed. de la
      Hutte, 1945. 32 p. [Salles de spectacle au temps de M.]
177. Chevalley, Sylvie. Album théâtre classique: la vie théâtrale sous Louis XIII
      et Louis XIV. Iconographie réunie et commentée par . . . Gallimard,
      1970. 340 p.
      rev. H. Coèle *in* RHT 22: 166–8, 1970.
178. Collinet, Jean-Pierre. A propos de René Le Pays. Deux énigmes grenobloises
      et moliéresques. RTG 3: 17–21, 1971. [Le Pays (1636–90) satirized by
      Boileau.]
179. Cosnier, Colette. Jodelet: un acteur du XVIIᵉ siècle devenu un type. RHLF
      62: 329–52, 1962.
      rev. C. Rizza *in* StF 18: 545, 1962.
180. Deierkauf-Holsboer, S. Wilma. Les difficultés d'une jeune compagnie au
      XVIIᵉ siècle. NL: 1–2, May, 22, 1952. *See no. 160.*
      rev. L. Chancerel *in* RHT 4: 270–1, 1952.
181. ——. Le théâtre de l'Hôtel de Bourgogne: v. 2. Le théâtre de la Troupe Royale,
      1638–1680; documents inédits, planches. Nizet, 1970. 239 p.
      rev. G. Mongrédien *in* RHT 22: 164–6, 1970.
182. Denoeu, François. M. et ses amis (et les gaîtés de la consigne). Aire-sur-la-
      Lys, Mordacq, 1950. 80 p.
183. Détharé, V. Un élève de M. (Baron) *in his* Images et pèlerinages littéraires
      (Ed. du Vieux Colombier, 1962): 34–7.
184. Guérin-Beaupré. François Raisin de la troupe de M. BSAl 7: 32–45, 1953.
185. Jurgens, Madeleine. Quelques amis et protégés de M. RHT 14: 22–8, 1962.
      [*Marriage contracts signed by M. in 1661 and 1662.*]
      rev. M. Richter *in* StF 19: 154, 1963.
186. Labracherie, Pierre. Les voyages de l'Illustre théâtre. CCRB 5: 97–106, 1954.
187. Larnac, Jean. *See no. 116.* [*M.'s relationship to Baron.*]
188. Lowe, Robert W. Marc-Antoine Charpentier, compositeur chez M. ECl
      33: 34–41, 1965.
      rev. H. G. Hall *in* StF 26: 356, 1965.
189. Ludovicy, Ernest. Racine et M., étude de quelques aspects apparemment
      commune à leurs oeuvres. Luxembourg, Imp. St. Paul, s.d. 65 p.
190. M. jugé par ses contemporains, avec une notice par A. Poulet-Malassis.
      [*Reprint of the 1877 ed.* Geneva, Slatkine, 1968. 175 p.]
191. Maurice-Amour, Mme. L. Comment Lully et ses poètes humanisent dieux
      et héros. CAIEF 17: 59–95, 1965.
192. Micolon, F. Un Brivadois dans la troupe de M.: Jean Meindre. AlB 46: 76–
      90, 1966.

193. Mongrédien, Georges. Notes sur quatre comédiens de l'Illustre Théâtre. RHLF 9: 309–10, 1957.
194. ———. Le meilleur ami de M.: Chapelle. MF 329: 86–109, 1957.
     rev. F. Simone *in* StF 6: 496, 1958.
195. ———. La vie quotidienne des comédiens au temps de M. Hachette, 1966. 288 p.
     rev. J. Scherer *in* RSH 128: 655, 1967.
196. ———. Dictionnaire biographique des comédiens français au XVIIe siècle, suivi d'un inventaire des troupes (1650–1710), d'après des documents inédits. CNRS, 1961. 239 p.
     rev. F. Simone *in* StF 22: 153–4, 1964.
197. Raeders, Georges & Bricio de Abreu. Tri-centenario de Illustre Théâtre de M. Rio-de-Janeiro, Praço Floriano, 1945. 112 p. [*Special no. of Dom Casmurro, Christmas,* 1945.]
198. Rat, Maurice. M. et Louis XIV ou les goûts du Roi et des Mortemart. IT 5: 27–30, 1956.
198a. Robert, Jean. Comédiens, musiciens et opéras à Avignon 1610–1715. RHT 15: 275–323, 1965.
     rev. G. Mirandola *in* StF 10: 150–1, 1966.
199. Whitefield, J. H. A note on M. and Mlle de Scudéry. Le parole e le idee (Naples) 5: 175–87, 1963.
200. Wortely, W. Victor. Tallemant des Réaux: a microcosmic M. LQ 4: 58–78, 1965.
     rev. W. Leiner *in* StF 32: 354–5, 1967.
201. Young, Edward. Michel Baron, acteur et auteur dramatique. *Reprint of 1904 ed.* Geneva, Slatkine, 1972.
202. Zarb, Mireille, *transcriptor.* La faillite de l'Illustre Théâtre. RHT 5: 286–9, 1953. *See no.* 182.

VII   THE CORNEILLE-MOLIÈRE-LOUIS XIV PROBLEM

203. Douchin, Jacques. Y-a-t-il une énigme M.? Blfr 12: 64–8, 1962.
204. Freudmann, Félix R. Is there *Un cas M.*? MLQ 19: 53–9, 1958.
     rev. F. Simone *in* StF 6: 495, 1958.
205. Garçon, Maurice. Sous le masque de M. Louis XIV est M. Traduit de l'anglais par J. M. Figuière, 1919. 32 p. *2d. ed.* Fayard, 1953. 62 p.
206. ———. Louis XIV est-il M.? Hist 74: 25–34, *and* 75: 174, 1953.
207. Landers, Y. Du nouveau sur M. RHis 232: 291–4, 1964.
208. Lavaud, Georges. Une énigme? Bayou 21: 533–41, 1957.
209. Lebois, André. Corneille sous le masque de M. RMéd 17: 563–7, 1957.
210. Lenôtre, George. M. était-il Louis XIV? Hist 18: 451–4, June, 1951.
211. Mongrédien, Georges. M. sous le masque. NL: 2, Jan. 9, 1964.
212. ———. Du nouveau sur M. RDDM 17: 397–405, 1964.
213. Poulaille, Henry. Corneille, auteur de *l'Amour médecin.* Aesculape (Paris): 146–60, July-Aug., 1951.
214. ———. *Tartuffe* ou la comédie de l'hypocrisie, présentée et préfacée par H. P. Amiot-Dumont, 1951. 270 p.
     See G. Mongrédien *in* EdN: May, 1951; 0. Saint-Girons *in* Arts: Sept., 1951: "*A propos de Tartuffe, réponse à Poulaille.*"
215. ———. Corneille, nègre de M. LM, April 15, 1950(?)

216.   ——. *Amphitryon,* M. ou Corneille? HM, Jan., 1952.
217.   ——. Corneille sous le masque de M. Grasset, 1957. 396 p.
        rev. A. Lebois *in* RHLF 59: 547–9, 1959; J. Lemarchand *in* FL: 2, Aug.
        17, 1957; G. Nicoletti *in* Sipario 138, 1957; J. P. Samson *in* Témoins (Zurich)
        17: 43, 1957; A. Lebois *in* France-Asie 14: 197–203, 1959. *See* CrB 2240.
218.   Viatte, A. Corneille a-t-il écrit les oeuvres de M.? Rlav 12: 588–603, 1957.

VIII   CRITICAL STUDIES: LANGUAGE, STYLE, TECHNIQUE, PSYCHOLOGY, COMEDY, IDEAS, SOURCES, INFLUENCES, REPUTATION.

219.   M. CCRB 15: 3–52, 1956.
        contents: Jacques Copeau. La voix de M., 3–9; Léon Chancerel. M. et le
        Siècle d'Or, 10–13; Alfred Simon. Les rites élémentaires de la comédie
        moliéresque, 14–28; Georges-Albert Astre. Un comique de l'absurde, 29–
        37; Michel Zeraffa. M. et l'essence du personnage, 38–43; Jean-Louis
        Bory. Une cuisine à la sauce M. (*Don Juan*), 44–50; Claude Cézan. M. et
        les cinq centres [*provincial theatre groups*], 51–2.
220.   "Le jeune M." Europe 39: 3–155, 1961.
        contents: Pierre Abraham. Un——.? Non, trois, 3–7; Antoine Adam. Vue
        perspective, 7–9; Emile Tersen. Le décor historique, 10–18; Maurice
        Bouvier-Ajam. Le décor économique et sociale, 18–28; Léon Chancerel.
        Les années d'apprentissage ou de Paris à Paris, 29–62; Pierre-Aimé
        Touchard. La vocation tragique de M., 62–74; Jean de Beer. Réalisme de
        M., 74–83; Daniel Sorano. *L'Etourdi,* 83–5; Gérard Milhaud. Les farces
        philosophiques, 85–97; Yves Sandre. M., source de M., 97–103; Georges
        Dupeyron. M. et les tricheurs, 103–8; Gisèle Casadesus. La jeune fille au
        théâtre, 109–15; Suzanne Rossat-Mignod. L'émancipation des femmes,
        de *Mélite* (1629) à *l'Ecole des femmes* (1662), 115–22; Madeleine Ozeray.
        Agnés, 123–31; Jacques Gaucheron. M. à l'heure des *Fâcheux,* 131–44;
        Lucien Psichari. Premier rendez-vous, 144–7; Rose-Marie Moudouès.
        Chronologie, 148–55.
        rev. O. Papadima *in* StHlf 10: 591–4, 1961; D. Dalla Valle *in* StF 20: 350–1,
        1963.
221.   M., combattant. Europe 44: 3–159, 1966.
        contents: Pierre Abraham. Dom Juan contre Alceste, 3–8; Maurice
        Bouvier-Ajam. Le décor historique, 8–20; Pierre Paraf. Dorine et Sgana-
        relle, 21–9; Jean Raymond. Nudité et dévoilement, 30–3; Sylvie Chevalley.
        Les Plaisirs de l'Île enchantée, 34–43; Suzanne Rossat-Mignod. La portée
        de *Tartuffe* à la fin du 17ᵉ siècle, 44–51; Guy Leclerc. *Dom Juan* dans la
        bataille de *Tartuffe,* 51–8; Annie Ubersfeld. Dom Juan et le noble vieillard,
        59–67; Marie-Louise Coudert. Dom Juan, Elvire et moi, 67–76; Ray-
        monde Temkine. Sganarelle et son arrière-neveu Matti (Brecht), 76–83;
        Dom Juan vu par les lycéens, 83–8; Françoise Han. L'avenir de Dom Juan
        —Dom Juan et la fidelité, 88–98; Georges Léon. De M. à Mozart ou le jeu
        des familles, 99–104; Georges Dupeyron. M. et les tricheurs (suite), 104–
        14; Mariane & Gérard Milhaud. M. face à la médecine de Thomas Diafoi-
        rus, 114–28; Jacques Guillerme. Bon sens et scepticisme chez M., 129–35;
        Hélène Henry. Toujours combattant ou le grand M. de Jacques Copeau

à Roger Planchon, 136–50; Juan Marey. L'espagnol Moratin à l'école de M., 151–6; Rose-Marie Moudouès. Chronologie, 156–9.

rev. H. G. Hall *in* StF 31: 144–6, 1967.

222. M. L'Esprit créateur 6: 137–216, 1966.

contents: Will G. Moore. M.'s theory of comedy, 137–44; Paul Saintonge. Theme and variations, 145–55; Francis L. Lawrence. The *raisonneur* in M., 156–66; Barbara C. Bowen. Some element of French farce in M., 167–75; Louis E. Auld. The music of the spheres in the comedy-ballets, 176–87; Marcel Gutwirth. Arnolphe et Horace, 188–96; James Doolittle. Bad writing in *l'Avare*, 197–206; Quentin M. Hope. M. and *Nicomède*, 207–16.

rev. H. G. Hall *in* StF 32: 352–3, 1967.

223. M., a collection of critical essays. *ed by* Jacques Guicharnaud. Englewood Cliffs, N. J., Prentice Hall, 1964. 186 p.

contents: Jacques Guicharnaud. Introduction, 1–13; René Bray. The actor, 14–9; Gustave Lanson. M. and farce, 20–8; Alfred Simon. The elementary rites of M.'s comedies, 29–39; Will G. Moore. Speech, 40–9; Ramon Fernandez. The comedy of will, 50–3; René Bray. World of imagination, 54–9; Paul Bénichou. The anti-bourgeois, 60–8; Lionel Gossman. The comic hero and his idols, 69–78; André Villiers. Dom Juan revisited, 79–89; James Doolittle. The humanity of M.'s Dom Juan, 90–102; H. Gaston Hall. A comic Dom Juan, 103–10; Robert J. Nelson. The reconstructed heroes of M., 111–35; Alfred Simon. From Alceste to Scapin, 136–49; Jacques Copeau. On *les Fourberies de Scapin*, 150–4; Charles Dullin. On *l'Avare*, 155–9; J. D. Hubert. The doctor's curse, 160–9; Jacques Audiberti. Poquelin and Chaplin, 170–2.

rev. W. G. Grubb *in* EsCr 6: 217–8, 1966; Q. M. Hope *in* MLJ 50: 53–4, 1966; W. D. Howarth *in* FS 20: 294–7, 1966; P. Saintonge *in* FR 39: 802–3, 1966.

223a. M. RHLF 72: 769–1093, 1972.

contents: Raymond Picard. M. comique ou tragique? Le cas d'Arnolphe, 769–85; Maurice Descotes. M. et le conflit des générations, 786–99; W. G. Moore. Raison et structure dans la comédie de M., 800–5; Fausta Garavini. La fantaisie verbale et le mimétisme dialectal dans le théâtre de M. A propos de *Monsieur de Pourceaugnac*, 806–20; J.M. Pelous. Les métamorphoses de Sganarelle: la permanence d'un type comique, 821–49; Jacques Scherer. Aventures des Précieuses, 850–62; Jean Mesnard. *Le Misanthrope* mise en question de l'art de plaire, 863–89; John Cairncross. *Tartuffe* ou M. hypocrite, 890–901; Jacqueline Plantié. M. et François de Sales (Du "docteur" de Madame Pernelle aux "vrais dévots" de Cléante), 902–27; Jacques Truchet. M. théologien dans *Dom Juan*, 928–38; Jean Morel. A propos de la "scène du pauvre" dans *Dom Juan*, 939–44; Edouard Guitton. M. juriste dans *Dom Juan*. 945–53; René Pintard. Un ami de M.: Jean de Henault, 954–75; Madeleine Jurgens. L'aventure de l'Illustre Théâtre, 976–1006; Roger Guichemerre. Situations et personnages "prémoliéresques," 1007–23; George Mongrédien. *Le cocu imaginaire* et la cocuë imaginaire, 1024–34; Sylvie Chevalley. Armande Béjart, comédienne, 1035–52; Henri Lagrave. M. à la Comédie-Française, 1680–1793, 1052–65; Gilbert Sigaux. Georges Monval et *le Moliériste*, 1066–71; Gilbert Sigaux. Notes pour une discographie de M., 1072–4; Alain et

Odette Virniaux. M., Jouvet, Ophuls: note sur un film interrompu, 1075–80; Jean-Jacques Roubine. Audiberti et M., 1082–93.

224. Abraham, Pierre. Un M.? Non, trois. *See no. 220.*

225. Adam, Antoine. M. *in his* Histoire de la littérature française (Domat, 1948–56) v. 3: 181–408.
   rev. J. Fonsy *in* ECl 22: 172–86, 1954.

226. ———. Une perspective. *See no. 220.*

227. Anouilh, Jean. Présence de M. CCRB 26: 3–7, 1959.
   rev. L. Derla *in* StF 16: 153, 1962.

228. ———. M. Julliard, 1959. 128 p.

229. Arnavon, Jacques. Morale de M. *Reprint* Geneva, Slatkine, 1970. 230 p.
   See CrB 2183.

230. Astre, Georges-Albert. Un comique de l'absurde. *See no. 219.*

231. Audiberti, Jacques. M., dramaturge, précédé de "La vie et la formation des instruments dramatiques, la troupe de M.," et suivi de "Répertoire des mise en scène." Mise au point rapide sur la critique moliéresque par Jean Duvignaud. L'Arche, 1954. 160 p.

232. ———. Poquelin et Chaplin. *See no. 223.*

233. Auld, Louis E. The music of the spheres in the comedy-ballets. *See no. 222.*

234. ———. The unity of M.'s comedy-ballets: a study of their structure, meaning, and values. (Thesis, Bryn Mawr, 1966) 266 p. Diss abs A 29: 3997–8, 1968/9.

235. Bailly, René. M., *enrichisseur* de la langue française. CCRB 10: 82–8, 1955.

236. Beer, Jean de. Réalisme de M. *See no. 220.*

237. Beigbéder, M. Comment on *démoliérise* M. Conf. 458–66, May, 1942.

238. Bénichou, Paul. M. *See* CrB 2188.

239. ———. M. *in his* Morales du Grand siècle (Gallimard, 1948): 156–218. [*See no. 223 for extract, translated as* "The anti-bourgeois."]

240. Berger, Françoise, Jacques Copeau, metteur en scène de M. (Thesis, Dip. Et. Sup., Univ. of Paris, Institut d'études théâtrales, 1965) 163 p.

241. Bernard, L. Léon. M. and the historian of French society. *See* CrB 2189.

242. Bertram-Cox, Jean de Sales. A definition of tradition in the production of M.'s plays. ETJ 17: 301–7, 1965.
   [*Interviews with Louis Seigner and Robert Manuel of the Comédie-Française.*]

243. Billefer, Regula. Les valeurs spectaculaires dans l'oeuvre de M. (Thesis, Univ. of Zurich). Boulogne s/Seine, Imp. Maleva, 1962. 44 p.

244. Blanc. A. La permanence de la farce dans l'oeuvre de M. (Thesis, Univ. of Paris, 1957.)

245. Bluwal, Marc. A la base du comique: la libération d'une angoisse. ThV 7: 1969.

246. Boiadziev, Grigorii. Mol'er istoricheski puti formirovaniia zhanra vysokoi komedii [M; voies historiques de la formation du genre de la haute comèdie.] Moscow, ed. Iskusstvo, 1967. 556 p.
   rev. L.L. Backès *in* RHLF 69: 691–3, 1969; N. Gourfinkel *in* RHT 21: 180–6. 1969.

247. Bonnet, H. M. HCl 41: 16–24, 1964.

248. Bonzon, Alfredo. O teatro de M. AnH 37: 228–37, 1960. *Also* BSPa 235(3), 1960. 156 p.
   rev. F. Simone *in* StF 14: 345–6, 1961.

249. Boulay, Henriette. M. pour les jeunes. Préface par Elie Ferrier. Le Havre,

Imp. de la Presse, 1959. 107 p.

250. Bowen, Barbara C. Some elements of French farce in M. *See no.* 222.

251. Bray, René. M., sur les tréteaux. MF 320: 5–15, 1954. *See* CrB 2191.

252. Brock-Sulzer. M. und die Farce. TrZ 5: 1–30, 1947.

253. Brody, Jules. Esthétique et société chez M. CSH v. 1: 307–27, 1968.
    rev. S. Crotto *in* StF 39: 547, 1969.

254. Brugmans, Hendrik. M. *in his* De Lach in de Franse literatuur (Amsterdam, 1955): 45–65.

255. Brunelli, Giuseppe Antoine. Luci barocche nel teatro antibarocco di M. RLMC 12: 129–43, 1959; *Also in his* Saggi critici, da Ronsard a M. (Messina, Peloritana, 1963): 108–43.
    rev. C. Rizza *in* StF 10: 148, 1960.

256. Bruyelle, Roland. Les personnages de la comédie de M. Debresse, 1946. 136 p. *See* CrB 2195.

257. ——. La société du XVIIe siècle à travers quelques pièces de M. NRped: 3–5, Feb. 15, 1965.

258. Burgess, G. S. M. and the pursuit of criteria. Sym 23: 5–15, 1969.

259. Busson, Henri. M. et la philosophie. *See* CrB 2196.

260. ——. La philosophie de M. *in his* La religion des classiques (Presses univertaires de France, 1948): 299–70.

261. Cairncross, John. *See no.* 70.

261. Calvet, Jean. M. est-il chrétien? Essai sur la séparation de la religion et de la vie. *See* CrB 2197.

263. Cap, Biruta. M.'s creative process studied through recurring patterns and techniques. (Thesis, Rutgers-State Univ. of N. J., 1968) 254 p. Diss abs A 29: 3999–4000, 1969/70.

264. Casadesus, Gisèle. La jeune fille au théâtre. *See no.* 220. *Also in* Conf, Feb., 1960.

265. Cento, Alberto. M. Naples, Liguari, 1965. 125 p. *Also in his* Studi di letteratura francese (Naples, Liguari, 1970): 147–232.
    rev. G. Giorgi *in* Bel 26: 235–9, 1971.

266. Centonze, Ferruccio. M. et la sua commedia. *See* CrB 2198.

267. Cézan, Claude. M. et les cinq centres. *See no.* 219.

268. Chamarat, Georges. Les personnages de Sganarelle dans les comédies de M. Conf 241: 36–47, 1970.

269. Chapman, Percy A. The spirit of M.: an interpretation. *ed. by* Jean-Albert Bédé, with an introduction by Christian Gauss. N.Y., Russell & Russell, 1965. *See* CrB 2199.

270. Charlier, Gustave. Sous le masque de M. RBP 32: 1017–26, 1954. *See also his* Du M. inédit *in* Le Soir, June 22 *and* Aug 14, 1954. *See no. 314.*

271. Chassex, Jean-Charles. Opinions contemporaines sur les sujets d'éducation traités par M. Le Bayou 25: 289–97, 1961.

272. Christout, M-F. Le ballet de cour de Louis XIV: 1643–1672. Picard, 1967. 274 p.
    rev. G. Mirandola *in* StF 33: 543, 1967.

273. Clubb, William G. M. and the baroque rhythm. (Thesis, Princeton Univ., 1956) 127 p. Diss abs A 17: 629, 1956/7.

274. Dalla Valle, Daniela. De Théophile à M. Aspectos de una continuidad. Santiago de Chile, M. Amstar, 1968. 2 v.
    rev. G. Hainsworth *in* FS 25: 195–6, 1971.

275. Davidson, Hugh M. Audience, words and art. Studies in seventeenth century French rhetoric. Columbus, Ohio, Ohio State Univ. Press. 1965. 198 p.
     rev. E. B. O. Borherhoff *in* FR 40: 146–7, 1966.
276. Delcourt, Marie. L'impartialité comique chez M. BALB 40: 303–24, 1962.
     rev. D. Della Valle *in* StF 22: 155, 1964.
277. ——. Les comiques antiques et le théâtre français. CB 62: 111–3, 1966.
278. De Nardis, Luigi. M., tra commedia et pantomina *in his* Il sorriso de Reims (Bologne, Cappelli, 1960): 87–103. *Also in* StLV 1: 333–45, 1961.
     rev. J. P. Chauveau *in* DDS 53: 67–8, 1961.
279. Descotes, Maurice. Les grands rôles de M. Presses Universitaires, 1960. 268 p.
     rev. F. Simone *in* StF 11: 347, 1960; Q. H. Hope *in* RR 52: 229–33, 1961; G. Gillain *in* LRo 16: 301–2, 1962.
280. ——. M. et sa fortune littéraire. Bordeaux, Ducros, 1970. 181 p.
     rev. P. Camarieri *in* CFr 17: 3701, 1970; H. G. Hall *in* StF 42: 549, 1970; R. Horville *in* RSH 143: 472–3, 1971; L. Gossman *in* FR 45: 270–1, 1971/2.
281. Doolittle, James. Human nature and institutions in M.'s plots. StMB: 153–64, 1962.
     rev. F. Simone *in* StF 23: 343–4, 1964.
282. Doyon, René Louis. M., panacée universitaire. I–III Chronique du Cyclope. La Connaissance, 1958. 59 p.
283. Dubeux, Albert. Cette mâle gaîté (le comique et les comédiens). RDDM 18: 494–510, 1965.
284. Dupeyron, Georges. M. et les tricheurs. *See no. 220, 221.*
285. Düwel, H. Über das Problem der Ironie und Parodie in M.s Komödie. WZ 2: 171–80, 1952/3.
286. Dux, Pierre. M. parmi nous. Conf 165: 5–23, 1964.
     rev. H. G. Hall *in* StF 24: 552, 1964.
287. Eerde, John van. The historicity of the valet role in French comedy during the reign of Louis XIV. RR 48: 185–96, 1957.
288. Emelina, Jean. Les valets et les servantes dans le théâtre de M. Aix-en-Provence, La pensée universitaire, 1958. 215 p. *See no. 329.*
     rev. E. Caramaschi *in* StF 9: 488, 1959.
289. Emery, Léon. M., du métier à la pensée. Lyon, Cahiers libres, 1956. 143 p.
290. Eneman, Daniel Lawrence. Unity in the plays of M. (Thesis, Univ. of Michigan, 1968) 186 p. Diss abs A 29: 2706–7, 1968/9.
291. Ernst, P. Plautus und M. *in his* Gedanken zur Weltliteratur (Gütersloh, 1959): 84–114. *First appeared in* Falke (Darmstadt) 1: 85–94, 160–7, 1916.
292. Escofet, José. *See no. 94.*
293. Fabre, Emile. Notre M. Albert Michel, 1951. 255 p.
294. Fargher, R. M. and his reasoners. StHWL: 105–20, 1968.
295. Fernandez, Ramon. M., the man seen through the plays. *Tr. by* Wilson D. Foller. N.Y., Hill & Wand, 1958. 212 p.
     rev. R. J. Nelson *in* RR 50: 289–90, 1958.
296. ——. M. *in* Tableau de la littérature française de Corneille à Chénier, *ed. by* André Gide. (Gallimard, 1962): 1962: 67–88. [*Reprint of 1939 ed. Also see no. 223.*]
297. Forsell, Lars. M. och den atonala teatern. DT 2: 17–20, 1966.
298. Fowlie, Wallace. M. today *in his* Dionysus in Paris: a guide to contemporary French theatre. (N.Y., Meridian Books, 1960): 247–64.

299. Gaillard de Champris, Henri. M. *in his* Les écrivains classiques (del Duca, 1960) v. 4: 89–141.
300. Garapon, Robert. Sur les dernières comédies de M. IL 10: 1–7, 1958.
301. ———. Le dialogue moliéresque. Contribution à l'étude de la stylistique de M. CAIEF 16: 204–17, 1964.
    rev. H. G. Hall *in* StF 24: 551, 1964.
302. García Mercadal, José. M., estudio y antología. Madrid, Compañía bibliografica española, 1963. 222 p.
303. Garreau, Albert. La religion de M. *in his* La religion des grands classiques français (Eds. du Cèdre, 1970): 19–30.
304. Glikman, Isaak Davidovitch. Mol'er; kritiko-biograficheskii ocherk. Moscow-Leningrad, Khudozh, 1966. 278 p.
305. Gossman, Lionel. Men and masks, a study of M. Baltimore, Johns Hopkins Press, 1963. 310 p. *See also no. 223.*
    rev. H. G. Hall *in* StF 24: 553–4, 1964. J. Morel *in* RHLF 65: 299–300, 1965; S. Pitou *in* Thought 39: 314–6, 1964; W. D. Howarth *in* FS 19: 185–6, 1965; H. W. Davidson *in* MLN 80: 379–82, 1965; P. J. Yarrow *in* MLR 60: 622–3, 1965; P. Saintonge *in* FR 39: 803–4, 1966; F. J. Drijkeningen *in* HFB 36: 195–6, 1966.
306. Grande-Ramos, María. M. Barcelon, Labor, 1952. 360 p.
307. Gravel, Cécile. Recherches sur les bruits et les jeux de lumières dans les comédies, tragi-comédies et pièces à machines de Pierre Corneille et de M. (Thesis, Maîtrise d'enseignement, Univ. of Paris, Institut d'études théâtrales, 1969) 159 p.
308. Grebanier, Bernard D. Barron's simplified approach to M. Woodbury, N.Y., Barron, 1965. 195 p.
309. Guicharnaud, Jacques. M. in the light of modern criticism. ASLH 21: 161–75, 1958.
310. ———. M., une aventure théâtrale: *Tartuffe, Dom Juan* et *le Misanthrope.* Gallimard, 1963. 550 p.
    rev. W. G. Moore *in* MLR 59: 476–8, 1964; R. Sudrin *in* NRF 23: 534–5, 1964; C. J. Nesmy *in* TR 202: 127–9, 1964; P. A. Wadsworth *in* RR 56: 136–8, 1965; L. Gossman *in* FR 38: 569–73, 1965; B. Bray *in* HFB 35: 119, 1965; S. Teroni *in* RLMC 18: 140–4, 1965; M. Jurgens-Connat *in* BECh 123: 230–1, 1965; W. D. Howarth *in* FS 20: 294–7, 1966; K. Choiński *in* KN 13: 92–5, 1966; P. Mélèse *in* RHT 18: 253–4, 1966; H. G. Hall *in* StF 29: 299–301, 1966.
311. Guichemerre, Roger. Une source peu connue de M.: le théâtre de Le Métel d'Ouville. RHLF 65: 92–102, 1965.
312. Guillerme, Jacques. Bon sens et scepticisme chez M. *See no. 221.*
313. Gutwirth, Marcel. M. ou l'invention comique; la métamorphose des thèmes, la création des types. Minard, 1966. 222 p.
    rev. L. Gossman *in* FR 29: 735–6, 1966; C. F. *in* BCLi 22: 107–8, 1967; H. G. Hall *in* StF 34: 151, 1968; P. Saintonge *in* MLQ 29: 491–3, 1968; P. Mélèse *in* RHT 22: 161, 1970.
313a. Hall, H. Gaston. Comedy and Romances in Moliere's "Dépits amoureux." AUMLA 8: 245–58, 1971.
314. Henkel, H. Das "dénouement" in den Komödien von M. (Thesis, Univ. of Tübingen, 1959) 123 p.
315. Henry, Hélène. Toujours combattant ou le grand M. de Jacques Copeau à

Roger Planchon. *See no. 221.*

316. Hénusse, Théo. Une pièce de M. inconnue. Bruxelles, Biblis, 1954. 555 p. *See* CrB 2212 *and* S. Jeune. RJ 7: 96–99, 1955.

317. Hertrich, Charles. La France immortelle, ses grandes forces spirituelles; M. et son théâtre. St. Etienne, Ed. des Flambeaux, 1943. 24 p.

318. Herzog, W. M. *in his* Große Gestalten der Geschichte (Munich, Bern, 1960): 73–84.

319. Hope, Quentin H. The scene of greeting in M. RR 50: 241–54, 1959.

320. ——. Animals in M. PLMA 79: 411–21, 1964.
     rev. H. G. Hall *in* StF 26: 355–6, 1965.

321. ——. M. and *Nicomède. See no. 222.*

322. ——. M.'s curtain line. FS 26: 143–55, 1972.

323. Hoy, Cyrus. M. *in his* The hyacinth room: an investigation into the nature of comedy, tragedy and tragi-comedy. (London, Chatto & Windus, 1964. 318 p.).

324. Hubert, Judd D. M. and the comedy of intellect. Berkeley, Cal., Univ. Press, 1962. 144 p.
     rev. P. Mélèse *in* RHT 14: 379–80, 1962; R. J. Nelson *in* FR: 36: 653–4, 1962/3; M. Bensimon *in* FS 7: 106–10, 1963; L. E. Harvey *in* EsCr 3: 46–8, 1963; W. G. Moore *in* MP 61: 245–6, 1964; J. Guicharnaud *in* RR 55: 126–7, 1964; F. P. *in* LSt 14: 40–1, 1965.

325. ——. M. et les deux styles burlesques. CAIEF 16: 235–48, 1964.
     rev. H. G. Hall *in* StF 24: 551, 1964.

326. Jasinski, René. M. Hatier, 1969. 290 p.
     rev. M. Françon *in* StF 39: 546, 1969; G. Mongrédien *in* RHLF 70: 313–4, 1970; P. Mélèse *in* RHT 22: 161–2, 1970; M. Piron *in* EL, Dec., 1970.

327. Jouhandeau, Marcel. M. in *his* Divertissements: mes préfaces, présentées par Bernard de Fallois (Gallimard, 1965): 87–99.

328. Jouvet, Louis. M. et la comédie classique. Gallimard, 1965. 304 p.
     rev. C. Cosnier *in* RHT 22: 162–4, 1970.

329. Kadlec, Oldrich. Dramatic portraits of M. RN 2: 36–41, 1960.
     rev. F. Simone *in* StF 14: 346, 1961.

330. Kentner, Heinz D. M.s tragische Satire in heutiger Inszenierung. MK 9: 114–31, 1963.

331. Kerman, Lâmia. Un personnage du théâtre classique: le valet de comédie; évolution du type. Ankara, Türk Tarih Kurumu, 1956. 190 p. *See no. 288.*

332. Klein, H. W. Die sprachliche Charakterisierung der Personen in einigen Komödien. NMit 21: 32–3, 1968.

333. Kleine, Winifred. Information und Informationsverhinderung in den Komödien M.s (Thesis, Univ. of Münster, 1970.) 217 p.

334. Klemperer, Victor. M., une introduction *in his* M. Komödien (Leipzig, Dietrich, 1950). *Also in his* Vor 33/nach 45 (Berlin, 1956): 171–95.

335. Klibbe, Lawrence H. The major plays of M. N.Y., Monarch Press, 1965. 126 p.

336. Kott, Jan. M. our contemporary. TDR 11 (35): 163–70, 1966/7.

337. Kourilsky, Françoise. La permanence de la structure de la farce dans les comédies de M. (Thesis, Dip. Et. Sup., Univ. of Paris, Institut d'études théâtrales, 1957.) 126 p.

338. Krailsheimer, A. J. M. *in his* Studies in self-interest (Oxford, Univ. Press, 1962): 152–72.

339. Krauss, Werner. M. und das Problem des Verstehens in der Welt des 17. Jahrhunderts. HMo 2 & 3: 104–6, 170–89, 1953.
340. Kreiss, Paul T. The valet in French comedy, 1670–1730. (Thesis, Northwestern Univ., 1968.) 995 p. Diss abs A 29: 2714, 1968/9.
341. Kuczyuski, Jürgen. M., Boisguillebert und die Gesellschaft des absolutistischen Feudalismus. WZH 2: 1–16, 1952/3.
342. Lafarge, Jacques. Les dialectes, parlers populaires et autres jargons, ou les bas langages' chez M. (Thesis, Univ. of Dijon, 1969).
343. Lane, C. W. French criticism of M. (Thesis, Univ. of Oxford, 1969).
344. Lanniel, Jean. L'homme riche et son rêve dans les pièces de famille de M. RLV 35: 357–67, 1969.
345. Lanson, Gustave. M. and farce. *See no. 223. Also* TDR 8: 144–54, 1963.
346. Lawrence. Francis L. The nature and function of the *raisonneur* in M. (Thesis, Tulane Univ., 1962.) 179 p. Diss abs A 23: 4685, 1962/3.
347. ——. The *raisonneur* in M. *See no. 222.*
348. ——. The roots of M. [La commedia dell'arte]. TSL 10: 151–64, 1965.
349. ——. M.; the comédy of unreason. New Orleans, Tulane Univ., 1968. 199 p.
      rev. G. R. Danner *in* MLJ 54: 288, 1970; B. Nicholas *in* MLR 65: 625–6, 1970; R. N. Nicolich *in* FR 44: 461–2, 1970/1; J. Weiss *in* StF 40: 156, 1970; R. Guichemerre *in* RHLF 71: 89, 1971.
350. Lebel, Maurice. M. MLEL 1: 47–65, 1964.
351. Lebèque, Raymond. Remarques sur M. et la farce. HomEC: 125–7.
352. ——. M. et la farce. CAIEF 16: 183–201, 1964.
      rev. H. G. Hall *in* StF 24: 551, 1964.
353. Le Hir, Yves. Remarques de poétique à propos de M. TLL 8: 135–40, 1970.
354. Lenôtre, G. L'énigme de M. *in his* L'énigme de M., suivi de 20 récits inédits (Geneva, La Palatine, 1968): 11–24.
355. Léon, Georges. De M. à Mozart. *See no. 221.*
356. Levi, Eugenio. M. e la comicità di carattere *in his* Il comico di carattere (Turin, G. Einaudi, 1959): 81–103.
357. Lewis, D. B. Wyndham. M.: the comic mask. London, Eyre Spottiswoode, 1959. 211 p. *Also* N.Y., Coward-McCaern, 1959. 214 p.
      rev. TLS 58: 663, 1959; R. Walker *in* TCL 167: 370–1, 1960; W. Fowlie *in* KR 22: 515–8, 1960.
358. Liebrecht, Henri. M., homme de théâtre. BALB 32: 67–77, 1954.
359. Lind, Th. Le comique étudié dans M. OrL 21: 255–72, 1966.
360. Lion, F. Möglichkeiten des Komischen; kleines M.-Brevier. AkZD 5: 389–98, 1958.
361. Lowenthal, Leo. M. *in his* Literature and the image of man, sociological studies of the European drama and novel, 1600–1900 (Boston, Beacon Press, 1967): 122–35.
362. McBride, Robert. The sceptical view of marriage and the comic vision in M. FMLS 5: 26–46, 1969.
      rev. H. G. Hall *in* StF 38: 348, 1969.
363. Machan, H. W. M.: the universal and timeless aspects of his comedies. KFLQ 4: 136–45, 1957.
364. Maranini, Lorenza. Il teatro francese dalle origini alla fondazione della Comédie Française. Pavia, Editrice succ. Fusi, 1969. 770 p.
      rev. RSH 110: 633, 1970.
365. Masters, Brian. A student's guide to M. London, Heinemann 1970. 92 p.

366. Mauron, Charles P. L'évolution créatrice de M. *in his* Des métaphores obsédantes au mythe personnel: introduction à la psycho-critique. (Corti, 1963): 270–98.

367. Melchinger, Siegfried. M. (1 & 2) *in his* Geschichte des politischen Theaters (Velber, Friedrich, 1971) 190–214.

368. Mélèse, Pierre. Rotrou et M. RHT 2: 259–63, 1950. *See* CrB 2228.

369. Meyer, G. Le *Francion* de Sorel (1622) et la comédie de M. Hmod 9: 24–5, 1966.

370. Micelli, S. La soubrette dans les oeuvres de M. Trapani, Corras, 1961. 79 p.

371. Mihály, Gabor. M. Budapest, Müvelt Nep, 1954. 158 p.

372. Mokul'sky, Stefan Stefanovitch. Molijer: *Tr. by* Ljubitsa Bauer-Protik. Belgrade, Zagreb, 1947. 110 p. *From his* 1935 Russian edition, 248 p.

373. M. CCAIEF 16: 181–303, 1964.

374. M. *in* I giganti della letteratura mondiale (Milan, Periodici Mondadori, 1969): 57–88. *Adapted in French by Annie Chaland.* Paris-Match, 1969. 136 p.

375. Mongrédien, Georges. M. et la société de son temps. RGB 2: 21–31, 1967.

376. Moore, Will G. M., a new criticism. Oxford, Clarendon Press, 1949. 136 p. *See* Crb 2231.

377. ——. M. in the melting pot. ML 36: 9–10, 1954/5.

378. ——. Poésie de M. CAIEF 16: 249–57, 1964.
    rev. H. G. Hall *in* StF 24: 551, 1964.

379. ——. M.'s theory of comedy. *See no.* 222.

380. ——. M. et la sottise. KFLQ 17: 335–43, 1970.

381. ——. The classical drama of France. London. Oxford Press, 1971. 138 p.
    rev. R. C. Knight *in* FS 261: 193–4, 1972.

382. Morel, Jacques. M. ou la dramaturgie de l'honnêteté. IL 15: 185–81, 1963.
    rev. H. G. Hall *in* StF 24: 551–2, 1964.

381. Mornet, Daniel. M. Boivin, 1943. 199 p. *4th ed.*, 1955. *See* CrB 2232.

384. Most, Woodrow L. Proverbes et blasons populaires dans les comédies de M. RLav 9: 685–706, 1955.

385. ——. Les traditions populaires dans les comédies de M. RLav 9: 606–22, 1955.

386. Muller, Armand. M. *in his* De Rabelais à Paul Valéry; les grands écrivains devant le christianisme (Foulon, 1969): 65–8.

387. Muller, Charles. Sur quelques scènes de M.: essai d'un indice du style familier. FMod 30: 99–108, 1962.

388. Müller, Franz W. M. und die "Anciens." RJ 10: 119–46, 1959.
    rev. J. Hösle *in* StF 13: 153, 1961.

389. Nadal, Octave. M. et le sens de la vie *in his* A mesure haute (Mercure de France, 1964): 91–108.

390. Nelson, Robert J. The unconstructed heroes of M. TDR 4: 14–37, 1960.
    See no. 223.

391. Nicholas, B. L. M. *in* French literature and its background: *ed. by* John Cruickhank (London, Oxford Press, 1969) v. 2: 98–118.

392. Nurse, Peter H. Le rire et la morale dans l'oeuvre de M. DSS 52: 20–35, 1961.

393. ——. Essai de définition du comique moliéresque. RSH 113: 9–14, 1964.

394. ——. M. and satire. UTQ 36: 113–28, 1967.
    rev. H. G. Hall *in* StF 32: 353–4, 1967.

395. ———. M. *in his* Classical voices; studies of Corneille, Racine, M., Madame de LaFayette (London, Harrap, 1971): 111–84.
rev. H. T. Barwell *in* StF 45: 545, 1971.

396. Obase, Takazo. Furansu koten kigeki seiritsu shi . . . (A history of the development of French classical comedy: a study of M. Tokyo, Hosei Univ. Press, 1970. 76 p.

397. Pauer, Monika. Der Monolog bei M. (Thesis, Univ. of Vienna, 1970). 156 p.

398. Pighi, Laura. M. e il teatro italiano in Francia. Bologna, Casa editrice Ricardo Patron, 1959. 122 p.

399. Plazolles, L. R. La pensée dramatique de M. APro 10: 114–20, 1957.

400. Pooré, Helje. From Tabarin to M.; a study of French comedy between 1612 and 1655. (Thesis, Univ. of Toronto, 1971). Diss abs A 32: 6999, 1971/2.

401. Portal, Georges. La saison des énergumènes. EcP 292: 121–8, 1970.

402. Potter, Edithe J. Principles of comedy in eight plays of M. (Thesis, Rice Univ., 1970) 188 p. Diss abs A 31: 2935, 1970/1.

403. Raibaud, Gabriel. Sur les lectures de M. RU 63: 83–8, 1954.

404. Rat, Maurice. M. parodiste. IT 6: 6–9, 1956.

405. Raymond, Jean. Nudité et dévoilement dans le théâtre de M. *See no. 221.*

406. Ribaric-Demers, M. M.: Les "hommes" et les "femmes" de M. *in his* Le valet et la soubrette de M. à la Révolution (Nizet, 1970) 23–38.

407. Ritchie, J. M. M., a critic of the ancien régime. (Thesis, Univ. of Nottingham, 1962.)

408. Robert, René. Des commentaires de première main sur les chefs-d'oeuvre les plus discutés de M. RSH 81: 19–49, 1956.
rev. F. Simone *in* StF 1: 141, 1957.

409. ———. Comment lire les grandes comédies de M. IL 10: 82–4, 1958.

410. Robra, K. J-B Molière, Philosophie und Gesellschaftskritik, Entlarvung und Entspannung. Tübingen, Elly Huth, 1969. 106 p.
rev. R. Pasch *in* StF 39: 546, 1969.

411. Romano, Danilo. Essai sur le comique de M. Berne, Franke, 1950. 155 p.
rev. H. C. Lancaster *in* MLN 67: 67–8, 1956; R. Bray *in* RHLF 56: 123–4, 1956; F. Simone *in* StF 1: 141–2, 1957.

412. Romero, Laurence, jr. M.: traditions in criticism 1900–1960. (Thesis, Yale Univ., 1969) 189 p. Diss abs A 31: 1290, 1970/1.

413. Ronin, Paul. De M. à nos jours (*le théâtre à St. Etienne*). Andrézieux, Imp. moderne, 1961. 127 p.

414. Rossat-Mignod, Suzanne. L'émancipation des femmes de *Mélite* (1629) à *l'Ecole des femmes* (1662). *See no. 220.*

415. ———. Les femmes chez M. Eur 354: 35–41, 1964.
rev. D. Dalla Valle *in* StF 25: 155, 1965.

416. Rossman, Sol. The stylistic status of the imperfect subjunctive in the drama of Corneille, M., and Racine. (Thesis, Univ. of Michigan, 1969) 238 p. Diss abs A 30: 3931, 1969/70.

417. Rouillard, Clarence D. The age of M. MSRC 51: 15–22, 1957.

418. Rudler, Gustave. M. FS 12: 3–4, 1958.
rev. F. Simone *in* StF 7, 141, 1959.

419. Saintonge, Paul. Theme and variations. *See no. 222.*

420. Salzmann, Wolfgang. M. und die lateinische Komödie. Ein Stil- und Strukturvergleich. Heidelberg, C. Winter, 1969. 272 p.

rev. H. Köhler *in* RHLF 70: 702–3, 1970; H. R. Picard *in* RFor 82: 634–7, 1970; C. N. Smith *in* FS 25: 455–6, 1971; W. G. Moore *in* MLR 66: 689, 1971; R. Pasch *in* StF 45: 546, 1971.

421. Sander, E. M. *in* Die Großen der Kunst, Literatur und Musik, Frankreich: [*ed. by* Herman Missenharter] (Stuttgart, Union Verlag, 1961): 126–37.
422. Sandre, Yves. M., source de M. *See no. 220.*
423. Sayce, Richard. Quelques réflexions sur le style comique de M. CAIEF 16: 219–33, 1964.
     rev. H. G. Hall *in* StF 24: 551, 1964.
424. Scherer, Jacques. Le théâtre de M. *in* StIS, v. 2: 1077–79.
     rev. H. G. Hall *in* StF 29: 301–2, 1966.
425. Schmidt, Julius. Was hat M. uns zu sagen? ZFSL 4: 332–8, 1967.
     rev. H. G. Hall *in* StF 37: 143, 1969.
426. Schwartz, Isadore A. The commedia dell' arte and its influence on French comedy in the seventeenth century. *See* CrB 2245 *and* 1555.
427. Sigler, Byron E. A critical examination of the major plays of M. in relation to the doctrine of poetic justice. (Thesis, Stanford Univ., 1964) 188 p. Diss abs A 25: 6119, 1964/5.
428. Simon, Alfred. Les rites élémentaires de la comédie moliéresque. *See no.* 219 *and* 223.
429. ———. La puissance comique. CCRB 26: 13–6, 1959.
430. Singer, Irving. The shadow of Dom Juan in M. MLN 85: 838–57, 1970.
431. Spink, John S. Literature and the sciences in the age of M. London, International Book Club, 1953. 26 p.
432. Spoerri, Theophil. Das Lächeln M.s. *See* CrB 2248.
433. Stoker, John T. M., writer of comedies. ML 37: 59–61, 1955/6.
434. ———. Le réel dans les oeuvres de M.: l'actuel et le démodé. Cult 31: 144–8, 232–7, 1970. *Also in* Le réel dans la littérature et dans la langue (FILLM, Strasbourg, 1966, *published* 1967).
435. Strozier, William A. Man in M.'s mirror. EUQ 16: 107–15, 1960.
436. Styan, John L. M. *in his* The dark comedy; the development of comic tragedy (Cambridge, Univ. Press, 1968): 24–31.
437. Swehla, Jaroslav. M. Prague, Skolaprozeny, 1952. 16 p.
438. Sylvius. A propos de M. Quo Vadis 92–4: 91–6, 1956.
439. Szogi, Alex. Truth-telling and truth-suggesting in M.'s theater. KFLQ 16: 209–19, 1969.
440. Tabart, Claude-André. Le théâtre de M. ou l'illusion comique. (Thesis, Dip. Et. Sup., Univ. of Paris, Institut d'études théâtrales, 1965) 130 p.
441. Taladoire, B. Discours de réception sur M. BAV 121: 96–101. 1961.
442. Taube, Nils E. M. Stockholm, Wahlstrom & Widstrand, 1947. 125 p.
443. Touchard, Pierre-Aimé. La vocation tragique de M. *See no.* 220. *Also in* LN 1: 8, 1961.
444. Truc, Gonzague. Eloge de M. Ec 52: 362, 403–4, 1960/1.
445. Tuiel, Paul. M. et la musique. BARB: 7–9, 1967.
446. Turnell, Martin. M. *See* CrB 2251.
447. Ungaro, Solange. Le monologue dans le théâtre de M. (Thesis, Dip. Et. Sup., Univ. of Paris, Institut d'études théâtrales, 1966) 101 p.
448. Urbani del Fabbretto, Angelo. M. Disegni di A.U. deF., testo di Alfredo Petrucci. A cura di Giorgio Moroni. Rome, 1951.
449. Wadsworth, Philip A. Exoticism in M. ASLH 40: 73–84, 1969.

450. Warner, Garret A. Le monologue chez M.; étude de stylistique et de dramaturgie. (Thesis, Univ. of Caen, 1966) 235 p.
451. Wells, David J. Comic atmosphere in selected comedies of M. (Thesis, Ohio
State Univ., 1969) 258 p. Diss abs A 30: 4602, 1969/70.
452. Wilson, C. J. Some aspects of M.'s style. (Thesis, Univ. of Cambridge, 1967).
453. Zeleński, Tadeuz. Molier. Pisma, v. 2. (Tom opracowal Jan Kott). Warsaw,
1958. 397 p.
454. Zeraffa, Michel. M. et l'essence du personnage. *See no. 219.*
455. Zwillenberg, Myrna K. Dramatic coherence and dynamics of closure in four
plays of M. (Thesis, Yale Univ., 1971) 259 p. Diss abs A 32: 3337, 1971/2.

IX   DOCTORS, APOTHECARIES AND MEDECINE

456. Bouvet, M. M. et les apothicaires. RHPh 138: 1–13, 1953. *Also* Cahors, A.
Coneslant, s.d. 15 p.
457. Cairncross, John. Impie en médecine. CAIEF 16: 269–84, 1964. *See also*
J. Rogers, 301–3.
   rev. H. G. Hall *in* StF 24: 551, 1964.
458. Chaumartin, A. Gens de M. Vienne, Ternet-Martin, 1963, 36 p.
459. Chauvois, L. M., Boileau, LaFontaine et la circulation du sang. PMed 62:
1219–20, 1954.
460. Drach, Luzie. Das medizinische Vokabular M.s. (Thesis, Univ. of Bonn,
1970.) 217 p.
461. François, Carlo. Médecine et religion chez M.: deux facette d'une même
absurdité. FR 42: 665–9, 1969.
452. Gill, A. The doctor in the farce and M. FS 2: 101–28, 1948.
453. Godlewski, Guy. Les médecins de M. et leurs modèles. SH 46: 3490–3500,
1970.
464. Jouhandeau, Marcel. Hommage à M. Médecine de France 164: 33–5, 1965.
465. Maxfield-Miller, Elizabeth. M., l'affaire Cressé and *le Médecin fouetté* et *le
Barbier cocu.* PMLA 72: 854–62, 1957.
466. Millepierres, François. La vie quotidienne des médecins au temps de M.
Hachette, 1964. 250 p.
   rev. E. Kanceff *in* StF 28: 150, 1966.
467. Pike, R. E. A. A contemporary judgement on M. *See* CrB 2239.
468. Plazolles, L. R. M. contre la médiocre [*sic*] [médecine] de son temps. Ec 53:
150, 191–2, 1961.
469. Raymond, Maurice. Les médecins au temps de M. PrMed 83: 105–10, 1955.
470. Savare, Jean. Apothicaires de comédie: deux oeuvres de Villiers, rival de
M. RHPh 43: 173–8, 1955.
471. Vialatte, Charles. M. a-t-il exagéré? ou la consultation du Cardinal (de
Fürstenberg) par François Aignan. HMed 3: 18–27, 1953.
472. Vivier, Robert. Notes sur les médecins et la médecine dans le théâtre de M.
BALB 42: 7–27, 1964.

X   INDIVIDUAL PLAYS: EDITIONS, PERFORMANCES

LE MÉDECIN VOLANT

473. Stegman, André. La source italienne du *Médecin volant* de M. RSH 88: 507–9, 1957.

    rev. F. Simone *in* StF 5: 314, 1958.

L'ÉTOURDI

474. ——. Ed by Pierre Mélèse. Geneva, Droz, 1951. 136 p. *See* CrB 2290.
475. ——. L'Arche, 1955, 1956.
476. Beck, Kirsten. Le jeune M. et la Commedia dell'arte: thèmes et aspects scéniques dans *l'Etourdi* et *le Dépit amoureux*. RRom 5: 1–16, 1970.
477. Dufeu, R. Texte commenté: Mascarille (*L'Etourdi,* Acte III, scène 1). Hmod 9: 17–21, 1966.
478. François, Carlo. *L'Etourdi* de M. ou l'illusion héroïque. RHLF 59: 87–91, 1959.

    rev. F, Simone *in* StF 8: 313, 1959.
479. Hope, Quentin M. M.'s coup d'essai. KFLQ 162: 163–78, 1969/70.
480. Sakharoff, Micheline. *L'Etourdi* de M. ou l'école des innocents. FR 43: 240–8, 1969.
481. Sorano, Daniel. *L'Etourdi. See no. 220.*
482. Wadsworth, Philip A. The Italian source of M.'s *l'Etourdi.* KFLQ 181: 319–31, 1971.

LE DÉPIT AMOUREUX

483. Chancerel, Léon. M. à Béziers. A propos du 300e anniversaire de la première du *Dépit amoureux.* IT 6: 13–5, 1956.

LES PRÉCIEUSES RIDICULES

484. ——. Introduction and notes by R. P. L. Ledésert. London, Harrap, 1948. 46 p.
485. ——. *and L'Impromptu de Versailles.* L'Arche, 1959. 60 p.
486. ——. *and les Femmes savantes* . . . par Jean J. Bourgeois et Pierre Charlot. Foucher, 1960. 81 p.
487. ——; *La Jalousie du Barbouillé, Sganarelle* . . . par Fernand Angué. Bordas, 1962, 1965, 1967. 111 & 128 p.
488. —— par Félix Guirand et Pierre Dussange. Larousse, 1962, 48 p.
489. —— par Jean Balcou. Larousse, 1965. 78 p.
490. —— par Hubert Carrier. Hachette, 1969. 38 p.
491. ——. Hatier, 1969. 64 p.
492. —— by Bronnie Treloar. London, E. Arnold, 1970. 57 p.

    rev. H. G. Hall *in* StF 41: 348, 1970; C. B. Thornton Smith *in* AUMLA 35: 128, 1971.
493. —— par Renato Tullio de Rosa. Naples, Instito ed. del Mezzo-giorno, 1970.
494. —— par Jean Balcou. Larousse, 1971. 107 p.
495. Brisson, Pierre. Le 3e centenaire des *Précieuses ridicules.* Hist 26: 513–17, 1959.
496. Giteau, Annie. Il y a trois cents ans, M. livrait et gagnait sa première bataille théâtre. Eaux-vives 201: 220–22, 1959.
497. Guibert, Albert Jean. Le tricentenaire des *Précieuses ridicules.* BouF, July 21, 1960.
498. Henriot, Emile. Le language des "Précieuses." Hist 26: 518–9, 1959.

499. Herval, René. Une pièce oubliée de M.: la *Farce des Précieuses*. CVo 19: 10–4, 1957.
500. Hope, Quentin M. Dramatic techniques in *les Précieuses ridicules*. RenWLW 140–50, 1968.
501. La Rosa, Tristán. M. . . . evocación de los desaparecido "salones" de las "preciosas" *in his* Paris: miscelanea par el week-end (La Vanguardia española (Barcelona), 1968.
502. Macchia, G. Follia del linguaggio e follia della recitazione *in his* La scuola dei sentimenti (Rome, Altanissella, 1963): 102–9.
503. Mongrédien, Georges. Les précieux et les précieuses. Introduction et choix de G. M. Mercure de France, 1963. 258 p.
504. Pintard, René. Pour le tricentenaire des *Précieuses ridicules*. Préciosité et classicisme. DSS 50: 8–20, 1961.
505. Pitou, Spire. A precious note: M. and Meunier. RN 6: 144–7, 1965.
     rev. H.G. Hall *in* StF 27: 547, 1965; E Hick *in* StF 28: 150, 1966.
506. Thérive, A. Les précieuses non ridicules. RDDM 12: 64–8. 1959.
507. Weinrich, Harald. Zur scène XI der *Précieuses ridicules*. RFor 79: 263–70, 1967.

SGANARELLE

508. Guibert, Albert-Jean. Un exemplaire corrigé de *Sganarelle*. BBB 4: 161–75, 1954.
509. Rau, Arthur. The first edition of M.'s *Sganarelle*. BC 9: 68–71, 1960.
510. Virolle, Roland. Sganarelle, bourgeois de Paris. Ec 53: 591–4, 1961/2.

DON GARCIE DE NAVARRE

511. Freudmann, Félix R. Le comique dans *Don Garcie de Navarre*. RR 60: 251–64, 1970.
     rev. G. Mirandola *in* StF 41: 348, 1970.
512. Gutwirth, Marcel. *Don Garcie de Navarre* et *le Misanthrope*. PLMA 83: 118–29. 1968.
     rev. H. G. Hall *in* StF 40: 157, 1970.
513. Howarth, W. D. *Don Garcie de Navarre* ou le Prince jaloux. *See* CrB 2266.
514. Hubert, Judd D. The comedy of incompatibility in M.'s *Don Garcie de Navarre*. MLQ 21: 228–34, 1960.
     rev. L. Derla *in* StF 13: 153, 1961.
515. Rountree, Benjamin. *Don Garcie de Navarre*: tentative de réconciliation avec les précieux. RR 56: 161–70, 1965.
516. Smith, Stephen. M.'s attitude toward *Don Garcie de Navarre*. RN 23: 301–5, 1971.

L'ÉCOLE DES MARIS

517. —— *Ed. by* Peter H. Nurse. London, Harrap, 1959. 78 p.
     rev. P. J. Yarrow *in* MLR 56: 146, 1961. W. D. Howarth *in* FS 15: 60–61, 1960/1.
518. —— *ed. by* Jean Boullé. Larousse, 1962. 84 p.
518a. Herreras, Domiciano. Fuentes españolas de *Escuela de los maridos de M.* Malaga, Grafs San Andrès, 1967.
519. Losse, Deborah N. Multiple masks in *l'Ecole des maris*. RN 12: 142–8, 1970.

LES FÂCHEUX

520.   Gaucheron, Jacques. M. à l'heure des *Fâcheux* (1661–1662). *See no. 220*.
521.   Walker, Hallam. *Les Fâcheux* and M.'s use of games. EsCr 11: 21–33, 1971.

L'ÉCOLE DES FEMMES

525.   —— L'Arche, 1958. 79 p.
523.   —— *ed. by* G. Sablayrolles. Larousse, 1959. 121 p.
524.   —— *ed. by* A. Nockels. London-N. Y., Macmillan, St. Martin's Press, 1960. 103 p.
525.   —— and *La critique de l'Ecole des femmes. ed. by* W. D. Howarth. Oxford, Blackwell, 1963. 142 p.
526.   —— *ed by* Pierre Cabanis. Bordas, 1963. 127 p.
527.   ——, suivi de *La critique de l'Ecole des femmes* et de *l'Impromptu de Versailles. ed. by* Suzanne Rossat-Mignod. Editions sociales, 1965. 212 p.
       rev. J. P. Chauveau *in* Il 17: 208, 1965.
528.   —— *ed. by* Gérard Sablayrolles. Larousse, 1965. 134 p.
529.   —— *ed. by* Alfred Simon *and* Hubert Gignoux. Hachette, 1970. 184 p.
530.   —— *ed. by* Lucie Cenarini. Rome, Signorelli, 1970. 142 p.
534.   Beck, William. Arnolphe et Monsieur de la Souche. FR 42: 254–61, 1968.
       rev. S. Crotto *in* StF 38: 348, 1969.
532.   Boylesve, René. Apologie d'Arnolphe *in his* Profiles littéraires (Nizet, 1962): 252–60. *Written in* 1913.
533.   Cismaru, Alfred. Agnès and Angélique: an attempt to settle the relationship. FR 35: 472–77, 1962.
534.   Doubrovsky, Serge. Arnolphe ou la chute du héros. MF 343: 111–8, 1961.
535.   Dumur, G. *L'Ecole des femmes* à la Comédie Française. Tpo 35: 95–7, 1959.
536.   Dussane, Béatrix. Vie et survie des héros de théâtre: Arnolphe et Agnès. Conf 66: 27–35, 1959.
537.   ——. La bataille de *l'Ecole des femmes*. Conf 70: 28–37, 1963.
538.   Ehrmann, J. Notes sur *l'Ecole des femmes*. RSH 109: 5–10, 1963.
539.   Gisselbrecht, A. *L'Ecole des femmes* au T. N. P. Tpo 34: 95–6, 1959.
540.   Grégoire, B. La querelle de *l'Ecole des femmes*. Fl 41: 672–86, 1958.
541.   Guillaume, Anne-Marie. Recherches sur l'iconographie de *l'Ecole des Femmes*. (Thesis, Dip. Et. Sup., Univ. of Paris, Institut d'études théâtrales, 1963.) 97 p.
542.   Gutwirth, Marcel. Arnolphe et Horace. *See no. 222*.
543.   Hall, H. Gaston. Parody in *l'Ecole des femmes:* Agnès's question. MLR 57: 63–5, 1962.
544.   Howarth, W. D. The sources of *l'Ecole des femmes*. MLR 58: 10–4, 1963.
545.   Hubert, Judd D. *L'Ecole des femmes*, tragédie burlesque. RSH 97: 41–52, 1960.
       rev. L. Derla *in* StF 11: 347–8, 1960.
546.   Louis Jouvet et sa compagnie dans *l'Ecole des femmes* de M. Société nouvelle Mercure, 1955. Inf 32 p.
547.   Magné, Bernard. *L'Ecole des femmes* ou la conquête de la parole. RSH 145: 125–40, 1972.
548.   Nicolich, Robert N. Door, window and balcony in *l'Ecole des femmes*. RN 12: 364–9, 1970/1.

549. Nurse, Peter H. The role of Chrysalde in *l'Ecole des femmes*. MLR 56: 167–71, 1961.
550. Ozeray, Madeleine. Agnès. *See no. 220.*
551. Pignault, L. Le vocabulaire d'Arnolphe dans *l'Ecole des femmes* de M. (avec index). BILAL 5: 1–29, 1961.
    rev. R. Rosellini *in* StF 21: 554, 1963.
552. Porter, Denis. Comic rhythm in *l'Ecole des femmes*. FMLS 5: 205–17, 1969.
553. Psichari, Lucien. Premier rendez-vous. *See no. 220.*

LA CRITIQUE DE L'ÉCOLE DES FEMMES

554. —— et l'Impromptu de Versailles. *ed. by* Georges Bonneville. Bordas, 1963. 127 p.
555. ——; l'Impromptu de Versailles, suivis d'un appendice sur la querelle de *l'Ecole des femmes . . . . ed. by* Pierre Mélèse. Larousse, 1962. 124 p.
556. ——; l'Impromptu de Versailles, suivis de documents sur la querelle de *l'Ecole des femmes . . . ed. by* André Tessier. Larousse, 1969. 174 p.
557. Brenner, Jacques. La guerre comique *in his* Les critiques dramatiques. (Flammarion, 1970): 55–65.
558. Chauveau, Jean-Pierre. *La critique de l'Ecole des femmes*. Ec 55: Jan. 1964.
559. Herland, Louis. Une source de *la Critique de l'Ecole des femmes*, ou M. lecteur de Balzac. *See* CrB 2288.
560. Leconte, Claude H. M. chez M. IT 4: 1–2, 1958.
561. Mongrédien, Georges. Donneau de Visé dans la "guerre comique" contre M. RGB 8: 57–68, 1970.
562. ——, éd. La querelle de *l'Ecole des femmes*: comédies de Donneau de Visé, E. Boursault, C. Robinet, A. M. Montfleury, J. Chevalier et P. de La Croix. Didier, 1971. 2 v. 457 p.
    rev. A. J. Guibert *in* NL 2326: 12, 1972.
563. Suzuki, Koji. Donneau de Visé et la querelle de *l'Ecole des femmes*. ELLF 6: 49–60, 1965.
    rev. G, Mirandola *in* StF 27: 547, 1965.

L'IMPROMPTU DE VERSAILLES

564. Carriat, Amédée. En marge de *l'Impromptu de Versailles*: La Feuillade et Montfleury. MSCr 36: 2ᵉ fasc., 1967.
565. Decaux, Alain. Quand Monsieur de M. jouait à Versailles un "impromptu." Versailles 6: 12, 1955.
566. Fumaroli, Marc. Microcosme comique et macrocosme scolaire: M., Louis XIV et *l'Impromptu de Versailles*. RSH 45: 95–114, 1972.
567. Mongrédien, Georges. La bataille des "impromptus" entre M. et Antoine Montfleury. RGB 105: 69–79, 1969.
568. Nelson, Robert J. *L'Impromptu de Versailles* reconsidered. FS 11: 305–14, 1957.
    rev. F. Simone *in* StF 4: 142, 1958.

LES PLAISIRS DE L'ÎLE ENCHANTÉE and LA PRINCESSE D'ÉLIDE

569. Bauer, R. Les métamorphoses de Diane (Augustin Moreto y Cabana. *El desdén con el desdén*, 1654) et *la Princesse d'Elide* (1664). WT: 294–314, 1963.

570. Chevalley, Sylvie. *Les Plaisirs de l'île enchantée*. *See no. 220.*
571. Dédéyan, Charles. La structure de la comédie-ballet dans *la Princesse d'Elide* et *l'Amour médecin*. IL 6: 127–32, 1954.
572. Premsela, Martin J. Nieuwe Molieriana. Neo 38: 94–100, 1954. [Is *Mélisse, le mariage sans mariage*, the origin of *la Princesse d'Elide?*]
573. Rousset, Jean. L'île enchantée. Fête de théâtre au XVIIe siècle. MelMB: 435–41, 1967.
       rev. S. Crotto *in* StF 34: 148, 1968.

LE TARTUFFE

574. —— *ed. by* Fernand Ledoux. *See* CrB 2320.
575. —— *ed. by* Suzanne Rossat-Mignod. Editions sociales, 1958. 165 p.
576. —— *ed. by* Pierre Cogny. Rome, Signorelli, 1958. 157 p.
577. —— *ed. by* H. Gaston Hall. London, Arnold, 1960. 63 p.
578. —— *ed.* by Pierre Clarac. Larousse, 1962. 114 p.
579. —— *ed.* by Jacques Guicharnaud. N. Y., Dell, 1962. 191 p.
       rev. H. G. Hall *in* StF 21: 554, 1963.
580. —— *ed.* by F. Cecchini. Naples, Mezzogiorno, 1963. 117 p.
581. —— *ed.* by H. P. Salomon; *preface by* Maurice Baudin. Didier, 1964, 65. 136 p.
582. —— *ed.* by Robert Jouanny. Hatier, 1965. 109 p.
583. —— *ed.* by Jean Pol Caput. Larousse, 1965. 143 p.
584. —— *ed.* by Fernand Ledoux. ASc 368: 13–53, 1966.
585. —— *ed.* by Pierre Brunet, *mise en scène by* Roger Planchon. Hachette, 1967, 201 p.
586. —— *ed.* by C. J. A. Akker. Groningen, Walters, 1967. 100 p.
587. —— *ed.* by Franco Petralia. Milan, Mursia, 1967. 214 p.
       rev. G. Mirandola *in* StF 32: 354, 1967.
588. —— *ed.* by Raymond Bernex. Bordas, 1968. 128 p.
589. —— *ed.* by Hallam Walker. Englewood Cliffs, N. J., Prentice Hall, 1969. 124 p.
       rev. B. E. Hicks *in* MLJ 55: 121, 1971.
590. —— *ed.* by Emile Lavielle. Hachette, 1970. 150 p.
591. Lettre sur la comédie de *l'Imposteur*. *Reprint*, Geneva, Slatkine, 1968. 81 p.
592. L'Univers des héros de M. ASc 368: 54–65, 1966.
       contents: Marcel Giraudet. Triomphe de Tartuffe, 54; Jean Anouilh. Dans la nuit profonde du 17e siècle au joyau noir, 55; Georges Bernanos. Doutes et certitude sur l'éternité de l'imposteur, 55–6; Paul-Emile Deiber. Orgon: autoritaire mais non veule, 56–7; Béatrix Dussane. L'évolution du rôle, 57–8; Louis Jouvet. Et voici Tartuffe, 58–9; *and* Plaidoyer pour l'amoralité, 59–60; Thierry Maulnier. La mise en accusation de la sottise, 60; Jean Meyer. Il doit être ridicule, 61; le Rev. Père Rouquet. Ce n'est pas une oeuvre anticléricale, 61; François Périer. Intelligence et séduction, 61–2; Albert Thibaudet. Julien Sorel et Tartuffe, 62–4; Claude Sainval. Orgon, méchant esprit et méchant coeur, 64–5.
593. Aastrup, Klaus. *Tartuffe* og den danske Kritik. Edda 3: 129–36, 1970.
594. Amadou, Anne Lise. *Tartuffe* ansirt og Essays om M. Oslo, Gryldendal, 1970. 134 p.
595. Barret, Gisèle. Recherches des mise en scène françaises du *Tartuffe* de M. aux XVIIe et XVIIIe siècles, d'après des documents iconographiques

contemporains. (Thesis, Dip. Et. Sup., Univ. of Paris, Institut d'études théâtrales, 1961.) 126 p.

596. Bastide, François R. *Le Tartuffe*: l'angélisme de l'ignoble. NL 2154: 12, Jan. 2, 1969.

597. Baudouin, Michèle. Le thème dramatique de la direction de conscience à travers *le Tartuffe*, *La Mère coupable* de Beaumarchais, et *l'Otage* de Claudel. CESCh 7: 81–113, 1969.

598. Berman, Lorna. The frightening message of *Tartuffe*. RLau 1 & 2: 129–31, 1968.

599. Blanch, Antonio. Acogida popular de *El Tartufo*. RyF 180: 428–30, 1969.

600. Bonnet, H. M.: *Tartuffe*, II, 3, texte commenté . . . . Hmod: 11–4, Jan. 1962.

601. Borgerhoff, E. B. O. *Tartuffe*. EsCr 11: 16–8, 1971.

602. Bouffard, Odorie, O. F. M. Tartuffe, faux monnayeur en dévotion. Cult 28: 341–58, 1962.

603. Bourdien, Pierre. Tartuffe ou le drame de la foi et de la mauvaise foi. RMéd 19: 453–8, 1959.

604. Brandwajn, Rachmael. Twarz i maska: rzecz o *Swietoszku* Moliera (Le visage et le masque: *le Tartuffe* de M.) Warsaw, 1965. 292 p.
    rev. J. Birnberg *in* StF 41: 303–9, 1970.

605. Brisson. Pierre. 1664–1669: les cinq années de *Tartuffe*. Hist 36: 99–108, 1964.

606. Brunelli, Giuseppe A. L'hypocrite amoureux: un modello di *Tartuffe* tra i "chierici folli" *in his* Saggi critici da Ronsard a M. (Messina, Peloritana, 1963): 97–107.

607. Bürger, Peter. M.: *Le Tartuffe*. FTBG: 227–46, 1968.

608. Butler, Philip F. Orgon le dirigé. EJHT: 103–20, 1969.

609. ———. *Tartuffe* et la direction spirituelle au XVIIe siècle. MMEV: 48–64, 1969.
    rev. G. Mirandola *in* StF 40: 157, 1970.

610. Cairncross, John. New light on M: *Tartuffe; Elomire hypocondre. See* CrB 2326.

611. Carteret, le chanoine L. I. Tartuffe était-il franc-comtois? ou encore Tartuffe était-il le Chanitois Jacques Cretenet? ASBe 172: 249–61, 1958.

612. Chill, E. S. *Tartuffe*, religion and courtly culture. FHS 3: 151–83, 1963.
    rev. H. G. Hall *in* StF 26: 354–5, 1965.

613. Couton, Georges. Réflexions sur *Tartuffe* et le péché d'hypocrise, *cas-réservé*. RHLF 69: 404–13, 1969.

614. Dainville. F. de. Une pièce au dossier de *Tartuffe*. *See* CrB 2327.

615. Défourneaux, Marceline. M. et l'inquisition espagnole. BHis 64: 30–42, 1962.
    rev. D. Dalla Valle *in* StF 22: 135–6, 1964.

616. Deguy, M. Un vrai Tartuffe, ou l'espace dramatique et la noirceur. Crit 204: 403–10, 1964.
    rev. H. G. Hall *in* StF 24: 553, 1964.

617. Delcourt, Marie. Tricentenaire de *Tartuffe*: ii. imposteur ou hypocrite. Mro 17: 205–6, 1967.

618. Derche, Roland. Encore un modèle de Tartuffe . . . *See* CrB 2328.

619. ———. Le problème de Tartuffe. Crat: 242–5, 1957.

620. Dubuc, André. Une représentation de *Tartuffe* au Havre sous le Second Empire. ANor 3: 202–3, 1953.

621. Dupriez, Bernard. Tartuffe et la sincérité. EtFr 1: 52–67, 1965.
    rev. H. G. Hall *in* StF 26: 355, 1965.

622. Dussane, Béatrix. Vie et survie des déhos de théâtre: Tartuffe et Orgon. Conf 103: 47–54, 1959.

623. Fernandez Santos, Angel. Un falso teatro politico (*Tartufo* di M., por la Companía di Adolfo Marsillach) Insula (Madrid) 25(279): 15, 1970.

624. Gaxotte, Pierre. Les trois *Tartuffe*. FL: 1–2, Feb 25, 1961.

625. Gossman, Lionel. M. and *Tartuffe*; law and order in the XVIIth century. FR 43: 901–12, 1969.

626. Guicharnaud, Jacques. *See no 310.*

627. Hall, H. Gaston. M.: *Tartuffe*. London, Studies in French literature 2, 1960. 63 p.

628. Hartley, K. H. Pietro Aretino and M. AUMLA 20: 309–17, 1963.

629. Hatzfeld, Helmut. *Le Tartuffe in his* Initiation à l'explication des textes français (Munich, Hueber, 1969): 27–34.

630. Hewitt, Barnard. *The haunted houses* (Plautus) and *Tartuffe*. HSTh: 4–5, Nov., 1942.

631. Jomaron, Jacqueline. A propos d'un document de mise en scène (*Tartuffe* par Louis Jouvet, 1950). RHT 18: 210–5, 1966.

632. Jouvet, Louis. Pourquoi j'ai monté *Tartuffe*. *See* CrB 2331.

633. Jubécourt, Gérard S. de. A propos du tricentenaire de *Tartuffe*: Versailles et son poète M. MCLB 8(1) 9–13, 1969.

634. Kasparek, Jerry L. M.'s *Tartuffe*: an interpretation based on significant parallels with traditions of Roman satiric literature. (Thesis, Vanderbilt Univ., 1971) 308 p. Diss abs A 32: 2660, 1971/2.

635. Kuczynski, Jürgen. M., Boisguillebert und die Gesellschaft des absoluten Feudalismus *in his* Zur politikökonomischen Ideologie in Frankreich. (Berlin, 1968): 115–26. *See no. 341.*

636. Laurent, M. Explication française: Dorine au secours de Mariane (*Le Tartuffe*, 11, 3). Ec 8: 441–2, Feb. 8, 1964.

637. Lawrence, Francis L. The norm in *Tartuffe*. ROtt 36: 698–701, 1966.

638. Leclerc, Guy. *Dom Juan* dans la bataille de *Tartuffe*. *See no. 221.*

639. Le Hir, J. Genres et procédés littéraires: le comique dans *le Tartuffe*. Ec 8: 438, 479–80, 483–4, 521–2, 1964.

640. Lemaître, Henri. *Le Tartuffe* de M. "transfiguré" par François Davant, 1673. RLav 19: 322–47, 1964.

641. Lemarchand, Jacques. Tartuffe à la Comédie-Française. M. c'est aussi un texte. FL 1184: 39–40, 1969.

642. Lorigiola, Pierre, s.j. Destin de Tartuffe. Et: 531–4, May, 1965.
    rev. H. G. Hall *in* StF 26: 355, 1965.

643. Louise, René. Recherches sur les documents figurés relatifs aux mises en scènes françaises du *Tartuffe* de M. jusqu'en 1850. (Thesis, Dip. Et. Sup., Univ. of Paris, Institut d'études théâtrales, 1964) 162 p.

644. Mazzara, Richard A. Unmasking the imposter: *Les lettres provinciales* and *Tartuffe*. FR 37: 664–72, 1963/4.

644a. Mégret, Christian, Tartuffe et Organ: une amitié particulière. Car: 21, Jan. 8, 1969.

645. Melchinger, Siegfried. M., gestern, heute, morgen. Im Hinblick auf zwei Aufführungen: *Der Geizige* in Stuttgart, *Tartuffe* in Wiesbaden. Thh 8: 22–5, 1967.

646. Mélèse, Pierre. Un épisode peu connu de la querelle de *Tartuffe*. DSS 53: 51–4, 1961.
    rev. F. Simone *in* StF 18: 554, 1962.

647. Mellot, Jean. A propos du tricentenaire du second *Tartuffe*. Hmod 99: 19–22, 1967.

648. Mongrédien, Georges. Autour de la querelle du *Tartuffe*. RGB 107: 49–56, 1971.

649. Mornet, Daniel. Un prototype de Tartuffe. *See* CrB 2333.

650. Nelson, Robert J. The unreconstructed heroes of M. (*Dom Juan, Tartuffe, le Misanthrope*). TDR 4: 14–37, 1960. *See nos. 223 and 390.*

651. Niderst, A. Traits, notes et remarques de Cideville: documents sur M. RHLF 69: 826, 1969. [*On the word Tartuffe.*]

652. Orwen, Gifford P. Tartuffe reconsidered. FR 41: 611–7, 1968.

653. Paraf, Pierre. Dorine et Sganarelle. *See no. 221.*

654. Petralia, Franco. Tartuffe, ipocrito da quattro soldi. Lst 15: 5–14, 1966.
     rev. S. Robiolio *in* StF 30: 559, 1966.

655. ———. La lotta al Tartuffe e la laicizzazione del personaggio. Lst 15: 1–18, 1966. *Also in his ed. of the play; See no. 587.*
     rev. S. Robiolio *in* StF 31: 146, 1967.

656. Pholien, Georges. Une défense du *Tartuffe*. Mro 17: 179–96, 1967.

657. Picard, Raymond. *Tartuffe*, production impie? MélRL: 227–39, 1969.

658. Picoche, Jacqueline. Le vocabulaire du mariage dans *Tartuffe*. Clex 7(2): 43–9, 1965.

659. Planchon, Richard. La mise en scène du *Tartuffe* par RP. (March, 1964).
     reviews: M. Deguy. Un vrai Tartuffe ou l'espace domestique de la noirceur. Crit 20: 403–10, 1964 (*see* H. G. Hall *in* StF 24, 553, 1964); A. Gisselbrecht. Entretien avec R. Planchon. NCr 159: 131–4, 1964; H. Gouhier. Tartuffe sans problème. TR 197: 122–7, 1964; G. Hourdin. Réflexion sur *le Tartuffe*. Stem 8: 33–5, 1964; H. Lemaître. *Le Tartuffe* de M. transfiguré par François Davant. RLav 19: 322–47, 1964/5; P. Lorigiola. Destin de *Tartuffe*. Et: 631–41, 1964; G. Macchia. Le "questions graves" in commedia *in his* La scuola dei sentimenti (Rome, Caltanisetta, 1964): 110–4; R. Natal. *Tartuffe*. Tpo 53: 131–6, 1964; G. Portal. Lettre à Robert Poulet sur les débordements du vulgaire. EcP 227: 123–9, 1964. J. M. Brosse. Planchon découvre *Tartuffe*. Csai 8: 317–8, 1964/5: Claude Roy. Sur *Tartuffe*. NRF 23: 897–908, 1964; Poirot-Delpech. Le Monde, Mar. 11, 1965; R. Abirached. Roger Planchon entre Aristote et Brecht. Et: 642–7, 1964.

660. ———. Postface à *Tartuffe*. LFr: 16–7, Mar. 24, 1966.

661. Rambaud, Alfred. La querelle du *Tartuffe* à Paris et à Québec. Rlav 8: 421–34, 1954.

661a. Rhonelle, André. Personnalité ou dissimulation: Tartuffe et Asmondée. Echoj: 1–2, Jan. 1966.

662. Rossat-Mignod, Suzanne. La bataille de *Tartuffe*. Rrat 166: 229–41, 1957.

663. ———. La portée de *Tartuffe* à la fin du XVIIe siècle. *See no. 221.*

664. Roy, Claude. Sur *Tartuffe*, NRF 12: 897–908, 1964. *See no. 659.*
     rev. F. Simone *in* StF 27: 547, 1965.

665. Salomon, Herman P. Tartuffe et la sénsibilité moderne. FrMon 21: 19–21, 1963.

666. ———. *Tartuffe* devant l'opinion française. (Thesis, N. Y. Univ., 1961) 288p. Diss abs A 28: 1085, 1961/2. Presses universitaires, 1962. 194 p.
     rev. M. Richter *in* StF 19: 154, 1963; J. v. d. L *in* LevT: 127–8, 1964; P. Saintonge *in* RR 55: 211–3, 1964.

667. Salvan, Paule. *Le Tartuffe* de M. et l'agitation anticléricale en 1825. RHT 12: 7–19, 1960.
    rev. M. Richter *in* StF 19: 154, 1963. J. A. Guérard *in* France littéraire 6: 177, 1960.
668. Sanzenbach, Simone. Histoire et analyse de *Tartuffe* et de *Dom Juan*. AtL: 46–70, Mar. 1963.
669. Schérer, Jacques. *Tartuffe*: histoire et structure. CDU, 1965, 124 p. dactylographiées.
670. ———. Structure de *Tartuffe*. Sedes, 1966. 263 p.
    rev. J. P. Chauveau *in* IL 18: 77, 1966; J. Morel *in* RSH 128: 653–4, 1967; W. G. Moore *in* MLR 62: 39–41, 1967; W. D. Howarth *in* FS 21: 159, 1967; R. Guichemerre *in* RHLF 68: 851–2, 1968; H. G. Hall *in* StF 29: 301–2, 1966, 34: 151–2, 1968.
671. ———. Aspects des mises en scènes de *Bajazet* et de *Tartuffe in his* Les mises en scènes des oeuvres du passé, présentés par J. Jacquet et A. Veinstein (CNRS, 1957): 211–6.
    rev. F. Simone *in* StF 8: 315, 1959.
672. Sénart, Philippe. *Tartuffe* à la Comédie-Française; mise en scène de Robert Hirsch. RDDM22: 626–8, 1969.
673. Simone, A *Il Don Pilone* di Girolamo Gigli e il *Tartuffe* di M. Git 13: 59–68, 1960.
    rev. F. Simone *in* StF 14: 346, 1961.
674. Sion, Georges. Comment était Tartuffe. RGB 102: 123–6, 1966.
675. Trahey, John T. *Tartuffe*; a study of the play in production. (Thesis, Northwestern Univ, 1967) 439 p. Diss abs A 28: 2378, 1967/8.
676. Vandermeulen-De Greef, Marie Thérèse. Tricentenaire de *Tartuffe*: Orgon. Mro 17: 197–205, 1967.
677. Vier, Jacques. L'affaire Tartuffe *in his* Littérature à l'emporte-pièce. (Ed du Cèdre, 1958): 12–32.
678. Wayne, Richard J. The relationship of Tartuffe and Orgon in M.'s *Tartuffe*. The problem posed by its symmetry. (Thesis, Johns Hopkins Univ., 1968) 184 p. Diss abs A 32: 6946, 1971/2.
679. Woodward, James B. Stanislavsky works with *Tartuffe*. DrS 5: 73–7, 1966.

DON JUAN, OU LE FESTIN DE PIERRE

680. ———. L'Arche, 1953. 1956. 61 p.
681. ——— *ed. by* Robert Jouanney. Hatier, 1957, 1965. 96 p.
682. ——— *ed. by* W. D. Howarth. Oxford, Blackwell, 1958. 100 p.
    rev. J. Marks *in* FS 13: 269–70, 1959.
683. ——— *ed. by* Guy Leclerc. Editions sociales, 1960. 133 p.
    rev. F. Simone *in* StF 14: 346, 1961;. J. F. LeNy *in* Pen 92: 152–3, 1960.
684. ——— *ed. by* Anne-Marie *and* Henri Marel. Bordas, 1963, 1965. 127 p.
685. ——— Lausanne, La Cité Editeur, 1965. 122 p.
686. ——— *ed. by* Léon Lajealle. Larousse, 1965, 123 p.
687. ——— *ed. by* Philippe Sellier. Hachette, 1969. 48 p.
688. ——— Photo de Michel Barbier. Avant-Quart, 1969. 174 p.
689. ——— Documentation spéciale. Larousse, 1971. 142 p.
690. ——— Mise en scène d'Antoine Bourseiller à la Comédie-Française, 1967.
    rev. H. Gouhier *in* TR 231: 121–3, 1967; D. Nores *in* LN 172–4, May-June, 1967; R. Saurel *in* TM 22: 1705–9, 1967; P. Sénart *in* RDDM 20: 284–7,

1967; J. Vier *in* PC 21: 78–83, 1967; J. Carat *in* Pre 194: 68–70, 1967; Thierry Maulnier *in* RP 74: 140–3, 1967.

691. —— Mise en scène par la Compagnie du Cothurne, Théâtre du 8e, Lyon et Sartrouville, 1968.

rev. R. Abirached *in* NRF 33: 595–600, 1969; J. Lemarchand *in* FL: 41, Fe. 10, 1969; G. Sandier *in* QL 66: 27–8, 1969; R. Saurel *in* TM 24: 1706–8, 1969.

692. —— Thème de l'art universel. Table Ronde 119: 9–177. *See* CrB 2264.

content: Henry de Montherlant. Don Juan (Acte I), 9–32; Ortega y Grasset (*tr. by Mathilde Romès*). La figure de Don Juan, 33–9; Esther van Loo. La conversion et la mort de Don Juan historique, 40–9; Jean Doresse. Don Juan, figure d'un siècle et de toujours, 50–6; René Depuis. De la naissance espagnole de Don Juan à sa maturité française (1630–1665). 57–66; Henri Gouhier. L'inhumain Don Juan, 67–73; René Pomeau. Beaumarchais ou le mariage de Don Juan, 74–9; Henri Guillernin. Clartés sur le mystère Byron, 80–9; Micheline Sauvage. L'ombre d'un séducteur: Kierkegaard et Don Juan, 108–13; Maurice Pradius. Les méprises de l'affectivité: la méprise de la douleur; la méprise du plaisir; les équivoques de l'amour; Don Juan; 114–27; Josep Palau. Idées pour un Don Juan, 128–33; Suzanne Lilar. Deuz mythes de l'amour: Don Juan, Tristan, 134–7; André Le Gall. Don Juan n'est pas un homme, 138–43; Maria Le Hardouin. Passage de Don Juan, 144–8; Henri d'Amfreville. Don Juan et la démoralisation de l'amour, 149–55; Robert Poulet. Un Don Juan en prose, 156–60; Claude Elsen. La fin d'un mythe, 161–6; Michel Déon. Postérité de Don Juan, 167–8; Christian Caprier. Don Juan vu par Montherlant, 169–77.

693. Notre dossier *Don Juan.* Approches, no. 10, 1969.

694. Aagaard, Anton. Dom Juan—sagnet, dets litteraere og musikalske behandling før Mozart. Copenhagen, G.E.C. Gad, 1956. 87 p.

695. Abraham, Pierre. Dom Juan contre Alceste. *See no. 221.*

696. Arnavon, Jacques. Le Don Juan de M. *See* CrB 2267.

697. Aubrun, Charles V. Le Don Juan de Tirso de Molina et celui de M. KN 61: 99–104, 1959.

698. Bihler, Heinrich. M: *Don Juan.* FTBG: 247–70, 392–6, 1968.

699. Bonnichou, André. *Le Dom Juan* de M.; un problème de mise en scène par André Villiers. Masques, 1947. 24 p.

700. Bory, Jean-Louis. Une cuisine à la sauce M. *See no. 219.*

701. Brahmer, Mieczyslaw. Uwagi o Don Juane Moliera. KN 1: 28–38, 1954.

702. Brody, Jules. *Dom Juan* and *le Misanthrope*, or the esthetics of individualism in M. PLMA 84: 559–76, 1969.

703. Caldarini, Ernesta. La retorica di Don Giovanni. Aevum 45: 409–29, 1971.

704. Castro, Américo. El Don Juan de Tirso y el de M. como personajes barrocos. HomEM: 93–111, 1939.

705. Chevalley, Sylvie. Publication de *Dom Juan*; la carrière de *Dom Juan* 1665–1967 . . . . Program notes, Comédie-Française, 1967.

706. Coe, Richard N. The ambiguity of Don Juan. AJFS 1: 23–36, 1964.

707. Copfermann, Emile. Quelques réflexions sur le *Dom Juan* de Chéreau. LFr 1269, 14–5, 1969.

708. Corbert, Charles. L'originalité du *Convive de pierre* de Pouchkine. RLC 291: 48–71, 1955.

709. Coudert, Marie-Louise. Don Juan, Elvire et moi. *See no. 221.*

710. Doolittle, James. The humanity of M.'s Don Juan. *See* CrB 2270; *also no. 223.*
711. Dreano, M. Monsieur de Queriolet (Pierre Le Gouvelle) et Don Juan. RHLF 62: 503–13, 1962.
712. Dresh, Odile. Les traductions anglaises du *Dom Juan* de M. (Thesis, Maîtrise d'enseignement, Univ. of Paris, Institut d'études théâtrales, 1968) 160 p.
713. Fiorentino, Liberato. *Dom Juan* de M. *in his* Essais de littérature française (Bari, 1965): 5–23.
714. Françon, Marcel. Sur un passage mal compris (*Dom Juan* éd. W. J. Howarth). BFol: 401, 1961.
715. Frémy, Pierre. *Don Juan* II, 2 (la scène du pauvre). Texte commenté. HCl 48: 19–24, 1969.
716. Gaudefroy-Demombynes, J. Don Juan et le problème du mal. EcP 278: 73–86, 1969.
717. Gaxotte, Pierre. Le *Don Juan* de M. et les autres. FL: 1–2, Aug 20, 1960.
718. Gouhier, Henri. *See no. 692.*
719. Grillet, Yveline. Mise en scène de *Don Juan* par Patrice Chéreau. (Thesis, Maîtrise d'enseignement, Unvi. of Paris, Institut d'études théâtrales, 1970) 72 p.
720. Grimsley, Ronald. Don Juan theme in M. and Kierkegaard. *See* CrB 2274.
721. ——. Kierkegaard and the Don Juan legend; Kierkegaard as a critic of M. *in his* Søren Kierkegaard and French literature (Cardiff, Univ. of Wales Press, 1966) 11–25.
    rev. R. Trousson *in* StF 35: 323–4, 1968.
722. Guicharnaud, Jacques. *See no. 310.*
723. Hall, H. Gaston. A comic Don Juan. YFS 23: 77–84, 1959. *See no. 223.*
724. ——. *Don Juan*, la scène du pauvre *in* The art of criticism, ed. by Peter H. Nurse (Edinburgh, Univ. Press, 1969): 69–87.
    rev. S. Crotto *in* StF 39: 546, 1969.
725. Han, Françoise. *See no. 221.*
726. Horn, Dieter. Le *Don Juan* de Brecht, une adaptation de M. RLau 2: 83–9, 1969.
727. Howarth, W. D. *Don Juan* reconsidered; a defense of the Amsterdam edition. FS 12: 222–33, 1958.
    rev. F. Simone *in* StF 7: 142, 1959.
728. Jaffré, Jean. Donjuanisme et tartufferie: à propos du *Don Juan* de M. Pen 146: 90–109, 1969.
729. Jouvet, Louis. *Don Juan* de M. retrouvera-t-il un public? *See* CrB 2275.
730. Jurgens, Madeleine. Don Juan dans ses meubles. NL 13: Mar. 25, 1965.
731. Klajn, H. Zganarel kac sluga dvaju gospodara i Don Žuan kao rasobiličitelj licemerja. Sav 14: 189–206, 1968. [Sganarelle en tant que valet de deux maîtres et Don Juan en tant qu'homme qui démasque l'hypocrisie.]
732. Krogh, Torben. M's *Don Juan* i Komediehuset på Kongens Nytorv. FestKU: 10102, 1964.
733. Laufer, Roger. Le comique du personnage de Don Juan de M. MLN 58: 15–20, 1963.
    rev. H. G. Hall *in* StF 25: 154–5, 1965.
734. Lawrence, Francis L. The ironic commentator in M.'s *Don Juan*. StF 35: 201–7, 1968.
735. Leclerc, Guy. *See no. 221.*
736. Levêque, André. Le "spectre en femme voilée" dans *Don Juan*. MLN 76: 742–8, 1961.

737. Macchia, Giovanni. Il *Don Juan* di M., con un scelta di testa da Tirso de Molina, Dorimon, Villers, Thomas Corneille. Rome, De Sanctis, 1967, 163 p.

738. Mandel, Oscar. The theatre of Don Juan: a collection of plays and views, 1630–1963. Lincoln, Neb., Univ. Press, 1963. 731 p.

739. Maranini, Lorenza. Morte e commedia di Don Juan, intorna a una commedia di M. Bologna, Zanichelli, 1937. 131 p.

740. Mercier, Vivien. From myth to idea—and back *in* John Gassner. Ideas in the drama (N.Y., Columbia Univ. Press, 1964): 60–3.

741. Mönch, Walter. *Don Juan*. Ein Drama der europäischen Bühne. Tirso de Molina, M., Mozart. RLC 35: 617–39, 1961.

742. Moore, Will G. *Don Juan* reconsidered. MLR 52: 510–17, 1957.

743. Munteanu, B. Un mare neliniştit Don Juan. Per F: 30–48, 1946.

744. Nelson, Robert J. *See nos. 223* and *390*.

745. Neri, Fernando. M. drammatico: *Don Juan in his* Saggi (Milan, 1964): 251–68. [*First published in* 1929].

746. Pholien, G. Le *Don Juan* de M.; essai d'interprétation. Mro 7: 11–8, 1957.

747. Pintard, René. Temps et lieux dans le *Don Juan* de M. StIS, v. 2: 997–1006, 1966.
    rev. H. G. Hall *in* StF 32: 353, 1967.

748. Rastier, François. Les niveaux d'ambiguïté des structures narratives (*Don Juan*) Semiotica (The Hague) 3: 289–42, 1971.

748a. Rioux, J.-C. La métamorphose romantique de Don Juan. EcoL: 762, 797–8, 811–2, May 17, 1969.

749. Robert, René. Le *Don Juan* a-t-il été interdit? RSH 81: 50–3, 1956.

750. Ropars-Wuillenmier, Marie-Claire. Explication de texte: *Don Juan*, I, 2. FrMon 58: 36–8, 1968.

751. Rousset, Jean. *Don Juan* et le baroque. Diogène (Genoa) 14: 3–21, 1956.
    rev. F. Simone *in* StF 7: 142, 1959.

752. ——. *Don Juan* et les métamorphoses d'une structure. NRF 15: 480–90, 1967.

753. Ruch, M. Le personnage de Sganarelle dans la comédie de *Don Juan*. Hmod 1: 24–5, 1957.

754. Sablé, J. Types universels de la littérature françaises: Don Juan ou le drame du libertin. Ec 20: 419–22, 465–6, 1962.

755. Saint-Paulien [Maurice Ivan Sicard]. Don Juan, myth et réalité. Plon 1967. 352 p.
    rev. J. E. d'Angers *in* DSS 84–5: 185–6, 1969/70.

756. Sanzenbach, Simone. *See no. 668*.

757. Sauvage, Micheline. Une énigme littéraire: l'Elvire de *Don Juan*. LN 2: 103–12, 1954.

758. ——. Le cas Don Juan. Ed. du Seuil, 1953, 208 p.
    rev. P. van Tieghen *in* RHLF 57: 104–5, 1957.

759. Scherer, Jacques. Surle *Don Juan* de M. Sedes, 1967, 199 p.
    rev. H.G. Hall *in* StF 36: 550, 1968; G. Leclerc *in* RHLF 69: 691, 1969.

760. Schmidt, M.D. Les incarnations de Don Juan dans la littérature françaises. Bfr: 150–4, Feb. 1960.

761. Serrano, Poncela. Pushkin y *Don Juan*. RNCul 185: 80–94, 1968.

762. Serres, Michel. *Don Juan* au palais des merveilles; sur les statues au XVIIᵉ siècle. Eph 21: 385–90, 1966.

763. ——. Le don de *Don Juan* ou la naissance de la comédie. Crit 24: 251–63, 1968.

764. Singer, Irving. The shadow of *Don Juan*. MLN 85: 838–57, 1970.

765. ——. *Don Juan.* HudR 24: 447–60, 1971.
766. Tan, H. G. Quelques observations de la fonction de la statue du commandant dans *Don Juan* de M. LevT: 346–52, 1968.
767. Teyssier, Jean-Marie. Réflexions sur le *Don Juan* de M. Nizet, 1970. 192 p.
     rev. P. Baroni *in* CFr 18: 296–7, 1971.
768. Ubersfeld, Annie. *See no. 221.*
769. Vier, Jacques. Où va le théâtre? Le *Don Juan* de M. en marge d'une reprise au Théâtre Français. PC 107: 78–83, 1967.
770. ——. L'actuel éternise: le *Don Juan* de M. *in* Le réel dans la littérature et dans la langue, ed. par Paul Vernois (Klincksieck, 1967); résumeé pages 251–2.
771. Villiers, André. Le *Don Juan* de M., un problème de mise au point. *See* CrB 2281.
772. Walker, Hallam. The self-creating hero in *Don Juan.* Fr 36: 167–74, 1962/3.
772a. Wurmser, A. Classiques sous la pluie, *Dom Juan.* Lmod: 4, Sept. 1, 1960.

L'AMOUR MÉDECIN

773. —— *ed. by* Robert Jouanny. Hatier, 1958. 95 p.
774. —— *adapted by* Paul Van Keymeulen. Antwerp, De Sikkel, 1969. 43 p.
775. Dédéyan, Charles. *See no. 571.*
776. Girard, Joseph. A propos de *l'Amour médecin*; M. et Louis-Henri Daguin. *See* CrB 2259.

LE MISANTHROPE

777. —— *ed. by* Ronald A. Wilson. London, Harrap, 1945. 98 p.
778. —— *ed. by* Gustave Rudler. *See* CrB 2305.
779. —— *ed. by* Fernand Angué. Bordas, 1961. 126 p.
780. —— *ed. by* Charles Bouton; *préf. by* René Jasinski. Didier, 1962, 1967. 96 p.
781. —— *ed. by* Félix Guirand. Larousse, 1962. 105 p.
782. ——, suivi de la Lettre sur la comédie du *Misanthrope. ed. by* Edouard Lop & André Sauvage. Editions sociales, 1963. 1964. 219 p.
     rev. H. G. Hall *in* StF 22: 154–5, 1964; R. Guichemère *in* RHLF 64: 482, 1964.
783. —— *ed. by* G. Sablayrolles. Larousse, 1963. 127 p.
784. —— *ed. by* Clément Borgal, *mise en scène by* Jacques Charon. Hachette, 1965. 172 p.
785. —— *ed. by* Robert Jouanny & Georges Chappon. Hatier, 1966. 95 p.
786. —— *ed. by* Paul Gauriat. Hachette, 1970. 126 p.
787. —— & le Bourgeois gentilhomme. *ed. by* Denis M. Calandra. Lincoln, Neb., Cliffs, 1967. 71 p.
788. Amadou, Anne-Lisa. M.s Alceste. Edda 54: 377–91, 1967.
789. Ampola, Filippo. Note sul *Misanthrope* di M. RLMC 13: 89–91, 1960.
     rev. L. Derla *in* StF 13: 153, 1961.
790. Bastide, François R. Le *Misanthrope.* NL 2167: 13, April 3, 1969.
791. Bihler, Heinrich. M.: le *Misanthrope.* FTBG: 271–89, 396–9, 1968.
792. Bogliolo, Giovanni. M., Alceste et la misantropia. Paragone (Florence) 20: 66–80, 1969.
     rev. S. Crotto *in* StF 40: 156–7, 1970.
793. Bonfantini, M. M. e il *Misanthrope.* Milan, La Goliardica, 1956. 176 p.
794. Bos, Charles. Analysez le *Misanthrope* et dégagez-en la signification. CaErom 2: 1–11, 1964.

795. Bourdat P. Une source cornélienne du *Misanthrope*: *la Veuve*. IL 20: 129–31, 1968.
     rev. H. G. Hall *in* StF 39: 547, 1969.
796. Brisson, Pierre. Il y a 300 ans *le Misanthrope* saisissait d'un amour déçu. Hist 235: 56–63, 1966.
797. Brody, Jules. *See no. 702.*
798. Calvet, Jean. Alceste *in his* Les types universels dans la littérature française v. 2 (Fernand Lanore, 1964): 23–4.
799. Cismaru, Alfred. *Les Sincères* (Marivaux) and *le Misanthrope*: an attempt to settle the relationship. FR 42: 865–70, 1969.
800. Cohen, Marcel. "Tant mieux, morbleu, tant mieux" (*Misanthrope*, I, 1) *in his* Les critiques dramatiques (Flammarion, 1970): 34–7.
801. Cohn, Dorrit. *The Misanthrope*: M. and Hofmannsthal. Arcadia 3: 292–8, 1968.
802. Crumbach, Franz. H. Der dramaturgische Aspekt exemplifiziert an M.s Komödie *Der Menschenhasser in his* Die Struktur des epischen Theaters (Braunschweig, 1960): 309–20.
803. Dorman, Peter J. Wycherley's adaptation of *Le Misanthrope*. Rest T 8: 54–9, 62, 1969.
804. Dussane, Béatrix. Vie et survie des héros de théâtre: Alceste et Célimène. Conf 100: 22–34, 1959.
805. Dutourd, Jean. Misanthropie *in his* Le fond et la forme (Gallimard, 1960): 153–5.
806. Edmunds, John. *Timon of Athens* blended with *le Misanthrope*: Shadwell's recipe for satirical tragedy. MLR 64: 500–7, 1969.
807. Ekelund. E. Traditionen och nuet. NTid 34: 159–66, 1958.
808. Elliott, Robert C. *Le Misanthrope in his* The power of satire. (Princeton, N.J., Univ. Press., 1960): 168–84.
809. Friedson, A. M. Wycherley and M.: satirical point of view in the *Plain Dealer*. MP 64: 189–97, 1967.
     rev. H.G. Hall *in* StF 39: 547, 1969.
810. Gevrey, H. C. Note on an influence of M.'s *Misanthrope* on Jean Barclay: *les Aventures d'Euphormion* (Antwerp, 1711). RN 7: 40–1, 1965.
     rev. W. Leiner *in* StF 30: 558–9, 1966.
811. Gossman, Lionel. Alceste, Orgon and le ridicule de la nature. BucR 10: 15–27, 1961.
812. Greive, Arthur. M. als Versdichter. Zum Alexandriner im *Misanthrope*. Arch 207: 81–93, 1970.
813. Guicharnaud, Jacques. *See no. 310.*
814. Gutwirth, Marcel. *See no. 512.*
815. Hall, H. Gaston. The literary context of M.'s *le Misanthrope*. StF 41: 20–38, 1970.
816. Hay, Gerhard. M.s *Misanthrope* und seine Rezeption *in his* Darstellung des Menschenhasses in der deutschen Literatur des 18. und 19. Jahrhunderts (Frankfort/M, Anthenäum Verlag, 1970): 49–62.
817. Hope, Quentin M. Society in *le Misanthrope*. FR 32: 329–36, 1958/9.
818. Hubert, Judd D. Futility and self-deception in *le Misanthrope*. StMB: 165–84.
     rev. F. Simone *in* StF 23: 343–4, 1964.
819. Jamet, Dominique. Le jour où Paris bouda *le Misanthrope* (4 juin, 1666): demi échec d'un auteur à succès. FL 1050: 10, June 2, 1966.

820. Jasinski, René. M. et *le Misanthrope*. *See* CrB 2312. *Reprint*: Nizet, 1963.
821. Kerr, Walter. M. and Eliot: love and jitters back to back (NY Times, D, 2–3, Oct. 20, 1968. [*Prod. of R. Wilbur's tran. and Eliot's Cocktail Party*]
822. Lavis, Georges. Un fragment du *Misanthrope* (Acte I, 1). CaAT 7: 49–61, 1965.
823. Lemarchand, Jacques. Un *Misanthrope* burlesque. FL 1296: 31, Mar. 19, 1971. [*Bourseiller's production at the Odéon.*]
824. Lichet, Raymond. *Le Misanthrope* et le langage. FrMon 46: 41–3, 1967.
825. Lindsay, Frank W. Alceste and the sonnet. *See* CrB 2313.
826. Magendie, M. Le véritable sens du *Misanthrope*. *See* CrB 2314.
827. Maggi, Gino. Trece'anni d'*Il Misantropo*: la morale di M. OsRom 3: 3, July 14, 1966.
828. Michel, Marc. Alceste ou le misanthrope? NRF 11: 316–23, 1963.
     rev. F, Simone *in* StF 27: 547, 1965.
829. Monod, Richard. Comment parler de Célimène. ANice 8: 85–99, 1969.
830. Moore, Will G. Reflection on *le Misanthrope*. AUMLA 4: 198–203, 1967.
831. Nelson, Robert J. *See nos. 223. and 390.*
832. Niderst, Alain. *Le Misanthrope* de M. Europe Edition, 1969. 100 p.
833. O'Regan, M. J. Two notes on French reminiscences in Restauration comedy. Hermathena 93: 63–70, 1959. [*See Michael J. O'Neil in Abstract of English Studies* 3: 113, 1960.]
834. Picard, M. Le personnage d'Alceste dans *le Misanthrope* IL 9; 134–7, 1957.
835. Premsela, Martin J. Twee Korte aantekeningen bij M.'s *Misanthrope*. LevT: 315–6, 1956.
836. Regosin, Richard L. Ambiguity and truth in *le Misanthrope*. RR 60: 265–72, 1969.
837. Renard, R. Alceste ou la bonne conscience. Rnou 35: 17–24, 1962.
838. Ristat, Jean. Le Misanthrope. La mis(e) en trop(e) ou la fascination du désert. LF 1372: 3–5, Feb. 10, 1971.
839. Roghi, Michèle. Recherches sur quelques mises en scènes du *Misanthrope* de M. depuis sa création jusqu'à nos jours. (Thesis, Dip. Et. Sup., Univ. of Paris, Institut d'études théâtrales, 1964.) 162 p.
840. Romains, Jules. Le coeur de M. NL: 1, 13, May 12, 1966. (Firmin-Didot, 1966, 6 p.)
841. Rouden, Alex. *Le Misanthrope* a trois siècles. RLLfr 14: 53–6, 1967.
842. Rudin, Seymour. M. and *le Misanthrope*. ETJ 17: 308–13, 1965.
843. Sablé, J. Types universels de la littérature française: Alceste ou la vertu irrascible. Ec 31: 635-8, 1962.
844. Santesson, C. G. En svårtolkad passage i M.s *le Misanthrope*. MSprak 50: 44–51, 1956.
845. Schmidt, Julius. *See no. 425.*
846. Schunk, Peter. Zur Wirkungsgeschichte des *Misanthrope*. GRM 21: 1–15, 1971.
847. Sénart, Philippe. *Le Misanthrope* au Théâtre de France. RDDM 24: 438–40, 1971.
848. Shepherd, James L. M. and Wycherley's *Plain Dealer*: further observations. SCB 23: 37–40, 1963.
849. ——. Arsinoé as Puppeteer. Fr 42: 262–71, 1968/9.
850. Smoot, Jean J. Alceste: the incomplete Don Quixote. RN 12: 169–73, 1970.
851. Stegman, André. Une source nouvelle de M.: *l'Honnête homme* de Faret,

et la scène des portraits. RHT 3: 416, 1951.
852. Strozier, William A. *See no. 435.*
853. Sullivan, Edward D. The actor's Alceste; evolution of the *Misanthrope.* See CrB 2316.
854. Teppe, Julien. Du sac de Scapin au cabinet d'Alceste. Vlan: 390–3, 1965.
855. Touchard, Pierre-Aimé. Célimène abusive. [Nouvelle mise en scène du *Misanthrope* pour le 300ᵉ anniversaire] Mon: 12, Dec. 22, 1966.
856. de Trooz, Charles. Alceste et nous *in his* Le concert dans la bibliothèque (Bruxelles, 1959): 37–52. *Also in* RGen 71: 443–60, 1935.
857. Ulrich, Leo. Goldonis *Locandiera* und M.s *Misanthrope,* zwei Motiventwicklungen. RFor 1–2: 323–65, 1958. *Part in* CL 2: 660–70, 1959; *also in his* Romanistische Aufsätze (Köln, Graz, 1966): 321–56.
858. Venesoen, C. M. tragédien? DSS 83: 25–34, 1969.
859. Walker, Hallam. Action and illusion in *le Misanthrope.* KFLQ 9: 150–61, 1962.
860. Winter, J. F. A forerunner of M.'s *Misanthrope.* MLN 74: 507–13, 1959.
861. Wurmser, A. Une leçon de critique (*le Misanthrope*). LF: 2, Mar. 5, 1964.
862. Yarrow, D. J. A reconsideration of Alceste. FS 13: 314–31, 1959.
     rev. F. Simone *in* StF 10: 149, 1960.

LE MÉDECIN MALGRÉ LUI

863. ——. L'Arche, 1953. 48 p.
864. —— *ed. by* Fernand Angué. Bordas, 1963. 110 p.
865. ——, suivi de Le Médecin volant. *ed. by* Jean Boullé. Larousse, 1970. 129 p.
866. Christmann, Hans H. M.s *Médecin malgré lui* und der Stoff vom Bauern als Arzt. NS 15: 7–20, 1966.

LE SICILIEN OU L'AMOUR PEINTRE

867. —— *ed. by* H. Th. Vlaanderen. Groningen, Wolters, 1967. 24 p.
868. Hubert, Judd D. Une source romanesque du *Sicilien.* RHT 22: 157–9, 1970.

AMPHITRYON

869. —— *ed. by* Pierre Mélèse. Droz, 1946, 1950. 121, 180 p.
     rev. W. C. Moore *in* FS 2: 90–1, 1948.
870. —— *ed. by* Claude Jodry. Larousse, 1961. 132 p.
871. —— *ed. by* Michel Autrand. Bordas, 1966, 1971. 128 p.
872. Ampola, Filippo. L'*Anfitrione* di M. *in his* Fra uomini e poeti. (Pisa, 1962): 9–54. *First in* CivM 2: 1070–1107, 1930.
873. Astre, Georges A. Magies d'*Amphitryon.* CCRB 10: 7081, 1955.
874. Bugliani, Ivanna. *Amphitryon* et l'oeuvre de M. MLN 84: 565–98, 1969.
875. Crumbach, Franz. H. *Der Geizige, Amphitryon in his* Die Struktur des epischen Theaters (Braunschweig, 1960): 82–7.
876. Delcourt, Marie. Les personnages de la comédie ancienne et le théâtre français [Rotrou, M.]. BGB 4: 103–10, 1964.
877. De Leeuwe, H. H. J. M.s und Kleists *Amphitryon.* Neo 31: 174–93, 1947.
878. Diez, Bernard. *Amphitryon* 1968. (Un acte en vers libres pour célébrer le 300ᵉ anniversaire de l'*Amphitryon.*) ASc 396: 37–43, 1968.
879. Gossman, Lionel. M.'s *Amphitryon.* PLMA 78: 201–13, 1963.
880. Hébert, R. L. An episode in M.'s *Amphitryon* and Cartesian epistemology. *See* CrB 2262.

881. Hill, J. K. *Amphitryon*: a critical study. (Thesis, Univ. of Wales, 1963).
882. Jasinski, René. Deux Alcmène: de M. à Giraudoux. MélPJ: 413–29, 1970.
883. Lindberger, Örjan. The transformation of *Amphitryon*. Stockholm, Almguist & Wissell, 1956. 233 p.
    rev. F. Simone *in* StF 4: 143, 1958; J. Voisine *in* OrL 14: 244–6, 1959.
884. Lübke, Diethard. Kleists Umarbeitung von M.s *Amphitryon*. EGer 231: 358–66, 1968.
885. Macchia, Giovanni. Il "cocuage" celeste *in his* La scuola dei sentimenti (Rome, Caltanessetta, 1963): 115–9.
886. Rat, Maurice. *Amphitryon*, plaisir royal. IL 4: 23–6, 1958.
887. Römer, Paul. M.s *Amphitryon* und sein gesellschaftlicher Hintergrund. Bonn, Romanisches Seminar der Unviserität, 1967. 248 p.
    rev. W. Drost *in* StF 35: 358, 1968; Sofer *in* NS 17: 468, 1968; F. Stock *in* Arch 206: 309–11, 1970; W. D. Howarth *in* FS 24: 290–1, 1970.
888. Sembdner, Helmut. Kleist und Falk. Zur Entstehungsgeschichte von Kleists *Amphitryon*. JSchil 13: 361–96, 1969.
889. Szondi, Peter. *L'Amphitryon* de Kleist, une comédie d'après M. RSH 113: 37–49, 1964. *First in* Euphorion 55: 249–59, 1961; *also in his* Satz und Gegensatz (Frankfort/M, Insel Verlag, 1964): 44–57.
    rev. W. Leiner *in* StF 18: 553, 1962.
890. Taladoire, B. A. *L'Amphitryon* de Plaute et celui de M.: étude dramatique comparée. HomJB: 672–77, 1964.
891. Truchet, Jacques. A propos de l'*Amphitryon* de M.: Alcmène et La Vallière. MélRL: 241–8, 1969.
892. Ulrich, Leo. M.s *Amphitryon* und seine Vorgänger *in his* Romanistische Aufsätz (Cologne, Gras, 1966): 46–73. *First appeared in* ZFSL 47: 377–402, 1925.
893. Voisine, Jacques. *L'Amphitryon*, sujet de parodie. CAIEF 12: 91–101, 1960.
    rev. C. Rizza *in* StF 12: 548, 1960.
894. Wittkowski, Wolfgang. Der neue Prometheus; Kleists *Amphitryon* zwischen M. und Giraudoux. *in* Kleist und Frankreich; im Auftrag der Heinrich-von-Kleist-Gesellschaft (Berlin, Erich Schmidt, 1969): 27–82. *Tr. by* Donald Riechel *as* The new Prometheus: M. and Kleist's *Amphitryon in* CLS 8: 109–24, 1971.

GEORGE DANDIN

885. ——— *ed. by* Claude Jodry. Larousse, 1960. 89 p.
896. ———, suivi du Grand Divertissement royal de Versailles (18 juillet, 1668). *ed. by* Jacques Monférier. Bordas, 1968. 128 p.
    rev. H. G. Hall *in* StF 38: 348, 1969.
897. Bottke, K. G. Torelli's adaptation of a play by M. Ital 33: 205–8, 1956.
    rev. F. Simone *in* StF 5: 317, 1957.
898. Coimbra Martins, Antonío. A proposito de uma tradução de *George Dandin* atribuída a Alexandre de Gusnão. Subsídios para o estudo da projecção de M. em Portugal. Arquivos do Centro cultural português (Fundaçao C. Gulbenkian). v. 1: 216–35, 1969.
899. Dort, Bernard. *Dandin* en situation. Tpo 32: 1958. *Also in his* Théâtre public (Ed. du Seuil, 1967): 30–3.
900. ———. *George Dandin ou le mari confondu* au Théâtre de la Cité, à Villeurbaune. Tpo 32: 124–8, 1958.

901. Planchon, Roger. Notes pour *Dandin*. Tpo 33: 47–50, 1959.
902. ———. Un metteur en scène présente *George Dandin. See no. 160 :* 259–62.

L'AVARE

903. ——— *ed. by* Charles Dullin. *See* CrB 2264.
904. ——— *ed. by* P. J. Yarrow. London, Univ. Press, 1959. 144 p.
905. ——— *ed. by* Fernand Angué. Bordas, 1962. 127 p.
906. ——— *ed. by* Gabriel Bonno. Larousse, 1962. 93 p.
907. ——— *ed. by* Gérard Delaisement. Didier, 1964, 1966. 142 p.
908. ——— *ed. by* Louis Forestier & Jacques Mauclair. Hachette, 1965. 224 p.
909. ——— *ed. by* Léon Lajealle. Larousse, 1965. 123 p.
910. ——— *ed. by* Henri Philibert. Hachette, 1965. 1968. 127 p.
911. ——— *ed. by* Georges Chappon. Hatier, 1966. 95 p.
912. ——— *ed. by* Giovanni Bianco. Milan-Rome, Dante Alighieri, 1966. 166 p.
913. ——— *ed. by* André Delaunoy. Antwerp, Nederlandsche Bookhandel. 1969, 116 p.
914. Bastide, Françis R. *L'Avare* de M. NL, Oct. 2, 1969. *Also in FR* 43: 654–6, 1969/70.
915. Chamarat, Georges. Harpagon est-il un personnage comique? Conf 157: 20–32, 1963.
    rev. H. G. Hall *in* StF 24: 552, 1964.
916. Crumbach, Franz. *See no. 875.*
917. Doolittle, James. Bad writing in *l'Avare. See no. 222.*
918. Dufrenne, Madeleine. Deux notes d'histoire littéraire: 1. M. sous les traits d'Harpagon. Fl 45: 54–8, 1962.
919. Dullin, Charles. *See no. 223.*
920. Gutwirth, Marcel. The unity of M.'s *l'Avare*. PLMA 76: 359–66, 1961.
    rev. L. Derla *in* StF 16: 152, 1962.
921. Hubert, Judd D. Theme and structure in *l'Avare*. PMLA 75: 31–6, 1960.
    rev. JD *in* DSS 49: 86–7, 1960; L. Derla *in* StF 12: 598, 1960.
922. Jauss, Hans R. M.: *l'Avare*. FTBG: 290–310, 1968.
923. Kilm, Jean-Jacques. Pierre Larivey, précurseur de M. BSAube 34: 4–9, 1963.
924. Melchinger, Siegfried. *See no. 645.*
925. Rochemay-Gordias, G. M. *See no. 152.*
926. Stoker, John T. Fénelon's errors concerning M.'s Harpagon. MLR 49: 472–3, 1954.
927. ———. Harpagon's "les autres." (*l'Avare* I, 2). Cult 27: 356–62, 1966.
928. Walker, Hallam. Action and ending in *l'Avare*. FR 34: 531–6, 1960/1. *See no. 921.*

MONSIEUR DE POURCEAUGNAC

929. ——— & la Comtesse d'Escarbagnas, *ed. by* Léon Lajealle. Larousse, 1958. 107 p.
930. Burger, Hilde. Hofmannsthal's debt to M. Monsieur de Pourceaugnac and Baron Ochs von Lerchenau. ML 39: 56–61, 1958.

LE BOURGEOIS GENTILHOMME.

931. ——— *ed. by* René d'Hermies. Larousse, 1962. 114 p.

932. —— *ed. by* René Jouanny & Georges Chappon. Hatier, 1966. 102 p.
933. —— *ed. by* Louis M. Moriarty. London-N.Y., Macmillan-St. Martins Press, 1962. 160 p.
934. —— *ed. by* Jean Thoraval. Bordas, 1963. 143 p.
935. —— *ed. by* A. C. Clapin. Cambridge, Univ. Press, 1963. 111 p.
936. —— *ed. by* Yves Hucher. Larousse, 1965. 134 p.
937. —— *ed. by* Gilles Sandier & Jean Meyer. Hachette, 1965. 224 p.
938. —— *ed. by* Claude K. Abraham. Englewood Cliffs, Prentice-Hall, 1966. 137 p.
      rev. J. Neustein *in* FR 40: 156–7, 1966/7: H. L. Robinson *in* MLJ 50: 517–8, 1966.
939. —— *ed. by* H. G. Hall. London, Univ. Press, 1966. 160 p.
      rev. F. Simone *in* StF 28: 149–50, 1966; J. Morel *in* DDS 76: 146–7, 1967; D. W. Howarth *in* FS 22: 156–7, 1968; Q. Hope *in* RR 59: 223, 1968.
940. —— *ed. by* Fernand Angué. Bordas, 1967. 128 p.
941. —— & la Comtesse d'Escarbagnas *ed. by* Jean Thoraval. Bordas, 1967. 192 p.
942. —— *ed. by* René Vaubourdolle. Hachette, 1935, 1968. 93 p.
943. —— *ed. by* Yves Brunsvick & Paul Ginestier; préf. de Paul van Tieghem. Didier, 1968. 152 p.
      rev. H. G. Hall *in* StF 38: 347, 1969.
944. Ayda, Adèle. M. et l'envoyé de la Sublime Porte. CAIEF 9: 103–16, 1957.
945. Chamarat, Georges. Un homme de bonne volonté: le bourgeois gentilhomme. Conf 252: 39–49, 1971.
946. Coulaudon, Aimé. De Royat à M. RSCler 14: 14–5, 1963.
      [Géraud de Cordemoy's *Discours physique de la parole* source for the prononciation scene.]
947. Falk, Eugene H. M., the indignant satirist: le *Bourgeois gentilhomme*. TDR 5: 73–8, 1960.
948. Ganz, Hans U. Zur Quellenfrage des *Bourgeois gentilhomme*. Alib 11: 238–45, 1963. *Published separately* Florence, Sansoni, 1964. 16 p. *Also in* MK 14: 310–7, 1968.
949. Garapon, Robert. La langue et le style des différents personnages du *Bourgeois gentilhomme*. FMod 26: 103–12, 1958.
950. Gil J. Note sur un piège de M. RMM 74: 263–7, 1969.
951. Laulan, Robert. *Le Bourgeois gentilhomme* et les circonstances de sa création. MF 332: 533–6, 1958.
952. Leroy, Maurice. Cordemoy et le *Bourgeois gentilhomme*. BARB 52: 76–95, 1966. *See no. 946.*
953. Maxfield-Miller, Elizabeth. The real M. Jourdain of le *Bourgeois gentilhomme*. SP 56: 62–73, 1959.
      rev. F. Simone *in* StF 8: 313, 1959.
954. Peixoto, Afranio. *Le Bourgeois gentilhomme* et le *Gentilhomme apprenti* (Dom Francesco Manoel, 1665). HomEM: 175–82, 1939.
955. Rat, Maurice. Le père Poquelin et son fils M., ont-ils servi de modèle à Monsieur Jourdain. Il 4: 23–8, 1955.
956. Rouillard, Clarence D. The background of the Turkish ceremony in le *Bourgeois gentilhomme*. UTQ 39: 33–52, 1969.
      rev. H. G. Hall in StF 42: 549, 1970; W. Leiner *in* StF 43: 151, 1971.
957. Stoker, John T. *Le Bourgeois gentilhomme*, 1670–1970. Cult 31: 338–49, 1970.

958. Walker, Hallam. Strength and style in *le Bourgeois gentilhomme*. FR 37: 282–7, 1963/4.
    rev. H. G. Hall *in* StF 24: 552, 1964.

PSYCHÉ

959. Derche, Roland. *Psyché* par M. *in his* Quatre mythes poétiques (Sedes, 1962): 126–37.
959b. Lapp, John C. Corneille's *Psyché* and the metamorphoses of love. FS 16: 395–404, 1972.
    Vanuxem, J. Les fêtes de Louis XIV et le baroque de la *Finta* Pazza à *Psyché*, 1645–71 *in* Le baroque au théâtre (Mautauban, 1967): 34–44.
    rev. F. Simone *in* StF 35:348, 1968.
960. Wadsworth, Philip A. The composition of *Psyché*. RUS 53: 69–76, 1967.

LES FOURBERIES DE SCAPIN

961. —— *ed. by* Jacques Copeau, 1951. *See* CrB 2297 *and no. 223.*
962. —— *ed. by* René d'Hermies. Larousse, 1962. 104 p.
963. —— *ed. by* Jacques Monférier. Larousse, 1964. 126 p.
964. —— *ed. by* Robert Jouanny. Hatier, 1965. 78 p.
965. —— *ed. by* Jean Fabre. Bordas, 1964, 1967. 127 p.
966. —— *ed. by* Georges Chappon. Hatier, 1968. 95 p.
967. —— *ed. by* Jean Lombard. Hachette, 1969. 64 p.
968. —— *ed. by* John T. Stoker. London, Univ. Press, 1971. 88 p.
    rev. H. G. Hall *in* STF 44: 350, 1971.
969. Claudel, Paul. Le ravissement de Scapin, d'après *les Fourberies de Scapain*. Op 55: 1–19, 1952.
910. Dussane, Béatrix. Vie et survie des héros de théâtre: Scapin et Dorine. Conf 104: 43–51, 1959.
971. Gorin, Carol. Contrasts in *les Fourberies de Scapin*. RN 9: 265–6, 1968.
972. Levin, Harry. From Terence to Tabarin: a note on *les Fourberies de Scapin*. YFS 38: 128–37, 1967.
973. Pujos, Charles. Cyrano et M. *in his* Le double visage de Cyrano de Bergerac (Agen, Imp. moderne, 1951): 171–84.
974. Simon, Alfred. La scapinade providentielle. CCRB 9: 81–6, 1955.

LA COMTESSE D'ESCARBAGNAS

975. ——. *See no. 929.*

LES FEMMES SAVANTES

976. —— *ed. by* Pierre Mélese, 1948. *See* CrB 2293.
977. —— l'Arche, 1956. 78 p.
978. —— *ed. by* Jean Pêcher & André Galan. Larousse, 1956. 113 p.
979. —— *ed. by* Jean Cordier & Charles Bruneau. Didier, 1959. 96 p.
    rev. L. Derla *in* StF 11: 348, 1960; W. D. Howarth *in* FS 15: 61–2. 1961.
980. —— *ed. by* Fernand Angué. Bordas, 1961. 127 p.
981. —— *ed. by* Jean Lecomte. Larousse, 1964. 159 p.
982. —— *ed. by* Fernand Angué. Bordas, 1965, 1967. 127 p.
983. —— *ed. by* Georges Chappon. Hatier, 1967. 96 p.
984. —— *ed. by* Herbert Carrier. Hachette, 1968. 127 p.

985.   —— *ed. by* Georges Chappon. Oxford, Pergamon Press, 1968. 95 p.

986.   —— *ed. by* Jean Meyer. ASc 409–10: 7–48, 1968. *Also separately*, 71 p. *Also contains*: Trois siècles jugent *les Femmes savantes*, 53–6; Les femmes et la société du 17e siècle, 57–8; Les personnages, 63–4; Sylvie Chevalley. L'interprétation des *Femmes savantes*, 65–7; *and* Robert Thomas. Rencontres boulevardières avec M., 68–9.

987.   ——, suivi d'*Un Caprice* (Musset). Avant-Scène, 1969. 94 p.

988.   —— *ed. by* Jean Cazalbou & Denise Sévely. Ed. sociales, 1971. 256 p.

989.   —— *ed. by* Jean Lecomte. Larousse, 1971. 170 p.

990.   Baldinger, K. Etwas über M., grammaire und grand'mère, WZFSU 5: 223–7, 1956.

991.   Cerney, Vaclav. Le "je ne sais quoi" de Trissotin. RHS 103: 367–78, 1961. *rev.* F. Simone *in* StF 15: 550, 1961.

992.   Chevalley, Sylvie. *Les Femmes savantes*: monographie. Collection de la Comédie-Française, 1962. 48 p.
       contents: list of productions, 1680–1960; De Visé's account of the first performance; G. Reynier. *Le style des Femmes savantes*; Pierre Mélese. *Les Femmes savantes* dans l'oeuvre de M; 5–14; J. Truchet. Les aspirations intellectuelles des femmes au XVIIe siècle, 15–22; S. Chevalley. *Les Femmes savantes* à la Comédie-Française, 29–34; S. Chevalley. L'interprétation des *Femmes savantes*, 35–46.
       rev. H. G. Hall *in* StF 26: 355, 1965.

993.   Cohen, Marcel. Philaminthe: Elle a insulté mon oreille . . . (II, 2). *in* Toujours des regards sur la langue française. (Ed. sociales, 1970); 19–24.

994.   Gossen, jr., Emmett J. *Les Femmes savantes*: métaphore et mouvement dramatique. FR 45: 37–45, 1971/2.

995.   Heisig, K. Trissotin und Vadius in M.s *Femmes savantes*. GMonat 12: 212–3, 1962.

996.   Jeune, S. M., le pédant et le pouvoir; note pour le commentaire des *Femmes savantes*. *See* CrB 2295.

997.   Maurel, Albert G. Notes sur un vers de M.: le livre de compte de Julien (IV. 5, 1394). Hmod, Mar., 1969.

998.   Michel, P. Montaigne-Chrysale. BSAM 18: 36–41, 1956.

999.   Morel, Jacques. La structure de Clitandre. RHT 2: 118–26, 1960.

1000.   Périvier, Jacques. Equivoques moliéresque: le sonnet de Trissotin. RSH. [to appear]

1001.   Perregaux, Béatrice. *Les Femmes savantes*, une mise en scène d'André Steiger. CAIEF 73–85, 1969. (Discussion: 270–8.)

1002.   Rat. Maurice. Trissotin-Cotin et Vadius-Ménage. EdN 10: 10–1, 1954.

1003.   Robinson, John K. French critical opinion of M.'s *les Femmes savantes* (1672–1968). (Thesis, Columbia Univ., 1970). 165 p. Diss Abs A 31: 2936, 1970/1.

1004.   Sénart, Philippe. *Les Femmes savantes* (au Théâtre de l'Est, Parisien). RDDM 21: 583–5, 1968.

1005.   ——. *Les Précieuses ridicules, les Femmes savantes* à la Comédie-Française. RDDM 25: 690–4, 1972.

1006.   Sion, Georges. *Les Femmes savantes* 1925 ou les coups de pieds qui se perdent. RGB 105: 115–7, 1969.

1007.   Timmermans, G. *Les Femmes savantes*; analyse littéraire. Hasselt (Bel.), Athénée royal, 1947.

1008. Tournaire, Georges. Causeries littéraires: *les Femmes savantes*. Plume d'Or, 1955. 159 p.
1009. Vier, Jacques. Des *Femmes savantes* à Mme Simone de Beauvoir. RLav 18: 608–26, 1964.

LE MALADE IMAGINAIRE

1010. —— *ed. by* Pierre Valde. 1946. 196 p. *See* CrB 2300.
1011. —— *ed. by* Daniel Mornet, 1947. 104 p. *See* CrB 2299.
1012. —— *ed. by* Jean-Louis Bory, *mise en scéne by* Robert Manuel. Hachette, 1956, 1965. 222 p.
1013. —— *ed. by* G. Eugène-Fasnacht. London-N.Y., Macmillan, St. Martins Press, 1961. 128 p.
1014. —— *ed. by* René de Messières. Larousse, 1962. 105 p.
1015. —— *ed. by* Alphonse Bouvet. Bordas, 1963. 143 p.
1016. —— *ed. by* Yves Hucher. Larousse, 1965. 159 p.
1017. —— *ed. by* Peter H. Nurse. Oxford,˙ Univ. Press, 1965. 162 p.
        rev. P. Voltz *in* RHLF 67: 815, 1967; H. G. Hall *in* StF 29: 353, 1966; J. Neustein *in* FR 41: 718, 1968.
1018. —— *ed. by* François Hinard. Hachette, 1970. 131 p.
1019. ——. Paris-Bruxelles-Montréal, Didier, 1971. 146 p.
1020. Cairncross, John. Note sur la genèse du *Malade imaginaire*. CAIEF 16: 282–4, 1964.
1021. Cismaru, Alfred. *See no. 533*.
1022. Couton, Georges. Quand Hippocrate collabore avec M. AUMLA: 65–9, 1969.
        rev. G. Mirandola *in* StF 41: 348, 1970.
1023. Dubarry, J. J. & Cl. Beausoleil. La cérémonie du doctorat en médicine avec M. Pméd: 57–9, 1957.
1024. Dumur, G. *Le Malade imaginaire* au T. N. P. Tpo 28: 81–4, 1958.
1025. Eckhardt, Alexandre. Un faux "Malade imaginaire". MélRL: 249–58, 1969.
1026. Engelberts, R. C. M.s *le Malade imaginaire* onder invloed van de *Aulularia* van Plautus. Neo 1: 44–60, 1954.
1027. Gilula, Dvora. The graduation ceremony of the medical school in the *Imaginary invalid*: M.'s use of Latin and its rendition in the Hebrew translation by N. Altermann. Hasefrut (Tel-Aviv) 1: 529–37, 1969.
1028. Hartley, K. H. An Italian source for part of the "premier intermède" in *le Malade imaginaire*. MLN 79: 309–11, 1964.
1029. Jeanne, J. Au chevet du *Malade imaginaire*. IT 5: 19–24, 1959.
1030. Knowlson, James R. *Le Malade imaginaire*: the "invention nouvelle" of Cléante. MLR 58: 69–70, 1963.
        rev. H. G. Hall *in* StF 25: 155, 1965.
1031. Lainé, Pascal. Petit Lacan illustré (extraits). CaCh 13: 152–62, 1971.
1032. Lowe, R. W. *See no. 188*.
1033. Mas, Raoul. Une oeuvre méconnue: *le Malade imaginaire*. Hum: 1–4, June 1962.
1034. Milhaud, M. & G. *See no. 221*.
1035. Pitou, Spire. *Le Malade imaginaire* and Grandval's *le Valet astrologue* (1710). RN 3: 30–2, 1961.
1036. Sénart, Philippe. *Le Malade imaginaire* à la Comédie Française. RDDM 15: 170–3, 1972.
1037. Stackelberg, Jürgen von. M.: *le Malade imaginaire*. FTBG: 311–2, 402–3, 1968.

1038. Stoker, John T. Toinette's age and temperament. MLR 37: 102–3, 1955/6.
1039. ———. Argan's sickness in M.'s *le Malade imaginaire*. Cult 30: 122–8, 1969.

LE REMERCIEMENT AU ROI

1040. Brin, Erwana. Le Remerciement au Roy de M., 1663. Humanisme actif 2: 187–9, 1968.
1041. Rountree, Benjamin. Narrative poetry as drama: M.'s *Remerciment au Roi*. RN 9: 260–4, 1968.

MAXIMES

1042. Leggevie, R. Maximes de M, présentées par . . . . The Hague, Martius Nijhoff, 1959. 80 p.
     rev. F. Simone *in* StF 11: 348, 1960; W. D. Howarth *in* FS 15: 163–4, 1961; P. J. Yarrow *in* MLR 56: 146, 1961; J. Hytier *in* RR 52: 231–3, 1961; S. Jeune *in* RHLF 62: 100, 1962.

Works Attributed

1043. Le docteur amoureux, comédie du 17ᵉ siècle présentée par A. J. Guibert. Paris-Geneva, Menard-Droz, 1960. 71 p.
     rev. F. Simone *in* StF 13: 153–4, 1961; L. Chancerel *in* RHT 14: 68–70, 1962. *See no. 160, 197–9.*
1044. La folle querelle ou la critique d'*Andromaque*, comédie attribuée à M. et à Subligny, . . . 1881. *Reprint*, Geneva, Slatkine, 1968. 83 p.
1045. Jogunet ou les vieillards dupés, comédie en trois actes par M. (Première forme des Fourberies de Scapin. . . .), 1816. *Reprint*, Geneva, Slatkine, 1968. 81 p.
1046. Marchand, Jean. *L'Eclogue*, esi-elle de M.? BSGuy 24: 48–9, 1954.
1047. ———. Une pièce inconnue attribuable à M., dans un rarissime ouvrage de François Colletet. BBB 5: 218–24, 1954.

XI   INFLUENCE ON FRENCH AND FOREIGN AUTHORS; PERFORMANCES AND INTERPRETATIONS IN FOREIGN COUNTRIES.

France and Belgium

1048. Ages, Arnold. M. *in his* The private Voltaire; three studies in the correspondence. StV 81: 7–125, 1971.
1049. Alsip, Barbara W. Fernand Crommelynck, spiritual heir of M. (Thesis, Emory Univ., 1971) 849 p. Diss abs A 32: 1500–1, 1971/2.
1050. Bismut, R. Une scène de M. dans *Madame Bovary*. BSFI 23: 14–7, 1963.
1051. Cismaru, Alfred G. The sources of Marivaux's theatre as derived from the theatre of M. (Thesis, N. Y. Univ., 1960) 151 p. Diss abs A 21: 3198, 1961/2.
1052. ———. *See no. 533.*
1053. ———. M.'s *le Tartuffe* in Marivaux's work. KFLQ 12: 142–54, 1965.
1054. ———. The moliéresque origins of *les Fausses confidences*. Cithara 7: 67–73, 1967. *Also in* KFLQ 15: 223–9, 1968.
1055. ———. *See no. 799.*
1055a. Desvignes, L. Marivaux et *La Méprise* (Plaute. *Menechmes* et M. *Amphi-*

tryon). Exploitation d'un thème antique. RLC 41: 166–79, 1967.

1056. Fellows, Otis. M. during the aftermath of the Enlightenment. KFLQ 14: 25–32, 1967.

1057. ———. M. à la fin du siècle de Lumière. StTB: 330–49, 1967. *Also in his* From Voltaire to "la nouvelle critique": problems and personalities (Geneva, Droz, 1970): 125–40.

1058. Garapon, Robert. Perspectives d'études sur La Bruyère: les sources littéraires des *Caractères*: LaBruyère et M. IL: 47–53, Mar.–April, 1965.

1059. Gevrey, H. C. *See no. 810.*

1060. Hope, Quentin M. M. and Saint-Evremond. PLMA 76: 200–4, 1961.
  rev. F. Simone *in* StF 16: 153, 1962.

1061. Hytier, Adrienne D. Diderot et M. DS 8: 77–103. 1966.

1062. Ince, W. M. Valéry on M.: an intellectual out of humor. MLR 60: 41–7, 1967.
  rev. H. G. Hall *in* StF 26: 354, 1965.

1063. Larnaudie, Suzanne. M. et Jean-Paul Sartre. ATou (Le Mirail) 18 (2), 1970.

1064. ———. M. et Jean-Paul Sartre: deux visages du donjuanisme. Littératures (Toulouse) 18: 67–85, 1971.
  rev. F. Simone *in* StF 44: 350, 1971.

1065. Lobet, Marcel. LaFontaine, M., et les moralistes français *in his* Classiques de l'an 2000 (Ed. de la Francité, 1970): 99–102.

1066. McBride, Robert. The sceptical vision of M.: a study in paradox (M. and La Mothe le Vayer). (Thesis, Queen's Univ., Belfast, 1970).

1067. ———. Un ami sceptique de M. StF 45: 1972.

1068. Müller, Franz W. Dancourts *Prologue des trois cousines*: Probleme der M.-Imitation in der Komödie der Frühaufklärung. Archiv 196: 113–44, 1960.

1069. Nurse, Peter H. M., précurseur de Marivaux. RSH 100: 379–84, 1960. *Also in* Marivaux and M. ML 15: 102–5, 1960.
  rev. L. Derla *in* StF 15: 551, 1961.

1070. Pellissier, Sidney L. The comic theatre of M. and of Ionesco: a comparative study. (Thesis, Louisiana State Univ., 1965) 215 p. Diss abs A 26: 4670–1. 1965/6.

1071. Pitou, Spire. *See no. 1035.*

1072. ———. M., Dancourt and Valentin. MLQ 23: 115–9, 1962.
  rev. G. Franceschetti *in* StF 16: 153, 1962.

1073. ———. *See no. 505.*

1074. Tournemille, J. M. et l'essai de Montaigne intitulé "De la ressemblance des enfants aux pères." BSAM 18: 42–4, 1956.

1075. Vier, Jacques. *See no. 1009.*

1076. ———. De M. à Jean-Paul Sartre *in his* Littérature à l'emporte-pièce (Eds. du Cèdre, v. 5, 1969): 15–21; *also in* L'homme nouveau: 18, Dec. 15, 1968.

1077. Wagner, Angelica M. M. and the age of Enlightenment. (Thesis, Columbia Univ., 1968) 353 p. Diss abs A 29: 1237, 1968/9.

1078. Watson, Harold. Saint-Beuve's M., a romantic Hamlet. FR 38: 606–18, 1965.
  rev. H. G. Hall *in* StF 26: 354, 1965.

1079. Wood, Paul W. A comparative study of Jean Anouilh and M.: the development of thought, characters and techniques in Anouilh's theatre considered in relation to M. (Thesis, Northwestern Univ., 1970) 223 p. Diss Abs A 31: 4801, 1970/1.

1080. Wurmser, André. Le maître de Balzac *in his* Conseils de révision (Gallimard, 1972): 9–15.

1081. Zanetta, Claire. Marmontel et M. EtJE: 105–16, 1970.

England

1082. Auffret, J. Etherege à l'école de M. CSH, v. 1: 395–407, 1968.
   rev. S. Crotto *in* StF 39: 547, 1969.
1083. Bean, Cecily M. M. and Wycherley, a comparative study of some aspects of their works. (Thesis, M. A., Westfield College, London, 1951).
1084. Coste, Brigitte. M. et Wycherley: deux génies comiques. (Thesis, M. A., Mount Holyoke College, 1967) 199 p.
1085. Danchin, P. Quatre adaptations de M. sur la scène anglaise à l'époque de la Restauration. CSH, v. 1: 327–71, 1968.
   rev. S. Crotto *in* StF 39: 547, 1969.
1086. Desvignes, Lucette. M. et Cyrano ont-ils connu Shakespeare. RLC 40: 110–21, 1966.
   rev. F. Simone *in* StF 29: 353–4, 1966.
1087. Dorman, Peter J. *See no. 803.*
1088. Edmunds, John. *See no. 806.*
1089. Engel, Claire E. Thomas Alcock and John Wilmot, Earl of Rochester: *The famous pathologists or the noble Mountebank.* RSH 105: 121–2, 1962.
1090. Friedson, A. M. *See no. 809.*
1091. Gassman, B. French sources for Goldsmith's *The goodnatur'd man.* PhQ 39: 56–65, 1960.
   rev. L. Derla *in* StF 11: 350, 1960.
1092. Guezennec, Gaële. L'éternel féminin chez M. et Congrève. (Thesis, M. A., Mount Holyoke College, 1967) 72 p.
1093. Hergešič, J. Shakespeare, M., Goethe. Zagreb, Zora, 1957. 300 p.
1094. Macey, Samuel L. Theatrical satire as a reflexion of changing tastes. (Thesis, Univ. of Washington, 1966) 226 p. Diss abs A 27: 3014, 1966/7. [*L'Impromptu de Versailles*, Sheridan's *Critic* and others as a genre.]
1095. Mandach, André de. M. et la comédie de moeurs en Angleterre (1660–1668). *See* CrB 2222.
1096. Mathieu-Arth, François. La *Psyché* de Thomas Shadwell d'après M. CSH, v. 1: 373–93, 1968.
1097. Mitra, D. Adaptations of the plays of M. for the English stage, 1660–1700. (Thesis, Bedford College, London, 1966/7).
1098. Moore, F. H. The composition of *Sir Martin Mar-all.* EDMac: 27–38, 1967.
   rev. H. G. Hall *in* StF 37: 146–7, 1969.
1099. Nelson, Judith K. Fielding and M. (Thesis, Rice Univ., 1971) 187 p. Diss abs A 32: 2064, 1971/2.
1100. Neri, Nicoletta. M. e il teatro inglese della Restaurazione. (Thesis, Univ. of Turin, 1966). Turin, Giappichelli, 1966. 58 p.
1101. Olson, Elder. Shakespeare and M. *in his* The theory of comedy (Bloomington, Ind., Univ. Press, 1968): 86–106.
1102. O'Regan, M. J. *See no. 833.*
1103. Rosenblithe, Anita R. A comparison of the moral and aesthetic vision of three seventeenth century dramatists: Corneille, M., and Ben Jonson. (Thesis, Univ. of Chicago, 1969) 235 p. Diss abs A 30: 2978–9, 1969/70.
1104. Rydals, Clyde deL. Browning's *Fifine at the Fair*: some further sources and influence. ELN 7: 46–51, 1969.

1105. Shelton, Frédéric V. M. et les écrivains comiques de la Restauration anglaise, 1664–1707. (Thesis, Univ. of Paris, 1964). *Résumé in* AUP 34: 418–9, 1964.
1106. Shepherd, James L. *See no. 848.*
1107. Stambusky, Alan A. Chaucer and M.: kindred patterns of the dramatic impulse in human comedy. LHR 1: 43–60, 1963. *See* S. J. Sackett *in* AbES 7: 283, 1964.
1108. Stern, Charles H. Jonson's satiric commentator and M.'s "raisonneur:" a study arising out of parallels in M. and Jonson. (Thesis, Columbia Univ., 1961) 273 p. Diss abs A 22: 3188–9, 1961/2.
1109. Stoll, Edgar S. M. and Shadwell. RR 35: 3–18, 1944.
1110. Suckling, Norman. M. and English Restauration comedy. RestT 43: 93–107, 1966.
1111. Sullivan, William A. Fielding's dramatic comedies: the influence of Congreve and M. (Thesis, Louisiana State Univ., 1971) 224 p. Diss abs A 32: 3966, 1971/2.
1112. Voisine, Jacques. Les Anglais comprennent-ils M.? RLM 9: 35–44, 1954.
1113. Walker, Ellen L. The varieties of comedy: a study of the dramatic comedies of M., Jonson and Shakespeare. (Thesis, Univ. of Connectocut, 1971) 237 p. Diss abs A 32: 2655, 1971/2.
1114. Wilcox, John. The relation of M. to Restauration comedy. *New ed.* N. Y., Blom, 1964. 240 p. *See* CrB 2256.
1115. Wood, John. M. in England. D 89: 33–6, 1968.

Germany and Austria

1116. Altenhofer, Norbet. Frei nach dem M.; zu Hofmannsthals Gesellschafts-komödie *Die Lästigen.* FestBB: 218–37, 1967.
1117. Burger, Hilde. *See no. 930.*
1118. Cohn, Dorrit. *See no. 801.*
1119. De Leeuwe, H. H. *See no. 877.*
1120. Fiedler, Leonhard M. Eine M.-Ausgabe von Hofmannsthal und Sternheim. Begegnungen und gemeinsame Pläne. Hofmannsthal-Blätter. 4: 289–93, 1970.
1121. Goldsmith, Ulrich K. Brecht as adaptor of M. ICLA, v. 2: 875–81, 1966.
1122. Hergešič, J. *See no. 1093.*
1123. Horn, Dieter. *See no. 726.*
1124. Lübke, Diethard. *See no. 884.*
1125. McClain, W. H. Kleist and M. as comic writers. *See* CrB 2227.
1126. Masson-Oussel, P. M. dévancier de Kant. REsth 1: 81–4, 1948.
1127. Mauser, W. Hugo von Hofmannsthal und M. Innsbruck, Beiträge zur Kulturwissenschaft, 1964. 16 p.
  rev. R. W. *in* NS 16: 251–2, 1967.
1128. Oswald, V. A. Hofmannsthal's collaboration with M. *See* CrB 2234.
1129. Roth, Michael A. The spirit of comedy in M. and Nestroy. (Thesis, Univ. of Indiana, 1967) 222 p. Diss abs A 28: 3682, 1967/8.
1130. Sembdner, Helmut. *See no. 888.*
1131. Steffen, H. Sprachkritik und Sprachhaltung bei M. und Lessing. WW: 383–97, 1961.
1132. Szondi, Peter. *See no. 889.*
1133. Temkine, Raymonde. *See no. 221.*

1134. Welti, L. Die erste österreichische M.-Aufführung (Bregenz, 1692). Mk 9: 87–93, 1963.
1135. Wittkowski, Wolfgang. *See no. 894.*
1136. Wucherpfenning, Wolf. *Der Schwierige* und *der Menschenfeind*; zur Auffassung des Individuums bei M. und Hofmannsthal. CG: 269–301, 1969.

Italy

1136a. Bottke, K. G. *See no. 897.*
1137. Hartley, K. H. *See no. 628.*
1138. Mignon, Maurice. M. et Goldoni. HomEC: 129–41, 1959.
1139. Pighi, Laura. M. e il teatro italiano in Francia. Bologna, Ed. Patron, 1958. 122 p.
1140. Simone, A. *See no. 673.*
1141. Ulrich, Leo. *See no. 857.*
1142. Whitefield, J. H. La Belle Charite III: Racine et M. and the *Pastor Fido.* ItS 24: 76–92, 1969.

Poland

1143. Brandwajn, Rachmiel. *See no. 604.*
1144. Kott, Jan. Bohomolec w termine u M. KStP: 435–43, 1961.
1145. Kowzan, Tadeuz. Littérature dramatique—littérature dérivée (Slowacki). KN 16: 9–43, 1969.
1146. Lasocka, Barbara, Anne Tatarkiewicz & Jerr Adamski. Z teatranych djiejòw Moliera *and* Powroty do Miera *and* Problem *Mizantropa.* Program Notes for the *Misanthrope.* National Theater, Warsaw, 1967.
1147. Szweykowski, Z. Stanislaw Boguslawski i jego *Lwy i lwice*; karta z dziejòw w plywu Moliera na komedie polska. KStP 435–43, 1961.

Portugal and Brazil

1148. Coimbra Martins, Antonío. *See no. 898.*
1149. Raeders, Georges. Oeuvres de Corneille, de Racine et de M. en portugais. RHLF 69: 662–3, 1969. *Slightly different text in* RHT 21: 285–7, 1969.
1150. Segal, Jenny Klabin. Teatro classico. São Paolo, Martins, 1966–9. [Includes translations of *Les Précieuses ridicules, l'Ecole des femmes, le Tartuffe* and *le Misanthrope.*]
1151. Sten, Holger. Les sources portugaises de M. OrL 1: 111–25, 1943.

Scandanavian Countries

1152. Grimsley, Ronald. *See no. 720.*
1153. ——. *See no. 721.*
1154. Heggelund, Kjell. M. i Ludvig Holbergs dikteriske gjennombrudd. Edda 53: 41–51, 1966.
1155. Jensen, Anne E. Holbergs Velslende Domne over M.s Komedier. Edda 44: 270–300, 1957.
1156. Krogh, Torben. *See no. 732.*
1157. Sauvage, Micheline. *See no. 692.*

Spain

1158. Aubrun, Charles V. *See no. 697.*
1159. Castro, Americo. *See no. 704.*
1160. Chancerel, Léon. *See no. 219.*
1161. Défourneaux, Marcelin. M. et l'Inquisition espagnole. Bhis 64: 1–2, 30–42, 1962.
    rev. D. Dalla Valle *in* StF 22: 155–6, 1964.
1162. ——. Une adaptation de *Tartuffe*: el Gasmono ou *Juan de buen amor* de Candido Maria Trigueres. Bhis 64: 43–60, 1962.
    rev. D. Dalla Valle *in* StF 22: 156, 1964.
1163. Domenech, Ricardo. *Les Femmes savantes* au Teatro español, Madrid. Gua 73: 420–8, Nov. 1969.
1164. Herreras, Domiciano. *See no. 518a.*
1165. Hesse, E. W. Influencia del tema de Dom Juan (bibliografia): Tirso de Molina. RevEs: 850–89, 1949.
1166. Marey, Juan. *See no. 221.*
1167. Quinto, José Maria de. *Las mujeres sabias* de M [Teatre español, Madrid]. Insula (Madrid) 253: 15–6, 1967.

U.S.A. and Canada

1168. Bertram-Cox. Jean De Sales. M. in New York: a comparison of productions of *le Malade imaginaire* and *le Bourgeois gentilhomme* on the New York professional stage, 1860–1961, with those by actors of the Comédie-Française, 1951–1959. (Thesis, Stanford Univ., 1963) 260p. Diss abs A 24: 3014, 1963/4.
1169. van Eerde, John. *Le Bourgeois gentilhomme* in New York, 1955. FR 29: 472–6. 1955/6.
1170. Fitzpatrick, Marjorie A. The fortunes of M. in Canada. (Thesis, Univ. of Toronto, 1968). Diss abs A 30: 4598, 1969/70.
1171. Lemaître, Henri. *See no. 640.*
1172. Mélèse, Pierre. *See no. 646.*
1173. Rambaud, Alfred. *See no. 661.*
1174. Santt, R. M. à Manhattan. Vieux-Virton (Belgium), Ed. de la Dryade, 1967.

U.S.S.R.

1175. Abensoir, Gérard. *Le Tartuffe* au théâtre de la Taganka à Moscou. RHT 23: 129–35, 1971.
1176. Corbet, Charles. *See no. 708.*
1177. Descaves, Pierre. M. en URSS. Amiot-Dumont, 1954. 220 p.
1178. Dobrovolski, O. M. et le théâtre russe au XVIIIe siècle.. ESov 124: 78, 1958.
1179. Leiste, Hans W. Gogol und M. Nuremberg, Carl, 1958. 62 p.
1180. Mandel, Oscar. M. et Turgenev: the literature of no-judgment. CL 11: 233–49, 1959.
    rev. F. Simone *in* StF 10: 149, 1960.
1181. Serrano, Poncela. *See no. 761.*
1182. Toporkov, Vasily O. K. S. Stanislavski na repetitsii . . . (*with special reference to* Gogol's *Mertvye Dushi* and M.'s *Tartuffe*.) Moscow, Iskusstvo, 1949, 189 p.

Other Countries

1183. Mladenhoff, Mladen. M. in Bulgarien. MK 11: 151–5, 1965.
1184. Brabec, Jean. *Les Précieuses ridicules* à Prague en 1718. RHLF 59: 49, 1959.
1185. Brett, Vladimir. *Préfaces and comments to his* Pièces choisies de M. Prague, Hry, 1953–6.
1186. ——.První ceský preklad *Smesných preciózek.* CasMF 49: 135–41, 1967. [*First translation of les Précieuses ridicules in Czech* (résumé: 141–2).]
1187. Petrovska-Giudici, Marija. M. à Prague. RN 12: 161–8, 1970. *Also in* DSS 89: 51–7, 1970.
1188. Benor, Y. M. en Guinée. LF 1: 8, Aug. 4, 1960.
1189. Nagy, Peter. Le théâtre classique en Hongrie (Corneille, M., Racine) ALASH 1–2: 39–54, 1969.
1190. Turbet-Delog, G. M. en Hongrie. It 6: 29–33, 1956.
1191. Suzuki, Koji R. M. au Japon. CAIEF 16: 260–7, 1964.
1192. Nastev, Bozidar. Trois traductions de M. en aroumain. AIFZa 14–7, 47–58, 1964/5.
1193. Oprescu, Eugenia. M. in Romania. StLBuch" 35–60, 1970. [*Résumé in French* 60–1.]
1194. Deanović, M. Le théâtre de M. à Raguse au XVIIIᵉ siècle. *See* CrB 2201.
1195. ——. M. à Dubrovnik. AIFZa 18–9: 127–30, 1966–7 [1968].

XII TRANSLATIONS, LISTED CHRONOLOGICALLY, AND ALPHABETICALLY BY COUNTRIES

Bulgarian

1196. Le Tartuffe, tr. by Asan Pastsvetnikov. Sofia, NarodnaProsveta, 1949. 133 p.

Chinese

1197. Les Précieuses ridicules, tr. into modern Chinese. Shanghai, K'ai Ming Bookshop, 1949. 41 p.
1198. Don Juan, tr. into modern Chinese. Shanghai, K'ai Ming Bookshop. 1949. 90 p.

Dutch

1199. Le Misanthrope, tr. by Jan Prins. Antwerp & Bilthoven, 1941, 1944. (Clandestinely printed. Date on title page is false)

English

1200. Copley, J. On translating M. into English. DurJ 52: 116–24, 1959/60.
1201. The Works. Reprint of the 1714 edition. N. Y. Blom, 1967. 6 v.
1202. The one act comedies of M., tr. by Albert Bermel. Cleveland, World, 1964. 177 p.
1203. Eight plays, tr. by Morris Bishop. N. Y., Modern Library, 1957, 399 p.
1204. Six prose comedies of M., tr. by George Gravely; introd. by W. G. Moore. London, Oxford Press, 1968. 378 p.
        rev. C. J. Wilson *in* FS 24: 176–8, 1970.

1205. Tartuffe, les Précieuses, l'Ecole des maris, l'Ecole des femmes, la Critique, l'Impromptu de Versailles, Don Juan, tr. by Donald M. Frame, N. Y., New American Library, 1967. 384 p.
1206. Le Misanthrope, le Médecin malgré lui, l'Avare, le Bourgeois gentilhomme, les Femmes savantes, le Malade imaginaire, tr. by Donald M. Frame. N. Y., New American Library, 1968. 512 p.
1207. L'Avare, le Bourgeois gentilhomme, les Fourberies de Scapin, l'Amour médecin, Don Juan, tr. by John Wood. Harmondsworth (Middlesex), Penguin, 1962. 251 p.
1208. L'Ecole des maris, le Médecin volant, le Cocu imaginaire, l'Amour médecin, tr. and adap. by Allan Clason. London, Heineman, 1969. 125 p.
1209. Le Tartuffe, le Bourgeois gentilhomme, tr. by H. Baker & J. Miller; introduction by Henri Peyre. N. Y., Heritage Press, 1964. 197 p.
1210. Le Tartuffe, le Misanthrope, le Malade imaginaire, tr. by Miles Malleson. London, Elek Books, 1950, 1957, 1959; N. Y., Coward-McCaer, 1960. 169 p.
1211. Les Précieuses ridicules, tr. by Herma Briffault. Great Neck, N. Y., Barrons, 1959. 39 p.
1212. Sganarelle, tr. by Milles Malleson in Plays of the year, v. 2, 1955: 337–78.
1213. L'Ecole des femmes, tr. by Miles Malleson. London, S. French, 1954. 102 p. *Also in* Plays of the year, v. 10, 1954: 109–222.
1214. ——, tr. in verse by Richard Wilbur. N. Y., Harcourt-Brace-Javanovich, 1971. 146 p.
1215. ——, adapted in verse by Eric M. Steel. Woodbury, N. Y., Barrons, 1971. 88 p.
1216. Le Tartuffe, tr. by Renée Walduiger. Great Neck, N. Y., Barrons, 1959. 97 p.
1217. ——, tr. by Haskell M. Block. N. Y., Appleteon-Century-Crofts, 1958. 82 p. [Film reproduction].
1218. ——, tr. in verse by James L. Rosenberg. San Francisco, Chandler, 1962. 62 p.
1219. ——, tr. in verse by Richard Wilbur. N. Y., Harcourt-Brace-World, 1963. 106 p.
   rev. V. Mercier *in* Mass Review 4: 582–96, 1962/3; Hudson Review 16: 634–6, 1963/4.
1220. ——, tr. by Robert W. Hartle. Indianapolis, Bobbs-Merrill, 1965. 84 p.
1221. ——, tr. by Joachim Neugroschel; introduction by Glen Willbern. N. Y., American R. D. M. Corp., 1967. 88 p.
1222. Don Juan, tr. by John Ozeel in Oscar Mandel. The theatre of Don Juan (Lincoln, Neb., Univ. Press, 1963): 118–63.
1223. ——, tr. by Wallace Fowlie. Great Neck, N. Y., Barrons, 1964. 83 p.
1224. Le Misanthrope, tr. in verse by Richard Wilbur. N. Y., Harcourt, Brace, 1955. 140 p. *See* CrB 2306.
1225. ——, tr. by Bernard D. N. Grebanier. Great Neck, N. Y., Barrons, 1959. 76 p.
1226. Le Médecin malgré lui, adapted by Victore François, tr. by Lisl Beer. Boston, Bruce Humphries, 1961. 22 p.
1227. ——, tr. and adapted by W. Hannan. London, Heineman, 1963. 31 p.
1228. ——, tr. by Osborne Ashby. Port-of-Spain, Univ. of the West Indies, 1966.
1229. L'Avare, based upon the 1739 translation of H. Baker & J. Miller, and arranged by Walter F. Kerr. Chicago, Dramatic Pub., 1942. 105 p.

1230.   ——, tr. by George R. Keruodle, with songs in the style of the period. Iowa City, Univ. of Iowa, 1946. 68 p.
1231.   ——, tr. Miles Malleson in Plays of the year, v. 1, 1948/9: 353–436.
1232.   ——, tr. by Katherine Cartledge. London, Oxford Press, 1962. 86 p.
1233.   ——, tr. by Donald Sutherland. Boulder, Colo., 1963. Mimeographed.
1234.   ——, tr. by Wallace Fowlie. Great Neck, N. Y., Barrons, 1964. 96 p.
1235.   Le Bourgeois gentilhomme, tr. by Roland Fernand. Chicago, Dramatic Club, 1946. 88 p. Director's manual.
1236.   ——, tr. by Miles Malleson, music by John Hotchilds. London, S. French, 1952. 72 p. Also in Plays of the year, v. 6, 1951: 141–231.
1237.   ——, tr. by Somerset Maugham. Theatre Arts 39: 49–64, 1955. [Special number devoted to the Comédie-Française.]
1238.   ——, tr. by Herma Briffault. Great Neck, N. Y., Barrons, 1957. 111 p.
1239.   ——, tr. by Henry S. Taylor. London, Ginn, 1959. 87 p. Also in Robert Saffron's Great farces, (1966): 65–120.
1240.   ——, tr. by J. S. Dugdale. Bath, J. Brodie, 1962. 94 p.
1241.   Les Fourberies de Scapin, tr. by Donald Sutherland. San Francisco, Chandler, 1962. 46 p.
1242.   Les Femmes savantes, tr. by Joachim Neugroschel.; introduction by Glen Willbern, N. Y., American R. D. M. Corp., 1966. 104 p.   .
1243.   Le Malade imaginaire, tr. by Barry Jackson in Plays of the year, v. 5. 1950/1: 217–96.
1244.   ——, based upon the 1739 translation of H. Baker and J. Miller in Vernon Loggins. 3 Great French plays (1961): 145–256.
1245.   ——, adapted by Kirk Denmark. Madison, Wis., Dane County Tille Co., 1961. Microfilm, 91 p. (Thesis, Univ. of Wisconsin, 1942).
1246.   ——, tr. by Morris Bishop. N. Y., Appleton-Century, 1950, 1964. 83 p.
1247.   ——, tr. by Bert Briscoe. Birmingham, Cambridge, 1967. 72 p.
1248.   The Kilkartan M.: l'Avare, le Médecin malgré lui, les Femmes savantes, tr. by Lady Gregory. N.Y., Blom, 1971. 231 p. Reprint of the 1910 edition.

Estonian

1249.   Le Tartuffe, tr. by Tõlkinud A. Sang. Tallinn, 1961. 119 p.
1250.   Le Misanthrope, tr. by Tõlkinud A. Sang. Tallinn, 1961. 102 p.

German

1251.   Bauer, Constantin. Die M.-Übersetzung von Heinrich Zschokke. NS 10: 286–91, 1961. [On translation into German.]
1252.   Weigel, Hans. Umgang mit M.; einige Bermerkungen über Probleme der Metrik und des Übersetzens im Hinblick auf Jean-Baptiste Poquelin genannt M. Der Monat 181: 62–72, 1963.
1253.   Werke, tr. by Arthur Luther, Rudolph A. Schröder & Ludwig Woldet. Wiesbaden, Insel-Verlag, 1954. 1079 p.
1254.   Sämtliche Werke, tr. by M. Beutler (et al.); ed. by Eugen Neresheimer. Berlin, Propyläenverlag, n. d. Reprint of the 1917–21 edition.
1255.   L'Ecole des femmes, le Tartuffe, les Femmes savantes, tr. in Alexandrines by Rudolph A. Schröder in his Gesammelte Werke (Berlin, 1958): 375–739.
1256.   L'Ecole des femmes, tr. by Rudolph A. Schröder. Stuttgart, Reclam, 1958, 1966. 72 p.

1257. ———, tr. in Alexandrines by Hans Weigel. Zurich, Diogenes Verlag, 1965. 99 p.
1258. Le Tartuffe, tr. by Reinhard Koester. Stuttgart, Reclam, 1954. 80 p.
1259. Don Juan, adapted by Bertolt Brecht, *et al.* Frankfort/M., 1959: *in* v. 12 *of his* collected works (Berlin-Frankfort, 1962, 1964).
1260. ———, tr. by Eugen Neresheimer. Frankfurt/M., Ullstein, 1965.
1261. Le Misanthrope, tr. in Alexandrines by Hans Weigel. Zurich, Diogenes Verlag, 1965. 99 p.
       rev. F-M Marbach. Eine neue M.-Übersetzung in gereimten Alexandrinern: Versuch einer sprachwissenschaftichen Interpretation. *in* LinAnt 2: 297–307, 1968.
1262. ———, tr. by Arthur Luther. Stuttgart, Reclam, 1966. 74 p.
1263. L'Avare, tr. by George Govert. Stuttgart, Reclam, 1954. 85 p.
1264. ———, tr. by W. Widmer; notice: zum Verständnis des Werkes von J. von Stackelberg. Hamburg, Klassiker der Literatur und Wissenschaft, 1962. 151 p.
1265. ———, tr. by Hans Weigel. Zurich, Diogenes Verlag, 1965. 101 p.
1266. Le Bourgeois gentilhomme, tr. by Arthur Luther. Stuttgart, Reclam, 1967. 85 p. *See* Stackelberg, Jürgen von. Nicht Pantoffel, nicht Kothurn *in* MK 14: 297–310, 1968.
1267. Monsieur de Pourceaugnac, tr. by Hans Weigel, Zurich, Diogenes Verlag, 1964. 73 p.
1268. Les Femmes savantes, tr. by Arthur Luther. Stuttgart, Reclam, 1966. 72 p.
1269. ———, tr. by Hans Weigel. Zurich, Diogenes Verlag, 1965. 108 p.
1270. Le Malade imaginaire, tr. by Johannes von Guenther. Stuttgart, Reclam, 1954, 1966. 80 p.
1271. ———, tr. by P. Pflug. Munich, H. Buehuer, 1955. 116 p.

Hebrew

1272. Comedies, tr. by Nathan Alterman. Tel-Aviv, Hakibutz Hame'uhad, 1967. 3 v.
1273. L'Ecole des femmes, tr. by Leah Goldberg. Jerusalem, Mosad Bialikm 1966, 111 p.
1274. Don Juan, tr. by Nathan Alterman and notes by Arie Navon. Tel-Aviv, Hakibutz Hame'uhad. 1965. 81 p.
1275. Le Malade imaginaire, tr. by Nathan Alterman and notes by Menachem Dorman. Tel-Aviv, Hakibutz Hame'uhad, 1958/9, 115p., 1967, 81 p. *See no. 1028.*

Hungarian

1276. Tartuffe, tr. by Jankovich Ferenc. Budapest, Müvelt nép Könuvizdó, 1954. 91 p.
1277. ———; pref. by Podor Laszlo, notes by Kassai Gyorgy. Budapest, Corvina, 1957.

Italian

1278. Le Tartuffe, le Malade imaginaire, & George Dandin, tr. by Mario Bonfantini, 2nd. ed. Turin, Unione tipografico-editrice tornese, 1959. 300 p.

1279. Le Tartuffe, tr. by Salvatore Quasimodo. Milan, Bompiani, 1958, 121 p., 1966, 1967, 213 p.
       rev. S. Crotto *in* StF 31: 146, 1967.
1280. ——, Act III, tr. by Cesare Garboli. Paragone 222: 55–71, 1968.
1281. Le Misanthrope, parts of Act III, IV and V, tr. by Vittorio Sermonti. Paragone 222: 71–8, 1968.
1282. Le Bourgeois gentilhomme, tr. by Cesare Levi. Florence, Sansoni, 1954. 199 p.
1283. Monsieur de Pourceaugnac, tr. by D. Valeri. Turin, Einaudi, 1965. 68 p.
1284. Les Femmes savantes, tr. by Giancarlo Giannozzi. Palc 54: 9–29, 1955.

India—Kannada–Kanarese

1285. Sganarelle, adapted by P. Narasingaräf. 1961. 24 p.

Papiamente, Lingua Franca of the Netherlands Antilles

1286. L'Avare, tr. by May Henriquez. Antilliaanse cahiers 5: 65–153. 1967.

Polish

1287. Complete works, tr. by Tadeuz Zaleński. Warsaw, Ksiazka i Wiedza, 1952. 6 v.
1288. Les Précieuse ridicules, tr. by Tadeuz Boy-Zeleński. Wroclaw, Zaklad im. Ossolińskich, 1950. 48 p.
1289. Le Tartuffe, tr. by Tadeuz Boy-Zeleński. Wroclaw, Zaki im. Ossolińskich, 1951, 1955, 1956, 136 p.
1290. ——, tr. by Tadeuz Boy-Zeleński. Warsaw, Czytelnik, 1951, 1955. 179 p.
1291. ——, tr. by Rachmiel Brandwajn. Warsaw, Panstwowe Zaklady wy dawnictw Szkolnych, 1968.
1292. Le Misanthrope, tr. by Tadeuz Boy-Zeleński. Warsaw, Biblioteka pisarzy polskich i obcych, 1947. 181 p.
1293. ——, tr. by Tadeuz Boy-Zeleński. Wroclaw, Biblioteka Narodowa, 1951. 109 p.
1294. ——, tr. by Jan Kott. Warsaw, 1967. 117 p.
1295. L'Avare, tr. by Tadeuz Boy-Zeleński. Wroclaw, Zaki im. Ossolińskich, 1954, 136 p.
1296. ——, tr. by Tadeuz Boy-Zaleński. Kraków, Wyawn, Biblioteka Narodowa, 194?, 125 p.

Portuguese

1297. L'Ecole des maris, tr. by Artur Azavedo. Rio-de-Janeiro, Ministério da Educação e Cultura, 1957. 111 p.
1298. Le Tartuffe, tr. by Guilherme Figueiredo. Rio-de-Janeiro, Imp. nacional, 1952. unpaged.
1299. Les Fourberies de Scapin, tr. by Carlos Drummond de Andrado. Rio-de-Janeiro, Ministério da Educação e Cultura, 1962. 91 p.

Russian

1300. Complete works, ed. by N. M. Liubimov; preface and notes by G. N. Boiadzhiev; tr. by different authors. Moscow, Iskusstvo, 1965–68. 4 v.

rev. N. Gourfinkel *in* RHT 21: 180, 1969.

1301. Les Précieuses ridicules, tr. by I. Iakovleva. Moscow, Iskusstvo, 1956. 46 p.
1302. Sganarelle, tr. by A. Onoshkovich-Iatsiny. Moscow, Iskusstvo, 1956. 51 p.
1303. Le Médecin maglré lui, tr. by I. Lubimov. Moscow, Iskusstvo, 1956. 46 p.

Slovak

1304. Comedies, Gosud, Izd-vo-Khudozh, 1957. 2 v.
1305. L'Avare, tr. by S. Kadlec. Praze, Uměnī Lidu, 1949. 156 p.
1306. ——, tr. by F. Kalma. Martin, Martica Slavenska, 1962. 113 p.

Spanish

1307. Comedies, illus. by Chico Prats. Barcelona, Ed. Maucci, 1962. 604 p.
1308. ——, tr. by Juan Gomez de Luaces. Barcelona, Iberia-J. Gil, 1966. 5 v.
1309. ——, tr. by Julio Gomez de la Serna. 5th ed. Madrid, Aguilar, 1966. 1153 p.
1310. Les Précieuses ridicules *in* F. C. Sainz de Robles, ed., El teatro español (Madrid, Aguilar, 1942/3) v. 5: 461–81.
1311. L'Avare, tr. by José López Rubio. Madrid Ed. Alfil, 1960. 80 p.
1312. Les Femmes savantes, tr. by Enrique Llovet, Madrid Ed. Alfil, 1968. 72 p.

Swahili

1313. Le Médecin maglré lui, adapted by A. Morrison for East African audiences. Dar es Salaam, East African Standard, 1945.
1314. Le Bourgeois gentilhomme, adapted by A. Morrison for East African audiences. Dar es Salaam, East African Literature Bureau, 1966. 75 p.

Swedish

1315. Le Tartuffe, tr. by Tor Hedberg; introd. by Hjakmar Alving. Stockholm, Bonnier, 1961. 80 p.
1316. Le Misanthrope, tr. by Allan Bergstrand. Stockholm, Svenska Riksteatern, 1968.
1317. L'Avare, tr. by Hjalmar Gullberg. Lund, Gleerup, 1963. 103 p.

Turkish

All of M.'s plays were translated by various authors and published separately by Maarif Matbassi of Ankara between 1941 and 1965. They will be listed chronologically under the French title with the name of the translator, the date and the number of pages.

1318. Le Médecin volant & La Jalousie du Barbouillé, tr. by Ali Süha Delibasi, 1943. 44 p.
1319. L'Etourdi, tr. by Behiç Enver Koryak. 1944. 93 p.
1320. Le Dépit amoureux, tr. by Güzin Dikel. 1944. 91 p.
1321. Les Précieuses ridicules, tr. by Galip Arcan. 1943. 42 p.
1322. Sganarelle, tr. by Teodar Kudret. 1965. 54 p.
1323. Don Garice de Navarre, tr. by Nuri Darago. 1949. 62 p.
1324. L'Ecole des maris, tr. by Vahdi Hatay. 1944. 62 p.
1325. Les Fâcheux, tr. by Yaşar Nabi Nayir. 1946. 41 p.
1326. L'Ecole des femmes, tr. by Sabahattin Eyüboğlu. 1941. 154 p.

1327. La Critique . . . . , tr. Sabahattin Eyüboğlu. 1944. 43 p.
1328. L'Impromptu de Versailles, tr. by Veli Kanik'la Azra Erhat. 1944. 36 p.
1329. Le Mariage forcé, tr. by Alif Obay. 1944. 42 p.
1330. Le Tartuffe, tr. by Veli Kanik. 1944. 98 p.
1331. Don Juan, tr. by Erel Güney & Melih Cevdet Anday. 1943. 91 p.
1332. L'Amour médecin, tr. by Oktay Refat. 1943. 36 p.
1333. Le Misanthrope, tr. by Ali Süha Delilbaşi. 1941. 159 p.
1334. Le Médecin malgré lui, tr. Sabiha Omay. 1943. 62 p.
1335. Le Sicilien, tr. by Orhan Veli Kanik. 1944. 34 p.
1336. Amphitryon, tr. by Ali Teoman. 1943. 84 p.
1337. George Dandin, tr. by Sabiha Omay. 1943. 73 p.
1338. L'Avare, tr. by Ali Süha. 1943. 90 p.
1339. Monsieur de Pourceaugnac, tr. by Erol Güney & Melin Ceudet. 1943. 84 p.
1340. Les Amants magnifiques, tr. by Oktay Refat. 1950. 82 p.
1341. Le Bourgeois gentilhomme, tr. by Ali Süha. 1943. 122 p.
1342. Les Fourberies de Scapin, tr. by Orhan Veli Kanik. 1944. 82 p.
1343. La Comtesse d'Escarbagnas, tr. by H. Fahri Ozansoy. 1943. 34 p.
1344. Les Femmes savantes, tr. by Ali Süha Delilbaşi. 1944. 106 p.
1345. Le Malade imaginaire, tr. by Ismail Hâmi Danişmend. 1943. 117 p.
1346. Le Bourgeois gentilhomme, French and Turkish texts by Adèle Ayda,
       Istambul, 1956. 62 p.

Ukranian

1347. Comedies, ed. by I. Liobimova. Moscow, Iskusstvo, 1954. 597 p.
1348. Comedies. Kiev, Ed. Art, 1958. 773 p.

XIII   PLAYS AND FICTION ABOUT MOLIÈRE.

1349. Anouilh, Jean. La petite M. Avant Scène, 1959. 42 p. *See* Jean-Louis
       Barrault. Depuis Chaptal . . . laisser la science aux docteurs de la ville.
       CCRB 26: 45–9, 1959; IT 5: 35–7, 1959; Richard Fenzl. J. Anouilhs M.-
       bild. NS 9: 242–7, 1960.
1350. Bulgakov, Michail A. Kabala sviatosh. Letchworth, Prudeaux, 1971. 70 p.
       Tr. by Paul Kalinine *as* La Cabale des dévots. Champs libre, 1972, *in* Le
       roman de Monsieur de M.; *tr. by* Carl R. Proffer & Ellender Proffer *as*
       Cabal of hypocrites *in their* The early plays of Mikhail Bulgakov (Indiana
       Univ. Press, 1972).
1351. Chabannes, Jacques. Monsieur et Madame Molière *in* Les Oeuvres libres
       30; 239–318, 1948.
1352. Davez, Arlette. Dans la loge de M. ASc 93: 13–36, 1954.
1353. Deiber, Paul E. La Troupe du Roy [Hommage à M. par les Comédiens
       Français.] ASc 269: 9–15, 1962.
1354. Farnoux-Reynaud, Lucien. La comédie des comédiens, ou M. à Lyon. Lyon,
       Impr. réunies, 1942, 4 fascicules gr in -8°: *also* Le Crocodile, 1942.
1355. Klefisch, Walter. Arzt in Liebessachen; ein übermütiges Singspiel nach M.,
       von Oskar Seidat; Musik von W. K, op. 27. Weinheim, Bergstrasse,
       Deutscher Laienspiel-Verlag, 1956. 45 p.

1356. La Barrogue-Reyssac, Claude. Célimène ou le retour d'Alceste. Debresse, 1956. 120 p.

1357. ——, La jeunesse de Philaminthe. L'Etrave [Revue de la nouvelle Pléïade], 1968. 152 p.

1358. O'Shaughnessey, Michael. Monsieur Molière, a novel. N. Y., Crowell, 1959. 280 p.

1359. Silzer, Erwin. Une soirée chez M., comédie; ein literarhistorisches Dokument aus den Manuskripten des romanischen Seminars. FestVK: 397–421, 1958.

1360. Simon, Alfred. L'Impromptu de M. *in his* M. par lui-même (Ed. du Seuil, 1957): 147–88.

XIV   MISCELLANEA

1361. Horn-Monval, Madeleine. Un historien du théâtre; le Moliériste Georges Monval. RHT 12: 137–46, 1960.

1362. LeClerc, Marcel. Louis Beffara, commissaire de police de la Révolution française, historien de M. et du théâtre lyrique (1751–1833). VIGILAT (Paris) 3: 2–3, 1953.

1363. Livet, Charles. Lexique de la langue de M. *Reprint*. Hildesheim-New York, Olms, 1970. 3 v.

XV   *Index*

LIST OF CONTRIBUTORS

ERICH A. ALBRECHT, Professor of German and co-director of the Max Kade German-American Document and Research Center at the University of Kansas, Lawrence, is primarily interested in the Age of Goethe and German-American Studies. His publications include *Deutschland im Umbruch*; *Primitivism and Related Ideas in German Lyric Poetry*; "Metamorphosis realiter," in *Homage to Charles Blaise Qualia*; and "Nordamerika," in *Goedekes Grundriß*. The recipient of several grants, Professor Albrecht was honored by the Order of Merit in 1960.

WARREN ANDERSON is Professor of Comparative Literature in the Department of Comparative Literature at the University of Massachusetts at Amherst. Professor Anderson has written approximately 40 articles on Greek and Roman literature and mythology in relation to music for the sixth edition of *Grove's Dictionary of Music and Musicians*. His major publications include *Aeschylus: Prometheus Bound*, translated, 1963; *Matthew Arnold and the Classical Tradition*, 1965; *Ethos and Education in Greek Music*, 1966; *Victorian Essays . . .*, co-editor, 1967; and *Theophrastus: The Character Sketches*, translated, 1970. Professor Anderson is a former Rhodes Scholar and is primarily concerned with classical influences on the major Victorian poets, translation theory, and ancient music.

ABRAHAM A. AVNI, Professor of English and Comparative Literature at California State College, Long Beach, is particularly interested in the influence of the Bible on European Romanticism. His publications include *The Bible and Romanticism: The Old Testament in German and French Romantic Poetry*, 1969; "The Old Testament in Novalis' Poetry," *Monatshefte*, 1964; "Inspiration in Plato and the Hebrew Prophets," *Comparative Literature*, 1968; and "The Bible and *Les Fleurs du mal*," *PMLA*, 1973.

ADELE BLOCH is Professor of Foreign Languages at Long Island University, Brooklyn. She is primarily interested in mythological themes in modern literature and has published articles dealing with literary archetypes.

BERNARD BRAY, who specializes in French literature of the seventeenth century, is Professor at the Romance Institute, University of Saarland, Saarbrücken, West Germany. Dr. Bray's major publications include *L'art de la lettre amoureuse, des manuels aux romans*, 1967; "Quelques aspects du système épistolaire de Mme de Sévigné," in *RHLF*, 1969; and "Le dialogue comme forme littéraire au XVIIe siècle," in *CAIEF*, 1972. Professor Bray is also the editor of *Jean Chapelain, 77 Lettres inédites à N. Heinsius*, 1966.

ALFRED CISMARU is a Professor of French in the Department of Classical and Romance Languages, Texas Tech University, Lubbock. Professor Cismaru's main interest of activity lies in the French literature of the eighteenth and twentieth centuries. He has published *Marguerite Duras* and *Boris Vian*, and numerous articles in *The French Review, The Texas Quarterly, Negro History Bulletin, The Antioch Review, Florida Quarterly, Modern Language Journal, Critique, Cimarron Review*, and others. Professor Cismaru is the recipient of some dozen research grants.

PETER V. CONROY, JR., Assistant Professor at the University of Illinois, Chicago, is primarily interested in the eighteenth-century novel. Contributions in his field include *Crébillon Fils: Techniques of the Novel* (1972); "The Hotel De Balber as a Church and Theater," in *Marcel Proust: A Critical Panorama*; and "Old and New in French Medieval Farce," *Romance Notes*. He has served as Resident Director of Illinois Year Abroad in France.

CHARLOTTE DELBO was secretary to Louis Jouvet from 1937 until 1941, when she was deported to Auschwitz. After the war, she resumed her place with Jouvet. She is an author and playwright and was the 1972 winner of the Quill award. Among Madame Delbo's works are *Mesure de nos Jours*, 1971, and *La Sentence*, 1972. She makes her home in Paris.

CHRISTOPHER DURER, who received the Marian Kister Award for the best Polish and English translation for *Madman and the Nun*, 1969–1970, is Associate Professor at the University of Wyoming. In 1968 he was co-editor and co-translator of *Madman and the Nun and Other Plays* by Stanislaw Ignacy Witkiewicz.

LEONHARD M. FIEDLER is Professor at the Deutsches Seminar of the University of Frankfurt. Well known as a comparatist and a student of European theater, he is also managing editor of the *Hofmannsthal-Blätter*. In addition to his extensive work on Hugo von Hofmannsthal, Professor Fiedler has published on Max Reinhardt, Molière, Nestroy, and Carl Sternheim.

MARJORIE A. FITZPATRICK is Visiting Assistant Professor of French in the French-Italian Department of the University of Massachusetts at Amherst. She is primarily interested in Molière and French-Canadian studies. The recipient of several scholarships and grants, Professor Fitzpatrick is a member of the Five-College Committee on Ethnic Studies.

FIORENZA DI FRANCO, the author of *Le théâtre de Salacrou*, 1970, is Assistant Professor in the Department of Modern Foreign Languages at the University of Missouri, St. Louis. She is particularly interested in French literature in the nineteenth and twentieth centuries, French drama from origins to the present, and Italian literature of the twentieth century. Professor Di Franco is presently working on a book on Eduardo de Filippo. She is the recipient of the Wright-Plaisance grant and an Italian government grant.

FRANCIS W. GRAVIT, Professor of French and Italian at Indiana University, Bloomington, is primarily interested in seventeenth-century French literature and the history of ideas. He has published on the Peiresc papers and contributed to the *Cabeen Bibliography*. Professor Gravit serves as editor of the French section of the *MLA International Bibliography*.

PETER HAFFTER is interested in Romance philology as a whole and currently concerns himself with the production of a Portuguese-Afrikaans dictionary and a

Portuguese grammar in Afrikaans. He has published on Voltaire, Labiche, and Dante. Mr. Haffter instructs in the Department of Romance Languages, University of South Africa, Pretoria.

CYNTHIA J. HAFT, Assistant Professor of French at Hunter College, New York City, is primarily interested in French literature of the twentieth century. Professor Haft has written a book on the theme of Nazi Concentration Camps in French literature and also various articles and short stories in *ELUL, Sh'ma, Jewish Currents, Jewish Digest, Le Monde*, and *Homme et Société*.

DOUGLAS ROWLAND HALL is Assistant Professor of French at the University of South Carolina, Columbia, and is especially interested in the psychological novel of seventeenth-century France. Professor Hall's publications include reviews and *The Chromium Agony: Substance and Style in André Perrin's Fiction*, 1973.

H. GASTON HALL, Senior Lecturer in French at the University of Warwick, Coventry, England, is primarily interested in seventeenth-century French studies. His publications include *Molière: Tartuffe*, 1960; editions of Molière, *Le Bourgeois Gentilhomme*, 1966, and *Les Femmes savantes*, 1973; a translation of Franco Simone, *The French Renaissance*, 1970; and contributions to *FS, MLR, YFS, SFr, YWMLS, AJFS*, and *Dizionario critico della lett. francese*. A former Fulbright Scholar at the University of Toulouse and a Rhodes Scholar at Oxford University, Professor Hall currently serves as volume editor of the Syracuse UP *Critical Bibliography of French Literature*.

ARTHUR R. HARNED of Mississippi State University received his degree in comparative literature from the Sorbonne with a thesis on the influence of Dante in England. Professor Harned is primarily interested in French and Italian literature.

JAMES F. HAMILTON, who is primarily interested in eighteenth-century French literature and Romanticism, is Assistant Professor in the Department of Romance Languages at the University of Cincinnati. He includes among his publications "Parallel Interpretations, Religious and Political, of Rousseau's *Discours sur l'inégalité*," *Studies on Voltaire and the Eighteenth Century*, 1972; "A Theory of Art in Rousseau's First *Discourse*," *Studies on Voltaire* (1972); and "Virtue in Rousseau's First *Discourse*," *Studies on Voltaire* (1972). Professor Hamilton is presently engaged in a study of Jean-Jacques Rousseau's socio-political theory of art.

CARL HAMMER, JR., won the Kentucky Foreign Language Conference Award for 1972 with a study entitled "Goethe and Rousseau: Resonances of the Mind." This honor adds luster to a scholarly career that has focused on Goethe. He is Horn Professor of German at Texas Tech University, Lubbock.

MIROSLAV JOHN HANAK, Professor of Spanish and Philosophy at East Texas State University, concerns himself primarily with comparative literature, literary history, and Existentialist philosophy. Professor Hanak has published essays in *JAAC, CLS, Romania, RF*, and other journals; he has read papers at a number of scholarly conferences.

MARION P. HOLT, Professor of Modern Languages and Literatures at Staten Island Community College, City University of New York, has edited two college texts: *López Rubio's La Venda En Los Ojos*, 1966, and *Ruiz Iriarte's El Carrusell*, 1970. In addition, he has edited *The Modern Spanish Stage: Four Plays*, 1970, and was the translator of Buero's *En La Ardiente Oscuridad* and López Rubio's *La Venda en Los Ojos*. Professor Holt has published articles on theater in *Modern Drama* and in *Hispania*.

WILLIAM D. HOWARTH is Professor of Classical French at the University of Bristol, England, and is primarily interested in French Classical drama and theater history. Himself General Editor of the Clarendon French Series, Professor Howarth is well known for his encouragement to those performing research in seventeenth-century French literature. He is co-editor of *Molière: Stage and Study. Essays in Honour of W. G. Moore* and has a number of other publications to his credit.

NORMA LOUISE HUTMAN, Chairman of the Humanities Division of Hartwick College, Oneonta, N.Y., established an experimental program in humanities and a major in comparative literature at Hartwick College. Her areas of specialization are comparative literature and literary criticism. A selection of her publications include *Machado: A Dialogue with Time*, 1969, and essays in *PMLA, MFS*, and *Modern Drama*. Professor Hutman has been the recipient of numerous fellowships and research grants.

ANNE E. JENSEN of the Institute of Nordic Philology, University of Copenhagen, is primarily interested in Danish literature and theater. Her publications include *Rahbek og de danske Digtere, Studier over Europaeisk Drama i Danmark 1722–1770*, and *Teatret i Lille Grønnegade, 1722–1728*.

ANNA KATONA, Chairman of the Department of English and Professor of English and American Literature at Kossuth University, Debrecen, Hungary, is a member of the Board of Trustees of the Dickens Society. She lists among her publications *George Eliot: Fiction and Reality*, and she has, in collaboration with two other scholars, written a history of English literature. Professor Katona has contributed several articles to *Hungarian Studies in English* and *Act LitH*.

FRANK J. KEARFUL is Visiting Professor of English at the University of Hamburg. He has held an Associate Professorship of English and Comparative Literature at the University of Washington and a Visiting Professorship of English at the University of Tübingen. He is also an assistant editor of the annual *Philological Quarterly* Eighteenth-Century Studies Bibliography. He has published articles on Jane Austen, Nicholas Rowe, Evelyn Waugh, William Faulkner, Thomas Mann, the Spanish picaresque novel, George Lillo, and John Dryden, and is the author of a forthcoming book on Lillo.

L. CLARK KEATING, recipient of Palmes Académiques, is Professor of French at the University of Kentucky in Lexington. He is primarily interested in French literature of the Renaissance and the twentieth century. Among his publications are *Studies on the Literary Salon in France 1550–1615* (Harvard), *Critic of Civilization: Georges Duhamel* (Kentucky), and individual works on André Maurois, Joachim Du Bellay, and Etienne Pasquier (Twayne Series).

EDITH KERN, Doris-Silbert Professor of Humanities at Smith College, Northampton, Massachusetts, is primarily concerned with the literature of seventeenth and twentieth century France. Among her major publications are *The Influence of Heinsius and Vossius Upon French Dramatic Theory*, 1949; *Sartre: A Collection of Critical Essays*, 1962; and *Existential Thought and Fictional Technique: Kierkegaard, Sartre, Beckett*, 1970. She collaborated in the 1962 production of the *Cabeen Bibliography* and participated in the writing of several other significant books, among them *The Hero in Literature*.

H.M. KLEIN is the translator and editor of a dual language text, *William Wycherley, The Country Wife/Die Unschuld vom Lande*, and the author of "Colman und Garrick: *The Clandestine Marriage*" in *Das englische Drama im 18. und 19. Jahrhundert*. He is currently working on *An Anthology of European Sonnets from the Thirteenth to the Seventeenth Centuries* and a book on English comedy of the eighteenth century. Educated largely in Germany, Mr. Klein holds the post of Lecturer in Comparative Literature at the University of East Anglia, Norwich, England.

MICHAEL S. KOPPISCH, Assistant Professor in the Department of Romance Languages, Michigan State University, East Lansing, is primarily interested in seventeenth-century French literature. Professor Koppisch's publications focus on La Bruyère, and he has in progress a book on seventeenth-century French literature from Molière to Marivaux.

EMILIE KOSTOROSKI-KADISH, who is primarily interested in Medieval and eighteenth-century French literature, is Assistant Professor of French at Case Western Reserve University. Among her publications are *The Eagle and the Dove: Corneille and Racine in the Literary Criticism of Eighteenth-Century France* and several recent essays.

JOHN THEODORE KRUMPELMANN, Emeritus Professor of German and Russian at Louisiana State University, is primarily interested in German classical literature and German-American literary relations. His scholarly work includes *Bayard Taylor and German Letters; Southern Scholars in Goethe's Germany*; Kleist's *The Broken Jug* (A verse translation); Schiller's *The Maiden of Orleans* (a verse translation); Sealsfield, *The Indian Chief*, vols. IV-V; and *Der Legitime und die Republikaner*, vols. VI-VII. Professor Krumpelmann is the recipient of numerous honors including Verdienstkreuz Erster Klasse, German Federal Republic, 1972, and is a former Fulbright Lecturer.

FRANCIS L. LAWRENCE, Professor and Chairman of the Department of French and Italian at Tulane University, is the author of *Molière: The Comedy of Unreason*, 1968. Professor Lawrence has published articles including: "Jean de Lacèppede and Ignatian Meditation" (*Comp. Lit.*, 1965); "La Princesse de Clèves Reconsidered" (*French Review*, 1965); "The Ironic Commentator in Molière's *Dom Juan*" (*Studi Francesi*, 1968); and "Our Alceste or Molière's" (*Revue des Langues vivantes*, 1972). He is also a bibliographer for studies in seventeenth-century French literature.

HANNA BALLIN LEWIS, Associate Professor of Modern Languages at Stephen F. Austin State University, Nacogdoches, Texas, is primarily interested in Anglo-German comparative literature and in that regard has written on Hofmannsthal and Browning, America, Milton, Shelley, and Keats.

BARBARA LIDE is a Ph.D. candidate in Comparative Literature at the University of Illinois, Urbana. Her interests lie in the fields of modern German and Scandinavian literature, and she is presently engaged in writing a dissertation on Strindberg's comedies.

YVETTE LOURIA, primarily interested in nineteenth-century European and twentieth-century French literature, is Professor of French and comparative literature at Queens College and the Graduate Center of the City University of New York. Professor Louria's publications include *La Convergence stylistique chez Proust*; "Ivan Goncharov's *Oblomov*: The Anti-Faust as Christian Hero" (co-authored); "Proust and Lunacharskii"; and "Eros and Thanatos dans *Bajazet*." She accomplished the first translation from Church Slavonic of Johann Gottfried Gregorii's *The Comedy of Artaxerxes*.

ANNE S. LUNDQUIST, Instructor in the Department of Scandinavian, University of Minnesota, Minneapolis, is primarily interested in Scandinavian literature and comparative drama. Her main publications include "Carl Michael Bellman, en Exegesis," (Translation) in *Scandinavian Studies*, 1972; and book reviews for *Books Abroad*, 1972 and 1973. She served as Swedish foreign correspondent from 1960 to 1961.

ELIZABETH MAXFIELD-MILLER is the recipient of many research grants and honors. Best known to students of Molière for her and Madeleine Jurgens' *Cent ans de recherches sur Molière*, she has also researched and translated Romansch poetry. Her home is Concord, Massachusetts, and she teaches at Concord Academy.

GITA MAY, Professor of French in the Department of French and Romance Philology at Columbia University, New York, specializes in French literature of the seventeenth, eighteenth and nineteenth centuries. Publications include *Diderot et Baudelaire, critiques d'art*, 1957; co-editor, with Otis Fellows, *Diderot Studies III*, 1961; *De Jean-Jacques Rousseau à Madame Roland*, 1964; *Madame Roland and the Age of Revolution*, 1970; and numerous articles and book reviews in academic journals on both sides of the Atlantic. Special honors of recognition include the Guggenheim Fellowship, Fulbright travel grant, Chevalier dans l'ordre des Palmes académiques, Senior Fellow-National Endowment for the Humanities, and the Vam Amringe Distinguished Book Award.

JAMES McGLATHERY specializes in German literature since Goethe and is Associate Professor of German at the University of Illinois, Urbana. He is especially interested in E. T. A. Hoffmann and has published on him, as well as on Kleist and Droste-Hülshoff. Professor McGlathery is co-editor of *JEGP*.

SIEGFRIED MEWS is the editor of the series, *University of North Carolina Studies in the Germanic Languages and Literatures*, and is Associate Professor of German at the University of North Carolina. Primarily interested in German literature of the nineteenth and twentieth centuries and in comparative literature, he has published extensively in scholarly journals. He edited *Studies in German Literature of the Nineteenth and Twentieth Centuries: Festschrift for Frederic E. Coenen*, 1970.

WOLFGANG F. MICHAEL is the recipient of the Goethe Medaille of the Goethe-Institut, Munich, and the Verdienstkreuz, Erster Klasse, of the Federal Republic. Professor of German at the University of Texas, Austin, he is primarily interested in the Renaissance and the Reformation and in drama. His major and distinguished publications include *Die geistlichen Prozessionsspiele in Deutschland, Frühformen der deutschen Bühne*, and *Das deutsche Drama des Mittelalters*.

WILLIAM A. MOULD, Assistant Professor of French at the University of South Carolina, is primarily interested in seventeenth-century French theater. Professor Mould's publications include "Jocaste: Mother of Evil," *L'Esprit créateur*, 1968; and "The *Innocent Strategème* of Racine's Andromaque," accepted for publication in the *French Review*, April, 1975.

TAKUO OBASE is Honor Professor of the Tokyo Metropolitain University, Tokyo, and is a Member of the Science Council of Japan. He is primarily concerned with French literature of the seventeenth and eighteenth centuries, especially Molière, Diderot, and Beaumarchais. His publications include *La Formation de la comédie classique en France*; *Molière, son temps et sa pensée*; *Dramaturgie de Molière*; and *Etude sur Diderot* (two volumes)—all appearing in Japanese.

FREDERIC O'BRADY, recently retired from the Department of Romance Languages and Literatures at Princeton University, is particularly interested in the history of French theater and the theater in general. His publications include several novels—*Extérieurs à Venise, Le ciel d'en face, Romarin pour le souvenir*, and *There's Always a Throgmorton*; an autobiography, *All Told*; and an advanced French textbook, *Propos Pertinents et Inpertinents*. He is currently Visiting Professor of the Humanities at the Eastman School of Music, University of Rochester.

SIDNEY LOUIS PELLISSIER enjoys acting and directing in theatrical productions, activities that complement his scholarly interests in Ionesco. He is Assistant Professor of French in the Department of Modern Languages, Purdue University.

HENRI PEYRE, Chairman of the Department of French at the Graduate Center, City University of New York, is undeniably one of the most widely respected French scholars today. He has published extensively on all aspects of French literature and is the recipient of numerous honorary degrees for his outstanding contributions to the fields of French literature and comparative literature.

ALICE RATHÉ is primarily interested in seventeenth- and eighteenth-century theater and seventeenth-century poetic language. She is Assistant Professor at Victoria College, University of Toronto, Canada.

CHRISTA REINIG, a free lance writer, makes her home in Munich. She is best known for her poèm collection *Die Steine von Finisterre* and her short story *Orion trat aus dem Haus*. Her chief interest is in the history of art, and she has served as consultant to the Märkische Museum in Berlin. Her special honors include the Rudolf-Alexander-Schroeder-Preis der Freien Hansestadt Bremen in 1964.

LAURENCE ROMERO is primarily interested in theater and is Assistant Professor of French at Tufts University in Medford, Massachusetts. The recipient of various grants, Professor Romero has written several articles on Molière and is also the author of *Molière: Traditions in Criticism, 1900–1970*.

PAUL SAINTONGE, Mary Lyon Professor and Professor of French Emeritus at Mt. Holyoke College, South Hadley, Massachusetts, concerns himself primarily with sixteenth- and seventeenth-century French literature and specializes in Molière. Professor Saintonge includes among his publications an extensive study, *Fifty Years of Molière Studies—A Bibliography, 1892–1941; Anthologie de la poésie française,* and several items on aspects of the French language.

JAMES B. SANDERS, Professor of French at the University of Western Ontario, is a member of the advisory board of *Nineteenth-Century French Studies* and the *Journal of the Humanities Association of Canada*. His main interest is in the French novel and theater of the nineteenth century, and he has published articles on Isben, Céard, Antoine, and Zola. In collaboration with D. G. Creighton he has edited a critical anthology entitled *A Travers les siècles*, 1967.

NORMAN R. SAVOIE, Assistant Professor in the Department of Languages and Philosophy, Utah State University, Logan, is primarily interested in seventeenth-century French literature. Professor Savoie has published several papers on the various uses French television has made of literature.

A. RICHARD SOGLIUZZO is an Assistant Professor in the Department of Theater at the State University of New York, Albany. Professor Sogliuzzo concerns himself primarily with contemporary Italian and American theater and drama and particularly with the drama of Luigi Pirandello. He is a member of the Executive Board of the Pirandello Society of New York, editor of the *Pirandello Newsletter*, and assistant editor of the *Theater Annual*.

SAMUEL SOLOMON, London, is a professional translator and author. He is perhaps best known for his translation of the complete plays of Jean Racine, selected plays of Corneille, and plays by Franz Grillparzer. His current work includes an original tragedy and translations of Molière, Louise Labé, and Heinrich Heine.

BERNARD STAMBLER, whose extensive publications on Dante include *Dante's Other World: The "Purgatorio" as Guide to the "Commedia,"* is Professor of English at Manhattan Community College. He has written librettos for three operas, among them *The Crucible*.

CARL STEINER, Associate Professor and Chairman of German at George Washington University, Washington, D.C., is primarily interested in nineteenth- and twentieth-century German literature. His publications include "Über Gottfried Kellers Verhältnis zur Demokratie," in *Monatshefte*; and "Frankreichbild und Katholizismus bei Joseph Roth," in *The German Quarterly*.

WINIFRED KERA STEVENS is Professora Colaborodora at the University of São Paulo, Brazil, where she pursues her interests in English and American literature, Luso-Brazilian literature, and comparative literature. She is co-author of *Curso Prático de Traducão, Inglês-Português, Português-Inglês*, and she has written articles on English, American, French, Portuguese, and Brazilian literature.

LEWIS A.M. SUMBERG, University Professor at the University of Tennessee, Chattanooga, is primarily interested in the humanities and interdisciplinary studies. He is the author of *La Chanson d'Antioche, une chronique en vers français de la première croisade par le pèlerin Richard*, 1968, and co-author of *Les grands écrivains français*, 1965. Professor Sumberg has been the recipient of several Faculty Research Fellowships and a grant of the Centre National de la Recherche Scientifique, Paris.

FREDERICK WRIGHT VOGLER is Associate Professor of French at the University of North Carolina at Chapel Hill. He includes among his publications *Vital d'Audiguier and the Early 17th Century French Novel*, 1964, and *Molière Mocked: Three Contemporary Hostile Comedies* (ed.), 1973. Professor Vogler is a former Fulbright Scholar, University of Strasbourg.

PHILIP A. WADSWORTH, Professor of French at the University of South Carolina, has published several books, including *The Novels of Gomberville*, 1942; *Young La Fontaine*, 1952; and an edition of Tristan l'Hermite, *Poésies*, 1962. He has written various articles on Montaigne, Malherbe, Scarron, Molière, La Rochefoucauld, and La Bruyère. Professor Wadsworth's honors include the Guggenheim Fellowship and the Folger Shakespeare Library Fellowship.

KENNETH S. WHITE is Professor in the Department of French and Italian at the University of Kansas, Lawrence. Professor White includes among his publications *School for Buffoons*, an American version of Ghelderode's play, with critical introduction and notes, 1968. He is the review editor in French of the *Modern Language Journal*, has served on the Executive Committee of the MMLA.

HANNELORE WIERSCHIN, patent librarian at the University of California, Central University Library, San Diego, is primarily interested in bibliography and research methods.

JYTTE WIINGAARD is lecturer at The Institute for Theater Research at the University of Copenhagen. Publications include "William Bloch og Holberg," "Den Yngste," "Skitser til Romantikkens teater," and "Forudsaetningerne for det moderne teater."

WOLFGANG WITTKOWSKI, Professor at Ohio State University, Columbus, is primarily interested in German literature. His publications include *Der junge Hebbel* (1969) and articles on Hebbel, Schiller, and Kleist. Professor Wittkowski has also published on Goethe's *Faust* in *Deutsche Vierteljahrsschrift für Literaturwissenschaft und Geistesgeschichte*, 1967, 1969; and on Molière and Giraudoux in *Kleist und Frankreich*, 1969, and *Comparative Literature Studies*, 1971.

INDEX

The following is a list of characters, names, and titles. Conventions for alphabetization are generally those of *The Oxford Companion to French Literature* by Sir Paul Harvey and J. E. Heseltine. Characters are listed by name as though they were real persons. Definite and indefinite articles are displaced in titles. The name "Molière" is not listed.

837